CONNECT FEATURES

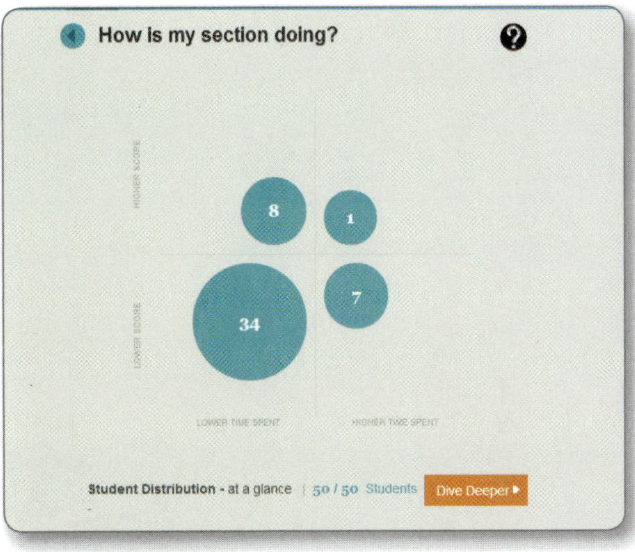

Connect Insight

The first and only analytics tool of its kind, Connect Insight is a series of visual data displays, each of which is framed by an intuitive question and provides at-a-glance information regarding how an instructor's class is performing. Connect Insight is available through Connect titles.

Tax Forms Problems

Updated for the 2016 edition, *Tax Forms Problems* are a set of requirements included in the end-of-chapter material that ask students to complete a tax form. These problems provide valuable experience and practice with filling out forms and are included in *Connect Accounting*. These requirements and their relevant forms are included in *Connect Accounting*.

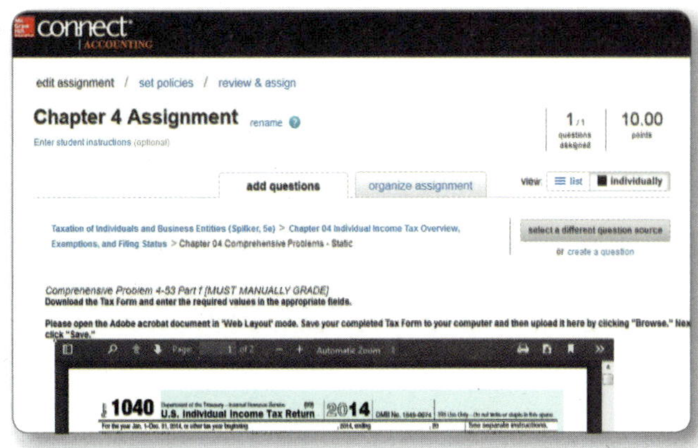

Through November, Tex has received gross income of $120,000. For December, Tex is considering whether to accept one more work engagement for the year. Engagement 1 will generate $7,000 of revenue at a cost of $4,000, which is deductible for AGI. In contrast, engagement 2 will generate $7,000 of revenue at a cost of $3,000, which is deductible as an itemized deduction. Tex files as a single taxpayer. (use the tax rate schedules.)

a. Calculate Tex's taxable income assuming he chooses engagement 1 and assuming he chooses engagement 2. Assume he has no itemized deductions other than those generated by engagement 2.

	Description	Engagement 1	Engagement 2
(1)	Gross income before new work engagement	$ 120,000	$ 120,000
(2)	Income from engagement	7,000	7,000
(3)	Additional for AGI deduction	(4,000)	
(4)	Adjusted gross income	$ 123,000	$ 127,000
(5)	Greater		
(6)	Greater of itemized deductions or standard deduction		

End-of-Chapter Material

McGraw-Hill Education redesigned the student interface for our end-of-chapter assessment content. The new interface provides improved answer acceptance to reduce students' frustration with formatting issues (such as rounding) and, for select questions, provides an expanded table that guides students through the process of solving the problem. Many questions have been redesigned to more fully test students' mastery of the content.

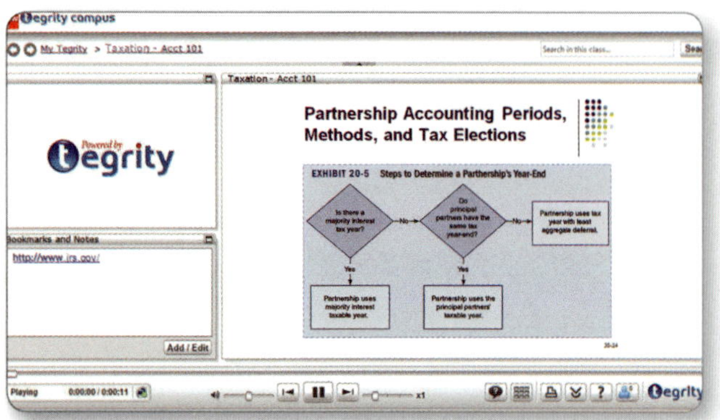

Tegrity

Make your classes available anytime, anywhere. With simple, one-click recording, students can search for a word or phrase and be taken to the exact place in your lecture that they need to review.

EASY TO USE

Learning Management System Integration

McGraw-Hill Campus is a one-stop teaching and learning experience available to use with any learning management system. McGraw-Hill Campus provides single sign-on to faculty and students for all McGraw-Hill material and technology from within the school website. McGraw-Hill Campus also allows instructors instant access to all supplements and teaching materials for all McGraw-Hill products.

Blackboard users also benefit from McGraw-Hill's industry-leading integration, providing single sign-on to access all Connect assignments and automatic feeding of assignment results to the Blackboard grade book.

POWERFUL REPORTING

Connect generates comprehensive reports and graphs that provide instructors with an instant view of the performance of individual students, a specific section, or multiple sections. Since all content is mapped to learning objectives, Connect reporting is ideal for accreditation or other administrative documentation.

McGraw-Hill's

Taxation of Individuals

Brian C. Spilker
Brigham Young University
Editor

Benjamin C. Ayers
The University of Georgia

Edmund Outslay
Michigan State University

Connie D. Weaver
Texas A&M University

John A. Barrick
Brigham Young University

John R. Robinson
The University of Texas–Austin

Ron G. Worsham
Brigham Young University

McGRAW-HILL'S TAXATION OF INDIVIDUALS, 2016 EDITION, SEVENTH EDITION

Published by McGraw-Hill Education, 2 Penn Plaza, New York, NY 10121.

This book is printed on acid-free paper.

1 2 3 4 5 6 7 8 9 0 DOW/DOW 1 0 9 8 7 6 5

ISBN 978-1-259-41550-0
MHID 1-259-41550-3
ISSN 1943-9318

Senior Vice President, Products & Markets: *Kurt L. Strand*
Vice President, General Manager, Products & Markets: *Marty Lange*
Vice President, Content Design & Delivery: *Kimberly Meriwether David*
Managing Director: *Tim Vertovec*
Marketing Director: *Brad Parkins*
Senior Brand Manager: *Kathleen Klehr*
Director, Product Development: *Rose Koos*
Director of Digital Content: *Patricia Plumb*
Lead Product Developer: *Ann Torbert*
Product Developer: *Danielle Andries*
Digital Product Developer: *Kevin Moran*
Digital Product Analyst: *Xin Lin*
Director, Content Design & Delivery: *Linda Avenarius*
Program Manager: *Daryl Horrocks*
Content Project Managers: *Lori Koetters, Brian Nacik*
Buyer: *Sue Culbertson*
Design: *Matt Diamond*
Content Licensing Specialists: *Keri Johnson, Rita Hingtgen*
Cover Image: *Paul Bradbury/Getty Images*
Compositor: *Aptara®, Inc.*
Printer: *R. R. Donnelley*

www.mhhe.com

Dedications

We dedicate this book to:

My children, Braxton, Cameron, Ethan, and Lauren, and to my parents, Ray and Janet. Last but not least, to my wife, Kim, for allowing me to take up valuable kitchen space while I was working on the project. I love you all.

Brian Spilker

My wife, Marilyn, daughters Margaret Lindley and Georgia, son Benjamin, and parents Bill and Linda.

Ben Ayers

My wife, Jill, and my children Annika, Corinne, Lina, Mitch, and Connor.

John Barrick

My family, Jane, Mark, Sarah, Chloe, Lily, and Jeff, and to Professor James E. Wheeler, my mentor and friend.

Ed Outslay

JES, Tommy, and Laura.

John Robinson

My family, Dan, Travis, Alix, and Alan.

Connie Weaver

My wife, Anne, sons Matthew and Daniel, and daughters Whitney and Hayley.

Ron Worsham

About the Authors

Brian Spilker (PhD, University of Texas at Austin, 1993) is the Robert Call/Deloitte Professor in the School of Accountancy at Brigham Young University. He teaches taxation in the graduate and undergraduate programs at Brigham Young University. He received both BS (Summa Cum Laude) and MAcc (tax emphasis) degrees from Brigham Young University before working as a tax consultant for Arthur Young & Co. (now Ernst & Young). After his professional work experience, Brian earned his PhD at the University of Texas at Austin. In 1996, he was selected as one of two nationwide recipients of the Price Waterhouse Fellowship in Tax Award. In 1998, he was a winner of the American Taxation Association and Arthur Andersen Teaching Innovation Award for his work in the classroom; he has also been awarded for his use of technology in the classroom at Brigham Young University. Brian researches issues relating to tax information search and professional tax judgment. His research has been published in journals such as *The Accounting Review, Organizational Behavior and Human Decision Processes, Journal of the American Taxation Association, Behavioral Research in Accounting, Journal of Accounting Education, Journal of Corporate Taxation,* and *Journal of Accountancy.*

Ben Ayers (PhD, University of Texas at Austin, 1996) holds the Earl Davis Chair in Taxation and is the Dean of the Terry College of Business at the University of Georgia. He received a PhD from the University of Texas at Austin and an MTA and BS from the University of Alabama. Prior to entering the PhD program at the University of Texas, Ben was a tax manager at KPMG in Tampa, Florida, and a contract manager with Complete Health, Inc., in Birmingham, Alabama.

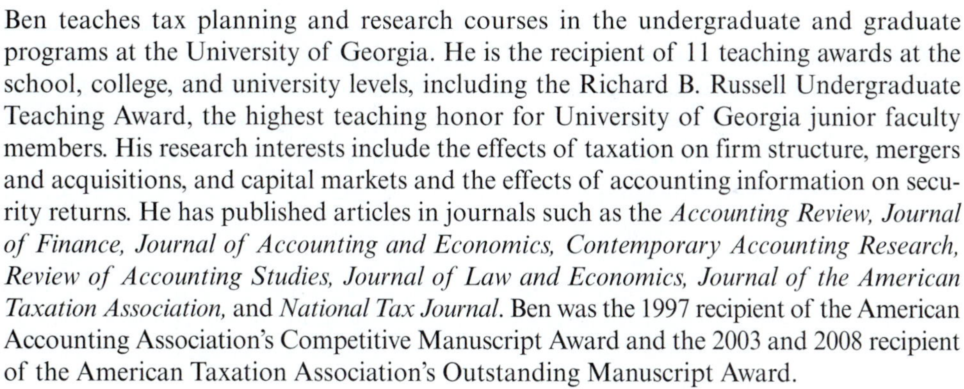

Ben teaches tax planning and research courses in the undergraduate and graduate programs at the University of Georgia. He is the recipient of 11 teaching awards at the school, college, and university levels, including the Richard B. Russell Undergraduate Teaching Award, the highest teaching honor for University of Georgia junior faculty members. His research interests include the effects of taxation on firm structure, mergers and acquisitions, and capital markets and the effects of accounting information on security returns. He has published articles in journals such as the *Accounting Review, Journal of Finance, Journal of Accounting and Economics, Contemporary Accounting Research, Review of Accounting Studies, Journal of Law and Economics, Journal of the American Taxation Association,* and *National Tax Journal.* Ben was the 1997 recipient of the American Accounting Association's Competitive Manuscript Award and the 2003 and 2008 recipient of the American Taxation Association's Outstanding Manuscript Award.

John Barrick (PhD, University of Nebraska at Lincoln, 1998) is currently an associate professor in the Marriott School at Brigham Young University. He served as an accountant at the United States Congress Joint Committee on Taxation for the 110th and 111th Congresses. He teaches taxation in the graduate and undergraduate programs at Brigham Young University. He received both BS and MAcc (tax emphasis) degrees from Brigham Young University before working as a tax consultant for Price Waterhouse (now PricewaterhouseCoopers). After his professional work experience, John earned his PhD at the University of Nebraska at Lincoln. He was the 1998 recipient of the American Accounting Association, Accounting, Behavior, and Organization Section's Outstanding Dissertation Award. John researches issues relating to professional tax judgment and tax information search. His research has been published in journals such as *Organizational Behavior and Human Decision Processes, Contemporary Accounting Research,* and *Journal of the American Taxation Association.*

Ed Outslay (PhD, University of Michigan, 1981) is a professor of accounting and the Deloitte/Michael Licata Endowed Professor of Taxation in the Department of Accounting and Information Systems at Michigan State University, where he has taught since 1981. He received a BA from Furman University in 1974 and an MBA and PhD from the University of Michigan in 1977 and 1981. Ed currently teaches graduate classes in corporate taxation, multiunit enterprises, accounting for income taxes, and international taxation. In February 2003, Ed testified before the Senate Finance Committee on the Joint Committee on Taxation's Report on Enron Corporation. MSU has honored Ed with the Presidential Award for Outstanding Community Service, Distinguished Faculty Award, John D. Withrow Teacher-Scholar Award, Roland H. Salmonson Outstanding Teaching Award, Senior Class Council Distinguished Faculty Award, MSU Teacher-Scholar Award, and MSU's 1st Annual Curricular Service-Learning and Civic Engagement Award in 2008. Ed received the Ray M. Sommerfeld Outstanding Tax Educator Award in 2004 and the lifetime Service Award in 2013 from the American Taxation Association. He has also received the ATA Outstanding Manuscript Award twice, the ATA/Deloitte Teaching Innovations Award, and the 2004 Distinguished Achievement in Accounting Education Award from the Michigan Association of CPAs. Ed has been recognized for his community service by the Greater Lansing Chapter of the Association of Government Accountants, the City of East Lansing (Crystal Award), and the East Lansing Education Foundation. He received a National Assistant Coach of the Year Award in 2003 from AFLAC and was named an Assistant High School Baseball Coach of the Year in 2002 by the Michigan High School Baseball Coaches Association.

John Robinson (PhD, University of Michigan, 1981) is the C. Aubrey Smith Professor of Accounting in the McCombs School of Business at the University of Texas at Austin. Prior to joining the faculty at Texas in 1985, he taught at the University of Kansas, where he was the Arthur Young Faculty Scholar from 1982–1984. John served as the Academic Fellow in the Division of Corporation Finance at the Securities and Exchange Commission for 2009–2010. He is the recipient of the Henry A. Bubb Award for outstanding teaching, the Texas Blazer's Faculty Excellence Award, and the MPA Council Outstanding Professor Award. John also received the 2012 Outstanding Service Award from the American Taxation Association (ATA). John conducts research in a broad variety of topics involving financial accounting, mergers and acquisitions, and the influence of taxes on financial structures and performance. His scholarly articles have appeared in *Accounting Review, Journal of Finance, National Tax Journal, Journal of Law and Economics, Journal of the American Taxation Association, The Journal of the American Bar Association,* and *The Journal of Taxation.* In addition, John was the editor of *The Journal of the American Taxation Association,* from 2002 through 2005, and he was a co-author of the articles honored with the 2003 and 2008 ATA Outstanding Manuscript Awards. John received his JD (*cum laude*) from the University of Michigan in 1979, and he was awarded his PhD in accounting from the University of Michigan in 1981. John teaches courses on individual and corporate taxation and advanced accounting at the University of Texas at Austin.

Connie Weaver Connie Weaver (PhD, Arizona State University, 1997) is the KPMG Professor of Accounting at Texas A&M University. She received a PhD from Arizona State University, an MPA from the University of Texas at Arlington, and a BS (chemical engineering) from the University of Texas at Austin. Prior to entering the PhD Program, Connie was a tax manager at Ernst & Young in Dallas, Texas, where she became licensed to practice as a CPA. She teaches taxation in the graduate and undergraduate programs at Texas A&M University. She has also taught undergraduate and graduate students at the University of Wisconsin-Madison and the University of Texas at Austin. She is the recipient of several teaching awards including the 2006 American Taxation Association/Deloitte Teaching Innovations and the David and Denise Baggett Teaching awards both recognizing innovation in teaching taxation. Connie's current research interests include the effects of tax and financial incentives on corporate decisions and reporting. She has published articles in journals such as the *Accounting Review, Contemporary Accounting Research, Journal of the American Taxation Association, Accounting Horizons, Journal of Corporate Finance,* and *Tax Notes*. She serves on the editorial board of Contemporary Accounting Research and Issues in Accounting Education and was the 1998 recipient of the American Taxation Association/Price Waterhouse Outstanding Dissertation award.

Ron Worsham (PhD, University of Florida, 1994) is an associate professor in the School of Accountancy at Brigham Young University. He teaches taxation in the graduate, undergraduate, MBA, and Executive MBA programs at Brigham Young University. He has also taught as a visiting professor at the University of Chicago. He received both BS and MAcc (tax emphasis) degrees from Brigham Young University before working as a tax consultant for Arthur Young & Co. (now Ernst & Young) in Dallas, Texas. While in Texas, he became licensed to practice as a CPA. After his professional work experience, Ron earned his PhD at the University of Florida. He has been honored for outstanding innovation in the classroom at Brigham Young University. Ron has published academic research in the areas of taxpayer compliance and professional tax judgment. He has also published legal research in a variety of areas. His work has been published in journals such as *Journal of the American Taxation Association, The Journal of International Taxation, The Tax Executive, Journal of Accountancy,* and *Practical Tax Strategies.*

TEACHING THE CODE IN CONTEXT

The basic approach to teaching taxation hasn't changed in decades. ***Today's student deserves a new approach.*** McGraw-Hill's Taxation of Individuals and Business Entities *is a bold and innovative series that has been adopted by over 300 schools across the country.*

McGraw-Hill's Taxation is designed to provide a unique, innovative, and engaging learning experience for students studying taxation. The breadth of the topical coverage, **the storyline approach to presenting the material,** the emphasis on the tax and nontax consequences of multiple parties involved in transactions, and the integration of financial and tax accounting topics make this book ideal for the modern tax curriculum.

> **This is the best tax book on the market.** It's very readable, student-friendly, and provides great supplements.
>
> – Ann Esarco, McHenry County College

> A lot of thought and planning went into the structure and content of the text, and a great product was achieved. **One of the most unique and helpful features is the common storyline** throughout each chapter.
>
> – Raymond J. Shaffer, Youngstown State University

Since the first manuscript was written in 2005, 400 professors have contributed 419 book reviews, in addition to 21 focus groups and symposia. Throughout this preface, their comments on the book's organization, pedagogy, and unique features are a testament to the **market-driven nature of *Taxation*'s development.**

> The Spilker text, in many ways, is a more logical approach than any other tax textbook. **The text makes great use of the latest learning technologies through Connect and LearnSmart.**
>
> – Ray Rodriguez, Southern Illinois University – Carbondale

A MODERN APPROACH FOR TODAY'S STUDENT

> **This text provides a new approach to the teaching of the technical material.** The style of the text material is easier to read and understand. The examples and storyline are interesting and informative. The arrangement makes more sense in the understanding of related topics.
>
> – Robert Bertucelli, Long Island University – Post

Spilker's taxation series was built around the following five core precepts:

1. **Storyline Approach:** Each chapter begins with a storyline that introduces a set of characters or a business entity facing specific tax-related situations. Each chapter's examples are related to the storyline, providing students with opportunities to **learn the code in context.**

2. **Conversational Writing Style:** The authors took special care to write *McGraw-Hill's Taxation* that fosters a friendly dialogue between the content and each individual student. The tone of the presentation is intentionally conversational—creating the impression of ***speaking with* the student,** as opposed to *lecturing to* the student.

3. **Superior Organization of Related Topics:** *McGraw-Hill's Taxation* takes a fresh approach to taxation by providing two alternative topic sequences. In the *McGraw-Hill's Taxation of Individuals and Business Entities,* topics are grouped in **theme chapters,** including separate chapters on home ownership, compensation, investments, and retirement savings and deferred compensation. However, in the *Essentials of Federal Taxation,* topics follow a more traditional sequence with topics presented in a life-cycle approach.

> I believe it **breaks down complex topics in a way that's easy to understand.** Definitely easier than other tax textbooks that I've had experience with.
>
> – Jacob Gatlin, Athens State University

4. **Real-World Focus:** Students learn best when they see how concepts are applied in the real world. For that reason, real-world examples and articles are included in **"Taxes in the Real World"** boxes throughout the book. These vignettes demonstrate current issues in taxation and show the relevance of tax issues in all areas of business.

5. **Integrated Examples:** The examples used throughout the chapter relate directly to the storyline presented at the beginning of each chapter, so students become familiar with one set of facts and learn how to apply those facts to different scenarios. In addition to providing in-context examples, we provide **"What if"** scenarios within many examples to **illustrate how variations in the facts might or might not change the answers.**

> **Excellent text; love the story line approach and integrated examples.** It's easy to read and understand explanations. The language of the text is very clear and straightforward.
>
> – Sandra Owen, Indiana University – Bloomington

A STORYLINE APPROACH THAT WILL RESONATE WITH STUDENTS

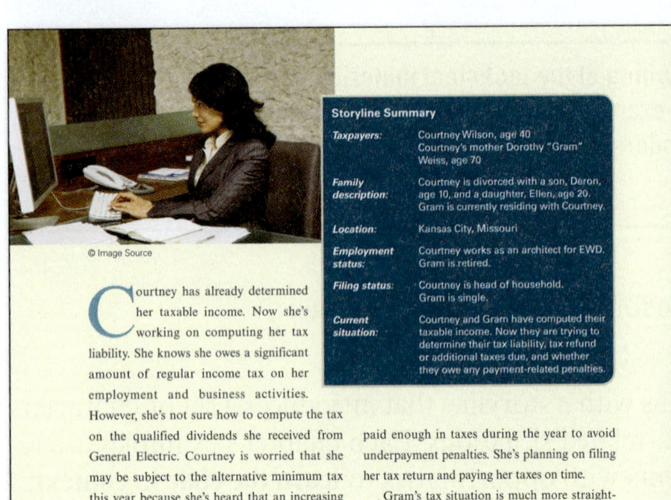

© Image Source

Storyline Summary

Taxpayers:	Courtney Wilson, age 40 Courtney's mother Dorothy "Gram" Weiss, age 70
Family description:	Courtney is divorced with a son, Deron, age 10, and a daughter, Ellen, age 20. Gram is currently residing with Courtney.
Location:	Kansas City, Missouri
Employment status:	Courtney works as an architect for EWD. Gram is retired.
Filing status:	Courtney is head of household. Gram is single.
Current situation:	Courtney and Gram have computed their taxable income. Now they are trying to determine their tax liability, tax refund or additional taxes due, and whether they owe any payment-related penalties.

Courtney has already determined her taxable income. Now she's working on computing her tax liability. She knows she owes a significant amount of regular income tax on her employment and business activities. However, she's not sure how to compute the tax on the qualified dividends she received from General Electric. Courtney is worried that she may be subject to the alternative minimum tax this year because she's heard that an increasing number of taxpayers in her income range must pay the tax. Finally, Courtney knows she owes some self-employment taxes on her business income. Courtney would like to determine whether she is eligible to claim any tax credits such as the child tax credit for her two children and education credits because she paid for a portion of her daughter Ellen's tuition at the University of Missouri–Kansas

paid enough in taxes during the year to avoid underpayment penalties. She's planning on filing her tax return and paying her taxes on time.

Gram's tax situation is much more straightforward. She needs to determine the regular income tax on her taxable income. Her income is so low she knows she need not worry about the alternative minimum tax, and she believes she doesn't owe any self-employment tax. Gram didn't prepay any taxes this year, so she is concerned that she might be required to pay an underpayment penalty. She also expects to file her tax return and pay her

Each chapter begins with a storyline that introduces a set of characters facing specific tax-related situations. This revolutionary approach to teaching tax emphasizes real people facing real tax dilemmas. Students learn to apply practical tax information to specific business and personal situations. The characters are brought further to life.

> The text provides very useful tools that students can read and understand, making it easier to **break the myth that "tax is hard."**
>
> – Daniel Hoops, Walsh College
>
> **I absolutely love this textbook.** This textbook makes my job of teaching so much easier.
>
> – Chuck Pier, Angelo State University

Examples

Examples are the cornerstone of any textbook covering taxation. For this reason, *McGraw-Hill's Taxation* authors took special care to create clear and helpful examples that relate to the storyline of the chapter. Students learn to refer to the facts presented in the storyline and apply them to other scenarios—in this way, they build a greater base of knowledge through application. Many examples also include "What if?" scenarios that add more complexity to the example or explore related tax concepts.

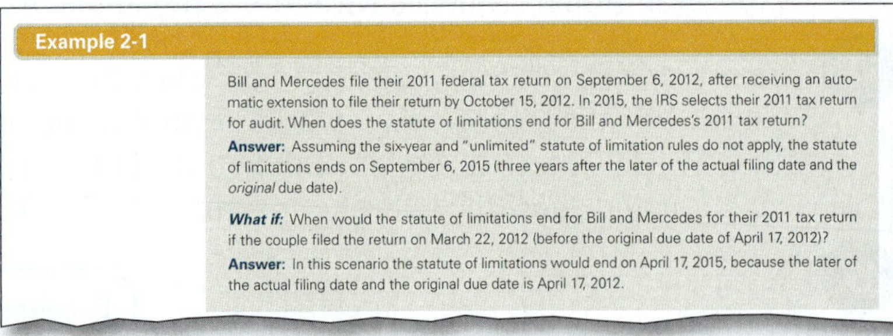

Example 2-1

Bill and Mercedes file their 2011 federal tax return on September 6, 2012, after receiving an automatic extension to file their return by October 15, 2012. In 2015, the IRS selects their 2011 tax return for audit. When does the statute of limitations end for Bill and Mercedes's 2011 tax return?

Answer: Assuming the six-year and "unlimited" statute of limitation rules do not apply, the statute of limitations ends on September 6, 2015 (three years after the later of the actual filing date and the *original* due date).

What if: When would the statute of limitations end for Bill and Mercedes for their 2011 tax return if the couple filed the return on March 22, 2012 (before the original due date of April 17, 2012)?

Answer: In this scenario the statute of limitations would end on April 17, 2015, because the later of the actual filing date and the original due date is April 17, 2012.

> The **case study approach is excellent** as you follow the taxpayers through the chapters.
>
> – Irwin Uhr, Hunter College

THE PEDAGOGY YOUR STUDENTS NEED TO PUT THE CODE IN CONTEXT

Taxes in the Real World

Taxes in the Real World are short boxes used throughout the book to demonstrate the real-world use of tax concepts. Current articles on tax issues, real-world application of chapter-specific tax rules, and short vignettes on popular news about tax are some of the issues covered in Taxes in the Real World boxes.

> The Spilker text makes tax easy for students to understand. **It integrates great real-world examples so students can see how topics will be applied in practice.** The integration of the tax form and exhibits of the tax forms in the text are outstanding.
>
> – Kristen Bigbee, Texas Tech University

TAXES IN THE REAL WORLD Republicans vs. Democrats

We often boil down the tax policy of our major political parties into its simplest form: Democrats raise taxes to fund social programs, and Republicans lower taxes to benefit big businesses and the wealthy. Both ideas simplify the policy of each party, yet both ideas are essentially true.

Whether you agree with more government spending or tax breaks for corporations, each party's agenda will affect your taxes.

Political Ideology: Republican

"We believe government should tax only to raise money for its essential functions." The Republicans state their case plainly on the Republican National Convention website. That is, Republicans believe government should spend money only to enforce contracts, maintain basic infrastructure and national security, and protect citizens against criminals.

The literature of the House Republican Conference goes on to illuminate the role of the government and how tax policies affect individuals: "The money the government spends does not belong to the government; it belongs to the taxpayers who earned it. Republicans believe Americans deserve to keep more of their own money to save and invest for the future, and low tax policies help drive a strong and healthy economy."

Tax relief is the Republican route to growing the economy. A Republican government would reduce taxes for businesses to allow businesses to grow and thus hire more employees. Republicans also seek to limit income taxes for individuals so that people can hold on to more disposable income, which they can then spend, save, or invest.

Political Ideology: Democrat

The tax policy for the Democratic Party calls for raising certain taxes to provide money for government spending, which in turn generates business. The party platform asserts that government spending provides "good jobs and will help the economy today."

Many Democrats are adherents to Keynesian economics, or aggregate demand, which holds that when the government funds programs, those programs pump new money into the economy. Keynesians believe that prices tend to stay relatively stable and therefore any kind of spending, whether by consumers or the government, will grow the economy.

Like the Republicans, Democrats believe the government should subsidize vital services that keep cities, states, and the country running: infrastructure such as road and bridge maintenance and repairs for schools. Democrats also call for tax cuts for the middle class. But who benefits most under each platform? The conventional wisdom is that corporations and the wealthy will benefit more with a Republican tax policy, while small businesses and middle-class households will benefit from a Democratic tax policy.

http://www.investopedia.com/articles/economics/09/us-parties-republican-democrat-taxes.asp

The Key Facts

Marginal Key Facts provide quick synopses of the critical pieces of information presented throughout each chapter.

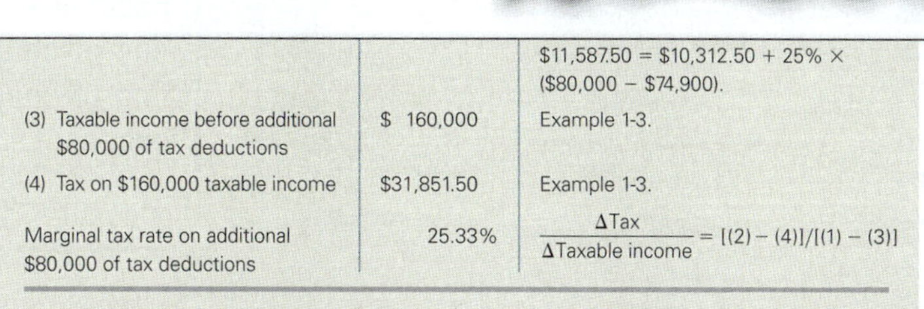

		\$11,587.50 = \$10,312.50 + 25% × (\$80,000 − \$74,900).
(3) Taxable income before additional \$80,000 of tax deductions	\$ 160,000	Example 1-3.
(4) Tax on \$160,000 taxable income	\$31,851.50	Example 1-3.
Marginal tax rate on additional \$80,000 of tax deductions	25.33%	$\frac{\Delta Tax}{\Delta Taxable\ income} = [(2) - (4)]/[(1) - (3)]$

THE KEY FACTS

Different Ways to Measure Tax Rates

- Marginal tax rate
  - The tax that applies to next increment of income or deduction.
  - $= \frac{\Delta Tax}{\Delta Taxable\ income}$

Exhibits

Today's students are visual learners, and *McGraw-Hill's Taxation* delivers by making appropriate use of charts, diagrams, and tabular demonstrations of key material.

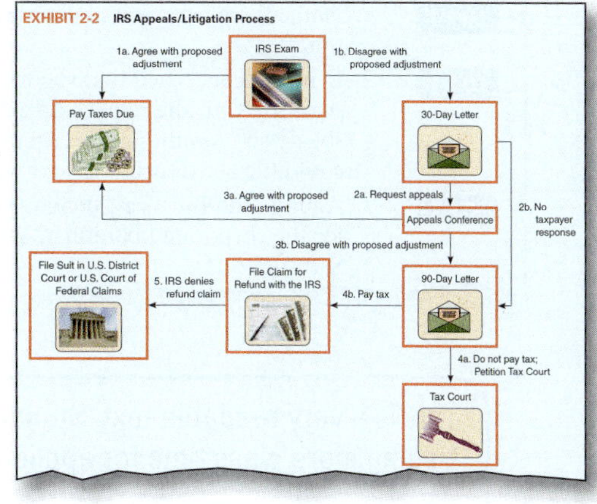

> A good textbook that uses **great examples throughout the chapters** to give a student an understanding of the tax theory and how it applies to the taxpayers.
>
> – Jennifer Wright, Drexel University

> Spilker's use of examples immediately following the concept is a **great way to reinforce the concepts.**
>
> – Karen Wisniewski, County College of Morris

PRACTICE MAKES PERFECT WITH A...

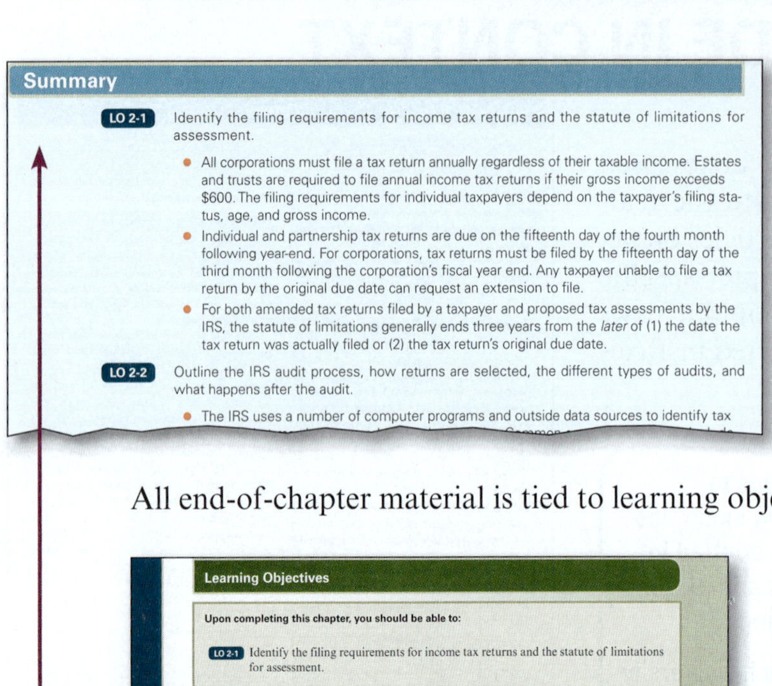

Summary

LO 2-1 Identify the filing requirements for income tax returns and the statute of limitations for assessment.

- All corporations must file a tax return annually regardless of their taxable income. Estates and trusts are required to file annual income tax returns if their gross income exceeds $600. The filing requirements for individual taxpayers depend on the taxpayer's filing status, age, and gross income.
- Individual and partnership tax returns are due on the fifteenth day of the fourth month following year-end. For corporations, tax returns must be filed by the fifteenth day of the third month following the corporation's fiscal year end. Any taxpayer unable to file a tax return by the original due date can request an extension to file.
- For both amended tax returns filed by a taxpayer and proposed tax assessments by the IRS, the statute of limitations generally ends three years from the *later* of (1) the date the tax return was actually filed or (2) the tax return's original due date.

LO 2-2 Outline the IRS audit process, how returns are selected, the different types of audits, and what happens after the audit.

- The IRS uses a number of computer programs and outside data sources to identify tax

Summary

A unique feature of *McGraw-Hill's Taxation* is the end-of-chapter summary organized around learning objectives. Each objective has a brief, bullet-point summary that covers the major topics and concepts for that chapter, including references to critical exhibits and examples.

All end-of-chapter material is tied to learning objectives:

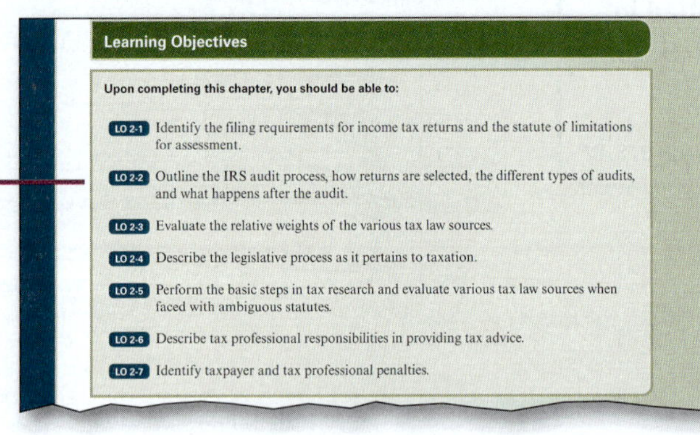

Learning Objectives

Upon completing this chapter, you should be able to:

LO 2-1 Identify the filing requirements for income tax returns and the statute of limitations for assessment.

LO 2-2 Outline the IRS audit process, how returns are selected, the different types of audits, and what happens after the audit.

LO 2-3 Evaluate the relative weights of the various tax law sources.

LO 2-4 Describe the legislative process as it pertains to taxation.

LO 2-5 Perform the basic steps in tax research and evaluate various tax law sources when faced with ambiguous statutes.

LO 2-6 Describe tax professional responsibilities in providing tax advice.

LO 2-7 Identify taxpayer and tax professional penalties.

You can tell the authors of this textbook are still in the classroom and responsible for the day-to-day education of accounting students. Examples are representative of the end-of-chapter problems, and the end-of-chapter summary is an excellent study tool.

– Debra Petrizzo, Franklin University

DISCUSSION QUESTIONS

LO 2-1 1. Name three factors that determine whether a tax return.

LO 2-1 2. Benita is concerned that she will not be able to co April 15. Can she request an extension to file her she do so? Assuming she requests an extension, w could file her return this year without penalty?

LO 2-1 3. Agua Linda Inc. is a calendar-year corporation. for the corporate tax return? What happens if the Saturday?

Discussion Questions are provided for each of the major concepts in each chapter, providing students with an opportunity to review key parts of the chapter and answer evocative questions about what they have learned.

This is a very readable text. **Students will understand it on their own,** generally, freeing more class time for application, practice, and student questions.

– Valrie Chambers,
Texas A&M University – Corpus Christi

...WIDE VARIETY OF ASSIGNMENT MATERIAL

Problems are designed to test the comprehension of more complex topics. Each problem at the end of the chapter is tied to one of that chapter's learning objectives, with multiple problems for critical topics.

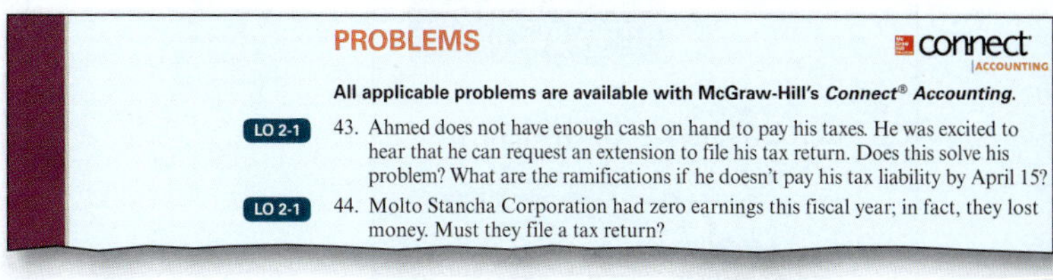
PROBLEMS connect ACCOUNTING

All applicable problems are available with McGraw-Hill's *Connect® Accounting*.

LO 2-1 43. Ahmed does not have enough cash on hand to pay his taxes. He was excited to hear that he can request an extension to file his tax return. Does this solve his problem? What are the ramifications if he doesn't pay his tax liability by April 15?

LO 2-1 44. Molto Stancha Corporation had zero earnings this fiscal year; in fact, they lost money. Must they file a tax return?

Tax Forms Problems are a set of requirements included in the end-of-chapter material of the 2016 edition. These problems require students to complete a tax form (or part of a tax form), providing students with valuable experience and practice with filling out these forms. These requirements—and their relevant forms—are also included in *Connect Accounting*. Each Tax Forms problem includes an icon to differentiate it from regular problems.

tax forms 70. Shauna Coleman is single. She is employed as an architectural designer for Streamline Design (SD). Shauna wanted to determine her taxable income for this year. She correctly calculated her AGI. However, she wasn't sure how to compute the rest of her taxable income. She provided the following information with hopes that you could use it to determine her taxable income.

a) Shauna paid $4,676 for medical expenses for care from a broken ankle. Also, Shauna's boyfriend, Blake, drove Shauna (in her car) a total of 115 miles to the doctor's office so she could receive care for her broken ankle.

b) Shauna paid a total of $3,400 in health insurance premiums during the year

Research Problems are special problems throughout the end of the chapter assignment material. These require students to do both basic and more complex research on topics outside of the scope of the book. Each Research Problem includes an icon to differentiate it from regular problems.

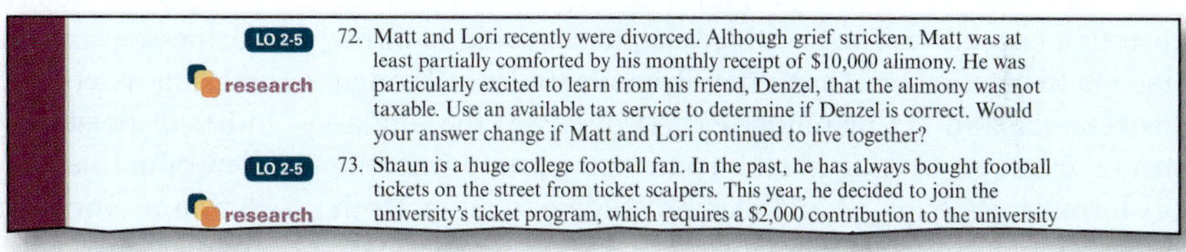
LO 2-5 research 72. Matt and Lori recently were divorced. Although grief stricken, Matt was at least partially comforted by his monthly receipt of $10,000 alimony. He was particularly excited to learn from his friend, Denzel, that the alimony was not taxable. Use an available tax service to determine if Denzel is correct. Would your answer change if Matt and Lori continued to live together?

LO 2-5 research 73. Shaun is a huge college football fan. In the past, he has always bought football tickets on the street from ticket scalpers. This year, he decided to join the university's ticket program, which requires a $2,000 contribution to the university

The textbook is comprehensive, uses an integrated approach to taxation, contains clear illustrations and examples in each chapter, and has **a wealth of end-of-chapter assignment material.**

– James P. Trebby, Marquette University

Planning Problems are another unique set of problems, also located at the end of the chapter assignment material. These require students to test their tax planning skills after covering the chapter topics. Each Planning Problem includes an icon to differentiate it from regular problems.

56. Jackie has a corporate client that has recently received a 30-day notice from the IRS with a $100,000 tax assessment. Her client is considering requesting an appeals conference to contest the assessment. What factors should Jackie advise her client to consider before requesting an appeals conference?

57. The IRS recently completed an audit of Shea's tax return and assessed $15,000 additional tax. Shea requested an appeals conference but was unable to settle the case at the conference. She is contemplating which trial court to choose to hear her case. Provide her a recommendation based on the following alternative facts:

a) Shea resides in the 2nd Circuit, and the 2nd Circuit has recently ruled against

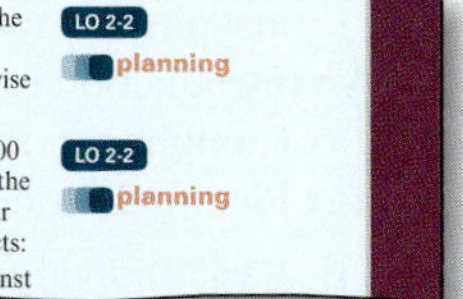

Comprehensive and Tax Return Problems address multiple concepts in a single problem. Comprehensive problems are ideal for cumulative topics; for this reason, they are located at the end of all chapters. In the end-of-book Appendix C, we include Tax Return Problems that cover multiple chapters. **Additional Tax Return Problems are also available on the *Connect Library*.**

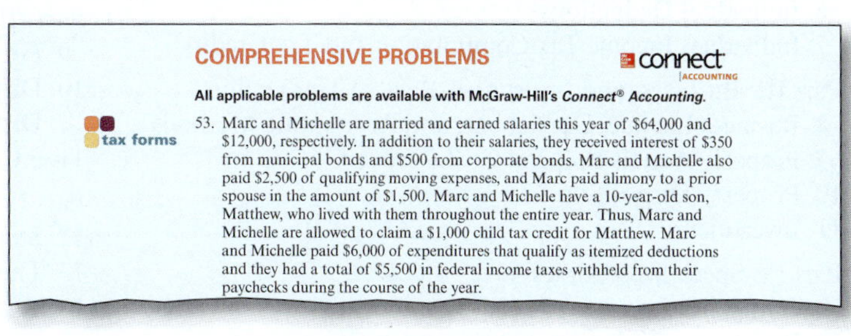
COMPREHENSIVE PROBLEMS connect ACCOUNTING

All applicable problems are available with McGraw-Hill's *Connect® Accounting*.

tax forms 53. Marc and Michelle are married and earned salaries this year of $64,000 and $12,000, respectively. In addition to their salaries, they received interest of $350 from municipal bonds and $500 from corporate bonds. Marc and Michelle also paid $2,500 of qualifying moving expenses, and Marc paid alimony to a prior spouse in the amount of $1,500. Marc and Michelle have a 10-year-old son, Matthew, who lived with them throughout the entire year. Thus, Marc and Michelle are allowed to claim a $1,000 child tax credit for Matthew. Marc and Michelle paid $6,000 of expenditures that qualify as itemized deductions and they had a total of $5,500 in federal income taxes withheld from their paychecks during the course of the year.

Four Volumes to Fit...

McGraw-Hill's Taxation of Individuals is organized to emphasize topics that are most important to undergraduates taking their first tax course. The first three chapters provide an introduction to taxation and then carefully guide students through tax research and tax planning. Part II discusses the fundamental elements of individual income tax, starting with the tax formula in Chapter 4 and then proceeding to more depth on individual topics in Chapters 5–7. Part III then discusses tax issues associated with business and investment activities. On the business side, it addresses business income and deductions, accounting methods, and tax consequences associated with purchasing assets and property dispositions (sales, trades, or other dispositions). For investments it covers portfolio-type investments such as stocks and bonds and business investments including loss limitations associated with these investments. Part IV is unique among tax textbooks; this section combines related tax issues for compensation, retirement savings, and home ownership.

Part I: Introduction to Taxation

1. An Introduction to Tax
2. Tax Compliance, the IRS, and Tax Authorities
3. Tax Planning Strategies and Related Limitations

Part II: Basic Individual Taxation

4. Individual Income Tax Overview
5. Gross Income and Exclusions
6. Individual Deductions
7. Individual Income Tax Computation and Tax Credits

Part III: Business- and Investment-Related Transactions

8. Business Income, Deductions, and Accounting Methods
9. Property Acquisition and Cost Recovery
10. Property Dispositions
11. Investments

Part IV: Specialized Topics

12. Compensation
13. Retirement Savings and Deferred Compensation
14. Tax Consequences of Home Ownership

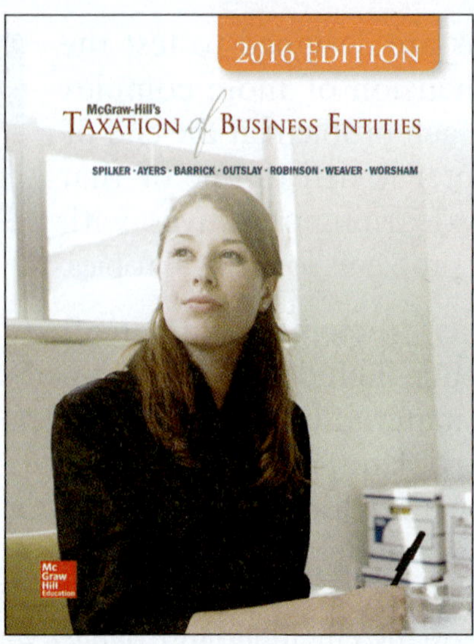

McGraw-Hill's Taxation of Business Entities begins with the process for determining gross income and deductions for businesses, and the tax consequences associated with purchasing assets and property dispositions (sales, trades, or other dispositions). Part II provides a comprehensive overview of entities, and the formation, reorganization, and liquidation of corporations. Unique to this series is a complete chapter on accounting for income taxes, which provides a primer on the basics of calculating the income tax provision. Included in the narrative is a discussion of temporary and permanent differences and their impact on a company's book "effective tax rate." Part III provides a detailed discussion of partnerships and S corporations. The last part of the book covers state and local taxation, multinational taxation, and transfer taxes and wealth planning.

Part I: Business- and Investment-Related Transactions

1. Business Income, Deductions, and Accounting Methods
2. Property Acquisition and Cost Recovery
3. Property Dispositions

Part II: Entity Overview and Taxation of C Corporations

4. Entities Overview
5. Corporate Operations
6. Accounting for Income Taxes
7. Corporate Taxation: Nonliquidating Distributions
8. Corporate Formation, Reorganization, and Liquidation

Part III: Taxation of Flow-Through Entities

9. Forming and Operating Partnerships
10. Dispositions of Partnership Interests and Partnership Distributions
11. S Corporations

Part IV: Multijurisdictional Taxation and Transfer Taxes

12. State and Local Taxes
13. The U.S. Taxation of Multinational Transactions
14. Transfer Taxes and Wealth Planning

...Four Course Approaches

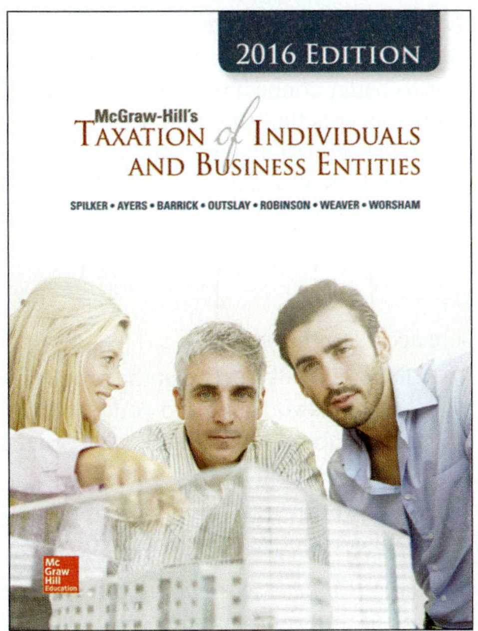

McGraw-Hill's Taxation of Individuals and Business Entities covers all chapters included in the two split volumes in one convenient volume.

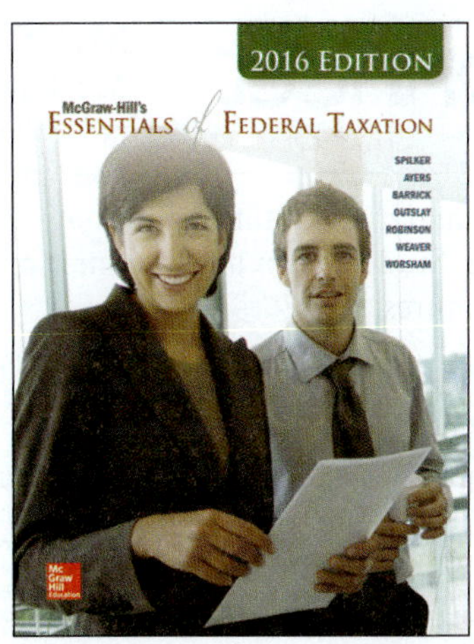

McGraw-Hill's Essentials of Federal Taxation is designed for a one-semester course, covering the basics of taxation of individuals and business entities. To facilitate a one-semester course, *McGraw-Hill's Essentials of Federal Taxation* folds the key topics from the investments, compensation, retirement savings, and home ownership chapters in *Taxation of Individuals* into three individual taxation chapters that discuss gross income and exclusions, for AGI deductions, and from AGI deductions, respectively. The essentials volume also includes a two-chapter C corporation sequence that uses a life-cycle approach covering corporate formations and then corporate operations in the first chapter and nonliquidating and liquidating corporate distributions in the second chapter. This volume is perfect for those teaching a one-semester course and for those who struggle to get through the 25-chapter comprehensive volume.

Part I: Introduction to Taxation

1. An Introduction to Tax
2. Tax Compliance, the IRS, and Tax Authorities
3. Tax Planning Strategies and Related Limitations

Part II: Individual Taxation

4. Individual Income Tax Overview
5. Gross Income and Exclusions
6. Individual for AGI Deductions
7. Individual from AGI Deductions
8. Individual Income Tax Computation and Tax Credits

Part III: Business-Related Transactions

9. Business Income, Deductions, and Accounting Methods
10. Property Acquisition and Cost Recovery
11. Property Dispositions

Part IV: Entity Overview and Taxation of C Corporations

12. Entities Overview
13. Corporate Formations and Operations
14. Corporate Nonliquidating and Liquidating Distributions

Part V: Taxation of Flow-Through Entities

15. Forming and Operating Partnerships
16. Dispositions of Partnership Interests and Partnership Distributions
17. S Corporations

How Can Technology Help...

McGRAW-HILL *CONNECT ACCOUNTING*

McGraw-Hill *Connect Accounting* is a digital teaching and learning environment that gives students the means to better connect with their coursework, their instructors, and the important concepts that they will need to know for success now and in the future. With *Connect Accounting*, instructors can deliver assignments, quizzes, and tests easily online. Students can review course material and practice important skills. *Connect Accounting* provides the following features:

- SmartBook and LearnSmart with additional learning resources.
- Auto-graded Online Homework.
- An integrated media-rich eBook, allowing for anytime, anywhere access to the textbook.

Through November, Tex has received gross income of $120,000. For December, Tex is considering whether to accept one more work engagement for the year. Engagement 1 will generate $7,000 of revenue at a cost of $4,000, which is deductible for AGI. In contrast, engagement 2 will generate $7,000 of revenue at a cost of $3,000, which is deductible as an itemized deduction. Tex files as a single taxpayer. (use the tax rate schedules.)

a. Calculate Tex's taxable income assuming he chooses engagement 1 and assuming he chooses engagement 2. Assume he has no itemized deductions other than those generated by engagement 2.

	Description	Engagement 1	Engagement 2
(1)	Gross income before new work engagement	$ 120,000	$ 120,000
(2)	Income from engagement	7,000	7,000
(3)	Additional for AGI deduction	(4,000)	
(4)	Adjusted gross income	$ 123,000	$ 127,000
(5)	Greater		
(6)	Greater of itemized deductions or standard deduction		

- Dynamic links between the problems or questions you assign to your students and the location in the eBook where that concept is covered.
- A powerful search function to pinpoint and connect key concepts to review.

In short, *Connect Accounting* offers students powerful tools and features that optimize their time and energy, enabling them to focus on learning.

For more information about *Connect Accounting,* go to **www.connect.mheducation.com,** or contact your local McGraw-Hill Higher Education representative.

SMARTBOOK™ SmartBook, powered by LearnSmart

LearnSmart™ is the market-leading adaptive study resource that is proven to strengthen memory recall, increase class retention, and boost grades. LearnSmart allows students to study more efficiently because they are made aware of what they know and don't know.

SmartBook™, which is powered by LearnSmart, is the first and only adaptive reading experience designed to change the way students read and learn. It creates a personalized reading experience by highlighting the most impactful concepts a student needs to learn at that moment in time. As a student engages with SmartBook, the reading experience continuously adapts by highlighting content based on what the student knows and doesn't know. This ensures that the focus is on the content he or she needs to learn, while simultaneously promoting long-term retention of material.

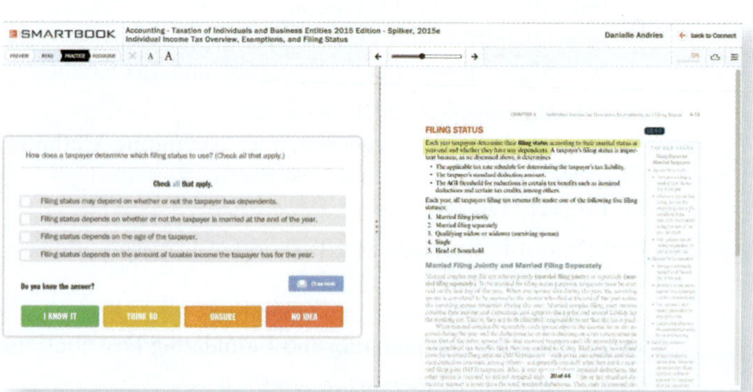

Use SmartBook's real-time reports to quickly identify the concepts that require more attention from individual students—or the entire class. The end result? Students are more engaged with course content, can better prioritize their time, and come to class ready to participate.

...Improve Student Success?

Online assignments

Connect Accounting helps students learn more efficiently by providing feedback and practice material when they need it, where they need it. *Connect* grades homework automatically and gives immediate feedback on any questions students may have missed. Our assignable, gradable end-of-chapter content includes a general journal application that looks and feels like what you would find in a general ledger software package. Also, select questions have been redesigned to test students' knowledge more fully. They now include tables for students to work through rather than requiring that all calculations be done offline.

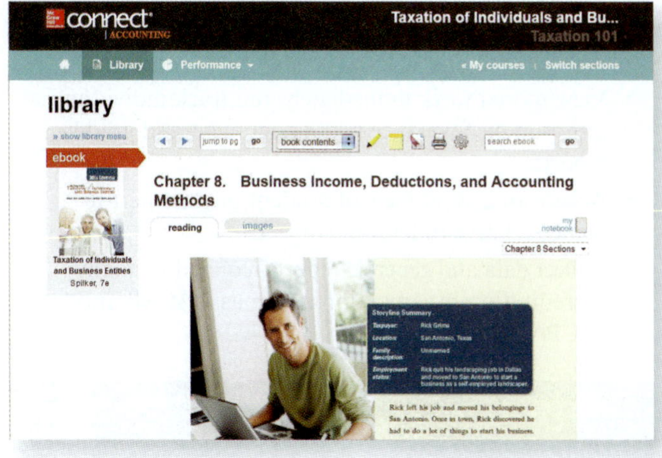

Student Resource Library

The *Connect Accounting* Student Resources give students access to additional resources such as recorded lectures, online practice materials, an eBook, and more.

McGRAW-HILL *CONNECT ACCOUNTING* FEATURES

Connect Accounting offers powerful tools, resources, and features to make managing assignments easier, so faculty can spend more time teaching.

Simple Assignment Management and Smart Grading With *Connect Accounting,* students can engage with their coursework anytime, anywhere, making the learning process more accessible and efficient.

- Create and deliver assignments easily with selectable end-of-chapter questions and test bank items.
- Have assignments scored automatically, giving students immediate feedback on their work and comparisons with correct answers.
- Access and review each response; manually change grades or leave comments for students to review.
- Reinforce classroom concepts with practice assignments, instant quizzes, and exams.

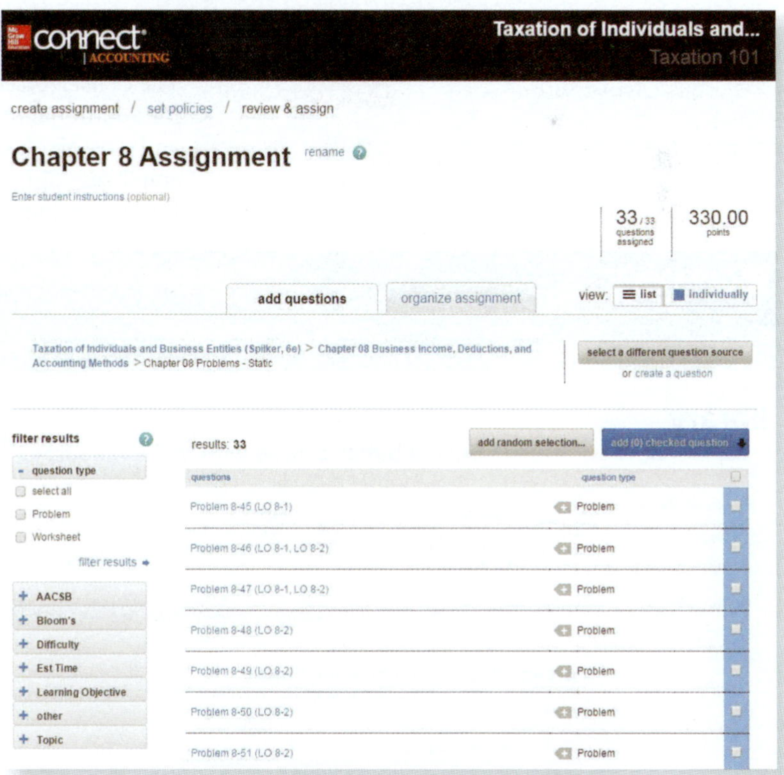

Powerful Instructor and Student Reports

Connect Accounting keeps instructors informed about how each student, section, and class is performing, allowing for more productive use of lecture and office hours. The reports tab enables you to:

- View scored work immediately and track individual or group performance with assignment and grade reports.
- Access an instant view of student or class performance relative to learning objectives.
- Collect data and generate reports required by many accreditation organizations, such as AACSB and AICPA.

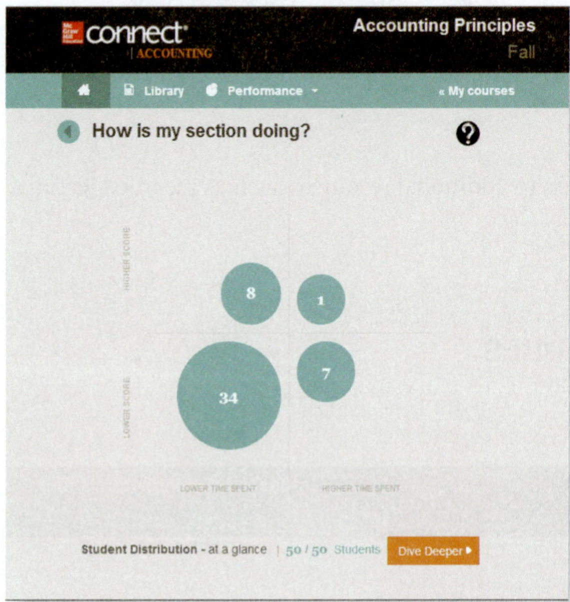

Connect Insight

The first and only analytics tool of its kind, Connect Insight™ is a series of visual data displays—each framed by an intuitive question—to provide at-a-glance information regarding how your class is doing.

Connect Insight™ provides an at-a-glance analysis on five key insights, available at a moment's notice from your tablet device.

- How are my students doing?
- How is my section doing?
- How is this student doing?
- How are my assignments doing?
- How is this assignment going?

Instructor Library

The *Connect Accounting* Instructor Library is your repository for additional resources to improve student engagement in and out of class. You can select and use any asset that enhances your lecture. The *Connect Accounting* Instructor Library includes access to:

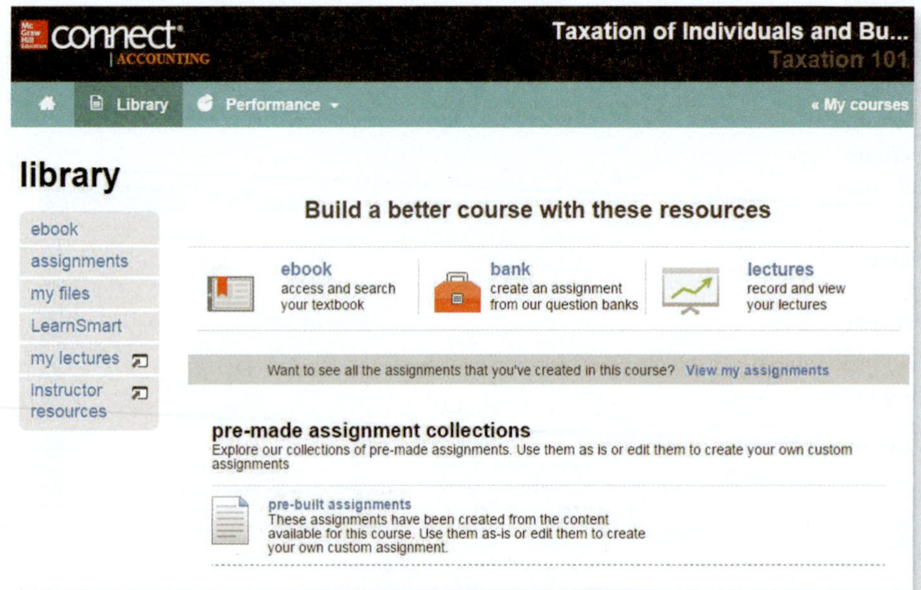

- Solutions Manual
- Instructor's Manual
- Test Bank
- Instructor PowerPoint® slides

TEGRITY CAMPUS: LECTURES 24/7

Tegrity Campus, is a service that makes class time available 24/7 by automatically capturing every lecture. With a simple one-click start-and-stop process, you capture all computer screens and corresponding audio in a format that is easily searchable, frame by frame. Students can replay any part of any class with easy-to-use browser-based viewing on a PC, Mac, or other mobile device.

Help turn your students' study time into learning moments immediately supported by your lecture. With Tegrity Campus, you also increase intent listening and class participation by easing students' concerns about note-taking. Lecture Capture will make it more likely you will see students' faces, not the tops of their heads. To learn more about Tegrity, watch a 2-minute Flash demo at **http://tegritycampus.mhhe.com.**

McGraw-Hill Campus

McGraw-Hill Campus™ is a new one-stop teaching and learning experience available to users of any learning management system. This institutional service allows faculty and students to enjoy single sign-on (SSO) access to all McGraw-Hill Higher Education materials, including the award-winning McGraw-Hill *Connect Plus* platform, from directly within the institution's website. To learn more about MH Campus, visit **http://mhcampus.mhhe.com.**

Custom Publishing through Create

McGraw-Hill Create™ is a new, self-service website that allows instructors to create custom course materials by drawing upon McGraw-Hill's comprehensive, cross-disciplinary content. Instructors can add their own content quickly and easily and tap into other rights-secured third-party sources as well, then arrange the content in a way that makes the most sense for their course. Instructors can even personalize their book with the course name and information and choose the best format for their students—color print, black-and-white print, or an eBook.

Through Create, instructors can

- Select and arrange the content in a way that makes the most sense for their course.
- Combine material from different sources and even upload their own content.
- Choose the best format for their students—print or eBook.
- Edit and update their course materials as often as they like.

Begin creating now at **www.mcgrawhillcreate.com.**

McGraw-Hill Customer Experience Group Contact Information

At McGraw-Hill, we understand that getting the most from new technology can be challenging. That's why our services don't stop after you purchase our products. You can contact our Product Specialists 24 hours a day to get product training online. Or you can search the knowledge bank of Frequently Asked Questions on our support website. For Customer Support, call **800-331-5094,** or visit **www.mhhe.com/support.** One of our Technical Support Analysts will be able to assist you in a timely fashion.

KAPLAN SIMULATIONS

CPA REVIEW

Apply the knowledge you've gained through *McGraw-Hill's Taxation* with CPA Review simulations from Kaplan and McGraw-Hill Education! Each CPA simulation demonstrates taxation concepts in a Web-based interface, identical to that used in the actual CPA exam. CPA simulations are found in the homework material after the very last case in selected chapters in your book.

TaxACT®

TaxACT

McGraw-Hill's Taxation can be packaged with tax software from TaxACT, one of the leading preparation software companies in the market today. The 2015 edition includes availability of both Individuals and Business Entities software, including the 1040 forms and TaxACT Preparer's Business 3-Pack (with Forms 1065, 1120, and 1120S).

SUPPLEMENTS FOR INSTRUCTORS

Assurance of Learning Ready

Many educational institutions today are focused on the notion of *assurance of learning*, an important element of many accreditation standards. *McGraw-Hill's Taxation* is designed specifically to support your assurance of learning initiatives with a simple, yet powerful, solution.

Each chapter in the book begins with a list of numbered learning objectives, which appear throughout the chapter as well as in the end-of-chapter assignments. Every Test Bank question for *McGraw-Hill's Taxation* maps to a specific chapter learning objective in the textbook. Each Test Bank question also identifies topic area, level of difficulty, Bloom's Taxonomy level, and AICPA and AACSB skill area. You can use our Test Bank software, *EZ Test Online*, or *Connect Accounting* to easily search for learning objectives that directly relate to the learning objectives for your course. You can then use the reporting features of *EZ Test* to aggregate student results in similar fashion, making the collection and presentation of Assurance of Learning data simple and easy.

AACSB Statement

McGraw-Hill/Irwin is a proud corporate member of AACSB International. Understanding the importance and value of AACSB accreditation, *McGraw-Hill's Taxation* recognizes the curricula guidelines detailed in the AACSB standards for business accreditation by connecting selected questions in the text and the Test Bank to the general knowledge and skill guidelines in the revised AACSB standards.

The statements contained in *McGraw-Hill's Taxation* are provided only as a guide for the users of this textbook. The AACSB leaves content coverage and assessment within the purview of individual schools, the mission of the school, and the faculty. While *McGraw-Hill's Taxation* and the teaching package make no claim of any specific AACSB qualification or evaluation, we have, within the text and test bank, labeled selected questions according to the eight general knowledge and skill areas.

McGraw-Hill's *Connect Accounting*

Connect Accounting offers a number of powerful tools and features to make managing your classroom easier. *Connect Accounting* with *McGraw-Hill's Taxation* offers enhanced features and technology to help both you and your students make the most of your time inside and outside the classroom.

EZ Test Online

This test bank in Word™ format contains multiple-choice questions, essay questions, and short problems. Each test item is coded for level of difficulty, learning objective, AACSB and AICPA skill area, and Bloom's Taxonomy level.

McGraw-Hill's EZ Test Online is a flexible and easy-to-use electronic testing program that allows instructors to create tests from book-specific items. EZ Test Online accommodates a wide range of question types and allows instructors to add their own questions. Multiple versions of the test can be created and any test can be exported for use with course management systems such as BlackBoard/WebCT. EZ Test Online gives instructors a place to easily administer exams and quizzes online. The program is available for Windows and Macintosh environments.

A HEARTFELT THANKS TO THE MANY COLLEAGUES WHO SHAPED THIS BOOK

The version of the book you are reading would not be the same book without the valuable suggestions, keen insights, and constructive criticisms of the list of reviewers below. Each professor listed here contributed in substantive ways to the organization of chapters, coverage of topics, and the use of pedagogy. We are grateful to them for taking the time to read chapters or attend reviewer conferences, focus groups, and symposia in support of the development for the book:

2015 Edition Reviewers

Kevin Baugess, *ICDC College*
Suzon Bridges, *Houston Community College*
Lisa Ekmekjian, *William Paterson University*
Ann Esarco, *Columbia College Columbia*
Robert Gary, *University of New Mexico*
Marcye Hampton, *University of Central Florida*
Melanie Hicks, *Liberty University*
Athena Jones, *University of Maryland University College*
Sandra Kemper, *Regis University*
Jack Lachman, *Brooklyn College*
Stacie Laplante, *University of Wisconsin Madison*
Stephanie Lewis, *Ohio State University Columbus*
Robert Lin, *California State University East Bay*
Anthony Masino, *East Tennessee State University*
Lisa McKinney, *University of Alabama at Birmingham*
Allison McLeod, *University of North Texas*
Frank Messina, *University of Alabama at Birmingham*
Michelle Moshier, *University at Albany*
Leslie Mostow, *University of Maryland, College Park*
Jackie Myers, *Sinclair Community College*
Jeff Paterson, *Florida State University*
James Pierson, *Franklin University*
Anthony Pochesci, *Rutgers University*
Terrie Stolte, *Columbus State Community College*
Marvin Williams, *University of Houston—Downtown*
Massood Yahya-Zadeh, *George Mason University*
Scott Yetmar, *Cleveland State University*

Acknowledgments

We would like to thank the many talented people who made valuable contributions to the creation of this sixth edition. William A. Padley of Madison Area Technical College, and Deanna Sharpe of the University of Missouri—Columbia checked the page proofs, Testbank, and Solutions Manual for accuracy; we greatly appreciate the hours they spent checking tax forms and double-checking our calculations throughout the book. Many thanks also to Jim Young for providing the tax numbers for 2015 well before the IRS made them available. Special thanks to Troy Lewis of Brigham Young University for his sharp eye and valuable feedback throughout the revision process. William A. Padley of Madison Area Technical College, Deanna Sharpe of the University of Missouri, Vivian Paige of Old Dominion University, and Teressa Farough greatly contributed to the accuracy of McGraw-Hill's *Connect Accounting* for the 2016 edition.

We also appreciate the expert attention given to this project by the staff at McGraw-Hill Education, especially Tim Vertovec, Managing Director; Kathleen Klehr, Senior Brand Manager; Danielle Andries, Product Developer; Lori Koetters, Brian Nacik, and Jill Eccher, Content Project Managers; Brad Parkins, Marketing Director; Matthew Diamond, Designer; and Sue Culbertson, Senior Buyer.

Changes in *Taxation of Individuals*, 2016 Edition

For the 2016 edition of McGraw Hill's *Taxation of Individuals,* many changes were made in response to feedback from reviewers and focus group participants:

- All **tax forms** have been **updated for the latest available tax form as of January 2015.** In addition, **chapter content** throughout the text has been **updated to reflect tax law changes through January 2015.**

Other notable changes in the 2016 edition include:

Chapter 2

- Updated for 2015 inflation adjustments and legislative changes.
- Revised discussion of Circular 230.
- Revised discussion of registered tax return preparers.
- Removed discussion of preparer tax identification number, related fees, and continuing education requirements due to recent judicial action.

Chapter 3

- Updated chapter for legislative changes.
- Updated Exhibit 3-3 for new tax rates.
- Added additional discussion relating to the conversion strategy and after-tax rates of returns.
- Added new example for conversion strategy.
- Added new Taxes in the Real World.
- Added ten new problems to end of chapter material.

Chapter 4

- Updated personal exemption amounts for 2014.
- Updated standard deduction amounts for 2014.
- Updated tax rates for 2014.
- Deleted portion of example referring to the tax tables.
- Deleted the appendix containing a sample page from the tax tables.

Chapter 5

- Updated for legislative changes.
- Updated for 2015 inflation adjustments.
- Updated for new tax forms.
- Revised Taxes in the Real World.
- Expanded discussion of 529 plans and Coverdell accounts.
- Expanded discussion of U.S. Series EE bonds.

Chapter 6

- Updated for legislative changes.
- Updated for 2015 inflation adjustments.
- Updated for new tax forms.
- Revised investment interest expense discussion.
- Revised actual cost method discussion for automobiles.

Chapter 7

- This chapter was formerly chapter 11 in previous editions and updated based on reviewer feedback.
- Modified chapter for new location in text
- Update chapter for legislative changes and new tax forms.
- Added new story line to improve flow and understanding of investments chapter
- Revised the Taxes in the Real World
- Eliminated discussion of tax-exempt income (now in chapter 5)
- Moved discussion of after-tax rates of return from investments to chapter 3 (conversion strategy).
- Added new examples for taxation of dividend income.
- Eliminated irrelevant end of chapter problems.

Chapter 8

- This chapter was formerly chapter 7 in previous editions and updated based on reviewer feedback.
- Updated for legislative changes.
- Updated for 2015 inflation adjustments.
- Revised Taxes in the Real World.
- Revised employee FICA tax discussion.
- Revised self-employment tax discussion and related examples.
- Updated for new tax forms.

Chapter 9

- This chapter was formerly chapter 8 in previous editions and updated based on reviewer feedback.
- Updated for 2015 inflation-adjusted limitations.
- Updated for new tax forms.

Chapter 10

- This chapter was formerly chapter 9 in previous editions and updated based on reviewer feedback.
- Updated chapter for legislative changes.
- Added new discussion and footnotes regarding depreciation amounts taken in last year of asset's recovery period.

- Added additional discussion to clarify business income for purposes of the §179 income limitation
- Clarified reporting requirements when taxpayer elects out of bonus depreciation.
- Added two new Taxes in the Real World.
- Added three new problems to end of chapter material.
- Eliminated unnecessary footnotes to streamline chapter.

Chapter 11

- This chapter was formerly chapter 10 in previous editions and updated based on reviewer feedback.
- Updated chapter for legislative changes.
- Revised examples affected by tax law changes.
- Revised discussion of depreciation recapture to clarify the concept

Chapter 13

- Updated inflation adjusted limits for defined benefit plans, defined contribution plans, and individually managed plans.
- Updated AGI phase-out thresholds for deductible contributions to traditional IRAs and contributions to Roth IRAs.
- Updated Saver's credit information.
- Updated Exhibit 13-6 describing Coca-Cola's nonqualified deferred compensation plan.
- Edited footnote to indicate that taxpayers who roll over funds from a traditional IRA (or other traditional retirement account) to a Roth must wait at least five years from the date of the rollover to withdraw the funds from the rollover in order to avoid a 10% penalty on the distribution.
- Removed Taxes in the Real World dealing with IRA to Roth IRA conversions.
- Added discussion comparing traditional and Roth IRAs, indicating that taxpayers can withdraw their Roth contributions tax free at any time without paying tax or paying a penalty. Taxpayers who withdraw their traditional IRA contributions are taxed on the distribution and potentially penalized.
- Updated and expanded flowchart on traditional IRA deduction limitations in Appendix A.
- Updated flowchart on Roth IRA contribution limits in Appendix B.

Chapter 14

- Added a footnote indicating that qualified mortgage interest is an itemized deduction that is subject to the overall phase-out of itemized deductions.
- Added a footnote indicating that real property tax deductions are itemized deductions that are subject to the overall phase-out of itemized deductions.
- Deleted the discussion of the First-Time Homebuyer Tax Credit and the related example. Also deleted mention of the First-Time Homebuyer Tax Credit from learning objective.
- Updated settlement statement in Appendix A.

As We Go to Press

The 2016 Edition is current through March 2, 2015. You can go to the *Connect Library* for updates that occur after this date.

Table of Contents

14 Tax Consequences of Home Ownership

McGraw-Hill's Taxation of Individuals

chapter

An Introduction to Tax

Learning Objectives

Upon completing this chapter, you should be able to:

- **LO 1-1** Demonstrate how taxes influence basic business, investment, personal, and political decisions.
- **LO 1-2** Discuss what constitutes a tax and the general objectives of taxes.
- **LO 1-3** Describe the different tax rate structures and calculate a tax.
- **LO 1-4** Identify the various federal, state, and local taxes.
- **LO 1-5** Apply appropriate criteria to evaluate alternate tax systems.

© Andrew Rich/Getty Images

Storyline Summary

Taxpayers:	Margaret
Employment status:	Margaret is a full-time student at the University of Georgia.
Current situation:	She is beginning her first tax class.

Margaret is a junior beginning her first tax course. She is excited about her career prospects as an accounting major but hasn't had much exposure to taxes. On her way to campus she runs into an old friend, Eddy, who is going to Washington, DC, to protest recent proposed changes to the U.S. tax system. Eddy is convinced the IRS is evil and that the current tax system is blatantly unfair and corrupt. He advocates a simpler, fairer way of taxation. Margaret is intrigued by Eddy's passion but questions whether he has a complete understanding of the U.S. tax system. She decides to withhold all judgments about it (or about pursuing a career in taxation) until the end of her tax course. ■

LO 1-1

WHO CARES ABOUT TAXES AND WHY?

A clear understanding of the role of taxes in everyday decisions will help you make an informed decision about the value of studying taxation or pursuing a career in taxation. One view of taxation is that it represents an inconvenience every April 15th (the annual due date for filing federal individual tax returns without extensions). However, the role of taxation is much more pervasive than this view suggests. Your study of this subject will provide you a unique opportunity to develop an informed opinion about taxation. As a business student, you can overcome the mystery that encompasses popular impressions of the tax system and perhaps, one day, share your expertise with friends or clients.

What are some common decisions you face that taxes may influence? In this course, we alert you to situations in which you can increase your return on investments by up to one third! Even the best lessons in finance courses can't approach the increase in risk-adjusted return that smart tax planning provides. Would you like to own your home someday? Tax deductions for home mortgage interest and real estate taxes can reduce the after-tax costs of owning a home relative to renting. Thus, when you face the decision to buy or rent, you can make an informed choice if you understand the relative tax advantages of home ownership. Would you like to retire someday? Understanding the tax-advantaged methods of saving for retirement can increase the after-tax value of your retirement nest egg—and thus increase the likelihood that you can afford to retire, and do so in style. Other common personal financial decisions that taxes influence include: choosing investments, evaluating alternative job offers, saving for education expenses, and doing gift or estate planning. Indeed, taxes are a part of everyday life and have a significant effect on many of the personal financial decisions all of us face.

The role of taxes is not limited to personal finance. Taxes play an equally important role in fundamental business decisions such as the following:

- What organizational form should a business use?
- Where should the business locate?
- How should business acquisitions be structured?
- How should the business compensate employees?
- What is the appropriate mix of debt and equity for the business?
- Should the business rent or own its equipment and property?
- How should the business distribute profits to its owners?

Savvy business decisions require owners and managers to consider all costs and benefits in order to evaluate the merits of a transaction. Although taxes don't necessarily dominate these decisions, they do represent large transaction costs that businesses should factor into the financial decision-making process.

Taxes also play a major part in the political process. U.S. presidential candidates often distinguish themselves from their opponents based upon their tax rhetoric. Indeed, the major political parties generally have very diverse views of the appropriate way to tax the public.[1] Determining who is taxed, what is taxed, and how much is taxed are tough questions with nontrivial answers. Voters must have a basic understanding of taxes to evaluate the merits of alternative tax proposals. Later in this chapter, we'll introduce criteria you can use to evaluate alternative tax proposals.

[1]The U.S. Department of the Treasury provides a "history of taxation" on its website (www.treasury.gov/resource-center/faqs/Taxes/Pages/historyrooseveltmessage.aspx). You may find it interesting to read this history in light of the various political parties in office at the time.

TAXES IN THE REAL WORLD Republicans vs. Democrats

We often boil down the tax policy of our major political parties into its simplest form: Democrats raise taxes to fund social programs, and Republicans lower taxes to benefit big businesses and the wealthy. Both ideas simplify the policy of each party, yet both ideas are essentially true.

Whether you agree with more government spending or tax breaks for corporations, each party's agenda will affect your taxes.

Political Ideology: Republican

"We believe government should tax only to raise money for its essential functions." The Republicans state their case plainly on the Republican National Convention website. That is, Republicans believe government should spend money only to enforce contracts, maintain basic infrastructure and national security, and protect citizens against criminals.

The literature of the House Republican Conference goes on to illuminate the role of the government and how tax policies affect individuals: "The money the government spends does not belong to the government; it belongs to the taxpayers who earned it. Republicans believe Americans deserve to keep more of their own money to save and invest for the future, and low tax policies help drive a strong and healthy economy."

Tax relief is the Republican route to growing the economy. A Republican government would reduce taxes for businesses to allow businesses to grow and thus hire more employees. Republicans also seek to limit income taxes for individuals so that people can hold on to more disposable income, which they can then spend, save, or invest.

Political Ideology: Democrat

The tax policy for the Democratic Party calls for raising certain taxes to provide money for government spending, which in turn generates business. The party platform asserts that government spending provides "good jobs and will help the economy today."

Many Democrats are adherents to Keynesian economics, or aggregate demand, which holds that when the government funds programs, those programs pump new money into the economy. Keynesians believe that prices tend to stay relatively stable and therefore any kind of spending, whether by consumers or the government, will grow the economy.

Like the Republicans, Democrats believe the government should subsidize vital services that keep cities, states, and the country running: infrastructure such as road and bridge maintenance and repairs for schools. Democrats also call for tax cuts for the middle class. But who benefits most under each platform? The conventional wisdom is that corporations and the wealthy will benefit more with a Republican tax policy, while small businesses and middle-class households will benefit from a Democratic tax policy.

http://www.investopedia.com/articles/economics/09/us-parties-republican-democrat-taxes.asp

In summary, taxes affect many aspects of personal, business, and political decisions. Developing a solid understanding of taxation should allow you to make informed decisions in these areas. Thus, Margaret can take comfort that her semester will likely prove useful to her personally. Who knows? Depending on her interest in business, investment, retirement planning, and the like, she may ultimately decide to pursue a career in taxation.

THE KEY FACTS

What Qualifies as a Tax?

- The general purpose of taxes is to fund government agencies.
- Unlike fines or penalties, taxes are not meant to punish or prevent illegal behavior; but *"sin taxes"* are meant to discourage some behaviors.
- The three criteria necessary to be a tax are that the payment is
  - required
  - imposed by a government
  - and not tied directly to the benefit received by the taxpayer.

WHAT QUALIFIES AS A TAX?

LO 1-2

"Taxes are the price we pay for a civilized society."—Oliver Wendell Holmes Jr.

Taxes have been described in many terms: some positive, some negative, some printable, some not. Let's go directly to a formal definition of a tax, which should prove useful in identifying alternative taxes and discussing alternative tax systems.

A **tax** *is a payment required by a government that is unrelated to any specific benefit or service received from the government.* The general purpose of a tax is to fund the operations of the government (to raise revenue). Taxes differ from fines and penalties in that taxes are not intended to punish or prevent illegal behavior. Nonetheless, by allowing deductions from income, our federal tax system does encourage

TAXES IN THE REAL WORLD Affordable Care Act

The Affordable Care Act has a new provision that takes effect in 2014. The provision requires individuals to be covered by a health insurance plan or to pay a tax—which is paid on the individual's income tax return. The adult annual dollar amount is phased in as follows: $95 for 2014; $325 for 2015; and $695 in 2016. The Congressional Budget Office and the Joint Committee on Taxation have jointly estimated that 5.9 million Americans will be subject to the penalty in 2016 and the provision will raise $6.9 billion in revenue in that year.

You may recall that one question the Supreme Court had to rule on was whether this provision was a "penalty" or a "tax." The Supreme Court held that the provision is a tax and answered as follows: "The payment is not so high that there is really no choice but to buy health insurance; the payment is not limited to willful violations, as penalties for unlawful acts often are; and the payment is collected solely by the (Internal Revenue Service) through the normal means of taxation," Chief Justice John Roberts wrote in the decision.

National Federation of Independent Business v. Sebelius, 132 S. Ct. 2566 (2012).

certain behaviors like charitable contributions, retirement savings, and research and development. Thus, we can view it as discouraging other legal behavior. For example, **sin taxes** impose relatively high surcharges on alcohol and tobacco products.[2] Another example is the shared-responsibility payment introduced by the Affordable Care Act. This payment was declared to be a "tax" by the Supreme Court. The tax is imposed on those who do not have minimum essential health care coverage.[3]

Key components of the definition of a tax are that

- the payment is required (it is not voluntary),
- the payment is imposed by a government agency (federal, state, or local), and
- the payment is not tied directly to the benefit received by the taxpayer.

This last point is not to say that taxpayers receive no benefits from the taxes they pay. They benefit from national defense, a judicial system, law enforcement, government-sponsored social programs, an interstate highway system, public schools, and many other government-provided programs and services. The distinction is that taxes paid are not *directly* related to any specific benefit received by the taxpayer. For example, the price of admission to Yellowstone National Park is a fee rather than a tax because a specific benefit is received.

Can taxes be assessed for special purposes, such as a 1 percent sales tax for education? Yes. Why is an **earmarked tax,** a tax that *is* assessed for a specific purpose, still considered a tax? Because the payment made by the taxpayer does not directly relate to the specific benefit *received by the taxpayer*.

Example 1-1

Margaret travels to Birmingham, Alabama, where she rents a hotel room and dines at several restaurants. The price she pays for her hotel room and meals includes an additional 2 percent city surcharge to fund roadway construction in Birmingham. Is this a tax?

Answer: Yes. The payment is required by a local government and does not directly relate to a specific benefit that Margaret receives.

[2]Sin taxes represent an interesting confluence of incentives. On the one hand, demand for such products as alcohol, tobacco, and gambling is often relatively inelastic because of their addictive quality. Thus, taxing such a product can raise substantial revenues. On the other hand, one of the arguments for sin taxes is frequently the social goal of *reducing* demand for such products.

[3]For details on the computation of the shared responsibility payment see Reg. §1.5000A-4.

Example 1-2

Margaret's parents, Bill and Mercedes, recently built a house and were assessed $1,000 by their county government to connect to the county sewer system. Is this a tax?

Answer: No. The assessment was mandatory and it was paid to a local government. However, the third criterion was not met since the payment directly relates to a specific benefit (sewer service) received by the payees. For the same reason, tolls, parking meter fees, and annual licensing fees are also not considered taxes.

HOW TO CALCULATE A TAX

LO 1-3

In its simplest form, the amount of tax equals the tax base multiplied by the tax rate:

Eq. 1-1 Tax = Tax base × Tax rate

The **tax base** defines what is actually taxed and is usually expressed in monetary terms, whereas the **tax rate** determines the level of taxes imposed on the tax base and is usually expressed as a percentage. For example, a sales tax rate of 6 percent on a purchase of $30 yields a tax of $1.80 ($1.80 = $30 × .06).

Federal, state, and local jurisdictions use a large variety of tax bases to collect tax. Some common tax bases (and related taxes) include taxable income (federal and state income taxes), purchases (sales tax), real estate values (real estate tax), and personal property values (personal property tax).

Different portions of a tax base may be taxed at different rates. A single tax applied to an entire base constitutes a **flat tax.** In the case of **graduated taxes,** the base is divided into a series of monetary amounts, or **brackets,** and each successive bracket is taxed at a different (gradually higher or gradually lower) percentage rate.

Calculating some taxes—income taxes for individuals or corporations, for example—can be quite complex. Advocates of flat taxes argue that the process should be simpler. But as we'll see throughout the text, most of the difficulty in calculating a tax rests in determining the tax *base,* not the tax rate. Indeed, there are only three basic tax rate structures (proportional, progressive, and regressive), and each can be mastered without much difficulty.

THE KEY FACTS

How to Calculate a Tax

- Tax = Tax base × Tax rate
- The tax base defines what is actually taxed and is usually expressed in monetary terms.
- The tax rate determines the level of taxes imposed on the tax base and is usually expressed as a percentage.
- Different portions of a tax base may be taxed at different rates.

DIFFERENT WAYS TO MEASURE TAX RATES

Before we discuss the alternative tax rate structures, let's first define three different tax rates that will be useful in contrasting the different tax rate structures: the marginal, average, and effective tax rates.

The **marginal tax rate** is the tax rate that applies to the *next additional increment* of a taxpayer's taxable income (or deductions). Specifically,

Eq. 1-2

$$\text{Marginal tax rate} = \frac{\Delta\text{Tax*}}{\Delta\text{Taxable income}} = \frac{(\text{New total tax} - \text{Old total tax})}{(\text{New taxable income} - \text{Old taxable income})}$$

*Δ means *change in*.

where "old" refers to the current tax and "new" refers to the revised tax after incorporating the additional income (or deductions) in question. In graduated income tax systems, additional income (deductions) can push a taxpayer into a higher (lower) tax bracket, thus changing the marginal tax rate.

Example 1-3

Margaret's parents, Bill and Mercedes, file a joint tax return. They have $160,000 of taxable income this year (after all tax deductions). Assuming the following federal tax rate schedule applies, how much federal income tax will they owe this year?[4]

2015 Federal Married Filing Jointly Tax Rate Schedule

If taxable income is over	But not over	The tax is:
$ 0	$ 18,150	10% of taxable income
18,450	74,900	$1,845.00 + 15% of taxable income in excess of $18,450
74,900	151,200	$10,312.50 + 25% of taxable income in excess of $74,900
151,200	230,450	$29,387.50 + 28% of taxable income in excess of $151,200
230,450	411,500	$51,577.50 + 33% of taxable income in excess of $230,450
411,500	464,850	$111,324.00 + 35% of taxable income in excess of $411,500
464,850	no limit	$129,996.50 + 39.6% of taxable income in excess of $464,850

Answer: Bill and Mercedes will owe $31,851.50 computed as follows:

$31,851.50 = $29,387.50 + 28% ($160,000 − $151,200)

Note that in this graduated tax rate structure, the first $18,450 of taxable income is taxed at 10 percent, the next $56,450 of taxable income (between $18,450 and $74,900) is taxed at 15 percent, and the next $76,300 of taxable income (between $74,900 and $151,200) is taxed at 25 percent. Bill and Mercedes's last $8,800 of taxable income (between $151,200 and $160,000) is taxed at 28 percent.

Many taxpayers incorrectly believe that all their income is taxed at their marginal rate. This mistake leads people to say, "I don't want to earn any additional money because it will put me in a higher tax bracket." Bill and Mercedes are currently in the 28 percent marginal tax rate bracket, but notice that *not* all their income is taxed at this rate. Their *marginal* tax rate is 28 percent. This means that small increases in income will be taxed at 28 percent, and small increases in tax deductions will generate tax *savings* of 28 percent. If Bill and Mercedes receive a large increase in income (or in deductions) such that they would change tax rate brackets, we cannot identify their marginal tax rate by simply identifying their current tax bracket.

Example 1-4

Bill, a well-known economics professor, signs a publishing contract with an $80,000 royalty advance. Using the rate schedule from Example 1-3, what would Bill and Mercedes's marginal tax rate be on this additional $80,000 of taxable income?

Answer: 28.60 percent, computed as follows:

Description	Amount	Explanation
(1) Taxable income with additional $80,000 of taxable income	$240,000	$80,000 plus $160,000 taxable income stated in Example 1-3.
(2) Tax on $240,000 taxable income	$ 54,729	Using the rate schedule in Example 1-3, $54,729 = $51,577.50 + 33% × ($240,000 − $230,450).

[4]The tax rate schedules for single, married filing jointly, married filing separately, and head of household are included inside the back cover of the text.

Description	Amount	Explanation
(3) Taxable income before additional $80,000 of taxable income	$ 160,000	Example 1-3.
(4) Tax on $160,000 taxable income	$31,851.50	Example 1-3.
Marginal tax rate on additional	28.60%	$\frac{\Delta\text{Tax}}{\Delta\text{Taxable income}} = [(2) - (4)]/[(1) - (3)]$

Note that Bill and Mercedes's marginal tax rate on the $80,000 increase in taxable income rests *between* the 28 percent and 33 percent bracket rates because a portion of the additional income ($230,450 − $160,000 = $70,450) is taxed at 28 percent with the remaining income ($240,000 − $230,450 = $9,550) taxed at 33 percent.

Example 1-5

Assume now that, instead of receiving a book advance, Bill and Mercedes start a new business that *loses* $80,000 this year (it results in $80,000 of additional tax deductions). What would be their marginal tax rate for these deductions?

Answer: 25.33 percent, computed as follows:

Description	Amount	Explanation
(1) Taxable income with additional $80,000 of tax deductions	$ 80,000	$160,000 taxable income stated in Example 1-3 less $80,000.
(2) Tax on $80,000 taxable income	$ 11,587.50	Using the rate schedule in Example 1-3, $11,587.50 = $10,312.50 + 25% × ($80,000 − $74,900).
(3) Taxable income before additional $80,000 of tax deductions	$ 160,000	Example 1-3.
(4) Tax on $160,000 taxable income	$31,851.50	Example 1-3.
Marginal tax rate on additional $80,000 of tax deductions	25.33%	$\frac{\Delta\text{Tax}}{\Delta\text{Taxable income}} = [(2) - (4)]/[(1) - (3)]$

Bill and Mercedes's marginal tax rate on $80,000 of additional deductions (25.33 percent) differs from their marginal tax rate on $80,000 of additional taxable income (28.60 percent) in these scenarios because of the relatively large increase in income and deductions. Taxpayers often will face the same marginal tax rates for small changes in income and deductions.

The marginal tax rate is particularly useful in tax planning because it represents the rate of taxation or savings that would apply to additional taxable income (or tax deductions). In Chapter 3, we discuss basic tax planning strategies that use the marginal tax rate.

The **average tax rate** represents a taxpayer's average level of taxation on each dollar of taxable income. Specifically,

Eq. 1-3

$$\text{Average tax rate} = \frac{\text{Total tax}}{\text{Taxable income}}$$

The average tax rate is often used in budgeting tax expense as a portion of income (what percent of taxable income earned is paid in tax).

THE KEY FACTS

Different Ways to Measure Tax Rates

- Marginal tax rate
  - The tax that applies to next increment of income or deduction.
  - $= \frac{\Delta\text{Tax}}{\Delta\text{Taxable income}}$
  - Useful in tax planning.
- Average tax rate
  - A taxpayer's average level of taxation on each dollar of *taxable* income.
  - $= \frac{\text{Total tax}}{\text{Total income}}$
  - Useful in budgeting tax expense.
- Effective tax rate
  - A taxpayer's average rate of taxation on each dollar of *total* income (taxable *and* nontaxable income).
  - $= \frac{\text{Total tax}}{\text{Total income}}$
  - Useful in comparing the relative tax burdens of taxpayers.

The **effective tax rate** represents the taxpayer's average rate of taxation on each dollar of total income (sometimes referred to as economic income), including taxable *and* nontaxable income. Specifically,

Eq. 1-4

$$\text{Effective tax rate} = \frac{\text{Total tax}}{\text{Total income}}$$

Relative to the average tax rate, the effective tax rate provides a better depiction of a taxpayer's tax burden because it depicts the taxpayer's total tax paid as a ratio of the sum of both taxable and nontaxable income earned.

Example 1-6

Assuming Bill and Mercedes have $160,000 of taxable income and $10,000 of nontaxable income, what is their average tax rate?

Answer: 19.91 percent, computed as follows:

Description	Amount	Explanation
(1) Taxable income	$ 160,000	
(2) Tax on $160,000 taxable income	$31,851.50	Example 1-3.
Average tax rate	19.91%	$\frac{\text{Total tax}}{\text{Taxable income}} = (2)/(1)$

We should not be surprised that Bill and Mercedes's average tax rate is lower than their marginal tax rate because, although they are currently in the 28 percent tax rate bracket, not all of their taxable income is subject to tax at 28 percent. The first $18,450 of their taxable income is taxed at 10 percent, their next $56,450 is taxed at 15 percent, their next $76,300 is taxed at 25 percent, and only their last $8,800 of taxable income is taxed at 28 percent. Thus, their average tax rate is considerably lower than their marginal tax rate.

Example 1-7

Again, given the same income figures as in Example 1-6 ($160,000 of taxable income and $10,000 of nontaxable income), what is Bill and Mercedes's effective tax rate?

Answer: 18.74 percent, computed as follows:

Description	Amount	Explanation
(1) Total income	$ 170,000	$160,000 taxable income plus $10,000 in nontaxable income (Example 1-6).
(2) Tax on $160,000 taxable income	$31,851.50	Example 1-3.
Effective tax rate	18.74%	$\frac{\text{Total tax}}{\text{Total income}} = (2)/(1)$

Should we be surprised that the effective tax rate is lower than the *average* tax rate? No, because except when the taxpayer has more nondeductible expenses (such as fines or penalties) than nontaxable income (such as tax-exempt interest), the effective tax rate will be equal to or less than the average tax rate.

TAX RATE STRUCTURES

There are three basic tax rate structures used to determine a tax: proportional, progressive, and regressive.

Proportional Tax Rate Structure

A **proportional tax rate structure,** also known as a flat tax, imposes a constant tax rate throughout the tax base. As the tax base increases, the taxes paid increase proportionally. Because this rate stays the same throughout all levels of the tax base, the marginal tax rate remains constant and, in fact, equals the average tax rate (see Exhibit 1-1). The most common example of a proportional tax is a sales tax, although Steve Forbes proposed a flat income tax as part of his 1996 and 2000 presidential campaigns.

To calculate the tax owed for a proportional tax, simply use Equation 1-1 to multiply the tax base by the tax rate.

$$\text{Proportional tax} = \text{Tax base} \times \text{Tax rate}$$

EXHIBIT 1-1 Proportional Tax Rate

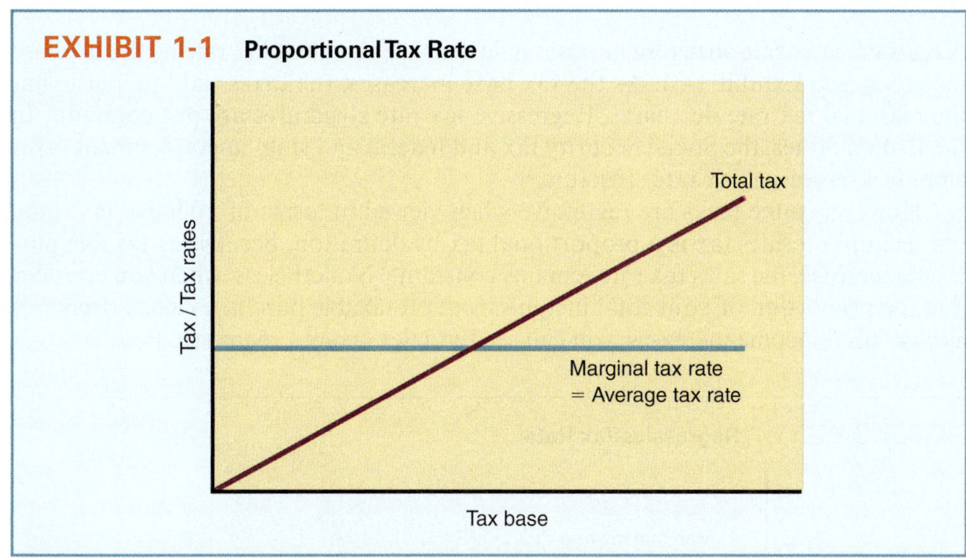

Example 1-8

Knowing her dad is a serious Bulldog fan, Margaret buys a $100 sweatshirt in downtown Athens. The city of Athens imposes a sales tax rate of 7 percent. How much tax does Margaret pay on the purchase?

Answer: $100 purchase (tax base) × 7% (tax rate) = $7

Progressive Tax Rate Structure

A **progressive tax rate structure** imposes an increasing marginal tax rate as the tax base increases. Thus as the tax base increases, both the marginal tax rate and the taxes paid increase. Common examples of progressive tax rate structures include federal and most state income taxes. The tax rate schedule in Example 1-3 is a progressive tax rate structure. As illustrated in Exhibit 1-2, the average tax rate in a progressive tax rate structure will always be less than or equal to the marginal tax rate.

EXHIBIT 1-2 **Progressive Tax Rate**

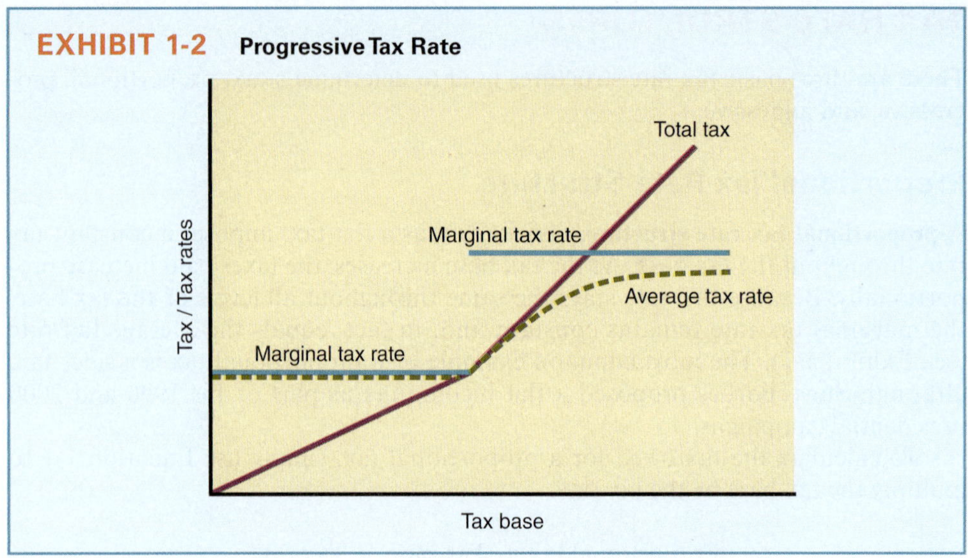

Regressive Tax Rate Structure

A **regressive tax rate structure** imposes a decreasing marginal tax rate as the tax base increases (see Exhibit 1-3). As the tax base increases, the taxes paid increase, but the marginal tax rate decreases. Regressive tax rate structures are not common. In the United States, the Social Security tax and federal and state unemployment taxes employ a regressive tax rate structure.[5]

However, some taxes are regressive when viewed in terms of effective tax rates. For example, a sales tax is a proportional tax by definition, because as taxable purchases increase, the sales tax rate remains constant.[6] Nonetheless, when you consider that the proportion of your total income spent on taxable purchases likely decreases as your total income increases, you can see the sales tax as a regressive tax.

EXHIBIT 1-3 **Regressive Tax Rate**

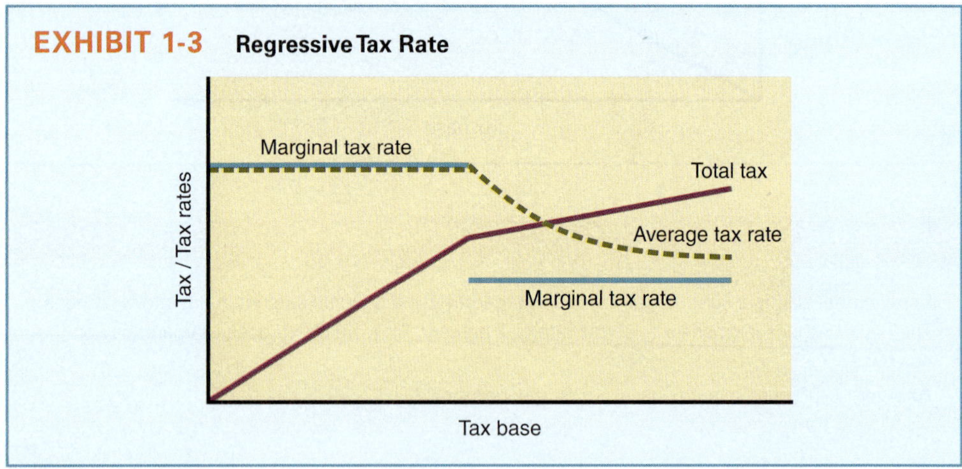

[5]Wages subject to the Social Security tax (6.2 percent in 2015) are capped each year ($118,500 in 2015). Wages in excess of the cap are not subject to the tax. As might be expected, the maximum Social Security retirement benefit is capped as a function of the maximum wage base. Likewise, the federal and state unemployment tax bases and related unemployment benefits are capped.

[6]For example, a destitute taxpayer likely spends all he makes on food and other items subject to the sales tax; thus, all of his income is subject to a sales tax. In contrast, a wealthy taxpayer likely spends only a small fraction of his income on items subject to sales tax (while saving the rest). Thus, less of wealthy taxpayers' total income is subject to the sales tax, which ultimately results in a lower effective tax rate.

Example 1-9

Bill and Mercedes have two single friends, Elizabeth and Marc, over for dinner. Elizabeth earns $300,000 as CFO of a company and spends $70,000 for purchases subject to the 7 percent sales tax. Marc, who earns $75,000 as a real estate agent, spends $30,000 of his income for taxable purchases. Let's compare their marginal, average, and effective tax rates for the sales tax with Bill and Mercedes, who spend $50,000 of their income for taxable purchases:

	Elizabeth	Bill and Mercedes	Marc
Total income (1)	$300,000	$170,000	$75,000
Total purchases subject to 7% sales tax (2)	$ 70,000	$ 50,000	$30,000
Sales tax paid (3)	$ 4,900	$ 3,500	$ 2,100
Marginal tax rate	7%	7%	7%
Average tax rate (3)/(2)	7%	7%	7%
Effective tax rate (3)/(1)	1.6%	2.1%	2.8%

Is the sales tax regressive?

Answer: Yes. In terms of *effective* tax rates.

When we consider the marginal and average tax rates in Example 1-9, the sales tax has a proportional tax rate structure. But when we look at the *effective* tax rates, the sales tax is a regressive tax. Indeed, Marc, who has the smallest total income, bears the highest effective tax rate, despite all three taxpayers being subject to the same marginal and average tax rates. Why do we see such a different picture when considering the effective tax rate? Because unlike the marginal and average tax rates, the effective tax rate captures the *incidence* of taxation, which relates to the ultimate economic burden of a tax. Thus, a comparison of effective tax rates is more informative about taxpayers' relative tax burdens.

THE KEY FACTS

Tax Rate Structures

- Proportional tax rate structure
  - Imposes a constant tax rate throughout the tax base.
  - As a taxpayer's tax base increases, the taxpayer's taxes increase proportionally.
  - The marginal tax rate remains constant and always equals the average tax rate.
- Progressive tax rate structure
  - Imposes an increasing marginal tax rate as the tax base increases.
  - As a taxpayer's tax base increases, both the marginal tax rate and the taxes paid increase.
- Regressive tax rate structure
  - Imposes a decreasing marginal tax rate as the tax base increases.
  - As a taxpayer's tax base increases, the marginal tax rate decreases while the total taxes paid increases.

LO 1-4

TYPES OF TAXES

"You can't live with 'em. You can't live without 'em." This statement has often been used in reference to bosses, parents, spouses, and significant others. To some degree, it applies equally as well to taxes. Although we all benefit in multiple ways from tax revenues, and all civilized nations impose them, it would be hard to find someone who *enjoys* paying them. Most people don't object to the idea of paying taxes. Instead, it's the way taxes are levied that many people, like Margaret's friend Eddy, dislike. Hence, the search for the "perfect" tax can be elusive. The following paragraphs describe the major types of taxes currently used by federal, state, and local governments. After this discussion, we describe the criteria for evaluating alternative tax systems.

Federal Taxes

The federal government imposes a variety of taxes to fund federal programs such as national defense, Social Security, an interstate highway system, educational programs, and Medicare. Major federal taxes include the individual and corporate income taxes, employment taxes, estate and gift taxes, and excise taxes (each discussed in detail in the following paragraphs). Noticeably absent from this list are a sales tax (a common tax for most state and local governments) and a **value-added tax** (a type

THE KEY FACTS

Federal Taxes

- Income taxes
  - The most significant tax assessed by the U.S. government is the income tax, representing approximately 60 percent of all tax revenues collected in the United States.
  - Levied on individuals, corporations, estates, and trusts.
- Employment and unemployment taxes
  - Second largest group of taxes imposed by the U.S. government.

(continued)

- Employment taxes consist of the Old Age, Survivors, and Disability Insurance (OASDI) tax, commonly called the Social Security tax, and the Medical Health Insurance (MHI) tax known as the Medicare tax.
- Unemployment taxes fund temporary unemployment benefits for individuals terminated from their jobs without cause.

- Excise taxes
  - Third largest group of taxes imposed by the U.S. government.
  - Levied on the *quantity* of products sold.
- Transfer taxes
  - Levied on the fair market values of wealth transfers upon death or by gift.

of sales tax also commonly referred to as a VAT). Value-added taxes are imposed on the producers of goods and services based on the value added to the goods and services at each stage of production. They are quite common in Europe.

Income Tax The most significant tax assessed by the U.S. government is the **income tax,** representing approximately 47.4 percent of all tax revenues collected in the United States in 2011. Despite the magnitude and importance of the federal income tax, its history is relatively short. Congress enacted the first U.S. personal income tax in 1861 to help fund the Civil War. This relatively minor tax (maximum tax rate of 5 percent) was allowed to expire in 1872. In 1892, Congress resurrected the income tax, but not without dissension among the states. In 1895, the income tax was challenged in *Pollock v. Farmers' Loan and Trust Company,* 157 U.S. 429 (1895). The U.S. Supreme Court ruled that the income tax was unconstitutional because direct taxes were prohibited by the Constitution unless the taxes were apportioned across states based upon their populations. This ruling, however, did not deter Congress. In July 1909, Congress sent a proposed constitutional amendment to the states to remove any doubt as to whether income taxes were allowed by the Constitution—and in February 1913, the 16th Amendment was ratified.

Congress then enacted the Revenue Act of 1913, which included a graduated income tax structure with a maximum rate of 7 percent. The income tax has been an important source of tax revenues for the U.S. government ever since. Today, income taxes are levied on individuals (maximum rate of 39.6 percent), corporations (maximum rate of 35 percent), estates (maximum rate of 39.6 percent), and trusts (maximum rate of 39.6 percent). New for 2013 and subsequent years is a 3.8 percent tax on net investment income for higher income taxpayers. As Exhibit 1-4 illustrates, the individual income tax and employment taxes represent the largest sources of federal tax revenues. We discuss each of these taxes in greater detail later in the text.

Employment and Unemployment Taxes Employment and unemployment taxes are the second largest group of taxes imposed by the U.S. government. **Employment taxes** consist of the Old Age, Survivors, and Disability Insurance (OASDI) tax, commonly called the Social Security tax, and the Medical Health Insurance (MHI) tax known as the Medicare tax. The **Social Security tax** pays the monthly retirement, survivor, and disability benefits for qualifying individuals, whereas the **Medicare tax** pays for medical insurance for individuals who are elderly or disabled. The tax base

EXHIBIT 1-4 U.S. Federal Tax Revenues

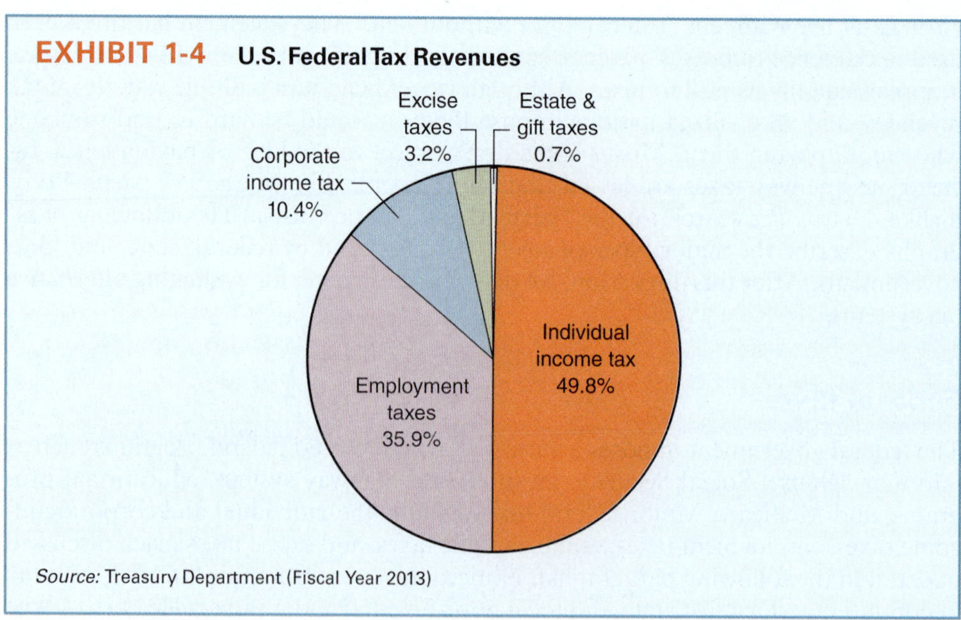

Source: Treasury Department (Fiscal Year 2013)

for the Social Security and Medicare taxes is wages or salary, and the rates are 12.4 percent and 2.9 percent, respectively, in 2015. In 2015, the tax base for the Social Security tax is capped at $118,500. The tax base for the Medicare tax is not capped. Employers and employees split these taxes equally. Self-employed individuals, however, must pay these taxes in their entirety. In this case, the tax is often referred to as the **self-employment tax.** We discuss these taxes in more depth later in the text. There is a 0.9 percent Additional Medicare Tax levied on employees (employers are exempt) on income exceeding the threshold amount (see Chapter 8 for details).

In addition to the Social Security and Medicare taxes, employers are also required to pay federal and state **unemployment taxes,** which fund temporary unemployment benefits for individuals terminated from their jobs without cause. As you might expect, the tax base for the unemployment taxes is also wages or salary. Currently, the Federal Unemployment Tax rate is 6.0 percent. The wage base is the first $7,000 of wages received during the year. The U.S. government allows a credit for state unemployment taxes paid up to 5.4 percent. Thus, the effective Federal Unemployment Tax rate may be as low as 0.6 percent (6.0% − 5.4% = 0.6%).[7]

Excise Taxes **Excise taxes** are taxes levied on the retail sale of particular products. They differ from other taxes in that the tax base for an excise tax typically depends on the *quantity* purchased, rather than a monetary amount. The federal government imposes a number of excise taxes on goods such as alcohol, diesel fuel, gasoline, and tobacco products and on services such as telephone use, air transportation, and tanning beds. In addition, states often impose excise taxes on these same items.

Example 1-10

On the drive home from Athens, Georgia, Margaret stops at Gasup-n-Go. On each gallon of gasoline she buys, Margaret pays 18.4 cents of federal excise tax and 7.5 cents of state excise tax (plus 4 percent sales tax). Could Margaret have avoided paying excise tax had she stopped in Florida instead?

Answer: No. Had she stopped in Florida instead, Margaret would have paid the same federal excise tax. Additionally, Florida imposes higher state taxes on gas.

Because the producer of the product pays the government the excise tax, many consumers are not even aware that businesses build these taxes into the prices consumers pay. Nonetheless, consumers bear the incidence of the taxes because of the higher price.

Transfer Taxes Although they are a relatively minor tax compared to the income tax in terms of revenues collected, federal **transfer taxes**—estate and gift taxes—can be substantial for certain individual taxpayers and have been the subject of much debate in recent years. The **estate tax** (labeled the "death tax" by its opponents) and **gift taxes** are based on the fair market values of wealth transfers upon death or by gift, respectively. The estate and gift tax rates have traditionally been high (maximum tax rate through 2009 was 45 percent) compared to income tax rates and can be burdensome without proper planning. In 2015, the maximum rate imposed on gifts is 40 percent. Most taxpayers, however, are not subject to estate and gift taxation because of the annual gift exclusion and gift and estate unified tax credits. The annual gift exclusion allows a taxpayer to transfer $14,000 of gifts per donee (gift recipient) each year without gift taxation. In 2015, the unified tax credit exempts from taxation

THE KEY FACTS

State and Local Taxes

- Sales and use taxes
  - The tax base for a sales tax is the retail sales of goods and some services.
  - The tax base for the use tax is the retail price of goods owned, possessed, or consumed within a state that were *not* purchased within the state.
- Property taxes
  - Property taxes are ad valorem taxes, meaning that the tax base for each is the fair market value of the property.

(continued)

[7]Although employers pay both federal and state unemployment taxes, all unemployment benefits actually are administered and paid by state governments.

- Real property taxes consist of taxes on land, structures, and improvements permanently attached to land.
- Personal property taxes include taxes on all other types of property, both tangible and intangible.
- Income taxes
  - Most state taxable income calculations largely conform to the federal taxable income calculations, with a limited number of modifications.
- Excise taxes
  - States typically impose excise taxes on items subject to federal excise tax.

EXHIBIT 1-5 Average State and Local Tax Revenues

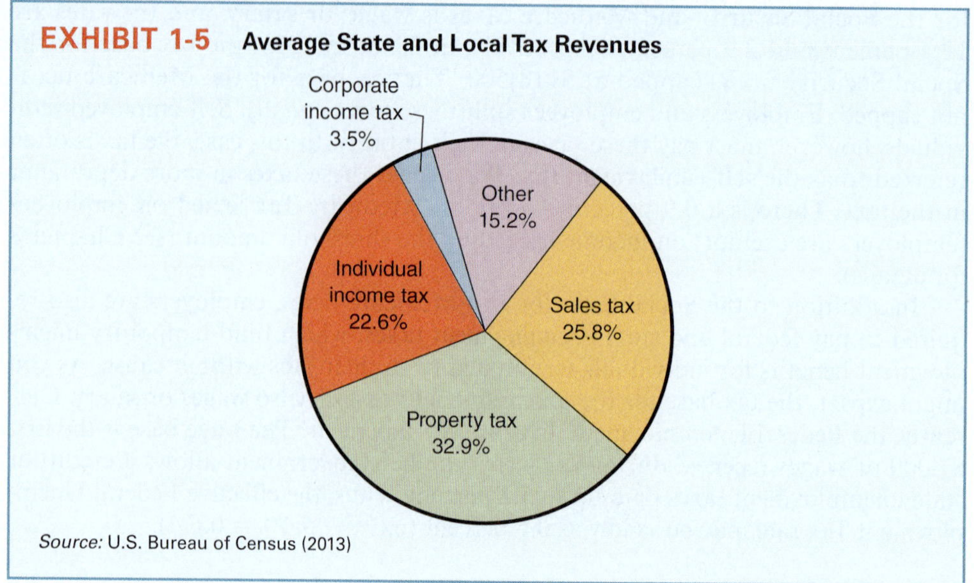

Source: U.S. Bureau of Census (2013)

$5,430,000 in bequests (transfers upon death) and gifts. Thus, only large transfers are subject to the gift and estate taxes.

State and Local Taxes

Like the federal government, state and local governments (such as counties, cities, and school districts) use a variety of taxes to generate revenues for their programs (such as education, highways, and police and fire departments). Some of the more common **state** and **local taxes** include income taxes, sales and use taxes, excise taxes, and property taxes. Typically, as shown in Exhibit 1-5, the largest state and local revenues are generated by state sales taxes and local property taxes—in contrast to federal revenues which rely primarily on income and employment taxes.

Income Taxes Currently, most states and the District of Columbia impose income taxes on individuals and corporations who either reside in or earn income within the state.[8] This requires individuals living in these states to file a state tax return in addition to the federal return they already file. Calculations of individual and corporate taxable income vary with state law. Nonetheless, most state taxable income calculations largely conform to the federal taxable income calculations, with a limited number of modifications, although the tax rates are significantly less than the federal rate. The state of California is a notable exception because it has numerous modifications. Certain local governments such as New York City also impose an income tax, and again, the local calculations generally follow the respective state taxable income calculation.

Sales and Use Taxes Most states, the District of Columbia, and local governments impose sales and use taxes. The tax base for a **sales tax** is the retail sales of goods and some services, and retailers are responsible for collecting and remitting

[8]Currently, Alaska, Florida, Nevada, South Dakota, Texas, Washington, and Wyoming have no personal income tax, and New Hampshire and Tennessee only tax individual dividend and interest income. Nevada and Wyoming do not impose taxes on corporate income, and South Dakota only taxes banks. Washington imposes a gross receipts tax instead of a corporate income tax. Texas and Ohio have an activity-based tax that is based on net income or gross receipts.

the tax; typically, sales tax is collected at the point of sale. The tax base for the **use tax** is the retail price of goods owned, possessed, or consumed within a state that were *not* purchased within the state. The purpose of a use tax is to discourage taxpayers from buying goods out of state in order to avoid or minimize the sales tax in their home state. At the same time, by eliminating the incentive to purchase goods out of state, a use tax removes any competitive disadvantage a retailer may incur from operating in a state with a high sales tax. States with a sales tax allow taxpayers to take a use tax credit on goods purchased out of state to mitigate the potential for double taxation on goods subject to sales tax in another state.

Example 1-11

Margaret buys three new Lands' End shirts for her dad for $100. Because Lands' End does not have a business presence in Florida, it does not collect Florida sales tax on the $100 purchase. Does Margaret's purchase escape Florida taxation?

Answer: No. Because Florida has a 6 percent use tax, Margaret is liable for $6 in use tax on the purchase ($6 = $100 × .06).

Despite the potential importance of the use tax as a source of state tax revenue, states have only recently begun to enforce it. Poor compliance is therefore not surprising; indeed, many individuals have never heard of the use tax. While it is relatively easy to enforce it on goods obtained out of state if they are subject to a registration requirement, such as automobiles, it is quite difficult for states to tax most other out-of-state purchases. The state of Florida is not likely to search your closet to look for tax-evaded Lands' End shirts. Note, however, that the majority of states have joined together (www.streamlinedsalestax.org) to try to subject all Internet sales to sales taxes.

Property Taxes State and local governments commonly use two types of property taxes as sources of revenue: **real property taxes** and **personal property taxes.** Both are **ad valorem** taxes, meaning that the tax base for each is the fair market value of the property, and both are generally collected annually (if imposed at all).

Real property consists of land, structures, and improvements permanently attached to land, whereas *personal property* includes all other types of property, both tangible and intangible. Common examples of tangible personal property potentially subject to state and local taxation include automobiles, boats, private planes, business inventory, equipment, and furniture. Intangible personal property potentially subject to state and local taxation includes stocks, bonds, and intellectual property. Relative to personal property tax, real property taxes are easier to administer because real property is not moveable and purchases often have to be registered with the state, thereby making it easy to identify the tax base and taxpayer. Furthermore, the taxing body can estimate market values for real property without much difficulty. In contrast, personal property is generally mobile (easier to hide) and may be more difficult to value, which make personal property taxes difficult to enforce. Accordingly, whereas all states and the District of Columbia provide for a real property tax, only a majority of states currently impose personal property taxes, most of which are assessed at the time of licensing or registration. However, most states collect personal property taxes on business property.

Excise Taxes We've said that the tax base for excise taxes is typically based on the quantity of an item or service purchased. States typically impose excise taxes on items subject to federal excise tax. Transactions subject to state excise tax often include the sale of alcohol, diesel fuel, gasoline, tobacco products, and telephone services.

Implicit Taxes

All the taxes discussed above are **explicit taxes;** that is, they are taxes directly imposed by a government and are easily quantified. **Implicit taxes,** on the other hand, are indirect taxes—not paid directly to the government—that result from a tax advantage the government grants to certain transactions to satisfy social, economic, or other objectives. Implicit taxes are defined as the reduced before-tax return that a tax-favored asset produces because of its tax-advantaged status. Let's examine this concept more closely.

First of all, what does it mean to be *tax-favored*? An asset is said to be tax-favored when the income the asset produces is either excluded from the tax base or subject to a lower (preferential) tax rate, or if the asset generates some other tax benefit such as large tax deductions. These tax benefits, *all other things equal,* result in higher after-tax profits (or lower after-tax costs) from investing in the tax-advantaged assets.

Why do tax-advantaged assets bear an implicit tax, or a reduced before-tax return as a result of the tax advantage? The answer is simple economics. The tax benefits associated with the tax-favored asset increase the demand for the asset. Increased demand drives up the price of the asset, which in turn reduces its before-tax return, which is an implicit tax by definition. Consider Example 1-12.

Example 1-12

Consider two bonds, one issued by the Coca-Cola Co. and the other issued by the state of Georgia. Both bonds have similar nontax characteristics (risk, for example), the same face value of $10,000, and the same market interest rate of 10 percent. The only difference between the two bonds is that the interest income from the Coca-Cola Co. bond is subject to a 20 percent income tax rate, whereas the interest income from the State of Georgia bond is tax-exempt with a 0 percent tax rate. Which of the two bonds is a better investment and should therefore have a higher demand?

	Price	Before-Tax* Return	Interest Income	Income† Tax	After-Tax Income	After-Tax† Return
Coca-Cola Bond	$10,000	10%	$1,000	$200	$ 800	8%
State of GA Bond	10,000	10	1,000	0	1,000	10

*Before-tax return is calculated as the before-tax income divided by the price of the bond. Likewise, after-tax return is calculated as the after-tax income divided by the price of the bond.

†Income tax equals the taxable interest income ($1,000) multiplied by the assumed income marginal tax rate (20 percent).

Answer: Compare the after-tax returns of the bonds. Given the difference between the return after taxes (10 percent vs. 8 percent), the better investment—again, all other investment features being equal—is the State of Georgia bond because it provides a higher *after*-tax return. Because all investors in this example should prefer to buy the State of Georgia bond, the demand for the bond will be high, and its price should increase. This increase in price leads to a lower before-tax return due to the bond's tax-favored status (this is an implicit tax).

Example 1-12 is a basic illustration of the need to consider the role of taxes in investment decisions. Without understanding the relative tax effects associated with each bond, we cannot correctly compare their after-tax returns.

At what point in Example 1-12 would you be indifferent between investing in the Coca-Cola Co. bond and the State of Georgia bond? Assuming each bond has the same nontax characteristics, you would be indifferent between them when they both provide the same after-tax rate of return. This could occur if the state of Georgia raised the price of its bond from $10,000 to $12,500 ($1,000 interest/$12,500 price = 8% return). Or the state of Georgia could lower its bond interest payment from $1,000 to $800 ($800 interest/$10,000 price = 8% return). Either way, the state of Georgia benefits from selling the tax-exempt bonds—either at a higher price or at a lower interest rate relative to other bonds. Let's look more closely at this latter option, because it is, in fact, what many tax-exempt bond issuers choose to do.

	Price	Before-Tax Return	Interest Income	Income Tax	After-Tax Income	After-Tax Return
Coca-Cola Bond	$10,000	10%	$1,000	$200	$800	8%
State of GA Bond	10,000	8	800	0	800	8

At this point, assuming each bond has the same nontax characteristics, an investor should be indifferent between the Coca-Cola Co. bond and the State of Georgia bond. What is the tax burden on investors choosing the Coca-Cola Co. bond? Coca-Cola Co. bond investors are paying $200 of income taxes (explicit taxes). What is the tax burden on investors choosing the State of Georgia bond? While it is true they are subject to zero income taxes (explicit taxes), they are subject to implicit taxes in the form of the $200 less in interest income they accept. This $200 reduced interest income (2 percent reduced before-tax rate of return) is an implicit tax. Although the investors in the State of Georgia bond are not paying this tax directly, they are paying it indirectly.

Does this happen in real life? Yes. Municipal bond interest income (interest income paid on bonds issued by state and local governments) generally is not subject to federal income taxation. Because of their tax-advantaged status, municipalities are able to pay a lower interest rate on their bond issuances and investors are willing to accept the lower rate. This type of indirect federal subsidy allows municipalities to raise money at a reduced cost without the need of direct federal subsidy or approval.

Although we were able to quantify the implicit taxes paid in the above example, in reality it is very difficult to estimate the amount of implicit taxes paid. For example, the federal government subsidizes housing by allowing taxpayers to deduct mortgage interest on their principal residence. Does this subsidy result in an implicit tax in the form of higher housing prices? Probably. Nonetheless, it would be difficult to quantify this implicit tax.

Despite the difficulty in quantifying implicit taxes, you should understand the concept of implicit taxes so you can make informed judgments about the attractiveness of alternative investments, and about the relative total tax burdens of tax-advantaged investments (considering both explicit and implicit taxes).

THE KEY FACTS

Implicit Taxes

- Implicit taxes are indirect taxes that result from a tax advantage the government grants to certain transactions to satisfy social, economic, or other objectives.
- Implicit taxes are defined as the reduced before-tax return that a tax-favored asset produces because of its tax-advantaged status.
- Implicit taxes are difficult to quantify, but are important to understand in evaluating the relative tax burdens of tax-advantaged investments.

EVALUATING ALTERNATIVE TAX SYSTEMS

LO 1-5

Although it may appear that tax systems are designed without much forethought, in truth lawmakers engage in continuous debate over the basic questions of whom to tax, what to tax, and how much to tax. Margaret's friend Eddy is obviously upset with what he views as an unfair tax system. But fairness, as we will discuss shortly, is often like beauty—it is in the eye of the beholder. What is fair to one may seem blatantly unfair to others. In the following paragraphs, we offer various criteria (sufficiency, equity, certainty, convenience, and economy) you can use to evaluate alternative tax systems.[9] Satisfying everyone at the same time is difficult. Hence, the spirited debate on tax reform.

[9]Adam Smith identified and described the latter four criteria in *The Wealth of Nations*.

Sufficiency

THE KEY FACTS

Evaluating Alternative Taxes—Sufficiency

- Sufficiency involves assessing the aggregate size of the tax revenues that must be generated and ensuring that the tax system provides these revenues.
- Static forecasting ignores how taxpayers may alter their activities in response to a proposed tax law change and bases projected tax revenues on the existing state of transactions.
- Dynamic forecasting attempts to account for possible taxpayer responses to a proposed tax law change.

Judging the **sufficiency** of a tax system means assessing the size of the tax revenues it must generate and ensuring that it provides them. For a tax system to be successful, it must provide sufficient revenues to pay for governmental expenditures for a defense system, social services, and so on. This sounds easy enough: Estimate the amount of government expenditures that will be required, and then design the system to generate enough revenues to pay for these expenses. In reality, however, accurately estimating governmental expenditures and revenues is a rather daunting and imprecise process. Estimating governmental expenditures is difficult because it is impossible to predict the unknown. For example, in recent years governmental expenditures have increased due to the terrorist attacks of September 11, 2001, the Afghanistan and Iraq Wars, natural disasters, economic stimulus, and health care. Likewise, estimating governmental revenues is difficult because tax revenues are the result of transactions influenced by these same national events, the economy, and other factors. Thus, precisely estimating and matching governmental expenditures with tax revenues is nearly impossible.

The task of estimating tax revenues becomes even more daunting when the government attempts to make significant changes to the existing tax system or design a new one. Whenever Congress proposes changing who is taxed, what is taxed, or how much is taxed, its members must consider the taxpayer response to the change. That affects the amount of tax collected, and how forecasters predict what taxpayers will do affects how much revenue they estimate.

Static vs. Dynamic Forecasting One option in forecasting revenue is to ignore how taxpayers may alter their activities in response to a tax law change and to base projected tax revenues on the existing state of transactions, a process referred to as **static forecasting.** However, this type of forecasting may result in a large discrepancy in projected versus actual tax revenues if taxpayers do change their behavior. The other choice is to attempt to account for possible taxpayer responses to the tax law change, a process referred to as **dynamic forecasting.** Dynamic forecasting is ultimately only as good as the assumptions underlying the forecasts and does not guarantee accurate results. Nonetheless, considering how taxpayers may alter their activities in response to a tax law change is a useful exercise to identify the potential ramifications of the change, even if the revenue projections ultimately miss the mark. For more information on the Congressional Revenue Estimating Process, including dynamic scoring, see the Joint Committee on Taxation explanation at https://www.jct.gov/publications.html?func=startdown&id=3720.

Example 1-13

The city of Heflin would like to increase tax revenues by $2,000,000 to pay for needed roadwork. A concerned taxpayer recently proposed increasing the cigarette excise tax from $1.00 per pack of cigarettes to $6.00 per pack to raise the additional needed revenue. Last year, 400,000 packs of cigarettes were sold in the city. Will the tax be successful in raising the $2,000,000 revenue?

Answer: Not likely. The proposed tax increase of $5, and the assumption that 400,000 packs will still be sold, is an example of static forecasting: It ignores that many taxpayers may respond to the tax change by quitting, cutting down, or buying cheaper cigarettes in the next town.

In some cases, static forecasting can lead to a tax consequence opposite the desired outcome. In Example 1-13, we might estimate that given Heflin's close proximity to other cities with a $1.00 cigarette tax, the number of packs of cigarettes sold within the city would drop significantly to, say, 50,000. In this case, the tax increase would actually *decrease* tax revenues by $100,000 ($400,000 existing tax − $300,000 new tax), not a good outcome if the goal was to increase tax revenues.

Income vs. Substitution Effects The example above described proposed changes in an excise tax, which is a proportional tax. In terms of a progressive tax such as an *income* tax, a tax rate increase or an expansion of the tax base can result in one of two taxpayer responses, both of which are important for dynamic forecasting. The **income effect** predicts that when taxpayers are taxed more (when, say, a tax rate increases from 25 to 28 percent), they will work harder to generate the same after-tax dollars. The **substitution effect** predicts that when taxpayers are taxed more, rather than work more, they will substitute nontaxable activities like leisure pursuits for taxable ones because the marginal value of taxable activities has decreased. Which view is accurate? The answer depends on the taxpayer. Consider the following examples.

Example 1-14

Margaret's friend George, who earns $40,000 taxable income as a mechanic, is taxed at an average rate of 10 percent ($4,000 of tax). If Congress increases the income tax rate such that George's average tax rate increases from 10 percent to 25 percent, how much more income tax will he pay?

Answer: It depends on whether the income effect or the substitution effect is operating. Assuming George is single and cannot afford a net decrease in his after-tax income, he will likely work more (the income effect rules). Prior to the tax rate increase, George had $36,000 of after-tax income ($40,000 taxable income less $4,000 tax). With the increased tax rate, George will have to earn $48,000 of taxable income to keep $36,000 after taxes [$48,000 − ($48,000 × .25) = $36,000]. Thus, if the income effect rules, the government will collect $12,000 of federal income tax from George, or $8,000 more than under the previous lower tax rate. In this scenario, the tax change increases government revenues because of the increased tax rate *and* the increased tax base.

Whether the substitution effect or the income effect will describe any individual taxpayer's reaction to a tax increase is something we can only guess. But some factors—such as having higher disposable income—are likely to correlate with the substitution effect.

Example 1-15

What if: Now let's assume that George is married and has two young children, both he and his wife work, and they file a tax return jointly with a 10 percent average tax rate. Either of their incomes is sufficient to meet necessities, even after the tax rate increase. But fixed child care costs make the marginal wage rate (the after-tax hourly wage less hourly child care cost) more sensitive to tax rate increases. In this case, the lower-earning spouse may choose to work less. Suppose George quits his full-time job and takes a part-time position that pays $10,000 to spend more time with his kids and to pursue his passion, reading sports novels. What are the taxes on George's income?

Answer: In this case, George will owe $2,500 tax ($10,000 × .25 = $2,500). Here, the substitution effect operates, and the government collects much less than it would have if George had maintained his full-time position, because the tax rate increase had a negative effect on the tax base.

As the previous examples illustrate, the response to a tax law change can vary by taxpayer and can greatly affect the magnitude of tax revenues generated by the change. Herein lies one of the challenges in significantly changing an existing tax system or designing a new one: If a tax system fails to generate sufficient revenues, the government must seek other sources to pay for governmental expenditures. The most common source of these additional funds for the federal government is the issuance of debt instruments such as Treasury bonds. This, however, is only a short-term solution to a budget deficit. Debt issuances require both interest and principal payments, which require the federal government to identify even more sources of revenue to service the debt issued, or to cut governmental spending (both of which may be unpopular choices with voters). A third option is for the government to default on its debt obligations. However, the costs of this option are potentially devastating. If the historical examples of Mexico, Brazil, Argentina, and Greece are any guide, a U.S. government default on its debt obligations would likely devalue the U.S. dollar severely and have extreme negative consequences for the U.S. capital markets.

The best option is for the government to match its revenues with its expenses—that is, not to spend more than it collects. State governments seem to be more successful in this endeavor than the U.S. federal government. Indeed, all states except Vermont require a balanced budget each year, whereas the federal government has had deficit spending for most of the last 40 years.

TAXES IN THE REAL WORLD National Debt

How much debt does the U.S. have today? About $17.9 trillion. Over $12.8 trillion of the national debt is held by public investors including: individual bondholders; institutional investors; and foreign governments such as China, the United Kingdom, and Brazil. The almost $5 trillion remaining amount represents intra-governmental holdings—primarily Social Security.

Is $17.9 trillion too much to handle? The key issue is fiscal sustainability: the ability to pay off a debt in the future. Rising debt also has other negative consequences, such as higher interest payments, a need for higher taxes, restricting policymaker's fiscal policy choices, and increasing the probability of a sudden fiscal crisis. If nothing is done to change the national debt trajectory, the debt will grow faster than the economy.

Is the national debt sustainable? The federal government has been recording budget deficits that are a larger share of the economy than any year since the end of World War II. With an aging population, Social Security and other benefits will require larger expenditures. By the end of the current decade, barring any significant policy shifts, the vast majority of federal tax revenue will be consumed by just four expenditures: interest on the debt, Medicare, Medicaid, and Social Security. To finance other government expenditures, including defense and all other discretionary programs, policymakers will have to borrow the money to pay for them.

Equity

We've looked at the challenges of designing a tax system that provides sufficient revenues to pay for governmental expenditures. An equally challenging issue is how the tax burden should be distributed across taxpayers. At the heart of this issue is the concept of **equity** or fairness. Fairness is inherently subject to personal interpretation, and informed minds often disagree about what is fair. There is no "one-size-fits-all" definition of equity or fairness. Nonetheless, it is informative to consider in broad terms what makes a fair or equitable tax system.

In general terms, a tax system is considered fair or equitable if the tax is based on the taxpayer's ability to pay. Taxpayers with a greater ability to pay tax, pay more tax. In broad terms, each of the federal, state, and local taxes we've discussed satisfies this criterion. For example, those individuals with greater taxable income, purchases, property, and estates (upon death) generally pay higher dollar amounts in federal income tax, sales tax, property tax, and estate tax. If this is the case, why is there so much debate over the fairness of the U.S. income tax system? The answer is that equity is more complex than our first definition suggests. Let's take a closer look.

Horizontal vs. Vertical Equity Two basic types of equity are relevant to tax systems. **Horizontal equity** means that two taxpayers in similar situations pay the same tax. In broad terms, each of the federal, state, and local taxes discussed satisfy this definition. Two individual taxpayers with the same taxable income, same purchases, same value of property, and same estate value pay the same federal income tax, sales tax, property tax, and estate tax. However, on closer inspection we might argue that each of these tax systems is *not* horizontally equitable. Here are some examples:

- Two individual taxpayers with the same income will not pay the same federal income tax if one individual's income was earned as salary and the other individual's income was tax-exempt municipal bond interest income, dividend income, or capital gain(s) income, which can be subject to a lower tax rate.
- Two individuals with the same dollar amount of purchases will not pay the same sales tax if one buys a higher proportion of goods that are subject to a lower sales tax rate, such as groceries.
- Two individuals with real estate of the same value will not pay the same property tax if one individual owns farmland, which is generally subject to a lower property tax rate.
- Finally, two individuals with estates of the same value will not pay the same estate tax if one individual bequeaths more of her property to charity or a spouse, because these transfers are not subject to estate tax.

These failures of horizontal equity are due to what we call *tax preferences.* Governments provide tax preferences for a variety of reasons, such as to encourage investment or further social objectives. Whether we view these tax preferences as appropriate greatly influences whether we consider a tax system to be fair in general and horizontally equitable in particular.

The second type of equity to consider in evaluating a tax system is **vertical equity.** Vertical equity is achieved when taxpayers with greater ability to pay tax, pay more tax than taxpayers with less ability to pay. We can think of vertical equity in terms of tax dollars paid or in terms of tax rates. Proponents of a flat income tax or of a sales tax—both of which are proportional tax rate structures—are more likely to argue that vertical equity is achieved when taxpayers with a greater ability to pay tax, simply pay more in tax *dollars*. Proponents of a progressive tax system are more likely to argue that taxpayers with a greater ability to pay should be subject to a higher tax *rate*. This view is based upon the argument that the *relative* burden of a flat tax rate decreases as a taxpayer's income increases. Which is the correct answer? There is no correct answer. Nonetheless, many feel very strongly regarding one view or the other.

Our discussion has focused on how we can view alternative tax rate structures in terms of vertical equity, ignoring the role that the tax base plays in determining vertical equity. Indeed, focusing on the tax rate structure in evaluating a tax system is appropriate only if the tax base chosen—whether it's taxable income, purchases, property owned, or something else—accurately portrays a taxpayer's ability to pay. This can be a rather strong assumption. Consider the sales tax in Example 1-9. Although taxable purchases in this example increase as the taxpayers' total incomes increase, total incomes increase at a much faster rate than taxable purchases. Thus, the gap between taxable purchases and total income widens as total income increases. The end result is that the effective tax rates for those with a greater ability to pay are *lower* than for those taxpayers with a lesser ability to pay, making this tax regressive. Regressive tax rate structures are generally considered not to satisfy vertical equity, unless you strongly believe that those with a greater ability to pay do so simply by paying more tax dollars, albeit at a lower tax rate. In sum, evaluating vertical equity in terms of effective tax rates may be much more informative than simply evaluating tax rate structures.

THE KEY FACTS

Evaluating Alternative Taxes—Equity

- Equity considers how the tax burden should be distributed across taxpayers.
- Horizontal equity means that two taxpayers in similar situations pay the same tax.
- Vertical equity is achieved when taxpayers with greater ability to pay tax, pay more tax relative to taxpayers with a lesser ability to pay tax.

Certainty

Certainty means that taxpayers should be able to determine when to pay the tax, where to pay the tax, and how to determine the tax. Determining when and where to pay each of the taxes previously discussed is relatively easy. For example, individual federal income tax returns and the remaining balance of taxes owed must be filed with the Internal Revenue Service each year on or before April 15th. Likewise, sales taxes, property taxes, and excise taxes are each determined with relative ease: Sales taxes are based on the value of taxable purchases, property taxes are generally based on assessed property values, and excise taxes are based on the number of taxable units purchased. Indeed, these taxes are calculated for the taxpayer and often charged at regular intervals or at the point of purchase; they do not require a tax return.

In contrast, income taxes are often criticized as being too complex. What are taxable vs. nontaxable forms of income? What are deductible/nondeductible expenses? When should income or expenses be reported? For wage earners with few investments, the answers to these questions are straightforward. For business owners and individuals with a lot of investments, the answers are nontrivial. Yearly tax law changes enacted by Congress can make it more difficult to determine a taxpayer's current tax liability, much less plan for the future.

THE KEY FACTS

Evaluating Alternative Taxes—Certainty, Convenience, and Economy

- Certainty
  - Means taxpayers should be able to determine when, where, and how much tax to pay.
  - Determining when and where to pay each of the taxes previously discussed is relatively easy.
  - The income tax has been criticized for its complexity in determining how much to pay.
- Convenience
  - Means a tax system should be designed to facilitate the collection of tax revenues without undue hardship on the taxpayer or the government.
  - Various tax systems meet this criterion by tying the collection of the tax as closely as possible to the transaction that generates it.
- Economy
  - Means a tax system should minimize its compliance and administration costs.
  - May be viewed from both the taxpayers' and the government's perspectives.

Convenience

Convenience suggests that a tax system should be designed to facilitate the collection of tax revenues without undue hardship on the taxpayer or the government. Various tax systems meet this criterion by tying the collection of the tax as closely as possible to the transaction that generates it. For example, retailers collect sales taxes when buyers purchase goods. Thus, it is difficult for the buyer to avoid paying sales tax, assuming she is transacting with an ethical retailer. Likewise, employers withhold federal income and Social Security taxes directly from wage earners' paychecks, which speeds the government's collection of the taxes and makes it difficult for the taxpayer to evade the taxes. If tax withholdings are not sufficient relative to the taxpayer's anticipated income tax liability, the taxpayer is required to make quarterly estimated tax installments. Individual quarterly estimated payments are due on April 15, June 15, September 15, and January 15, whereas corporate estimated tax payments are due on the 15th day of the third, sixth, ninth, and twelfth months of the corporation's fiscal year.

Economy

Economy requires that a good tax system should minimize the compliance and administration costs associated with the tax system. We can view economy from both the taxpayers' and the government's perspectives. Believe it or not, most tax systems fare well in terms of economy, at least from the government's perspective. For example, the current IRS budget represents approximately $\frac{1}{2}$ of a percent of every tax dollar collected. Compared to the typical costs of a collection agency, this is quite low.

How about from the taxpayer's perspective? Here the picture is a bit different. The sales tax imposes no administrative burden on the taxpayer and only small administrative costs on the local retailer. However, out-of-state sellers argue that collecting and remitting use taxes for thousands of state and city jurisdictions would be a substantial burden. Other taxes such as excise taxes and property taxes also impose minimal administrative costs on the taxpayer. In contrast, as we've seen, the income tax is often criticized for the compliance costs imposed on the taxpayer. Indeed, for certain taxpayers, record-keeping costs, accountant fees, attorney fees, and so on can be substantial. Advocates of alternative tax systems often challenge the income tax on this criterion.

Evaluating Tax Systems—The Trade-Off

At the heart of any debate on tax reform are fundamental decisions and concessions based on the five criteria we've just discussed. Interestingly enough, much of the debate regarding alternative tax systems reduces to a choice between simplicity and fairness. Those taxes that generally are simpler and easier to administer, such as the sales tax, are typically viewed as less fair. Those taxes that may be viewed as more fair, such as the federal income tax, often are more complex to administer. Thus, Margaret's friend Eddy faces a difficult choice about which type of tax system to advocate, as do all taxpayers. An understanding of the evaluative criteria should be helpful to anyone trying to reconcile the trade-offs among alternative tax proposals.

CONCLUSION

In almost any society taxes are a part of life. They influence decisions about personal finance, investment, business, and politics. In this chapter, we introduced the basic concepts of why one should study tax, what is a tax, and how to calculate a tax. We also discussed various tax rates, tax rate structures, and different types of taxes imposed by federal, state, and local governments. Finally, we discussed the criteria that one might use to evaluate alternative tax rate systems. To make informed personal finance, investment, business, and political decisions, one must have a basic understanding of these items. In the following chapters we expand the discussion of how taxes influence these decisions while providing a basic understanding of our federal income tax system. Read on and learn more!

Summary

Demonstrate how taxes influence basic business, investment, personal, and political decisions. LO 1-1

- Taxes are significant costs that influence many basic business, investment, and personal decisions.
  - *Business decisions:* what organization form to take; where to locate; how to compensate employees; appropriate debt mix; owning vs. renting equipment and property; how to distribute profits, and so forth.
  - *Investment decisions:* alternative methods for saving for education or retirement, and so forth.
  - *Personal finance decisions:* evaluating job offers; gift or estate planning; owning vs. renting home, and so forth.
- Taxes also play a major part in the political process. Major parties typically have very diverse views on whom, what, and how much to tax.

Discuss what constitutes a tax and the general objectives of taxes. LO 1-2

- The general purpose of taxes is to fund the government. Unlike fines or penalties, taxes are not meant to punish or prevent illegal behavior; but "*sin taxes*" (on alcohol, tobacco, tanning beds, etc.) are meant to discourage some behaviors.
- The three criteria necessary to be a tax are that the payment is (1) required (it is not voluntary), (2) imposed by a government (federal, state, or local), and (3) not tied directly to the benefit received by the taxpayer.

Describe the different tax rate structures and calculate a tax. LO 1-3

- Tax = Tax rate × Tax base, where the tax base is what is taxed and the tax rate is the level of taxes imposed on the base. Different portions of a tax base may be taxed at different rates.

- There are three different tax rates that are useful in contrasting the different tax rate structures, tax planning, and/or assessing the tax burden of a taxpayer: the marginal, average, and effective tax rates.
- The marginal tax rate is the tax that applies to the next increment of income or deduction. The average tax rate represents a taxpayer's average level of taxation on each dollar of taxable income. The effective tax rate represents the taxpayer's average rate of taxation on each dollar of total income (taxable *and* nontaxable income).
- The three basic tax rate structures are proportional, progressive, and regressive.
  - A *proportional tax rate* structure imposes a constant tax rate throughout the tax base. As a taxpayer's tax base increases, the taxpayer's taxes increase proportionally. The marginal tax rate remains constant and always equals the average tax rate. A common example is a sales tax.
  - A *progressive tax rate* imposes an increasing marginal tax rate as the tax base increases. As a taxpayer's tax base increases, both the marginal tax rate and the taxes paid increase. A common example is the U.S. federal income tax.
  - A *regressive tax rate* imposes a decreasing marginal tax rate as the tax base increases. As a taxpayer's tax base increases, the marginal tax rate decreases while the total taxes paid increases.

LO 1-4 Identify the various federal, state, and local taxes.

- Federal taxes include the income tax, employment taxes (Social Security and Medicare taxes), unemployment taxes, excise taxes (levied on quantity purchased), and transfer taxes (estate and gift taxes).
- State and local taxes include the income tax (levied by most states), sales tax (levied on retail sales of goods and some services), use tax (levied on the retail price of goods owned or consumed within a state that were purchased out of state), property taxes (levied on fair market value of real and personal property), and excise taxes.
- Implicit taxes are indirect taxes that result from a tax advantage the government grants to certain transactions to satisfy social, economic, or other objectives. They are defined as the reduced before-tax return that a tax-favored asset produces because of its tax-advantaged status.

LO 1-5 Apply appropriate criteria to evaluate alternate tax systems.

- Sufficiency involves assessing the aggregate size of the tax revenues that must be generated and ensuring that the tax system provides these revenues. Static forecasting ignores how taxpayers may alter their activities in response to a proposed tax law change and bases projected tax revenues on the existing state of transactions. Dynamic forecasting attempts to account for possible taxpayer responses to a proposed tax law change.
- Equity considers how the tax burden should be distributed across taxpayers. Generally, a tax system is considered fair or equitable if the tax is based on the taxpayer's ability to pay—that is, taxpayers with a greater ability to pay tax, pay more tax. Horizontal equity means that two taxpayers in similar situations pay the same tax. Vertical equity is achieved when taxpayers with greater ability to pay tax, pay more tax relative to taxpayers with a lesser ability to pay tax.
- Certainty means taxpayers should be able to determine when, where, and how much tax to pay.
- Convenience means a tax system should be designed to facilitate the collection of tax revenues without undue hardship on the taxpayer or the government.
- Economy means a tax system should minimize its compliance and administration costs.

KEY TERMS

ad valorem (1-15)
average tax rate (1-7)
bracket (1-5)
certainty (1-22)
convenience (1-22)
dynamic forecasting (1-18)
earmarked tax (1-4)
economy (1-22)
effective tax rate (1-8)
employment taxes (1-12)
equity (1-20)
estate tax (1-13)

excise taxes (1-13)
explicit tax (1-16)
flat tax (1-5)
gift tax (1-13)
graduated taxes (1-5)
horizontal equity (1-21)
implicit tax (1-16)
income effect (1-19)
income tax (1-12)
local tax (1-14)
marginal tax rate (1-5)
Medicare tax (1-12)
personal property tax (1-15)
progressive tax rate structure (1-9)
proportional tax rate structure (1-9)
real property tax (1-15)
regressive tax rate structure (1-10)
sales tax (1-14)
self-employment tax (1-13)
sin taxes (1-4)
Social Security tax (1-12)
state tax (1-14)
static forecasting (1-18)
substitution effect (1-19)
sufficiency (1-18)
tax (1-3)
tax base (1-5)
tax rate (1-5)
transfer taxes (1-13)
unemployment tax (1-13)
use tax (1-15)
value-added tax (1-11)
vertical equity (1-21)

DISCUSSION QUESTIONS

1. Jessica's friend Zachary once stated that he couldn't understand why someone would take a tax course. Why is this a rather naïve view? LO 1-1
2. What are some aspects of business that require knowledge of taxation? What are some aspects of personal finance that require knowledge of taxation? LO 1-1
3. Describe some ways in which taxes affect the political process in the United States. LO 1-1
4. Courtney recently received a speeding ticket on her way to the university. Her fine was $200. Is this considered a tax? Why or why not? LO 1-2
5. Marlon and Latoya recently started building a house. They had to pay $300 to the county government for a building permit. Is the $300 payment a tax? Why or why not? LO 1-2
6. The city of Birmingham recently enacted a 1 percent surcharge on hotel rooms that will help pay for the city's new stadium. Is this a tax? Why or why not? LO 1-2
7. As noted in Example 1-2, tolls, parking meter fees, and annual licensing fees are not considered taxes. Can you identify other fees that are similar? LO 1-2
8. If the general objective of our tax system is to raise revenue, why does the income tax allow deductions for charitable contributions and retirement plan contributions? LO 1-2
9. One common argument for imposing so-called sin taxes is the social goal of *reducing* demand for such products. Using cigarettes as an example, is there a segment of the population that might be sensitive to price and for whom high taxes might discourage purchases? LO 1-2
10. Dontae stated that he didn't want to earn any more money because it would "put him in a higher tax bracket." What is wrong with Dontae's reasoning? LO 1-3
11. Describe the three different tax rates discussed in the chapter and how taxpayers might use them. LO 1-3
12. Which is a more appropriate tax rate to use to compare taxpayers' tax burdens—the average or the effective tax rate? Why? LO 1-3
13. Describe the differences between a proportional, progressive, and regressive tax rate structure. LO 1-3
14. Arnold and Lilly have recently had a heated discussion about whether a sales tax is a proportional tax or a regressive tax. Arnold argues that a sales tax is regressive. Lilly counters that the sales tax is a flat tax. Who is correct? LO 1-3
15. Which is the largest tax collected by the U.S. government? What types of taxpayers are subject to this tax? LO 1-4

LO 1-4 16. What is the tax base for the Social Security and Medicare taxes for an employee or employer? What is the tax base for Social Security and Medicare taxes for a self-employed individual? Is the self-employment tax in addition to or in lieu of federal income tax?

LO 1-4 17. What are unemployment taxes?

LO 1-4 18. What is the distinguishing feature of an excise tax?

LO 1-4 19. What are some of the taxes that currently are unique to state and local governments? What are some of the taxes that the federal, state, and local governments each utilize?

LO 1-4 20. The state of Georgia recently increased its tax on a pack of cigarettes by $2.00. What type of tax is this? Why might Georgia choose this type of tax?

LO 1-4 21. What is the difference between a sales tax and a use tax?

LO 1-4 22. What is an ad valorem tax? Name an example of this type of tax.

LO 1-4 23. What are the differences between an explicit and an implicit tax?

LO 1-4 24. When we calculate average and effective tax rates, do we consider implicit taxes? What effect does this have on taxpayers' perception of equity?

LO 1-4 25. Benjamin recently bought a truck in Alabama for his business in Georgia. What different types of federal and state taxes may affect this transaction?

LO 1-5 26. Kobe strongly dislikes SUVs and is appalled that so many are on the road. He proposes to eliminate the federal income tax and replace it with a $50,000 annual tax per SUV. Based on the number of SUVs currently owned in the United States, he estimates the tax will generate exactly the amount of tax revenue currently collected from the income tax. What is wrong with Kobe's proposal? What type of forecasting is Kobe likely using?

LO 1-5 27. What is the difference between the income and substitution effects? For which types of taxpayers is the income effect more likely descriptive? For which types of taxpayers is the substitution effect more likely descriptive?

LO 1-5 28. What is the difference between horizontal and vertical equity? How do tax preferences affect people's view of horizontal equity?

LO 1-3 LO 1-5 29. Montel argues that a flat income tax rate system is vertically equitable. Oprah argues that a progressive tax rate structure is vertically equitable. How do their arguments differ? Who is correct?

LO 1-3 LO 1-5 30. Discuss why evaluating vertical equity simply based on tax rate structure may be less than optimal.

LO 1-4 LO 1-5 31. Compare the federal income tax to sales taxes using the "certainty" criterion.

LO 1-5 32. Many years ago a famous member of Congress proposed eliminating federal income tax withholding. What criterion for evaluating tax systems did this proposal violate? What would likely have been the result of eliminating withholding?

LO 1-5 33. "The federal income tax scores very high on the economy criterion because the current IRS budget is relatively low compared to the costs of a typical collection agency." Explain why this statement may be considered wrong.

PROBLEMS

All applicable problems are available with McGraw-Hill's *Connect*® *Accounting*.

LO 1-3 34. Chuck, a single taxpayer, earns $75,000 in taxable income and $10,000 in interest from an investment in City of Heflin bonds. Using the U.S. tax rate schedule, how much federal tax will he owe? What is his average tax rate? What is his effective tax rate? What is his current marginal tax rate?

35. Using the facts in the previous problem, if Chuck earns an additional $40,000 of taxable income, what is his marginal tax rate on this income? What is his marginal rate if, instead, he had $40,000 of additional deductions? LO 1-3

36. In reviewing the tax rate schedule for a single taxpayer, Chuck notes that the tax on $75,000 is $5,156.25 plus 25 percent of the taxable income over $37,450. What does the $5,156.25 represent? LO 1-3

37. Campbell, a single taxpayer, earns $400,000 in taxable income and $2,000 in interest from an investment in State of New York bonds. Using the U.S. tax rate schedule, how much federal tax will she owe? What is her average tax rate? What is her effective tax rate? What is her current marginal tax rate? LO 1-3

38. Using the facts in the previous problem, if Campbell earns an additional $15,000 of taxable income, what is her marginal tax rate on this income? What is her marginal rate if, instead, she had $15,000 of additional deductions? LO 1-3

39. Jorge and Anita, married taxpayers, earn $150,000 in taxable income and $40,000 in interest from an investment in City of Heflin bonds. Using the U.S. tax rate schedule for married filing jointly, how much federal tax will they owe? What is their average tax rate? What is their effective tax rate? What is their current marginal tax rate? LO 1-3

40. Using the facts in the previous problem, if Jorge and Anita earn an additional $100,000 of taxable income, what is their marginal tax rate on this income? What is their marginal rate if, instead, they reported an additional $100,000 in deductions? LO 1-3

41. In reviewing the tax rate schedule for married filing jointly, Jorge and Anita note that the tax on $155,000 is $29,387.50 plus 28 percent of the taxable income over $151,200. What does the $29,387.50 represent? LO 1-3

42. Scot and Vidia, married taxpayers, earn $240,000 in taxable income and $5,000 in interest from an investment in City of Tampa bonds. Using the U.S. tax rate schedule for married filing jointly, how much federal tax will they owe? What is their average tax rate? What is their effective tax rate? What is their current marginal tax rate? LO 1-3

43. Using the facts in the previous problem, if Scot and Vidia earn an additional $70,000 of taxable income, what is their marginal tax rate on this income? How would your answer differ if they, instead, had $70,000 of additional deductions? LO 1-3

44. Melinda invests $200,000 in a City of Heflin bond that pays 6 percent interest. Alternatively, Melinda could have invested the $200,000 in a bond recently issued by Surething Inc., that pays 8 percent interest with similar risk and other nontax characteristics to the City of Heflin bond. Assume Melinda's marginal tax rate is 25 percent. LO 1-3 LO 1-4
    a) What is her after-tax rate of return for the City of Heflin bond?
    b) How much explicit tax does Melinda pay on the City of Heflin bond?
    c) How much implicit tax does she pay on the City of Heflin bond?
    d) How much explicit tax would she have paid on the Surething Inc. bond?
    e) What is her after-tax rate of return on the Surething Inc. bond?

45. Hugh has the choice between investing in a City of Heflin bond at 6 percent or a Surething bond at 9 percent. Assuming that both bonds have the same nontax characteristics and that Hugh has a 40 percent marginal tax rate, in which bond should he invest? LO 1-3 LO 1-4 planning

46. Using the facts in the previous problem, what interest rate does Surething Inc., need to offer to make Hugh indifferent between investing in the two bonds? LO 1-3 LO 1-4 planning

LO 1-3 LO 1-4 planning

47. Fergie has the choice between investing in a State of New York bond at 5 percent and a Surething bond at 8 percent. Assuming that both bonds have the same nontax characteristics and that Fergie has a 30 percent marginal tax rate, in which bond should she invest?

LO 1-3 LO 1-4 planning

48. Using the facts in the previous problem, what interest rate does the state of New York need to offer to make Fergie indifferent between investing in the two bonds?

LO 1-3

49. Given the following tax structure, what minimum tax would need to be assessed on Shameika to make the tax progressive with respect to average tax rates?

Taxpayer	Salary	Muni-Bond Interest	Total Tax
Mihwah	$10,000	$10,000	$600
Shameika	50,000	30,000	???

LO 1-3

50. Using the facts in the previous problem, what minimum tax would need to be assessed on Shameika to make the tax progressive with respect to effective tax rates?

LO 1-3 LO 1-5

51. Song earns $100,000 taxable income as an interior designer and is taxed at an average rate of 20 percent (i.e., $20,000 of tax). If Congress increases the income tax rate such that Song's average tax rate increases from 20 percent to 25 percent, how much more income tax will she pay assuming that the income effect is descriptive? What effect will this tax rate change have on the tax base and tax collected?

LO 1-3 LO 1-5

52. Using the facts from the previous problem, what will happen to the government's tax revenues if Song chooses to spend more time pursuing her other passions besides work in response to the tax rate change and earns only $75,000 in taxable income? What is the term that describes this type of reaction to a tax rate increase? What types of taxpayers are likely to respond in this manner?

LO 1-5

53. Given the following tax structure, what tax would need to be assessed on Venita to make the tax horizontally equitable?

Taxpayer	Salary	Total Tax
Mae	$10,000	$ 600
Pedro	20,000	1,500
Venita	10,000	???

LO 1-5

54. Using the facts in the previous problem, what is the minimum tax that Pedro should pay to make the tax structure vertically equitable based on the tax rate paid? This would result in what type of tax rate structure?

LO 1-5

55. Using the facts in the previous problem, what is the minimum tax that Pedro should pay to make the tax structure vertically equitable with respect to the amount of tax paid? This would result in what type of tax rate structure?

LO 1-5

56. Consider the following tax rate structure. Is it horizontally equitable? Why or why not? Is it vertically equitable? Why or why not?

Taxpayer	Salary	Total Tax
Rajiv	$10,000	$600
LaMarcus	20,000	600
Dory	10,000	600

57. Consider the following tax rate structure. Is it horizontally equitable? Why or why not? Is it vertically equitable? Why or why not?

LO 1-5

Taxpayer	Salary	Total Tax
Marilyn	$10,000	$ 600
Kobe	20,000	3,000
Alfonso	30,000	6,000

58. Consider the following tax rate structure. Is it horizontally equitable? Why or why not? Is it vertically equitable? Why or why not?

LO 1-5

Taxpayer	Salary	Total Tax
Rodney	$10,000	$600
Keisha	10,000	600

59. Lorenzo is considering starting a trucking company either in Texas or Oklahoma. He will relocate his family, which includes his wife, children, and parents, to reside in the same state as his business. What types of taxes may influence his decision of where to locate his business?

LO 1-1 LO 1-4 planning

60. Congress would like to increase tax revenues by 10 percent. Assume that the average taxpayer in the United States earns $65,000 and pays an average tax rate of 15 percent. If the income effect is in effect for all taxpayers, what average tax rate will result in a 10 percent increase in tax revenues? This is an example of what type of forecasting?

LO 1-3 LO 1-5 planning

61. Locate the IRS website at www.irs.gov/. For every $100 the IRS collected, how much was spent on the IRS collection efforts? What tax system criterion does this information help you to evaluate with respect to the current U.S. tax system?

LO 1-5
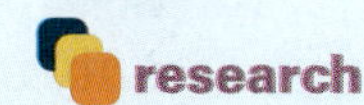

62. Using the Internet, find a comparison of income tax rates across states. What state currently has the highest income tax rate? In considering individual tax burdens across states, what other taxes should you consider?

LO 1-4
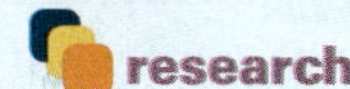

chapter

2 Tax Compliance, the IRS, and Tax Authorities

Learning Objectives

Upon completing this chapter, you should be able to:

- **LO 2-1** Identify the filing requirements for income tax returns and the statute of limitations for assessment.
- **LO 2-2** Outline the IRS audit process, how returns are selected, the different types of audits, and what happens after the audit.
- **LO 2-3** Evaluate the relative weights of the various tax law sources.
- **LO 2-4** Describe the legislative process as it pertains to taxation.
- **LO 2-5** Perform the basic steps in tax research and evaluate various tax law sources when faced with ambiguous statutes.
- **LO 2-6** Describe tax professional responsibilities in providing tax advice.
- **LO 2-7** Identify taxpayer and tax professional penalties.

© Blend Images

Storyline Summary

Taxpayers:	Bill and Mercedes
Family description:	Bill and Mercedes are married with one daughter, Margaret.
Employment status:	Bill is an economics professor; Mercedes is a small business owner.
Filing status:	Married, filing jointly
Current situation:	Bill and Mercedes face an IRS audit involving a previous year's interest deductions.

Bill and Mercedes received a notice from the Internal Revenue Service (IRS) that their return is under audit for certain interest deductions. As you might expect, they are quite concerned, especially because it has been several years since they claimed the deductions and they worry that all their supporting documentation may not be in place. Several questions run through their minds. How could the IRS audit a return that was filed so long ago? Why was their tax return selected, and what should they expect during the audit? The interest deductions they reported were based on advice from their CPA. What would cause the IRS and a CPA to interpret the law differently? What is their financial exposure if the deductions are ultimately disallowed?

Will they have to pay interest and penalties in addition to the tax they might owe? ■

Even the most conservative taxpayer is likely to feel anxiety after receiving an IRS notice. This chapter will help answer Bill and Mercedes's questions and provide an overview of the audit process and tax research. While all taxpayers should understand these basics of our tax system, aspiring accountants should be especially familiar with them.

LO 2-1

TAXPAYER FILING REQUIREMENTS

To file or not to file? Unlike Hamlet's "to be or not to be," this question has a pretty straightforward answer. Filing requirements are specified by law for each type of taxpayer. All corporations must file a tax return annually regardless of their taxable income. Estates and trusts are required to file annual income tax returns if their gross income exceeds $600.[1]

The filing requirements for individual taxpayers are a little more complex. Specifically, they depend on the taxpayer's filing status (single, married filing jointly, and so on, discussed in more detail in Chapter 4), age, and gross income (income before deductions). Exhibit 2-1 lists the 2015 gross income thresholds for taxpayers based on their filing status, gross income, and age. As detailed in Exhibit 2-1, the gross income thresholds are calculated as the sum of the standard deduction, additional deductions for taxpayers age 65 or older, and personal exemption(s) that apply to each respective filing status.[2] These amounts are indexed for inflation and thus change each year. For certain taxpayers such as the self-employed and those claimed as dependents by another taxpayer, lower gross income thresholds apply.

EXHIBIT 2-1 **2015 Gross Income Thresholds by Filing Status**

Filing Status and Age (in 2015)	2015 Gross Income	Explanation
Single	$10,300	$6,300 standard deduction + $4,000 personal exemption
Single, 65 or older	$11,850	$6,300 standard deduction + $1,550 additional deduction + $4,000 personal exemption
Married, filing a joint return	$20,600	$12,600 standard deduction + $8,000 personal exemptions (2)
Married, filing a joint return, one spouse 65 or older	$21,850	$12,600 standard deduction + $1,250 additional deduction + $8,000 personal exemptions (2)
Married, filing a joint return, both spouses 65 or older	$23,100	$12,600 standard deduction + $2,500 additional deductions (2) + $8,000 personal exemptions (2)
Married, filing a separate return	$ 4,000	$4,000 personal exemption
Head of household	$13,250	$9,250 standard deduction + $4,000 personal exemption
Head of household, 65 or older	$14,800	$9,250 standard deduction + $1,550 additional deduction + $4,000 personal exemption
Surviving spouse with a dependent child	$16,600	$12,600 standard deduction + $4,000 personal exemption
Surviving spouse, 65 or older, with a dependent child	$17,850	$12,600 standard deduction + $1,250 additional deduction + $4,000 personal exemption

Whether a taxpayer is due a refund (which occurs when taxes paid exceed tax liability) does *not* determine whether a taxpayer must file a tax return. Gross income determines whether a tax return is required. Further, note that a taxpayer whose

[1]Estates file income tax returns during the administration period (i.e., before all of the estate assets are distributed).

[2]IRC §6012. We describe the standard deduction and personal exemptions in detail later in the text.

gross income falls below the respective threshold is not precluded from filing a tax return. Indeed, taxpayers due a refund *should* file a tax return to receive the refund (or claim a refundable tax credit), even if they are not required to file a tax return.

Tax Return Due Date and Extensions

Like the filing requirements, due dates for tax returns vary based on the type of taxpayer. Individual tax returns are due on the fifteenth day of the fourth month following year-end—that is, April 15 for calendar year individuals. (Due dates that fall on a Saturday, Sunday, or holidays are automatically extended to the next day that is not a Saturday, Sunday, or holiday.) Similarly, partnership returns are also due on the fifteenth day of the fourth month following the partnership's year-end. For corporations, tax returns must be filed by the fifteenth day of the third month following the corporation's year-end (March 15 for calendar-year corporations). Any individual or corporation unable to file a tax return by the original due date can, by that same deadline, request a six-month extension to file, which is granted automatically by the IRS. Similarly, partnerships may request an automatic five-month extension to file.

An extension allows the taxpayer to delay filing a tax return but does *not* extend the due date for tax payments. Thus, when a taxpayer files an extension, she must estimate how much tax will be owed. If a taxpayer fails to pay the entire balance of tax owed by the original due date of the tax return, the IRS charges the taxpayer interest on the underpayment from the due date of the return until the taxpayer pays the tax.[3] The interest rate charged depends on taxpayer type (individual or corporation) and varies quarterly with the federal short-term interest rate.[4] For example, the interest rate for tax underpayments for individuals equals the federal short-term rate plus three percentage points.[5]

What happens if the taxpayer does not file a tax return by the time required, whether April 15 or an extended deadline? As you might guess, the IRS imposes penalties on taxpayers failing to comply with the tax law. In many cases, the penalties can be quite substantial (see later discussion in this chapter). In the case of failure to file a tax return, the penalty equals 5 percent of the tax due for each month (or partial month) that the return is late. However, the maximum penalty is generally 25 percent of the tax owed, and the failure to file penalty does not apply if the taxpayer owes no tax.

THE KEY FACTS

Filing Requirements and Due Dates

- Filing requirements
  - Specified by law for each type of taxpayer.
  - For individuals, filing requirements vary by filing status, gross income, and age.
  - Gross income thresholds are indexed each year for inflation.
- Due dates
  - The due date for tax returns varies based on the type of taxpayer.
  - Individual tax returns are due on April 15 for calendar-year individuals.
  - Due dates that fall on a Saturday, Sunday, or holiday are automatically extended to the next day that is not a Saturday, Sunday, or holiday.
  - Any taxpayer unable to file a tax return by the original due date can request an extension to file.
  - An extension allows the taxpayer to delay filing a tax return but does *not* extend the due date for tax payments.

Statute of Limitations

Despite the diligent efforts of taxpayers and tax professionals, it is quite common for tax returns to contain mistakes. Some may be to the taxpayer's advantage and others may be to the government's advantage. Regardless of the nature of the mistake, the taxpayer is obligated to file an amended return to correct the error (and request a refund or pay a deficiency) if the statute of limitations has not expired for the tax return. Likewise, the IRS can propose adjustments to the taxpayer's return if the statute of limitations for the return has not expired.

By law, the **statute of limitations** defines the period in which the taxpayer can file an amended tax return or the IRS can assess a tax deficiency for a specific tax year. For both amended tax returns filed by a taxpayer and proposed tax assessments by the IRS, the statute of limitations generally ends three years from the *later* of (1) the date the tax return was actually filed or (2) the tax return's original due date.

The statute of limitations for IRS assessment can be extended in certain circumstances. For example, a six-year statute of limitations applies to IRS assessments if the taxpayer omits items of gross income that exceed 25 percent of the gross income

[3]The tax law also imposes a penalty for late payment in addition to the interest charged on the underpayment. We briefly discuss this penalty later in the chapter and in Chapter 8.

[4]The federal short-term rate is determined from a one-month average of the market yields from marketable obligations of the United States with maturities of three years or less.

[5]This same interest rate applies to individuals who overpay their taxes (i.e., receive a tax refund and interest payment as a result of an IRS audit or from filing an amended tax return).

reported on the tax return. For fraudulent returns, or if the taxpayer fails to file a tax return, the news is understandably worse. The statute of limitations remains open indefinitely in these cases.

Example 2-1

Bill and Mercedes file their 2011 federal tax return on September 6, 2012, after receiving an automatic extension to file their return by October 15, 2012. In 2015, the IRS selects their 2011 tax return for audit. When does the statute of limitations end for Bill and Mercedes's 2011 tax return?

Answer: Assuming the six-year and "unlimited" statute of limitation rules do not apply, the statute of limitations ends on September 6, 2015 (three years after the later of the actual filing date and the *original* due date).

What if: When would the statute of limitations end for Bill and Mercedes for their 2011 tax return if the couple filed the return on March 22, 2012 (before the original due date of April 17, 2012)?

Answer: In this scenario the statute of limitations would end on April 17, 2015, because the later of the actual filing date and the original due date is April 17, 2012.

Taxpayers should prepare for the possibility of an audit by retaining all supporting documents (receipts, cancelled checks, etc.) for a tax return until the statute of limitations expires. After the statute of limitations expires, taxpayers can discard the majority of supporting documents but should still keep a copy of the tax return itself, as well as any documents that may have ongoing significance, such as those establishing the taxpayer's *basis* or original investment in existing assets like personal residences and long-term investments.

LO 2-2 IRS AUDIT SELECTION

Why me? This is a recurring question in life and definitely a common taxpayer question after receiving an IRS audit notice. The answer, in general, is that a taxpayer's return is selected for audit because the IRS has data suggesting the taxpayer's tax return has a high probability of a significant understated tax liability. Budget constraints limit the IRS's ability to audit a majority or even a large minority of tax returns. Currently, fewer than 2 percent of all tax returns are audited. Thus, the IRS must be strategic in selecting returns for audit in an effort to promote the highest level of voluntary taxpayer compliance and increase tax revenues.

Specifically, how does the IRS select tax returns for audit? The IRS uses a number of computer programs and outside data sources (newspapers, financial statement disclosures, informants, and other public and private sources) to identify tax returns that may have an understated tax liability. Common computer initiatives include the **DIF (Discriminant Function) system, document perfection program,** and **information matching program.** The most important of these initiatives is the DIF system. The DIF system assigns a score to each tax return that represents the probability the tax liability on the return has been underreported (a higher score = a higher likelihood of underreporting). The IRS derives the weights assigned to specific tax return attributes from historical IRS audit adjustment data from the National Research Program.[6] The DIF system then uses these (undisclosed) weights to score each tax return based on the tax return's characteristics. Returns with higher DIF scores are then reviewed to determine whether an audit is the best course of action.

[6]Similar to its predecessor, the Taxpayer Compliance Measurement Program, the National Research Program (NRP) analyzes a large sample of tax returns that are randomly selected for audit. From these randomly selected returns, the IRS identifies tax return characteristics (e.g., deductions for a home office, unusually high tax deductions relative to a taxpayer's income) associated with underreported liabilities, weights these characteristics, and then incorporates them into the DIF system. The NRP analyzes randomly selected returns to ensure that the DIF scorings are representative of the population of tax returns.

All returns are checked for mathematical and tax calculation errors, a process referred to as the document perfection program. Individual returns are also subject to the information matching program. This program compares the taxpayer's tax return to information submitted to the IRS from other taxpayers like banks, employers, mutual funds, brokerage companies, and mortgage companies. Information matched includes items such as wages (Form W-2 submitted by employers), interest income (Form 1099-INT submitted by banks), and dividend income (Form 1099-DIV submitted by brokerage companies). For tax returns identified as incorrect via the document perfection and information matching programs, the IRS recalculates the taxpayer's tax liability and sends a notice explaining the adjustment. If the taxpayer owes tax, the IRS will request payment of the tax due. If the taxpayer overpaid tax, the IRS will send the taxpayer a refund of the overpayment.

In addition to computer-based methods for identifying tax returns for audit, the IRS may use a number of other audit initiatives that target taxpayers in certain industries, engaged in certain transactions like the acquisition of other companies, or having specific attributes like home office deductions. Taxpayers of a given size and complexity, such as large publicly traded companies, may be audited every year.

THE KEY FACTS

IRS Audit Selection

- The IRS uses a number of computer programs and outside data sources to identify tax returns that may have an understated tax liability.
- Common computer initiatives include the DIF (Discriminant Function) system, document perfection program, and information matching program.
- The DIF system assigns a score to each tax return that represents the probability the tax liability on the return has been underreported.
- The document perfection program checks all returns for mathematical and tax calculation errors.
- The information matching program compares the taxpayer's tax return to information submitted to the IRS from other taxpayers.

TAXES IN THE REAL WORLD Turning in Your Neighbor Can Pay Big Bucks

The Wall Street Journal reported that in April 2011 the IRS paid its first payment under its new taxpayer whistleblower program that promises large rewards for turning in tax cheats. Under the large-award whistleblower program (where unpaid taxes, interest, and penalties exceed $2 million and the tax cheat, if an individual, had gross income exceeding $200,000 in at least one year), whistleblowers can be paid between 15 and 30 percent of the taxes, interest, and penalties collected by the IRS. Under the small-award whistleblower program (tax, interest, and penalty underpayments of $2 million or less), the IRS may pay whistleblowers up to 15 percent of the unpaid taxes and interest collected. Whistleblowers use IRS Form 211 (www.IRS.gov) to apply for the program, and as you might expect, all whistleblower payments received are fully taxable. In its first payment, the IRS paid $4.5 million to a former in-house accountant for a large financial services firm. Given the potential windfall to whistleblowers, you might expect a long line of "concerned" citizens applying for the program. You would be correct. As of August 2014, the IRS Commissioner announced that the IRS has paid out more than $186 million in awards in the preceding three years, on collection of more than $1 billion based on whistleblower information.

Based on: "Taxes: How to Turn in Your Neighbor to the IRS," *The Wall Street Journal*, WSJ.com, September 3, 2011.

How was Bill and Mercedes's tax return selected for audit? Given the audit focus on certain deductions, the IRS likely selected their return for audit because the amount or type of the deductions resulted in a high DIF score. IRS personnel then determined that the deductions warranted further review and, thus, selected the tax return for audit.

ETHICS

After Bill and Mercedes's tax return was selected for audit, Bill read on the Internet speculation that filing a paper copy tax return (instead of filing electronically) and extending a tax return decrease the chance of IRS audit. Bill has convinced Mercedes that they need to use these strategies going forward and look for other ways to avoid audit. Has Bill crossed an ethical boundary?

Types of Audits

The three types of IRS audits are correspondence, office, and field examinations. **Correspondence examinations** are the most common. These audits, as the name suggests, are conducted by mail and generally are limited to one or two items on the taxpayer's return. Of the three types of audits, correspondence audits are generally the narrowest in scope and the least complex. The IRS typically requests supporting documentation for one or more items on the taxpayer's return, like charitable contributions deducted, for example. When appropriate documentation is promptly supplied, these audits typically can be concluded relatively quickly. Of course, they can also be expanded to address other issues that arise as a result of the IRS's inspection of taxpayer documents.

Office examinations are the second most common audit. As the name suggests, the IRS conducts them at its local office. These audits are typically broader in scope and more complex than correspondence examinations. Small businesses, taxpayers operating sole proprietorships, and middle- to high-income individual taxpayers are more likely, if audited, to have office examinations. In these examinations, the taxpayer receives a notice that identifies the items subject to audit; requests substantiation for these items as necessary; and notifies the taxpayer of the date, time, and location of the exam. Taxpayers may attend the examination alone, with representation, such as their tax adviser or attorney, or simply let their tax adviser or attorney attend on the taxpayer's behalf.

Field examinations are the least common audit. The IRS conducts these at the taxpayer's place of business or the location where the taxpayer's books, records, and source documents are maintained. Field examinations are generally the broadest in scope and the most complex of the three audit types. They can last months to years and generally are limited to business returns and the most complex individual returns.

What type of exam do you think Bill and Mercedes will have? Because their return is an individual tax return and the audit is restricted to a relatively narrow set of deductions, their return will likely be subject to a correspondence audit. If the audit were broader in scope, an office examination would be more likely.

After the Audit After the examination, the IRS agent provides a list of proposed adjustments (if any) to the taxpayer for review. If he or she agrees to the proposed changes, the taxpayer signs an agreement form (Form 870) and pays the additional tax owed or receives the proposed refund. If the taxpayer disputes the proposed changes, the taxpayer will receive a **30-day letter** giving him or her 30 days to either (1) request a conference with an appeals officer, who is independent and resides in a separate IRS division from the examining agent, or (2) agree to the proposed adjustment. An appeals officer would consider the merits of the unresolved issues as well as the "hazards of litigation"—that is, the probability that the IRS will lose if the case is brought to court and the resulting costs of a taxpayer-favorable ruling. If the taxpayer chooses the appeals conference and reaches an agreement with the IRS there, the taxpayer can then sign the Form 870. If the taxpayer and IRS still do not agree on the proposed adjustment at the appeals conference, or the taxpayer chooses not to request an appeals conference, the IRS will send the taxpayer a 90-day letter. See Exhibit 2-2.

THE KEY FACTS

IRS Audits

- The three types of IRS audits are correspondence, office, and field examinations.
- After the audit, the IRS will send the taxpayer a 30-day letter, which provides the taxpayer the opportunity to pay the proposed assessment or request an appeals conference.
- If an agreement is not reached at appeals or the taxpayer does not pay the proposed assessment, the IRS will send the taxpayer a 90-day letter.
- After receiving the 90-day letter, the taxpayer may pay the tax or petition the U.S. Tax Court to hear the case.
- If the taxpayer chooses to pay the tax, the taxpayer may then request a refund of the tax and eventually sue the IRS for refund in the U.S. District Court or the U.S. Court of Federal Claims.

The **90-day letter** (also known as a *statutory notice of deficiency*) explains that the taxpayer has 90 days to either (1) pay the proposed deficiency or (2) file a petition in the U.S. Tax Court to hear the case.[7] The **U.S. Tax Court** is a national court whose judges are tax experts and who hear only tax cases. If the taxpayer would like to litigate the case but prefers it to be heard in the local **U.S. District Court** or the **U.S. Court of Federal Claims,** the taxpayer must pay the tax deficiency first, then request a refund from the IRS, and then sue the IRS for refund in the court after the IRS denies the refund claim.

Why would a taxpayer prefer one trial court over others? To understand this, we must appreciate the basic distinguishing factors of each. First and foremost, it is relatively common for the U.S. Tax Court, local U.S. District Court, or the U.S. Court of Federal Claims to interpret and rule differently on the same basic tax issue. Given a choice of courts, the taxpayer should prefer the court most likely to rule favorably on

[7]If the taxpayer lacks the funds to pay the assessed tax, there is legitimate doubt as to whether the taxpayer owes part or all of the assessed tax, or collection of the tax would cause the taxpayer economic hardship or be unfair or inequitable, the taxpayer can request an offer in compromise with the IRS to settle the tax liability for less than the full amount assessed by completing Form 656.

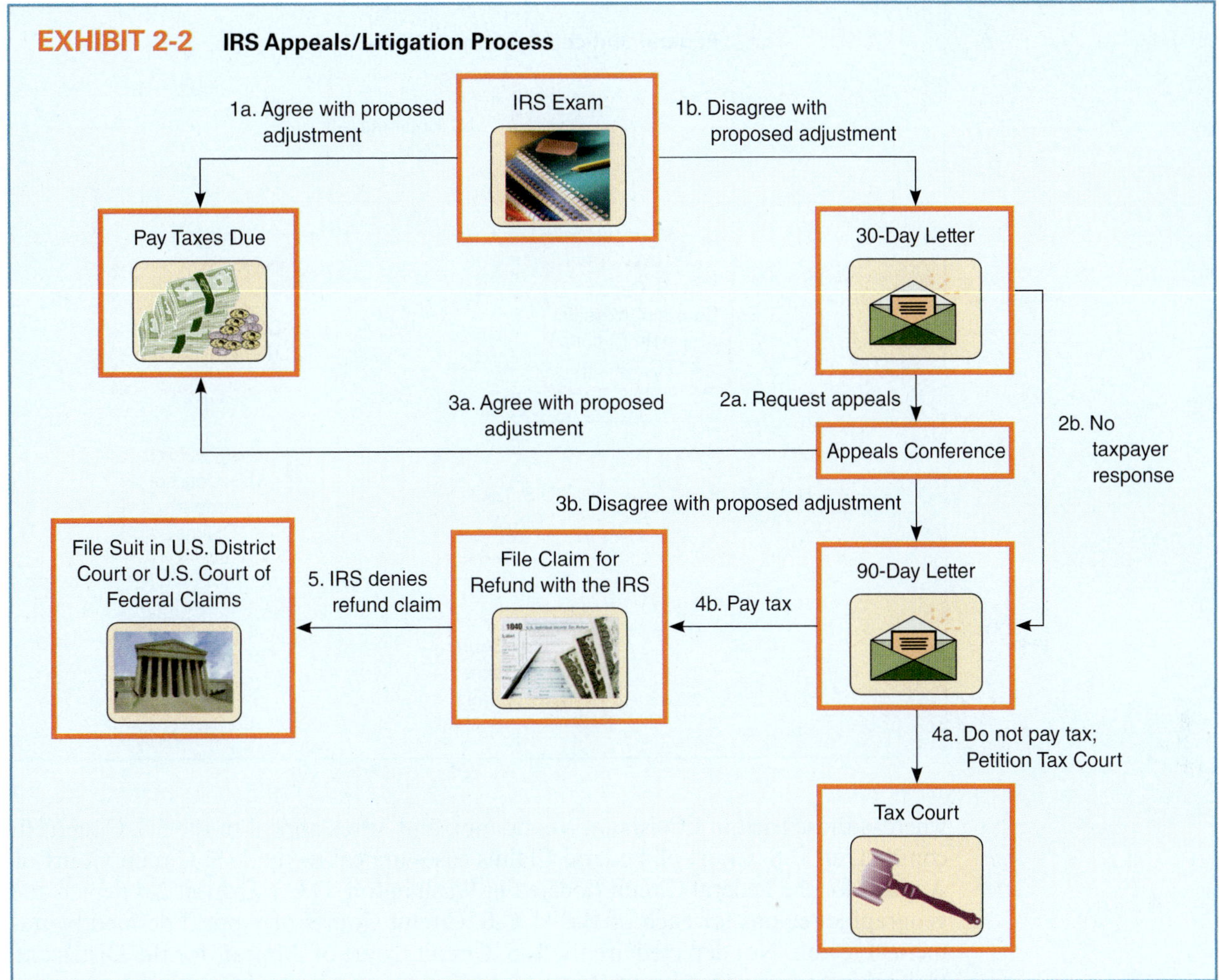

IRS Exam: © Royalty-Free/Corbis, Supreme Court: ©The McGraw-Hill Companies, Inc./Jill Braaten, photographer, File Claim: © Michael A. Keller/Corbis

his or her particular issues. The courts also differ in other ways. For example, the U.S. District Court is the only court that provides for a jury trial; the U.S. Tax Court is the only court that allows tax cases to be heard *before* the taxpayer pays the disputed liability and the only court with a small claims division (hearing claims involving disputed liabilities of $50,000 or less); the U.S. Tax Court judges are tax experts, whereas the U.S. District Court and U.S. Court of Federal Claims judges are generalists. The taxpayer should consider each of these factors in choosing a trial court. For example, if the taxpayer feels very confident in her tax return position but does not have sufficient funds to pay the disputed liability, she will prefer the U.S. Tax Court. If, instead, the taxpayer is litigating a tax return position that is low on technical merit but high on emotional appeal, a jury trial in the local U.S. District Court may be the best option.

What happens after the taxpayer's case is decided in a trial court? The process may not be quite finished. After the trial court's verdict, the losing party has the right to request one of the 13 **U.S. Circuit Courts of Appeals** to hear the case. Exhibit 2-3 depicts the specific appellant courts for each lower-level court. Both the U.S. Tax Court and local U.S. District Court cases are appealed to the specific U.S. Circuit Court of Appeals based on the taxpayer's residence.[8] Cases litigated in Alabama, Florida, and Georgia, for example, appeal to the U.S. Circuit Court of Appeals for the 11th Circuit;

[8]Decisions rendered by the U.S. Tax Court Small Claims Division cannot be appealed by the taxpayer or the IRS.

EXHIBIT 2-3 Federal Judicial System

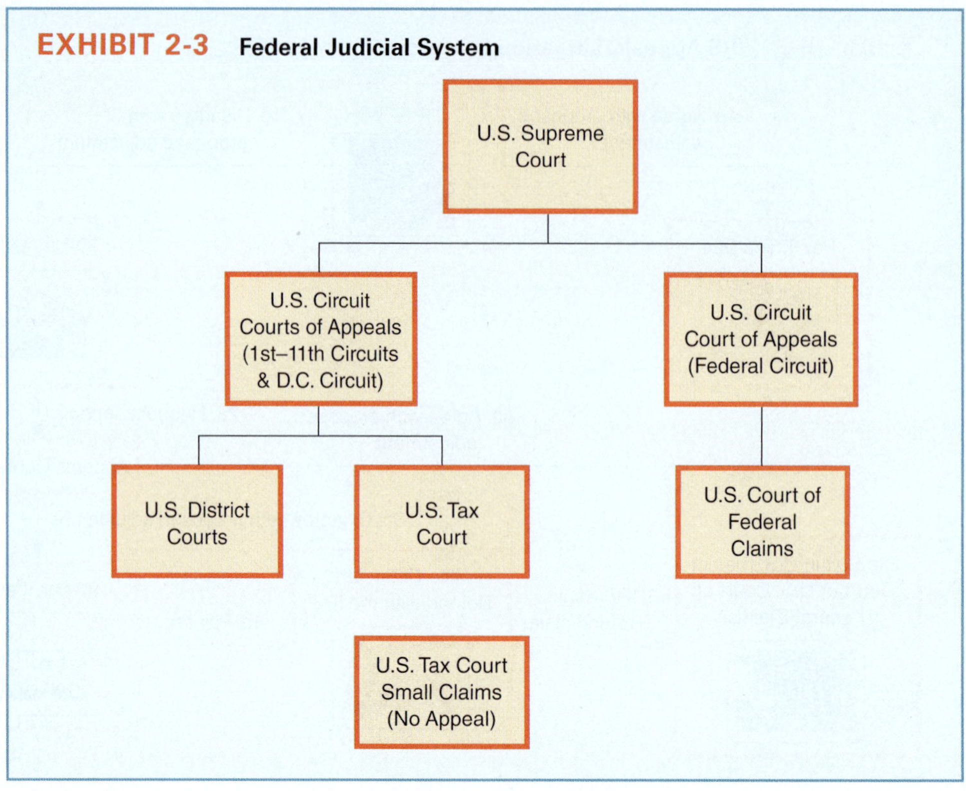

whereas those tried in Louisiana, Mississippi, and Texas appeal to the 5th Circuit. In contrast, all U.S. Court of Federal Claims cases appeal to the U.S. Circuit Court of Appeals for the Federal Circuit (located in Washington, D.C.). Exhibit 2-4 depicts the geographic regions for each of the 11 U.S. Circuit Courts of Appeal defined by numerical region. Not depicted are the U.S. Circuit Court of Appeals for the District of Columbia and the U.S. Circuit Court of Appeals for the Federal Circuit.

Through the initial selection of a trial court—U.S. District Court, U.S. Tax Court, or U.S. Court of Federal Claims—the taxpayer has the ability to determine which circuit court would hear an appeal of the case (the U.S. Circuit Court of Appeals based on residence or the U.S. Circuit Court of Appeals for the Federal Circuit). Because alternative circuit courts may interpret the law differently, the taxpayer should consider in choosing a trial-level court the relevant circuit courts' judicial histories to determine which circuit court (and thus, which trial court) would be more likely to rule in his or her favor.

After an appeals court hears a case, the losing party has one last option to receive a favorable ruling: a petition to the **U.S. Supreme Court** to hear the case. However, given the quantity of other cases appealed to the U.S. Supreme Court that are of national importance, the Supreme Court agrees to hear only a few tax cases a year with great significance to a broad cross-section of taxpayers, or cases litigating issues in which there has been disagreement among the circuit courts. For most tax cases, the Supreme Court refuses to hear the case (denies the ***writ of certiorari***) and litigation ends with the circuit court decision.

Although litigation of tax disputes is quite common, taxpayers should carefully consider the pros and cons. Litigation can be very costly financially and emotionally, and thus it is more appropriately used as an option of last resort, after all other appeal efforts have been exhausted.

What is the likely course of action for Bill and Mercedes's audit? It is too soon to tell. Before you can assess the likely outcome of their audit, you need a better understanding of both the audit issue and the relevant tax laws that apply to the issue. The next section explains alternative tax law sources. After we discuss the various sources

EXHIBIT 2-4 Geographic Boundaries for the U.S. Circuit Courts of Appeal

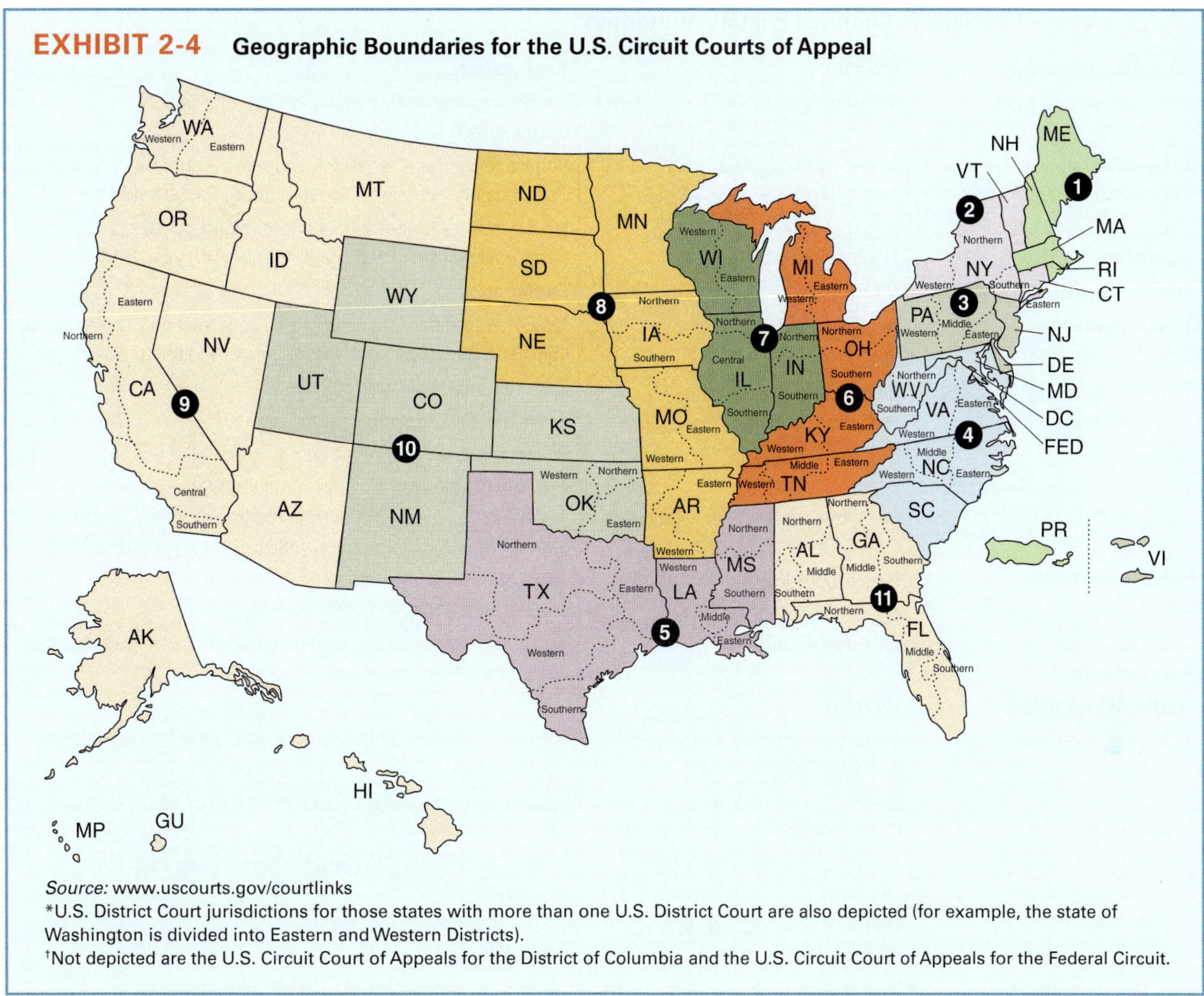

Source: www.uscourts.gov/courtlinks

*U.S. District Court jurisdictions for those states with more than one U.S. District Court are also depicted (for example, the state of Washington is divided into Eastern and Western Districts).

†Not depicted are the U.S. Circuit Court of Appeals for the District of Columbia and the U.S. Circuit Court of Appeals for the Federal Circuit.

of our tax laws, we'll describe how Bill and Mercedes (or their CPA) can research the sources to identify the best possible course of action.[9]

TAX LAW SOURCES

LO 2-3 LO 2-4

There are two broad categories of tax authorities: primary authorities and secondary authorities. **Primary authorities** are official sources of the tax law generated by the legislative branch (statutory authority issued by Congress), judicial branch (rulings by the U.S. District Court, U.S. Tax Court, U.S. Court of Federal Claims, U.S. Circuit Court of Appeals, or U.S. Supreme Court), and executive/administrative branch (Treasury and IRS pronouncements). Exhibit 2-5 displays the most common primary sources, their respective citations, and related explanations. We'll discuss each of these authorities below.

Secondary authorities are unofficial tax authorities that interpret and explain the primary authorities, such as tax research services (discussed below), tax articles from professional journals and law reviews, newsletters, and textbooks. For quick questions, practitioners often use the *CCH Master Tax Guide* or *RIA Federal Tax Handbook*. Secondary authorities may be very helpful in understanding a tax issue, but

[9]Accountants should be mindful to not engage in the unauthorized practice of law. In years past, several court cases have addressed this issue without providing a clear understanding between practicing tax accounting and the unauthorized practice of law. At present, tax accountants are not likely to overstep their responsibilities if they limit their advice to tax issues and leave the general legal advice and drafting of legal documents to attorneys.

EXHIBIT 2-5 Citations to Common Primary Authorities

Statutory Authorities:	***Citation:***	***Explanation:***
Internal Revenue Code	IRC Sec. 162(e)(2)(B)(i)	Section number 162, subsection e, paragraph 2, subparagraph B, clause i
Committee Reports: Senate Finance Committee Report	S. Rep. No. 353, 82d Cong., 1st Sess. 14 (1951).	Senate report number 353, Congress number 82, Congressional session 1, page number 14, year 1951
House Ways and Means Committee Report	H. Rep. No. 242, 82d Cong., 1st Sess. 40 (1951)	House report number 242, Congress number 82, Congressional session 1, page number 40, year 1951
Administrative Authorities:	***Citation:***	***Explanation:***
Final Regulation	Reg. Sec. 1.217-2(c)(1)	Type of regulation (1 = income tax), code section 217, regulation number 2, paragraph number c, subparagraph number 1
Temporary Regulation	Temp. Reg. Sec. 1.217-2(c)(1)	Same as final regulation
Proposed Regulation	Prop. Reg. Sec. 1.217-2(c)(1)	Same as final regulation
Revenue Ruling	Rev. Rul. 77-262, 1977-2 C.B. 41	Ruling number 77-262 (262nd ruling of 1977), volume number of cumulative bulletin 1977-2, page number 41
Revenue Procedure	Rev. Proc. 99-10, 1999-1 C.B. 272	Procedure number 99-10 (10th procedure of 1999), volume number of cumulative bulletin 1999-1, page number 272
Private Letter Ruling	PLR 200601001	Year 2006, week number 01 (1st week of 2006), ruling number 001 (1st ruling of the week)
Technical Advice Memorandum	TAM 200402001	Year 2004, week number 02 (2nd week of 2004), ruling number 001 (1st ruling of the week)
Judicial Authorities:	***Citation:***	
U.S. Supreme Court	*Comm. v. Kowalski*, 434 U.S. 77 (S. Ct., 1977)	Volume 434 of the GPO court reporter, page 77, year 1977
	Comm. v. Kowalski, 98 S. Ct. 315 (S. Ct., 1977)	Volume 98 of the West court reporter, page 315, year 1977
	Comm. v. Kowalski, 77-2 USTC par. 9,748 (S. Ct., 1977)	Volume 77-2 of the CCH court reporter, paragraph 9,748, year 1977
	Comm. v. Kowalski, 40 AFTR2d 77-6128 (S. Ct., 1977)	Volume 40 of the RIA AFTR2d court reporter, paragraph 77-6128, year 1977
U.S. Circuit Court of Appeals	*Azar Nut Co. v. Comm.*, 931 F.2d 314 (5th Cir., 1991)	Volume 931 of the West F.2d court reporter, page 314, circuit 5th, year 1991
	Azar Nut Co. v. Comm., 91-1 USTC par. 50,257 (5th Cir., 1991)	Volume 91-1 of the CCH USTC court reporter, paragraph 50,257, circuit 5th, year 1991
	Azar Nut Co. v. Comm., 67 AFTR2d 91-987 (5th Cir., 1991)	Volume 67 of the RIA AFTR2d court reporter, paragraph 77-6128, year 1977
U.S. Tax Court—Regular decision	*L.A. Beeghly*, 36 TC 154 (1962)	Volume 36 of the Tax Court reporter, page 154, year 1962
U.S. Tax Court—Memorandum decision	*Robert Rodriguez*, RIA TC Memo 2005-012	Paragraph number 2005-012 of the RIA Tax Court Memorandum reporter
	Robert Rodriguez, 85 TCM 1162 (2005)	Volume 85 of the CCH Tax Court Memorandum reporter, page 1162, year 2005
U.S. Court of Federal Claims	*J.R. Cohen v. U.S.*, 510 F. Supp. 297 (Fed. Cl., 1993)	Volume 510 of the West F. Supp. court reporter, page 297, year 1993
	J.R. Cohen v. U.S., 72 AFTR2d 93-5124 (Fed. Cl., 1993)	Volume 72 of the RIA AFTR2d court reporter, paragraph 93-5124, year 1993
	J.R. Cohen v. U.S., 93-1 USTC par. 50,354 (Fed. Cl., 1993)	Volume 93-1 of the CCH USTC court reporter, paragraph 50,354, year 1993
U.S. District Court	*Waxler Towing Co., Inc. v. U.S.*, 510 F. Supp. 297 (W.D, TN, 1981)	Volume 510 of the West F. Supp. court reporter, page 297, Western District (W.D.), state Tennessee, year 1981
	Waxler Towing Co., Inc. v. U.S., 81-2 USTC par. 9,541 (W.D., TN, 1981)	Volume 81-2 of the CCH USTC court reporter, paragraph 9,541, Western District (W.D.), state Tennessee, year 1981
	Waxler Towing Co., Inc. v. U.S., 48 AFTR2d 81-5274 (W.D., TN, 1981)	Volume 48 of the RIA AFTR2d court reporter, paragraph 81-5274, Western District (W.D.), state Tennessee, year 1981

EXHIBIT 2-6 Common Secondary Tax Authorities

Tax Research Services:	***Professional Journals:***
BNA Tax Management Portfolios	*Journal of Accountancy*
CCH Standard Federal Tax Reporter	*Journal of Taxation*
CCH Tax Research Consultant	*Practical Tax Strategies*
RIA Federal Tax Coordinator	*Taxes*
RIA United States Tax Reporter	*Tax Adviser*
Newsletters:	***Quick Reference Sources:***
Daily Tax Report	*IRS Publications*
Federal Tax Weekly Alert	*CCH Master Tax Guide*
Tax Notes	*RIA Federal Tax Handbook*
Law Reviews:	***Textbooks:***
Tax Law Review (New York University School of Law)	*McGraw-Hill's Taxation of Individuals and Business Entities*
Virginia Tax Review (University of Virginia School of Law)	*McGraw-Hill's Essentials of Federal Taxation*

they hold little weight in a tax dispute (hence their "unofficial" status). Thus, tax advisers should always be careful to verify their understanding of tax law by examining primary authorities directly and to *never* cite secondary authority in a research memo. Exhibit 2-6 lists some of the common sources of secondary authority.

TAXES IN THE REAL WORLD Google: Not Authoritative on Tax Matters

While Internet super giant Google may be the king of all cyberspace knowledge, the Tax Court ruled in *Woodard v. Comm.*, TC Summary Opinion 2009-150, that a Google search does not constitute reasonable cause to excuse a Harvard MBA/CPA from taking an incorrect tax return position. The Tax Court noted that although the taxpayer had not worked as an accountant for years before filing his tax return, "his accounting degree, MBA, and CPA training, no matter how stale, undoubtedly taught him what sources could be relied upon as definitive; such as, for example, the Internal Revenue Code and the income tax regulations, both of which are readily available on the Internet."

Legislative Sources: Congress and the Constitution

The three legislative or statutory tax authorities are the U.S. Constitution, the Internal Revenue Code, and tax treaties. The **U.S. Constitution** is the highest authority in the United States, but it provides very little in the way of tax law since it contains no discussion of tax rates, taxable income, or other details. Instead, the 16th Amendment provides Congress the ability to tax income directly, from whatever source derived, without apportionment across the states.

Various attempts to amend the U.S. Constitution with regard to taxation—for example, one effort to repeal the 16th Amendment entirely and one to require a two-thirds majority in both houses to raise taxes—have so far met with failure.

Internal Revenue Code The second (and main) statutory authority is the **Internal Revenue Code of 1986,** as amended, known as the Code. The Internal Revenue Code has the same authoritative weight as tax treaties and Supreme Court rulings. Thus, a taxpayer should feel very confident in a tax return position, such as taking a deduction that is specifically allowed by the Code. The Internal Revenue Code is unique in that every other authority—all administrative and judicial authorities except tax treaties

EXHIBIT 2-7 Tax Legislation Process

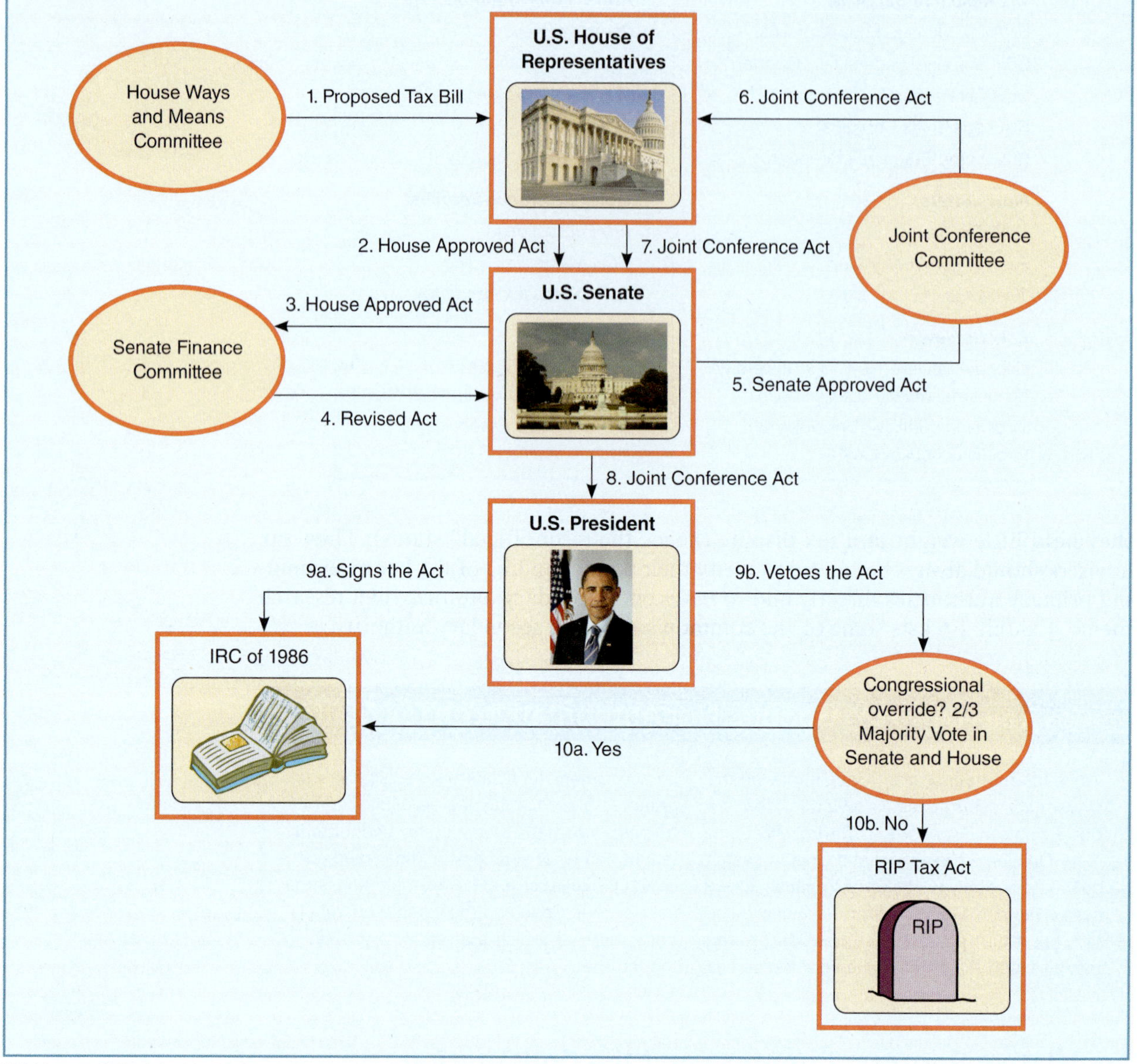

House Ways and Means Committee
1. Proposed Tax Bill
U.S. House of Representatives
6. Joint Conference Act
Joint Conference Committee
2. House Approved Act
7. Joint Conference Act
U.S. Senate
3. House Approved Act
Senate Finance Committee
4. Revised Act
5. Senate Approved Act
8. Joint Conference Act
U.S. President
9a. Signs the Act
9b. Vetoes the Act
IRC of 1986
Congressional override? 2/3 Majority Vote in Senate and House
10a. Yes
10b. No
RIP Tax Act
RIP

US House: © Dwight Nadig/Getty Images, US Senate: © Brand X Pictures/PunchStock, President: Library of Congress Prints and Photographs Division [LC-DIG-ppbd-00358]

and the Constitution—can be seen as an interpretation of it. Hence, understanding the relevant code section(s) is critical to being an efficient and effective tax professional.

Congress enacts tax legislation virtually every year that changes the Code; 1986 was simply the last major overhaul. Prior to 1986, tax law changes were incorporated into the Internal Revenue Code of 1954, the year a new numbering system and other significant changes were introduced. Before that, tax law changes were incorporated into the Internal Revenue Code of 1939, which was the year of the first Code.

The Legislative Process for Tax Laws Exhibit 2-7 illustrates the legislative process for enacting tax laws. As required by the U.S. Constitution (Article 1, Section 7), "All bills for raising revenue shall originate in the House of Representatives." The Senate may propose tax legislation, but the first to formally consider a bill will be the House, typically within its Ways and Means Committee. After the committee debates the proposed legislation and drafts a bill, the bill goes to the House of Representatives floor for debate and ultimately a vote (either yea or nay without modification). If the bill is approved, it becomes an *act* and is sent to the Senate, which typically refers the act to the Senate Finance Committee. Not to be outdone by the House, the Senate Finance Committee usually amends the act during its deliberations. After the revised act passes the Senate Finance Committee, it goes to the Senate for debate and vote. Unlike representatives, senators may modify the proposed legislation during their debate.

If the Senate passes the act, both the House and Senate versions of the legislation are sent to the Joint Conference Committee, which consists of members of the House Ways and Means Committee and the Senate Finance Committee. During the Joint Conference Committee deliberations, committee members debate the two versions of the proposed legislation. Possible outcomes for any specific provision in the proposed legislation include adoption of the Senate version, the House version, or some compromise version of the two acts. Likewise, the Joint Conference Committee may simply choose to eliminate specific provisions from the proposed legislation or fail to reach a compromise, thereby terminating the legislation.

After the Joint Conference Committee approves the act, the revised legislation is sent to the House and Senate for vote. If both the House and Senate approve it, the act is sent to the president for his or her signature. If the president signs the act, it becomes law and is incorporated into the Internal Revenue Code of 1986 (Title 26 of the U.S. Code, which contains *all* codified laws of the United States). If the president vetoes the legislation, Congress may override the veto with a two-thirds positive vote in both the House and the Senate.

The House Ways and Means Committee, Senate Finance Committee, and Joint Conference Committee each produce a committee report that explains the current tax law, proposed change in the law, and reasons for the change. These committee reports are considered statutory sources of the tax law and may be very useful in interpreting tax law changes and understanding congressional intent. This is especially important after new legislation has been enacted because, with the exception of the Code, there will be very little authority interpreting the new law (i.e., no judicial or administrative authorities because of the time it takes for the new law to be litigated or for the IRS to issue interpretative guidance).

Basic Organization of the Code The Internal Revenue Code is segregated into subtitles, chapters, subchapters, parts, subparts, and sections. All existing and any new tax laws are placed in the Code within a specific subtitle, chapter, subchapter, part, subpart, and section of the Code. When referencing a tax law, the researcher generally refers to the law simply by its code section. Code sections are numbered from 1 to 9833, with gaps in the section numbers to allow new code sections to be added to the appropriate parts of the Code as needed. Each code section is further segregated into subsections, paragraphs, subparagraphs, and clauses to allow more specific reference or citation. See Exhibit 2-5 for an example code citation and explanation.

Memorizing the various subtitles and chapters of the Code has limited value (except to impress your friends at parties). However, understanding the *organization* of the Code is important, especially for the aspiring tax accountant. (See Exhibit 2-8.) First, you must understand the organization of a code section, its subsections, paragraphs, subparagraphs, and clauses to be able to cite the respective law correctly as, for example, IRC Sec. 162(b)(2). Second, note that many provisions in the Code apply only to specific parts of the Code. For example, it is quite common for a code section to include the phrase "for purposes of this chapter, ..." If you do not understand what laws are encompassed in the chapter, it would be very difficult for you to interpret the code section and determine its applicability to a research question.

Finally, remember that code sections addressing similar transactions, such as deductions, or topics, such as C corporations, are grouped together. Consider a researcher faced with the question of whether an item of income is taxable. If the researcher understands the organization of the Code, she can quickly focus her research on code sections 61–140, which provide a broad definition of gross income, list items specifically included in gross income, and identify items specifically excluded from gross income.

THE KEY FACTS

Statutory Authorities

- U.S. Constitution
  - The 16th Amendment provides Congress the ability to tax income directly, from whatever source derived, without apportionment across the states.
- Internal Revenue Code
  - The main statutory authority is the Internal Revenue Code of 1986.
  - The Internal Revenue Code has the same authoritative weight as tax treaties and Supreme Court rulings.
  - Changes to the Code are passed by the House of Representatives and Senate and signed into law by the president.
  - The House Ways and Means Committee and Senate Finance Committee oversee tax legislation in the House of Representatives and Senate, respectively.
  - When referencing a tax law, the researcher generally refers to the law by its code section.
- Treaties
  - Tax treaties are agreements negotiated between countries that describe the tax treatment of entities subject to tax in both countries.

EXHIBIT 2-8 Example of Code Organization

Subtitle A—Income Taxes
Chapter 1—Income Taxes
Subchapter A—Determination of Tax Liability
Part I—Definition of Gross Income, Adjusted Gross Income, Taxable Income, etc. (Sec. 61–68)
Sec. 61—Gross Income Defined
Sec. 62—Adjusted Gross Income Defined
Sec. 63—Taxable Income Defined
Subsection 63(c)—Standard Deduction
Paragraph 63(c)(2)—Basic Standard Deduction
Subparagraph 63(c)(2)(A) . . .
Clause 63(c)(2)(A)(i) . . .
Part II—Items Specifically Included in Gross Income (Sec. 71–90)
Sec. 71—Alimony
Sec. 72—Annuities
Sec. 73—Services of Child
Sec. 74—Prizes & Awards - . . .
Part III—Items Specifically Excluded from Gross Income (Sec. 101–140)
Sec. 101—Certain Death Benefits
Sec. 102—Gifts and Inheritances
Sec. 103—Interest on State & Local Bonds

Tax Treaties **Tax treaties** are negotiated agreements between countries that describe the tax treatment of entities subject to tax in both countries, such as U.S. citizens earning investment income in Spain. The U.S. president has the authority to enter into a tax treaty with another country after receiving the Senate's advice. If you are a U.S. citizen earning income abroad or an accountant with international clients, you need knowledge of U.S. tax laws, the foreign country's tax laws, and the respective tax treaty between the U.S. and the foreign country for efficient tax planning. Because the focus in this text is on U.S. tax laws, we only briefly mention the importance of tax treaties as a statutory authority.

Example 2-2

Bill recently spent a summer in Milan, Italy, teaching a graduate level economics course. While in Italy he earned a $20,000 stipend from Bocconi University and some interest in a temporary banking account that he established for the trip. What tax laws must Bill consider to determine the taxation of his $20,000 stipend?

Answer: U.S. tax laws, Italian tax laws, and the U.S.–Italy tax treaty will determine the tax consequences of the amounts Bill earned in Italy.

THE KEY FACTS

Judicial Authorities

- Our judicial system is tasked with the ultimate authority to interpret the Internal Revenue Code and settle disputes between taxpayers and the IRS.
- The Supreme Court is the highest judicial authority.
- Beneath the Supreme Court, the decisions of the 13 Circuit Courts of Appeal represent the next highest judicial authority.

(continued)

Judicial Sources: The Courts

Our judicial system has the ultimate authority to interpret the Internal Revenue Code and settle disputes between the IRS and taxpayers. As Exhibit 2-3 illustrates, there are five basic sources of judicial authority (three trial-level courts, 13 U.S. Circuit Courts of Appeal, and the Supreme Court). We've noted that the Supreme Court, along with the Code, represents the highest tax-specific authority. An important distinction between the two, however, is that the Supreme Court does not establish law, but instead simply interprets and applies the Code (along with other authorities). Thus, the Code and the Supreme Court should never be in conflict.[10]

[10]The Supreme Court does have the authority to declare a Code provision unconstitutional.

Below the Supreme Court, the decisions of the 13 U.S. Circuit Courts of Appeal represent the next highest judicial authority. The lowest level of judicial authority consists of three different types of trial-level courts (94 U.S. District Courts that hear cases involving taxpayers that reside within their respective district, the U.S. Court of Federal Claims, and the U.S. Tax Court). Given that the U.S. Tax Court hears only tax cases and that its judges are "tax experts," its decisions typically have more weight than those rendered by a district court or the U.S. Court of Federal Claims.[11] Likewise, because the U.S. Court of Federal Claims hears a much narrower set of issues than U.S. District Courts (only monetary claims against the U.S. government), its decisions have more weight than district court decisions.

In rendering court decisions, all courts apply the judicial doctrine of ***stare decisis.*** This doctrine means that a court will rule consistently with (a) its previous rulings (unless, due to evolving interpretations of the tax law over time, the court decides to overturn an earlier decision) and (b) the rulings of higher courts with appellate jurisdiction (the courts its cases are appealed to). The implication of *stare decisis* is that a circuit court will abide by Supreme Court rulings and its own rulings, whereas a trial-level court will abide by Supreme Court rulings, its respective circuit court's rulings, and its own rulings. For example, a district court in California would follow U.S. 9th Circuit and Supreme Court rulings as well as the court's own rulings.

The doctrine of *stare decisis* presents a special problem for the U.S. Tax Court because it appeals to different circuit courts based on the taxpayer's residence. To implement the doctrine of *stare decisis,* the tax court applies the **Golsen rule.**[12] The Golsen rule simply states that the tax court will abide by rulings of the circuit court that has appellate jurisdiction for a case.

- The lowest level of judicial authority consists of three different types of trial-level courts (U.S. District Courts, U.S. Court of Federal Claims, and the U.S. Tax Court).
- U.S. Tax Court decisions typically are considered to have more authoritative weight than decisions rendered by a district court or the U.S. Court of Federal Claims.
- All courts apply the judicial doctrine of *stare decisis,* which means that a court will rule consistently with its previous rulings and the rulings of higher courts with appellate jurisdiction.

Example 2-3

What if: If Bill and Mercedes opt to litigate their case in tax court, by which circuit court's rulings will the tax court abide?

Answer: Because Bill and Mercedes live in Florida, the U.S. Tax Court will abide the circuit court with appellate jurisdiction in Florida, which happens to be U.S. 11th Circuit Court.

Administrative Sources: The U.S. Treasury

Regulations, Revenue Rulings, and Revenue Procedures The Treasury Department, of which the IRS is a bureau, is charged with administering and interpreting the tax laws of the United States, among other duties such as printing money and advising the president on economic issues. **Regulations** are the Treasury Department's official interpretation of the Internal Revenue Code, have the highest authoritative weight, and often contain examples of the application of the Code that may be particularly helpful to the tax researcher. Regulations are issued in three different forms: final, temporary, and proposed. The names are very descriptive. **Final regulations** are regulations that have been issued in final form, and thus, unless or until revoked, they represent the Treasury's interpretation of the Code. **Temporary regulations** have a limited life (three years for regulations issued after November 20, 1988). Nonetheless, during their life, they carry the same authoritative weight as final regulations. Finally, all regulations are issued in the form of **proposed regulations** first, to allow public comment on them. Proposed regulations do not carry the same authoritative weight as temporary or final regulations.

In addition to being issued in three different forms, regulations also serve three basic purposes: interpretative, procedural, and legislative. Most regulations are issued as

THE KEY FACTS

Administrative Authorities

- The Treasury Department is charged with administering and interpreting the tax laws.
- Regulations
  - Regulations are the Treasury Department's official interpretation of the Internal Revenue Code and have the highest authoritative weight.
  - Regulations are issued in three different forms (proposed, temporary, and final) and serve three basic purposes (interpretative, procedural, and legislative).

(continued)

[11]The Tax Court renders both "regular" and "memorandum" decisions. Regular decisions involve new or unusual points of law, whereas memorandum decisions involve questions of fact or the application of existing law. Both decisions have similar authoritative weight. Decisions issued by the Tax Court's Small Claims division may not be cited as precedent.

[12]54 TC 742 (1970).

- Revenue rulings and revenue procedures
  - Revenue rulings and revenue procedures are second in administrative authoritative weight after regulations.
  - Revenue rulings address the application of the Code and regulations to a specific factual situation.
  - Revenue procedures explain in greater detail IRS practice and procedures in administering the tax law.
- Letter rulings
  - Letter rulings are less authoritative but more specific than revenue rulings and regulations.
  - Private letter rulings represent the IRS's application of the Code and other tax authorities to a specific transaction and taxpayer.

interpretative or procedural regulations. As the names suggest, **interpretative regulations** represent the Treasury's interpretation of the Code. In Bill and Mercedes's case, these might be the regulations issued under IRC Sec. 163, which discuss interest deductions. **Procedural regulations** explain Treasury Department procedures as they relate to administering the Code. Again, for Bill and Mercedes's case, these might be the regulations issued under IRC Sec. 6501 regarding the statute of limitations for IRS assessment and collection. **Legislative regulations,** the rarest type, are issued when Congress specifically directs the Treasury Department to create regulations to address an issue in an area of law. In these instances, the Treasury is actually writing the law instead of interpreting the Code. Because legislative regulations represent tax law instead of interpretation of tax law, legislative regulations generally have been viewed to have more authoritative weight than interpretative and procedural regulations. However, in *Mayo Foundation for Medical Education & Research v. U.S.*, 131 S.Ct. 704 (2011), the Supreme Court held (subject to specific conditions) that all Treasury regulations warrant deference. Accordingly, it is a very difficult process to challenge any regulation and thus, taxpayers are cautioned not to take tax return positions inconsistent with regulations.

Revenue rulings and revenue procedures are second in administrative authoritative weight after regulations. But unlike regulations, revenue rulings address the application of the Code and regulations to a specific factual situation. Thus, while **revenue rulings** have less authoritative weight, they provide a much more detailed interpretation of the Code as it applies to a specific transaction and fact pattern. For example, Rev. Rul. 87-22 discusses the deductions of prepaid interest (points) a taxpayer may claim when refinancing the mortgage for a principal residence, whereas the Code and regulations do not specifically address this issue. Although revenue rulings are binding on the IRS (until revoked, superseded, or modified), courts may agree or disagree with a revenue ruling. Thus, while revenue rulings should be carefully evaluated as they represent the IRS's interpretation, courts may provide a different interpretation of the tax law that a taxpayer might choose to follow. **Revenue procedures** are also much more detailed than regulations. They explain in greater detail IRS practice and procedures in administering the tax law. For example, Rev. Proc. 87-56 provides the specific depreciation lives for depreciable assets (discussed in Chapter 10). As with revenue rulings, revenue procedures are binding on the IRS until revoked, modified, or superseded.

Letter Rulings Below revenue rulings and revenue procedures in authoritative weight rest letter rulings. As you might guess, letter rulings are less authoritative but more specific than revenue rulings and regulations. Letter rulings generally may not be used as precedent by taxpayers. However, they may be cited as authority to avoid the substantial understatement of tax penalty under IRC Sec. 6662 imposed on taxpayers and the related tax practitioner penalty under IRC Sec. 6694 (discussed later in this chapter). **Private letter rulings** represent the IRS's application of the Code and other tax authorities to a specific transaction and taxpayer. Private letter rulings are issued in response to a taxpayer request and are common for proposed transactions with potentially large tax implications. For example, companies commonly request a private letter ruling to ensure that a proposed corporate acquisition meets the definition of a tax-free exchange. However, the IRS also maintains a list of certain issues on which it refuses to rule, such as the tax consequences of proposed federal tax legislation. Each year, the IRS publishes an updated list of these transactions in a revenue procedure.

Other types of letter rulings include determination letters and technical advice memorandums. **Determination letters,** issued by local IRS directors, are generally not controversial. An example of a determination letter is the request by an employer for the IRS to rule that the taxpayer's retirement plan is a "qualified plan." **Technical advice memorandums** differ from private letter rulings in that they are generated for completed transactions and usually are requested by an IRS agent during an IRS audit.

Is this a comprehensive list of IRS pronouncements? No. In addition to the pronouncements listed above, the IRS issues several less common types, which are beyond the scope of this text. A couple of other pronouncements, however, warrant some discussion. As we mentioned above, the IRS and taxpayers litigate tax cases in a number of courts and jurisdictions. Obviously, the IRS wins some and loses some of these cases. Except for Supreme Court cases, whenever the IRS loses, it may issue an **acquiescence** or **nonacquiescence** as guidance for how the IRS intends to respond to the loss. Although an acquiescence indicates that the IRS has decided to *follow* the court's adverse ruling in the future, it does not mean that the IRS *agrees* with it. Instead, it simply means that the IRS will no longer litigate this issue. A nonacquiescence has the exact opposite implications and alerts taxpayers that the IRS does plan to continue to litigate this issue. Finally, the IRS also issues **actions on decisions,** which explain the background reasoning behind an IRS acquiescence or nonacquiescence.[13] What are noticeably absent from the list of administrative authorities? IRS publications and tax return form instructions. *Neither can be cited as precedent or relied upon to avoid taxpayer or tax practitioner penalties.*

TAX RESEARCH

LO 2-5

Now that you have a basic understanding of the different types of tax authority, why do you think that the IRS and taxpayers disagree with respect to the tax treatment of a transaction? In other words, why would the IRS and Bill and Mercedes's CPA reach different conclusions regarding the deductibility of certain expenses? The answer is that, because the Code does not specifically address the tax consequences of each transaction type or every possible variation of a particular transaction, the application of the tax law is subject to debate and differing interpretations by the IRS, courts, tax professionals, taxpayers, and so on. Tax research, therefore, plays a vital role in allowing us to identify and understand the varying authorities that provide guidance on an issue, to assess the relative weights of differing authorities, to understand the risks associated with different tax return positions, and ultimately to draw an appropriate conclusion regarding the application of the tax law to the issue. The following paragraphs describe the basic process of tax research that tax professionals use to identify and analyze tax authorities to answer tax questions. We will then revisit Bill and Mercedes's issue and view the research memo prepared by their CPA.

Step 1: Understand Facts

To answer a tax question, you must understand the question. To understand the question, you must know the facts. There are two basic types of facts: open facts and closed facts. Open facts have not yet occurred, such as the facts associated with a proposed transaction. Closed facts have already occurred. The distinction between open and closed facts is important because, unlike closed facts, open facts can be altered, and different facts may result in very different tax consequences. Open facts allow the taxpayer to arrange a transaction to achieve the most advantageous outcome. Thus, they are especially important in tax planning.

How do you determine the facts for a research question? Interview clients, speak with third parties such as attorneys and brokers, and review client documents such as contracts, prior tax returns, wills, trust documents, deeds, and corporate minutes. When interviewing clients, remember that not many are tax experts. Thus, it is up to the tax professional to ask the correct initial and follow-up questions to obtain all the relevant facts. Also consider nontax factors, such as a client's personal values or objectives, as these often put constraints on tax planning strategies.

Step 2: Identify Issues

A tax professional's ability to identify issues is largely a function of his or her type of tax expertise. A tax expert in a particular area will typically be able to identify quickly the

THE KEY FACTS

Tax Research

- The five steps in tax research are (1) understand the facts, (2) identify issues, (3) locate relevant authorities, (4) analyze the tax authorities, and (5) document and communicate research results.
- The two types of tax services that tax professionals use in tax research are annotated tax services, arranged by code section, and topical services, arranged by topic.
- Research questions often consist of questions of fact or questions of law.
    - The answer to a question of fact hinges upon the facts and circumstances of the taxpayer's transaction.
    - The answer to a question of law hinges upon the interpretation of the law, such as interpreting a particular phrase in a code section.
- When the researcher identifies that different authorities have conflicting views, she should evaluate the "hierarchy," jurisdiction, and age of the authorities.
- Once the tax researcher has identified relevant authorities, she must make sure that the authorities are still valid and up to date.

(continued)

[13] Actions on decisions have no precedential value but may be cited as authority to avoid the substantial understatement of tax penalty under IRC Sec. 6662 imposed on taxpayers and the related tax practitioner penalty under IRC Sec. 6694 (discussed later in this chapter).

- The most common end product of a research question is a research memo, which has five basic parts: (1) facts, (2) issues, (3) authority list, (4) conclusion, and (5) analysis.

specific tax issues that relate to transactions in that area. For example, an expert in corporate acquisitions would quickly identify the tax consequences and specific issues of alternative acquisition types. A novice, on the other hand, would likely identify broader issues first and then more specific issues as he or she researched the relevant tax law.

What's the best method to identify tax issues? First of all, get a good understanding of the client's facts. Then, combine your understanding of the facts with your knowledge of the tax law. Let's consider the example of Bill and Mercedes's interest deduction. For an expert in this particular area, the issues will be immediately evident. For a novice, the initial response may take the form of a series of general questions: (1) Is this item of expense deductible? (2) Is that item of income taxable? (3) In what year should the expense be deducted? (4) In what year should the item of income be taxed? After you identify these types of general issues, your research will enable you to identify the more specific issues that ultimately determine the tax ramifications of the transaction.

Example 2-4

Elizabeth, Bill and Mercedes's friend who is a shareholder and the CFO of a company, loaned money to her company to help prevent the company from declaring bankruptcy. Despite Elizabeth's loan, the company did file bankruptcy, and Elizabeth was not repaid the loan. What issues would a researcher consider?

Answer: The first questions to ask are whether Elizabeth can deduct the bad debt expense and, if so, as what type of deduction? As the researcher delves more into the general issue, he would identify that the type of deduction depends on whether Elizabeth's debt is considered a business or nonbusiness bad debt. This more specific issue depends on whether Elizabeth loaned the money to the company to protect her job (business bad debt) or to protect her stock investment in the company (nonbusiness bad debt). Bad debt expenses incurred for nonbusiness debts (investment-related debts) are deducted as capital losses and thus subject to limitations (discussed in Chapter 7), whereas bad debt expenses for business debts (business-related debts) are ordinary deductions and not limited.

Why might this case be a good one to litigate in U.S. District Court?

Answer: Because a jury might be more likely to be convinced to assess Elizabeth's motives favorably.

Step 3: Locate Relevant Authorities

Step three in the research process is to locate the relevant authorities (code sections, regulations, court cases, revenue rulings) that address the tax issue. Luckily, tax services can aid the researcher in identifying relevant authorities. Most, if not all, of these services are available on the Internet (with a subscription), and thus offer the flexibility to conduct research almost anywhere.[14]

There are two basic types of tax services: annotated and topical. **Annotated tax services** are arranged by Internal Revenue Code Section. That is, for each code section, an annotated service includes the code section; a listing of the code section history; copies of congressional committee reports that explain changes to the code section; a copy of all the regulations issued for the specific code section; the service's unofficial explanation of the code section; and brief summaries (called annotations) of relevant court cases, revenue rulings, revenue procedures, and letter rulings that address issues specific to the code section. Two examples of annotated tax services are Commerce Clearing House's (CCH) Standard Federal Tax Reporter and Research Institute of America's (RIA) United States Tax Reporter.

[14]www.IRS.gov contains a lot of information (tax forms, IRS publications, etc.) that may be especially useful for answering basic tax questions. In addition, tax publishers, such as CCH and RIA, produce quick reference tax guides (e.g., the *CCH Master Tax Guide* or the *RIA Tax Handbook*) that may be used to answer basic tax questions.

Topical tax services are arranged by topic, such as taxable forms of income, tax-exempt income, and trade or business expenses. For each topic, the services identify tax issues that relate to each topic, and then explain and cite authorities relevant to the issue (code sections, regulations, court cases, revenue rulings, etc.). Beginning tax researchers often prefer topical services, because they generally are easier to read. Some examples of topical federal tax services include BNA's Tax Management Portfolios, CCH's Tax Research Consultant, and RIA's Federal Tax Coordinator.

How does a researcher use these services? An expert would probably go directly to the relevant portions of an annotated or topical service. A novice may conduct a keyword search in the service, use the tax service's topical index, or "browse" the tax service to identify the relevant portions. Some suggestions for identifying keywords: Try to describe the transaction in three to five words. An ideal keyword search typically includes (1) the relevant area of law and (2) a fact or two that describes the transaction. Try to avoid keywords that are too broad (income, deduction, taxable) or that may be too narrow.

Example 2-5

Bill and Mercedes refinanced the mortgage on their principal residence a couple of years ago when their original mortgage's four-year balloon payment came due. Their mortgage institution charged Bill and Mercedes $3,000 of points (prepaid interest) upon the refinancing in order to give them a reduced interest rate. On their CPA's advice, Bill and Mercedes deducted the $3,000 in the year they paid it, but upon audit, the IRS disallowed the deduction. What is the research issue?

Answer: The issue is, should Bill and Mercedes have deducted the $3,000 of points in the year they paid it?

What are some keywords that could identify relevant tax authority?

Answer: Points (area of law), interest (area of law), refinancing (fact that describes the transaction).

Keyword searching is more an art than an exact science. As you gain a better understanding of different areas of the tax law, you'll become much more efficient at using keywords. If keyword searching is not proving beneficial, check your spelling, make sure you're searching within the correct database, rethink your keywords, use another research method, use another tax service, or as a last resort, take a break.

While utilizing keyword searches or other research methods to identify potentially relevant areas of law and tax authorities, constantly ask yourself whether you are indeed in the correct area of law. Once the answer to this question is an authoritative yes, you can delve deeper into the area of law and related authorities to answer the question.

Step 4: Analyze Tax Authorities

Once a researcher identifies relevant authorities, she must read carefully to ensure she fully understands them, as well as their application to the research problem. Two basic types of issues researchers will encounter are questions of fact and questions of law.

The answer to a **question of fact** hinges upon the facts and circumstances of the taxpayer's transaction. For example, whether a trade or business expense is "ordinary," "necessary," "reasonable," and thus deductible, is a question of fact. If you're researching a question of fact, understand *which* facts determine the answer—in this case, which facts make an expense "ordinary," "necessary," and "reasonable" and which do not. In this type of question, the researcher will focus on understanding how various facts affect the research answer and identifying authorities with fact patterns similar to her client's.

The answer to a **question of law** hinges upon the interpretation of the law, such as interpreting a particular phrase in a code section (see the sample research memo in Exhibit 2-9 for an example of a question of law). If a researcher is faced with this type of question, she will spend much of her time researching the various interpretations of the code section and take note of which authorities interpret the code differently and why.

For many tax questions, the answer is clear with no opposing interpretations or contrary authorities. For other questions, the researcher may identify that different authorities have conflicting views. In this situation, the tax researcher should evaluate the hierarchical level, jurisdiction, and age of the authorities, placing more weight on higher and newer authorities that have jurisdiction over the taxpayer. A tax researcher will become more adept at this process as she gains experience.

Once the tax researcher has identified relevant authorities, she must make sure the authorities are still valid and up to date. For court cases, a **citator,** which is a research tool that allows you to check the status of several types of tax authorities, will review the history of the case to find out, for example, whether it was subsequently appealed and overturned, and to identify subsequent cases that cite the case. Favorable citations strengthen a case, while unfavorable ones weaken it. Citators can also check the status of revenue rulings, revenue procedures, and other IRS pronouncements. Checking the status of the Code is fairly simple: just locate the current version. Checking the status of regulations is a little more complicated. Most tax services alert researchers if a regulation has not been updated for certain changes in the Code. If this is the case, the researcher should evaluate whether the changes in the Code make the regulation obsolete.

As you will see in the analysis section of the sample research memo drafted by Bill and Mercedes's CPA (see Exhibit 2-9), the question whether they should amortize or currently deduct the points paid to refinance the mortgage on their principal residence is a question of law that ultimately depends upon the interpretation of a particular phrase: "in connection with the purchase or improvement of" found in IRC Sec. 461(g)(2). Is there a correct answer to this question? No. There is no clear-cut answer. Rather, this is a situation where the tax professional must use professional judgment. Because there is substantial authority supporting the current deduction of the points (discussed in detail in the sample memo), Bill and Mercedes should be able to deduct the points currently without risk of penalty. However, Bill and Mercedes should be aware that the IRS has clearly stated in an action on decision that it will fight this issue outside the 8th Circuit—for example, in the 11th Circuit, where Bill and Mercedes live.

Step 5: Document and Communicate the Results

After a researcher finishes her research, the final step of the process is to document and communicate the results. The most common end product of a research question is the internal research memo the researcher drafts for her supervisor's attention. The memo has five basic parts: (1) facts, (2) issues, (3) authority list, (4) conclusion, and (5) analysis. The purpose of the memo is to inform the reader of the answer to a research question, and thus, it should be written in an objective manner by discussing all relevant authorities to the research question, including those authorities that support, as well as those that conflict with, the answer. Below are some suggestions for each part of the memo. Compare these to the execution within the sample internal research memo presented in Exhibit 2-9.

Facts Discuss facts relevant to the question presented—that is, facts that provide necessary background of the transaction (generally, who, what, when, where, and how much) and those facts that may influence the research answer. Keeping the fact discussion relatively brief will focus the reader's attention on the relevant characteristics of the transaction.

Issues State the specific issues that the memo addresses. This section confirms that you understand the research question, reminds the reader of the question being analyzed, and allows future researchers to determine whether the analysis in the

EXHIBIT 2-9 Sample Internal Research Memo

Below is the memo that Bill and Mercedes's CPA drafted after researching their issue.

Date: July 8, 2015

Preparer: Joe Staff

Reviewer: Sandra Miller

Subject: Deductibility of Points Paid in Refinancing

Facts: Four years ago Bill and Mercedes's credit union provided them a $250,000 mortgage loan for their new home. The mortgage loan was a four-year interest-only note with a balloon payment at the end of four years. Bill and Mercedes (Floridians residing in the 11th Circuit) chose this type of loan to allow them to minimize their mortgage payment until their previous house was sold. After 18 months, Bill and Mercedes sold their previous house and refinanced their original short-term loan with a 15-year conventional mortgage. The credit union charged Bill and Mercedes $3,000 in points (prepaid interest) upon the refinancing.

Issue: Can Bill and Mercedes deduct the points in the year they paid them?

Authorities: IRC Sec. 461(g)
Rev. Rul. 87-22, 1987-1 CB 146.
J.R. Huntsman v. Comm. (8 Cir., 1990), 90-2 USTC par. 50,340, rev'g 91 TC 917 (1988).
AOD 1991-002.
P.G. Cao v. Comm. (9 Cir., 1996), 96-1 USTC par. 50,167, aff'g 67 TCM 2171 (1994)

Conclusion: Because Bill and Mercedes's refinancing represents an integrated step in securing permanent financing for their home, substantial authority supports their deduction of the $3,000 in points this year.

Analysis: IRC Sec. 461(g)(1) provides that cash-method taxpayers (Bill and Mercedes) must amortize prepaid interest (points) over the life of the loan instead of receiving a current deduction. IRC Sec. 461(g)(2) provides an exception to the general rule of Sec. 461(g)(1). Specifically, IRC Sec. 461(g)(2) allows cash-method taxpayers to deduct points in the year paid if the related debt was incurred "in connection with the purchase or improvement of," and secured by, the taxpayer's principal residence. The question whether Bill and Mercedes should amortize or currently deduct the points paid to refinance the mortgage on their principal residence depends upon the interpretation of "in connection with the purchase or improvement of" found in IRC Sec. 461(g)(2).

There are two basic interpretations of "in connection with the purchase or improvement of." In Revenue Ruling 87-22, the IRS rules that points incurred in refinancing a mortgage on a taxpayer's residence are deductible in the year paid to the extent that the taxpayer uses the loan proceeds to improve the taxpayer's residence. Thus, points paid to simply refinance an existing mortgage without improving the residence must be amortized over the life of the loan.

In contrast, in *J.R. Huntsman v. Comm.*, the 8th Circuit Court interpreted the phrase "in connection with the purchase or improvement of" much more broadly and held that points incurred to refinance a mortgage on the taxpayer's principal residence are currently deductible if the refinancing represents an *integrated step to secure permanent financing* for the taxpayer's residence. The facts in *J.R. Huntsman v. Comm.* are very similar to Bill and Mercedes's facts. Like Bill and Mercedes, the taxpayers in *J.R. Huntsman v. Comm.* also purchased their principal residence using a short-term loan with a "balloon" payment. When the balloon payment came due, the taxpayers obtained a permanent mortgage on their home (a 30-year conventional mortgage). The 8th Circuit Court held that in this case the permanent mortgage was acquired to extinguish the short-term financing and finalize the purchase of the home. "Thus, where taxpayers purchase a principal residence with a short-term three-year loan secured by a mortgage on the residence, and replace the loan with permanent financing . . . , the permanent mortgage obtained is sufficiently in connection with the purchase of the home to fall within the exception provided for by section 461(g)(2)."

In Action on Decision 1991-002, the IRS has indicated that it will not follow the *J.R. Huntsman v. Comm.* decision outside the 8th Circuit (in the 11th Circuit where Bill and Mercedes live). Nonetheless, other courts (the 9th Circuit in *P.G. Cao v. Comm.*) have indicated a willingness to apply the 8th Circuit's interpretation of IRC Sec. 461(g)(2). That is, they have allowed deductibility of points incurred in refinancing if the refinancing occurred to secure permanent financing, instead of for some other reason such as to secure a lower interest rate.

Given the similarity in facts between Bill and Mercedes's refinancing and those in *J.R. Huntsman v. Comm.* (refinancing of a short-term note to secure permanent financing), substantial authority supports a current deduction of the points paid.

memo is relevant. Issues should be written as specifically as possible and be limited to one or two sentences per issue.

Authorities In this section, the researcher cites the relevant tax authorities that apply to the issue, such as the IRC, court cases, and revenue rulings. How many authorities should you cite? Enough to provide a clear understanding of the issue and interpretation of the law. Remember, in order to reach an accurate assessment of the strength of your conclusion, you should consider authorities that may support your desired conclusion, as well as those that may go against it.

Conclusion There should be one conclusion per issue. Each conclusion should answer the question as briefly as possible, and preferably indicate why the answer is what it is.

Analysis The goal of the analysis is for the researcher to provide the reader a clear understanding of the area of law and specific authorities that apply. Typically, an analysis will be organized to discuss the general area(s) of law first (the code section) and then the specific authorities (court cases, revenue rulings) that apply to the research question. How many authorities should you discuss? As many as necessary to provide the reader an understanding of the issue and relevant authorities. After you discuss the relevant authorities, apply the authorities to your client's transaction and explain how the authorities result in your conclusion.

Client Letters In addition to internal research memos, tax professionals often send their clients letters that summarize their research and recommendations. Basic components of the client letter include: (1) research question and limitations, (2) facts, (3) analysis, and (4) closing. Below are some suggestions for each part of the client letter. Compare these to the execution within the sample client letter presented in Exhibit 2-10.

Research Question and Limitations After the salutation (Dear Bill and Mercedes) and social graces (I enjoyed seeing you last week at the Tampa Bay Boys and Girls Clubs charity auction. What a great event for such a worthy cause!), clearly state the research question addressed and any disclaimers related to the work performed. This portion of the letter ensures that the tax professional and client have a mutual understanding of the question researched and any limitations on the research performed. As with a memo, issues should be written as specifically as possible and be limited to one or two sentences. Most accounting firms have standard boilerplate language regarding the limitations on work performed that is included in every client letter.

Facts Briefly summarize the facts relevant to the question presented—that is, facts that provide necessary background of the transaction and those facts that may influence the research answer. Keeping the fact discussion relatively brief will focus the client's attention on the relevant characteristics of the transaction.

Analysis Summarize the relevant authorities (including citations in most situations) and their implications for the client's research question using precise language appropriate for the client's level of tax expertise. The length of this portion of the letter will vary with the complexity of the research question and client's interest in understanding the specific research details.

Closing In this section, summarize the key outcome(s) of the research conducted and any recommended client action, thank the client for requesting your service, and remind the client to contact you with additional questions or for further assistance.

In the case of Bill and Mercedes's interest deduction, their CPA recommended a tax return position that the IRS disallowed upon audit. Did their CPA violate her professional responsibilities by recommending a position the IRS disallowed? Good question. Let's take a look at the rules governing tax professional responsibilities.

EXHIBIT 2-10 Sample Client Letter

Below is the client letter that Bill and Mercedes's CPA sent to them.

Dear Bill and Mercedes,

I enjoyed seeing you last week at the Tampa Bay Boys and Girls Clubs charity auction. What a great event for such a worthy cause! Thank you for requesting my advice concerning the tax treatment of the points paid when refinancing your mortgage.

My research is based upon the federal income tax laws that apply as of the date of this letter and the facts that you have provided as follows. Four years ago your credit union provided you a $250,000 interest-only note on your home that required a balloon payment at the end of four years. You chose this type of loan to minimize your mortgage payment until your previous house sold. After 18 months, you sold your previous house and refinanced the original short-term loan with a 15-year conventional mortgage. The credit union charged you $3,000 in points upon the refinancing.

After a thorough review of the applicable tax authority, there is substantial authority that supports a current deduction of the $3,000 points paid. IRC Sec. 461(g)(2) allows cash-method taxpayers to deduct points in the year paid if the related debt was incurred "in connection with the purchase or improvement of," and secured by, the taxpayer's principal residence. There are two basic interpretations of "in connection with the purchase or improvement of." The IRS has ruled (Revenue Ruling 87-22) that points paid to simply refinance an existing mortgage without improving the residence must be amortized over the life of the loan. In contrast, in *J.R. Huntsman v. Comm.*, the 8th Circuit Court held that points incurred to refinance a mortgage on the taxpayer's principal residence are currently deductible if the refinancing represents an *integrated step to secure permanent financing* for the taxpayer's residence.

The facts in *J.R. Huntsman v. Comm.* are very similar to your facts. Like you, the taxpayers in *J.R. Huntsman v. Comm.* purchased their principal residence using a short-term loan with a "balloon" payment. When the balloon payment came due, the taxpayers obtained a permanent mortgage on their home. The 8th Circuit Court held that in this case the permanent mortgage was acquired to finalize the purchase of the home and allowed the current deduction of the points.

J.R. Huntsman v. Comm. provides substantial authority to support a current deduction of the $3,000 points paid to refinance your initial short-term mortgage. In addition, other courts have applied the 8th Circuit's interpretation of IRC Sec. 461(g)(2), which adds "strength" to the 8th Circuit decision. However, the IRS has indicated that it will not follow the *J.R. Huntsman v. Comm.* decision outside the 8th Circuit (in the 11th Circuit where you live). Accordingly, the IRS would likely disallow the $3,000 deduction upon audit, and thus, while you have substantial authority to deduct the points currently, there is risk in doing so.

I would be happy to discuss this issue with you in more depth as these types of issues are always difficult. Likewise, if you have any other questions or issues with which I may assist you, please do not hesitate to contact me. Thank you again for requesting my advice.

Sincerely,

Sandra Miller, CPA

TAX PROFESSIONAL RESPONSIBILITIES

LO 2-6

Tax practitioners are subject to a variety of statutes, rules, and codes of professional conduct. Some examples include the American Institute of CPAs (AICPA) Code of Professional Conduct, the AICPA **Statements on Standards for Tax Services (SSTS),** the IRS's Circular 230, and statutes enacted by a CPA's specific state board of accountancy. Tax practitioners should absolutely have a working knowledge of these statutes, rules, and guidelines because (1) they establish the professional standards for the practitioner and (2) failure to comply with the standards could result in adverse consequences for the tax professional, such as being admonished, suspended, or barred from practicing before the IRS; being admonished, suspended, or expelled from the

AICPA; or suffering suspension or revocation of the CPA license. Given the voluminous nature of applicable statutes, rules, and codes, we will simply provide a brief overview of the major common sources of tax professional standards.

CPAs who are members of the AICPA are bound by the AICPA Code of Professional Conduct and Statements on Standards for Tax Services. Other tax professionals use these provisions as guidance of professional standards. The AICPA Code of Professional Conduct is not specific to tax practice and provides broader professional standards that are especially relevant for auditors—that is, for those independent CPAs charged with examining an entity's financial statements. Provisions included in the Code of Professional Conduct address the importance of a CPA maintaining independence from the client and using due professional care in carrying out responsibilities. Additional provisions limit the acceptance of contingent fees, preclude discreditable acts such as signing a false return, and prohibit false advertising and charging commissions. Most of these provisions rightly fall under the heading of common sense. Nonetheless, a regular review should prove useful to the practicing CPA.

The AICPA's Statements on Standards for Tax Services **(SSTS)** recommend appropriate standards of practice for tax professionals and are intended to complement other provisions that govern tax practice (e.g., Circular 230 discussed below). One objective of these standards is to encourage increased understanding by the Treasury, IRS, and the public of a CPA's professional standards. Many state boards of accountancy have adopted similar standards, thus making the SSTS especially important. Currently, seven SSTS describe the tax professional standards when recommending a tax return position, answering questions on a tax return, preparing a tax return using data supplied by a client, using estimates on a tax return, taking a tax return position inconsistent with a previous year's tax return, discovering a tax return error, and giving tax advice to taxpayers. Exhibit 2-11 provides a brief summary of each SSTS. Most important from a research perspective, SSTS No. 1 provides that a tax professional must comply with the standards imposed by the applicable tax authority when recommending a tax return position or preparing or signing a tax return. IRC Sec. 6694 provides these standards for federal tax purposes.

IRC Sec. 6694 imposes a penalty on a *tax practitioner* for any position that is not supported by **substantial authority.**[15] A good tax professional evaluates whether supporting authority is substantial based upon the supporting and opposing authorities' weight and relevance. Substantial authority suggests the probability that the taxpayer's position is sustained upon audit or litigation is in the 35 to 40 percent range or above. The tax practitioner can also avoid penalty under IRC Sec. 6694 if the tax return position has at least a reasonable basis (i.e., supported by one or more tax authorities) and the position is disclosed on the taxpayer's return.

Example 2-6

Did Bill and Mercedes's CPA meet her professional standards as provided by SSTS No. 1?

Answer: Yes. Based on *J.R. Huntsman v. Comm.*, it is safe to conclude that there is a 35 to 40 percent or greater probability that the current points deduction will be sustained upon judicial review. Specifically, Bill and Mercedes's facts are very similar to those in *J.R. Huntsman v. Comm.*, and subsequent courts have interpreted the phrase "in connection with" consistently with *J.R. Huntsman v. Comm.*

Circular 230, issued by the IRS, provides regulations governing tax practice and applies to all persons practicing before the IRS. There are five parts of Circular 230: Subpart A describes who may practice before the IRS (CPAs, attorneys, enrolled agents)

[15]The "more likely than not" standard, defined as a greater than 50 percent chance of a position being sustained on its merits, applies to tax shelters and other reportable transactions specified by the IRS.

EXHIBIT 2-11 Summary of the AICPA Statements on Standards for Tax Services

SSTS No 1: Tax Return Positions

A tax professional should comply with the standards, if any, imposed by the applicable tax authority for recommending a tax return position, or preparing or signing a tax return. If the tax authority has no written standards (or if they are lower than the following standard), the tax professional may recommend a tax return position or prepare or sign a return when she has a good-faith belief that the position has a realistic possibility of being sustained if challenged, or if there is a reasonable basis for the position and it is *adequately disclosed* on the tax return.

SSTS No. 2: Answers to Questions on Returns

A tax professional should make a reasonable effort to obtain from the taxpayer the information necessary to answer all questions on a tax return.

SSTS No. 3: Certain Procedural Aspects of Preparing Returns

In preparing or signing a tax return, a tax professional may rely without verification on information that a taxpayer or a third party has provided, unless the information appears to be incorrect, incomplete, or inconsistent.

SSTS No. 4: Use of Estimates

Unless prohibited by statute or rule, a tax professional may use taxpayer estimates in preparing a tax return if it is impractical to obtain exact data and if the estimated amounts appear reasonable based on the facts and circumstances known by the professional.

SSTS No. 5: Departure from a Position Previously Concluded in an Administrative Proceeding or Court Decision

A tax professional may sign a tax return that contains a departure from a position previously concluded in an administrative or court proceeding if the tax professional adheres to the standards of SSTS No. 1. This rule does not apply if the taxpayer is bound to a specific tax treatment in the later year, such as by a formal closing agreement with the IRS.

SSTS No. 6: Knowledge of Error: Return Preparation and Administrative Proceedings

A tax professional must advise the taxpayer promptly of an error and its potential consequences when she learns of an error in a previously filed tax return, an administrative hearing (such as an audit), or the taxpayer's failure to file a required return. The tax professional should include a recommendation for appropriate measures the taxpayer should take. The professional is not obligated to inform the IRS of the error, nor may she do so without the taxpayer's permission, except when required by law. However, in an administrative proceeding only, the tax professional should request the taxpayer's agreement to disclose the error to the IRS. If the taxpayer refuses to disclose the error to the IRS, the professional may consider terminating the professional relationship with the taxpayer.

SSTS No. 7: Form and Content of Advice to Taxpayers

In providing advice to taxpayers, tax professionals must use judgment that reflects professional competence and serves the taxpayer's needs. The professional should ensure that the standards under SSTS No. 1 are satisfied for all advice rendered. The professional is not obligated to communicate with a taxpayer when subsequent events affect advice previously provided except when implementing plans associated with the advice provided or when the professional is obligated to do so by specific agreement.

and what practicing before the IRS means (tax return preparation, representing clients before the IRS, and so on).[16] Subpart B describes the duties and restrictions that apply to individuals governed by Circular 230. Included in Subpart B are provisions discussing the submission of records to the IRS, guidelines when a practitioner discovers a tax return error, restrictions on charging contingency fees, prohibition of sharing employment with someone suspended from practicing before the IRS, stringent rules relating to providing advice for tax shelters, and standards for when a practitioner can recommend a

THE KEY FACTS

Tax Professional Responsibilities

- Tax practitioners are subject to a variety of statutes, rules, and codes of professional conduct.
- The AICPA's seven Statements on Standards for Tax Services (SSTS) recommend appropriate standards of practice for tax professionals.
  - Many state boards of accountancy have adopted similar standards to the SSTS standards.
- Circular 230 provides regulations governing tax practice and applies to all persons practicing before the IRS.
  - There is a good bit of overlap between Circular 230 and the AICPA SSTS.

[16]Similar to attorneys and CPAs, enrolled agents and registered tax return preparers can represent taxpayers before the IRS. To become an enrolled agent, you must have either worked for the IRS for five years or pass a comprehensive examination. Registered tax return preparers must pay an annual registration fee and complete continuing education requirements designated by the IRS.

tax return position.[17] Subparts C and D explain sanctions and disciplinary proceedings for practitioners violating the Circular 230 provisions. Subpart E concludes with a few miscellaneous provisions (such as the Circular 230 effective date). There is a good bit of overlap between Circular 230 and the AICPA SSTS.

Although Circular 230 provides many rules governing tax practice, the Internal Revenue Code and other Treasury Regulations often contain requirements specific to tax professionals. Thus, it is important for tax professionals to keep abreast of all applicable guidance, regardless of the specific authoritative source. A good example of this is the tax-preparer registration requirement in Reg. §1.6109-2. Reg. §1.6109-2 requires that all paid tax-return preparers apply for and receive a preparer tax identification number (PTIN) and pay an annual fee, as prescribed by the IRS. Although not a particularly daunting registration requirement, it is important nonetheless as failure to include the tax-return preparer's PTIN on tax returns is subject to a $50 penalty per violation.

LO 2-7

TAXPAYER AND TAX PRACTITIONER PENALTIES

THE KEY FACTS

Taxpayer and Tax Practitioner Penalties

- The IRS can impose both criminal and civil penalties to encourage tax compliance by both tax professionals and taxpayers.
- The standard of conviction is higher in a criminal trial, but the penalties are also much higher.
- A taxpayer will not be subject to an underpayment penalty if there is substantial authority that supports the tax return position.
- A tax practitioner will also not be subject to penalty for recommending a tax return position if there is substantial authority that supports the position.

In addition to motivating good behavior via tax professional standards, the IRS can impose both criminal and civil penalties to encourage tax compliance by both tax professionals and taxpayers. **Civil penalties** are much more common, generally come in the form of monetary penalties, and may be imposed when tax practitioners or taxpayers violate tax statutes without reasonable cause—say, as the result of negligence, intentional disregard of pertinent rules, willful disobedience, or outright fraud. Some common examples of civil penalties are listed in Exhibit 2-12.

Criminal penalties are much less common than civil penalties, although they have been used to incarcerate some of the most notorious criminals. (Notorious mobster Al Capone was convicted and put in prison for tax evasion.) They are commonly charged in tax evasion cases, which include willful intent to defraud the government, but are imposed only after normal due process, including a trial. Compared to civil cases, the standard of conviction is higher in a criminal trial; guilt must be proven beyond a reasonable doubt (versus a "clear and convincing evidence" standard for civil tax fraud). However, the penalties are also much higher, such as fines up to $100,000 for individuals plus a prison sentence.

Assuming the IRS assesses additional tax upon audit, will the taxpayer always be subject to penalty? No. While the taxpayer will have to pay interest on the underpayment, he or she will *not* be subject to an underpayment penalty *if there is* substantial authority *that supports the tax return position*.[18] As previously discussed, substantial authority suggests the probability that the taxpayer's position is sustained upon audit or litigation is in the 35 to 40 percent range or above.

Example 2-7

What is Bill and Mercedes's exposure to penalties in their IRS audit?

Answer: None. Why? Because "substantial tax authority" supports their tax return position and the disputed tax liability is relatively small (the tax savings on a $3,000 tax deduction), Bill and Mercedes have no penalty exposure. Nonetheless, Bill and Mercedes will owe interest on the disputed tax liability unless the IRS recants its position in the audit or appeals process (or if the case is litigated and Bill and Mercedes win).

[17]In 2011, Circular 230 was revised to reflect the tax practitioner standards in IRC Sec. 6694 for when a tax practitioner generally may recommend a tax return position (substantial authority and no disclosure or reasonable basis with disclosure).

[18]The taxpayer can also avoid penalty if the tax return position has at least a reasonable basis (i.e., supported by one or more tax authorities) and the position is disclosed on the taxpayer's return (IRC Sec. 6662).

EXHIBIT 2-12 Civil Penalties Imposed for Tax Violations

Taxpayers		Tax Practitioners	
Failure to file a tax return.	5% of tax due per month (or partial month). Maximum penalty is 25% of net tax due. If the tax return is not filed within 60 days of the due date (including extensions), the minimum penalty is the smaller of $135 or 100% of the unpaid tax.	Failure to provide a copy of the tax return to a taxpayer.	$50 per violation.
Failure to pay tax owed.	.5% of tax due per month (or partial month). Reduces the failure to file a tax return penalty, if applicable. Maximum combined failure to file and failure to pay tax penalty is 5% of net tax due per month not to exceed 25% of net tax due. Minimum combined penalty if the tax return is not filed within 60 days of the due date (including extensions) is the smaller of $135 or 100% of the unpaid tax.	Failure to sign a tax return.	$50 per violation.
Failure to make estimated payments.	Penalty varies with federal short-term interest rate and underpayment.	Failure to include the tax practitioner's ID number on the tax return.	$50 per violation.
Substantial understatement of tax.	20% of understatement.	Failure to keep a listing of taxpayers or tax returns.	$50 per violation.
Underpayment of tax due to transactions lacking economic substance.	20% or 40% of understatement.		
Providing false withholding information.	$500.	Failure to keep a listing of employees.	$50 per violation.
Fraud.	75% of liability attributable to fraud.	Understatement due to unreasonable position.	Greater of $1,000 or 50% of income derived from preparing the taxpayer's tax return.
		Willful understatement of tax.	Greater of $5,000 or 50% of income derived from preparing the taxpayer's tax return.
		Organizing, promoting, etc. an abusive tax shelter.	Lesser of $1,000 or 100% of gross income derived from tax shelter. If activity is based on fraudulent statements, the penalty equals 50% of gross income derived from tax shelter.
		Aiding and abetting the understatement of a tax liability.	$1,000.

As we explained in Example 2-6, Bill and Mercedes's CPA met her professional standards (as defined currently in SSTS No. 1) by recommending a tax return position that meets the "Substantial Authority" standard. Likewise, because substantial tax authority supports the tax return position, Bill and Mercedes's CPA should also not have penalty exposure under IRC Sec. 6694.

CONCLUSION

Now that we have a full understanding of the issue under audit for Bill and Mercedes, what is their likely outcome? Another good question. The IRS has stated that it will continue to disallow a current deduction for points incurred for refinanced mortgages. Nonetheless, the courts appear to follow *J.R. Huntsman v. Comm.*, and therefore, the IRS stands a strong possibility of losing this case if litigated. In an IRS appeals conference, the appeals officer may consider the hazards of litigation. Accordingly, Bill and Mercedes have a good likelihood of a favorable resolution at the appeals conference.

In this chapter we discussed several of the fundamentals of tax practice and procedure: taxpayer filing requirements, the statute of limitations, the IRS audit process, the primary tax authorities, tax research, tax professional standards, and taxpayer and tax practitioner penalties. For the tax accountant, these fundamentals form the basis for much of her work. Likewise, tax research forms the basis of much of a tax professional's compliance and planning services. Even for the accountant who doesn't specialize in tax accounting, gaining a basic understanding of tax practice and procedure is important, as assisting clients with the IRS audit process is a valued service that accountants provide, and clients expect all accountants to understand basic tax procedure issues and how to research basic tax issues.

Summary

LO 2-1 Identify the filing requirements for income tax returns and the statute of limitations for assessment.

- All corporations must file a tax return annually regardless of their taxable income. Estates and trusts are required to file annual income tax returns if their gross income exceeds $600. The filing requirements for individual taxpayers depend on the taxpayer's filing status, age, and gross income.
- Individual and partnership tax returns are due on the fifteenth day of the fourth month following year-end. For corporations, tax returns must be filed by the fifteenth day of the third month following the corporation's fiscal year end. Any taxpayer unable to file a tax return by the original due date can request an extension to file.
- For both amended tax returns filed by a taxpayer and proposed tax assessments by the IRS, the statute of limitations generally ends three years from the *later* of (1) the date the tax return was actually filed or (2) the tax return's original due date.

LO 2-2 Outline the IRS audit process, how returns are selected, the different types of audits, and what happens after the audit.

- The IRS uses a number of computer programs and outside data sources to identify tax returns that may have an understated tax liability. Common computer initiatives include the DIF (Discriminant Function) system, document perfection program, and information matching program.
- The three types of IRS audits consist of correspondence, office, and field examinations.
- After the audit, the IRS will send the taxpayer a 30-day letter, which provides the taxpayer the opportunity to pay the proposed assessment or request an appeals conference. If an agreement is not reached at appeals or the taxpayer does not pay the proposed assessment, the IRS will send the taxpayer a 90-day letter. At this time, the taxpayer may pay

the tax or petition the U.S. Tax Court to hear the case. If the taxpayer chooses to pay the tax, the taxpayer may then request a refund of the tax and eventually sue the IRS for a refund in the U.S. District Court or the U.S. Court of Federal Claims.

Evaluate the relative weights of the various tax law sources. LO 2-3

- Primary authorities are official sources of the tax law generated by the legislative branch (statutory authority issued by Congress), judicial branch (rulings by the U.S. District Court, U.S. Tax Court, U.S. Court of Federal Claims, U.S. Circuit Court of Appeals, or U.S. Supreme Court), or executive/administrative branch (Treasury and IRS pronouncements). Secondary authorities are unofficial tax authorities that interpret and explain the primary authorities.

Describe the legislative process as it pertains to taxation. LO 2-4

- Exhibit 2-7 illustrates the legislative process for enacting tax law changes. Bills proceed from the House Ways and Means Committee to the House of Representatives. If approved, the act is sent to the Senate Finance Committee with a revised version then sent to the U.S. Senate. If approved, the Joint Conference Committee considers the acts passed by the House of Representative and Senate. If a compromise is reached, the revised act is sent to the House of Representatives, if approved then to the Senate, and if approved then to the president. If signed by the president, the act is incorporated into the IRC of 1986. If the president vetoes the legislation, Congress may override the veto with a two-thirds positive vote in both the House of Representatives and Senate.

Perform the basic steps in tax research and evaluate various tax law sources when faced with ambiguous statutes. LO 2-5

- The five basic steps in tax research are (1) understand the facts, (2) identify issues, (3) locate relevant authorities, (4) analyze the tax authorities, and (5) document and communicate research results.
- When the researcher identifies that different authorities have conflicting views, she should evaluate the "hierarchy," jurisdiction, and age of the authorities, placing more weight on higher and newer authorities that have jurisdiction over the taxpayer.

Describe tax professional responsibilities in providing tax advice. LO 2-6

- Tax practitioners are subject to a variety of statutes, rules, and codes of professional conduct. Some examples include the American Institute of CPAs (AICPA) Code of Professional Conduct, the AICPA Statements on Standards for Tax Services (SSTS), the IRS's Circular 230, and statutes enacted by a CPA's specific state board of accountancy.
- The AICPA's Statements on Standards for Tax Services (SSTS) recommend appropriate standards of practice for tax professionals. Many state boards of accountancy have adopted similar standards, thus making the SSTS especially important. Currently, there are seven SSTS summarized in Exhibit 2-11 that describe the tax professional standards.
- Circular 230 provides regulations governing tax practice and applies to all persons practicing before the IRS. There is a good bit of overlap between Circular 230 and the AICPA SSTS.

Identify taxpayer and tax professional penalties. LO 2-7

- The IRS can impose both criminal and civil penalties to encourage tax compliance by both tax professionals and taxpayers. Civil penalties are much more common, generally come in the form of monetary penalties, and may be imposed when tax practitioners or taxpayers violate tax statutes without reasonable cause. Some common examples of civil penalties are listed in Exhibit 2-12.

- Criminal penalties are much less common than civil penalties and are commonly charged in tax evasion cases. Compared to civil cases, the standard of conviction is higher in a criminal trial, but the penalties are also much higher.
- A taxpayer will not be subject to an underpayment penalty if there is substantial authority that supports the tax return position.
- A tax practitioner will also not be subject to penalty for recommending a tax return position if there is substantial authority that supports the position.

KEY TERMS

30-day letter (2-6)
90-day letter (2-6)
acquiescence (2-17)
action on decision (2-17)
annotated tax service (2-18)
Circular 230 (2-24)
citator (2-20)
civil penalties (2-26)
correspondence examination (2-5)
criminal penalties (2-26)
determination letters (2-16)
DIF (Discriminant Function) system (2-4)
document perfection program (2-4)
field examination (2-6)
final regulations (2-15)
Golsen rule (2-15)
information matching program (2-4)
Internal Revenue Code of 1986 (2-11)
interpretative regulations (2-16)
legislative regulations (2-16)
nonacquiescence (2-17)
office examination (2-6)
primary authority (2-9)
private letter rulings (2-16)
procedural regulations (2-16)
proposed regulations (2-15)
question of fact (2-19)
question of law (2-19)
regulations (2-15)
revenue procedures (2-16)
revenue rulings (2-16)
secondary authority (2-9)
***stare decisis* (2-15)**
Statements on Standards for Tax Services (SSTS) (2-23)
statute of limitations (2-3)
substantial authority (2-24)
tax treaties (2-14)
technical advice memorandum (2-16)
temporary regulations (2-15)
topical tax service (2-19)
U.S. Circuit Courts of Appeal (2-7)
U.S. Constitution (2-11)
U.S. Court of Federal Claims (2-6)
U.S. District Court (2-6)
U.S. Supreme Court (2-8)
U.S. Tax Court (2-6)
***writ of certiorari* (2-8)**

DISCUSSION QUESTIONS

LO 2-1 1. Name three factors that determine whether a taxpayer is required to file a tax return.

LO 2-1 2. Benita is concerned that she will not be able to complete her tax return by April 15. Can she request an extension to file her return? By what date must she do so? Assuming she requests an extension, what is the latest date that she could file her return this year without penalty?

LO 2-1 3. Agua Linda Inc. is a calendar-year corporation. What is the original due date for the corporate tax return? What happens if the original due date falls on a Saturday?

LO 2-2 4. Approximately what percentage of tax returns does the IRS audit? What are the implications of this number for the IRS's strategy in selecting returns for audit?

LO 2-2 5. Explain the difference between the DIF system and the National Research Program. How do they relate to each other?

LO 2-2 6. Describe the differences between the three types of audits in terms of their scope and taxpayer type.

LO 2-2 7. Simon just received a 30-day letter from the IRS indicating a proposed assessment. Does he have to pay the additional tax? What are his options?

LO 2-2 8. Compare and contrast the three trial-level courts.

LO 2-3 9. Compare and contrast the three types of tax law sources and give examples of each.

10. The U.S. Constitution is the highest tax authority but provides very little in the way of tax laws. What are the next highest tax authorities beneath the U.S. Constitution? LO 2-3
11. Jackie has just opened her copy of the Code for the first time. She looks at the table of contents and wonders why it is organized the way it is. She questions whether it makes sense to try and understand the Code's organization. What are some reasons why understanding the organization of the Internal Revenue Code may prove useful? LO 2-3
12. Laura Li, a U.S. resident, works for three months this summer in Hong Kong. What type of tax authority may be especially useful in determining the tax consequences of her foreign income? LO 2-3
13. What are the basic differences between regulations, revenue rulings, and private letter rulings? LO 2-3
14. Under what circumstance would the IRS issue an acquiescence? A nonacquiescence? An action on decision? LO 2-3
15. Carlos has located a regulation that appears to answer his tax research question. He is concerned because the regulation is a temporary regulation. Evaluate the authoritative weight of this type of regulation. Should he feel more or less confident in his answer if the regulation was a proposed regulation? LO 2-3
16. Tyrone recently read a regulation that Congress specifically requested the IRS to issue. What type of regulation is this? How does this regulation's authoritative weight compare to other regulations? LO 2-3
17. In researching a tax question, you find only one authority (a trial-level court opinion) that is directly on point. Which court would you least prefer to have heard this case and why? LO 2-3
18. What is *stare decisis* and how does it relate to the Golsen rule? LO 2-3
19. Mason was shocked to learn that the current Code is the Internal Revenue Code of 1986. He thought that U.S. tax laws change more frequently. What is wrong with Mason's perception? LO 2-4
20. Describe in general the process by which new tax legislation is enacted. LO 2-4
21. What are the three committees that debate proposed tax legislation? What documents do these committees generate, and how might they be used? LO 2-4
22. The president recently vetoed a tax act passed by the House and Senate. Is the tax act dead? If not, what will it take for the act to be passed? LO 2-4
23. What are the five basic parts of an internal research memo? LO 2-5
24. What is the difference between primary and secondary authorities? Explain the role of each authority type in conducting tax research. LO 2-5
25. Jorge is puzzled that the IRS and his CPA could legitimately reach different conclusions on a tax issue. Why does this happen? LO 2-5
26. What is the difference between open and closed facts? How is this distinction important in conducting tax research? LO 2-5
27. In writing a research memo, what types of facts should be included in the memo? LO 2-5
28. Amber is a tax expert, whereas Rob is a tax novice. Explain how their process in identifying tax issues may differ. LO 2-5
29. Discuss the basic differences between annotated and topical tax services. How are these services used in tax research? LO 2-5
30. In constructing a keyword search, what should the keyword search include? LO 2-5
31. Lindley has become very frustrated in researching a tax issue using keyword searches. What suggestions can you give her? LO 2-5

LO 2-5 32. Nola, a tax novice, has a fairly simple tax question. Besides tax services, what are some sources that she can use to answer her question?

LO 2-5 33. Armando identifies a tax research question as being a question of fact. What types of authorities should he attempt to locate in his research?

LO 2-5 34. How are citators used in tax research?

LO 2-5 35. What is the general rule for how many authorities a research memo should discuss?

LO 2-6 36. Identify some of the sources for tax professional standards. What are the potential ramifications of failing to comply with these standards?

LO 2-6 37. Levi is recommending a tax return position to his client. What standard must he meet to satisfy his professional standards? What is the source of this professional standard?

LO 2-6 38. What is Circular 230?

LO 2-7 39. What are the basic differences between civil and criminal tax penalties?

LO 2-7 40. What are some of the most common civil penalties imposed on taxpayers?

LO 2-7 41. What are the taxpayer's standards to avoid the substantial understatement of tax penalty?

LO 2-7 42. What are the tax practitioner's standards to avoid a penalty for recommending a tax return position?

PROBLEMS

All applicable problems are available with McGraw-Hill's *Connect® Accounting*.

LO 2-1 43. Ahmed does not have enough cash on hand to pay his taxes. He was excited to hear that he can request an extension to file his tax return. Does this solve his problem? What are the ramifications if he doesn't pay his tax liability by April 15?

LO 2-1 44. Molto Stancha Corporation had zero earnings this fiscal year; in fact, they lost money. Must they file a tax return?

LO 2-1 45. The estate of Monique Chablis earned $450 of income this year. Is the estate required to file an income tax return?

LO 2-1 46. Jamarcus, a full-time student, earned $2,500 this year from a summer job. He had no other income this year and will have zero federal income tax liability this year. His employer withheld $300 of federal income tax from his summer pay. Is Jamarcus required to file a tax return? Should Jamarcus file a tax return?

LO 2-1 47. Shane has never filed a tax return despite earning excessive sums of money as a gambler. When does the statute of limitations expire for the years in which Shane has not filed a tax return?

LO 2-1 48. Latoya filed her tax return on February 10 this year. When will the statute of limitations expire for this tax return?

LO 2-1 49. Using the facts from the previous problem, how would your answer change if Latoya understated her income by 40 percent? How would your answer change if Latoya intentionally failed to report as taxable income any cash payments she received from her clients?

LO 2-2 50. Paula could not reach an agreement with the IRS at her appeals conference and has just received a 90-day letter. If she wants to litigate the issue but does not have sufficient cash to pay the proposed deficiency, what is her best court choice?

LO 2-2 51. In choosing a trial-level court, how should a court's previous rulings influence the choice? How should circuit court rulings influence the taxpayer's choice of a trial-level court?

52. Sophia recently won a tax case litigated in the 7th Circuit. She recently heard that the Supreme Court denied the *writ of certiorari*. Should she be happy or not, and why? LO 2-2

53. Campbell's tax return was audited because she failed to report interest she earned on her tax return. What IRS audit selection method identified her tax return? LO 2-2

54. Yong's tax return was audited because he calculated his tax liability incorrectly. What IRS audit procedure identified his tax return for audit? LO 2-2

55. Randy deducted a high level of itemized deductions two years ago relative to his income level. He recently received an IRS notice requesting documentation for his itemized deductions. What audit procedure likely identified his tax return for audit? LO 2-2

56. Jackie has a corporate client that has recently received a 30-day notice from the IRS with a $100,000 tax assessment. Her client is considering requesting an appeals conference to contest the assessment. What factors should Jackie advise her client to consider before requesting an appeals conference? LO 2-2 planning

57. The IRS recently completed an audit of Shea's tax return and assessed $15,000 additional tax. Shea requested an appeals conference but was unable to settle the case at the conference. She is contemplating which trial court to choose to hear her case. Provide her a recommendation based on the following alternative facts: LO 2-2 planning
    a) Shea resides in the 2nd Circuit, and the 2nd Circuit has recently ruled against the position Shea is litigating.
    b) The Federal Circuit Court of Appeals has recently ruled in favor of Shea's position.
    c) The issue being litigated involves a question of fact. Shea has a very appealing story to tell but little favorable case law to support her position.
    d) The issue being litigated is highly technical, and Shea believes strongly in her interpretation of the law.
    e) Shea is a local elected official and would prefer to minimize any local publicity regarding the case.

58. Juanita, a Texas resident (5th Circuit), is researching a tax question and finds a 5th Circuit case ruling that is favorable and a 9th Circuit case that is unfavorable. Which circuit case has more "authoritative weight" and why? How would your answer change if Juanita were a Kentucky resident (6th Circuit)? LO 2-3

59. Faith, a resident of Florida (11th Circuit) recently found a circuit court case that is favorable to her research question. Which two circuits would she prefer to have issued the opinion? LO 2-3

60. Robert has found a "favorable" authority directly on point for his tax question. If the authority is a court case, which court would he prefer to have issued the opinion? Which court would he least prefer to have issued the opinion? LO 2-3

61. Jamareo has found a "favorable" authority directly on point for his tax question. If the authority is an administrative authority, which specific type of authority would he prefer to answer his question? Which administrative authority would he least prefer to answer his question? LO 2-3

62. For each of the following citations, identify the type of authority (statutory, administrative, or judicial) and explain the citation. LO 2-3
    a) Reg. Sec. 1.111-1(b)
    b) IRC Sec. 469(c)(7)(B)(i)
    c) Rev. Rul. 82-204, 1982-2 C.B. 192
    d) *Amdahl Corp.*, 108 TC 507 (1997)
    e) PLR 9727004
    f) *Hills v. Comm.*, 50 AFTR2d 82-6070 (11th Cir., 1982)

LO 2-3 63. For each of the following citations, identify the type of authority (statutory, administrative, or judicial) and explain the citation.

a) IRC Sec. 280A(c)(5)

b) Rev. Proc. 2004-34, 2004-1 C.B. 911

c) *Lakewood Associates,* RIA TC Memo 95-3566

d) TAM 200427004

e) *U.S. v. Muncy,* 2008-2 USTC par. 50,449 (E.D., AR, 2008)

LO 2-4 64. Justine would like to clarify her understanding of a code section recently enacted by Congress. What tax law sources are available to assist Justine?

LO 2-5 65. Aldina has identified conflicting authorities that address her research question. How should she evaluate these authorities to make a conclusion?

LO 2-5 66. Georgette has identified a 1983 court case that appears to answer her research question. What must she do to determine if the case still represents "current" law?

LO 2-5 67. Sandy has determined that her research question depends upon the interpretation of the phrase "not compensated by insurance." What type of research question is this?

LO 2-5 research 68. J. C. has been a professional gambler for many years. He loves this line of work and believes the income is tax-free.

a) Use an available tax research service to determine whether J. C.'s thinking is correct. Is the answer to this question found in the Internal Revenue Code? If not, what type of authority answers this question?

b) Write a memo communicating the results of your research.

LO 2-5 research 69. Katie recently won a ceramic dalmatian valued at $800 on a television game show. She questions whether this prize is taxable since it was a "gift" she won on the show.

a) Use an available tax research service to answer Katie's question.

b) Write a letter to Katie communicating the results of your research.

LO 2-5 research 70. Pierre recently received a tax penalty for failing to file a tax return. He was upset to receive the penalty, but he was comforted by the thought that he will get a tax deduction for paying the penalty.

a) Use an available tax research service to determine if Pierre is correct.

b) Write a memo communicating the results of your research.

LO 2-5 research 71. Paris was happy to provide a contribution to her friend Nicole's campaign for mayor, especially after she learned that charitable contributions are tax deductible.

a) Use an available tax service to determine whether Paris can deduct this contribution.

b) Write a memo communicating the results of your research.

LO 2-5 research 72. Matt and Lori recently were divorced. Although grief stricken, Matt was at least partially comforted by his monthly receipt of $10,000 alimony. He was particularly excited to learn from his friend, Denzel, that the alimony was not taxable. Use an available tax service to determine if Denzel is correct. Would your answer change if Matt and Lori continued to live together?

LO 2-5 research 73. Shaun is a huge college football fan. In the past, he has always bought football tickets on the street from ticket scalpers. This year, he decided to join the university's ticket program, which requires a $2,000 contribution to the university for the "right" to purchase tickets. Shaun will then pay $400 per season ticket. Shaun understands that the price paid for the season tickets is not tax deductible as a charitable contribution. However, contributions to a university are typically tax deductible.

a) Use an available tax service to determine how much, if any, of Shaun's $2,000 contribution for the right to purchase tickets is tax deductible.

b) Write a letter to Shaun communicating the results of your research.

74. Latrell recently used his Delta Skymiles to purchase a free roundtrip ticket to Milan, Italy (value $1,200). The frequent flyer miles used to purchase the ticket were generated from Latrell's business travel as a CPA. Latrell's employer paid for his business trips, and he was not taxed on the travel reimbursement. LO 2-5 research

a) Use an available tax research service to determine how much income, if any, does Latrell have to recognize as a result of purchasing an airline ticket with Skymiles earned from business travel.

b) Write a memo communicating the results of your research.

75. Benjamin, a new staff accountant for Local Firm CPAs LLC takes a CPA review course to help prepare for the CPA exam. Benjamin is not reimbursed for the cost of the course ($1,500), but his firm expects him to take and pass the exam. LO 2-5 research

a) Use an available tax research service to determine if Benjamin may deduct the cost of the CPA exam course.

b) Write a memo communicating the results of your research.

76. Randy has found conflicting authorities that address a research question for one of his clients. The majority of the authorities provide an unfavorable answer for his client. Randy estimates that if the client takes the more favorable position on its tax return that there is approximately a 48 percent chance that the position will be sustained upon audit or judicial proceeding. If the client takes this position on its tax return, will Randy be subject to penalty? Will the client potentially be subject to penalty? LO 2-6

77. Using the same facts from the previous problem, how would your answer change if Randy estimates that there is only a 20 percent chance that the position will be sustained upon audit or judicial proceeding? LO 2-6

78. Sasha owes additional tax imposed in a recent audit. In addition to the tax, will she be assessed other amounts? If so, how will these amounts be determined? LO 2-7

79. Maurice has a client that recently asked him about the odds of the IRS detecting cash transactions not reported on a tax return. What are some of the issues that Maurice should discuss with his client? LO 2-7

chapter 3

Tax Planning Strategies and Related Limitations

Learning Objectives

Upon completing this chapter, you should be able to:

- LO 3-1 Identify the objectives of basic tax planning strategies.
- LO 3-2 Apply the timing strategy and describe its applications and limitations.
- LO 3-3 Apply the concept of present value to tax planning.
- LO 3-4 Apply the strategy of income shifting, provide examples, and describe its limitations.
- LO 3-5 Apply the conversion strategy, provide examples, and describe its limitations.
- LO 3-6 Describe basic judicial doctrines that limit tax planning strategies.
- LO 3-7 Contrast tax avoidance and tax evasion.

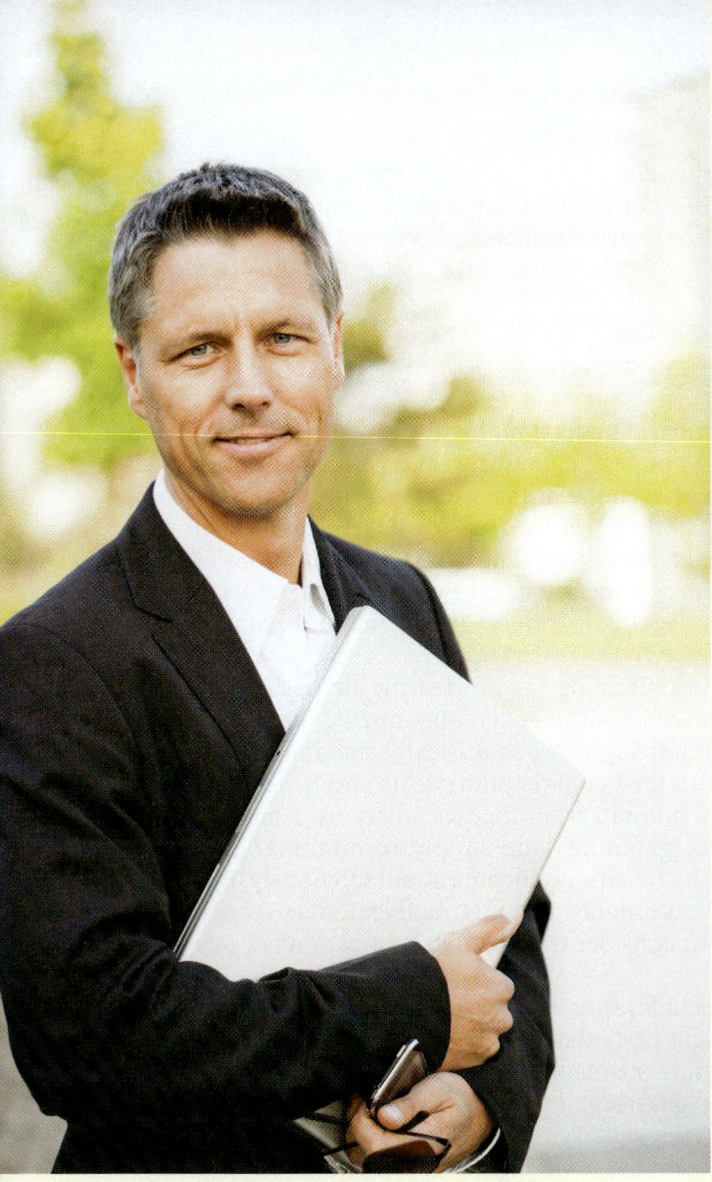
© Cultura RF/Getty Images

Storyline Summary

Taxpayers:	Bill and Mercedes
Family description:	Bill and Mercedes are married with one daughter, Margaret.
Employment status:	Bill is an economics professor; Mercedes is a small-business owner.
Filing status:	Married, filing jointly
Current situation:	Bill and Mercedes want to engage in less risky tax planning strategies.

While working with their CPA during their audit, Bill and Mercedes decide to inquire about less risky tax planning opportunities. Specifically, they would like to gain a better understanding of how to maximize their after-tax returns without increasing their potential for another audit. (Although it was fun and educational, one audit is enough!) Mercedes is convinced that, as a small-business owner (Lavish Interior Designs Inc.), she pays more than her fair share of taxes. Likewise, Bill, an avid investor, wonders whether he is missing the mark by not considering taxes in his investment decisions. ■

Bill and Mercedes have come to the right place. This chapter describes the basic tax planning concepts that form the basis of the simplest to most complex tax planning transactions. In the process we also discuss the judicial doctrines that serve as basic limits on tax planning.

LO 3-1

BASIC TAX PLANNING OVERVIEW

Effective tax planning requires a basic understanding of the roles that taxes and nontax factors play in structuring business, investment, and personal decisions. Although taxes may not be the sole or even the primary determinant of a transaction or its structure, taxes can significantly affect the costs or benefits associated with business, investment, and personal transactions. Thus, the tax implications of competing transactions warrant careful consideration. Likewise, nontax factors, such as the taxpayer's financial goals or legal constraints, are an integral part of every transaction.

In general terms, effective tax planning maximizes the taxpayer's after-tax wealth while achieving the taxpayer's nontax goals. Maximizing after-tax wealth is not necessarily the same as minimizing taxes. Specifically, maximizing after-tax wealth requires us to consider both the tax and nontax costs and benefits of alternative transactions, whereas tax minimization focuses solely on a single cost—taxes. Indeed, if the goal of tax planning were simply to minimize taxes, the simplest way to achieve it would be to earn no income at all. Obviously, this strategy has potential limitations—most notably, the unattractive nontax consequence of poverty. Thus, it is necessary to consider the nontax ramifications of any planning strategy.

THE KEY FACTS

The Basics of Tax Planning

- Effective tax planning maximizes the taxpayer's after-tax wealth while achieving the taxpayer's nontax goals.
- Virtually every transaction includes three parties: the taxpayer, the other transacting party, and the uninvited silent party that specifies the tax consequences of the transaction—the government.
- Astute tax planning requires an understanding of the tax and nontax costs from the taxpayer's *and* the other party's perspectives.

Virtually every transaction includes three parties: the taxpayer, the other transacting party, and the uninvited silent party that specifies the tax consequences of the transaction—the government. Astute tax planning requires an understanding of the tax and nontax costs from the taxpayer's *and* the other party's perspective. For example, as discussed in Chapter 12, it would be impossible for an employer to develop an effective compensation plan without considering the tax and nontax costs associated with different compensation arrangements from both the employer's and the employees' perspectives. With sound tax planning, the employer can design a compensation package that generates value for employees while reducing costs for the employer. (One way to achieve this goal is through the use of nontaxable fringe benefits, such as health insurance, which are deductible by the employer but not taxable income to employees.) Throughout the text, we highlight situations where this multilateral approach to tax planning is especially important.

In this chapter we discuss three basic tax planning strategies that represent the building blocks of tax planning:

1. *Timing* (deferring or accelerating taxable income and tax deductions).
2. *Income shifting* (shifting income from high to low tax rate taxpayers).
3. *Conversion* (converting income from high to low tax rate activities).

LO 3-2 LO 3-3 LO 3-6

TIMING STRATEGIES

One of the cornerstones of basic tax planning is the idea of *timing. When* income is taxed or an expense is deducted affects the associated "real" tax costs or savings. This is true for two reasons. First, the timing of when income is taxed or an expense is deducted affects the *present value* of the taxes paid on income or the tax savings on deductions. Second, the tax costs of income and tax savings of deductions vary as *tax rates* change. The tax costs on income are higher when tax rates are higher and lower when tax rates are lower. Likewise, the tax savings on deductions are higher when tax rates are higher and lower when tax rates are lower. Let's look at the effects of present value and tax rates on the timing strategy.

Present Value of Money

The concept of **present value**—also known as the time value of money—basically states that \$1 today is worth *more* than \$1 in the future. Is this true, or is this some type of new math?

It's true. Assuming an investor can earn a positive **after-tax rate of return** such as 5 percent, \$1 invested today should be worth \$1.05 in one year.[1] Specifically

Eq. 3-1

$$\text{Future Value} = \text{Present Value} \times (1 + r)^n$$
$$= \$1 \times (1 + .05)^1 = \$1.05$$

where \$1 is the present value, r is the after-tax rate of return (5 percent), and n is the investment period (1 year). Hence, \$1 today is equivalent to \$1.05 in one year. The implication of the time value of money for tax planning is that the timing of a cash inflow or a cash outflow affects the present value of the income or expense.

Example 3-1

Bill is given the choice of receiving a \$1,000 nontaxable gift today or a \$1,000 nontaxable gift in one year. Which would Bill prefer? Assume Bill could invest \$1,000 today and earn an 8 percent return after taxes in one year. If he receives the gift today, how much would the \$1,000 be worth in one year?

Answer: The \$1,000 gift today would be worth \$1,080 in one year and thus, Bill should prefer to receive the gift today. Specifically,

$$\text{Future Value} = \text{Present Value} \times (1 + r)^n$$
$$= \$1{,}000 \times (1 + .08)^1 = \$1{,}080$$

In terms of *future value,* the choice in the above example of receiving either \$1,000 today or \$1,000 in one year simplifies to a choice of \$1,080 or \$1,000. For even the least materialistic individual, choosing \$1,080—that is, \$1,000 *today*—should be straightforward.

Often tax planners find it useful to consider sums not in terms of future value, but rather in terms of present value. How would we restate the choice in Example 3-1 in terms of present value? Obviously, the present value of receiving \$1,000 today is \$1,000, but what is the *present value* of \$1,000 received in one year? The answer depends on the **discount factor,** which we derive from the taxpayer's expected after-tax rate of return. The discount factor is very useful for calculating the present value of future inflows or outflows of cash. We can derive the discount factor for a given rate of return simply by rearranging the future value equation (Eq. 3-1) from above:

Eq. 3-2

$$\text{Present Value} = \text{Future Value}/(1 + r)^n$$
$$= \$1/(1 + .08)^1 = \$0.926$$
$$\text{Therefore, the discount factor} = 0.926$$

THE KEY FACTS

Present Value of Money

- The concept of present value—also known as the time value of money—states that \$1 today is worth *more* than \$1 in the future.
- The implication of the time value of money for tax planning is that the timing of a cash inflow or a cash outflow affects the present value of the income or expense.
- Present Value = Future Value/$(1 + r)^n$.
- When considering cash inflows, higher present values are preferred; when considering cash outflows, lower present values are preferred.

[1] Assuming a constant marginal tax rate (t), after-tax rate of return (r) may be calculated as follows: $r = R \times (1 - t)$, where R is the taxpayer's before-tax rate of return.

EXHIBIT 3-1 Present Value of a Single Payment at Various Annual Rates of Return

Year	4%	5%	6%	7%	8%	9%	10%	11%	12%
1	.962	.952	.943	.935	.926	.917	.909	.901	.893
2	.925	.907	.890	.873	.857	.842	.826	.812	.797
3	.889	.864	.840	.816	.794	.772	.751	.731	.712
4	.855	.823	.792	.763	.735	.708	.683	.659	.636
5	.822	.784	.747	.713	.681	.650	.621	.593	.567
6	.790	.746	.705	.666	.630	.596	.564	.535	.507
7	.760	.711	.665	.623	.583	.547	.513	.482	.452
8	.731	.677	.627	.582	.540	.502	.467	.434	.404
9	.703	.645	.592	.544	.500	.460	.424	.391	.361
10	.676	.614	.558	.508	.463	.422	.386	.352	.322
11	.650	.585	.527	.475	.429	.388	.350	.317	.287
12	.625	.557	.497	.444	.397	.356	.319	.286	.257
13	.601	.530	.469	.415	.368	.326	.290	.258	.229
14	.577	.505	.442	.388	.340	.299	.263	.232	.205
15	.555	.481	.417	.362	.315	.275	.239	.209	.183

Applying the discount factor, we can see that $1,000 received in one year is worth $926 in today's dollars. Thus, in terms of present value, Bill's choice in Example 3-1 simplifies to a choice between a cash inflow of $1,000 today and a cash inflow worth $926 today. Again, choosing $1,000 today is pretty straightforward.

Exhibit 3-1 provides the discount factors for a lump sum (single payment) received in *n* periods using various rates of return. Tax planners frequently utilize such tables for quick reference in calculating present value for sums under consideration.

Example 3-2

At a recent holiday sale, Bill and Mercedes purchased $1,000 worth of furniture with "no money down and no payments for one year!" How much money is this deal really worth? (Assume their after-tax rate of return on investments is 10 percent.)

Answer: The discount factor of .909 (Exhibit 3-1, 10% Rate of Return column, Year 1 row) means the present value of $1,000 is $909 ($1,000 × .909 = $909)—so Bill and Mercedes save $91 ($1,000 − $909 = $91).

While Example 3-1 considers a $1,000 cash inflow, Example 3-2 addresses a $1,000 cash *outflow.* In terms of present value, a choice between $1,000 paid today and $1,000 paid in a year simplifies to incurring a cash outflow of either $1,000 (by paying today) or $909 (by paying in one year). Most people would prefer to pay $909. Indeed, financial planners always keep the following general rule of thumb in mind: When considering *cash inflows, prefer higher present values;* when considering *cash outflows, prefer lower present values.*

The Timing Strategy When Tax Rates Are Constant

In terms of tax planning, remember that *taxes paid* represent cash *outflows,* while *tax savings* generated from tax deductions are cash *inflows*. This perspective leads us to two basic tax-related timing strategies when tax rates are constant (not changing):

1. Accelerate tax deductions (deduct in an earlier period).
2. Defer recognizing taxable income (recognize in a later period).

Accelerating tax deductions to an earlier period increases the present value of the tax savings from the deduction. That is, tax savings received now have a higher present value than the same amount received a year from now.

Deferring income to a later period decreases the present value of the tax cost of the income. That is, taxes paid a year from now have a lower present value than taxes paid today. These two strategies are summarized in Exhibit 3-2.

EXHIBIT 3-2 The Timing Tax Strategy When Tax Rates Are Constant

Item	Recommendation	Why?
Tax deductions	Accelerate tax deductions into earlier years.	Maximizes the present value of tax savings from deductions.
Taxable income	Defer taxable income into later tax years.	Minimizes the present value of taxes paid.

Example 3-3

Mercedes, a calendar-year taxpayer, uses the cash method of accounting for her small business.[2] On December 28, she receives a $10,000 bill from her accountant for consulting services related to her small business. She can avoid late payment charges by paying the $10,000 bill before January 10 of next year. Let's assume that Mercedes's marginal tax rate is 30 percent *this year and next* and that she can earn an after-tax rate of return of 10 percent on her investments. When should she pay the $10,000 bill—this year or next?

Answer: If Mercedes pays the bill this year, she will receive a tax deduction on this year's tax return.[3] If she pays the bill in January, she will receive a tax deduction on next year's tax return (one year later). She needs to compare the after-tax cost of the accounting service using the present value of the tax savings for each scenario:

Present Value Comparison

Description	Option 1: Pay $10,000 bill *this year*	Option 2: Pay $10,000 bill *next year*
Tax deduction	$10,000	$10,000
Marginal tax rate	× 30%	× 30%
Tax savings	$ 3,000	$ 3,000
Discount factor	× 1	× .909
Present value tax savings	$ 3,000	$ 2,727
After-tax cost of accounting services:		
Before-tax cost	$10,000	$10,000
Less: Present value tax savings	− 3,000	− 2,727
After-tax cost of accounting services	$ 7,000	$ 7,273

Since Mercedes would surely rather spend $7,000 than $7,273 for accounting services, paying the bill in December is the clear winner.

[2] In Chapter 9, we discuss the basic accounting methods (e.g., cash vs. the accrual method), which influence the timing of when income and deductions are recognized for tax purposes.

[3] Accelerating her payment from January 10 to December 31 will increase the present value of the $10,000 cash outflow by 10 days. Thus, there is a minor present value cost associated with accelerating her payment.

In terms of accelerating deductions, the intent of the timing strategy is to accelerate the tax deduction significantly *without* accelerating the actual cash outflow that generates the expense. Indeed, if we assume a marginal rate of 30 percent and an after-tax return of 8 percent, accelerating a $1,000 cash outflow by one year to realize $300 in tax savings actually *increases* the after-tax *cost* of the expense from $648.20 to $700.

Present Value Comparison

Description	Present value of net cash outflow *today*	Present value of net cash outflow in *one year*
Cash outflow	$1,000	$ 1,000
Less: Tax savings (outflow × 30% tax rate)	− 300	− 300
Net cash outflow	$ 700	$ 700
Present value factor	× 1	× .926
Present value of net cash outflow today	$ 700	$648.20

Generally speaking, whenever a taxpayer can accelerate a deduction without also accelerating the cash outflow, the timing strategy will be more beneficial.

Is the accelerating deductions strategy utilized in the real world? Yes. While the strategy is particularly effective for cash-method taxpayers who can often control the year in which they pay their expenses, all taxpayers have *some* latitude in timing deductions. Common examples of the timing strategy include accelerating depreciation deductions for depreciable assets, using LIFO instead of FIFO for inventory, and accelerating the deduction of certain prepaid expenses.[4] For large corporations, the benefits associated with this timing strategy can be quite substantial. Thus, tax planners spend considerable time evaluating the proper period in which to recognize expenses and identifying opportunities to accelerate deductions.

Are there certain taxpayer or transaction attributes that enhance the advantages of accelerating deductions? Absolutely. Higher tax rates, higher rates of return, larger transaction amounts, and the ability to accelerate deductions by two or more years all increase the benefits of accelerating deductions. To demonstrate this for yourself, simply rework Example 3-3 and substitute any of the following: 50 percent tax rate, 12 percent after-tax rate of return, $100,000 expense, or a five-year period difference in the timing of the expense deduction. The benefits of accelerating deductions become much more prominent with these changes.

Deferring income recognition is an equally beneficial timing strategy, especially when the taxpayer can defer the recognition of income significantly without deferring the actual receipt of income very much. Consider the following example.

Example 3-4

In early December, Bill decides he would like to sell $100,000 of his Dell Inc. stock, which cost $20,000 10 years ago. Assume Bill's tax rate on the $80,000 gain will be 15 percent and his typical after-tax rate of return on investments is 7 percent. What effect would deferring the sale to January have on Bill's after-tax income on the sale?

[4]See the discussion of accounting methods in Chapter 9.

Answer:

Present Value Comparison		
Description	**Option 1: Sell the $100,000 stock in *December*[5]**	**Option 2: Sell the $100,000 stock in *January*[6]**
Sales price	$100,000	$100,000
Less: Cost of stock	− 20,000	− 20,000
Gain on sale	$ 80,000	$ 80,000
Marginal tax rate	× 15%	× 15%
Tax on gain	$ 12,000	$ 12,000
Discount factor	× 1	× .935
Present value tax cost	$ 12,000	$ 11,220
After-tax income from sale:		
Before-tax income	$100,000	$100,000
Less: Present value tax cost	− 12,000	− 11,220
After-tax income from sale	$ 88,000	$ 88,780

Bill would doubtlessly prefer to earn $88,780 to $88,000, so from a tax perspective, selling the Dell Inc. stock in January is preferable. An important nontax issue for Bill to consider is the possibility that the stock price may fluctuate between December and January.

Income deferral represents an important aspect of investment planning (Chapter 7), retirement planning (Chapter 13), and certain property transactions (Chapter 11). Income-related timing considerations also affect tax planning for everyday business operations, such as determining the appropriate period in which to recognize sales income (upon product shipment, on delivery, or on customer acceptance).

TAXES IN THE REAL WORLD Deferring Bonuses? Maybe Not!

The top statutory tax rate in the UK decreased from 50 to 45 percent on April 6, 2013. As one would expect, many companies including Aon, Goldman Sachs, Credit Suisse, Virgin Media, and Lloyds considered delaying top employees' bonus payments until after the lower tax rate came into effect. This tax avoidance strategy however came under harsh criticism by taxing authorities and other government officials. Speaking before the Treasury select committee, Sir Mervyn King, governor of the Bank of England, said that he found it "a bit depressing that people who earn so much find it would be even more exciting to adjust their pay-outs to benefit from the tax rate, knowing that this must have an impact on the rest of society, which is suffering most from the consequences of the financial crisis." Bowing to public and political pressure, Goldman Sachs publicly abandoned the tax avoidance strategy citing potential damage to its reputation. This U-turn in plans highlights the importance of considering the nontax costs of tax planning strategies.

[5]This will require Bill to pay the tax on the gain no later than April 15 of the following year (i.e., three months after the sale). If Bill and Mercedes's current-year withholding and estimated payments do not equal or exceed 110 percent of their previous year's tax liability, they will have to make an estimated payment by January 15 to avoid the failure to make estimated tax payment penalty discussed later in Chapter 8. This example assumes that Bill and Mercedes can avoid the underpayment of estimated tax penalty discussed in Chapter 8 by paying 110 percent of their previous year's tax liability in both options 1 and 2. Thus, they can defer paying the tax on the gain until April 15 of the year following the sale.

[6]This will require Bill to pay the tax on the gain no later than April 15 of the following year (i.e., 15 months after the sale).

Do certain taxpayer or transaction attributes enhance the advantages of deferring income? Yes. The list is very similar to that for accelerating deductions: Higher tax rates, higher rates of return, larger transaction amounts, and the ability to defer revenue recognition for longer periods of time increase the benefits of deferral. To demonstrate this for yourself, simply rework Example 3-4 using any of the following: 50 percent tax rate, 12 percent after-tax rate of return on investments, or \$200,000 gain.[7]

THE KEY FACTS

The Timing Strategy

- The timing of when income is taxed or an expense is deducted affects the *present value* of the taxes paid on income or tax savings on deductions.
- The tax costs of income and tax savings of deductions vary as *tax rates* change.
- When tax rates are constant, tax planners prefer to defer income and accelerate deductions.
- When tax rates are increasing, the taxpayer must calculate the optimal tax strategies for deductions and income.
- When tax rates are decreasing, taxpayers should accelerate tax deductions into earlier years and defer taxable income to later years.

The Timing Strategy When Tax Rates Change

When tax rates change, the timing strategy requires a little more consideration because the tax costs of income and the tax savings from deductions will now vary. The higher the tax rate, the higher the tax savings for a tax deduction. The lower the tax rate, the lower the tax costs for taxable income. *All other things being equal, taxpayers should prefer to recognize deductions during high-tax-rate years and income during low-tax-rate years.* The implication is that before a taxpayer implements the timing strategies suggested above (accelerate deductions, defer income), she should consider whether her tax rates are likely to change. In fact, as we discuss below, increasing tax rates may even suggest the taxpayer should *accelerate* income and *defer* deductions.

What would cause a taxpayer's marginal tax rate to change? The taxpayer's taxable income can change, perhaps due to changing jobs, retiring, or starting a new business. Indeed, in Chapter 1, we demonstrated how a taxpayer's marginal tax rate changes as income or deductions change. Marginal tax rates can also change because of tax legislation. We discussed the tax legislative process in Chapter 2 and noted that Congress frequently enacts tax legislation because lawmakers use taxes to raise revenue, stimulate the economy, and so on. In the last 30 years, Congress has changed the maximum statutory tax rates that apply to ordinary income, such as wages and business income, or capital gains, such as gains from the sale of stock, for individual taxpayers no fewer than nine times (see Exhibit 3-3).

EXHIBIT 3-3 Historical Maximum Ordinary and Capital Gains Tax Rates for Individuals Since 1982

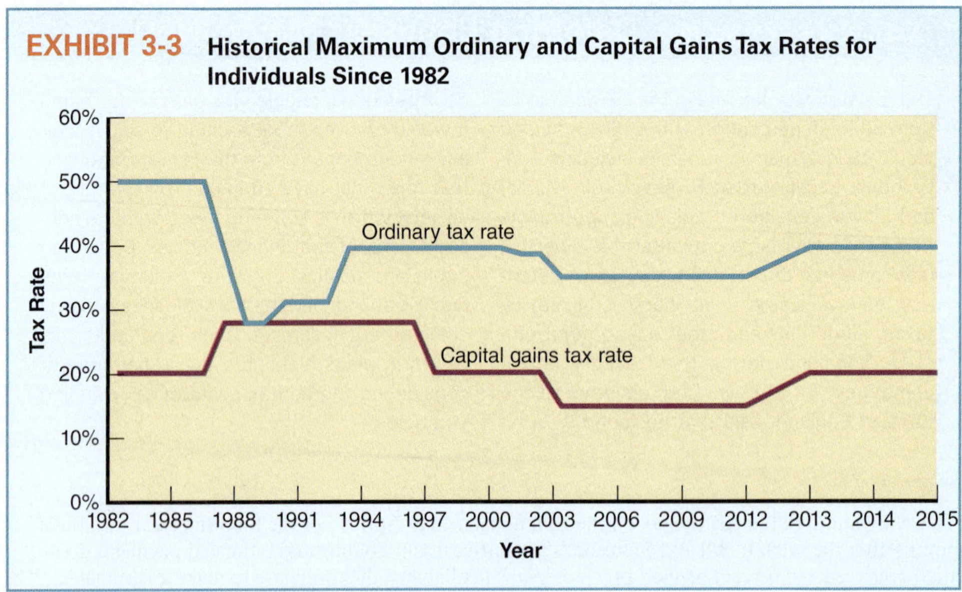

[7]In Example 3-4, increasing the deferral period (e.g., from one to five years) also increases the benefits of tax deferral but requires additional assumptions regarding the expected five-year return of the Dell Inc. stock (assuming he does not sell the stock for five years) and his new investment (assuming he sells the Dell Inc. stock and immediately reinvests the after-tax proceeds).

EXHIBIT 3-4 The Timing Tax Strategy When Tax Rates Are *Increasing*

Item	Recommendation	Why?
Tax deductions	Requires calculation to determine optimal strategy.	The taxpayer must calculate whether the benefit of accelerating deductions outweighs the disadvantage of recognizing deductions in a *lower*-tax-rate year.
Taxable income	Requires calculation to determine optimal strategy.	The taxpayer must calculate whether the benefit of deferring income outweighs the disadvantage of recognizing income in a *higher*-tax-rate year.

Let's take a look at how changing tax rates affect the timing strategy recommendations. Exhibit 3-4 presents recommendations when tax rates are increasing. The taxpayer must actually calculate the optimal tax strategies for deductions and income when tax rates are increasing. Specifically, because accelerating deductions causes them to be recognized in a *lower*-tax-rate year, the taxpayer must calculate whether the benefit of accelerating the deduction outweighs the disadvantage. Likewise, because deferring income causes income to be recognized in a *higher*-tax-rate year, the taxpayer must calculate whether the benefit of deferring it outweighs the disadvantage.

Example 3-5

Having decided she needs new equipment for her business, Mercedes is now considering whether to make the purchase and claim a corresponding $10,000 deduction at year-end or next year. Mercedes anticipates that, with the new machinery, her business income will rise such that her marginal rate will increase from 20 percent this year to 28 percent next year. Assuming her after-tax rate of return is 8 percent, what should Mercedes do?

Answer: Given rising tax rates, Mercedes must calculate the after-tax cost of the equipment for *both* options and compare present values.

Present Value Comparison

Description	Option 1: Pay $10,000 bill *this year*	Option 2: Pay $10,000 bill *next year*
Tax deduction	$10,000	$10,000
Marginal tax rate	× 20%	× 28%
Tax savings	$ 2,000	$ 2,800
Discount factor	× 1	× .926
Present value tax savings	$ 2,000	$ 2,593
After-tax cost of equipment:		
Before-tax cost	$10,000	$10,000
Less: Present value tax savings	− 2,000	− 2,593
After-tax cost of equipment	$ 8,000	$ 7,407

Paying the $10,000 in January is the clear winner.

In the above example, if the choice were either to recognize $10,000 of *income* this year or next, the *amounts* would be exactly the same but the conclusion would be different, and Mercedes would prefer to receive $8,000 of after-tax income this year instead of $7,407. (Remember, when considering cash *inflows,* we prefer the *higher* present value.) Are these always the answers when tax rates are increasing? No, the answer will depend both on the taxpayer's after-tax rate of return and on the magnitude of the tax rate increase.

EXHIBIT 3-5 The Timing Tax Strategy When Tax Rates Are *Decreasing*

Item	Recommendation	Why?
Tax deductions	Accelerate tax deductions into earlier years.	Maximizes the present value of tax savings from deductions due to the acceleration of the deductions into *earlier* years with a *higher*-tax-rate year.
Taxable income	Defer taxable income into later tax years.	Minimizes the present value of taxes paid due to the deferral of the income to later years with a *lower* tax rate.

Now let's consider the recommendations when tax rates are *decreasing*—a common scenario when an individual reaches retirement. Exhibit 3-5 presents the timing strategy recommendations in this case. The recommendations are clear. Taxpayers should accelerate tax deductions into earlier years to reap the tax savings from *accelerating* deductions to *higher*-tax-rate years. Likewise, taxpayers should defer taxable income to later years to enjoy the tax benefits of *deferring* taxable income to *lower*-tax-rate years.

Limitations to Timing Strategies Timing strategies contain certain inherent limitations. First, tax laws generally require taxpayers to continue their investment in an asset in order to defer income recognition for tax purposes. In other words, deferral is generally not an option if a taxpayer has "cashed out" of an investment.[8] For example, Bill could not sell his Dell stock in December and then choose not to recognize the income until January. A deferral strategy may not be optimal (1) if the taxpayer has severe cash flow needs, (2) if continuing the investment would generate a low rate of return compared to other investments, or (3) if the current investment would subject the taxpayer to unnecessary risk. For example, the risk that the value of Bill's investment in Dell Inc. will decline from December to January in Example 3-4 may lead Bill to forgo deferring his stock sale until January. Again, the astute taxpayer considers both the tax *and* nontax ramifications of deferring income.

A second limitation results from the **constructive receipt doctrine,** which also restricts income deferral for cash-method taxpayers.[9] Unlike accrual-method taxpayers, cash-method taxpayers report income for tax purposes when the income is *received,* whether it is in the form of cash, property, or services.[10] The cash method affords taxpayers some leeway in determining when to recognize income because such taxpayers can control when they bill their clients. However, the constructive receipt doctrine provides that a taxpayer must recognize income when it is actually *or* constructively received. Constructive receipt is deemed to have occurred if the income has been credited to the taxpayer's account or if the income is unconditionally available to the taxpayer, the taxpayer is aware of the income's availability, and there are no restrictions on the taxpayer's control over the income.

THE KEY FACTS

Limitation on the Timing Strategy

- Timing strategies contain several inherent limitations.
- Whenever a taxpayer is unable to accelerate a deduction without also accelerating the cash outflow, the timing strategy will be less beneficial.
- Tax law generally requires taxpayers to continue their investment in an asset in order to defer income recognition for tax purposes.
- A deferral strategy may not be optimal if the taxpayer has severe cash flow needs, if continuing the investment would generate a low rate of return compared to other investments, if the current investment would subject the taxpayer to unnecessary risk, and so on.
- The constructive receipt doctrine, which provides that a taxpayer must recognize income when it is actually *or* constructively received, also restricts income deferral for cash-method taxpayers.

[8]See the discussions of like-kind exchanges in Chapter 11, investment planning in Chapter 7, and retirement planning in Chapter 13.

[9]Later in this chapter we discuss other judicial doctrines that apply to all planning strategies.

[10]As we discuss in depth in Chapter 9, accrual-method taxpayers report income when it is earned. In general, income is deemed earned when all events have occurred that fix the taxpayer's right to the income and the income can be estimated with reasonable accuracy. Thus, income recognition for accrual-method taxpayers generally is not tied to payment. Receipt of prepaid income by accrual-method taxpayers may trigger income recognition in certain circumstances. The constructive receipt doctrine may apply in these situations.

Example 3-6

Mercedes's brother-in-law, Carlos, works for King Acura, which recently instituted a bonus plan that pays year-end bonuses each December to employees rated above average for their customer service. Carlos is expecting a $10,000 bonus this year that will be paid on December 31. Thinking he'd prefer to defer this income until next year, Carlos plans to take a vacation on December 30 so that he will not receive his bonus check until January. Will Carlos's strategy work?

Answer: No, the constructive receipt doctrine applies here. Because Carlos's check was unconditionally available to him on December 31, he was aware of its availability, and there were no restrictions on his control over the income on that date, Carlos must report the income in the current year.

What could taxpayers do to avoid Carlos's problem in the future? They could request that their employer institute a company policy of paying bonuses on January 1, which would allow all employees to report the bonus income in that year. However, if the employer is a cash-method taxpayer, this creates a potential conflict with its employees.[11] Such an employer would most likely prefer to deduct the bonus in the current year, which requires the bonuses to be paid in December. This conflict would not exist if the employer were an accrual-method taxpayer, because paying the bonuses in January would not affect its ability to deduct the bonuses in the previous year.[12]

ETHICS

When Carlos, Mercedes's brother, began work at King Acura he was required to complete a Form W-4 that provides his employer information to determine how much to withhold from his paycheck for income taxes. He originally claimed four exemptions but would like to increase this number to 15 because he has recently been having some cash flow problems and the larger number of exemptions would result in fewer taxes being withheld from his paycheck. He intends to make up any withholding deficiency by the end of the year. Would you advise Carlos to change his W-4? Would your advice change if Carlos cannot make up the deficiency by year-end?

INCOME-SHIFTING STRATEGIES

LO 3-4 LO 3-6

We've seen that the value of a tax deduction, or the tax cost of income, varies with the marginal tax rate. We've also seen that tax rates can vary across time, which leads to basic tax planning strategies regarding when to recognize deductions and income. Tax rates can also vary across *taxpayers* or *jurisdictions* (states, countries), which leads to still other tax planning strategies—for example, shifting income from high-tax-rate taxpayers to low-tax-rate taxpayers or shifting deductions from low-tax-rate taxpayers to high-tax-rate taxpayers.

[11]Because King Acura carries inventory, the cash method is not allowed for transactions related to its inventory (e.g., cost of goods sold, sales, etc.). However, King Acura is permitted to use the cash method for other transactions. This mixed method is referred to the "hybrid" method of accounting.

[12]When an employee/shareholder and an employer/corporation are related (i.e., the employee/shareholder owns more than 50 percent of the value of the employer corporation), the corporation is not allowed to deduct the compensation expense until the employee/shareholder includes the payment in income. §267(a)(2).

The type of taxpayers who benefit most from this strategy are (1) related parties, such as family members or businesses and their owners, who have varying marginal tax rates and are willing to shift income for the benefit of the group; and (2) taxpayers operating in multiple jurisdictions with different marginal tax rates. In any case, tax planners should seek only legitimate methods of shifting income that will withstand IRS scrutiny. In the following section we discuss transactions between family members, followed by a discussion of transactions between owners and their businesses, and finally a discussion of income shifting across jurisdictions.

Transactions between Family Members and Limitations

One of the most common examples of income shifting is high-tax-rate parents shifting income to low-tax-rate children. For example, Bill and Mercedes have a 30 percent marginal tax rate, whereas their daughter, Margaret, has a 10 percent marginal tax rate. Assuming their marginal tax rates remain constant with relatively modest changes in income, every $1 of income that Bill and Mercedes shift to Margaret reduces the family's tax liability by 20 cents [$1 × (30% − 10%)]. Thus, if Bill and Mercedes shift $10,000 of taxable income to Margaret, the family's after-tax income will increase by $2,000. Can taxpayers legally do this? Yes and no. As you might expect, there are limitations on this type of income shifting.

The **assignment of income doctrine** requires income to be taxed to the taxpayer who actually earns it.[13] Merely attributing your paycheck or dividend to another taxpayer does not transfer the tax liability associated with the income. The assignment of income doctrine implies that, in order to shift income to a taxpayer, that taxpayer must actually earn the income. For example, if Mercedes would like to shift some of her business income to Margaret, Margaret must actually earn it. One way to accomplish this would be for Mercedes to employ Margaret in her business and pay her a $10,000 salary. The effects of this transaction are to decrease Mercedes's taxable income by $10,000 because of tax-deductible salary expense, and increase Margaret's income by the $10,000 taxable salary. What if Margaret is paid $10,000 to answer Mercedes's business phone one Saturday afternoon every month? Does this seem reasonable? Not likely. The IRS frowns upon this type of aggressive strategy.

Indeed, the IRS closely scrutinizes such **related-party transactions**—that is, financial activities among family members (also among owners and their businesses, or among businesses owned by the same owners). Unlike **arm's-length transactions,** where each transacting party negotiates for his or her own benefit, related-party transactions involve taxpayers who are much more willing to negotiate for their own common good to the detriment of the IRS. For example, would Mercedes pay an unrelated party $10,000 to answer the phone once a month? Doubtful.[14]

Are there other ways to shift income to children? For example, could Bill shift some of his investment income to Margaret? Yes, but there's a catch. The assignment of income applies what is referred to as the "fruit and the tree" analogy [*Lucas v. Earl* (S. Ct., 1930), 8 AFTR 10287]. For the owner to avoid being taxed on the fruit from the tree (the income), the owner must transfer the tree. Thus, to shift investment income, Bill would also have to transfer ownership in the underlying investment assets to Margaret.[15] Is there a problem with this requirement? Not for Margaret. However, Bill would likely prefer to maintain his wealth. The nontax disadvantages of transferring wealth to implement the income-shifting strategy often outweigh the tax

[13]Later in this chapter we discuss other judicial doctrines that apply to all planning strategies.

[14]The Internal Revenue Code also contains specific provisions to curtail benefits from related-party transactions. For example, as we discuss in Chapter 11, §267 disallows a tax deduction for losses on sales to related parties (even if the sale was consummated at the asset's fair market value).

[15]Further, as we discuss in Chapter 8, the "kiddie tax" may apply when parents shift too much investment income to children. The kiddie tax restricts the amount of a child's investment income that can be taxed at the child's (lower) tax rate instead of the parents' (higher) tax rate.

benefits of the transfer. For example, most parents either could not afford to or would have serious reservations about transferring significant wealth to their children—a prime example of how nontax costs may override tax considerations.

Transactions between Owners and Their Businesses and Limitations

Income shifting is not limited to transactions within a family unit. One of the most common examples occurs between owners and their businesses. Let's consider Mercedes's interior design business. Currently, Mercedes operates her business as a sole proprietorship. A sole proprietorship (unlike a C corporation) is not a separate reporting entity, and thus, Mercedes reports her business income and deductions on her individual tax return. Shifting income to or from her sole proprietorship offers little benefit, because all of her sole proprietorship income is reported on her tax return regardless of whether it is attributed to her personally or to her business. On the other hand, if Mercedes operated her interior design business as a C corporation, shifting income to or from the C corporation may make good financial sense because the corporation would be a separate entity with tax rates distinct from Mercedes's individual tax rate. Shifting income to herself may allow Mercedes to decrease the tax on her business profits, thereby increasing her after-tax income. Example 3-7 illustrates the savings obtainable from this strategy.

In order to shift income from the corporation to the owner, the corporation must create a tax deduction for itself in the process. Compensation paid to employee–owners is the most common method of shifting income from corporations to their owners. Compensation expense is deductible by the corporation and is generally taxable to the employee. (See Chapter 12 for a broader discussion of nontaxable compensation benefits.) Having the business owner rent property to the corporation or loan money to the corporation are also effective income-shifting methods, because both transactions generate tax deductions for the corporation and income for the shareholder. Because corporations don't get a tax deduction for dividends paid, paying dividends is *not* an effective way to shift income. Having a corporation pay dividends actually results in "double taxation"—the profits generating the dividends are taxed first at the corporate level, and then at the shareholder level. Recommending this tax planning strategy may not be a good way to keep your job as a tax consultant.

Example 3-7

Mercedes is considering incorporating her interior design business. She projects $200,000 of business profit next year. Excluding this profit, Bill and Mercedes expect $160,000 of taxable income next year. If Mercedes would like to minimize her current-year tax liability, should she incorporate her business? [Use the married filing jointly and corporate tax rates inside the back cover of the book to answer this question.]

Answer: If Mercedes does not incorporate her business, the first $70,450 of her business profits will be taxed at 28 percent (from $160,000 to $230,450 of taxable income, the marginal tax rate is 28 percent). The remaining $129,550 (from $230,450 to $360,000 of taxable income) would be taxed at 33 percent. Upon reviewing the corporate tax rate schedule, you should note that the first two corporate tax rates (15 and 25 percent) are lower than Bill and Mercedes's current marginal tax rate of 33 percent. Thus, there appears to be some opportunity for Mercedes to reduce her current year tax exposure by incorporating her business.[16]

[16]Note that this is a simplified discussion of one of many tax issues associated with incorporating a business. For example, as discussed later in this chapter, Mercedes must consider the judicial doctrines (economic substance, business purpose, etc.) in making this decision and for further tax planning opportunities described in the following example.

After a taxpayer identifies the opportunity and appropriate method to shift income (compensation paid to a related party), he or she can easily determine the optimal amount to shift depending on the taxpayers' marginal tax rates.

Example 3-8

Assuming Mercedes's goal is to minimize her current year federal income tax liability, how much of the $200,000 business income should her corporation report?

Answer: It should report $75,000. Comparing the two tax rate schedules reveals how to calculate this number.

Step 1: Would Mercedes rather have income taxed at 15 percent (the corporation's marginal tax rate from zero to $50,000 taxable income) or 28 percent (Bill and Mercedes's marginal tax rate before recognizing any profit from Mercedes's business)? 15 percent is the obvious answer. To take advantage of the 15 percent corporate tax bracket, Mercedes should retain $50,000 of the expected $200,000 in profits in the corporation, because $50,000 is the width of the 15 percent corporate tax bracket.

Step 2: Assuming the corporation reports $50,000 of income, its marginal tax rate will now be 25 percent, and thus Mercedes's choice is to have any additional income taxed at 25 percent (the corporation's marginal tax rate) or at 28 percent (Bill and Mercedes's marginal tax rate before recognizing any profit from Mercedes's business). Twenty-five percent is the clear answer. To take advantage of the 25 percent corporate tax bracket, the corporation should retain another $25,000 of the expected $200,000 in profits. ($25,000 is the width of the 25 percent corporate tax bracket.) The corporation's marginal tax rate will now be 34 percent.

Step 3: Continuing this same decision process, Mercedes should shift the remaining $125,000 of profits ($70,450 taxed at 28 percent and $54,550 taxed at 33 percent) to herself and Bill—via a salary paid to Mercedes—because their marginal tax rates (28 percent and 33 percent) will be lower than the corporation's marginal tax rate (34 percent).

How much current federal income tax does this strategy save Bill and Mercedes? The corporation's and Bill and Mercedes's combined federal income tax liability will be $83,329 ($13,750 for the corporation plus $69,579 for Bill and Mercedes) compared to $94,329 for Bill and Mercedes if the business is operated as a sole proprietorship. Thus, they will save $11,000.[17]

Are there nontax disadvantages of the income-shifting-via-incorporating strategy? Yes. For example, one nontax disadvantage for Mercedes is that her new corporation now has $61,250 of her after-tax profits ($75,000 profits less $13,750 of corporate tax). If Mercedes has personal cash flow needs that require use of the $61,250, this is not a viable strategy. Indeed, it's advantageous only if the business owner intends to reinvest the business profits into the business. Furthermore, any subsequent transactions between Mercedes and the corporation would clearly be related-party transactions. Thus, Mercedes should be prepared for IRS scrutiny.[18] If the salary, rent, and other costs are deemed to be unreasonable, the IRS may reclassify any excess payments above the value of services and property provided as nondeductible corporate dividends. In this scenario, the corporation and Mercedes would both pay income tax on each dollar of deemed dividend payment. This is not a good outcome for Mercedes or any business owner.

[17]This strategy will result in the eventual double taxation of the income retained in Mercedes's corporation. Specifically, Mercedes will eventually have to pay tax on the income retained by the corporation, either in the form of taxable dividends from the corporation or a taxable gain when she sells or liquidates the corporation. The present value of this additional layer of tax reduces the tax savings from this strategy. The longer that the second layer of tax is deferred, the more advantageous this strategy will be. This calculation is beyond the scope of this chapter.

[18]The taxpayer should maintain documentation for related-party transactions (e.g., notes for related-party loans and contemporaneous documentation of reasonable compensation paid to related parties).

Example 3-9

Upon reviewing Bill and Mercedes's tax return, the IRS reclassifies $65,000 of Mercedes's $125,000 salary in Example 3-8 as a dividend. What are the tax consequences of this reclassification?

Answer: (1) The corporation's taxable income will increase from $75,000 to $140,000 because dividends are not deductible, thereby increasing the corporation's tax liability from $13,750 to $37,850; and (2) Bill and Mercedes's taxable income will remain the same, except $65,000 of their $285,000 of taxable income will be dividends taxed at a preferential 15 percent tax rate.[19] Thus, Bill and Mercedes will have $220,000 of taxable income taxed at their ordinary tax rates ($48,652 of tax) and $65,000 of dividend income taxed at 15 percent ($9,750 of tax), resulting in a tax liability of $58,402.

Under this scenario, the combined tax liabilities of the corporation and Bill and Mercedes will be $96,252, which is $1,923 *higher* than Bill and Mercedes's $94,329 tax liability had they not incorporated Mercedes's business.[20]

As the above examples illustrate, tax-avoiding strategies can be quite beneficial, but they also entail some financial risks if the structure fails to pass muster with the IRS.

Income Shifting across Jurisdictions and Limitations

Taxpayers that operate in multiple jurisdictions (states, countries) also apply the income-shifting strategy. Specifically, income earned in different jurisdictions—whether in the United States or abroad, and for state income tax purposes, income earned in different states—is often taxed very differently. With a proper understanding of the differences in tax laws across jurisdictions, taxpayers can use these differences to maximize their after-tax wealth.

Example 3-10

Carlos's employer, King Acura, has two locations. Its main location is in South Dakota (a state with no corporate tax), with a secondary location in North Dakota (maximum corporate state tax rate of 4.53 percent). What tax planning strategy may save money for King Acura?

Answer: The most obvious strategy is to shift income from the North Dakota location to the South Dakota location, thereby reducing King Acura's state income tax liability by about 4.53 cents for every dollar of income shifted.[21]

A number of possibilities exist to execute a strategy such as King Acura's in Example 3-10. Assuming that the North Dakota and South Dakota locations exchange cars, the firm could shift income via *transfer pricing* (using the price the South Dakota location charges the North Dakota location for cars transferred to North Dakota). Likewise, if the South Dakota location (the corporate headquarters) provides a legitimate support function for the North Dakota location, the firm should allocate a portion of the overhead and administrative expenses from the South Dakota location to the North Dakota location.

What are some of the limitations of income shifting across jurisdictions? First, taxing authorities are fully aware of the tax benefits of strategically structuring transactions

[19]Bill and Mercedes may also be subject to an additional 3.8% Net Investment Income Tax on some of the reclassified dividends, which would increase the combined tax liabilities if Bill and Mercedes incorporate the business.

[20]Chapter 12 discusses the consequences of unreasonable compensation to employee–owners.

[21]Because state taxes are deductible for federal tax purposes, every dollar of state taxes reduced with this strategy will increase King Acura's federal income tax liability by its federal marginal tax rate (e.g., 35 percent). Thus, the net tax savings for every dollar of income shifted from North Dakota to South Dakota will be 2.94 percent, which equals the state tax savings (4.53 percent) less the federal tax increase resulting from the lost state tax deduction (4.53% × 35%).

across tax borders (across countries or states). Thus, the IRS closely examines transfer pricing on international transactions. Similarly, state tax authorities scrutinize interstate transactions between related taxpayers. Second, when taxpayers locate in low-tax-rate jurisdictions to, in effect, shift income to a tax-advantaged jurisdiction, they may bear **implicit taxes** (i.e., additional costs attributable to the jurisdiction's tax advantage). For example, the demand for workers, services, or property in low-tax-rate jurisdictions, whether a foreign country or a low-tax state, may increase the nontax costs associated with operating a business there enough to offset the tax advantages. Finally, negative publicity from moving operations (and jobs) from the United States to a lower-tax jurisdiction may more than offset any tax benefits associated with these strategies.

THE KEY FACTS

The Income Shifting Strategy

- Income shifting exploits the differences in tax rates across taxpayers or jurisdictions.
- Common examples of income shifting include high-tax-rate parents shifting income to low-tax-rate children, businesses shifting income to their owners, and taxpayers shifting income from high-tax jurisdictions to low-tax jurisdictions. The assignment of income doctrine requires income to be taxed to the taxpayer who actually earns the income.
- The IRS also closely monitors related-party transactions.

TAXES IN THE REAL WORLD Fleeing from Taxes

What do Phil Mickelson, Rafael Nadal, Usain Bolt, and Tiger Woods have in common? The obvious answer is that they are all well-known sports figures. The less obvious answer is that they share a sensitivity to tax rules that affects where they work and live. For Nadal and Bolt, the UK's tax system has caused them to forgo events held in the UK. Nadal believes that the UK tax system is too harshly weighted against visiting athletes in individual sports. As a result, he has decided not to renew his agreement to play at London's Queen's Club, instead signing with a tournament in Halle, Germany. Bolt pulled out of the London Grand Prix at Crystal Palace amidst similar concerns.

In the golfing world, Phil Mickelson created quite a stir when he hinted that new California tax burdens might drive him out of the state and possibly out of professional golf after the Humana Challenge in January 2013. His win at the British Open brought his concerns back into the spotlight. So what's the issue? Mickelson earned about £1,445,000 (equivalent to about $2,167,500) in July 2013 for his wins in the Scottish Open and the British Open. The UK will tax his earnings at roughly 44 percent PLUS the UK will tax a portion of his worldwide endorsement income for the two weeks Mickelson was in Scotland and any bonuses he receives for winning the tournaments at 45 percent. However, Mickelson is also subject to U.S. tax on his income earned worldwide. The good news is that he can take a foreign tax credit so he is not double-taxed at the federal level on his income. The bad news? The foreign tax credit does not apply to self-employment taxes (2.9 percent) or the additional Medicare tax on earned income (0.9 percent) and California does not have a foreign tax credit, so Mickelson pays 13.3 percent on his earnings there. All this adds up to a tax rate over 60 percent before considering expenses. After Mickelson's initial comments in January about his high tax burden, Tiger Woods spoke out and admitted that the reason he left California for Florida in the mid-90s was because California's taxes were too high.

LO 3-5

CONVERSION STRATEGIES

We've now seen how tax rates can vary across time and taxpayers. They can also vary across different *activities*. For example, ordinary income such as salary, interest income, and business income received by individual taxpayers is taxed at their ordinary marginal tax rates, whereas long-term capital gains, which are gains from the sale of investment assets held longer than one year, and dividends are taxed at lower tax rates (currently a maximum of 20 percent), and still other forms of income like nontaxable compensation benefits and municipal bond interest are tax-exempt. Expenses from different types of activities may also be treated very differently for tax purposes. Business expenses are generally fully tax deductible, whereas tax deductions for investment expenses may be limited, and tax deductions for personal expenses may be completely disallowed. In sum, the tax law does not treat all types of income or deductions the same. This understanding forms the basis for the conversion strategy—recasting income and expenses to receive the most favorable tax treatment.

To implement the conversion strategy, the taxpayer must be aware of the underlying differences in tax treatment across various types of income, expenses, and activities and have some ability to alter the nature of the income or expense to receive the more advantageous tax treatment. What are some common examples of the conversion strategy? In Chapter 4, we explain character differences in income and deductions. In

THE KEY FACTS

The Conversion Strategy

- The conversion strategy is based on the understanding that the tax law does not treat all types of income or deductions the same.
- To implement the conversion strategy, one must be aware of the underlying differences in tax treatment across various types of income, expenses, and activities, and have some ability to alter the nature of the income or expense to receive the more advantageous tax treatment.

(continued)

Chapter 7, we consider investment planning and the advantages of investing in assets that generate preferentially taxed income. In Chapter 9, we explain the basic differences between business and investment activities and what characteristics result in the more favorable "business" designation for expense deductions. In Chapters 12 and 13, we discuss compensation planning and the benefits of restructuring employee compensation from currently taxable compensation to nontaxable or tax-deferred forms of compensation, such as employer-provided health insurance and retirement contributions.

- The Internal Revenue Code contains specific provisions that prevent the taxpayer from changing the nature of expenses, income, or activities to a more tax-advantaged status.
- Implicit taxes may also reduce or eliminate the advantages of conversion strategies.

To analyze the benefits of the conversion strategy, you often compare the after-tax returns of alternative investments. Given a stationary marginal tax rate, you can calculate an investment's after-tax rate of return as follows:

Eq. 3-3

After-Tax Return = **Before-Tax Return** − (Before-Tax Return × Marginal Tax Rate)

which simplifies to:

Eq. 3-4

After-Tax Return = Before-Tax Return × (1 − Marginal Tax Rate)

Example 3-11

Bill is contemplating three different investments, each with the same amount of risk:

1. A high-dividend stock that pays 8.5 percent dividends annually but has no appreciation potential.
2. Taxable corporate bonds that pay 9 percent interest annually.
3. Tax-exempt municipal bonds that pay 6 percent interest annually.

Assuming that dividends are taxed at 20 percent and that Bill's marginal tax rate on ordinary income is 30 percent, which investment should Bill choose?

Answer: To answer this question, we must compute Bill's after-tax rate of return for each investment. The after-tax returns for the three investments are:

Investment Choice	Computation	After-Tax Return
High-dividend stock	8.5% × (1 − 20%) =	6.8%
Corporate bond	9% × (1 − 30%) =	6.3
Municipal bond	6% × (1 − 0%) =	6.0

Accordingly, Bill should choose the dividend-yielding stock.

What marginal tax rate on ordinary income would make Bill indifferent between the dividend-yielding stock and the corporate bond?

Answer: The dividend-yielding stock has an after-tax rate return of 6.8 percent. For Bill to be indifferent between this stock and the corporate bond, the corporate bond would need a 6.8 percent after-tax rate of return. We can use Eq. 3-4 above to solve for the marginal tax rate.

After-Tax Return = Before-Tax Return × (1 − Marginal Tax Rate)
6.8% = 9% × (1 − Marginal Tax Rate)
Marginal Tax Rate = 24.44%

Let's check this answer: After-Tax Return = 9% × (1 − 24.44%) = 6.8%

The example above shows how taxpayers may compare investments when the investment period is one year. However, when taxpayers hold investments for more than a year they potentially receive benefits from combining the timing strategy and the conversion strategy. First they may be able to defer recognizing gains on the assets until they sell them—the longer the deferral period, the lower the present value of the tax when taxpayers ultimately sell the assets. Second, they may pay taxes on the gains at preferential rates. For example, taxpayers who invest in a corporate stock (capital asset) that does not pay dividends will defer gain on any stock appreciation until they sell the stock; and because it is a capital asset held longer than one year, gains will be taxed at the lower preferential tax rate for long-term capital gains. These tax advantages provide taxpayers with a greater after-tax rate of return on these investments than they would obtain from less tax-favored assets that earn equivalent before-tax rates of return. Investors who quickly sell investments pay taxes on gains at higher, ordinary rates and incur significantly greater transaction costs. Nevertheless, taxpayers should balance the tax benefits available for holding assets with the risk that the asset values will have declined by the time they want to sell the assets.

To enable comparison of investments with differing time horizons, taxpayers use the annualized after-tax rate of return. In general, the after-tax rate of return on any investment is $(FV/I)^{1/n} - 1$ where *FV* is the future value after taxes, *I* is the investment, and *n* is the number of investment periods.[22]

Example 3-12

What if: Assume Bill decides to purchase Intel stock for $50,000 and hold the shares for five years. If the Intel stock grows at a constant 8 percent before-tax rate and does not pay any dividends, how much cash will Bill accumulate after taxes after five years assuming a long-term capital gains tax rate of 20 percent?

Answer: $68,773, computed as follows:

Description	Amount	Explanation
(1) Proceeds from sale	$73,466	[$50,000 × $(1 + 0.08)^5$]
(2) Basis in shares	50,000	This is the investment in the shares.
(3) Gain realized on sale	$23,466	(1) − (2)
(4) Tax rate on gain	× 20%	Low rate for long-term capital gain*
(5) Tax on gain	$ 4,693	(3) × (4)
After-tax cash after 5 years	**$68,773**	(1) − (5)

*Assumes Bill doesn't have any capital losses.

What annual after-tax rate of return will Bill earn on the money invested?

Answer: 6.58 percent [$(\$68{,}773/\$50{,}000)^{1/5} - 1$].

What if: What would be the after-tax rate of return if Bill held the stock for 18 years?

Answer: 7.03 percent, computed as follows:

Description	Amount	Explanation
(1) Proceeds from sale	$199,801	[$50,000 × $(1 + 0.08)^{18}$]
(2) Basis in shares	50,000	This is the investment in the shares.
(3) Gain realized on sale	$149,801	(1) − (2)
(4) Tax rate on gain	× 20%	Low rate for long-term capital gain*
(5) Tax on gain	$ 29,960	(3) × (4)
After-tax cash after 18 years	$169,841	(1) − (5)
After-tax rate of return after 18 years	**7.03**	[$(\$169{,}841/\$50{,}000)^{1/18} - 1$]

*Assumes Bill doesn't have any capital losses.

What if: How does Bill's rate of return on the Intel stock held for five years compare to a taxable corporate bond that pays 9 percent interest annually and is held for five years?

Answer: The annualized rate of return on the stock held for five years is 6.58 percent as shown above. Because the interest on the taxable corporate bond is taxed annually, the annual after-tax rate of return does not change with the investment horizon and will equal 6.3 percent as shown in example 3-11 [9% × (1−30%)]. In this situation, the combined tax benefits from the timing and conversion strategies causes the stock investment to generate a higher annualized after tax return than the taxable corporate bond even though its pretax return is lower.

[22]Financial calculators designate this calculation as the IRR or internal rate of return.

TAXES IN THE REAL WORLD Turning Losses into Gains

"Attention, investors: Uncle Sam will share your pain—if you let him."

Many investors have seen their investments plummet in value in recent years due to the economic downturn. However, financial advisers remind us that even in the midst of such seemingly bad news, there is good news. The tax code allows individuals to reduce or eliminate tax on their current gains using these losses, which in turn raises overall returns.

Using capital losses to offset capital gains (or even up to $3,000 of ordinary income) is a term investment advisers call *tax-loss harvesting,*" says Joel Dickson, a tax specialist at Vanguard Group, "and we urge investors to take Uncle Sam up on it." Many investors do. As an example New York's billionaire former mayor, Michael Bloomberg disclosed that he will declare no net capital gains on his 2010 tax return.

So, how much can loss harvesting improve your returns? Investment advisers have differing predictions, but claim that loss harvesting can add up to 2 percentage points over a 10-year period. Pretty good considering that the Standard & Poor's 500 stock index's annualized total return for the period has been under 2 percent.

Source: The Wall Street Journal, Laura Saunders, August 20, 2011.

Limitations of Conversion Strategies

Like other tax planning strategies, conversion strategies face potential limitations. The Code itself also contains several specific provisions that prevent the taxpayer from changing the nature of expenses, income, or activities to a more tax-advantaged status, including (among many others) the depreciation recapture rules discussed in Chapter 11 and the luxury auto depreciation rules discussed in Chapter 10. In addition, as discussed in Chapter 1, implicit taxes may reduce or eliminate the advantages of tax-preferred investments (such as municipal bonds or any investment taxed at preferential tax rates) by decreasing their before-tax rate of returns. Thus, implicit taxes may reduce the advantages of the conversion strategy.

ADDITIONAL LIMITATIONS TO TAX PLANNING STRATEGIES: JUDICIAL DOCTRINES

LO 3-6

The IRS also has several other doctrines at its disposal for situations where it expects taxpayer abuse. These doctrines apply across a wide variety of transactions and planning strategies (timing, income shifting, and conversion). The **business purpose doctrine,** for instance, allows the IRS to challenge and disallow business expenses for transactions with no underlying business motivation, such as the travel cost of a spouse accompanying a taxpayer on a business trip. The **step-transaction doctrine** allows the IRS to collapse a series of related transactions into one transaction to determine the tax consequences of the transaction. The **substance-over-form doctrine** allows the IRS to consider the transaction's substance regardless of its form, and where appropriate, to reclassify the transaction according to its substance. Finally, the **economic substance doctrine** requires transactions to meet two criteria to obtain tax benefits. First, a transaction must meaningfully change a taxpayer's economic position (excluding any federal income tax effects). Second, the taxpayer must have a substantial purpose (other than tax avoidance) for the transaction. Economic substance is clearly related to several other doctrines such as business purpose, step-transaction, and substance-over-form doctrine; however, its codification standardizes the requirement for transactions to meet both tests. The courts had been inconsistent with the application of the tests with some requiring the transaction to meet either the business purpose or economic substance and others requiring that both tests be met. A key part of the codification is the strict penalty of 40 percent—reduced to 20 percent if the taxpayer makes adequate disclosure—of the underpayment for failing to meet the requirements. In Chapter 2,

THE KEY FACTS

Additional Limitations to Tax Planning Strategies: Judicial Doctrines

- Certain judicial doctrines restrict the common tax planning strategies (timing, income shifting, and conversion).
  - The business purpose doctrine allows the IRS to challenge and disallow business expenses for transactions with no underlying business motivation.

(continued)

- The step-transaction doctrine allows the IRS to collapse a series of related transactions into one transaction to determine the tax consequences of the transaction.
- The substance-over-form doctrine allows the IRS to reclassify a transaction according to its substance.

we noted that the Internal Revenue Code is the ultimate tax authority. The business purpose, step-transaction, substance-over-form, and economic substance doctrines allow the IRS to determine the tax consequences of transactions that follow only the form of the Internal Revenue Code and not the spirit.

You can often assess whether the business purpose, step-transaction, or substance-over-form doctrines apply by using the "smell test." If the transaction "smells bad," one of these doctrines likely applies. (Transactions usually smell bad when the primary purpose is to avoid taxes and not to accomplish an independent business objective.) For example, using the substance-over-form doctrine, the IRS would likely reclassify most of the $10,000 paid to Margaret for answering the phone one Saturday afternoon a month as a gift from Mercedes to Margaret (see the earlier discussion of income shifting and transactions between family members), even though the transaction was structured as compensation and Margaret did do some work for her mother. This recharacterization would unwind the income-shifting benefits for the amount considered to be a gift, as gifts to family members are not tax deductible. In sum, the *substance* of the transaction must be justifiable, not just the form.

LO 3-7

TAX AVOIDANCE VERSUS TAX EVASION

Each of the tax planning strategies discussed in this book falls within the confines of legal **tax avoidance.** Tax avoidance has long been endorsed by the courts and even Congress. For example, remember that Congress specifically encouraged tax avoidance by excluding municipal bond income from taxation, preferentially taxing dividend and capital gain income, and other strategies. Likewise, the courts have often made it quite clear that taxpayers are under no moral obligation to pay more taxes than required by law. As an example, in *Commissioner v. Newman,* 159 F.2d 848 (2 Cir., 1947), which considered a taxpayer's ability to shift income to his children using trusts, Judge Learned Hand included the following statement in his dissenting opinion:

> Over and over again courts have said that there is nothing sinister in so arranging one's affairs as to keep taxes as low as possible. Everybody does so, rich or poor; and all do right, for nobody owes any public duty to pay more than the law demands: taxes are enforced exactions, not voluntary contributions. To demand more in the name of morals is mere cant.

In contrast to tax avoidance, **tax evasion**—that is, the willful attempt to defraud the government—falls outside the confines of legal tax avoidance and thus may land the perpetrator within the confines of a federal prison. (Recall from Chapter 2 that the rewards of tax evasion include stiff monetary penalties and imprisonment.) When does tax avoidance become tax evasion? Very good question. In many cases a clear distinction exists between avoidance (such as not paying tax on municipal bond interest) and evasion (not paying tax on a $1,000,000 game show prize). In other cases, the line is less clear. In these situations, professional judgment, the use of a smell test, and consideration of the business purpose, step-transaction, and substance-over-form doctrines may prove useful.

THE KEY FACTS

Tax Evasion versus Tax Avoidance

- Tax avoidance is the legal act of arranging one's transactions to minimize taxes paid.
- Tax evasion is the willful attempt to defraud the government by not paying taxes legally owed.
- Tax evasion falls outside the confines of legal tax avoidance.

As you might expect, tax evasion is a major area of concern and focus for the IRS. While the IRS vigorously prosecutes suspected tax evaders, its actions alone have not been able to solve this problem. Is tax evasion a victimless crime? No. Because the federal government must replace lost tax revenues by imposing higher taxes on others, honest taxpayers are the true victims of tax evasion. Currently, the federal government estimates that tax evasion costs the federal government annually more than $450 billion in lost tax revenues. As citizens and residents of the United States, each of us must recognize our obligation to support our country. As future accountants and business professionals, we also must recognize the inherent value of high ethical standards, which call for us to do the right thing in *all* situations. As business professionals have learned over and over, the costs of doing otherwise far exceed any short-term gains.

CONCLUSION

In this chapter we discussed three basic tax planning strategies—timing, income shifting, and conversion—and their related limitations. Each of these strategies exploits the variation in taxation across different dimensions. The timing strategy exploits the variation in taxation across time: The "real" tax costs of income decrease as taxation is deferred; the "real" tax savings associated with tax deductions increase as tax deductions are accelerated. However, because tax rates may change over time and the tax costs of income and tax savings of deductions vary with tax rates, tax planning should consider the effects of such changes on the timing strategy. The income-shifting strategy exploits the variation in taxation across taxpayers or jurisdictions. The assignment of income doctrine limits aggressive attempts to shift income across taxpayers. In addition, related-party transactions receive close IRS attention given the increased likelihood of taxpayer abuses in these transactions. Finally, the conversion strategy exploits the variation in taxation rates across activities although implicit taxes may reduce the advantages of this strategy. In addition to limitations specific to each planning strategy, the judicial doctrines of business purpose, step-transaction, and substance-over-form broadly apply to a wide range of transactions and planning strategies.

The timing, income-shifting, and conversion strategies represent the building blocks for the more sophisticated tax strategies that tax professionals employ on a daily basis. Combining an understanding of these basic tax planning strategies with knowledge of our tax law will provide you with the tools necessary to identify, evaluate, and implement tax planning strategies. Throughout the remainder of the text, we will discuss how these strategies can be applied to different transactions.

Summary

Identify the objectives of basic tax planning strategies. **LO 3-1**

- Effective tax planning maximizes the taxpayer's after-tax wealth while achieving the taxpayer's nontax goals. Maximizing after-tax wealth is not necessarily the same as tax minimization. Maximizing after-tax wealth requires one to consider both the tax and nontax costs and benefits of alternative transactions, whereas tax minimization focuses solely on a single cost (i.e., taxes).
- Virtually every transaction involves three parties: the taxpayer, the other transacting party, and the uninvited silent party that specifies the tax consequences of the transaction (i.e., the government). Astute tax planning requires an understanding of the tax and nontax costs from the taxpayer's *and* the other party's perspectives.

Apply the timing strategy and describe its applications and limitations. **LO 3-2**

- One of the cornerstones of basic tax planning involves the idea of *timing*—that is, *when* income is taxed or an expense is deducted affects the associated "real" tax costs or savings. This is true for two reasons. First, the timing of when income is taxed or an expense is deducted affects the *present value* of the taxes paid on income or tax savings on deductions. Second, the tax costs of income and tax savings income vary as *tax rates* change.
- When tax rates are constant, tax planners prefer to defer income (i.e., to reduce the present value of taxes paid) and accelerate deductions (i.e., to increase the present value of tax savings). Higher tax rates, higher rates of return, larger transaction amounts, and the ability to accelerate deductions or defer income by two or more years increase the benefits of the timing strategy.
- When tax rates change, the timing strategy requires a little more consideration because the tax costs of income and the tax savings from deductions vary as *tax rates* change. When tax rates are increasing, the taxpayer must calculate the optimal tax strategies for deductions and income. When tax rates are decreasing, the recommendations are clear. Taxpayers should accelerate tax deductions into earlier years and defer taxable income to later years.

- Timing strategies contain several inherent limitations. Generally speaking, whenever a taxpayer must accelerate a cash outflow to accelerate a deduction, the timing strategy will be less beneficial. Tax law generally requires taxpayers to continue their investment in an asset in order to defer income recognition for tax purposes. A deferral strategy may not be optimal if the taxpayer has severe cash flow needs, if continuing the investment would generate a low rate of return compared to other investments, if the current investment would subject the taxpayer to unnecessary risk, and so on. The constructive receipt doctrine, which provides that a taxpayer must recognize income when it is actually or constructively received, also restricts income deferral for cash-method taxpayers.

LO 3-3 Apply the concept of present value to tax planning.

- The concept of present value—also known as the time value of money—basically states that $1 today is worth *more* than $1 in the future. For example, assuming an investor can earn a positive return (e.g., 5 percent after taxes), $1 invested today should be worth $1.05 in one year. Hence, $1 today is equivalent to $1.05 in one year.
- The implication of the time value of money for tax planning is that the timing of a cash inflow or a cash outflow affects the present value of the income or expense.

LO 3-4 Apply the strategy of income shifting, provide examples, and describe its limitations.

- The income-shifting strategy exploits the differences in tax rates across taxpayers or jurisdictions. Three of the most common examples of income shifting are high-tax-rate parents shifting income to low-tax-rate children, businesses shifting income to their owners, and taxpayers shifting income from high-tax jurisdictions to low-tax jurisdictions.
- The assignment of income doctrine requires income to be taxed to the taxpayer who actually earns the income. In addition, the IRS closely monitors such related-party transactions—that is, financial activities among family members, among owners and their businesses, or among businesses owned by the same owners. Implicit taxes may also limit the benefits of income shifting via locating in tax-advantaged jurisdictions.

LO 3-5 Apply the conversion strategy, provide examples, and describe its limitations.

- Tax law does not treat all types of income or deductions the same. This understanding forms the basis for the conversion strategy—recasting income and expenses to receive the most favorable tax treatment. To implement the conversion strategy, one must be aware of the underlying differences in tax treatment across various types of income, expenses, and activities, and have some ability to alter the nature of the income or expense to receive the more advantageous tax treatment.
- Common examples of the conversion strategy include investment planning to invest in assets that generate preferentially taxed income, compensation planning to restructure employee compensation from currently taxable compensation to nontaxable or tax-deferred forms of compensation, and corporate distribution planning to structure corporate distributions to receive the most advantageous tax treatment.
- The Internal Revenue Code contains specific provisions that prevent the taxpayer from changing the nature of expenses, income, or activities to a more tax-advantaged status. Implicit taxes may also reduce or eliminate the advantages of conversion strategies.

LO 3-6 Describe basic judicial doctrines that limit tax planning strategies.

- The constructive receipt doctrine, which may limit the timing strategy, provides that a taxpayer must recognize income when it is actually *or* constructively received. Constructive receipt is deemed to have occurred if the income has been credited to the taxpayer's account or if the income is unconditionally available to the taxpayer, the taxpayer is aware of the income's availability, and there are no restrictions on the taxpayer's control over the income.
- The assignment of income doctrine requires income to be taxed to the taxpayer who actually earns the income. The assignment of income doctrine implies that, in order to shift income to a taxpayer, that taxpayer must actually earn the income.

- The business purpose, step-transaction, and substance-over-form doctrines apply across a wide variety of transactions and planning strategies (timing, income shifting, and conversion).
- The business purpose doctrine allows the IRS to challenge and disallow business expenses for transactions with no underlying business motivation, such as a travel cost of a spouse accompanying a taxpayer on a business trip.
- The step-transaction doctrine allows the IRS to collapse a series of related transactions into one transaction to determine the tax consequences of the transaction.
- The substance-over-form doctrine allows the IRS to consider the transaction's substance regardless of its form, and where appropriate, reclassify the transaction according to its substance.
- The codified economic substance doctrine requires transactions to have a substantial purpose and to meaningfully change a taxpayer's economic position in order for a taxpayer to obtain tax benefits.

Contrast tax avoidance and tax evasion. LO 3-7

- Tax avoidance is the legal act of arranging one's transactions, and so on, to minimize taxes paid. Tax evasion is the willful attempt to defraud the government (i.e., by not paying taxes legally owed). Tax evasion falls outside the confines of legal tax avoidance.
- In many cases a clear distinction exists between avoidance (e.g., not paying tax on municipal bond interest) and evasion (e.g., not paying tax on a $1,000,000 game show prize). In other cases, the line between tax avoidance and evasion is less clear. In these situations, professional judgment, the use of a "smell test," and consideration of the business purpose, step-transaction, and substance-over-form doctrines may prove useful.

KEY TERMS

after-tax rate of return (3-3)
arm's-length transaction (3-12)
assignment of income doctrine (3-12)
before-tax rate of return (3-17)
business purpose doctrine (3-19)
constructive receipt doctrine (3-10)
discount factor (3-3)
economic substance doctrine (3-19)
implicit tax (3-16)
present value (3-3)
related-party transaction (3-12)
step-transaction doctrine (3-19)
substance-over-form doctrine (3-19)
tax avoidance (3-20)
tax evasion (3-20)

DISCUSSION QUESTIONS

1. "The goal of tax planning is to minimize taxes." Explain why this statement is not true. LO 3-1
2. Describe the three parties engaged in every business transaction and how understanding taxes may aid in structuring transactions. LO 3-1
3. In this chapter we discuss three basic tax planning strategies. What different features of taxation does each of these strategies exploit? LO 3-1
4. What are the two basic timing strategies? What is the intent of each? LO 3-2
5. Why is the timing strategy particularly effective for cash-method taxpayers? LO 3-2
6. What are some common examples of the timing strategy? LO 3-2
7. What factors increase the benefits of accelerating deductions or deferring income? LO 3-2
8. How do changing tax rates affect the timing strategy? What information do you need to determine the appropriate timing strategy when tax rates change? LO 3-2 LO 3-3
9. Describe the ways in which the timing strategy has limitations. LO 3-2 LO 3-6

LO 3-3 10. The concept of the time value of money suggests that $1 today is not equal to $1 in the future. Explain why this is true.

LO 3-3 11. Why is understanding the time value of money important for tax planning?

LO 3-3 12. What two factors increase the difference between present and future values?

LO 3-4 13. What factors have to be present for income shifting to be a viable strategy?

LO 3-4 14. Name three common types of income shifting.

LO 3-4 15. What are some ways that a parent could effectively shift income to a child? What are some of the disadvantages of these methods?

LO 3-4 16. What is the key factor in shifting income from a business to its owners? What are some methods of shifting income in this context?

LO 3-4 17. Explain why paying dividends is not an effective way to shift income from a corporation to its owners.

LO 3-5 18. What are some of the common examples of the conversion strategy?

LO 3-5 19. What is needed to implement the conversion strategy?

LO 3-5 20. Explain how implicit taxes may limit the benefits of the conversion strategy.

LO 3-5 planning LO 3-6 21. Clark owns stock in BCS Corporation that he purchased in January of the current year. The stock has appreciated significantly during the year. It is now December of the current year, and Clark is deciding whether or not he should sell the stock. What tax and nontax factors should Clark consider before making the decision on whether to sell the stock now?

LO 3-5 22. Do after-tax rates of return for investments in either interest or dividend paying securities increase with the length of the investment? Why or why not?

LO 3-5 23. Cameron purchases stock in Corporation X and in Corporation Y. Neither corporation pays dividends. The stocks both earn an identical before-tax rate of return. Cameron sells stock in Corporation X after three years and he sells the stock in Corporation Y after five years. Which investment likely earned a greater after-tax return? Why?

LO 3-5 24. Under what circumstances would you expect the after-tax return from an investment in a capital asset to approach that of tax-exempt assets assuming equal before-tax rates of return?

LO 3-5 planning 25. Laurie is thinking about investing in one or several of the following investment options:

Corporate bonds (ordinary interest paid annually)
Dividend-paying stock (qualified dividends)
Life insurance (tax-exempt)
Savings account
Growth stock

a) Assuming all of the options earn similar returns before taxes, rank Laurie's investment options from highest to lowest according to their after-tax returns.

b) Which of the investments employ the deferral and/or conversion tax planning strategies?

c) How does the time period of the investment affect the returns from these alternatives?

d) How do these alternative investments differ in terms of their nontax characteristics?

LO 3-5 26. What is an "implicit tax" and how does it affect a taxpayer's decision to purchase municipal bonds?

27. Several judicial doctrines limit basic tax planning strategies. What are they? Which planning strategies do they limit? LO 3-6
28. What is the constructive receipt doctrine? What types of taxpayers does this doctrine generally affect? For what tax planning strategy is the constructive receipt doctrine a potential limitation? LO 3-6
29. Explain the assignment of income doctrine. In what situations would this doctrine potentially apply? LO 3-6
30. Relative to arm's-length transactions, why do related-party transactions receive more IRS scrutiny? LO 3-6
31. Describe the business purpose, step-transaction, and substance-over-form doctrines. What types of tax planning strategies may these doctrines inhibit? LO 3-6
32. What is the difference between tax avoidance and tax evasion? LO 3-7
33. What are the rewards of tax avoidance? What are the rewards of tax evasion? LO 3-7
34. "Tax avoidance is discouraged by the courts and Congress." Is this statement true or false? Please explain. LO 3-7

PROBLEMS

connect ACCOUNTING

All applicable problems are available with McGraw-Hill's *Connect® Accounting*.

35. Yong recently paid his accountant $10,000 for elaborate tax planning strategies that exploit the timing strategy. Assuming this is an election year and there could be a power shift in the White House and Congress, what is a potential risk associated with Yong's strategies? LO 3-2 planning
36. Billups, a physician and cash-method taxpayer, is new to the concept of tax planning and recently learned of the timing strategy. To implement the timing strategy, Billups plans to establish a new policy that allows all his clients to wait two years to pay their co-pays. Assume that Billups does not expect his marginal tax rates to change. What is wrong with his strategy? LO 3-2 LO 3-3 planning
37. Tesha works for a company that pays a year-end bonus in January of each year (instead of December of the preceding year) to allow employees to defer the bonus income. Assume Congress recently passed tax legislation that decreases individual tax rates as of next year. Does this increase or decrease the benefits of the bonus deferral this year? What if Congress passed legislation that increased tax rates next year? Should Tesha ask the company to change its policy this year? What additional information do you need to answer this question? LO 3-2 LO 3-3 planning
38. Isabel, a calendar-year taxpayer, uses the cash method of accounting for her sole proprietorship. In late December she received a $20,000 bill from her accountant for consulting services related to her small business. Isabel can pay the $20,000 bill anytime before January 30 of next year without penalty. Assume her marginal tax rate is 40 percent this year and next year, and that she can earn an after-tax rate of return of 12 percent on her investments. When should she pay the $20,000 bill—this year or next? LO 3-2 LO 3-3 planning
39. Using the facts from the previous problem, how would your answer change if Isabel's after-tax rate of return were 8 percent? LO 3-2 LO 3-3 planning
40. Manny, a calendar-year taxpayer, uses the cash method of accounting for his sole proprietorship. In late December he performed $20,000 of legal services for a client. Manny typically requires his clients to pay his bills immediately upon receipt. Assume Manny's marginal tax rate is 40 percent this year and next year, and that he can earn an after-tax rate of return of 12 percent on his investments. Should Manny send his client the bill in December or January? LO 3-2 LO 3-3 planning

LO 3-2 LO 3-3 planning

41. Using the facts from the previous problem, how would your answer change if Manny's after-tax rate of return were 8 percent?

LO 3-2 LO 3-3 planning

42. Reese, a calendar-year taxpayer, uses the cash method of accounting for her sole proprietorship. In late December, she received a $20,000 bill from her accountant for consulting services related to her small business. Reese can pay the $20,000 bill anytime before January 30 of next year without penalty. Assume Reese's marginal tax rate is 30 percent this year and will be 40 percent next year, and that she can earn an after-tax rate of return of 12 percent on her investments. When should she pay the $20,000 bill—this year or next?

LO 3-2 LO 3-3 planning

43. Using the facts from the previous problem, when should Reese pay the bill if she expects her marginal tax rate to be 33 percent next year? 25 percent next year?

LO 3-2 LO 3-3 planning

44. Hank, a calendar-year taxpayer, uses the cash method of accounting for his sole proprietorship. In late December, he performed $20,000 of legal services for a client. Hank typically requires his clients to pay his bills immediately upon receipt. Assume his marginal tax rate is 30 percent this year and will be 40 percent next year, and that he can earn an after-tax rate of return of 12 percent on his investments. Should Hank send his client the bill in December or January?

LO 3-2 LO 3-3 planning

45. Using the facts from the previous problem, when should Hank send the bill if he expects his marginal tax rate to be 33 percent next year? 25 percent next year?

LO 3-3

46. Geraldo recently won a lottery and chose to receive $100,000 today instead of an equivalent amount in 10 years, computed using an 8 percent rate of return. Today, he learned that interest rates are expected to increase in the future. Is this good news for Geraldo given his decision?

LO 3-3 planning

47. Assume Rafael can earn an 8 percent after-tax rate of return. Would he prefer $1,000 today or $1,500 in five years?

LO 3-3 planning

48. Assume Ellina earns a 10 percent after-tax rate of return, and that she owes a friend $1,200. Would she prefer to pay the friend $1,200 today or $1,750 in four years?

LO 3-3 planning

49. Jonah has the choice of paying Rita $10,000 today or $40,000 in 10 years. Assume Jonah can earn a 12 percent after-tax rate of return. Which should he choose?

LO 3-3 planning

50. Bob's Lottery Inc. has decided to offer winners a choice of $100,000 in 10 years or some amount currently. Assume that Bob's Lottery Inc. earns a 10 percent after-tax rate of return. What amount should Bob offer lottery winners currently, in order for him to be indifferent between the two choices?

LO 3-4 planning

51. Tawana owns and operates a sole proprietorship and has a 40 percent marginal tax rate. She provides her son, Jonathon, $8,000 a year for college expenses. Jonathon works as a pizza delivery person every fall and has a marginal tax rate of 15 percent.
    a) What could Tawana do to reduce her family tax burden?
    b) How much pretax income does it currently take Tawana to generate the $8,000 after-taxes given to Jonathon?
    c) If Jonathon worked for his mother's sole proprietorship, what salary would she have to pay him to generate $8,000 after taxes (ignoring any Social Security, Medicare, or self-employment tax issues)?
    d) How much money would this strategy save?

LO 3-4 planning

52. Moana is a single taxpayer who operates a sole proprietorship. She expects her taxable income next year to be $250,000, of which $200,000 is attributed to her sole proprietorship. Moana is contemplating incorporating her sole proprietorship. Using the single individual tax brackets and the corporate tax brackets, find out how much current tax this strategy could save Moana (ignore any Social Security, Medicare, or self-employment tax issues). How much income should be left in the corporation?

53. Orie and Jane, husband and wife, operate a sole proprietorship. They expect their taxable income next year to be $300,000, of which $125,000 is attributed to the sole proprietorship. Orie and Jane are contemplating incorporating their sole proprietorship. Using the married-joint tax brackets and the corporate tax brackets, find out how much current tax this strategy could save Orie and Jane. How much income should be left in the corporation? LO 3-4 planning

54. Hyundai is considering opening a plant in two neighboring states. One state has a corporate tax rate of 10 percent. If operated in this state, the plant is expected to generate $1,000,000 pretax profit. The other state has a corporate tax rate of 2 percent. If operated in this state, the plant is expected to generate $930,000 of pretax profit. Which state should Hyundai choose? Why do you think the plant in the state with a lower tax rate would produce a lower before-tax income? LO 3-4 planning

55. Bendetta, a high-tax-rate taxpayer, owns several rental properties and would like to shift some income to her daughter, Jenine. Bendetta instructs her tenants to send their rent checks to Jenine so Jenine can report the rental income. Will this shift the income from Bendetta to Jenine? Why, or why not? LO 3-4 LO 3-6 planning

56. Using the facts in the previous problem, what are some ways that Bendetta could shift some of the rental income to Jenine? What are the disadvantages associated with these income-shifting strategies? LO 3-4 LO 3-6 planning

57. Daniel is considering selling two stocks that have not fared well over recent years. A friend recently informed Daniel that one of his stocks has a special designation, which allows him to treat a loss up to $50,000 on this stock as an ordinary loss rather than the typical capital loss. Daniel figures that he has a loss of $60,000 on each stock. If Daniel's marginal tax rate is 35 percent and he has $120,000 of other capital gains (taxed at 15 percent), what is the tax savings from the special tax treatment? LO 3-5 planning

58. Dennis is currently considering investing in municipal bonds that earn 6 percent interest, or in taxable bonds issued by the Coca-Cola Company that pay 8 percent. If Dennis's tax rate is 20 percent, which bond should he choose? Which bond should he choose if his tax rate is 30 percent? At what tax rate would he be indifferent between the bonds? What strategy is this decision based upon? LO 3-5 planning

59. Helen holds 1,000 shares of Fizbo Inc. stock that she purchased 11 months ago. The stock has done very well and has appreciated $20/share since Helen bought the stock. When sold, the stock will be taxed at capital gains rates (long-term rate is 15 percent and short-term rate is the taxpayer's marginal tax rate). If Helen's marginal tax rate is 35 percent, how much would she save by holding the stock an additional month before selling? What might prevent Helen from waiting to sell? LO 3-5 planning

60. Anne's marginal income tax rate is 30 percent. She purchases a corporate bond for $10,000 and the maturity, or face value, of the bond is $10,000. If the bond pays 5 percent per year before taxes, what is Anne's annual after-tax rate of return from the bond if the bond matures in one year? What is her annual after-tax rate of return if the bond matures in 10 years? LO 3-5

61. Irene is saving for a new car she hopes to purchase either four or six years from now. Irene invests $10,000 in a growth stock that does not pay dividends and expects a 6 percent annual before-tax return (the investment is tax deferred). When she cashes in the investment after either four or six years, she expects the applicable marginal tax rate on long-term capital gains to be 25 percent. LO 3-5 planning
    a) What will be the value of this investment four and six years from now?
    b) When Irene sells the investment, how much cash will she have after taxes to purchase the new car (four and six years from now)?

LO 3-5 planning

62. Komiko Tanaka invests $12,000 in LymaBean, Inc. LymaBean does not pay any dividends. Komiko projects that her investment will generate a 10 percent before-tax rate of return. She plans to invest for the long term.

a) How much cash will Komiko retain, after-taxes, if she holds the investment for 5 years and then she sells it when the long-term capital gains rate is 15 percent?

b) What is Komiko's after-tax rate of return on her investment in part (a)?

c) How much cash will Komiko retain, after-taxes, if she holds the investment for 5 years and then sells when the long-term capital gains rate is 25 percent?

d) What is Komiko's after-tax rate of return on her investment in part (c)?

e) How much cash will Komiko retain, after taxes, if she holds the investment for 15 years and then she sells when the long-term capital gains rate is 15 percent?

f) What is Komiko's after-tax rate of return on her investment in part (e)?

LO 3-5

63. Alan inherited $100,000 with the stipulation that he "invest it to financially benefit his family." Alan and Alice decided they would invest the inheritance to help them accomplish two financial goals: purchasing a Park City vacation home and saving for their son, Cooper's, education.

	Vacation Home	Cooper's Education
Initial investment	$50,000	$50,000
Investment horizon	5 years	18 years

Alan and Alice have a marginal income tax rate of 30 percent (capital gains rate of 15 percent) and have decided to investigate the following investment opportunities.

	5 Years	Annual After-Tax Rate of Return	18 Years	Annual After-Tax Rate of Return
Corporate bonds (ordinary interest taxed annually)	5.75%		4.75%	
Dividend-paying stock (no appreciation and dividends are taxed at 15%)	3.50%		3.50%	
Growth stock	Future value is $65,000		Future value is $140,000	
Municipal bond (tax-exempt)	3.20%		3.10%	

Complete the two annual after-tax rates of return columns for each investment and provide investment recommendations for Alan and Alice.

LO 3-7

64. Duff is really interested in decreasing his tax liability, and by his very nature he is somewhat aggressive. A friend of a friend told him that cash transactions are more difficult for the IRS to identify and, thus, tax. Duff is contemplating using this "strategy" of not reporting cash collected in his business to minimize his tax liability. Is this tax planning? What are the risks with this strategy?

LO 3-7

65. Using the facts from the previous problem, how would your answer change if instead, Duff adopted the cash method of accounting to allow him to better control the timing of his cash receipts and disbursements?

LO 3-2 LO 3-4 LO 3-5 planning research

66. Using an available tax service or the Internet, identify three basic tax planning ideas or tax tips suggested for year-end tax planning. Which basic tax strategy from this chapter does each planning idea employ?

67. Jayanna, an advertising consultant, is contemplating instructing some of her clients to pay her in cash so that she does not have to report the income on her tax return. Use an available tax service to identify the three basic elements of tax evasion and penalties associated with tax evasion. Write a memo to Jayanna explaining tax evasion and the risks associated with her actions. LO 3-7 research

68. Using the IRS website (www.irs.gov/index.html), how large is the current estimated "tax gap" (i.e., the amount of tax underpaid by taxpayers annually)? What group of taxpayers represents the largest "contributors" to the tax gap? LO 3-7 research

chapter

4 Individual Income Tax Overview, Exemptions, and Filing Status

Learning Objectives

Upon completing this chapter, you should be able to:

LO 4-1 Describe the formula for calculating an individual taxpayer's taxes payable or refund and generally explain each formula component.

LO 4-2 Explain the requirements for determining a taxpayer's personal and dependency exemptions.

LO 4-3 Determine a taxpayer's filing status.

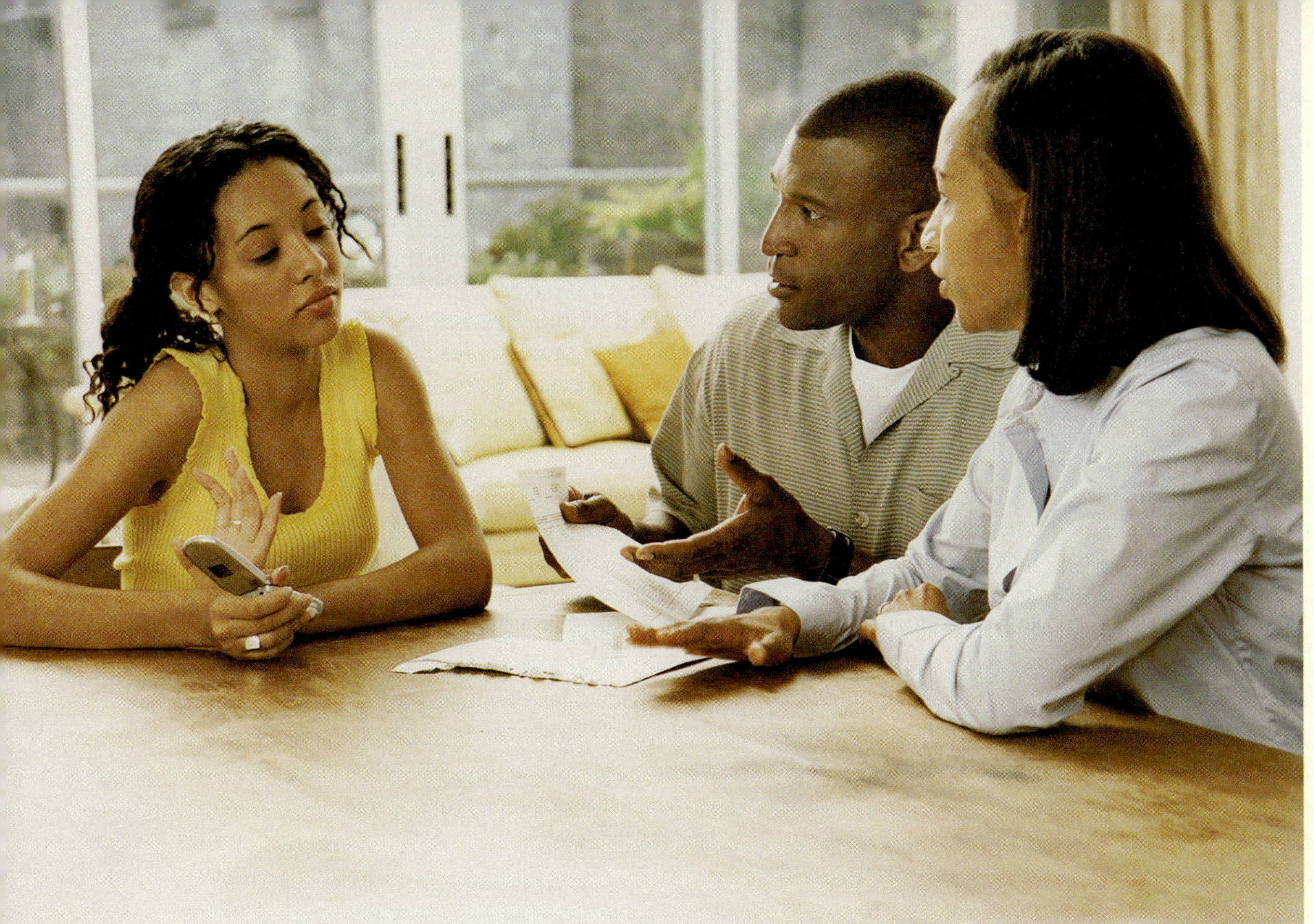

© Getty Images/Digital Vision

Tara Hall just completed a unit on individual taxation in her undergraduate tax class at South Dakota State University. She was excited to share her knowledge with her parents, Rodney and Anita Hall, as they prepared their tax return. Rodney and Anita have been married for over 25 years, and they have filed a joint tax return each year. The Halls' 12-year-old son Braxton lives at home but Tara, who is 21, lives nearby in the university dorms. Further, in January of this year, Rodney's younger brother Shawn moved in with the Halls. They expect Shawn to live with them for at least one year and maybe two. Every year Rodney and Anita use tax-preparation software to complete their tax return, but they are not always sure they understand the final result. This year, with Tara's help, they hope that will change. ■

Storyline Summary

Taxpayers:	Rodney and Anita Hall
Other household members:	Tara, their 21-year-old daughter, and Braxton, their 12-year-old son. Shawn, Rodney's brother, also lives with the Halls.
Location:	Brookings, South Dakota
Employment status:	Rodney is a manager for a regional grocery chain. His salary is $64,000. Anita works part-time as a purchasing-card auditor at South Dakota State University. Her salary is $46,000.
Current situation:	Determining their tax liability

This chapter and the next four discuss the fundamental elements of the individual income tax formula. This is the overview chapter; the other chapters provide more depth on individual income tax topics. Here we introduce the individual income tax formula, summarize its components, describe requirements for dependency exemptions, and explain how to determine a taxpayer's filing status. Chapter 5 explains gross income, Chapter 6 describes deductible expenses to determine adjusted gross income and taxable income, and Chapter 7 discusses tax issues associated with income from investments. Finally, Chapter 8 addresses issues associated with calculating a taxpayer's tax liability and discusses tax return filing concerns.

LO 4-1

THE INDIVIDUAL INCOME TAX FORMULA

Each year, individuals file tax returns to report their **taxable income,** the tax base for the individual income tax, to the Internal Revenue Service.[1] Exhibit 4-1 presents a simplified formula for calculating taxable income.

EXHIBIT 4-1 Individual Tax Formula

	Gross income
Minus:	*For* AGI deductions
Equals:	Adjusted gross income (AGI)
Minus:	*From* AGI deductions:
	(1) *Greater* of
	(a) Standard deduction or
	(b) Itemized deductions and
	(2) Personal and dependency exemptions
Equals:	Taxable income
Times:	Tax rates
Equals:	Income tax liability
Plus:	Other taxes
Equals:	Total tax
Minus:	Credits
Minus:	Prepayments
Equals:	Taxes due or (refund)

Beginning with gross income, this formula is imbedded in the first two pages of the individual income tax Form 1040, the form individuals generally use to report their taxable income.[2] Exhibit 4-2 presents the first two pages from the form (throughout the text we use 2014 tax forms because 2015 forms were unavailable when the book went to press). The last line on page 1 of Form 1040 is **adjusted gross income (AGI),** an important reference point in the income tax formula.

Let's look at the components of the individual tax formula and provide a brief description of each of the key elements.

Gross Income

The U.S. tax laws are based on the **all-inclusive income concept.** Under this concept, **gross income** generally includes all **realized income** from *whatever source derived.*[3] Realized income is generated in a transaction with a second party in which there is a measurable change in property rights between parties (appreciation in a stock

[1]See Exhibit 2-1 (in Chapter 2) for a description of who must file a tax return.

[2]To see the 1913 version of the individual tax form, go to http://www.irs.gov/pub/irs-utl/1913.pdf

[3]§61(a).

EXHIBIT 4-2 Form 1040, pages 1 and 2

Form **1040** Department of the Treasury—Internal Revenue Service (99) **U.S. Individual Income Tax Return** **2014** OMB No. 1545-0074 IRS Use Only—Do not write or staple in this space.

For the year Jan. 1–Dec. 31, 2014, or other tax year beginning , 2014, ending , 20 See separate instructions.

Your first name and initial	Last name	Your social security number
If a joint return, spouse's first name and initial	Last name	Spouse's social security number
Home address (number and street). If you have a P.O. box, see instructions.	Apt. no.	▲ Make sure the SSN(s) above and on line 6c are correct.
City, town or post office, state, and ZIP code. If you have a foreign address, also complete spaces below (see instructions).		**Presidential Election Campaign** Check here if you, or your spouse if filing jointly, want $3 to go to this fund. Checking a box below will not change your tax or refund. ☐ You ☐ Spouse
Foreign country name	Foreign province/state/county	Foreign postal code

Filing Status

Check only one box.

1 ☐ Single
2 ☐ Married filing jointly (even if only one had income)
3 ☐ Married filing separately. Enter spouse's SSN above and full name here. ▶
4 ☐ Head of household (with qualifying person). (See instructions.) If the qualifying person is a child but not your dependent, enter this child's name here. ▶
5 ☐ Qualifying widow(er) with dependent child

Exemptions

6a ☐ **Yourself.** If someone can claim you as a dependent, **do not** check box 6a
b ☐ **Spouse**

Boxes checked on 6a and 6b
No. of children on 6c who:
• lived with you
• did not live with you due to divorce or separation (see instructions)
Dependents on 6c not entered above
Add numbers on lines above ▶

c **Dependents:**

(1) First name Last name	(2) Dependent's social security number	(3) Dependent's relationship to you	(4) ✓ if child under age 17 qualifying for child tax credit (see instructions)
			☐
			☐
			☐
			☐

If more than four dependents, see instructions and check here ▶ ☐

d Total number of exemptions claimed

Income

Attach Form(s) W-2 here. Also attach Forms W-2G and 1099-R if tax was withheld.

If you did not get a W-2, see instructions.

7	Wages, salaries, tips, etc. Attach Form(s) W-2		7
8a	**Taxable** interest. Attach Schedule B if required		8a
b	**Tax-exempt** interest. **Do not** include on line 8a	8b	
9a	Ordinary dividends. Attach Schedule B if required		9a
b	Qualified dividends	9b	
10	Taxable refunds, credits, or offsets of state and local income taxes		10
11	Alimony received		11
12	Business income or (loss). Attach Schedule C or C-EZ		12
13	Capital gain or (loss). Attach Schedule D if required. If not required, check here ▶ ☐		13
14	Other gains or (losses). Attach Form 4797		14
15a	IRA distributions 15a	b Taxable amount	15b
16a	Pensions and annuities 16a	b Taxable amount	16b
17	Rental real estate, royalties, partnerships, S corporations, trusts, etc. Attach Schedule E		17
18	Farm income or (loss). Attach Schedule F		18
19	Unemployment compensation		19
20a	Social security benefits 20a	b Taxable amount	20b
21	Other income. List type and amount		21
22	Combine the amounts in the far right column for lines 7 through 21. This is your **total income** ▶		22

Adjusted Gross Income

23	Educator expenses	23	
24	Certain business expenses of reservists, performing artists, and fee-basis government officials. Attach Form 2106 or 2106-EZ	24	
25	Health savings account deduction. Attach Form 8889	25	
26	Moving expenses. Attach Form 3903	26	
27	Deductible part of self-employment tax. Attach Schedule SE	27	
28	Self-employed SEP, SIMPLE, and qualified plans	28	
29	Self-employed health insurance deduction	29	
30	Penalty on early withdrawal of savings	30	
31a	Alimony paid **b** Recipient's SSN ▶	31a	
32	IRA deduction	32	
33	Student loan interest deduction	33	
34	Tuition and fees. Attach Form 8917	34	
35	Domestic production activities deduction. Attach Form 8903	35	
36	Add lines 23 through 35		36
37	Subtract line 36 from line 22. This is your **adjusted gross income** ▶		37

For Disclosure, Privacy Act, and Paperwork Reduction Act Notice, see separate instructions. Cat. No. 11320B Form **1040** (2014)

(continued)

EXHIBIT 4-2 Form 1040, pages 1 and 2 (*continued*)

Form 1040 (2014) Page **2**

Tax and Credits

38	Amount from line 37 (adjusted gross income)	38	
39a	Check if: ☐ **You** were born before January 2, 1950, ☐ Blind. ☐ **Spouse** was born before January 2, 1950, ☐ Blind. **Total boxes checked ▶ 39a**		
b	If your spouse itemizes on a separate return or you were a dual-status alien, check here▶ 39b☐		
40	**Itemized deductions** (from Schedule A) **or** your **standard deduction** (see left margin)	40	
41	Subtract line 40 from line 38	41	
42	**Exemptions.** If line 38 is $152,525 or less, multiply $3,950 by the number on line 6d. Otherwise, see instructions	42	
43	**Taxable income.** Subtract line 42 from line 41. If line 42 is more than line 41, enter -0-	43	
44	**Tax** (see instructions). Check if any from: **a** ☐ Form(s) 8814 **b** ☐ Form 4972 **c** ☐	44	
45	**Alternative minimum tax** (see instructions). Attach Form 6251	45	
46	Excess advance premium tax credit repayment. Attach Form 8962	46	
47	Add lines 44, 45, and 46 ▶	47	
48	Foreign tax credit. Attach Form 1116 if required	48	
49	Credit for child and dependent care expenses. Attach Form 2441	49	
50	Education credits from Form 8863, line 19	50	
51	Retirement savings contributions credit. Attach Form 8880	51	
52	Child tax credit. Attach Schedule 8812, if required	52	
53	Residential energy credits. Attach Form 5695	53	
54	Other credits from Form: **a** ☐ 3800 **b** ☐ 8801 **c** ☐	54	
55	Add lines 48 through 54. These are your **total credits**	55	
56	Subtract line 55 from line 47. If line 55 is more than line 47, enter -0- ▶	56	

Standard Deduction for—
• People who check any box on line 39a or 39b **or** who can be claimed as a dependent, see instructions.
• All others:
Single or Married filing separately, $6,200
Married filing jointly or Qualifying widow(er), $12,400
Head of household, $9,100

Other Taxes

57	Self-employment tax. Attach Schedule SE	57	
58	Unreported social security and Medicare tax from Form: **a** ☐ 4137 **b** ☐ 8919	58	
59	Additional tax on IRAs, other qualified retirement plans, etc. Attach Form 5329 if required	59	
60a	Household employment taxes from Schedule H	60a	
b	First-time homebuyer credit repayment. Attach Form 5405 if required	60b	
61	Health care: individual responsibility (see instructions) Full-year coverage ☐	61	
62	Taxes from: **a** ☐ Form 8959 **b** ☐ Form 8960 **c** ☐ Instructions; enter code(s)	62	
63	Add lines 56 through 62. This is your **total tax** ▶	63	

Payments

64	Federal income tax withheld from Forms W-2 and 1099	64	
65	2014 estimated tax payments and amount applied from 2013 return	65	
66a	**Earned income credit (EIC)**	66a	
b	Nontaxable combat pay election 66b		
67	Additional child tax credit. Attach Schedule 8812	67	
68	American opportunity credit from Form 8863, line 8	68	
69	Net premium tax credit. Attach Form 8962	69	
70	Amount paid with request for extension to file	70	
71	Excess social security and tier 1 RRTA tax withheld	71	
72	Credit for federal tax on fuels. Attach Form 4136	72	
73	Credits from Form: **a** ☐ 2439 **b** ☐ Reserved **c** ☐ Reserved **d** ☐	73	
74	Add lines 64, 65, 66a, and 67 through 73. These are your **total payments** ▶	74	

If you have a qualifying child, attach Schedule EIC.

Refund

75	If line 74 is more than line 63, subtract line 63 from line 74. This is the amount you **overpaid**	75	
76a	Amount of line 75 you want **refunded to you.** If Form 8888 is attached, check here ▶☐	76a	
▶ b	Routing number ▶ c Type: ☐ Checking ☐ Savings		
▶ d	Account number		
77	Amount of line 75 you want **applied to your 2015 estimated tax** ▶ 77		

Direct deposit? See instructions.

Amount You Owe

78	**Amount you owe.** Subtract line 74 from line 63. For details on how to pay, see instructions ▶	78	
79	Estimated tax penalty (see instructions) 79		

Third Party Designee

Do you want to allow another person to discuss this return with the IRS (see instructions)? ☐ **Yes.** Complete below. ☐ **No**

Designee's name ▶ Phone no. ▶ Personal identification number (PIN) ▶

Sign Here

Under penalties of perjury, I declare that I have examined this return and accompanying schedules and statements, and to the best of my knowledge and belief, they are true, correct, and complete. Declaration of preparer (other than taxpayer) is based on all information of which preparer has any knowledge.

Joint return? See instructions. Keep a copy for your records.

Your signature	Date	Your occupation	Daytime phone number
Spouse's signature. If a joint return, **both** must sign.	Date	Spouse's occupation	If the IRS sent you an Identity Protection PIN, enter it here (see inst.)

Paid Preparer Use Only

Print/Type preparer's name	Preparer's signature	Date	Check ☐ if self-employed	PTIN
Firm's name ▶			Firm's EIN ▶	
Firm's address ▶			Phone no.	

www.irs.gov/form1040 Form **1040** (2014)

investment would not represent realized income unless the taxpayer sold the stock). Certain tax provisions allow taxpayers to permanently exclude specific types of realized income from gross income (the income items are never taxable) and other provisions allow taxpayers to defer including certain types of realized income items in gross income until a subsequent year (the income item is included in gross income in a later year). Realized income items that taxpayers permanently exclude from taxation are referred to as **exclusions.** Realized income items that taxpayers include in gross income in a subsequent year are called **deferrals.** Exhibit 4-3 provides a

EXHIBIT 4-3 Partial Listing of Common Income Items

Income Item	Character	Discussed in More Detail in
Compensation for services including fringe benefits	Ordinary	Chapters 5 and 12
Business income	Ordinary	Chapter 9
Gains from selling property	Ordinary or Capital[4]	Chapters 7 and 11
Interest and dividends	Ordinary or Qualified Dividend	Chapters 5 and 7
Rents and royalties	Ordinary	Chapters 5, 7, and 14
Alimony received and annuities	Ordinary	Chapter 5
Retirement income	Ordinary	Chapter 13
Income from the discharge of indebtedness	Ordinary	Chapter 5

partial listing of common income items included in gross income, their character (discussed below), and where in the text we provide more detail on each income item. Exhibit 4-4 provides a partial listing of common exclusions and deferrals and indicates where in the text we discuss each in more detail.

EXHIBIT 4-4 Partial Listing of Common Exclusions and Deferrals

Exclusion or Deferral Item	Exclusion or Deferral	Discussed in
Interest income from municipal bonds	Exclusion	Chapter 5
Gifts and inheritances	Exclusion	Chapter 5
Gain on sale of personal residence	Exclusion	Chapters 5 and 14
Life insurance proceeds	Exclusion	Chapter 5
Installment sale	Deferral	Chapter 11
Like-kind exchange	Deferral	Chapter 11

Character of Income While gross income increases taxable income dollar for dollar, it is important to note that not all types of income are treated equally. In fact, the *type* of income (commonly referred to as the **character of income**) determines the rate at which the income will be taxed. The different types or characters of income are as follows:

- Tax-exempt: This is income realized during the year that is excluded from gross income and is never taxed (income qualifies as an exclusion).

[4]Dispositions of assets used in a trade or business for more than a year generate an intermediate character of income called § 1231 gain or loss. Ultimately, § 1231 gains and losses are treated as either ordinary or capital on the tax return.

- Tax deferred: This is income realized during the year that is not included in gross income until a later year(s) (the current year tax rate is zero). That is, the income is not taxed in the current year but will be taxed in a subsequent year or years when certain events take place (the income qualifies as a deferral).
- Ordinary: This is income included in gross income (or loss subtracted in determining gross income) in the current year and taxed at the ordinary rates provided in the tax rate schedules.
- Qualified dividend: Shareholders receiving dividends from corporations include the dividend income in gross income. If the dividend meets the qualified dividend requirements, it is taxed at a rate of 15 percent (20 percent for high income taxpayers and 0 percent for low income taxpayers). If the dividend does not meet these requirements, it is taxed as ordinary income. Because qualified dividends are subject to a lower rate than ordinary income (a **preferential tax rate**), qualified dividends can be referred to as **preferentially taxed income.** A qualified dividend generally includes dividends distributed by a U.S. corporation if the shareholder meets certain holding requirements for the stock.[5] These requirements are discussed in more detail in Chapter 7.
- Capital: These are gains or losses on the disposition or sale of capital assets. In general, capital assets are all assets *other than*

  1. Accounts receivable from the sale of goods or services.
  2. Inventory and other assets held for sale in the ordinary course of business.
  3. Assets used in a trade or business, including supplies.[6]

  Thus, personal use assets such as a personal automobile or personal residence and assets held for investment such as stocks and bonds are capital assets. Gain on the sale of a capital asset is generally included in gross income. If the gain is a long-term capital gain (the taxpayer owned the capital asset for more than a year before selling it), it is taxed at a 15 percent tax rate (20 percent for high income taxpayers and 0 percent for low income taxpayers). If the gain is a short-term capital gain (the taxpayer holds the asset for a year or less before selling it), the gain is taxed at ordinary income rates. Note that even though short-term capital gains are taxed at ordinary rates, they are still considered to be capital gains and not ordinary income.

  Loss on the sale of a capital asset (no matter how long the taxpayer held it before selling) is a *for* AGI deduction in the year of sale. However, the deduction for a capital loss in a particular year is limited to $3,000 (losses in excess of the limit are carried forward indefinitely). If the taxpayer sells a personal use asset (like a personal automobile or personal residence) at a loss, the loss is not deductible. When a taxpayer sells more than one capital asset during the year, the gains and losses are netted together. A net loss is subject to the $3,000 annual *for* AGI deduction limit. A net gain may be taxed at of 15, 20, or 0 percent or at the ordinary rates depending on the outcome of the netting process and the taxpayer's taxable income. We discuss the netting process in detail in Chapter 7.[7]

Example 4-1

Rodney earned a salary of $64,000, and Anita earned a salary of $46,000 working part-time. The Halls also received $600 of interest income from investments in corporate bonds and $300 of interest income from investments in municipal bonds. This was their only income during the year. What is the Halls' gross income?

[5]Dividends from "qualified foreign corporations" may also qualify [see §1(h)(11)(B)].

[6]See §1221(a) for the definition of a capital asset.

[7]As we discover in Chapter 7, certain capital gains may be taxed at a maximum rate of 28 percent or 25 percent.

Answer: $110,600, computed as follows:

Description	Amount	Explanation
(1) Rodney's salary	$ 64,000	
(2) Anita's salary	46,000	
(3) Interest from corporate bonds	600	
Gross income	**$110,600***	(1) + (2) + (3).

*The $300 of interest income from municipal bonds is excluded from gross income.

What is the character of the salary, the interest income from the corporate bonds, and the interest income from the investments in municipal bonds?

Answer: The salary and interest income from corporate bonds are ordinary income. The interest income from the municipal bonds is tax-exempt income.

What if: Suppose this year the Halls sold stock at a $4,000 gain. They purchased the stock three years ago. What would be the character of the gain? At what rate would the gain be taxed?

Answer: Long-term capital gain because stock is a capital asset and the Halls owned the stock for more than a year before selling. The gain would be taxed at a maximum rate of 15 percent.

What if: Suppose this year the Halls sold stock at a $4,000 loss (their only transaction involving a capital asset). They purchased the stock three years ago. What would be the character of the loss? How much of the loss may the Halls deduct in the current year?

Answer: Long-term capital loss because the stock is a capital asset and the Halls owned the stock for more than a year before selling. The Halls can deduct $3,000 of the loss as a *for* AGI deduction this year. The remaining $1,000 loss is carried over to next year.

What if: Suppose this year the Halls sold a personal automobile at a $4,000 loss. They purchased the automobile three years ago. What is the character of the loss? How much of the loss may the Halls deduct in the current year?

Answer: Long-term capital loss because the automobile is a capital asset and the Halls owned the auto for more than a year before selling. However, the Halls are not allowed to deduct any of the $4,000 loss this year or any year because the automobile is a personal use asset.

Deductions

Deductions reduce a taxpayer's taxable income. However, they are not necessarily easy to come by because, in contrast to the all-inclusive treatment of income, taxpayers are *not allowed to deduct anything unless a specific tax provision allows them to do so*. Thus, deductions are a matter of **legislative grace.** The tax laws provide for two distinct types of deductions in the individual tax formula: *for adjusted gross income (AGI) deductions* and *from AGI deductions.* As indicated in the individual tax formula, gross income minus ***for*** **AGI deductions** equals AGI and AGI minus ***from*** **AGI deductions** equals taxable income. When it enacts new legislation that grants deductions, Congress identifies whether the deductions are *for* or *from* AGI. The distinction between the deduction types is particularly important because AGI is an important reference point that is often used in other tax-related calculations. Specifically, limits on certain *from* AGI deductions depend on AGI (certain *from* AGI deductions are reduced as a taxpayer's AGI increases). Because *for* AGI deductions decrease AGI, they *increase* the deductibility of *from* AGI deductions subject to AGI limitations.

THE KEY FACTS

For **and** ***From*** **AGI Deductions**

- *For* AGI deductions
  - Deduct in determining AGI.
  - Deduction "above the line."
  - Generally more valuable than *from* AGI deductions.
- *From* AGI deductions
  - Deducted *from* AGI to determine taxable income.
  - Deduction "below the line."
  - Generally less valuable than *for* AGI deductions.

For AGI Deductions

For AGI deductions tend to be deductions associated with business activities and certain investing activities. Because *for* AGI deductions are subtracted in determining AGI (deducted on page 1 of Form 1040), they are referred to as **"deductions above the line."** The "line" in this case is AGI, which is the last line on page 1 of Form 1040 (see Exhibit 4-2). Exhibit 4-5 provides a partial listing of common *for* AGI deductions and indicates where in the text we discuss them.

EXHIBIT 4-5 Partial Listing of Common *for* AGI Deductions

For AGI Deduction	Discussed in
Alimony paid	Chapter 6
Health insurance deduction for self-employed taxpayers	Chapter 6
Moving expenses	Chapter 6
Rental and royalty expenses	Chapter 6
Capital losses (*net* losses limited to $3,000 for the year)	Chapter 7
One-half of self-employment taxes paid	Chapter 8
Business expenses	Chapter 9
Losses on dispositions of assets used in a trade or business	Chapter 11
Contributions to qualified retirement accounts	Chapter 13

Example 4-2

The Halls paid $5,000 of deductible moving expenses (*for* AGI) when the family relocated due to an employment transfer for Rodney. What is the Halls' adjusted gross income?

Answer: $105,600, computed as follows:

Description	Amount	Explanation
(1) Gross income	$ 110,600	Example 4-1.
(2) Moving expenses	(5,000)	*For* AGI deduction (see Exhibit 4-5).
Adjusted gross income	**$105,600**	(1) + (2).

***From* AGI Deductions** In contrast to *for* AGI deductions, *from* AGI deductions tend to be personal in nature. *From* AGI deductions are commonly referred to as **"deductions below the line"** because they are deducted after AGI has been determined (deducted on page 2 of Form 1040). *From* AGI deductions include **itemized deductions,** the **standard deduction,** and **exemptions.** In a given year, individuals have the choice of deducting *either* their itemized deductions *or* deducting a fixed amount called the standard deduction. As we discuss in Chapter 6, itemized deductions are partially phased out for taxpayers with AGI over a certain threshold. They generally deduct the higher of the two (after the itemized deductions phase out, if any). Exhibit 4-6 identifies the primary categories of itemized deductions.

EXHIBIT 4-6 Primary Categories of Itemized Deductions

- *Medical and dental expenses:* Deductible to the extent these expenses exceed 10 percent of AGI for taxpayers under age 65 at year end and 7.5 percent otherwise.
- *Taxes:* State and local income taxes, real estate taxes, personal property taxes, and other taxes.
- *Interest expense:* Mortgage, home equity, and investment interest expense.
- *Gifts to charity (charitable contributions).*
- *Casualty and theft losses:* Deductible to the extent they exceed 10 percent of AGI.
- *Job expenses and certain miscellaneous deductions:* Deductible to the extent the sum of these expenses exceeds 2 percent of AGI.
- *Other miscellaneous deductions:* Gambling losses (to the extent of gambling winnings) and certain other deductions not subject to AGI limitation.

Note: Itemized deductions are detailed on Schedule A of Form 1040. We discuss itemized deductions in more depth in Chapter 6.

The amount of the standard deduction varies by taxpayer filing status (we discuss filing status in more detail later in the chapter); the government indexes this deduction for inflation. Exhibit 4-7 presents the basic standard deduction amounts by filing status for 2014 and 2015. Special rules may alter the allowable standard deduction

EXHIBIT 4-7 Standard Deduction Amounts by Filing Status*

	2014	2015
Married filing jointly	$12,400	$12,600
Qualifying widow or widower	12,400	12,600
Married filing separately	6,200	6,300
Head of household	9,100	9,250
Single	6,200	6,300

*Married taxpayers 65 years of age or over and/or blind are entitled to an additional standard deduction of $1,250 ($1,250 for age and another $1,250 for blindness); single and head of household taxpayers 65 years of age or over and/or blind are entitled to an additional standard deduction of $1,550 (one for age and another for blindness). (See Chapter 6 for more detail.) For individuals claimed as a dependent on another tax return, the 2015 standard deduction is the greater of (1) $1,050 or (2) $350 plus earned income not to exceed the standard deduction amount for those who are not dependents (see Chapter 8 for more detail).

for certain taxpayers. We discuss these departures from the basic standard deduction amounts in Chapter 6.

The final *from* AGI deduction is the deduction for exemptions. An exemption is a flat deduction allowed for the taxpayer, the taxpayer's spouse, and each person who qualifies as a dependent of the taxpayer. The exemptions for the taxpayer(s) filing the tax return are called **personal exemptions,** while the others are referred to as **dependency exemptions.** In 2015, the amount of the exemption deduction is $4,000 for both exemption types. As we discuss in Chapter 6, deductions for exemptions are phased out over a range of AGI for taxpayers with AGI over a certain threshold. We discuss the dependency qualification requirements later in this chapter.

Example 4-3

Tara's parents, Rodney and Anita, annually file a joint tax return. Tara determined that her parents paid a total of $14,000 for expenditures that qualify as itemized deductions. Assuming Tara and her younger brother Braxton qualify as Rodney and Anita's dependents, what is the total amount of *from* AGI deductions Rodney and Anita are allowed to deduct on their tax return?

Answer: $30,000, computed as follows:

Description	Amount	Explanation
(1) Standard deduction	$12,600	Married filing joint filing status (see Exhibit 4-7).
(2) Itemized deductions	14,000	
(3) Greater of (1) or (2)	14,000	Itemized deductions exceed the standard deduction.
(4) Personal and dependency exemptions	16,000	($4,000 × 4) One exemption each for Rodney, Anita, Tara, and Braxton.
Total deductions from AGI	**$30,000**	(3) + (4). (Also referred to as deductions "below the line.")

What if: What would be the amount of the Halls' *from* AGI deductions if, instead of the original facts, Rodney and Anita had paid a total of $8,000 in expenditures that qualified as itemized deductions, such as interest expense and gifts to charity?

Answer: $28,600, computed as follows:

Description	Amount	Explanation
(1) Standard deduction	$12,600	Married filing joint filing status (see Exhibit 4-7).
(2) Itemized deductions	8,000	
(3) Greater of (1) or (2)	12,600	The standard deduction exceeds itemized deductions.
(4) Personal and dependency exemptions	16,000	($4,000 × 4) One personal exemption each for Rodney, Anita, Tara, and Braxton.
Total deductions from AGI	**$28,600**	(3) + (4).

Income Tax Calculation

After determining taxable income, taxpayers can generally calculate their regular income tax liability using either a **tax table** or a **tax rate schedule,** depending on their filing status and income level (see inside back cover for the regular tax rate schedules). Taxpayers with taxable income under $100,000 generally must use the tax tables.[8] However, as we discussed above, certain types of income that are included in taxable income are taxed at rates different from the rates embedded in the tables or published in the tax rate schedules.

Example 4-4

With Tara's help, the Halls determined their taxable income to be $75,600 as follows:

Description	Amount	Explanation
(1) Adjusted gross income	$105,600	Example 4-2.
(2) *From* AGI deductions	(30,000)	Example 4-3.
Taxable income	$ 75,600	(1) + (2).

They have also determined that all of their income is ordinary income. What is their tax liability (use the tax rate schedule rather than the tax tables to answer the question)?

Answer: $10,487.50. See the married filing jointly tax rate schedule inside the back cover. [$10,312.50 + $175 {25% × ($75,600 − $74,900)}].

What if: Using the tax rate schedules, what would the Halls' tax liability be if their taxable income was $12,000 (all ordinary income)?

Answer: $1,200 ($12,000 × 10%).

What if: Assume that in addition to the $75,600 of ordinary income, the Halls also reported $5,000 of long-term capital gain subject to a 15 percent tax rate. How much tax would they pay on the additional $5,000 gain?

Answer: $750 ($5,000 × 15%). Long-term capital gains (gains on the sale of a capital asset owned for more than a year) are generally taxed at a 15 percent rate. Note that the Halls' taxable income is $80,600. $75,600 of the income is taxed at ordinary rates and $5,000 is taxed at the preferential 15 percent rate.

Other Taxes

In addition to the individual income tax, individuals may also be required to pay other taxes such as the **alternative minimum tax (AMT)** or **self-employment taxes.** These taxes are imposed on tax bases other than the individual's regular taxable income. Furthermore, taxpayers with relatively high AGI are subject to a 3.8% net investment income tax and a .9% additional Medicare tax on earned income. We discuss these taxes in more detail in Chapter 8.

Tax Credits

Individual taxpayers may reduce their tax liabilities by **tax credits** to determine their total taxes payable. Like deductions, tax credits are specifically granted by Congress and are narrowly defined. Unlike deductions, which reduce *taxable income,* tax credits *directly reduce taxes payable*. Thus, a $1 deduction reduces taxes payable

[8]For administrative convenience and to prevent low- and middle-income taxpayers from making mathematical errors using a rate schedule, the IRS provides tax tables that present the gross tax for various amounts of taxable income. For simplicity, we use the tax rate schedule to determine tax liabilities in the examples presented in this text.

by $1 times the marginal tax rate while a $1 credit reduces taxes payable by $1. Common credits include the child tax credit ($1,000 per child that qualifies for the credit), the child and dependent care credit, the earned income credit, the American opportunity credit, and the lifetime learning credit. We discuss credits in more detail in Chapter 8.

Tax Prepayments

After calculating the total tax and subtracting their available credits, taxpayers determine their taxes due (or tax refund) by subtracting tax prepayments from the total tax remaining after credits. Tax prepayments include (1) **withholdings,** or income taxes withheld from the taxpayer's salary or wages by her employer; (2) **estimated tax payments** the taxpayer makes for the year (paid directly to the IRS), and (3) taxes the taxpayer overpaid on the prior year tax return that the taxpayer elects to apply as an estimated payment for the next tax year instead of receiving the overpayment as a refund.

If tax prepayments exceed the total tax after subtracting credits, the taxpayer receives a tax refund for the difference. If tax prepayments are less than the total tax after credits, the taxpayer owes additional tax and potentially a penalty for the underpayment.

Example 4-5

Based on their calculation in Example 4-4, Rodney and Anita Hall's tax liability is $10,487.50. The Halls had $9,800 of federal income taxes withheld by their employers from their paychecks and are able to claim a $1,000 child tax credit for their 12-year-old son Braxton (Tara is too old to qualify). What is the Halls' tax due or tax refund?

Answer: $312.50 tax refund, computed as follows:

Description	Amount	Explanation
(1) Tax liability	$10,487.50	Example 4-4.
(2) Tax credits	(1,000)	$1,000 child tax credit for 12-year old son Braxton.
(3) Tax prepayments	(9,800)	
Tax refund	**$ 312.50**	(1) + (2) + (3).

Although not explicitly stated in the individual tax formula, a taxpayer's filing status affects many parts of the tax formula, including the standard deduction amount and the applicable income tax rate schedule among others. Below, we describe the rules for determining a taxpayer's filing status. However, because a taxpayer's filing status may depend on whether the taxpayer has dependents for tax purposes, we discuss how to determine who qualifies as a taxpayer's dependent before we address filing status.

PERSONAL AND DEPENDENCY EXEMPTIONS

LO 4-2

In 2015, taxpayers are allowed to deduct $4,000 for each personal and dependency exemption they are entitled to claim. Individual taxpayers generally may deduct a personal exemption for themselves. Married couples filing jointly may claim two personal exemptions (one for each spouse).[9] Further, to provide some tax relief for taxpayers supporting others, individuals may claim additional exemptions for each person who qualifies as the taxpayer's dependent.[10] Individuals who qualify as a

[9]§151(b).
[10]§151(c).

dependent of another taxpayer may *not* claim a personal exemption for themselves on their own individual tax returns and they may not claim a dependency exemption for someone else.[11, 12]

Example 4-6

Assume that Tara (the Halls' 21-year-old daughter who is a full-time college student) qualifies as Rodney and Anita's dependent. Tara earned $9,000 at a summer job this year, and she files her own tax return. Is Tara allowed to claim a personal exemption for herself on her own tax return?

Answer: No. Because Tara qualifies as the Halls' dependent, the Halls may deduct a dependency exemption for Tara, but Tara may *not* deduct a personal exemption for herself.

Dependency Requirements

Taxpayers (who are not dependents of another) may claim exemptions only for persons qualifying as their **dependents.** To qualify as a dependent of another, an individual

1. Must be a citizen of the United States or a resident of the United States, Canada, or Mexico.
2. Must *not* file a joint return with the individual's spouse unless there is no tax liability on the couple's joint return and there would not have been any tax liability on either spouse's tax return if they had filed separately.[13]
3. Must be considered either a **qualifying child** of the taxpayer *or* a **qualifying relative** of the taxpayer.[14]

While the requirements for determining a qualifying child and a qualifying relative have some similarities, the qualifying relative requirements are broader in scope than the qualifying child requirements.

Qualifying Child

To be considered a qualifying child of a taxpayer, an individual must satisfy the following four tests: (1) relationship, (2) age, (3) residence, and (4) support.[15]

Relationship test. A qualifying child must be an eligible relative of the taxpayer. Eligible relatives include the taxpayer's

- Child or descendant of a child. For this purpose, a child includes a taxpayer's adopted child, stepchild, and eligible foster child.
- Sibling or descendant of sibling. For this purpose, a sibling includes a taxpayer's half-brother, half-sister, stepbrother, or stepsister.

Under this definition, the taxpayer's grandchild would qualify as an eligible relative as would the taxpayer's sister's grandchild.

Age test. A qualifying child must be younger than the taxpayer and *either* (1) under age 19 at the end of the year or (2) under age 24 at the end of the year *and* a full-time

[11]§151(b)

[12]See Publication 17, "Your Federal Income Tax," for information relating to personal and dependency exemptions.

[13]Rev. Rul. 54-567, 1954-2 C.B. 108.

[14]§152.

[15]Technically, an individual is not eligible to be a qualifying child of another if she filed a joint return with her spouse (other than to claim a refund) [see §151(c)(2)(e)]. However, because this is also a requirement to be claimed as a dependent, we do not discuss the requirement separately here.

student.[16] A person is a full-time student if she was in school full-time during any part of each of five calendar months during the calendar year.[17] An individual who is permanently and totally disabled is deemed to have met the age test.[18]

Residence test. A qualifying child must have the same principal residence as the taxpayer for *more* than half the year. Time that a child (or the taxpayer) is temporarily away from the taxpayer's home because the child (or taxpayer) is ill, is pursuing an education, or has other special circumstances is counted as though the child (or taxpayer) were living in the taxpayer's home.[19]

Support test. A qualifying child must *not* have provided more than half his or her *own* support (living expenses) for the year. When determining who provided the support for a *child* of the taxpayer who is a full-time student, scholarships are excluded from the computation.[20] Otherwise, support generally includes

- Food, school lunches, toilet articles, and haircuts.
- Clothing.
- Recreation—including toys, summer camp, horseback riding, entertainment, and vacation expenses.
- Medical and dental care.
- Child care expenses.
- Allowances and gifts.
- Wedding costs.
- Lodging.
- Education—including board, uniforms at military schools, and tuition.

Example 4-7

Rodney and Anita have two children: Braxton, age 12, who lives at home and Tara, age 21, who is a full-time student and does not live at home. Tara earned $9,000 in a summer job, but she did *not* provide more than half of her own support during the year. Are Braxton and Tara qualifying children of Rodney and Anita?

Answer: Yes, see analysis of factors below:

Test	Braxton	Tara
Relationship	Yes, son.	Yes, daughter.
Age	Yes, under age 19 at end of year (and younger than his parents).	Yes, under age 24 at year-end *and* full-time student (and younger than her parents).
Residence	Yes, lived at home entire year.	Yes, time away at college is considered as time at home if Tara plans to live in her parent's home again at some point (it is a temporary absence).
Support	Yes, does not provide more than half of own support.	Yes, does not provide more than half of own support.

(continued on page 4-14)

[16]§152(c)(3)(A).
[17]§152(f)(2).
[18]§151(c)(3)(B).
[19]Reg. §1.152-1(b).
[20]§152(f)(5) and §152(f)(1). This provision requires that the student be a son, daughter, stepson, stepdaughter, or an eligible foster child of the taxpayer.

Because they both meet all the requirements, Braxton and Tara are qualifying children to the Halls. So, the Halls may claim one dependency exemption for Braxton and one for Tara.

What if: Suppose Tara provided more than half of her own support, would she be considered a qualifying child of her parents?

Answer: No. She would fail the support test.

What if: Assume the original facts except that Tara was age 25. Would Tara be considered a qualifying child of her parents?

Answer: No. She would fail the age test. Note, however, that Tara could still qualify as her parents' dependent as a qualifying relative (see Example 4-9 below).

What if: Assume the original facts except that Braxton was Anita's stepbrother's son. Would Braxton be considered a qualifying child of Rodney and Anita?

Answer: Yes. Braxton meets the relationship test because he is the descendant of Anita's stepbrother (sibling).

Tiebreaking rules. The requirements for determining who is a qualifying child leave open the possibility that one person could be a qualifying child to more than one taxpayer. In these circumstances, the taxpayer who has priority for claiming the dependency exemption is based on the following tiebreaking rules:

1. If the person is a qualifying child of a parent, the parent is entitled to the dependency exemption for the child. This situation could arise, for example, when a child lives with her mother *and* her grandparents. In this case, the mother has priority for claiming the dependency exemption over the grandparents.
2. If the individual is a qualifying child to both parents, the parent with whom the child has resided for the longest period of time during the year has priority for claiming the dependency exemption. This situation may arise in a year when the child lives with both parents for more than half of the year, but the parents divorce in the latter part of the year. Note, however, that the dependency exemption for a child of divorced parents can be claimed by the noncustodial parent if the custodial parent (the parent entitled to claim the exemption) releases the exemption to the noncustodial parent through a written declaration and the noncustodial parent attaches the declaration to his or her tax return.[21]
3. Finally, if the child resides with both parents for the same amount of time during the year or the qualifying child resides with taxpayers who are not the parents, the taxpayer with the *highest AGI* has priority for claiming the dependency exemption for the child.[22]

Example 4-8

In the previous example, we determined that Braxton (Rodney and Anita's son) is Rodney and Anita's qualifying child. Braxton's Uncle Shawn (Rodney's brother) lived in the Halls' home (the same home Braxton lived in) for more than 11 months during the year. Does Braxton meet the requirements to be considered Shawn's qualifying child?

[21]See §152(e). The custodial parent releases the exemption to the noncustodial parent with a signature on Form 8332.

[22]However, if the parents may claim the child as a qualifying child but no parent does so, another taxpayer may claim the individual as a qualifying child but only if the other individual's AGI is higher than the AGI of any parent of the child [§152(c)(4)(C)].

Answer: Yes, see analysis of factors below.

Test	Braxton
Relationship	Yes, son of Shawn's brother.
Age	Yes, under age 19 at end of year (and younger than Shawn).
Residence	Yes, lived in same residence as Shawn for more than half the year.
Support	Yes, does not provide more than half of own support.

Thus, Braxton is considered to be Rodney and Anita's qualifying child *and* he is considered to be Shawn's qualifying child. Under the tiebreaker rules, who is allowed to claim Braxton as a dependent for the year?

Answer: Rodney and Anita. Under the first tiebreaking rule, Rodney and Anita are allowed to claim the dependency exemption for Braxton because they are Braxton's parents.

What if: Suppose that Shawn is Rodney's cousin. Would Braxton be Shawn's qualifying child?

Answer: No, Braxton does not meet the relationship test for Shawn. Braxton is not the descendent of Shawn's sibling.

Qualifying Relative A qualifying relative is a person who is *not* a qualifying child *and* satisfies (1) a relationship test, (2) a support test, and (3) a gross income test.

Relationship test. As you might expect, the relationship test for a qualifying relative is more inclusive than the relationship test for a qualifying child. In fact, as described below, a qualifying relative may include a person who is *unrelated* (through a qualifying family relationship) to the taxpayer. A person is "related" to the taxpayer under the qualifying relative relationship test if the person is

- A descendant or ancestor of the taxpayer. For this purpose, a child includes a taxpayer's adopted child, stepchild, and eligible foster child; and a parent includes a stepmother and stepfather.
- A sibling of the taxpayer, including a stepbrother or a stepsister.
- A son or daughter of the brother or sister of the taxpayer (cousins do not qualify).
- A sibling of the taxpayer's mother or father.
- An in-law (mother-in-law, father-in-law, sister-in-law, brother-in-law, son-in-law, or daughter-in-law) of the taxpayer.
- Any person who has the same principal place of abode as the taxpayer for the *entire* year (*even if not related through a qualifying family relationship*).[23] This test is commonly referred to as the "member of the household" test for qualifying relative.

Support test. The support test generally requires that the taxpayer pay more than half the qualifying relative's living expenses (note that this is a different support test than the support test for a qualifying child). As we discussed above, living expenses include rent, food, medicine, and clothes, among other things. Just as with the qualifying child support test, scholarships of children of a taxpayer who are full-time students are excluded from the support test.[24] Under a multiple support agreement, taxpayers

[23] A person is considered to live with the taxpayer for the entire year if he or she was either born during the year or died during the year and resided with the taxpayer for the remaining part of the year.

[24] §152(f)(5) and §152(f)(1). Just as with a qualifying child, this provision requires that the student be a son, daughter, stepson, stepdaughter, or an eligible foster child of the taxpayer.

who don't pay over half of an individual's support may still be allowed to claim the individual as a dependent under the qualifying relative rules if the following apply:[25]

1. No one taxpayer paid over one-half of the individual's support.
2. The taxpayer and at least one other person provided more than half the support of the individual, and the taxpayer and the other person(s) would have been allowed to claim the individual as a dependent except for the fact that they did not provide over half of the support of the individual.
3. The taxpayer contributed *over* 10 percent of the individual's support for the year.
4. Each other person who provided *over* 10 percent of the individual's support (see requirement (2) above) provides a signed statement to the taxpayer agreeing not to claim the individual as a dependent. The taxpayer includes the names, addresses, and Social Security numbers of each other person on a Form 2120, which the taxpayer attaches to her Form 1040.

Multiple support agreements are commonly used in situations where siblings support elderly parents.

Gross income test. The gross income test requires that a qualifying relative's gross income for the year be *less* than the personal exemption amount. As we noted above, the personal exemption amount for 2015 is $4,000.

Example 4-9

What if: Suppose Tara is age 25, is a full-time student, and does not live with her parents. Tara earned $3,000 in a summer job, and her parents provided more than half her support. Does Tara qualify as her parents' dependent?

Answer: Yes, as their qualifying relative. She is too old to be their qualifying child.

Test	Explanation
Relationship	Yes, Rodney and Anita's daughter.
Support	Yes, the Halls provide more than half of Tara's support.
Gross income	Yes, Tara's gross income for the year is less than the exemption amount.

Tara's parents may claim a dependency exemption for Tara. Tara is not allowed to claim a personal exemption for herself. Note that if Tara's gross income exceeded the exemption amount, she would not qualify as her parents' dependent, and she would claim a personal exemption for herself.

Example 4-10

In determining their dependency exemptions for the year, Rodney and Anita evaluated whether Shawn is their *qualifying relative.* Assuming Shawn's gross income for the year is $42,000, the Halls provided food and lodging for Shawn valued at $8,000, and Shawn paid for his other living expenses valued at $14,000, is Shawn a qualifying relative of the Halls?

Answer: No, as analyzed below.

Test	Explanation
Relationship	Yes, Rodney's brother.
Support	No, the Halls provided $8,000 of support to Shawn, but Shawn provided $14,000 of his own support. Because the Halls provided less than half of Shawn's support, Shawn does not pass the support test.
Gross income	No, Shawn's gross income for the year is $42,000, which exceeds the exemption amount, so Shawn fails the gross income test.

[25]§152(d)(3).

Because Shawn fails the support test and the gross income test, he is not a qualifying relative of the Halls. Consequently, they cannot claim a dependency exemption for him. Thus, Shawn can claim a personal exemption for himself on his own tax return.

What if: Assume that Shawn received $5,000 of tax-exempt interest during the year and that this is his only source of income. Does he fail the gross income test?

Answer: No. Because tax-exempt interest is excluded from gross income, Shawn's gross income is $0, so he passes the gross income test.

What if: Assume the original facts in the example except that Shawn paid for his $14,000 of living expenses with interest he had received from tax-exempt bonds. Would Shawn pass the support test?

Answer: No. The Halls would not have provided more than half of Shawn's support. The fact that Shawn received the money he spent on his support from tax-exempt income does not matter. All that matters is that he provided more than half of his own support.

What if: Assume that Anita's 92-year-old grandfather Juan lives in an apartment by himself near the Halls' residence. His gross income for the year is $3,000. Assuming the Halls provide more than half of Juan's living expenses for the year, would Juan be a qualifying relative of the Halls?

Answer: Yes, as analyzed below.

Test	Explanation
Relationship	Yes, Anita's grandfather.
Support	Yes, as assumed in the facts, the Halls provide more than half of Juan's support.
Gross income	Yes, Juan's gross income for the year is $3,000, which is below the exemption amount, so Juan passes the gross income test.

What if: Assume that Anita's 92-year-old grandfather Juan lives in an apartment by himself and reports gross income for the year of $3,000. Anita provided 40 percent of Juan's support, Juan provided 25 percent of his own support, Anita's brother Carlos provides 30 percent of the support, and Anita's sister Kamella provided 5 percent of Juan's support. Who is eligible to claim Juan as a dependent under a multiple support agreement?

Answer: Anita and Carlos. Anita and Carlos are eligible because (1) no one taxpayer provided more than half of Juan's support, (2) Anita and Carlos together provided more than half of Juan's support and Juan would have been both Anita's and Carlos's qualifying relative except for the fact that neither provided over half of Juan's support, and (3) Anita and Carlos each provided over 10 percent of Juan's support (Kamella provided only 5 percent of Juan's support so she is not eligible). Anita and Carlos would need to agree on who would claim the dependency exemption for Juan. Assuming they agree that Anita would claim the exemption, she would need to receive a signed statement from Carlos agreeing not to claim the exemption and she would need to attach a Form 2120 to her (and Rodney's) tax return providing Carlos's name, address, and Social Security number.

What if: Assume Juan was a friend of the family but was not related to either Rodney or Anita, that his gross income is $3,000, and that the Halls provided over half of his support. Is Juan a qualifying relative of the Halls?

Answer: No, as analyzed below.

Test	Explanation
Relationship	No, not related to Halls and his principal place of abode was not in the Halls' household for the *entire* year. If the Halls' home was his principal place of abode for the entire year, he would have met the relationship test even though he's not actually related to anyone in the Hall family.
Support	Yes, as assumed in the facts, the Halls provide more than half of Juan's support.
Gross income	Yes, Juan's gross income for the year is $3,000, which is below the exemption amount, so Juan passes the gross income test.

The Halls would not be able to claim an exemption for Juan as a qualifying relative because he fails the relationship test under this set of facts.

The rules for determining who qualifies as a dependent as a qualifying child and who qualifies as a dependent as a qualifying relative overlap to some extent. The primary differences between the two are

1. The relationship requirement is more broadly defined for qualifying relatives than qualifying children.
2. Qualifying children are subject to age restrictions while qualifying relatives are not.
3. Qualifying relatives are subject to a gross income restriction while qualifying children are not.
4. Taxpayers need not provide more than half a qualifying child's support (though the child cannot provide more than half of her own support), but they must provide more than half the support of a qualifying relative.
5. Qualifying children are subject to a residence test (they must have the same primary residence as the taxpayer for more than half the year) while qualifying relatives are not. Exhibit 4-8 summarizes the dependency requirements.

EXHIBIT 4-8 Summary of Dependency Requirements

Test	Qualifying Child	Qualifying Relative
Relationship	Taxpayer's child, stepchild, foster child, sibling, half-brother or sister, stepbrother or sister, or a descendant of any of these relatives.	Taxpayer's descendant or ancestor, sibling, stepmother, stepfather, stepbrother or stepsister, son or daughter of taxpayer's sibling, sibling of the taxpayer's mother or father, in-laws, and anyone else who has the same principal place of abode as the taxpayer for the entire year (even if not otherwise related).
Age	Younger than the taxpayer claiming the individual as a qualifying child and under age 19 or a full-time student under age 24. Also anyone totally and permanently disabled.	Not applicable.
Residence	Lives with taxpayer for more than half of the year (includes temporary absences for things such as illness and education).	Not applicable.
Support	The qualifying child must not provide more than half of his or her own support.	Taxpayer must have provided more than half of the support for the qualifying relative.
Gross income	Not applicable.	Gross income less than exemption amount ($4,000 in 2015).
Other	Not applicable.	Not a qualifying child.

Appendix A provides a flowchart for determining whether an individual qualifies as the taxpayer's dependent.

ETHICS

Blake is 21 years of age at the end of the year. During the year, Blake was a full-time college student. He also worked part-time and earned $8,000, which he used to pay all of his $6,000 of living expenses. Blake's parents, Troy and Camille, claimed Blake as a dependent on their joint tax return. After filing the joint tax return, Troy told Blake they owed him $3,001 for his annual living expenses. What do you think of Troy and Camille's strategy to claim a dependency exemption for Blake?

FILING STATUS

LO 4-3

Each year taxpayers determine their **filing status** according to their marital status at year-end and whether they have any dependents. A taxpayer's filing status is important because, as we discussed above, it determines

- The applicable tax rate schedule for determining the taxpayer's tax liability.
- The taxpayer's standard deduction amount.
- The AGI threshold for reductions in certain tax benefits such as itemized deductions and certain tax credits, among others.

Each year, all taxpayers filing tax returns file under one of the following five filing statuses:

1. Married filing jointly
2. Married filing separately
3. Qualifying widow or widower (surviving spouse)
4. Single
5. Head of household

Married Filing Jointly and Married Filing Separately

Married couples may file tax returns jointly **(married filing jointly)** or separately **(married filing separately)**. To be married for filing status purposes, taxpayers must be married on the last day of the year. When one spouse dies during the year, the surviving spouse is considered to be *married* to the spouse who died at the end of the year unless the surviving spouse remarries during the year. Married couples filing joint returns combine their income and deductions and agree to share joint and several liability for the resulting tax. That is, they are both ultimately responsible to see that the tax is paid.

When married couples file separately, each spouse reports the income he or she received during the year and the deductions he or she is claiming on a tax return separate from that of the other spouse.[26] So that married taxpayers can't file separately to gain more combined tax benefits than they are entitled to if they filed jointly, tax-related items for married filing separate (MFS) taxpayers—such as tax rate schedules and standard deduction amounts, among others—are generally one-half what they are for married filing joint (MFJ) taxpayers. Also, if one spouse deducts itemized deductions, the other spouse is required to deduct itemized deductions even if his or her standard deduction amount is more than the total itemized deductions. Thus, only in unusual circumstances does it make sense for *tax* purposes for married couples to file separately.

However, it may be wise for married couples to file separately for *nontax* reasons. For example, a spouse who does not want to be liable for the other spouse's income tax liability, or a spouse who is not in contact with the other spouse, may want to file separately (see abandoned spouse discussion below).

THE KEY FACTS

Filing Status for Married Taxpayers

- Married filing jointly
  - Taxpayers are legally married as of the last day of the year.
  - When one spouse dies during the year the surviving spouse is still considered to be married for tax purposes during the year of the spouse's death.
  - Both spouses are ultimately responsible for paying the joint tax.
- Married filing separately
  - Taxpayers are legally married as of the last day of the year.
  - Generally no tax advantage to filing separately (usually a disadvantage).
  - Each spouse is ultimately responsible for paying own tax.
  - Couples may choose to file separately (generally for nontax reasons).
- Qualifying widow or widower
  - When a taxpayer's spouse dies, the surviving spouse can file as qualifying widow or widower for two years after the year of the spouse's death if the surviving spouse remains unmarried and maintains a household for a dependent child.

Example 4-11

Rodney and Anita Hall are married at the end of the year. What is their filing status?

Answer: Married filing jointly, unless they choose to file separately.

What if: Assume that in 2015 the Halls file a joint return. In 2016, Rodney and Anita divorce and the IRS audits their 2015 tax return and determines that due to overstating their deductions, the Halls underpaid their taxes by $2,000. Who must pay the tax?

Answer: Both Rodney and Anita are responsible for paying. If the IRS can't locate Rodney, it can require Anita to pay the full $2,000 even though Anita earned $46,000 and Rodney earned $64,000.

(continued on page 4-20)

[26]As we discuss in the next chapter, under community property laws of certain states, one spouse may be treated as receiving income earned by the other spouse.

What if: Assume that in 2015 the Halls file separate tax returns. In 2016, Rodney and Anita divorce and the IRS audits the Halls' separate tax returns. It determines that by overstating deductions, Rodney understated his tax liability by $1,500 and Anita understated her tax liability by $500. Further, the IRS cannot locate Rodney. What is the maximum amount of taxes Anita is liable for?

Answer: $500. Because she filed a separate return, she is responsible for the tax liability associated with her separate tax return, and she is not responsible for the taxes associated with Rodney's tax return.

TAXES IN THE REAL WORLD Tax Status for Same-Sex Married Couples

In June of 2013, the Supreme Court struck down the federal "Defense of Marriage Act" (DOMA). Under DOMA, no federal agency, including the IRS, was allowed to recognize same-sex marriages. Now that the Supreme Court Justices have struck down DOMA, same-sex married couples that were married in a state that authorizes and recognizes same-sex marriages will be treated as married for federal income tax purposes. However, couples who have entered into a registered domestic partnership, civil union, or other similar formal relationship recognized under state law will not be recognized as married for federal income tax purposes. Whether same-sex couples are considered as married for federal income tax purposes is important for determining filing status and has implications for other areas of the tax law (estate and gift tax, for example).

Source: Rev. Rul. 2013-17.

Qualifying Widow or Widower (Surviving Spouse)

When a taxpayer's spouse dies during the year, the taxpayer is no longer legally married. However, to provide tax relief for widows and widowers *with dependents,* taxpayers who meet certain requirements qualify for the **qualifying widow or widower** (also referred to as surviving spouse) filing status for up to two years *after* the end of the year in which the other spouse died (recall that for tax purposes, they are still considered to be married for the year of the spouse's death). Taxpayers are eligible for qualifying widow or widower filing status if they (1) remain unmarried and (2) pay over half the cost of maintaining a household where a dependent child lived for the entire year (except for temporary absences).[27] The dependent child must be a child or stepchild (including an adopted child) for whom the taxpayer may claim an exemption (not a foster child). A qualifying widow or widower is not considered to be married for tax purposes. Consequently, a qualifying widow or widower is allowed to claim one personal exemption (recall that taxpayers who are married filing jointly are allowed to claim two personal exemptions).

Example 4-12

What if: Assume that last year Rodney passed away, and during the current year Anita did not remarry but maintained a household for Braxton and Tara, her dependent children. Under these circumstances, what would Anita's filing status be?

Answer: Qualifying widow. Last year, the year of Rodney's death, Anita qualified to file a joint return with Rodney. This year, Anita qualifies as a qualifying widow (also referred to as a surviving spouse) because she has not remarried and she maintains a household for the entire year for her dependent children. She will qualify as a surviving spouse next year (two years after Rodney's death) if she does not remarry and she continues to maintain a household for Braxton and/or Tara for the entire year. Anita will claim three exemptions. One personal exemption and two dependency exemptions (for Braxton and Tara).

[27]§2(a).

Single

Unmarried taxpayers who do not qualify for head of household status (discussed below) file as **single** taxpayers. As we discuss below, an unmarried taxpayer generally must be able to claim an exemption for a dependent in order to qualify for head of household status.

Example 4-13

Shawn Hall, Rodney's brother, was divorced in January and is unmarried at the end of the year. Shawn does not claim any dependency exemptions. What is his filing status?

Answer: Single. Because Shawn is unmarried at the end of the year, and he does not have any dependents, his filing status is single.

THE KEY FACTS

Filing Status for Unmarried Taxpayers

- Single
  - Unmarried taxpayers at year-end who do not qualify for head of household.
- Head of household
  - Unmarried taxpayers or taxpayers considered to be unmarried at year end.
  - Must pay more than half of the costs of maintaining a household in which a qualifying person lives for more than half of the tax year or must pay more than half of the costs for maintaining a separate household for a parent who qualifies as taxpayer's dependent.

Head of Household

In terms of tax rate schedules and standard deduction amounts, the **head of household** filing status is less favorable than the married filing jointly and qualifying widow or widower filing statuses. However, it is more favorable than married filing separately and single filing statuses (see tax rates and standard deduction amounts provided inside the back cover). To qualify for head of household filing status, a taxpayer must

- Be unmarried (or considered to be unmarried under the provisions discussed below) at the end of the year.
- Not be a qualifying widow or widower.
- Pay more than half the costs of keeping up a home for the year.
- Have a "qualifying person" live in the taxpayer's home for more than half the year (except for temporary absences such as military service, illness, or schooling). However, if the qualifying person is the taxpayer's *dependent* parent, the parent is not required to live with the taxpayer. A qualifying person may not

Example 4-14

What if: Assume Rodney and Anita divorced last year. During the current year, Braxton lives with Anita for the entire year and Anita pays all the costs of maintaining the household for herself and Braxton. Under these circumstances, what is Anita's filing status for the year?

Answer: Head of household. Anita is unmarried at the end of the year, she provides more than half the costs of maintaining her household, Braxton lives with her for more than half the year, and Braxton is her qualifying child.

What if: Assume Rodney and Anita divorced last year. During the current year, Braxton lives with Anita for the entire year, and Anita pays all the costs of maintaining the household for herself and Braxton. Assume that Anita released the dependency exemption to Rodney under the divorce decree. Under these circumstances, what is Anita's filing status for the year?

Answer: Head of household. Braxton is a qualifying person for Anita (the custodial parent) even though Anita is not claiming the dependency exemption for Braxton. Braxton is not a qualifying person for Rodney (the noncustodial parent).

What if: Assume that Rodney and Anita divorced last year, Braxton is Anita's cousin, and Braxton lived with Anita in her home from June 15 through December 31. What is Anita's filing status for the year?

(continued on page 4-22)

Answer: Single. Anita does not qualify for head of household filing status because Braxton is not Anita's qualifying child (fails relationship test) or qualifying relative (fails relationship test because he did not live in Anita's home for the entire year, and he does not have a qualifying family relationship with Anita because he is Anita's cousin).

What if: Assume that Rodney and Anita divorced last year, Braxton is Anita's cousin, and Braxton lived with Anita in her home for the entire year. What is Anita's filing status for the year?

Answer: Single. Even though Braxton is Anita's qualifying relative, Braxton meets the qualifying relative relationship test only because he lived with Anita for the entire year (not because he had a qualifying family relationship with Anita). Therefore, while Anita may claim a dependency exemption for Braxton, she does not qualify for the head of household filing status.

What if: Assume Shawn (Rodney's brother) lived with the Halls, but Shawn paid more than half the costs of maintaining a separate apartment that is the principal residence of his mother, Sharon, whose gross income is $1,500. Because Shawn provided more than half of Sharon's support during the year, and because Sharon's gross income was only $1,500, she qualifies as Shawn's dependent (as a qualifying relative). In these circumstances, what is Shawn's filing status?

Answer: Head of household. Shawn paid more than half the costs of maintaining a separate household where his mother resides, and his mother qualifies as his dependent.

If Sharon's gross income exceeded the exemption amount she would fail the dependency gross income test and would not qualify as Shawn's dependent. If she did not qualify as his dependent she would not be a qualifying person, and Shawn would not qualify for the head of household filing status. Also, if Sharon were Shawn's grandmother rather than his mother, she would not be a qualifying person (no matter the amount of her gross income) and Shawn would not qualify for head of household status—Sharon must be Shawn's parent for him to qualify as a head of household.

qualify more than one person for head of household filing status. Exhibit 4-9 describes who is a qualifying person for purposes of head of household filing status.[28]

Married Individuals Treated as Unmarried (Abandoned Spouse) In certain situations a couple may be legally married at the end of the year, but living apart. Although the couple could technically file a joint tax return, this is often not desirable from a nontax perspective, because each spouse would be assuming responsibility for paying tax on income earned by either spouse whether it was reported or not. However, because both spouses are married at the end of the year, their only other option is to file under the tax-unfavorable married filing separately filing status.

To provide tax relief in these situations, the tax laws treat a married taxpayer *as though he or she were unmarried* at the end of the year if the taxpayer meets the following requirements:

- The taxpayer is married at the end of the year (or is not *legally* separated from the other spouse).
- The taxpayer does not file a joint tax return with the other spouse.
- The taxpayer pays *more than half* the costs of maintaining his or her home for the entire year, and this home is the principal residence for a child (who qualifies as the taxpayer's dependent[29]) for *more than half* the year (the child must be a child of the taxpayer, including adopted child, stepchild, or eligible foster child[30]).

[28]§2(b).

[29]A taxpayer meets this test if the taxpayer (custodial parent) cannot claim an exemption for the child only because he or she released the exemption to the noncustodial parent under a divorce agreement.

[30]§152(f).

EXHIBIT 4-9 Who Is a Qualifying Person for Determining Head of Household Filing Status? (Adapted from Table 4 in IRS Publication 501)

IF the person is the taxpayer's . . .	And . . .	THEN the person is . . .
qualifying child	the person is single.	a qualifying person, whether or not the taxpayer can claim an exemption for the person.*
	the person is married and the taxpayer may claim a dependency exemption for the person.	a qualifying person.*
	the person is married and the taxpayer may not claim a dependency exemption for the person.	not a qualifying person.
qualifying relative who is the taxpayer's mother or father	the taxpayer may claim a dependency exemption for the taxpayer's father or mother.	a qualifying person even if the taxpayer's mother or father did not live with the taxpayer. However, the taxpayer must have paid more than half the costs to maintain the household of the mother or father.
	the taxpayer may not claim a dependency exemption for the mother or father.	not a qualifying person.
qualifying relative other than the taxpayer's mother or father	the person did not live with the taxpayer for more than half the year.	not a qualifying person.
	the taxpayer can claim a dependency exemption for the person, the person lived with the taxpayer for more than half the year and the person is related to the taxpayer through a qualifying family relationship.	a qualifying person.
	the person is the taxpayer's qualifying relative only because the person lived with the taxpayer as a member of the taxpayer's household for the entire year (the person does not have a qualifying family relationship with the taxpayer).	not a qualifying person.
	the taxpayer cannot claim a dependency exemption for the person or the taxpayer can claim a dependency exemption only because of a multiple support agreement.	not a qualifying person.

*If a custodial parent releases the exemption deduction of a qualifying child to a noncustodial parent, the child is still considered to be a qualifying person of the custodial parent for purposes of determining head of household filing status for the custodial parent. However, the qualifying child is not a qualifying person of the noncustodial parent for head of household filing status purposes even though the noncustodial parent is entitled to claim the exemption for the child.

- The taxpayer lived apart from the other spouse for the last six months of the year (the other spouse did not live at all in the taxpayer's home during the last six months—temporary absences due to illness, education, business, vacation, or military service count as though the spouse still lived in the taxpayer's home).

If the taxpayer meets these requirements, he or she also meets the head of household filing status requirements and may file as head of household for the year. The primary objective of this tax rule is to provide tax relief to one spouse who has been abandoned by or separated from the other spouse and left to care for a dependent child. Thus, the married spouse who qualifies as unmarried under this provision is frequently referred to as an **abandoned spouse.** Nevertheless, the provision may still apply even when no spouse has been abandoned. For example, a couple may separate by mutual consent. Further, if both spouses meet the requirements, both spouses may qualify as being unmarried in the same year and thus both may qualify for head of household filing status.

Example 4-15

What if: Assume that last year, Rodney and Anita informally separated (they did not *legally* separate). Rodney moved out of the home and into his own apartment. Anita stayed in the Halls' home with Braxton. During the current year, Anita paid more than half the costs of maintaining the home for herself and Braxton. Even though Rodney and Anita were legally married at the end of the year, they filed separate tax returns. Under these circumstances, is Anita considered to be married or unmarried for tax purposes?

Answer: Unmarried. Anita meets the requirements for being treated as unmarried determined as follows (see requirements above):

- Anita is married to Rodney at the end of the year.
- Anita filed a tax return separate from Rodney's.
- Anita paid more than half the costs of maintaining her home, and her home was the principal residence for Braxton who is her dependent child.
- Rodney did not live in Anita's home for the last six months of the year (in fact, he didn't live there at any time during the entire year).

What if: Given that Anita meets the requirements for being treated as unmarried, what is her filing status?

Answer: Head of household. Since Anita meets the abandoned spouse requirements she also meets the head of household filing status requirements. Without the abandoned spouse rule, Anita would have been required to file as married filing separately. Rodney's filing status, however, is married filing separately. Note, however, that if Rodney's new residence became Tara's principal residence, Rodney would also be treated as unmarried and would be eligible for head of household filing status.

Appendix B includes a flowchart for determining a taxpayer's filing status.

SUMMARY OF INCOME TAX FORMULA

Tara crunched some numbers and put together a summary of her parents' taxable income calculation. She determined that her parents will receive a $312.50 tax refund when they file their tax return. Tara's summary is provided in Exhibit 4-10, and Exhibit 4-11 presents pages 1 and 2 of the Halls' Form 1040.

CONCLUSION

This chapter presents an overview of the individual income tax formula and provides rules for determining a taxpayer's filing status and who qualifies as a taxpayer's dependents. In Chapter 5, we turn our attention to determining gross income. In Chapter 6, we describe deductions available to taxpayers when computing their taxable income. In Chapter 7, we conclude our review of the individual income tax formula by determining how to compute a taxpayer's tax liability and her taxes due or tax refund.

EXHIBIT 4-10 Taxable Income and Tax Calculation Summary for Rodney and Anita Hall

Description	Amount	Explanation
(1) Gross income	110,600	Example 4-1.
(2) For AGI deductions	(5,000)	Example 4-2, line (2).
(3) Adjusted gross income	$105,600	(1) + (2).
(4) Itemized deductions	(14,000)	Example 4-3, line (2).
(5) Personal and dependency exemptions	(16,000)	Example 4-3, line (4).
(6) Taxable income	$ 75,600	(3) + (4) + (5).
(7) Income tax liability	$ 10,487.50	Example 4-4.
(8) Other taxes	0	
(9) Total tax	$ 10,487.50	(7) + (8).
(10) Credits	(1,000)	Example 4-5, line (2).
(11) Prepayments	(9,800)	Example 4-5, line (3).
Tax refund	$ 312.50	(9) + (10) + (11).

EXHIBIT 4-11

Form 1040 Department of the Treasury—Internal Revenue Service (99)
U.S. Individual Income Tax Return **2014** OMB No. 1545-0074 IRS Use Only—Do not write or staple in this space.

For the year Jan. 1–Dec. 31, 2014, or other tax year beginning , 2014, ending , 20 See separate instructions.

Your first name and initial	Last name	Your social security number
Rodney	Hall	224-56-1245
If a joint return, spouse's first name and initial	Last name	Spouse's social security number
Anita	Hall	324-43-3478
Home address (number and street). If you have a P.O. box, see instructions.	Apt. no.	▲ Make sure the SSN(s) above and on line 6c are correct.
665 Henry Avenue		
City, town or post office, state, and ZIP code. If you have a foreign address, also complete spaces below (see instructions).		**Presidential Election Campaign** Check here if you, or your spouse if filing jointly, want $3 to go to this fund. Checking a box below will not change your tax or refund. ☐ You ☐ Spouse
Brookings, SD 57007		
Foreign country name	Foreign province/state/county	Foreign postal code

Filing Status

Check only one box.

1 ☐ Single
2 ☑ Married filing jointly (even if only one had income)
3 ☐ Married filing separately. Enter spouse's SSN above and full name here. ▶
4 ☐ Head of household (with qualifying person). (See instructions.) If the qualifying person is a child but not your dependent, enter this child's name here. ▶
5 ☐ Qualifying widow(er) with dependent child

Exemptions

6a ☑ **Yourself.** If someone can claim you as a dependent, **do not** check box 6a
b ☑ **Spouse**

Boxes checked on 6a and 6b: 2

c **Dependents:**

(1) First name Last name	(2) Dependent's social security number	(3) Dependent's relationship to you	(4) ✓ if child under age 17 qualifying for child tax credit (see instructions)
Tara Hall	242-68-9945	Daughter	☐
Braxton Hall	242-23-7845	Son	☑
			☐
			☐

If more than four dependents, see instructions and check here ▶ ☐

No. of children on 6c who:
• lived with you: 2
• did not live with you due to divorce or separation (see instructions):
Dependents on 6c not entered above:

d Total number of exemptions claimed — Add numbers on lines above ▶ 4

Income

Attach Form(s) W-2 here. Also attach Forms W-2G and 1099-R if tax was withheld.

If you did not get a W-2, see instructions.

7	Wages, salaries, tips, etc. Attach Form(s) W-2	7	110,000
8a	**Taxable** interest. Attach Schedule B if required	8a	600
b	**Tax-exempt** interest. **Do not** include on line 8a — 8b: 300		
9a	Ordinary dividends. Attach Schedule B if required	9a	
b	Qualified dividends — 9b		
10	Taxable refunds, credits, or offsets of state and local income taxes	10	
11	Alimony received	11	
12	Business income or (loss). Attach Schedule C or C-EZ	12	
13	Capital gain or (loss). Attach Schedule D if required. If not required, check here ▶ ☐	13	
14	Other gains or (losses). Attach Form 4797	14	
15a	IRA distributions — 15a; b Taxable amount	15b	
16a	Pensions and annuities — 16a; b Taxable amount	16b	
17	Rental real estate, royalties, partnerships, S corporations, trusts, etc. Attach Schedule E	17	
18	Farm income or (loss). Attach Schedule F	18	
19	Unemployment compensation	19	
20a	Social security benefits — 20a; b Taxable amount	20b	
21	Other income. List type and amount	21	
22	Combine the amounts in the far right column for lines 7 through 21. This is your **total income** ▶	22	110,600

Adjusted Gross Income

23	Educator expenses	23			
24	Certain business expenses of reservists, performing artists, and fee-basis government officials. Attach Form 2106 or 2106-EZ	24			
25	Health savings account deduction. Attach Form 8889	25			
26	Moving expenses. Attach Form 3903	26	5,000		
27	Deductible part of self-employment tax. Attach Schedule SE	27			
28	Self-employed SEP, SIMPLE, and qualified plans	28			
29	Self-employed health insurance deduction	29			
30	Penalty on early withdrawal of savings	30			
31a	Alimony paid b Recipient's SSN ▶	31a			
32	IRA deduction	32			
33	Student loan interest deduction	33			
34	Tuition and fees. Attach Form 8917	34			
35	Domestic production activities deduction. Attach Form 8903	35			
36	Add lines 23 through 35			36	5,000
37	Subtract line 36 from line 22. This is your **adjusted gross income** ▶			37	105,600

For Disclosure, Privacy Act, and Paperwork Reduction Act Notice, see separate instructions. Cat. No. 11320B Form **1040** (2014)

(continued)

EXHIBIT 4-11 *(continued)*

Form 1040 (2014) Page **2**

	38	Amount from line 37 (adjusted gross income)			38	105,600
Tax and Credits	39a	Check if: ☐ **You** were born before January 2, 1950, ☐ Blind. ☐ **Spouse** was born before January 2, 1950, ☐ Blind. } **Total boxes checked ▶ 39a** ☐				
	b	If your spouse itemizes on a separate return or you were a dual-status alien, check here ▶ 39b☐				
	40	**Itemized deductions** (from Schedule A) **or** your **standard deduction** (see left margin)			40	14,000
	41	Subtract line 40 from line 38			41	91,600
	42	**Exemptions.** If line 38 is $152,525 or less, multiply $3,950 by the number on line 6d. Otherwise, see instructions			42	16,000
	43	**Taxable income.** Subtract line 42 from line 41. If line 42 is more than line 41, enter -0-			43	75,600
	44	**Tax** (see instructions). Check if any from: **a** ☐ Form(s) 8814 **b** ☐ Form 4972 **c** ☐			44	10,488
	45	**Alternative minimum tax** (see instructions). Attach Form 6251			45	
	46	Excess advance premium tax credit repayment. Attach Form 8962			46	
	47	Add lines 44, 45, and 46 ▶			47	10,488
	48	Foreign tax credit. Attach Form 1116 if required	48			
	49	Credit for child and dependent care expenses. Attach Form 2441	49			
	50	Education credits from Form 8863, line 19	50			
	51	Retirement savings contributions credit. Attach Form 8880	51			
	52	Child tax credit. Attach Schedule 8812, if required	52	1,000		
	53	Residential energy credits. Attach Form 5695	53			
	54	Other credits from Form: **a** ☐ 3800 **b** ☐ 8801 **c** ☐	54			
	55	Add lines 48 through 54. These are your **total credits**			55	1,000
	56	Subtract line 55 from line 47. If line 55 is more than line 47, enter -0- ▶			56	9,488
Other Taxes	57	Self-employment tax. Attach Schedule SE			57	
	58	Unreported social security and Medicare tax from Form: **a** ☐ 4137 **b** ☐ 8919			58	
	59	Additional tax on IRAs, other qualified retirement plans, etc. Attach Form 5329 if required			59	
	60a	Household employment taxes from Schedule H			60a	
	b	First-time homebuyer credit repayment. Attach Form 5405 if required			60b	
	61	Health care: individual responsibility (see instructions) Full-year coverage ☐			61	
	62	Taxes from: **a** ☐ Form 8959 **b** ☐ Form 8960 **c** ☐ Instructions; enter code(s)			62	
	63	Add lines 56 through 62. This is your **total tax** ▶			63	9,488
Payments	64	Federal income tax withheld from Forms W-2 and 1099	64	9,800		
	65	2014 estimated tax payments and amount applied from 2013 return	65			
	66a	**Earned income credit (EIC)**	66a			
	b	Nontaxable combat pay election 66b				
	67	Additional child tax credit. Attach Schedule 8812	67			
	68	American opportunity credit from Form 8863, line 8	68			
	69	Net premium tax credit. Attach Form 8962	69			
	70	Amount paid with request for extension to file	70			
	71	Excess social security and tier 1 RRTA tax withheld	71			
	72	Credit for federal tax on fuels. Attach Form 4136	72			
	73	Credits from Form: **a** ☐ 2439 **b** ☐ Reserved **c** ☐ Reserved **d** ☐	73			
	74	Add lines 64, 65, 66a, and 67 through 73. These are your **total payments** ▶			74	9,800
Refund	75	If line 74 is more than line 63, subtract line 63 from line 74. This is the amount you **overpaid**			75	312
	76a	Amount of line 75 you want **refunded to you.** If Form 8888 is attached, check here ▶☐			76a	312
	▶ b	Routing number ▶ c Type: ☐ Checking ☐ Savings				
	▶ d	Account number				
	77	Amount of line 75 you want **applied to your 2015 estimated tax** ▶	77			
Amount You Owe	78	**Amount you owe.** Subtract line 74 from line 63. For details on how to pay, see instructions ▶			78	
	79	Estimated tax penalty (see instructions)	79			

Standard Deduction for—
• People who check any box on line 39a or 39b **or** who can be claimed as a dependent, see instructions.
• All others:
Single or Married filing separately, $6,200
Married filing jointly or Qualifying widow(er), $12,400
Head of household, $9,100

If you have a qualifying child, attach Schedule EIC.

Direct deposit? See instructions.

Third Party Designee Do you want to allow another person to discuss this return with the IRS (see instructions)? ☐ **Yes.** Complete below. ☐ **No**

Designee's name ▶ Phone no. ▶ Personal identification number (PIN) ▶

Sign Here Under penalties of perjury, I declare that I have examined this return and accompanying schedules and statements, and to the best of my knowledge and belief, they are true, correct, and complete. Declaration of preparer (other than taxpayer) is based on all information of which preparer has any knowledge.

Joint return? See instructions. Keep a copy for your records.

Your signature	Date	Your occupation	Daytime phone number
Spouse's signature. If a joint return, **both** must sign.	Date	Spouse's occupation	If the IRS sent you an Identity Protection PIN, enter it here (see inst.)

Paid Preparer Use Only

Print/Type preparer's name	Preparer's signature	Date	Check ☐ if self-employed	PTIN
Firm's name ▶			Firm's EIN ▶	
Firm's address ▶			Phone no.	

www.irs.gov/form1040 Form **1040** (2014)

Appendix A Dependency Exemption Flowchart (Part I)

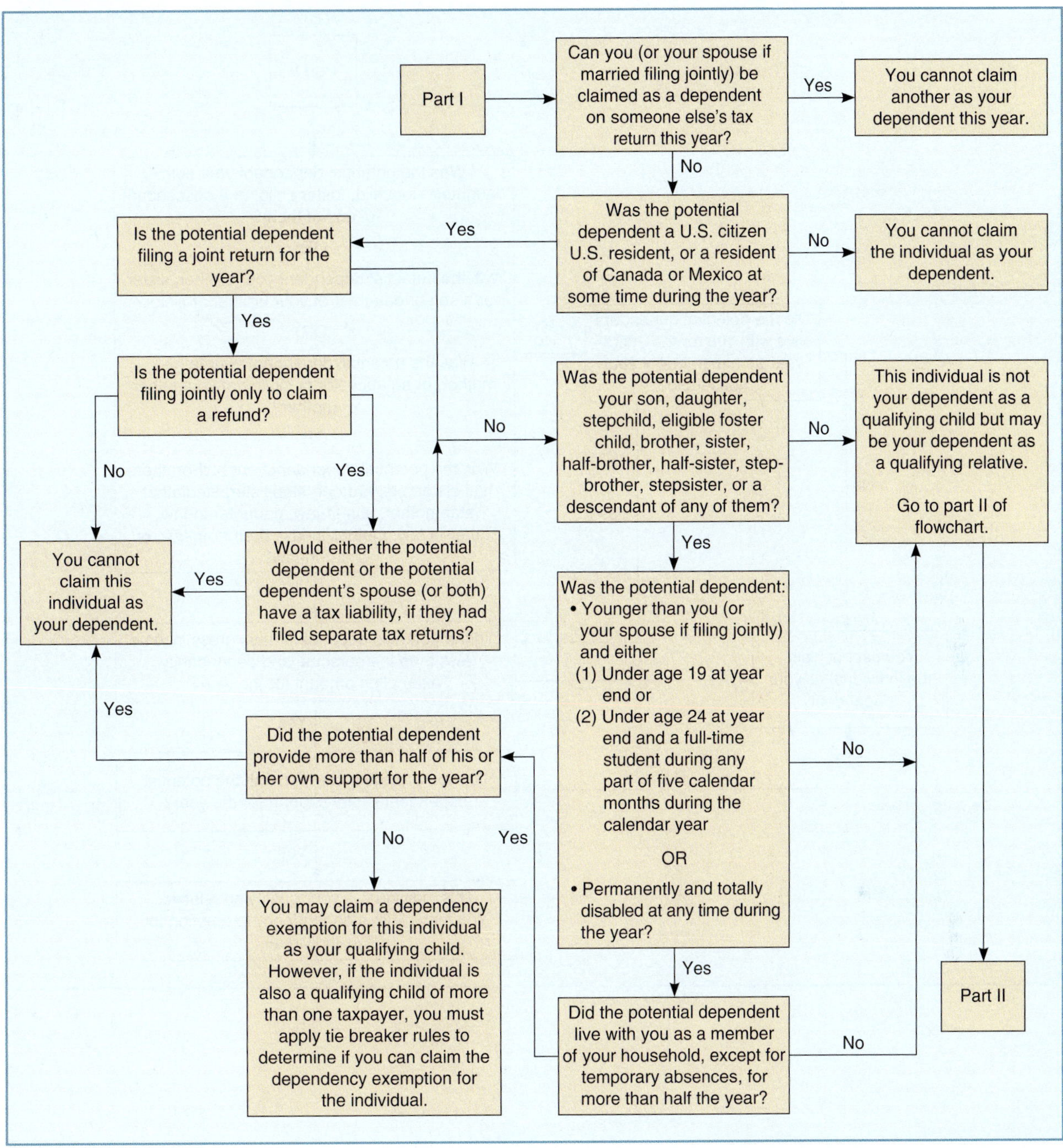

Appendix A (Part II)

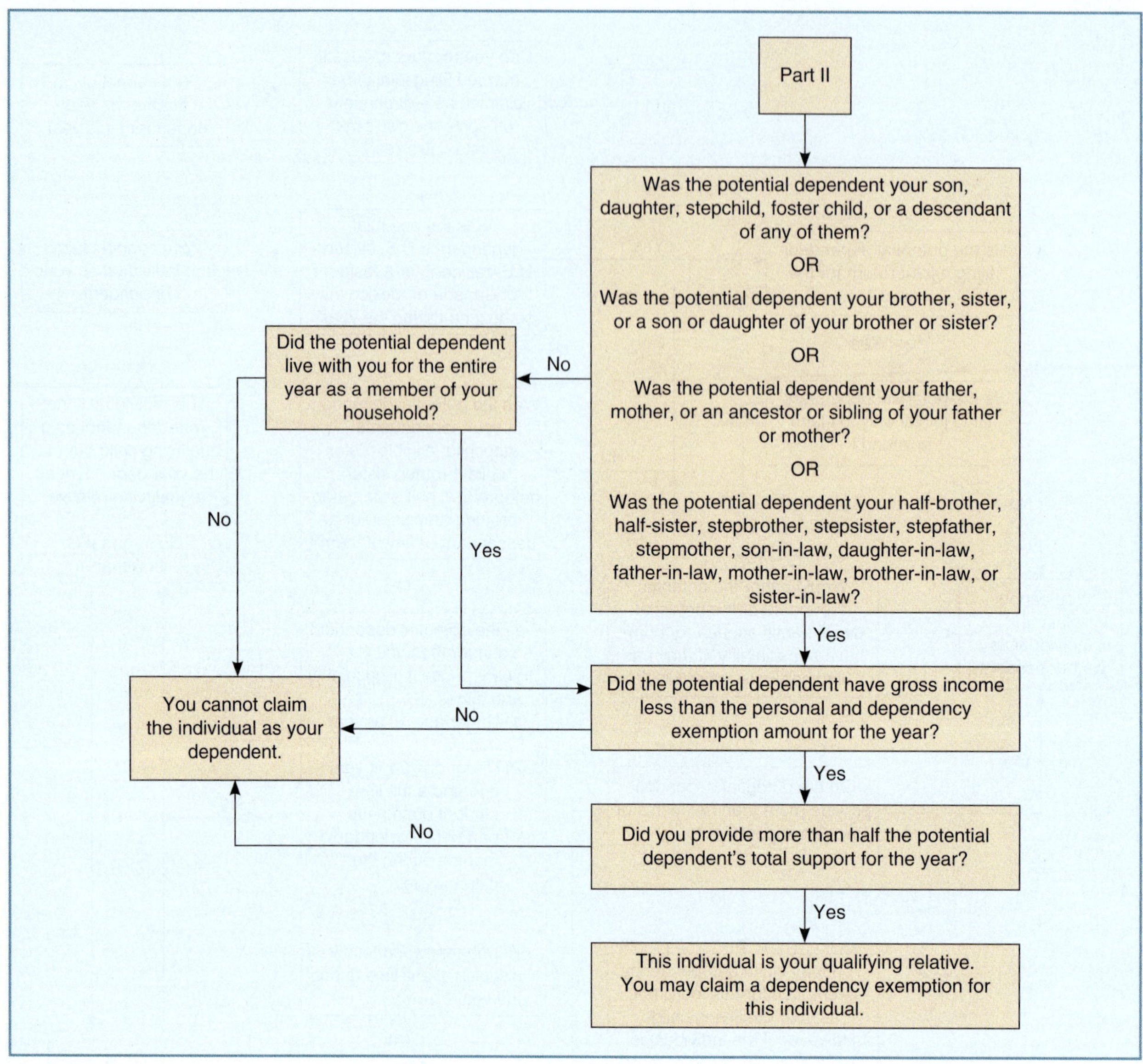

Appendix B Qualifying Person for Head of Household Filing Status

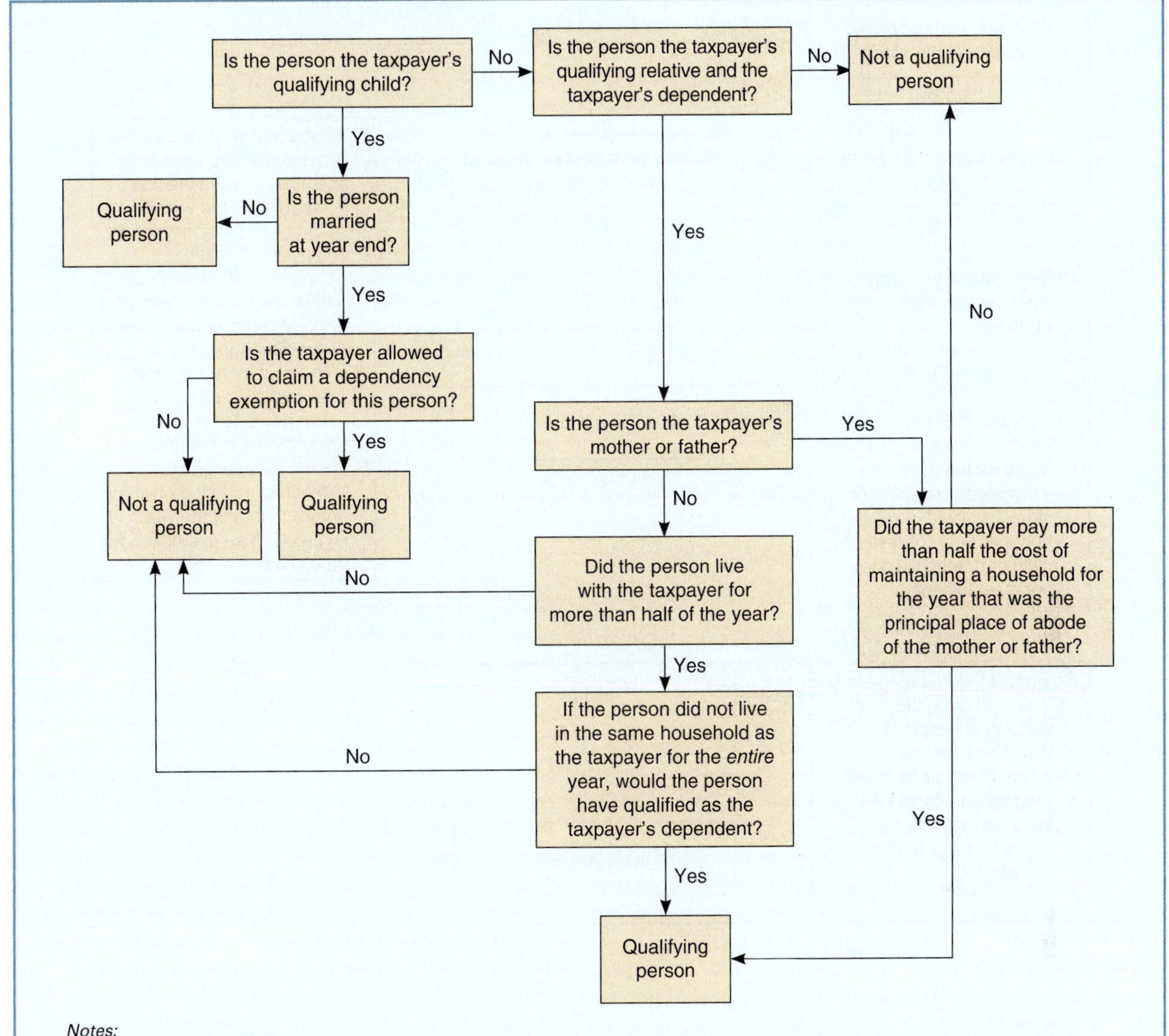

Notes:

- If a custodial parent releases the exemption for the person under a divorce decree the person is still a qualifying person to the custodial parent. The person is not a qualifying person to the noncustodial parent.
- If the taxpayer can claim an exemption for the person only because of a multiple support agreement, that person is not a qualifying person.
- One qualifying person may not qualify more than one person for head of household filing status.

Appendix C Determination of Filing Status Flowchart

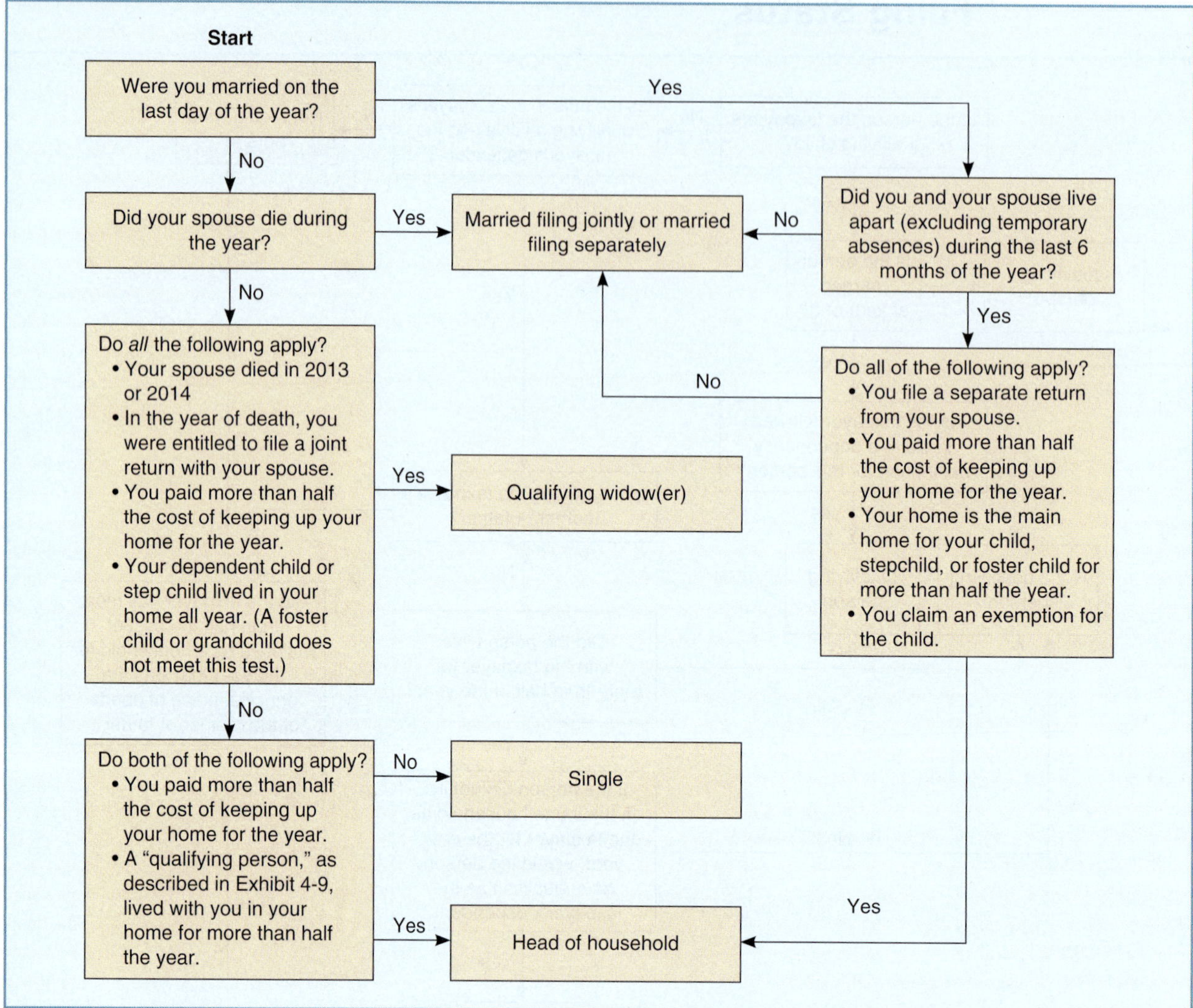

Summary

LO 4-1 Describe the formula for calculating an individual taxpayer's taxes payable or refund and generally explain each formula component.

- Generally, taxpayers are taxed on all income they realize during the year, no matter the source. However, the tax laws allow taxpayers to permanently exclude or to defer to a later year certain types of income they realize during the year.
- Income items that taxpayers are allowed to permanently exclude from income are called exclusions. Realized income items that taxpayers are not taxed on until a future period are called deferrals.
- Taxpayers include gross income on their tax returns.
- The rate at which items of income are taxed depends on the type or character of the income.

- Tax-exempt income is never taxed (excluded from gross income); tax deferred income is realized in the current year but included in gross income in a subsequent year; ordinary income is income taxed at the rates provided in the tax rate schedules; qualified dividends and long-term capital gains are taxed at a maximum rate of 15 or 20 percent, depending on the taxpayer's taxable income.
- Capital gains and losses arise from the sale or disposition of capital assets. In general a capital asset is any asset other than accounts receivable from the sale of goods or services, inventory, and assets used in a trade or business. If a capital asset is owned for more than a year before it is sold, the capital gain or loss is long-term. Otherwise, it is short-term.
- Taxpayers may deduct up to $3,000 of net capital loss for the year (excess of capital losses over capital gains for the year) against ordinary income. The remainder is suspended and carried over to the next year.
- Even though a personal use asset meets the capital asset definition, a taxpayer is not allowed to deduct a loss on the sale or disposition of a personal use asset.
- Deductions reduce a taxpayer's taxable income. The two types of deductions are *for* AGI deductions and *from* AGI deductions.
- Gross income minus *for* AGI deductions equals adjusted gross income (AGI). *For* AGI deductions are deductions "above the line," the last line on the front page of the individual tax Form 1040.
- *For* AGI deductions tend to relate to business activities and certain investment activities.
- AGI minus *from* AGI deductions equals taxable income.
- *From* AGI deductions include itemized deductions, the standard deduction, and exemptions. *From* AGI deductions are referred to as "deductions below the line."
- AGI is an important reference point in the individual tax formula because it is often used in other tax-related calculations, including determining limitations on *from* AGI deductions.
- Taxpayers generally deduct itemized deductions when the amount of the itemized deductions exceeds the standard deduction. The standard deduction varies by filing status and is indexed for inflation. Special rules may alter the standard deduction amount for certain taxpayers.
- Taxpayers are allowed to deduct personal exemptions for themselves (and their spouses if they file jointly) and dependency exemptions for those who qualify as their dependents.
- Taxpayers generally calculate the tax on their taxable income by referring to tax tables or tax rate schedules.
- Taxpayers may be required to pay the alternative minimum tax (AMT), self-employment tax, the 3.8% net investment income tax, and/or the .9% additional Medicare tax on earned income in addition to their regular income tax.
- Tax credits reduce taxpayers' tax liability dollar for dollar, while deductions decrease taxable income dollar for dollar.
- Taxpayers prepay taxes during the year through withholdings by employers, estimated tax payments, or prior year overpayments applied toward the current year tax liability.
- If tax prepayments exceed the taxpayer's total tax after credits, the taxpayer receives a refund. If tax prepayments are less than the total tax after credits, the taxpayer owes additional tax with his or her tax return.

Explain the requirements for determining a taxpayer's personal and dependency exemptions. **LO 4-2**

- For 2015, taxpayers are allowed to deduct $4,000 for each personal and dependency exemption they are entitled to claim.
- Individuals may claim a personal exemption for themselves (and for their spouses if they are married and file jointly). They may also claim dependency exemptions for each person who qualifies as their dependent.
- If an individual qualifies as a dependent of another taxpayer, the individual may not deduct a personal exemption for him- or herself on his or her individual return. Also, the individual may not claim any dependency exemptions.

- Taxpayers may claim dependency exemptions for those who (1) are citizens of the United States or residents of the United States, Canada, or Mexico; and (2) meet the joint tax return test, and are considered either a qualifying child or a qualifying relative of the taxpayer.
- A child must meet a relationship test, an age test, a residence test, and a support test to qualify as a qualifying child.
- A person who is not a qualifying child may be considered a qualifying relative by meeting a relationship test, a support test, and a gross income test.

LO 4-3 Determine a taxpayer's filing status.

- Taxpayers may file their tax returns as married filing jointly, married filing separately, qualifying widow or widower (also referred to as surviving spouse), single, or head of household.
- Married taxpayers may file a joint return or they may file separately. It is generally more advantageous for tax purposes to file jointly, if married. However, for nontax reasons, it may be advantageous to file separately.
- Each spouse is ultimately responsible for paying the tax on a joint return no matter who received the income.
- For two years after the year in which one spouse dies, the surviving spouse may file as a qualifying widow or widower as long as he or she (1) remains unmarried and (2) maintains a household for a dependent child (child, stepchild, or adopted child). However, the surviving spouse is not allowed to claim a dependency exemption for the deceased spouse beyond the year of the spouse's death. That is, a qualifying widow or widower (surviving spouse) may claim only one personal exemption.
- Unmarried taxpayers who do not qualify for head of household status file as single taxpayers.
- An unmarried taxpayer who is not a qualifying widow or widower may file as head of household if the person pays more than half the costs of maintaining a household that is, for *more* than half the taxable year, the principal place of abode for a qualifying person (if the qualifying person is a parent, the parent need not reside with the taxpayer). In general, for an individual to be a qualifying person, the taxpayer must be able to claim an exemption for that individual and the individual must be considered to be related to the taxpayer even if the individual does not live with the taxpayer for the entire year. That is, the taxpayer and the individual must be related through a qualifying family relationship. See Exhibit 4-9 for a flowchart for determining whether an individual is a qualifying person for determining head of household filing status.

KEY TERMS

abandoned spouse (4-23)
adjusted gross income (AGI) (4-2)
all-inclusive income concept (4-2)
alternative minimum tax (AMT) (4-10)
character of income (4-5)
deductions (4-7)
deductions above the line (4-7)
deductions below the line (4-8)
deferrals (4-5)
dependency exemptions (4-9)
dependent (4-12)
estimated tax payments (4-11)
exclusions (4-5)
exemptions (4-8)
filing status (4-19)
***for* AGI deductions (4-7)**
***from* AGI deductions (4-7)**
gross income (4-2)
head of household (4-21)
itemized deductions (4-8)
legislative grace (4-7)
married filing jointly (4-19)
married filing separately (4-19)
personal exemptions (4-9)
preferential tax rate (4-6)
preferentially taxed income (4-6)
qualifying child (4-12)
qualifying relative (4-12)
qualifying widow or widower (4-20)
realized income (4-2)
single (4-21)
self-employment taxes (4-10)
standard deduction (4-8)
taxable income (4-2)
tax credits (4-10)
tax rate schedule (4-10)
tax tables (4-10)
withholdings (4-11)

DISCUSSION QUESTIONS

1. How are realized income, gross income, and taxable income similar, and how are they different? LO 4-1
2. Are taxpayers required to include all realized income in gross income? Explain. LO 4-1
3. All else being equal, should taxpayers prefer to exclude income or to defer it? Why? LO 4-1
4. Why should a taxpayer be interested in the character of income received? LO 4-1
5. Is it easier to describe what a capital asset is or what it is not? Explain. LO 4-1
6. Are all capital gains (gains on the sale or disposition of capital assets) taxed at the same rate? Explain. LO 4-1
7. Are taxpayers allowed to deduct net capital losses (capital losses in excess of capital gains)? Explain. LO 4-1
8. Compare and contrast *for* and *from* AGI deductions. Why are *for* AGI deductions likely more valuable to taxpayers than *from* AGI deductions? LO 4-1
9. What is the difference between gross income and adjusted gross income, and what is the difference between adjusted gross income and taxable income? LO 4-1
10. How do taxpayers determine whether they should deduct their itemized deductions or utilize the standard deduction? LO 4-1
11. Why are some deductions called "above the line" deductions and others are called "below the line" deductions? What is the "line"? LO 4-1
12. What is the difference between a tax deduction and a tax credit? Is one more beneficial than the other? Explain. LO 4-1
13. What types of federal income-based taxes, other than the regular income tax, might taxpayers be required to pay? In general terms, what is the tax base for each of these other taxes on income? LO 4-1
14. Identify three ways taxpayers can pay their income taxes to the government. LO 4-1
15. If a person is considered to be a qualifying child or qualifying relative of a taxpayer, is the taxpayer automatically entitled to claim a dependency exemption for the person? LO 4-1
16. Emily and Tony are recently married college students. Can Emily qualify as her parents' dependent? Explain. LO 4-2
17. Compare and contrast the relationship test requirements for a qualifying child with the relationship requirements for a qualifying relative. LO 4-1
18. In general terms, what are the differences in the rules for determining who is a qualifying child and who qualifies as a dependent as a qualifying relative? Is it possible for someone to be a qualifying child and a qualifying relative of the same taxpayer? Why or why not? LO 4-2
19. How do two taxpayers determine who has priority to claim the dependency exemption for a qualifying child of both taxpayers when neither taxpayer is a parent of the child (assume the child does not qualify as a qualifying child of either parent)? How do parents determine who gets to deduct the dependency exemption for a qualifying child of both parents when the parents are divorced or file separate returns? LO 4-2
20. Isabella provides 30 percent of the support for her father Hastings who lives in an apartment by himself and has no gross income. Is it possible for Isabella to claim a dependency exemption for her father? Explain. LO 4-2
21. What requirements do an abandoned spouse and qualifying widow or widower have in common? LO 4-3

LO 4-3 22. True or False. For purposes of determining head of household filing status, the taxpayer's mother or father is considered to be a qualifying person of the taxpayer (even if the mother or father does not qualify as the taxpayer's dependent) as long as the taxpayer pays more than half the costs of maintaining the household of the mother or father. Explain.

LO 4-3 23. Is a qualifying relative always a qualifying person for purposes of determining head of household filing status?

LO 4-3 24. For tax purposes, why is the married filing jointly tax status generally preferable to the married filing separately filing status? Why might a married taxpayer prefer *not* to file a joint return with the taxpayer's spouse?

LO 4-3 25. What does it mean to say that a married couple filing a joint tax return has joint and several liability for the taxes associated with the return?

PROBLEMS

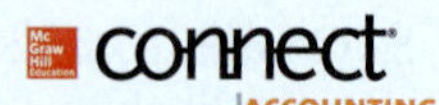

All applicable problems are available with McGraw-Hill's *Connect® Accounting*.

LO 4-1 26. Jeremy earned $100,000 in salary and $6,000 in interest income during the year. Jeremy has two qualifying dependent children who live with him. He qualifies to file as head of household and has $17,000 in itemized deductions. Neither of his dependents qualifies for the child tax credit.

a) Use the 2015 tax rate schedules to determine Jeremy's taxes due.

b) Assume that in addition to the original facts, Jeremy has a long-term capital gain of $4,000. What is Jeremy's tax liability including the tax on the capital gain?

c) Assume the original facts except that Jeremy had only $7,000 in itemized deductions. What is Jeremy's total income tax liability?

LO 4-1 27. David and Lilly Fernandez have determined their tax liability on their joint tax return to be $1,700. They have made prepayments of $1,500 and also have a child tax credit of $1,000. What is the amount of their tax refund or taxes due?

LO 4-1 planning 28. Rick, who is single, has been offered a position as a city landscape consultant. The position pays $125,000 in cash wages. Assume Rick files single and is entitled to one personal exemption. Rick deducts the standard deduction instead of itemized deductions.

a) What is the amount of Rick's after-tax compensation (ignore payroll taxes)?

b) Suppose Rick receives a competing job offer of $120,000 in cash compensation and nontaxable (excluded) benefits worth $4,000. What is the amount of Rick's after-tax compensation for the competing offer? Which job should he take if taxes were the only concern?

LO 4-1 planning 29. Through November, Tex has received gross income of $120,000. For December, Tex is considering whether to accept one more work engagement for the year. Engagement 1 will generate $7,000 of revenue at a cost of $4,000 which is deductible for AGI. In contrast, engagement 2 will generate $7,000 of revenue at a cost of $3,000, which is deductible as an itemized deduction. Tex files as a single taxpayer.

a) Calculate Tex's taxable income assuming he chooses engagement 1 and assuming he chooses engagement 2. Assume he has no itemized deductions other than those generated by engagement 2.

b) Calculate Tex's taxable income assuming he chooses engagement 1 and assuming he chooses engagement 2. Assume he has $4,500 of itemized deductions other than those generated by engagement 2.

c) Calculate Tex's taxable income assuming he chooses engagement 1 and assuming he chooses engagement 2. Assume he has $7,000 of itemized deductions other than those generated by engagement 2.

30. Matteo, who is single and has no dependents, was planning on spending the weekend repairing his car. On Friday, Matteo's employer called and offered him $500 in overtime pay if he would agree to work over the weekend. Matteo could get his car repaired over the weekend at Autofix for $400. If Matteo works over the weekend, he will have to pay the $400 to have his car repaired but he will earn $500. Assume Matteo pays tax at a flat 15 percent rate. LO 4-1 planning

a) Strictly considering tax factors, should Matteo work or repair his car if the $400 he must pay to have his car fixed is not deductible?

b) Strictly considering tax factors, should Matteo work or repair his car if the $400 he must pay to have his car fixed is deductible for AGI?

31. Rank the following three single taxpayers in order of the magnitude of taxable income (from lowest to highest) and explain your results. LO 4-1 LO 4-2

	Ahmed	Baker	Chin
Gross income	$80,000	$80,000	$80,000
Deductions *for* AGI	8,000	4,000	0
Itemized deductions	0	4,000	8,000

32. Aishwarya's husband passed away in 2014. She needs to determine whether Jasmine, her 17-year-old stepdaughter, who is single, qualifies as her dependent in 2015. Jasmine is a resident but not a citizen of the United States. She lived in Aishwarya's home from June 15 through December 31, 2015. Aishwarya provided more than half of Jasmine's support for 2015. LO 4-2

a) Is Aishwarya allowed to claim a dependency exemption for Jasmine for 2015?

b) Would Aishwarya be allowed to claim a dependency exemption for Jasmine for 2015 if Aishwarya provided more than half of Jasmine's support in 2015, Jasmine lived in Aishwarya's home from July 15 through December 31 of 2015, and Jasmine reported gross income of $5,000 in 2015?

c) Would Aishwarya be allowed to claim a dependency exemption for Jasmine for 2015 if Aishwarya provided more than half of Jasmine's support in 2015, Jasmine lived in Aishwarya's home from July 15 through December 31 of 2015, and Jasmine reported gross income of $2,500 in 2015?

33. The Samsons are trying to determine whether they can claim their 22-year-old adopted son, Jason, as a dependent. Jason is currently a full-time student at an out-of-state university. Jason lived in his parents' home for three months of the year and he was away at school for the rest of the year. He received $9,500 in scholarships this year for his outstanding academic performance and earned $4,800 of income working a part-time job during the year. The Samsons paid a total of $5,000 to support Jason while he was away at college. Jason used the scholarship, the earnings from the part-time job, and the money from the Samsons as his only sources of support. LO 4-2

a) Can the Samsons claim Jason as their dependent?

b) Assume the original facts except that Jason's grandparents, not the Samsons, provided him with the $5,000 worth of support. Can the Samsons (Jason's parents) claim Jason as their dependent? Why or why not?

c) Assume the original facts except substitute Jason's grandparents for his parents. Determine whether Jason's grandparents can claim Jason as a dependent.

d) Assume the original facts except that Jason earned $5,500 while working part-time and used this amount for his support. Can the Samsons claim Jason as their dependent? Why or why not?

LO 4-2

34. John and Tara Smith are married and have lived in the same home for over 20 years. John's uncle Tim, who is 64 years old, has lived with the Smiths since March of this year. Tim is searching for employment but has been unable to find any—his gross income for the year is $2,000. Tim used all $2,000 toward his own support. The Smiths provided the rest of Tim's support by providing him with lodging valued at $5,000 and food valued at $2,200.
    a) Are the Smiths able to claim a dependency exemption for Tim?
    b) Assume the original facts except that Tim earned $10,000 and used all the funds for his own support. Are the Smiths able to claim Tim as a dependent?
    c) Assume the original facts except that Tim is a friend of the family and not John's uncle.
    d) Assume the original facts except that Tim is a friend of the family and not John's uncle and Tim lived with the Smiths for the entire year.

LO 4-2

35. Francine's mother Donna and her father Darren separated and divorced in September of this year. Francine lived with both parents until the separation. Francine does *not* provide more than half of her own support. Francine is 15 years old at the end of the year.
    a) Is Francine a qualifying child to Donna?
    b) Is Francine a qualifying child to Darren?
    c) Assume Francine spends more time living with Darren than Donna after the separation. Who may claim Francine as a dependency exemption for tax purposes?
    d) Assume Francine spends an equal number of days with her mother and her father and that Donna has AGI of $52,000 and Darren has AGI of $50,000. Who may claim a dependency exemption for Francine?

LO 4-2

36. Jamel and Jennifer have been married 30 years and have filed a joint return every year of their marriage. Their three daughters, Jade, Lindsay, and Abbi, are ages 12, 17, and 22, respectively, and all live at home. None of the daughters provides more than half of her own support. Abbi is a full-time student at a local university and does not have any gross income.
    a) How many personal and dependency exemptions are Jamel and Jennifer allowed to claim?
    b) Assume the original facts except that Abbi is married. She and her husband live with Jamel and Jennifer while attending school and they file a joint return. Abbi and her husband reported a $1,000 tax liability on their tax return. If all parties are willing, can Jamel and Jennifer claim Abbi as a dependent on their tax return? Why or why not?
    c) Assume the same facts as part (b), except that Abbi and her husband report a $0 tax liability on their joint tax return. Also, if the couple had filed separately, Abbi would have not had a tax liability on her return but her husband would have had a $250 tax liability on his separate return. Can Jamel and Jennifer claim Abbi as a dependent on their tax return? Why or why not?
    d) Assume the original facts except that Abbi is married. Abbi files a separate tax return. Abbi's husband files a separate tax return and reports a $250 tax liability on the return. Can Jamel and Jennifer claim Abbi as a dependent?

LO 4-2 LO 4-3

37. Dean Kastner is 78 years old and lives by himself in an apartment in Chicago. Dean's gross income for the year is $2,500. Dean's support is provided as follows: Himself (5 percent), his daughters Camille (25 percent) and Rachel (30 percent), his son Zander (5 percent), his friend Frankie (15 percent), and his niece Sharon (20 percent).
    a) Absent a multiple support agreement, of the parties mentioned in the problem, who may claim a dependency exemption for Dean as a qualifying relative?

b) Under a multiple support agreement, who is eligible to claim a dependency exemption for Dean as a qualifying relative? Explain.

c) Assume that Camille is allowed to claim Dean as a dependent under a multiple support agreement. Camille is single, and Dean is her only dependent. What is Camille's filing status?

38. Mel and Cindy Gibson's 12-year-old daughter Rachel was abducted on her way home from school on March 15, 2015. Police reports indicated that a stranger had physically dragged Rachel into a waiting car and sped away. Everyone hoped that the kidnapper and Rachel would be located quickly. However, as of the end of the year, Rachel was still missing. The police were still pursuing several promising leads and had every reason to believe that Rachel was still alive. In 2016, Rachel was returned safely to her parents. LO 4-2 research

a) Are the Gibsons allowed to claim an exemption deduction for Rachel in 2015 even though she only lived in the Gibson's home for two-and-one-half months? Explain and cite your authority.

b) Assume the original facts except that Rachel is unrelated to the Gibsons but she has been living with them since January 2010. The Gibsons have claimed a dependency exemption for Rachel for the years 2010 through 2014. Are the Gibsons allowed to claim a dependency exemption for Rachel in 2015? Explain and cite your authority.

39. Bob Ryan filed his tax return and claimed a dependency exemption for his 16-year-old son Dylan. Both Bob and Dylan are citizens and residents of the United States. Dylan meets all the necessary requirements to be considered a qualifying child; however, when Bob filed the tax return he didn't know Dylan's Social Security number and, therefore, didn't include an identifying number for his son on the tax return. Instead, Bob submitted an affidavit with his tax return stating he had requested Dylan's Social Security number from Dylan's birth state. Is Bob allowed to claim a dependency exemption for Dylan without including Dylan's identifying number on the return? LO 4-2 research

40. Kimberly is divorced and the custodial parent of a 3-year-old girl named Bailey. Kimberly and Bailey live with Kimberly's parents, who pay all the costs of maintaining the household (such as mortgage, property taxes, and food). Kimberly pays for Bailey's clothing, entertainment, and health insurance costs. These costs comprised only a small part of the total costs of maintaining the household. Kimberly does not qualify as her parent's dependent. LO 4-2 LO 4-3

a) Determine the appropriate filing status for Kimberly.

b) What if Kimberly lived in her own home and provided all the costs of maintaining the household?

c) Assume Kimberly qualifies as her parents' dependent. How many personal and dependency exemptions may Kimberly claim on her tax return?

41. Lee is 30 years old and single. Lee paid all the costs of maintaining his household for the entire year. Determine Lee's filing status in each of the following alternative situations: LO 4-2 LO 4-3

a) Lee is Ashton's uncle. Ashton is 15 years old and has gross income of $5,000. Ashton lived in Lee's home from April 1 through the end of the year.

b) Lee is Ashton's uncle. Ashton is 20 years old, not a full-time student, and has gross income of $7,000. Ashton lived in Lee's home from April 1 through the end of the year.

c) Lee is Ashton's uncle. Ashton is 22 years old and was a full-time student from January through April. Ashton's gross income was $5,000. Ashton lived in Lee's home from April 1 through the end of the year.

d) Lee is Ashton's cousin. Ashton is 18 years old, has gross income of $3,000, and is not a full-time student. Ashton lived in Lee's home from April 1 through the end of the year.

e) Lee and Ashton are cousins. Ashton is 18 years old, has gross income of $3,000, and is not a full-time student. Ashton lived in Lee's home for the entire year.

LO 4-2 LO 4-3

42. Ray Albertson is 72 years old and lives by himself in an apartment in Salt Lake City. Ray's gross income for the year is $3,000. Ray's support is provided as follows: himself (11 percent), his daughters Diane (20 percent) and Karen (15 percent), his sons Mike (20 percent) and Kenneth (10 percent), his friend Milt (14 percent), and his cousin Henry (12 percent).

a) Absent a multiple support agreement, of the parties mentioned in the problem, who may claim a dependency exemption for Ray as a qualifying relative?

b) Under a multiple support agreement, who is eligible to claim a dependency exemption for Ray as a qualifying relative? Explain.

c) Assume that under a multiple support agreement, Diane claims a dependency exemption for Ray. Diane is single with no other dependents. What is her filing status?

LO 4-3

43. Juan and Bonita are married and have two dependent children living at home. This year, Juan is killed in an avalanche while skiing.

a) What is Bonita's filing status this year?

b) Assuming Bonita doesn't remarry and still has two dependent children living at home, what will her filing status be next year?

c) Assuming Bonita doesn't remarry and doesn't have any dependents next year, what will her filing status be next year?

LO 4-3

44. Gary and Lakesha were married on December 31 last year. They are now preparing their taxes for the April 15 deadline and are unsure of their filing status.

a) What filing status options do Gary and Lakesha have for last year?

b) Assume instead that Gary and Lakesha were married on January 1 of this year. What is their filing status for last year (neither has been married before and neither had any dependents last year)?

LO 4-3

45. Elroy, who is single, has taken over the care of his mother Irene in her old age. Elroy pays the bills relating to Irene's home. He also buys all her groceries and provides the rest of her support. Irene has no gross income.

a) What is Elroy's filing status?

b) Assume the original facts except that Elroy has taken over the care of his grandmother, Renae, instead of his mother. What is Elroy's filing status?

c) Assume the original facts except that Elroy's mother, Irene, lives with him and that she receives an annual $4,500 taxable distribution from her retirement account. Elroy still pays all the costs to maintain the household. What is his filing status?

LO 4-3

46. Kano and his wife, Hoshi, have been married for 10 years and have two children under the age of 12. The couple has been living apart for the last two years and both children live with Kano. Kano has provided all the means necessary to support himself and his children. Kano and Hoshi do not file a joint return.

a) What is Kano's filing status?

b) Assume the original facts except that Kano and Hoshi separated in May of the current year. What is Kano's filing status?

c) Assume the original facts except that Kano and Hoshi separated in November of this year. What is Kano's filing status?

d) Assume the original facts except that Kano's parents, not Kano, paid more than half of the cost of maintaining the home in which Kano and his children live. What is Kano's filing status?

47. Horatio and Kelly were divorced at the end of last year. Neither Horatio nor Kelly remarried during the current year and Horatio moved out of state. Determine the filing status of Horatio and Kelly for the current year in the following independent situations: LO 4-3
   a) Horatio and Kelly did not have any children and neither reported any dependents in the current year.
   b) Horatio and Kelly had one child, Amy, who turned 10 years of age in the current year. Amy lived with Kelly for all of the current year and Kelly provided all of her support.
   c) Assume the same facts as in part (b), but Kelly released the exemption for Amy to Horatio even though Amy did not reside with him at all during the current year.
   d) Assume the original facts except that during the current year Madison, a 17-year-old friend of the family, lived with Kelly (for the entire year) and was fully supported by Kelly.
   e) Assume the original facts except that during the current year Kelly's mother, Janet, lived with Kelly. For the current year, Kelly was able to claim a dependency exemption for her mother under a multiple support agreement.
48. In each of the following *independent* situations, determine the taxpayer's filing status and the number of personal and dependency exemptions the taxpayer is allowed to claim. LO 4-2 LO 4-3
   a) Frank is single and supports his 17-year-old brother, Bill. Bill earned $3,000 and did not live with Frank.
   b) Geneva and her spouse reside with their son, Steve, who is a 20-year-old undergraduate student at State University. Steve earned $13,100 at a part-time summer job, but he deposited this money in a savings account for graduate school. Geneva paid all of the $12,000 cost of supporting Steve.
   c) Hamish's spouse died last year and Hamish has not remarried. Hamish supports his father, Reggie, age 78, who lives in a nursing home and had interest income this year of $2,500.
   d) Irene is married but has not seen her spouse since February. She supports her spouse's 18-year-old child, Dolores, who lives with Irene. Dolores earned $4,500 this year.
   e) Assume the same facts as in part (d). Also, assume that Craig is Irene's husband. Craig supports his 12-year-old son Ethan, who lives with Craig. Ethan did not earn any income.
49. In each of the following *independent* cases, determine the taxpayer's filing status and the number of personal and dependency exemptions the taxpayer is allowed to claim. LO 4-2 LO 4-3
   a) Alexandra is a blind widow (her spouse died five years ago) who provides a home for her 18-year-old nephew, Newt. Newt's parents are dead and so Newt supports himself. Newt's gross income is $5,000.
   b) Bharati supports and maintains a home for her daughter, Daru, and son-in-law, Sam. Sam earned $15,000 and filed a joint return with Daru, who had no income.
   c) Charlie intended to file a joint return with his spouse, Sally. However, Sally died in December. Charlie has not remarried.
   d) Deshi cannot convince his spouse to consent to signing a joint return. The couple has not separated.
   e) Edith and her spouse support their 35-year-old son, Slim. Slim is a full-time college student who earned $5,500 over the summer in part-time work.
50. Jasper and Crewella Dahvill were married in year 0. They filed joint tax returns in years 1 and 2. In year 3, their relationship was strained and Jasper insisted LO 4-3

on filing a separate tax return. In year 4, the couple divorced. Both Jasper and Crewella filed single tax returns in year 4. In year 5, the IRS audited the couple's joint year 2 tax return and each spouse's separate year 3 tax returns. The IRS determined that the year 2 joint return and Crewella's separate year 3 tax return understated Crewella's self-employment income causing the joint return year 2 tax liability to be understated by $4,000 and Crewella's year 3 separate return tax liability to be understated by $6,000. The IRS also assessed penalties and interest on both of these tax returns. Try as it might, the IRS has not been able to locate Crewella, but they have been able to find Jasper.

a) What amount of tax can the IRS require Jasper to pay for the Dahvill's year 2 joint return? Explain.

b) What amount of tax can the IRS require Jasper to pay for Crewella's year 3 separate tax return? Explain.

LO 4-3 research

51. Janice Traylor is single. She has an 18-year-old son named Marty. Marty is Janice's only child. Marty has lived with Janice his entire life. However, Marty recently joined the Marines and was sent on a special assignment to Australia. During the current year, Marty spent nine months in Australia. Marty was extremely homesick while in Australia, since he had never lived away from home. However, Marty knew this assignment was only temporary, and he couldn't wait to come home and find his room just the way he left it. Janice has always filed as head of household, and Marty has always been considered a qualifying child (and he continues to meet all the tests with the possible exception of the residence test due to his stay in Australia). However, this year Janice is unsure whether she qualifies as head of household due to Marty's nine-month absence during the year. Janice has come to you for advice on whether she qualifies for head of household filing status. What do you tell her?

LO 4-3 research

52. Doug Jones timely submitted his 2015 tax return and elected married filing jointly status with his wife, Darlene. Doug and Darlene did not request an extension for their 2015 tax return. Doug and Darlene owed and paid the IRS $124,000 for their 2015 tax year. Two years later, Doug amended his return and claimed married filing separate status. By changing his filing status, Doug sought a refund for an overpayment for the tax year 2015 (he paid more tax in the original joint return than he owed on a separate return). Is Doug allowed to change his filing status for the 2015 tax year and receive a tax refund with his amended return?

COMPREHENSIVE PROBLEMS

All applicable problems are available with McGraw-Hill's *Connect® Accounting*.

53. Marc and Michelle are married and earned salaries this year of $64,000 and $12,000, respectively. In addition to their salaries, they received interest of $350 from municipal bonds and $500 from corporate bonds. Marc and Michelle also paid $2,500 of qualifying moving expenses, and Marc paid alimony to a prior spouse in the amount of $1,500. Marc and Michelle have a 10-year-old son, Matthew, who lived with them throughout the entire year. Thus, Marc and Michelle are allowed to claim a $1,000 child tax credit for Matthew. Marc and Michelle paid $6,000 of expenditures that qualify as itemized deductions and they had a total of $5,500 in federal income taxes withheld from their paychecks during the course of the year.

a) What is Marc and Michelle's gross income?

b) What is Marc and Michelle's adjusted gross income?

c) What is the total amount of Marc and Michelle's deductions *from* AGI?

d) What is Marc and Michelle's taxable income?

e) What is Marc and Michelle's taxes payable or refund due for the year? (Use the tax rate schedules.)

f) Complete the first two pages of Marc and Michelle's Form 1040 (use 2014 forms if 2015 forms are unavailable).

54. Demarco and Janine Jackson have been married for 20 years and have four children who qualify as their dependents (Damarcus, Janine, Michael, and Candice). The couple received salary income of $100,000 and they sold their home this year. They initially purchased the home three years ago for $200,000 and they sold it for $250,000. The gain on the sale qualified for the exclusion from the sale of a principal residence. The Jacksons incurred $16,500 of itemized deductions, and they had $6,250 withheld from their paychecks for federal taxes. They are also allowed to claim a child tax credit for each of their children.

a) What is the Jacksons' taxable income, and what is their tax liability or (refund)?

b) Complete the first two pages of the Jacksons' 1040 (use 2014 forms if 2015 forms are unavailable).

c) What would their taxable income be if their itemized deductions totaled $6,000 instead of $16,500?

d) What would their taxable income be if they had $0 itemized deductions and $6,000 of *for* AGI deductions?

e) Assume the original facts except that they also incurred a loss of $5,000 on the sale of some of their investment assets. What effect does the $5,000 loss have on their *taxable income*?

f) Assume the original facts except that the Jacksons owned investments that appreciated by $10,000 during the year. The Jacksons believe the investments will continue to appreciate, so they did not sell the investments during this year. What is the Jacksons' taxable income?

55. Camille Sikorski was divorced last year. She currently owns and provides a home for her 15-year-old daughter, Kaly, and 18-year-old son, Parker. Both children lived in Camille's home for the entire year, and Camille paid for all the costs of maintaining the home. She received a salary of $105,000 and contributed $6,000 of it to a qualified retirement account (a *for* AGI deduction). She also received $10,000 of alimony from her former husband. Finally, Camille paid $5,000 of expenditures that qualified as itemized deductions.

a) What is Camille's taxable income?

b) What would Camille's taxable income be if she incurred $14,000 of itemized deductions instead of $5,000?

c) Assume the original facts except that Camille's daughter, Kaly, is 25 years old and a full-time student. Kaly's gross income for the year was $5,000. Kaly provided $3,000 of her own support, and Camille provided $5,000 of support. What is Camille's taxable income?

56. Tiffany is unmarried and has a 15-year-old qualifying child. Tiffany has determined her tax liability to be $3,525, and her employer has withheld $1,500 of federal taxes from her paycheck. Tiffany is allowed to claim a $1,000 child credit for her qualifying child. What amount of taxes will Tiffany owe (or what amount will she receive as a refund) when she files her tax return?

chapter

5 Gross Income and Exclusions

Learning Objectives

Upon completing this chapter, you should be able to:

- **LO 5-1** Apply the concept of realization and explain when taxpayers recognize gross income.
- **LO 5-2** Understand the distinctions between the various sources of income, including income from services and property.
- **LO 5-3** Apply basic income exclusion provisions to compute gross income.

© Image Source

Storyline Summary

Taxpayers:	Courtney Wilson, age 40 Courtney's mother, Dorothy "Gram" Weiss, age 70
Family description:	Courtney is divorced with a son, Deron, age 10, and a daughter, Ellen, age 20. Gram is currently residing with Courtney.
Location:	Kansas City, Missouri
Employment status:	Courtney works as an architect for EWD. Her salary is $98,000. Gram is unemployed.
Current situation:	Determining what income is taxable

The past year was a year of change for Courtney Wilson. After her divorce from Al Wilson, Courtney assumed sole custody of their 10-year-old son, Deron, and their 20-year-old daughter, Ellen. Looking for a fresh start in January, Courtney quit her job as an architect in Cincinnati, Ohio, and moved to Kansas City, Missouri. Courtney wanted to pursue several promising job opportunities in Kansas City and be close to Ellen while she attends the University of Missouri-Kansas City. Courtney's 70-year-old mother "Gram" also lives in Kansas City and is in relatively good health. However, Courtney's father, "Gramps," passed away last December from cancer. At Courtney's insistence, Gram moved in with Courtney and Deron in April.

In late April, Courtney broke her wrist in a mountain biking accident and was unable to work for two weeks. Thankfully, Courtney's disability insurance paid her for lost wages during her time away from work.

While her personal life has been in disarray, Courtney's financial prospects have been improving. Shortly after arriving in Kansas City, Courtney was fortunate to land a job as an architect with Earth Wise Design (EWD). EWD provided Courtney the following compensation and benefits this year:

- Salary $98,000.
- Medical and life insurance premiums.
- Contribution of 10 percent of her base salary to her qualified retirement account.
- No-interest loan with a promise to forgive the loan principal over time if she continues her employment with EWD.
- Performance bonus for her first year on the job.

Courtney also received other payments unrelated to her employment with EWD as follows:

- Alimony from her ex-husband Al.
- Child support from her ex-husband Al.
- Consulting income.
- Dividend, interest, and rental income.
- Refund of state taxes she paid last year.

Before Gram moved in with Courtney, she lived alone in an apartment in Kansas City. After Gramps died, Gram was dependent on her Social Security benefits. In March, Gram's landlord agreed to allow Gram to babysit his infant son in lieu of paying rent. In early April, Gram received the proceeds from Gramps's life insurance policy. She invested part of the proceeds in an annuity contract that will pay Gram a fixed amount per year. Gram also invested some of the proceeds in the stock of a local corporation. She used the rest of the life insurance proceeds to purchase a certificate of deposit and start a savings account. Gram also spent some of her spare time completing sweepstakes entries. Her hard work paid off when she won a WaveRunner in a sweepstakes contest.

Until their divorce, Courtney's husband always prepared their income tax return. Since EWD hired her, Courtney has become anxious about her income tax and whether her withholding will be sufficient to cover her tax bill. Courtney is also worried about Gram's tax situation, because Gram did not make any tax payments this year. ■

In the previous chapter, we presented an overview of individual taxation. In this chapter, we begin to dig deeper into the tax formula to determine a taxpayer's gross income. We focus on whether income is included or excluded from a taxpayer's gross income rather than the rate at which the income is taxed. In the next three chapters, we continue to work through the individual tax formula to determine the tax liabilities for Courtney and Gram. Chapter 6 describes deductible expenses to determine adjusted gross income and taxable income, Chapter 7 discusses the taxation of investments, and Chapter 8 addresses issues associated with calculating the tax liability, tax credits, and tax return filing concerns.

LO 5-1

REALIZATION AND RECOGNITION OF INCOME

As we learned in the previous chapter, **gross income** is income that taxpayers realize, recognize, and report on their tax returns for the year. In the previous chapter, we discussed gross income in general terms. In this chapter we explain the requirements for taxpayers to recognize gross income, and we discuss the most common sources of gross income.

What Is Included in Gross Income?

The definition of gross income for tax purposes is provided in §61(a) as follows:

> General Definition.—Except as otherwise provided in this subtitle, gross income means all income *from whatever source derived* (emphasis added).

In addition to providing this **all-inclusive definition of income,** §61 includes a list of examples of gross income such as compensation for services, business income, rents, royalties, interest, and dividends. However, it is clear that unless a tax provision says otherwise, gross income includes *all* income. Thus, gross income is *broadly* defined. Reg. §1.61-(a) provides further insight into the definition of gross income as follows:

> Gross income means all income from whatever source derived, unless excluded by law. Gross income includes income realized in any form, whether in money, property, or services.

Based on §61(a), Reg. §1.61-(a), and various judicial rulings, taxpayers *recognize* gross income when (1) they receive an economic benefit, (2) they realize the income, *and* (3) no tax provision allows them to exclude or defer the income from gross income for that year.[1] Let's address each of these three requirements for recognizing gross income.

Economic Benefit Taxpayers must receive an economic benefit (i.e., receive an item of value) to have gross income. Common examples where a taxpayer receives economic benefit include being paid for services rendered (typically cash received, but includes property or even services), proceeds from property sales (typically cash, property, or debt relief), and income from investments or business activities (such as business income, rents, interest, and dividends). How about when a taxpayer borrows money? Is the economic benefit criterion met? No, because when a taxpayer borrows money, the economic benefit received (the cash received) is completely offset by the liability the taxpayer is required to pay from borrowing the funds (the debt amount).

Realization Principle As indicated in Reg. §1.61-(a), the tax definition of income adopts the **realization principle.** Under this principle, income is realized when (1) a taxpayer engages in a transaction with another party, and (2) the transaction results in a measurable change in property rights. In other words, assets or services are exchanged for cash, claims to cash, or other assets with determinable value.

The concept of realization for tax purposes closely parallels the concept of realization for financial accounting purposes. Requiring a transaction to trigger realization reduces the uncertainty associated with determining the *amount* of income because a change in rights can typically be traced to a specific moment in time and is generally accompanied by legal documentation.

Example 5-1

In April, Gram used part of the life insurance proceeds she received from Gramps's death to purchase 50 shares in Acme Corporation for $30 per share. From April to the end of December, the value of the shares fluctuated between $40 and $25, but on December 31, the shares were worth $35. If Gram does *not* sell the shares, how much income from her stockholdings in Acme Corporation does she *realize for* the year?

Answer: $0. Unless Gram sells the stock, she does not enter into a transaction resulting in a measurable change of property rights with a second party. Thus, she does not realize income even though she experienced an economic benefit from the appreciation of the stock from $30 per share to $35 per share.

Adopting the realization principle for defining gross income provides two major advantages. First, because parties to the transaction must agree to the value of the exchanged property rights, the transaction allows the income to be measured objectively. Second, the transaction often provides the taxpayer with the **wherewithal to pay** taxes (at least when the taxpayer receives cash in the transaction). That is, the transaction itself provides the taxpayer with the funds to pay taxes on income generated by the transaction. Thus, it reduces the possibility that the taxpayer will be required to sell other assets to pay the taxes on the income from the transaction. Note, however, when taxpayers receive property or services in a transaction (instead of cash), realization has also occurred (despite the absence of wherewithal to pay).

[1]For tax purposes it matters not whether income is obtained through legal or illegal activities (e.g., embezzlement). See *Eugene James v. U.S.* (1961, S. Ct.), 7 AFTR 2d 1361.

Recognition Taxpayers who realize an economic benefit must include the benefit in gross income unless a specific provision of the tax code says otherwise. That is, taxpayers are generally required to *recognize* all realized income by reporting it as gross income on their tax returns. However, as we describe later in this chapter, through exclusions Congress allows taxpayers to permanently exclude certain types of income from gross income and through deferrals they allow taxpayers to defer certain types of income from gross income until a subsequent year. Thus, it is important to distinguish between realized and recognized income.

Other Income Concepts

The tax laws, administrative authority, and judicial rulings have established several other concepts important for determining an individual's gross income.

Form of Receipt A common misperception is that taxpayers must receive cash to realize and recognize gross income. However, Reg. §1.61-(a) indicates that taxpayers realize income whether they receive money, property, *or* services in a transaction. For example, **barter clubs** facilitate the exchange of rights to goods and services between members, many of whom have the mistaken belief that they need not recognize income on the exchanges. However, when members exchange property, they realize and recognize income at the market price, the amount that outsiders are willing to pay for the goods or services. Also, other taxpayers who exchange or trade goods or services with each other must recognize the value of the goods or services as income, even when they do not receive any cash. Indeed, taxpayers have the legal and ethical responsibility to report realized income no matter the form of its receipt or whether the IRS knows the taxpayer received the income.

Example 5-2

During March, Gram paid no rent to her neighbor (also her landlord). Although the neighbor typically charges $350 per month for rent, he allowed Gram to live rent free in exchange for babysitting his infant son. What income must Gram and Gram's neighbor realize and recognize on this exchange?

Answer: $350. Gram and the neighbor each must recognize $350 of income for March. The neighbor recognizes $350 of rental receipts because this is the value of the babysitting services the neighbor received in lieu of a cash payment for rent from Gram (an economic benefit the neighbor realized through the exchange). Gram recognizes $350 of babysitting income, because this is the value of the services provided to her neighbor (an economic benefit was realized because Gram was not required to pay rent).

Return of Capital Principle When taxpayers sell assets, they must determine the extent to which they include the sale proceeds in gross income. Initially, the IRS was convinced that Congress's all-inclusive definition of income required taxpayers to include *all* sale proceeds in gross income. Taxpayers, on the other hand, argued that a portion of proceeds from a sale represented a return of the cost or capital investment in the underlying property (called **tax basis**). The courts determined that when receiving a payment for property, taxpayers are allowed to recover the cost of the property tax free. Consequently, when taxpayers sell property, they are allowed to reduce the sale proceeds by their unrecovered investment in the property to determine the realized gain from the sale.[2] When the tax basis exceeds

[2]§1001(a).

the sale proceeds, the **return of capital** principle generally applies to the extent of the sale proceeds. The excess of basis over sale proceeds is generally not considered to be a return of capital, but rather a loss that is deductible only if specifically authorized by the tax code. Below, we revisit the return of capital principle when we discuss asset dispositions.

The return of capital principle gets complicated when taxpayers sell assets and collect the sale proceeds over several periods. In these cases, the principle is usually modified by law to provide that the return of capital occurs evenly (pro rata) over the collection period. We discuss this issue in more detail later in this chapter when we discuss the taxation of annuities.

Recovery of Amounts Previously Deducted A refund is not typically included in gross income because it usually represents a return of capital. For example, a refund of $1,000 on an auto purchased for $12,000 simply reduces the net cost of the vehicle to $11,000. Likewise, a $200 refund of a $700 business expense is not included in gross income but instead reduces the net expense to $500. However, if the refund is made for an expenditure deducted in a *previous* year, then under the **tax benefit rule** the refund is included in gross income to the extent that the prior deduction produced a tax benefit.[3] For example, suppose an individual paid a $1,000 business expense claimed as a *for* AGI deduction in 2015, but $250 of the expense was subsequently reimbursed in 2016. Because the $250 business deduction produced a tax benefit in 2015 (reduced taxable income), the $250 refund in 2016 would be included in income.

The application of the tax benefit rule is more complex for individuals who itemize deductions. An itemized deduction only produces a tax benefit to the extent that total itemized deductions exceed the standard deduction. For example, suppose that an individual's total itemized deductions exceeded the standard deduction by $100. A refund of $150 of itemized deductions would cause the individual's itemized deductions to fall $50 beneath the standard deduction. If the refund occurred in the same year as the expense, the individual would have elected the standard deduction, and the refund would have only caused taxable income to decline by $100 (the difference between claiming the standard deduction and the total itemized deductions that would have been claimed in the absence of any refund). If the refund occurs the year after the deduction is claimed, then only $100 of the $150 refund would be included in gross income under the tax benefit rule. The $100 is added to taxable income in the year of the refund because this is the increment in taxable income that would have resulted if the refund was issued in the year the itemized deduction was claimed.

Example 5-3

In 2014 Courtney paid $3,500 in Ohio state income taxes, and she included this payment with her other itemized deductions when she filed her federal income tax return in March of 2015. Courtney filed her 2014 federal return as a head of household and claimed $15,500 of itemized deductions. She also filed an Ohio state income tax return in March of 2015 and discovered she only owed $3,080 in Ohio income tax for 2014. Hence, Courtney received a $420 refund of her Ohio income tax in June of 2015. How much of the $420 refund, if any, is Courtney required to include in her gross income in 2015? The answer depends upon the standard deduction for 2014. Help Courtney apply the tax benefit rule (the standard deduction for head of household filling status in 2014 was $9,100).

Answer: All $420. Courtney is required to include the entire refund in her 2015 gross income because her itemized deduction for the $420 of state income taxes that she overpaid last year reduced her taxable income by $420. Accordingly, because she received a tax benefit (deduction) for the entire

(continued on page 5-6)

[3]§111.

$420 overpayment, she must include it all in gross income in 2015. See the following for the calculation of the amount of tax benefit Courtney received from the $420 overpayment of taxes in 2014.

Deduction	Amount	Explanation
(1) Itemized deduction	$15,500	
(2) 2014 standard deduction	9,100	Head of household filing status.
(3) Reduction in taxable income	15,500	Greater of (1) and (2).
(4) Itemized deductions adjusted for the $420 refund	15,080	(1) − $420.
(5) Reduction in taxable income after adjustment for the $420 refund	15,080	Greater of (2) and (4).
Tax benefit due to prior deduction or $420 refund	$ 420	(3) − (5).

What if: Let's consider *alternative* fact patterns provided in Scenarios A and B to further illustrate the application of the tax benefit rule.

Scenario A: In 2014 Courtney's itemized deductions, including $3,500 in state taxes, were $5,500.

Scenario B: In 2014 Courtney's itemized deductions, including $3,500 in state taxes, were $9,300.

How much of the $420 refund would Courtney include in her 2015 gross income in Scenarios A and B?

Answer Scenario A: $0. As computed below, Courtney received $0 tax benefit from the $420 tax overpayment in 2014, so she need not include any of the refund in her gross income.

Answer Scenario B: $200. As computed below, Courtney received a $200 tax benefit (reduction in taxable income) from the $420 state tax overpayment in 2014, so she must include $200 of the refund in her 2015 gross income.

Deduction	Scenario A Amount	Scenario B Amount	Explanation
(1) Itemized deductions	$5,500	$9,300	
(2) 2014 standard deduction	9,100	9,100	Head of household filing status.
(3) Reduction in taxable income	9,100	9,300	Greater of (1) and (2).
(4) Itemized deductions adjusted for the $420 refund	5,080	8,880	(1) − $420.
(5) Reduction in taxable income adjusted for the $420 refund	9,100	9,100	Greater of (2) and (4).
Tax benefit due to prior deduction of $420 refund	$ 0	$ 200	(3) − (5).

When Do Taxpayers Recognize Income?

Individual taxpayers generally file tax returns reporting their taxable income for a calendar-year period, whereas corporations often use a fiscal year-end. In either case, the taxpayer's method of accounting generally determines the year in which realized income is recognized and included in gross income.

Accounting Methods Most large corporations use the accrual method of accounting. Under the **accrual method,** income is generally recognized when earned, and expenses are generally deducted in the period when liabilities are incurred. In contrast, most individuals use the **cash method** as their overall method of accounting.[4] Under the cash method, taxpayers recognize income in the period they receive it (in the form of cash, property, or services), rather than when they actually earn it. Likewise,

[4]Taxpayers involved in a business may use the accrual or hybrid overall method of accounting. We discuss these methods in Chapter 9.

cash-method taxpayers claim deductions when they make expenditures, rather than when they incur liabilities. The cash method greatly simplifies the computation of income for the overwhelming majority of individuals, many of whom have neither the time nor the training to apply the accrual method. Another advantage of the cash method is that taxpayers may have some control over when income is received and expenses are paid. Because of this control, taxpayers can more easily use the timing tax planning strategy (described in Chapter 3) to lower the present value of their tax bill.

THE KEY FACTS

Income Recognition

- Cash-method taxpayers recognize income when it is received.
- Income is realized regardless of whether payments are received in money, property, *or* services.
- Income is taxed in the period in which a cash-method taxpayer has a right to receive payment without substantial restrictions.

Constructive Receipt Taxpayers using the cash method of accounting may try to shift income from the current year to the next year when they receive payments near year-end. For instance, taxpayers may merely delay cashing a check or avoid picking up a compensation payment until after year-end. The courts responded to this ploy by devising the **constructive receipt doctrine.**[5] The constructive receipt doctrine states that a taxpayer realizes and recognizes income when it is actually or *constructively* received. Constructive receipt is deemed to occur when the income has been credited to the taxpayer's account or when the income is unconditionally available to the taxpayer, the taxpayer is aware of the income's availability, and there are no restrictions on the taxpayer's control over the income.

Example 5-4

Courtney is a cash-method taxpayer. Based on her outstanding performance, Courtney earned a $4,800 year-end bonus. On December 28, Courtney's supervisor told her that her bonus was issued as a separate check and that Courtney could pick up the check in the accounting office anytime. Courtney did not pick up the check until January 2 of next year, and she did not cash it until late January. When does Courtney realize and recognize the $4,800 income?

Answer: On December 28 of the current year. Courtney *constructively* received the check this year because it was unconditionally available to her on December 28, she was aware of the check's availability, and there were no restrictions on her control over the check. Courtney must include the $4,800 bonus in gross income this year, even though she did not actually receive the funds until late January of next year.[6]

Claim of Right The **claim of right doctrine** is another judicial doctrine created to address the timing of income recognition. This doctrine was conceived when a taxpayer received income in one period but was required to return the payment in a subsequent period. The claim of right doctrine states that income has been realized if a taxpayer receives income and there are no restrictions on the taxpayer's use of the income (e.g., the taxpayer does not have an obligation to repay the amount). A common example of the claim of right doctrine is a cash bonus paid to employees based on company earnings. Despite *potentially* having to repay the bonuses (e.g., if there is a "clawback" provision that requires repayment if the company has an earnings restatement), the employees would include the bonuses in gross income in the year received because there are no restrictions on their use of the income.[7]

[5]Justice Holmes summarized this doctrine as follows: "The income that is subject to a man's unfettered command and that he is free to enjoy at his own option may be taxed to him as his income, whether he sees fit to enjoy it or not." *Corliss v. Bowers,* 281 US 378 (1930).

[6]Note also that Courtney's employer would include her bonus on Courtney's W-2 for the year in which it issued the check.

[7]§1341 provides relief for a taxpayer who recognizes taxable income because of the claim of right doctrine and in a later year determines that she does not have a claim of right. Specifically, §1341 provides that if a taxpayer recognizes taxable income because she has a "claim of right" (unrestricted right) to the income received, a deduction is allowable in a later year because she did not have an unrestricted right to the income, and the related tax deduction exceeds $3,000, then the tax imposed in the later year is the lesser of (1) the tax for the taxable year computed with the deduction or (2) the tax for the taxable year computed without the deduction, less a tax credit for the previous tax paid on the item of income.

Who Recognizes the Income?

In addition to determining when taxpayers realize and recognize income, it is important to consider *who* (which taxpayer) recognizes the income. This question often arises when taxpayers attempt to shift income to other related taxpayers through the income-shifting strategy. For example, a father (with a high marginal income tax rate) might wish to assign his paycheck to his baby daughter (with a low marginal income tax rate) to minimize their collective tax burden.

Assignment of Income The courts developed the **assignment of income doctrine** to prevent taxpayers from arbitrarily transferring the taxation on their income to others. In essence, the assignment of income doctrine holds that the taxpayer who earns income from services must recognize the income. Likewise, income from property, such as dividends and interest, is taxable to the person who actually owns the income-producing property.[8] For example, interest income from a bond is taxable to the person who owns the bond during the time the interest income accrues. Thus, to shift income from property to another person, a taxpayer must also transfer the *ownership* in the property to the other person.

Example 5-5

What if: Courtney would like to begin saving for Deron's college tuition. If Courtney were to direct EWD to deposit part of her salary in Deron's bank account, who would pay tax on the salary income?

Answer: Courtney would be taxed on her entire salary as income because she earned the income.[9] The payment to Deron would be treated as a gift and would not be taxable to him (gifts are excluded from the recipient's income as discussed later in the chapter).

What if: Suppose that Courtney wanted to shift her rental income to Deron. What would Courtney need to do to ensure that her rental income is taxed to Deron?

Answer: Courtney would have to transfer her ownership in the rental property to Deron in order for Deron to be taxed on the rental income.[10]

Community Property Systems While most states use a common law system, nine states (Arizona, California, Idaho, Louisiana, Nevada, New Mexico, Texas, Washington, and Wisconsin) implement **community property systems.** Under community property systems, the income earned from services by one spouse is treated as though it was earned equally by both spouses. Also, property acquired by either spouse during the marriage is usually community property and is treated as though it is owned equally by each spouse.[11] Property that a spouse brings into a marriage is treated as that spouse's separate property. For federal income tax purposes, the community property system has the following consequences:

- Half of the income earned from the *services* of one spouse is included in the gross income of the other spouse.
- Half of the income from property held as *community* property by the married couple is included in the gross income of each spouse.

[8]This rule of thumb is also referred to as the "fruit and the tree" doctrine because of the analogy to fruit belonging to the tree upon which it was grown. See *Lucas v. Earl* (1930) 281 US 111 and *Helvering v. Horst* (1940) 311 US 112.

[9]Note also that EWD has the responsibility of issuing a W-2 to the taxpayer who provided the services—Courtney in this case.

[10]As explained in Chapter 8, the tax savings from such a transfer would be mitigated in the calculation of Deron's tax by the so-called "kiddie" tax. Likewise, Courtney should consider the gift tax implications of this transfer before transferring the property to Deron.

[11]Property acquired during the marriage via gift or inheritance or purchased with a spouse's separate property is considered separate property.

- In five community property states (Arizona, California, Nevada, New Mexico, and Washington), all of the income from property owned *separately* by one spouse is included in that spouse's gross income.
- In Texas, Louisiana, Wisconsin, and Idaho, half of the income from property owned *separately* by one spouse is included in the gross income of each spouse.

In contrast, for federal income tax purposes, the common law system has the following consequences:

- All of the income earned from the *services* of one spouse is included in the gross income of the spouse who earned it.
- For property owned *separately,* all of the income from the separately owned property is included in that spouse's gross income.
- For property owned *jointly* (i.e., not separately), each co-owner is taxed on the income attributable to his or her share of the property. For example, suppose that a parcel of property is jointly owned by husband and wife. One-half would be included in the gross income of each spouse. Similarly, income from property owned by three or more persons would be included in the gross income of each co-owner based on his or her respective ownership share.

Example 5-6

In the year of their divorce, Courtney and Al Wilson lived in Ohio, a common law state. The divorce was finalized on October 1 of that year, and up to that date Al had earned $90,000 of annual salary and Courtney had earned $60,000. How much of the income earned by Al and by Courtney in the year of the divorce did Al report on his individual tax return? How much income did Courtney report on her individual tax return?

Answer: Because they resided in a common law state, Al reports the $90,000 that he earned through September (and all the income he earned through the end of the year) on his own return, and Courtney reports the entire $60,000 she earned through September (and all the income she earned through the rest of the year) on her own tax return.

What if: How much of this income would Al have been required to include on his individual tax return, and how much of this income would Courtney have been required to report on her individual tax return if they lived in California, a community property state?

Answer: If they resided in a community property state, both Al and Courtney would have included $75,000 of the $150,000 the couple had jointly earned through September [(Al's $90,000 + Courtney's $60,000)/2] on their respective individual tax returns. Whether they resided in a community property state or not, Al and Courtney also would have included on their respective individual tax returns the income they individually earned and received from October through December.

If a couple files a joint tax return, the community property rules do not affect the aggregate taxes payable by the couple, because the income of both spouses is aggregated on the return. However, when couples file separate tax returns, their combined tax liability may depend on whether they live in a common law state, a community property state that shares income from separate property equally between spouses, or a community property state that does not split income from separate property between spouses.[12]

TYPES OF INCOME

LO 5-2

Now that we have a basic understanding of the general definition of gross income and related concepts, let's turn our attention to specific *types* of income subject to taxation. Our discussion is organized around income from services, income from property, and other sources of income.

[12]§66 provides rules that allow spouses living apart in community property states to be taxed on his or her own income from services if (1) the taxpayers live apart for the entire year, (2) they do not file a joint tax return with each other, and (3) they do not transfer any of the income from services between each other.

Income from Services

Income from labor is one of the most common sources of gross income, and it is rarely exempt from taxation. Payments for services including salary, wages, and fees that a taxpayer earns through services in a nonemployee capacity are all considered income from services and so is unemployment compensation. Income from services is often referred to as **earned income** because it is generated by the efforts of the taxpayer (this also includes business income earned by a taxpayer even if the taxpayer's business is selling inventory).

Example 5-7

EWD pays Courtney a salary of $98,000. In addition, Courtney earned and received $19,500 of fees from consulting work she did on weekends independent of her employment with EWD. She incurred $1,500 of miscellaneous expenses for supplies and transportation while doing the consulting work. What is Courtney's *income* from services (earned income) from her employment and her self-employment activities?

Answer: $116,000, consisting of her $98,000 of salary and $19,500 of her business income from her consulting activities, less the $1,500 of expenses related to her consulting activities. Note that business deductions are *for* AGI deductions that taxpayers subtract from their gross business income to derive net business income or loss reported on page 1 of Form 1040. We discuss *for* AGI deductions in greater detail in Chapter 6.

Income from Property

Income from property, often referred to as **unearned income,** may take different forms, such as gain or losses from the sale of property, dividends, interest, rents, royalties, and annuities.[13] The tax treatment of unearned income depends upon the type of income and, in some circumstances, the type of the transaction generating the income. For example, as discussed in Chapter 4, qualified dividends and long-term capital gains are taxed at preferential tax rates, whereas other unearned income is generally taxed at ordinary tax rates. Likewise, while gains or losses are typically recognized in the current period, certain types of gains and losses are postponed indefinitely. We discuss annuity income and property dispositions briefly in the following paragraphs. We discuss income from property in more detail in subsequent chapters.

Example 5-8

Courtney owns 1,000 shares of GE stock that she registered in a dividend reinvestment plan. Under this plan, all dividends are automatically used to purchase more shares of the stock. This year, GE declared and paid $700 in dividends on Courtney's stock. Must Courtney include the dividend in her gross income for the year?

Answer: Yes. Courtney includes the $700 of dividends (unearned income) in her gross income. The fact that Courtney chose to reinvest the dividends does not affect their taxability because she received an economic benefit and change in property rights associated with the dividend.

Example 5-9

Gram purchased a $100,000, three-year certificate of deposit (CD) with a portion of the life insurance proceeds she received on Gramps's death. At year-end, her CD account is credited with $4,100 of interest, and her savings account is credited with $300 of interest. Courtney had a total of $567 of interest credited to her savings account and $50 credited to her checking account during the year. How much interest must Gram and Courtney include in their gross income for the year?

[13]The tax definition of unearned income is different from the financial accounting definition. Unearned income for financial accounting purposes is a liability that represents advance payments for goods or services.

Answer: Gram must include the $4,100 of interest credited to her CD account and the $300 of interest credited to her savings account this year regardless of whether she withdraws the interest or not. Courtney must include the $567 of interest credited to her savings account and the $50 credited to her checking account regardless of whether she withdraws the interest or not.

Example 5-10

Courtney owns a condo in town that she rents to tenants. This year, the condo generated $14,000 of rental revenue. Courtney incurred $4,000 in real estate taxes, $2,500 in utility expenses, $500 in advertising expenses, and $2,000 of depreciation and other expenses associated with the rental. What effect does the rental have on Courtney's *gross income*? What effect does the rental have on Courtney's *taxable income*?

Answer: The rent increases Courtney's *gross income* by $14,000. However, after considering her allowable deductions for the rental, Courtney will only report $5,000 of *taxable income* from rental activities computed as follows:

Description	Amount	
Rental revenue		$14,000
Less allowable deductions:		
Real estate taxes	(4,000)	
Utilities	(2,500)	
Advertising	(500)	
Depreciation and other expenses	(2,000)	
Total rental expenses		(9,000)
Net rental income		$ 5,000

Annuities An **annuity** is an investment that pays a stream of equal payments over time. Individuals often purchase annuities as a means of generating a fixed income stream during retirement. There are two basic types of annuities: (1) annuities paid over a fixed period and (2) annuities paid over a person's life (for as long as the person lives). The challenge from a tax perspective is to determine how much of each annuity payment represents gross income (income taxed at ordinary tax rates) and how much represents a nontaxable *return of capital* (return of the original investment). For both types of annuities, the tax law deems a *portion* of each annuity payment as a nontaxable return of capital and the remainder as gross income. Taxpayers use the annuity *exclusion* ratio to determine the portion of each payment that is a nontaxable return of capital.

$$\text{Annuity exclusion ratio} = \frac{\textit{Original investment}}{\textit{Expected value of annuity}} = \text{Return of capital } \textit{percentage}$$

For fixed annuities, the expected value is the number of payments times the amount of the payment. In other words, for an annuity payable over a fixed term the return of capital is simply the original investment divided by the number of payments. The number of payments, however, is uncertain for annuities paid over a person's life. For these annuities, taxpayers must use IRS tables to determine the expected value based upon the taxpayer's life expectancy at the start of the annuity.[14] To calculate the

[14]See Reg. §1.72-9. Special rules under §72(d) apply to annuities from qualified retirement plans. These rules only apply when a taxpayer makes an after-tax contribution to a qualified employer retirement plan (which is uncommon). In most cases, taxpayers only make pretax contributions to qualified retirement plans, which results in fully taxable annuity distributions.

expected value of the annuity, the number of annual payments from the table (referred to as the expected return multiple) is multiplied by the annual payment amount. Taxpayers with an annuity paid over the life of one person (a single-life annuity) use the expected return multiple from the table, a portion of which is presented in Exhibit 5-1.

EXHIBIT 5-1 Table for Expected Return Multiple for Ordinary Single-Life Annuity

Age at Annuity Starting Date	Expected Return Multiple
68	17.6
69	16.8
70	16.0
71	15.3
72	14.6

Some annuities provide payments over the lives of two people. For example, a taxpayer may purchase an annuity that provides an annual payment each year until both the taxpayer *and* the taxpayer's spouse pass away. This type of annuity is called a joint-life annuity. The IRS provides a separate table for determining the expected number of payments from joint-life annuities.

A taxpayer receiving a life annuity who lives longer than his or her estimated life expectancy will ultimately receive more than the expected number of payments. The entire amount of these "extra" payments is included in the taxpayer's gross income because the taxpayer has completely recovered her investment in the annuity by the time she receives them. If the taxpayer dies *before* receiving the expected number of payments, the amount of the unrecovered investment (the initial investment less the amounts received that is treated as a nontaxable return of capital) is deducted on the taxpayer's final income tax return.[15]

Example 5-11

In January of this year, Gram purchased an annuity from UBET Insurance Co. that will pay her $10,000 per year for the next 15 years. Gram received the first $10,000 payment in December. Gram paid $99,000 for the annuity and will receive $150,000 over the life of the annuity (15 years × $10,000 per year). How much of the $10,000 payment Gram receives in December should she include in her gross income?

Answer: $3,400. Because Gram purchased a fixed-payment annuity, the portion of the annuity payment included in gross income is calculated as follows:

Description	Amount	Explanation
(1) Investment in annuity contract	$99,000	
(2) Number of payments	15	
(3) Return of capital per payment	$ 6,600	(1)/(2).
(4) Amount of each payment:	$10,000	
Gross income per payment	**$ 3,400**	(4) − (3).

What if: Assume the annuity Gram purchased pays her $1,000 per month over the remainder of her life. Gram (70 years old) paid $99,000 for the annuity, and she received her first $1,000 payment in December of this year. How much income would she recognize on the $1,000 payment?

[15]The unrecovered cost of the annuity is deducted as a miscellaneous itemized deduction not subject to the 2 percent of AGI floor. See §72(b)(3) and §67(b)(10).

Answer: $484.40, computed as follows:

Description	Amount	Explanation
(1) Investment in annuity contract	$ 99,000	
(2) Expected return multiple	16	Exhibit 5-1, 70 years old.
(3) Amount of each payment	$ 1,000	
(4) Expected return	$192,000	(2) × (3) × 12 months.
(5) Return of capital percentage	51.56%	(1)/(4).
(6) Return of capital per payment	$ 515.60	(3) × (5).
Taxable income per payment	$ 484.40	(3) − (6).

After Gram receives her entire $99,000 as a return of capital, each subsequent $1,000 annuity payment would be fully taxable.

Property Dispositions Taxpayers can realize a gain or loss when disposing of an asset. Consistent with the return of capital principle we discussed above, taxpayers are allowed to recover their investment in property (tax basis) before they realize any gain. A loss is realized when the proceeds are less than the tax basis in the property. Because the return of capital principle generally applies only to the extent of the sale proceeds, a loss does not necessarily reduce the taxpayer's taxable income. A loss will only reduce the taxpayer's taxable income if the loss is deductible. Exhibit 5-2 presents a general formula for computing the gain or loss from a sale of an asset.

THE KEY FACTS

Return of Capital

- Taxpayers are allowed to recover the capital invested in property tax free.
- Payments from purchased annuities are part income and part return of capital.
- When property is sold or disposed, the realized gain or loss equals the sale proceeds reduced by the tax basis of the property.

EXHIBIT 5-2 Formula for Calculating Gain (Loss) from Sale of an Asset

Sales proceeds
Less: Selling expenses
= Amount realized
Less: Basis (investment) in property sold
= Gain (Loss) on sale

The rate at which taxpayers are taxed on *gains* from property dispositions and the extent to which they can deduct *losses* from property dispositions depends on whether the taxpayer used the asset for business purposes, investment purposes, or personal purposes. For example, as we discussed in Chapter 4, long-term capital gains realized by individuals are taxed at preferential tax rates, and deductions for net capital losses realized by individuals are limited to $3,000 per year. In contrast, losses realized on assets used for personal purposes are generally not deductible. We discuss specific rules associated with property dispositions in Chapters 7 and 11.

Example 5-12

On December 31, Gram sold her 50 shares of Acme Corporation stock for $40 per share. Gram also paid $150 of broker's commissions on the sale. Gram originally purchased the shares in April of this year for $30 per share. How much gross income does Gram recognize from the stock sale?

Answer: Gram recognizes $350 gross income on the sale, computed as follows:

Sales proceeds ($40 × 50 shares)	$2,000
Less: Selling expenses	−150
= Amount realized	$1,850
Less: Tax basis (investment) in property sold ($30 × 50 shares)	−1,500
Gain (Loss) on sale	$ 350

Other Sources of Gross Income

Taxpayers may receive income from sources other than their efforts (earned income from wages or business) and their property (unearned income such as dividends and interest). In this section we briefly summarize other common types of gross income. If by chance you encounter other types of income that are not specifically discussed here, remember that the tax law is based upon the all-inclusive income concept. That is, unless a specific provision grants exclusion or deferral, economic benefits that are realized generate gross income. This basic understanding of the structure of our tax law (and research skills to investigate the taxability of specific income types) will serve you well as you evaluate whether realized income should be included in gross income.

Income from Flow-through Entities Individuals may invest in various business entities. The legal form of the business affects how the income generated by the business is taxed. For example, income earned by a corporation (other than an S corporation) is taxed at the entity level as opposed to the owner level. In contrast, the income and deductions from a **flow-through entity,** such as a partnership or S corporation (a corporation electing S corporation status), "flow through" to the owners of the entity (partners or shareholders). That is, the owners report income or deductions as though they operated a portion of the business personally. Specifically, each partner or S corporation shareholder reports his or her share of the entity's income and deductions, generally in proportion to his or her ownership percentage, on his or her individual tax return.[16]

Because different types of income and deductions may be treated differently for tax purposes (e.g., qualified dividends are eligible for a special low tax rate), each item the partners or shareholders report on their tax returns retains its underlying tax characteristics. That is, the partners are treated as if they personally received their share of each item of the flow-through entity's income. For example, corporate dividend income paid to a partnership is reported and taxed as dividend income on the partners' individual tax returns. Also, it is important to note that owners of flow-through entities are taxed on their share of the entity's income whether or not cash is distributed to them. When owners receive cash distributions from the entity, the distributions are generally treated as a return of capital to the extent of their investment (tax basis) in the entity and, therefore, not included in the owner's gross income. Distributions in excess of basis are taxable. Partnerships and S corporations report to each partner or shareholder, that partner's or shareholder's share of partnership and S corporation income (or loss) on Schedule K-1 filed with the partnership and S corporation's annual information returns (Form 1065 and 1120S, respectively).[17]

Example 5-13

What if: Suppose that Courtney is a 40 percent partner in KJZ partnership. KJZ reported $20,000 of business income and $3,000 of interest income for the year. KJZ also distributed $1,000 of cash to Courtney. What amount of gross income from her ownership in KJZ partnership would Courtney report for the current year?

Answer: $9,200, consisting of $8,000 of business income ($20,000 × 40%) and $1,200 of interest income ($3,000 × 40%). Courtney would not include the $1,000 distribution in her gross income because it was a return of her investment.

Alimony When couples legally separate or divorce, one spouse may be required to provide financial support to the other in the form of **alimony.** The tax law defines alimony as (1) a transfer of *cash* made under a written separation agreement or divorce decree, (2) the separation or divorce decree does not designate the payment as something

[16]The deduction of losses from partnerships and S corporations are subject to several limitations that we discuss in Chapter 7.

[17]See Forms 1065 and 1120S on the IRS website, www.IRS.gov.

other than alimony, (3) in the case of legally separated (or divorced) taxpayers under a separation or divorce decree, the spouses do not live together when the payment is made, and (4) the payments cannot continue after the death of the recipient.[18]

For tax purposes, a transfer between former spouses represents alimony only if it meets this definition. If the payment is alimony, then the amount of the payment is included in the gross income of the person receiving it and is deductible *for* AGI by the person paying it. Thus, alimony shifts income from one spouse to the other.

Example 5-14

In addition to paying child support, under the divorce decree Al is required to pay Courtney $20,000 cash each year until she dies. The decree does not designate the payment as a payment for something other than alimony, and Al and Courtney do not live together. Does this payment qualify as alimony?

Answer: Yes. These payments qualify as alimony for tax purposes because they are (1) cash payments made under a divorce decree, (2) the payments are not designated as something other than alimony, (3) Al and Courtney do not live together, and (4) the payments cease on Courtney's death. In the current year, Al made a $20,000 alimony payment to Courtney. Courtney includes all $20,000 in her gross income. To ensure that the income is taxed only once, Al is allowed to deduct the entire payment as a deduction *for* AGI.

There may be other types of payments that *do not qualify as alimony*. These include (1) property divisions (e.g., who gets the car, house, or china?) and (2) child support payments fixed by the divorce or separation agreement.[19] In any event, if a transfer of property between spouses does *not* meet the definition of alimony, the *recipient* of the transfer *excludes* the value of the transfer from income, and the person transferring the property is not allowed to deduct the value of the property transferred.

Example 5-15

As required by the divorce decree, Al made $10,000 in child support payments during the year to Courtney to help her support Deron. Al is required to make child support payments until Deron is 18 years old. Is the current-year payment considered alimony?

Answer: No. The $10,000 of child support payments are not income to Courtney. The payments are not alimony because the divorce decree specifies that the payments are for child support. Consequently, Courtney does not include these payments in gross income, and Al does not deduct them.

The objective definition of alimony eliminates uncertainty regarding which transfers are treated as alimony. However, it creates a second problem. Since the purpose of the transfer is irrelevant to the tax consequences, it is possible to use alimony transfers to assign income from the (higher tax rate) payer of the alimony to the (lower tax rate) recipient. For example, instead of transferring ownership of an asset to the recipient as a nondeductible/nontaxable property settlement, the payer could claim an alimony deduction by making a transfer that meets the alimony requirements. The spouses can share the tax savings from this transaction if they can agree on structuring the payments to qualify as alimony (although cooperations may be a little difficult for a couple going through a divorce). To address this tax-avoidance opportunity, Congress enacted a complex set of restrictions called the *anti-front loading* rules that make it difficult for taxpayers to disguise property payments as alimony payments. In general terms, when taxpayers attempt to disguise property payments as alimony payments (large alimony payments shortly after the divorce, followed by smaller alimony payments in

[18]§71(b). In addition, certain payments to third parties on behalf of the spouse, such as mortgage payments, can also qualify as payments in cash.

[19]§71(c). A payment that is not specifically designated as child support may nonetheless be treated as child support if the payment is reduced on the happening of a specific contingency related to the child. For example, a payment that ceases once a child reaches the age of 18 would be treated as child support.

subsequent years), the tax laws may require the taxpayers to recharacterize (or "recapture") part of the alimony payments as nondeductible property transfers.[20]

Example 5-16

As part of the divorce agreement, Al transferred his interest in their joint residence to Courtney. The couple did not have any outstanding debt on the home. At the time of the divorce, the home was valued at $500,000 and Al's share was valued at $250,000. What are the tax consequences of the home ownership transfer to Courtney?

Answer: Because the transfer is not a cash transfer, it does not qualify as alimony. Consequently, Courtney does not recognize the $250,000 as income, and Al is not allowed to deduct the $250,000 transfer.

What if: Assume that Al's marginal tax rate is 35 percent and Courtney's marginal tax rate is 15 percent. To generate tax savings, in lieu of transferring his share of the ownership in the home, Al and Courtney agreed that Al would make a $250,000 cash transfer to Courtney. The divorce agreement stipulated that this payment was alimony. What are Al and Courtney trying to accomplish under this arrangement? Will they be successful?

Answer: They are trying to convert a property payment into alimony that is deductible by Al (at a high tax rate) and includible in Courtney's income (at a lower tax rate). As we discussed above, under a complex set of alimony recapture rules, it is likely that a portion of this payment will be treated as a nonalimony property settlement.

Prizes, Awards, and Gambling Winnings Prizes, awards, and gambling winnings, such as raffle or sweepstake prizes or lottery winnings, are included in gross income.

Example 5-17

After devoting much of her free time during the year to filling out sweepstakes entries, Gram hit the jackpot. She won a WaveRunner worth $7,500 in a sweepstakes sponsored by *Reader's Digest*. How much of the prize, if any, must Gram include in her gross income?

Answer: Gram must include the full $7,500 value of the WaveRunner in her gross income. Note that because she must pay taxes on the winnings, she's not really getting the WaveRunner for "free."

There are two specific, narrowly defined exceptions to this rule. First, awards for scientific, literary, or charitable achievement such as the Nobel Prize are excluded from gross income, *but only if* (1) the recipient was selected without any action on his part to enter the contest or proceeding, (2) the recipient is not required to render substantial future services as a condition to receive the prize or award, and (3) the payor of the prize or award transfers the prize or award to a federal, state, or local governmental unit or qualified charity such as a church, school, or charitable organization designated by the taxpayer.[21] The obvious downside of this exception is that the award recipient does not actually get to receive or keep the cash from the award. However, for tax purposes it is more beneficial for the recipient to exclude the award from income entirely by immediately transferring it to a charitable organization than it is to receive the award, recognize the income, and then contribute funds to a charity for a charitable deduction. Designating the award for payment to a federal, state, or local governmental unit or qualified charity has the same effect as claiming the transfer as a deduction *for* AGI. However, by receiving the award, recognizing the income, and then contributing funds to a charity, the taxpayer is deducting the donation as a deduction *from* AGI. As we discussed in Chapter 4, deductions *for* AGI are likely more advantageous than deductions *from* AGI.

[20]These rules apply when alimony decreases by more than $15,000 between years 1 and 3 after the divorce. See §71(f) for details.

[21]§74(b).

The second exception is for employee *awards for length of service or safety achievement.*[22] These nontaxable awards are limited to $400 of tangible property *other than cash* per employee per year.[23] The award is not excluded from the employee's income if circumstances suggest it is disguised compensation.[24]

TAXES IN THE REAL WORLD You Get a Car! And You Get a Car!

Remember when Oprah gave out cars like other people give out refrigerator magnets and foam cup holders?. Audience members were thrilled with her generosity—until they realized that they had to pay income tax on their newfound luck. That's because there's literally no such thing as a free lunch—unless that lunch is served up with a heap of exceptions that make the IRS happy.

So in her last go-round, Oprah had her ducks in a row. When she gave her entire audience an all-expense-paid trip to Australia in honor of her 25th and final season, she really meant *all* expenses. Including taxes. A CPA was said to be waiting in the wings to settle all of the tax issues associated with the trip. Reportedly, Oprah took care of paying the taxes associated with the fabulous prize.

Source: Kelly Phillips Erb, "The Oprah of Oz," *TaxGirl .com,* September 18, 2010.

Taxpayers must include the *gross* amount of their gambling winnings for the year in gross income.[25] Taxpayers are allowed to deduct their gambling losses to the extent of their gambling winnings, but the losses are usually deductible as miscellaneous itemized deductions.[26] For professional gamblers, however, the losses are deductible (to the extent of gambling winnings) *for* AGI.

ETHICS

While vacationing you find a $100 bill on the beach. Nobody saw you find it. Assuming the find meets the definition of gross income, would you report it as taxable income? Why or why not? Would your answer differ if you found $100,000 instead of $100?

Social Security Benefits Over the last 30 years, the taxation of Social Security benefits has changed considerably. Thirty years ago, Social Security benefits were completely excluded from income. Today, taxpayers may be required to include *up to* 85 percent of the benefits in gross income *depending* on the amount of the taxpayer's filing status, Social Security benefits, and *modified* AGI.[27] Modified AGI is regular AGI (excluding Social Security benefits) plus tax-exempt interest income, excluded foreign income (discussed later in the chapter), and certain other deductions *for* AGI.[28] The calculation of the amount of Social Security benefits to be included in income is depicted on the IRS worksheet in the appendix at the end of this chapter.[29]

[22]Prizes or awards from an employer-sponsored contest are fully taxable.

[23]§74(c).

[24]The $400 limit is increased to $1,600 for qualified award plans (written plans that do not discriminate in favor of highly compensated employees). However, the *average* cost of all qualified plan awards from an employer is limited to $400. Managers, administrators, clerical employees, or professional employees are not eligible for an exclusion for a safety award.

[25]Subject to de minimis rules, payers of gambling winnings report winnings to recipients and the IRS on Form W-2G.

[26]See Rev. Rul. 83-130, 1983-2 CB 148.

[27]§86(d) applies to monthly benefits under title II of the Social Security Act and tier 1 railroad retirement benefits. The Social Security Administration reports Social Security benefits on Form SSA-1099.

[28]See §86(b)(2).

[29]Because the 2015 worksheet was not available at the time the book went to press, we include the 2014 worksheet in the appendix at the end of the chapter. The 2014 worksheet can be used to determine the taxable portion of Social Security benefits received in 2015.

The calculation is complex, to say the least. However, the taxability of Social Security benefits can be summarized as follows:

Single taxpayers:

1. If modified AGI + 50 percent of Social Security benefits ≤ $25,000, Social Security benefits are not taxable.
2. If $25,000 < modified AGI + 50 percent of Social Security benefits ≤ $34,000, taxable Social Security benefits are the lesser of (a) 50 percent of the Social Security benefits or (b) 50 percent of (modified AGI + 50 percent of Social Security benefits − $25,000).
3. If modified AGI + 50 percent of Social Security benefits > $34,000, taxable Social Security benefits are the lesser of (a) 85 percent of Social Security benefits or (b) 85 percent of (modified AGI + 50 percent of Social Security benefits − $34,000), plus the lesser of (1) $4,500 or (2) 50 percent of Social Security benefits.

Taxpayers filing married separate:

Taxable Social Security benefits are the lesser of (a) 85 percent of the Social Security benefits or (b) 85 percent of the taxpayer's modified AGI + 50 percent of Social Security benefits.

Taxpayers filing married joint:

1. If modified AGI + 50 percent of Social Security benefits ≤ $32,000, Social Security benefits are not taxable.
2. If $32,000 < modified AGI + 50 percent of Social Security benefits ≤ $44,000, taxable Social Security benefits are the lesser of (a) 50 percent of the Social Security benefits or (b) 50 percent of (modified AGI + 50 percent of Social Security benefits − $32,000).
3. If modified AGI + 50 percent of Social Security benefits > $44,000, taxable Social Security benefits are the lesser of (a) 85 percent of Social Security benefits or (b) 85 percent of (modified AGI + 50 percent of Social Security benefits − $44,000), plus the lesser of (1) $6,000 or (2) 50 percent of Social Security benefits.

The implications of the above calculations are that the Social Security benefits of taxpayers with relatively low taxable income are not taxable and that 85 percent of the Social Security benefits of taxpayers with moderate to high taxable income is taxable.

Example 5-18

Gram received $7,200 of Social Security benefits this year. Suppose that Gram's modified AGI is $16,000. What amount of the Social Security benefits must Gram include in her gross income?

Answer: $0. Gram's modified AGI plus one-half of her Social Security benefits is $19,600, which is below $25,000. Hence, Gram may *exclude* the entire $7,200 of Social Security income from gross income.

What if: Assume that Gram received $7,200 of Social Security benefits this year and that her modified AGI is $50,000. What amount of benefits must Gram include in her gross income?

Answer: $6,120 ($7,200 × 85%).

What if: Assume that Gram received $7,200 of Social Security benefits this year and that her modified AGI is $26,400. What amount of benefits must Gram include in her gross income?

Answer: $2,500. Gram is single and her modified AGI + 50 percent of Social Security benefits falls between $25,000 and $34,000. Her taxable Social Security benefits are the lesser of (a) 50 percent of the Social Security benefits ($7,200 × 50% = $3,600) or (b) 50 percent of [$26,400 modified AGI + $3,600 (50 percent of Social Security benefits) − $25,000] = $2,500. Thus, her taxable Social Security benefits are $2,500.

What if: Assume that Gram received $7,200 of Social Security benefits this year and that her modified AGI is $31,400. What amount of benefits must Gram include in her gross income?

Answer: $4,450. Gram is single and her modified AGI + 50 percent of Social Security benefits exceeds $34,000. Her taxable Social Security benefits are the lesser of (a) 85 percent of Social Security benefits ($7,200 × 85% = $6,120) or (b) 85 percent of [$31,400 modified AGI + $3,600 (50 percent of Social Security benefits) − $34,000] = $850, plus the lesser of (1) $4,500 or (2) 50 percent of Social Security benefits (50% × $7,200 = $3,600). This calculation simplifies to the lesser of (a) $6,120 or (b) $4,450 ($850 + lesser of (1) $4,500 or (2) $3,600). Thus, Gram's taxable Social Security benefits are $4,450.

Imputed Income Besides realizing *direct* economic benefits like wages and interest, taxpayers sometimes realize *indirect* economic benefits that they must include in gross income as **imputed income.** Bargain purchases (such as an employer selling a good to an employee at a discount) and below-market loans (such as an employer lending an employee money at a zero or unusually low interest rate) are two common examples of taxable indirect economic benefits. Both bargain purchases and below-market loans generally result in gross income if the purchase or loan transaction takes place between related parties (such as an employer and employee, owner and entity, or transactions among family members). For bargain purchases, the general rule is that the discount received on the purchase from a related party is taxable, but the tax consequences vary based on the relationship of the parties. For example, a bargain purchase by an employee from an employer results in taxable compensation income to the employee, a bargain purchase by a shareholder from a corporation results in a taxable dividend to the shareholder, and a bargain purchase between family members is deemed to be a gift from one family member to the other (as discussed later in the chapter, gifts are nontaxable for income tax purposes but potentially subject to gift tax to be paid by the person making the gift).

Although the general rule is that bargain purchases by an employee from an employer creates taxable compensation income to the employee, the tax law does provide a limited exclusion for employee bargain purchases. Specifically, employees may exclude (a) a discount on employer-provided goods as long as the discount does not exceed the employer's gross profit percentage on all property offered to sale to customers and (b) up to 20 percent employer-provided discount on services. Discounts in excess of these amounts are taxable as compensation.[30]

Example 5-19

As part of her compensation package, EWD agreed to provide Courtney with EWD architectural design services (to create more space for Gram) at a substantial discount. EWD provided Courtney with services valued at $35,000 but charged her only $22,000 for the services. How much of the discount must Courtney include in gross income?

Answer: $6,000, computed as follows:

Description	Amount	Explanation
(1) Value of services EWD provided to Courtney	$35,000	
(2) Courtney's cost of the services	22,000	
(3) Discount on services	$13,000	(1) − (2).
(4) Excludable discount	7,000	(1) × 20%.
Discount in excess of 20% is included in gross income	**$ 6,000**	(3) − (4).

For below-market loans, the indirect economic benefit conveyed to the borrower (such as an employee, shareholder, or family member) is a function of the amount of the loan and the difference in the market interest rate and the rate actually charged by the lender (such as an employer, corporation, or family member). To eliminate

[30]§132(a)(2).

any tax advantages of below-market loans, the tax law generally requires the lender and borrower to treat the transaction as if

1. The borrower paid the lender the difference between the applicable federal interest rate (compounded semiannually) and the actual interest paid (this difference is called *imputed interest*).
2. The lender then returned the imputed interest to the borrower.

The deemed "payment" of the imputed interest in these transactions is treated as interest income to the lender and interest expense to the borrower. The deductibility of the interest expense for the borrower depends on how she used the loan proceeds (for business, investment, or personal purposes). As we learn in the next chapter, business interest expense is a deduction *for* AGI, investment interest expense is an itemized deduction subject to limitations, and personal interest is generally not deductible. The tax consequences of the "return" of the imputed interest from the lender to the borrower vary based on the relationship of the parties (similar to a bargain purchase). For example, the return of the imputed interest from an employer lender to an employee borrower is treated by both parties as taxable compensation paid to the employee, the return of the imputed interest from a corporation to a shareholder is considered a dividend, and a return of imputed interest by a family member to another family member is considered a gift. The imputed interest rules generally do not apply to aggregate loans of $10,000 or less between the lender and borrower [§7872(c)].[31]

Example 5-20

At the beginning of January, EWD provides Courtney with a $100,000 zero-interest loan. Assume that the applicable federal interest rate (compounded semiannually) is 4 percent. Courtney used the loan proceeds to acquire several personal-use assets (an automobile and other items). What amount is Courtney required to include in gross income in the current year?

Answer: $4,000, computed as follows:

Description	Amount	Explanation
(1) Loan principal	$100,000	
(2) Applicable federal interest rate compounded semiannually	4%	
(3) Interest on loan principal at federal rate	$ 4,000	(1) × (2).
(4) Interest paid by Courtney	0	
Imputed interest included in Courtney's gross income	**$ 4,000**	(3) − (4).

Courtney will also incur an imputed interest expense of $4,000 for the year, and EWD will also (a) deduct $4,000 of compensation expense and (b) report $4,000 of interest income. In this example, we assume Courtney used the proceeds for personal purposes so she is not allowed to deduct the interest expense.

What if: Assume the same facts except that EWD had loaned Courtney $10,000 at a zero-interest rate. How much imputed interest income would Courtney be required to include in her gross income for the year?

Answer: $0. The imputed interest rules don't apply because the loan did not exceed $10,000.

THE KEY FACTS

Other Sources of Income

- Alimony is taxable to recipient when paid in cash, pursuant to written agreement or decree, the spouses do not live together, and the payment is contingent on life of the recipient.
- Awards are included in gross income unless they meet one of two narrowly defined exceptions.
- A maximum of 85 percent of Social Security benefits are included in gross income depending on level of AGI.
- Discharge of debt is included in gross income unless taxpayer is insolvent before and after forgiveness.

Discharge of Indebtedness In general, when a taxpayer's debt is forgiven by a lender (the debt is discharged), the taxpayer must include the amount of debt relief in gross income.[32]

[31]For "gift" loans (loans between family members), the $10,000 de minimis exception is not available for loan proceeds used to purchase or carry income-producing assets. Likewise, the $10,000 de minimis exception is not available for compensation-related loans or corporate-shareholder loans where the principal purpose of the loans is to avoid federal tax. For gift loans of $100,000 or less, the imputed interest is limited to the borrower's net investment income (investment income, such as interest income or other investment income not taxed at preferential rates, less related investment expenses). If the borrower's net investment income is $1,000 or less, the imputed interest rules do not apply. §7872(d). The exception for gift loans of $100,000 or less is not available for loans where the principal purpose of the loans is to avoid federal tax.

[32]§61(a)(12). Income from discharge of indebtedness is also realized when debt is forgiven by lenders other than employers such as banks and credit card companies.

Example 5-21

In the previous example, Courtney borrowed $100,000 from EWD. Because EWD wants to keep Courtney as an employee, it agreed to forgive $10,000 of loan principal at the end of each year that Courtney stays on board. On December 31 of this year, EWD formally cancels $10,000 of Courtney's indebtedness. How much of this debt relief is Courtney required to include in gross income?

Answer: All $10,000 is included in Courtney's gross income.

To provide tax relief for insolvent taxpayers—taxpayers with liabilities, including tax liabilities, exceeding their assets—a **discharge of indebtedness** is *not* taxable if the taxpayer is insolvent before *and* after the debt forgiveness.[33] If the discharge of indebtedness makes the taxpayer solvent, the taxpayer recognizes gross income to the extent of his solvency.[34] For example, if a taxpayer is discharged of $30,000 of debt and this causes him to be solvent by $10,000 (after the debt relief, the taxpayer's assets exceed his liabilities by $10,000), the taxpayer must include $10,000 in gross income.[35]

EXCLUSION PROVISIONS

LO 5-3

So far in this chapter, we've discussed various types of income taxpayers must realize and recognize by reporting it on their tax returns in the current year. However, there are specific types of income that taxpayers realize but are allowed to permanently *exclude* from gross income or temporarily defer from gross income until a subsequent period. As we discussed in the previous chapter, *exclusions* and *deferrals* are the result of *specific congressional action* and are *narrowly defined*. Because taxpayers are not required to recognize income that is excluded or deferred, we refer to tax laws allowing exclusions or deferrals as **nonrecognition provisions.** Nonrecognition provisions result from various policy objectives. In very general terms, Congress allows most exclusions and deferrals for two primary reasons: (1) to subsidize or encourage particular activities or (2) to be fair to taxpayers (such as mitigating the inequity of double taxation). Our discussion in this chapter focuses on exclusions.

Common Exclusions

Because exclusion provisions allow taxpayers to permanently remove certain income items from their tax base, they are particularly taxpayer friendly. We begin by introducing three common exclusion provisions, the exclusions of municipal interest, gain on the sale of a personal residence, and fringe benefits. We continue with a survey of other exclusion provisions based on their underlying purpose: education, double taxation, and sickness and injury.[36]

Municipal Interest The most common example of an exclusion provision is the exclusion of interest on **municipal bonds.** Municipal bonds include bonds issued by state and local governments located in the United States, and this exclusion is generally recognized as a subsidy to state and local governments (the exclusion allows state and local governments to offer bonds at a lower before-tax interest rate). In

[33]§108(a)(1)(B).

[34]§108(a)(3).

[35]Other circumstances in which taxpayers may exclude a discharge of indebtedness are beyond the scope of this chapter. See §108(f)(2) for discussion of the limited exclusion of student loan forgiveness for loans requiring students to work for a specified time in certain professions. See §108(a)(1)(E) for discussion of the exclusion of up to $2,000,000 of home mortgage forgiveness from 2007 through 2014. See §108(i) for a discussion for the deferral of debt forgiveness income for businesses reacquiring debt at a discounted price in 2009 and 2010. This provision allows taxpayer to recognize the debt forgiveness income ratably over the five-year period 2014 through 2018.

[36]Another common exclusion we discuss in detail in Chapter 13 is the exclusion of earnings on "Roth" retirement savings accounts.

contrast, interest on U.S. government obligations (such as Treasury bills) is taxable for federal tax purposes but is tax-exempt for state and local tax purposes.

Example 5-22

Courtney holds a $10,000 City of Cincinnati municipal bond. The bond pays 5 percent interest annually. Courtney acquired the bond a few years ago. The city used the proceeds from the bond issuance to help pay for renovations on a major league baseball stadium. In late December, Courtney received $500 of interest income from the bond for the year. How much of the $500 interest from the municipal bond may Courtney *exclude* from her gross income?

Answer: All $500 because the interest is from a municipal bond.

Gains on the Sale of Personal Residence The tax law provides several provisions that encourage or subsidize home ownership, and the exclusion of the gain on the sale of a personal residence is a common example of one such provision. Specifically, taxpayers meeting certain home ownership *and* use requirements can permanently exclude up to $250,000 ($500,000 if married filing jointly) of realized gain on the sale of their principal residence.[37] Gain in excess of the excludable amount generally qualifies as long-term capital gain subject to tax at preferential rates. To satisfy the ownership test, the taxpayer must have owned the residence (house, condominium, trailer, or houseboat) for a total of two or more years during the five-year period ending on the date of the sale. To satisfy the use test, the taxpayer must have *used* the property as her principal residence for a total of two or more years (noncontiguous use is permissible) during the five-year period ending on the date of the sale. The tax law limits each taxpayer to one exclusion every two years. Married couples filing joint returns are eligible for the full $500,000 exclusion if *either* spouse meets the ownership test and *both* spouses meet the principal-use test. However, if *either* spouse is ineligible for the exclusion because he or she personally used the $250,000 exclusion on another home sale during the two years before the date of the current sale, the couple's available exclusion is reduced to $250,000.[38]

Example 5-23

What if: Assume that in October of this year, Courtney sold her prior home in Cincinnati. Courtney and her ex-husband purchased the home four years ago for $400,000, and Courtney received the house in the divorce. Courtney lived in the home until she moved to Kansas City in January. Courtney sold the home for $550,000. How much taxable gain does she recognize on the sale of the home?

Answer: $0. Because Courtney satisfies the two-year ownership and two-year use test, she may exclude up to $250,000 of gain from the sale of her home. Thus, Courtney may exclude the entire $150,000 gain that she realized on the sale ($550,000 sales price less $400,000 basis).

What if: Assume the same facts except Courtney sold the home for $700,000. How much taxable gain does she recognize on the sale of the home?

Answer: $50,000. Because Courtney satisfies the two-year ownership and two-year use test, she may exclude $250,000 of the $300,000 gain from the sale of her home ($700,000 sales price less $400,000 basis). Thus, Courtney recognizes a $50,000 taxable gain on the sale.

[37]§121.

[38]We discuss the rules for sale of principal residence in more detail in Chapter 14, including relief rules for taxpayers who cannot meet the ownership and use test due to unusual or hardship circumstances and the limitation on the gain exclusion for taxpayers using a home for something other than a principal residence for a period (nonqualified *use*) before using the home as a principal residence.

Fringe Benefits In addition to paying salary and wages, many employers provide employees with **fringe benefits.** For example, an employer may provide an employee with an automobile to use for personal purposes, pay for an employee to join a health club, or pay for an employee's home security. In general, the value of these benefits is *included* in the employee's gross income as compensation for services. However, certain fringe benefits, called "qualifying" fringe benefits, are excluded from gross income.[39] Exhibit 5-3 lists some of the most common fringe benefits that are excluded from an employee's gross income. In addition to excluded fringe benefits, many employers make contributions to retirement plans on behalf of their employees. Subject to specific rules that we discuss in Chapter 13, these contributions (as well as employee contributions from salary) are not currently included in the employee's gross income but are deferred until the employee withdraws the contributions and related earnings from the plan. We discuss fringe benefits in more depth in Chapter 12.

Example 5-24

EWD paid $6,000 this year for Courtney's health insurance premiums and $150 in premiums for her $40,000 group-term life insurance policy. How much of the $6,150 in benefits can Courtney exclude from her gross income?

Answer: Courtney can exclude all $6,150 in benefits from her gross income. All health insurance premiums paid by an employer on an employee's behalf are excluded from the employee's income. In addition, premiums employers pay on an employee's behalf for group-term life insurance (up to $50,000 of coverage) are also excluded from the employee's gross income.

Example 5-25

In December, Courtney mailed a newsletter to several dozen friends and relatives with a recent picture of her son, daughter, and grandmother. Courtney printed both the newsletter and the photos on printers at work (with permission of EWD). Courtney would have paid $55 for the duplicate newsletters and photos at a nearby copy center. How much of this $55 benefit that Courtney received from EWD may Courtney *exclude* from her gross income?

Answer: All $55 is excluded. The $55 benefit is considered a nontaxable de minimis fringe benefit because it is small in amount and infrequent.

TAXES IN THE REAL WORLD Have Phone, Will Call Tax-Free

In years past, the IRS classified employee cell phones issued by employers as a taxable benefit (i.e., taxable compensation), and required employees to keep detailed records to substantiate business versus personal use of the phone. As you might expect, the classification and record-keeping requirements were not met with great enthusiasm. In 2011, the IRS reversed its course and now considers an employer-issued cell phone as an excludible fringe benefit (both the business and personal use) when the phone is provided primarily for noncompensatory business reasons. Even better, the IRS no longer requires record-keeping to receive the tax-free treatment. See Notice 2011-72.

[39]Most nontaxable fringe benefits are listed with "items specifically excluded from gross income" in §§101-140 of the Internal Revenue Code. Employers are generally prohibited from discriminating among employees with respect to nontaxable fringe benefits (i.e., they cannot offer them only to executives).

EXHIBIT 5-3 Common Qualifying Fringe Benefits (excluded from employee's gross income)

Item	Description
Medical and dental health insurance coverage (§106)	An employee may exclude from income the cost of medical and insurance coverage and dental health insurance premiums the employer pays on an employee's behalf.[40]
Life insurance coverage (§79)	Employees may exclude from income the value of life insurance premiums the employer pays on an employee's behalf for up to $50,000 of group-term life insurance.
De minimis (small) benefits (§132(a)(4))	As a matter of administrative convenience, Congress allows employees to exclude from income relatively small and infrequent benefits employees receive at work (such as limited use of a business copy machine).
Meals and lodging for the employer's provided convenience (§119)	Employees may exclude employer-provided meals and lodging if they (1) are provided on the employer's business premises to the employee (and spouse and dependents); (2) are provided for the employer's convenience (such as allowing the employee to be on-call 24 hours a day or continue working on-site over lunch); and (3) for lodging only, the employee must accept the lodging as a condition of employment.
Employee educational assistance programs (§127)	Employees may exclude up to $5,250 of employer-provided educational assistance benefits covering tuition, books, and fees for any instruction that improves the taxpayer's capabilities, whether or not job-related or part of a degree program.
No additional cost services (§132(a)(1))	Employees may exclude the value of services provided by an employer that generate no substantial costs to the employer (such as free flight benefits for airline employees on a space-available basis or free hotel service for hotel employees).
Qualified employee discounts (§132(a)(2))	Employees may exclude (a) a discount on employer-provided goods as long as the discount does not exceed the employer's gross profit percentage on all property offered to sale to customers and (b) up to 20 percent employer-provided discount on services. Discounts in excess of these amounts are taxable as compensation. See Example 5-19.
Dependent care benefits (§129)	Employees may exclude up to $5,000 for benefits paid or reimbursed by employers for caring for children under age 13 or dependents or spouses who are physically or mentally unable to care for themselves.
Working condition fringe benefits (§132(a)(3))	Employees may exclude from income any benefit or reimbursement of a benefit provided by an employer that would be deductible as an ordinary and necessary expense by the employee if the employee had paid the expense.
Qualified transportation benefits (§132(a)(5))	Employees may exclude up to $250 per month of employer-provided parking and up to $130 per month of the combined value of employer-provided mass transit passes and the value of a car pool vehicle for employee use.[41]
Qualified moving expenses (§132(a)(6))	Employees may exclude employer reimbursement for qualified moving expenses (cost of moving household items and costs of travel, including lodging, to a new home for employee and dependents) that would otherwise be deductible by the employee. We discuss deductible moving expenses in Chapter 6.
Cafeteria plans (§125)	A plan where employees choose among various nontaxable fringe benefits (such as health insurance and dental insurance) or cash. Tax-free to the extent the taxpayer chooses nontaxable fringe benefits; taxable to the extent the employee receives cash.
Flexible Spending Accounts (§125)	Allow employees to set a portion of their before-tax salary for payment of either health and/or dependent-care benefits. Amounts set aside must be used by the end of the year or within the first two and a half months of the next plan year, or employees forfeit the unused balance. In lieu of the two and a half month grace period each year for health-care flexible spending accounts, employers instead can allow employees to carry over up to $500 of unused amounts to be used anytime during the next year (i.e., it is the employer's choice). This option does not apply to dependent-care flexible spending accounts. For 2015, the amount of before-tax salary that an employee may set aside for medical expenses is limited to $2,550 and for dependent-care expenses is limited to $5,000.

[40]The cost of medical coverage paid by an employer and offered through a health insurance exchange is not an excludible benefit unless the employer is a small employer that elects to make all of its full-time employees eligible for plans offered through the small business health options program (SHOP). For this purpose, a small employer is an employer that employed an average of at least one but 100 or fewer employees during business days in the prior year, and employs at least one employee on the first day of the plan year. In 2015, SHOP is open to employers with 50 or fewer full-time equivalent employees. Beginning in 2016, all SHOPs will be open to employers with up to 100 full-time equivalent employees.

[41]In 2014, employees may exclude up to $250 per month of the combined value of employer-provided mass transit passes and the value of a car pool vehicle for employee use. At press time, this exclusion was scheduled to be reduced to $130 per month in 2015.

Education-Related Exclusions

As an incentive for taxpayers to participate in higher education (education beyond high school), Congress excludes certain types of income if the funds are used for higher education. In the following paragraphs, we discuss exclusions for scholarships and exclusions for certain types of investment plans used to save for college.[42]

Scholarships College students seeking a degree can exclude from gross income scholarships (including Pell grants) that pay for tuition, fees, books, supplies, and other equipment *required* for the student's courses.[43] Any excess scholarship amounts (such as for room or meals) are fully taxable. The scholarship exclusion applies only if the recipient is *not* required to perform services in exchange for receiving the scholarship. "Scholarships" that represent compensation for past, current, or future services are fully taxable. However, tuition waivers or reductions provided by an educational institution for undergraduate courses for student employees or for graduate courses for teaching or research assistants are not taxable.

What about athletic scholarships? Good question. The IRS has ruled that the value of athletic scholarships—which may not exceed expenses for tuition, fees, room, board, and necessary supplies; are awarded to students by a university that *expects* but *does not require* the students to participate in a particular sport; require no particular activity in lieu of participation; and are not cancelled if the student cannot participate—is excludable from gross income.[44]

Example 5-26

Ellen, Courtney's daughter, received a $700 scholarship from the University of Missouri–Kansas City that pays $400 of her tuition and provides $300 cash for books. Ellen spent $350 on books. How much of the scholarship may she exclude from gross income?

Answer: All $700 is excluded. Ellen may exclude all of the scholarship for tuition and she may exclude the $300 cash she received for books because she spent all $300 purchasing her books for school.

What if: How much is Ellen allowed to exclude if she spent only $250 on books?

Answer: $650 is excluded. Ellen excludes all of the scholarship for her tuition and $250 of the $300 in cash payments because she spent $250 on books. She must include the excess cash payment of $50 ($300 − $250) in her gross income.

THE KEY FACTS

Education Exclusions

- Students seeking a college degree can exclude scholarships that pay for required tuition, fees, books, and supplies.
- Taxpayers can elect to exclude interest earned on Series EE savings bonds when the redemption proceeds are used to pay qualified higher education expenses.
- The exclusion of interest on Series EE savings bonds is restricted to taxpayers with modified AGI below specific limits.

Other Educational Subsidies Taxpayers are allowed to exclude from gross income earnings on investments in qualified education plans such as 529 plans and Coverdell education savings accounts as long as they use the earnings to pay for qualifying educational expenditures.

529 plans allow parents, grandparents, and other individuals to contribute up to the maximum allowed by state-sponsored 529 plans to fund the qualified educational costs of future *college* students.[45] Earnings in 529 plans are distributed tax-free provided they are used for qualified *higher* education expenses. If, on the other hand, distributions are made to the beneficiary for other purposes, investment returns are taxed to the beneficiary at the beneficiary's tax rate and are subject to an additional 10 percent penalty while distributions to the beneficiary in excess of investment

[42]A detailed explanation is available in IRS Publication 970 *Tax Benefits for Education* available on the IRS website at www.IRS.gov.

[43]§117(b)(2).

[44]Rev. Rul. 77-263, 1977-2 CB 47.

[45]Contribution limits vary according to the state administering the 529 plan. In addition, more than half the states offer a state tax deduction or credit to residents contributing to the 529 plan sponsored by the state in which the contributors reside.

returns are treated as gifts.[46] Distributions to contributors (e.g., parents, grandparents) in excess of their contributions are included in contributors' gross income and are also subject to the 10 percent penalty.

With a Coverdell account, yearly contributions to the account are limited to $2,000 for each beneficiary, and distributions may be used to pay for qualified educational costs of kindergarten through 12th grade and qualified higher education expenses such as tuition, books, fees, supplies, and reasonable room and board.[47] The $2,000 contribution limit for Coverdell accounts phases out as AGI (modified to include certain types of excluded foreign income) increases from $190,000 to $220,000 for married filing jointly taxpayers, and from $95,000 to $110,000 for all other taxpayers.

U.S. Series EE bonds The federal government issues bonds that allow taxpayers to acquire the bonds at a discount and redeem the bonds for a fixed amount over stated time intervals. These bonds don't generate any cash in the form of interest until the taxpayer redeems the bond. At redemption, the amount of the redemption price in excess of the acquisition price is interest included in gross income.[48] U.S. Series EE bonds fall into this category. However, an exclusion is available for interest from Series EE bonds. This exclusion requires that the redemption proceeds be used to pay for higher education expenses of the taxpayer, the taxpayer's spouse, or a dependent of the taxpayer. Qualified higher education expenses include the tuition and fees required for enrollment or attendance at an eligible educational institution. Taxpayers may also exclude the interest income if they contribute the proceeds to a qualified tuition program.

The exclusion is partially reduced or eliminated for taxpayers exceeding a fixed level of modified adjusted gross income (adjusted gross income before the educational savings bond exclusion, the foreign earned income exclusion, and certain other deductions).[49] If the taxpayer's modified AGI exceeds the thresholds in the redemption year, the exclusion is phased out (gradually reduced) until all of the interest from the bonds is taxed.[50]

Exclusions That Mitigate Double Taxation

Congress provides certain exclusions that eliminate the potential double tax that may arise for gifts, inheritances, and life insurance proceeds.

Gifts and Inheritances Individuals may transfer property to other taxpayers without receiving or expecting to receive value in return. If the *transferor* is alive at the time of the transfer, the property transfer is called a **gift.** If the property is transferred from the decedent's estate (*transferor* is deceased), it is called an **inheritance.** These transfers are generally subject to a federal transfer tax, *not* the income tax. Gifts are typically subject to the federal gift tax and inheritances are typically subject to a federal estate tax.[51] Thus, gift and estate taxes are imposed on *transfer* of the

[46]Under §529(c)(3), multiple distributions received under these circumstances are treated as annuities. As a result, a portion of each distribution would be treated as a gift with the remainder treated as income.

[47]§530(b). This definition of qualified higher education expenses is consistent with the definition used in §221(d)(2) to determine if interest paid on education-related loans is deductible (see Chapter 6).

[48]Alternatively, taxpayers can elect to include the annual increase in the redemption value in gross income rather than waiting to recognize all the income on redemption. See §454(a).

[49]§135(c)(4).

[50]In 2015, the phase-out range begins at $115,750 of modified adjusted gross income for married taxpayers filing joint returns. For all other taxpayers, the phase-out range begins at $77,200.

[51]As a general rule, the federal gift tax does not apply to relatively small gifts ($14,000 or less), and the federal estate tax does not apply to transfers from relatively small estates (under $5,430,000).

property and *not included in income by the recipient.* The exclusion of gifts and inheritances from income taxation avoids the potential double taxation (transfer and income taxation) on these transfers.

Example 5-27

Ellen graduated from high school last year. As a graduation present, Gram purchased a $1,500 travel package for Ellen, so that Ellen could go on a Caribbean cruise. Last year, Ellen also received an inheritance of $2,000 from Gramps's estate. How much gross income does Ellen recognize on the $1,500 gift she received from Gram and the $2,000 inheritance she received from Gramps's estate?

Answer: $0. Ellen is allowed to exclude the entire gift and the entire amount of the inheritance from her gross income. Consequently, she does not recognize any gross income from these transactions.

Life Insurance Proceeds In some ways, life insurance proceeds are similar to inheritances. When the owner of the life insurance policy dies, the beneficiary receives the death benefit proceeds. The decedent (or the decedent's estate) is generally subject to estate taxation on the amount of the insurance proceeds. In order to avoid potential double taxation on the life insurance proceeds, the tax laws allow taxpayers receiving life insurance proceeds to exclude the proceeds from gross income.[52] However, when the insurance proceeds are paid over a period of time rather than in a lump sum, a portion of the payments represents interest and must be included in gross income. In addition, the life insurance proceeds exclusion generally does not apply when a life insurance policy is transferred to another party for valuable consideration. In this case, the eventual life insurance proceeds collected by the purchaser are excluded up to the sum of the purchase price of the policy and any subsequent premiums with remaining proceeds taxable as ordinary income.[53]

What happens if a taxpayer cashes out a policy before death? The tax treatment varies based on the specific facts. Generally, if a taxpayer simply cancels a life insurance contract and is paid the policy's cash surrender value, she would recognize ordinary income to the extent the proceeds received exceed previous premiums paid. If premiums paid exceed the proceeds received, the loss is not deductible. If, however, the taxpayer is terminally ill (medically certified with an illness expected to cause death within 24 months), early receipt of life insurance proceeds **(accelerated death benefits)** are not taxable. If a taxpayer is chronically ill (medically certified to require substantial assistance for daily living activities or due to cognitive impairment), life insurance proceeds are not taxable to the extent they are used to pay for the taxpayer's long-term care.

Example 5-28

What if: Gramps received $200,000 of accelerated death benefits from a life insurance policy last year when he was diagnosed with terminal cancer with an expected life of less than one year. How much gross income would the $200,000 payment generate?

Answer: None, because Gramps was medically certified as terminally ill with an illness expected to cause death within 24 months. *(continued on page 5-28)*

[52]§101. The exclusion does not apply if the insurance policy is sold by the owner.

[53]This exception to the exclusion does not apply if the recipient of the policy is the insured, a partner of the insured, a partnership in which the insured is a partner, or a corporation in which the insured is an officer or shareholder. This exception also does not apply to policies transferred by gift or tax-free exchange. §101(a)(2).

What if: Due to financial issues, Gramps several years ago transferred a $100,000 life insurance policy on his life to a business associate for $5,000. Since that time, the business associate continued to pay the annual premiums on the policy (totaling $20,000 before Gramps's death). Upon Gramps's death, the life insurance company paid the business associate the policy's $100,000 face value. How much of the $100,000 payment is taxable?

Answer: $75,000. Because the business associate purchased the life insurance policy from Gramps for valuable consideration, she may exclude the $100,000 proceeds up to the sum of the purchase price of the policy ($5,000) and any subsequent premiums ($20,000) with the remaining proceeds ($100,000 − $5,000 − $20,000 = $75,000) taxable as ordinary income.

THE KEY FACTS

Exclusions to Mitigate Double Taxation

- Gifts and inheritances are subject to federal transfer taxes and are, therefore, excluded from the income of the recipient.
- A maximum of $100,800 (2015) of foreign earned income can be excluded from gross income for qualifying individuals.
- To be eligible for the foreign earned income exclusion, the taxpayer must live in the foreign country for 330 days in a consecutive 12-month period.

Foreign-Earned Income U.S. citizens are subject to tax on all income whether it is generated in the United States or in foreign countries. Because most foreign countries also impose tax on income earned within their borders, U.S. citizens could be subject to both U.S. and foreign taxation on income earned abroad. To provide relief from this potential double taxation, Congress allows taxpayers to exclude foreign-earned income (income from foreign sources for personal services performed) up to an annual maximum amount. Income from pensions, annuities, salary paid by the U.S. government, or deferred compensation does not qualify for the exclusion. The maximum exclusion is indexed for inflation, and in 2015 the maximum is $100,800. Rather than claim this exclusion, taxpayers may deduct foreign taxes paid as itemized deductions or they may claim the foreign tax credit for foreign taxes paid on their foreign-earned income.[54] To determine whether claiming the annual exclusion, the deduction, or the foreign tax credit is most advantageous, taxpayers should compare the tax effects of each option. To claim the annual exclusion instead of the foreign tax deduction or credit, the taxpayer must elect to do so using Form 2555. Taxpayers who elect to use the exclusion may revoke the election for later years and use the foreign tax credit or deduct foreign taxes paid. However, once a taxpayer revokes the exclusion election, she may not reelect to use the exclusion before the sixth tax year after the tax year the revocation was made.

As you might expect, individuals must meet certain requirements to qualify for the foreign-earned income exclusion. To be eligible for the annual exclusion, a taxpayer must have her tax home in a foreign country and (1) be considered a resident of the foreign country or (2) live in the foreign country for 330 days in a consecutive 12-month period. However, because the exclusion is computed on a *daily* basis, the *maximum* exclusion is reduced pro rata for each day during the calendar year the taxpayer is not considered to be a resident of the foreign country or does not actually live in the foreign country. Taxpayers meeting the requirement for the foreign-earned income exclusion may also exclude from income reasonable housing costs (provided by an employer) that exceed 16 percent of the statutory foreign-earned income exclusion amount for the year (exceed 16 percent × $100,800 = $16,128 in 2015). The exclusion, however, is limited to a maximum of 14 percent of the statutory exclusion amount (14 percent × $100,800 = $14,112 in 2015). Thus, in 2015, if a taxpayer incurs housing costs (provided by an employer) exceeding $16,128, she may exclude such excess costs up to $14,112 (thus, the first $16,128 of employer-provided housing costs are included in gross income).[55] The housing exclusion limit is also subject to daily proration if the taxpayer is not considered a resident of the foreign country for the entire year or does not actually live in the foreign country the entire year.

[54]See §911(b)(2) and Chapters 6 and 8.

[55]§911(c).

Example 5-29

What if: Assume that Courtney is considering a transfer to EWD's overseas affiliate. If Courtney transfers, she anticipates she will earn approximately $120,000 in salary. How much of her expected $120,000 salary will Courtney be allowed to exclude from her gross income assuming she meets the residency requirements?

Answer: She is eligible to exclude $100,800 of her $120,000 of compensation from U.S. taxation in 2015. However, her entire $120,000 salary may be subject to the foreign country's income tax.

What if: Assume that Courtney decides to transfer but she expects to live in the foreign country for only 340 days in the first year. How much of her expected $120,000 salary will she be allowed to exclude from gross income?

Answer: $93,896 [$100,800 full exclusion × 340/365 (days in foreign country/days in year)].

What if: Assume that Courtney expects to live in the foreign country for 340 days in the first year and that she expects her salary to be $60,000. How much of her expected $60,000 salary will she be allowed to exclude from gross income?

Answer: All $60,000. She can exclude up to $93,896 of salary from income (see above computation).

What if: Assume that if Courtney transfers, EWD's overseas affiliate will also pay for her housing while overseas ($25,000). How much of the $25,000 housing payments may Courtney exclude?

Answer: $8,872. Since Courtney meets the requirements for the foreign-earned income exclusion, she may exclude the employer-provided housing costs that exceed $16,128 (16% × $100,800), up to a maximum exclusion of $14,112 (14% × $100,800). Thus, Courtney may exclude $8,872 (the lesser of (a) ($25,000 housing cost less $16,128 = $8,872 or (b) $14,112).

Sickness and Injury-Related Exclusions

The tax laws provide several exclusion provisions for taxpayers who are sick or injured. One explanation for these exclusions is that payments for sickness or injury are considered returns of (human) capital.

Workers' Compensation The provision for workers' compensation is relatively straightforward. Taxpayers receive workers' compensation benefits when they are unable to work because of a work-related injury. Any payments a taxpayer receives from a state-sponsored workers' compensation plan are excluded from the taxpayer's income.[56] Note that this treatment is *opposite* that of *unemployment* compensation, which is fully taxable.

Payments Associated with Personal Injury Historically, the question of which payments associated with a personal injury were excludible was controversial. In 1996 Congress settled the matter by deciding that all payments associated with compensating a taxpayer for a *physical* injury (including payments for past, current, and future lost wages) are excluded from gross income. That is, the tax laws specify that any *compensatory damages* on account of a *physical injury* or *physical sickness* are nontaxable. Thus, damages taxpayers receive for emotional distress associated with a physical injury are excluded. In contrast, *punitive damages* are *fully taxable,* because they are intended to punish the harm-doer rather than to compensate the taxpayer for injuries. Likewise, taxpayers receiving damages for emotional distress that are not associated with a physical injury must include those payments in income. In general, all other awards (those that do not relate to physical injury or sickness or are payments for the medical costs of treating emotional distress) are included in gross income.

[56]§104.

Example 5-30

In February, Courtney's cousin, Kelsey, was struck and injured by a bus while walking in a crosswalk. Because the bus driver was negligent, the bus company settled Kelsey's claim by paying her $1,500 for medical expenses and $500 for emotional distress associated with the accident. How much of the $2,000 Kelsey received from the bus company may she *exclude* from her gross income?

Answer: All $2,000. Kelsey may exclude the $1,500 she received for medical expenses and the $500 payment she received for emotional distress because these damages were associated with Kelsey's physical injury.

What if: Assume Kelsey sued the bus company and was awarded $5,000 in punitive damages. How much of the $5,000 would Kelsey be able to exclude from her gross income?

Answer: $0. Payments for punitive damages are not excludable. Kelsey would be required to include the entire $5,000 in her gross income.

THE KEY FACTS

Exclusions Related to Sickness and Injury

- Payments from workers' compensation plans are excluded from gross income.
- Payments received as compensation for a *physical* injury are excluded from gross income, but punitive damages are included in gross income.
- Reimbursements by health and accident insurance policies for medical expenses paid by the taxpayer are excluded from gross income.
- Disability payments received from an *employee-purchased* policy are excluded from gross income.

Health Care Reimbursement Any reimbursement a taxpayer receives from a health and accident insurance policy for medical expenses paid by the taxpayer during the current year is excluded from gross income. The exclusion applies regardless of whether the taxpayer, her employer, or someone else purchased the health and accident policy for the taxpayer. Of course, the tax benefit rule may require inclusion of reimbursements of medical expenses that were deducted by the taxpayer in a prior year.

Disability Insurance The exclusion provisions for **disability insurance** are more restrictive than those for workers' compensation payments or reimbursements from a health and accident insurance plan. Disability insurance, sometimes called wage replacement insurance, pays the insured individual for wages lost when the individual misses work due to injury or disability. If an individual purchases disability insurance directly, the cost of the policy is not deductible, but any disability benefits are excluded from gross income.

Disability insurance may also be purchased on an individual's behalf by an employer. When an employer pays disability insurance premiums, the employer may allow employees to choose whether the payments on their behalf are to be considered taxable compensation or a nontaxable fringe benefit. If the premiums paid on the employee's behalf are taxable compensation to the employee, the policy is considered to have been purchased by the employee. If the premium paid for by the employer is a nontaxable fringe benefit to the employee, the policy is considered to have been purchased by the employer. This distinction is important because only payments taxpayers receive from an *employee-purchased* policy are excluded from an employee's gross income. If the employer pays the premiums for an employee as a nontaxable fringe benefit, the employee must include all disability benefits in gross income.

Example 5-31

Courtney purchased disability insurance last year. In late April of this year, she broke her wrist in a mountain biking accident and could not work for two weeks. Courtney's doctor bills totaled $2,000, of which $1,600 were reimbursed by her health insurance purchased by EWD. How much of the $1,600 health insurance reimbursement for medical expenses is Courtney allowed to *exclude* from her gross income?

Answer: All $1,600 is excluded. All medical expense reimbursements from health insurance are excluded from a taxpayer's gross income.

Courtney also received $600 for lost wages due to the accident from her disability insurance policy. How much of the $600 is Courtney allowed to exclude from her gross income?

Answer: All $600 is excluded. Courtney can exclude the entire amount because she paid the premiums on the policy.

What if: How much of the $600 payment for lost wages from the disability insurance policy would Courtney exclude if EWD paid the disability insurance premium on her behalf as a nontaxable fringe benefit?

Answer: $0 is excluded. In this circumstance the policy would be considered to be purchased by the employer, so Courtney would not be allowed to exclude any of the payment from gross income. She would include the payment in gross income and be taxed on the entire $600.

What if: How much of the $600 payment for lost wages from the disability insurance policy would Courtney be allowed to exclude if she paid half the cost of the policy with after-tax dollars and EWD paid the other half as a taxable fringe benefit?

Answer: All $600 is excluded. Because Courtney paid for the entire cost of the policy with after-tax dollars, she is allowed to exclude all of the disability insurance benefit. Note that if EWD had paid for half the cost of the policy as a nontaxable fringe benefit, Courtney would have been able to exclude $300 not $600.

Deferral Provisions

We've described exclusion provisions that allow taxpayers to permanently eliminate certain types of income from their tax base. Other code sections, called *deferral provisions,* allow taxpayers to defer (but not permanently exclude) the recognition of certain types of realized income. Transactions generating deferred income include **installment sales,** like-kind exchanges, involuntary conversions, and contributions to non-Roth **qualified retirement accounts.** We "defer" our detailed discussion of these transactions to subsequent chapters.

INCOME SUMMARY

At the end of the year, Courtney calculated her income and Gram's income. Exhibit 5-4 presents Courtney's income calculation, Exhibit 5-5 displays how this income would be reported on the front page of Courtney's tax return, and Exhibit 5-6 presents Gram's income calculation. Note that Courtney's actual *gross* income equals her total income on page 1 of her Form 1040 plus her $1,500 consulting expenses (see Example 5-7) and her $9,000 deductions for rental expenses (see Example 5-10), which are both *for* AGI deductions. Because Gram doesn't have any business, rental, or royalty deductions, her gross income is equal to her total income on line 22 of page 1 of her tax return.

EXHIBIT 5-4 Courtney's Income

Description	Amount	Reference
(1) Salary (line 7, 1040 page 1)	$ 98,000	Example 5-7.
(2) Employment bonus award (line 7, 1040 page 1)	4,800	Example 5-4.
(3) Discount architectural design services (line 7, 1040 page 1)	6,000	Example 5-19.
(4) Compensation on below market loan from EWD (line 7, 1040 page 1)	4,000	Example 5-20.
(5) Discharge of indebtedness (line 7, 1040 page 1)	10,000	Example 5-21.
(6) Interest income (line 8a, 1040 page 1)	617	Example 5-9.
(7) Dividends (line 9a and 9b, 1040 page 1)	700	Example 5-8.
(8) State tax refund (line 10, 1040 page 1)	420	Example 5-3.
(9) Alimony (line 11, 1040 page 1)	20,000	Example 5-14.
(10) Net business income (line 12, 1040 page 1)	18,000	Example 5-7.
(11) Net rental income (line 17, 1040 page 1)	5,000	Example 5-10.
Total income as presented on line 22 of front page of 1040 (see Exhibit 5-5)	**$167,537**	Sum of (1) through (11).

EXHIBIT 5-5 **Courtney's Tax Return**
(total income as reported on 1040 page 1, lines 7–22)

If more than four dependents, see instructions and check here ▶ ☐				(see instructions)	
				Dependents on 6c not entered above	
	d	Total number of exemptions claimed		Add numbers on lines above ▶	
Income	7	Wages, salaries, tips, etc. Attach Form(s) W-2		7	122,800
	8a	**Taxable** interest. Attach Schedule B if required		8a	617
	b	**Tax-exempt** interest. **Do not** include on line 8a	8b 500		
Attach Form(s) W-2 here. Also attach Forms W-2G and 1099-R if tax was withheld.	9a	Ordinary dividends. Attach Schedule B if required		9a	700
	b	Qualified dividends	9b 700		
	10	Taxable refunds, credits, or offsets of state and local income taxes		10	420
	11	Alimony received		11	20,000
	12	Business income or (loss). Attach Schedule C or C-EZ		12	18,000
If you did not get a W-2, see instructions.	13	Capital gain or (loss). Attach Schedule D if required. If not required, check here ▶ ☐		13	
	14	Other gains or (losses). Attach Form 4797		14	
	15a	IRA distributions 15a	b Taxable amount	15b	
	16a	Pensions and annuities 16a	b Taxable amount	16b	
	17	Rental real estate, royalties, partnerships, S corporations, trusts, etc. Attach Schedule E		17	5,000
	18	Farm income or (loss). Attach Schedule F		18	
	19	Unemployment compensation		19	
	20a	Social security benefits 20a	b Taxable amount	20b	
	21	Other income. List type and amount		21	
	22	Combine the amounts in the far right column for lines 7 through 21. This is your **total income** ▶		22	167,537
Adjusted Gross Income	23	Educator expenses	23		
	24	Certain business expenses of reservists, performing artists, and fee-basis government officials. Attach Form 2106 or 2106-EZ	24		
	25	Health savings account deduction. Attach Form 8889	25		
	26	Moving expenses. Attach Form 3903	26		

EXHIBIT 5-6 **Gram's Income**

Description	Amount	Reference
Babysitting services	$ 350	Example 5-2.
Interest income	4,400	Example 5-9.
Annuity income	3,400	Example 5-11.
Gain on stock sale	350	Example 5-12.
Sweepstakes winnings (WaveRunner)	7,500	Example 5-17.
Income for current year	$16,000	

CONCLUSION

In this chapter we explained the basic concepts of income realization and recognition, identified and discussed the major types of income, and described the most common income exclusions. We discovered that many exclusions are related to specific congressional objectives, but that absent a specific exclusion, realized income should be included in gross income. In the next chapter, we turn our attention to the deductions available to taxpayers when computing their taxable income. We will continue to follow Courtney and Gram in their quest to determine their taxable income and corresponding tax liability.

Appendix 2014 Social Security Worksheet from Form 1040

2014 Form 1040—Lines 20a and 20b

Social Security Benefits Worksheet—Lines 20a and 20b

Keep for Your Records

Before you begin:
- ✓ Complete Form 1040, lines 21 and 23 through 32, if they apply to you.
- ✓ Figure any write-in adjustments to be entered on the dotted line next to line 36 (see the instructions for line 36).
- ✓ If you are married filing separately and you lived apart from your spouse for all of 2014, enter "D" to the right of the word "benefits" on line 20a. If you do not, you may get a math error notice from the IRS.
- ✓ Be sure you have read the **Exception** in the line 20a and 20b instructions to see if you can use this worksheet instead of a publication to find out if any of your benefits are taxable.

1. Enter the total amount from **box 5** of **all** your **Forms SSA-1099** and **Forms RRB-1099.** Also, enter this amount on Form 1040, line 20a .... **1.** ________

2. Enter one-half of line 1 .... **2.** ________

3. Combine the amounts from Form 1040, lines 7, 8a, 9a, 10 through 14, 15b, 16b, 17 through 19, and 21 .... **3.** ________

4. Enter the amount, if any, from Form 1040, line 8b .... **4.** ________

5. Combine lines 2, 3, and 4 .... **5.** ________

6. Enter the total of the amounts from Form 1040, lines 23 through 32, plus any write-in adjustments you entered on the dotted line next to line 36 .... **6.** ________

7. Is the amount on line 6 less than the amount on line 5?

☐ **No.** STOP None of your social security benefits are taxable. Enter -0- on Form 1040, line 20b.

☐ **Yes.** Subtract line 6 from line 5 .... **7.** ________

8. If you are:
- Married filing jointly, enter $32,000
- Single, head of household, qualifying widow(er), or married filing separately and you **lived apart** from your spouse for all of 2014, enter $25,000
- Married filing separately and you lived with your spouse at any time in 2014, skip lines 8 through 15; multiply line 7 by 85% (.85) and enter the result on line 16. Then go to line 17

.... **8.** ________

9. Is the amount on line 8 less than the amount on line 7?

☐ **No.** STOP None of your social security benefits are taxable. Enter -0- on Form 1040, line 20b. If you are married filing separately and you **lived apart** from your spouse for all of 2014, be sure you entered "D" to the right of the word "benefits" on line 20a.

☐ **Yes.** Subtract line 8 from line 7 .... **9.** ________

10. Enter: $12,000 if married filing jointly; $9,000 if single, head of household, qualifying widow(er), or married filing separately and you **lived apart** from your spouse for all of 2014 .... **10.** ________

11. Subtract line 10 from line 9. If zero or less, enter -0- .... **11.** ________

12. Enter the **smaller** of line 9 or line 10 .... **12.** ________

13. Enter one-half of line 12 .... **13.** ________

14. Enter the **smaller** of line 2 or line 13 .... **14.** ________

15. Multiply line 11 by 85% (.85). If line 11 is zero, enter -0- .... **15.** ________

16. Add lines 14 and 15 .... **16.** ________

17. Multiply line 1 by 85% (.85) .... **17.** ________

18. **Taxable social security benefits.** Enter the **smaller** of line 16 or line 17. Also enter this amount on Form 1040, line 20b .... **18.** ________

TIP *If any of your benefits are taxable for 2014* ***and*** *they include a lump-sum benefit payment that was for an earlier year, you may be able to reduce the taxable amount. See* Lump-Sum Election *in Pub. 915 for details.*

Summary

LO 5-1 Apply the concept of realization and explain when taxpayers recognize gross income.

- Income is typically realized with a transaction that allows economic benefit to be identified and measured.
- Unless realized income is deferred or excluded, it is included in gross income in the period dictated by the taxpayer's accounting method.
- The accrual method of accounting recognizes income in the period it is earned, and this method is typically used by large corporations.
- The cash method of accounting recognizes income in the period received, and this method offers a simple and flexible method of accounting typically used by individuals.
- The return of capital principle, constructive receipt doctrine, and assignment of income doctrine affect how much income is recognized, when income is recognized, and who recognizes income, respectively.

LO 5-2 Understand the distinctions between the various sources of income, including income from services and property.

- Income from services is called earned income, whereas income from property is called unearned income.
- A portion of annuity payments and proceeds from sales of property is a nontaxable return of capital.
- Earned and unearned income generated by flow-through business entities is reported by partners and Subchapter S shareholders.
- Other sources of income include alimony payments, unemployment compensation, Social Security benefits, prizes and awards, bargain purchases, imputed interest on below-market loans, and discharge of indebtedness.

LO 5-3 Apply basic income exclusion provisions to compute gross income.

- Interest received from holding state and local indebtedness (municipal interest) is excluded from gross income.
- A taxpayer satisfying certain home ownership and use requirements can permanently exclude up to $250,000 ($500,000 if married filing jointly) of realized gain on the sale of her principal residence.
- Employment-related nonrecognition provisions include a variety of excludable fringe benefits.
- Gifts, inheritances, life insurance proceeds, and foreign earned income are excluded from gross income in order to mitigate the effects of double taxation.
- Common injury-related nonrecognition provisions include the exclusions for worker's compensation, personal injury payments and reimbursements from health insurance policies, and certain payments from disability policies.

KEY TERMS

accelerated death benefits (5-27)
accrual method (5-6)
alimony (5-14)
all-inclusive definition of income (5-2)
annuity (5-11)
assignment of income doctrine (5-8)
barter clubs (5-4)
cash method (5-6)
claim of right doctrine (5-7)
community property systems (5-8)
constructive receipt doctrine (5-7)
disability insurance (5-30)
discharge of indebtedness (5-21)
earned income (5-10)
flow-through entity (5-14)
fringe benefits (5-22)
gift (5-26)
gross income (5-2)
imputed income (5-19)
inheritance (5-26)
installment sale (5-31)
municipal bond (5-21)
nonrecognition provisions (5-21)
qualified retirement accounts (5-31)
realization principle (5-3)
return of capital (5-5)
tax basis (5-4)
tax benefit rule (5-5)
unearned income (5-10)
wherewithal to pay (5-3)

DISCUSSION QUESTIONS

1. Based on the definition of gross income in §61 and related regulations, what is the general presumption regarding the taxability of income realized? LO 5-1
2. Based on the definition of gross income in §61, related regulations, and judicial rulings, what are the three criteria for recognizing taxable income? LO 5-1
3. Describe the concept of realization for tax purposes. LO 5-1
4. Compare and contrast realization of income with recognition of income. LO 5-1
5. Tim is a plumber who joined a barter club. This year Tim exchanges plumbing services for a new roof. The roof is properly valued at $2,500, but Tim would have only billed $2,200 for the plumbing services. What amount of income should Tim recognize on the exchange of his services for a roof? Would your answer change if Tim would have normally billed $3,000 for his services? LO 5-1
6. Andre constructs and installs cabinets in homes. Blair sells and installs carpet in apartments. Andre and Blair worked out an arrangement whereby Andre installed cabinets in Blair's home and Blair installed carpet in Andre's home. Neither Andre nor Blair believes they are required to recognize any gross income on this exchange because neither received cash. Do you agree with them? Explain. LO 5-1
7. What issue precipitated the return of capital principle? Explain. LO 5-1
8. Compare how the return of capital principle applies when (1) a taxpayer sells an asset and collects the sale proceeds immediately and (2) a taxpayer sells an asset and collects the sale proceeds over several periods (an installment sale). If Congress wanted to maximize revenue from installment sales, how would they have applied the return of capital principle for installment sales? LO 5-1
9. This year Jorge received a refund of property taxes that he deducted on his tax return last year. Jorge is not sure whether he should include the refund in his gross income. What would you tell him? LO 5-1
10. Describe in general how the cash method of accounting differs from the accrual method of accounting. LO 5-1
11. Janet is cash-method calendar-year taxpayer. She received a check for services provided in the mail during the last week of December. However, rather than cash the check, Janet decided to wait until the following January because she believes that her delay will cause the income to be realized and recognized next year. What would you tell her? Would it matter if she didn't open the envelope? Would it matter if she refused to check her mail during the last week of December? Explain. LO 5-1
12. The cash method of accounting means that taxpayers don't recognize income unless they receive cash or cash equivalents. True or false? Explain. LO 5-1
13. Contrast the constructive receipt doctrine with the claim of right doctrine. LO 5-1
14. Dewey is a lawyer who uses the cash method of accounting. Last year Dewey provided a client with legal services worth $55,000, but the client could not pay the fee. This year Dewey requested that in lieu of paying Dewey $55,000 for the services, the client could make a $45,000 gift to Dewey's daughter. Dewey's daughter received the check for $45,000 and deposited it in her bank account. How much of this income is taxed, if any, to Dewey? Explain. LO 5-1
15. Clyde and Bonnie were married this year. Clyde has a steady job that will pay him about $37,000, while Bonnie does odd jobs that will produce about $28,000 of income. They also have a joint savings account that will pay about $400 of interest. If Clyde and Bonnie reside in a community property state and file married-separate tax returns, how much gross income will Clyde and Bonnie each report? Any difference if they reside in a common law state? Explain. LO 5-1

LO 5-2 16. Distinguish earned income from unearned income, and provide an example of each.

LO 5-2 17. Jim purchased 100 shares of stock this year and elected to participate in a dividend reinvestment program. This program automatically uses dividends to purchase additional shares of stock. This year Jim's shares paid $350 of dividends and he used these funds to purchase additional shares of stock. These additional shares are worth $375 at year-end. What amount of dividends, if any, should Jim declare as income this year? Explain.

LO 5-2 18. Jerry has a certificate of deposit at the local bank. The interest on this certificate was credited to his account on December 31 of last year, but he didn't withdraw the interest until January of this year. When is the interest income taxed?

LO 5-2 19. Conceptually, when taxpayers receive annuity payments, how do they determine the amount of the payment they must include in gross income?

LO 5-2 20. George purchased a life annuity to provide him monthly payments for as long as he lives. Based on IRS tables, George's life expectancy is 100 months. Is George able to recover his cost of the annuity if he dies before he receives 100 monthly payments? Explain. What happens for tax purposes if George receives more than 100 payments?

LO 5-2 21. Brad purchased land for $45,000 this year. At year-end Brad sold the land for $51,700 and paid a sales commission of $450. What effect does this transaction have on Brad's gross income? Explain.

LO 5-2 22. Tomiko is a 50 percent owner (partner) in the Tanaka partnership. During the year, the partnership reported $1,000 of interest income and $2,000 of dividends. How much of this income must Tomiko include in her gross income?

LO 5-2 23. Clem and Ida have been married for several years, but this year they decided to get divorced. In the divorce decree, Clem agreed to deed his car to Ida and pay Ida $10,000 per year for four years. Will either of these transfers qualify as alimony for tax purposes? Explain.

LO 5-2 planning 24. Otto and Fiona are negotiating the terms of their divorce. Otto has agreed to transfer property to Fiona over the next two years, but he has reserved the right to make cash payments in lieu of property transfers. Will tax considerations play a role in Otto's decision to transfer property or pay cash? How will Otto's choice affect the combined gross income and income taxes paid by Otto and Fiona? Explain.

LO 5-2 25. Larry Bounds has won the gold bat award for hitting the longest home run in major league baseball this year. The bat is worth almost $35,000. Under what conditions can Larry exclude the award from his gross income? Explain.

LO 5-2 26. Rory and Nicholi, single taxpayers, each annually receive Social Security benefits of $15,000. Rory's taxable income from sources other than Social Security exceeds $200,000. In contrast, the Social Security benefits are Nicholi's only source of income. What percentage of the Social Security benefits must Rory include in his gross income? What percentage of Social Security benefits is Nicholi required to include in his gross income?

LO 5-2 27. Rolando purchases a golf cart from his employer, E-Z-Go Golf Carts, for a sizable discount. Explain the rules for determining if Rolando's purchase results in taxable income for him.

LO 5-2 28. When an employer makes a below-market loan to an employee, what are the tax consequences to the employer and employee?

LO 5-2 29. Explain why an insolvent taxpayer is allowed to exclude income from the discharge of indebtedness if the taxpayer remains insolvent after receiving the debt relief.

LO 5-3 30. What are the basic requirements to exclude the gain on the sale of a personal residence?

31. Cassie works in an office and has access to several professional color printers. Her employer allows Cassie and her fellow employees to use the printers to print color postcards for the holidays. This year Cassie printed out two dozen postcards worth almost $76. Must Cassie include this amount in her gross income this year? Explain your answer. LO 5-3
32. What are some common examples of taxable and tax-free fringe benefits? LO 5-3
33. Explain how state and local governments benefit from the provisions that allow taxpayers to exclude interest on state and local bonds from their gross income. LO 5-3
34. Explain why taxpayers are allowed to exclude gifts and inheritances from gross income even though these payments are realized and clearly provide taxpayers with the wherewithal to pay. LO 5-3
35. Describe the kinds of insurance premiums an employer can pay on behalf of an employee without triggering includible compensation to the employee. LO 5-3
36. How are state-sponsored 529 educational savings plans taxed if investment returns are used for educational purposes? Are the returns taxed differently if they are not ultimately used to pay for education costs? LO 5-3
37. Jim was injured in an accident and his surgeon botched the medical procedure. Jim recovered $5,000 from the doctors for pain and suffering and $2,000 for emotional distress. Determine the taxability of these payments and briefly explain to Jim the apparent rationale for including or excluding these payments from gross income. LO 5-3
38. Tom was just hired by Acme Corporation and has decided to purchase disability insurance. This insurance promises to pay him weekly benefits to replace his salary should he be unable to work because of disability. Disability insurance is also available through Acme as part of its compensation plan. Acme pays these premiums as a nontaxable fringe benefit, but the plan promises to pay about 10 percent less in benefits. If Tom elects to have Acme pay the premiums, then his compensation will be reduced by an equivalent amount. Should tax considerations play a role in Tom's choice to buy disability insurance through Acme or on his own? Explain. LO 5-3

PROBLEMS

connect ACCOUNTING

All applicable problems are available with McGraw-Hill's *Connect® Accounting*.

39. For the following independent cases, determine whether economic income is present and, if so, whether it must be included in gross income (i.e., is it realized and recognized for tax purposes?). LO 5-1
    a) Asia owns stock that is listed on the New York Stock Exchange, and this year the stock increased in value by $20,000.
    b) Ben sold stock for $10,000 and paid a sales commission of $250. Ben purchased the stock several years ago for $4,000.
    c) Bessie is a partner in SULU Enterprises LLC. This year SULU reported that Bessie's share of rental income was $2,700 and her share of municipal interest was $750.
40. Devon owns 1,000 shares of stock worth $10,000. This year he received 200 additional shares of this stock from a stock dividend. His 1,200 shares are now worth $12,500. Must Devon include the dividend paid in stock in income? LO 5-1 research
41. XYZ declared a $1 per share dividend on August 15. The date of record for the dividend was September 1 (the stock began selling *ex-dividend* on September 2). The dividend was paid on September 10. Ellis is a cash-method taxpayer. Determine if he must include the dividends in gross income under the following independent circumstances. LO 5-1 research
    a) Ellis bought 100 shares of XYZ stock on August 1 for $21 per share. Ellis received $100 on September 10. Ellis still owns the shares at year-end.

b) Ellis bought 100 shares of XYZ stock on August 1 for $21 per share. Ellis sold his XYZ shares on September 5 for $23 per share. Ellis received the $100 dividend on September 10 (note that even though Ellis didn't own the stock on September 10, he still received the dividend because he was the shareholder on the record date).

c) Ellis bought 100 shares of XYZ stock for $22 per share on August 20. Ellis received the $100 dividend on September 10. Ellis still owns the shares at year-end.

LO 5-1 research

42. For the following independent cases, determine whether economic income is present and, if so, whether it must be included in gross income. Identify a tax authority that supports your analysis.

a) Hermione discovered a gold nugget (valued at $10,000) on her land.

b) Jay embezzled $20,000 from his employer and has not yet been apprehended.

c) Keisha found $1,000 inside an old dresser. She purchased the dresser at a discount furniture store at the end of last year and found the money after the beginning of the new year. No one has claimed the money.

LO 5-1

43. Although Hank is retired, he is an excellent handyman and often works part-time on small projects for neighbors and friends. Last week his neighbor, Mike, offered to pay Hank $500 for minor repairs to his house. Hank completed the repairs in December of this year. Hank uses the cash method of accounting and is a calendar-year taxpayer. Compute Hank's gross income for this year from each of the following alternative transactions:

a) Mike paid Hank $200 in cash in December of this year and promised to pay the remaining $300 with interest in three months.

b) Mike paid Hank $100 in cash in December of this year and gave him a negotiable promissory note for $400 due in three months with interest. Hank sold the note in January for $350.

c) Mike gave Hank tickets to the big game in January. The tickets have a face value of $50 but Hank could sell them for $400. Hank went to the game with his son.

d) Mike bought Hank a new set of snow tires. The tires typically sell for $500, but Mike bought them on sale for $450.

LO 5-1

44. Jim recently joined the Austin Barter Club, an organization that facilitates the exchange of services between its members. This year Jim provided lawn-mowing services to other club members. Jim received the following from the barter club. Determine the amount, if any, Jim should include in his gross income in each of the following situations:

a) Jim received $275 of car repair services from another member of the club.

b) Jim received a $150 credit that gave him the option of receiving a season pass at a local ski resort from another member of the club. However, he forgot to request the pass by the end of the ski season and his credit expired.

c) Jim received a $450 credit that can only be applied for goods or services from club members next year.

LO 5-1 research

45. Last year Acme paid Ralph $15,000 to install a new air-conditioning unit at its headquarters building. The air conditioner did not function properly, and this year Acme requested that Ralph return the payment. Because Ralph could not repair one critical part in the unit, he refunded the cost of the repair, $5,000, to Acme.

a) Is Ralph required to include the $15,000 payment he received last year in his gross income from last year?

b) What are the tax implications of the repayment if Ralph was in the 35 percent tax bracket when he received the $15,000 payment from Acme, but was in the 28 percent tax bracket when he refunded $5,000 to Acme?

c) How would you answer the question in part (b) if Ralph refunded $2,500 to Acme and not $5,000?

46. Louis files as a single taxpayer. In April of this year he received a $900 refund of state income taxes that he paid last year. How much of the refund, if any, must Louis include in gross income under the following independent scenarios? Assume the standard deduction last year was $6,200. LO 5-1

a) Last year Louis claimed itemized deductions of $6,450. Louis's itemized deductions included state income taxes paid of $1,750.

b) Last year Louis had itemized deductions of $4,800 and he chose to claim the standard deduction. Louis's itemized deductions included state income taxes paid of $1,750.

c) Last year Louis claimed itemized deductions of $7,640. Louis's itemized deductions included state income taxes paid of $2,750.

47. L. A. and Paula file as married taxpayers. In August of this year, they received a $5,200 refund of state income taxes that they paid last year. How much of the refund, if any, must L. A. and Paula include in gross income under the following independent scenarios? Assume the standard deduction last year was $12,400. LO 5-1

a) Last year L. A. and Paula had itemized deductions of $10,200, and they chose to claim the standard deduction.

b) Last year L. A. and Paula claimed itemized deductions of $23,200. Their itemized deductions included state income taxes paid of $7,500.

c) Last year L. A. and Paula claimed itemized deductions of $15,200. Their itemized deductions included state income taxes paid of $10,500.

48. Clyde is a cash-method taxpayer who reports on a calendar-year basis. This year Paylate Corporation has decided to pay Clyde a year-end bonus of $1,000. Determine the amount Clyde should include in his gross income this year under the following circumstances: LO 5-1

a) Paylate Corporation wrote the check and put it in his office mail slot on December 30 of this year, but Clyde did not bother to stop by the office to pick it up until after year-end.

b) Paylate Corporation mistakenly wrote the check for $100. Clyde received the remaining $900 after year-end.

c) Paylate Corporation mailed the check to Clyde before the end of the year, (and it was delivered before year end). Although Clyde expected the bonus payment, he decided not to collect his mail until after year-end.

d) Clyde picked up the check in December, but the check could not be cashed immediately because it was postdated January 10.

49. Identify the amount, if any, that these individuals must include in gross income in the following independent cases. Assume that the individuals are on the cash method of accounting and report income on a calendar-year basis. LO 5-1

a) Elmer was an extremely diligent employee this year and his employer gave him three additional days off with pay (Elmer's gross pay for the three days totaled $1,200, but his net pay was only $948).

b) Amax purchased new office furniture and allowed each employee to take home old office furniture valued at $250.

50. Ralph owns a building that he is trying to lease. Ralph is a calendar-year, cash-method taxpayer and is trying to evaluate the tax consequences of three different lease arrangements. Under lease 1 the building rents for $500 per month, payable on the first of the next month, and the tenant must make a $500 security deposit that is refunded at the end of the lease. Under lease 2 the building rents for $5,500 per year, payable at the time the lease is signed, but no security deposit is required. Under lease 3 the building rents for $500 per month, payable at the beginning of each month, and the tenant must pay a security deposit of $1,000 that is to be applied toward the rent for the last two months of the lease. LO 5-2

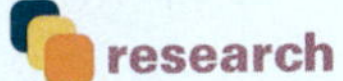

a) What amounts are included in Ralph's gross income this year if a tenant signs lease 1 on December 1 and makes timely payments under that lease?
b) What amounts are included in Ralph's gross income this year if the tenant signs lease 2 on December 31 and makes timely payments under that lease?
c) What amounts are included in Ralph's gross income this year if the tenant signs lease 3 on November 30 and makes timely payments under that lease?

LO 5-2

51. Anne purchased an annuity from an insurance company that promised to pay her $20,000 per year for the next ten years. Anne paid $145,000 for the annuity, and in exchange she will receive $200,000 over the term of the annuity.
a) How much of the first $20,000 payment should Anne include in gross income?
b) How much income will Anne recognize over the term of the annuity?

LO 5-2

52. Larry purchased an annuity from an insurance company that promises to pay him $1,500 per month for the rest of his life. Larry paid $170,820 for the annuity. Larry is in good health and he is 72 years old. Larry received the first annuity payment of $1,500 this month. Use the expected number of payments in Exhibit 5-1 for this problem.
a) How much of the first payment should Larry include in gross income?
b) If Larry lives more than 15 years after purchasing the annuity, how much of each additional payment should he include in gross income?
c) What are the tax consequences if Larry dies just after he receives the 100th payment?

53. Gramps purchased a joint survivor annuity that pays $500 monthly over his remaining life and that of his wife, Gram. Gramps is 70 years old and Gram is 65 years old. Gramps paid $97,020 for the contract. How much income will Gramps recognize on the first payment?

LO 5-2

54. Lanny and Shirley are recently divorced and do not live together. Shirley has custody of their child, Art, and Lanny pays Shirley $22,000 per year. All property was divided equally.
a) How much should Shirley include in income if Lanny's payments are made in cash but will cease if Shirley dies or remarries?
b) How much should Shirley include in income if $12,000 of Lanny's payments is designated as "nonalimony" in the divorce decree?
c) How much should Shirley include in income if Lanny's payments drop to $15,000 once Art reaches the age of 18?

LO 5-2
planning

55. Todd and Margo are seeking a divorce and no longer live together. Margo has offered to pay Todd $42,000 per year for five years if Margo receives sole title to the art collection. This collection cost them $100,000 but is now worth $360,000. All other property is to be divided equally.
a) If Margo's payments cease in the event of Todd's death, how are the payments treated for tax purposes?
b) How much of the gain would be taxed to Todd if Margo sells the art at the end of five years?
c) Compute the tax cost (benefit) to Todd (Margo) if the payments qualify as alimony. Assume that Todd (Margo) has a marginal tax rate of 15 percent (35 percent), and ignore the time value of money.
d) How much more over the five-year period should Todd demand in order to agree to allow the payments to cease in the event of his death? (How much more will make him indifferent between receiving $42,000 a year in nonalimony payments and receiving higher payments that are considered to be alimony?)

56. For each of the following independent situations, indicate the amount the taxpayer must include in gross income and explain your answer: LO 5-2
    a) Phil won $500 in the scratch-off state lottery. There is no state income tax.
    b) Ted won a compact car worth $17,000 in a TV game show. Ted plans to sell the car next year.
    c) Al Bore won the Nobel Peace Prize of $500,000 this year. Rather than take the prize, Al designated that the entire award should go to Weatherhead Charity, a tax-exempt organization.
    d) Jerry was awarded $2,500 from his employer, Acme Toons, when he was selected most handsome employee for Valentine's Day this year.
    e) Ellen won a $1,000 cash prize in a school essay contest. The school is a tax-exempt entity, and Ellen plans to use the funds to pay her college education.
    f) Gene won $400 in the office March Madness pool.
57. Grady received $8,200 of Social Security benefits this year. Grady also reported salary and interest income this year. What amount of the benefits must Grady include in his gross income under the following five independent situations? LO 5-2
    a) Grady files single and reports salary of $12,100 and interest income of $250.
    b) Grady files single and reports salary of $22,000 and interest income of $600.
    c) Grady files married joint and reports salary of $75,000 and interest income of $500.
    d) Grady files married joint and reports salary of $44,000 and interest income of $700.
    e) Grady files married separate and reports salary of $22,000 and interest income of $600.
58. George and Weezy received $30,200 of Social Security benefits this year ($12,000 for George; $18,200 for Weezy). They also received $5,000 of interest from jointly owned City of Ranburne bonds and dividend income. What amount of the Social Security benefits must George and Weezy include in their gross income under the following independent situations? LO 5-2
    a) George and Weezy file married joint and receive $8,000 of dividend income from stocks owned by George.
    b) George and Weezy file married separate and receive $8,000 of dividend income from stocks owned by George.
    c) George and Weezy file married joint and receive $30,000 of dividend income from stocks owned by George.
    d) George and Weezy file married joint and receive $15,000 of dividend income from stocks owned by George.
59. Nikki works for the Shine Company, a retailer of upscale jewelry. How much taxable income does Nikki recognize under the following scenarios? LO 5-2
    a) Nikki buys a diamond ring from Shine Company for $10,000 (normal sales price, $14,000; Shine Company's gross profit percentage is 40%).
    b) Nikki receives a 25 percent discount on jewelry restoration services offered by Shine Company. This year, Nikki had Shine Company repair a set of antique earrings (normal repair cost $500; discounted price $375).
60. Wally is employed as an executive with Pay More Incorporated. To entice Wally to work for Pay More, the corporation loaned him $20,000 at the beginning of the year at a simple interest rate of 1 percent. Wally would have paid interest of $2,400 this year if the interest rate on the loan had been set at the prevailing federal interest rate. LO 5-2

a) Wally used the funds as a down payment on a speedboat and repaid the $20,000 loan (including $200 of interest) at year-end. Does this loan result in any income to either party, and if so, how much?

b) Assume instead that Pay More forgave the loan and interest on December 31. What amount of gross income does Wally recognize this year? Explain.

LO 5-3

61. Jimmy has fallen on hard times recently. Last year he borrowed $250,000 and added an additional $50,000 of his own funds to purchase $300,000 of undeveloped real estate. This year the value of the real estate dropped dramatically, and Jimmy's lender agreed to reduce the loan amount to $230,000. For each of the following independent situations, indicate the amount Jimmy must include in gross income and explain your answer:

a) The real estate is worth $175,000 and Jimmy has no other assets or liabilities.

b) The real estate is worth $235,000 and Jimmy has no other assets or liabilities.

c) The real estate is worth $200,000 and Jimmy has $45,000 in other assets but no other liabilities.

LO 5-3

research

62. Grady is a 45-year-old employee with AMUCK Garbage Corporation. AMUCK pays group-term life insurance premiums for employees, and Grady chose the maximum face amount of $120,000. What amount, if any, of the premium AMUCK paid on his behalf, must Grady include in his gross income for the year? Provide a tax authority to support your answer.

LO 5-3

63. Fred currently earns $9,000 per month. Fred has been offered the chance to transfer for three to five years to an overseas affiliate. His employer is willing to pay Fred $10,000 per month if he accepts the assignment. Assume that the maximum foreign earned income exclusion for next year is $100,800.

a) How much U.S. gross income will Fred report if he accepts the assignment abroad on January 1 of next year and works overseas for the entire year? If Fred's employer also provides him free housing (cost of $18,000), how much of the $18,000 is excludible from Fred's income?

b) Suppose that Fred's employer has offered Fred only a six-month overseas assignment beginning on January 1 of next year. How much U.S. gross income will Fred report next year if he accepts the six-month assignment abroad and returns home on July 1 of next year?

c) Suppose that Fred's employer offers Fred a permanent overseas assignment beginning on March 1 of next year. How much U.S. gross income will Fred report next year if he accepts the permanent assignment abroad? Assume that Fred will be abroad for 305 days out of 365 days next year. If Fred's employer also provides him free housing (cost of $16,000 next year), how much of the $16,000 is excludible from Fred's income?

LO 5-3

64. For each of the following situations, indicate how much the taxpayer is required to include in gross income and explain your answer:

a) Steve was awarded a $5,000 scholarship to attend State Law School. The scholarship pays Steve's tuition and fees.

b) Hal was awarded a $15,000 scholarship to attend State Hotel School. All scholarship students must work 20 hours per week at the school residency during the term.

LO 5-3

65. Cecil cashed in a Series EE savings bond with a redemption value of $14,000 and an original cost of $9,800. For each of the following independent scenarios, calculate the amount of interest Cecil will include in his gross income assuming he files as a single taxpayer:

a) Cecil plans to spend all of the proceeds to pay his son's tuition at State University. Cecil's son is a full-time student, and Cecil claims his son as a dependent. Cecil estimates his modified adjusted gross income at $63,100.

b) Assume the same facts in part (a), except Cecil plans to spend $4,200 of the proceeds to pay his son's tuition at State University, and Cecil estimates his modified adjusted gross income at $60,600.

66. Grady is a member of a large family and received the following payments this year. For each payment, determine whether the payment constitutes realized income and determine the amount of each payment Grady must include in his gross income. LO 5-3
   a) A gift of $20,000 from Grady's grandfather.
   b) 1,000 shares of GM stock worth $120 per share inherited from Grady's uncle. The uncle purchased the shares for $25 each, and the shares are worth $125 at year-end.
   c) A gift of $50,000 of Ford Motor Bonds. Grady received the bonds on October 31, and he received $1,500 of semiannual interest from the bonds on December 31.
   d) A loan of $5,000 for school expenses from Grady's aunt.

67. Bart is the favorite nephew of his aunt Thelma. Thelma transferred several items of value to Bart. For each of the following transactions, determine the effect on Bart's gross income. LO 5-3
   a) Thelma gave Bart an auto worth $22,000. Thelma purchased the auto three years ago for $17,000.
   b) Thelma elects to cancel her life insurance policy, and she gives the cash surrender value of $15,000 to Bart.
   c) Bart is the beneficiary of a $100,000 whole life insurance policy on the life of Thelma. Thelma died this year, and Bart received $100,000 in cash.
   d) Bart inherited 500 shares of stock from Thelma's estate. Thelma purchased the shares many years ago for $1,200, and the shares are worth $45,000 at her death.

68. Terry was ill for three months and missed work during this period. During his illness, Terry received $4,500 in sick pay from a disability insurance policy. What amounts are included in Terry's gross income under the following independent circumstances? LO 5-3
   a) Terry has disability insurance provided by his employer as a nontaxable fringe benefit. Terry's employer paid $2,800 in disability premiums for Terry this year.
   b) Terry paid $2,800 in premiums for his disability insurance this year.
   c) Terry's employer paid the $2,800 in premiums for Terry, but Terry elected to have his employer include the $2,800 as compensation on Terry's W-2.
   d) Terry has disability insurance whose cost is shared with his employer. Terry's employer paid $1,800 in disability premiums for Terry this year as a nontaxable fringe benefit, and Terry paid the remaining $1,000 of premiums from his after-tax salary.

69. Tim's parents plan to provide him with $50,000 to support him while he establishes a new landscaping business. In exchange for the support, Tim will maintain the landscape at his father's business. Under what conditions will the transfer of $50,000 be included in Tim's gross income? Explain. Do you have a recommendation for Tim and his parents? LO 5-3 planning

70. What amounts are included in gross income for the following taxpayers? Explain your answers. LO 5-3
   a) Janus sued Tiny Toys for personal injuries from swallowing a toy. Janus was paid $30,000 for medical costs and $250,000 for punitive damages.
   b) Carl was injured in a car accident. Carl's insurance paid him $500 to reimburse his medical expenses and an additional $250 for the emotional distress Carl suffered as a result of the accident.

c) Ajax published a story about Pete and as a result Pete sued Ajax for damage to his reputation. Ajax lost in court and paid Pete an award of $20,000.

d) Bevis was laid off from his job last month. This month he drew $800 in unemployment benefits.

LO 5-3 71. This year, Janelle received $200,000 in life insurance proceeds. Under the following scenarios, how much of the $200,000 is taxable?

a) Janelle received the proceeds upon the death of her father, Julio.

b) Janelle received the $200,000 proceeds because she was diagnosed with colon cancer (life expectancy of 6 months), and she needed the proceeds for her care.

c) The proceeds related to a life insurance policy she purchased for $35,000 from a friend in need. After purchase, Janelle paid annual premiums that total $22,000.

LO 5-3 72. This year, Leron and Sheena sold their home for $750,000 after all selling costs. Under the following scenarios, how much taxable gain does the home sale generate for Leron and Sheena?

a) Leron and Sheena bought the home three years ago for $150,000 and lived in the home until it sold.

b) Leron and Sheena bought the home one year ago for $600,000 and lived in the home until it sold.

c) Leron and Sheena bought the home five years ago for $500,000. They lived in the home for three years until they decided to buy a smaller home. Their home has been vacant for the past two years.

LO 5-3 73. Dontae's employer has offered him the following employment package. What is Dontae's gross income from his employment?

Salary	$400,000
Health insurance	10,000
Dental insurance	1,500
Membership to Heflin Country Club	20,000
Season tickets to Atlanta Braves games	5,000
Tuition reimbursement for graduate courses	4,000
Housing allowance (for a McMansion in his neighborhood of choice)	40,000

COMPREHENSIVE PROBLEMS

All applicable problems are available with McGraw-Hill's *Connect® Accounting.*

74. Charlie was hired by Ajax this year as a corporate executive and a member of the board of directors. During the current year, Charlie received the following payments or benefits paid on his behalf.

Salary payments	$92,000
Contributions to qualified pension plan	10,200
Qualified health insurance premiums	8,400
Year-end bonus	15,000
Annual director's fee	10,000
Group-term life insurance premiums (face = $40,000)	750
Whole life insurance premiums (face = $100,000)	1,420
Disability insurance premiums (no special elections)	4,350

a) Charlie uses the cash method and calendar year for tax purposes. Calculate Charlie's gross income for the current year.

b) Suppose that Ajax agrees to pay Charlie an additional $100,000 once Charlie completes five years of employment. Will this agreement alter Charlie's gross income this year relative to your part (a) answer? Explain.

c) Suppose that in exchange for his promise to remain with the firm for the next four years, Ajax paid Charlie four years of director's fees in advance. Will this arrangement alter Charlie's gross income this year relative to your part (a) answer? Explain.

d) Assume that in lieu of a year-end bonus Ajax transferred 500 shares of Bell stock to Charlie as compensation. Further assume that the stock was listed at $35 per share and Charlie would sell the shares by year-end, at which time he expected the price to be $37 per share. Will this arrangement alter Charlie's gross income this year relative to your part (a) answer? Explain.

e) Suppose that in lieu of a year-end bonus Ajax made Charlie's house payments (a total of $23,000). Will this arrangement alter Charlie's gross income this year relative to your part (a) answer? Explain.

75. Irene is disabled and receives payments from a number of sources. The interest payments are from bonds that Irene purchased over past years and a disability insurance policy that Irene purchased herself. Calculate Irene's gross income.

Interest, bonds issued by City of Austin, Texas	$2,000
Social Security benefits	8,200
Interest, U.S. Treasury bills	1,300
Interest, bonds issued by Ford Motor Company	1,500
Interest, bonds issued by City of Quebec, Canada	750
Disability insurance benefits	19,500
Distributions from qualified pension plan	5,400

76. Ken is 63 years old and unmarried. He retired at age 55 when he sold his business, Understock.com. Though Ken is retired, he is still very active. Ken reported the following financial information this year. *Assume* Ken files as a single taxpayer. Determine Ken's gross income and complete page 1 of Form 1040 for Ken.

a) Ken won $1,200 in an illegal game of poker (the game was played in Utah, where gambling is illegal).

b) Ken sold 1,000 shares of stock for $32 a share. He inherited the stock two years ago. His tax basis (or investment) in the stock was $31 per share.

c) Ken received $25,000 from an annuity he purchased eight years ago. He purchased the annuity, to be paid annually for 20 years, for $210,000.

d) Ken received $13,000 in disability benefits for the year. He purchased the disability insurance policy last year.

e) Ken decided to go back to school to learn about European history. He received a $500 cash scholarship to attend. He used $300 to pay for his books and tuition, and he applied the rest toward his new car payment.

f) Ken's son, Mike, instructed his employer to make half of his final paycheck of the year payable to Ken. Ken received the check on December 30 in the amount of $1,100.

g) Ken received a $610 refund of the $3,600 in state income taxes his employer withheld from his pay last year. Ken claimed $6,250 in itemized deductions last year (the standard deduction for a single filer was $6,200).

h) Ken received $30,000 of interest from corporate bonds and money market accounts.

77. Consider the following letter and answer Shady's question.

To my friendly student tax preparer:

Hello, my name is Shady Slim. I understand you are going to help me figure out my gross income for the year . . . whatever that means. It's been a busy year and I'm a busy man, so let me give you the lowdown on my life and you can do your thing.

I was unemployed at the beginning of the year and got $2,000 in unemployment compensation. I later got a job as a manager for Roca Cola. I earned $55,000 in base salary this year. My boss gave me a $5,000 Christmas bonus check on December 22. I decided to hold on to that check and not cash it until next year, so I won't have to pay taxes on it this year. Pretty smart, huh? My job's pretty cool. I get a lot of fringe benefits like a membership to the gym that costs $400 a year and all the Roca Cola I can drink, although I can't really drink a whole lot.

As part of my manager duties, I get to decide on certain things like contracts for the company. My good buddy, Eddie, runs a bottling company. I made sure that he won the bottling contract for Roca Cola for this year (even though his contract wasn't quite the best). Eddie bought me a Corvette this year for being such a good friend. The Corvette cost $50,000 and he bought it for me out of the goodness of his own heart. What a great guy!

Here's a bit of good luck for the year. Upon leaving my office one day, I found $8,000 lying in the street! Well, one person's bad luck is my good luck, right?

I like to gamble a lot. I won a $22,000 poker tournament in Las Vegas this year. I also won about $5,000 over the year playing the guys at our Friday night poker game. Can you believe that I didn't lose anything this year?

Speaking of the guys, one of them hit me with his car as we were leaving the game one night. He must have been pretty ticked that he lost! I broke my right leg and my left arm. I sued the guy and got $11,000 for my medical expenses, $3,000 to pay my psychotherapist for the emotional problems I had relating to the injuries (I got really depressed!), and I won $12,000 in punitive damages. That'll teach him that he's not so tough without his car!

Another bit of bad luck. My uncle Monty died this year. I really liked the guy, but the $200,000 inheritance I received from him made me feel a little better about the loss. I did the smart thing with the money and invested it in stocks and bonds and socked a little into my savings account. As a result, I received $600 in dividends from the stock, $200 in interest from the municipal bonds, and $300 in interest from my savings account.

My ex-wife, Alice, is still paying me alimony. She's a lawyer who divorced me a few years ago because I was "unethical" or something like that. Since she was making so much money and I was unemployed at the time, the judge ruled that she had to pay ME alimony. Isn't that something? She sent me $3,000 in alimony payments this year. She still kind of likes me, though. She sent me a check for $500 as a Christmas gift this year. I didn't get her anything, though.

So there you go. That's this year in a nutshell. Can you figure out my gross income and complete page 1 of Form 1040 for me? And since you're a student, this is free, right? Thanks, I owe you one! Let me know if I can get you a six-pack of Roca Cola or something.

78. Diana and Ryan Workman were married on January 1 of last year. Diana has an eight-year-old son, Jorge, from her previous marriage. Ryan works as a computer programmer at Datafile Inc. (DI) earning a salary of $96,000. Diana is self-employed and runs a day care center. The Workmans reported the following financial information pertaining to their activities during the current year.

a) Ryan earned a $96,000 salary for the year.

b) Ryan borrowed $12,000 from DI to purchase a car. DI charged him 2 percent interest on the loan, which Ryan paid on December 31. DI would have charged Ryan $720 if interest had been calculated at the applicable federal interest rate.

c) Diana received $2,000 in alimony and $4,500 in child support payments from her former husband.

d) Diana won a $900 cash prize at her church-sponsored Bingo game.
e) The Workmans received $500 of interest from corporate bonds and $250 of interest from a municipal bond. Diana owned these bonds before she married Ryan.
f) The couple bought 50 shares of ABC Inc. stock for $40 per share on July 2. The stock was worth $47 a share on December 31. The stock paid a dividend of $1.00 per share on December 1.
g) Diana's father passed away on April 14. She inherited cash of $50,000 and his baseball card collection, valued at $2,000. As the beneficiary of her father's life insurance policy, Diana also received $150,000.
h) The couple spent a weekend in Atlantic City in November and came home with gambling winnings of $1,200.
i) Ryan received $400 cash for reaching 10 years of continuous service at DI.
j) Ryan was hit and injured by a drunk driver while crossing a street at a crosswalk. He was unable to work for a month. He received $6,000 from his disability insurance. DI paid the premiums for Ryan, but they reported the amount of the premiums as compensation to Ryan on his year-end W-2.
k) The drunk driver who hit Ryan in part (j) was required to pay his $2,000 medical costs, $1,500 for the emotional trauma he suffered from the accident, and $5,000 for punitive damages.
l) For meeting his performance goals this year, Ryan was informed on December 27 that he would receive a $5,000 year-end bonus. DI (located in Houston, Texas) mailed Ryan's bonus check from its payroll processing center (Tampa, Florida) on December 28. Ryan didn't receive the check at his home until January 2.
m) Diana is a 10 percent owner of MNO Inc., a Subchapter S corporation. The company reported ordinary business income for the year of $92,000. Diana acquired the MNO stock last year.
n) Diana's day care business collected $35,000 in revenues. In addition, customers owed her $3,000 at year-end. During the year, Diana spent $5,500 for supplies, $1,500 for utilities, $15,000 for rent, and $500 for miscellaneous expenses. One customer gave her use of his vacation home for a week (worth $2,500) in exchange for Diana allowing his child to attend the day care center free of charge. Diana accounts for her business activities using the cash method of accounting.
o) Ryan's employer pays the couple's annual health insurance premiums of $5,500 for a qualified plan.

Required:

A) Assuming the Workmans file a joint tax return, determine their gross income.
B) Using your answer in part A, complete page 1 of Form 1040 through line 22 for the Workmans.
C) Assuming the Workmans live in California, a community property state, and that Diana and Ryan file separately, what is Ryan's gross income?
D) Using your answer in part C, complete page 1 of Form 1040 through line 22 for Ryan Workman.

chapter

6 Individual Deductions

Learning Objectives

Upon completing this chapter, you should be able to:

LO 6-1 Identify the common deductions necessary for calculating adjusted gross income (AGI).

LO 6-2 Describe the different types of itemized deductions available to individuals and compute itemized deductions.

LO 6-3 Explain the operation of the standard deduction, determine the deduction for personal and dependency exemptions, and compute taxable income.

Storyline Summary

Taxpayers:	Courtney Wilson, age 40 Courtney's mother, Dorothy "Gram" Weiss, age 70
Family description:	Courtney is divorced with a son, Deron, age 10, and a daughter, Ellen, age 20. Gram is currently residing with Courtney. Ellen is currently a full-time student.
Location:	Kansas City, Missouri
Employment status:	Courtney works as an architect for EWD. Gram is retired.
Filing status:	Courtney files as head-of-household. Gram files as a single taxpayer.
Current situation:	Courtney and Gram are trying to determine their allowable deductions and compute taxable income.

Now that Courtney has determined her gross income, she still must determine her deductions to compute taxable income. Fortunately, Courtney keeps detailed records of all the expenditures she believes to be deductible. Besides expenses associated with her weekend consulting work and rental property, Courtney incurred some significant costs moving from Cincinnati to Kansas City. She also paid self-employment taxes on her consulting income and paid tuition for Ellen to attend summer school. Courtney is confident most of these items are deductible, but she isn't quite sure about the tuition.

Based on her review of prior-year tax returns, Courtney has a pretty good handle on her itemized deductions. She incurred some extra medical expenses to treat a broken wrist from a mountain biking accident and had additional state income taxes withheld from her paycheck. Courtney paid real estate taxes for her personal residence and investment property and interest expense on loans secured by her new home. She also donated (cash and property) to her favorite charities. Courtney experienced losses when her purse was stolen and when she damaged her car in an accident. She isn't sure if these losses are deductible.

In a push to improve her job performance, Courtney incurred costs to attend motivational seminars and travel to other parts of the country to study different architectural designs. Despite the fact that she was trying to improve her job performance, EWD did not reimburse her for these costs.

Gram wasn't as busy as Courtney this year. Gram paid a penalty for cashing in her certificate of deposit early. She also paid some medical expenses and donated money to her local church. Gram is a little frustrated because she doesn't incur enough itemized deductions to exceed the standard deduction amount. Gram recently heard that she might be able to save taxes by "bunching" her itemized deductions into one year. She's hoping to learn a little bit more about this technique. In any event, Gram didn't pay any taxes during the year and she wants to learn how much she's going to owe. ■

In the previous chapter, we determined *gross income* for both Courtney and Gram. To compute their taxable income, however, we need to identify their deductions. As emphasized previously, taxpayers are not allowed to deduct expenditures unless there is a specific tax law authorizing the deductions. And as we learn in this chapter, Congress grants many deductions for taxpayers for a variety of reasons.

As we discussed in Chapter 4, deductions appear in one of two places in the individual income tax formula. Deductions "for AGI" (also called deductions "above the line") are subtracted directly from gross income.[1] Next, deductions "from AGI" (also called deductions "below the line" or "itemized" deductions) are subtracted directly from AGI, resulting in taxable income. Deductions for AGI are generally preferred over deductions from AGI because deductions above the line reduce taxable income dollar for dollar. In contrast, deductions from AGI sometimes have no effect on taxable income. Further, because many of the limitations on tax benefits for higher income taxpayers are based upon AGI, deductions for AGI often reduce these limitations thereby increasing potential tax benefits. Thus, it's important to determine both the amount of the deduction and whether it's a deduction *for* AGI or *from* AGI. We begin our discussion of deductions by describing deductions for AGI, and we conclude by tackling itemized deductions, the standard deduction, and exemptions.

LO 6-1 DEDUCTIONS FOR AGI

Congress allows taxpayers to claim a variety of deductions for AGI.[2] To provide an overview, we select a cross section of deductions for AGI and classify them into three categories:

1. Deductions *directly* related to **business activities.**
2. Deductions *indirectly* related to business activities.
3. Deductions subsidizing specific activities.

We've organized our discussion around these categories to illustrate the variety of deductions for AGI and explain why Congress provides preferential treatment for certain deductions.

Deductions Directly Related to Business Activities

As a matter of equity, Congress allows taxpayers involved in business activities to deduct expenses incurred to generate business income. That is, because taxpayers include the revenue they receive from doing business in gross income, they should be allowed to deduct against gross income the expenses they incur to generate those revenues.

To begin, we must define "business activities" and, for reasons we discuss below, we must distinguish business activities from **investment activities.** In general, for tax

[1]Most, but not all, deductions for AGI appear on lines 23 through 35 on page 1 of Form 1040. The term "above the line" refers to the placement of deductions for AGI before the last line of the first page of Form 1040. This last line is the taxpayer's AGI.

[2]§62 identifies deductions for AGI.

purposes activities are either *profit-motivated* or motivated by personal objectives. Profit-motivated activities are, in turn, classified as either (1) business activities or (2) investment activities. Business activities are sometimes referred to as a **trade or business,** and these activities require a relatively high level of involvement or effort. For example, if an individual is a full-time employee, the individual is in the business of being an employee. Self-employed individuals are also engaged in business activities. Unlike business activities, investment activities are profit-motivated activities that *don't* require a high degree of involvement or effort.[3] Instead, investment activities involve investing in property for appreciation or for income payments. An individual who occasionally buys land or stock in anticipation of appreciation or dividend payments would be engaged in an investment activity.

Example 6-1

Suppose that Courtney purchased a parcel of land for its appreciation potential. Would her ownership in the land be considered a business or investment activity?

Answer: Courtney's activity would most likely be considered an investment activity, because she acquired the land for its appreciation potential and she does not plan to exercise any special effort to develop the property or to become actively involved in other real estate speculation.

What if: Suppose that Courtney frequently buys and sells land or develops land to sell in small parcels to those wanting to build homes. Would Courtney's activity be considered a business or investment activity?

Answer: Courtney's activity would most likely be considered a business activity because she is actively involved in generating profits from the land by developing it rather than simply holding the land for appreciation.

The distinction between business and investment activities is critical for determining whether a deduction associated with the activity is above the line or below. With one exception, business expenses are deducted for AGI. The lone exception is unreimbursed employee business expenses, which are deductible as miscellaneous itemized deductions (from AGI deduction).[4] In contrast, investment expenses are deductible as itemized deductions, with one exception. Expenses associated with rental and royalty activities are deductible for AGI regardless of whether the activity qualifies as an investment or a business. Exhibit 6-1 summarizes the rules for classifying business and investment expenses as for and from AGI deductions.

EXHIBIT 6-1 Individual Business and Investment Expense Deductions for AGI and from AGI

	Deduction Type	
Activity Type	**Deduction for AGI**	**Deduction from AGI** (itemized deduction)
Business activities	Self-employed business expenses	Unreimbursed employee business expenses
Investment activities	Rental and royalty expenses	Other investment expenses

[3]§162 authorizes trade or business expense deductions, while §212 authorizes deductions for investment activities. The distinction between these activities is discussed in Chapter 9.

[4]For example, an employee may use her own automobile to make a business delivery for her employer. The expenses she incurs to make the delivery (cost of operating the automobile and parking) are business expenses that are deducted from AGI as miscellaneous itemized deductions.

Trade or Business Expenses Congress limits business deductions to expenses directly related to the business activity and those that are **ordinary and necessary** for the activity.[5] This means that deductible expenses must be appropriate and helpful for generating a profit. Although business deductions are one of the most common deductions for AGI, they are not readily visible on the front page of Form 1040. Instead, these deductions are reported with business revenues on Schedule C of Form 1040. Schedule C, presented in Exhibit 6-2, is essentially an income statement for the business that identifies typical ordinary and necessary business expenses. Taxpayers transfer the *net* income or loss from Schedule C to Form 1040 (page 1), line 12.

EXHIBIT 6-2 Parts I and II from Schedule C Profit or Loss from Business

Part I Income

1	Gross receipts or sales. See instructions for line 1 and check the box if this income was reported to you on Form W-2 and the "Statutory employee" box on that form was checked . . . . ▶ ☐	1	
2	Returns and allowances	2	
3	Subtract line 2 from line 1	3	
4	Cost of goods sold (from line 42)	4	
5	**Gross profit.** Subtract line 4 from line 3	5	
6	Other income, including federal and state gasoline or fuel tax credit or refund (see instructions)	6	
7	**Gross income.** Add lines 5 and 6 . . . . ▶	7	

Part II Expenses. Enter expenses for business use of your home **only** on line 30.

8	Advertising	8		18	Office expense (see instructions)	18	
9	Car and truck expenses (see instructions)	9		19	Pension and profit-sharing plans .	19	
				20	Rent or lease (see instructions):		
10	Commissions and fees .	10		a	Vehicles, machinery, and equipment	20a	
11	Contract labor (see instructions)	11		b	Other business property . . .	20b	
12	Depletion	12		21	Repairs and maintenance . . .	21	
13	Depreciation and section 179 expense deduction (not included in Part III) (see instructions)	13		22	Supplies (not included in Part III) .	22	
				23	Taxes and licenses	23	
				24	Travel, meals, and entertainment:		
14	Employee benefit programs (other than on line 19) . .	14		a	Travel	24a	
15	Insurance (other than health)	15		b	Deductible meals and entertainment (see instructions) .	24b	
16	Interest:			25	Utilities	25	
a	Mortgage (paid to banks, etc.)	16a		26	Wages (less employment credits) .	26	
b	Other	16b		27a	Other expenses (from line 48) . .	27a	
17	Legal and professional services	17		b	**Reserved for future use** . . .	27b	

28	**Total expenses** before expenses for business use of home. Add lines 8 through 27a . . . . . . ▶	28	
29	Tentative profit or (loss). Subtract line 28 from line 7	29	
30	Expenses for business use of your home. Do not report these expenses elsewhere. Attach Form 8829 unless using the simplified method (see instructions). **Simplified method filers only:** enter the total square footage of: (a) your home: ______ and (b) the part of your home used for business: ______ . Use the Simplified Method Worksheet in the instructions to figure the amount to enter on line 30	30	
31	**Net profit or (loss).** Subtract line 30 from line 29. • If a profit, enter on both **Form 1040, line 12** (or **Form 1040NR, line 13**) and on **Schedule SE, line 2.** (If you checked the box on line 1, see instructions). Estates and trusts, enter on **Form 1041, line 3.** • If a loss, you **must** go to line 32.	31	
32	If you have a loss, check the box that describes your investment in this activity (see instructions). • If you checked 32a, enter the loss on both **Form 1040, line 12,** (or **Form 1040NR, line 13**) and on **Schedule SE, line 2.** (If you checked the box on line 1, see the line 31 instructions). Estates and trusts, enter on **Form 1041, line 3.** • If you checked 32b, you **must** attach **Form 6198.** Your loss may be limited.	32a ☐ All investment is at risk. 32b ☐ Some investment is not at risk.	

For Paperwork Reduction Act Notice, see the separate instructions. Cat. No. 11334P **Schedule C (Form 1040) 2014**

Example 6-2

Besides being employed by EWD, Courtney is also a self-employed consultant (a business activity). This year her consulting activity generated $19,500 of revenue and incurred $1,500 in expenses (primarily travel and transportation expenses). How does she report the revenue and deductions from the activity?

Answer: Courtney reports the $19,500 of revenue and deducts the $1,500 of business expenses for AGI on her Schedule C. Her net income of $18,000 from her consulting activities is included on the front page (line 12) of her individual tax return.

[5]§162. In Chapter 9, we address the requirements for deductible business expenses in detail.

Rental and Royalty Expenses Taxpayers are allowed to deduct their expenses associated with generating rental or royalty income for AGI.[6] Similar to business expenses, rental and royalty expenses do not appear directly on the front page of Form 1040. Instead, rental and royalty deductions are reported with rental and royalty revenues on Schedule E of Form 1040.[7] Schedule E, presented in Exhibit 6-3, is essentially an income statement for the taxpayer's rental or royalty activities. Taxpayers transfer the *net* income or loss from Schedule E to Form 1040 (page 1), line 17.

Rental and royalty endeavors are most commonly considered to be investment activities, but like trade or business expenses, rental and royalty deductions are claimed above the line.[8] Perhaps rental and royalty expenses are deductible for AGI because Congress believed that these activities usually require more taxpayer involvement than other types of investment activities. Despite this preferential treatment, the deductibility of rental losses (where expenses exceed income) are subject to limitations (basis, at-risk, and passive loss rules). We discuss these limitations in Chapter 7 when we discuss similar limitations that apply to investments in flow-through entities.

EXHIBIT 6-3 **Page 1 of Schedule E Rental or Royalty Income**

	Income: **Properties:**		A	B	C
3	Rents received	3			
4	Royalties received	4			
Expenses:					
5	Advertising	5			
6	Auto and travel (see instructions)	6			
7	Cleaning and maintenance	7			
8	Commissions.	8			
9	Insurance	9			
10	Legal and other professional fees	10			
11	Management fees	11			
12	Mortgage interest paid to banks, etc. (see instructions)	12			
13	Other interest.	13			
14	Repairs.	14			
15	Supplies	15			
16	Taxes	16			
17	Utilities.	17			
18	Depreciation expense or depletion	18			
19	Other (list) ▶	19			
20	Total expenses. Add lines 5 through 19	20			
21	Subtract line 20 from line 3 (rents) and/or 4 (royalties). If result is a (loss), see instructions to find out if you must file **Form 6198**	21			
22	Deductible rental real estate loss after limitation, if any, on **Form 8582** (see instructions)	22	( )	( )	( )
23a	Total of all amounts reported on line 3 for all rental properties	23a			
b	Total of all amounts reported on line 4 for all royalty properties	23b			
c	Total of all amounts reported on line 12 for all properties	23c			
d	Total of all amounts reported on line 18 for all properties	23d			
e	Total of all amounts reported on line 20 for all properties	23e			
24	**Income.** Add positive amounts shown on line 21. **Do not** include any losses	24			
25	**Losses.** Add royalty losses from line 21 and rental real estate losses from line 22. Enter total losses here	25	( )		
26	**Total rental real estate and royalty income or (loss).** Combine lines 24 and 25. Enter the result here. If Parts II, III, IV, and line 40 on page 2 do not apply to you, also enter this amount on Form 1040, line 17, or Form 1040NR, line 18. Otherwise, include this amount in the total on line 41 on page 2. . . .	26			

For Paperwork Reduction Act Notice, see the separate instructions. Cat. No. 11344L **Schedule E (Form 1040) 2014**

[6]§212(a)(4).

[7]Rental income and expenses for renting personal property (e.g., equipment, furniture, etc.) instead of real property is generally reported on Schedule C (not Schedule E). If the rental of personal property is not considered a trade or business, the rental income and expenses are reported on lines 21 and 36, respectively, of Form 1040.

[8]Royalties are received for allowing others to use property or rights to property. For example, royalties are paid for allowing others to use or sell copyrighted material such as books or plays, or extract natural resources from property. The amount of the royalty is often a percentage of total revenues derived from the property or rights to property.

Example 6-3

Courtney owns a condominium that she rents to tenants. This year she received $14,000 in rental revenue and incurred $9,000 of expenses associated with the rental, including management fees, maintenance, and depreciation. How does she report the revenue and expenses for tax purposes?

Answer: Courtney reports the $14,000 of rental receipts and deducts the $9,000 of rental expenses for AGI on Schedule E. The net rental income of $5,000 is reported on the front page (line 17) of her individual tax return.

Losses As we discuss in more detail in Chapter 11, taxpayers disposing of business assets at a loss are allowed to deduct the losses for AGI. Also, individual taxpayers selling investment (capital) assets at a loss are allowed to deduct the "capital" losses against other capital gains. If the capital losses exceed the capital gains, they can deduct up to $3,000 as a net capital loss in a particular year. Losses in excess of the $3,000 limit are carried forward indefinitely to subsequent years when they are deductible subject to the same limitations.

Flow-through Entities Income from flow-through entities such as partnerships, LLCs, and S corporations passes through to the owners of those entities and is reported on Schedule E of the tax returns of the owners. Similarly, any expenses and losses incurred by the entity pass through to the entity owners, who typically treat them as deductions for AGI, subject to certain restrictions (basis, at-risk, and passive loss rules) that we discuss in Chapter 7.

Deductions Indirectly Related to Business Activities

Taxpayers can incur expenses in activities that are not directly related to making money but that they would not have incurred if they were not involved in a business activity. Taxpayers are allowed to deduct several of these expenses that are indirectly related to business activities as deductions for AGI. We describe several of these deductions below.

Moving Expenses The cost of moving personal possessions is not a direct cost of doing business or being employed. Nonetheless, individuals qualify for a moving expense deduction if they move *and* change their principal place of work. Specifically, individuals can deduct moving expenses as deductions for AGI if they meet two tests: (1) a distance test and (2) a time test associated with the move.[9]

To satisfy the distance test, the distance from the taxpayer's old residence to the new place of work must be at least 50 miles more than the distance from the old residence to the old place of work. In other words, if the taxpayer were staying in her old home, the new place of work must increase her commute by at least 50 miles, thereby justifying a move to a new residence. To satisfy the time test, the taxpayer must either be employed full-time for 39 of the first 52 weeks after the move or be self-employed for 78 of the first 104 weeks after the move. A taxpayer can deduct moving expenses on her return if she expects to meet the time test but has not yet

[9]§217. Moving expenses are deducted on Form 3903.

done so at year-end. If the taxpayer later fails to meet the time test, she must either amend her prior return to eliminate the moving expense deduction or include the previous moving expense deduction as other income on her return in the year the time test was not met.

Individuals need not change employers if they meet both tests. Indeed, taxpayers can qualify for a moving expense deduction by beginning their first job, by beginning a job after a prolonged absence from the workforce, or by changing locations with the same employer. In addition, a taxpayer's reasons for moving may be entirely personal, such as wanting to move to a milder climate; business-related, such as wanting to change jobs or start a new business; or some of both.

Example 6-4

Before moving to Kansas City, Courtney lived in Cincinnati, Ohio, where she commuted 10 miles to her place of work. The distance from Courtney's home in Cincinnati to EWD in Kansas City, her new place of work, is 580 miles. Can Courtney deduct the expenses of moving her residence to Kansas City?

Answer: Yes. Courtney meets both the distance and the time tests because 580 miles is more than 60 miles (her original 10-mile commute from her former residence to her former place of work, plus 50 miles), and because she worked for EWD for the requisite 39 weeks during her first 52 weeks after her move (she worked from mid-January through December 31).

What if: Suppose that Courtney started a new job at an office just outside of Cincinnati and moved into a new residence. The distance from Courtney's former residence to her former place of work was 12 miles. The distance from Courtney's former residence to her new place of work is 55 miles. Does Courtney meet the distance test for moving expenses?

Answer: No, because if she had stayed in her former residence her commute would have increased by only 43 miles. To qualify, the commute from her former residence to her new work must be at least 50 miles longer than her commute from her former residence to her former place of work. Note that the location of her new residence is irrelevant to the distance test.

What if: Suppose that Courtney started a new job at an office just outside of Cincinnati and moved into a new residence. If the distance from Courtney's former residence to her former place of work was 12 miles, and the distance from her former residence to her new work place was 80 miles, would Courtney meet the distance test for moving expenses?

Answer: Yes, the commute from her former residence to her new job is 68 miles longer than the commute from her former residence to her old job.

Deductible moving expenses are limited to reasonable expenses associated with moving personal possessions and traveling to the new residence, including transportation and lodging. Taxpayers are allowed to deduct a mileage rate in lieu of the actual costs of driving their personal automobiles during the move. In 2015, taxpayers are allowed to deduct 23 cents a mile for driving their personal automobiles during a move. Taxpayers may also deduct the cost of moving their personal belongings and the belongings of members of their households. Taxpayers are *not* allowed to deduct costs such as meals during the move or costs associated with house-hunting trips. Taxpayers who are reimbursed by their employers for actual moving expenses exclude the reimbursement from income but do not deduct the reimbursed expenses. However, taxpayers who receive a flat amount as a moving allowance from their employers (i.e., without a requirement to document actual moving expenses to the employer) are required to include the allowance in gross income, and can deduct their actual moving expenses for AGI.

THE KEY FACTS

Moving Expenses

- Deductible for AGI for individuals who pass a mileage test and a time test.
- Mileage test: New job site must extend existing commute by at least 50 miles.
- Time test: Taxpayer must be employed at least 39 of 52 weeks or be self-employed for 78 of the 104 weeks following the move.

Example 6-5

Courtney drove 691 miles in her move from Cincinnati to Kansas City and incurred the following expenses related to the move:

Description	Amount
Moving company (personal belongings)	$5,000
Lodging (one night en route)	137
Meals en route	75
House-hunting trip	520

What amount can Courtney deduct as moving expenses?

Answer: Courtney can deduct $5,296 computed as follows:

Description	Deduction
Transportation (23¢ per mile times 691 miles)	$ 159
Moving company (personal belongings)	5,000
Lodging (one night en route)	137
Total deduction	**$5,296**

The meals and house-hunting are not deductible.

What if: Suppose that EWD agreed to reimburse Courtney for moving expenses up to a maximum of $2,000. What amount would Courtney deduct for moving expenses?

Answer: $3,296. Courtney would deduct $3,296 in moving expenses ($5,296 minus $2,000 reimbursement). She would not include the reimbursement in income and would not deduct the $2,000 of expenses for which she was reimbursed.

Health Insurance Deduction by Self-Employed Taxpayers The cost of health insurance is essentially a personal expense. However, *employers* often pay a portion of health insurance premiums for employees as a qualified fringe benefit. Employers are allowed to deduct health insurance premiums as compensation expense while employees are allowed to *exclude* these premiums from gross income. In contrast to employees, the health insurance fringe benefit does not apply to self-employed taxpayers because they are not "employees." To provide equitable treatment, Congress allows self-employed taxpayers to claim personal health insurance premiums for the taxpayer, the taxpayer's spouse, the taxpayer's dependents, and taxpayer's children under age 27 (regardless of whether or not the child is a dependent of the taxpayer) as deductions for AGI, but only to the extent of the self-employment income derived from the specific trade or business.[10]

This deduction is intended to help self-employed taxpayers who must pay their own insurance premiums. Consequently, self-employed taxpayers are *not* allowed to deduct health care insurance premiums if the taxpayer is *eligible* to participate in an employer-provided health plan. This restriction applies regardless of whether the health plan is sponsored by either an employer of the taxpayer or an employer of the taxpayer's spouse, and it is irrelevant whether the taxpayer actually participates in the plan.[11]

[10]§162(l). As we'll explain shortly, health insurance premiums also qualify as itemized deductions as medical expenses, but itemizing these deductions may not produce any tax benefits. To the extent that self-employed taxpayers do not have sufficient self-employment income to deduct all of their health insurance premiums as a for AGI deduction, they may deduct the remaining premiums as an itemized deduction. Finally, subject to certain restrictions, self-employed taxpayers who purchase health insurance through an exchange, have household incomes below 400% of the poverty line, and are not eligible for affordable coverage through an employer health plan that provides at least 60% of the expected costs for covered services can receive a premium tax credit under §36B. Any premiums offset by the tax credit cannot be deducted as either a for AGI or itemized deduction.

[11]§162(l)(2)(B).

Self-Employment Tax Deduction Employees and employers each pay Social Security and Medicare tax on employee salaries. Employers deduct the Social Security and Medicare taxes they pay on employee salaries. In contrast, because self-employed individuals do not have an employer, these individuals are required to pay self-employment tax. This tax represents both the employee's *and* the employer's share of the Social Security and Medicare taxes. Unfortunately for the self-employed, the self-employment tax is *not* considered a business expense. To put self-employed individuals on somewhat equal footing with other employers who are allowed to deduct the *employer's* share of the Social Security and Medicare taxes, self-employed taxpayers are allowed to deduct the employer portion of the self-employment tax they pay.

Example 6-6

As we indicated in Example 6-2, Courtney reported $18,000 of net income from her self-employed consulting activities. She paid $482 in self-employment taxes on this income, with $241 representing the employer portion of the self-employment tax.[12] What amount of self-employment tax can she deduct this year?

Answer: $241 (the employer portion of the self-employment tax).

Penalty for Early Withdrawal of Savings This provision allows a deduction for AGI for any interest income an individual forfeits to a bank as a penalty for prematurely withdrawing a certificate of deposit or similar deposit. This deduction reduces the taxpayer's net interest income to the amount she actually received. Otherwise, taxpayers would be required to report the full amount of interest income as taxable income and could deduct only the forfeited interest as an investment-expense miscellaneous itemized deduction. As we discuss below, investment expenses deducted as miscellaneous itemized deductions are subject to limitations that substantially reduce their tax benefits.

Example 6-7

Gram invested $100,000 in a three-year certificate of deposit (CD). On December 31, she decided to cash out the certificate of deposit after holding it for less than a year. She receives the $4,100 of interest income the CD had generated up to the withdrawal date, less a $410 early withdrawal penalty. How will Gram report the interest and early withdrawal for tax purposes?

Answer: Gram reports $4,100 as interest income this year and deducts the $410 early withdrawal penalty as a deduction for AGI.

Deductions Subsidizing Specific Activities

To address specific policy objectives, Congress provides that certain expenditures are deductible for AGI. For example, alimony payments are deductible for AGI to maintain equity and contributions to retirement savings are deductible for AGI to encourage savings.[13] Further, Congress created two important deductions for AGI to encourage and subsidize higher education. Taxpayers are allowed to deduct for AGI, subject to certain limitations, (1) interest expense on **qualified educational loans** and (2) **qualified educational expenses.**[14] As we discuss throughout the text, Congress has

[12]In this case, Courtney uses the following equation to determine her total self-employment tax $18,000 × .9235 × .029 (Courtney's business income is subject to the Medicare tax but not the Social Security tax due to the level of her salary). Of the total self-employment tax, the employer portion is calculated as $18,000 × .9235 × .0145 = $241. We discuss how to compute the self-employment tax in detail in Chapter 8.

[13]See Chapter 5 for detailed discussion of alimony and Chapter 13 for detailed discussion of the tax consequences of retirement savings.

[14]See §221 and §222.

THE KEY FACTS

Interest on Education Loans

- Up to $2,500 of interest on education loans is deductible for AGI.
- A loan qualifies as an education loan if the proceeds are used to fund qualified education.
- The interest deduction is phased-out for taxpayers with AGI exceeding $65,000 ($130,000 married filing jointly).

also created a number of related provisions, including education tax credits, to encourage and subsidize higher education.

Deduction for Interest on Qualified Education Loans Qualified education loans are loans whose proceeds are used to pay qualified education expenses.[15] Qualified education expenses encompass expenses paid for the education of the taxpayer, the taxpayer's spouse, or a taxpayer's dependent to attend a postsecondary institution of higher education.[16] These expenses include tuition and fees, books and expenses required for enrollment, room and board, and other necessary supplies and expenses including travel.

The deduction for interest expense on qualified education loans is the amount of interest paid up to $2,500. However, the deduction is reduced (phased-out) for taxpayers depending on the taxpayer's filing status and **modified AGI.** Modified AGI for this purpose is AGI *before* deducting interest expense on the qualified education loans and *before* deducting qualified education expenses (discussed below). Married individuals who file separately are not allowed to deduct this expense under any circumstance. The deduction limitations for other taxpayers are summarized in Exhibit 6-4 as follows:

EXHIBIT 6-4 Summary of Limitations on Deduction of Interest on Education Loans

Panel A: AGI limitations

Modified AGI Level	Deduction
Not over $65,000 ($130,000 for married filing jointly)	Amount paid up to $2,500
Above $65,000 ($130,000 for married filing jointly) but below $80,000 ($160,000 for married filing jointly)	Amount paid up to $2,500 reduced by the phase-out amount. The phase-out amount is the amount paid up to $2,500 times the phase-out percentage (see Panel B for the phase-out percentage computation).
Equal to or above $80,000 ($160,000 for married filing jointly)	Zero

Panel B: Phase-out Percentage*

Filing Status	Phase-out Percentage
Single or head of household	(Modified AGI − $65,000)/$15,000
Married filing jointly	(Modified AGI − $130,000)/$30,000

*Married taxpayers filing separately are ineligible for the deduction.

Example 6-8

What if: Assume that Courtney's brother Jason paid interest on a qualified education loan that he used to pay the tuition and fees for his three daughters to attend State University. In 2015, Jason was married and filed a joint return, paid $2,000 of interest expense on the loan, and reported modified AGI of $142,000. What amount of interest expense on the education loan is Jason allowed to deduct as a for AGI deduction?

[15]Home equity loans cannot qualify as education loans regardless of how the loan proceeds are spent.

[16]Postsecondary education includes courses at a university, college, or vocational school including internship programs leading to a degree or certificate. Qualifying costs claimed as deductions for AGI cannot be reimbursed by scholarships or Coverdell education savings accounts and are also ineligible for American opportunity and lifetime learning credit purposes.

Answer: $1,200, computed as follows:

Description	Amount	Explanation
(1) Modified AGI	$142,000	AGI before higher education deductions.
(2) Amount of interest paid up to $2,500	2,000	Lesser of amount paid ($2,000) or $2,500.
(3) Phase-out (reduction) percentage	40%	[(1) − $130,000]/30,000).
(4) Phase-out amount (reduction in maximum)	800	(2) × (3).
Deductible interest expense	$ 1,200	(2) − (4).

Deduction for Qualified Education Expenses This deduction subsidizes tuition payments for higher education. For purposes of this deduction, qualified education expenses are limited to the tuition and fees required for enrollment at a postsecondary institution of higher education. Thus, the definition of qualifying expenses is more restrictive for the qualified education expense deduction than it is for the education loan interest expense deduction. However, similar to the education interest expense deduction, the amount of the maximum education expense deduction depends on filing status and level of modified AGI. For purposes of the qualified education expense deduction, modified AGI is AGI *after* deducting the education loan interest expense but *before* deducting qualified education expenses. Just as with the qualified education loan interest deduction, married individuals filing separately are ineligible for the qualified education expense deduction. The rules for determining the allowable education expense deduction for taxpayers who qualify for the deduction are summarized in Exhibit 6-5.[17]

EXHIBIT 6-5 Summary of 2014 Limitations on Qualified Education Expenses

Modified AGI Level	Deduction
Not over $65,000 ($130,000 for married filing jointly)	Amount paid up to $4,000
Above $65,000 ($130,000 for married filing jointly) but less than or equal to $80,000 ($160,000)	Lesser of amount paid or $2,000
Above 80,000 ($160,000 for married filing jointly)	Zero

A taxpayer generally may only deduct the qualified education expenses that he or she pays. To deduct a dependent's education expense, the taxpayer must actually pay the expense and claim the student as a dependent. If a student pays his or her own education expenses and is eligible to be claimed as another taxpayer's dependent, no taxpayer (including the dependent) may deduct the education expense. In contrast, if another taxpayer pays a student's education expenses and the student is not considered the taxpayer's dependent, the payment of the student's education expense is considered a gift and the student can deduct the expenses.

There are two important differences between the AGI limits on the interest on education loans deduction (summarized in Exhibit 6-4) and the AGI limits on the educational expense deduction (summarized in Exhibit 6-5). First, the definition of modified AGI for qualified education expenses in Exhibit 6-5 includes the deduction for interest on education loans. Second, the interest expense on education loans is phased out gradually over a range of AGI but the deduction for qualified education expenses is phased out in specific AGI increments (the phase-out applies in steps).

[17]At press time, the deduction for qualified education expenses is scheduled to expire after 2014.

Example 6-9

Courtney paid $2,100 of tuition for Ellen to attend the University of Missouri–Kansas City during the summer. How much of this payment can Courtney deduct as a qualifying education expense?

Answer: None. The cost of the tuition is a qualified education expense, but Courtney's modified AGI exceeds $80,000. (Courtney files as a head of household.) Hence, Courtney is not allowed to deduct any of the cost of the tuition she paid for Ellen.

What if: Assume the same facts except that Courtney is married filing jointly and her modified AGI is $57,000. What amount can Courtney deduct as a qualifying education expense in this situation?

Answer: $2,100. She can deduct the full amount of the expenditure (limited to $4,000) because she is married filing jointly and her modified AGI is less than $130,000.

What if: Assume the original facts except that Courtney's modified AGI is $77,000. How much of the $2,100 tuition for Ellen would Courtney be allowed to deduct as a for AGI qualified education expense?

Answer: $2,000. Because Courtney's AGI is greater than $65,000 but not greater than $80,000 (she files as head of household) her deduction is the lesser of (1) her actual qualified education expenditures and (2) $2,000. Since Courtney's actual education expenditures were $2,100, her deduction is $2,000.

THE KEY FACTS

Education Expenses

- Up to $4,000 of qualified education expenses can be deducted for AGI.
- Qualified education expenses include tuition and related costs for postsecondary or higher education.
- The deduction is reduced for taxpayers with modified AGI over $65,000 ($130,000 married filing jointly) and eliminated for taxpayers with modified AGI exceeding $80,000 ($160,000 married filing jointly).

Because there are several education-related tax incentives, individuals can sometimes select among different tax benefits. For example, certain education expenses that qualify as deductions for AGI may also qualify for an education tax credit (see Chapter 8) or employee business expenses (deductible as miscellaneous itemized deductions discussed later in the chapter). Likewise, as shown in Chapter 5, up to $5,250 of education expenses paid by an employer's educational assistance program may be excluded from an employee's gross income (but not deducted or claimed as a credit by the employee). Typically, a single expenditure *cannot* generate multiple tax benefits. Consequently, individuals should select the tax provision to apply to the expenses that generates the most benefit.

Summary: Deductions for AGI

Business expenses and rental and royalty expenses are two of the most important deductions for AGI. There are other important deductions for AGI that are indirectly related to business or provided to subsidize certain activities. After we have determined the deductions for AGI, we can compute AGI. Exhibits 6-6 and 6-7 summarize the computation of AGI for Courtney and Gram. Exhibit 6-8 shows Courtney's AGI calculation as presented on the front page of her Form 1040.

EXHIBIT 6-6 Courtney's Adjusted Gross Income

Description	Amount	Reference
Gross income for current year	$178,037	Exhibit 5-4.
Deductions for AGI:		
Business expenses	(1,500)	Example 6-2.
Rental expenses	(9,000)	Example 6-3.
Moving expenses	(5,296)	Example 6-5.
Employer-portion of self-employment taxes	(241)	Example 6-6.
Adjusted gross income	**$162,000**	

EXHIBIT 6-7 Gram's Adjusted Gross Income

Description	Amount	Reference
Gross income for current year	$16,000	Exhibit 5-6.
Deduction for AGI:		
Penalty for early withdrawal of savings	(410)	Example 6-7.
Adjusted gross income	**$15,590**	

EXHIBIT 6-8 Courtney's AGI Computation on Form 1040, Page 1

Income	7	Wages, salaries, tips, etc. Attach Form(s) W-2			7	122,800
	8a	**Taxable** interest. Attach Schedule B if required			8a	617
	b	**Tax-exempt** interest. **Do not** include on line 8a	8b	500		
Attach Form(s) W-2 here. Also attach Forms W-2G and 1099-R if tax was withheld.	9a	Ordinary dividends. Attach Schedule B if required			9a	700
	b	Qualified dividends	9b	700		
	10	Taxable refunds, credits, or offsets of state and local income taxes			10	420
	11	Alimony received			11	20,000
	12	Business income or (loss). Attach Schedule C or C-EZ			12	18,000
	13	Capital gain or (loss). Attach Schedule D if required. If not required, check here ▶ ☐			13	
If you did not get a W-2, see instructions.	14	Other gains or (losses). Attach Form 4797			14	
	15a	IRA distributions	15a	b Taxable amount	15b	
	16a	Pensions and annuities	16a	b Taxable amount	16b	
	17	Rental real estate, royalties, partnerships, S corporations, trusts, etc. Attach Schedule E			17	5,000
	18	Farm income or (loss). Attach Schedule F			18	
	19	Unemployment compensation			19	
	20a	Social security benefits	20a	b Taxable amount	20b	
	21	Other income. List type and amount			21	
	22	Combine the amounts in the far right column for lines 7 through 21. This is your **total income** ▶			22	167,537
Adjusted Gross Income	23	Educator expenses	23			
	24	Certain business expenses of reservists, performing artists, and fee-basis government officials. Attach Form 2106 or 2106-EZ	24			
	25	Health savings account deduction. Attach Form 8889	25			
	26	Moving expenses. Attach Form 3903	26	5,296		
	27	Deductible part of self-employment tax. Attach Schedule SE	27	241		
	28	Self-employed SEP, SIMPLE, and qualified plans	28			
	29	Self-employed health insurance deduction	29			
	30	Penalty on early withdrawal of savings	30			
	31a	Alimony paid b Recipient's SSN ▶	31a			
	32	IRA deduction	32			
	33	Student loan interest deduction	33			
	34	Tuition and fees. Attach Form 8917	34			
	35	Domestic production activities deduction. Attach Form 8903	35			
	36	Add lines 23 through 35			36	5,537
	37	Subtract line 36 from line 22. This is your **adjusted gross income** ▶			37	162,000

For Disclosure, Privacy Act, and Paperwork Reduction Act Notice, see separate instructions. Cat. No. 11320B Form **1040** (2014)

Once we have determined AGI, we calculate taxable income by identifying deductions *from* AGI. These deductions consist of (1) the greater of itemized deductions or the standard deduction and (2) personal and dependency exemption deductions. We address itemized deductions next.

DEDUCTIONS FROM AGI: ITEMIZED DEDUCTIONS

LO 6-2

There is a variety of itemized deductions, a few of which relate to profit-motivated activities (employee business expenses and investment expenses that are unrelated to rental or royalty activities). Many itemized deductions are personal in nature but are allowed to subsidize desirable activities such as home ownership and charitable giving. Other itemized deductions, such as medical expenses and casualty losses, provide relief for taxpayers whose ability to pay taxes has been involuntarily reduced. We discuss itemized deductions in the order they appear on the individual tax return, Form 1040, Schedule A.

Medical Expenses

The medical expense deduction is designed to provide relief for taxpayers whose ability to pay taxes is seriously hindered by health-related circumstances. Qualifying medical expenses include any payments for the care, prevention, diagnosis, or cure of injury, disease, or bodily function that are not reimbursed by health insurance or are not paid for through a "flexible spending account."[18] Taxpayers may also deduct medical expenses incurred to treat their spouses and their dependents.[19] Common medical expenses include:

- Prescription medication, insulin, and medical aids such as eyeglasses, contact lenses, and wheelchairs. Over-the-counter medicines are generally not deductible.

[18]Taxpayers participating in flexible spending accounts are allowed to direct that a fixed amount of their salary be placed in an account to pay for medical expenses. The salary paid into these accounts is excluded from gross income and used to pay for medical expenses. See Chapter 12.

[19]For the purpose of deducting medical expenses, a dependent need not meet the gross income test [§213(a)], and a child of divorced parents is considered a dependent of both parents [§213(d)(5)]. We discuss the general requirements for dependency in Chapter 4.

- Payments to medical care *providers* such as doctors, dentists, and nurses and medical care *facilities* such as hospitals.
- Transportation for medical purposes.
- Long-term care facilities.
- Health insurance premiums (if not deducted for AGI by self-employed taxpayers) and insurance for long-term care services.[20,21]

Example 6-10

In April, Courtney broke her wrist in a mountain biking accident. She paid $2,000 for a visit to the hospital emergency room and follow-up visits with her doctor. While she recuperated, Courtney paid $300 for prescription medicine and $700 to a therapist for rehabilitation. Courtney's insurance reimbursed her $1,840 for these expenses. What is the amount of Courtney's qualifying medical expenses?

Answer: $1,160, computed as follows:

Description	Deduction
Emergency room and doctor visits	$2,000
Prescription medication	300
Physical therapy	700
Total qualifying medical expenses	$3,000
Less insurance reimbursement	−1,840
Qualifying medical expenses from the accident	**$1,160**

Medical expenses for cosmetic surgery or other similar procedures are not deductible unless the surgery or procedure is necessary to ameliorate a deformity arising from, or directly related to, a congenital abnormality, a personal injury resulting from an accident or trauma, or disfiguring disease.[22]

TAXES IN THE REAL WORLD Are Discretionary Medical Expenses Deductible?

While cosmetic surgery is generally not deductible, discretionary medical costs may be deducted where the procedure affects the structure or function of the body. Take, for example, procedures that facilitate pregnancy by overcoming infertility. In IRS Letter Ruling 200318017, the IRS ruled that egg donor fees and expenses related to obtaining a willing donor, paid by a taxpayer who could not conceive using her own eggs, qualified as deductible medical expenses because they were incurred in preparation of the taxpayer's medical procedure (the implantation of a donated egg). Deductible expenses included the donor's fee for her time and expense in following the procedures to ensure successful egg retrieval, the agency's fee for procuring the donor and coordinating the transaction, expenses for medical and psychological testing and assistance of the donor before and after the procedure, and legal fees for preparing a contract between the taxpayer and the donor.

What about the same type of expenses paid by a single male to father a child through a surrogate? Are those expenses deductible? No, because in that situation, the expenses are not related to an underlying medical condition or defect of the taxpayer nor are they affecting any structure or function of his body. See *William Magdalin*, TC Memo 2008-293.

[20]This includes the annual cost of Medicare and prescription insurance withheld from Social Security recipient's benefits checks.

[21]The portion of any premiums for health insurance purchased through an exchange and offset by a premium tax credit under §36B is not deductible as an itemized deduction.

[22]§213(d)(9)(A).

Transportation and Travel for Medical Purposes Taxpayers traveling for the primary purpose of receiving essential and deductible medical care may deduct the cost of lodging while away from home overnight (with certain restrictions) and transportation.[23] Taxpayers using personal automobiles for medical transportation purposes may deduct a standard mileage allowance in lieu of actual costs. For 2015, the mileage rate is 23 cents a mile.

Example 6-11

Gram drove Courtney, *in Courtney's car,* 110 miles back and forth from the doctor's office and the physical therapist's facility during the period Courtney was being treated for her broken wrist. What is the amount of Courtney's qualifying medical expense for her trips to the doctor's office?

Answer: $25 (110 × $0.23, rounded).

Hospitals and Long-Term Care Facilities Taxpayers may deduct the cost of meals and lodging at hospitals. However, the cost of meals and lodging at other types of facilities such as nursing homes are deductible only when the principal purpose for the stay is medical care rather than convenience.[24] Of course, taxpayers may deduct the costs of actual medical care whether the care is provided at hospitals or other long-term care facilities.

Example 6-12

Gram considered moving into a long-term care facility before she decided she would move in with Courtney. The facility was not primarily for medical care and would have cost Gram $36,000 a year. During discussions with facility administrators, Gram learned that typically 20 percent of the total cost for the facility is allocable to medical care. If Gram were to stay in the facility for an entire year, what amount of the long-term care costs would qualify as a medical expense for Gram?

Answer: $7,200 ($36,000 × 20% allocable to medical care).

Medical Expense Deduction Limitation The deduction for medical expenses is limited to the amount of unreimbursed qualifying medical expenses paid during the year (no matter when the services were provided) *reduced* by 10 percent of the taxpayer's AGI. If a taxpayer or his or her spouse is age 65 or older at the end of the tax year, the 10 percent AGI floor is reduced to 7.5 percent of AGI through 2016. This restriction is called a **floor limitation** because it eliminates any deduction for amounts below the floor. The purpose of a floor limitation is to restrict a deduction to taxpayers with substantial qualifying expenses. Because this floor limitation is set at a high percentage of AGI, unreimbursed medical expenses rarely produce tax benefits, especially for high income taxpayers.

[23]The cost of travel for and essential to medical care, including lodging (with certain limitations) is also deductible if the expense is not extravagant and the travel has no significant element of personal pleasure. However, under §213(d)(2) the deduction for the cost of lodging is limited to $50 per night per individual.

[24]Taxpayers may deduct the cost of long-term care facilities if they are chronically ill under a prescribed plan of care. A taxpayer is deemed to be chronically ill, generally, if she or he cannot perform at least two daily living tasks (eating, bathing, dressing, toileting, transferring, continence) for 90 days or more. §7702B. Taxpayers may also deduct long-term care insurance premiums, which are limited annually based on the age of the taxpayer.

Example 6-13

This year Courtney incurred $2,400 in unreimbursed qualifying medical expenses (including the $1,160 of qualifying medical expenses associated with the accident and the $25 transportation deduction for mileage). Given that Courtney's AGI is $162,000, what is the amount of Courtney's itemized medical expense deduction?

Answer: $0 computed as follows:

Description	Expense
Total unreimbursed qualifying medical expenses	$ 2,400
Minus: 10% of AGI ($162,000 × 10%)	(16,200)
Medical expense itemized deduction	**$ 0**

What if: What amount of medical expenses would Courtney be allowed to deduct if her AGI was $20,000?

Answer: $400, computed as follows:

Description	Expense
Total unreimbursed qualifying medical expenses	$ 2,400
Minus: 10% of AGI ($20,000 × 10%)	(2,000)
Medical expense itemized deduction	**$ 400**

Taxes

Individuals may deduct as itemized deductions payments made during the year for the following taxes:

- State, local, and foreign *income* taxes, including state and local taxes paid during the year through employer withholding, estimated tax payments, and overpayments on the prior year return that the taxpayer applies to the current year (the taxpayer asks the state to keep the overpayment rather than refund it).
- Real estate taxes on property held for personal or investment purposes.
- Personal property taxes that are assessed on the *value* of the specific property.[25]

Taxpayers may elect to deduct state and local sales taxes *instead* of deducting state and local income taxes.[26] This election is particularly advantageous for taxpayers in states that don't have an individual state income tax.[27]

Example 6-14

During the year, Courtney paid $6,700 of state income taxes through withholding from her paycheck. She also paid $2,700 of real estate taxes on her personal residence and $980 of real estate taxes on an investment property she owns in Oklahoma. Finally, Courtney paid $180 as a registration fee for her automobile (the fee is based on the year the automobile was manufactured, not its value). What amount of these payments can Courtney deduct as itemized deductions?

[25]§164.

[26]At press time, the deduction for state and local sales taxes is set to expire after 2014.

[27]The deduction can be based upon either the amount paid or the amount published in the IRS tables (IRS Publication 600) based upon the state of residence, income, and number of exemptions. The states with no income tax are Alaska, Florida, Nevada, South Dakota, Texas, Washington, and Wyoming. Tennessee and New Hampshire have no state income tax on wages, but do impose a tax on unearned income.

Answer: $10,380 ($6,700 state taxes + $2,700 real estate taxes on residence + $980 real estate taxes on investment property). Courtney is not allowed to deduct the registration fee for her car because the fee is not based on the value of the automobile.

What if: Suppose that on April 1, 2015, Courtney filed her 2014 state tax return and was due a refund from the state in the amount of $420. However, Courtney elected to have the state keep the overpayment and apply it to her 2015 tax payments. What amount of state income taxes is Courtney allowed to deduct as an itemized deduction in 2015?

Answer: $7,120 ($6,700 withholding + $420 overpayment applied to 2015). The treatment of the overpayment is the same as if Courtney had received the refund in 2015 and then remitted it to the state as payment of 2015 taxes. Because she paid the tax in 2015, she is allowed to deduct the tax in 2015. Recall that under the tax benefit rule (see Chapter 5), Courtney was required to include the $420 in her 2015 gross income.

Interest

There are two itemized deductions for interest expense.[28] First, subject to limitations described in more detail in Chapter 14, individuals can deduct interest paid on acquisition indebtedness and home-equity indebtedness secured by a qualified residence (the taxpayer's principal residence and one other residence).[29] Acquisition indebtedness is any debt secured by a qualified residence that is incurred in acquiring, constructing, or substantially improving the residence.[30] Home-equity indebtedness is any other debt secured by the taxpayer's qualified residence. Two rules limit the mortgage interest deduction: (1) Taxpayers may only deduct mortgage interest on up to $1,000,000 of acquisition indebtedness and (2) The amount of qualified home-equity indebtedness is limited to the *lesser* of (a) the fair market value of the qualified residence(s) in excess of the acquisition debt related to the residence(s) (determined when the home-equity loan is executed) and (b) $100,000 ($50,000 for married filing separately). In combination, these limitations allow taxpayers to deduct interest on up to $100,000 of home-equity debt (no matter what the taxpayer does with the proceeds from the home-equity loan) plus interest on up to $1,000,000 acquisition debt.[31]

As we discuss in more detail in Chapter 7, individuals can also deduct interest paid on loans used to purchase investment assets such as stocks, bonds, or land (investment interest expense). The deduction of investment interest is limited to a taxpayer's net investment income (investment income minus investment expenses). Any investment interest in excess of the net investment income limitation carries forward to the subsequent year. Taxpayers are not allowed to deduct interest on personal credit card debt or on loans to acquire (and secured by) personal-use automobiles.

[28]Interest paid on loans where the proceeds are used in a trade or business is fully deductible as a business expense deduction for AGI.

[29]In Chapter 8, we note that interest expense on home-equity loans not used to purchase or substantially improve the home is not deductible for AMT purposes.

[30]Subject to rules discussed in Chapter 14, points paid on indebtedness incurred in acquiring a home are also generally deductible as mortgage interest expense in the year the loan originates and points to refinance a home mortgage are typically amortized and deducted over the life of the loan (but see research memo in Chapter 2 for an exception).

[31]Taxpayers can also deduct premiums paid or accrued on mortgage insurance (insurance premiums paid by the borrower to protect the lender against the borrower defaulting on the loan) as qualified residence interest expense. At press time, the deduction for mortgage insurance premiums is set to expire after 2014.

Example 6-15

Courtney acquired her home in Kansas City in January of this year for $300,000 (also its value throughout the year). She purchased it by paying $40,000 as a down payment and borrowing $260,000 from a credit union. Her home is the collateral for the loan. During the year, Courtney paid $15,800 in interest on the loan. How much of this interest may Courtney deduct?

Answer: $15,800. Because Courtney's home mortgage is secured by her home, she is allowed to deduct the interest expense on the home as an itemized deduction.

What if: Suppose Courtney paid $3,000 in interest this year on a $60,000 home-equity loan. When Courtney secured the home-equity loan her house was worth $450,000 and her acquisition indebtedness was $250,000. How much of the $3,000 interest is deductible?

Answer: $3,000. Because the $60,000 home-equity loan does not exceed the lesser of (a) the fair market value of the residence in excess of the acquisition debt ($450,000 − $250,000 = $200,000) or (b) $100,000, Courtney may deduct the $3,000 interest paid.

What if: Suppose Courtney paid $6,000 in interest this year on a $120,000 home-equity loan (the average balance for the year). When Courtney secured the home-equity loan her house was worth $450,000 and her acquisition indebtedness was $250,000. How much of the $6,000 interest is deductible?

Answer: $5,000. Courtney is limited to deducting interest on $100,000 of the home-equity debt, which is the lesser of (a) the fair market value of the residence in excess of the acquisition debt ($450,000 − $250,000 = $200,000) or (b) $100,000. The deductible interest on the home-equity debt is calculated as: $6,000 interest paid × ($100,000 home-equity limit/$120,000 home-equity debt) = $5,000.

What if: Suppose that Courtney borrowed $26,000 to purchase a new car (the loan was secured by the car). Would she be allowed to deduct the interest on the loan?

Answer: No, the loan was not used to purchase a personal residence or investment assets.

Charitable Contributions

Congress encourages donations to charities by allowing taxpayers to deduct contributions of money and other property to *qualified* domestic charitable organizations. Qualifying charitable organizations include organizations that engage in educational, religious, scientific, governmental, and other public activities.[32] Political and campaign contributions are not deductible even though they arguably indirectly support the government (contributions to which are generally deductible).

Example 6-16

This year Courtney donated $1,700 to the Red Cross. She also gave $200 in cash to various homeless people she met on the streets during the year. What amount of these donations is Courtney allowed to deduct as a charitable contribution?

Answer: $1,700. Because the Red Cross is a public charity recognized by the IRS, Courtney may deduct her $1,700 charitable contribution to it as an itemized deduction. However, despite Courtney's charitable intent, her donations to the homeless are not deductible as charitable contributions because individuals do not qualify as charitable organizations.

What if: Suppose that instead of transferring cash to homeless people on the streets, Courtney donated $200 cash to a local food bank that is listed in IRS Publication 78 as a qualified charity. The food bank provides meals to those in need. Would Courtney be allowed to deduct this contribution?

Answer: Yes, because the food bank is a qualified charity.

[32]§170(c). IRS Publication 78 lists the organizations that the IRS has determined to be qualified charities.

The *amount* of the charitable contribution deduction depends on whether the taxpayer contributes money or other property to the charity. Note that in virtually all circumstances, donations are only deductible if the contribution is substantiated by written records.[33]

Contributions of Money Cash contributions are deductible in the year paid, including donations of cash or by check, electronic funds transfers, credit card charges, and payroll deductions.[34] Taxpayers are also considered as making monetary contributions for the cost of transportation and travel for charitable purposes if there is no significant element of pleasure or entertainment in the travel. When taxpayers use their personal vehicles for charitable transportation purposes, they may deduct, as a cash contribution, a standard mileage allowance for each mile driven (14 cents a mile in 2015). While taxpayers are allowed to deduct their transportation costs and other out-of-pocket costs of providing services for charities, they are not allowed to deduct the value of the services they provide for charities.

Example 6-17

Once a month, Courtney does volunteer work at a Goodwill Industries outlet about 20 miles from her home. Altogether, Courtney traveled 500 miles during the year driving to and from the Goodwill outlet. Courtney has determined that the services she provided during the year are reasonably valued at $1,500. What amount is Courtney allowed to deduct for her volunteer work with Goodwill Industries?

Answer: $70. Courtney is *not* allowed to deduct the value of the services she provides to Goodwill. However, she is allowed to deduct the $70 cost of her transportation to and from the Goodwill outlet (500 miles × 14 cents per mile).

Taxpayers receiving goods or services from a charity in exchange for a contribution may only deduct the amount of the contribution *in excess of the fair market value of the goods or services they receive* in exchange for their contribution.[35]

Contributions of Property Other Than Money When a taxpayer donates *property* to charity, the *amount* the taxpayer is allowed to deduct depends on whether the property is **capital gain property** or **ordinary income property.**

Capital gain property. In general, taxpayers are allowed to deduct the *fair market value* of capital gain property on the date of the donation. Capital gain property is

[33]For example, to deduct monetary donations, taxpayers must keep a bank record or a written communication from the charity showing the name of the charity and the date and amount of the contribution. In addition, to deduct charitable contributions for cash or noncash contributions of $250 or more, a taxpayer must receive a written acknowledgment from the charity that shows the amount of cash and a description of any property contributed. The acknowledgment must also state whether the donee organization provided any goods or services to the donor for the contribution and if so, either include a description and estimate of the value of the goods or services provided by the donee organization or, if applicable, a statement that the goods or services provided by the donee organization consist entirely of intangible religious benefits. See Publication 526 for more information.

[34]When individual taxpayers mail a contribution, they are allowed to deduct the contribution when they place the payment in the mail. When they pay via credit card, they are allowed to deduct the contribution on the day of the charge. Rev. Rul. 78-38, 1978-1 CB 67.

[35]Reg. §1.170A-1(h). To help with this determination, a charity that provides goods or services in return for a contribution of more than $75 must provide contributors with a written statement estimating the value of goods and services that the charity has provided to the donor.

any appreciated asset that would have generated a *long-term* capital gain if the taxpayer had sold the property for its fair market value instead of contributing the asset to charity. To qualify as long-term, the taxpayer must have held the asset for more than a year. Capital assets include the following assets:

- Investment assets (stocks, bonds, land held for investment, paintings, etc.).
- Business assets (to the extent that gain on the sale of the business asset would *not* have been considered ordinary income).[36]
- Personal-use assets.

Contributing capital gain property is a particularly tax-efficient way to make charitable contributions, because taxpayers are allowed to deduct the fair market value of the property, and they are *not* required to include the appreciation on the asset in gross income.

Example 6-18

In December of the current year, Courtney donated 100 shares of stock in JBD Corp. to her church, a qualified charity. Courtney purchased the stock several years ago for $2,600, but the shares were worth $10,600 at the time of the donation. What is the amount of Courtney's charitable deduction for donating the stock?

Answer: $10,600. Because the stock is an appreciated investment asset held for more than a year, it qualifies as capital gain property. Hence, Courtney is allowed to deduct the $10,600 fair market value of the stock, and she is *not* required to recognize any of the $8,000 realized gain ($10,600 − $2,600).

Certain contributions of capital gain property do not qualify for a fair market value deduction. The deduction for capital gain property that is *tangible personal property* is limited to the *adjusted basis* of the property if the charity uses the property for a purpose that is *unrelated* to its charitable purpose.[37] That is, this restriction applies to capital gains property that is (1) tangible, (2) personal property (not realty), and (3) unrelated to the charity's operations. The third requirement does not apply if, at the time of the donation, the taxpayer reasonably anticipates that the charity will put the property to a related use.

Example 6-19

What if: Suppose that Courtney donated a religious-themed painting to her church. Courtney purchased the painting several years ago for $2,600, but the painting was worth $10,600 at the time of the donation. When Courtney contributed the painting, she reasonably expected the church to hang the painting in the church chapel. What would be the amount of Courtney's charitable contribution deduction?

Answer: $10,600. Because Courtney reasonably expected the church to use the painting in a manner related to its tax-exempt purpose, Courtney is allowed to deduct the full fair market value of the painting without recognizing the $8,000 realized gain.

[36]These assets are considered to be §1231(b) assets. We discuss the tax treatment of dispositions of business assets in Chapter 11.

[37]Reg. §1.170A-4(b)(2). The taxpayer's deduction for donating capital gain property is also limited to basis if the taxpayer contributes capital gain property other than publicly traded stock to a private nonoperating foundation. There are also other exceptions in which capital gain property might not otherwise qualify for deduction at value such as the subsequent sales of donated property by the charity. These exceptions are beyond the scope of this text.

What if: Suppose that Courtney was told at the time she donated the painting that the church intended to sell it and use the cash to help fund expansion of the church building. What would be Courtney's charitable contribution deduction?

Answer: $2,600, the adjusted basis of the property. Because the church expects to sell it, the painting is being used for a purpose unrelated to the charitable purpose of the church. Thus, Courtney may deduct only the tax basis of the painting.

What if: Suppose that Courtney donated stock to her church and the church informed her that it intended to immediately sell the stock. What would be the amount of Courtney's charitable contribution deduction?

Answer: $10,600. Stock is intangible property, not tangible personal property. Hence, Courtney would deduct the fair market value of the stock.

Ordinary income property. Taxpayers contributing ordinary income property can only deduct the *lesser* of (1) the property's fair market value or (2) the property's adjusted basis. Ordinary income property consists of all assets other than capital gain property. That is, ordinary income property is property that if sold would generate income taxed at ordinary rates. This includes the following types of assets:

- Assets the taxpayer has held for a year or less.
- Inventory the taxpayer sells in a trade or business.
- Business assets held for more than a year to the extent the taxpayer would recognize ordinary income under the depreciation recapture rules if the taxpayer had sold the property.[38]
- Assets, including investment assets and personal-use assets, with a value *less than* the taxpayer's basis in the assets (assets that have declined in value).

Example 6-20

Before her move from Cincinnati, Courtney decided to donate her excess possessions to Goodwill Industries. Courtney estimated that she paid over $900 for these items, including clothing, a table, and a couch. However, although the items were in excellent condition, they were worth only $160. What amount can Courtney deduct for her donation of these items?

Answer: $160. Because Courtney's possessions have declined in value, they are considered to be ordinary income property. Consequently, Courtney may deduct the lesser of (1) the fair market value of $160 or (2) her tax basis in the property of $900.

Charitable Contribution Deduction Limitations The amount of a taxpayer's charitable contribution deduction for the year is limited to a **ceiling** or maximum deduction. The ceiling depends upon the type of property the taxpayer donates and the nature of the charity receiving the donation; donations to public charities (charities that are publicly supported such as churches and schools) and **private operating foundations** (privately sponsored foundations that actually fund and conduct charitable activities) are subject to less stringent restrictions than other charities. In general, cash and property donations to public charities and private operating foundations are limited to 50 percent of the taxpayer's AGI. Deductions for contributions of capital gain property to public charities and private operating foundations are generally limited to 30 percent of the taxpayer's AGI. Deductions for cash and property contributions to **private nonoperating foundations** (privately sponsored foundations that disburse funds to other charities, such as the Bill and Melinda Gates Foundation) are limited to 30 percent of the taxpayer's AGI. Finally, deductions for

[38]We discuss depreciation recapture in Chapter 11.

contributions of capital gain property to private nonoperating foundations are limited to 20 percent of the taxpayer's AGI. Exhibit 6-9 summarizes the charitable contribution limitations for individual taxpayers.

When taxpayers make contributions that are subject to different percentage limitations, they apply the AGI limitations in the following sequence:

Step 1: Determine the limitation for the 50 percent contributions.

Step 2: Apply the limitations to the 30 percent contributions. The 30 percent contribution limit is the *lesser* of (a) AGI × 30% or (b) AGI × 50% minus the contributions subject to the 50 percent limit.

Step 3: Apply the limitations to the 20 percent contributions. The 20 percent contribution limit is the *lesser* of (a) AGI × 20%, (b) AGI × 30% minus contributions subject to 30 percent limit, or (c) AGI × 50% minus the contributions subject to 50 percent and the contributions subject to the 30 percent limit.

EXHIBIT 6-9 Summary of Charitable Contribution Limitation Rules

Contribution Type	Public Charity and Private Operating Foundation	Private Nonoperating Foundation
Cash:		
Amount	Cash amount	Cash amount
AGI limit	50%	30%
Capital gain property:		
Amount	FMV	Basis*
AGI limit	30%	20%
Ordinary income property:		
Amount	Lesser of Basis or FMV	Lesser of Basis or FMV
AGI limit	50%	30%

*FMV if the stock is publicly traded [§170(e)(5)].

When a taxpayer's contributions exceed the AGI ceiling limitation for the year, the excess contribution is treated as though it were made in the subsequent tax year and is subject to the same AGI limitations in the next year. The excess contribution can be carried forward for five years before it expires. If a charitable contribution deduction is carried forward, the current year contributions must first be considered when applying the AGI percentage limitations. However, because the ceiling limitations are fairly generous, taxpayers exceed the ceiling limitations only in unusual circumstances.

Example 6-21

This year Courtney made the following contributions to qualified charities:

Organization	Amount	Type	AGI Limitation	Reference
Red Cross	$ 1,700	Cash	50%	Example 6-16.
Goodwill Industries	70	Cash-mileage	50	Example 6-17.
Goodwill	160	Ordinary income property	50	Example 6-20.
Church	10,600	Capital gain property	30	Example 6-18.
Total contributions	$12,530			

After applying the AGI limitations, how much of the $12,530 in contributions is Courtney allowed to deduct?

Answer: $12,530, computed as follows:

Description	Amount	Explanation
(1) AGI	$162,000	Exhibit 6-6.
(2) 50% contributions	1,930	($1,700 + 70 + 160).
(3) 50% AGI contribution limit	81,000	(1) × 50%.
(4) Allowable 50% deductions	**1,930**	Lesser of (2) or (3).
(5) 30% contributions	10,600	
(6) 30% AGI contribution limit	48,600	(1) × 30%.
(7) Remaining 50% AGI limitation	79,070	(3) − (4).
(8) Allowable 30% deductions	**10,600**	Least of (5), (6), or (7).
Deductible charitable contributions	**$ 12,530**	(4) + (8).

What if: Suppose that Courtney's AGI was $30,000. After applying the AGI limitations, how much of the $12,530 in contributions would Courtney be allowed to deduct?

Answer: $10,930, computed as follows:

Description	Amount	Explanation
(1) AGI	$30,000	
(2) 50% contributions	1,930	
(3) 50% AGI contribution limit	15,000	(1) × 50%.
(4) Allowable 50% deductions	**1,930**	Lesser of (2) and (3).
(5) 30% contributions	10,600	
(6) 30% AGI contribution limit	9,000	(1) × 30%.
(7) Remaining 50% AGI limitation	13,070	(3) − (4).
(8) Allowable 30% deductions	**9,000**	Least of (5), (6), or (7).
Deductible charitable contributions	**$10,930**	(4) + (8).

Courtney would not be allowed to deduct this year $1,600 of her $10,600 capital gain property contribution to her church. However, she will carry forward the $1,600 to next year (and up to four years after that, if necessary) and treat it as though she made a $1,600 contribution next year subject to the 30 percent of AGI limitation.

ETHICS

Sabrina loves the latest fashions, but she is also very charitable. Every year she donates her previous year's clothing to Goodwill to make room in her closet for this year's fashion. Sabrina estimates the value of her donation to be approximately $6,000. Sabrina recently learned that because her donation exceeds $5,000, she must support her donation with an appraisal and signed statement by the appraiser on Form 8283. Sabrina decides to claim a charitable deduction of $4,900 to avoid the appraisal requirement. What do you think of Sabrina's decision? Do you think nationally that there is an abnormally large number of charitable contributions valued just under $5,000?

Casualty and Theft Losses on Personal-Use Assets

Individuals cannot deduct losses they realize when they sell or dispose of assets used for personal purposes (personal-use assets as opposed to business or investment assets). However, individuals *are* allowed to deduct casualty and theft losses realized on personal-use assets.[39] A **casualty loss** is defined as a loss arising from a *sudden, unexpected,* or *unusual* event such as a "fire, storm, or shipwreck" or loss from theft.[40] Taxpayers may deduct casualty losses in the year the casualty occurs or in the year the theft of an asset is discovered.

Tax Loss from Casualties Congress allows deductions for unreimbursed casualty and theft losses because these losses may substantially reduce a taxpayer's ability to pay taxes. However, limitations on the deduction generally ensure that taxpayers receive a tax benefit from such losses only when the losses are relatively large. The *amount* of the tax loss from any *specific casualty event* (including theft) is the *lesser* of (1) the decline in value of the property caused by the casualty or (2) the taxpayer's tax basis in the damaged or stolen asset. The loss is reduced by any reimbursements the individual is eligible to receive, such as insurance reimbursements. Likewise, any deductible loss reduces the taxpayer's basis in the underlying asset.

Example 6-22

In June, Courtney had a bad day at a nearby lake. Her purse containing $200 in cash was stolen, and she wrecked her car on the way home. Courtney purchased her purse for $150 and it was worth $125 at the time of the theft ($325 in total value was stolen). Courtney purchased her car earlier in the year for $22,000 and had to pay $2,000 to have it repaired. Courtney's insurance company reimbursed her $1,400 for the repairs. What is the amount of Courtney's casualty tax loss before considering deductibility limitations?

Answer: $925 ($325 theft + $600 accident). The theft and the automobile accident are considered to be two separate casualty events generating two different casualty losses. The amount of each casualty loss, before considering deductibility limitations, is computed as follows:

	Theft	Accident
Fair market value (FMV) before casualty	$325	
FMV after the casualty	−0	
(1) Decline in FMV (cost to repair)	325	$ 2,000
(2) Tax basis in property before casualty	350	22,000
Loss before reimbursement [lesser of (1) or (2)]	325	2,000
Insurance reimbursement	−0	−1,400
Unreimbursed casualty losses	$325	$ 600

Casualty Loss Deduction Floor Limitations Casualty losses must exceed two separate floor limitations to qualify as itemized deductions. The first floor is $100 for *each* casualty event during the year. This floor eliminates deductions for small losses. The second floor limitation is 10 percent of AGI, and it applies to the sum of all casualty losses for the year (after applying the $100 floor). In other words, the itemized deduction is the aggregate amount of casualty losses that exceeds 10 percent of AGI.

[39]§165. As we discuss in more detail in Chapter 9, businesses may deduct casualty and theft losses of business property as a deduction for AGI. Further, casualty or theft losses on investment assets are deductible as a miscellaneous itemized deduction not subject to the 2 percent of AGI floor.

[40]§165(c)(3). See also IRS Publication No. 547.

Example 6-23

Courtney's total casualty loss before applying the deduction limitations is $925. What amount of the $925 loss is Courtney allowed to deduct after applying the two floor limitations?

Answer: $0, computed as follows:

	Theft	Accident	Total
Losses before limitations	$325	$600	
Less $100 per casualty floor	−100	−100	
Casualty loss before AGI limit	$225	$500	$ 725
Less 10% of $162,000			−16,200
Casualty loss deduction after AGI limit			$ 0

What if: Suppose that Courtney's automobile was worth $20,000, and that it was completely destroyed in the accident. What would be Courtney's casualty loss deduction if she received only $3,100 of insurance reimbursement for her loss?

Answer: $825, computed as follows:

	Theft	Accident	Total
Fair market value (FMV) before casualty	$325	$20,000	
FMV after the casualty	0	0	
(1) Decline in FMV (cost to repair)	$325	$20,000	
(2) Tax basis in property before casualty	$350	$22,000	
Loss before reimbursement [lesser of (1) or (2)]	$325	$20,000	
Less Insurance reimbursement	−0	−3,100	
Less $100 per casualty floor	−100	−100	
Unreimbursed casualty losses	$225	$16,800	$17,025
Less 10% of $162,000			−16,200
Casualty loss deduction after AGI limit			$ 825

TAXES IN THE REAL WORLD "The Trilogy of the Rings"

In order to qualify for a casualty loss deduction, a taxpayer's personal loss must be sudden or unexpected. Taxpayers and the IRS sometimes disagree about what is a casualty. Consider the following three case summaries (sometimes called the "trilogy of the rings") and, for each case, see whether you can determine whether the taxpayer or the IRS was victorious.

Case 1

Nancy Carpenter cleaned her wedding ring by placing it in some ammonia near the kitchen sink. Nancy's husband, William, later emptied the ammonia into the drain along with the ring while doing the dishes. He then turned on the garbage disposal, destroying the ring [*William H. Carpenter,* decided by the Tax Court in 1966, 25 TCM 1186].

Case 2

John lovingly helped his wife Agnes from the car and started to shut the door. Agnes, upon realizing she had left something on the seat, reached her hand back toward the car only to have the door shut directly on her engagement ring. The setting of the ring broke on impact and the diamond was flung into the leaf-covered driveway as she retracted her hand. Despite all their efforts, John and Agnes never found the stone [*John P. White,* decided by the Tax Court in 1967, 48 TC 430].

Case 3

Mr. and Mrs. Keenan spent the night at a hotel. Mr. Keenan, who was suffering from a stuffy nose, used tissues he had placed near his bed throughout the night. During the night

(*continued on page 6-26*)

Mrs. Keenan removed her rings and placed them within a tissue at the bedside. Mr. Keenan awoke before his wife the following morning, and he gathered the tissues, including the ring, and flushed them down the toilet [*Keenan v. Bowers*, decided in 1950 by the South Carolina District Court, 50-2 USTC ¶9444].

So, what do you think?

The taxpayers won Case 1 and Case 2 because the losses were deemed to be "sudden and unexpected" in nature. However, the taxpayer lost Case 3 because the loss was due to a "chain of events on the parts of Mrs. Keenan and Mr. Keenan." Thus, the loss was not considered to be sudden in nature.

Miscellaneous Itemized Deductions Subject to AGI Floor

There are a variety of deductions that address specific objectives but do not fit easily into any category. Congress called these deductions **miscellaneous itemized deductions** and subjected most of these deductions to an AGI floor (only amounts over the floor are deductible). Miscellaneous itemized deductions subject to the floor limitation include employee business expenses, investment expenses, and certain other expenses. These miscellaneous deductions are summed together and are deductible only to the extent that their sum *exceeds* 2 percent of the taxpayer's AGI.

Employee Business Expenses While most business expenses are typically deductible as deductions for AGI, employee business expenses are deductible as miscellaneous itemized deductions. Expenses that qualify include those that are appropriate and helpful for the employee's work such as the cost of professional dues, uniforms (unless suitable as normal attire), union dues, and subscriptions to publications related to employment.

Example 6-24

Courtney subscribes to several architectural publications at an annual cost of $410. She finds these publications helpful, and it is certainly appropriate that an architect read current publications to keep up with new trends. Her employer does not reimburse Courtney for the cost of the subscriptions. What amount, if any, qualifies as a deductible employee business expense?

Answer: All $410 qualifies as a deductible employee business expense because the expense is appropriate and helpful to Courtney's employment.

Several types of employee expenses are restricted. For example, the costs of job hunting qualify if the job is in the employee's current trade or business, but not for the individual's first job. In addition, the cost of education qualifies if it serves to maintain or improve the employee's skill in the business, but not if the education is *required* to qualify for a new business or profession.[41] Thus, a high school teacher would not be able to deduct the cost of attending law school because a law degree would qualify him for a different profession.

Example 6-25

During the year, Courtney paid $1,529 to attend motivational seminars sponsored by a continuing education provider. Courtney has found these seminars helpful, and her employer has encouraged Courtney to attend. How much of the cost of the seminars qualifies as a deductible employee business expense?

Answer: All $1,529. The cost qualifies as an employee business expense because the courses are appropriate and helpful and do not qualify Courtney for a new business.

[41]If a taxpayer is self-employed (instead of an employee), the cost of education that maintains or improves his or her skills (but is not required for a new business or profession) is deductible on Schedule C (not on Schedule A as a miscellaneous itemized deduction).

TAXES IN THE REAL WORLD Is the Cost of an MBA Deductible?

Is the cost of an MBA deductible? That is a very good question with differing answers depending on the taxpayer's specific facts. The nature of an MBA degree lends itself to vigorous disputes as to whether the degree qualifies a taxpayer to engage in a new trade or business. On the one hand, an MBA degree is typically not a foundational requirement to practice in a profession. On the other hand, the knowledge and skills obtained in an MBA program may be stepping stones to opportunities that otherwise may have been out of reach to the taxpayer. As a result, the determination of whether MBA expenditures are deductible is fact intensive. From a purely objective standpoint, an MBA degree surely qualifies its recipient for a new trade or business somewhere and someplace. The courts, however, have not focused on this fact. Instead, the courts have focused on the relationship of the MBA curriculum to the taxpayer's duties and responsibilities in his or her profession *before* and *after* he or she receives the degree. Thus, in the typical situation where students enter an MBA program to change career paths, the deductibility of the education is not likely to pass muster. For a taxpayer working in the same profession before and after the MBA degree (the more typical situation for an Executive MBA program), the result is much more favorable.

Source: Matthew A. Melone, "Tax Court Upholds Deduction for MBA Tuition," *Practical Tax Strategies,* March 2010.

Travel and transportation. The cost of travel and transportation associated with the employee's work responsibilities may also qualify as miscellaneous itemized deductions. The cost of travel is deductible if the primary purpose of the trip is business. However, the cost of **commuting**—traveling from a residence to the place of business—is personal and never deductible.[42] When employees drive their personal automobiles for business purposes, they may deduct a standard mileage rate in lieu of deducting actual costs.[43] In 2015, the standard business mileage rate is 57.5 cents per mile. When employees travel on business trips long enough to be away from home overnight, meals and lodging also qualify as employee business expenses. Although meals and lodging are deductible employee business expenses, employees are allowed to deduct only half the cost of the meals. When the travel has both business and personal aspects, the deductibility of transportation costs depends on the primary purpose of the trip. If the primary purpose is business, the transportation costs to arrive at the location are fully deductible. If the primary purpose is personal, the transportation costs to arrive at the location are not deductible. For travel with both business and personal aspects, the meals (50 percent), lodging, transportation while at the location, and incidental expenses are deductible for the business portion of the trip (that is, for the business days of the trip).

Example 6-26

Because Courtney is extremely motivated to reach her potential as an architect (the seminars are doing wonders), she spent a week in September, at her own expense, driving her personal car to several large cities to study different architectural designs. During the trip, she drove a total of 2,134 miles,

(continued on page 6-28)

[42]Costs of commuting to and from a temporary place of work are deductible and costs of commuting from a first job to a second job are deductible. Employees may take *temporary* business trips that last for months. For these trips, the costs of the travel, including meals and lodging, are deductible for the duration of the trip. However, because trips in excess of one year are deemed to be *permanent,* the cost of travel on indefinite trips is *not* deductible.

[43]If an employee chooses to deduct actual automobile costs instead, she would deduct the automobile depreciation or lease payments (see Chapter 10 for applicable depreciation limits), gas, oil, repairs, license, and insurance attributable to business use. Expenses are allocated to business use based on the proportion of business miles to total miles driven for the year. Once a taxpayer chooses the actual cost method, she cannot switch to using the standard business mileage rate.

spent $753 on lodging, and paid $500 for meals. What amount can Courtney deduct as unreimbursed employee business expenses before considering the 2 percent of AGI floor?

Answer: $2,230, computed as follows:

Description	Expense	Calculation
Transportation	$1,227	2,134 miles × 57.5 cents
Lodging	753	
Meals	250	$500 × 50%
Total employee business expense from trip	$2,230	

Employee expense reimbursements. Many employees are reimbursed for their business expenses by their employers. As a general rule, employees *include* reimbursements in gross income and deduct employee business expenses as miscellaneous itemized deductions. However, if an employee is required to submit documentation supporting expenses to receive reimbursement and the employer reimburses only legitimate business expenses, then the employer's reimbursement plan qualifies as an **accountable plan.** Under an accountable plan (which is the most common method for reimbursement) employees *exclude* expense reimbursements from gross income and do *not* deduct the reimbursed expenses. If the expenses exceed the reimbursements, the excess (unreimbursed) portion of each expense is deductible as an employee business expense. Thus, miscellaneous itemized deductions for employee business expenses are commonly referred to as deductions for *unreimbursed* employee business expenses.

Example 6-27

In November, Courtney went on a business trip to Los Angeles to meet with a prospective client and spent $1,700 on business travel including meals and lodging. EWD reimbursed Courtney for the entire $1,700 cost of the trip under an accountable plan. What amount can Courtney deduct?

Answer: $0. Because EWD's reimbursement is made under an accountable plan, Courtney ignores the reimbursement and the expenses for tax purposes; the reimbursement and expenses completely offset each other.

What if: Suppose that EWD provided Courtney with a flat amount of $2,000 to cover her expenses for the trip and did not require her to account for expenditures. How would Courtney treat the reimbursement and the expenses for tax purposes?

Answer: Courtney would include the $2,000 in gross income and claim the $1,700 from the trip from AGI as an employee business expense, miscellaneous itemized deduction subject to the 2 percent of AGI floor (and 50 percent meals limitation). The reimbursement was not made under an accountable plan because Courtney was not required to substantiate her expenses.

Investment Expenses As previously explained, investment expenses are itemized deductions. These expenses are classified as miscellaneous itemized deductions and include expenditures necessary for the production or collection of income, or for the management, conservation, or maintenance of property held for the production of income.[44] Common investment expenses include:

- Expenses associated with investment income or property.
- Investment advisory fees.
- Safe-deposit box fees.
- Subscriptions to investment-related publications.

[44]§212. As we discussed earlier in the chapter, rental and royalty expenses are the only investment expenses that qualify as a deduction for AGI.

Tax Preparation Fees Ordinary and necessary expenses incurred in connection with determining tax obligations imposed by federal, state, municipal, or foreign authorities are also deductible as miscellaneous itemized deductions subject to the 2 percent of AGI floor.[45] While the most common tax preparation fees are the costs of preparing taxpayers' tax returns, taxpayers may also deduct other related expenses such as the cost of property appraisals for tax purposes and the costs of contesting tax liabilities.

Example 6-28

In 2015, Courtney paid Quick Taxes Inc. $250 to prepare her 2014 income tax return. What amount of this expenditure can Courtney deduct before considering the 2 percent of AGI floor?

Answer: $250. The entire amount qualifies as a miscellaneous itemized deduction for 2015.

Hobby Losses As stated previously, individuals engaged in *business* activities are allowed to deduct their business expenses as deductions for AGI. However, taxpayers may engage in certain activities for primarily personal enjoyment but these activities may also generate revenue. For tax purposes, this type of activity is considered a **hobby** rather than a business. Hobby expenses are deductible only to the extent of the revenue generated by the hobby. Sometimes referred to as the *hobby loss limitation,* this limit is less taxpayer-friendly for a hobby than the limits on business expenses. Thus, it's important to determine whether an activity should be considered a business or a hobby for tax purposes. This determination hinges upon whether the taxpayer is engaged in the activity *primarily* to make a profit or *primarily* for personal enjoyment.

To help make this subjective determination, the regulations provide a list of the following factors to consider.[46]

- The manner in which the taxpayer carries on the activity.
- The expertise of the taxpayer or his advisors.
- The time and effort expended by the taxpayer in carrying on the activity.
- The expectation that assets used in the activity may appreciate in value.
- The success of the taxpayer in carrying on other, similar activities.
- The taxpayer's history of income or losses with respect to the activity.
- The amount of occasional profits, if any.
- The financial status of the taxpayer.
- The elements of personal pleasure or recreation.

One of the most important factors is the taxpayer's history of income or loss in the activity. In fact, the tax law explicitly presumes that an activity is a business if it generates a profit in three of five consecutive years.[47] This presumption is difficult for the IRS to overcome in disputes with taxpayers.

If an activity is determined to be a hobby, the taxpayer must *include* the revenue from the activity in gross income and may deduct the expenses, to the extent of the gross income from the activity, as itemized deductions (mortgage interest, real estate taxes, and *miscellaneous itemized deductions*). When hobby expenses exceed revenue, the expenses must be deducted in a particular sequence. Taxpayers first deduct

[45]§212.

[46]See Reg. §1.183-2.

[47]For activities involving breeding, training, or racing horses, the taxpayer need show a profit in only two of seven years for the activity to be presumed to be a business.

expenses that are deductible anyway, such as mortgage interest or property taxes. Second, taxpayers deduct all other hobby expenses except depreciation expense (deducted as miscellaneous itemized deductions). Finally, they deduct depreciation expense (also deducted as a miscellaneous itemized deduction). As discussed below, miscellaneous itemized deductions are only deductible to the extent they exceed 2 percent of AGI. Thus, the revenue from the activity increases the taxpayer's AGI (and taxable income) dollar for dollar. However, the hobby deductions may or may not decrease taxable income depending on whether and the extent to which the taxpayer's itemized deductions exceed her standard deduction and her miscellaneous itemized deductions exceed the 2 percent of AGI floor.

Example 6-29

Courtney's cousin, Phil T. Thrill, played golf at Arizona State University. He turned pro and tried to qualify for the PGA tour when he graduated from college. Unfortunately, he couldn't support his family playing golf and is currently employed as a high school physical education instructor. Every summer, Phil plays in several local and a few regional professional golf tournaments. His only source of revenue from golf is the prize money he wins in these tournaments. Phil has managed to earn prize money in excess of his expenses in only one of the previous five years. This year Phil received golf revenues of $3,200 and incurred golf-related expenses of $8,800 consisting of tournament entry fees, equipment, food, transportation, clothing, and lodging. For tax purposes, are Phil's golf activities considered to be a business or a hobby? If Phil's golfing activities are determined to be a *hobby,* how does Phil account for his revenues and expenses for tax purposes?

Answer: It could go either way. We need more facts regarding his golf activities to make a more clear determination. See *Donald C. Kimbrough,* TC Memo 1988-185, for an example of the Tax Court ruling in a somewhat similar setting that the golfer was engaged in a business. Nonetheless, because Phil has only generated golf revenue in excess of expenses in one of the past five years, the activity is not presumed to be a business activity. To qualify as a business, Phil would have to convince the IRS that he is primarily engaging in golf activities to make a profit rather than for personal enjoyment. If the activity is determined to be a hobby, Phil includes the $3,200 of revenue in gross income as miscellaneous income. He is allowed to deduct $3,200 of his expenses as miscellaneous itemized deductions subject to the 2 percent floor (the deduction is limited to gross income from the activity).

What if: Suppose that Phil's golfing activities are determined to be a hobby and (1) his AGI is $70,000 before considering the effects of his golfing activity, (2) he has itemized deductions of $10,000 that are unrelated to the golf activity, (3) the applicable standard deduction is $6,200, and (4) he has no miscellaneous itemized deductions other than his golfing expenses. What is the effect of his golfing activities on his AGI and taxable income this year?

Answer: The golfing activities will increase Phil's AGI by $3,200 and his taxable income by $1,464 because the full amount of the revenue is included in gross income but his expense deductions are limited. Phil's AGI and taxable income are computed as follows:

Description	Amounts without Hobby	Amounts with Hobby	Explanation
(1) AGI before activity	$70,000	$70,000	
(2) Golf revenue (increase in AGI)		3,200	
(3) AGI after activity	70,000	73,200	(1) + (2).
(4) Golf expenses	0	8,800	
(5) Golf expenses after revenue limit	0	3,200	Lesser of (2) or (4).
(6) 2% of AGI floor	0	1,464	(3) × 2%.
(7) Deductible golf expenses (as miscellaneous itemized deduction)	0	1,736	(5) − (6).
(8) Other itemized deductions	10,000	10,000	
(9) Total itemized deductions	10,000	11,736	(7) + (8).
(10) Taxable income (ignoring exemptions)	60,000	61,464	(3) − (9).
Increase in taxable income		**$ 1,464**	Difference in line (10).

What if: Suppose the same preceding facts, except that Phil does not have the $10,000 of itemized deductions unrelated to the golf activity. What is the effect of his golfing activities on his AGI and taxable income this year?

Answer: The golfing activities will increase Phil's AGI and taxable income by $3,200 because the full amount of the revenue is included in gross income but none of his expense deductions are deductible because his itemized deductions (including the $1,736 of golf expenses that exceed 2 percent of AGI) do not exceed the standard deduction. Thus, the $3,200 golf revenue increases his AGI and taxable income, but he gets no tax deduction for his related expenses because his itemized deductions do not exceed the standard deduction.

Limitation on Miscellaneous Itemized Deductions (2 percent of AGI Floor) To apply the 2 percent floor limit and determine the miscellaneous itemized deduction, the sum of all deductions subject to the 2 percent floor limitation is reduced by 2 percent of AGI. If the 2 percent floor equals or exceeds the sum of miscellaneous itemized deductions, the deductions do not increase the taxpayer's itemized deductions (they don't provide any tax benefit). The 2 percent floor limitation makes it likely that most taxpayers will receive limited, if any, tax benefit from the deductions subject to the floor.

Example 6-30

What amount is Courtney's deduction for miscellaneous itemized deductions that are subject to the 2 percent floor?

Answer: $1,179, computed as follows:

Description	Amount	Reference
Subscriptions to publications	$ 410	Example 6-24.
Educational costs	1,529	Example 6-25.
Business trip to observe architecture	2,230	Example 6-26.
Tax preparation fees	250	Example 6-28.
Total deductions subject to 2% floor	$4,419	
2% of AGI floor (162,000 × 2%)	−3,240	
Total miscellaneous itemized deductions	$1,179	

Courtney incurred a total of $4,419 of miscellaneous itemized deductions, but she can deduct only $1,179 of them due to the 2 percent of AGI restriction.

THE KEY FACTS

Miscellaneous Itemized Deductions

- Employee business expenses not reimbursed by an accountable plan.
- Investment expenses if not in a rental or royalty activity.
- Tax preparation fees and allowable hobby expenses.
- Total miscellaneous itemized deductions are subject to a 2 percent of AGI floor limit.

Miscellaneous Itemized Deductions *Not* Subject to AGI Floor

Several deductions are considered to be miscellaneous itemized deductions but are not subject to the 2 percent of AGI floor. Perhaps because gambling includes a significant element of personal enjoyment (losers may think otherwise), individuals include all gambling winnings for the year in gross income but may also deduct gambling losses *to the extent of gambling winnings* for the year.[48] The deductible gambling losses are miscellaneous itemized deductions; therefore, *losses don't directly offset*

[48]§165(d).

winnings.[49] However, unlike other miscellaneous itemized deductions, gambling losses are *not* subject to the 2 percent of AGI floor. Casualty and theft losses on property held for investment and the unrecovered cost of a life annuity (the taxpayer died before recovering the full cost of the annuity) also qualify as miscellaneous itemized deductions not subject to the AGI floor.

Phase-out of Itemized Deductions

In addition to limits on specific deductions, the amount of a taxpayer's *total* itemized deductions *other than* medical expenses, casualty losses, investment *interest* expense, and gambling losses is subject to a phase-out. That is, when AGI exceeds a certain threshold, itemized deductions are reduced. In 2015, the threshold begins at $309,900 for married taxpayers filing joint, $284,050 for heads of household, $258,250 for single taxpayers, and $154,950 for married taxpayers filing separately. We provide the computation details of the phase-out in Appendix A to this chapter.

Summary of Itemized Deductions

This part of the chapter examined the various itemized deductions (deductions from AGI). We found that both medical expense and casualty loss deductions are designed to reduce the tax burden on individuals whose ability to pay has been involuntarily impaired, but because of large floor limitations these itemized deductions are unlikely to produce tax benefits. Most miscellaneous itemized deductions, including unreimbursed employee business expense and investment expenses (excluding rental and royalty expenses), are likewise hampered by a relatively large floor limitation.

Example 6-31

Given Courtney's current year AGI of $162,000, what is the amount of her total itemized deductions she may claim on her tax return?

Answer: Courtney's itemized deductions for the year are $39,889 calculated as follows:

Description	Amount	Reference
Taxes	$10,380	Example 6-14.
Interest on loans secured by residence	15,800	Example 6-15.
Charitable contributions	12,530	Example 6-21.
Miscellaneous itemized deductions	+1,179	Example 6-30.
Total itemized deductions	$39,889	

*Because Courtney's AGI of $162,000 is below the phase-out threshold of $284,050 for taxpayers filing as a head of household, none of her itemized deductions is phased-out.

Exhibit 6-10 presents Courtney's itemized deductions on Form 1040, Schedule A.

[49]If gambling is deemed to be a business activity (see *Linda M. Myers,* TC Summary Opinion 2007-194), then the taxpayer reports gambling winnings and losses on Schedule C (not as a miscellaneous itemized deduction). However, gambling losses remain only deductible to the extent of gambling winnings.

EXHIBIT 6-10 Courtney's Form 1040, Schedule A

SCHEDULE A (Form 1040)
Department of the Treasury Internal Revenue Service (99)

Itemized Deductions

▶ Information about Schedule A and its separate instructions is at *www.irs.gov/schedulea*.
▶ Attach to Form 1040.

OMB No. 1545-0074
2014
Attachment Sequence No. 07

Name(s) shown on Form 1040: Courtney Wilson
Your social security number: 123-45-6789

Medical and Dental Expenses		**Caution.** Do not include expenses reimbursed or paid by others.				
	1	Medical and dental expenses (see instructions)	1	2,400		
	2	Enter amount from Form 1040, line 38 [2] 162,000				
	3	Multiply line 2 by 10% (.10). But if either you or your spouse was born before January 2, 1950, multiply line 2 by 7.5% (.075) instead	3	16,200		
	4	Subtract line 3 from line 1. If line 3 is more than line 1, enter -0-			4	0
Taxes You Paid	5	State and local **(check only one box):**				
		a ☑ Income taxes, **or** / b ☐ General sales taxes	5	6,700		
	6	Real estate taxes (see instructions)	6	3,680		
	7	Personal property taxes	7			
	8	Other taxes. List type and amount ▶	8			
	9	Add lines 5 through 8			9	10,380
Interest You Paid	10	Home mortgage interest and points reported to you on Form 1098	10	15,800		
Note. Your mortgage interest deduction may be limited (see instructions).	11	Home mortgage interest not reported to you on Form 1098. If paid to the person from whom you bought the home, see instructions and show that person's name, identifying no., and address ▶	11			
	12	Points not reported to you on Form 1098. See instructions for special rules	12			
	13	Mortgage insurance premiums (see instructions)	13			
	14	Investment interest. Attach Form 4952 if required. (See instructions.)	14			
	15	Add lines 10 through 14			15	15,800
Gifts to Charity	16	Gifts by cash or check. If you made any gift of $250 or more, see instructions	16	1,770		
If you made a gift and got a benefit for it, see instructions.	17	Other than by cash or check. If any gift of $250 or more, see instructions. You **must** attach Form 8283 if over $500	17	10,760		
	18	Carryover from prior year	18			
	19	Add lines 16 through 18			19	12,530
Casualty and Theft Losses	20	Casualty or theft loss(es). Attach Form 4684. (See instructions.)			20	
Job Expenses and Certain Miscellaneous Deductions	21	Unreimbursed employee expenses—job travel, union dues, job education, etc. Attach Form 2106 or 2106-EZ if required. (See instructions.) ▶	21	3,759		
	22	Tax preparation fees	22	250		
	23	Other expenses—investment, safe deposit box, etc. List type and amount ▶ Subscription to Business Publications	23	410		
	24	Add lines 21 through 23	24	4,419		
	25	Enter amount from Form 1040, line 38 [25] 162,000				
	26	Multiply line 25 by 2% (.02)	26	3,240		
	27	Subtract line 26 from line 24. If line 26 is more than line 24, enter -0-			27	1,179
Other Miscellaneous Deductions	28	Other—from list in instructions. List type and amount ▶			28	
Total Itemized Deductions	29	Is Form 1040, line 38, over $152,525? ☐ **No.** Your deduction is not limited. Add the amounts in the far right column for lines 4 through 28. Also, enter this amount on Form 1040, line 40. ☑ **Yes.** Your deduction may be limited. See the Itemized Deductions Worksheet in the instructions to figure the amount to enter.			29	39,889
	30	If you elect to itemize deductions even though they are less than your standard deduction, check here ▶ ☐				

For Paperwork Reduction Act Notice, see Form 1040 instructions. Cat. No. 17145C Schedule A (Form 1040) 2014

LO 6-3

THE STANDARD DEDUCTION AND EXEMPTIONS

Standard Deduction

The **standard deduction** is a flat amount that most individuals can elect to deduct *instead* of deducting their itemized deductions (if any). That is, taxpayers generally *deduct the greater of their standard deduction or their itemized deductions.*

The amount of the standard deduction varies according to the taxpayer's filing status, age, and eyesight. The basic standard deduction is greater for married taxpayers filing jointly and those supporting a family (head of household) than it is for married taxpayers filing separately and unmarried taxpayers not supporting a family. Taxpayers who are at least 65 years of age on the last day of the year or blind are entitled to additional standard deduction amounts above and beyond their basic standard deduction.[50] Exhibit 6-11 summarizes the standard deduction amounts.[51]

EXHIBIT 6-11 Standard Deduction Amounts*

2014 Amounts		
Filing Status	**Basic Standard Deduction**	**Additional Standard Deduction for Age and/or Blindness at End of Year**
Married filing jointly	$12,400	$1,200
Head of household	9,100	1,550
Single	6,200	1,550
Married filing separately	6,200	1,200

2015 Amounts		
Filing Status	**Basic Standard Deduction**	**Additional Standard Deduction for Age and/or Blindness at End of Year**
Married filing jointly	$12,600	$1,250
Head of household	9,250	1,550
Single	6,300	1,550
Married filing separately	6,300	1,250

*For individuals claimed as a dependent on another return, the 2015 standard deduction is the greater of (1) $1,050 or (2) $350 plus earned income not to exceed the standard deduction amount of those who are not dependents.

For 2015, the additional standard deduction for either age and/or blindness is $1,250 for married taxpayers and $1,550 for taxpayers who are not married. Thus, a blind individual who is 65 years old and single is entitled to a standard deduction of $9,400 (6,300 + 1,550 + 1,550). A married couple filing a joint return with one spouse over age 65 and one spouse considered legally blind is entitled to a standard deduction of $15,100 (12,600 + 1,250 + 1,250). Finally, for an individual who is eligible to be claimed as a dependent on another's return, the standard deduction is the greater of (1) $1,050 or (2) $350 plus the individual's earned income limited to the regular standard deduction. The additional standard deduction amounts for age and blindness, if any, are not impacted by the preceding limitation for eligible dependents.

[50]Taxpayers are considered 65 on the day before their 65th birthday. Taxpayers are considered to be blind if they have a certified statement from their eye doctor or registered optometrist that their corrected vision of their better eye is no better than 20/200 or their field of vision is 20 degrees or less.

[51]The standard deduction amount is indexed for inflation.

Example 6-32

What is Courtney's standard deduction for the year?

Answer: $9,250. Because Courtney is unmarried at the end of the year and she maintains a household for more than six months for Deron and Ellen who both qualify as her dependents (as qualifying children), Courtney's filing status is head of household, which allows her to claim a standard deduction of $9,250.

Given that Courtney's itemized deductions are $39,889, will Courtney deduct her itemized deductions or her standard deduction?

Answer: She will deduct her itemized deductions because they exceed her standard deduction.

What if: Suppose that Courtney's 10-year-old son, Deron, earned $600 this summer by mowing lawns for neighbors. If Courtney claims a dependency exemption for Deron, what amount of standard deduction can Deron claim on his individual return?

Answer: Deron claims a minimum standard deduction of $1,050 because he is claimed as a dependent on Courtney's return. Hence, Deron would not pay any income tax because his taxable income is reduced to zero by the standard deduction.[52]

What if: Any difference in amount of the standard deduction if Deron earned $2,100?

Answer: Because of the amount of his earnings, Deron claims a standard deduction in the amount of his earned income plus $350. Hence, Deron claims a standard deduction of $2,450 and he would not pay any income tax.[53]

What if: Suppose that Deron earned $8,600?

Answer: Again, Deron claims a standard deduction in the amount of his earned income plus $350. However, Deron's standard deduction is limited to $6,300, the maximum allowable standard deduction for a taxpayer filing single and claimed as a dependent on another return. Hence, Deron would report taxable income of $2,300.

From the government's standpoint, the standard deduction serves two purposes. First, to help taxpayers with lower income, it automatically provides a minimum amount of income that is not subject to taxation. Second, it eliminates the need for the IRS to verify and audit itemized deductions for those taxpayers who chose to deduct the standard deduction. From the taxpayers' perspective, the standard deduction allows them to avoid taxation on a portion of their income, and for those not planning to itemize deductions, it eliminates the need to substantiate and collect information about them. The standard deduction, however, is a double-edged sword. While it reduces taxes by offsetting income with an automatic deduction, it eliminates the tax benefits of itemized deductions up to the amount of the standard deduction. This is a very important point to consider when evaluating the tax benefits of itemized deductions.

Example 6-33

In Example 6-31, we determined that Courtney is entitled to deduct $39,889 of itemized deductions this year. How much do Courtney's itemized deductions reduce her taxable income relative to a situation in which she had $0 itemized deductions?

Answer: $30,639. Because Courtney files as a head of household, she would have been able to deduct $9,250 as a standard deduction even if she had not incurred *any* itemized deductions. Consequently, her itemized deductions reduce her taxable income by only $30,639 ($39,889 − $9,250) beyond what her taxable income would have been if she did not itemize deductions.

[52]Deron will need to file a tax return because his self-employment income exceeds $400 and, as explained in Chapter 8, he will likely owe self-employment tax.

[53]As mentioned previously, Deron will need to file a tax return because his self-employment income exceeds $400 and, as explained in Chapter 8, he will likely owe self-employment taxes.

Bunching Itemized Deductions Some taxpayers may deduct the standard deduction every year because their itemized deductions always fall just short of the standard deduction amount and thus never produce any tax benefit. They may gain some tax benefit from their itemized deductions by implementing a simple timing tax planning strategy called **bunching itemized deductions.** The basic strategy consists of shifting itemized deductions into one year such that the amount of itemized deductions exceeds the standard deduction for the year, and then deducting the standard deduction in the next year (or vice versa).

Because individuals are cash-method taxpayers, they may shift certain itemized deductions by accelerating payment into the current year. For example, a taxpayer could make charitable contributions at the end of December rather than at the beginning of January in the following year. Taxpayers' ability to shift itemized deductions is limited because the timing of these payments is not completely discretionary. For example, real estate taxes have due dates, state taxes are generally paid throughout the year via withholding, and employees may incur and be required to pay business expenses throughout the year. However, taxpayers who annually make a certain amount of charitable contributions, for example, may consider lumping contributions for two years into one year and not contributing in the next year.[54]

Example 6-34

What if: Gram is 70 years old and files as a single taxpayer. Last year Gram paid deductible medical expenses (after the AGI floor limitation) of $4,000. She also contributed $3,000 to her local church. Last year her total itemized deductions were $7,000 ($4,000 medical + 3,000 charitable). Assuming Gram has similar expenditures this year, what amount of additional deductions would Gram have been able to deduct last year if she had bunched her deductions by making her 2014 and 2015 charitable contributions in 2015?

Answer: $2,150, computed as follows:

	No Bunching		Bunching	
	2014	**2015**	**2014**	**2015**
(1) Standard deduction*	$7,750	$7,850	$7,750	$ 7,850
(2) Itemized deductions	7,000	7,000	4,000	10,000
Greater of (1) and (2)	$7,750	$7,850	$7,750	$10,000
Total deductions (combined years)	$15,600 ($7,750 + $7,850)		$17,750 ($7,750 + $10,000)	
Deductions gained through bunching	$2,150 ($17,750 bunching deductions − $15,600 nonbunching deductions)			

*For 2014, her standard deduction is the $6,200 standard deduction for single taxpayers plus an additional $1,550 standard deduction amount for age. For 2015, her standard deduction is the $6,300 standard deduction plus an additional $1,550 standard deduction amount for age.

Deduction for Personal and Dependency Exemptions

As we learned in Chapter 4, taxpayers are generally allowed to deduct $4,000 in 2015 for each **personal** and **dependency exemption.** In general, then, a taxpayer's from AGI deduction for personal and dependency exemptions is $4,000 multiplied by the number of the taxpayer's **exemptions.** However, just as with itemized deductions, a taxpayer's total exemption deduction is phased out based on AGI for relatively high income taxpayers. The AGI threshold for the beginning of the phase-out and the AGI for the maximum phase-out depends on the taxpayer's filing status. The amounts for 2015 are presented in Exhibit 6-12. We discuss the computational details of the phase-out in Appendix B to this chapter.

[54]Of course, as we discussed in Chapter 3, taxpayers adopting this strategy must also consider the time value of money for the contributions amounts they pay in advance to determine whether a tax planning strategy designed to save taxes makes economic sense.

EXHIBIT 6-12 Maximum Phase-out Range for Personal and Dependency Exemptions for 2015

Filing Status	Threshold	AGI Maximum Phase-out
Married filing jointly	$309,900	$432,401
Head of household	284,050	406,551
Single	258,250	380,751
Married filing separately	154,950	216,201

Example 6-35

This year, Courtney is allowed to claim a personal exemption for herself and dependency exemptions for her daughter Ellen and her son Deron. Courtney's filing status is head of household. What amount is Courtney allowed to deduct for her personal and dependency exemptions?

Answer: $12,000 ($4,000 × 3). Because Courtney's AGI is $162,000 and she files as a head of household, her AGI is below the $284,050 threshold for the exemption phase-out. Thus, she is allowed to deduct her full exemption amounts without phase-out.

Taxable Income Summary

We now have enough information to calculate Courtney's and Gram's taxable income. Exhibit 6-13 shows Courtney's taxable income calculation and Exhibit 6-14 illustrates how this information would be displayed on page 2 of Courtney's Form 1040.

Exhibit 6-15 provides Gram's taxable income calculation.

EXHIBIT 6-13 Courtney's Taxable Income

Description	Amount	Reference
AGI	$162,000	Exhibit 6-6.
Less: Greater of (1) itemized deductions ($39,889) or (2) standard deduction ($9,250)	(39,889)	Example 6-31.
Less: Personal and dependency exemptions	(12,000)	Example 6-35.
Taxable income	$ 110,111	

EXHIBIT 6-14 Courtney's Taxable Income Computation as Presented on Form 1040, Page 2

Form 1040 (2014) Page **2**

Tax and Credits	38	Amount from line 37 (adjusted gross income)	38	162,000
	39a	Check if: { ☐ **You** were born before January 2, 1950, ☐ Blind. ☐ **Spouse** was born before January 2, 1950, ☐ Blind. } **Total boxes checked ▶ 39a** ☐		
	b	If your spouse itemizes on a separate return or you were a dual-status alien, check here ▶ 39b☐		
Standard Deduction for— • People who check any box on line	40	**Itemized deductions** (from Schedule A) **or** your **standard deduction** (see left margin) . .	40	39,889
	41	Subtract line 40 from line 38	41	122,111
	42	**Exemptions.** If line 38 is $152,525 or less, multiply $3,950 by the number on line 6d. Otherwise, see instructions	42	12,000
	43	**Taxable income.** Subtract line 42 from line 41. If line 42 is more than line 41, enter -0- . .	43	110,111

EXHIBIT 6-15 Gram's Taxable Income

Description	Amount	Explanation
(1) AGI	$15,590	Exhibit 6-7.
(2) Greater of (a) itemized deductions ($7,000) or (b) standard deduction ($7,850)	(7,850)	Example 6-34.
(3) Personal and dependency exemptions	(4,000)	One exemption.
Taxable income	$ 3,740	(1) + (2) + (3).

Note that because Gram's gross income of $16,000 (Exhibit 5-6) is more than the sum of her basic standard deduction amount plus her personal and dependency exemption ($11,850), she is required to file a tax return.

CONCLUSION

We started this chapter with Courtney's and Gram's gross incomes. In this chapter, we first identified the duo's separate *deductions for AGI* and we computed their AGI. We then determined their *from* AGI deductions. Courtney deducted her itemized deductions because they exceeded her standard deduction. Gram, on the other hand, deducted her standard deduction. Finally, Courtney deducted three exemptions: a personal exemption for herself and dependency exemptions for each of her two children, Deron and Ellen. Gram deducted one personal exemption for herself. By subtracting their *from* AGI deductions from their AGI, we determined taxable income for both Courtney and Gram. With this knowledge, we proceed to the next two chapters and address issues relating to investments and determining the amount of tax Courtney and Gram are required to pay on their taxable income.

Appendix A Calculation of Itemized Deduction Phase-out for 2015

The amount of the itemized deduction phase-out for 2015 is the lesser of:

(1) 3 percent × [AGI minus $309,900 ($284,050 for heads of household, $258,250 for single taxpayers, and $154,950 for married taxpayers filing separately)] or

(2) 80 percent of the total itemized deductions subject to phase-out.

Example 6-1A

What if: Suppose Courtney's AGI was $320,000. What would be the amount of her total itemized deductions she may claim on her tax return after computing the itemized deduction phase-out?

Answer: Courtney's itemized deductions for the year are $38,810, calculated as follows:

Description	Amount	Reference
Taxes	$ 10,380	Example 6-14.
Interest on loans secured by residence	15,800	Example 6-15.
Charitable contributions	12,530	Example 6-21.
Miscellaneous itemized deductions	1,179	Example 6-30.
Total itemized deductions subject to phase-out	$ 39,889	
Less phase-out of itemized deductions	−$1,079	See calculation below.
Total itemized deductions	$ 38,810	

Calculation of the phase-out:

Lesser of :

(1) 3 percent × (AGI minus $284,050) = 3 percent × ($320,000 − $284,050) = $1,079 or

(2) 80 percent of the total itemized deductions subject to phase-out ($39,889) = $31,911

APPENDIX B Personal Exemption Phase-out Computation for 2015

The process of determining the amount of the phase-out involves the following five steps.

Step 1: Subtract the taxpayer's AGI from the AGI threshold based on the taxpayer's filing status. If the threshold equals or exceeds the taxpayer's AGI, the taxpayer deducts her full personal and dependency exemption.

Step 2: Divide the excess AGI (the amount from Step 1) by 2,500. If the result is not a whole number (i.e., the excess AGI is not evenly divisible by 2,500), round *up* to the next whole number. [For married filing separate taxpayers, replace the 2,500 amount with 1,250).

Step 3: Multiply the outcome of Step 2 by 2 percent, but limit the product to 100 percent.

Step 4: Multiply the percentage determined in Step 3 by the taxpayer's total personal and dependency exemptions (i.e., number of personal and dependency exemptions times $4,000 in 2015). The product is the amount of personal and dependency exemption that is phased-out (i.e., the taxpayer is *not* allowed to deduct this amount).

Step 5: Subtract the Step 4 result from the taxpayer's total personal and dependency exemptions that would be deductible without any phase-out (i.e., number of personal and dependency exemptions times $4,000 in 2015).

Example 6-1B

What if: Suppose that Courtney's AGI was $339,550 and her personal and dependency exemptions total $12,000 ($4,000 × 3). What amount of personal and dependency exemptions would she be allowed to deduct with the phase-out?

Answer: $6,480, computed as follows:

	Amount	Explanation
Step 1:	$55,500	$339,550 – $284,050 (Excess AGI).
Step 2:	23	Divide $55,500 by 2,500 and round up to nearest whole number $55,500/2,500 = 22.2 → 23.
Step 3:	46%	Multiply the amount in Step 2 by 2% (i.e., 23 × 2%).
Step 4:	$ 5,520	Multiply the Step 3 result by the total exemption amount (i.e., $12,000 × 46%). This is the amount of the phase-out.
Step 5:	$ 6,480	Subtract the Step 4 result from the total exemption amount (i.e., $12,000 – $5,520). This is the deductible exemption amount.

Summary

Identify the common deductions necessary for calculating adjusted gross income (AGI). LO 6-1

- Deductions for AGI may be categorized into those that are directly or indirectly business-related and those that address specific policy issues.
- The business-related deductions for AGI include business expenses, rent and royalty expenses, self-employment taxes, moving expenses, medical and health insurance by self-employed taxpayers, and forfeited interest.
- Other common deductions for AGI include the deductions for alimony, interest on student loans, qualified education expenses, and early withdrawal penalties.

LO 6-2 Describe the different types of itemized deductions available to individuals and compute itemized deductions.

- The medical expense and casualty loss deductions are designed to provide tax benefits to needy individuals but both are subject to significant floor limitations.
- The itemized deduction for interest is limited to interest related to a personal residence and investment interest, and the latter is limited by net investment income.
- The deduction for charitable contributions extends to contributions of money and property to qualifying charities. The charitable deduction is subject to ceiling limitations, which are more restrictive for donations of property.
- The deduction for taxes includes state income and property taxes. Sales taxes can be deducted in lieu of deducting state and local income taxes.
- Employee business expenses and investment expenses (except rental and royalty expenses) are miscellaneous itemized deductions subject to a 2 percent of AGI floor limitation.

LO 6-3 Explain the operation of the standard deduction, determine the deduction for personal and dependency exemptions, and compute taxable income.

- Itemized deductions do not produce any tax benefit unless the total itemized deductions exceed the standard deduction.
- Certain itemized deductions are subject to a phase-out for high income taxpayers.
- Personal exemptions are allowed for the taxpayer and spouse (if married filing jointly).
- Personal and dependency exemptions are subject to a phase-out for high income taxpayers.

KEY TERMS

accountable plan (6-28)
bunching itemized deductions (6-36)
business activities (6-2)
capital gain property (6-19)
casualty loss (6-24)
ceiling (6-21)
commuting (6-27)
dependency exemption (6-36)
exemption (6-36)
floor limitation (6-15)
hobby (6-29)
investment activities (6-2)
miscellaneous itemized deductions (6-26)
modified AGI (6-10)
ordinary and necessary (6-4)
ordinary income property (6-19)
personal exemption (6-36)
private nonoperating foundations (6-21)
private operating foundations (6-21)
qualified educational expenses (6-9)
qualified educational loans (6-9)
standard deduction (6-34)
trade or business (6-3)

DISCUSSION QUESTIONS

LO 6-1 1. It has been suggested that tax policy favors deductions for AGI compared to itemized deductions. Describe two ways in which deductions for AGI are treated more favorably than itemized deductions.

LO 6-1 2. How is a business activity distinguished from an investment activity? Why is this distinction important for the purpose of calculating federal income taxes?

LO 6-1 3. Describe how a business element is reflected in the requirements to deduct moving expenses and how Congress limited this deduction to substantial moves.

LO 6-1 4. Explain why Congress allows self-employed taxpayers to deduct the cost of health insurance above the line (for AGI) when employees can only itemize this cost as a medical expense. Would a self-employed taxpayer ever prefer to claim health insurance premiums as an itemized deduction rather than a deduction for AGI? Explain.

5. Explain why Congress allows self-employed taxpayers to deduct the employer portion of their self-employment tax. LO 6-1

6. Using the Internal Revenue Code, describe two deductions for AGI that are not discussed in this chapter. LO 6-1 research

7. Explain why Congress allows taxpayers to deduct interest forfeited as a penalty on the premature withdrawal from a certificate of deposit. LO 6-1

8. Describe the mechanical limitation on the deduction for interest on qualified educational loans. LO 6-1

9. Explain why the medical expense and casualty loss provisions are sometimes referred to as "wherewithal" deductions and how this rationale is reflected in the limits on these deductions. LO 6-2

10. Describe the type of medical expenditures that qualify for the medical expense deduction. Does the cost of meals consumed while hospitalized qualify for the deduction? Do over-the-counter drugs and medicines qualify for the deduction? LO 6-2

11. Under what circumstances can a taxpayer deduct medical expenses paid for a member of his family? Does it matter if the family member reports significant amounts of gross income and cannot be claimed as a dependent? LO 6-2

12. What types of taxes qualify to be deducted as itemized deductions? Would a vehicle registration fee qualify as a deductible tax? LO 6-2

13. Compare and contrast the limits on the deduction of interest on home acquisition indebtedness versus home equity loans. Are these limits consistent with horizontal equity? Explain. LO 6-2

14. Explain the argument that the deductions for charitable contributions and home mortgage interest represent indirect subsidies for these activities. LO 6-2

15. Cash donations to charity are subject to a number of very specific substantiation requirements. Describe these requirements and how charitable gifts can be substantiated. Describe the substantiation requirements for property donations. LO 6-2 research

16. Describe the conditions in which a donation of property to a charity will result in a charitable contribution deduction of fair market value and when it will result in a deduction of the tax basis of the property. LO 6-2

17. Describe the type of event that qualifies as a casualty for tax purposes. LO 6-2

18. A casualty loss from the complete destruction of a personal asset is limited to the lesser of fair market value or the property's adjusted basis. Explain the rationale for this rule as opposed to just allowing a deduction for the basis of the asset. LO 6-2

19. This week Jim's residence was heavily damaged by a storm system that spread destruction throughout the region. While Jim's property insurance covers some of the damage, there is a significant amount of uninsured loss. The governor of Jim's state has requested that the president declare the region a federal disaster area and provide federal disaster assistance. Explain to Jim the income tax implications of such a declaration and any associated tax planning possibilities. LO 6-2 research

20. Describe the types of expenses that constitute miscellaneous itemized deductions and explain why these expenses rarely produce any tax benefits. LO 6-2

21. Explain why the cost of commuting from home to work is not deductible as a business expense. LO 6-2

22. When is the cost of education deductible as an employee business expense? LO 6-2

23. How might the reimbursement of a portion of an employee expense influence the deductibility of the expense for the employee? LO 6-2

LO 6-2 24. Explain why an employee should be concerned about whether his employer reimburses business expenses using an "accountable" plan?

LO 6-2 25. Jake is a retired jockey who takes monthly trips to Las Vegas to gamble on horse races. Jake also trains race horses part time at his Louisville ranch. So far this year, Jake has won almost $47,500 during his trips to Las Vegas while spending $27,250 on travel expenses and incurring $62,400 of gambling losses. Jake also received $60,000 in revenue from his training activities and he incurred $72,000 of associated costs. Explain how Jake's gambling winnings and related costs will be treated for tax purposes. Describe the factors that will influence how Jake's ranch expenses are treated for tax purposes.

LO 6-2 research 26. Frank paid $3,700 in fees for an accountant to tabulate business information (Frank operates as a self-employed contractor and files a Schedule C). The accountant also spent time tabulating Frank's income from his investments and determining Frank's personal itemized deductions. Explain to Frank whether or not he can deduct the $3,700 as a business expense or as an itemized deduction, and provide a citation to an authority that supports your conclusion.

LO 6-2 27. Contrast ceiling and floor limitations, and give an example of each.

LO 6-2 28. Identify which itemized deductions are subject to floor limitations, ceiling limitations, or some combination of these limits.

LO 6-3 29. Describe the tax benefits from "bunching" itemized deductions in one year. Describe the characteristics of the taxpayers who are most likely to benefit from using bunching and explain why this is so.

LO 6-3 30. Explain how the standard deduction is rationalized and why the standard deduction might be viewed as a floor limit on itemized deductions.

LO 6-3 31. Explain how the calculation of the standard deduction limits the ability to shift income to a dependent.

LO 6-3 32. Explain why the overall phase-out of itemized deductions has been described as a "haircut" of itemized deductions. Explain whether it is possible for a taxpayer to lose all their itemized deductions under the phase-out rules.

LO 6-3 33. Describe the mechanism for phasing out exemptions. Can a taxpayer lose the benefit of all of her personal and dependency exemptions?

LO 6-3 research 34. Determine if a taxpayer can change his election to itemize deductions once a return is filed. (*Hint:* Read about itemization under Reg. §1.63-1.)

LO 6-3 research 35. Determine whether a taxpayer who is claimed as a dependent on another return is entitled to an addition to the standard deduction for age or blindness. (*Hint:* Read the calculation of the standard deduction under IRC §63.)

PROBLEMS

All applicable problems are available with McGraw-Hill's *Connect*® *Accounting*.

LO 6-1 36. Clem is married and is a skilled carpenter. Clem's wife, Wanda, works part-time as a substitute grade school teacher. Determine the amount of Clem's expenses that are deductible *for AGI* this year (if any) under the following independent circumstances:

a) Clem is self-employed and this year he incurred $525 for tools and supplies related to his job. Since neither were covered by a qualified health plan, Wanda paid health insurance premiums of $3,600 to provide coverage for herself and Clem (not through an exchange).

b) Clem and Wanda own a garage downtown that they rent to a local business for storage. This year they incurred $1,250 in utilities and depreciation of $780.

c) Clem paid self-employment tax of $15,300 (the employer portion is $7,650), and Wanda had $3,000 of Social Security taxes withheld from her pay.

d) Clem paid $45 to rent a safe deposit box to store his coin collection. Clem has collected coins intermittently since he was a boy, and he expects to sell his collection when he retires.

37. Clyde currently commutes 55 miles to work in the city. He is considering a new assignment in the suburbs on the other side of the city that would increase his commute considerably. He would like to accept the assignment, but he thinks it might require that he move to the other side of the city. Determine if Clyde's move qualifies for a moving expense deduction and calculate the amount (if any) under the following circumstances: LO 6-1

a) Clyde estimates that unless he moves across town, his new commute would be almost 70 miles. He also estimates the costs of a move as follows:

Lodging while searching for an apartment	$ 126
Transportation—auto (100 miles @ 23 cents/mile, rounded)	23
Mover's fee (furniture and possessions)	1,500
Meals while en route	35

b) Same as part (a), except Clyde estimates that unless he moves across town, his new commute would be almost 115 miles.

c) Same as part (a), except Clyde's new commute would be almost 150 miles and the movers intend to impose a $450 surcharge on the moving fee for the additional distance.

38. Smithers is a self-employed individual who earns $30,000 per year in self-employment income. Smithers pays $2,200 in annual health insurance premiums (not through an exchange) for his own medical care. In each of the following situations, determine the amount of the deductible health insurance premium for Smithers before any AGI limitation. LO 6-1

a) Smithers is single and the self-employment income is his only source of income.

b) Smithers is single, but besides being self-employed, Smithers is also employed part-time by SF Power Corporation. This year Smithers elected not to participate in SF's health plan.

c) Smithers is self-employed and he is also married. Smithers's spouse, Samantha, is employed full-time by SF Power Corporation and is covered by SF's health plan. Smithers is not eligible to participate in SF's health plan.

d) Smithers is self-employed and he is also married. Smithers's spouse, Samantha, is employed full-time by SF Power Corporation and is covered by SF's health plan. Smithers elected not to participate in SF's health plan.

39. Hardaway earned $100,000 of compensation this year. He also paid (or had paid for him) $3,000 of health insurance (not through an exchange). What is Hardaway's AGI in each of the following situations (ignore the effects of Social Security and self-employment taxes)? LO 6-1

a) Hardaway is an employee and his employer paid Hardaway's $3,000 of health insurance for him as a nontaxable fringe benefit. Consequently, Hardaway received $97,000 of taxable compensation and $3,000 of non-taxable compensation.

b) Hardaway is a self-employed taxpayer, and he paid $3,000 of health insurance himself. He is not eligible to participate in an employer-sponsored plan.

40. Betty operates a beauty salon as a sole proprietorship. Betty also owns and rents an apartment building. This year Betty had the following income and expenses. Determine Betty's AGI and complete page 1 of Form 1040 for Betty. You may assume that Betty will owe $2,502 in self-employment tax on her salon income.

Interest income	$11,255
Salon sales and revenue	86,360
Salaries paid to beauticians	45,250
Beauty salon supplies	23,400
Alimony paid to her ex-husband, Rocky	6,000
Rental revenue from apartment building	31,220
Depreciation on apartment building	12,900
Real estate taxes paid on apartment building	11,100
Real estate taxes paid on personal residence	6,241
Contributions to charity	4,237

41. Lionel is an unmarried law student at State University Law School, a qualified educational institution. This year Lionel borrowed $24,000 from Counti Bank and paid interest of $1,440. Lionel used the loan proceeds to pay his law school tuition. Calculate the amounts Lionel can deduct for higher education expenses and interest on higher education loans under the following circumstances (assume the 2014 rules apply for purposes of the qualified education expense deduction):

a) Lionel's AGI before deducting interest on higher education loans is $50,000.

b) Lionel's AGI before deducting interest on higher education loans is $74,000.

c) Lionel's AGI before deducting interest on higher education loans is $90,000.

42. This year Jack intends to file a married-joint return with two dependents. Jack received $162,500 of salary and paid $5,000 of interest on loans used to pay qualified tuition costs for his dependent daughter, Deb. This year Jack has also paid qualified moving expenses of $4,300 and $24,000 of alimony.

a) What is Jack's adjusted gross income? Assume that Jack will opt to treat tax items in a manner to minimize his AGI.

b) Suppose that Jack also reported income of $8,800 from a half share of profits from a partnership. Disregard any potential self-employment taxes on this income. What AGI would Jack report under these circumstances? Again, assume that Jack will opt to treat tax items in a manner to minimize his AGI.

LO 6-1 LO 6-2

43. In each of the following independent cases, indicate the amount (1) deductible *for* AGI, (2) deductible *from* AGI, and (3) neither deductible for nor from AGI before considering income limitations or the standard deduction.

a) Ted paid $8 rent on a safety deposit box at the bank. In this box he kept the few shares of stock that he owned.

b) Tyler paid $85 for minor repairs to the fence at a rental house he owned.

c) Timmy paid $545 for health insurance premiums this year (not through an exchange). Timmy is employed full-time and his employer paid the remaining premiums as a qualified fringe benefit.

d) Tess paid $1,150 of state income taxes on her consulting income.

44. In each of the following independent cases, indicate the amount (1) deductible *for* AGI, (2) deductible *from* AGI, and (3) neither deductible for nor deductible from AGI before considering income limitations or the standard deduction. LO 6-1 LO 6-2

a) Fran spent $90 for uniforms for use on her job. Her employer reimbursed her for $75 of this amount under an accountable plan.

b) Timothy, a plumber employed by ACE Plumbing, spent $65 for small tools to be used on his job, but he was not reimbursed by ACE.

c) Jake is a perfume salesperson. Because of his high pay, he receives no allowance or reimbursement from his employer for advertising expenses even though his position requires him to advertise frequently. During the year, he spent $2,200 on legitimate business advertisements.

d) Trey is a self-employed special-duty nurse. He spent $120 for uniforms.

e) Mary, a professor at a community college, spent $340 for magazine subscriptions. The magazines were helpful for her research activities, but she was not reimbursed for the expenditures.

f) Wayne lost $325 on the bets he made at the race track, but he won $57 playing slot machines.

45. Ted is a successful attorney, but when he turned 50 years old he decided to retire from his law practice and become a professional golfer. Ted has been a very successful amateur golfer, so beginning this year Ted began competing in professional golf tournaments. At year-end, Ted reported the following expenses associated with competing in 15 professional events: LO 6-2

Transportation from his home to various tournaments	$25,000
Lodging for the 15 weeks on the road	18,200
Meals while traveling and during golf tournaments	5,200
Entry fees	7,500
Lessons from various golf teachers	12,500
Golf supplies (balls, tees, etc.)	783
Total expenses	$69,183

a) Suppose that Ted reports $175,000 in gross income from his pension and various investments. Describe the various considerations that will dictate the extent to which Ted can deduct the expenses associated with professional golf.

b) Calculate Ted's deduction for golf expenses assuming that the IRS and the courts are convinced that Ted engages in competitive golf primarily for enjoyment rather than the expectation of making a profit. Assume Ted wins $10,000 this year and his AGI is $185,000 (including the golf revenues).

46. Penny, a full-time biochemist, loves stock car racing. To feed her passion, she bought a used dirt track car and has started entering some local dirt track races. The prize money is pretty small ($1,000 for the winner), but she really is not in it for the money. Penny reported the following income and expenses from her nights at the track: LO 6-2

Prize money	$2,500
Expenses:	
Transportation from her home to the races	1,000
Depreciation on the dirt track car	4,000
Entry fees	3,500
Oil, gas, supplies, repairs for the dirt track car	2,050

Calculate Penny's deduction for the racing expenses assuming that the racing activity is a hobby, and Penny's AGI is $97,500 *before* considering the prize money.

LO 6-2

47. Simpson is a single individual who is employed full-time by Duff Corporation. This year Simpson reports AGI of $50,000 and has incurred the following medical expenses:

Dentist charges	$ 900
Physician's charges	1,800
Optical charges	500
Cost of eyeglasses	300
Hospital charges	2,100
Prescription drugs	250
Over-the-counter drugs	450
Medical insurance premiums (not through an exchange)	775

a) Calculate the amount of medical expenses that will be included with Simpson's itemized deductions after any applicable limitations.

b) Suppose that Simpson was reimbursed for $250 of the physician's charges and $1,200 for the hospital costs. Calculate the amount of medical expenses that will be included with Simpson's itemized deductions after any applicable limitations.

LO 6-2

48. This year Tim is age 45 and is considering enrolling in an insurance program that provides for long-term care insurance. He is curious about whether the insurance premiums are deductible as a medical expense and, if so, what is the maximum amount that can be deducted in any year.

LO 6-2

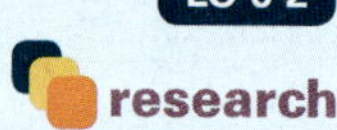

49. Doctor Bones prescribed physical therapy in a pool to treat Jack's broken back. In response to this advice (and for no other reason), Jack built a swimming pool in his backyard and strictly limited use of the pool to physical therapy. Jack paid $25,000 to build the pool, but he wondered if this amount could be deducted as a medical expense. Determine if a capital expenditure such as the cost of a swimming pool qualifies for the medical expense deduction.

LO 6-1 LO 6-2

50. Charles has AGI of $50,000 and has made the following payments related to (1) land he inherited from his deceased aunt and (2) a personal vacation taken last year. Calculate the amount of taxes Charles may include in his itemized deductions for the year under the following circumstances:

State inheritance tax on the land	$1,200
County real estate tax on the land	1,500
School district tax on the land	690
City special assessment on the land (replacing curbs and gutters)	700
State tax on airline tickets (paid on vacation)	125
Local hotel tax (paid during vacation)	195

a) Suppose that Charles holds the land for appreciation.

b) Suppose that Charles holds the land for rent.

c) Suppose that the vacation was actually a business trip.

LO 6-2

51. Dan has AGI of $50,000 and paid the following taxes during this tax year. Calculate how much Dan can deduct for taxes as an itemized deduction this year.

State income tax withholding	$1,400
State income tax estimated payments	750
Federal income tax withholding	3,000
Social Security tax withheld from wages	2,100
State excise tax on liquor	400
Automobile license (based on the car's weight)	300
State sales tax paid	475

52. Tim is a single, cash method taxpayer with one personal exemption and an AGI of $50,000. In April of this year Tim paid $1,020 with his state income tax return for the previous year. During the year, Tim had $5,400 of state income tax and $18,250 of federal income tax withheld from his salary. In addition, Tim made estimated payments of $1,360 and $1,900 of state and federal income taxes, respectively. Finally, Tim expects to receive a refund of $500 for state income taxes when he files his state tax return for this year in April next year. What is the amount of taxes that Tim can deduct as an itemized deduction? LO 6-1 LO 6-2

53. This year Randy paid $28,000 of interest. (Randy borrowed $450,000 to buy his residence, which is currently worth $500,000.) Randy also paid $2,500 of interest on his car loan and $4,200 of margin interest to his stockbroker (investment interest expense). How much of this interest expense can Randy deduct as an itemized deduction under the following circumstances? LO 6-2

a) Randy received $2,200 of interest this year and no other investment income or expenses. His AGI is $75,000.

b) Randy had no investment income this year, and his AGI is $75,000.

54. This year, Major Healy paid $40,000 of interest on a mortgage on his home (Major Healy borrowed $800,000 to buy the residence; $900,000 original purchase price and value at purchase; $1,000,000 current worth), $6,000 of interest on a $120,000 home equity loan on his home (loan proceeds were used to buy antique cars), and $10,000 of interest on a mortgage on his vacation home (loan of $200,000; home purchased for $500,000). Major Healy's AGI is $220,000. LO 6-2

a) How much interest expense can Major Healy deduct as an itemized deduction?

b) Assume the original facts, except that Major Healy's home had a fair market value of $1,000,000 when he purchased the home and took out the home equity debt, but now the home is worth $500,000. How much interest expense can Major Healy deduct as an itemized deduction?

55. Ray Ray made the following contributions this year. LO 6-2

Charity	Property	Cost	FMV
Athens Academy School	cash	$ 5,000	$ 5,000
United Way	cash	4,000	4,000
American Heart Association	Antique painting	15,000	75,000
First Methodist Church	Coca-Cola stock	12,000	20,000

Determine the maximum amount of charitable deduction for each of these contributions *ignoring* the AGI ceiling on charitable contributions and assuming that the American Heart Association plans to sell the antique painting to fund its operations. Ray Ray has owned the painting and Coca-Cola stock since 1990.

56. Calvin reviewed his cancelled checks and receipts this year for charitable contributions. He has owned the IBM stock and painting since 2005. Calculate Calvin's charitable contribution deduction and carryover (if any) under the following circumstances. LO 6-2

Donee	Item	Cost	FMV
Hobbs Medical Center	IBM stock	$5,000	$22,000
State Museum	painting	5,000	3,000
A needy family	food and clothes	400	250
United Way	cash	8,000	8,000

a) Calvin's AGI is $100,000.

b) Calvin's AGI is $100,000 but the State Museum told Calvin that it plans to sell the painting.

c) Calvin's AGI is $50,000.

d) Calvin's AGI is $100,000 and Hobbs is a nonoperating private foundation.

e) Calvin's AGI is $100,000 but the painting is worth $10,000.

LO 6-2

57. In addition to cash contributions to charity, Dean decided to donate shares of stock and a portrait painted during the earlier part of the last century. Dean purchased the stock and portrait many years ago as investments. Dean reported the following recipients:

Charity	Property	Cost	FMV
State University	cash	$15,000	$15,000
Red Cross	cash	14,500	14,500
State History Museum	painting	5,000	82,000
City Medical Center	Dell stock	28,000	17,000

a) Determine the maximum amount of charitable deduction for each of these contributions *ignoring* the AGI ceiling on charitable contributions.

b) Assume that Dean's AGI this year is $150,000. Determine Dean's itemized deduction for his charitable contributions this year and any carryover.

c) Assume that Dean's AGI this year is $240,000. Determine Dean's itemized deduction for his charitable contributions this year and any carryover.

d) Suppose Dean is a dealer in antique paintings and had held the paintings for sale before the contribution. What is Dean's charitable contribution deduction for the paintings in this situation (ignoring AGI limitations)?

e) Suppose that Dean's objective with the donation to the museum was to finance expansion of the historical collection. Hence, Dean was not surprised when the museum announced the sale of the portrait because of its limited historical value. What is Dean's charitable contribution deduction for the paintings in this situation (ignoring AGI limitations)?

LO 6-2

58. Tim suffered greatly this year. In January a freak storm damaged his sailboat and in July Tim's motorcycle was stolen from his vacation home. Tim originally paid $27,000 for the boat, but he was able to repair the damage for $6,200. Tim paid $15,500 for the motorcycle, but it was worth $17,000 before it was stolen. Insurance reimbursed $1,000 for the boat repairs and the cycle was uninsured.

a) Calculate Tim's deductible casualty loss if his AGI is $50,000.

b) Calculate Tim's deductible casualty loss if his AGI is $150,000.

c) How would you answer (a) if Tim received an additional $65,000 in interest from municipal bonds this year?

LO 6-2
planning

59. Trevor is a single individual who is a cash-method calendar-year taxpayer. For each of the next two years (year 1 and year 2), Trevor expects to report AGI of $80,000, contribute $3,500 to charity, and pay $2,500 in state income taxes.

a) Estimate Trevor's taxable income for year 1 and year 2 using the 2015 amounts for the standard deduction and personal exemption for both years.

b) Now assume that Trevor combines his anticipated charitable contributions for the next two years and makes the combined contribution in December of year 1. Estimate Trevor's taxable income for each of the next two years using the 2015 amounts for the standard deduction and personal exemption. Reconcile the total taxable income to your solution to part (a).

c) Trevor plans to purchase a residence next year, and he estimates that additional property taxes and residential interest will each cost $4,000 annually ($8,000 in total annually). Estimate Trevor's taxable income for each of the next two years (year 1 and year 2) using the 2015 amounts for the standard deduction and personal exemption and also assuming Trevor makes the charitable contribution of $3,500 and state tax payments of $2,500 in each year.

d) Assume that Trevor makes the charitable contribution for year 2 and pays the real estate taxes for year 2 in December of year 1. Estimate Trevor's taxable income for year 1 and year 2 using the 2015 amounts for the standard deduction and personal exemption. Reconcile the total taxable income to your solution to part (c).

e) Explain the conditions in which the bunching strategy in part (d) will generate tax savings for Trevor.

60. Baker paid $775 for the preparation of his tax return and incurred $375 of employee business expenses, of which $60 was reimbursed by his employer through an accountable plan. Baker also paid a $100 fee for investment advice. Calculate the amount of these expenses that Baker is able to deduct assuming he itemizes his deductions in each of the following situations: **LO 6-2**

a) Baker's AGI is $50,000.

b) Baker's AGI is $100,000.

61. Simon lost $5,000 gambling this year on a trip to Las Vegas. In addition, he paid $2,000 to his broker for managing his $200,000 portfolio and $1,500 to his accountant for preparing his tax return. In addition, Simon incurred $2,500 in transportation costs commuting back and forth from his home to his employer's office, which were not reimbursed. Calculate the amount of these expenses that Simon is able to deduct, assuming he itemizes his deductions, in each of the following situations: **LO 6-2**

a) Simon's AGI is $40,000.

b) Simon's AGI is $200,000.

62. Zack is employed as a full-time airport security guard. This year Zack's employer transferred him from Dallas to Houston. At year-end, Zack discovered a number of unreimbursed expenses related to his employment in Dallas prior to his move to Houston. Identify which expenses are deductible and whether the deductions are *for* or *from* AGI. **LO 6-2**

Cost of bus transportation from his home to the airport	$ 150
Subscription to *Journal of Security Guards*	52
Lunch with colleagues	195
Cost of self-defense course at local community center	500
Cost of lunch with supervisor during evaluations	383
Total	$1,280

63. Stephanie is a twelve-year-old who often assists neighbors on weekends by babysitting their children. Calculate the 2015 standard deduction Stephanie will claim under the following independent circumstances (assume that Stephanie's parents will claim her as a dependent). **LO 6-3**

a) Stephanie reported $850 of earnings from her babysitting.

b) Stephanie reported $1,500 of earnings from her babysitting.

c) Stephanie reported $8,000 of earnings from her babysitting.

LO 6-1 LO 6-2 LO 6-3

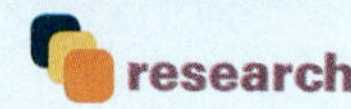

64. Tammy teaches elementary school history for the Metro School District. In 2015 she has incurred the following expenses associated with her job:

Noncredit correspondence course on history	$ 900
Teaching cases for classroom use	1,800
Tuition for university graduate course in physics	1,200
Transportation between school and home	750
Photocopying class materials	100
Transportation from school to extracurricular activities	110
Cost of lunches eaten during study halls	540

Tammy receives a base salary of $45,000 and a $200 salary supplement to help her cover expenses associated with her school extracurricular activities.

a) Identify the amount and type (*for* AGI or *from* AGI) of deductible expenses (assume the 2014 rules apply for purposes of the qualified education expense deduction and the educator expense deduction).

b) Calculate Tammy's AGI and taxable income for 2015 assuming she files single with one personal exemption (assume the 2014 rules apply for purposes of the qualified education expense deduction and the educator expense deduction).

LO 6-3

65. In 2015, Jeff, who is single, is entitled to the following deductions before phase-outs:

State income taxes	$7,850
Real estate taxes	1,900
Home mortgage interest	8,200
Charitable contributions	1,700

a) Assume that Jeff's AGI is $280,000. Calculate Jeff's itemized deductions after considering the overall phase-out of itemized deductions.

b) Suppose that Jeff's AGI increases to $1,280,000. Calculate Jeff's itemized deductions after considering the overall phase-out of itemized deductions.

LO 6-3

66. Jim is single and has three dependent children. Calculate his deductible total personal and dependency exemptions under the following independent conditions:

a) Jim has AGI of $150,000.

b) Jim has AGI of $303,000.

c) Jim has AGI of $450,000.

COMPREHENSIVE PROBLEMS

All applicable problems are available with McGraw-Hill's *Connect*® *Accounting*.

67. Evan graduated from college, and took a job as a deliveryman in the city. Evan was paid a salary of $68,500 and he received $700 in hourly pay for part-time work over the weekends. Evan summarized his expenses below.

Cost of moving his possessions to the city (125 miles away)	$1,200
Interest paid on accumulated student loans	2,800
Cost of purchasing a delivery uniform	1,400
Contribution to State University deliveryman program	1,300

Calculate Evan's AGI and taxable income if he files single with one personal exemption.

68. Read the following letter and help Shady Slim with his tax situation. Please assume that his gross income is $172,900 (which consists only of salary) for purposes of this problem.

December 31, 2015

To the friendly student tax preparer:

Hi, it's Shady Slim again. I just got back from my 55th birthday party, and I'm told that you need some more information from me in order to complete my tax return. I'm an open book! I'll tell you whatever I think you need to know.

Let me tell you a few more things about my life. As you may recall, I am divorced from my wife, Alice. I know that it's unusual, but I have custody of my son, Shady, Jr. The judge owed me a few favors and I really love the kid. He lives with me full-time and my wife gets him every other weekend. I pay the vast majority of my son's expenses. I think Alice should have to pay some child support, but she doesn't have to pay a dime. The judge didn't owe me that much, I guess.

I had to move this year after getting my job at Roca Cola. We moved on February 3 of this year, and I worked my job at Roca Cola for the rest of the year. I still live in the same state, but I moved 500 miles away from my old house. I left a little bit early to go on a house-hunting trip that cost me a total of $450. I hired a moving company to move our stuff at a cost of $2,300, and I drove Junior in my car. Junior and I got a hotel room along the way that cost us $45 (I love Super 8!). We spent $35 on meals on the way to our new home. Oh yeah, I took Junior to a movie on the way and that cost $20.

Can you believe I'm still paying off my student loans, even after 15 years? I paid a total of $900 in interest on my old student loans this year.

Remember when I told you about that guy that hit me with his car? I had a bunch of medical expenses that were not reimbursed by the lawsuit or by my insurance. I incurred a total of $20,000 in medical expenses, and I was only reimbursed for $11,000. Good thing I can write off medical expenses, right?

I contributed a lot of money to charity this year (and have receipt documentation for all contributions). I'm such a nice guy! I gave $1,000 in cash to the March of Dimes. I contributed some of my old furniture to the church. It was some good stuff! I contributed a red velvet couch and my old recliner. The furniture is considered vintage and is worth $5,000 today (the appraiser surprised me!), even though I only paid $1,000 for it back in the day. When I contributed the furniture, the pastor said he didn't like the fabric and was going to sell the furniture to pay for some more pews in the church. Oh well, some people just have no taste, right? Roca Cola had a charity drive for the United Way this year and I contributed $90. Turns out, I don't even miss it, because Roca Cola takes it right off my paycheck every month . . . $15 a month starting in July. My pay stub verifies that I contributed the $90 to the United Way. Oh, one other bit of charity from me this year. An old buddy of mine was down on his luck. He lost his job and his house. I gave him $500 to help him out.

I paid a lot of money in interest this year. I paid a total of $950 in personal credit card interest. I also paid $13,000 in interest on my home mortgage. I also paid $2,000 in real estate taxes for my new house.

A few other things I want to tell you about this year. Someone broke into my house and stole my kid's brand new bicycle and my set of golf clubs. The total loss from theft was $900. I paid $125 in union dues this year. I had to pay $1,200 for new suits for my job. Roca Cola requires its managers to wear suits every day on the job. I spent a total of $1,300 to pay for gas to commute to my job this year.

Oh, this is pretty cool. I've always wanted to be a firefighter. I spent $1,400 in tuition to go to the local firefighter's school. I did this because someone told me that I can deduct the tuition as an itemized deduction, so the money would be coming back to me.

That should be all the information you need right now. Please calculate my taxable income and complete pages 1 and 2 of Form 1040 (through taxable income, line 43) and Schedule A. You're still doing this for free, right?

69. Jeremy and Alyssa Johnson have been married for five years and do not have any children. Jeremy was married previously and has one child from the prior

marriage. He is self-employed and operates his own computer repair store. For the first two months of the year, Alyssa worked for Office Depot as an employee. In March, Alyssa accepted a new job with Super Toys Inc. (ST), where she worked for the remainder of the year. This year, the Johnsons received $255,000 of gross income. Determine the Johnsons' AGI given the following information (assume the 2014 rules apply for purposes of the qualified education expense deduction):

a) Expenses associated with Jeremy's store include $40,000 in salary (and employment taxes) to employees, $45,000 of supplies, and $18,000 in rent and other administrative expenses.

b) As a salesperson, Alyssa incurred $2,000 in travel expenses related to her employment that were not reimbursed by her employer.

c) The Johnsons own a piece of raw land held as an investment. They paid $500 of real property taxes on the property and they incurred $200 of expenses in travel costs to see the property and to evaluate other similar potential investment properties.

d) The Johnsons own a rental home. They incurred $8,500 of expenses associated with the property.

e) The Johnsons' home was only five miles from the Office Depot store where Alyssa worked in January and February. The ST store was 60 miles from their home, so the Johnsons decided to move to make the commute easier for Alyssa. The Johnsons' new home was only ten miles from the ST store. However, their new home was 50 miles from their former residence. The Johnsons paid a moving company $2,000 to move their possessions to the new location. They also drove the 50 miles to their new residence. They stopped along the way for lunch and spent $60 eating at Denny's. None of the moving expenses were reimbursed by ST.

f) Jeremy paid $4,500 for health insurance coverage for himself (not through an exchange). Alyssa was covered by health plans provided by her employer, but Jeremy is not eligible for the plan until next year.

g) Jeremy paid $2,500 in self-employment taxes ($1,250 represents the employer portion of the self-employment taxes).

h) Jeremy paid $5,000 in alimony and $3,000 in child support from his prior marriage.

i) Alyssa paid $3,100 of tuition and fees to attend night classes at a local university. The Johnsons would like to deduct as much of this expenditure as possible rather than claim a credit.

j) The Johnsons donated $2,000 to their favorite charity.

70. Shauna Coleman is single. She is employed as an architectural designer for Streamline Design (SD). Shauna wanted to determine her taxable income for this year. She correctly calculated her AGI. However, she wasn't sure how to compute the rest of her taxable income. She provided the following information with hopes that you could use it to determine her taxable income.

a) Shauna paid $4,676 for medical expenses for care from a broken ankle. Also, Shauna's boyfriend, Blake, drove Shauna (in her car) a total of 115 miles to the doctor's office so she could receive care for her broken ankle.

b) Shauna paid a total of $3,400 in health insurance premiums during the year (not through an exchange). SD did not reimburse any of this expense. Besides the health insurance premiums and the medical expenses for her broken ankle, Shauna had Lasik eye surgery last year and she paid $3,000 for the surgery (she received no insurance reimbursement). She also incurred $450 of other medical expenses for the year.

c) SD withheld $1,800 of state income tax, $7,495 of Social Security tax, and $14,500 of federal income tax from Shauna's paychecks throughout the year.

d) In 2015, Shauna was due a refund of $250 for overpaying her 2014 state taxes. On her 2014 state tax return that she filed in April 2015, she applied the overpayment toward her 2015 state tax liability. She estimated that her state tax liability for 2015 will be $2,300.

e) Shauna paid $3,200 of property taxes on her personal residence. She also paid $500 to the developer of her subdivision, because he had to replace the sidewalk in certain areas of the subdivision.

f) Shauna paid a $200 property tax based on the state's estimate of the value of her car.

g) Shauna has a home mortgage loan in the amount of $220,000 that she secured when she purchased her home. The home is worth about $400,000. Shauna paid interest of $12,300 on the loan this year.

h) Shauna made several charitable contributions throughout the year. She contributed stock in ZYX Corp. to the Red Cross. On the date of the contribution, the fair market value of the donated shares was $1,000 and her basis in the shares was $400. Shauna originally bought the ZYX Corp. stock in 2008. Shauna also contributed $300 cash to State University and religious artifacts she has held for several years to her church. The artifacts were valued at $500 and Shauna's basis in the items was $300. Shauna had every reason to believe the church would keep them on display indefinitely. Shauna also drove 200 miles doing church-related errands for her minister. Finally, Shauna contributed $1,200 of services to her church last year.

i) Shauna's car was totaled in a wreck in January. The car was worth $14,000 and her cost basis in the car was $16,000. The car was a complete loss. Shauna received $2,000 in insurance reimbursements for the loss.

j) Shauna paid $300 for architectural design publications, $100 for continuing education courses to keep her up to date on the latest design technology, and $200 for professional dues to maintain her status in a professional designer's organization.

k) Shauna paid $250 in investment advisory fees and another $150 to have her tax return prepared (that is, she paid $150 in 2015 to have her 2014 tax return prepared).

l) Shauna is involved in horse racing as a hobby. During the year, she won $2,500 in prize money and incurred $10,000 in expenses. She has never had a profitable year with her horse racing activities, so she acknowledges that this is a hobby for federal income tax purposes.

m) Shauna sustained $2,000 in gambling losses over the year (mostly horse-racing bets) and only had $200 in winnings.

Required

A) Determine Shauna's taxable income and complete page 2 of Form 1040 (through taxable income, line 43) and Schedule A assuming her AGI is $107,000.

B) Determine Shauna's taxable income and complete page 2 of Form 1040 (through taxable income, line 43) and Schedule A assuming her AGI is $207,000.

71. Joe and Jessie are married and have one dependent child, Lizzie. Lizzie is currently in college at State University. Joe works as a design engineer for a manufacturing firm while Jessie runs a craft business from their home. Jessie's craft business consists of making craft items for sale at craft shows that are held periodically at various locations. Jessie spends considerable time and effort on her craft business and it has been consistently profitable over the years. Joe and

Jessie own a home and pay interest on their home loan (balance of $220,000) and a personal loan to pay for Lizzie's college expenses (balance of $35,000). Neither Joe nor Jessie is blind or over age 65, and they plan to file as married-joint. Based on their estimates, determine Joe and Jessie's AGI and taxable income for the year and complete pages 1 and 2 of Form 1040 (through taxable income, line 43) and Schedule A. Assume the 2014 rules apply for purposes of the qualified education expense deduction and that the employer portion of the self-employment tax on Jessie's income is $808. Joe and Jessie have summarized the income and expenses they expect to report this year as follows:

Income:	
Joe's salary	$119,100
Jessie's craft sales	18,400
Interest from certificate of deposit	1,650
Interest from Treasury bond funds	727
Interest from municipal bond funds	920
Expenditures:	
Federal income tax withheld from Joe's wages	$13,700
State income tax withheld from Joe's wages	6,400
Social Security tax withheld from Joe's wages	7,482
Real estate taxes on residence	6,200
Automobile licenses (based on weight)	310
State sales tax paid	1,150
Home mortgage interest	14,000
Interest on Masterdebt credit card	2,300
Medical expenses (unreimbursed)	1,690
Joe's employee expenses (unreimbursed)	2,400
Cost of Jessie's craft supplies	4,260
Postage for mailing crafts	145
Travel and lodging for craft shows	2,230
Meals during craft shows	670
Self-employment tax on Jessie's craft income	1,615
College tuition paid for Lizzie	5,780
Interest on loans to pay Lizzie's tuition	3,200
Lizzie's room and board at college	12,620
Cash contributions to the Red Cross	525

KAPLAN CPA SIMULATIONS

KAPLAN CPA REVIEW

Please visit the *Connect Library* to access the following Kaplan CPA Simulations:

- **Mr. Frank** is currently employed and a single taxpayer. Determine which of several interest expenses paid by Mr. Frank during the year are tax deductible and which are personal, nondeductible expenses.
- **Mr. Jones** is currently employed and a single taxpayer. Determine which of several medical and health-related expenses paid by Mr. Jones on behalf of himself and his mother during the year are tax deductible and which are personal, nondeductible expenses.

chapter

7 Investments

Learning Objectives

Upon completing this chapter, you should be able to:

LO 7-1 Explain how interest income and dividend income are taxed.

LO 7-2 Compute the tax consequences associated with the disposition of capital assets, including the netting process for calculating gains and losses.

LO 7-3 Calculate the deduction for portfolio investment-related expenses, including investment expenses and investment interest expense.

LO 7-4 Understand the distinction between portfolio investments and passive investments and apply tax basis, at-risk, and passive activity loss limits to losses from passive investments.

© Image Source

Storyline Summary

Taxpayers:	Courtney Wilson, age 40 Courtney's uncle, Jeb Landers, age 65
Family description:	Courtney is divorced with a son, Deron, age 10, and a daughter, Ellen, age 20. Jeb is single.
Location:	Kansas City, Missouri
Employment status:	Courtney works as an architect for EWD. Her salary is $98,000. Jeb is recently retired.
Current situation:	Courtney is deciding how to invest her inheritance. Jeb is concerned about the tax effects of selling investment assets.

Courtney has settled into her new Kansas City location and is now focusing on her investment portfolio. When her father, "Gramps," passed away last December, he left Courtney an inheritance of $100,000 with the stipulation that she "invest it to financially benefit her family." After considerable thought, Courtney decided to invest the inheritance to accomplish two financial goals. First, she wants to save for her son Deron's college education. She figures that if she immediately invests $50,000 of the inheritance for his college education, she should have a significant sum accumulated when Deron starts college in eight years. Second, she decided that she will immediately invest the remaining $50,000 for five years and use the accumulation to make a significant down payment on a vacation home in Park City, Utah, a town she fell in love with during a college ski trip. Courtney is concerned about how different investment choices will be taxed and how this might affect her ability to meet her financial goals.

Courtney's Uncle Jeb, who is single, has sold several investments during the year with the hope that he could use the proceeds to fulfill his lifelong dream of owning a sailboat. He is uncertain about how much tax he will owe after selling the assets. ■

INVESTMENTS OVERVIEW

THE KEY FACTS

Investments Overview

- After-tax rate of return of investment depends on:
  - Before-tax rate of return.
  - When investment income and gains are taxed.
    - Taxed annually
    - Tax deferred
    - Tax-exempt
  - When investment losses are deducted.
    - Deduction annually
    - Deduction deferred
  - Rate at which investment income or gains/expenses or losses are taxed/deducted.
    - Ordinary tax rates
    - Preferential tax rates
    - Zero tax rate

Investors are attracted to certain investments according to their investment philosophy and their appetite for risk, among other things. Some prefer investments that provide a consistent income stream. Others prefer investments that have significant appreciation potential but provide no current cash flows. These investment attributes affect the before-tax returns on investments. However, taxes are levied on **investment income,** and thus, it would be unwise to make an investment without considering the tax cost. For example, it is possible that two investments with identical before-tax rates of return will generate different after-tax rates of return because the investments are taxed differently. Indeed, it is possible that an investment with a lower before-tax rate of return compared to an alternative investment will have a higher after-tax rate of return because income from the investment is taxed at a later date or taxed at a lower rate than the alternative investment.

Two key tax characteristics that affect after-tax returns from investments are (1) the timing of tax payments or tax benefits and (2) the rate at which investment income or gains are taxed or deductible expenses or losses generate tax savings. Not surprisingly, these variables are directly related to the timing and conversion tax planning strategies introduced in Chapter 3.

Income from **portfolio investments** (investments producing **dividends,** interest, royalties, annuities, or capital gains) may be taxed at ordinary rates, preferential rates, or may be exempt from taxation. Further, depending on the type of investment, tax on income from a portfolio investment may be imposed annually or may be deferred until the taxpayer sells the investment. Losses from portfolio investments are deferred until the investment is sold and are typically subject to limitations.

In contrast to portfolio investments, **passive investments** generate **operating income** and **operating losses.** Operating income is always taxed annually at ordinary rates while operating losses are either deducted annually at ordinary rates or deferred and deducted later at ordinary rates depending on the investor's circumstances. Losses from passive investments are also subject to limitations.

This chapter explores several common portfolio and passive investments, discusses important tax and nontax considerations relevant for those investments, and compares investment returns on an after-tax basis.

LO 7-1

PORTFOLIO INCOME: INTEREST AND DIVIDENDS

THE KEY FACTS

Interest and Dividend Income

- Interest
  - Interest is taxed at ordinary rates.
  - Cash interest payments are taxed annually.
  - Accrued market discount is taxed at sale or maturity.
  - Savings bonds are taxed at sale or maturity.
  - Original issue discount is taxed annually.

(continued)

Taxpayers who desire current cash flows from their investments may choose investments that generate interest or regular dividends. Investments generating interest income include **certificates of deposit** (CDs), savings accounts, corporate **bonds,** and governmental bonds. Investments generating dividend income include direct equity investments in corporate stocks or investments in **mutual funds** that invest in corporate stock.[1] Although all of these investments generate current cash flows, they differ significantly in terms of their economic and tax consequences.

By lending money to banks, governmental entities, or corporations, investors essentially become debt holders. As such, they are legally entitled to receive periodic interest payments *and* to recover the amount of principal loaned (in the case of bonds, principal is the **maturity value** or **face value** of the bonds). Interest payments and the time and manner of repayment of the loan principal are defined either contractually for CDs and savings accounts or by bond covenants for loans made either to governments or corporations. In contrast, investors who purchase stocks become shareholders (also called equity holders) of a corporation. As shareholders, they are entitled to receive dividends if the company declares dividends and to *indirectly*

[1]Mutual funds are portfolios of investment assets managed by professional money managers. Generally, the income earned by mutual funds flows through to the owners of mutual fund shares who pay the resulting taxes due. The nature of the assets held by the mutual fund determines the character of the income.

share in either the future appreciation or depreciation in the value of a corporation through stock ownership. Unlike debt holders, shareholders are not legally entitled to receive dividend payments or to recover their initial investment. Thus, from an investor's perspective, debt tends to be less risky than equity.

For tax purposes, individual investors typically are taxed on both interest and dividend income when they receive it. However, interest income is taxed at ordinary rates while dividend income is generally taxed at lower capital gains rates.

- Dividends
  - Dividends are taxed annually.
  - Qualified dividends are taxed at preferential rates.

Interest

In general, taxpayers recognize interest income from investments when they receive the interest payments.[2] Taxpayers investing in savings accounts, money market accounts, CDs, and most bonds receive interest payments based on a stated annual rate of return at yearly or more frequent intervals.

Special rules apply for determining the timing and amount of interest from bonds when there is a **bond discount** (bonds are issued at an amount below the maturity value) or a **bond premium** (bonds are issued at an amount above the maturity value). Below we discuss these rules as they apply to corporate, U.S. Treasury bonds, and **U.S. savings bonds.**

Corporate and U.S. Treasury Bonds

Both corporations and the U.S. Treasury raise money from debt markets by issuing bonds.[3] Corporate bonds, **Treasury bonds,** and **Treasury notes** are issued at maturity value, at a discount, or at a premium, depending on prevailing interest rates.[4] Treasury bonds and Treasury notes pay a stated rate of interest semiannually.[5] However, corporate bonds may pay interest at a stated "coupon" rate or they may not provide any periodic interest payments. Corporate bonds that do not pay periodic interest are called **zero-coupon bonds.** Overall, the consequences of holding corporate or Treasury bonds are very similar. The two primary differences are that (1) interest from Treasury bonds is exempt from *state* taxation while interest from corporate bonds is not and (2) Treasury bonds always pay interest periodically while corporate bonds may or may not. The tax rules for determining the timing and amount of interest income from corporate and U.S. Treasury bonds are as follows:

- Taxpayers include the actual interest payments they receive in gross income.
- If the bond was issued at a discount, special **original issue discount** (OID) rules apply. Taxpayers are required to amortize the discount and include the amount of the current year **amortization** in gross income in addition to any interest payments the taxpayer actually receives.[6] In the case of corporate zero-coupon bonds, this means taxpayers must report and pay taxes on income related to the bonds even though they did not receive *any* payments from the bonds. Bond issuers or brokers are responsible for calculating the yearly amortization of original issue discount and providing this information to investors using Form 1099-OID.

[2]Interest income is reported on Part I of Schedule B filed with taxpayers' Form 1040.

[3]Investors in corporate bonds assume more risk than investors in Treasury securities because they are relying on the creditworthiness of the corporation issuing the bonds. To compensate bondholders for this additional risk, corporate bonds usually yield higher before-tax rates of return than Treasury securities.

[4]The bonds are issued at a discount (premium) if the market interest rate is higher (lower) than the stated rate on the bonds.

[5]Treasury notes and bonds differ in terms of their maturities. Treasury notes are issued with two-, five-, and ten-year maturities. In contrast, Treasury bonds are issued with maturities greater than ten years. From this point forward, we use the term Treasury bonds to refer to both Treasury notes and Treasury bonds.

[6]§1272. Original issue discount is amortized semiannually under the constant yield method, which is consistent with the approach used to amortize bond discount under GAAP.

- If the bond was issued at a premium, taxpayers may *elect* to amortize the premium.[7] Taxpayers or their advisors are responsible for determining the yearly amortization of bond premium if the election to amortize the premium has been made. The amount of the current year amortization offsets a portion of the actual interest payments that taxpayers must include in gross income. The original tax basis of the bond includes the premium and is reduced by any amortization of bond premium over the life of the bond.
- If the bond is purchased in the secondary bond market at a discount, the taxpayer treats some of or all of the **market discount** as interest income *when she sells the bond or the bond matures.*[8] If the bond is sold prior to **maturity,** a ratable amount of the market discount (based on the number of days the bond is held over the number of days until maturity when the bond is purchased), called the **accrued market discount,** is treated as interest income on the date of sale.[9] If the bond is held to maturity, the entire bond discount is treated as interest income at maturity.
- If the bond is purchased in the secondary bond market at a premium, the premium is treated exactly like original issue bond premiums. As a result, the taxpayer may elect to amortize the **market premium** to reduce the annual interest income received from the bond. Otherwise, the premium remains as part of the tax basis of the bond and affects the capital gain or loss the taxpayer recognizes when the taxpayer sells or redeems the bond.

U.S. Savings Bonds U.S. savings bonds such as Series EE or Series I bonds are issued at either face value or at a discount. These bonds do not pay periodic interest; rather, interest accumulates over the term of the bonds and is paid when investors redeem them at maturity or earlier.[10] That is, the amount of interest income taxpayers recognize *when they redeem* the bonds is the excess of the bond proceeds over the taxpayer's **basis** (purchase price) in the bonds. Taxpayers may elect to include the increase in the bond redemption value in income each year, but this is generally not advisable because it accelerates the income from the bond without providing any cash to pay the taxes.[11] Finally, interest from Series EE and Series I bonds may be excluded from gross income to the extent the bond proceeds are used to pay qualifying educational expenses. However, this exclusion benefit is subject to phase-out based on the taxpayer's AGI.

Example 7-1

What if: *Assume* that Courtney was deciding whether to invest the $50,000 earmarked for the Park City vacation home in (1) Series EE savings bonds that mature in exactly five years, (2) original issue AMD Corporation *zero-coupon* bonds that mature in exactly five years, or (3) U.S. Treasury bonds that pay $46,250 at maturity in five years trading in the secondary bond market with a stated annual interest rate of 10 percent. Further, assume that all bonds yield 8 percent annual before-tax returns compounded semiannually. At the end of the first year, the redemption value of the EE savings bond would be $54,080, or Courtney would receive a Form 1099-OID from AMD

[7]§171. Like an original issue discount, a bond premium is amortized semiannually under the constant yield method—the same method used to amortize bond premiums under GAAP. Unlike premiums on taxable bonds, premiums on tax-exempt bonds must always be amortized.

[8]§1276(a). Under §1278(b)(1), taxpayers may elect to include the amortization of market discount in their income annually. However, this election accelerates the recognition of income from the market discount and is therefore usually not advisable.

[9]§1276(b).

[10]Series EE savings bonds are issued at a discount and Series I savings bonds are issued at maturity value. EE bonds provide a constant rate of return while Series I bonds provide a return that is indexed for inflation and thus increases over time.

[11]§454(a). Investors that make this election report the annual increase in the redemption value of their savings bonds using savings bond redemption tables published by the Treasury Department.

reporting $4,080 of OID amortization for the year, or she would receive two semiannual interest payments of $2,312.50 from the Treasury bonds. Under the general rules, how much interest income from each bond would Courtney report at the end of the first year?

Answer: $0 from the Series EE savings bonds, $4,080 from the AMD bonds, and $4,625 (two semiannual payments of $2,312.50) from the Treasury bonds. Note, however, that Courtney could *elect* to include the $4,080 increase in redemption value of the Series EE bond in interest income even though she did not receive any interest payments on the bond (probably not optimal). She also could *elect* to amortize $637.50 of the $3,750 premium ($50,000 purchase price less the $46,250 maturity value) on the Treasury bond to offset the $4,625 in actual interest payments she received on the bond (probably a good idea). The calculations required to amortize the premium on the Treasury bond for the first year are reflected in the following table:

Semiannual Period	(A) Adjusted Basis of Bond at Beginning of Semiannual Period	(B) Interest Received and Reported ($46,250 × 10% × .5)	(C) Interest Earned (A) × 8% × .5	Premium Amortization (B) − (C)
1	$50,000.00	$2,312.50	$2,000.00	$312.50
2	49,687.50	2,312.50	1,987.50	325.00
Yearly Total		4,625.00	3,987.50	637.50

Intuitively, would Courtney be better or worse off purchasing the Series EE savings bonds rather than a corporate bond to save for the Park City home?

Answer: She would better off in two respects. First, she wouldn't have to pay state income taxes on the interest earned from the savings bonds. Second, she would be able to defer paying taxes on the accumulated interest from the savings bonds until the savings bonds are cashed in at maturity. This will increase the after-tax returns from the savings bonds relative to a corporate bond.

Intuitively, would Courtney be better or worse off purchasing the AMD zero-coupon bonds rather than a corporate bond to save for the Park City home?

Answer: She will be worse off because she will have to pay taxes currently from the OID amortization on the AMD bonds without receiving any cash flow from the bonds to pay the taxes due. This will reduce the after-tax returns from the AMD bonds relative to a corporate bond.

Example 7-2

What if: Assume that on January 1, Courtney used the $50,000 earmarked for the Park City vacation home to purchase AMD zero-coupon bonds in the *secondary bond market* almost immediately after they were originally issued. If the bonds mature in exactly five years and have a maturity value of $74,000, how much interest income will Courtney report at the end of the first year and in the year the bonds mature?

Answer: $0 in the first year and $24,000 in the year the bonds mature. Because the AMD zero-coupon bonds were not purchased at original issue, the entire $24,000 market discount on the bonds will be reported as interest income when the bonds mature. Thus, Courtney will not report any income related to the AMD bonds until the year the bonds mature.

What if: Assume the same facts as above, except Courtney purchased a U.S. Series EE bond instead of an AMD zero-coupon bond to fund the Park City vacation home in five years. How much interest income will she report at the end of the first year and in the year the bonds mature?

Answer: $0 in the first year and $24,000 in the year the EE savings bonds mature; exactly the same outcome as the investment in the AMD zero-coupon bonds.

As our discussion suggests, for certain types of investments such as savings accounts, money market accounts, and CDs, computing the annual taxable interest income is relatively straightforward. However, for investments in bonds, the process is much more involved. Exhibit 7-1 summarizes the general rule and exceptions for the timing of interest payments and related tax payments.

EXHIBIT 7-1 Timing of Interest Payments and Taxes

General Rule	Exception	Exception
Interest Received Annually and Taxed Annually	**Interest Received at Sale or Maturity and Taxed at Sale or Maturity**	**Interest Received at Sale or Maturity but Taxed Annually**
• Savings accounts • CDs • Money market accounts • Bond interest payments actually received in the year	• Accrued market discount on bonds • Interest earned on U.S. savings bonds	• Original issue discount (OID) on corporate and Treasury bonds

Dividends

Historically, dividends received by investors have been taxed at the same rate as interest income. However, in 2003, Congress changed the law for dividends to mitigate the so-called "double tax" on dividend income.[12] Consistent with the general rule for taxing interest income, dividend payments (including reinvested dividends) are taxed annually.[13] However, as we discuss in Chapter 8, **qualified dividends** are taxed at a preferential rate: 0, 15, or 20 percent, depending on the rate at which the dividends would be taxed if they were ordinary income.[14] Qualified dividends are those paid by domestic or certain qualified foreign corporations provided investors hold the dividend-paying stock for *more than* 60 days during the 121-day period that begins 60 days before the **ex-dividend date** (the first day on which the purchaser of the stock would not be entitled to receive a declared dividend on the stock).[15] Exhibit 7-2 illustrates the 121-day period surrounding the ex-dividend date. Nonqualified dividends are not eligible for the reduced rate and are therefore taxed at ordinary rates. Corporations report the amounts of the dividends and indicate whether the dividends are potentially eligible for the preferential rate when they send Form 1099-DIV to shareholders after year-end. However, shareholders ultimately must determine if they qualify for the preferential rate by confirming they held the stock for the required number of days around the ex-dividend date.

EXHIBIT 7-2 Holding Period for Qualified Dividends

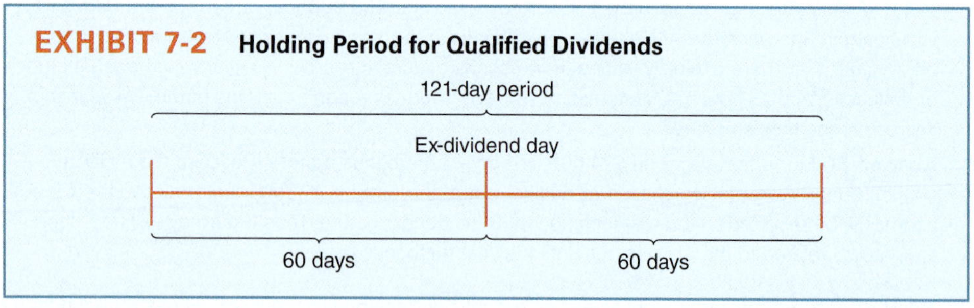

[12]Because corporations pay income taxes, dividends are taxed once at the corporate level when the income used to pay dividends is earned by the corporation, and a second time when dividends are received by investors.

[13]Dividends are reported on Part II of Schedule B filed with taxpayers' Form 1040.

[14]Qualified dividends that would have been taxed at 10 or 15 percent if they were ordinary income are taxed at 0 percent, qualified dividends that would have been taxed at 39.6 percent as ordinary income are taxed at 20 percent, and all other qualified dividends are taxed at 15 percent.

[15]Qualified foreign corporations are those incorporated in a U.S. possession (e.g., Puerto Rico, U.S. Virgin Islands), those eligible for the benefits of a comprehensive income tax treaty with the United States, or those whose shares are readily traded on an established U.S. securities market.

Example 7-3

What if: Assume Courtney decides to purchase dividend-paying stocks to achieve her financial objectives. She invests $50,000 in Xerox stock, which she intends to hold for five years and then sell it to fund the Park City home down payment. She invests another $50,000 in Coca-Cola stock, which she intends to hold for eight years and then sell it to fund her son's education. How much dividend income will Courtney report at the end of the first year if the dividend payments provide an 8 percent return on her investments?[16]

Answer: Courtney will report $4,000 ($50,000 × .08) of dividend income from the Xerox stock for the first year of her investment and $4,000 ($50,000 × .08) of dividend income from the Coca-Cola stock for a total of $8,000 of dividend income.

What if: Assume Courtney's ordinary marginal tax rate is 30 percent. How much tax would Courtney owe on her dividend income if the dividends are nonqualified?

Answer: Courtney would owe $240 ($8,000 × 30%) of tax if the dividends are nonqualified because the income would be taxed at her ordinary income tax rate.

What if: What amount of tax would Courtney owe if the dividends are qualified?

Answer: Courtney would owe $120 ($8,000 × 15%) of tax if the dividends are qualified because qualified dividends are taxed at preferential rates. Courtney's dividends are taxed at 15 percent because her ordinary tax rate is more than 15 percent but less than 39.6 percent.

Because dividend income is taxed generally at lower rates than interest income, it appears that taxpayers seeking current cash flows from their investments should favor dividend-paying investments over interest-paying investments. This raises the question of why anyone would ever prefer investments paying interest over those paying dividends. Remember, though, that savvy investors also should consider nontax factors such as before-tax rates of return, risk, and liquidity needs when choosing among alternative investments. These fundamental differences explain why investors may continue to seek out interest income in spite of the associated tax disadvantages.

LO 7-2

PORTFOLIO INCOME: CAPITAL GAINS AND LOSSES

Investors who don't need annual cash flows from their investments may prefer to invest in assets with the expectation that the investments will appreciate in value over time, providing cash at some point in the future when they sell the assets. Investors also may be willing to assume greater risk in exchange for greater returns than those provided by interest or dividend-paying investments. For example, they might purchase raw land, fine art, rare coins, precious gems or metals, growth stocks (stock in corporations that reinvest their earnings to grow the company as opposed to distributing earnings to shareholders in the form of dividends), mutual fund shares, or even vintage automobiles. Purchasing any such asset is not without risk. Indeed, investments held solely for appreciation potential *may* actually decline in value.

When taxpayers buy and hold assets with appreciation potential, they typically are investing in **capital assets.** As we discussed in Chapter 4, capital assets are typically investment-type assets and personal-use assets.[17] Thus, artwork, corporate stock, bonds, your personal residence, and even your iPod are capital assets.

[16]Annual returns from dividend-paying stocks are typically lower than the return from taxable bonds. However, it is assumed here that the returns are equal for the sake of comparability.

[17]§1221 defines capital assets in the negative. This code section excludes inventory, depreciable property or real property used in a trade or business, certain self-created intangibles, accounts or notes receivable, U.S. government publications, certain commodities derivative financial instruments, certain hedging transactions, and supplies from the definition of a capital asset.

While it may be enjoyable to view collectible fine art in your home or watch a stock portfolio grow in value on quarterly brokerage statements, from a tax perspective the real advantages of investing in capital assets are (1) gains are deferred for tax purposes until the taxpayer sells or otherwise disposes of the assets[18] and (2) gains generally are taxed at preferential rates relative to ordinary income.[19] Why the favorable treatment? One reason is that taxpayers may not have the wherewithal (cash) to pay the tax on their gains until they sell the investment. Another is that the preferential tax rate provides an incentive for taxpayers to invest in assets that may stimulate the economy. Investors can capture these tax benefits when they sell capital assets at a gain. However, when they sell capital assets at a loss, their ability to deduct the loss may be limited.

When a taxpayer sells a capital asset for more than its **tax basis,** the taxpayer recognizes a capital gain; if a taxpayer sells a capital asset for less than its tax basis, the taxpayer recognizes a capital loss (to the extent the loss is deductible).[20] The amount realized or selling price of a capital asset includes the cash and fair market value of other property received, less broker's fees and other selling costs. The basis of any asset, including a capital asset, is generally the taxpayer's "cost" of acquiring the asset, including the initial purchase price and other costs incurred to purchase or improve the asset.[21] Thus, the tax basis of corporate stock purchased from a stockbroker includes the cost of the stock and any additional brokerage fees paid by the taxpayer to acquire the stock. Also, the tax basis in a personal residence includes the initial purchase price plus the cost of subsequent improvements to the home.

TAXES IN THE REAL WORLD Creative Genius

The tax code defines capital assets by listing assets that are *not* capital assets in §1221. Listed among the assets not to be treated as capital are copyrights and literary, musical, and artistic compositions. This placed those who create intangible products on par with those who produce tangible products because §1221 also defines inventory as not a capital asset. Back in 2005, Congress passed temporary legislation (later made permanent in 2006) that permits musicians to treat the sale of their creative works as the sale of capital assets. In 2011, the IRS issued final regulations on making this election. As a result of making this election, a composer who sells copyrighted material will pay tax on any gain at the lower capital gains tax rates.

Source: Federal Tax Updates on Checkpoint Newsstand tab, February 7, 2011.

Because a taxpayer cannot accurately compute the gain or loss on the sale of a capital asset without knowing its basis, it is important for taxpayers to maintain accurate records to track their basis in capital assets. This process is relatively

[18]Similarly, interest related to market discount on bonds and the original issue discount on U.S. EE savings bonds accumulates free of tax until the bonds mature or are sold. However, ordinary rather than capital gains rates apply when the tax must finally be paid.

[19]Mutual funds that generate current income by regularly selling capital assets or by holding income-producing securities are an exception to this general rule. However, tax-efficient mutual funds that only buy and hold growth stocks are treated more like other capital assets for tax purposes (capital gains are deferred until mutual fund shares are sold).

[20]As discussed below, losses on personal assets are not deductible for tax purposes.

[21]For stocks acquired on or after January 1, 2011, brokers are required to report to the IRS the tax basis of securities their customers sell. Starting January 1, 2012, brokers are required to report cost basis information for sales associated with shares of mutual funds and dividend reinvestment plans that were purchased on or after January 1, 2012. Finally, for all other securities not previously mentioned, starting for sales after January 1, 2013, cost basis information must be reported if the securities were purchased on or after January 1, 2013.

straightforward for unique assets such as a taxpayer's personal residence or individual jewels in a taxpayer's jewelry collection. However, capital assets such as shares of stock are much more homogeneous and difficult to track. For example, a taxpayer may purchase blocks of stock in a given corporation at different times over a period of several years, paying a different price per share for each block of stock acquired. When the taxpayer sells shares of this stock in subsequent years, what basis does she use to compute gain or loss? By default, taxpayers are required to use the **first-in first-out (FIFO) method** of determining the basis of the shares they sell.[22] However, if they (or their broker) track the basis of their stock, taxpayers can sell (or instruct their broker to sell) specific shares using the **specific identification method** to determine the basis of the shares they sell. Taxpayers using the specific identification method can choose to sell their high-basis stock first, minimizing their gains or increasing their losses on stock dispositions.

Example 7-4

After Courtney's car broke down, she decided to buy a new one. To fund the down payment, she sold 200 shares of Cisco stock at the current market price of $40 per share for a total amount realized of $8,000. Courtney held the following blocks of Cisco stock at the time of the sale:

Cisco Corporation Stock Ownership

Holding Period	(1) Cost per share	(2) Shares	(1) × (2) Basis	Basis of 200 shares sold	Explanation
5 years	$25	250	$6,250	$5,000	FIFO basis ($25 × 200)
2 years	$32	250	$8,000	$6,400	Specific ID basis ($32 × 200)

How much capital gain will Courtney recognize if she uses the FIFO method of computing the basis in the Cisco shares sold?

Answer: $3,000. $8,000 amount realized ($40 × 200) minus $5,000 FIFO basis ($25 × 200). As indicated in the table above, under the FIFO (oldest first) method, they are treated as though she sold the stock held for five years.

What if: How much capital gain will Courtney recognize if they use the specific identification method of computing the basis in the shares sold to minimize the taxable gain on the sale?

Answer: $1,600. $8,000 amount realized ($40 × 200) minus $6,400 ($32 × 200). To minimize her gain on the sale under the specific identification method, Courtney would choose to sell the 200 shares with the highest basis. As indicated in the table above, the shares with the higher basis are those acquired and held two years for $32 per share.

Note in the above example that Courtney receives $8,000 from the stock sale ($40 per share × 200 shares sold) regardless of the method she uses to compute the basis of the shares she sells. The difference between the FIFO and specific identification methods lies in the amount of taxable gain on the *current* sale. Over time, as taxpayers sell all of their stock, both methods will ultimately allow taxpayers to fully recover their cost in the investments. However, applying the specific identification method will result in lower capital gains taxes currently and thereby minimize the present value of the taxes paid on stock sales.

[22]Reg. §1.1012-1(c)(1).

Types of Capital Gains and Losses

Taxpayers selling capital assets that they hold for a year or less recognize **short-term capital gains or losses.**[23] Alternatively, taxpayers selling capital assets they hold for more than a year recognize **long-term capital gains or losses.** Short-term capital gains are taxed at ordinary rather than preferential rates. In contrast, long-term capital gains are taxed at preferential rates. However, not all long-term capital gains are created equal. Just like dividends, most long-term capital gains are taxed at either 0 percent, 15 percent, or 20 percent depending on the rate at which the gains would be taxed if they were ordinary income. Long-term capital gains that would be taxed at 10 or 15 percent as ordinary income are taxed at 0 percent, gains that would be taxed at 39.6 percent as ordinary income are taxed at 20 percent, and other long-term capital gains are taxed at 15 percent. However, certain long-term capital gains are taxed at a maximum rate of 25 percent and others are taxed at a maximum 28 percent rate for tax policy reasons.

Unrecaptured §1250 Gain When individuals sell depreciable real property at a gain, some or all of the gain is subject to a maximum tax rate of 25 percent. As we will discuss in Chapter 11 the amount of this **unrecaptured §1250 gain** is generally the *lesser* of (1) the recognized gain or (2) the accumulated depreciation on the property. Gains from depreciable real property in excess of this unrecaptured §1250 gain amount may be treated as long-term capital gains subject to a maximum 0/15/20 percent tax rate. Thus, even though unrecaptured §1250 gains are treated as long-term capital gains, they are taxed at a maximum rate higher than most other long-term capital gains.[24] Unrecaptured §1250 gains are taxed at higher capital gains rates because the depreciation deductions responsible for these gains previously reduced the seller's ordinary income taxable at higher ordinary rates.

Example 7-5

What if: Assume Jeb Landers (single), Courtney's uncle, recently sold a rental home for $160,000. He originally acquired the home many years ago for $100,000, and he has fully depreciated it for tax purposes. Assuming Jeb's marginal ordinary tax rate is 35 percent, what tax does he owe on the gain if he did not sell any other property during the year?

Answer: $34,000. Because Jeb's tax basis in the home is $0 (he has fully depreciated it), his gain on the sale is $160,000. As we discuss in more detail in Chapter 11, all of the gain qualifies as §1231 gain because Jeb held the rental home for more than one year. This gain will ultimately be treated as long-term capital gain because Jeb does not have any §1231 losses during the year. The unrecaptured §1250 gain is $100,000, which is the lesser of (1) the $160,000 gain recognized on the sale or (2) the $100,000 accumulated depreciation. Thus, Jeb must pay $25,000 in tax on this portion of the gain ($100,000 × 25%). The remaining $60,000 of gain is taxed at 15 percent, so he owes $9,000 of tax on this portion ($60,000 × 15%). In total, he owes $34,000 of tax on the sale ($25,000 + $9,000).

What if: Suppose Jeb's marginal ordinary tax rate is 39.6 percent rather than 35 percent. What tax does he owe on the gain?

Answer: $37,000. The unrecaptured §1250 gain of $100,000 is taxed at 25 percent for a tax of $25,000. The remaining $60,000 of gain is taxed at 20 percent because it would have been taxed at 39.6 percent if it were ordinary income. Consequently, he owes $12,000 of tax on this portion ($60,000 × 20%). In total, Jeb owes $37,000 of tax on the sale ($25,000 + $12,000).

[23]Nonbusiness bad debt is treated as a short-term capital loss no matter how long the debt was outstanding before it became worthless. Whether a bad debt is considered to be a business bad debt for individuals depends on the facts and circumstances. In general, if the taxpayer experiencing the loss is in the business of loaning money, the bad debt should be considered to be business bad debt; otherwise, the bad debt will likely be considered nonbusiness bad debt.

[24]As we discuss in Chapter 11, unrecaptured §1250 gain is technically a §1231 gain.

Collectibles and §1202 Gain Gains from two types of capital assets are taxable at a maximum 28 percent rate. The first type, **collectibles,** consists of works of art, any rug or antique, any metal or gem, any stamp or coin, any alcoholic beverage, or other similar items held for more than one year.[25] The second type is **qualified small business stock** held for *more than five years.*[26] In general, §1202 defines qualified small business stock as stock received at *original issue* from a C corporation with a gross tax basis in its assets both before and after the issuance of no more than $50,000,000 and with at least 80 percent of the value of its assets used in the active conduct of certain qualified trades or businesses. Under this definition, many investors and employees who hold stock in closely held corporations are likely to hold qualified small business stock. When taxpayers sell qualified small business stock after holding it for more than five years, they may exclude a portion of the gain on the sale from regular taxation. The excluded portion depends on the date the taxpayer acquired the stock.

EXHIBIT 7-3 Exclusion for §1202 Stock Held More Than Five Years

Acquisition Date	Exclusion	Effective Capital Gains Tax Rate
After December 31, 2013	50%	14%
After September 27, 2010 and before January 1, 2014	100%	0%
After February 17, 2009 and before September 28, 2010	75%	7%
After August 10, 1993 and before February 18, 2009	50%	14%

The capital gain not excluded from income is taxed at 28 percent. After the exclusion is taken into account, the effective capital gains tax rate is 14 percent on stock acquired after December 31, 2013 and held five years.[27]

Example 7-6

What if: Assume that Jeb sold his stock in Gangbusters Inc., a qualified small business stock, for $200,000 after holding it for six years. His basis in the stock is $50,000. How much tax will he owe on the sale if his ordinary marginal rate is 35 percent, the stock was acquired on February 17, 2014, and he is not subject to the alternative minimum tax?

Answer: $21,000. Because Jeb held the qualified small business stock for more than five years and because he acquired the stock in 2014, he will exclude $75,000 of the gain from income (one-half), and he will be taxed on the other $75,000 at 28%.

What if: Assume instead that Jeb sold his Gangbusters stock after holding it for only two years, how much tax will he owe on the sale?

Answer: $22,500. Because Jeb didn't hold the stock for more than five years, he must recognize all $150,000 of long-term capital gain. This gain is taxed at 15 percent, yielding a total tax due of $22,500.

Exhibit 7-4 presents the maximum tax rates applicable to capital gains.

[25]§408(m).

[26]§1(h)(7).

[27]The maximum exclusion is the greater of $10,000,000 ($5,000,000 for married taxpayers filing separately) or 10 times the adjusted basis of the stock [see §1202(b)(1)]. Generally, the amount of gain excluded from the sale of qualified small business stock is an AMT preference item. Consequently, the gain otherwise excludable for regular tax purposes may be taxed under the AMT system. However, gain excluded from the sale of qualified small business stock acquired after September 27, 2010, and before January 1, 2014, is not an AMT preference item.

EXHIBIT 7-4 Classification of Capital Gains by Maximum Applicable Tax Rates

Short-Term or Long-Term	Type	Maximum Rate
Short-term	All	39.6%*
Long-term	Collectibles	28*
Held > 5 years	Qualified small business stock	14%
Long-term	Unrecaptured §1250 gain from depreciable realty	25*
Long-term	All remaining capital (and §1231 gains) gain not included elsewhere	20†

*Lower rates will apply when the taxpayer's ordinary rate is less than the rates reflected in this exhibit.
†This gain is taxed at 0 percent to the extent it would have been taxed at a rate of 15 percent or less if it were ordinary income, taxed at 20 percent to the extent it would have been taxed at 39.6 percent as ordinary income, and taxed at 15 percent otherwise.

Netting Process for Gains and Losses To this point, our discussion of applicable tax rates for capital gains hasn't considered situations in which taxpayers recognize both capital gains and capital losses in the same year. To determine the appropriate tax treatment for the capital gains and losses recognized during the year, the taxpayer must complete a netting process. This netting process can be complex when taxpayers recognize capital losses and long-term capital gains subject to different maximum tax rates. We first describe the netting steps for taxpayers *who do not recognize any 25 percent or 28 percent rate long-term capital gains.*

Step 1: Net all short-term gains and short-term losses, including any short-term capital loss carried forward from a prior year. If the net amount is positive, it is termed a **net short-term capital gain** (NSTCG). If the net amount is negative, it is called a **net short-term capital loss** (NSTCL).

Step 2: Net long-term gains and losses, including any long-term capital loss carried forward from a prior year. If the net amount is positive, the amount is called a **net long-term capital gain** (NLTCG). If negative, the amount is termed a **net long-term capital loss** (NLTCL).

Step 3: If Step 1 and Step 2 both yield gains—*or* if they both yield losses—the netting process ends. Otherwise, net the short- and long-term outcomes against each other to yield a final net gain or net loss, which may be either classified as short-term (if the NSTCG exceeds the NLTCL or if the NSTCL exceeds the NLTCG) or long-term (if the NLTCG exceeds the NSTCL or if the NLTCL exceeds the NSTCG). When net long-term capital gains exceed net short-term capital losses, if any, the taxpayer is said to have a **net capital gain.**

Example 7-7

Jeb Landers has recently retired and now wants to pursue his life-long dream of owning a sailboat. To come up with the necessary cash, he sells the following investments:

Stock	Market Value	Basis	Capital Gain/Loss	Scenario 1 Type	Scenario 2 Type
A	$40,000	$ 5,000	$35,000	Long	Short
B	20,000	30,000	(10,000)	Long	Short
C	20,000	12,000	8,000	Short	Long
D	17,000	28,000	(11,000)	Short	Long

What is the amount and nature of Jeb's capital gains and losses (Scenario 1)?

Answer: $22,000 net capital gain (treated as long-term capital gain), computed as follows:

Step 1: Net short-term gains and short-term losses. The $8,000 short-term gain on stock C is netted against the $11,000 short-term loss on stock D, yielding a NSTCL of $3,000.

Step 2: Net long-term gains and long-term losses. The $35,000 long-term gain on stock A is netted against the $10,000 long-term loss on stock B, producing a NLTCG of $25,000.

Step 3: Net the results of Step 1 and Step 2. The NSTCL from Step 1 is netted with the NLTCG from Step 2 yielding a $22,000 net capital gain [($3,000) + $25,000] taxable at long-term capital gains rates.

What if: Consider the original facts, except that Scenario 2 dictates the long- and short-term capital gains. What is the amount and character of Jeb's net gain (or loss) on the sale of the shares in this situation?

Answer: $22,000 net short-term capital gain computed as follows:

Step 1: The gain from stock A would first be netted with the loss from stock B to produce a $25,000 NSTCG [$35,000 + ($10,000)]

Step 2: The loss from stock D and the gain from stock C are combined to provide a $3,000 NLTCL [($11,000) + $8,000].

Step 3: The results from Step 1 and Step 2 are netted to reach a $22,000 net short-term capital gain [$25,000 NSTCG + ($3,000) NLTCL].

After completing the netting process, taxpayers must calculate the tax consequences of the resulting outcomes. Net short-term capital gains are taxed as ordinary income. Net long-term capital gains are taxed at 20 percent to the extent the gains would have been taxed at 39.6 percent if they were ordinary income, at 15 percent to the extent the gains would have been taxed between 15 and 39.6 percent if they were ordinary income, and at 0 percent to the extent they would have been taxed at a rate of 15 percent or lower if they were ordinary income. Taxpayers can deduct up to $3,000 ($1,500 if married filing separately) of net capital losses against ordinary income. Net capital losses in excess of $3,000 ($1,500 if married filing separately) retain their short- or long-term character and are carried forward and treated as though they were incurred in the subsequent year. Short-term losses are applied first to reduce ordinary income when the taxpayer recognizes both short- and long-term net capital losses. Capital loss carryovers for individuals never expire.

Reporting capital gains. When taxpayers sell capital assets, they report the details of their sales on Form 8949 (dates of sale and purchase are additional items provided on Form 8949). After listing their sales on Form 8949, taxpayers then use Schedule D to summarize the sales and apply the basic capital gains netting process. Exhibits 7-5 and 7-6 illustrate how Jeb would report his stock sales in Example 7-7, Scenario 1.

Netting gains and losses from 0/15/20 percent, 25 percent, and 28 percent capital assets. When taxpayers sell long-term capital assets and recognize gains subject to the 25 percent and/or 28 percent capital gains rates, we must expand the basic netting process we've just described.[28] In these situations, apply the following steps to determine the amount of gain taxable at the different tax rates:

Step 1: Net all short-term gains and short-term losses, including any short-term capital loss carried forward from a prior year. If the net amount is positive, it is a net short-term capital gain. If the net amount is negative, it is a net short-term capital loss.

Step 2: Determine whether long-term capital losses, including any long-term capital losses carried forward from a prior year, exceed long-term capital gains. If they do, proceed to Step 3; otherwise, ignore Step 3 and proceed to Step 4.

[28]§1(h).

EXHIBIT 7-5 Jeb's Form 8949

Form **8949**

Department of the Treasury
Internal Revenue Service

Sales and Other Dispositions of Capital Assets

▶ Information about Form 8949 and its separate instructions is at *www.irs.gov/form8949.*
▶ File with your Schedule D to list your transactions for lines 1b, 2, 3, 8b, 9, and 10 of Schedule D.

OMB No. 1545-0074
2014
Attachment Sequence No. **12A**

Name(s) shown on return	Social security number or taxpayer identification number
Jeb Landers	

Before you check Box A, B, or C below, see whether you received any Form(s) 1099-B or substitute statement(s) from your broker. A substitute statement will have the same information as Form 1099-B. Either may show your basis (usually your cost) even if your broker did not report it to the IRS. Brokers must report basis to the IRS for most stock you bought in 2011 or later (and for certain debt instruments you bought in 2014 or later).

Part I **Short-Term.** Transactions involving capital assets you held 1 year or less are short term. For long-term transactions, see page 2.

Note. You may aggregate all short-term transactions reported on Form(s) 1099-B showing basis was reported to the IRS and for which no adjustments or codes are required. Enter the total directly on Schedule D, line 1a; you are not required to report these transactions on Form 8949 (see instructions).

You *must* check Box A, B, *or* C below. Check only one box. If more than one box applies for your short-term transactions, complete a separate Form 8949, page 1, for each applicable box. If you have more short-term transactions than will fit on this page for one or more of the boxes, complete as many forms with the same box checked as you need.

- [x] **(A)** Short-term transactions reported on Form(s) 1099-B showing basis was reported to the IRS (see **Note** above)
- [ ] **(B)** Short-term transactions reported on Form(s) 1099-B showing basis was **not** reported to the IRS
- [ ] **(C)** Short-term transactions not reported to you on Form 1099-B

1 (a) Description of property (Example: 100 sh. XYZ Co.)	(b) Date acquired (Mo., day, yr.)	(c) Date sold or disposed (Mo., day, yr.)	(d) Proceeds (sales price) (see instructions)	(e) Cost or other basis. See the **Note** below and see *Column (e)* in the separate instructions	Adjustment, if any, to gain or loss. If you enter an amount in column (g), enter a code in column (f). **See the separate instructions.** (f) Code(s) from instructions	(g) Amount of adjustment	(h) **Gain or (loss).** Subtract column (e) from column (d) and combine the result with column (g)
Stock C	**3/01/14**	**11/15/14**	**20,000**	**12,000**			**8,000**
Stock D	**2/01/14**	**6/09/14**	**17,000**	**28,000**			**(11,000)**
2 Totals. Add the amounts in columns (d), (e), (g), and (h) (subtract negative amounts). Enter each total here and include on your Schedule D, **line 1b** (if **Box A** above is checked), **line 2** (if **Box B** above is checked), or **line 3** (if **Box C** above is checked) ▶			**37,000**	**40,000**			**(3,000)**

Note. If you checked Box A above but the basis reported to the IRS was incorrect, enter in column (e) the basis as reported to the IRS, and enter an adjustment in column (g) to correct the basis. See *Column (g)* in the separate instructions for how to figure the amount of the adjustment.

For Paperwork Reduction Act Notice, see your tax return instructions. Cat. No. 37768Z Form **8949** (2014)

EXHIBIT 7-5 Jeb's Form 8949 (*continued*)

Form 8949 (2014) Attachment Sequence No. **12A** Page **2**

Name(s) shown on return. Name and SSN or taxpayer identification no. not required if shown on other side	**Social security number or taxpayer identification number**
Jeb Landers	

Before you check Box D, E, or F below, see whether you received any Form(s) 1099-B or substitute statement(s) from your broker. A substitute statement will have the same information as Form 1099-B. Either may show your basis (usually your cost) even if your broker did not report it to the IRS. Brokers must report basis to the IRS for most stock you bought in 2011 or later (and for certain debt instruments you bought in 2014 or later).

Part II **Long-Term.** Transactions involving capital assets you held more than 1 year are long term. For short-term transactions, see page 1.

Note. You may aggregate all long-term transactions reported on Form(s) 1099-B showing basis was reported to the IRS and for which no adjustments or codes are required. Enter the total directly on Schedule D, line 8a; you are not required to report these transactions on Form 8949 (see instructions).

You *must* check Box D, E, *or* F below. Check only one box. If more than one box applies for your long-term transactions, complete a separate Form 8949, page 2, for each applicable box. If you have more long-term transactions than will fit on this page for one or more of the boxes, complete as many forms with the same box checked as you need.

- ☑ **(D)** Long-term transactions reported on Form(s) 1099-B showing basis was reported to the IRS (see **Note** above)
- ☐ **(E)** Long-term transactions reported on Form(s) 1099-B showing basis was **not** reported to the IRS
- ☐ **(F)** Long-term transactions not reported to you on Form 1099-B

1 (a) Description of property (Example: 100 sh. XYZ Co.)	(b) Date acquired (Mo., day, yr.)	(c) Date sold or disposed (Mo., day, yr.)	(d) Proceeds (sales price) (see instructions)	(e) Cost or other basis. See the **Note** below and see *Column (e)* in the separate instructions	Adjustment, if any, to gain or loss. If you enter an amount in column (g), enter a code in column (f). See the separate instructions. (f) Code(s) from instructions	(g) Amount of adjustment	(h) **Gain or (loss).** Subtract column (e) from column (d) and combine the result with column (g)
Stock A	**11/07/12**	**3/06/14**	**40,000**	**5,000**			**35,000**
Stock B	**7/09/11**	**9/01/14**	**20,000**	**30,000**			**(10,000)**
2 Totals. Add the amounts in columns (d), (e), (g), and (h) (subtract negative amounts). Enter each total here and include on your Schedule D, **line 8b** (if **Box D** above is checked), **line 9** (if **Box E** above is checked), or **line 10** (if **Box F** above is checked) ▶			**60,000**	**35,000**			**25,000**

Note. If you checked Box D above but the basis reported to the IRS was incorrect, enter in column (e) the basis as reported to the IRS, and enter an adjustment in column (g) to correct the basis. See *Column (g)* in the separate instructions for how to figure the amount of the adjustment.

Form **8949** (2014)

EXHIBIT 7-6 Jeb's Schedule D

SCHEDULE D (Form 1040)

Department of the Treasury Internal Revenue Service (99)

Capital Gains and Losses

▶ Attach to Form 1040 or Form 1040NR.
▶ Information about Schedule D and its separate instructions is at *www.irs.gov/scheduled*.
▶ Use Form 8949 to list your transactions for lines 1b, 2, 3, 8b, 9, and 10.

OMB No. 1545-0074

2014

Attachment Sequence No. 12

Name(s) shown on return: Jeb Landers | Your social security number

Part I Short-Term Capital Gains and Losses—Assets Held One Year or Less

See instructions for how to figure the amounts to enter on the lines below. This form may be easier to complete if you round off cents to whole dollars.	(d) Proceeds (sales price)	(e) Cost (or other basis)	(g) Adjustments to gain or loss from Form(s) 8949, Part I, line 2, column (g)	(h) Gain or (loss) Subtract column (e) from column (d) and combine the result with column (g)
1a Totals for all short-term transactions reported on Form 1099-B for which basis was reported to the IRS and for which you have no adjustments (see instructions). However, if you choose to report all these transactions on Form 8949, leave this line blank and go to line 1b .				
1b Totals for all transactions reported on Form(s) 8949 with **Box A** checked	37,000	40,000		(3,000)
2 Totals for all transactions reported on Form(s) 8949 with **Box B** checked				
3 Totals for all transactions reported on Form(s) 8949 with **Box C** checked				

4 Short-term gain from Form 6252 and short-term gain or (loss) from Forms 4684, 6781, and 8824 .	4	
5 Net short-term gain or (loss) from partnerships, S corporations, estates, and trusts from Schedule(s) K-1	5	
6 Short-term capital loss carryover. Enter the amount, if any, from line 8 of your **Capital Loss Carryover Worksheet** in the instructions	6	( )
7 **Net short-term capital gain or (loss).** Combine lines 1a through 6 in column (h). If you have any long-term capital gains or losses, go to Part II below. Otherwise, go to Part III on the back	7	(3,000)

Part II Long-Term Capital Gains and Losses—Assets Held More Than One Year

See instructions for how to figure the amounts to enter on the lines below. This form may be easier to complete if you round off cents to whole dollars.	(d) Proceeds (sales price)	(e) Cost (or other basis)	(g) Adjustments to gain or loss from Form(s) 8949, Part II, line 2, column (g)	(h) Gain or (loss) Subtract column (e) from column (d) and combine the result with column (g)
8a Totals for all long-term transactions reported on Form 1099-B for which basis was reported to the IRS and for which you have no adjustments (see instructions). However, if you choose to report all these transactions on Form 8949, leave this line blank and go to line 8b .				
8b Totals for all transactions reported on Form(s) 8949 with **Box D** checked	60,000	35,000		25,000
9 Totals for all transactions reported on Form(s) 8949 with **Box E** checked				
10 Totals for all transactions reported on Form(s) 8949 with **Box F** checked.				

11 Gain from Form 4797, Part I; long-term gain from Forms 2439 and 6252; and long-term gain or (loss) from Forms 4684, 6781, and 8824	11	
12 Net long-term gain or (loss) from partnerships, S corporations, estates, and trusts from Schedule(s) K-1	12	
13 Capital gain distributions. See the instructions	13	
14 Long-term capital loss carryover. Enter the amount, if any, from line 13 of your **Capital Loss Carryover Worksheet** in the instructions	14	( )
15 **Net long-term capital gain or (loss).** Combine lines 8a through 14 in column (h). Then go to Part III on the back	15	25,000

For Paperwork Reduction Act Notice, see your tax return instructions. Cat. No. 11338H **Schedule D (Form 1040) 2014**

Step 3: If Step 1 generated a gain, net the gain against the loss from Step 2. If the outcome is a gain, the gain is a net short-term gain and you can ignore Steps 4–9. If the outcome is a loss, it is a net long-term capital loss and you can ignore Steps 4–9. If Step 1 generated a loss, you have both a net short-term and net long-term capital loss; apply the capital loss deduction limitations we described previously, and ignore Steps 4–9.

Step 4: Separate all long-term capital gains and losses into the three separate rate groups (0/15/20 percent, 25 percent, and 28 percent). Any long-term capital loss carried forward from the previous year is placed in the 28 percent group. Also, note that by definition the 25 percent group includes only gains.

Step 5: Net the gains and losses in the 0/15/20 percent group. If the result is a net loss, move the net loss into the 28 percent group. If the result is a net gain, leave the net gain in the 0/15/20 percent group and proceed to Step 9.

Step 6: *If the Step 1 result is a short-term capital loss,* move the loss into the 28 percent rate group. Otherwise, ignore this step.

Step 7: Net the gains and losses in the 28 percent rate group to determine if there is a net gain or loss in this group. Net gains in this group are taxed at a maximum rate of 28 percent. Net losses move to the 25 percent group.

Step 8: Net the 25 percent gains with the net loss determined in Step 7. Net gains are taxed at a maximum rate of 25 percent. Net losses move to the 0/15/20 percent rate group.

Step 9: Net the 0/15/20 percent net gain from Step 5 with the net loss from Step 8. This gain is taxed at a maximum 0/15/20 percent rate.

Steps 4 through 9 are designed to maximize the tax benefits of net short-term capital losses, long-term capital loss carryovers, and current year net losses in the 0/15/20 percent and 28 percent rate groups.

Example 7-8

What if: Assume that in addition to selling stocks, Jeb sold gold coins and a rental home (with $50,000 of accumulated depreciation) as follows:

Capital Asset	Market Value	Tax Basis	Capital Gain/Loss	Scenario 1 Type
A stock	$ 40,000	$ 5,000	$ 35,000	Long 0/15/20%
B stock	20,000	30,000	(10,000)	Long 0/15/20%
C stock	20,000	12,000	8,000	Short
D stock	17,000	28,000	(11,000)	Short
Gold coins	4,000	3,000	1,000	Long 28%
Rental home	200,000	80,000	120,000	Long 25% and 0/15/20%*
Overall gain			$143,000	

*$50,000 of the gain is 25 percent gain (from accumulated depreciation on the property) and the remaining $70,000 is 0/15/20 percent gain.

Assuming Jeb did not sell any other capital assets during the year, he recognizes an overall capital gain of $143,000. What is (are) the maximum tax rate(s) applicable to this gain?

Answer: $95,000 of gain subject to a 0/15/20 percent maximum rate and $48,000 of gain is subject to a 25 percent rate, computed as follows:

Step 1: $3,000 net short-term capital loss [$8,000 + ($11,000)].

Step 2: $146,000 overall net long-term capital gain, so ignore Step 3 and proceed to Step 4.

Step 3: Not required.

(continued on page 7-18)

THE KEY FACTS

28 Percent and 25 Percent Rate Capital Gains

- Certain capital gains are taxable at maximum rates of 25 percent or 28 percent.
  - Unrecaptured §1250 gains are taxed at a maximum rate of 25 percent.
  - Gains from collectibles and from qualified small business stock not held for 5 years are taxed at a maximum rate of 28 percent.
- When taxpayers have 25 percent or 28 percent rate capital gains, an expanded netting process applies.
  - The expanded netting process generally requires that losses be applied to higher rate groups before lower rate groups.
- When taxable income without long-term capital gains would be taxed in the 28 percent or higher ordinary income rate bracket, the capital gains in each rate group are simply taxed according to the capital gains rate applicable to each group. Otherwise applicable capital gains rates must be adjusted to reflect their inclusion in lower ordinary income rate brackets.

Step 4: The $35,000 gain on the A stock, the $10,000 loss on the B stock, and $70,000 ($120,000 − $50,000) of gain from the rental home are placed in the 0/15/20 percent group. $50,000 of the gain from the rental property is placed in the 25 percent group, and $1,000 gain on the gold coins is placed in the 28 percent group.

Step 5: *$95,000 net gain in the 0/15/20 percent group* [$35,000 A stock + (10,000) B stock + $70,000 rental property].

Step 6: Move the $3,000 loss from Step 1 into the 28 percent group.

Step 7: $2,000 net loss in 28 percent group [$1,000 gain on gold + ($3,000) short-term loss from Step 1]. Move the $2,000 net loss to the 25 percent group.

Step 8: *$48,000 net gain in the 25 percent group* [$50,000 25 percent gain on rental + ($2,000) loss from Step 7].

Step 9: Not required.

Jeb's netting process is reflected in the following table:

Description	Short-Term	Long-Term Overall	Long-Term 28%	Long-Term 25%	Long-Term 0/15/20%
Stock C	$ 8,000				
Stock D	(11,000)				
Step 1:	(3,000)				
Coins		$ 1,000	1,000		
Unrecaptured §1250 Gain		50,000		50,000	
Remaining Gain from Rental Property		70,000			70,000
Stock A		35,000			35,000
Stock B		(10,000)			(10,000)
Step 2:		$146,000			
Steps 4 and 5:			$1,000	$50,000	$95,000
Step 6:	(3,000) →		(3,000)		
Step 7			(2,000) →	(2,000)	
Step 8				48,000	
Summary				$48,000	$95,000
Applicable Rate				25%	0/15/20%

So, we've learned how to determine the *maximum* tax rates applicable to different types of capital gains. How do we go about actually calculating the effect these gains have on the taxpayer's tax liability? Follow these basic guidelines:

- If the long-term capital gains would have been taxed at a rate of 39.6 percent if they were ordinary income, the gain is taxed at the maximum rate for their group (0/15/20 percent, 25 percent, or 28 percent).
- To the extent the long-term capital gains would have been taxed at a rate of 15 percent or lower if they were ordinary income, the 0/15/20 percent gains are taxed at 0 percent, and the 25 percent and 28 percent gains are taxed at the taxpayer's ordinary rate.
- For other situations, use the following steps to determine the tax on the gains:[29]

  Step 1: Fill up the 10, 15, 25, 28, 35, and 39.6 percent tax rate brackets with taxable income, exclusive of long-term capital gains subject to preferential rates.

  Step 2: Next, if there is any remaining space in the 10 or 15 percent brackets, add any 25 percent rate capital gains to these brackets to the extent room remains in either of these brackets after Step 1. Twenty-five percent rate capital gains included in these brackets are taxed at the ordinary rates applicable to these brackets.

[29]§1(h).

Step 3: Next, if there is any remaining space in the 10 or 15 percent brackets, add any 28 percent rate capital gains to these brackets to the extent room remains in either of these brackets after Step 2. Twenty-eight percent rate capital gains included in these brackets are taxed at the ordinary rates applicable to these brackets.

Step 4: Next, add any 0/15/20 percent rate capital gains to either the 10 percent or 15 percent brackets to the extent room remains in either of these brackets after Step 3. 0/15/20 percent rate capital gains included in these brackets are taxed at 0 percent.

Step 5: Add any remaining 0/15/20 percent rate capital gains (those not taxed in Step 4) to the 25, 28, 33, 35, and 39.6) percent brackets. The 0/15/20 percent rate capital gains included in brackets below 39.6 percent are taxed at 15 percent. The 0/15/20 percent rate capital gains included in the 39.6 percent bracket are taxed at 20 percent.

Step 6: Any remaining 25 percent rate capital gains (those not taxed in Step 2) are taxed at 25 percent. Any remaining 28 percent rate capital gains are taxed at 28 percent. [This means that 28 percent rate capital gains that would have been taxed at 25 percent if they were ordinary income are taxed at the higher 28 percent rate. If however, a taxpayer's tax liability would be lower using the regular tax rates for all ordinary income and capital gains (which is possible but not typical), the taxpayer would simply owe tax based on the regular tax rates.]

Example 7-9

What if: Let's return to the facts of the previous example where Jeb recognized a $48,000 25 percent net capital gain and a $95,000 0/15/20 percent net capital gain. Also, assume that Jeb's taxable income for 2015 before considering the net capital gains is $10,000. Jeb's filing status is single. What is Jeb's gross tax liability for the year?

Answer: $24,543.75, computed as follows:

Amount and Type of Income	Applicable Rate	Tax	Explanation
$9,225; ordinary	10%	$ 922.50	$9,225 × 10%. The first $9,225 of Jeb's $10,000 of ordinary income is taxed at 10 percent (see single tax rate schedule for this and other computations).
$775	15%	116.25	$775 × 15%. Jeb's remaining $775 of ordinary income ($10,000 − $9,225) is taxed at 15 percent.
$27,450; 25 percent rate capital gains	15%	4,117.50	$27,450 × 15%. The end of the 15 percent bracket is $37,450 minus $10,000 ($9,225 + $775) already taxed.
$20,550; 25 percent rate capital gains	25%	5,137.50	$20,550 × 25%. $48,000 total 25% gain minus $27,450 25 percent gain already taxed at 15 percent.
$95,000; 15 percent rate capital gains	15%	14,250.00	$95,000 × 15%. All of the 15 percent gain would have been taxed at a rate higher than 15 percent but less than 39.6%, so it is all taxed at 15 percent.
Gross tax liability		**$24,543.75**	

(continued on page 7-20)

What if: Suppose Jeb's 0/15/20 percent capital gain was $400,000 rather than $95,000. What is Jeb's gross tax liability for the year?

Answer: $72,533.75, computed as follows:

Amount and Type of Income	Applicable Rate	Tax	Explanation
$9,225; ordinary	10%	$922.50	$9,225 × 10%. The first $9,225 of Jeb's $10,000 of ordinary income is taxed at 10 percent (see single tax rate schedule for this and other computations).
$775	15%	116.25	$775 × 15%. Jeb's remaining $775 of ordinary income ($10,000 − $9,225) is taxed at 15 percent.
$27,450; 25 percent rate capital gains	15%	4,117.50	$27,450 × 15%. The end of the 15 percent bracket is $37,450 minus $10,000 ($9,225 + $775) already taxed.
$20,550; 25 percent rate capital gains	25%	5,137.50	$20,550 × 25%. $48,000 total 25% gain minus $27,450 25 percent gain already taxed at 15 percent.
$355,200; 0/15/20 percent rate capital gains	15%	53,280.00	$355,200 × 15%. $355,200 represents the 0/15/20 percent gain that would have been taxed at 25, 28, 33, or 35 percent if it were ordinary. This gain is taxed at 15 percent.
$44,800; 0/15/20 percent rate capital gains	20%	8,960.00	$44,800 × 20%. The remaining 0/15/20 percent gain that would have been taxed at 39.6 percent had it been ordinary is taxed at the maximum 20 percent.
Gross tax liability		**$72,533.75**	

Limitations on Capital Losses

We've previously discussed the general rule that taxpayers may deduct capital losses against capital gains in the netting process and that individual taxpayers may deduct up to $3,000 ($1,500 if married filing separately) of net capital losses against ordinary income in a given year. This general rule, however, is subject to certain exceptions as described below.

Losses on the Sale of Personal-Use Assets As previously described, personal-use assets fall within the category of capital assets. When taxpayers sell personal-use assets, what are the tax consequences? Consider an engaged taxpayer who calls off the wedding plans. After getting the ring back from his former fiancée, the taxpayer sells the engagement ring for more than its purchase price. Does he recognize a taxable gain? Absolutely—the gain from the sale of a personal-use asset is taxable even though it was not purchased for its appreciation potential. The tax rate on the gain depends on the amount of time between the date the taxpayer purchased the ring and the date he sold it and on the netting process involving the seller's other capital gains and losses during the year. What if a taxpayer sold her car for less than she paid for it? Does she get to deduct the capital loss? Unfortunately, no—losses on the sale of personal-use assets are *not* deductible, and therefore never become part of the netting process.

Capital Losses on Sales to Related Parties When taxpayers sell capital assets at a loss to related parties, they are not able to deduct the loss.[30] As we described in detail in Chapter 11, the related party acquiring the asset may eventually be allowed to deduct all, a portion, or none of the disallowed loss on a subsequent sale.

Wash Sales Consider the case of a taxpayer attempting to do some tax planning near the end of the year: She has invested in the stock of several corporations; some of these investments have appreciated while others have declined in value. The taxpayer wants to capture the tax benefit of the stock losses in the current year to offset ordinary income (up to $3,000) or to offset other capital gains she has already recognized during the year. However, she can't deduct the losses until she sells the stock. Why might this be a problem? If the taxpayer believes that the stocks with unrealized losses are likely to appreciate in the near future, she may prefer *not* to sell those stocks but rather to keep them in her investment portfolio. What might this taxpayer do to deduct the losses while continuing to hold the investment in the stocks? For one, she might be tempted to sell the stocks and then immediately buy them back. Or, she might buy more of the same stock and then sell the stock she originally held to recognize the losses. With this strategy, she hopes to realize (and then recognize or deduct) the losses and, at the end of the day, still hold the stocks in her investment portfolio.

Although this might sound like a great plan, certain **wash sale** tax rules prevent this strategy from accomplishing the taxpayer's objective. A wash sale occurs when an investor sells or trades stock or securities at a loss *and* within 30 days *either before or after* the day of sale buys substantially identical stocks or securities.[31] Because the day of sale is included, the 30 days before and after period creates a 61-day window during which the wash sale provisions may apply.[32] When the wash sale provisions apply to a sale of stock, realized losses are not recognized; instead, the amount of *the unrecognized loss is added to the basis of the newly acquired stock.* Congress created this rule to prevent taxpayers from accelerating losses on securities that have declined in value without actually altering their investment in the securities. The 61-day period ensures that taxpayers cannot deduct losses from stock sales without exposing themselves to the risk that the stock they sold will subsequently increase in value.

Example 7-10

What if: Suppose Courtney owns 100 shares of Cisco stock that she purchased in June 2013 for $50 a share. On December 21, 2015, Courtney sells the shares for $40 a share to generate cash for the holidays. This sale generates a capital loss of $1,000 [$4,000 sale proceeds (100 × $40) − $5,000 tax basis ($50 × 100)]. Later, however, Courtney decides that Cisco might be a good long-term investment. On January 3, 2016 (13 days later), Courtney purchases 100 shares of Cisco stock for $41 a share ($4,100). Does Courtney *realize* a short- or long-term capital loss on the December 21 sale?

Answer: Long-term capital loss. She held the stock for more than one year (June 2013 to December 2015) before selling.

How much of the realized $1,000 long-term capital loss can Courtney recognize or deduct on her 2015 tax return?

(continued on page 7-22)

[30] §267(a).

[31] Substantially identical stocks or securities include contracts or options to buy substantially identical securities. However, corporate bonds and preferred stock are not generally considered substantially identical to common stock of the same corporation.

[32] §1091.

THE KEY FACTS

Capital Gains and Losses

- Tax on the appreciation of capital assets is deferred until the asset is sold.
  - The longer the holding period, the greater the after-tax rate of return for a given before-tax rate of return.
- Tracking the basis of stock sold.
  - FIFO method is the default.
  - Specific identification is allowed.
- Capital gains and losses.
  - Long-term capital gain if the asset is held more than a year before sold; short-term otherwise.
  - Net long-term capital gains are taxed at the maximum 0/15/20 percent rate.
  - ($3,000) net capital loss is deductible annually against ordinary income.
  - Losses on personal-use assets are not deductible.
  - Losses on wash sales are not deductible but are added to the basis of new shares acquired.
- Basic tax planning strategies.
  - Hold capital assets for more than a year before selling.
  - Sell loss capital assets to offset gains.

Answer: Zero. Because Courtney sold the stock at a loss and purchased the same stock within the 61-day period centered on the date of sale (30 days before December 21, and 30 days after December 21), the wash sale rules disallow the loss in 2015. Had Courtney waited just another 18 days to repurchase the Cisco shares, she could have avoided the wash sale rules. In that case, under the general rules for capital loss deductibility, Courtney *would* be able to deduct the $1,000 capital loss from the sale against her ordinary income on her 2014 income tax return.

What tax basis will Courtney have in the Cisco stock she purchased (or repurchased) on January 3, 2016?

Answer: $5,100. Under the wash sale rules, Courtney adds the $1,000 disallowed loss to the basis of the stock she purchased on January 3. Thus, she now owns 100 shares of Cisco stock with a $5,100 basis in the shares, which is $1,000 more than she paid for it.

What if: How much of the $1,000 realized loss would Courtney have recognized if she had only purchased 40 shares of Cisco stock instead of 100 shares on January 3, 2016?

Answer: $600. The wash sale rules disallow the loss to the extent taxpayers acquire other shares in the 61-day window. In this situation, Courtney only acquired 40 percent (40 of 100) of the shares she sold at a loss within the window. Consequently, she must disallow 40 percent, or $400, of the loss, and she is allowed to deduct the remaining $600 loss.

ETHICS

In December, T. D. Weber evaluated his stock portfolio and found that his DLW Inc. common stock had declined in value since T. D. purchased it. He strategizes to sell the DLW stock on December 15. However, T. D. figures that he'd like to retain an interest in the company. So, knowing that he needs to avoid the wash sale rules, when he sells the common stock on December 15th he simultaneously purchased an equivalent amount of preferred stock in DLW Inc. On January 17 of the next year, T. D. sells the preferred stock and repurchases DLW common stock. What do you think of his strategy?

Balancing Tax Planning Strategies for Capital Assets with Other Goals

When taxpayers invest in capital assets and hold the assets for more than a year, they receive at least two benefits. First, they are able to defer recognizing gains on the assets until they sell them—the longer the deferral period, the lower the present value of the capital gains tax when taxpayers ultimately sell the assets. Second, they pay taxes on the gains at preferential rates. These tax advantages provide taxpayers with a greater after-tax rate of return on these investments than they would obtain from less tax-favored assets that earn equivalent before-tax rates of return. Investors who quickly sell investments pay taxes on gains at higher, ordinary rates and incur significantly greater transaction costs. Nevertheless, taxpayers should balance the tax benefits available for holding assets with the risk that the asset values will have declined by the time they want to sell the assets.

Example 7-11

What if: Assume Courtney decides to purchase Intel stock for $100,000 and hold half of the shares for 5 years to purchase the Park City home and the other half for 18 years to pay for Deron's education. If the Intel stock grows at a constant 8 percent before-tax rate and does not pay any dividends, how much cash will Courtney accumulate after taxes for the Park City home?

Answer: $69,946, computed as follows:

Description	Amount	Explanation
(1) Proceeds from sale	$73,466	[$50,000 × (1 + .08)^{5}].
(2) Basis in fund shares	50,000	This is the nondeductible investment in the shares.
(3) Gain realized on sale	$23,466	(1) − (2).
(4) Tax rate on gain	× 15%	Low rate for long-term capital gain.*
(5) Tax on gain	$ 3,520	(3) × (4).
After-tax cash for Park City home	**$69,946**	(1) − (5).

*Assumes Courtney doesn't have any capital losses.

How much cash will Courtney accumulate after taxes for Deron's education?

Answer: $177,331, computed as follows:

Description	Amount	Explanation
(1) Proceeds from sale	$199,801	[$50,000 × (1 + .08)^{18}].
(2) Basis in fund shares	50,000	This is the nondeductible investment in the shares.
(3) Gain realized on sale	$149,801	(1) − (2).
(4) Tax rate on gain	× 15%	Low rate for long-term capital gain.*
(5) Tax on gain	$ 22,470	(3) × (4).
After-tax cash for education goal	**$177,331**	(1) − (5).

*Assumes Courtney doesn't have capital losses.

TAXES IN THE REAL WORLD Turning Losses into Gains

Many investors have seen their investments plummet in value in recent years due to the economic downturn. However, financial advisers remind us that even in the midst of such seemingly bad news, there is good news. The tax code allows individuals to reduce or eliminate tax on their current gains using these losses, which in turn raises overall returns. Using capital losses to offset capital gains (or even up to $3,000 of ordinary income) is a term investment advisers call *tax-loss harvesting*. Tax advisers encourage investors to take advantage of the available capital loss offset and many investors do. For example, New York's billionaire mayor, Michael Bloomberg, disclosed that he will declare no net capital gains on his 2010 tax return. So, how much can loss harvesting improve your returns? Investment advisers have differing predictions but claim that loss harvesting can add up to 2 percentage points over a ten-year period. Pretty good considering that the Standard & Poor's 500 stock index's annualized total return for the period has been under 2 percent.

Source: The Wall Street Journal, Laura Saunders, August 20, 2011.

When investing in capital assets, taxpayers run the risk that some of their investments may decline in value. Thus, a productive strategy for managing investments in capital assets is to sell investments with built-in losses. This strategy is commonly referred to as "loss harvesting." By selectively selling loss assets, taxpayers can reduce their taxes by deducting up to $3,000 against their ordinary income and by reducing the amount of capital gains that would otherwise be subject to tax during the year. This is particularly beneficial for taxpayers who have short-term capital gains that will be taxed at higher ordinary rates absent offsetting capital losses. Note, however, that taxpayers should not sell investments to gain tax benefits if they believe that the potential economic benefit of holding the investment outweighs the tax benefits of selling the stock. Also, keep in mind that capital losses on stock sales may not be deductible due to the wash sale rules discussed above.

PORTFOLIO INCOME SUMMARY

As we've discussed the tax consequences of various investments up to this point in the chapter, we have proceeded from the least tax-advantaged (taxed annually at ordinary rates) to more tax-advantaged (capital gains). By moving along this continuum from investments taxed annually at ordinary rates (corporate bonds[33]) to investments taxed annually at capital gains rates (dividend-paying stock), investors are in essence employing the conversion planning strategy referred to repeatedly throughout this text. As taxpayers move from dividend-paying stock to growth stock, which provides tax deferral in addition to preferential tax rates, taxpayers combine the conversion strategy with the basic strategy of shifting income from one time period to another.

In this chapter and elsewhere in this text, we emphasize that tax planning must not be done in a vacuum without considering all relevant parties and taxpayers' economic and personal objectives. Because investments typically are not designed to accommodate the specific needs of each individual investor, considering the other party in the deal is not as relevant when investing as it is in other transactions. However, it is vital that investors carefully balance the tax characteristics of their investment options with the other attributes of their investment options such as risk and liquidity.

LO 7-3

PORTFOLIO INVESTMENT EXPENSES

Now that we've discussed how *income* from various forms of investments is taxed, let's explore the deductibility of expenses taxpayers incur to acquire or maintain their investments. We first discuss tax consequences associated with **investment expenses,** and we conclude by discussing the deductibility of **investment interest expense.** Even though the names of these two deductions sound very similar, investment expenses and investment interest expense are two different deductions with different deductibility limitations. So, when you are reading about an investment-related expense, pay careful attention to whether the expense is an *investment expense* or *investment interest expense*. Exhibit 7-7 provides a description of these expenses and the limitations on the deductibility of the expenses.

EXHIBIT 7-7 Summary of Investment-Related Expenses

Item	Investment Expense	Investment *Interest* Expense
Description	Expenses (other than interest) incurred to generate investment income.	Interest expense on loans used to acquire investments.
Deduction type	Miscellaneous itemized deduction (subject to 2 percent of AGI floor).	Interest expense itemized deduction.
Deduction limitations	Deductible only when investment expenses and other miscellaneous itemized deductions exceed 2 percent of AGI floor.	Deduction limited to taxpayer's net investment income for the year. Net investment income is gross investment income reduced by *deductible investment expenses*.
Nondeductible amounts due to limitations	Deduct it in the year incurred or lose it.	Carryover indefinitely.

Investment Expenses

Just as taxpayers can deduct ordinary and necessary business expenditures when conducting business activities, individual taxpayers are allowed to deduct ordinary and necessary expenses they incur in investment activities to produce or collect income and

[33]We refer here to corporate bonds issued or acquired at face value.

for expenses they pay or incur to manage property held for producing income—such as safe deposit box rental fees, attorney and accounting fees that are necessary to produce investment income, and expenses for investment advice, among other things.[34]

The arrangement makes sense if you think about it: The government taxes investment income, so it is willing to allow taxpayers to deduct expenses they incur to generate investment income. Conversely, to the extent taxpayers incur expenses to produce tax-exempt income, such as municipal bond interest, they are not allowed to deduct the related expenses.[35] For example, a taxpayer who keeps a fully taxable corporate bond in a safe deposit box would be allowed an investment expense deduction for the cost of renting the box, but one who keeps a tax-exempt municipal bond in a safe deposit box would not.

The bad news here for taxpayers is that investment expenses are treated as miscellaneous itemized deductions subject to the 2 percent of AGI floor.[36] Thus, taxpayers with investment expenses will only realize tax benefits from these expenses if they itemize deductions *and* their total miscellaneous itemized deductions (fees for investment advice, tax return preparation fees, an employee's job-related magazine subscriptions, and other unreimbursed employee business expenses—see Chapter 6)—including investment expenses—exceed 2 percent of their AGI. Consequently, it is likely that taxpayers with taxable investments and investment expenses will receive little tax benefit, if any, from the expenses.

THE KEY FACTS

Investment-Related Expenses

- Investment expenses deducted as miscellaneous itemized deductions are subject to the 2 percent of AGI floor.
  - Expenses other than interest incurred to generate investment income.
  - No carryover of amounts not currently deductible.

Example 7-12

What if: Suppose Courtney met with a financial planner who advised her about her investment decisions. Courtney paid the advisor $500 for her services. Also, during the year Courtney paid a CPA $250 to prepare her tax return. Courtney had no other miscellaneous itemized deductions for the year. Does Courtney gain any tax benefit from the $500 she paid to the financial planner (her AGI is $162,000)?

Answer: No. The $500 payment is a deductible investment expense for Courtney. However, to receive any tax benefit from the payment, her total miscellaneous itemized deductions must exceed 2 percent of her AGI. The computation for her deductible investment expense is as follows:

Description	Amount
Investment expenses	$ 500
Tax return preparation fees	250
Total miscellaneous itemized deductions	750
Less: 2 percent of AGI ($162,000 × 2%)	3,240
Miscellaneous itemized deductions over 2 percent of AGI floor	0

Because her miscellaneous itemized deductions are less than 2 percent of her AGI, Courtney does not gain any tax benefit from the $500 investment expense (it does not reduce taxable income).

In fact, Courtney could have paid another $2,490 of investment expenses before she would have exceeded the 2 percent of AGI threshold and received any tax benefit from the payment ($3,290 − $750).

Investment Interest Expense

When taxpayers borrow money to acquire investments, the interest expense they pay on the loan is investment interest expense. For example, if you borrow funds to buy stock, any interest you pay on the loan would be considered investment interest expense.

[34]IRC §212. Rental expenses are also deductible under §212 as we discuss in Chapter 6.

[35]§265.

[36]See Chapter 6 for a discussion of the tax treatment of miscellaneous itemized deductions. Also note that as we discussed in Chapter 6, investment expenses from rental and royalty-related activities are deductible as *for* AGI and not as itemized deductions.

Investment interest expense may be deductible as an itemized deduction.[37] Unlike investment expenses, the investment interest expense deduction is *not* a miscellaneous itemized deduction subject to the 2 percent of AGI floor. It is, however, subject to a different limitation. A taxpayer's investment interest expense deduction for the year is limited to the taxpayer's **net investment income** for the year.[38]

Net Investment Income Net investment income is gross investment income reduced by *deductible* investment expenses. Deductible investment expenses are investment expenses that actually reduce taxable income *after* applying the 2 percent of AGI floor.[39] Gross investment income includes interest, annuity, and royalty income not derived in the ordinary course of a trade or business. It also includes net *short*-term capital gains, and nonqualified dividends. However, investment income generally does not include net long-term capital gains and qualified dividends because this income is taxed at a preferential rate.

Example 7-13

What if: Suppose that during the year, Courtney recognized the following income from investments: $3,000 of qualified dividends and $500 of taxable interest. What is Courtney's gross investment income?

Answer: $500. The taxable interest is included, and the qualified dividends are excluded because they are taxed at a preferential rate.

What is Courtney's *net* investment income?

Answer: $500. Recall that net investment income is gross investment income minus deductible (taxable income reducing) investment expenses. In Example 7-12, we found that Courtney's deductible investment expenses were $0. Thus, her net investment income is $500 ($500 − $0).

Taxpayers may deduct their investment interest expense up to the amount of their net investment income. Any investment interest expense in excess of net investment income is carried over and treated as though it was incurred in the next year when it is subject to the same limitations. The carryover amount never expires. That is, taxpayers can carry over the excess investment interest expense until they generate sufficient net investment income to deduct it.

Example 7-14

What if: Suppose that in July of this year, Courtney purchased a parcel of undeveloped land as an investment for $120,000. She made a $20,000 down payment and financed the remaining $100,000 with a loan from her local credit union. The interest rate on the loan was 9 percent, payable annually. During the year, Courtney paid $4,500 in interest expense on the loan. Because the loan was used to purchase an investment, the interest expense is investment interest expense. What amount of this investment interest expense is Courtney allowed to deduct this year?

Answer: $500. Although she incurred $4,500 of investment interest expense, her deduction for the current year is limited to her $500 net investment income (see Example 7-13). The $4,000 of investment interest expense that is not deductible this year is carried forward until Courtney generates enough net investment income to deduct it.

[37]§163.

[38]The investment interest expense limitation is calculated on Form 4952. Note that taxpayers can avoid the limitations on investment interest expense by acquiring the investment assets with funds from a qualified home equity loan. As we discuss in Chapter 14, interest on home equity loans is generally fully deductible.

[39]When taxpayers have both investment expenses and other miscellaneous itemized deductions subject to the 2 percent of AGI floor, deductible amounts in excess of the 2 percent of AGI floor are considered to first come from investment expenses up to the total amount of investment expenses and then from other miscellaneous itemized deductions.

Congress allows taxpayers to *elect to include* preferentially taxed income in investment income if they are willing to subject this income to tax at the ordinary (not preferential) tax rates. Taxpayers who make this election benefit from increasing their net investment income and thus increasing their current year investment interest expense deduction. But, this additional deduction comes at a price because they must subject their net long-term capital gains and qualified dividends included in investment income to ordinary tax rates.[40]

Example 7-15

In Examples 7-13 and 7-14, we discovered that Courtney paid $4,500 of investment interest expense during the year but was only able to deduct $500 of the interest expense because her net investment income was only $500. However, as indicated in Example 7-13, Courtney also received $3,000 of qualified dividends that were *excluded* from the net investment income computation. Courtney may elect to increase her investment income by the amount of the qualified dividends (and increase her investment interest expense deduction), but by doing so, she must subject the qualified dividends to her ordinary tax rate (30 percent) instead of the preferential rate (15 percent). Thus, Courtney is faced with a choice of whether to include the $3,000 dividend in investment income and tax it at ordinary rates (Alternative 1) or to exclude it from investment income and tax it at preferential rates (Alternative 2). How much more investment interest expense is she allowed to deduct under Alternative 1 than Alternative 2?

Answer: $3,000 more under Alternative 1, computed as follows:

Alternative 1: *Include the $3,000 dividends in investment income.*

Description	Amount	Explanation
(1) Increase in net investment income	$3,000	Elect to include dividends in net investment income.
(2) Increase in investment interest expense deduction	**3,000**	Investment interest expense deduction increased from $500 to $3,500.
(3) Tax benefit from additional deduction	900	(2) × 30%.
(4) Tax cost of taxing dividends at ordinary rate	450	(1) × (30% − 15%).
(5) Current savings from election to include dividends in net investment income	450	(3) − (4).
Investment interest expense carryforward	$1,000	$4,500 total − $3,500 deducted.

Alternative 2: *Exclude the $3,000 dividends from investment income.*

Description	Amount	Explanation
Forgone tax benefit available *this year* under Alternative 1	$ 450	Under Alternative 2, Courtney doesn't receive the tax savings available under Alternative 1.
(1) Increase in investment interest expense carryforward	3,000	Investment interest expense not deducted under Alternative 2.
Total investment interest expense carryforward	$4,000	(1) + $1,000 investment interest expense carryforward under Alternative 1.

THE KEY FACTS

Investment-Related Expenses

- Investment *interest* expense.
  - Itemized deduction not subject to the 2 percent of AGI floor.
  - Interest expense on loans used to purchase taxable investments.
  - Deductible to the extent of net investment income.
  - Net investment income is gross investment income minus deductible investment expenses.
  - Investment income includes interest, annuity, and other investment-type income not taxed at the preferential rate (long-term capital gains and qualified dividends).
  - Taxpayers can elect to include long-term capital gains and dividends in investment income but must tax them at the ordinary not the preferential rate.
  - Investment interest expense not deducted carries forward indefinitely.

Whether or not it makes sense to elect to include net long-term capital gains and qualified dividends in investment income depends on the taxpayers' circumstances and their personal preferences. As we see in Example 7-15, Courtney could

[40]Note that the election is not an all-or-nothing proposition. Taxpayers can elect to include all or only a portion of their net long-term capital gains and qualifying dividends in investment income. However, the amount they include in investment income is subject to tax at ordinary tax rates.

save $450 this year by electing to include this income in investment income. However, by doing so, she is forgoing $3,000 of investment interest expense carryforward ($4,000 − $1,000) that would be available to offset ordinary income in future years.

Net Investment Income Tax

For years after 2012, a net investment income tax is imposed on net investment income. The tax imposed is 3.8 percent of the lesser of (a) net investment income or (b) the excess of modified adjusted gross income over $250,000 for married-joint filers and surviving spouses, $125,000 for married separate filers, and $200,000 for other taxpayers. Modified adjusted gross income equals adjusted gross income increased by income excluded under the foreign earned income exclusion less any disallowed deductions associated with the foreign earned income exclusion. Additional details and examples of the tax are provided in Chapter 8.

LO 7-4

PASSIVE ACTIVITY INCOME AND LOSSES

Thus far we have discussed how taxpayers may invest in business- and income-producing activities and earn various forms of income that are taxed as *portfolio income.* For example, taxpayers acquiring stock in a **C corporation** that files tax returns and pays taxes or purchasing bonds issued by a taxable corporation are taxed on the portfolio income these investments generate in the form of dividends and interest. On the other hand, a taxpayer may invest directly in an income-producing enterprise by purchasing rental property or by forming a business as a sole proprietor. Similarly, a taxpayer could invest in a partial interest in a trade or business or rental activity by acquiring an ownership interest in a **flow-through entity** that doesn't pay taxes such as a partnership, limited liability company (taxed as a partnership), or an S corporation (taxed similar to a partnership by shareholders' election). No matter whether an investor makes a direct investment in rental property or in a sole proprietorship or makes an indirect investment in a business or rental activity through a partnership, limited liability company, or S corporation, the *actual operating income or loss* from these investments flows through to the taxpayer as it is earned and is treated as ordinary income or ordinary loss. If trade or business or rental activities (held either directly or indirectly through flow-through entities) generate ordinary operating income, taxpayers report it on their tax returns and it is taxed at ordinary rates. However, if these activities generate operating losses, the operating losses must clear three hurdles to be deductible currently. The three loss limits are the tax basis, at-risk, and the passive loss limits.

The tax basis hurdle limits a taxpayer's deductible operating losses to the taxpayer's tax basis in the business or rental activity. This limitation is very similar to loss limitations that apply when a taxpayer sells an investment asset such as corporate stock or other similar capital asset. Recall that the formula for determining gain or loss on an exchange is the amount realized less the taxpayer's adjusted basis in the property. If a taxpayer were to sell an asset for nothing, the loss would be the amount of her tax basis in the property, but no more.

Obviously, in order to apply the tax basis loss limitation, we must first determine the taxpayer's tax basis in the activity. Very generally speaking, the tax basis is the taxpayer's investment in the activity adjusted for certain items (namely, income, debt, and investments). The adjustments are beyond the scope of this chapter; however, tax basis is discussed in later chapters relating to flow-through entities.

When a loss from a business or business-related activity clears the tax basis hurdle, it next must clear an **at-risk** hurdle on its journey toward deductibility.[41] The at-risk rules are meant to limit the ability of investors to deduct "artificial"

[41]§465.

ordinary losses produced with certain types of debt. These rules serve to limit ordinary losses to a taxpayer's economic risk in an activity. Generally, a taxpayer is considered to be at risk in an activity to the extent of any cash personally contributed to the activity and certain other adjustments similar (but not identical) to those for tax basis.[42] Because the computation of tax basis and at-risk amount are so similar, a taxpayer's tax basis and her at-risk amount in the activity are frequently the same so that when she clears the tax basis hurdle for deducting a loss, she also clears the at-risk hurdle. If the at-risk amount does differ from the tax basis, the at-risk amount will be less than the tax basis. Losses that do not clear the at-risk hurdle are suspended until the taxpayer generates more at-risk amounts to absorb the loss or until the activity is sold, when they may offset the seller's gain from the disposition of the activity.

Example 7-16

What if: Assume that instead of investing solely in assets that generate portfolio income, Courtney used $10,000 of the inheritance from "Gramps" to acquire a 5 percent interest in a limited partnership (a flow-through entity) called Color Comfort Sheets (CCS). Courtney's share of CCS's loss for the year is $15,000. What amount of this loss is Courtney allowed to deduct after applying the tax basis and at-risk limitations?

Answer: $10,000. Since Courtney's tax basis and at-risk amount in her CCS interest are both $10,000 (the amount of cash invested), the tax basis and at-risk amount limitations result in the same limitation. Thus, Courtney may deduct $10,000 of the $15,000 loss before considering the passive activity loss limits discussed below.

Even when a taxpayer has sufficient tax basis and sufficient amounts at risk to absorb a loss from a business-related activity, the loss may still be limited by the passive activity loss rules. Prior to 1986, investors were able to use ordinary losses from certain passive activities to offset portfolio income (interest, dividends, and capital gains), salary income, and self-employment income, including income from other trades or businesses they were actively involved in managing. During this time, a **tax shelter** industry thrived by marketing investments to wealthy investors designed primarily to generate ordinary losses that could be used to shield other income from tax. To combat this practice, Congress introduced the passive activity loss rules.[43] Specifically, these rules limit the ability of investors in certain passive activities involving interests in trade or businesses and in rental property, including real estate, to use their ordinary losses from these activities currently to reduce taxable income from other sources.[44] The passive activity loss rules are applied to any losses remaining *after* applying the tax basis and at-risk loss limits.

Passive Activity Definition

The **passive activity loss rules** define a passive activity as "any activity which involves the conduct of a trade or business, and in which the taxpayer does not materially participate." According to the tax code, participants in rental activities, including rental real estate, and limited partners in partnerships are generally deemed to be passive participants, and participants in all other trade or business activities are passive

[42]A detailed discussion of these adjustments is beyond the scope of this chapter.

[43]§469.

[44]Before passage of the passive activity loss rules, the "at-risk rules" in §465 were adopted in an attempt to limit the ability of investors to deduct "artificial" ordinary losses. Given the similarity of the at-risk and tax basis computations, especially for real estate investments, the at-risk rules were not entirely successful at accomplishing this objective. The passive activity loss rules were adopted as a backstop to the at-risk rules and both sets of rules may potentially apply to a given activity.

unless their involvement in an activity is "regular, continuous, and substantial." Clearly, these terms are quite subjective and difficult to apply. Fortunately, regulations provide more certainty in this area by listing seven separate tests for material participation.[45] An individual, other than a limited partner, can be classified as a material participant in an activity by meeting any one of the seven tests in Exhibit 7-8. Therefore, investors who purchase rental property or an interest in a trade or business without intending to be involved in the management of the trade or business are classified as passive participants, and these activities are classified as passive activities with respect to them.

EXHIBIT 7-8 Tests for Material Participation

Individuals are generally considered material participants for the activity if they meet any *one* of these tests:

1. The individual participates in the activity more than 500 hours during the year.
2. The individual's activity constitutes substantially all of the participation in such activity by all individuals including nonowners.
3. The individual participates more than 100 hours during the year, and the individual's participation is not less than any other individual's participation in the activity.
4. The activity qualifies as a "significant participation activity" (more than 100 hours spent during the year) and the aggregate of all "significant participation activities" is greater than 500 hours for the year.
5. The individual materially participated in the activity for any 5 of the preceding 10 taxable years.
6. The individual materially participated for any three preceding years in any personal service activity (personal services in health, law, accounting, architecture, etc.)
7. Taking into account all the facts and circumstances, the individual participates on a regular, continuous, and substantial basis during the year.

Income and Loss Categories

Under the passive activity loss rules, each item of a taxpayer's income or loss for the year is placed in one of three categories. Losses from *the passive category* cannot offset income from other categories. The three different categories are as follows (see Exhibit 7-9):

1. *Passive activity income or loss*—income or loss from an activity in which the taxpayer is not a material participant.

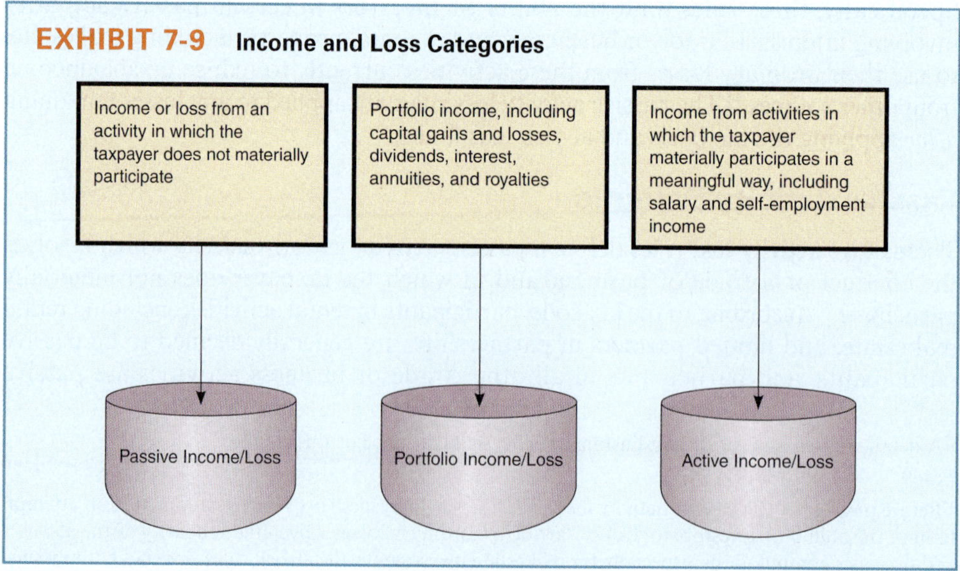

[45]§1.469-5T.

2. *Portfolio income*—income from investments including capital gains and losses, dividends, interest, annuities, and royalties.
3. *Active business income*—income from sources in which the taxpayer is a material participant. For individuals, this includes salary and self-employment income. Thus, an individual with income in this category is no longer an investor with respect to this source of income given that we define investors in this chapter as individuals with portfolio and/or passive income and losses.

The impact of segregating taxpayers' income in these categories is to limit their ability to apply passive activity losses against income in the other two categories. In effect, passive activity losses are suspended and remain in the passive income or loss category until the taxpayer generates passive income, either from the passive activity producing the loss or from some other passive activity, or until the taxpayer sells the entire activity that generated the passive loss in a taxable transaction. On the sale, current and suspended passive losses from the activity are first applied to reduce gain from the sale of the activity, then to reduce net passive income from other passive activities, and then to reduce nonpassive income.[46]

Example 7-17

What if: Let's return to the facts in the previous example where Courtney's share of CCS loss was $15,000, her tax basis in their CCS interest is $10,000, and her at-risk amount in the activity is also $10,000. Further assume that Courtney received $170,000 in combined salary, $4,000 of taxable interest income from corporate bonds, $3,000 of dividends, and $5,000 of long-term capital gains. Finally, assume that Courtney also owned a rental condominium that generated $8,000 of net income. How would each of these income or loss items be allocated among the passive, portfolio, and active income and loss categories?

Answer: Courtney's $10,000 loss from CCS remaining after applying the tax basis and at-risk loss limits is placed in the passive category because, as a limited partner, Courtney did not materially participate in the activity. Further, her $8,000 of net income from her rental property is included in the passive category because rental activities are generally considered to be passive. The $4,000 of taxable interest income, $3,000 of dividends, and $5,000 of long-term capital gains are all included in the portfolio income category. Finally, the $170,000 of salary is included in the active income category.

What if: What is Courtney's AGI for the year assuming, other than the items described above, no other items affect her AGI?

Answer: $182,000, computed as follows:

Description	Amount	Explanation
(1) Active income	$170,000	Salary
(2) Portfolio income	12,000	Interest of $4,000; dividends of $3,000; $5,000 of long-term capital gains.
(3) Passive income	0	$10,000 passive loss that clears tax basis and at-risk hurdles and $8,000 of passive income. However, the passive loss clearing the basis and at-risk hurdles is deductible only to the extent of passive income. The suspended passive loss is ($2,000).
AGI	$182,000	(1) + (2) + (3).

What if: Assume the facts above and that at the beginning of next year Courtney sells her limited partnership interest for $12,000. If Courtney's tax basis on the date of sale is $0, what effect does the sale have on her AGI?

(continued on page 7-32)

THE KEY FACTS

Passive Activities

- Ordinary losses from flow-though entities and other enterprises will be classified as passive if the taxpayer is not a material participant.
- Losses from limited partnerships and from rental activities, including rental real estate, are generally deemed to be passive losses.
- Passive loss rules limit losses from passive activities to passive income from other sources.
  - Active business income such as salary and self-employment income is not passive income.
  - Investment-type income such as interest and dividends is portfolio income, not passive income.

(continued)

[46]§469(g).

- Passive losses in excess of passive income are suspended and deductible against passive income in the future or when the taxpayer sells the passive activity generating the loss.
- Income from passive activities is subject to the net investment income tax.

Answer: $10,000 increase in AGI, computed as follows:

Description	Amount	Explanation
(1) Capital gain	$12,000	Gain recognized = $12,000 − $0 tax basis.
(2) Ordinary loss	0	The ($5,000) loss that was suspended at the basis level is not deductible on the sale. This loss expires unused. There was no loss suspended at the at-risk level or it would have been deductible on the sale.
(3) Ordinary loss	(2,000)	This is the loss that was suspended at the passive loss level last year.
Increase in AGI	$10,000	(1) + (2) + (3).

THE KEY FACTS

Rental Real Estate Losses

- Rental real estate exception to passive loss rules.
  - Applies to active participants in rental property.
  - Deduct up to $25,000 of rental real estate loss against ordinary income.
  - $25,000 maximum deduction phased out by 50 cents for every dollar of AGI over $100,000 (excluding the rental loss deduction).
  - Fully phased out at $150,000 of AGI.

Rental Real Estate Exception to the Passive Activity Loss Rules

Tax laws are renowned for exceptions to rules and, not surprisingly, the general rule that passive activity losses cannot be used to offset nonpassive types of income is subject to a few important exceptions. The one we choose to discuss here applies to lower-to-middle income individuals with rental real estate.[47] A taxpayer who is an **active participant in a rental activity** may be allowed to deduct up to $25,000 of the rental loss against other types of income. To be considered an active participant, the taxpayer must (1) own at least 10 percent of the rental property, and (2) participate in the process of making management decisions such as approving new tenants, deciding on rental terms, and approving repairs and capital expenditures.

Consistent with a number of tax benefits, the exception amount for active owners is phased out as adjusted gross income increases: The $25,000 maximum exception amount is phased out by 50 cents for every dollar the taxpayer's adjusted gross income (before considering the rental loss) exceeds $100,000. Consequently, the entire $25,000 deduction is phased out when the taxpayer's adjusted gross income reaches $150,000.

Example 7-18

What if: Assume that Jeb Landers, Courtney's uncle, owns and rents a condominium. Jeb is involved in approving new tenants for the rental home and in managing its maintenance. During the year, he reported a net loss of $5,000 from the rental activity, and he had sufficient tax basis and at-risk amounts to absorb the loss. Further, his only sources of income during the year were $126,000 of salary and $22,000 of long-term capital gains. Given Jeb's $5,000 loss from his rental home, how much of the loss could he deduct currently and what would be his passive loss carryforward?

Answer: $1,000. Because Jeb meets the definition of an "active participant" and has adjusted gross income of less than $150,000, before considering his rental loss, he may deduct a portion of the loss against his other income. His $1,000 deduction is computed as follows:

Description	Amount	Explanation
(1) Maximum deduction available before phase-out	$25,000	
(2) Phase-out of maximum deduction	24,000	[($148,000 − 100,000) × .5].
(3) Maximum deduction in current year	$ 1,000	(1) − (2).
(4) Rental loss in current year	$ 5,000	
(5) Rental loss deductible in current year	**1,000**	Lesser of (3) or (4).
Passive loss carryforward	**$ 4,000**	(4) − (3).

[47]§469(b)(7) provides another important exception to the general rule that all real estate activities are passive. To overcome this presumption, taxpayers must spend more than half their time working in real estate trades or businesses and for more than 750 hours during the year. This exception benefits individuals that spend a substantial amount of time in activities like real estate development and construction.

What if: Assume that Jeb's salary for the year had been $50,000 and he reported $22,000 from the sale of his stock, how much of his rental loss could he deduct currently?

Answer: Because Jeb's adjusted gross income would only be $72,000 under this scenario, he could deduct his entire $5,000 rental loss during the year.

Net Investment Income Tax on Net Passive Income

Earlier in this chapter we noted that taxpayers with modified AGI over certain thresholds are required to pay a 3.8 percent tax on their net investment income (in addition to the income tax). In calculating net investment income for this tax, taxpayers must include their net passive income.

Example 7-19

What if: Suppose Courtney has income from her salary of $170,000. Assume that in addition to this income, Courtney also owns 50 percent of an S corporation in which she does not materially participate. The S corporation is profitable and generates $100,000 of flow-through income to her this year. How much net investment income tax will Courtney owe?

Answer: $760, calculated as follows:

Description	Amount	Explanation
(1) Net investment income	$100,000	Income from passive investment.
(2) Modified AGI	270,000	$170,000 salaries + $100,000 LLC income.
(3) Modified AGI threshold	250,000	
(4) Excess modified AGI above threshold	20,000	(2) − (3).
(5) Net investment income tax base	20,000	Lesser of (1) or (4).
Net investment income tax	760	(5) × 3.8%.

What if: Assume that Courtney spends 525 hours participating in the activity during the year. How much net investment income tax will she owe?

Answer: $0. Because Courtney materially participates in the S corporation, the flow-through income is no longer passive income and she will not be subject to the net investment income tax.

CONCLUSION

Investors and their advisors face numerous tax rules that apply to investment income and expenses. Understanding these rules is important, not only to comply with the tax law, but also to make wise investment choices. Investments differ in terms of their potential for implementing the conversion and shifting tax planning strategies. Failing to consider these strategies when investing will lead to less than optimal results. By carefully weighing nontax investment objectives along with the tax characteristics of different investment options, informed investors will be better equipped to select investments appropriate for them.

Summary

LO 7-1 Explain how interest income and dividend income are taxed.

- Investors seeking current income invest in interest-bearing securities or dividend-paying stocks.
- Interest income received from certificates of deposit, U.S. Treasury securities, corporate bonds, and other similar investments is typically taxed annually at ordinary rates.
- Accrued market discount on bonds and interest earned on U.S. savings bonds is taxed at sale or maturity, while original issue discount on bonds is taxed annually.
- Bond premiums increase the tax basis of bonds and affect the amount of capital gains or losses investors report.
- Taxpayers may elect to amortize bond premiums to reduce the amount of annual interest reported on bonds purchased at a premium.
- Dividend income, like interest income, is taxed annually when it is received. However, most dividend income currently is taxed at preferential capital gains rates.

LO 7-2 Compute the tax consequences associated with the disposition of capital assets, including the netting process for calculating gains and losses.

- When taxpayers sell stock, they may determine the basis of the stock using the specific identification method or the FIFO method.
- Capital assets held for more than one year generate long-term capital gains or losses on sale or disposition. Other capital assets generate short-term capital gains or losses on sale or disposition.
- Generally, net long-term capital gains in excess of net short-term losses are taxed at a maximum 20 percent tax rate.
- Unrecaptured §1250 gain is taxed at a maximum 25 percent rate, and gains from collectibles and §1202 stock are taxed at a maximum 28 percent rate.
- Up to $3,000 of net capital losses are deductible against ordinary income for the year.
- A taxpayer's capital gains and losses for the year are reported on Schedule D of Form 1040.
- Wash sale provisions prevent taxpayers from selling stock at a loss, deducting the loss, and replacing the stock sold with the same stock or substantially identical securities within 30 days either before or after the day of sale.
- Losses on the disposition of property held for personal use are not deductible.
- Because of the deferral of the capital gains tax, after-tax returns from capital assets will increase as an investor's investment horizon increases.

LO 7-3 Calculate the deduction for portfolio investment-related expenses, including investment expenses and investment interest expense.

- Investment expenses are miscellaneous itemized deductions subject to the 2 percent of AGI floor.
- Investment interest expense is deductible to the extent of net investment income.
- Net investment income is investment income minus deductible investment expenses.
- Net long-term capital gains and qualified dividends are not included in investment income unless the taxpayer elects to tax them as ordinary income.

LO 7-4 Understand the distinction between portfolio investments and passive investments and apply tax basis, at-risk, and passive activity loss limits to losses from passive investments.

- A taxpayer's share of operating losses from flow-through entities and other trade or business activities are deductible to the extent they clear the tax basis, at-risk, and passive activity loss hurdles.
- A taxpayer's ordinary losses from flow-through entities and other trade or business activities may be classified as passive if the taxpayer's involvement is not regular, continuous, and substantial.
- A taxpayer's operating losses from rental activities are, with limited exceptions, deemed to be passive regardless of taxpayer's activity level.

- A taxpayer's passive losses from an activity are limited to passive income from all other sources until disposition of the activity. On disposition, current and prior passive losses from an activity can be used without limitation.
- A rental real estate exception allows taxpayers to deduct up to $25,000 of operating losses from rental real estate annually provided they are actively involved in managing the rental real estate and have adjusted gross income of less than $150,000.

KEY TERMS

accrued market discount (7-4)
active participant in a rental activity (7-32)
amortization (7-3)
at-risk (7-28)
basis (7-4)
bond (7-2)
bond discount (7-3)
bond premium (7-3)
C corporation (7-28)
capital asset (7-7)
certificate of deposit (7-2)
collectibles (7-11)
dividend (7-2)
ex-dividend date (7-6)
face value (7-2)
first-in first-out (FIFO) method (7-9)
flow-through entity (7-28)
investment expenses (7-24)
investment income (7-2)
investment interest expense (7-24)
long-term capital gains or losses (7-10)
market discount (7-4)
market premium (7-4)
maturity (7-4)
maturity value (7-2)
mutual fund (7-2)
net capital gain (7-12)
net investment income (7-26)
net long-term capital gain (7-12)
net long-term capital loss (7-12)
net short-term capital gain (7-12)
net short-term capital loss (7-12)
operating income (7-2)
operating loss (7-2)
original issue discount (7-3)
passive activity loss rules (7-29)
passive investments (7-2)
portfolio investments (7-2)
qualified dividends (7-6)
qualified small business stock (7-11)
short-term capital gains or losses (7-10)
specific identification method (7-9)
tax basis (7-8)
tax shelter (7-29)
Treasury bond (7-3)
Treasury note (7-3)
unrecaptured §1250 gain (7-10)
U.S. savings bonds (7-3)
wash sale (7-21)
zero-coupon bonds (7-3)

DISCUSSION QUESTIONS

1. Describe how interest income and dividend income are taxed. What are the similarities and differences in their tax treatment? LO 7-1
2. What is the underlying policy rationale for the current tax rules applicable to interest income and dividend income? LO 7-1
3. Compare and contrast the tax treatment of interest from a Treasury bond and qualified dividends from corporate stock. LO 7-1
4. How are Treasury notes and Treasury bonds treated for federal and state income tax purposes? LO 7-1
5. Why would taxpayers generally prefer the tax treatment of market discount to the treatment of original issue discount on corporate bonds? LO 7-1
6. In what ways are U.S. savings bonds treated more favorably for tax purposes than corporate bonds? LO 7-1
7. When should investors consider making an election to amortize market discount on a bond into income annually? [*Hint:* See §1278(b).] LO 7-1 research
8. Why might investors purchase interest-paying securities rather than dividend-paying stocks? LO 7-1 planning
9. Compare and contrast the tax treatment of dividend-paying stocks and growth stocks. LO 7-1
10. What is the definition of a capital asset? Give three examples of capital assets. LO 7-2
11. Why does the tax law allow a taxpayer to defer gains accrued on a capital asset until the taxpayer actually sells the asset? LO 7-2
12. Why does the tax law provide preferential rates on certain capital gains? LO 7-2

LO 7-2 13. What is the deciding factor in determining whether a capital gain is a short-term or long-term capital gain?

LO 7-2 14. What methods may taxpayers use to determine the adjusted basis of stock they have sold?

LO 7-2 15. What tax rate applies to net short-term capital gains?

LO 7-2 16. What limitations are placed on the deductibility of capital losses for individual taxpayers?

LO 7-2 17. What happens to capital losses that are not deductible in the current year?

LO 7-2 18. Are all long-term capital gains taxable at the same maximum rate? If not, what rates may apply to long-term capital gains?

planning LO 7-2 19. This year, David, a taxpayer in the highest tax rate bracket, has the option to purchase either stock in a Fortune 500 company or qualified small business stock in his friend's corporation. All else equal, which of the two will he prefer from a tax perspective if he intends to hold the stock for six years? Which would he prefer if he only plans to hold the stock for two years?

LO 7-2 20. What is a "wash sale"? What is the purpose of the wash sale tax rules?

LO 7-2 21. Nick does not use his car for business purposes. If he sells his car for less than he paid for it, does he get to deduct the loss for tax purposes? Why or why not?

LO 7-2 22. Describe three basic tax planning strategies available to taxpayers investing in capital assets.

planning LO 7-2 23. Clark owns stock in BCS Corporation that he purchased in January of the current year. The stock has appreciated significantly during the year. It is now December of the current year, and Clark is deciding whether or not he should sell the stock. What tax and nontax factors should Clark consider before making the decision on whether to sell the stock now?

LO 7-3 24. Are dividends and capital gains considered to be investment income for purposes of determining the amount of a taxpayer's deductible investment interest expense for the year?

LO 7-3 25. How is the amount of net investment income determined for a taxpayer with investment expenses and other noninvestment miscellaneous itemized deductions?

LO 7-3 26. What limitations are placed on the deductibility of investment interest expense? What happens to investment interest expense that is not deductible because of the limitations?

LO 7-3 27. When taxpayers borrow money to buy municipal bonds, are they allowed to deduct interest expense on the loan? Why or why not?

LO 7-3 28. What types of losses may potentially be characterized as passive losses?

LO 7-4 29. What are the implications of treating losses as passive?

LO 7-4 30. What tests are applied to determine if losses should be characterized as passive?

planning LO 7-4 31. All else being equal, would a taxpayer with passive losses rather have wage income or passive income?

PROBLEMS

All applicable problems are available with McGraw-Hill's *Connect*® *Accounting*.

LO 7-1 32. Matt recently deposited $20,000 in a savings account paying a guaranteed interest rate of 4 percent for the next 10 years. If Matt expects his marginal tax rate to be 20 percent for the next 10 years, how much interest will he earn after-tax for the first year of his investment? How much interest will he earn after-tax for the second year of his investment if he withdraws enough cash every year to pay the tax on the interest he earns? How much will he have in the account after 4 years? How much will he have in the account after 7 years?

33. Dana intends to invest $30,000 in either a Treasury bond or a corporate bond. The Treasury bond yields 5 percent before tax and the corporate bond yields 6 percent before tax. Assuming Dana's federal marginal rate is 25 percent and her marginal state rate is 5 percent, which of the two options should she choose? If she were to move to another state where her marginal state rate would be 10 percent, would her choice be any different? Assume that Dana itemizes deductions. LO 7-1

34. At the beginning of his current tax year David invests $12,000 in original issue U.S. Treasury bonds with a $10,000 face value that mature in exactly 10 years. David receives $700 in interest ($350 every six months) from the Treasury bonds during the current year, and the yield to maturity on the bonds is 5 percent. LO 7-1
    a) How much interest income will he report this year if he elects to amortize the bond premium?
    b) How much interest will he report this year if he does not elect to amortize the bond premium?

35. Seth invested $20,000 in Series EE savings bonds on April 1. By December 31, the published redemption value of the bonds had increased to $20,700. How much interest income will Seth report from the savings bonds in the current year absent any special election? LO 7-1

36. At the beginning of her current tax year, Angela purchased a zero-coupon corporate bond at original issue for $30,000 with a yield to maturity of 6 percent. Given that she will not actually receive any interest payments until the bond matures in 10 years, how much interest income will she report this year assuming semiannual compounding of interest? LO 7-1

37. At the beginning of his current tax year, Eric bought a corporate bond with a maturity value of $50,000 from the secondary market for $45,000. The bond has a stated annual interest rate of 5 percent payable on June 30 and December 31, and it matures in five years on December 31. Absent any special tax elections, how much interest income will Eric report from the bond this year and in the year the bond matures? LO 7-1

38. Hayley recently invested $50,000 in a public utility stock paying a 3 percent annual dividend. If Hayley reinvests the annual dividend she receives net of any taxes owed on the dividend, how much will her investment be worth in four years if the dividends paid are qualified dividends? (Hayley's marginal income tax rate is 28 percent.) What will her investment be worth in four years if the dividends are nonqualified? LO 7-1

39. Five years ago, Kate purchased a dividend-paying stock for $10,000. For all five years, the stock paid an annual dividend of 4 percent before tax and Kate's marginal tax rate was 25 percent. Every year Kate reinvested her after-tax dividends in the same stock. For the first two years of her investment, the dividends qualified for the 15 percent capital gains rate; however, for the last three years the 15 percent dividend rate was repealed and dividends were taxed at ordinary rates. LO 7-1 planning
    a) What is the current value (at the beginning of year 6) of Kate's investment assuming the stock has not appreciated in value?
    b) What will Kate's investment be worth three years from now (at the beginning of year 9) assuming her marginal tax rate increases to 35 percent for the next three years?

40. John bought 1,000 shares of Intel stock on October 18, 2012, for $30 per share plus a $750 commission he paid to his broker. On December 12, 2015, he sells the shares for $42.50 per share. He also incurs a $1,000 fee for this transaction. LO 7-2
    a) What is John's adjusted basis in the 1,000 shares of Intel stock?
    b) What amount does John realize when he sells the 1,000 shares?
    c) What is the gain/loss for John on the sale of his Intel stock? What is the character of the gain/loss?

LO 7-2

41. Dahlia is in the 28 percent tax rate bracket and has purchased the following shares of Microsoft common stock over the years:

Date Purchased	Shares	Basis
7/10/2005	400	$12,000
4/20/2006	300	10,750
1/29/2007	500	12,230
11/02/2009	250	7,300

If Dahlia sells 800 shares of Microsoft for $40,000 on December 20, 2015, what is her capital gain or loss in each of the following assumptions?

a) She uses the FIFO method.

b) She uses the specific identification method and she wants to minimize her current year capital gain.

LO 7-2

42. Karyn loaned $20,000 to her co-worker to begin a new business several years ago. If her co-worker declares bankruptcy on June 22nd of the current year, is Karyn allowed to deduct the bad debt loss this year? If she can deduct the loss, what is the character of the loss?

LO 7-2

research

43. Sue has 5,000 shares of Sony stock that has an adjusted basis of $27,500. She sold the 5,000 shares of stock for cash of $10,000, and she also received a piece of land as part of the proceeds. The land was valued at $20,000 and had an adjusted basis to the buyer of $12,000. What is Sue's gain or loss on the sale of 5,000 shares of Sony stock?

LO 7-2

44. Matt and Meg Comer are married. They do not have any children. Matt works as a history professor at a local university and earns a salary of $64,000. Meg works part-time at the same university. She earns $21,000 a year. The couple does not itemize deductions. Other than salary, the Comers' only other source of income is from the disposition of various capital assets (mostly stocks).

a) What is the Comers' tax liability for 2015 if they report the following capital gains and losses for the year?

Short-term capital gains	$ 9,000
Short-term capital losses	(2,000)
Long-term capital gains	15,000
Long-term capital losses	(6,000)

b) What is the Comers' tax liability for 2015 if they report the following capital gains and losses for the year?

Short-term capital gains	$ 1,500
Short-term capital losses	0
Long-term capital gains	13,000
Long-term capital losses	(10,000)

LO 7-2

45. Grayson is in the 25 percent tax rate bracket and has the sold the following stocks in 2015:

	Date Purchased	Basis	Date Sold	Amount Realized
Stock A	1/23/1991	$ 7,250	7/22/2015	$ 4,500
Stock B	4/10/2015	14,000	9/13/2015	17,500
Stock C	8/23/2013	10,750	10/12/2015	15,300
Stock D	5/19/2005	5,230	10/12/2015	12,400
Stock E	8/20/2015	7,300	11/14/2015	3,500

a) What is Grayson's net short-term capital gain or loss from these transactions?

b) What is Grayson's net long-term gain or loss from these transactions?

c) What is Grayson's overall net gain or loss from these transactions?

d) What amount of the gain, if any, is subject to the preferential rate for certain capital gains?

46. George bought the following amounts of Stock A over the years: LO 7-2

	Date Purchased	Number of Shares	Adjusted Basis
Stock A	11/21/1989	1,000	$24,000
Stock A	3/18/1995	500	9,000
Stock A	5/22/2004	750	27,000

On October 12, 2015, he sold 1,200 of his shares of Stock A for $38 per share.

a) How much gain/loss will George have to recognize if he uses the FIFO method of accounting for the shares sold?

b) How much gain/loss will George have to recognize if he specifically identifies the shares to be sold by telling his broker to sell all 750 shares from the 5/22/2004 purchase and 450 shares from the 11/21/1989 purchase?

47. During the current year, Ron and Anne sold the following assets: LO 7-2

Capital Asset	Market Value	Tax Basis	Holding Period
L stock	$ 50,000	$41,000	> 1 year
M stock	28,000	39,000	> 1 year
N stock	30,000	22,000	< 1 year
O stock	26,000	33,000	< 1 year
Antiques	7,000	4,000	> 1 year
Rental home	300,000*	90,000	> 1 year

*$30,000 of the gain is 25 percent gain (from accumulated depreciation on the property).

a) Given that Ron and Anne have taxable income of only $20,000 (all ordinary) before considering the tax effect of their asset sales, what is their gross tax liability for 2015 assuming they file a joint return?

b) Given that Ron and Anne have taxable income of $400,000 (all ordinary) before considering the tax effect of their asset sales, what is their gross tax liability for 2015 assuming they file a joint return?

48. In 2015, Tom and Amanda Jackson (married filing jointly) have $200,000 of taxable income before considering the following events: LO 7-2

a) On May 12, 2015, they sold a painting (art) for $110,000 that was inherited from Grandma on July 23, 2013. The fair market value on the date of Grandma's death was $90,000 and Grandma's adjusted basis of the painting was $25,000.

b) Applied a long-term capital loss carryover from 2014 of $10,000.

c) Recognized a $12,000 loss on 11/1/2015 sale of bonds (acquired on 5/12/2005).

d) Recognized a $4,000 gain on 12/12/2015 sale of IBM stock (acquired on 2/5/2015).

e) Recognized a $17,000 gain on the 10/17/2015 sale of rental property (the only §1231 transaction) of which $8,000 is reportable as gain subject to the 25 percent maximum rate and the remaining $9,000 is subject to the 15 percent maximum rate (the property was acquired on 8/2/2009).

f) Recognized a $12,000 loss on 12/20/2015 sale of bonds (acquired on 1/18/2015).

g) Recognized a $7,000 gain on 6/27/2015 sale of BH stock (acquired on 7/30/2006).

h) Recognized an $11,000 loss on 6/13/2015 sale of QuikCo stock (acquired on 3/20/2008).

i) Received $500 of qualified dividends on 7/15/2015.

Complete the required capital gains netting procedures and calculate the Jacksons' 2015 tax liability.

LO 7-2

49. For 2015, Sherri has a short-term loss of $2,500 and a long-term loss of $4,750.

a) How much loss can Sherri deduct in 2015?

b) How much loss will Sherri carryover to 2016, and what is the character of the loss carryover?

LO 7-2

50. Three years ago, Adrian purchased 100 shares of stock in X Corp. for $10,000. On December 30 of year 4, Adrian sells the 100 shares for $6,000.

a) Assuming Adrian has no other capital gains or losses, how much of the loss is Adrian able to deduct on her year 4 tax return?

b) Assume the same facts as in part (a), except that on January 20 of year 5, Adrian purchases 100 shares of X Corp. stock for $6,000. How much loss from the sale on December 30 of year 4 is deductible on Adrian's year 4 tax return? What basis does Adrian take in the stock purchased on January 20 of year 5?

LO 7-2

51. Christopher sold 100 shares of Cisco stock for $5,500 in the current year. He purchased the shares several years ago for $2,200. Assuming his ordinary income tax rate is 28 percent, and he has no other capital gains or losses, how much tax will he pay on this gain?

LO 7-2

52. Christina, who is single, purchased 100 shares of Apple Inc. stock several years ago for $3,500. During her year-end tax planning, she decided to sell 50 shares of Apple for $1,500 on December 30. However, two weeks later, Apple introduced its latest iPhone, and she decided that she should buy the 50 shares (cost of $1,600) of Apple back before prices skyrocket.

a) What is Christina's deductible loss on the sale of 50 shares? What is her basis in the 50 new shares?

b) Assume the same facts, except that Christina repurchased only 25 shares for $800. What is Christina's deductible loss on the sale of 50 shares? What is her basis in the 25 new shares?

LO 7-2
research

53. Arden purchased 300 shares of AMC common stock several years ago for $1,500. On April 30, Arden sold the shares of AMC common for $500 and then purchased 250 shares of AMC preferred stock two days later for $700. The AMC preferred stock is not convertible into AMC common stock. What is Arden's deductible loss from the sale of the 300 shares of AMC common stock?

LO 7-2
planning

54. Shaun bought 300 shares of Dental Equipment Inc. several years ago for $10,000. Currently the stock is worth $8,000. Shaun's marginal tax rate this year is 25 percent, and he has no other capital gains or losses. Shaun expects to have a marginal rate of 30 percent next year, but also expects to have a long-term capital gain of $10,000. To minimize taxes, should Shaun sell the stock on December 31 of this year or January 1 of next year (ignore the time value of money)?

LO 7-2
research

55. Becky recently discovered some high-tech cooking technology that has advantages over microwave and traditional ovens. She received a patent on the technology that gives her exclusive rights to the technology for 20 years. Becky would

prefer to retain the patent, but she doesn't want to deal with the manufacturing and marketing of the technology. She was able to reach a compromise. A little over a year after she secured the patent, Becky signed a contract with DEF Company giving DEF control to manufacture and market the technology. In exchange, Becky is to receive a royalty based on the sales of the technology. For tax purposes, Becky is not sure how to treat her arrangement with DEF. If the exchange with DEF is treated as a sale, she will recognize long-term capital gain because the patent is a capital asset held for more than a year. If the exchange is not treated as a sale, Becky will recognize ordinary income as she receives the royalties. (*Hint:* IRC §1235 and www.aicpa.org/pubs/taxadv/online/aug2000/clinic5a.htm)

a) Is it possible for Becky to treat the exchange with DEF as a sale even though she never relinquishes actual title of the patent? If so, what requirements must she meet to treat the contract as a sale for tax purposes?

b) Does your answer to the question above change if Becky's contract with DEF gave DEF Company control over the income from the patent for the next 10 years of the patent's remaining 19-year life?

56. Rich and Shauna Nielson file a joint tax return, and they itemize deductions. Assume their marginal tax rate on ordinary income is 25 percent. The Nielsons incur $2,000 in miscellaneous itemized deductions, excluding investment expenses. They also incur $1,000 in noninterest investment expenses during the year. What tax savings do they receive from the investment expenses under the following assumptions: LO 7-3

a) Their AGI is $90,000.

b) Their AGI is $130,000.

57. Mickey and Jenny Porter file a joint tax return, and they itemize deductions. The Porters incur $2,000 in employment-related miscellaneous itemized deductions. They also incur $3,000 of investment interest expense during the year. The Porters' income for the year consists of $150,000 in salary, and $2,500 of interest income. LO 7-3

a) What is the amount of the Porters' investment interest expense deduction for the year?

b) What would their investment interest expense deduction be if they also had a ($2,000) long-term capital loss?

58. On January 1 of year 1, Nick and Rachel Sutton purchased a parcel of undeveloped land as an investment. The purchase price of the land was $150,000. They paid for the property by making a down payment of $50,000 and borrowing $100,000 from the bank at an interest rate of 6 percent per year. At the end of the first year, the Suttons paid $6,000 of interest to the bank. During year 1, the Suttons' only source of income was salary. On December 31 of year 2, the Suttons paid $6,000 of interest to the bank and sold the land for $210,000. They used $100,000 of the sale proceeds to pay off the $100,000 loan. The Suttons itemize deductions and are subject to a marginal ordinary income tax rate of 35 percent. LO 7-3 planning

a) Should the Suttons treat the capital gain from the land sale as investment income in year 2 in order to minimize their year 2 tax bill? If so, how much?

b) How much does this cost or save them in year 2?

59. George recently received a great stock tip from his friend, Mason. George didn't have any cash on hand to invest, so he decided to take out a $20,000 loan to facilitate the stock acquisition. The loan terms are 8 percent interest with interest-only payments due each year for five years. At the end of the LO 7-3

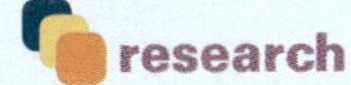

five-year period the entire loan principal is due. When George closed on the loan on April 1, 2015, he decided to invest $16,000 in stock and to use the remaining $4,000 to purchase a four-wheel recreation vehicle. George is unsure how he will treat the interest paid on the $20,000 loan. In 2015, George paid $1,200 interest expense on the loan. For tax purposes, how should he treat the 2015 interest expense? (*Hint:* Visit www.irs.gov and consider IRS Publication 550.)

LO 7-4

60. Larry recently invested $20,000 (tax basis) in purchasing a limited partnership interest. His at-risk amount is also $20,000. In addition, Larry's share of the limited partnership loss for the year is $2,000, his share of income from a different limited partnership was $1,000, and he had $3,000 of dividend income from the stock he owns. How much of Larry's $2,000 loss from the limited partnership can he deduct in the current year?

LO 7-4

61. Rubio recently invested $20,000 (tax basis) in purchasing a limited partnership interest. His at-risk amount is $15,000. In addition, Rubio's share of the limited partnership loss for the year is $22,000, his share of income from a different limited partnership was $5,000, and he had $40,000 in wage income and $10,000 in long-term capital gains.
   a) How much of Rubio's $22,000 loss is allowed considering only the tax basis loss limitations?
   b) How much of the loss from part (a) is allowed under the at-risk limitations?
   c) How much of Rubio's $22,000 loss from the limited partnership can he deduct in the current year considering all limitations?

LO 7-4

62. Molly Grey (single) acquired a 30 percent limited partnership interest in Beau Geste LLP several years ago for $48,000. At the beginning of year 1, Molly has tax basis and an at-risk amount of $20,000. In year 1, Beau Geste incurs a loss of $180,000 and does not make any distributions to the partners.
   - In year 1, Molly's AGI (excluding any income or loss from Beau Geste) is $60,000. This includes $10,000 of passive income from other passive activities.
   - In year 2, Beau Geste earns income of $30,000. In addition, Molly contributes an additional $30,000 to Beau Geste during year 2. Molly's AGI in year 2 is $63,000 (excluding any income or loss from Beau Geste). This amount includes $8,000 in income from her other passive investments.

   a) Based on the above information, determine the following amounts:
      - At-risk amount at the end of year 1
      - At-risk amount at the end of year 2
      - Losses allowed under the at-risk rules in year 2
      - Total suspended passive losses at the end of year 1
      - Total suspended at-risk losses at the end of year 2
      - Deductible losses in year 1
      - Year 2 AGI after considering Beau Geste events
   b) Briefly describe actions Molly Grey could undertake in year 2 to utilize any suspended passive losses from year 1.

LO 7-4

63. Anwar owns a rental home and is involved in maintaining it and approving renters. During the year he has a net loss of $8,000 from renting the home. His other sources of income during the year were a salary of $111,000 and $34,000 of long-term capital gains. How much of Anwar's $8,000 rental loss can he deduct currently if he has no sources of passive income?

COMPREHENSIVE PROBLEMS

All applicable problems are available with McGraw-Hill's *Connect® Accounting*.

64. During 2015, your clients, Mr. and Mrs. Howell, owned the following investment assets:

Investment Assets	Date Acquired	Purchase Price	Broker's Commission Paid at Time of Purchase
300 shares of IBM common	11/22/12	$ 10,350	$ 100
200 shares of IBM common	4/3/13	43,250	300
3,000 shares of Apple preferred	12/12/13	147,000	1,300
2,100 shares of Cisco common	8/14/14	52,500	550
420 shares of Vanguard mutual fund	3/2/15	14,700	No load fund*

*No commissions are charged when no load mutual funds are bought and sold.

Because of the downturn in the stock market, Mr. and Mrs. Howell decided to sell most of their stocks and mutual fund in 2015 and to reinvest in municipal bonds. The following investment assets were sold in 2015:

Investment Assets	Date Sold	Sale Price	Broker's Commission Paid at Time of Sale
300 shares of IBM common	5/6/15	$ 13,700	$ 100
3,000 shares of Apple preferred	10/5/15	221,400	2,000
2,100 shares of Cisco common	8/15/15	63,250	650
451 Shares of Vanguard mutual fund	12/21/15	15,700	No load fund*

*No commissions are charged when no load mutual funds are bought and sold.

The Howells' broker issued them a Form 1099 showing the sales proceeds net of the commissions paid. For example, the IBM sales proceeds were reported as $13,600 on the Form 1099 they received.

In addition to the sales reflected in the table above, the Howells provided you with the following additional information concerning 2015:

- The Howells received a Form 1099 from the Vanguard mutual fund reporting a $900 long-term capital gain distribution. This distribution was reinvested in 31 additional Vanguard mutual fund shares on 6/30/2015.
- In 2010, Mrs. Howell loaned $6,000 to a friend who was starting a new multilevel marketing company called LD3. The friend declared bankruptcy in 2015, and Mrs. Howell has been notified she will not be receiving any repayment of the loan.
- The Howells have a $2,300 short-term capital loss carryover and a $4,800 long-term capital loss carryover from prior years.
- The Howells did not instruct their broker to sell any particular lot of IBM stock.
- The Howells earned $3,000 in municipal bond interest, $3,000 in interest from corporate bonds, and $4,000 in qualified dividends.
- Assume the Howells have $130,000 of wage income during the year.

a) Go to the IRS website (www.IRS.gov) and download the most current version of Form 8949 and Schedule D. Use Form 8949 and page 1 of Schedule D to compute net long-term and short-term capital gains. Then, compute the Howells' tax liability for the year (ignoring the alternative minimum tax and any phase-out provisions) assuming they file a joint return, they have no dependents, they don't make any special tax elections, and their itemized deductions total $25,000. Assume that asset bases are reported to the IRS.

b) Are there any tax planning recommendations related to the stock sales that you should have shared with the Howells before their decision to sell?
c) Assume the Howells' short-term capital loss carryover from prior years is $82,300 rather than $2,300 as indicated above. If this is the case, how much short-term and long-term capital loss carryover remains to be carried beyond 2015 to future tax years?

KAPLAN CPA SIMULATION

KAPLAN CPA REVIEW

Please visit the *Connect Library* to access the following Kaplan CPA Simulation:

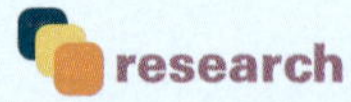

The simulation for **Honestown Securities** deals with researching the appropriate section of the Internal Revenue Code in which this commodities dealer can elect to value its securities at fair market value instead of historical cost.

chapter **8**

Individual Income Tax Computation and Tax Credits

Learning Objectives

Upon completing this chapter, you should be able to:

LO 8-1 Determine a taxpayer's regular tax liability and identify tax issues associated with the process.

LO 8-2 Compute a taxpayer's alternative minimum tax liability and describe the tax characteristics of taxpayers most likely to owe the alternative minimum tax.

LO 8-3 Calculate a taxpayer's employment and self-employment taxes payable and explain tax considerations relating to whether a taxpayer is considered to be an employee or a self-employed independent contractor.

LO 8-4 Describe the different general types of tax credits, identify specific tax credits, and compute a taxpayer's allowable child tax credit, child and dependent care credit, American opportunity credit, lifetime learning credit, and earned income credit.

LO 8-5 Explain taxpayer filing and tax payment requirements and describe in general terms how to compute a taxpayer's underpayment, late filing, and late payment penalties.

© Image Source

Storyline Summary

Taxpayers:	Courtney Wilson, age 40 Courtney's mother Dorothy "Gram" Weiss, age 70
Family description:	Courtney is divorced with a son, Deron, age 10, and a daughter, Ellen, age 20. Gram is currently residing with Courtney.
Location:	Kansas City, Missouri
Employment status:	Courtney works as an architect for EWD. Gram is retired.
Filing status:	Courtney is head of household. Gram is single.
Current situation:	Courtney and Gram have computed their taxable income. Now they are trying to determine their tax liability, tax refund or additional taxes due, and whether they owe any payment-related penalties.

Courtney has already determined her taxable income. Now she's working on computing her tax liability. She knows she owes a significant amount of regular income tax on her employment and business activities. However, she's not sure how to compute the tax on the qualified dividends she received from General Electric. Courtney is worried that she may be subject to the alternative minimum tax this year because she's heard that an increasing number of taxpayers in her income range must pay the tax. Finally, Courtney knows she owes some self-employment taxes on her business income. Courtney would like to determine whether she is eligible to claim any tax credits such as the child tax credit for her two children and education credits because she paid for a portion of her daughter Ellen's tuition at the University of Missouri–Kansas City this year. Courtney is hoping that she has paid enough in taxes during the year to avoid underpayment penalties. She's planning on filing her tax return and paying her taxes on time.

Gram's tax situation is much more straightforward. She needs to determine the regular income tax on her taxable income. Her income is so low she knows she need not worry about the alternative minimum tax, and she believes she doesn't owe any self-employment tax. Gram didn't prepay any taxes this year, so she is concerned that she might be required to pay an underpayment penalty. She also expects to file her tax return and pay her taxes by the looming due date.

to be continued . . .

In prior chapters we've learned how to compute taxable income for taxpayers such as Courtney and Gram. This chapter describes how to determine a taxpayer's tax liability for the year. We discover that the process is not as easy as simply applying taxable income to the applicable tax rate schedule or tax table. Taxpayers may generate taxable income that is taxed at rates not provided in the tax rate schedules or tax tables. We will learn that they may also be required to pay taxes in addition to the regular income tax. We also describe tax credits taxpayers may use to reduce their gross taxes payable. We conclude the chapter by describing taxpayer filing requirements and identifying certain penalties taxpayers may be required to pay when they underpay or are late paying their taxes. We start our coverage by explaining how to compute one's regular tax liability.

LO 8-1

REGULAR FEDERAL INCOME TAX COMPUTATION

When taxpayers have determined their taxable income, they are ready to compute their gross tax from a series of progressive tax rates called a **tax rate schedule.**

Tax Rate Schedules

Congress has constructed four different tax rate schedules for individuals. The applicable tax rate schedule is determined by the taxpayer's filing status, which we discussed in depth in Chapter 4. Recall that a taxpayer's filing status is one of the following:

1. Married filing jointly.
2. Qualifying widow or widower, also referred to as surviving spouse.
3. Married filing separately.
4. Head of household.
5. Single.

As we describe in Chapter 1, a tax rate schedule is composed of several ranges of income taxed at different (increasing) rates. Each separate range of income subject to a different tax rate is referred to as a **tax bracket.** While each filing status has its own tax rate schedule (married filing jointly and qualifying widow or widower use the same rate schedule), all tax rate schedules consist of tax brackets taxed at 10 percent, 15 percent, 25 percent, 28 percent, 33 percent, 35 percent, and 39.6 percent. However, the width or range of income within each bracket varies by filing status. In general, the tax brackets are widest and higher levels of income are taxed at the lowest rates for the married filing jointly filing status, followed by the head of household filing status, single filing status, and finally, the married filing separately filing status.

The tax rate schedule for each filing status is provided inside the back cover of this book. Notice that the married filing separately schedule is the same as the married filing jointly schedule except that the taxable income levels listed in the schedule are exactly one-half the taxable income levels for married filing jointly.

Example 8-1

As we determined in Chapter 6, Courtney files under the head of household filing status and her 2015 taxable income is $110,111 (see Exhibit 6-14).

What if: For now, let's *assume* that all of Courtney's income is taxed as ordinary income. That is, assume that none of her income is taxed at a preferential rate (some is, but we'll address this in a bit). What is the tax on her taxable income?

Answer: $21,850. Using the head of household tax rate schedule, her taxable income falls in the 25 percent marginal tax rate bracket, in between $50,200 and $129,600, so her tax is computed as follows:

Description	Amount	Explanation
(1) Base tax	$ 6,872.50	From head of household tax rate schedule for taxpayer with taxable income in 25% bracket.
(2) Income taxed at marginal tax rate	59,911	$110,111 − 50,200 from head of household tax rate schedule.
(3) Marginal tax rate	25%	From head of household tax rate schedule.
(4) Tax on income at marginal tax rate	14,977.75	(2) × (3).
Tax on taxable income	**$21,850**	(1) + (4), rounded.

Example 8-2

As we determined in Chapter 6, Gram files under the single filing status. In Chapter 6 we calculated her 2015 taxable income to be $3,740 (see Exhibit 6-15). None of her income is taxed at a preferential rate. What is the tax on her taxable income using the tax rate schedules?

Answer: $374 ($3,740 × 10%)

For administrative convenience and to prevent low and middle income taxpayers from making mathematical errors using a tax rate schedule, the IRS provides **tax tables** that present the gross tax for various amounts of taxable income under $100,000 and filing status (it's impractical to provide a table for essentially unlimited amounts of income). Taxpayers with taxable income less than $100,000 generally must use the tax tables to determine their tax liability.[1]

Because the tax tables generate nearly the same tax as calculated from the tax rate schedule, we use the tax rate schedules throughout this chapter.

Marriage Penalty or Benefit

An interesting artifact of the tax rate schedules is that they can impose what some refer to as a **marriage penalty,** but they may actually produce a **marriage benefit.** A marriage penalty (benefit) occurs when, for a given level of income, a married couple has a greater (lesser) tax liability when they use the married filing jointly tax rate schedule to determine the tax on their joint income than they would have owed (in total) if each spouse would have used the single tax rate schedule to compute the tax on each spouse's individual income. Exhibit 8-1 explores the marriage penalty in a scenario in which both spouses earn income and another in which only one spouse earns income. As the exhibit illustrates, the marriage penalty applies to couples with two wage earners, but a marriage benefit applies to couples with single breadwinners.

Exceptions to the Basic Tax Computation

In certain circumstances, taxpayers cannot completely determine their final tax liability from their tax rate schedule or tax table. Taxpayers must perform additional computations to determine their tax liability (1) when they recognize long-term capital gains or receive dividends that are taxed at preferential (lower) rates, (2) when they receive investment income subject to the net investment income tax, or (3) when the taxpayer is a child and the child's unearned income is taxed at her parent's **marginal tax rate.** We describe these additional computations in detail below.

[1]Exceptions to this requirement include taxpayers subject to the kiddie tax, with qualified dividends or capital gains, or claiming the foreign earned income exclusion. You may view the tax tables in the instructions for Form 1040 located at www.irs.gov/.

EXHIBIT 8-1 2015 Marriage Penalty (Benefit) Two Income vs. Single Income Married Couple*

Married Couple	Taxable Income	Tax if File Jointly (1)	Tax if File Single[†] (2)	Marriage Penalty (Benefit) (1) − (2)
Scenario 1: *Two wage-earners*				
Wife	$100,000		$21,071.25	
Husband	100,000		$21,071.25	
Combined	$200,000	$43,051.50	$42,142.50	$909
Scenario 2: *One wage-earner*				
Wife	$200,000		$49,606.25	
Husband	0		0	
Combined	$200,000	$43,051.50	$49,606.25	($6,554.75)

*This analysis assumes the taxpayers do not owe any alternative minimum tax (discussed below).
[†]Married couples do not actually have the option of filing as single. If they choose not to file jointly they must file as married filing separately.

Preferential Tax Rates for Capital Gains and Dividends As we described in detail in Chapter 7, certain capital gains and certain dividends are taxed at a lower or **preferential tax rate** relative to other types of income. In general, the preferential tax rate is 0 percent, 15 percent, or 20 percent. The preferential tax rate is 0 percent *to the extent* the income would have been taxed in the 10 percent or 15 percent tax rate bracket if it were ordinary income, 20 percent to the extent the income would have been taxed in the 39.6 percent tax rate bracket if it were ordinary income, and 15 percent for all other taxpayers.[2] The tax rate tables and tax rate schedules allow taxpayers to compute their tax on ordinary but not **preferentially taxed income.** This is true even though preferentially taxed income is included in adjusted gross income (AGI) and in taxable income. Taxpayers with income subject to the preferential rate (long-term capital gains and qualified dividends) can use the following three-step process to determine their tax liability.

Step 1: Split taxable income into the portion that is subject to the preferential rate and the portion taxed at the ordinary rates.

Step 2: Compute the tax separately on each type of income. Note that the income that is not taxed at the preferential rate is taxed at the ordinary tax rates using the tax rate schedule for the taxpayer's filing status.

Step 3: Add the tax on the income subject to the preferential tax rates and the tax on the income subject to the ordinary rates. This is the taxpayer's regular tax liability.

Example 8-3

Courtney's taxable income of $110,111 includes $700 of qualified dividends from GE (Exhibit 5-4). What is her tax liability on her taxable income?

Answer: $21,780, computed at head of household rates as follows:

Description	Amount	Explanation
(1) Taxable income	$ 110,111	Exhibit 6-14.
(2) Preferentially taxed income	700	Exhibit 5-4.
(3) Income taxed at ordinary rates	$109,411	(1) − (2).

[2]As we discovered in Chapter 7, some types of income may be taxed at a preferential rate of 28 percent or 25 percent. In addition, as we discuss later in this chapter, dividends and capital gains for higher income taxpayers are subject to the 3.8% net investment income tax.

Description	Amount	Explanation
(4) Tax on income taxed at ordinary rates	21,675	[$6,872.50 + (109,411 − 50,200) × 25%], rounded.
(5) Tax on preferentially taxed income	105	(2) × 15% [Note that if (2) were ordinary income it would have been taxed at 25 percent.]
Tax on taxable income	**$21,780**	(4) + (5).

In this example, what is Courtney's tax savings from having the dividends taxed at the preferential rate rather than the ordinary rate?

Answer: $70. $700 × (25% − 15%). This is the amount of the dividend times the difference in the ordinary and preferential tax rate.

What if: Assume that Courtney's taxable income is $449,000 including $15,000 of qualified dividends taxed at the preferential rate. What would be Courtney's tax liability under these circumstances?

Answer: $126,362, computed using the head of household tax rate schedule as follows:

Description	Amount	Explanation
(1) Taxable income	$449,000	
(2) Preferentially taxed income	15,000	
(3) Income taxed at ordinary rates	434,000	(1) − (2).
(4) Tax on income at ordinary tax rates	123,612	$115,737 + [($434,000 − $411,500) × 35%] (see tax rate schedule for head of household).
(5) Tax on preferentially taxed income	2,750	[($5,000 × 15%) + ($10,000 × 20%)].*
Tax	**$126,362**	(4) + (5).

*Courtney had $15,000 of preferentially taxed income. If this income was ordinary income, $5,000 would have been taxed at 35 percent [$439,000 (end of 35 percent bracket) − $434,000 (ordinary taxable income)] and the remaining $10,000 would have been taxed at 39.6 percent [$449,000 (total taxable income) − $439,000 (end of 35 percent bracket)]. Consequently, $5,000 of the preferential income is taxed at 15 percent and the remaining $10,000 is taxed at 20 percent.

Net Investment Income Tax For years after 2012, a 3.8 percent tax is imposed on net investment income. For purposes of this tax, net investment income equals the sum of:

1. Gross income from interest, dividends, annuities, royalties, and rents (unless these items are derived in a trade or business to which the net investment income tax does not apply).
2. Income from a trade or business that is a passive activity or a trade or business of trading financial instruments or commodities.
3. Net gain from disposing of property (other than property held in a trade or business in which the net investment income tax does not apply).[3]
4. Less the allowable deductions that are allocable to items 1, 2, and 3.

Tax-exempt interest, veterans' benefits, excluded gain from the sale of a principal residence, distributions from qualified retirement plans, and any amounts subject to self-employment tax are not subject to the net investment income tax.

The tax imposed is 3.8 percent of the lesser of (1) net investment income or (2) the excess of modified adjusted gross income over $250,000 for married-joint filers and surviving spouses, $125,000 for married separate filers, and $200,000 for other

[3]However, the income, gain, or loss attributable to invested working capital of a trade or business is subject to the net investment income tax. §1411(c)(3).

taxpayers. Modified adjusted gross income equals adjusted gross income increased by income excluded under the foreign earned income exclusion less any disallowed deductions associated with the foreign earned income exclusion.[4]

Example 8-4

Courtney's AGI (and modified AGI) is $162,000, and her investment income consists of $617 of taxable interest, $700 of dividends, and $5,000 of rental income. How much net investment income tax will Courtney owe?

Answer: $0. Because Courtney's modified AGI ($162,000) is less than the $200,000 threshold for the net investment income tax for a taxpayer filing as head of household, she will not be subject to the tax.

What if: Assume that Courtney's AGI (and modified AGI) is $225,000. How much net investment income tax will Courtney owe?

Answer: $240, calculated as follows.

Description	Amount	Explanation
(1) Net investment income	$ 6,317	$617 interest + $700 dividends + $5,000 rental income.
(2) Modified AGI	225,000	
(3) Modified AGI threshold	200,000	
(4) Excess modified AGI above threshold	25,000	(2) − (3).
(5) Net investment income tax base	6,317	Lesser of (1) or (4).
Net investment income tax	**240**	(5) × 3.8%.

Kiddie Tax Parents can reduce their family's income tax bill by shifting income that would otherwise be taxed at their higher tax rates to their children whose income is taxed at lower rates. However, as we described in Chapter 5, under the assignment of income doctrine, taxpayers cannot simply assign or transfer income to other parties. Earned income, or income from services or labor, is taxed to the person who earns it. Thus, it's difficult for a parent to shift *earned* income to a child. However, unearned income or income from property such as dividends from stocks or interest from bonds is taxed to the *owner* of the property. Thus, a parent can shift unearned income to a child by transferring actual ownership of the income-producing property to the child. By transferring ownership, the parent runs the risk that the child will sell the asset or use it in a way unintended by the parent. However, this risk is relatively small for parents transferring property ownership to younger children.

The tax laws reduce parents' ability to shift unearned income to children through the so-called **kiddie tax.** The kiddie tax provisions apply (or potentially apply) to a child if (1) the child is under 18 years old at year end, (2) the child is 18 at year end but her earned income does *not* exceed half of her support, or (3) the child is over age 18 but under age 24 at year end, is a full-time student during the year, and her earned income does not exceed half of her support (excluding scholarships).[5]

In general terms, if the kiddie tax applies, children must pay tax on a certain amount of their unearned income (their **net unearned income,** discussed below) at their parents' marginal tax rate rather than at their own marginal tax rate, unless the parents' marginal tax rate on the income (the preferential tax rate if the income is long-term capital gain or qualified dividends) would be lower than the child's marginal tax rate.[6] When the parents of the child are not married, this

[4]Taxpayers compute the net investment income tax using Form 8960.

[5]§1(g)(2)(A).

[6]§1(g).

provision applies to the custodial parent.[7] That is, the kiddie tax will never allow children to pay less tax than they would have been required to pay without the kiddie tax provision.

The kiddie tax base is the child's net unearned income. Net unearned income is the *lesser* of (1) the child's gross *unearned income* minus $2,100[8] or (2) the child's taxable income (the child is not taxed on more than her taxable income).[9] Consequently, the kiddie tax does not apply unless the child has *unearned* income in *excess* of $2,100.[10] Thus the kiddie tax significantly limits, but does not eliminate, the tax benefit gained by a family unit when parents transfer income-producing assets to children.

Example 8-5

What if: Suppose that during 2015, Deron received $1,100 in interest from the IBM bond, and he received another $2,200 in interest income from a money market account that his parents have been contributing to over the years. Is Deron potentially subject to the kiddie tax?

Answer: Yes, Deron is younger than 18 years old at the end of the year and his net unearned income exceeds $2,100.

What is Deron's taxable income and corresponding tax liability?

Answer: $2,250 taxable income and $405 tax liability, calculated as follows:

Description	Amount	Explanation
(1) Gross income/AGI	$3,300	$1,100 interest from IBM bond + $2,200 interest. All unearned income.
(2) Standard deduction	1,050	Minimum for taxpayer claimed as a dependent on another return (no earned income, so must use minimum). See Chapter 6.
(3) Personal exemption	0	Claimed as a dependent on Courtney's return.
(4) Taxable income	**$2,250**	(1) − (2) − (3).
(5) Gross unearned income minus $2,100	1,200	(1) − 2,100.
(6) Net unearned income	$1,200	Lesser of (4) or (5).
(7) Courtney's ordinary marginal rate	25%	See Example 8-3 (use Courtney's rate because she is the custodial parent).
(8) Kiddie tax	$ 300	(6) × (7) (Deron's income taxed at Courtney's marginal rate.)
(9) Taxable income taxed at Deron's rate	1,050	(4) − (6).
(10) Tax on taxable income using Deron's tax rates	$ 105	(9) × 10% (See single filing status, $1,050 taxable income.)
Deron's total tax liability	**$ 405**	(8) + (10).

What if: Assume Deron's only source of income is qualified dividends of $2,200 (unearned income). What is his taxable income and tax liability?

(continued on page 8-8)

THE KEY FACTS

Tax Rates

- Regular tax rates
  - Schedule depends on filing status.
  - Progressive tax rate schedules with tax rates ranging from 10 percent to 39.6 percent.
  - Marriage penalty (benefit) occurs because dual earning spouses pay more (less) combined tax than if they each filed single.
- Preferential tax rates
  - Net long-term capital gains and qualified dividends generally taxed at 0 percent, 15 percent, or 20 percent.
- Net Investment income tax
  - 3.8 percent tax on lesser of (a) net investment income or (b) excess of modified AGI over applicable threshold based on filing status.
- Kiddie tax
  - Unearned income in excess of $2,100 is taxed at parent's marginal tax rate if child is (1) under age 18, (2) 18 but earned income does not exceed one-half of support, or (3) over 18 and under 24, full-time student, and earned income does not exceed one-half of support.

[7]§1(g)(5).

[8]The $2,100 consists of $1,050 of the child's standard deduction (even if the child is entitled to a larger standard deduction) plus an *extra* $1,050. See Chapter 6 for a discussion of the standard deduction for the dependent of another taxpayer. If the child itemizes deductions, then the calculation becomes more complex and is beyond the scope of this text.

[9]§1(g)(4).

[10]Under §1(g)(7), subject to certain requirements, parents may elect to include their child's unearned income on their own tax return (on Form 8814).

Answer: Taxable income is $1,150; tax liability is $15, computed as follows:

Description	Amount	Explanation
(1) Gross income/(AGI)	$2,200	Qualified dividends, all unearned income.
(2) Minimum standard deduction	1,050	Minimum for taxpayer claimed as a dependent on another return (all unearned income, so must use minimum). See Chapter 6.
(3) Personal exemption	0	Claimed as a dependent on Courtney's return.
(4) Taxable income	**$1,150**	(1) − (2) − (3).
(5) Gross unearned income minus $2,100	100	(1) − $2,100.
(6) Net unearned income	$ 100	Lesser of (4) or (5).
Description	**Amount**	**Explanation**
(7) Courtney's marginal tax rate on qualified dividend income	15%	See Example 8-3 (her marginal rate on ordinary income is 25%, so her marginal rate on preferentially taxed income is 15%).
(8) Kiddie tax	$ 15	(6) × (7) (Deron's income taxed at Courtney's marginal rate on the dividend income.)
(9) Taxable income taxed at Deron's rate	1,050	(4) − (6).
(10) Tax on taxable income using Deron's tax rates	$ 0	(9) × 0% (Deron's marginal rate on the dividend would be 10% if it were ordinary income, so he qualifies for 0% rate on dividend.)
Deron's total tax liability	**$ 15**	(8) + (10).

As we've just described, all individual taxpayers must pay federal income taxes on their federal taxable income. However, taxpayers may be liable for other federal taxes in addition to the regular tax liability. Many taxpayers are also required to pay the alternative minimum tax, and some working taxpayers are required to pay employment or self-employment taxes. We delve into these additional taxes below.

LO 8-2

ALTERNATIVE MINIMUM TAX

Each year, a number of taxpayers are required to pay the **alternative minimum tax (AMT)** in *addition to* their *regular* tax liability. The **alternative minimum tax system** was implemented in 1986 (earlier variations date back to the late 1960s) to ensure that taxpayers generating income pay some *minimum* amount of income tax each year. The tax was originally targeted at higher-income taxpayers who were benefiting from or were perceived by the public to be benefiting from the *excessive* use (more than Congress intended) of tax preference items such as exclusions, deferrals, and deductions to reduce or even eliminate their tax liabilities. However, as currently structured, the tax forces many taxpayers who don't fit this description to pay the tax.

In general terms, the alternative minimum tax is a tax on an *alternative* tax base meant to more closely reflect economic income than the regular income tax base. Thus the **AMT base** is more inclusive (or more broadly defined) than is the regular income tax base. To compute their AMT, taxpayers first compute their regular income tax liability. Then, they compute the AMT base and multiply the base by the applicable alternative tax rate.[11] They must pay the AMT only when the tax on the AMT base exceeds their regular tax liability.

[11]The rate of the alternative minimum tax (AMT) was set below that of the income tax with the objective of avoiding the perception that the AMT was an additional assessment.

Alternative Minimum Tax Formula

Regular taxable income is the starting point for determining the alternative minimum tax. As the AMT formula in Exhibit 8-2 illustrates, taxpayers make several "plus" and "minus" adjustments to regular taxable income to compute alternative minimum taxable income (AMTI). They then arrive at the AMT base by subtracting an AMT exemption from AMTI. Taxpayers multiply the AMT base by the AMT rate to determine their **tentative minimum tax.** Finally, to determine their alternative minimum tax, taxpayers subtract their regular tax liability from the tentative minimum tax. The alternative minimum tax is the *excess* of the tentative minimum tax over the regular tax. If the regular tax liability equals or exceeds the tentative minimum tax, taxpayers need not pay any AMT. Individual taxpayers compute their AMT on Form 6251 (see Exhibit 8-3).

Alternative Minimum Taxable Income (AMTI) In order to compute alternative minimum taxable income (AMTI), taxpayers make several **alternative minimum tax adjustments** to regular taxable income. Many of these are plus adjustments that are added to regular taxable income to reach AMTI and some are minus adjustments that are subtracted from regular taxable income to determine AMTI. Consequently, these adjustments tend to expand the regular income tax base to more closely reflect economic income.

Exemptions, standard deduction, and itemized deduction phase-out. Taxpayers first add back to regular taxable income the amount of personal and dependency exemptions they actually deducted, after considering phase-outs, in determining their regular taxable income. The exemption deduction is added back because it does not represent an actual economic outflow. Next, taxpayers add back the standard deduction amount, but only *if they deducted it* in determining taxable income. Again, just like exemptions, taxpayers add back the standard deduction because it is a deduction that does not reflect an actual economic outflow from the taxpayer.[12] Finally, taxpayers *subtract* the amount of itemized deductions they incurred but did not deduct because the deductions were phased-out or reduced for regular tax purposes (see discussion in Chapter 6). The phase-out is subtracted because it represents an economic outflow that did not reduce taxable income.

EXHIBIT 8-2 Formula for Computing the Alternative Minimum Tax

	Regular Taxable Income
Plus:	Personal exemptions and standard deduction if taxpayer deducted the standard deduction in computing regular taxable income
Minus:	Phase-out of itemized deductions for regular tax purposes (if applicable)
Plus or *Minus:*	Other adjustments*
	Alternative minimum taxable income
Minus:	AMT exemption amount (if any)
Equals:	Tax base for AMT
Times:	AMT rate
Equals:	Tentative minimum tax
Minus:	Regular tax
Equals:	Alternative minimum tax

*Technically, some of these adjustments are referred to as preference items and some are referred to as adjustments. We refer to all of these items as adjustments for simplicity's sake.

[12]The AMT add back of personal and dependency exemptions and the standard deduction is accomplished on Form 6251 by beginning with taxable income before personal and dependency exemptions (and before the standard deduction if the taxpayer does not itemize).

EXHIBIT 8-3 **2014 Form 6251 (Page 1 of 2)**

Form **6251**

Department of the Treasury
Internal Revenue Service (99)

Alternative Minimum Tax—Individuals

▶ **Information about Form 6251 and its separate instructions is at *www.irs.gov/form6251.***
▶ **Attach to Form 1040 or Form 1040NR.**

OMB No. 1545-0074
2014
Attachment Sequence No. **32**

Name(s) shown on Form 1040 or Form 1040NR | **Your social security number**

Part I Alternative Minimum Taxable Income (See instructions for how to complete each line.)

1	If filing Schedule A (Form 1040), enter the amount from Form 1040, line 41, and go to line 2. Otherwise, enter the amount from Form 1040, line 38, and go to line 7. (If less than zero, enter as a negative amount.)	1	
2	Medical and dental. If you or your spouse was 65 or older, enter the **smaller** of Schedule A (Form 1040), line 4, **or** 2.5% (.025) of Form 1040, line 38. If zero or less, enter -0-	2	
3	Taxes from Schedule A (Form 1040), line 9	3	
4	Enter the home mortgage interest adjustment, if any, from line 6 of the worksheet in the instructions for this line	4	
5	Miscellaneous deductions from Schedule A (Form 1040), line 27	5	
6	If Form 1040, line 38, is $152,525 or less, enter -0-. Otherwise, see instructions	6	( )
7	Tax refund from Form 1040, line 10 or line 21	7	( )
8	Investment interest expense (difference between regular tax and AMT)	8	
9	Depletion (difference between regular tax and AMT)	9	
10	Net operating loss deduction from Form 1040, line 21. Enter as a positive amount	10	
11	Alternative tax net operating loss deduction	11	( )
12	Interest from specified private activity bonds exempt from the regular tax	12	
13	Qualified small business stock (7% of gain excluded under section 1202)	13	
14	Exercise of incentive stock options (excess of AMT income over regular tax income)	14	
15	Estates and trusts (amount from Schedule K-1 (Form 1041), box 12, code A)	15	
16	Electing large partnerships (amount from Schedule K-1 (Form 1065-B), box 6)	16	
17	Disposition of property (difference between AMT and regular tax gain or loss)	17	
18	Depreciation on assets placed in service after 1986 (difference between regular tax and AMT)	18	
19	Passive activities (difference between AMT and regular tax income or loss)	19	
20	Loss limitations (difference between AMT and regular tax income or loss)	20	
21	Circulation costs (difference between regular tax and AMT)	21	
22	Long-term contracts (difference between AMT and regular tax income)	22	
23	Mining costs (difference between regular tax and AMT)	23	
24	Research and experimental costs (difference between regular tax and AMT)	24	
25	Income from certain installment sales before January 1, 1987	25	( )
26	Intangible drilling costs preference	26	
27	Other adjustments, including income-based related adjustments	27	
28	**Alternative minimum taxable income.** Combine lines 1 through 27. (If married filing separately and line 28 is more than $242,450, see instructions.)	28	

Part II Alternative Minimum Tax (AMT)

29 Exemption. (If you were under age 24 at the end of 2014, see instructions.)

IF your filing status is . . .	**AND line 28 is not over . . .**	**THEN enter on line 29 . . .**
Single or head of household	$117,300	$52,800
Married filing jointly or qualifying widow(er)	156,500	82,100
Married filing separately	78,250	41,050

If line 28 is **over** the amount shown above for your filing status, see instructions. . . . **29**

30	Subtract line 29 from line 28. If more than zero, go to line 31. If zero or less, enter -0- here and on lines 31, 33, and 35, and go to line 34	30	
31	• If you are filing Form 2555 or 2555-EZ, see instructions for the amount to enter. • If you reported capital gain distributions directly on Form 1040, line 13; you reported qualified dividends on Form 1040, line 9b; **or** you had a gain on both lines 15 and 16 of Schedule D (Form 1040) (as refigured for the AMT, if necessary), complete Part III on the back and enter the amount from line 64 here. • **All others:** If line 30 is $182,500 or less ($91,250 or less if married filing separately), multiply line 30 by 26% (.26). Otherwise, multiply line 30 by 28% (.28) and subtract $3,650 ($1,825 if married filing separately) from the result.	31	
32	Alternative minimum tax foreign tax credit (see instructions)	32	
33	Tentative minimum tax. Subtract line 32 from line 31	33	
34	Add Form 1040, line 44 (minus any tax from Form 4972), and Form 1040, line 46. Subtract from the result any foreign tax credit from Form 1040, line 48. If you used Schedule J to figure your tax on Form 1040, line 44, refigure that tax without using Schedule J before completing this line (see instructions)	34	
35	**AMT.** Subtract line 34 from line 33. If zero or less, enter -0-. Enter here and on Form 1040, line 45	35	

For Paperwork Reduction Act Notice, see your tax return instructions. Cat. No. 13600G Form **6251** (2014)

Example 8-6

Courtney started the process of determining whether she owed any AMT by adjusting her regular taxable income for her exemptions. What is Courtney's AMTI before other adjustments?

Answer: $122,111, computed as follows:

Description	Amount	Explanation
(1) Taxable income	$110,111	Exhibit 6-14.
(2) Exemptions	12,000	Exhibit 6-14.
AMTI before other adjustments	**$122,111**	(1) + (2).

Other adjustments. Taxpayers are required to make several other adjustments to compute AMTI. Exhibit 8-4 describes the most common of these adjustments.

EXHIBIT 8-4 Common AMT Adjustments

Adjustment	Description
Plus adjustments:	
Tax-exempt interest from private activity bonds	Taxpayers must add back interest income that was excluded for regular tax purposes if the bonds were used to fund private activities (privately owned baseball stadium or private business subsidies) and not for the public good (build or repair public roads). However, taxpayers do not add back interest income from private activity bonds if the bonds were issued in either 2009 or 2010.
Real property and personal property taxes deducted as itemized deductions	Deductible for regular tax purposes, but not for AMT purposes.
State income or sales taxes[13]	Deductible for regular tax purposes, but not for AMT purposes.
Home-equity interest expense	This is *not deductible* for AMT purposes if the proceeds from the loan are used for *purposes other than to acquire or substantially improve the home.*
Miscellaneous itemized deductions (subject to the 2 percent floor) in excess of the 2 percent floor	Deductible for regular tax purposes but not for AMT purposes.
Plus or Minus adjustment:	
Depreciation	Taxpayers must compute their depreciation expense for AMT purposes. For certain types of assets, the regular tax method is more accelerated than the AMT method. In any event, if the regular tax depreciation exceeds the AMT depreciation, this is a plus adjustment. If the AMT depreciation exceeds the regular tax depreciation, this is a minus adjustment.
Minus adjustments:	
State income tax refunds included in regular taxable income	Because state income taxes paid are not deductible for AMT purposes, refunds are not taxable (they do not increase the AMT base).
Gain or loss on sale of depreciable assets	Due to differences in regular tax and AMT depreciation methods, taxpayers may have a different adjusted basis (cost minus accumulated depreciation) for regular tax and for AMT purposes. Thus, they may have a different gain or loss for regular tax purposes than they do for AMT purposes. If regular tax gain exceeds AMT gain, this is a minus adjustment. Because AMT accumulated depreciation will never exceed regular tax accumulated depreciation, this would never be a plus adjustment.

[13]At press time, the deduction for state and local sales taxes is set to expire after 2014.

As Exhibit 8-4 indicates, several itemized deductions are not deductible for AMT purposes. The major itemized deductions that are deductible for both regular tax and AMT purposes using the *same limitations* are

- Casualty and theft losses.
- Charitable contributions.
- Home mortgage interest expenses.
- Gambling losses.

Deductions that are deductible for regular tax and AMT purposes but have *different limitations* are

- Medical expenses [10 percent of AGI floor for AMT purposes rather than 7.5 percent for regular tax purposes if the taxpayer (or his or her spouse) is age 65 or older]. Note that for regular tax and AMT purposes, all other taxpayers have a 10 percent AGI floor for medical expenses.
- Home-equity interest (interest not deductible for AMT purposes unless loan proceeds used to acquire or substantially improve the home).
- Investment interest expense (interest income that is tax exempt for regular tax purposes but included in the AMT base is included in investment income for determining the AMT investment interest expense deduction).

Example 8-7

Courtney continued to work on her AMT computation by determining the other adjustments she needs to make to determine her alternative minimum taxable income (AMTI). What is Courtney's AMTI?

Answer: $133,750, computed as follows:

Description	Amount	Explanation
(1) AMTI before other adjustments	$ 122,111	Example 8-6.
Plus adjustments:		
(2) Tax-exempt interest on Cincinnati bond used to pay for renovations to major league baseball stadium (Private activity bond: issued in 2005)	500	Example 5-22.
(3) Real estate property taxes	3,680	Example 6-14.
(4) State income taxes	6,700	Example 6-14.
(5) Miscellaneous itemized deductions in excess of 2 percent floor	1,179	Example 6-30.
Minus adjustments:		
(6) State income tax refund	(420)	Example 5-3.
Alternative minimum taxable income	$133,750	Sum of (1) through (6).

AMT Exemption To help ensure that low-income taxpayers aren't required to pay the alternative minimum tax, Congress allows taxpayers to deduct an **alternative minimum tax (AMT) exemption** amount to determine their alternative minimum tax base.[14] The amount of the exemption depends on the taxpayer's filing status. The exemption is phased-out (reduced) by 25 cents for every dollar the AMTI exceeds the threshold amount. Exhibit 8-5 identifies, by filing status, the base exemption amount, the phase-out threshold, and the range of AMTI over which the exemption is phased out for 2015.

[14]Similar to exemption and standard deduction amounts, the AMT exemption is indexed for inflation. The phase-out threshold amounts are also indexed annually for inflation.

EXHIBIT 8-5 2015 AMT Exemptions

Filing Status	Exemption	Phase-out Begins at This Level of AMTI	Phase-out Complete for This Level of AMTI
Married filing jointly	$83,400	$158,900	$492,500
Married filing separately	41,700	79,450	246,250
Head of household and Single	53,600	119,200	333,600

Example 8-8

What is Courtney's AMT base?

Answer: $83,788 computed by subtracting her allowable exemption amount from her AMTI as follows:

Description	Amount	Explanation
(1) AMTI	$133,750	Example 8-7.
(2) Full AMT Exemption (head of household):	53,600	Exhibit 8-5.
(3) Exemption phase-out threshold	119,200	
(4) AMTI in excess of exemption phase-out threshold	14,550	(1) – (3).
(5) Exemption phase-out percentage	25%	
(6) Exemption phase-out amount	3,638	(4) × (5).
(7) Deductible exemption amount	49,962	(2) – (6).
AMT base	**$ 83,788**	(1) – (7).

Tentative Minimum Tax and AMT Computation Taxpayers compute the tentative minimum tax by multiplying the AMT base by the applicable AMT rates. The 2015 AMT rate schedule consists of just two regular brackets as follows:

- 26 percent on the first $185,400 (indexed for inflation annually) of AMT base for all taxpayers other than married taxpayers filing separately ($92,700, indexed for inflation annually, for married taxpayers filing separately).
- 28 percent on AMT base in excess of $185,400 (indexed for inflation annually) for all taxpayers other than married taxpayers filing separately ($92,700, indexed for inflation annually, for married taxpayers filing separately).

However, for AMT purposes long-term capital gains and dividends are taxed at the same preferential rate as they were taxed for regular tax purposes (generally 0 percent, 15 percent, or 20 percent).

Example 8-9

Courtney's AMT base is $83,788. However, Courtney also received $700 in dividends that are included in the base but are subject to a tax rate of 15 percent even under the AMT system. The remaining $83,088 ($83,788 – $700) is taxed at the normal AMT rates. What is Courtney's tentative minimum tax?

Answer: $21,708, computed as follows:

Description	Amount	Reference
(1) AMT base	$83,788	Example 8-8.
(2) Dividends taxed at preferential rate	700	Example 8-3.
(3) Tax rate applicable to dividends	15%	
(4) Tax on dividends	105	(2) × (3).
(5) AMT base taxed at regular AMT rates	83,088	(1) – (2).
(6) Regular AMT tax rate	26%	For AMT base below $185,400.
(7) Tax on AMT base taxed at regular AMT rates	21,603	(5) × (6), rounded.
Tentative minimum tax	**$21,708**	(4) + (7).

Taxpayers subtract their regular tax liability from their tentative minimum tax to determine their AMT.[15] If the taxpayer's regular tax liability is equal to or exceeds the tentative minimum tax liability, the taxpayer does not owe any AMT.

Example 8-10

What is Courtney's alternative minimum tax liability?

Answer: $0, computed as follows:

Description	Amount	Reference
(1) Tentative minimum tax	$21,708	Example 8-9.
(2) Regular tax liability	21,780	Example 8-3.
Alternative minimum tax	$ 0	(1) − (2), $0 if negative.

Courtney does not owe alternative minimum tax because her regular tax liability exceeds her tentative minimum tax.

THE KEY FACTS

Alternative Minimum Tax (AMT)

- Implemented to ensure taxpayers pay some minimum level of income tax.
- AMT base
  - More broad than regular income tax base.
  - No deductions for exemptions, standard deduction, state income taxes, property taxes, and others.
- AMT exemption amounts for 2015
  - $83,400 married filing jointly.
  - $41,700 married filing separately.
  - $53,600 other.
  - Phased-out by 25 cents for each dollar of AMTI over threshold.
- AMT rates
  - 26 percent on first $185,400 of AMT base.
  - 28 percent on AMT base in excess of $185,400.
  - Net long-term capital gains and qualified dividends taxed at same preferential rates used for regular tax purposes.
- AMT is the excess of tentative minimum tax (tax on AMT base) over regular tax liability.

In some situations, taxpayers who pay the AMT are entitled to a **minimum tax credit** to use when the regular tax exceeds the tentative minimum tax. They can use the credit to offset regular tax but not below the tentative minimum tax for that year.[16]

General AMT Planning Strategies Based on the nature of the adjustments we've explained, it's clear that the taxpayers who tend to get hit the hardest by AMT are taxpayers who (1) have many dependents, (2) live in a high-income-tax state (they deduct state taxes for regular tax purposes but not AMT purposes), (3) pay high real estate or other property taxes, and/or (4) have relatively high capital gains (the capital gains increase AMTI, which reduces the exemption amount and thus exposes more income to the AMT). In certain circumstances, taxpayers can implement tax planning strategies to mitigate the impact of the AMT. For example, consistent with the tax rate timing strategy we discussed in Chapter 3, taxpayers who pay AMT at 26 percent (or 28 percent) one year and expect to pay regular tax at 35 percent in the next year may want to consider accelerating income into the AMT year to ensure that it is taxed at a lower rate than it would be in a regular tax year. In any event, taxpayers who either pay or may pay the AMT should consider their tax situation to determine whether and how to use timing tax planning strategies to reduce their combined tax burden (regular tax and AMT) given their circumstances.

EMPLOYMENT AND SELF-EMPLOYMENT TAXES

LO 8-3

As we discussed in Chapter 1, employees and self-employed taxpayers must pay employment (or self-employment) taxes known as **FICA** taxes.[17] The FICA tax consists of a Social Security and a Medicare component that are payable by both employees and employers. The **Social Security tax** is intended to provide basic pension coverage for the retired and disabled. The **Medicare tax** helps pay medical costs for qualifying individuals. Because Social Security and Medicare taxes are paid by working taxpayers

[15]As might be expected, self-employment taxes and the 3.8% net investment income tax are not considered as part of a taxpayer's regular tax liability in determining whether a taxpayer owes AMT.

[16]The credit applies only when the taxpayer has positive adjustments that will reverse and become negative adjustments in the future. For example, depreciation, gain or loss on asset sales, and incentive stock option bargain element adjustments (see Chapter 12) fall into this category. Due to the nature of her adjustments, Courtney does not qualify for the minimum tax credit.

[17]FICA stands for Federal Insurance Contributions Act.

but received by retired taxpayers, Social Security and Medicare taxes represent intergenerational transfers. The Social Security tax rate is 12.4 percent on the tax base (limited to $118,500 in 2015). The Medicare tax rate is 2.9 percent on the tax base up to $200,000 ($125,000 for married filing separately; $250,000 for married filing jointly) and is 3.8 percent on the tax base in excess of $200,000 ($125,000 for married filing separately; $250,000 for married filing jointly). The party responsible for paying the tax and the tax base depends on whether the taxpayer is an employee or whether the taxpayer is self-employed.

THE KEY FACTS

Employee FICA Tax

- Social Security tax
  - 6.2 percent rate on wage base.
  - 2015 wage base limit is $118,500.
- Medicare tax
  - 1.45 percent rate on wage base up to $200,000 ($125,000 for married filing separately; $250,000 for married filing jointly). 2.35 percent rate on excess wage base.
  - Wage base unlimited.

Employee FICA Taxes Payable

Both employees and employers have to pay **FICA taxes** on employee salary, wages, and other compensation paid by employers. The Social Security tax rate for employees is 6.2 percent of their salary or wages (wage base limited to $118,500 in 2015). The Medicare tax rate for employees is 1.45 percent on salary or wages up to $200,000 ($125,000 for married filing separate; $250,000 of combined salary or wages for married filing joint) and is 2.35 percent on salary or wages in excess of $200,000 ($125,000 for married filing separate; $250,000 of combined salary or wages for married filing joint). Employers withhold the employees' FICA tax liabilities from the employees' paychecks for both the Social Security tax and the Medicare tax. For the Medicare tax, employers are required to withhold the tax at a rate of 1.45 percent on salary or wages up to $200,000 and at a rate of 2.35 percent for any salary or wages above $200,000, irrespective of the taxpayer's filing status (e.g., single, married filing separate, married filing joint, or head of household).[18] Taxpayers use Form 8959 to determine their liability for the .9 percent additional Medicare tax and report all of the .9 percent additional Medicare tax withheld as a tax payment on Form 1040 (line 62).

Employers must also pay their portion of the Social Security tax (6.2 percent of employee salary or wages) and Medicare tax (1.45 percent of employee salary or wages, regardless of the amount of salary or wages). In contrast to employees, employers are not subject to the .9 percent additional Medicare tax on employee salary or wages.

Example 8-11

While she was attending school full-time, Ellen received $15,000 in wages working part-time for an off-campus employer during 2015. How much in FICA taxes should Ellen's employer have withheld from her paychecks during the year?

Answer: $1,148, computed as follows:

Description	Amount	Reference
(1) Wages	$15,000	
(2) Social Security tax rate	6.2%	
(3) Social Security tax	930	(1) × (2).
(4) Medicare tax rate	1.45%	
(5) Medicare tax	218	(1) × (4).
FICA taxes withheld	$ 1,148	(3) + (5).

The wage base for Social Security taxes is limited to an annually determined amount, reflecting the fact that the benefits the employee may ultimately receive are also capped. The limits apply to *each* taxpayer's wages regardless of marital or tax filing status. That is, the earnings of each spouse are subject to a *separate* limit. The 2015

[18]To avoid potential underpayment penalty, taxpayers can request additional income tax withholding or make estimated tax payments to pay any Medicare tax that otherwise would have been owed upon filing their tax return.

limit is $118,500. There is no wage base limit for the Medicare component of the FICA tax, but as previously discussed, the Medicare tax rate varies with the taxpayer's salary or wages (or combined salary or wages for married filing joint taxpayers).

Example 8-12

During 2015, Courtney received a total of $122,800 in employee compensation from EWD. Recall that the compensation consisted of $98,000 in wages, $4,800 performance bonus, $6,000 discount for architectural design services, $4,000 compensation for a below-market loan, and $10,000 forgiveness of debt (see Exhibit 5-4). What is her FICA tax liability on this income?

Answer: $9,128, computed as follows:

Description	Amount	Reference
(1) Compensation subject to FICA tax	$122,800	
(2) Social Security tax base limit for 2015	118,500	
(3) Compensation subject to Social Security tax	118,500	Lesser of (1) or (2).
(4) Social Security tax rate	6.2%	
(5) Social Security tax	7,347	(3) × (4).
(6) Medicare tax rate on compensation up to $200,000	1.45%	
(7) Medicare tax	1,781	(1) × (6).
FICA taxes	$ 9,128	(5) + (7).

What amount of FICA taxes for the year must EWD pay on Courtney's behalf?

Answer: $9,128, which includes $7,347 of Social Security tax ($118,500 × 6.2%) and $1,781 of Medicare tax ($122,800 × 1.45%).

What if: Courtney received a total of $220,000 in employee compensation. What is her FICA tax liability on this income?

Answer: $10,717, computed as follows:

Description	Amount	Reference
(1) Compensation subject to FICA tax	$220,000	
(2) Social Security tax base limit for 2015	118,500	
(3) Compensation subject to Social Security tax	118,500	Lesser of (1) or (2).
(4) Social Security tax rate	6.2%	
(5) Social Security tax	7,347	(3) × (4).
(6) Medicare tax rate on compensation up to $200,000	1.45%	
(7) Compensation subject to 1.45% Medicare tax	200,000	Lesser of (1) or $200,000.
(8) Medicare tax rate on compensation in excess of $200,000	2.35%	
(9) Compensation subject to 2.35% Medicare tax	20,000	Greater of [((1) – $200,000) or $0].
(10) Medicare tax	3,370	[(6) × (7)] + [(8) × (9)].
FICA taxes	**10,717**	(5) + (10).

What amount of FICA taxes for the year must EWD pay on Courtney's behalf?

Answer: $10,537, which includes $7,347 of Social Security tax ($118,500 × 6.2%) and $3,190 of Medicare tax ($220,000 × 1.45%).

Employees who work for multiple employers within a calendar year may receive aggregate compensation that exceeds the Social Security wage base. Because each employer is required to withhold Social Security taxes on the employee's wages until the employee has reached the wage base limit *with that employer,* the employee may end up paying Social Security tax in *excess* of the required maximum. Similar to situations in which excess Medicare tax has been withheld, the IRS treats the excess Social Security tax paid through withholding as an additional federal income tax payment (or credit) on Page 2 of Form 1040 (line 69). The government refunds the excess withholding to the employee through either lower taxes payable with the tax return or a greater tax refund. Employers, on the other hand, are *not* able to recover excess Social Security taxes paid on behalf of their employees.

Example 8-13

What if: Suppose that Courtney worked for her former employer Landmark Architects Inc. (LA), in Cincinnati for two weeks in January 2015 before moving to Kansas City. During those two weeks, Courtney would have earned $4,000 in salary. LA would have withheld $306 in FICA taxes from her final paycheck consisting of $248 of Social Security taxes ($4,000 × 6.2%) and $58 of Medicare taxes ($4,000 × 1.45%). How much excess Social Security tax would have been withheld from Courtney's combined salaries from LA and EWD during 2015?

Answer: $248 ($4,000 wages earned with LA × 6.2% Social Security rate). Due to the $118,500 Social Security tax wage base for the year, Courtney's Social Security tax liability is limited to $7,347 ($118,500 × 6.2%). However, through employer withholding, she would have paid a total of $7,595 in Social Security taxes, consisting of $248 withheld by LA ($4,000 × 6.2%) and $7,347 withheld by EWD ($118,500 × 6.2%). Thus, given these facts, Courtney's *excess* Social Security tax withheld was $248 ($7,595 − $7,347). Courtney would get this amount back from the government through either lower taxes payable with her tax return or a greater tax refund.

Self-Employment Taxes

While employees share their FICA (Social Security and Medicare) tax burden with employers, self-employed taxpayers must pay the *entire* FICA tax burden on their self-employment earnings.[19] Just as it is with FICA taxes for employees, self-employment taxes consist of both Social Security and Medicare taxes. Because their FICA taxes are based on their self-employment earnings, FICA taxes for self-employed taxpayers are referred to as **self-employment taxes.** Just as it is with employees, the base for the Social Security component of the self-employment tax is limited to $118,500. The base for the Medicare portion of the self-employment tax is unlimited. Taxpayers use the Schedule SE to determine their Social Security tax and 2.9% Medicare tax on self-employment earnings and Form 8959 to determine the .9 percent additional Medicare tax on self-employment earnings. The process for determining the taxpayer's self-employment taxes payable requires the following steps:

Step 1: Compute the amount of the taxpayer's net income from self-employment activities (this is generally the taxpayer's net income from **Schedule C** of Form 1040—Schedule C reports the taxpayers self-employment-related income and expenses) that is subject to self-employment taxes.

Step 2: Multiply the amount from Step (1) by 92.35 percent. The product is called **net earnings from self-employment.** Because self-employed taxpayers are responsible for paying the *entire* amount of their FICA taxes, they are allowed an implicit deduction for the 7.65 percent "employer's portion" of the taxes, leaving 92.35 percent (100% − 7.65%) of the full amount subject to self-employment taxes. Note that

[19]As we discussed in Chapters 5 and 6, self-employed taxpayers report their self-employment earnings on Schedule C of Form 1040. Individuals who are partners in partnerships and who are actively involved in the partnerships' business activities may be required to pay self-employment taxes on the income they are allocated from the partnerships. They would report these earnings on Schedule E of Form 1040.

the 7.65 percent consists of the 6.2 percent Social Security tax and 1.45 percent Medicare tax. Net earnings from self-employment is the base for the self-employment tax. If net earnings from self-employment is less than $400, the taxpayer is not subject to self-employment tax (but the taxpayer is still subject to income tax on the earnings).

Step 3: **Social Security tax.** The Social Security tax component of the self-employment tax equals 12.4 percent [the combined Social Security tax rate for employer and employee (6.2% + 6.2% = 12.4%)] multiplied by the lesser of (a) the taxpayer's net earnings from self-employment (from step 2) or (b) $118,500 (the maximum tax base for the Social Security tax).

Step 4: **Medicare tax.** The Medicare tax component of the self-employment tax equals 2.9 percent [the combined Medicare tax rate for employer and employee (1.45% + 1.45% = 2.9%)] multiplied by the net earnings from self-employment (from Step 2).

Step 5: **.9 Percent Additional Medicare tax.** The .9 percent additional Medicare tax due on net self-employment earnings equals .9 percent multiplied by the greater of (1) zero or (2) net earnings from self-employment (from Step 2) less $200,000 ($125,000 for married filing separately; $250,000 for married filing jointly). The .9 percent additional Medicare tax is considered an "employee" tax.

Note that as we discussed in Chapter 6, taxpayers are allowed to deduct the employer portion of their self-employment taxes as a *for* AGI deduction. For years prior to 2011, the employer and employee portions of self-employment tax were equal. Since 2011, the employer and employee portions potentially vary based on the level of self-employment earnings. Nonetheless, the employer portion is simple to calculate if you know the Social Security and Medicare tax rates that apply to employers.

Example 8-14

What if: Assume that Courtney's only income for the year is her $18,000 in net self-employment income from her weekend consulting business. What amount of self-employment taxes would Courtney be required to pay on this income?

Answer: $2,543, computed as follows:

Step 1: $18,000 of net self-employment income subject to self-employment taxes.

Step 2: $18,000 × .9235 = $16,623. This is net earnings from self-employment.

Step 3: $16,623 × 12.4% = $2,061. This is Courtney's Social Security tax payable for her self-employment income.

Step 4: $16,623 × 2.9% = $482. This is Courtney's Medicare tax payable for self-employment income.

Step 5: $2,543. The sum of the Social Security and Medicare taxes in Steps 3 and 4.

Under these circumstances, Courtney would be able to deduct $1,272 as a *for* AGI deduction for the employer portion of self-employment taxes she paid [i.e., $16,623 × (6.2% + 1.45%)].

When a taxpayer receives *both* employee compensation and self-employment earnings in the same year, the calculation of self-employment tax is a bit more complicated. For the Social Security tax component, the taxpayer's *total earnings* subject to the Social Security tax are capped at $118,500. In these situations, the taxpayer's Social Security tax liability on the employee compensation is determined as if the employee had no self-employment income. The taxpayer then computes her Social Security tax on her net self-employment earnings. This ordering is favorable for taxpayers because it allows them to use up all or a portion of the Social Security wage base limit with their employee income (taxed at 6.2 percent) before they determine the Social Security tax on their net earnings from self-employment (taxed at 12.4 percent). Consequently, if an employee's wages exceed the Social Security tax wage base limitation, she would not be required to pay any Social Security tax on her self-employment earnings.

Likewise, the Medicare tax calculation is more complicated when (1) the taxpayer receives both employee compensation and self-employment earnings or (2) the taxpayer files married jointly with a spouse receiving employee compensation or net self-employment earnings. Specifically, while the employer portion of the Medicare tax is 1.45 percent regardless of the level of net self-employment earnings, the employee portion of the Medicare tax varies based on the combined amount of employee compensation and net self-employment earnings for the taxpayer (or the taxpayer and his or her spouse, if they file married jointly). For taxpayers not filing married jointly, the employee portion of the Medicare tax rate is 1.45 percent on the taxpayer's salary or wages and net self-employment earnings up to $200,000 ($125,000 for married filing separately) and is 2.35 percent on salary or wages and net self-employment earnings in excess of $200,000 ($125,000 for married filing separately). For married filing jointly taxpayers, the employee portion of the Medicare tax rate is 1.45 percent on the taxpayer's and his or her spouse's salary or wages and net self-employment earnings up to $250,000 and is 2.35 percent on the taxpayer's and his or her spouse's salary or wages and net self-employment earnings in excess of $250,000.

The calculation of the taxpayer's FICA taxes on self-employment earnings in these settings can be determined as follows:[20]

Social Security Tax:

Step 1: Determine the limit on the Social Security portion of the self-employment tax base by subtracting the employee compensation from the Social Security wage base ($118,500 in 2015) (not below $0).

Step 2: Determine the net earnings from self-employment (self-employment earnings times 92.35 percent).

Step 3: Multiply the lesser of Steps (1) and (2) by 12.4 percent. This is the amount of Social Security taxes due on the self-employment income.

Medicare Tax:

Step 4: Multiply the amount from Step (2) by 2.9 percent, the combined Medicare tax rate for employer and employee.

.9 Percent Additional Medicare Tax:

Step 5: Add the amount from Step (2) and the taxpayer's compensation. If married filing jointly, also add the spouse's compensation and net earnings from self-employment (spouse's self-employment earnings times 92.35 percent).

Step 6: Multiply the greater of [(a) zero or (b) the amount from Step (5) minus $200,000 ($125,000 for married filing separately; $250,000 for married filing jointly)] by .9 percent.

Step 7: Take the amount from Step 6 and subtract the amount of the .9 percent additional Medicare tax withheld by the taxpayer's employer (and his or her spouse's employer if married filing jointly). This is the .9 percent additional Medicare tax due on the self-employment income.

[20]If net earnings from self-employment is less than $400, the taxpayer is *not* subject to self-employment tax (but the taxpayer is still subject to income tax on the earnings).

Example 8-15

In 2015, Courtney received $122,800 in taxable compensation from EWD (see Example 8-12) and $18,000 in self-employment income from her weekend consulting activities (see Example 6-2). What are Courtney's *self-employment taxes* payable on her $18,000 of income from self-employment? Assume that Courtney's employer correctly withheld $7,347 of Social Security tax and $1,781 of Medicare tax.

Answer: $482, computed as follows:

Description	Amount	Explanation
(1) Social Security wage base limit less employee compensation subject to Social Security tax	$ 0	$118,500 − $122,800, limited to $0.
(2) Net earnings from self-employment	16,623	$18,000 × 92.35%.
(3) Social Security portion of self-employment tax	0	[Lesser of Step (1) or (2)] × 12.4%.
(4) Medicare tax	482	Step (2) × 2.9%.
(5) Sum of taxpayer's compensation and net earnings from self-employment	139,423	$122,800 + Step (2).
(6) [Greater of (a) zero or (b) the amount from Step (5) minus $200,000] × 0.9%.	0	0 × 0.9%.
(7) Step (6) less any .9 percent additional Medicare tax withheld by Courtney's employer.	0	0 − 0.
(8) Steps (3) + (4) + (7)	482	0 + 482 + 0.

As we reported in Chapter 6, Courtney is entitled to a $241 *for* AGI deduction for the employer portion of the $482 self-employment taxes she incurred during the year ($16,623 × 1.45% employer portion of the Medicare tax rate = $241).

Example 8-16

What if: Let's change the facts and assume that Courtney received $100,000 of taxable compensation from EWD in 2015, and she received $180,000 in self-employment income from her weekend consulting activities. What amount of self-employment taxes is Courtney required to pay on her $180,000 of business income? Assume that Courtney's employer correctly withheld $6,200 of Social Security tax, $1,450 of Medicare tax, and $0 of .9 percent additional Medicare tax.

Answer: $7,710, computed as follows:

Description	Amount	Explanation
(1) Social Security wage base limit less employee compensation subject to Social Security tax	$ 18,500	$118,500 − $100,000, limited to $0.
(2) Net earnings from self-employment	166,230	$180,000 × 92.35%.
(3) Social Security portion of self-employment tax	2,294	[Lesser of Step (1) or (2)] × 12.4%.
(4) Medicare tax	4,820	Step (2) × 2.9%.

Description	Amount	Explanation
(5) Sum of taxpayer's compensation and net earnings from self-employment	266,230	$100,000 + Step (2).
(6) [Greater of (a) zero or (b) the amount from Step (5) minus $200,000] × 0.9%.	596	66,230 × 0.9%.
(7) Step (6) less any .9 percent additional Medicare tax withheld by Courtney's employer.	596	596 − 0.
(8) Steps (3) + (4) + (7)	7,710	2,294 + 4,820 + 596.

What if: Now let's assume that Courtney is married and files jointly. Assume that Courtney received $100,000 of taxable compensation from EWD in 2015 and $180,000 in self-employment income from her weekend consulting activities. In addition, her husband received $75,000 of taxable compensation from his employer. What amount of self-employment taxes is Courtney required to pay on her $180,000 of business income? Assume that Courtney's employer correctly withheld $6,200 of Social Security tax, $1,450 of Medicare tax, and $0 .9 percent additional Medicare tax and that her husband's employer correctly withheld $4,650 of Social Security tax, $1,088 of Medicare tax, and $0 of .9 percent additional Medicare tax.

Answer: $7,935, computed as follows:

Description	Amount	Explanation
(1) Social Security wage base limit less employee compensation subject to Social Security tax	$ 18,500	$118,500 − $100,000, limited to $0.
(2) Net earnings from self-employment	166,230	$180,000 × 92.35%.
(3) Social Security portion of self-employment tax	2,294	[Lesser of Step (1) or (2)] × 12.4%.
(4) Medicare tax	4,820	Step (2) × 2.9%.
(5) Sum of taxpayer's and spouse's compensation and net earnings from self-employment	341,230	$100,000 + $75,000 + Step (2).
(6) [Greater of (a) zero or (b) the amount from Step (5) minus $250,000] × 0.9%.	821	91,230 × 0.9%.
(7) Step (6) less any .9 percent additional Medicare tax withheld by Courtney's employer and her husband's employer.	821	821 − 0.
(8) Steps (3) + (4) + (7)	7,935	2,294 + 4,820 + 821.

Unlike employees, whose employers withhold tax throughout the year on their behalf, self-employed taxpayers must satisfy their self-employment tax obligations through periodic, usually quarterly, estimated tax payments. Taxpayers who are employed and self-employed (an employee with a business on the side, like Courtney) may have their employers withhold enough taxes to cover both their income and self-employment tax obligations. Any self-employment taxes not paid through these mechanisms must be paid with the self-employed taxpayer's individual tax return.

continued from page 8-1...

Courtney was enjoying her work with EWD but she also really liked her weekend consulting work. A couple of months ago, after Courtney had played an integral part in completing a successful project, Courtney's boss jokingly mentioned that, if Courtney ever decided to leave EWD to work for herself as a full-time consultant, EWD would love to hire her back for contract work. This caused Courtney to start thinking about the possibilities of starting her own consulting business. She's always had some interest in working for herself, but she is not at a point in her life where she can take significant financial risks even if it might mean a more satisfying career. Courtney knew that before making such a move she would need to seriously consider the nontax issues associated with self-employment and she would need to learn more about the tax consequences of working as an independent contractor. She was particularly interested in the tax consequences of working for EWD as an independent contractor (contract worker) relative to working for EWD as an employee. ■

Employee vs. Self-Employed (Independent Contractor)

Determining whether an individual is taxed as an **employee** or as an **independent contractor** can be straightforward or quite complex, depending on the specific arrangement between the parties. In its published guidance, the IRS stipulates that an employer/employee relationship exists when the party for whom services are performed has the right to direct or control the individual performing services.[21] To assist taxpayers in deciding whether the party receiving services has the requisite amount of control over the individual providing services, the IRS has published a list of 20 factors to consider.[22] A few of the factors suggesting independent contractor rather than employee status include the contractor's ability to

1. Set her own working hours.
2. Work part-time.
3. Work for more than one firm.
4. Realize either a profit or a loss from the activities.
5. Perform work somewhere other than on an employer's premises.
6. Work without frequent oversight.

When these factors are absent, individuals are more likely to be classified as employees. Rather than simply summing the number of factors in favor of independent contractor status and those in favor of employee status, however, taxpayers and their advisors should use the factors as guides in determining the overall substance of the contractual relationship.

Whether a taxpayer is classified as an employee or as an independent contractor (self-employed) has both tax and nontax consequences to the employer and the taxpayer. The best classification for the taxpayer is situation specific.

Employee vs. Independent Contractor Comparison

The two primary *tax* differences between independent contractors and employees relate to (1) the amount of their FICA taxes payable and (2) the deductibility of their business expenses.[23] However, there are several nontax factors to consider as well. In the previous section,

[21]IRS Publication 1779. Independent Contractor or Employee brochure.

[22]Rev. Rul. 87-41, 1987-1 CB 296.

[23]Also, independent contractors generally receive a Form 1099 from each client reporting the gross income they received from the client during the year. Employees receive Form W-2 reporting the compensation the employee received from the employer during the year.

we detailed how to determine the FICA taxes payable for employees and independent contractors (self-employed taxpayers). In terms of the deductibility of business expenses, as we discussed in Chapter 6, *employees* who incur unreimbursed business expenses relating to their employment can deduct these expenses as miscellaneous itemized deductions subject to 2 percent of AGI floor. This floor means, in many cases, that employees receive little or no tax benefit for their employee business expenses. In contrast, as we also described in Chapter 6, self-employed independent contractors are able to deduct expenses relating to their business activities as *for* AGI deductions, which they can deduct without restriction. While these factors appear to favor independent contractor status over employee status, note that employees generally don't incur many unreimbursed expenses relating to their employment. Thus, even though independent contractors may be able to deduct more expenses than employees, they typically incur more costs in doing business.

When taxpayers are classified as independent contractors rather than employees, they are not eligible for nontaxable fringe benefits available to employees, such as health care insurance, retirement plan benefits, and other fringe benefits provided to employees. Further, independent contractors are responsible for paying their estimated tax liability throughout the year through estimated tax payments because the employer does not withhold taxes from an independent contractor's pay. However, as we mentioned above, taxpayers are allowed to deduct the employer portion of the self-employment taxes they pay.

From the employer's perspective, it is generally less costly to hire an independent contractor than an employee because the employer need not provide these benefits and the employer need not withhold or pay any FICA taxes on behalf of an independent contractor. As a result, an employer may be willing to offer an apparently higher level of taxable compensation to an independent contractor than a similarly situated employee. However, after considering all relevant factors, the taxpayer may do better receiving less compensation as an employee than slightly higher compensation as an independent contractor.

ETHICS

Sudipta is an accounting major who works during the day and takes classes in the evening. He was excited to finally land his first accounting job doing the books for a local dry cleaners. In his new job, Sudipta works 30 hours a week at the dry cleaners' main office. His excitement quickly dampened when he realized that his new employer was not withholding any income taxes or FICA taxes from his paycheck. Apparently, Sudipta's employer is treating him as an independent contractor. Sudipta likes his job, loves the money that he is earning, but recognizes that he should be treated as an employee instead of an independent contractor. What would you do if you were Sudipta?

Example 8-17

What if: Let's compare Courtney's compensation as an employee with EWD to her compensation if she were to work for EWD as an independent contractor. *Assume* that Courtney works an average of 40 hours per week for 50 weeks per year to earn a salary of $100,000; in addition she receives fringe benefits including a 5 percent contribution to her retirement plan, life insurance coverage, and health insurance coverage. Would Courtney be "made whole" in terms of her hourly rate if EWD agreed to pay her $55 an hour for her contract work (10 percent more than her hourly rate as an employee)?

Answer: Not very likely. As an independent contractor, Courtney must pay more costly self-employment taxes (at nearly twice the rate of employment taxes) under the new arrangement. In addition, she will be ineligible for the nontaxable fringe benefits (retirement plan contributions, life insurance, and health coverage) she was receiving as an employee and will not receive as a contractor.

THE KEY FACTS

Employee vs. Independent Contractor

- Employees
  - Less control over how, when, and where to perform duties.
  - Pay 6.2 percent Social Security tax subject to limit.

(continued)

- Pay Medicare tax from 1.45 percent to 2.35 percent.
- Independent contractors
  - More control over how, when, and where to perform duties.
  - Report income and expenses on Form 1040, Schedule C.
  - Pay 12.4 percent self-employment (Social Security) tax subject to limit.
  - Pay self-employment (Medicare tax) tax from 2.9 percent to 3.8 percent.
  - Self-employment tax base is 92.35 percent of net self-employment income.
  - Deduct the employer portion of self-employment taxes paid for AGI.

We've described how to calculate a taxpayer's regular tax liability, alternative minimum tax liability, and self-employment tax liability. These tax liabilities sum to a taxpayer's gross tax liability. While Gram's gross tax is simply her regular income tax liability of $374 (see Example 8-2), Courtney's gross tax includes other taxes. Courtney's gross tax liability is calculated in Exhibit 8-6.

EXHIBIT 8-6 Courtney's Gross Tax

Description	Amount	Explanation
(1) Regular federal income tax	$ 21,780	Example 8-3.
(2) Alternative minimum tax	0	Example 8-10.
(3) Self-employment tax	482	Example 8-15.
Gross tax (rounded)	$ 22,262	(1) + (2) + (3).

Taxpayers reduce their gross tax by tax credits and tax prepayments (withholding and estimated tax payments) for the year. As indicated in Exhibit 8-7, if the gross tax exceeds the tax credits and prepayments, the taxpayer owes additional

EXHIBIT 8-7 Formula for Computing Net Tax Due or Refund

Gross tax
Minus: Tax credits
Minus: Prepayments
Net tax due (refund)

taxes when she files her tax return. In contrast, if the prepayments exceed the gross tax after applying tax credits, the taxpayer is entitled to a tax refund. We next explore available tax credits and conclude the chapter by dealing with taxpayer prepayments.

LO 8-4

TAX CREDITS

Congress provides a considerable number of credits for taxpayers. **Tax credits** reduce a taxpayer's *tax liability* dollar for dollar. In contrast, deductions reduce *taxable income* dollar for dollar, but the tax savings deductions generated depend on the taxpayer's marginal tax rate. Because tax credits generate tax savings *independent of* a taxpayer's marginal tax rate, they are a popular tax policy tool for avoiding the perception that tax benefits for certain tax policies are distributed disproportionately to taxpayers with higher incomes and corresponding higher marginal tax rates. Further, tax credits are powerful tax policy tools because they directly affect taxes due. By using tax credits, policy makers can adjust the magnitude of the tax effects of tax policy without changing tax rates.

Tax credits may be either nonrefundable or refundable. A **nonrefundable credit** may reduce a taxpayer's gross tax liability to zero, but if the amount of the credit exceeds the amount of the taxpayer's gross tax liability, the credit in excess of the gross tax liability is not refunded to the taxpayer and expires without ever providing tax benefits (unless the unused credit can be carried over to a different year). Refundable credits in excess of a taxpayer's gross tax liability are refunded to the taxpayer.

Tax credits are generally classified into one of three categories: nonrefundable personal, refundable personal, or business credits, depending on the nature of the credit. The primary exception to this general rule is the foreign tax credit. The foreign tax credit is a hybrid between personal and business credits because, like nonrefundable personal credits, it reduces the taxpayer's liability before business credits but, like business credits, unused foreign tax credits can be carried over to use in other years.

Nonrefundable Personal Credits

Congress provides many nonrefundable personal tax credits to generate tax relief for certain groups of individuals. For example, the child tax credit (partially refundable) provides tax relief for taxpayers who provide a home for dependent children and the child and dependent care credit provides tax relief for taxpayers who incur expenses to care for their children and other dependents in order to work. The American opportunity credit (partially refundable) and the lifetime learning credit help taxpayers pay for the cost of higher education. Because the child tax credit, the child and dependent care credit, and the American opportunity and lifetime learning credits are some of the most common nonrefundable personal credits, we discuss them in detail.

THE KEY FACTS

Child Tax Credit

- Taxpayers may claim a $1,000 credit for each qualifying child under age 17.
- Credit is phased out for taxpayers with AGI above threshold.
  - Lose $50 for every $1,000 or portion thereof that AGI exceeds threshold.

Child Tax Credit Taxpayers may claim a $1,000 **child tax credit** for *each qualifying child* (same definition for dependency exemption purposes—see §152(c) and Chapter 4) who is under age 17 at the end of the year and who is claimed as their dependent.[24] The credit is subject to phase-out based on the taxpayer's AGI. The phase-out threshold depends on the taxpayer's filing status and is provided in Exhibit 8-8.

EXHIBIT 8-8 **Child Tax Credit Phase-out Threshold**

Filing Status	Phase-out Threshold
Married filing jointly	$110,000
Married filing separately	55,000
Head of household and single	75,000

The total amount of the credit ($1,000 × number of qualifying children) is phased-out, but not below zero, by $50 for each $1,000 *or portion thereof* by which the taxpayer's AGI exceeds the applicable threshold. Taxpayers can determine their allowable child tax credit after the phase-out by using the following four steps:

Step 1: Determine the excess AGI by subtracting the threshold amount (see Exhibit 8-8) from the taxpayer's AGI.

Step 2: Divide the excess AGI from step (1) by 1,000 and round up to the next whole number.

Step 3: Multiply the amount from step (2) by $50. This is the amount of the total credit that is phased-out or disallowed.

Step 4: Subtract the amount from step (3) from the total credit before phase-out (limited to $0) to determine the allowable child tax credit.

Because the phase-out is based upon a fixed amount ($50) rather than a percentage, the phase-out range varies according to the amount of credit claimed.[25]

[24]§24(a).

[25]The child tax credit is partially refundable. In 2015, the refundable portion of the credit is the lesser of (1) the taxpayer's earned income in excess of $3,000 times 15 percent, or (2) the amount of the unclaimed portion of the otherwise nonrefundable credit. Thus, if a taxpayer has enough tax liability to absorb the nonrefundable portion of the credit, the refundable portion is reduced to zero. The computation is modified for taxpayers with three or more qualifying children. See IRS Publication 972 for more information relating to the child tax credit.

Example 8-18

Both Ellen and Deron are Courtney's qualifying children. Courtney may claim a child tax credit for Deron but she may *not* claim a child tax credit for Ellen because Ellen is not under age 17 at the end of the year. What amount of child tax credit is Courtney allowed to claim for Deron after accounting for the credit phase-out?

Answer: $0. Because Courtney's AGI of $162,000 exceeds the $75,000 AGI phase-out threshold, she must determine her credit after the phase-out. Her phase-out is computed as follows:

1. $162,000 AGI (Exhibit 6-6) − $75,000 head of household threshold (Exhibit 8-8) = $87,000.
2. $87,000 excess AGI divided by 1,000 = 87 (if her AGI was $87,001, this would be 88).
3. 87 × $50 = $4,350. This is the amount of the phase-out.
4. $1,000 allowable credit minus $4,350 = $0 (limited to $0).

Courtney is *not able to claim any child tax credit* because the entire amount is phased out.

What if: How much child tax credit would Courtney be able to claim after the phase-out if she had claimed five qualifying children under the age of 17 as dependents?

Answer: $650. Her total child tax credit before phase-outs would be $5,000 ($1,000 × 5). Assuming the same AGI of $162,000, she would be required to phase-out $4,350 of the credit. Consequently, she would still be able to reduce her taxes by the $650 portion of the credit that was not phased-out ($5,000 − $4,350).

Child and Dependent Care Credit The child and dependent care credit is a tax subsidy to help taxpayers pay the cost of providing care for their dependents to allow taxpayers to work or look for work. The amount of the credit is based on the amount of the taxpayer's expenditures to provide care for one or more qualifying persons. A qualifying person includes (1) a dependent under the age of 13, and (2) a dependent or spouse who is physically or mentally incapable of caring for herself or himself and who lives in the taxpayer's home for more than half the year.

The amount of expenditures eligible for the credit is the *least* of the following three amounts:

1. The total amount of dependent care expenditures for the year.
2. $3,000 for one qualifying person or $6,000 for two or more qualifying persons.
3. The taxpayer's earned income including wage, salary, or other taxable employee compensation, or net earnings from self-employment. Married taxpayers must file a joint tax return and the amount of earned income for purposes of the dependent care credit limitation is the earned income of the lesser-earning spouse.[26]

THE KEY FACTS

Child and Dependent Care Credit

- Designed to help taxpayers who work or seek work when they must provide care for dependents.
- Nonrefundable.
- Based on maximum qualifying expenditures multiplied by the rate based on AGI.
  - Maximum expenditures are $3,000 for one qualifying person or $6,000 for two or more qualifying persons.
  - Rate is 35 percent for the lowest AGI taxpayers and 20 percent for the highest.

Expenditures for care qualify whether the care is provided outside or within the home. But, expenditures for care do *not* qualify if the caregiver is a dependent relative or child of the taxpayer.[27] The amount of the credit is calculated by multiplying qualifying expenditures by the appropriate credit percentage. The credit percentage is based upon the taxpayer's AGI level and begins at 35 percent for taxpayers with AGI of $15,000 or less. The minimum dependent care credit is 20 percent for taxpayers with AGI over $43,000. Exhibit 8-9 provides the dependent care credit percentage for different levels of AGI.

[26]If the lesser-earning spouse cannot work due to a disability or is a full-time student, the lesser-earning spouse is *deemed* to have earned $250 a month if the couple is computing the credit for one qualifying person or $500 a month if the couple is computing the credit for more than one qualifying person.

[27]§21(e)(6). Also, the regulations indicate that the costs of summer school and tutoring programs are indistinguishable from general education and, therefore, do not qualify for the credit [See Reg. §1.21-1(b)].

EXHIBIT 8-9 Child and Dependent Care Credit Percentage

If AGI is over	but not over	then the percentage is
$ 0	15,000	35%
15,000	17,000	34
17,000	19,000	33
19,000	21,000	32
21,000	23,000	31
23,000	25,000	30
25,000	27,000	29
27,000	29,000	28
29,000	31,000	27
31,000	33,000	26
33,000	35,000	25
35,000	37,000	24
37,000	39,000	23
39,000	41,000	22
41,000	43,000	21
43,000	No limit	20

Example 8-19

What if: Suppose that this year, Courtney paid a neighbor $3,200 to care for her 10-year-old son, Deron, so Courtney could work. Would Courtney be allowed to claim the child and dependent care credit for the expenditures she made for Deron's care?

Answer: Yes. (1) Courtney paid for Deron's care to allow her to work, and (2) Deron is a qualifying person for purposes of the credit because (a) he is Courtney's dependent and (b) he is under 13 years of age at the end of the year.

What amount of child and dependent care credit, if any, would Courtney be allowed to claim for the $3,200 she spent to provide Deron's care given her AGI is $162,000?

Answer: $600, computed as follows:

Description	Amount	Explanation
(1) Dependent care expenditures	$ 3,200	
(2) Limit on qualifying expenditures for one dependent	3,000	
(3) Courtney's earned income	140,800	$122,800 compensation from EWD + $18,000 business income (see Example 8-15).
(4) Expenditures eligible for credit	3,000	Least of (1), (2), and (3).
(5) Credit percentage rate	20%	AGI over $43,000 (see Exhibit 8-9).
Dependent care credit	**$ 600**	(4) × (5).

What if: If Courtney's AGI (and her earned income) was only $31,500, what would be her child and dependent care credit?

Answer: $780, computed as follows:

Description	Amount	Explanation
(1) Dependent care expenditures	$ 3,200	
(2) Limit on qualifying expenditures for one dependent	3,000	
(3) Courtney's earned income	31,500	
(4) Expenditures eligible for credit	3,000	Least of (1), (2), and (3).
(5) Credit percentage rate	26%	See table for AGI between $31,000 and $33,000.
Dependent care credit	**$ 780**	(4) × (5).

Education Credits Congress provides the American opportunity credit (AOC) (formerly called the Hope scholarship credit) and the lifetime learning credit to encourage taxpayers and their dependents to obtain higher education by reducing the costs of the education. In contrast to the payment rules discussed in Chapter 6 for the deduction for Qualified Education Expense, taxpayers may claim credits for eligible expenditures made by them personally, their dependents, and third parties on behalf of the taxpayers' dependents.[28] If a student is claimed as a dependent of another taxpayer, only that taxpayer may claim the education credits (even if the dependent or another third party actually pays the education expenses).[29] Married taxpayers filing separate returns are not eligible for the AOC or the lifetime learning credit.

The AOC is available for students in their *first four years* of postsecondary (post high school) education. To qualify, students must be enrolled in a qualified postsecondary educational institution at least half time.[30] For 2015, the amount of the credit is 100 percent of the first $2,000 of eligible expenses paid by the taxpayer (or another person) plus 25 percent of the next $2,000 of eligible expenses paid by the taxpayer (or another person). Thus, the maximum AOC for eligible expenses paid in 2015 for any one person is $2,500 [$2,000 + (25% × $2,000)]. To be eligible for the 2015 credit, taxpayers must pay the eligible expenses in 2015 for any academic period beginning in 2015 or in the first three months of 2016.[31] Eligible expenses for the AOC include tuition, fees, and course materials (cost of books and other materials) needed for courses of instruction at an eligible educational institution.[32] The AOC is applied on a *per student* basis. Consequently, a taxpayer with three eligible dependents can claim a maximum AOC of $2,500 for *each* dependent. The AOC is subject to phase-out based on the taxpayer's AGI. For 2015, the credit is phased out pro rata for taxpayers with AGI between $80,000 and $90,000 ($160,000 − $180,000 for married taxpayers filing jointly).[33] For 2015, 40 percent of a taxpayer's allowable AOC is refundable.[34]

Example 8-20

Courtney paid $2,000 of tuition and $300 for books for Ellen to attend the University of Missouri–Kansas City during the summer at the end of her freshman year. What is the maximum American opportunity credit (AOC) (before phase-out) Courtney may claim for these expenses?

Answer: $2,075. Because the cost of tuition and books is an eligible expense Courtney may claim a maximum AOC before phase-out of $2,075 [($2,000 × 100%) + ($2,300 − $2,000) × 25%].

How much AOC is Courtney allowed to claim on her 2015 tax return (how much can she claim after applying the phase-out)?

Answer: $0. Because Courtney's AGI exceeds the head of household limit of $90,000, she is not allowed to claim any AOC.

THE KEY FACTS

Education Credits

- American opportunity credit
  - Qualifying expenses include tuition for a qualifying student incurred during the first four years at a qualifying institution of higher education.
  - In 2015, maximum credit of $2,500 per student calculated as percentage of maximum of $4,000 qualifying expenses.

(continued)

[28]§25A(g)(3).

[29]If a third party pays the education expenses of a student claimed as a dependent by another taxpayer, the dependent is deemed to have paid the education expenses and the taxpayer claiming the student as a dependent is allowed to claim the credit for the expenses.

[30]§25A(b). Generally, eligible institutions are those eligible to participate in the federal student loan program [§25A(f)(2)].

[31]Reg. §1.25A-3(e).

[32]§25A(i)(3). Eligible expenses for both the AOC and the lifetime learning credit must be reduced by scholarships received to pay for these expenses or other amounts received as reimbursements for the expenses (Pell grants, employer-sponsored reimbursement plans, Educational IRAs, 529 plans, and the like). The cost of room and board or other personal expenses do not qualify as eligible expenses for either the AOC or the lifetime learning credit.

[33]§25A(i)(4).

[34]§25A(i)(6).

What if: How much AOC would Courtney have been allowed to claim on her 2015 tax return if she were married and filed a joint return with her husband (assuming the couple's AGI is $162,000)?

Answer: $1,867, computed as follows:

Description	Amount	Explanation
(1) AOC before phase-out	$ 2,075	
(2) AGI	162,000	
(3) Phase-out threshold	160,000	
(4) Excess AGI	2,000	(2) − (3).
(5) Phase-out range for taxpayer filing for married filing jointly	20,000	$180,000 − 160,000.
(6) Phase-out percentage	10%	(4)/(5).
(7) Phase-out amount	208	(1) × (6).
AOC after phase-out	$ 1,867	(1) − (7).

What if: Suppose Courtney could claim a $1,867 AOC in 2015 (after phase-out). How much of this credit would be refundable?

Answer: $747 ($1,867 × 40%).

- Subject to phase-out for taxpayers with AGI in excess of $80,000 ($160,000 MFJ).
- Lifetime learning credit
  - Qualifying expenses include costs at a qualifying institution associated with acquiring or improving job skills.
  - Maximum credit of $2,000 per taxpayer calculated as percentage of maximum of $10,000 in annual expenses.
  - Subject to phase-out for taxpayers with AGI in excess of $55,000 ($110,000 MFJ).

The lifetime learning credit is a nonrefundable credit that applies to the cost of tuition and fees (but generally not books) for any course of instruction to acquire or improve a taxpayer's job skills.[35] This includes the cost of professional or graduate school tuition (expenses are not limited to those incurred in the first four years of postsecondary education). The credit is equal to 20 percent of eligible expenses up to an annual maximum of $10,000 of eligible expenses (maximum of $2,000). The credit for a year is based on the amount paid during that year for an academic period beginning in that year or the first three months of the following year. In contrast to the American opportunity credit, the lifetime learning credit limit applies to the taxpayer (a married couple filing a joint return may claim only $2,000 of lifetime learning credit). Thus, a taxpayer with multiple eligible dependents can claim a maximum lifetime learning credit of only $2,000. Finally, the credit is phased out pro rata for taxpayers with AGI between $55,000 and $65,000 ($110,000 and $130,000) for married taxpayers filing jointly).[36]

Example 8-21

Courtney paid $1,550 to attend motivational seminars to help her improve her job skills. Courtney could elect to claim the lifetime learning credit for these expenses instead of deducting them as miscellaneous itemized deductions. If Courtney decided to claim a credit for these expenditures, what would be her maximum lifetime learning credit (before phase-out)?

Answer: $310 ($1,550 × 20%)

How much lifetime learning credit is Courtney allowed to claim on her 2015 tax return (how much can she claim after applying the phase-out)?

Answer: $0. Because Courtney's AGI exceeds the head of household limit of $65,000 she is not allowed to claim any lifetime learning credit.

For expenses that qualify for both the AOC and lifetime learning credit (tuition and fees during the first four years of postsecondary education), taxpayers may

[35]§25A(f)(1).

[36]§25A(d).

choose which credit to use, but they may not claim both credits for the same student in the same year. In addition, taxpayers may choose to *either* (1) deduct qualifying education expenses of an individual as a *for* AGI deduction (see discussion of this *for* AGI deduction in Chapter 6) or claim an education credit for the individual's expenses.[37] However, if a taxpayer claims *any* educational credit for an individual's educational expenditures, the taxpayer may not claim *any* for AGI deduction for that individual's qualifying expenditures (and vice versa).[38]

Example 8-22

What if: Suppose Courtney paid $5,000 of tuition for Ellen to attend the University of Missouri–Kansas City during the summer at the end of her freshman year. Further assume that Courtney's AGI is $45,000, so her education credits are not subject to phase-out. Courtney would be allowed to claim the maximum AOC of $2,500 on the first $4,000 of the qualifying educational expenditures. Assuming Courtney used $4,000 of the educational expenses to claim the maximum AOC, would she be allowed to deduct (or claim the lifetime credit on) the remaining $1,000 of tuition costs ($5,000 total expenses − $4,000 maximum AOC expenses)? Assume the 2014 rules apply for purposes of the qualified education expense deduction.

Answer: No. If Courtney claims any AOC for Ellen's expenditures, she is not allowed to deduct or claim a lifetime learning credit for Ellen's expenditures (even for the expenses not used in computing the AOC).

What if: Assume that both Ellen and Deron were in their first year of college, and that Courtney paid tuition for both Ellen and Deron. Further, assume that Courtney's AGI is below the phase-out threshold. Is Courtney allowed to claim a AOC for Ellen's expenses and claim a *for* AGI educational expense deduction for Deron's expenses?

Answer: Yes. Courtney may claim an AOC or a deduction for Ellen's expenses, and she may claim an AOC or a deduction for Deron's expenses.

Example 8-23

What if: Assume that Courtney paid $8,000 tuition for Ellen to attend graduate school at the University of Missouri–Kansas City (assume this is her fifth year at the university and that Ellen still qualifies as Courtney's dependent). Further assume that Courtney's AGI is $60,000, so her potential lifetime learning credit for Ellen would be phased out by 50 percent (assume Courtney did not claim the credit for herself). Before phase-out, Courtney would be allowed to claim a $1,600 lifetime learning credit ($8,000 tuition × 20% credit percentage). After the phase-out, however, Courtney would be able to claim an $800 lifetime learning credit ($1,600 full credit × 1–50% phase-out percentage). If Courtney claims the $800 lifetime learning credit for Ellen's tuition, is she allowed to claim any for AGI deduction for Ellen's tuition since half of the lifetime learning credit is phased out based on Courtney's AGI? Assume the 2014 rules apply for purposes of the qualified education expense deduction.

Answer: No. As we discussed above, if Courtney claims *any* lifetime learning credit for Ellen's expenditures, she is not allowed to deduct any *for* AGI deduction for Ellen's expenditures (even the portion of the expenses that provided no tax benefit because the credit was partially phased out).

What if: Assume the same facts as above and that Courtney's marginal tax rate is 15%. Would Courtney be better off claiming an $800 lifetime learning credit or a $4,000 *for* AGI qualified education expense deduction for the cost of Ellen's tuition?

Answer: The $800 lifetime learning credit. The credit saves Courtney $800 while the qualified education expense deduction would save her $600 ($4,000 × 15%).

[37]At press time, the deduction for qualified education expenses is scheduled to expire after 2014.
[38]§222(c)(2)(A).

Refundable Personal Credits

Several personal credits are refundable, the most common of which is the earned income credit, which we discuss in this chapter.

Earned Income Credit The **earned income credit** is a refundable credit that is designed to help offset the effect of employment taxes on compensation paid to low-income taxpayers and to encourage lower-income taxpayers to seek employment. Because it is refundable (if the credit exceeds the tax after considering nonrefundable credits the taxpayer receives a refund for the excess), it is sometimes referred to as a *negative income tax.* The credit is available for qualified individuals who have earned income for the year.[39] Qualified individuals generally include (1) any individual who has at least one qualifying child (same definition of qualifying child for dependent purposes—see Chapter 4) or (2) any individual who does not have a qualifying child for the taxable year, but who lives in the United States for more than half the year, is at least 25 years old but younger than 65 years old at the end of the year, and is not a dependent of another taxpayer. Earned income includes wages, salaries, tips, and other employee compensation included in gross income and net earnings from self-employment. Taxpayers with investment income such as interest, dividends, and capital gains in excess of $3,400 are ineligible for the credit.[40]

The amount of the credit depends on the taxpayer's filing status, the number of the taxpayer's qualifying children who live in the home for more than half of the year, and the amount of the taxpayer's earned income. To be eligible for the credit, married taxpayers must file a joint tax return. The credit is computed by multiplying the appropriate credit percentage times the taxpayer's earned income up to a maximum amount. The credit percentage depends upon the number of qualifying children in the home and is subject to a phase-out based upon AGI (or earned income if greater). As summarized in Exhibit 8-10, the earned income credit increases as taxpayers receive earned income up to the maximum amount of earned income eligible for the credit. However, as taxpayers earn more income, the credit begins to phase out and is completely eliminated once taxpayers' earned income reaches established levels.

EXHIBIT 8-10 **2015 Earned Income Credit Table**

Qualifying Children	(1) Maximum Earned Income Eligible for Credit	(2) Credit %	(3) Maximum Credit (1) × (2)	(4) Credit Phase-out for AGI (or earned income if greater) Over This Amount	(5) Phase-out Percentage	No Credit When AGI (or earned income if greater) Equals or Exceeds This Amount (4) + [(3)/(5)]
Married taxpayers filing joint returns						
0	$ 6,580	7.65%	$ 503	$13,750	7.65%	$20,330
1	9,880	34	3,359	23,630	15.98	44,651
2	13,870	40	5,548	23,630	21.06	49,974
3+	13,870	45	6,242	23,630	21.06	53,267
All taxpayers *except* married taxpayers filing joint returns						
0	$ 6,580	7.65%	$ 503	$ 8,240	7.65%	$14,820
1	9,880	34	3,359	18,110	15.98	39,131
2	13,870	40	5,548	18,110	21.06	44,454
3+	13,870	45	6,242	18,110	21.06	47,747

[39]§32.

[40]§32(i).

Example 8-24

Courtney's earned income for the year is $140,800 (Example 8-19) and her AGI is $162,000 (Exhibit 6-6). Deron and Ellen both qualify as Courtney's qualifying children. What amount of earned income credit is Courtney entitled to claim on her 2015 tax return?

Answer: $0. Courtney's AGI (which is greater than her earned income) exceeds the $44,454 limit for unmarried taxpayers with two or more qualifying children. Consequently, Courtney is not allowed to claim any earned income credit.

What if: Assume that Courtney's only source of income for the year was $30,000 in salary. Also assume Courtney's AGI for the year was $30,000. What would be Courtney's earned income credit in these circumstances?

Answer: $3,044, computed as follows

Description	Amount	Explanation
(1) Earned income	$ 30,000	
(2) Maximum earned income eligible for earned income credit for taxpayers filing as head of household with two qualifying children	13,870	Exhibit 8-10.
(3) Earned income eligible for credit	13,870	Lesser of (1) and (2).
(4) Earned income credit percentage for taxpayer with two qualifying children	40%	
(5) Earned income credit before phase-out	5,548	(3) × (4).
(6) Phase-out threshold begins at this level of AGI (or earned income if greater)	18,110	See Exhibit 8-11 for head of household filing status and two qualifying children.
(7) Greater of (a) AGI or (b) earned income, less the phase-out threshold	11,890	(1) − (6). In this example AGI equals earned income.
(8) Phase-out percentage	21.06%	See Exhibit 8-11.
(9) Credit phase-out amount	2,504	(7) × (8).
Earned income credit after phase-out	**$ 3,044**	(5) − (9).

TAXES IN THE REAL WORLD *Taking a Bite Out of Earned Income Tax Credit Abuse*

In 2011, the IRS imposed new filing requirements (Form 8867) for tax professionals filing tax returns that include an earned income tax credit. Form 8867, the Paid Preparer's Earned Income Credit Checklist, is intended to ensure that tax professionals use appropriate due diligence in determining a taxpayer's eligibility for, and the amount of, the earned income tax credit.

Why the extra concern with the earned income tax credit? Because the earned income tax credit is a refundable tax credit, the potential for abuse (fraudulent claim) is quite high. Only paid tax preparers are required to complete the form, and failure to do so could result in a $500 penalty for each failure. See Form 8867 and IRC Sec. 6695(g).

Other Refundable Personal Credits Other refundable personal tax credits include a portion of the child tax credit (discussed above), excess FICA withholdings (see discussion above under FICA taxes), and taxes withheld on wages and estimated tax payments. We address withholdings and estimated taxes below when we discuss tax prepayments.

Business Tax Credits

Business tax credits are designed to provide incentives for taxpayers to hire certain types of individuals or to participate in certain business activities. For example, Congress provides the employment tax credit to encourage businesses to hire certain unemployed individuals, and it provides the research and development credit to encourage businesses to expend funds to develop new technology. Business tax credits are *nonrefundable* credits. However, when business credits other than the foreign tax credit (discussed below), exceed the taxpayer's gross tax for the year, the credits are carried *back* one year and forward 20 years to use in years when the taxpayer has sufficient gross tax liability to use the credits.

Why discuss business credits in an individual tax chapter? We discuss business credits here because self-employed individuals may qualify for these credits. Also, individuals may be allocated business credits from flow-through entities (partnerships, LLCs, and S corporations). Finally, individuals working as employees overseas or receiving dividends from investments in foreign securities may qualify for the foreign tax credit.

Foreign Tax Credit U.S. citizens must pay U.S. tax on their worldwide income. However, when they generate some or all of their income in other countries, they generally are required to pay income taxes to the foreign country where they earned their income. Without some form of tax relief, taxpayers earning income overseas would be double-taxed on this income. When taxpayers pay income taxes to foreign countries, for U.S. tax purposes, they may treat the payment in one of three ways: (1) as we discussed in Chapter 5 when we introduced the foreign earned income exclusion, taxpayers may exclude the foreign earned income from U.S. taxation (in which case they would *not* deduct or receive a credit for any foreign taxes paid); (2) taxpayers may include the foreign income in their gross income and deduct the foreign taxes paid as itemized deductions; or (3) taxpayers may include foreign income in gross income and claim a foreign tax credit for the foreign taxes paid. Here, we discuss the foreign tax credit.

The foreign tax credit helps reduce the double tax taxpayers may pay when they pay income taxes on foreign earned income to the United States and to foreign countries. Taxpayers are allowed to claim a foreign tax credit, against their U.S. tax liability, for the income taxes they pay to foreign countries.[41] In certain situations, taxpayers may not be able to claim the full amount of foreign tax paid as a credit. This restriction may apply when the taxpayer's effective foreign tax rate is higher than the effective U.S. tax rate on the foreign earnings. Taxpayers generally benefit from claiming credits rather than deductions for foreign taxes paid because credits reduce their liabilities dollar for dollar. However, in circumstances when the foreign tax credit is restricted (see above), taxpayers may benefit by claiming deductions for the taxes paid instead of credits.

As we discussed above, the foreign tax credit may be limited in circumstances where a taxpayer's effective foreign tax rate exceeds her U.S. tax rate. In addition, as a nonrefundable credit, it may only reduce the taxpayer's tax liability to zero. When the use of a foreign tax credit is limited, taxpayers may carry back their unused credits one year and carry forward the credits up to 10 years.[42]

[41]§904.

[42]See IRS Publication 514 "Foreign Tax Credit for Individuals" for more information about the foreign tax credit.

Tax Credit Summary

Exhibit 8-11 identifies several tax credits and for each credit identifies the credit type, notes the IRC section allowing the credit, and describes the credit.

EXHIBIT 8-11 Summary of Selected Tax Credits

Credit	Type of Credit	IRC	Description
Child and dependent care credit	Nonrefundable personal	§21	Credit for taxpayers who pay dependent care expenses due to their employment activities.
Credit for elderly and disabled	Nonrefundable personal	§22	Credit for elderly low-income taxpayers who retired because of a disability.
Adoption expense credit	Nonrefundable personal	§23	Credit for qualified adoption-related expenses.
Child tax credit	Nonrefundable and refundable personal	§24	Credit for providing home for dependent children under the age of 17.
American opportunity credit	Nonrefundable and refundable personal	§25A	Credit for higher education expenses for the first four years of postsecondary education.
Lifetime learning credit	Nonrefundable personal	§25A	Credit for higher education expenses.
Saver's credit	Nonrefundable personal	§25B	Credit for contributing to qualified retirement plans.
Residential energy efficient property credit	Nonrefundable personal	§25D	Credit for qualified expenditures for solar water heating property, fuel cell property, wind energy property, and qualified geothermal heat pump property.
Earned income credit	Refundable personal	§32	Credit to encourage low-income taxpayers to work.
Premium tax credit	Refundable personal	§36B	Credit for health insurance purchased through an exchange for individuals and families with household incomes between 100% and 400% of the poverty line.
Credit for increasing research activities	Business	§41	Credit to encourage research and development.
Employer-provided child care credit	Business	§45F	Credit for providing child care for employees.
Small employer health insurance credit	Business	§45R	Credit to encourage employer-provided health insurance.
Rehabilitation credit	Business	§47	Credit for expenditures to renovate or restore older business buildings.
Energy credit	Business	§48	Credit for businesses that invest in energy conservation measures.
Work opportunity credit	Business	§51	Credit for hiring certain qualified veterans.
Foreign tax credit	Hybrid business and personal	§904	Credit to reduce effects of double taxation of foreign income.

Credit Application Sequence

As we've discussed, credits are applied against a taxpayer's gross tax. However, we still must describe what happens when the taxpayer's allowable credits exceed the taxpayer's gross tax. To set up this discussion, it is important to understand that nonrefundable personal credits and business credits may be used to reduce a taxpayer's gross tax to zero, but not below zero.[43] In contrast, by definition, a refundable credit may reduce a taxpayer's gross tax below zero. This excess refundable credit generates a tax refund for the taxpayer.

When a nonrefundable personal credit exceeds the taxpayer's gross tax, it reduces the gross tax to zero, but the excess credit (credit in excess of the taxpayer's gross tax) disappears. That is, the taxpayer may *not* carry over any excess nonrefundable personal credits to use in other years. However, when a business credit or foreign tax credit exceeds the gross tax, it reduces the taxpayer's gross tax to zero, but the excess credit may be carried forward or back to be used in other years when the taxpayer has sufficient gross tax to use the credit (subject to certain time restrictions discussed above).

Because the tax treatment of excess credits depends on the type of credit, it is important to identify the sequence in which taxpayers apply the credits when they have more than one type of credit for the year. When taxpayers have multiple credit types in the same year, they apply the credits against their gross tax in the following order: (1) nonrefundable personal credits, (2) business credits, and (3) refundable credits. This sequence maximizes the chances that taxpayers will receive full benefit for their tax credits.

Because, as we discuss above, the foreign tax credit is a hybrid credit subject to a unique set of application rules, we exclude it from our general discussion on applying credits. Exhibit 8-12 summarizes the order in which the credits are applied against gross tax and indicates the tax treatment of any excess credits.

EXHIBIT 8-12 Credit Application

Credit Type	Order Applied	Excess Credit
Nonrefundable personal	First	Lost
Business	Second	Carryback and carryover
Refundable personal	Last	Refunded

Example 8-25

What if: As we describe in Example 8-2, Gram's gross tax liability is $374. For illustrative purposes, let's *assume* that Gram is entitled to an $800 nonrefundable personal tax credit, a $700 business tax credit, and a $600 refundable personal tax credit. What is the amount of Gram's refund or taxes due?

Answer: $600 refund. Gram would apply these credits as follows:

Description	Amount	Treatment of Excess Credit
Gross tax liability	$ 374	Example 8-2.
Nonrefundable personal credits	(374)	$426 ($800 − $374) excess credit expires unused.
Business credits	0	$700 carried back one year or forward 20 years (10 years for foreign tax credit).
Refundable personal credits	**(600)**	**Generates $600 tax refund to Gram.**

TAXPAYER PREPAYMENTS AND FILING REQUIREMENTS

LO 8-5

Even after determining their tax liabilities, taxpayers must still file a tax return and pay any additional tax due or receive a refund. When taxpayers don't pay enough taxes during the year or when they are late filing their tax return or late paying their taxes due, they may be subject to certain penalties.

[43]In general, nonrefundable personal credits can offset a taxpayer's regular tax and AMT (§26) but not self-employment tax. The limitation on business credits is more complex. We limit our discussion here to basic concepts. See §38(c) for the detailed limitations.

Prepayments

The income tax must be paid on a *pay-as-you-go* basis. This means that the tax must be prepaid via **withholding** from salary or through periodic **estimated tax payments** during the tax year. Employees pay tax through withholding, and self-employed taxpayers generally pay taxes through estimated tax payments. Employers are required to withhold taxes from an employee's wages based upon the employee's marital status, exemptions, and estimated annual pay. Wages include both cash and noncash remuneration for services, and employers remit withholdings to the government on behalf of employees. At the end of the year employers report the amounts withheld to each employee via Form W-2. Estimated tax payments are required only if withholdings are insufficient to meet the taxpayer's tax liability. For calendar-year taxpayers, estimated tax payments are due on April 15, June 15, and September 15 of the current year and January 15 of the following year. If the due date falls on a Saturday, Sunday, or holiday, it is automatically extended to the next day that is not a Saturday, Sunday, or holiday.

Example 8-26

Courtney's gross tax liability for the year including federal income tax, alternative minimum tax, and self-employment taxes is $22,262 (see Exhibit 8-6). However, because she had only $19,432 withheld from her paycheck by EWD, she underpaid $2,830 for the year ($22,262 − $19,432). If she had been aware that her withholding would be insufficient, she could have increased her withholding at any time during the year (even in her December paycheck) or made estimated tax payments of $707.50 on April 15, June 15, and September 15 in 2015 and January 15, 2016 ($2,830/4).

What if: If Courtney was self-employed (instead of employed by EWD) and thus had no tax withholdings by an employer, she would be *required* to pay quarterly estimated tax payments. In this scenario, she would need to pay $5,565.50 ($22,262/4 = $5,565.50) by April 15, June 15, and September 15 of 2015 and $5,565.50 by January 15 of 2016 to cover her gross tax liability of $22,262.

Underpayment Penalties When taxpayers like Courtney fall behind on their tax prepayments, they may be subject to an **underpayment penalty.**[44] Taxpayers with unpredictable income streams may be particularly susceptible to this penalty because it is difficult for them to accurately estimate their tax liability for the year. To help taxpayers who may not be able to predict their earnings for the year and to provide some margin of error for those who can, the tax laws provide some **safe-harbor provisions.** Under these provisions taxpayers can avoid underpayment penalties if their withholdings and estimated tax payments equal or exceed one of the following two safe harbors: (1) 90 percent of their *current tax liability* or (2) 100 percent of their *previous year tax liability* (110 percent for individuals with AGI greater than $150,000).

These two safe harbors determine on a quarterly basis the minimum tax prepayments that a taxpayer must have made to avoid the underpayment penalty. The first safe harbor requires that a taxpayer must have paid at least 22.5 percent (90 percent/4 = 22.5 percent) of the *current* year liability via withholdings or estimated tax payments by April 15 to avoid the underpayment penalty for the first quarter. Similarly by June 15, September 15, and January 15, the taxpayer must have paid 45 percent (22.5 percent × 2), 67.5 percent (22.5 percent × 3), and 90 percent (22.5 percent × 4), respectively, of the current year liability via withholding or estimated tax payments to avoid the underpayment penalty in the second, third, and

[44]§6654.

fourth quarters.[45] In determining taxpayers' prepayments for a quarter, tax withholdings are generally treated as though they are withheld evenly through the year. In contrast, estimated tax payments are credited to the taxpayer's account when they are remitted.

Example 8-27

Because all of Courtney's prepayments were made through withholding by EWD, the payments are treated as though they were made evenly throughout the year. What are Courtney's actual and required withholdings under the 90 percent safe-harbor provision throughout the year?

Answer: See the following table:

Dates	(1) Actual Withholding	(2) Required Withholding	(1) − (2) Over (Under) Withheld
April 15, 2015	$4,858 ($19,432 × .25)	$5,009 ($22,262 × .9 × .25)	($151)
June 15, 2015	$9,716 ($19,432 × .50)	$10,018 ($22,262 × .9 × .50)	(302)
September 15, 2015	$14,574 ($19,432 × .75)	$15,027 ($22,262 × .9 × .75)	(453)
January 15, 2016	$19,432	$20,036 ($22,262 × .9 × 1)	(604)

It looks like Courtney is underwithheld in each quarter.

The second safe harbor requires that by April 15, June 15, September 15, and January 15, the taxpayer must have paid 25 percent, 50 percent (25 percent × 2), 75 percent (25 percent × 3), and 100 percent (25 percent × 4), respectively, of the *previous* year tax liability via withholding or estimated tax payments to avoid the underpayment penalty in the first, second, third, and fourth quarters.

If the taxpayer does not satisfy either of the safe harbor provisions, the taxpayer can compute the underpayment penalty owed using Form 2210. The underpayment penalty is determined by multiplying the **federal short-term interest rate** plus 3 percentage points by the amount of tax underpayment per quarter. For purposes of this computation, the quarterly tax underpayment is the difference between the taxpayer's quarterly withholding and estimated tax payments and the required minimum tax payment under the first or second safe harbor (whichever is less). If the taxpayer does not complete Form 2210 and remit the underpayment penalty with the taxpayer's tax return, the IRS will compute and assess the penalty for the taxpayer.

Example 8-28

In the previous example, we discovered that Courtney was underwithheld in each quarter based on the first (90 percent of current year) safe-harbor provision. Assuming Courtney was underwithheld by even more under the second (100 percent of prior year) safe-harbor provision, she is required to pay an underpayment penalty based on the underpayments determined using the first safe harbor. Assuming the federal short-term rate is 5 percent, what is Courtney's underpayment penalty for 2015?

(continued on page 8-38)

[45]As an alternative method of estimating safe harbor, (1) taxpayers can compute 90 percent of the current liability using the seasonal method. This method allows the taxpayer to estimate 90 percent of their current tax liability by annualizing their taxable income earned through the month prior to the payment date (e.g., through March for April 15, May for June 15, and August for September 15). Taxpayers with uneven taxable income throughout the year with smaller taxable income earlier in the year benefit from this method.

Answer: $30, computed as follows:

Description	First Quarter	Second Quarter	Third Quarter	Fourth Quarter
Underpayment	$ 151	$302	$453	$ 604
Times: federal rate + 3% (5% + 3%)	× 8%	× 8%	× 8%	× 8%
	$ 12	$ 24	$ 36	$ 48
Times one quarter of a year[46]	× 25%	× 25%	× 25%	× 25%
Underpayment penalty per quarter	$ 3	$ 6	$ 9	$ 12

That's a lot of work to figure out a $30 penalty: (3 + 6 + 9 + 12 = $30)

As a matter of administrative convenience, taxpayers who either (1) had no tax liability in the previous year or (2) whose tax payable after subtracting their withholding amounts (but not estimated payments) is less than $1,000 are not subject to underpayment penalties.

Example 8-29

Gram's tax liability for the year is $374 (Example 8-2), but she did not have any taxes withheld during the year, and she did not make any estimated tax payments. What is Gram's underpayment penalty?

Answer: $0. Because Gram's $374 tax payable after subtracting her withholding amounts ($374 tax − $0 withholding) is less than $1,000, she is not subject to an underpayment penalty.

THE KEY FACTS

Taxpayer Prepayments and Underpayment Penalties

- Taxpayers prepay their tax via withholding from salary or through periodic estimated tax payments during the tax year.
- Estimated tax payments are required only if withholdings are insufficient to meet the taxpayer's tax liability.
- For calendar-year taxpayers, estimated tax payments are due on April 15, June 15, and September 15 of the current year and January 15 of the following year.
- Taxpayers can avoid an underpayment penalty if their withholdings and estimated tax payments equal or exceed one of two safe harbors.
- The underpayment penalty is determined by multiplying the federal short-term interest rate plus 3 percentage points by the amount of tax underpayment per quarter.

Filing Requirements

Individual taxpayers are required to file a tax return only if their *gross income* exceeds certain thresholds, which vary based on the taxpayer's filing status and age. However, a taxpayer may prefer to file a tax return even when she is not required to do so. For example, a taxpayer with gross income less than the threshold may want to file a tax return to receive a refund of income taxes withheld. In general, the thresholds are simply the applicable standard deduction amount for the different filing statuses plus the personal exemption amount (twice the personal exemption amount of married taxpayers filing jointly).[47]

Individual tax returns are due on April 15 for calendar-year individuals (the fifteenth day of the fourth month following year-end). If the due date falls on a Saturday, Sunday, or holiday, it is automatically extended to the next day that is not a Saturday, Sunday, or holiday. Taxpayers unable to file a tax return by the original due date can request (by that same deadline) a six-month extension to file, which is granted automatically by the IRS. The extension gives the taxpayer additional time to file the tax return, but does *not* extend the due date for paying the tax.

Late Filing Penalty The tax law imposes a penalty on taxpayers that do not file a tax return by the required date (the original due date plus extension).[48] The

[46]Form 2210 actually computes the penalty per quarter based on the number of days in the quarter divided by the number of days in the year. For simplicity, we assume this ratio is $\frac{1}{4}$ per quarter.

[47]§6012. Filing requirements for individuals who are dependents of other taxpayers are subject to special rules that consider the individual's unearned income, earned income, and gross income. See IRS Publication 17 "Your Federal Income Tax."

[48]§6651.

penalty equals 5 percent of the amount of tax owed for each month (or fraction thereof) that the tax return is late, with a maximum penalty of 25 percent. For fraudulent failure to file, the penalty is 15 percent of the amount of tax owed per month with a maximum penalty of 75 percent. If the taxpayer owes no tax as of the due date of the tax return (plus extension), the tax law does not impose a **late filing penalty.**

Late Payment Penalty An extension allows the taxpayer to delay filing a tax return but does *not* extend the due date for tax payments. If a taxpayer fails to pay the entire balance of tax owed by the original due date of the tax return, the tax law imposes a **late payment penalty** from the due date of the return until the taxpayer pays the tax.[49] The late payment penalty equals .5 percent of the amount of tax owed for each month (or fraction thereof) that the tax is not paid.

The *combined* maximum penalty that may be imposed for late payment and late filing (nonfraudulent) is 5 percent per month (25 percent in total). For late payment and filing due to fraud, the combined maximum penalty for late payment and late filing is 15 percent per month (75 percent in total).

Example 8-30

Courtney filed her tax return on April 10 and included a check with the return for $2,860 made payable to the United States Treasury. The $2,860 consisted of her underpaid tax liability of $2,830 (Example 8-26) and her $30 underpayment penalty (Example 8-28).

What if: If Courtney had waited until May 1 to file her return and pay her taxes, what late filing and late payment penalties would she owe?

Answer: Her combined *late filing penalty* and *late payment penalty* would be $142 ($2,830 late payment × 5 percent × 1 month or portion thereof—the combined penalty is limited to 5 percent per month).

THE KEY FACTS

Filing Requirements and Filing-related Penalties

- Filing requirements vary based on the taxpayer's filing status, age, and gross income.
- Individual tax returns are due on April 15 for calendar-year individuals.
- Taxpayers unable to file a tax return by the original due date can request a six-month extension to file.
- The tax law imposes penalties on taxpayers who do not file a tax return (by the original due date plus extension) or pay the tax owed (by the original due date).

TAX SUMMARY

Courtney's and Gram's net taxes due, including an underpayment penalty for Courtney, are provided in Exhibits 8-13 and 8-15, respectively. Exhibit 8-14 illustrates how this information would be presented on Courtney's tax return by providing Courtney's Form 1040, page 2.

EXHIBIT 8-13 Courtney's Net Tax Payable

Description	Amount	Reference
(1) Regular federal income tax	$21,780	Example 8-3.
(2) Alternative minimum tax	0	Example 8-10.
(3) Self-employment tax	482	Example 8-15.
(4) Gross tax	$22,262	(1) + (2) + (3).
(5) Tax credits	0	Examples 8-18, 8-20, 8-21, and 8-24.
(6) Prepayments	($19,432)	Example 8-27.
(7) Underpayment penalties	30	Example 8-28.
Tax and penalties due with tax return	$ 2,860	

[49]§6651. As we discussed in Chapter 2, the tax law also assesses interest on any tax underpayments until the tax is paid (§6601).

EXHIBIT 8-14 Courtney's Net Tax Payable (as presented on her Form 1040, page 2)

Form 1040 (2014) Page 2

Tax and Credits	38	Amount from line 37 (adjusted gross income)			38	162,000
	39a	Check if: ☐ You were born before January 2, 1950, ☐ Blind. ☐ Spouse was born before January 2, 1950, ☐ Blind. Total boxes checked ▶ 39a				
	b	If your spouse itemizes on a separate return or you were a dual-status alien, check here▶ 39b☐				
Standard Deduction for— • People who check any box on line 39a or 39b **or** who can be claimed as a dependent, see instructions. • All others: Single or Married filing separately, $6,200 Married filing jointly or Qualifying widow(er), $12,400 Head of household, $9,100	40	**Itemized deductions** (from Schedule A) **or** your **standard deduction** (see left margin)			40	39,889
	41	Subtract line 40 from line 38			41	122,111
	42	**Exemptions.** If line 38 is $152,525 or less, multiply $3,950 by the number on line 6d. Otherwise, see instructions			42	12,000
	43	**Taxable income.** Subtract line 42 from line 41. If line 42 is more than line 41, enter -0-			43	110,111
	44	**Tax** (see instructions). Check if any from: **a** ☐ Form(s) 8814 **b** ☐ Form 4972 **c** ☐			44	21,780
	45	**Alternative minimum tax** (see instructions). Attach Form 6251			45	0
	46	Excess advance premium tax credit repayment. Attach Form 8962			46	
	47	Add lines 44, 45, and 46 ▶			47	21,780
	48	Foreign tax credit. Attach Form 1116 if required	48			
	49	Credit for child and dependent care expenses. Attach Form 2441	49			
	50	Education credits from Form 8863, line 19	50			
	51	Retirement savings contributions credit. Attach Form 8880	51			
	52	Child tax credit. Attach Schedule 8812, if required	52			
	53	Residential energy credits. Attach Form 5695	53			
	54	Other credits from Form: **a** ☐ 3800 **b** ☐ 8801 **c** ☐	54			
	55	Add lines 48 through 54. These are your **total credits**			55	
	56	Subtract line 55 from line 47. If line 55 is more than line 47, enter -0- ▶			56	21,780
Other Taxes	57	Self-employment tax. Attach Schedule SE			57	482
	58	Unreported social security and Medicare tax from Form: **a** ☐ 4137 **b** ☐ 8919			58	
	59	Additional tax on IRAs, other qualified retirement plans, etc. Attach Form 5329 if required			59	
	60a	Household employment taxes from Schedule H			60a	
	b	First-time homebuyer credit repayment. Attach Form 5405 if required			60b	
	61	Health care: individual responsibility (see instructions) Full-year coverage ☐			61	
	62	Taxes from: **a** ☐ Form 8959 **b** ☐ Form 8960 **c** ☐ Instructions; enter code(s)			62	
	63	Add lines 56 through 62. This is your **total tax** ▶			63	22,262
Payments	64	Federal income tax withheld from Forms W-2 and 1099	64	19,432		
If you have a qualifying child, attach Schedule EIC.	65	2014 estimated tax payments and amount applied from 2013 return	65			
	66a	**Earned income credit (EIC)**	66a			
	b	Nontaxable combat pay election 66b				
	67	Additional child tax credit. Attach Schedule 8812	67			
	68	American opportunity credit from Form 8863, line 8	68			
	69	Net premium tax credit. Attach Form 8962	69			
	70	Amount paid with request for extension to file	70			
	71	Excess social security and tier 1 RRTA tax withheld	71			
	72	Credit for federal tax on fuels. Attach Form 4136	72			
	73	Credits from Form: **a** ☐ 2439 **b** Reserved **c** Reserved **d** ☐	73			
	74	Add lines 64, 65, 66a, and 67 through 73. These are your **total payments** ▶			74	19,432
Refund	75	If line 74 is more than line 63, subtract line 63 from line 74. This is the amount you **overpaid**			75	
	76a	Amount of line 75 you want **refunded to you.** If Form 8888 is attached, check here ▶☐			76a	
Direct deposit? See instructions.	▶ b	Routing number ▶ c Type: ☐ Checking ☐ Savings				
	▶ d	Account number				
	77	Amount of line 75 you want **applied to your 2015 estimated tax** ▶	77			
Amount You Owe	78	**Amount you owe.** Subtract line 74 from line 63. For details on how to pay, see instructions ▶			78	2,830
	79	Estimated tax penalty (see instructions)	79	30		

Third Party Designee Do you want to allow another person to discuss this return with the IRS (see instructions)? ☐ **Yes.** Complete below. ☐ **No**
Designee's name ▶ Phone no. ▶ Personal identification number (PIN) ▶

Sign Here Under penalties of perjury, I declare that I have examined this return and accompanying schedules and statements, and to the best of my knowledge and belief, they are true, correct, and complete. Declaration of preparer (other than taxpayer) is based on all information of which preparer has any knowledge.
Joint return? See instructions. Keep a copy for your records.
Your signature | Date | Your occupation | Daytime phone number
Spouse's signature. If a joint return, **both** must sign. | Date | Spouse's occupation | If the IRS sent you an Identity Protection PIN, enter it here (see inst.)

Paid Preparer Use Only Print/Type preparer's name | Preparer's signature | Date | Check ☐ if self-employed | PTIN
Firm's name ▶ | Firm's EIN ▶
Firm's address ▶ | Phone no.

www.irs.gov/form1040 Form **1040** (2014)

EXHIBIT 8-15 Gram's Tax Payable

Description	Amount	Explanation
(1) Gross tax	$374	Example 8-2.
(2) Alternative minimum tax	0	
(3) Self-employment tax	0	
(4) Gross tax	$374	(1) + (2) + (3).
(5) Tax credits	0	
(6) Prepayments	0	
(7) Penalties	0	
Tax due with return	$374	(4) − (5) − (6) − (7).

CONCLUSION

This chapter reviewed the process for determining an individual's gross and net tax liability. We discovered that taxpayers may be required to pay regular federal income tax, alternative minimum tax, and employment-related tax. Taxpayers are able to offset their gross tax liability dollar for dollar with various types of tax credits and by the amount of tax they prepay during the year. Taxpayers must pay additional taxes with their tax return or they may receive a refund when they file their tax return depending on their gross tax liability and their available tax credits and tax prepayments. The prior three chapters have covered the basic individual tax formula. The next three chapters (9–11) address issues relevant for taxpayers involved in business activities. In Chapters 12–14, we dig a little deeper into certain individual income taxation issues.

Summary

Determine a taxpayer's regular tax liability and identify tax issues associated with the process. LO 8-1

- Individual income is taxed using progressive tax rate schedules with rates ranging from 10 percent to 39.6 percent.
- Marginal tax rates depend on filing status and amount of taxable income.
- Progressive tax rate schedules may lead to either a marriage penalty or a marriage benefit for married taxpayers.
- Long-term capital gains and qualified dividends are taxed at either 0 percent, 15 percent, or 20 percent depending on the amount of taxable income.
- A 3.8 percent tax is levied on net investment income for higher income taxpayers.
- Strategies to shift investment income from parents to children are limited by the "kiddie tax" whereby children's investment income is taxed at the parents' marginal tax rate.

Compute a taxpayer's alternative minimum tax liability and describe the tax characteristics of taxpayers most likely to owe the alternative minimum tax. LO 8-2

- The AMT was designed to ensure that higher-income taxpayers pay some minimum level of income tax.
- The AMT base is broader than the regular income tax base. The AMT base is designed to more closely reflect economic income than is regular taxable income.
- The starting point for calculating AMT is regular taxable income. To compute AMTI, taxpayers add back items not deductible for AMT purposes. In some cases, taxpayers may subtract items not includible in AMTI and items deductible for AMT but not for regular tax purposes. Taxpayers then subtract the allowable AMT exemption to generate the AMT base. They then apply the AMT rates and compare the product (the tentative minimum tax) to their regular tax liability. They owe AMT if the tentative minimum tax exceeds the regular tax liability.
- The 2015 AMT exemption depends on the taxpayer's filing status and is subject to phase-out of 25 cents for each dollar of AMTI over the specific thresholds based on filing status.
- The 2015 AMT tax rates are 26 percent (up to $185,400 of AMT base) and 28 percent thereafter. However, long-term capital gains and qualified dividends are subject to the same preferential rate they are taxed at for regular tax purposes.
- The amount of the AMT is the excess of the tentative minimum tax over the taxpayer's regular tax liability.

Calculate a taxpayer's employment and self-employment taxes payable and explain tax considerations relating to whether a taxpayer is considered to be an employee or a self-employed independent contractor. LO 8-3

- Employees' wages are subject to FICA tax. The Social Security component is 6.2 percent and the Medicare component ranges from 1.45 percent to 2.35 percent for employees.

For employers, the Social Security component is 6.2 percent and the Medicare component is 1.45 percent. The Social Security tax applies to the first $118,500 of salary or wages in 2015. The wage base on the Medicare tax is unlimited.

- Self-employed taxpayers pay self-employment tax on their net self-employment income (92.35 percent of their net Schedule C income). They pay Social Security tax of 12.4 percent and Medicare tax of 2.9 percent to 3.8 percent on their net self-employment income. The Social Security tax applies to the first $118,500 of net Schedule C income in 2015. The base for the Medicare tax is unlimited.
- The decision of whether a worker should be treated as an independent contractor or as an employee for tax purposes is a subjective test based in large part on the extent of control the worker has over things such as the nature, timing, and location of work performed.
- Independent contractors are able to deduct ordinary and necessary business expenses as *for* AGI deductions. Employees incurring unreimbursed business expenses must deduct the items as miscellaneous itemized deductions subject to the 2 percent of AGI floor.
- Independent contractors may deduct the employer portion of their self-employment taxes paid during the year. Employees may not deduct their FICA taxes.
- Independent contractors are required to pay self-employment tax, which represents the employer and employee portions of FICA taxes. Further, independent contractors must pay estimated taxes on their income because the employer does not withhold taxes from the independent contractor's paychecks.
- Hiring independent contractors is generally less costly for employers than is hiring employees. Employers do not pay FICA taxes, withhold taxes, or provide fringe benefits for independent contractors.

LO 8-4 Describe the different general types of tax credits, identify specific tax credits, and compute a taxpayer's allowable child tax credit, child and dependent care credit, American opportunity credit, lifetime learning credit, and earned income credit.

- Tax credits are generally classified into one of three categories: business, nonrefundable personal, or refundable personal credits.
- Nonrefundable personal tax credits provide tax relief to specified groups of individuals.
- The child tax credit is a $1,000 credit for low-income taxpayers who provide a home for dependent children under the age of 17.
- The child and dependent care credit is provided to help taxpayers pay the cost of providing care for their dependents to allow taxpayers to work or to look for work.
- The American opportunity credit provides a credit for a percentage of the costs of the first four years of a student's college education. Forty percent of the credit is refundable.
- The lifetime learning credit provides a credit for a percentage of the costs for instruction in a postsecondary degree program, or to acquire or improve a taxpayer's job skills.
- Nonrefundable credits are first used to reduce a taxpayer's gross tax but cannot reduce the gross tax below zero. Any excess credit is lost unless it is allowed to be carried to a different tax year.
- The earned income credit is refundable but subject to a very complex calculation.
- Business credits reduce the tax after applying nonrefundable credits. Any credit in excess of the remaining tax is generally allowed to be carried over or back to be used in other years.
- Refundable credits are the last credit applied to the tax after applying nonrefundable and business credits. Any refundable credit in excess of the remaining tax is treated as an overpayment and refunded to the taxpayer.

LO 8-5 Explain taxpayer filing and tax payment requirements and describe in general terms how to compute a taxpayer's underpayment, late filing, and late payment penalties.

- The income tax must be prepaid via withholding from salary or through periodic estimated tax payments during the tax year. Estimated tax payments are required only if withholdings are insufficient to meet the taxpayer's tax liability. For calendar-year taxpayers, estimated tax payments are due on April 15, June 15, and September 15 of the current year and January 15 of the following year.

- Taxpayers can avoid an underpayment penalty if their withholdings and estimated tax payments equal or exceed one of two safe harbors (90 percent of current year tax, 100 percent of previous year tax, or 110 percent if AGI exceeds $150,000). If the taxpayer does not satisfy either of the safe-harbor provisions, the underpayment penalty is determined by multiplying the federal short-term interest rate plus 3 percentage points by the amount of tax underpayment per quarter.
- Individual taxpayers are required to file a tax return only if their *gross income* exceeds certain thresholds, which vary based on the taxpayer's filing status, age, and gross income.
- Individual tax returns are due on April 15 for calendar-year individuals. Taxpayers unable to file a tax return by the original due date can request a six-month extension to file.
- The tax law imposes penalties on taxpayers that do not file a tax return (by the original due date plus extension) or pay the tax owed (by the original due date). The failure to file penalty equals 5 percent of the amount of tax owed for each month (or fraction thereof) that the tax return is late with a maximum penalty of 25 percent. The late payment penalty equals .5 percent of the amount of tax owed for each month (or fraction thereof) that the tax is not paid. The combined maximum penalty that may be imposed for late filing and late payment is 5 percent per month (25 percent in total). The late filing and late payment penalties are higher if fraud is involved.

KEY TERMS

alternative minimum tax (AMT) (8-8)
alternative minimum tax adjustments (8-9)
alternative minimum tax base (AMT base) (8-8)
alternative minimum tax (AMT) exemption (8-12)
alternative minimum tax system (8-8)
business tax credits (8-33)
child tax credits (8-25)
earned income credit (8-31)
employee (8-22)
estimated tax payments (8-36)
federal short-term interest rate (8-37)
FICA taxes (8-15)
independent contractor (8-22)
kiddie tax (8-6)
late filing penalty (8-39)
late payment penalty (8-39)
marginal tax rate (8-3)
marriage benefit (8-3)
marriage penalty (8-3)
Medicare tax (8-14)
minimum tax credit (8-14)
net earnings from self-employment (8-17)
net investment income tax (8-6)
net unearned income (8-6)
nonrefundable credit (8-24)
preferential tax rate (8-4)
preferentially taxed income (8-4)
safe-harbor provisions (8-36)
Schedule C (8-17)
self-employment taxes (8-17)
Social Security tax (8-14)
tax bracket (8-2)
tax credits (8-24)
tax rate schedule (8-2)
tax tables (8-3)
tentative minimum tax (8-9)
underpayment penalty (8-36)
withholding (8-36)

DISCUSSION QUESTIONS

1. What is a tax bracket? What is the relationship between filing status and the width of the tax brackets in the tax rate schedule? LO 8-1
2. In 2015, for a taxpayer with $50,000 of taxable income, without doing any actual computations, which filing status do you expect to provide the lowest tax liability? Which filing status provides the highest tax liability? LO 8-1
3. What is the tax marriage penalty and when does it apply? Under what circumstances would a couple experience a tax marriage benefit? LO 8-1
4. Once they've computed their taxable income, how do taxpayers determine their regular tax liability? What additional steps must taxpayers take to compute their tax liability when they have preferentially taxed income? LO 8-1
5. Are there circumstances in which preferentially taxed income (long-term capital gains and qualified dividends) is taxed at the same rate as ordinary income? Explain. LO 8-1

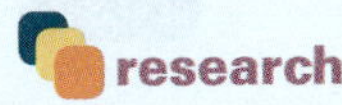

LO 8-1 6. Augustana received $10,000 of qualified dividends this year. Under what circumstances would all $10,000 be taxed at the same rate? Under what circumstances might the entire $10,000 of income not be taxed at the same rate?

LO 8-1 7. What is the difference between earned and unearned income?

LO 8-1 8. Does the kiddie tax eliminate the tax benefits gained by a family when parents transfer income-producing assets to children? Explain.

LO 8-1 9. Does the kiddie tax apply to all children no matter their age? Explain.

LO 8-1 10. What is the kiddie tax and on whose tax return is the kiddie tax liability reported? Explain.

LO 8-1 11. Lauren is 17 years old. She reports earned income of $3,000 and unearned income of $2,200. Is it likely that she is subject to the kiddie tax? Explain.

LO 8-2 12. In very general terms, how is the alternative minimum tax system different from the regular income tax system? How is it similar?

LO 8-2 13. Describe, in general terms, why Congress implemented the AMT.

LO 8-2 14. Do taxpayers always add back the standard deduction when computing alternative minimum taxable income? Explain.

LO 8-2 15. The starting point for computing alternative minimum taxable income is regular taxable income. What are some of the plus adjustments, plus or minus adjustments, and minus adjustments to regular taxable income to compute alternative minimum taxable income?

LO 8-2 16. Describe what the AMT exemption is and who is and isn't allowed to deduct the exemption. How is it similar to the standard deduction and how is it dissimilar?

LO 8-1 LO 8-2 17. How do the AMT tax rates compare to the regular income tax rates?

LO 8-2 18. Is it possible for a taxpayer who pays AMT to have a marginal tax rate higher than the stated AMT rate? Explain.

LO 8-2 19. What is the difference between the tentative minimum tax (TMT) and the AMT?

LO 8-2 planning 20. Lee is single and he runs his own business. He uses the cash method of accounting to determine his business income. Near the end of the year, Lee performed work that he needs to bill a client for. The value of his services is $5,000. Lee figures that if he immediately takes the time to put the bill together and send it out, the client will pay him before year-end. However, if he doesn't send out the bill for one week, he won't receive the client's payment until the beginning of next year. Lee expects that he will owe AMT this year and that his AMT base will be around $200,000 before counting any of the additional business income. Further, Lee anticipates that he will not owe AMT next year. He anticipates his regular taxable income next year will be in the $200,000 range. Would you advise Lee to immediately bill his client or to wait? What factors would you consider in making your recommendation?

LO 8-3 21. Are an employee's entire wages subject to the FICA tax? Explain.

LO 8-3 22. Bobbie works as an employee for Altron Corp. for the first half of the year and for Betel Inc. for the rest of the year. She is relatively well paid. What FICA tax issues is she likely to encounter? What FICA tax issues do Altron Corp. and Betel Inc. need to consider?

LO 8-3 23. Compare and contrast an employee's FICA tax payment responsibilities with those of a self-employed taxpayer.

24. When a taxpayer works as an employee and as a self-employed independent contractor during the year, how does the taxpayer determine her employment and self-employment taxes payable? LO 8-3
25. What are the primary factors to consider when deciding whether a worker should be considered an employee or a self-employed taxpayer for tax purposes? LO 8-3
26. How do the tax consequences of being an employee differ from those of being self-employed? LO 8-3
27. Mike wanted to work for a CPA firm but he also wanted to work on his father's farm in Montana. Because the CPA firm wanted Mike to be happy, they offered to let him work for them as an independent contractor during the fall and winter and let him return to Montana to work for his father during the spring and summer. He was very excited to hear that they were also going to give him a 5 percent higher "salary" for the six months he would be working for the firm over what he would have made over the same six-month period if he worked full-time as an employee (i.e., an increase from $30,000 to $31,500). Should Mike be excited about his 5 percent raise? Why or why not? What counteroffer could Mike reasonably suggest? LO 8-3 planning
28. How are tax credits and tax deductions similar? How are they dissimilar? LO 8-4
29. What are the three types of tax credits, and explain why it is important to distinguish between the different types of tax credits. LO 8-4
30. Explain why there is such a large number and variety of tax credits. LO 8-4
31. What is the difference between a refundable and nonrefundable tax credit? LO 8-4
32. Is the child tax credit a refundable or nonrefundable credit? Explain. LO 8-4
33. Diane has a job working three-quarter time. She hired her mother to take care of her two small children so Diane could work. Do Diane's child care payments to her mother qualify for the child and dependent care credit? Explain. LO 8-4
34. The amount of the child and dependent care credit is based on the amount of the taxpayer's expenditures to provide care for one or more qualifying persons. Who is considered to be a qualifying person for this purpose? LO 8-4
35. Compare and contrast the lifetime learning credit with the American opportunity credit. LO 8-4
36. Jennie's grandfather paid her tuition this fall to State University (an eligible educational institution). Jennie is claimed as a dependent by her parents, but she also files her own tax return. Can Jennie claim an education credit for the tuition paid by her grandfather? What difference would it make, if any, if Jennie did not qualify as a dependent of her parents (or anyone else)? LO 8-4 research
37. Why is the earned income credit referred to as a negative income tax? LO 8-4
38. Under what circumstances can a college student qualify for the earned income credit? LO 8-4
39. How are business credits similar to personal credits? How are they dissimilar? LO 8-4
40. Is the foreign tax credit a personal credit or a business credit? Explain. LO 8-4
41. When a U.S. taxpayer pays income taxes to a foreign government, what options does the taxpayer have when determining how to treat the expenditure on her U.S. individual income tax return? LO 8-4
42. Describe the order in which different types of tax credits are applied to reduce a taxpayer's tax liability. LO 8-4
43. Describe the two methods that taxpayers use to prepay their taxes. LO 8-5

LO 8-5 44. What are the consequences of a taxpayer underpaying his or her tax liability throughout the year? Explain the safe-harbor provisions that may apply in this situation.

LO 8-5 45. Describe how the underpayment penalty is calculated.

LO 8-5 46. What determines if a taxpayer is required to file a tax return? If a taxpayer is not required to file a tax return, does this mean that the taxpayer should not file a tax return?

LO 8-5 47. What is the due date for individual tax returns? What extensions are available?

LO 8-5 48. Describe the consequences for failing to file a tax return and for paying tax owed late.

PROBLEMS

All applicable problems are available with McGraw-Hill's *Connect*® *Accounting*.

LO 8-1 49. Whitney received $75,000 of taxable income in 2015. All of the income was salary from her employer. What is her income tax liability in each of the following alternative situations?

a) She files under the single filing status.

b) She files a joint tax return with her spouse. Together their taxable income is $75,000.

c) She is married but files a separate tax return. Her taxable income is $75,000.

d) She files as a head of household.

LO 8-1 50. In 2015, Lisa and Fred, a married couple, have taxable income of $300,000. If they were to file separate tax returns, Lisa would have reported taxable income of $125,000 and Fred would have reported taxable income of $175,000. What is the couple's marriage penalty or benefit?

LO 8-1 51. In 2015, Jasmine and Thomas, a married couple, have taxable income of $150,000. If they were to file separate tax returns, Jasmine would have reported taxable income of $140,000 and Thomas would have reported taxable income of $10,000. What is the couple's marriage penalty or benefit?

LO 8-1 52. Lacy is a single taxpayer. In 2015, her taxable income is $40,000. What is her tax liability in each of the following alternative situations?

a) All of her income is salary from her employer.

b) Her $40,000 of taxable income includes $1,000 of qualified dividends.

c) Her $40,000 of taxable income includes $5,000 of qualified dividends.

LO 8-1 53. Henrich is a single taxpayer. In 2015, his taxable income is $425,000. What is his income tax and net investment income tax liability in each of the following alternative scenarios?

a) All of his income is salary from his employer.

b) His $425,000 of taxable income includes $2,000 of long-term capital gain that is taxed at preferential rates.

c) His $425,000 of taxable income includes $55,000 of long-term capital gain that is taxed at preferential rates.

d) Henrich has $195,000 of taxable income, which includes $50,000 of long-term capital gain that is taxed at preferential rates. Assume his modified AGI is $210,000.

54. In 2015, Sheryl is claimed as a dependent on her parents' tax return. Her parents' ordinary income marginal tax rate is 35 percent. Sheryl did not provide more than half her own support. What is Sheryl's tax liability for the year in each of the following alternative circumstances? LO 8-1
    a) She received $7,000 from a part-time job. This was her only source of income. She is 16 years old at year-end.
    b) She received $7,000 of interest income from corporate bonds she received several years ago. This is her only source of income. She is 16 years old at year-end.
    c) She received $7,000 of interest income from corporate bonds she received several years ago. This is her only source of income. She is 20 years old at year-end and is a full-time student.
    d) She received $7,000 of qualified dividend income. This is her only source of income. She is 16 years old at year-end.

55. In 2015, Carson is claimed as a dependent on his parent's tax return. His parents' ordinary income marginal tax rate is 28 percent. Carson's parents provided most of his support. What is Carson's tax liability for the year in each of the following alternative circumstances? LO 8-1
    a) Carson is 17 years old at year-end and earned $12,000 from his summer job and part-time job after school. This was his only source of income.
    b) Carson is 23 years old at year-end. He is a full-time student and earned $12,000 from his summer internship and part-time job. He also received $5,000 of qualified dividend income.

56. Brooklyn files as a head of household for 2015 and claims a total of three exemptions (3 × $4,000 = $12,000). She claimed the standard deduction of $9,250 for regular tax purposes. Her regular taxable income was $80,000. What is Brooklyn's AMTI? LO 8-2

57. Sylvester files as a single taxpayer during 2015 and claims one personal exemption. He itemizes deductions for regular tax purposes. He paid charitable contributions of $7,000, real estate taxes of $1,000, state income taxes of $4,000, and interest on a home-equity loan of $2,000. Sylvester's regular taxable income is $100,000. LO 8-2
    a) What is Sylvester's AMTI if he used the home-equity proceeds to purchase a car?
    b) What is Sylvester's AMTI if he used the home-equity loan proceeds to build a new garage next to his home?

58. In 2015, Nadia has $100,000 of regular taxable income. She itemizes her deductions as follows: real property taxes of $1,500, state income taxes of $2,000, and mortgage interest expense of $10,000 (not a home-equity loan). In addition, she receives tax-exempt interest of $1,000 from a municipal bond (issued in 2006) that was used to fund a new business building for a (formerly) out-of-state employer. Finally, she received a state tax refund of $300 from the prior year. LO 8-2

    a) What is Nadia's AMTI this year if she deducted $15,000 of itemized deductions last year (she did not owe any AMT last year)? Complete Form 6251 (through line 28) for Nadia.
    b) What is Nadia's AMTI this year if she deducted the standard deduction last year (she did not owe any AMT last year)? Complete Form 6251 (through line 28) for Nadia.

LO 8-2

tax forms

59. In 2015, Sven is single and has $120,000 of regular taxable income. He itemizes his deductions as follows: real property tax of $2,000, state income tax of $4,000, mortgage interest expense of $15,000 (not a home-equity loan). He also paid $2,000 in tax preparation fees and has a positive AMT depreciation adjustment of $500. What is Sven's alternative minimum taxable income (AMTI)? Complete Form 6251 (through line 28) for Sven.

LO 8-2

60. Olga is married and files a joint tax return with her husband. What amount of AMT exemption may she deduct under each of the following alternative circumstances?

a) Her AMTI is $90,000.

b) Her AMTI is $180,000.

c) Her AMTI is $500,000.

LO 8-2

61. Corbett's AMTI is $130,000. What is his AMT exemption under the following alternative circumstances?

a) He is married and files a joint return.

b) He is married and files a separate return.

c) His filing status is single.

d) His filing status is head of household.

LO 8-2

62. In 2015, Juanita is married and files a joint tax return with her husband. What is her tentative minimum tax in each of the following alternative circumstances?

a) Her AMT base is $100,000, all ordinary income.

b) Her AMT base is $250,000, all ordinary income.

c) Her AMT base is $100,000, which includes $10,000 of qualified dividends.

d) Her AMT base is $250,000, which includes $10,000 of qualified dividends.

LO 8-2

63. Steve's tentative minimum tax (TMT) for 2015 is $15,000. What is his AMT if

a) His regular tax is $10,000?

b) His regular tax is $20,000?

LO 8-2

tax forms

64. In 2015, Janet and Ray are married filing jointly. They have five dependent children under 18 years of age. Janet and Ray's taxable income is $140,000, and they itemize their deductions as follows: real property taxes of $5,000, state income taxes of $9,000, and mortgage interest expense of $15,000 (not a home-equity loan). What is Janet and Ray's AMT? Complete Form 6251 for Janet and Ray.

LO 8-2

65. In 2015, Deon and NeNe are married filing jointly. They have three dependent children under 18 years of age. Deon and NeNe's AGI is $809,900, their taxable income is $718,850, and they itemize their deductions as follows: real property taxes of $10,000, state income taxes of $40,000, miscellaneous itemized deductions of $4,000 (subject to but in excess of 2 percent AGI floor), charitable contributions of $6,000, and mortgage interest expense of $41,000 ($11,000 of which is attributable to a home-equity loan used to buy a new car). What is Deon and NeNe's AMT? Complete Form 6251 for Deon and NeNe.

LO 8-3

66. Brooke works for Company A for all of 2015, earning a salary of $50,000.

a) What is her FICA tax obligation for the year?

b) Assume Brooke works for Company A for half of 2015, earning $50,000 in salary, and she works for Company B for the second half of 2015, earning $70,000 in salary. What is Brooke's FICA tax obligation for the year?

67. Rasheed works for Company A, earning $350,000 in salary during 2015. Assuming he has no other sources of income, what amount of FICA tax will Rasheed pay for the year? LO 8-3

68. Alice is self-employed in 2015. Her net business profit on her Schedule C for the year is $140,000. What is her self-employment tax liability for 2015? LO 8-3

69. Kyle worked as a free-lance software engineer for the first three months of 2015. During that time, he earned $44,000 of self-employment income. On April 1, 2015, Kyle took a job as a full-time software engineer with one of his former clients, Hoogle Inc. From April through the end of the year, Kyle earned $178,000 in salary. What amount of FICA taxes (self-employment and employment related) does Kyle owe for the year? LO 8-3

70. Eva received $60,000 in compensation payments from JAZZ Corp. during 2015. Eva incurred $5,000 in business expenses relating to her work for JAZZ Corp. JAZZ did not reimburse Eva for any of these expenses. Eva is single and she deducts a standard deduction of $6,300 and a personal exemption of $4,000. Based on these facts answer the following questions: LO 8-3
    a) Assume that Eva is considered to be an *employee*. What amount of FICA taxes is she required to pay for the year?
    b) Assume that Eva is considered to be an *employee*. What is her regular income tax liability for the year?
    c) Assume that Eva is considered to be a *self-employed contractor*. What is her self-employment tax liability for the year?
    d) Assume that Eva is considered to be a *self-employed contractor*. What is her regular tax liability for the year?

71. Terry Hutchison worked as a self-employed lawyer until two years ago when he retired. He used the cash method of accounting in his business for tax purposes. Five years ago, Terry represented his client ABC corporation in an antitrust lawsuit against XYZ corporation. During that year, Terry paid self-employment taxes on all of his income. ABC won the lawsuit but Terry and ABC could not agree on the amount of his earnings. Finally, this year, the issue got resolved and ABC paid Terry $90,000 for the services he provided five years ago. Terry plans to include the payment in his gross income, but because he spends most of his time playing golf and absolutely no time working on legal matters, he does not intend to pay self-employment taxes on the income. Is Terry subject to self-employment taxes on this income? LO 8-3 research

72. Trey claims a dependency exemption for both of his daughters, ages 14 and 17, at year-end. Trey files a joint return with his wife. What amount of child credit will Trey be able to claim for his daughters under each of the following alternative situations? LO 8-4
    a) His AGI is $100,000.
    b) His AGI is $120,000.
    c) His AGI is $122,100, and his daughters are ages 10 and 12.

73. Julie paid a day care center to watch her two-year-old son while she worked as a computer programmer for a local start-up company. What amount of child and dependent care credit can Julie claim in each of the following alternative scenarios? LO 8-4
    a) Julie paid $2,000 to the day care center and her AGI is $50,000 (all salary).
    b) Julie paid $5,000 to the day care center and her AGI is $50,000 (all salary).

c) Julie paid $4,000 to the day care center and her AGI is $25,000 (all salary).

d) Julie paid $2,000 to the day care center and her AGI is $14,000 (all salary).

e) Julie paid $4,000 to the day care center and her AGI is $14,000 ($2,000 salary and $12,000 unearned income).

LO 8-4

74. In 2015, Elaine paid $2,800 of tuition and $600 for books for her dependent son to attend State University this past fall as a freshman. Elaine files a joint return with her husband. What is the maximum American opportunity credit that Elaine can claim for the tuition payment and books in each of the following alternative situations?

a) Elaine's AGI is $80,000.

b) Elaine's AGI is $168,000.

c) Elaine's AGI is $184,000.

LO 8-4

planning

75. In 2015, Laureen is currently single. She paid $2,800 of qualified tuition and related expenses for each of her twin daughters Sheri and Meri to attend State University as freshmen ($2,800 each for a total of $5,600). Sheri and Meri qualify as Laureen's dependents. Laureen also paid $1,900 for her son Ryan's (also Laureen's dependent) tuition and related expenses to attend his junior year at State University. Finally, Laureen paid $1,200 for herself to attend seminars at a community college to help her improve her job skills. What is the maximum amount of education credits Laureen can claim for these expenditures in each of the following alternative scenarios? Assume the 2014 rules apply for purposes of the qualified education expense deduction.

a) Laureen's AGI is $45,000. If Laureen claims education credits is she allowed to deduct as *for* AGI expenses tuition costs for her daughters that do not generate credits? Explain.

b) Laureen's AGI is $95,000. What options does Laureen have for deducting her continuing education costs to the extent the costs don't generate a credit?

c) Laureen's AGI is $45,000 and Laureen paid $12,000 (not $1,900) for Ryan to attend graduate school (his fifth year not his junior year).

LO 8-4

76. In 2015, Amanda and Jaxon Stuart have a daughter who is one year old. The Stuarts are full-time students and they are both 23 years old. Their only sources of income are gains from stock they held for three years before selling and wages from part-time jobs. What is their earned income credit in the following alternative scenarios if they file jointly?

a) Their AGI is $15,000, consisting of $5,000 of capital gains and $10,000 of wages.

b) Their AGI is $15,000, consisting of $10,000 of lottery winnings (unearned income) and $5,000 of wages.

c) Their AGI is $25,000, consisting of $20,000 of wages and $5,000 of lottery winnings (unearned income).

d) Their AGI is $25,000, consisting of $5,000 of wages and $20,000 of lottery winnings (unearned income).

e) Their AGI is $10,000, consisting of $10,000 of lottery winnings (unearned income).

LO 8-4

77. In 2015, Zach is single with no dependents. He is not claimed as a dependent on another's return. All of his income is from salary and he does not have

any *for* AGI deductions. What is his earned income credit in the following alternative scenarios?

a) Zach is 29 years old and his AGI is $5,000.

b) Zach is 29 years old and his AGI is $10,000.

c) Zach is 29 years old and his AGI is $19,000.

d) Zach is 24 years old and his AGI is $5,000.

78. This year Luke has calculated his gross tax liability at $1,800. Luke is entitled to a $2,400 nonrefundable personal tax credit, a $1,500 business tax credit, and a $600 refundable personal tax credit. In addition, Luke has had $2,300 of income taxes withheld from his salary. What is Luke's net tax due or refund? LO 8-4

79. This year Lloyd, a single taxpayer, estimates that his tax liability will be $10,000. Last year, his total tax liability was $15,000. He estimates that his tax withholding from his employer will be $7,800. LO 8-5 planning

a) Is Lloyd required to increase his withholding or make estimated tax payments this year to avoid the underpayment penalty? If so, how much?

b) Assuming Lloyd does not make any additional payments, what is the amount of his underpayment penalty? Assume the federal short-term rate is 5 percent.

80. This year, Paula and Simon (married filing jointly) estimate that their tax liability will be $200,000. Last year, their total tax liability was $170,000. They estimate that their tax withholding from their employers will be $175,000. Are Paula and Simon required to increase their withholdings or make estimated tax payments this year to avoid the underpayment penalty? If so, how much? LO 8-5 planning

81. This year, Santhosh, a single taxpayer, estimates that his tax liability will be $100,000. Last year, his total tax liability was $15,000. He estimates that his tax withholding from his employer will be $35,000. Is Santhosh required to increase his withholding or make estimated tax payments this year to avoid the underpayment penalty? If so, how much? LO 8-5 planning

82. For the following taxpayers, determine if they are required to file a tax return in 2015. LO 8-5

a) Ricko, single taxpayer, with gross income of $12,000.

b) Fantasia, head of household, with gross income of $17,500.

c) Ken and Barbie, married taxpayers with no dependents, with gross income of $12,000.

d) Dorothy and Rudolf, married taxpayers, both age 68, with gross income of $19,000.

e) Janyce, single taxpayer, age 73, with gross income of $12,500.

83. For the following taxpayers, determine the due date of their tax returns. LO 8-5

a) Jerome, a single taxpayer, is not requesting an extension this year. Assume the due date falls on a Tuesday.

b) Lashaunda, a single taxpayer, requests an extension this year. Assume the extended due date falls on a Wednesday.

c) Barney and Betty, married taxpayers, do not request an extension this year. Assume the due date falls on a Sunday.

d) Fred and Wilma, married taxpayers, request an extension this year. Assume the extended date falls on a Saturday.

LO 8-5

84. Determine the amount of the late filing and late payment penalties that apply for the following taxpayers.
    a) Jolene filed her tax return by its original due date but did not pay the $2,000 in taxes she owed with the return until one and a half months later.
    b) Oscar filed his tax return and paid his $3,000 tax liability seven months late.
    c) Wilfred, attempting to evade his taxes, did not file a tax return or pay his $10,000 in taxes for several years.

COMPREHENSIVE PROBLEMS

All applicable problems are available with McGraw-Hill's *Connect*® *Accounting*.

85. In 2015, Jack and Diane Heart are married with two children, ages 10 and 12. Jack works full-time and earns an annual salary of $75,000, while Diane works as a substitute teacher and earns approximately $25,000 per year. Jack and Diane expect to file jointly and do not itemize their deductions. In the fall of this year, Diane was offered a full-time teaching position that would pay her an additional $20,000.
    a) Calculate the marginal tax rate on the additional income, *excluding employment taxes,* to help Jack and Diane evaluate the offer.
    b) Calculate the marginal tax rate on the additional income, *including employment taxes,* to help Jack and Diane evaluate the offer.
    c) Calculate the marginal tax rate on the additional income, *including self-employment taxes,* if Diane earned an additional $20,000 as a self-employed contractor ($20,000 self-employment income in addition to the $25,000 as an employee).

planning

86. Matt and Carrie are married, have two children, and file a joint return. Their daughter Katie is 19 years old and was a full-time student at State University. During 2015, she completed her freshman year and one semester as a sophomore. Katie's expenses while she was away at school during the year were as follows:

Tuition	$5,000
Class fees	300
Books	500
Room and board	4,500

Katie received a half-tuition scholarship that paid for $2,500 of her tuition costs. Katie's parents paid the rest of these expenses. Matt and Carrie are able to claim Katie as a dependent on their tax return.

Matt and Carrie's 23-year-old son Todd also attended graduate school (fifth year of college) full time at a nearby college. Todd's expenses while away at school were as follows:

Tuition	$3,000
Class fees	0
Books	250
Room and board	4,000

Matt and Carrie paid for Todd's tuition, books, and room and board.

Since Matt and Carrie still benefit from claiming Todd as a dependent on their tax return, they decided to provide Todd with additional financial assistance by making the payments on Todd's outstanding student loans. Besides paying off some of the loan principal, Matt and Carrie paid a total of $900 of interest on the loan.

This year Carrie decided to take some classes at the local community college to help improve her skills as a schoolteacher. The community college is considered to be a qualifying postsecondary institution of higher education. Carrie spent a total of $1,300 on tuition for the classes, and she was not reimbursed by her employer. Matt and Carrie's AGI for 2015 before any education-related tax deductions is $120,000 and their taxable income before considering any education-related tax benefits is $80,000. Matt and Carrie incurred $500 of miscellaneous itemized deductions subject to the 2 percent floor not counting any education-related expenses.

Required:

Determine the mix of tax benefits that maximize tax savings for Matt and Carrie. Assume the 2014 rules apply for purposes of the qualified education expense deduction. Their options for credits for each student are as follows:

a) They may claim either a credit or a qualified education deduction for Katie's expenses.

b) They may claim either a credit or a qualified education deduction for Todd.

c) They may claim (1) a credit or (2) a qualified education deduction for Carrie. They may deduct any amount not included in (1) or (2) as a miscellaneous itemized deduction subject to the 2 percent of AGI floor.

Remember to apply any applicable limits or phase-outs in your computations.

87. Reba Dixon is a fifth-grade schoolteacher who earned a salary of $38,000 in 2015. She is 45 years old and has been divorced for four years. She received $1,200 of alimony payments each month from her former husband. Reba also rents out a small apartment building. This year Reba received $30,000 of rental payments from tenants and she incurred $19,500 of expenses associated with the rental.

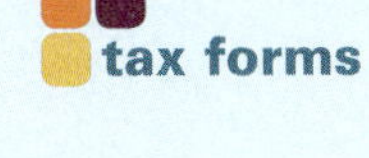

Reba and her daughter Heather (20 years old at the end of the year) moved to Georgia in January of this year. Reba provides more than one-half of Heather's support. They had been living in Colorado for the past 15 years, but ever since her divorce, Reba has been wanting to move back to Georgia to be closer to her family. Luckily, last December, a teaching position opened up and Reba and Heather decided to make the move. Reba paid a moving company $2,010 to move their personal belongings, and she and Heather spent two days driving the 1,426 miles to Georgia. During the trip, Reba paid $143 for lodging and $85 for meals. Reba's mother was so excited to have her daughter and granddaughter move back to Georgia that she gave Reba $3,000 to help out with the moving costs.

Reba rented a home in Georgia. Heather decided to continue living at home with her mom, but she started attending school full-time in January at a nearby university. She was awarded a $3,000 partial tuition scholarship this year, and Reba helped out by paying the remaining $500 tuition cost. If possible, Reba thought it would be best to claim the education credit for these expenses.

Reba wasn't sure if she would have enough items to help her benefit from itemizing on her tax return. However, she kept track of several expenses this year that she thought might qualify if she was able to itemize. Reba paid $2,800 in state income taxes and $6,500 in charitable contributions during the year. She also paid the following medical-related expenses for her and Heather:

Insurance premiums	$4,795
Medical care expenses	1,100
Prescription medicine	350
Nonprescription medicine	100
New contact lenses for Heather	200

Shortly after the move, Reba got distracted while driving and she ran into a street sign. The accident caused $900 in damage to the car and gave her whiplash. Because the repairs were less than her insurance deductible, she paid the entire cost of the repairs. Reba wasn't able to work for two months after the accident. Fortunately, she received $2,000 from her disability insurance. Her employer, the Central Georgia School District, paid 60 percent of the premiums on the policy as a nontaxable fringe benefit and Reba paid the remaining 40 percent portion.

A few years ago, Reba acquired several investments with her portion of the divorce settlement. This year she reported the following income from her investments: $2,200 of interest income from corporate bonds and $1,500 interest income from City of Denver municipal bonds. Overall, Reba's stock portfolio appreciated by $12,000 but she did not sell any of her stocks.

Heather reported $3,200 of interest income from corporate bonds she received as gifts from her father over the last several years. This was Heather's only source of income for the year.

Reba had $10,000 of federal income taxes withheld by her employer. Heather made $500 of estimated tax payments during the year. Reba did not make any estimated payments. Reba had qualifying insurance for purposes of the Affordable Care Act (ACA).

Required:

a) Determine Reba's federal income taxes due or taxes payable for the current year. Complete pages 1 and 2 of Form 1040 for Reba.

b) Is Reba allowed to file as a head of household or single?

c) Determine the amount of FICA taxes Reba was required to pay on her salary.

d) Determine Heather's federal income taxes due or payable.

88. John and Sandy Ferguson got married eight years ago and have a seven-year-old daughter Samantha. In 2015, John worked as a computer technician at a local university earning a salary of $52,000, and Sandy worked part-time as a receptionist for a law firm earning a salary of $29,000. John also does some Web design work on the side and reported revenues of $4,000 and associated expenses of $750. The Fergusons received $800 in qualified dividends and a $200 refund of their state income taxes. The Fergusons always itemize their deductions and their itemized deductions were well over the standard deduction amount last year. The Fergusons had qualifying insurance for purposes of the Affordable Care Act (ACA).

The Fergusons reported making the following payments during the year:

- State income taxes of $4,400. Federal tax withholding of $4,000.
- Alimony payments to John's former wife of $10,000.
- Child support payments for John's child with his former wife of $4,100.
- $3,200 of real property taxes.
- Sandy was reimbursed $600 for employee business expenses she incurred. She was required to provide documentation for her expenses to her employer.

- In addition to the $750 of Web design expenses, John attended a conference to improve his skills associated with his Web design work. His trip was for three days and he incurred the following expenses: airfare $370, total taxi fares for trip $180, meals $80, and conference fee of $200.
- $3,600 to Kid Care day care center for Samantha's care while John and Sandy worked.
- $14,000 interest on their home mortgage.
- $3,000 interest on a $40,000 home-equity loan. They used the loan to pay for family vacation and new car.
- $6,000 cash charitable contributions to qualified charities.
- Donation of used furniture to Goodwill. The furniture had a fair market value of $400 and cost $2,000.

Required:

What is the Fergusons' 2015 federal income taxes payable or refund, including any self-employment tax and AMT, if applicable? Complete pages 1 and 2 of Form 1040 and Form 6251 for John and Sandy.

chapter 9

Business Income, Deductions, and Accounting Methods

Learning Objectives

Upon completing this chapter, you should be able to:

- **LO 9-1** Describe the general requirements for deducting business expenses and identify common business deductions.
- **LO 9-2** Apply the limitations on business deductions to distinguish between deductible and nondeductible business expenses.
- **LO 9-3** Identify and explain special business deductions specifically permitted under the tax laws.
- **LO 9-4** Explain the concept of an accounting period and describe accounting periods available to businesses.
- **LO 9-5** Identify and describe accounting methods available to businesses and apply cash and accrual methods to determine business income and expense deductions.

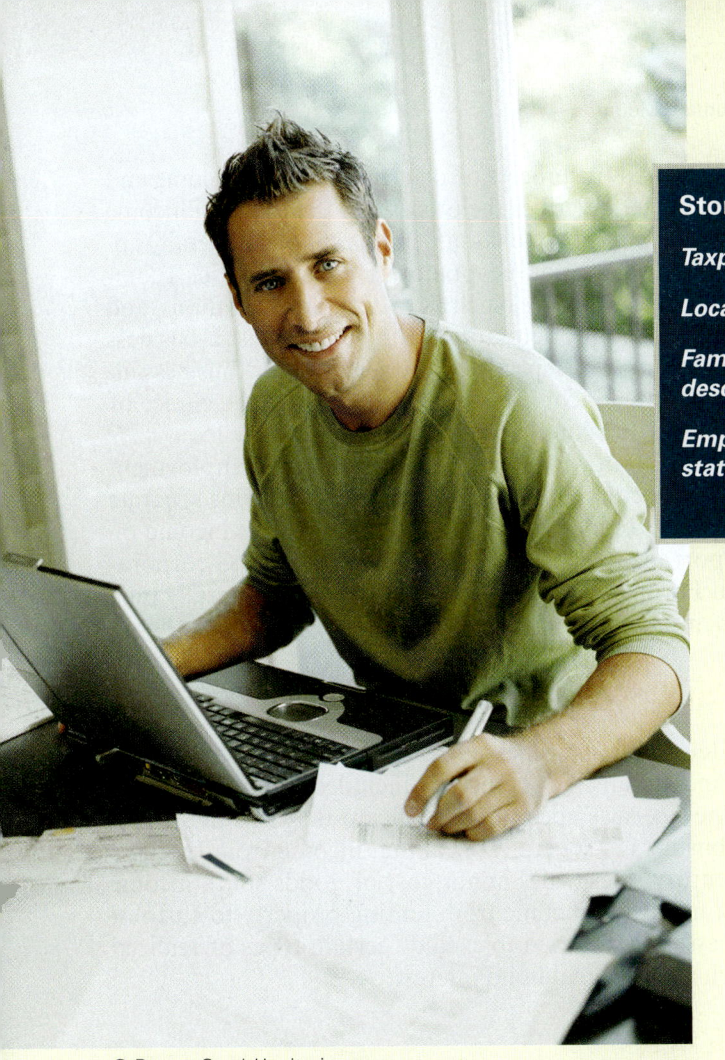

© BananaStock/Jupiterimages

Storyline Summary

Taxpayer:	Rick Grime
Location:	San Antonio, Texas
Family description:	Unmarried
Employment status:	Rick quit his landscaping job in Dallas and moved to San Antonio to start a business as a self-employed landscaper.

Rick Grime graduated from Texas A&M University with a degree in agronomy, and for the past few years he has been employed by a landscape architect in Dallas. Nearly every day that Rick went to work, he shared ideas with his employer about improving the business. Rick finally decided to take his ideas and start his own landscaping business in his hometown of San Antonio, Texas. In mid-April, Rick left his job and moved his belongings to San Antonio. Once in town, Rick discovered he had to do a lot of things to start his business. First, he registered his new business name (Green Acres Landscaping) and established a bank account for the business. Next, he rented a used sport utility vehicle (SUV) and a shop for his place of business. Rick didn't know much about accounting for business activities, so he hired a CPA, Jane Bronson, to help him. Jane and Rick decided that Green Acres would operate as a sole proprietorship, but Jane suggested that as the business grew, he might want to consider organizing it as a different type of legal entity. Operating as a corporation, for instance, would allow him to invite new investors or business partners to help fund future expansion. Rick formally started his business on May 1. He spent a lot of time attracting new customers, and he figured he would hire employees as he needed them.

to be continued . . .

In previous chapters, we've emphasized the process of determining gross income and deductions for *individuals*. This chapter describes the process for determining income for *businesses*. Keep in mind that the concepts we discuss in this chapter generally apply to all types of business entities including sole proprietorships (such as Rick's company, Green Acres), partnerships, hybrid entities (such as LLCs), S corporations, and C corporations.[1] Because Rick is a sole proprietor, our examples emphasize business income and deductions from his personal perspective. Proprietors report business income on Schedule C of their individual income tax returns. However, the choice of the organizational form is a complex decision that is described in Chapter 15.

Schedule C income is subject to both individual income and self-employment taxes. Entities other than sole proprietorships report income on tax forms separate from the owners' tax returns. For example, partnerships report taxable income on Form 1065, S corporations report taxable income on Form 1120S, and C corporations report taxable income on Form 1120. Of all these entity types, generally only C corporations pay taxes on their income.

BUSINESS GROSS INCOME

In most respects, the rules for determining business gross income are the same as for determining gross income for individuals. Gross income includes "all income from whatever source derived."[2] The tax laws specifically indicate that this definition includes gross income from "business." Generally speaking, income from business includes gross profit from inventory sales (sales minus cost of goods sold), income from services provided to customers, and income from renting property to customers. Just like individuals, businesses are allowed to exclude certain types of realized income from gross income, such as municipal bond interest.

LO 9-1

BUSINESS DEDUCTIONS

THE KEY FACTS

Business Expenses

- Business expenses must be incurred in pursuit of profits, not personal goals.
- Only reasonable amounts are allowed as deductions.
- A deduction must be ordinary and necessary (appropriate and helpful).

Because Congress intended for taxable income to reflect the *net* increase in wealth from a business, it is only fair that businesses be allowed to deduct expenses incurred to generate business income. Typically, Congress provides *specific* statutory rules authorizing deductions. However, as you can see from the following excerpt from IRC §162, the provision authorizing business deductions is relatively broad and ambiguous:

> There shall be allowed as a deduction all the ordinary and necessary expenses paid or incurred during the taxable year in carrying on any trade or business . . .

This provision authorizes taxpayers to deduct expenses for "trade or business" activities.[3] The tax code does not define the phrase "trade or business," but it's clear that the objective of business activities is to make a profit. Thus, the tax law requires that a business expense be made in the pursuit of profits rather than the pursuit of other, presumably personal, motives.

When a taxpayer's activity does not meet the "for profit" requirement, it is treated as a hobby, an activity motivated by personal objectives. A taxpayer engaged in a hobby that generates revenues includes all revenues from the activity in gross

[1]Both S corporations and C corporations are incorporated for state law purposes. However, S corporations are taxed as flow-through entities (S corporation income is taxed to its owners) while C corporations (or taxable corporations) are taxed as separate taxable entities. Hybrid entities may opt to be taxed as either flow-through entities or taxable corporations.

[2]§61(a).

[3]§212 contains a sister provision to §162 allowing deductions for ordinary and necessary expenses incurred for the production of income ("investment expenses") and for the management and maintenance of property (including expenses incurred in renting property in situations when the rental activity is not considered to be a trade or business). Recall from Chapter 6 that a business activity, sometimes referred to as a trade or business, requires a relatively high level of involvement or effort from the taxpayer. Unlike business activities, investments are profit-motivated activities that don't require a high degree of taxpayer involvement or effort.

income and deducts associated expenses to the extent of gross income from the activity as *miscellaneous itemized deductions* (subject to the 2 percent of AGI floor).

Ordinary and Necessary

Business expenditures must be both **ordinary and necessary** to be deductible. An *ordinary* expense is an expense that is normal or appropriate for the business under the circumstances.[4] An expense is *not* necessarily required to be typical or repetitive in nature to be considered ordinary. For example, a business could deduct the legal fees it expends to defend itself in an antitrust suit. Although an antitrust suit would be atypical and unusual for most businesses, defending the suit would probably be deemed ordinary, because it would be expected under the circumstances. A *necessary* expense is an expense that is helpful or conducive to the business activity, but the expenditure need not be essential or indispensable. For example, a deduction for metric tools would qualify as ordinary and necessary even if there was only a small chance that a repairman might need these tools. The "ordinary and necessary" requirements are applied on a case-by-case basis, and while the deduction depends on individual circumstances, the IRS is often reluctant to second-guess business decisions. Exhibit 9-1 presents examples of expenditures that are ordinary and necessary for typical businesses.

EXHIBIT 9-1 Examples of Typical Ordinary and Necessary Business Expenses

- Advertising
- Car and truck expenses
- Depreciation
- Employee compensation and benefits
- Insurance
- Interest
- Legal fees
- Office expenses
- Rent
- Repairs
- Supplies
- Travel
- Utilities
- Wages

Example 9-1

Outside Rick's office is a small waiting room for clients. Rick paid $50 for several books to occupy clients while waiting for appointments. These are hardcover books with photographs and illustrations of landscape designs. Rick believes that the books will inspire new designs and will alleviate boredom for potential clients, and he deducted the $50 cost as a business expense. Is he correct?

Answer: Under the code and regulations, expenses directly connected to a business are deductible if the expenditure is ordinary and necessary. The phrase *ordinary and necessary* is interpreted as *helpful or conducive to business activity.* In Rick's situation, it seems highly unlikely that the IRS or a court would conclude that the cost of these books is not ordinary and necessary. What do you think?

What if: Suppose that Rick's hobby was pre-Columbian Maya civilization. Do you think Rick would be able to deduct the cost of a new treatise on translating Maya script if he placed the book in his waiting room? Why or why not?

ETHICS

Sheri is a lawyer who operates as a sole practitioner. Despite her busy schedule, in the past Sheri found time for her family. This year Sheri took on two new important clients, and she hired a personal assistant to help her manage her schedule and make timely court filings. Occasionally, Sheri asked her assistant to assist her with personal tasks such as having her car serviced or buying groceries. Do you think that Sheri should treat her assistant's entire salary as a business expense? Would your answer be any different if personal assistants commonly perform these tasks for busy attorneys?

[4] *Welch v. Helvering* (1933), 290 US 111.

Reasonable in Amount

Ordinary and necessary business expenses are deductible only *to the extent* they are also **reasonable in amount.** The courts have interpreted this requirement to mean that an expenditure is not reasonable when it is extravagant or exorbitant.[5] If the expenditure is extravagant in amount, the courts presume the excess amount is spent for personal rather than business reasons and is not deductible.

Determining whether an expenditure is reasonable is not an exact science and, not surprisingly, taxpayers and the IRS may have different opinions. Generally, the courts and the IRS test for extravagance by comparing the amount of the expense to a market price or an **arm's length amount.** If the amount of the expense is the amount typically charged in the market by unrelated parties, the amount is considered to be reasonable. The underlying issue is *why* a profit-motivated taxpayer would pay an extravagant amount. Hence, reasonableness is most likely to be an issue when a payment is made to an individual related to the taxpayer, or the taxpayer enjoys some incidental benefit from the expenditure, such as entertainment value.

Example 9-2

During the busy part of the year, Rick could not keep up with all the work. Therefore, he hired four part-time employees and paid them $10 an hour to mow lawns and pull weeds for an average of 20 hours a week. When things finally slowed down in late fall, Rick released his four part-time employees. Rick paid a total of $22,000 in compensation to the four employees. He still needed some extra help now and then, so he hired his brother, Tom, on a part-time basis. Tom performed the same duties as the prior part-time employees (his quality of work was about the same). However, Rick paid Tom $25 per hour because Tom is a college student and Rick wanted to provide some additional support for Tom's education. At year-end, Tom had worked a total of 100 hours and received $2,500 from Rick. What amount can Rick deduct for the compensation he paid to his employees?

Answer: $23,000. Rick can deduct the $22,000 paid to part-time employees. However, he can only deduct $10 an hour for Tom's compensation because the extra $15 per hour Rick paid Tom is unreasonable in amount.[6] The remaining $15 per hour is considered a personal (nondeductible) gift from Rick to Tom. Hence, Rick can deduct a total of $23,000 for compensation expense this year [$22,000 + ($10 × 100)].

TAXES IN THE REAL WORLD What Qualifies as a "Business"?

Richard Bagley earned an MS in accounting from UCLA and was the chief financial manager for TRW's space and technology group. Bagley became aware of false claims made by TRW to the government and discussed these false claims with supervisors. Bagley was subsequently fired. Bagley retained attorneys to help him file a False Claims Act (FCA) suit against his employer.

Over a nine-year period, Bagley exclusively worked on his FCA prosecution activity. Bagley maintained a contemporaneous log of hours that showed he spent over 21,000 hours prosecuting the FCA suits. Besides numerous meetings, Bagley drafted and/or edited at least 73 documents in furtherance of the FCA litigation activity. According to Bagley, he was actively involved with the litigation because the lawyers "weren't accountants and . . . didn't have an in-depth understanding of TRW's accounting system."

Bagley considered himself to be in a trade or business as a "Private Attorney General," but Bagley never filed any business registration or

[5]§162(a) and *Comm. v. Lincoln Electric Co.* (CA-6, 1949), 176 F.2d 815.

[6]In practice, this distinction is rarely cut and dried. Rick may be able to argue for various reasons that Tom's work is worth more than $10 an hour but perhaps not as much as $25 per hour. We use this example to illustrate the issue of reasonable expenses and not to discuss the merits of what actually is reasonable compensation to Tom.

notice anywhere with a city or the state. Furthermore, Bagley did not advertise his business nor did he keep accounting books, but he ultimately received an award of $36,651,295. On his amended federal tax refund claim, Bagley reported the income as attributable to his "trade or business" and deducted $18,477,815 in attorney's fees as ordinary and necessary business expenses. The IRS denied Bagley's refund claim.

The District Court, however, rejected the government's claim that a one-time pursuit of an FCA claim with a large payout was not indicative of a for-profit business. The court held that Bagley's litigation activities, and the regular, continuous way he undertook them, combined with skill and a good-faith effort to make a profit, indicated a trade or business. Further, the individual's litigation expenses were ordinary and necessary expenses paid in relation to his trade or business of prosecuting the FCA lawsuits. Without hiring the attorneys, the individual could not have engaged in his business.

Source: Richard D. Bagley v. U.S. (DC CA), 2013-2 U.S.T.C. 50,462.

LIMITATIONS ON BUSINESS DEDUCTIONS

LO 9-2

For a variety of reasons, Congress specifically prohibits or limits a business's ability to deduct certain expenditures that appear to otherwise meet the general business expense deductibility requirements.

THE KEY FACTS

Limitations on Business Deductions

- No business deductions are allowable for expenditures against public policy (bribes) or political contributions.
- Expenditures that benefit a period longer than 12 months generally must be capitalized.
- No deductions are allowable for expenditures associated with the production of tax-exempt income.
- Personal expenditures are not deductible.

Expenditures against Public Policy

Businesses occasionally incur fines and penalties and may even pay illegal bribes and kickbacks. However, these payments are not deductible for tax purposes.[7] Congress disallows these expenditures under the rationale that allowing them would subsidize illegal activities and frustrate public policy. Interestingly enough, businesses conducting illegal activities (selling stolen goods or conducting illegal gambling activities) are allowed to deduct their cost of goods sold and their ordinary and necessary business expenses in conducting the business activities (note, however, that they are not allowed to deduct fines, penalties, illegal bribes, or illegal kickbacks).[8] Of course, the IRS is probably more concerned that many illegal businesses fail to report *any* income than that illegal businesses overstate deductions.[9]

Political Contributions and Lobbying Costs

Perhaps to avoid the perception that the federal government subsidizes taxpayer efforts to influence politics, the tax laws disallow deductions for political contributions and most lobbying expenses.[10] An exception exists to the prohibition of lobbying expenses. Under §162(e), deductions are allowed for reasonable costs incurred in conjunction with the submission of statements to a local council with respect to proposed legislation of direct interest to the taxpayer.

[7]§162(c) and Reg. §1.162-21. This prohibition applies to fines and penalties imposed by a government or governmental unit. Fines and penalties imposed by other organizations, such as a NASCAR fine, would be fully deductible if the payment otherwise qualified as an ordinary and necessary business expense.

[8]*Comm. v. Sullivan* (1958), 356 US 27.

[9]§280E explicitly prohibits drug dealers from deducting any business expenses associated with this "business" activity. However, drug dealers are able to deduct cost of goods sold because cost of goods sold is technically a reduction in gross income and not a business expense. See Reg. §1.61-3(a).

[10]§162(e).

Example 9-3

In July, the city fined Rick $200 for violating the city's watering ban when he watered a newly installed landscape. Later, Rick donated $250 to the mayor's campaign for reelection. Can Rick deduct these expenditures?

Answer: No. Rick cannot deduct either the fine or the political contribution as a business expense because the tax laws specifically prohibit deductions for these expenditures.

What if: Suppose that Rick had paid $250 for an economist to help Rick prepare a presentation to the city council on a proposed ordinance restricting water usage. Rick's presentation demonstrated to the council how the ordinance on water restrictions could affect area landscapers.

Answer: It is likely that this expenditure would qualify for deduction as a business expense under the exception in §162(e)(2).

Capital Expenditures

Whether a business uses the cash or the accrual method of accounting, it must capitalize expenditures for *tangible* assets such as buildings, machinery and equipment, furniture and fixtures, and similar property that have useful lives of more than one year (12 months).[11] For tax purposes, businesses recover the cost of capitalized tangible assets (other than land) through depreciation.

Businesses also capitalize the cost to create or acquire *intangible* assets such as patents, goodwill, start-up costs, and organizational expenditures.[12] They recover the costs of capitalized intangible assets either through amortization (when the tax laws allow them to do so) or upon disposition of the assets. Prepaid expenses are also subject to capitalization, but there is a special exception that we discuss under accounting methods later in this chapter.[13]

Expenses Associated with the Production of Tax-Exempt Income

Expenses that do not help businesses generate *taxable* income are not allowed to offset taxable income. For example, this restriction disallows interest expense deductions for businesses that borrow money and invest the loan proceeds in municipal (tax-exempt) bonds. It also disallows deductions for life insurance premiums businesses pay on policies that cover the lives of officers or other key employees and compensate the business for the disruption and lost income they may experience due to a key employee's death. Because the death benefit from the life insurance policy is not taxable, the business is not allowed to deduct the insurance premium expense associated with this nontaxable income.

Example 9-4

Rick employs Joan, an arborist who specializes in trimming trees and treating local tree ailments. Joan generates a great deal of revenue for Rick's business, but is in her mid-60s and suffers from diabetes. In November, Rick purchased a "key-employee" term-life insurance policy on Joan's life. The policy cost Rick $720 and will pay Rick (Green Acres) a $20,000 death benefit if Joan passes away during the next 12 months. What amount of life insurance policy premium can Rick deduct?

Answer: $0. Rick cannot deduct the $720 premium on the life insurance policy because the life insurance proceeds from the policy are tax-exempt.

[11]Reg. §1.263(a)-2(d)(4). The act of recording the asset is sometimes referred to as *capitalizing* the expenditure.

[12]Reg. §1.263(a)-4(b). The extent to which expenditures for intangible assets must be capitalized is explored in *Indopco v. Comm.* (1992), 503 US 79.

[13]See §195, §197, and §248 for provisions that allow taxpayers to amortize the cost of certain intangible assets.

What if: Suppose Rick purchased the life insurance policy on Joan's life and allowed Joan to name the beneficiary. The policy cost Rick $720 and will pay the beneficiary a $20,000 death benefit if Joan passes away during the next 12 months. What amount of life insurance policy premium can Rick deduct?

Answer: $720. In this scenario, Rick can deduct the entire premium of $720 as a *compensation* expense because the benefit of the policy inures to Joan and not to Rick's business.

Personal Expenditures

Taxpayers are not allowed to deduct **personal expenses** unless the expenses are "expressly" authorized by a provision in the law.[14] While the tax laws do not define personal expenses, they imply the scope of personal expenses by stating that "personal, living, or family expenses" are not deductible. Therefore, at a minimum, the costs of food, clothing, and shelter are assumed to be personal and nondeductible. Of course, there are the inevitable exceptions when otherwise personal items are specially adapted to business use. For example, taxpayers may deduct the cost of uniforms or special clothing they purchase for use in their business, if the clothing is not appropriate to wear as ordinary clothing outside the place of business. When the clothing is adaptable as ordinary clothing, the cost of the clothing is a nondeductible personal expenditure.[15]

Example 9-5

Rick spent $500 to purchase special coveralls that identify his landscaping service and provide a professional appearance. How much of the cost for the clothing can Rick deduct as a business expense?

Answer: All $500. While the cost of clothing is inherently personal, Rick can deduct the $500 cost of the coveralls because, due to the design and labeling on the coveralls, they are not suitable for ordinary use.

Many business owners, particularly small business owners such as sole proprietors, may be in a position to use business funds to pay for items that are entirely personal in nature. For example, a sole proprietor could use the business checking account to pay for family groceries. These expenditures, even though funded by the business, are not deductible.

Expenditures made by a taxpayer for education, such as tuition and books, are often related to a taxpayer's business aspirations. However, educational expenditures are not deductible as business expenses unless the education: (1) maintains or improves skills required by the individual in his employment or other trade or business, or (2) meets the express requirements of the individual's employer, or the requirements of applicable law or regulations, imposed as a condition to the retention by the individual of an established employment relationship, status, or rate of compensation. Education necessary to meet minimum requirements for an occupation are not deductible. For example, tuition payments for courses to satisfy the education requirement to sit for the CPA exam are not deductible. This is an example of education that qualifies the taxpayer for a new trade or business rather than improving his skills in an existing trade or business.

[14]§262(a).

[15]An employee who purchases clothing for work would go through a similar analysis to determine if the cost of the clothing qualifies as an employee business expense.

THE KEY FACTS

Mixed-Motive Expenditures

- Special limits are imposed on expenditures that have both personal and business benefits.
- Only 50 percent of business meals and entertainment are deductible.
- Contemporaneous written records of business purpose are required.

Mixed-Motive Expenditures

Business owners in general, and owners of small or closely held businesses in particular, often make expenditures that are motivated by *both* business and personal concerns. These **mixed-motive expenditures** are of particular concern to lawmakers and the IRS because of the tax incentive to disguise nondeductible personal expenses as deductible business expenses. Thus, deductions for business expenditures with potential personal motives are closely monitored and restricted. The rules for determining the amount of *deductible* mixed-motive expenditures depend on the type of the expenditure. Here we review the rules for determining the deductible portion of mixed-motive expenditures for meals and entertainment, travel and transportation, and the use of property for both business and personal purposes.

Meals and Entertainment Because everyone needs to eat, even business meals contain a significant personal element. To allow for this personal element, taxpayers may only deduct 50 percent of actual business meals. In addition, to deduct any portion of the cost of a meal as a business expense, (1) the amount must be reasonable under the circumstances, (2) the taxpayer (or an employee) must be present when the meal is furnished, and (3) the meal must be directly associated with the active conduct of the taxpayer's business.

Similar to business meals, entertainment associated with business activities contains a significant element of enjoyment. Hence, only 50 percent of allowable business entertainment may be deducted as a business expense.[16] Further, entertainment deductions are allowable only if (1) "business associates" are entertained, (2) the amounts paid are reasonable in amount, and (3) the entertainment is either "directly related" or "associated with" the active conduct of business.

Business associates are individuals with whom the taxpayer reasonably expects to do business, such as customers, suppliers, employees, or advisors. Entertainment is directly related to business if there is an active discussion aimed at generating revenue or fees or the discussion occurs in a clear business setting (such as a hospitality room). The cost of entertainment that occurs in a setting with little possibility of conducting a business discussion, such as a theater or sports venue, will only be deductible if the entertainment directly precedes or follows a substantial business discussion, thereby satisfying the "associated with" test. In addition, to deduct the cost of meals and entertainment, taxpayers generally must meet strict record-keeping requirements we discuss below.[17]

Example 9-6

Rick went out to dinner with a prospective client to discuss Rick's ideas for landscaping the homeowner's yard. After dinner, Rick and the prospective client attended the theater. Rick paid $190 for the meal and $350 for the tickets, amounts that were reasonable under the circumstances. What amount of these expenditures can Rick deduct as a business expense?

Answer: Rick can deduct $270 [($190 + $350) × 50%], representing half the cost of the meal and entertainment, as a business expense, as long as Rick can substantiate the business purpose and substantial nature of the dinner discussion.

[16]§274 also provides some exceptions to the 50 percent reduction for meals and entertainment, such as meals and entertainment provided for special events or as employee compensation. Taxpayers can also use a *per diem* rate (an automatic, flat amount per meal) in lieu of actual expenditures to determine the amount of the deduction. There are special limits placed on entertainment expenses associated with spouses.

[17]Under §274, there are special limits placed on certain entertainment expenditures, such as those related to spouses, club dues and entertainment facilities, skyboxes, and entertainment associated with corporate officers, directors, and large shareholders.

What if: Suppose that Rick did not discuss business with the client either before, during, or after the meal. What amount of the expenditures can Rick deduct as a business expense?

Answer: $0. In this scenario, Rick cannot deduct the costs of the meal or entertainment because the activity was not directly related to or associated with a substantial business discussion.

Travel and Transportation Under certain conditions, sole proprietors and self-employed taxpayers may deduct the cost of travel and transportation for business purposes. Transportation expenses include the direct cost of transporting the taxpayer to and from business sites. However, the cost of commuting between the taxpayer's home and regular place of business is personal and, therefore, not deductible. If the taxpayer uses a vehicle for business, the taxpayer can deduct the costs of operating the vehicle plus depreciation on the vehicle's tax basis. Alternatively, in lieu of deducting these costs, the taxpayer may simply deduct a standard amount for each business mile driven. The standard mileage rate represents the per-mile cost of operating an automobile (including depreciation or lease payments).[18] For 2015 the standard mileage rate has been set at 57.5 cents per mile. To be deductible, the transportation must be for business reasons. If the transportation is primarily for personal purposes, the cost is not deductible.

Example 9-7

Rick leases an SUV to drive between his shop and various work sites. Rick carefully documents the business use of the SUV (8,100 miles this year) and his $5,335 of operating expenses ($3,935 for gas, oil, and repairs and $1,400 for lease payments). At no time does Rick use the SUV for personal purposes. What amount of these expenses may Rick deduct as business expenses?

Answer: $5,335. Since Rick uses the SUV in his business activities, he can deduct (1) the $5,335 cost of operating and leasing the SUV or (2) $4,658 for the 8,100 business miles he drove (57.5 cents per mile × 8,100 miles). Assuming Rick chooses to deduct operating expenses and lease payments in lieu of using the mileage rate, he can deduct $5,335.

In contrast to transportation expenses, travel expenses are only deductible if the taxpayer is *away from home* overnight while traveling. This distinction is important because, besides the cost of transportation, the deduction for **travel expenses** includes meals (50 percent), lodging, and incidental expenses. A taxpayer is considered to be away from home overnight if the travel is away from the primary place of business and of sufficient duration to require sleep or rest (typically this will be overnight). When a taxpayer travels solely for business purposes, *all* of the costs of travel are deductible (but only 50 percent of meals). When the travel has both business and personal aspects, the deductibility of the transportation costs depends upon whether business is the *primary* purpose for the trip. If the primary purpose of a trip is business, the transportation costs are fully deductible, but meals (50 percent), lodging, and incidental expenditures are limited to those incurred during the business portion of the travel.[19] If the taxpayer's primary purpose for the trip is personal, the taxpayer may not deduct *any* transportation costs to arrive at the location but may deduct meals (50 percent), lodging, transportation, and incidental expenditures for the *business* portion of the trip. The primary purpose of a trip depends upon facts and circumstances and is often the subject of dispute.

[18]This mileage rate is updated periodically (sometimes two or three times within a year) to reflect changes in the cost of operating a vehicle. The mileage option is only available for vehicles not previously depreciated, vehicles previously depreciated on the straight-line method, or for leased vehicles where this method has been used throughout the term of the lease.

[19]Special limitations apply to a number of travel expenses that are potentially abusive, such as luxury water travel, foreign conventions, conventions on cruise ships, and travel expenses associated with taking a companion.

The rule for business travel is modified somewhat if a trip abroad includes both business and personal activities. Like the rule for domestic travel, if foreign travel is primarily for personal purposes, then only those expenses directly associated with business activities are deductible. However, unlike the rule for domestic travel, when foreign travel is primarily for business purposes, a portion of the roundtrip transportation costs is not deductible. The nondeductible portion is typically computed based on a time ratio such as the proportion of personal days to total days (travel days count as business days).[20]

Example 9-8

Rick paid a $300 registration fee for a three-day course in landscape design. The course was held in New York (Rick paid $700 for airfare to attend) and he spent four days in New York. He spent the last day sightseeing. During the trip, Rick paid $150 a night for three nights' lodging, $50 a day for meals, and $70 a day for a rental car. What amount of these travel-related expenditures may Rick deduct as business expenses?

Answer: $1,435 for business travel and $300 for business education. The primary purpose for the trip appears to be business because Rick spent three days on business activities versus one personal day. He can deduct travel costs, computed as follows:

Deductible Travel Costs

Description	Amount	Explanation
Airfare to New York	$ 700	Primary purpose is business.
Lodging in New York	450	3 business days × $150 a day.
Meals	75	3 business days × $50 a day × 50% limit.
Rental car	210	3 business days × $70 a day.
Total business travel expenses	$1,435	

What if: Assume Rick stayed in New York for ten days, spending three days at the seminar and seven days sightseeing. What amount could he deduct?

Answer: In this scenario Rick can deduct $735 for business travel and $300 for business education. Rick would not be able to deduct the $700 cost of airfare because the trip is primarily personal, as evidenced by the seven days of personal activities compared to only three days of business activities.

Deductible Travel Costs

Description	Amount	Explanation
Airfare to New York	$ 0	Primary purpose is personal.
Lodging in New York	450	3 business days × $150 a day.
Meals	75	3 business days × $50 a day × 50% limit.
Rental car	210	3 business days × $70 a day.
Total business travel expenses	$735	

What if: Assume the original facts in the example except Rick traveled to London (rather than New York) for ten days spending six days at the seminar and four days sightseeing. What amount could he deduct?

Answer: In this scenario Rick can deduct $1,890 for travel (computed below) and $300 for business education.

[20]Foreign transportation expense is deductible without prorating under special circumstances authorized in §274(c). For example, the cost of getting abroad is fully deductible if the travel is for one week or less or if the personal activity constitutes less than one-fourth of the travel time.

Deductible Travel Costs

Description	Amount	Explanation
Airfare to London	$ 420	6 business days/10 total days × $700.
Lodging in London	900	6 business days × $150 a day.
Meals	150	6 business days × $50 a day × 50% limit.
Rental car	420	6 business days × $70 a day.
Total business travel expenses	$1,890	

Rick is allowed to deduct $420 of the $700 airfare (60 percent) because he spent 6 of the 10 days on the trip conducting business activities.

Property Use Several types of property may be used for both business and personal purposes. For example, business owners often use automobiles, computers, or cell phones for both business and personal purposes.[21] However, because expenses relating to these assets are deductible only to the extent the assets are used for business purposes, taxpayers must allocate the expenses between the business and personal use portions. The calculation of depreciation on mixed-use assets is discussed in the next chapter and with specific topics, such as the office in the home deduction.

Example 9-9

Rick occasionally uses his personal auto (a BMW) to drive to interviews with prospective clients and to drive back and forth between his shop and various work sites. This year Rick carefully recorded that the BMW was driven 532 miles for business activities and 10,500 miles in total. What expenses associated with the BMW may Rick deduct?

Answer: $306. Based on the standard mileage rate of 57.5 cents per mile, Rick can deduct $306 (532 × 57.5 cents) for business use of his BMW. Alternatively, Rick can track the operating expenses of the BMW (including depreciation) and deduct the business portion [based upon the percentage of business miles driven to total miles driven (532 business miles/10,500 total miles)].

When taxpayers use other business assets for both business and personal purposes, the deductible business expense is determined by prorating the expenses based upon the percentage of the time the asset is used for business purposes. For example, if a full year's expense for a business asset is $1,000, but the asset is only used for business purposes 90 percent of the time, then only $900 of expense can be deducted ($1,000 × 90%). Special rules apply when the business usage for an asset drops below 50 percent. We discuss these issues in the next chapter.

Record Keeping and Other Requirements Because distinguishing business purposes from personal purposes is a difficult and subjective task, the tax laws include provisions designed to help the courts and the IRS determine the business element of mixed-motive transactions. Under these provisions, taxpayers must maintain specific, written, contemporaneous records (of time, amount, and business purpose) for mixed-motive expenses. For example, as we discussed above, the tax laws prohibit any deductions for business meals and entertainment unless substantial business discussions accompany the entertainment activity. Consequently, when taxpayers incur

[21]These types of assets are referred to as "listed property." Note that cell phones are specifically exempted from the definition of listed property (§280F(d)(4)(A), as amended by the 2010 Small Business Act §2043(a)).

meals and entertainment expenses, they must document the business purpose and the extent of the discussion to deduct any of the expenditures.[22]

LO 9-3

SPECIFIC BUSINESS DEDUCTIONS

As we discussed above, the tax code provides general guidelines for determining whether business expenditures are deductible. We learned that to be deductible, business expenditures must be ordinary, necessary, and reasonable in amount. In some cases, however, the tax laws identify specific items businesses are allowed to deduct. We discuss several of these deductions below.

THE KEY FACTS

Domestic Production Activities Deduction

- A subsidy for the cost of producing goods or certain construction services within the United States.
- 9 percent of qualified production activity income.
- Limited to overall income (AGI for individuals) and 50 percent of wages associated with the production.

Domestic Production Activities Deduction

Businesses that manufacture goods are allowed to deduct an *artificial* business deduction for tax purposes called the U.S. **domestic production activities deduction (DPAD).** This deduction is designed to reduce the tax burden on domestic manufacturers to make investments in domestic manufacturing facilities more attractive. The DPAD provides a special tax deduction for businesses, large and small, that "manufacture, produce, grow or extract" tangible products entirely or in significant part within the United States.[23] This deduction is artificial because it does not represent an expenditure per se, but merely serves to reduce the income taxes the business must pay and thereby increase the after-tax profitability of domestic manufacturing.

The formula for computing the DPAD is 9 percent times the *lesser* of (1) the business's taxable income before the deduction (or modified AGI for individuals) or (2) **qualified production activities income (QPAI).**[24] Generally speaking, QPAI is the *net* income from selling or leasing property that was manufactured in the United States. Thus, to compute QPAI, businesses need to determine the amount of revenues, cost of goods sold, and expenses attributable to U.S. production activities. Obviously, the calculation of the income allocable to domestic production can be exceedingly complex, especially in the case of large multinational businesses. The final deduction cannot exceed 50 percent of the wages the business paid to employees for working in qualifying production activities during the year.[25]

Example 9-10

This fall Rick constructed a greenhouse that qualified for the domestic production activities deduction. Rick received $5,000 for the construction project from his client and allocated $4,000 in expenses to the project. These expenses included $2,000 of qualified wages. Thus, the greenhouse project generated $1,000 of qualified production activity income (QPAI) for Rick ($5,000 minus $4,000). What is Rick's domestic production activities deduction for this project?

Answer: $90. Assuming Rick's QPAI of $1,000 is less than his modified AGI, the DPAD is $90, calculated by multiplying 9 percent times $1,000 of QPAI. The entire computation is summarized as follows:

[22]§274 requires substantiation of all elements of travel and entertainment including sufficient corroborating evidence. Although there are a few exceptions to this rule, approximations and estimates are generally not sufficient. Also, taxpayers must maintain records to deduct the business portion of mixed-use assets such as cars used for both business and personal purposes. Note that when the taxpayer is unable to substantiate other deductions, the court may estimate the deductible amount under the Cohan rule (*George Cohan v. Com.*, (1930, CA2), 39 F2d 540).

[23]§199 also allows this deduction for qualifying taxpayers in the domestic film and sound recording industries, those engaged in a construction business in the United States, and engineering and architectural firms providing services for U.S. construction projects. Because the domestic production activities deduction does not represent a real expenditure, the deduction is not an expense for financial accounting purposes.

[24]See §199(d)(2). Modified AGI is AGI before the DPAD and certain other specified deductions.

[25]Taxpayers report the deduction computations on Form 8903.

DPAD Calculation

Description	Amount	Explanation
Qualified domestic gross receipts	$5,000	Must be a qualified activity.
Allocable costs and expenses	−4,000	Allocate to qualified activity.
Qualified production activity income	$1,000	Limited to modified AGI.
Statutory percentage	× 9%	
Domestic production activities deduction	$ 90	Limited to 50% of wages.

The 50 percent wage limitation is $1,000 (50% × $2,000 in wages Rick paid to employees working on the project). Thus, Rick is allowed to deduct the entire $90 domestic production activities deduction even though the $90 deduction doesn't represent a specific liability or payment to anyone.

TAXES IN THE REAL WORLD Decorative Packaging as a Manufacturing Process

Houdini, Inc., designs, assembles, and sells gift baskets and gift "towers" (stacked decorative boxes of food). Houdini has two facilities and maintains about 300 employees and additional temporary workers during the holidays. Houdini selects gift baskets and the items to be placed inside, such as candy or wine, as well as the "void fill" that holds everything together. Houdini's Packaging Department takes food items that are in small, food-safe containers and places them in other packaging, such as a small, colorful box.

Houdini claimed the domestic production activities deduction contending that designing a gift basket is a complicated process that involves steps like determining appropriate container sizes and colors, selecting materials, ensuring quality control, and reviewing packaging. The IRS filed to recover the taxes relating to the DPAD deductions asserting that Houdini merely packaged the items in its gift baskets and towers. To qualify for the deduction, the gift baskets must be items that are "manufactured, produced, grown, or extracted" (MPGE). The regulations hold that "packaging, repackaging, labeling, or minor assembly" doesn't qualify as MPGE but only if the taxpayer engages in no other MPGE activity.

The court determined that Houdini's production qualifies as manufacturing or producing, but also qualifies as packaging or repackaging. To reconcile this contradiction, the court found that Houdini's production process changes "the form of an article" under the regulations. Houdini uses assembly line workers and machines and ultimately produces a final product (i.e., a gift) that is distinct in form and purpose from the individual items inside (i.e., grocery-type items). The court rejected the IRS's argument that Houdini's packaging and repackaging are mere services. The court held that, rather than merely enhancing an existing product, Houdini creates a new product with a different demand.

U.S. v. Dean (DC CA), 112 AFTR 2d 2013-5164.

Losses on Dispositions of Business Property

Besides operating expenses, businesses are generally allowed to deduct losses incurred when selling or disposing of business assets.[26] The calculation of losses from business property dispositions can be complex, but the main idea is that businesses realize and recognize a loss when the asset's tax basis exceeds the sale proceeds. We will discuss the rules governing the tax treatment of gains and losses on asset disposition in more detail in Chapter 11.

[26]In most circumstances businesses may *not* deduct losses on assets sold to related parties. We describe who qualifies as a related party later in this chapter.

Example 9-11

What if: Assume that in late October, Rick purchased a used trailer to transport equipment to work sites. Rick bought the trailer for what he thought was a bargain price of $1,000. However, shortly after Rick acquired it , the axle snapped and was not repairable. Rick was forced to sell the trailer to a parts shop for $325. What amount can Rick deduct as a loss from the trailer sale?

Answer: $675, because the trailer was a business asset (amount realized of $325 minus adjusted basis of $1,000). (Note, as we discuss in the next chapter, Rick is not allowed to deduct depreciation on the trailer because he disposed of it in the same year he acquired it.)

Business Casualty Losses

Besides selling assets, businesses can incur losses when their assets are stolen, damaged, or completely destroyed by a force outside the control of the business. These events are called casualties.[27] Businesses may deduct **casualty losses** in the year the casualty occurs or in the year the theft of an asset is discovered. The amount of the loss deduction depends on whether the asset is (1) completely destroyed or stolen or (2) only partially destroyed. When its asset is *completely* destroyed or stolen, the business calculates the amount of the loss as though it sold the asset for the insurance proceeds, if any. That is, the loss is the amount of insurance proceeds minus the adjusted tax basis of the asset. If the asset is damaged but not completely destroyed, the amount of the loss is the amount of the insurance proceeds minus the *lesser* of (1) the asset's tax basis or (2) the decline in the value of the asset due to the casualty. While individuals deduct business casualty losses and casualty losses associated with rentals and royalties as deductions *for* AGI, casualty and theft losses of assets used for the production of income (investments) and personal-use assets are generally deductible as itemized deductions.[28] We summarize the casualty and theft loss rules for business, production of income, and personal-use assets in Exhibit 9-2, which appears on the following page.

Example 9-12

What if: Suppose Rick acquired a personal-use asset several years ago for $9,000. Suppose further that a casualty event destroyed the asset, and at that time the asset was worth $1,000 and insured for $250. What is the amount of Rick's casualty loss (before applying the per casualty floor and the AGI restriction)?

Answer: $750, computed as follows:

Insurance proceeds		$250
Minus the *lesser* of:		
(1) adjusted tax basis or	$9,000	
(2) value at time of casualty	1,000	−1,000
Casualty loss deduction (before limitations)		($750)

Suppose instead that Rick's asset was a business-use asset and Rick had deducted $4,000 of depreciation expense against the asset. Hence, the asset's tax basis was $5,000 ($9,000 − $4,000). What would be the amount of his business casualty loss?

Answer: $4,750, computed as follows:

Insurance proceeds	$ 250
Minus adjusted tax basis	−5,000
Casualty loss deduction	($4,750)

[27]Casualties are unexpected events driven by forces outside the control of the taxpayer that damage or destroy a taxpayer's property. Section 165 lists "fire, storm, and shipwreck" as examples of casualties.

[28]For example, a taxpayer with a coin collection that is stolen or valuable antique collection that burns is potentially eligible for a casualty loss deduction on assets used for the production of income. Under §165(h)(5), personal casualty losses are allowed to offset personal casualty gains in computing AGI.

EXHIBIT 9-2 Comparison of Casualty and Theft Loss Rules for Property Used in Business, for Production of Income, and for Personal Purposes

	Property Used in Business (including losses from rental and royalty property)	Property Used for the Production of Income	Property Used for Personal Purposes
Amount of loss if property completely destroyed or stolen	Insurance proceeds minus adjusted basis	Same as business	Insurance proceeds minus lesser of (1) adjusted basis or (2) decline in asset's value due to casualty or theft.
Amount of loss if property is not completely destroyed	Insurance proceeds minus lesser of (1) adjusted basis or (2) decline in asset's value	Same as business	Same as business
Loss limitation	None	None	A per casualty floor limitation and 10 percent of AGI floor for total casualty losses for year.
Type of deduction	For AGI	Miscellaneous itemized deduction (not subject to 2 percent floor)	Itemized deduction

ACCOUNTING PERIODS

LO 9-4

So far we've discussed how to determine a business's income and how to determine its deductible business expenses. In this section, we will discuss accounting periods, which affect when taxpayers determine their income and deductions. Businesses must report their income and deductions over a fixed **accounting period** or **tax year.** A full tax year consists of 12 full months. A tax year can consist of a period less than 12 months (a short tax year) in certain circumstances. For instance, a business may report income for such a short year in its first year of existence (for example, it reports income on a calendar year-end and starts business after January 1) or in its final year of existence (for example, a calendar-year business ends its business before December 31). Short tax years in a business's initial or final year are treated the same as full years. A business may also have a short year when it changes its tax year, and this can occur when the business is acquired by new owners. In these situations, special rules may apply for computing the tax liability of the business.[29]

There are three types of tax years, each with different year-ends:

1. A calendar year ends on December 31.
2. A **fiscal year** ends on the last day of a month other than December.
3. A 52/53 week-year ends on the same day of the week every year. In other words, a 52/53 week-year could end on the same day of the week that is the last such day in the month or on the same day of the week nearest the end of the month. For example, a business could adopt a 52/53-week fiscal year that (1) ends on the last Saturday in July each year or (2) ends on the Saturday closest to the end of July (although this Saturday might be in August rather than July).[30]

[29]§443. Discussion of tax consequences associated with these short years is beyond the scope of this text.

[30]Businesses with inventories may benefit from 52/53 year-ends to facilitate an inventory count when the store is closed (e.g., over a weekend).

THE KEY FACTS

Accounting Periods

- Individuals and proprietorships account for income on a calendar year.
- Corporations are allowed to choose a fiscal year.
- Partnerships and other flow-through entities generally use a required year.

Not all types of tax years are available to all types of businesses. The rules for determining the tax years available to the business depends on whether the business is a sole proprietorship, a **flow-through entity,** or a C corporation. These rules are summarized as follows:

- *Sole proprietorships:* Because individual proprietors must report their business income on their individual returns, proprietorships use a calendar year-end to report their business income.[31]
- *Flow-through entities:* Partnerships and S corporations are flow-through entities (partners and S corporation owners report the entity's income directly on their own tax returns), and these entities generally must adopt tax years consistent with the owners' tax years.[32] Because owners are allocated income from flow-through entities on the last day of the entity's taxable year, the tax laws impose the tax year consistency requirement to minimize income tax deferral opportunities for the owners.
- *C corporations:* C corporations are generally allowed to select a calendar, fiscal, or 52/53-week year-end.

A business adopts a calendar year-end or fiscal year-end by filing its initial tax return. In contrast, a business adopts a 52/53-week year-end by filing a special election with the IRS. Once a business establishes its tax year, it generally must receive permission from the IRS to change.

Example 9-13

Rick is a calendar-year taxpayer. What tax year must Rick use to report income from his business Green Acres?

Answer: Calendar year. This is true even though Rick began his business in May of this year. He will calculate income and expense for his landscaping business over the calendar year and include the net business income from May through December of this year on Schedule C of his individual tax return.

What if: Suppose that Rick incorporated Green Acres at the time he began his business. What tax year could Green Acres adopt?

Answer: If Green Acres was operated as a C corporation, it could elect a calendar year-end, a fiscal year-end, or a 52/53-week year-end. If it were an S corporation, it likely would use a calendar year-end.

LO 9-5 ACCOUNTING METHODS

Once a business adopts a tax year, it must determine which items of income and deduction to recognize during a particular year. Generally speaking, the taxpayer's **accounting methods** determine the tax year in which a business recognizes a particular item of income or deduction. Because accounting methods affect the *timing* of when a taxpayer reports income and deductions, these methods are very important for taxpayers using a timing tax strategy to defer income or accelerate deductions.[33]

[31]Virtually all individual taxpayers use a calendar-year tax year.

[32]See §706 for the specific restrictions on year-ends for partnerships and §1378 for restrictions on S corporations. If they can show a business purpose (not easy to do), both partnerships and S corporations may adopt year-ends other than those used by their owners.

[33]Accounting methods do not determine *whether* an item of income is taxable or an expense is deductible. Accordingly, accounting methods generally do not affect the total income or deductions recognized over the lifetime of the business.

Financial and Tax Accounting Methods

Many businesses are required to generate financial statements for nontax reasons. For example, publicly traded corporations must file financial statements with the Securities and Exchange Commission (SEC) based on generally accepted accounting principles (GAAP). Also, privately owned businesses borrowing money from banks are often required to generate financial statements under GAAP, so that the lender can evaluate the business's creditworthiness. In reporting financial statement income, businesses have incentives to select accounting methods permissible under GAAP that accelerate income and defer deductions. In contrast, for tax planning purposes, businesses have incentives to choose accounting methods that *defer income* and *accelerate deductions*. This natural tension between financial reporting incentives and tax reporting incentives may be the reason the tax laws sometimes require businesses to use the same accounting methods for tax purposes that they use for financial accounting purposes. In other words, in many circumstances, if businesses want to defer taxable income, they must also defer book income.[34]

Sometimes the tax laws require businesses to use different, presumably more appropriate, accounting methods for tax purposes. Consequently, for policy and administrative reasons, the tax laws also identify several circumstances when businesses must use specific tax accounting methods to determine taxable income no matter what accounting method they use for financial reporting purposes. We will now turn our attention to accounting methods prescribed by the tax laws. With certain restrictions, businesses are able to select their *overall* accounting methods and accounting methods for *specific* items or transactions. We will cover each of these in turn.

Overall Accounting Method

Businesses must choose an overall method of accounting to track and report their business activities for tax purposes. The overriding requirement for any tax accounting method is that the method must "clearly reflect income" and be applied consistently.[35] The two primary overall methods are the cash method and the accrual method. Businesses may also choose a hybrid method (some accounts on the cash method and others on the accrual method).

Cash Method A taxpayer (or business) using the cash method of accounting recognizes revenue when property or services are actually or constructively received. This is generally true no matter when the business sells the good or performs the service that generates the revenue. Likewise, a business adopting the cash method generally recognizes deductions when the expense is paid. Thus, the timing of the liability giving rise to the expense is usually irrelevant.

Keep in mind that a cash-method business receiving payments in *noncash* form (as property or services) must recognize the noncash payments as gross income. Also, in certain circumstances, a business expending cash on ordinary and necessary business expenses may not be allowed to *currently* deduct the expense at the time of the payment. For example, cash-method taxpayers (and accrual-method taxpayers) are not allowed to deduct prepaid interest expense and cannot usually deduct prepaid expenses or payments that create a tangible or intangible asset.[36] However, the regulations provide a **12-month rule** for prepaid business expenses to simplify the process of determining whether to capitalize or immediately expense payments that create benefits for a relatively brief period of time, such as insurance, security, rent, and

[34]§446(a). Businesses that use different accounting methods for book and tax must typically file a form M-1 that reconciles the results from the two accounting methods.

[35]§446(b).

[36]§461(g).

warranty service contracts. When a business prepays business expenses, it may *immediately* deduct the prepayment if (1) the contract period does not last more than a year *and* (2) the contract period does not extend beyond the end of the taxable year following the tax year in which the taxpayer makes the payment.[37] If the prepaid expense does not meet both of these criteria, the business must capitalize the prepaid amount and amortize it over the length of the contract whether the business uses the cash or accrual method of accounting.[38]

Example 9-14

On July 1 of this year, Rick paid $1,200 for a 12-month insurance policy that covers his business property from accidents and casualties from July 1 of this year, through June 30 of next year. How much of the $1,200 expenditure may Rick deduct this year if he uses the cash method of accounting for his business activities?

Answer: $1,200. Because the insurance coverage does not exceed 12 months and does not extend beyond the end of next year, Rick is allowed to deduct the entire premium payment under the 12-month rule.

What if: Suppose the insurance policy was for 12 months but the policy ran from February 1 of next year, through January 31 of the following year. How much of the expenditure may Rick deduct this year if he uses the cash method of accounting for his business activities?

Answer: $0. Even though the contract period is 12 months or less, Rick is required to capitalize the cost of the prepayment for the insurance policy because the contract period extends beyond the end of next year.

What if: Suppose Rick had paid $1,200 for an *18-month* policy beginning July 1 of this year, and ending December 31 of next year. How much may he deduct this year if he uses the cash method of accounting for his business activities?

Answer: $400. In this scenario, because the policy exceeds 12 months, Rick is allowed to deduct the portion of the premium pertaining to this year. Hence, this year, he would deduct $400 (6 months/18 months × $1,200). He would deduct the remaining $800 in the next year.

Accrual Method Businesses using the accrual method to determine taxable income follow rules similar to GAAP with two basic differences. First, as we discuss below, requirements for recognizing taxable income tend to be structured to recognize income earlier than the recognition rules for financial accounting. Second, requirements for accruing tax deductions tend to be structured to recognize less accrued expenses than the recognition rules for financial reporting purposes. These differences reflect the underlying objectives of financial accounting income and taxable income. The objective of financial accounting is to provide useful information to stakeholders such as creditors, prospective investors, and shareholders. Because financial accounting methods are designed to guard against businesses overstating their profitability to these users, financial accounting tends to bias against *overstating* income. In contrast, the government's main objective for writing tax laws is to collect revenues. Thus, tax accounting rules for accrual-method businesses tend to bias against *understating* income. These differences will become apparent as we describe tax accounting rules for businesses.

[37]This 12-month rule applies to both cash-method and accrual-method taxpayers. However, for accrual-method taxpayers to deduct prepaid expenses, they must meet both the 12-month rule requirements and the economic performance requirements that we discuss in the next section.

[38]Reg. §1.263(a)-4(f).

continued from page 9-1...
Rick's CPA, Jane, informed him that he needs to select an overall method of accounting for Green Acres to compute its taxable income. Jane advised Rick to use the cash method. However, Rick wanted to prepare GAAP financial statements and use the accrual method of accounting. He decided that if Green Acres was going to become a big business, it needed to act like a big business. Finally, after much discussion, Rick and Jane reached a compromise. For the first year, they would track Green Acres's business activities using both the cash *and* the accrual methods. In addition, they would also keep GAAP-based books for financial purposes. When filing time comes, Rick would decide which method to use in reporting taxable income. Jane told Rick that he could wait until he filed his tax return to select the accounting method for tax purposes. ■

Accrual Income

Businesses using the accrual method of accounting generally recognize income when they meet the all-events test.

All-Events Test for Income The all-events test requires that businesses recognize income when (1) all events have occurred that determine or fix their right to receive the income and (2) the amount of the income can be determined with reasonable accuracy.[39] Assuming the amount of income can be determined with reasonable accuracy, businesses meet the all-events requirement on the *earliest* of the following three dates:

1. When they complete the task required to earn the income. Businesses earn income for services as they provide the services, and they generally earn income from selling property when the title of the property passes to the buyer.
2. When the payment for the task is due from the customer.
3. When the business receives payment for the task.

Example 9-15

In early fall, Rick contracted with a dozen homeowners to landscape their yards. Rick agreed to do the work for an aggregate of $11,000. Rick and his crew started in the fall and completed the jobs in December of this year. However, he didn't mail the bills until after the holidays and didn't receive any payments until the following January. When must Rick recognize the income from this work?

Answer: Under the accrual method, Rick must recognize the entire $11,000 as income this year because his right to the income is fixed when Rick and his crew had completed the work by year-end. Under the cash method, however, Rick would not recognize the $11,000 as income until next year when he received it.

Taxation of Advance Payments of Income (Unearned Income)

In some cases, businesses receive income payments *before* they actually earn the income (they receive a prepayment). *When* the business must recognize a prepayment as income depends on the type of income. The rule for interest and rental income is

[39]Reg. §1.451-1(a). The all-events test is sometimes called the "fixed and determinable" test because the right to payment must be fixed and the amount determinable with reasonable accuracy.

THE KEY FACTS

Revenue Recognition Under the Accrual Method

- Income is recognized when earned (all-events) or received (if earlier).
- The all-events test requires that the business has the right to income.
- Taxpayers can generally elect to defer recognition of prepaid income for services (for one year) and goods.

relatively strict. Businesses must recognize unearned rental and unearned interest income *immediately* upon receipt (the income is recognized before it is earned). However, businesses are not required to recognize security deposits received from rental customers because they incur a liability to return the deposits when they receive the payments.[40] The income recognition rules are less strict when businesses receive advance payments for services or goods.

Unearned Service Revenue For financial reporting purposes, a business does not immediately recognize income on payments it receives for services to be provided in the future. For financial reporting purposes, an advance payment for services is recorded as a debit for cash received and a credit to a liability account (unearned income). The business then recognizes the *financial* income from the services as it performs the services. In contrast, for tax purposes, the all-events test generally requires businesses receiving *advance* payments for services to recognize the income when they receive the payment, rather than when they perform the services.

The IRS provides an exception to this immediate recognition general rule. Specifically, businesses receiving advance payments for services may *defer* recognizing the *prepayment* as income until the tax year *following* the year they receive the payment.[41] This one-year deferral does *not* apply (1) if (or the extent to which) the income is actually earned by the end of the year of receipt, (2) if the prepayment was included in financial reporting income, or (3) if the prepayment was for interest or rent (taxpayers must recognize unearned interest and rental income on receipt).

Advance Payment for Goods When an accrual-method business receives an advance payment for *goods* it will provide to customers in the future, the business may account for the prepayment for tax purposes under the **full-inclusion method** or the **deferral method.**[42] A business electing the full-inclusion method will *immediately* recognize an advance payment as income. In contrast, a business using the deferral method will recognize advance payments for goods by the earlier of (1) when the business would recognize the income for tax purposes if it had not received the *advance* payment or (2) when it recognizes the income for financial reporting purposes. Thus, the deferral method is comparable to the deferral allowed for advance payments received for future services. However, unlike the treatment of advance payments for services, advance payments for goods could be deferred for more than a year if the business defers the income for financial reporting purposes for more than a year.

Example 9-16

In late November 2015, Rick received a $7,200 payment from a client for monthly landscaping services from December 1, 2015, through November 30, 2017 ($300 a month for 24 months). When must Rick recognize the income from the advance payment for services?

Answer: Under the accrual method, Rick would initially recognize the $300 income he earned in December 2015. In 2016, he would recognize the remaining $6,900 (rather than only the $3,600

[40]*Comm. v. Indianapolis Power & Light Co.* (1990), 493 US 203. Customer deposits required by a public utility weren't taxable income because the right to keep the deposits depended on events outside of the taxpayer's control, such as the decision to have the deposit applied to future bills.

[41]Rev Proc. 2004-34, 2004-1 CB 991.

[42]Reg. §1.451-5. This exception does not apply to goods held for sale in the ordinary course of business (inventory).

related to 2016) because he is not allowed to defer the prepayments for services for more than a year. Under the cash method, Rick must recognize the entire prepayment, $7,200, as income upon receipt in 2015.

What if: Suppose the $7,200 prepayment was for the delivery of 15 pallets of sod (not inventory) at a cost to Rick of $1,800. Suppose further that five pallets were to be delivered in 2016 and the remainder was to be delivered in 2017. When would Rick recognize the income from the advance payment of goods under the accrual method?

Answer: If Rick elected the full-inclusion method, then he would recognize the entire prepayment of $7,200 as income (minus his cost of goods sold of $1,800) in 2015. However, if Rick elected the deferral method, then he would recognize the income as the sod is delivered, $2,400 in 2016 (minus $600 cost of goods sold) and $4,800 in 2017 (minus $1,200 cost of goods sold).

Inventories

THE KEY FACTS

Inventories

- Businesses must use the accrual method to account for substantial inventories.
- The UNICAP rules require capitalization of most indirect costs of production.
- The LIFO method is allowed if also used for financial reporting purposes.

Many businesses generate income by selling products they acquire for resale or products they manufacture. When selling inventory is a material income-producing factor, a business generally must account for gross profit (sales minus cost of goods sold) using the accrual method, even if they are a cash-method taxpayer.

An exception to this general rule is that a cash-method business is allowed to use the cash method to account for gross profit if the average annual gross receipts for the three-year period prior to the current year do not exceed $10 million. In addition, the primary business activity must be to provide services to customers and the sales of products is a secondary or small part of its services.[43] However, the business is not allowed to deduct the cost of the inventory to the extent it has the product at the end of the year. How does this exception benefit a cash-method business if the business is not allowed to fully deduct the cost of inventory until it sells the inventory? It may be beneficial because it allows the business to use the cash method to account for sales revenue. Without the exception, cash-method service businesses would be required to account for sales revenue from inventory sales on the accrual method, which means they may be required to recognize revenue before they actually receive it. With the exception, they are allowed to defer the revenue recognition until they receive the payments from customers.

Businesses selling inventory must determine their inventory costs to accurately compute taxable income. This requires businesses to maintain records of balances for finished goods inventory and, if applicable, for partially finished goods and raw materials. Inventory costs include the purchase price of raw materials (minus any discounts), shipping costs, and any indirect costs it allocates to the inventory under the **uniform cost capitalization rules (UNICAP rules).**[44]

Uniform Capitalization The tax laws require businesses to capitalize certain direct and indirect costs associated with inventories.[45] Congress enacted these rules primarily for two reasons. First, the rules accelerate tax revenues for the government by deferring deductions for the capitalized costs until the business sells the associated inventory. Thus, there is generally a one-year lag between when businesses initially capitalize the costs and when they deduct them. Second, Congress

[43]Rev. Proc. 2002-28, 2002-1 CB 815. There are other exceptions to this general rule. For example, certain cash-method taxpayers (average annual receipts of $1 million or less) can qualify to account for merchandise for sale as materials and supplies under Rev. Proc. 2001-10, 2001-1 CB 272.

[44]Inventory valuation allowances are generally not allowed, but taxpayers can adopt the lower of cost or market method of inventory valuation. In addition, under certain conditions specific goods not salable at normal prices can be valued at bona fide selling prices less direct cost of disposition.

[45]§263A(a).

designed the "uniform" rules to reduce variation in the costs businesses include in inventory. Congress intended the UNICAP provisions to apply to manufacturers and large resalers. Consequently, businesses that resell personal property are not required to use the UNICAP rules if they report average annual gross receipts of $10 million or less over the three-year period ending with the taxable year prior to the current year.

Under these uniform cost capitalization rules, large businesses are generally required to capitalize more costs to inventory for tax purposes than they capitalize under financial accounting rules. Under GAAP, businesses generally include in inventory only those costs incurred within their production facility. In contrast, the UNICAP rules require businesses to allocate to inventory the costs they incur inside the production facility and the costs they incur outside the facility to support production (or inventory acquisition) activities. For example, under the UNICAP provisions, a business must capitalize at least a portion of the compensation paid to employees in its purchasing department, general and administrative department, and even its information technology department, to the extent these groups provide support for the production process. In contrast, businesses immediately expense these items as period costs for financial accounting purposes. The regulations provide guidance on the costs that must be allocated to inventory. Selling, advertising, and research are specifically identified as costs that do not have to be allocated to inventory under the UNICAP provisions.[46]

Example 9-17

What if: Green Acres sells trees but Rick anticipates selling flowers, shrubs, and other plants in future years. Ken is Rick's employee in charge of purchasing inventory. Ken's compensation this year is $30,000, and Rick estimates that Ken spends about 5 percent of his time acquiring inventory and the remaining time working on landscaping projects. How would Rick allocate Ken's compensation under the UNICAP rules?

Answer: If the UNICAP rules applied to Green Acres, Rick would allocate $1,500 ($30,000 × 5%) of Ken's compensation to the cost of the inventory Green Acres acquired this year. In contrast, Ken's entire salary would be expensed as a period cost for financial accounting purposes. (Note, however, because Green Acres's gross receipts for the year are under $10,000,000, it is not *required* to apply the UNICAP rules.)

Inventory Cost-Flow Methods Once a business determines the cost of its inventory, it must use an inventory cost-flow method to determine its cost of goods sold. Three primary cost-flow methods are (1) first-in, first-out (**FIFO**), (2) last-in, first-out (**LIFO**), and (3) **specific identification.** Businesses might be inclined to use FIFO or LIFO methods when they sell similar, relatively low-cost, high-volume products such as cans of soup or barrels of oil. These methods simplify inventory accounting because the business need not track the individual cost of each item it sells. In contrast, businesses that sell distinct, relatively high-cost, low-volume products might be more likely to adopt the specific identification method. For example, jewelry and used-car businesses would likely use the specific identification method to account for their cost of sales. In general terms, when costs are increasing, a business using the FIFO method will report a higher gross margin than if it used the LIFO method. The opposite is true if costs are decreasing.

[46]Reg. §1.263A–1(e)(3)(iii).

Example 9-18

In late August, Rick purchased 10 oak saplings (immature trees) for a total purchase price of $3,000. In September, he purchased 12 more for a total price of $3,900, and in late October, he purchased 15 more for $5,000. The total cost of each lot of trees was determined as follows:

Purchase Date	Trees	Direct Cost	Other Costs	Total Cost
August 20	10	$ 3,000	$200	$ 3,200
September 15	12	3,900	300	4,200
October 22	15	5,000	400	5,400
Totals	37	$11,900	$900	$12,800

Before the end of the year, Green Acres sold 20 of the oak saplings (5 from the August lot, 5 from the September lot, and 10 from the October lot) for cash. What is Green Acres's gross profit from sales of oak saplings if the sales revenue totaled $14,000 (all collected by year-end), and what is its ending oak sapling inventory under the accrual and the cash method of accounting?

Answer: Under the accrual method, Green Acres's gross profit from sapling sales and its ending inventory balance for the remaining oak saplings under the FIFO, LIFO, and specific identification cost-flow methods is as follows:

	FIFO	LIFO	Specific ID
Sales	$14,000	$14,000	$14,000
Cost of goods sold	−6,700	−7,150	−6,950
Gross profit	$ 7,300	$ 6,850	$ 7,050
Ending inventory:			
August 20 trees	$ 0	$ 3,200	$ 1,600
September 15 trees	700	2,450	2,450
October 22 trees	5,400	0	1,800
Total ending inventory	$ 6,100	$ 5,650	$ 5,850

Using the cash method, the answer is the same as it is under the accrual method. Green Acres is not allowed to deduct the cost of its ending inventory even if it qualifies to use the cash method to account for gross profit under the small business ($10M) exception.

What if: Assume the same original facts except that Green Acres received $10,000 sales revenue from customers this year and the remaining $4,000 early next year. Assuming Green Acres qualifies to use the cash method to account for gross profit under the small business ($10M) exception, what is the amount of Green Acres's gross profit this year if it uses the specific identification method of accounting for its ending inventory?

Answer: $3,050 ($10,000 revenue minus $6,950 cost of goods sold). In this situation Green Acres would be allowed to defer $4,000 of the sales revenue until it collected it next year.

When costs are subject to inflation over time, a business would get the best of both worlds if it adopted the FIFO method for financial reporting purposes and the LIFO method for tax purposes. Not surprisingly, the tax laws require that a business can use LIFO for tax purposes only if it also uses LIFO for financial reporting purposes.[47] While this "conformity" requirement may not matter to entities not required to generate financial reports, it can be very restrictive to publicly traded corporations.

[47]§472(c).

Accrual Deductions

Generally, when accrual-method businesses incur a liability relating to a business expense, they account for it by crediting a liability account (or cash if they pay the liability at the time they incur it) and debiting an expense account. However, to record an expense and the corresponding deduction for tax purposes, the business must meet (1) an **all-events test** for the liability *and* (2) an **economic performance test** with respect to the liability.[48] While the all-events test for recognizing deductions is similar to the all-events test for recognizing income, the additional economic performance requirement makes the deduction recognition rules more stringent than the income recognition rules. The deduction rules generally preclude businesses from deducting estimated expenses or reserves.

All-Events Test for Deductions For a business to recognize a deduction, all events that establish its liability giving rise to the deduction must have occurred, and it must be able to determine the amount of the liability with reasonable accuracy.[49]

Example 9-19

On November of this year, Rick agreed to a one-year $6,000 contract with Ace Advertising to produce a radio ad campaign. Ace agreed that Rick would owe nothing under the contract unless his sales increase a minimum of 25 percent over the next six months. What amount, if any, may Rick deduct this year for this contract under the accrual and cash methods?

Answer: Under the accrual method, Green Acres is not allowed to recognize *any* deduction this year for the liability. Even though Ace will have completed two months of advertising for Green Acres by the end of the year, its guarantee means that Rick's liability is not fixed until and unless his sales increase by 25 percent. Under the cash method, Rick would not deduct any of the cost of the campaign this year because he has not paid anything to Ace.

Economic Performance Even when businesses meet the all-events test, they still must clear the economic performance hurdle to recognize the tax deduction. Congress added the economic performance requirement because in some situations taxpayers claimed current deductions and delayed paying the associated cash expenditures for years. Thus, the delayed payment reduced the real (present value) cost of the deduction. This requirement specifies that businesses may not recognize a deduction for an expense until the underlying activity generating the associated liability has occurred. Thus, an accrual-method business would not be allowed to deduct a prepaid business expense even if it qualified to do so under the 12-month rule (discussed above) unless it also met the economic performance test with respect to the liability associated with the expense.

The specific requirements for the economic performance test differ based on whether the liability arose from

- Receiving goods or services *from* another party.
- Use of property.
- Providing goods or services *to* another party.
- Certain activities creating **payment liabilities.**

THE KEY FACTS

Accrual of Business-Expense Deductions

- Both all-events and economic performance are required for deducting accrued business expenses.
- The all-events test requires that the business be liable for the payment.
- Economic performance generally requires that underlying activity generating liability has occurred in order for the associated expense to be deductible.

[48]§461(h).
[49]§461.

Receiving goods and (or) services from another party. When a business agrees to pay another party for goods or services the other party will provide, the business deducts the expense associated with the liability as the other party provides the goods or services (assuming the all-events test is met for the liability). An exception to this general rule occurs when a business hires another party to provide goods or services, and the business actually *pays* the liability before the other party provides the goods or services. In this circumstance, the business may treat the *actual payment* as economic performance as long as it *reasonably expects* the other party to provide the goods or all of the services within three and one-half months after the payment.[50]

Example 9-20

On December 15, 2015, Rick hires Your New Fence LLC (YNF) to install a concrete wall for one of his clients by paying $1,000 of the cost as a down payment and agreeing to pay the remaining $7,000 when YNF finishes the wall. YNF was not going to start building the wall until early 2016, so as of the end of the year Rick has not billed his client for the wall. Rick expects YNF to finish the wall by the end of April. What amount associated with his liability to YNF is Rick allowed to deduct in 2015 and 2016?

Answer: Under the accrual method, Rick is not entitled to a deduction in 2015. Rick will deduct his full $8,000 cost of the wall in 2016 when YNF builds the wall, because economic performance occurs as YNF provides the services, even though Rick paid for part of the goods and services in 2015. Under the cash method, Rick would deduct $1,000 (his down payment) in 2015 and the remainder in 2016 when he pays the remainder on the contract.

What if: Assume that Rick expected YNF to finish building the wall by the end of January 2016. What amount associated with this liability to YNF is Rick allowed to deduct in 2015 and 2016?

Answer: Under the accrual method, Rick is allowed to deduct $1,000 in 2015 because Rick actually paid this amount in 2015 and he reasonably expected YNF to finish its work on the wall within 3½ months after he made the payment to YNF on December 15. Rick would deduct the remaining $7,000 cost of the wall in 2016 when YNF builds the wall. Under the cash method, Rick deducts the $1,000 down payment in 2015 and the remaining $7,000 when he makes the payment in 2016.

Renting or leasing property from another party. When a business enters into an agreement to rent or lease property from another party, economic performance occurs over the rental period. Thus, the business is allowed to deduct the rental expense over the lease.

Example 9-21

On May 1, 2015, Rick paid $7,200 in advance to rent his shop for 12 months ($600 per month). What amount may Rick deduct for rent in 2015 if he accounts for his business activities using the accrual method?

Answer: $4,800 ($600 × 8 months use). Even though the rent is a prepaid business expense under the 12-month rule (the contract period is for 12 months and the contract period does not extend beyond 2016), he must deduct the rent expense over the term of the lease because that is when economic performance occurs.

What if: Assuming the original facts, what amount of the $7,200 rental payment may Rick deduct in 2015 if he is using the cash method of accounting for his business?

Answer: $7,200. In this case, Rick may deduct the expense under the 12-month rule. He does not have to meet the economic performance requirement to deduct the expense because the economic performance requirements apply to accrual—not cash-method taxpayers.

[50]Reg. §1.461-4(d)(6).

Example 9-22

On November 1, 2015, Rick paid $2,400 to rent a trailer for 24 months. What amount of this payment may Rick deduct and when may he deduct it?

Answer: Under the accrual method, even though Rick paid the entire rental fee in advance, economic performance occurs over the 24-month rental period. Thus, Green Acres deducts $200 for the trailer rental in 2015, $1,200 in 2016, and $1,000 in 2017. Because the rental period exceeds 12 months, the amount and timing of the deductions are the same under the cash method.

Providing goods and services to another party. Businesses liable for providing goods and services to other parties meet the economic performance test as they provide the goods or services that satisfy the liability.

Example 9-23

In the summer, Rick landscaped a city park. As part of this service, Rick agreed to remove a fountain from the park at the option of the city parks committee. In December 2015, the committee decided to have Rick remove the fountain. Rick began the removal in December and completed the removal in the spring of 2016. Rick paid a part-time employee $850 for the removal work in December and an additional $685 to complete the removal the following spring. What is the amount and timing of Rick's deductions for the removal project?

Answer: Under the accrual method, Rick is allowed to deduct his costs as he provides the services. Consequently, in 2015 Rick can deduct $850 for the cost of the services provided by his employee in 2015. In 2016, Rick can deduct the remaining $685 cost of the services provided by his employee in 2016. Under the cash method, the amount and timing of his deductions would be the same as it is under the accrual method.

Payment liabilities. Economic performance occurs for certain liabilities only when the business actually *pays* the liability. Thus, accrual-method businesses incurring payment liabilities are essentially on the *cash method* for deducting the associated expenses. Exhibit 9-3 describes different categories of these payment liabilities.

EXHIBIT 9-3 Categories of Payment Liabilities

Economic performance occurs when taxpayer pays liability associated with:

- Worker's compensation, tort, breach of contract, or violation of law.
- Rebates and refunds.
- Awards, prizes, and jackpots.
- Insurance, warranties, and service contracts provided *to* the business. (Note: This is insurance, warranties, and product service contracts that cover the taxpayer and *not* a warranty that the taxpayer provides to others.)
- Taxes.[51]
- Other liabilities not provided for elsewhere.

Recurring item exception. One of the most common exceptions to economic performance is the **recurring item** exception. This exception is designed to minimize the cost of applying economic performance to relatively small expenses that occur on a regular basis. Under §461(h)(3), accrual method taxpayers can deduct certain accrued

[51]While taxes are generally not deducted until they are paid, §461(c) allows businesses to elect to accrue the deduction for real property taxes ratably over the tax period instead of deducting them when they actually pay them.

expenses even if economic performance has not occurred by year-end. A recurring item is a liability that is expected to persist in future years, and is either not material in amount or deducting the expense currently matches with revenue. In addition, the all-events test must be satisfied at year-end and actual economic performance must occur within a reasonable time after year-end (but prior to the filing of the tax return which could be up to 8½ months with an extension). As a final note, the recurring item exception does not apply to worker's compensation or tort liabilities.

Example 9-24

If clients are not completely satisfied with Green Acres's landscaping work, Rick offers a $200 refund with no questions asked. Near the end of the year, Rick had four clients request refunds. Rick incurred the liability for the refunds this year. However, Rick was busy during the holiday season, so he didn't pay the refunds until January 2016. When should Rick deduct the customer refunds?

Answer: Because refunds are payment liabilities, economic performance does not occur until Rick actually pays the refunds. Consequently, Rick deducts the $800 of refunds in 2016 even though the liability for the refunds met the all-events test in 2015. Under the cash method, Rick would not deduct the refunds until he paid them in 2016.

What if: Suppose that Rick expected that $800 of refunds would typically be accrued at year-end. Under what conditions could Rick deduct the refunds in 2015 if he elects to use accrual accounting?

Answer: If the accrued refunds are not material in amount and Rick expects actual economic performance within a reasonable time after year-end (but not longer than 8½ months or filing of the tax return), then Rick can elect to deduct the refunds in 2015 using the recurring item exception.

Accrual-method taxpayers that prepay business expenses for *payment liabilities* (insurance contracts, warranties, and product service contracts provided to the taxpayer) are allowed to immediately deduct the prepayments subject to the 12-month rule for prepaid expenses. Thus, the deductible amounts for Rick's prepaid insurance contracts in Example 9-14 are the same for both the cash method and accrual method of accounting. Exhibit 9-4 describes the requirements for economic performance for the different types of liabilities.

EXHIBIT 9-4 Economic Performance

Taxpayer incurs liability from	Economic performance occurs
Receiving goods and services *from* another party	When the goods or services are provided to the taxpayer or with payment if the taxpayer reasonably expects actual performance within 3½ months.
Renting or leasing property *from* another party	Ratably over the time period during which the taxpayer is entitled to use the property or money.
Providing goods and services *to* another party	When the taxpayer incurs costs to satisfy the liability or provide the goods and services.
Activities creating "payment" liabilities	When the business actually makes payment.
Interest expense	As accrued. This technically does not fall within the economic performance rules but it is a similar concept.

Bad Debt Expense When accrual method businesses sell a product or a service on credit, they debit accounts receivable and credit sales revenue for both financial and tax purposes. However, because businesses usually are unable to collect the full amount of their accounts receivable, they incur bad debt expense (a customer owes them a debt that the customer will not pay). For financial reporting purposes, the business estimates the amount of the bad debt, debits bad debt expense, and credits an allowance for doubtful accounts. However, for tax purposes, businesses are allowed to deduct bad debt expense only when the debt actually becomes worthless within the taxable year.[52] Consequently, for tax purposes, businesses determine which debts are uncollectible and write them off by debiting bad debt expense and *directly* crediting the actual account receivable account that is uncollectible. This required method of determining bad debt expense for tax purposes is called the **direct write-off method.** In contrast, the method used for financial reporting purposes is called the **allowance method.** Businesses reporting taxable income on the cash method of accounting are *not* allowed to deduct bad debt expenses, because they do not include receivables in taxable income (they do not credit revenue until they actually receive payment).

Example 9-25

At year-end, Rick estimates that about $900 of the receivables from his landscaping services will be uncollectible, but he has identified only one client, Jared, who will definitely not pay his bill. Jared, who has skipped town, owes Rick $280 for landscaping this fall. What amount of bad debt expense may Rick deduct for the year?

Answer: For financial reporting purposes, Rick recognizes a $900 bad debt expense. However, for tax purposes, under the accrual method, Rick can only deduct $280—the amount associated with specifically writing off Jared's receivable. Under the cash method, Rick would not be able to claim any deduction, because he did not receive a payment from Jared and thus did not recognize income on the amount Jared owed him.

Limitations on Accruals to Related Parties To prevent businesses and related parties from working together to defer taxes, the tax laws prevent an accrual-method business from accruing (and deducting) an expense for a liability owed to a related party using the cash method until the related party recognizes the income associated with the payment.[53] For this purpose, related parties include

- Family members including parents, siblings, and spouses.
- Shareholders and C corporations when the shareholder owns more than 50 percent of the corporation's stock.[54]
- Owners of partnerships and S corporations no matter the ownership percentage.[55]

This issue frequently arises in situations in which a business employs the owner or a relative of an owner. The business is not allowed to deduct compensation expense owed to the related party until the year in which the related party includes the compensation in income. However, this related-party limit extends beyond compensation to *any* accrued expense the business owes to a related cash-method taxpayer.

Example 9-26

In December, Rick asked his retired father, Henry, to help him finish a landscaping job. By the end of the year, Rick owed Henry $2,000 of (reasonable) compensation for his efforts, which he paid in January 2016. What amount of this compensation may Rick deduct and when may he deduct it?

Answer: If Rick uses the accrual method and Henry the cash method, Rick will not be able to deduct the $2,000 compensation expense until 2016. Rick is Henry's son, so Rick and Henry are "related" parties for tax purposes. Consequently, Rick can deduct the compensation only when Henry includes the payment in his taxable income in 2016. If Rick uses the cash method, he will deduct the expense when he pays it in January 2016.

[52]§166(a).

[53]§267(a).

[54]Certain constructive ownership rules apply in determining ownership percentages for this purpose. See §267(c).

[55]See §267(b) for related-party definitions.

Comparison of Accrual and Cash Methods

From a business perspective, the two primary advantages of adopting the cash method over the accrual method are that (1) the cash method provides the business with more flexibility to time income and deductions by accelerating or deferring payments (timing tax planning strategy) and (2) bookkeeping for the cash method is easier. For example, a cash-method taxpayer could defer revenue by waiting to bill clients for goods or services until after year-end, thereby increasing the likelihood that customers would send payment after year-end. There are some concerns with this tax strategy. For example, delaying the bills might increase the likelihood that the customers will not pay their bills at all.

The primary advantage of the accrual method over the cash method is that it better matches revenues and expenses. For that reason, external financial statement users who want to evaluate a business's financial performance prefer the accrual method. Consistent with this idea, the cash method is not allowed for financial reporting under GAAP.

Although the cash method is by far the predominate accounting method among sole proprietors, it is less common in other types of businesses. In fact, tax laws generally prohibit C corporations and partnerships with corporate partners from using the cash method of accounting.[56] Exhibit 9-5 details the basic differences in accounting for income and deductions under the accrual and the cash method of accounting.

EXHIBIT 9-5 Comparison of Cash and Accrual Methods

Income or Expense Item	Cash Method	Accrual Method
Income recognition	Actually or constructively received.	Taxable once the all-events test is satisfied.
Unearned rental and interest income	Taxable on receipt.	Taxable on receipt.
Advance payment for services	Taxable on receipt.	Taxed when received or under the deferral method in the following year of receipt if not earned by end of year of receipt.
Advance payment for goods	Taxable on receipt.	Full-inclusion is taxed on receipt but deferral election allows taxation when earned.
Deduction recognition	Deduct when paid; economic performance does not apply.	Deduct once all-events test and economic performance test are both satisfied.
Expenditures for tangible assets with a useful life more than one year	Capitalize and apply cost recovery.	Same as the cash method.
Expenditures for intangible assets other than prepaid business expenses	Capitalize and amortize if provision in code allows it.	Same as the cash method.
Prepaid business expenses	Immediately deductible unless contract period exceeds 12 months or extends beyond the end of the next taxable year.	Same as cash method for payment liabilities; otherwise, apply all-events and economic performance tests to ascertain when to capitalize and amortize.
Prepaid interest expense	Not deductible until interest accrues.	Same as the cash method.
Bad debt expense	Not deductible because sales on account not included in income.	Deduct under direct write-off method.

[56]These entities are able to adopt the cash method if their average annual gross receipts for the three tax years ending with the prior tax year do not exceed $5 million (see §448).

Example 9-27

At year-end, Rick determined that Green Acres had collected a total of $71,000 of service revenue (not described elsewhere in examples). Rick is debating whether to adopt the cash or accrual method. To help him resolve his dilemma, Jane includes these revenues in a calculation of Green Acres's taxable income under the cash and accrual methods (Exhibit 9-6). What are the differences between the two calculations?

Answer: Jane provided the following summary of the differences between taxable income under the cash method and taxable income under the accrual method:

Description	(1) Cash	(2) Accrual	(1) − (2) Difference	Example
Revenue:				
Credit sales	0	11,000	−11,000	8-15
Prepaid revenue	7,200	300	+6,900	8-16
Expenses:				
Prepaid services	−1,000	0	−1,000	8-20
Prepaid rent expense	−7,200	−4,800	−2,400	8-21
Bad debts	0	−280	+280	8-25
Total difference (accrual income > cash income)			**−7,220**	

Jane explains that by comparing the revenue and expenses recognized under the two accounting methods, the selection of the accrual method for Green Acres means that Rick will be taxed on an additional $7,220 of income this year than if Green Acres adopts the cash method.

The business income for Green Acres under the accrual and cash methods is summarized in Exhibit 9-6. After reflecting on these numbers and realizing that he would recognize $7,220 more taxable income (and self-employment income subject to self-employment tax) this year under the accrual method than under the cash method, Rick determined it made sense to adopt the cash method of accounting for Green Acres's first tax return. Meanwhile, he knew he had to include Green Acres's business income on Schedule C of his individual tax return. Exhibit 9-7 presents Rick's Schedule C for Green Acres using the cash method of accounting.

Adopting an Accounting Method

We've seen that businesses use overall accounting methods (cash, accrual, or hybrid) and many specific accounting methods (inventory cost-flow assumption, methods of accounting for prepaid income for goods, and methods for accounting for prepaid expenses, among other methods) to account for their business activities. For tax purposes, it's important to understand how and when a business technically *adopts* an accounting method because once it does so, it must get the IRS's permission to change the method.

Businesses generally elect their accounting methods by using them on their tax returns. However, *when* the business technically adopts a method depends on whether it is a **permissible accounting method** or an **impermissible accounting method.** So far, our discussion has emphasized accounting methods permissible under the tax laws. A business adopts a permissible accounting method by using and reporting the tax results of the method for at least one year. However, businesses may

EXHIBIT 9-6 **Green Acres's Net Business Income**

Description	Cash	Accrual	Example
Income			
Service revenue:			
Greenhouse construction	$ 5,000	$ 5,000	8-10
December landscape service	0	11,000	8-15
Prepaid landscape services	7,200	300	8-16
Landscaping revenue	71,000	71,000	8-27
Sales of inventory:			
Tree sales	14,000	14,000	8-18
Cost of goods sold (LIFO method)	−7,150	−7,150	8-18
Gross Profit	**$90,050**	**$94,150**	
Car and truck expense:			
SUV operating expense	$ 5,335	$ 5,335	8-7
BMW operating expense	306	306	8-9
Insurance	1,200	1,200	8-14
Rent			
Shop	7,200	4,800	8-21
Trailer	200	200	8-22
Travel, meals, and entertainment:			
Travel to NY seminar	1,435	1,435	8-8
Dinner and theater with client	270	270	8-6
Wages and subcontractor fees:			
Part-time employees	23,000	23,000	8-2
Full time employee (Ken)	30,000	30,000	8-17
Fountain removal (part-time employee)	850	850	8-23
Fence installation (prepaid subcontractor)	1,000	0	8-20
Other expenses:			
Education—meditation class	50	50	8-1
Education—seminar	300	300	8-8
Domestic production activities deduction	90	90	8-10
Uniforms	500	500	8-5
Bad debts	0	280	8-25
Other expenses not in examples:			
Advertising	1,100	1,200	
Depreciation	4,000	4,000	
Interest	300	300	
Legal and professional services	1,100	1,100	
Office expense	1,500	1,500	
Repairs and maintenance	1,975	1,975	
Taxes and licenses	400	400	
Utilities	2,200	2,200	
Total deductions	**$84,311**	**$81,191**	
Net Business Income	**$ 5,739**	**$12,959**	

unwittingly (or intentionally) use impermissible accounting methods. For example, a business using the allowance method for determining bad debt expense for tax purposes is using an impermissible accounting method because the tax laws prescribe the use of the direct write-off method for determining bad debt expense. A business *adopts* an *impermissible* method by using and reporting the results of the method for *two consecutive years*.

EXHIBIT 9-7 Green Acres Schedule C

SCHEDULE C (Form 1040)
Department of the Treasury Internal Revenue Service (99)

Profit or Loss From Business
(Sole Proprietorship)

▶ Information about Schedule C and its separate instructions is at *www.irs.gov/schedulec*.
▶ Attach to Form 1040, 1040NR, or 1041; partnerships generally must file Form 1065.

OMB No. 1545-0074
2014
Attachment Sequence No. 09

Name of proprietor: RICK GRIME
Social security number (SSN): 000-00-0000

A Principal business or profession, including product or service (see instructions): LANDSCAPER
B Enter code from instructions ▶ 5 7 1 6 3 0

C Business name. If no separate business name, leave blank.: GREEN ACRES LANDSCAPING
D Employer ID number (EIN), (see instr.): 4 6 0 0 0 0 0 0 0

E Business address (including suite or room no.) ▶ BUCKSNORT STREET
City, town or post office, state, and ZIP code: SAN ANTONIO, TEXAS 78208

F Accounting method: (1) ☑ Cash (2) ☐ Accrual (3) ☐ Other (specify) ▶
G Did you "materially participate" in the operation of this business during 2014? If "No," see instructions for limit on losses . ☑ Yes ☐ No
H If you started or acquired this business during 2014, check here . . . ▶ ☑
I Did you make any payments in 2014 that would require you to file Form(s) 1099? (see instructions) . . . ☐ Yes ☑ No
J If "Yes," did you or will you file required Forms 1099? . . . ☐ Yes ☐ No

Part I Income

1	Gross receipts or sales. See instructions for line 1 and check the box if this income was reported to you on Form W-2 and the "Statutory employee" box on that form was checked . . . ▶ ☐	1	97,200
2	Returns and allowances	2	
3	Subtract line 2 from line 1	3	
4	Cost of goods sold (from line 42)	4	7,150
5	**Gross profit.** Subtract line 4 from line 3	5	90,050
6	Other income, including federal and state gasoline or fuel tax credit or refund (see instructions)	6	
7	**Gross income.** Add lines 5 and 6 . . . ▶	7	90,050

Part II Expenses. Enter expenses for business use of your home **only** on line 30.

		Line	Amount			Line	Amount
8	Advertising	8	1,100	18	Office expense (see instructions)	18	1,500
9	Car and truck expenses (see instructions)	9	5,641	19	Pension and profit-sharing plans	19	
10	Commissions and fees	10		20	Rent or lease (see instructions):		
11	Contract labor (see instructions)	11	1,000	a	Vehicles, machinery, and equipment	20a	7,400
12	Depletion	12		b	Other business property	20b	
13	Depreciation and section 179 expense deduction (not included in Part III) (see instructions)	13	4,000	21	Repairs and maintenance	21	1,975
				22	Supplies (not included in Part III)	22	
				23	Taxes and licenses	23	400
				24	Travel, meals, and entertainment:		
14	Employee benefit programs (other than on line 19)	14		a	Travel	24a	1,435
15	Insurance (other than health)	15	1,200	b	Deductible meals and entertainment (see instructions)	24b	270
16	Interest:			25	Utilities	25	2,200
a	Mortgage (paid to banks, etc.)	16a	300	26	Wages (less employment credits)	26	58,850
b	Other	16b		27a	Other expenses (from line 48)	27a	940
17	Legal and professional services	17	1,100	b	**Reserved for future use**	27b	

28	**Total expenses** before expenses for business use of home. Add lines 8 through 27a . . . ▶	28	84,311
29	Tentative profit or (loss). Subtract line 28 from line 7	29	5,739
30	Expenses for business use of your home. Do not report these expenses elsewhere. Attach Form 8829 unless using the simplified method (see instructions). **Simplified method filers only:** enter the total square footage of: (a) your home: ________ and (b) the part of your home used for business: ________ . Use the Simplified Method Worksheet in the instructions to figure the amount to enter on line 30	30	
31	**Net profit or (loss).** Subtract line 30 from line 29. • If a profit, enter on both **Form 1040, line 12** (or **Form 1040NR, line 13**) and on **Schedule SE, line 2.** (If you checked the box on line 1, see instructions). Estates and trusts, enter on **Form 1041, line 3.** • If a loss, you **must** go to line 32.	31	5,739

32 If you have a loss, check the box that describes your investment in this activity (see instructions).
• If you checked 32a, enter the loss on both **Form 1040, line 12,** (or **Form 1040NR, line 13**) and on **Schedule SE, line 2.** (If you checked the box on line 1, see the line 31 instructions). Estates and trusts, enter on **Form 1041, line 3.**
• If you checked 32b, you **must** attach **Form 6198.** Your loss may be limited.

32a ☑ All investment is at risk.
32b ☐ Some investment is not at risk.

For Paperwork Reduction Act Notice, see the separate instructions. Cat. No. 11334P **Schedule C (Form 1040) 2014**

Changing Accounting Methods

Once a business has adopted an accounting method, it must receive permission to change the method, regardless of whether it is a permissible or an impermissible method. A taxpayer requests permission to change accounting methods by filing Form 3115 with the IRS. The IRS automatically approves certain types of accounting method changes, but for others the business must provide a good business purpose for the change and pay a fee. The IRS also requires permission when a business must change from using an impermissible method; this requirement helps the IRS to certify that the business properly makes the transition to a permissible method. In essence, the IRS requires the business to report its own noncompliance. Why would a business do so? Besides complying with the tax laws, a business might report its own noncompliance to receive leniency from the IRS. Without getting into the details, the IRS is likely to assess fewer penalties and less interest expense for noncompliance when the business reports the noncompliance before the IRS discovers it on its own.

Tax Consequences of Changing Accounting Method When a business changes from one accounting method to another, the business determines its taxable income for the year of change using the new method. Furthermore, the business must make an adjustment to taxable income that effectively represents the *cumulative difference,* as of the beginning of the tax year, between the amount of income (or deductions) recognized under the old accounting method and the amount that would have been recognized for all prior years if the new method had been applied. This adjustment is called a **§481 adjustment.** The §481 adjustment prevents the duplication or omission of items of income or deduction due to a change in accounting method. If the §481 adjustment *increases* taxable income, the taxpayer recognizes it over *four years* beginning with the year of the change (25 percent of the full adjustment each year). If the adjustment *decreases* taxable income, the taxpayer recognizes it *entirely in the year of change.*

Example 9-28

What if: Suppose that at the end of 2015, Green Acres has $24,000 of accounts receivable. Assuming Green Acres uses the cash method of accounting in 2015, it would not include the $24,000 of receivables in income in determining its 2015 taxable income. Suppose further that Rick decides to switch Green Acres to the accrual method of accounting in 2016 by filing a Form 3115 and receiving permission from the IRS. What is Rick's §481 adjustment for his change in accounting method from the cash to the accrual method?

Answer: $24,000 increase to income ($6,000 in 2016 and each of the subsequent three years). Since Rick would use the accrual method in 2016, he would *not* include payments he receives for the $24,000 receivables as income because he earned this income in 2015 (not 2016). Instead, Rick would be required to make a §481 adjustment to ensure that he does not *omit* these items from taxable income. His total §481 adjustment is to increase net income by $24,000. Because this is an income-increasing adjustment, Rick includes $6,000 of the adjustment (25 percent) in Green Acres's taxable income in 2016. He would likewise include a $6,000 §481 adjustment in each of the subsequent three years.

What if: Suppose that at the end of 2015, Green Acres has $4,000 of accounts payable instead of $24,000 of accounts receivable. What is Rick's §481 adjustment for his change in accounting method from the cash to the accrual method?

Answer: In this instance Green Acres would have a negative (income-decreasing) §481 adjustment of $4,000 because the $4,000 of expenses would have accrued in 2015 but would not have been deducted. Hence, Green Acres would be entitled to deduct the full $4,000 as a negative §481 adjustment amount in 2016.

CONCLUSION

This chapter discussed issues relating to business income and deductions. We learned that the income rules for businesses are very similar to those for individuals, and that businesses may deduct only ordinary and necessary business expenses and other business expenses specifically authorized by law. We also described several business expense limitations and discussed the accounting periods and methods businesses may use in reporting taxable income to the IRS. The issues described in this chapter are widely applicable to all types of business entities including sole proprietorships, partnerships, S corporations, and C corporations. In the next chapter, we determine how businesses recover the costs of assets they use in their business activities.

Summary

LO 9-1 Describe the general requirements for deducting business expenses and identify common business deductions.

- Ordinary and necessary business expenses are allowed as deductions to calculate net income from activities entered into with a profit motive.
- Only reasonable amounts are allowed as business expense deductions. Extravagant or excessive amounts are likely to be characterized by personal motives and are disallowed.

LO 9-2 Apply the limitations on business deductions to distinguish between deductible and nondeductible business expenses.

- The law specifically prohibits deducting expenses against public policy (such as fines or bribes) and expenses that produce tax-exempt income.
- Expenses benefiting multiple periods must be capitalized and special limits and recordkeeping requirements are applied to business expenses that may have personal benefits, such as entertainment and meals.

LO 9-3 Identify and explain special business deductions specifically permitted under the tax laws.

- Special calculations are necessary for deductions such as bad debt expenses, the domestic production activities deduction, and casualty losses.

LO 9-4 Explain the concept of an accounting period and describe accounting periods available to businesses.

- Accounting periods and methods are chosen at the time of filing the first tax return.
- There are three types of tax years, calendar year, fiscal year, and 52/53-week year, and each tax year is distinguished by year-end.

LO 9-5 Identify and describe accounting methods available to businesses and apply cash and accrual methods to determine business income and expense deductions.

- Under the cash method, taxpayers recognize revenue when they actually or constructively receive property or services and recognize deductions when they actually pay the expense.
- Under the accrual method, the all-events test requires that income be recognized when all the events have occurred that are necessary to fix the right to receive payments and the amount of the payments can be determined with reasonable accuracy.
- The accrual method must be used to account for sales and purchases for businesses where inventories are an income-producing factor.
- Under the accrual method, accrued expenses can only be deducted once both the all-events test and the economic performance tests are met. The application of the economic performance test depends, in part, on the type of business expense.
- Changes in accounting method or accounting period typically require the consent of the IRS and a §481 adjustment to taxable income.

KEY TERMS

12-month rule (9-17)
accounting method (9-16)
accounting period (9-15)
all-events test (9-24)
allowance method (9-28)
arm's length amount (9-4)
casualty losses (9-14)
deferral method (9-20)
direct write-off method (9-28)
domestic production activities deduction (DPAD) (9-12)
economic performance test (9-24)
FIFO (9-22)
fiscal year (9-15)
flow-through entities (9-16)
full-inclusion method (9-20)
impermissible accounting method (9-30)
LIFO (9-22)
mixed-motive expenditures (9-8)
ordinary and necessary (9-3)
payment liabilities (9-24)
permissible accounting method (9-30)
personal expenses (9-7)
qualified production activities income (QPAI) (9-12)
reasonable in amount (9-4)
recurring item (9-26)
§481 adjustment (9-33)
specific identification (9-22)
tax year (9-15)
travel expenses (9-9)
uniform cost capitalization rules (UNICAP rules) (9-21)

DISCUSSION QUESTIONS

1. What is an "ordinary and necessary" business expenditure? LO 9-1
2. Is cost of goods sold deductible as a business expense for a business selling inventory? Explain. LO 9-1
3. Tom is an attorney who often represents individuals injured while working (worker liability claims). This year Tom spent $50 on a book entitled *Plumbing for Dummies* and paid $500 to take a course on plumbing residences and rental housing. Can you imagine circumstances in which these expenditures would be deductible as "ordinary and necessary" for an attorney? Explain. LO 9-1
4. Jake is a professional dog trainer who purchases and trains dogs for use by law enforcement agencies. Last year Jake purchased 500 bags of dog food from a large pet food company at an average cost of $30 per bag. This year, however, Jake purchased 500 bags of dog food from a local pet food company at an average cost of $45 per bag. Under what circumstances would the IRS likely challenge the cost of Jake's dog food as unreasonable? LO 9-1
5. What kinds of deductions are prohibited as a matter of public policy? Why might Congress deem it important to disallow deductions for expenditures against public policy? LO 9-2
6. Provide an example of an expense associated with the production of tax-exempt income, and explain what might happen if Congress repealed the prohibition against deducting expenses incurred to produce tax-exempt income. LO 9-2
7. Jerry is a self-employed rock star and this year he expended $1,000 on special "flashy" clothes and outfits. Jerry would like to deduct the cost of these clothes as work-related because the clothes are not acceptable to Jerry's sense of fashion. Under what circumstances can Jerry deduct the cost of these work clothes? LO 9-2 research
8. Jimmy is a sole proprietor of a small dry cleaning business. This month Jimmy paid for his groceries by writing checks from the checking account dedicated to the dry cleaning business. Why do you suppose Jimmy is using his business checking account rather than his personal checking account to pay for personal expenditures? LO 9-2
9. Tim employs three sales representatives who often take clients to dinner and provide entertainment in order to increase sales. This year Tim reimbursed the representatives $2,500 for the cost of meals and $8,250 for the cost of LO 9-2

entertaining clients. Describe the conditions under which Tim can claim deductions for meals and entertainment.

LO 9-2 10. Jenny uses her car for both business and personal purposes. She purchased the auto this year and drove 11,000 miles on business trips and 9,000 miles for personal transportation. Describe how Jenny will determine the amount of deductible expenses associated with the auto.

LO 9-1 LO 9-2 11. What expenses are deductible when a taxpayer combines both business and personal activities on a trip? How do the rules for international travel differ from the rules for domestic travel?

LO 9-2 12. Clyde lives and operates a sole proprietorship in Dallas, Texas. This year Clyde found it necessary to travel to Fort Worth (about 25 miles away) for legitimate business reasons. Is Clyde's trip likely to qualify as "away from home," and why would this designation matter?

LO 9-2 13. Describe the record-keeping requirements for business deductions expenses including mixed-motive expenditures.

LO 9-3 14. Explain why the domestic production activities deduction is sometimes described as an "artificial" expense and the apparent rationale for this deduction. How might a business begin to determine the domestic portion of revenues and expenses for products that are assembled in the United States from parts made overseas?

LO 9-3 15. Describe the calculation of the domestic production activities deduction.

LO 9-3 16. Describe the limits placed on the domestic production activities deduction, and explain the apparent reason for each limitation.

LO 9-3 17. Explain the difference between calculating a loss deduction for a business asset that was partially damaged in an accident and a loss deduction for a business asset that was stolen or completely destroyed in an accident.

LO 9-3 18. How do casualty loss deductions differ when a business asset is completely destroyed as opposed to the destruction of a personal-use asset?

LO 9-4 19. What is the difference between a full tax year and a short tax year? Describe circumstances in which a business may have a short tax year.

LO 9-4 20. Explain why a taxpayer might choose one tax year over another if given a choice.

LO 9-4 21. Compare and contrast the different year-ends available to sole proprietorships, flow-through entities, and C corporations.

LO 9-4 22. Why does the law generally require partnerships to adopt a tax year consistent with the year used by the partners?

LO 9-4 23. How does an entity choose its tax year? Is it the same process no matter the type of tax year-end the taxpayer adopts?

LO 9-5 24. Explain when an expenditure should be "capitalized" rather than expensed based upon accounting principles. From time to time, it is suggested that all business expenditures should be expensed for tax purposes. Do you agree with this proposition, and if so, why?

LO 9-5 25. Describe the 12-month rule for determining whether and to what extent businesses should capitalize or immediately deduct prepaid expenses such as insurance or security contracts. Explain the apparent rationale for this rule.

LO 9-5 26. Explain why Congress sometimes mandates that businesses use particular accounting methods while other times Congress is content to require businesses to use the same accounting methods for tax purposes that they use for financial accounting purposes.

LO 9-5 27. Why is it not surprising that specific rules differ between tax accounting and financial accounting?

28. Fred is considering using the accrual method for his next business venture. Explain to Fred the conditions for recognizing income for tax purposes under the accrual method. LO 9-5
29. Describe the all-events test for determining income and describe how to determine the date on which the all-events test has been met. LO 9-5
30. Compare and contrast the tax treatment for rental income received in advance and advance payments for services. LO 9-5
31. Compare and contrast the rules for determining the tax treatment of advance payments for services versus advance payments for goods. LO 9-5
32. Jack operates a plumbing business as a sole proprietorship on the cash method. Besides providing plumbing services, Jack also sells plumbing supplies to homeowners and other plumbers. The sales of plumbing supplies constitute less than $20,000 per year, and this is such a small portion of Jack's income that he does not keep physical inventories for the supplies. Describe the conditions in which Jack must account for sales and purchases of plumbing supplies on the accrual method. LO 9-5 research
33. Explain why Congress enacted the UNICAP rules and describe the burdens these rules place on taxpayers. LO 9-5
34. Compare and contrast financial accounting rules with the tax rules under UNICAP (§263A). Explain whether the UNICAP rules tend to accelerate or defer income relative to the financial accounting rules. LO 9-5
35. Compare and contrast the tests for accruing income and those for accruing deductions for tax purposes. LO 9-5
36. Compare and contrast when taxpayers are allowed to deduct amounts for warranties provided by others to the taxpayer and when taxpayers are allowed to deduct expenses associated with warranties they provide to others. LO 9-5
37. Describe when economic performance occurs for the following expenses: LO 9-5

    Worker's compensation

    Rebates and refunds

    Insurance, warranties, and service contracts provided *to* the business

    Taxes
38. On December 31 of the current year, a taxpayer prepays an advertising company to provide advertising services for the next 10 months. Using the 12-month rule and the economic performance rules, contrast when the taxpayer would be able to deduct the expenditure if the taxpayer uses the cash method of accounting versus if the taxpayer uses the accrual method of accounting. LO 9-5
39. Compare and contrast how bad debt expense is determined for financial accounting purposes and how the deduction for bad debts is determined for accrual-method taxpayers. How do cash-method taxpayers determine their bad debt expense for accounts receivable? LO 9-5
40. Describe the related-party limitation on accrued deductions. What tax savings strategy is this limitation designed to thwart? LO 9-5
41. What are the relative advantages of the cash and accrual methods of accounting? LO 9-5
42. Describe how a business adopts a permissible accounting method. Explain whether a taxpayer can adopt an impermissible accounting method. LO 9-5
43. Describe why the IRS might be skeptical of permitting requests for changes in accounting method without a good business purpose. LO 9-5
44. What is a §481 adjustment and what is its purpose? LO 9-5

PROBLEMS

All applicable problems are available with McGraw-Hill's *Connect® Accounting*.

LO 9-1

45. Manny hired his brother's firm to provide accounting services to his business. During the current year, Manny paid his brother's firm $82,000 for services even though other firms were willing to provide the same services for $40,000. How much of this expenditure, if any, is deductible as an ordinary and necessary business expenditure?

LO 9-1 LO 9-2

46. Indicate the amount (if any) that Michael can deduct as ordinary and necessary business deductions in each of the following situations and explain your solution.
    a) From time to time, Michael rents a dump truck for his business. While hauling gravel to a job site, Michael was stopped for speeding. He paid a fine of $125 for speeding and a fine of $80 for carrying an overweight load.
    b) Michael paid a part-time employee $750 to drive his rented dump truck. Michael reimbursed the employee $35 for gasoline for the truck.
    c) Michael gave a member of the city council a new watch, which cost $200. He hopes that the city councilman will "throw" some contracts to his business.

LO 9-1 LO 9-2

47. Indicate the amount (if any) that Josh can deduct as ordinary and necessary business deductions in each of the following situations and explain your solution.
    a) Josh borrowed $50,000 from the First State Bank using his business assets as collateral. He used the money to buy City of Blanksville bonds. Over the course of a year, Josh paid interest of $4,200 on the borrowed funds, but he received $3,500 of interest on the bonds.
    b) Josh purchased a piece of land for $45,000 in order to get a location to expand his business. He also paid $3,200 to construct a new driveway for access to the property.
    c) This year Josh paid $15,000 to employ the mayor's son in the business. Josh would typically pay an employee with these responsibilities about $10,000 but the mayor assured Josh that after his son was hired, some city business would be coming his way.
    d) Josh paid his brother, a mechanic, $3,000 to install a robotic machine for Josh's business. The amount he paid to his brother is comparable to what he would have paid to an unrelated party to do the same work. Once the installation was completed by his brother, Josh began calibrating the machine for operation. However, by the end of the year, he had not started using the machine in his business.

LO 9-2

48. Ralph invited a potential client to dinner and the theater. Ralph paid $250 for the dinner and $220 for the theater tickets in advance. They first went to dinner and then they went to the theater.
    a) What amount can Ralph deduct if, prior to the dinner, he met with the potential client to discuss future business prospects?
    b) What amount can Ralph deduct if he and the client only discussed business during the course of the dinner?
    c) What amount can Ralph deduct if he and the potential client tried to discuss business during the course of the theater performance but did not discuss business at any other time?
    d) What amount can Ralph deduct if the potential client declined Ralph's invitation, so Ralph took his accountant to dinner and the theater to reward his accountant for a hard day at work? At dinner, they discussed the accountant's workload and upcoming assignments.

49. Melissa recently paid $400 for round-trip airfare to San Francisco to attend a business conference for three days. Melissa also paid the following expenses: $250 fee to register for the conference, $300 per night for three nights' lodging, $200 for meals, and $150 for cab fare. LO 9-2
    a) What amount of the travel costs can Melissa deduct as business expenses?
    b) Suppose that while Melissa was on the coast, she also spent two days sightseeing the national parks in the area. To do the sightseeing, she paid $1,000 for transportation, $800 for lodging, and $450 for meals during this part of her trip, which she considers personal in nature. What amount of the travel costs can Melissa deduct as business expenses?
    c) Suppose that Melissa made the trip to San Francisco primarily to visit the national parks and only attended the business conference as an incidental benefit of being present on the coast at that time. What amount of the airfare can Melissa deduct as a business expense?
    d) Suppose that Melissa's permanent residence and business was located in San Francisco. She attended the conference in San Francisco and paid $250 for the registration fee. She drove 100 miles over the course of three days and paid $90 for parking at the conference hotel. In addition, she spent $150 for breakfast and dinner over the three days of the conference. She bought breakfast on the way to the conference hotel and she bought dinner on her way home each night from the conference. What amount of the travel costs can Melissa deduct as business expenses?
50. Kimberly is a self-employed taxpayer. She recently spent $1,000 for airfare to travel to Italy. What amount of the airfare is deductible in each of the following alternative scenarios? LO 9-2
    a) Her trip was entirely for personal purposes.
    b) On the trip, she spent eight days on personal activities and two days on business activities.
    c) On the trip, she spent seven days on business activities and three days on personal activities.
    d) Her trip was entirely for business purposes.
51. Ryan is self-employed. This year Ryan used his personal auto for several long business trips. Ryan paid $1,500 for gasoline on these trips. His depreciation on the car if he was using it fully for business purposes would be $3,000. During the year, he drove his car a total of 12,000 miles (a combination of business and personal travel). LO 9-2
    a) Ryan can provide written documentation of the business purpose for trips totaling 3,000 miles. What business expense amount can Ryan deduct (if any) for these trips?
    b) Ryan estimates that he drove approximately 1,300 miles on business trips, but he can only provide written documentation of the business purpose for trips totaling 820 miles. What business expense amount can Ryan deduct (if any) for these trips?
52. Christopher is a cash-method, calendar-year taxpayer, and he made the following cash payments related to his business this year. Calculate the after-tax cost of each payment assuming he has a 30 percent marginal tax rate. LO 9-1 LO 9-2
    a) $500 fine for speeding while traveling to a client meeting.
    b) $240 of interest on a short-term loan incurred in September and repaid in November. Half of the loan proceeds were used immediately to pay salaries and the other half was invested in municipal bonds until November.

c) $600 for office supplies in May of this year. He used half of the supplies this year and he will use the remaining half by February of next year.

d) $450 for several pairs of work boots. Christopher expects to use the boots about 80 percent of the time in his business and the remainder of the time for hiking. Consider the boots to be a form of clothing.

LO 9-2 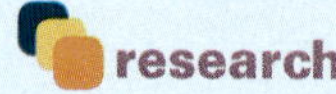

53. Heather paid $15,000 to join a country club in order to meet potential clients. This year she paid $4,300 in greens fees when golfing with clients. Under what circumstances, if any, can Heather deduct the $15,000 cost of country club dues and the costs of the golf played with clients?

LO 9-1 LO 9-2

54. Assume Sarah is a cash-method, calendar-year taxpayer, and she is considering making the following cash payments related to her business. Calculate the after-tax cost of each payment assuming she has a 25 percent marginal tax rate.

a) $2,000 payment for next year's property taxes on her place of business.

b) $800 to reimburse the cost of meals incurred by employees while traveling for the business.

c) $1,200 for football tickets to entertain out-of-town clients during contract negotiations.

d) $500 contribution to the mayor's re-election campaign.

LO 9-3

55. Renee manufactured and sold a "gadget," a specialized asset used by auto manufacturers that qualifies for the domestic production activities deduction. Renee incurred $15,000 in direct expenses in the project, which includes $2,000 of wages Renee paid to employees in the manufacturing of the gadget. What is Renee's domestic production activities deduction for the gadget in each of the following alternative scenarios?

a) Renee sold the gadget for $25,000 and she reported AGI of $75,000 before considering the manufacturing deduction.

b) Renee sold the gadget for $25,000 and she reported AGI of $5,000 before considering the manufacturing deduction.

c) Renee sold the gadget for $40,000 and she reported AGI of $50,000 before considering the manufacturing deduction.

LO 9-3 planning

56. Andrew is considering starting a business of constructing and selling prefabricated greenhouses. There are three very different methods to constructing these greenhouses, and each method results in different revenue and cost projections. Below, Andrew has projected the qualifying revenue and costs for each method. The selling price includes qualifying receipts. The allocable expenses include wages and allocable expenses are included in total costs.

Method	Selling Price	Qualifying Receipts	Total Cost	Allocable Expenses	Allocable Wages
#1	$13,000	$ 9,000	$6,500	$2,500	$2,000
#2	14,000	9,000	7,400	5,500	1,500
#3	15,000	14,000	8,600	2,000	1,000

a) Estimate the tax benefit from the domestic production activities deduction for each construction technique. You may assume that Andrew has sufficient AGI to utilize the deduction and that his marginal tax rate is 30 percent.

b) Which construction technique should Andrew use if his marginal tax rate is 30 percent?

57. This year Amy purchased $2,000 of equipment for use in her business. However, the machine was damaged in a traffic accident while Amy was transporting the equipment to her business. Note that because Amy did not place the equipment into service during the year, she does not claim any depreciation expense for the equipment. LO 9-3

a) After the accident, Amy had the choice of repairing the equipment for $1,800 or selling the equipment to a junk shop for $300. Amy sold the equipment. What amount can Amy deduct for the loss of the equipment?

b) After the accident, Amy repaired the equipment for $800. What amount can Amy deduct for the loss of the equipment?

c) After the accident, Amy could not replace the equipment so she had the equipment repaired for $2,300. What amount can Amy deduct for the loss of the equipment?

58. In July of this year, Stephen started a proprietorship called ECR (which stands for electric car repair). ECR uses the cash method of accounting and Stephen has produced the following financial information for this year. LO 9-3 tax forms

ECR collected $81,000 in cash for repairs completed during the year and an additional $3,200 in cash for repairs that will commence after year end. Customers owe ECR $14,300 for repairs completed this year, and while Stephen isn't sure which bills will eventually be paid, he expects to collect all but about $1,900 of these revenues next year.

ECR has made the following expenditures:

Interest expense	$ 1,250
Shop rent ($1,500 per month)	27,000
Utilities	1,075
Contract labor	8,250
Compensation	21,100
Liability insurance premiums ($350 per month)	4,200
Term life insurance premiums ($150 per month)	1,800

The interest paid relates to interest accrued on a $54,000 loan made to Stephen in July of this year. Stephen used half of the loan to pay for 18 months of shop rent, and the remainder he used to upgrade his personal wardrobe. In July, Stephen purchased 12 months of liability insurance to protect against liability should anyone be injured in the shop. ECR has only one employee (the remaining workers are contract labor), and this employee thoroughly understands how to repair an electric propulsion system. On November 1 of this year, Stephen purchased a 12-month term-life policy that insures the life of this "key" employee. Stephen paid Gecko Insurance Company $1,800; in return, Gecko promises to pay Stephen a $40,000 death benefit if this employee dies any time during the next 12 months.

Fill out a draft of the front page of Stephen's Schedule C.

59. Nicole is a calendar-year taxpayer who accounts for her business using the cash method. On average, Nicole sends out bills for about $12,000 of her services at the first of each month. The bills are due by the end of the month, and typically 70 percent of the bills are paid on time and 98 percent are paid within 60 days. LO 9-5

a) Suppose that Nicole is expecting a 2 percent reduction in her marginal tax rate next year. Ignoring the time value of money, estimate the tax savings for Nicole if she postpones mailing of bills for December until January 1 of next year.

b) Describe how the time value of money affects your calculations.

c) Would this tax savings strategy create any additional business risks? Explain.

LO 9-5

60. Jeremy is a calendar-year taxpayer who sometimes leases his business equipment to local organizations. He recorded the following receipts this year. Indicate the extent to which these payments are taxable income to Jeremy this year if Jeremy is (1) a cash-method taxpayer and (2) he is an accrual-method taxpayer.
   a) $1,000 deposit from the Ladies' Club, which wants to lease a trailer. The club will receive the entire deposit back when the trailer is returned undamaged.
   b) $800 from the Ladies' Club for leasing the trailer from December of this year through March of next year ($200 per month).
   c) $300 lease payment received from the Men's Club this year for renting Jeremy's trailer last year. Jeremy billed the club last year but recently he determined that the Men's Club would never pay him, so he was surprised when he received the check.

LO 9-5

61. Brown Thumb Landscaping is a calendar-year, accrual-method taxpayer. In September, Brown Thumb negotiated a $14,000 contract for services it would provide to the city in November of the current year. The contract specifies that Brown Thumb will receive $4,000 in October as a down payment for these services and it will receive the remaining $10,000 in January of next year.
   a) How much income from this $14,000 contract will Brown Thumb recognize in the current year? Explain.
   b) How much income from this $14,000 contract will Brown Thumb recognize in the current year if it uses the cash method of accounting?
   c) Suppose that the total amount to be paid under the contract with the city is estimated at $14,000 but may be adjusted to $12,000 next year during the review of the city budget. What amount from the contract, if any, should Brown Thumb recognize as income this year? Explain.
   d) Suppose that in addition to the basic contract, Brown Thumb will be paid an additional $3,000 if its city landscape design wins the annual design competition next year. Should Brown Thumb accrue $3,000 revenue this year? Why or why not?

LO 9-5

62. In January of year 0, Justin paid $4,800 for an insurance policy that covers his business property for accidents and casualties. Justin is a calendar-year taxpayer who uses the cash method of accounting. What amount of the insurance premium may Justin deduct in year 0 in each of the following alternative scenarios?
   a) The policy covers the business property from April 1 of year 0 through March 31 of year 1.
   b) The policy begins on February 1 of year 1 and extends through January 31 of year 2.
   c) Assume Justin paid $6,000 for a 24-month policy that covers from April 1, year 0 through March 31, year 2.
   d) Assume that instead of paying an insurance premium, Justin paid $4,800 to rent his business property from April 1 of year 0 through March 31 of year 1.

LO 9-5

63. Ben teaches golf lessons at a country club under a business called Ben's Pure Swings (BPS). He operates this business as a sole proprietorship on the accrual basis of accounting. Ben's trusty accountant, Brian, has produced the following accounting information for BPS:

   This year BPS billed clients for $86,700 and collected $61,000 in cash for golf lessons completed during the year. In addition, BPS collected an additional $14,500 in cash for lessons that will commence after year-end. Ben hopes to collect about half of the outstanding billings next year but the rest will likely be written off.

   Besides providing private golf lessons, BPS also contracted with the country club to staff the driving range. This year, BPS billed the country club $27,200 for the service. The club paid $17,000 of the amount but disputed the remainder. By year-end, the dispute had not been resolved, and while Ben believes he is entitled to the money, he has still not collected the remaining $10,200.

BPS has accrued the following expenses (explained below):

Advertising (in the clubhouse)	$13,150
Pro Golf Teachers Membership Fees	860
Supplies (golf tees, balls, etc.)	4,720
Club rental	6,800
Malpractice insurance	2,400
Accounting fees	8,820

The expenditures were all paid for this calendar year with several exceptions. First, Ben initiated his golfer's malpractice insurance on June 1 of this year. The $2,400 insurance bill covers the last six months of this calendar year and the first six months of next year. At year-end, Ben had only paid $600, but he has assured the insurance agent he would pay the remaining $1,800 early next year. Second, the amount paid for club rental ($100 per week) represents rental charges for the last 6 weeks of the previous year, for the 52 weeks in this calendar year, and the first 10 weeks of next year. Ben has also mentioned that BPS only pays for supplies that are used at the club. Although BPS could buy the supplies for half the cost elsewhere, Ben likes to "throw some business" to the golf pro shop because it is operated by his brother.

Fill out a draft of the front page of a Schedule C for BPS.

64. On April 1 of year 0 Stephanie received a $9,000 payment for full payment on a three-year service contract (under the contract Stephanie is obligated to provide advisory services for the next three years). LO 9-5
   a) What amount of income should Stephanie recognize in year 0 if she uses the accrual method of accounting (she recognized $2,250 for financial accounting purposes)?
   b) What amount of income will Stephanie recognize in year 1 if she uses the accrual method of accounting?
   c) What amount of income will Stephanie recognize in year 2 if she uses the accrual method of accounting?
   d) What amount of income will Stephanie recognize in year 0 if she recognizes $5,000 of income from the contract for financial statement purposes?

65. In October of year 0, Janine received a $6,000 payment from a client for 25 months of security services she will provide starting on November 1 of year 0. This amounts to $240 per month. LO 9-5
   a) When must Janine recognize the income from the $6,000 advance payment for services if she uses the cash method of accounting?
   b) When must Janine recognize the income from the $6,000 advance payment for services if she uses the accrual method of accounting?
   c) Suppose that instead of services, Janine received the payment for a security system (inventory) that she will deliver and install in year 2. When would Janine recognize the income from the advance payment for inventory sale if she uses the accrual method of accounting and she uses the deferral method for reporting income from advance payments? For financial accounting purposes, she reports the income when the inventory is delivered.
   d) Suppose that instead of services, Janine received the payment for the delivery of inventory to be delivered next year. When would Janine recognize the income from the advance payment for sale of goods if she uses the accrual method of accounting and she uses the full-inclusion method for advance payments?

LO 9-5 66. Nicole's business uses the accrual method of accounting and accounts for inventory with specific identification. In year 0, Nicole received a $4,500 payment with an order for inventory to be delivered to the client early next year. Nicole has the inventory ready for delivery at the end of year 0 (she purchased the inventory in year 0 for $2,300).

a) When does Nicole recognize the $2,200 of gross profit ($4,500 revenue minus $2,300 cost of the inventory) if she uses the full-inclusion method?

b) When does Nicole recognize the $2,200 of gross profit from the inventory sale if she uses the deferral method?

c) How would Nicole account for the inventory-related transactions if she uses the cash method of accounting and her annual sales are usually less than $100,000?

d) How would Nicole account for the inventory-related transactions if she uses the cash method of accounting and her annual sales are usually over $2,000,000 per year?

LO 9-5 67. This year Amber opened a factory to process and package landscape mulch. At the end of the year, Amber's accountant prepared the following schedule for allocating manufacturing costs to the mulch inventory, but her accountant is unsure of what costs need to be allocated to the inventory under UNICAP. Approximately 20 percent of management time, space, and expenses are spent on this manufacturing process.

		Costs	Tax Inventory
Material:	Mulch and packaging	$ 5,000	?
	Administrative supplies	250	?
Salaries:	Factory labor	12,000	?
	Sales & advertising	3,500	?
	Administration	5,200	?
Property taxes:	Factory	4,600	?
	Offices	2,700	?
Depreciation:	Factory	8,000	?
	Offices	1,500	?

a) At the end of the year, Amber's accountant indicated that the business had processed 10,000 bags of mulch but only 1,000 bags remained in the ending inventory. What is Amber's tax basis in her ending inventory after applying the UNICAP rules to allocate indirect costs to inventory? (Assume direct costs are allocated to inventory according to the level of ending inventory. In contrast, indirect costs are first allocated by time spent and then according to level of ending inventory.)

b) Under what conditions could Amber's business avoid having to apply UNICAP to allocate indirect costs to inventory for tax purposes?

LO 9-5 68. Suppose that David adopted the last-in, first-out (LIFO) inventory-flow method for his business inventory of widgets (purchase prices below).

Widget	Purchase Date	Direct Cost	Other Costs	Total Cost
#1	August 15	$2,100	$100	$2,200
#2	October 30	2,200	150	2,350
#3	November 10	2,300	100	2,400

In late December, David sold widget #2 and next year David expects to purchase three more widgets at the following estimated prices:

Widget	Purchase Date	Estimated Cost
#4	Early spring	$2,600
#5	Summer	2,260
#6	Fall	2,400

a) What cost of goods sold and ending inventory would David record if he elects to use the LIFO method this year?
b) If David sells two widgets next year, what will be his cost of goods sold and ending inventory next year under the LIFO method?
c) How would you answer (a) and (b) if David had initially selected the first-in, first-out (FIFO) method instead of LIFO?
d) Suppose that David initially adopted the LIFO method, but wants to apply for a change to FIFO next year. What would be his §481 adjustment for this change, and in what year(s) would he make the adjustment?

69. On November 1 of year 0, Jaxon borrowed $50,000 from Bucksnort Savings and Loan for use in his business. In December, Jaxon paid interest of $4,500 relating to the 12-month period from November of year 0 through October of year 1. LO 9-5
a) How much interest, if any, can Jaxon deduct in year 0 if his business uses the cash method of accounting for tax purposes?
b) How much interest, if any, can Jaxon deduct in year 0 if his business uses the accrual method of accounting for tax purposes?

70. Matt hired Apex Services to repair his business equipment. On November 1 of year 0, Matt paid $2,000 for the repairs that he expects to begin in early March of year 1. LO 9-5
a) What amount of the cost of the repairs can Matt deduct in year 0 if he uses the cash method of accounting for his business?
b) What amount of the cost of the repairs can Matt deduct in year 0 if he uses the accrual method of accounting for his business?
c) What amount of the cost of the repairs can Matt deduct in year 0 if he uses the accrual method and he expects the repairs to be done by early February?
d) What amount of the cost of the repairs can Matt deduct in year 0 if he uses the cash method of accounting and he expects the repairs to be done by early February?

71. Circuit Corporation (CC) is a calendar-year, accrual-method taxpayer. CC manufactures and sells electronic circuitry. On November 15, year 0, CC enters into a contract with Equip Corp (EC) that provides CC with exclusive use of EC's specialized manufacturing equipment for the five-year period beginning on January 1 of year 1. Pursuant to the contract, CC pays EC $100,000 on December 30, year 0. How much of this expenditure is CC allowed to deduct in year 0 and in year 1? LO 9-5

72. This year (year 0) Elizabeth agreed to a three-year service contract with an engineering consulting firm to improve efficiency in her factory. The contract requires Elizabeth to pay the consulting firm $1,500 for each instance that Elizabeth requests their assistance. The contract also provides that Elizabeth only pays the consultants if its advice increases efficiency as measured 12 months from the date of service. This year Elizabeth requested advice on three occasions and she has not yet made any payments to the consultants. LO 9-5

a) How much should Elizabeth deduct in year 0 under this service contract if she uses the accrual method of accounting?

b) How much should Elizabeth deduct in year 0 under this service contract if she uses the cash method of accounting?

LO 9-5

73. Travis is a professional landscaper. He provides his clients with a one-year (12-month) warranty for retaining walls he installs. In June of year 1, Travis installed a wall for an important client, Sheila. In early November, Sheila informed Travis that the retaining wall had failed. To repair the wall, Travis paid $700 cash for additional stone that he delivered to Sheila's location. Travis also offered to pay a mason $800 to repair the wall on November 20 of year 1. Due to some bad weather and the mason's work backlog, the mason agreed to finish the work by the end of January of year 2. Even though Travis expected the mason to finish the project by the end of February, Travis informed the mason that he would pay the mason the $800 when he completed the job.

a) Assuming Travis is an accrual-method taxpayer, how much can he deduct in year 1 from these activities?

b) Assuming Travis is a cash-method taxpayer, how much can he deduct in year 1 from these activities?

LO 9-5

research

74. Adam elects the accrual method of accounting for his business. What amount of deductions does Adam recognize in year 0 for the following transactions?

a) Adam guarantees that he will refund the cost of any goods sold to a client if the goods fail within a year of delivery. In December of year 0, Adam agreed to refund $2,400 to clients, and he expects to make payment in January of year 1.

b) On December 1 of year 0, Adam paid $480 for a one-year contract with CleanUP Services to clean his store. The agreement calls for services to be provided on a weekly basis.

c) Adam was billed $240 for annual personal property taxes on his delivery van. Because this was the first time Adam was billed for these taxes, he did not make payment until January. However, he considers the amounts immaterial.

LO 9-5

75. Rebecca is a calendar-year taxpayer who operates a business. She made the following business-related expenditures in December of year 0. Indicate the amount of these payments that she may deduct in year 0 under both the cash method of accounting and the accrual method of accounting.

a) $2,000 for an accountant to evaluate the accounting system of Rebecca's business. The accountant spent three weeks in January of year 1 working on the evaluation.

b) $2,500 for new office furniture. The furniture was delivered on January 15, year 1.

c) $3,000 for property taxes payable on her factory.

d) $1,500 for interest on a short-term bank loan relating to the period from November 1, year 0 through March 31, year 31.

LO 9-5

76. BCS Corporation is a calendar-year, accrual-method taxpayer. BCS was formed and started its business activities on January 1, year 0. It reported the following information for year 0. Indicate BCS's deductible amount for year 0 in each of the following alternative scenarios.

a) BCS provides two-year warranties on products it sells to customers. For its year 0 sales, BCS estimated and accrued $200,000 in warranty expense for financial accounting purposes. During year 0, BCS actually spent $30,000 repairing its product under the warranty.

b) BCS accrued an expense for $50,000 for amounts it anticipated it would be required to pay under the workers' compensation act. During year 0, BCS actually paid $10,000 for workers' compensation–related liabilities.

c) In June of year 0, a display of BCS's product located in its showroom fell on and injured a customer. The customer sued BCS for $500,000. The case is scheduled to go to trial next year. BCS anticipates that it will lose the case and accrued a $500,000 expense on its financial statements.

d) Assume the same facts as in (c) except that BCS was required to pay $500,000 to a court-appointed escrow fund in year 0. If BCS loses the case in year 1, the money from the escrow fund will be transferred to the customer suing BCS.

e) On December 1 of year 0, BCS acquired equipment from Equip Company. As part of the purchase, BCS signed a warranty agreement with Equip so that Equip would warranty the equipment for two years (from December 1 of year 0 through November 30 of year 2). The cost of the warranty was $12,000. BCS paid Equip for the warranty in January of year 1.

77. This year William provided $4,200 of services to a large client on credit. Unfortunately, this client has recently encountered financial difficulties and has been unable to pay William for the services. Moreover, William does not expect to collect for his services. William has "written off" the account and would like to claim a deduction for tax purposes. **LO 9-5**

a) What amount of deduction for bad debt expense can William claim this year if he uses the accrual method?

b) What amount of deduction for bad debt expense can William claim this year if he uses the cash method?

78. Dustin has a contract to provide services to Dado Enterprises. In November of year 0, Dustin billed Dado $10,000 for the services he rendered during the year. Dado is an accrual-method proprietorship that is owned and operated by Dustin's father. **LO 9-5**

a) What amount of revenue must Dustin recognize in year 0 if Dustin uses the cash method and Dado remits payment for the services in December of year 0? What amount can Dado deduct in year 0?

b) What amount of revenue must Dustin recognize in year 0 if Dustin uses the accrual method and Dado remits payment for the services in December of year 0? What amount can Dado deduct in year 0?

c) What amount of revenue must Dustin recognize in year 0 if Dustin uses the cash method and Dado remits payment for the services in January of year 1? What amount can Dado deduct in year 0?

d) What amount of revenue must Dustin recognize in year 0 if Dustin uses the accrual method and Dado remits payment for the services in January of year 1? What amount can Dado deduct in year 0?

79. Nancy operates a business that uses the accrual method of accounting. In December, Nancy asked her brother, Hank, to provide her business with consulting advice. Hank billed Nancy for $5,000 of consulting services in year 0 (a reasonable amount), but Nancy was only able to pay $3,000 of the bill by the end of year 0. However, Nancy paid the remainder of the bill in year 1. **LO 9-5**

a) How much of the $5,000 consulting services will Hank include in his income in year 0 if he uses the cash method of accounting? What amount can Nancy deduct in year 0 for the consulting services?

b) How much of the $5,000 consulting services will Hank include in his income in year 0 if he uses the accrual method of accounting? What amount can Nancy deduct in year 0 for the consulting services?

LO 9-5

80. Erin is considering switching her business from the cash method to the accrual method at the beginning of next year (year 1). Determine the amount and timing of her §481 adjustment assuming the IRS grants Erin's request in the following alternative scenarios.

a) At the end of year 0/beginning of year 1, Erin's business has $15,000 of accounts receivables and $18,000 of accounts payables that have not been recorded for tax purposes.

b) At the end of year 0/beginning of year 1, Erin's business reports $25,000 of accounts receivables and $9,000 of accounts payables that have not been recorded for tax purposes.

COMPREHENSIVE PROBLEMS

All applicable problems are available with McGraw-Hill's *Connect® Accounting*.

81. Joe operates a business that locates and purchases specialized assets for clients, among other activities. Joe uses the accrual method of accounting but he doesn't keep any significant inventories of the specialized assets that he sells. Joe reported the following financial information for his business activities during year 0. Determine the effect of each of the following transactions on the taxable business income.

a) Joe has signed a contract to sell gadgets to the city. The contract provides that sales of gadgets are dependent upon a test sample of gadgets operating successfully. In December, Joe delivers $12,000 worth of gadgets to the city that will be tested in March. Joe purchased the gadgets especially for this contract and paid $8,500.

b) Joe paid $180 for entertaining a visiting out-of-town client. The client didn't discuss business with Joe during this visit, but Joe wants to maintain good relations to encourage additional business next year.

c) On November 1, Joe paid $600 for premiums providing for $40,000 of "key man" insurance on the life of Joe's accountant over the next 12 months.

d) At the end of year 0, Joe's business reports $9,000 of accounts receivable. Based upon past experience, Joe believes that at least $2,000 of his new receivables will be uncollectible.

e) In December of year 0, Joe rented equipment to complete a large job. Joe paid $3,000 in December because the rental agency required a minimum rental of three months ($1,000 per month). Joe completed the job before year-end, but he returned the equipment at the end of the lease.

f) Joe hired a new sales representative as an employee and sent her to Dallas for a week to contact prospective out-of-state clients. Joe ended up reimbursing his employee $300 for airfare, $350 for lodging, $250 for meals, and $150 for entertainment (Joe provided adequate documentation to substantiate the business purpose for the meals and entertainment). Joe requires the employee to account for all expenditures in order to be reimbursed.

g) Joe uses his BMW (a personal auto) to travel to and from his residence to his factory. However, he switches to a business vehicle if he needs to travel after he reaches the factory. Last month, the business vehicle broke down and he was forced to use the BMW both to travel to and from the factory and to visit work sites. He drove 120 miles visiting work sites and 46 miles driving to and from the factory from his home. Joe uses the standard mileage rate to determine his auto-related business expenses.

h) Joe paid a visit to his parents in Dallas over the Christmas holidays. While he was in the city, Joe spent $50 to attend a half-day business symposium. Joe paid $200 for airfare, $50 for meals during the symposium, and $20 on cab fare to the symposium.

82. Jack, a geologist, had been debating for years whether or not to venture out on his own and operate his own business. He had developed a lot of solid relationships with clients and he believed that many of them would follow him if he were to leave his current employer. As part of a New Year's resolution, Jack decided he would finally do it. In January, Jack put his business plan together and in February opened his doors for business as a C corporation called Geo-Jack (GJ). Jack is the sole shareholder. Jack reported the following financial information for the year (assume GJ reports on a calendar year and uses the accrual method of accounting).

    a) In January, GJ rented a small business office about 12 miles from Jack's home. GJ paid $10,000 which represented a damage deposit of $4,000 and rent for two years ($3,000 annually).
    b) GJ earned and collected $290,000 performing geological-related services and selling its specialized digging tool [see part (i)].
    c) GJ received $50 interest from municipal bonds and $2,100 interest from other investments.
    d) GJ purchased some new equipment in February for $42,500. It claimed depreciation on these assets during the year in the amount of $6,540.
    e) GJ paid $7,000 to buy luxury season tickets for Jack's parents for State U football games.
    f) GJ paid Jack's father $10,000 for services that would have cost no more than $6,000 if Jack had hired any other local business to perform the services. While Jack's dad was competent, he does not command such a premium from his other clients.
    g) In an attempt to get his name and new business recognized, GJ paid $7,000 for a one-page ad in the *Geologic Survey.* It also paid $15,000 in radio ads to be run through the end of December.
    h) GJ leased additional office space in a building downtown. GJ paid rent of $27,000 for the year.
    i) In August, GJ began manufacturing a special geological digging tool that it sells to wholesalers. GJ's QPAI from the activity for the year is $100,000 [included in revenues reported in part (b)]. GJ paid $10,000 of wages to the employees working on the project during the year and its cost of goods sold on the sales is $15,000. (Assume that taxable income does not limit the amount of the DPAD, and that no wages should be included in cost of goods sold.) Remember that cost of goods sold and wages reduce taxable income.
    j) In November, Jack's office was broken into and equipment valued at $5,000 was stolen. The tax basis of the equipment was $5,500. Jack received $2,000 of insurance proceeds from the theft.
    k) GJ incurred a $4,000 fine from the state government for digging in an unauthorized digging zone.
    l) GJ contributed $3,000 to lobbyists for their help in persuading the state government to authorize certain unauthorized digging zones.
    m) On July 1, GJ paid $1,800 for an 18-month insurance policy for its business equipment. The policy covers the period July 1 of this year through December 31 of next year.
    n) GJ borrowed $20,000 to help with the company's initial funding needs. GJ used $2,000 of funds to invest in municipal bonds. At the end of the year, GJ paid the $1,200 of interest expense that accrued on the loan during the year.
    o) Jack lives 12 miles from the office. He carefully tracked his mileage and drove his truck 6,280 miles between the office and his home. He also drove an additional 7,200 miles between the office and traveling to client sites. Jack did not use the truck for any other purposes. He did not keep track of the specific expenses associated with the truck. However, while traveling to a client

site, Jack received a $150 speeding ticket. GJ reimbursed Jack for business mileage and for the speeding ticket.

p) GJ purchased two season tickets (20 games) to attend State U baseball games for a total of $1,100. Jack took existing and prospective clients to the games to maintain contact and find further work. This was very successful for Jack as GJ gained many new projects through substantial discussions with the clients following the games.

q) GJ reimbursed employee-salespersons $3,500 for meals involving substantial business discussion.

r) GJ had a client who needed Jack to perform work in Florida. Because Jack had never been to Florida before, he booked an extra day and night for sightseeing. Jack spent $400 for airfare and booked a hotel for 3 nights ($120/night). (Jack stayed two days for business purposes and one day for personal purposes.) He also rented a car for $45 per day. The client arranged for Jack's meals while Jack was doing business. GJ reimbursed Jack for all expenses.

Required:

A) What is GJ's net business income for tax purposes for the year?

B) As a C corporation, does GJ have a required tax year? If so, what would it be?

C) If GJ were a sole proprietorship, would it have a required tax year-end? If so, what would it be?

D) If GJ were an S corporation, would it have a required tax year-end? If so, what would it be?

83. Rex loves to work with his hands and is very good at making small figurines. Three years ago, Rex opened Bronze Age Miniatures (BAM) for business as a sole proprietorship. BAM produces miniature characters ranging from sci-fi characters (his favorite) to historical characters like George Washington (the most popular). Business has been going very well for him, and he has provided the following information relating to his business. Calculate the business taxable income for BAM.

a) Rex received approval from the IRS to switch from the cash method of accounting to the accrual method of accounting effective January 1 of this year. At year-end of last year, BAM reported accounts receivable that had not been included in income under the accrual method of $14,000 and accounts payable that had not been deducted under the accrual method of $5,000.

b) In March, BAM sold 5,000 miniature historical figures to History R Us Inc. (HRU), a retailer of historical artifacts and figurines, for $75,000.

c) HRU was so impressed with the figurines that it purchased in March that it wanted to contract with BAM to continue to produce the figurines for them for the next three years. HRU paid BAM $216,000 ($12 per figurine) on October 30 of this year, to produce 500 figurines per month for 36 months beginning on November 1 of this year. BAM delivered 500 figurines on November 30 and again on December 30. Rex elects to use the deferral method to account for the transaction.

d) Though the sci-fi figurines were not quite as popular, BAM sold 400 figurines at a sci-fi convention in April. Rex accepted cash only and received $11,000 for these sales.

e) In January, BAM determined that it would not be able to collect on $2,000 of its beginning-of-the-year receivables, so it wrote off $2,000 of specific receivables. BAM sold 100,000 other figurines on credit for $120,000. BAM estimates that it will be unable to collect 5 percent of the sales revenue from these sales but it has not been able to specifically identify any accounts to write off.

f) Assume that BAM correctly determined that its cost of goods sold this year is $54,000.

g) The sci-fi convention in April was held in Chicago, Illinois. Rex attended the convention because he felt it was a good opportunity to gain new customers and to get new ideas for figurines. He paid $350 round-trip airfare, $100 for entrance to the convention, $210 for lodging, $65 for cab fare, and $110 for meals during the trip. He was busy with business activities the entire trip.

h) On August 1, BAM purchased a 12-month insurance policy that covers its business property for accidents and casualties through July 31 of next year. The policy cost BAM $3,600.

i) BAM reported depreciation expense of $8,200 for this year.

j) Rex had previously operated his business out of his garage, but in January he decided to rent a larger space. He entered into a lease agreement on February 1 and paid $14,400 ($1,200 per month) to possess the space for the next 12 months (February of this year through January of next year).

k) Before he opened his doors for business, Rex spent $30,000 investigating and otherwise getting ready to do business. He expensed $5,000 immediately and is amortizing the remainder using the straight-line method over 180 months.

l) In December, BAM agreed to a 12-month $8,000 contract with Advertise-With-Us (AWU) to produce a radio ad campaign. BAM paid $3,000 up front (in December of this year) and AWU agreed that BAM would owe the remaining $5,000 only if BAM's sales increased by 15 percent over the nine-month period after the contract was signed.

m) In November of this year, BAM paid $2,500 in business property taxes (based on asset values) covering the period December 1 of this year through November 30 of next year. In November of last year, BAM paid $1,500 for business property taxes (based on asset values) covering the period December 1 of last year through November 30 of this year.

84. Bryan followed in his father's footsteps and entered into the carpet business. He owns and operates I Do Carpet (IDC). Bryan prefers to install carpet only, but in order to earn additional revenue, he also cleans carpets and sells carpet cleaning supplies. Compute his taxable income for the current year considering the following items:

a) IDC contracted with a homebuilder in December of last year to install carpet in 10 new homes being built. The contract price of $80,000 includes $50,000 for materials (carpet). The remaining $30,000 is for IDC's service of installing the carpet. The contract also stated that all money was to be paid up front. The homebuilder paid IDC in full on December 28 of last year. The contract required IDC to complete the work by January 31 of this year. Bryan purchased the necessary carpet on January 2 and began working on the first home January 4. He completed the last home on January 27 of this year.

b) IDC entered into several other contracts this year and completed the work before year-end. The work cost $130,000 in materials. Bryan billed out $240,000 but only collected $220,000 by year-end. Of the $20,000 still owed to him, Bryan wrote off $3,000 he didn't expect to collect as a bad debt from a customer experiencing extreme financial difficulties.

c) IDC entered into a three-year contract to clean the carpets of an office building. The contract specified that IDC would clean the carpets monthly from July 1 of this year through June 30 three years hence. IDC received payment in full of $8,640 ($240 a month for 36 months) on June 30 of this year.

d) IDC sold 100 bottles of carpet stain remover this year for $5 per bottle (it collected $500). Rex sold 40 bottles on June 1 and 60 bottles on November 2. IDC had the following carpet cleaning supplies on hand for this year and it uses the LIFO method of accounting for inventory under a perpetual inventory system:

Purchase Date	Bottles	Total Cost
November last year	40	$120
February this year	35	112
July this year	25	85
August this year	40	140
Totals	140	$457

e) On August 1 of this year, IDC needed more room for storage and paid $900 to rent a garage for 12 months.

f) On November 30 of this year, Bryan decided it was time to get his logo on the sides of his work van. IDC hired We Paint Anything Inc. (WPA) to do the job. It paid $500 down and agreed to pay the remaining $1,500 upon completion of the job. WPA indicated it wouldn't be able to begin the job until January 15 of next year, but the job would only take one week to complete. Due to circumstances beyond its control, WPA wasn't able to complete the job until April 1 of next year, at which time IDC paid the remaining $1,500.

g) In December, Bryan's son, Aiden, helped him finish some carpeting jobs. IDC owed Aiden $600 (reasonable) compensation for his work. However, Aiden did not receive the payment until January of next year.

h) IDC also paid $1,000 for interest on a short-term bank loan relating to the period from November 1 of this year through March 31 of next year.

85. Hank started a new business in June of last year, Hank's Donut World (HW for short). He has requested your advice on the following specific tax matters associated with HW's first year of operations. Hank has estimated HW's income for the first year as follows:

Revenue:		
Donut sales	$252,000	
Catering revenues	71,550	$323,550
Expenditures:		
Donut supplies	$124,240	
Catering expense	27,910	
Salaries to shop employees	52,500	
Rent expense	40,050	
Accident insurance premiums	8,400	
Other business expenditures	6,850	−259,950
Net Income		$ 63,600

HW operates as a sole proprietorship and Hank reports on a calendar year. Hank uses the cash method of accounting and plans to do the same with HW (HW has no inventory of donuts because unsold donuts are not salable). HW does not purchase donut supplies on credit nor does it generally make sales on credit. Hank has provided the following details for specific first-year transactions.

- A small minority of HW clients complained about the catering service. To mitigate these complaints, Hank's policy is to refund dissatisfied clients 50 percent of the catering fee. By the end of the first year, only two HW clients had complained but had not yet been paid refunds. The expected refunds amount to $1,700, and Hank reduced the reported catering fees for the first year to reflect the expected refund.
- In the first year, HW received a $6,750 payment from a client for catering a monthly breakfast for 30 consecutive months beginning in December. Because the payment didn't relate to last year, Hank excluded the entire amount when he calculated catering revenues.

- In July, HW paid $1,500 to ADMAN Co. for an advertising campaign to distribute fliers advertising HW's catering service. Unfortunately, this campaign violated a city code restricting advertising by fliers, and the city fined HW $250 for the violation. HW paid the fine, and Hank included the fine and the cost of the campaign in "other business" expenditures.
- In July, HW also paid $8,400 for a 24-month insurance policy that covers HW for accidents and casualties beginning on August 1 of the first year. Hank deducted the entire $8,400 as accident insurance premiums.
- On May of the first year, Hank signed a contract to lease the HW donut shop for 10 months. In conjunction with the contract, Hank paid $2,000 as a damage deposit and $8,050 for rent ($805 per month). Hank explained that the damage deposit was refundable at the end of the lease. At this time, Hank also paid $30,000 to lease kitchen equipment for 24 months ($1,250 per month). Both leases began on June 1 of the first year. In his estimate, Hank deducted these amounts ($40,050 in total) as rent expense.
- Hank signed a contract hiring WEGO Catering to help cater breakfasts. At year-end, WEGO asked Hank to hold the last catering payment for the year, $9,250, until after January 1 (apparently because WEGO didn't want to report the income on its tax return). The last check was delivered to WEGO in January after the end of the first year. However, because the payment related to the first year of operations, Hank included the $9,250 in last year's catering expense.
- Hank believes that the key to the success of HW has been hiring Jimbo Jones to supervise the donut production and manage the shop. Because Jimbo is such an important employee, HW purchased a "key-employee" term-life insurance policy on his life. HW paid a $5,100 premium for this policy and it will pay HW a $40,000 death benefit if Jimbo passes away any time during the next 12 months. The term of the policy began on September 1 of last year and this payment was included in "other business" expenditures.
- In the first year, HW catered a large breakfast event to celebrate the city's anniversary. The city agreed to pay $7,100 for the event, but Hank forgot to notify the city of the outstanding bill until January of this year. When he mailed the bill in January, Hank decided to discount the charge to $5,500. On the bill, Hank thanked the mayor and the city council for their patronage and asked them to "send a little more business our way." This bill is not reflected in Hank's estimate of HW's income for the first year of operations.

Required:

A) Hank files his personal tax return on a calendar year, but he has not yet filed last year's personal tax return nor has he filed a tax return reporting HW's results for the first year of operations. Explain when Hank should file the tax return for HW and calculate the amount of taxable income generated by HW last year.

B) Determine the taxable income that HW will generate if Hank chooses to account for the business under the accrual method.

C) Describe how your solution might change if Hank incorporated HW before he commenced business last year.

86. R.E.M., a calendar-year corporation and Athens, Georgia, band, recently sold tickets ($20,000,000) for concerts scheduled in the United States for next year and the following year. For financial statement purposes, R.E.M. will recognize the income from the ticket sales when it performs the concerts. For tax purposes, it uses the accrual method and would prefer to defer the income from the ticket sales until after the concerts are performed. This is the first time that it has sold tickets one or two years in advance. Michael Stipe has asked your advice. Write a memo to Michael explaining your findings. 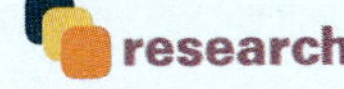

chapter

10 Property Acquisition and Cost Recovery

Learning Objectives

Upon completing this chapter, you should be able to:

LO 10-1 Explain the concept of basis and adjusted basis and describe the cost recovery methods used under the tax law to recover the cost of personal property, real property, intangible assets, and natural resources.

LO 10-2 Determine the applicable cost recovery (depreciation) life, method, and convention for tangible personal and real property and calculate the deduction allowable under basic MACRS.

LO 10-3 Explain the additional special cost recovery rules (§179, bonus, listed property) and calculate the deduction allowable under these rules.

LO 10-4 Explain the rationale behind amortization, describe the four categories of amortizable intangible assets, and calculate amortization expense.

LO 10-5 Explain cost recovery of natural resources and the allowable depletion methods.

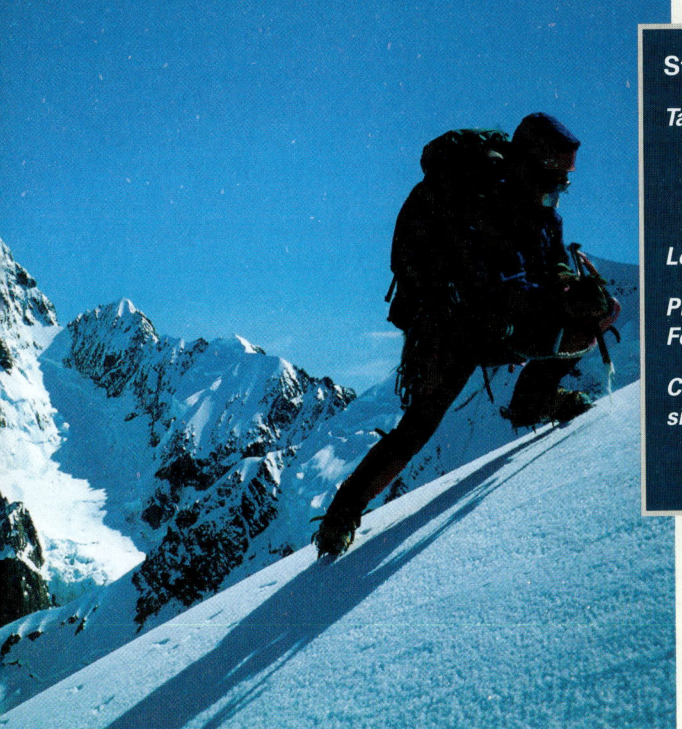

© Brand X Pictures/SuperStock

Storyline Summary

Taxpayer:	Teton Mountaineering Technology, LLC (Teton)—a calendar-year single-member LLC (treated as a sole proprietorship for tax purposes)
Location:	Cody, Wyoming
President/ Founder:	Steve Dallimore
Current situation:	Teton must acquire property to start manufacturing operations and wants to understand the tax consequences of property acquisitions.

Two years ago while climbing the Black Ice Couloir (pronounced "cool-wahr") in Grand Teton National Park, Steve Dallimore and his buddy got into a desperate situation. The climbers planned to move fast and light and to be home before an approaching storm reached the Teton. But just shy of the summit, climbing conditions forced them to turn back. Huddled in a wet sleeping bag in a dark snow cave waiting for the tempest to pass, Steve had an epiphany—a design for a better ice-climbing tool. Since that moment, Steve has been quietly consumed with making his dream—designing and selling his own line of climbing equipment—a reality. Although his current sales career is challenging and financially rewarding, Steve has too often found himself watching the clock and dreaming of a more fulfilling and adventurous career based upon his early training as a mechanical engineer. Steve decided to exercise his stock options, leave his current position, and start Teton. The only problem is that Steve has no employees, no business location, and no manufacturing equipment.

to be continued . . .

Steve obviously has many issues to resolve and decisions to make. In this chapter, we focus on the tax issues relating to the assets Steve will acquire for use in his new business. In particular, we explain how Teton will determine its cost recovery (depreciation, amortization, and depletion) deductions for the assets in the year the business begins and in subsequent years.[1] These deductions can generate significant tax savings for companies in capital-intensive industries.

This chapter explores the tax consequences of acquiring new or used property, depreciation methods businesses may use to recover the cost of their assets, and other special cost recovery incentives. Along the way, we compare and contrast the process of computing depreciation for tax purposes and for financial accounting purposes. We also address the tax consequences of using intangible assets and natural resources in business activities.

LO 10-1 COST RECOVERY AND BASIS FOR COST RECOVERY

Most businesses make a significant investment in property, plant, and equipment that is expected to provide benefits over a number of years. For both financial accounting and tax accounting purposes, businesses must capitalize the cost of assets with a useful life of more than one year (on the balance sheet) rather than expense the cost immediately. Businesses are allowed to use various methods to allocate the cost of these assets over time because the assets are subject to wear, tear, and obsolescence.

The method of **cost recovery** depends on the nature of the underlying asset. **Depreciation** is the method of deducting the cost of *tangible* personal and real property (other than land) over a specific time period. **Amortization** is the method of deducting the cost of **intangible assets** over a specific time period. Finally, **depletion** is the method of deducting the cost of natural resources over time. Exhibit 10-1 summarizes these concepts.

Generally, a significant portion of a firm's assets comprises property, plant, equipment, intangibles, or even natural resources. In most cases, this holds true for small businesses like Teton and also for large publicly traded companies. For example, Exhibit 10-2 describes the assets held by Weyerhaeuser, a publicly traded timber company. As indicated in Exhibit 10-2, Weyerhaeuser has almost $3 billion in property and equipment (net of depreciation) and $6 billion in timber (net of depletion), comprising roughly 60 percent of its assets.

Businesses must choose accounting methods for the assets acquired during the year from among the allowable cost recovery alternatives we describe in this chapter. Attention to detail is important because the basis of an asset must be reduced by the

EXHIBIT 10-1 Assets and Cost Recovery

Asset Type	Cost Recovery Method
Personal property is comprised of tangible assets such as automobiles, equipment, and machinery.	Depreciation
Real property is comprised of buildings and land (although land is nondepreciable).	Depreciation
Intangible assets are nonphysical assets such as goodwill and patents.	Amortization
Natural resources are commodities that are considered valuable in their natural form such as oil, coal, timber, and gold.	Depletion

[1]Cost recovery is the common term used to describe the process by which businesses allocate the cost of their fixed assets over the time period in which the assets are used.

EXHIBIT 10-2 Weyerhaeuser Assets

Assets (in millions) per 2012 10-K Statement	2013	2012
Total current assets	$ 2,326	$ 2,407
Property and equipment, net (Note 6)	2,704	2,872
Construction in progress	112	50
Timber and timberlands at cost, less depletion charged to disposals	6,580	3,961
Investments in and advances to equity affiliates (Note 7)	211	213
Goodwill	42	40
Deferred tax assets	41	368
Restricted assets held by special purpose entities (Note 9)	615	615
Other	1,867	2,066
Total Assets	$14,498	$12,592

cost recovery deductions allowed or *allowable*.[2] This means that if a business fails to deduct (by mistake or error) the allowable amount of depreciation expense for the year, the business must still reduce the asset's basis by the depreciation expense the taxpayer could have deducted under the method the business is using to depreciate the asset (this reduces the future depreciation deductions for the asset).

Basis for Cost Recovery

Businesses may begin recouping the cost of purchased business assets (cost basis) once they begin using the asset in their business (place it in service).[3] Once the business establishes its cost basis in an asset, the basis is reduced as the business recovers the cost of the asset through cost recovery deductions such as depreciation, amortization, or depletion. The amount of an asset's cost that has yet to be recovered through cost recovery deductions is called the asset's **adjusted basis** or **tax basis.** An asset's adjusted basis can be computed by subtracting the accumulated depreciation (or amortization or depletion) from the asset's initial cost or historical basis.[4]

For most assets, the initial basis is the cost plus all of the expenses to purchase, prepare it for use, and begin using the asset. These costs may include sales tax, shipping, and installation. The financial accounting and tax rules for computing an asset's basis are very similar. Thus, a purchased asset's initial basis for both tax and book purposes is generally the same.[5]

When a business incurs additional costs associated with an asset after the asset has been placed in service, how are the additional costs treated for tax purposes? In December 2011, the Treasury issued regulations to help guide taxpayers on this question. In general, the answer depends on whether the expense constitutes routine maintenance on the asset or whether it results in a "betterment, restoration, or new or different use for the property."[6] Routine maintenance costs are immediately deductible as ordinary business expenses. For example, Teton would immediately deduct a $35 cost to have a delivery truck's oil changed as routine maintenance. Alternatively, if an additional cost significantly extends an asset's useful life or increases

THE KEY FACTS

Cost Basis

- An asset's cost basis includes all costs needed to purchase the asset, prepare it for use, and begin using it.
- Cost basis is usually the same for book and tax purposes.
- Special basis rules apply when personal use assets are converted to business use and when assets are acquired through nontaxable transactions, gifts, or inheritances.

[2]If a business discovers that it failed to claim allowable depreciation in a previous year, it cannot currently deduct the depreciation attributable to prior years. Rather, the business must file amended returns—assuming the statute of limitations is still open—to claim the depreciation expense. Additionally, Reg. §1.446-1 indicates other situations that will result in an accounting method change.

[3]Cost basis is defined under §1012. The mere purchase of an asset does not trigger cost recovery deductions. A business must begin using the asset for business purposes (place it in service) in order to depreciate the asset. However, because businesses generally acquire and place assets in service at the same time, we refer to these terms interchangeably throughout the chapter.

[4]§1011.

[5]However, special basis rules apply when an asset is acquired through a nontaxable transaction. See discussion in Chapter 11.

[6]Reg. §1.263(a)-1T.

the value of the asset, the expenditure generates a new asset (for cost recovery purposes) separate from the original asset.[7] For example, if Teton spends $3,000 on a rebuilt engine for a delivery truck in an attempt to add 50,000 miles to the truck's useful life, the cost of the engine would be accounted for as a separate, new asset.

When a business acquires multiple assets for one purchase price, the tax laws require the business to determine a cost basis for each separate asset. For example, if Teton were to acquire land and a building on the land, Teton must treat the building and land as separate assets. In these types of acquisitions, businesses determine the cost basis of each asset by allocating a portion of the purchase price to each asset based on that asset's value relative to the total value of all the assets the business acquired in the same purchase. The asset values are generally determined by an appraisal.[8]

Example 10-1

Steve determined that he needed machinery and office furniture for a manufacturing facility and a design studio (located in Cody, Wyoming). During the year, Steve purchased the following assets and incurred the following costs to prepare the assets for business use. His cost basis in each asset is determined as follows:

Asset	Date Acquired	(1) Purchase Price	(2) Business Preparation Costs	(1) + (2) Cost Basis
Office furniture	2/3/15	$ 10,000		$ 10,000
Warehouse	5/1/15	270,000*	$5,000 (minor modifications)	275,000
Land (10 acres)	5/1/15	75,000*		75,000
Machinery	7/22/15	500,000	$10,000 (delivery and setup)	510,000
Delivery truck (used)	8/17/15	15,000		15,000

*Note that the warehouse and the land were purchased together for $345,000. Steve and the seller determined that the value (and cost) of the warehouse was $270,000 and the value (and cost) of the land was $75,000.

Special rules apply when determining the tax basis of assets converted from personal to business use or assets acquired through a nontaxable exchange, gift, or inheritance. If an asset is used for personal purposes and is later converted to business (or rental) use, the basis for cost recovery purposes is the *lesser* of (1) the cost basis of the asset or (2) the fair market value of the asset on the date of conversion to business use.[9] This rule prevents taxpayers from converting a nondeductible personal loss into a deductible business loss. For example, if Steve had purchased a truck for $20,000 several years ago for personal use but decided to use it as a delivery truck when its value had declined to $15,000, his basis in the truck for cost recovery purposes would be $15,000. The $5,000 decline in the truck's value from $20,000 to $15,000 would be a nondeductible personal loss to Steve, and the reduction in basis ensures that he will not be allowed to deduct the loss as a business loss. Assets acquired through a nontaxable exchange such as a like-kind exchange generally take the same basis the taxpayer had in the property the taxpayer transferred in the transaction. Assets acquired by gift have a carryover basis. This means that the taxpayer's basis in property received through a gift is generally the same basis the transferor had in the property.[10] For example, if Steve's parents gave him equipment worth

[7]§168(i)(6).

[8]Reg. §1.167(a)-5.

[9]Reg. §§1.167(g)-1 and 1.168(i)-4(b). However, this rule creates an interesting situation when selling converted assets. The taxpayer uses the lower of the adjusted basis or the fair market value at the time of the conversion for computing loss but uses the adjusted basis to compute a gain when selling converted assets.

[10]§1015. The basis may be increased if the transferor is required to pay gift tax on the transfer [see §1015(d)]. In addition, special dual basis rules apply if the basis in the gifted property at the gift date is greater than its fair market value.

$45,000 to help him start his business and his parents had purchased the equipment 10 years earlier for $25,000, Steve's basis in the equipment would be $25,000 (the same basis his parents had in the equipment). Assets acquired through inheritance generally receive a basis equal to the fair market value on the transferor's date of death.[11] For example, if Steve inherited a building worth $90,000 from his grandfather who originally paid $3,500 for it, Steve's basis would be $90,000 (its fair market value at date of death) because Steve acquired it through an inheritance.

ETHICS

Catherine Travis is starting a new business. She has several assets that she wants to use in her business that she has been using personally. Since she plans to convert several assets from personal to business use, she will need to find out how much each asset is worth so she can determine her basis for depreciating the assets. Catherine has decided to obtain two appraisals and take the better of the two figures for each asset. What do you think of Catherine's strategy for determining her business asset bases?

DEPRECIATION

LO 10-2

THE KEY FACTS

Tax Depreciation

- To depreciate an asset, a business must determine:
  - Original basis
  - Depreciation method
  - Recovery period
  - Depreciation convention

Before 1981, tax depreciation methods closely resembled financial accounting methods. For both financial accounting and tax purposes, businesses were allowed to choose from among a wide range of depreciation methods and **recovery periods.** Computing both tax and financial accounting depreciation required businesses to determine the assets' useful lives and "salvage values." In 1981, tax and financial accounting depreciation methods parted ways when Congress introduced the **Accelerated Cost Recovery System (ACRS)** for computing depreciation expense. Under ACRS, businesses used accelerated depreciation methods to depreciate assets over predetermined, fixed recovery periods.

Today, businesses calculate their tax depreciation using the **Modified Accelerated Cost Recovery System (MACRS)**—which is pronounced "makers" by tax accountants.[12] Compared to financial (book) depreciation, MACRS tax depreciation is quite simple. To compute MACRS depreciation for an asset, the business need only know the asset's *original cost,* the applicable *depreciation method,* the asset's *recovery period* (or depreciable "life"), and the applicable depreciation *convention* (the amount of depreciation deductible in the year of acquisition and the year of disposition). The method, recovery, period, and convention vary based on whether the asset is **personal property** or **real property.** The tax depreciation laws also include several special rules, which we discuss following the basic MACRS rules. We first turn our attention to determining depreciation expense for personal property.

Personal Property Depreciation

Personal property includes all tangible property, such as computers, automobiles, furniture, machinery, and equipment, other than real property. Note that personal property and *personal-use* property are *not* the same thing. Personal property denotes any property that is not real property (e.g., building and land) while personal-use property is any property used for personal purposes (e.g., a personal residence is personal-use property even though it is real property). Personal property is relatively short-lived and subject to obsolescence as compared to real property.

[11]§1014. In certain circumstances, the estate can elect an alternative valuation date six months after death.

[12]IRS Publication 946 provides a useful summary of MACRS depreciation.

Depreciation Method MACRS provides three acceptable methods for depreciating personal property: 200 percent (double) declining balance (DB), 150 percent declining balance, and straight-line.[13] The 200 percent declining balance method is the default method. This method takes twice the straight-line amount of depreciation in the first year and continues to take twice the straight-line percentage on the asset's declining basis until switching to the straight-line method in the year that the straight-line method over the remaining life provides a greater depreciation expense. Fortunately, as we describe below, the IRS provides depreciation tables to simplify the calculations.

Profitable businesses with relatively high marginal tax rates generally choose to use the 200 percent declining balance method because it generates the largest depreciation expense in the early years of the assets' lives and, thus, the highest current year after-tax cash flows. For tax planning purposes, companies that currently have lower marginal tax rates but expect their marginal tax rates to increase in the near future may elect the straight-line method because that method generates less depreciation expense in the early years of the asset's life, relatively, and more depreciation expense in the later years when their marginal tax rates may increase.

Example 10-2

If Teton wants to accelerate its current depreciation deductions to the extent possible, what method should it use to depreciate its office furniture, machinery, and delivery truck?

Answer: The 200 percent declining balance method (default). Teton could elect to use either the 150 percent declining balance or the straight-line method, if it wants a less accelerated method for determining its depreciation deductions.

Each year, businesses elect the depreciation method for the assets placed in service during *that year*. Specifically, businesses elect one depreciation method for all similar assets they acquired that year.[14] Thus, if a business acquires several different machines during the year, it must use the same method to depreciate all of the machines. However, the methods may differ for machines acquired in different tax years.

Depreciation Recovery Period For financial accounting purposes, an asset's recovery period (depreciable life) is based on its taxpayer-determined estimated useful life. In contrast, for tax purposes an asset's recovery period is predetermined by the IRS in Rev. Proc. 87-56. This revenue procedure helps taxpayers categorize each of their assets based upon the property's description. Once the business has determined the appropriate categories for its assets, it can use the Revenue Procedure to identify the recovery period for all assets in a particular category. For example, Teton placed office furniture in service during the year. By examining the excerpt from Rev. Proc. 87-56 provided in Exhibit 10-3, you can see that Category or Asset Class 00.11 includes office furniture and that assets in this category, including Teton's office furniture, have a recovery period of seven years (emphasis in excerpt added through bold text).[15]

[13]For personal property, the 200 percent DB is often referred to as the General Depreciation System (GDS) while the 150 percent DB or straight-line methods are referred to as the Alternative Depreciation System (ADS).

[14]Technically, similar assets are assets in the same asset class. We discuss asset classes below.

[15]The "alternative" recovery period in Rev. Proc. 87-56 refers to an asset's life under the alternative depreciation system (which was discussed earlier under depreciation methods). The Class Life referred to in Rev. Proc. 87-56 refers to the midpoint of asset depreciation range (ADR) applicable under pre-ACRS and has little or no meaning under MACRS.

EXHIBIT 10-3 Excerpt from Revenue Procedure 87-56

Description of Assets Included	Years		
Specific depreciable assets used in all business activities, except as noted:	**Class Life**	**General Recovery Period**	**Alternative Recovery Period**
00.11 Office Furniture, Fixtures, and Equipment: Includes furniture and fixtures that are not a structural component of a building. Includes such assets as desks, files, safes, and communications equipment. Does not include communications equipment that is included in other classes.	10	7	10
00.241 Light General Purpose Trucks: Includes trucks for use over the road (actual unloaded weight less than 13,000 pounds) . . .	4	5	5
34.0 Manufacture of Fabricated Metal Products Special Tools: Includes assets used in the production of metal cans, tinware . . .	12	7	12

While even this small excerpt from Rev. Proc. 87-56 may seem a bit intimidating, you can classify the vast majority of business assets acquired by knowing a few common recovery periods. Exhibit 10-4 lists the most commonly purchased assets and their recovery periods.

EXHIBIT 10-4 Recovery Period for Most Common Business Assets

Asset Description (summary of Rev. Proc. 87-56)	Recovery Period
Cars, light general-purpose trucks, and computers and peripheral equipment.	5-year
Office furniture, fixtures, and equipment.	7-year

To this point, our discussion has emphasized computing depreciation for new assets. Does the process change when businesses acquire used assets? No, it is exactly the same. For example, Teton purchased a *used* delivery truck. The fact that the truck is used does not change its MACRS recovery period. No matter how long the previous owner used the truck, Teton will restart the five-year recovery period for light general purpose trucks (see Exhibit 10-4).

Under MACRS, the tax recovery period for machinery and equipment is seven years. Using Rev. Proc. 87-56, Teton has determined the cost recovery periods for the personal property it purchased and placed in service during the year. Exhibit 10-5 summarizes this information.

EXHIBIT 10-5 Teton Personal Property Summary (Base Scenario)

Asset	Date Acquired	Quarter Acquired	Cost Basis	Recovery Period	Reference
Office furniture	2/3/15	1st	$ 10,000	7	Example 10-1; Exhibit 10-3.
Machinery	7/22/15	3rd	$510,000	7	Example 10-1; Exhibit 10-3.
Delivery truck	8/17/15	3rd	15,000	5	Example 10-1; Exhibit 10-3.
Total personal property			**$535,000**		

Depreciation Conventions Once a business has determined the depreciation methods and recovery periods for the assets it placed in service during the year, it must also determine the applicable depreciation conventions. The depreciation convention specifies the portion of a full year's depreciation the business can deduct for an asset in the year the asset is first placed in service *and* in the year the asset is sold. For *personal property,* taxpayers must use either the **half-year convention** or the **mid-quarter convention.** But, as we discuss below, taxpayers are *not* free to choose between the two conventions. The half-year convention applies most of the time; however, under certain conditions taxpayers will be required to use the mid-quarter convention.

THE KEY FACTS

Half-Year Convention

- One-half of a year's depreciation is allowed in the first and the last year of an asset's life.
- The IRS depreciation tables automatically account for the half-year convention in the acquisition year.
- If an asset is disposed of before it is fully depreciated, only one-half of the table's applicable depreciation percentage is allowed in the year of disposition.

Half-year convention. The half-year convention allows one-half of a full year's depreciation in the year the asset is placed in service, regardless of when it was actually placed in service. For example, when the half-year convention applies to a calendar-year business, an asset placed in service on either February 3 or August 17 is treated as though it was placed in service on July 1, which is the middle of the calendar year. Thus, under this convention, Teton would deduct one-half of a year's worth of depreciation for the machinery, office furniture, and delivery truck even though it acquired the machinery, delivery truck, and office furniture at various times during the year (see Exhibit 10-5). The half-year convention is built into the depreciation tables provided by the IRS, which simplifies the depreciation calculation for the year the asset is placed into service.

The original ACRS system required the use of the half-year convention for all personal property placed in service during the year. However, Congress believed that many businesses took unfair advantage of the half-year convention by purposely acquiring assets at the end of the year that they otherwise would have acquired at the beginning of the next taxable year. Thus, businesses received one-half of a year's worth of depreciation for assets that they only used for a small portion of the year. Even though the half-year convention is the default convention, policy makers introduced the *mid-quarter convention* under MACRS to limit or prevent this type of opportunistic behavior.

Calculating Depreciation for Personal Property Once a business has identified the applicable method, recovery period, and convention for personal property, tax depreciation is relatively easy to calculate because the Internal Revenue Service provides depreciation percentage tables in Rev. Proc. 87-57. The percentages in the depreciation tables for tangible personal property incorporate the method and convention [accordingly there are separate tables for each combination of depreciation method (200 percent declining balance, 150 percent declining balance, and straight-line) and convention (half-year and mid-quarter; each quarter has its own table)]. To determine the depreciation for an asset for the year, use the following three steps:

Step 1: Locate the applicable table provided in Rev. Proc. 87-57.

Step 2: Select the column that corresponds with the asset's recovery period.

Step 3: Find the row identifying the year of the asset's recovery period.

The tables are constructed so that the intersection of the row and column provides the percentage of the asset's *original basis* that is deductible as depreciation expense for the particular year. Thus, depreciation expense for a particular asset is the product of the percentage from the table and the asset's *original basis.*

Applying the Half-Year Convention Consider Table 1 in the appendix at the end of the chapter that shows the depreciation percentages for MACRS 200 percent declining balance using the half-year convention. If a seven-year asset is placed into service during the current year, the depreciation percentage is 14.29 percent [the intersection of row 1 (year 1) and the seven-year property column].

Notice from Table 1 that the depreciation percentages for five-year property extend for six years and the percentages for seven-year property extend for eight years.

Why does it take six years to fully depreciate an asset with a five-year recovery period and eight years for a seven-year asset? Because the business does not deduct a full year's depreciation in the first year (businesses must use either the half-year or mid-quarter convention), an entire year of depreciation is effectively split between the first and last year. For example, when the half-year convention applies to a five-year asset, the taxpayer deducts one-half of a year's depreciation in year 1 and one-half of a year's depreciation in year 6.

Example 10-3

Teton is using the 200 percent declining balance method and half-year convention to compute depreciation expense on its current year personal property additions. What is Teton's depreciation expense for these assets?

Answer: $77,308, computed as follows:

Asset	Date Placed in Service	(1) Original Basis	(2) Rate	(1) × (2) Depreciation
Office furniture	February 3	$ 10,000	14.29%	$ 1,429
Machinery	July 22	510,000	14.29	72,879
Used delivery truck	August 17	15,000	20.00	3,000
Total				$77,308

Because the office furniture and machinery have a seven-year recovery period and it is the first year for depreciation, the depreciation rate is 14.29 percent (see Table 1). The depreciation rate for the used delivery truck (five-year property) is determined in a similar manner.

Calculating depreciation for assets in years after the year of acquisition is also relatively simple. Again, using Table 1 to compute depreciation for the second year, the taxpayer would multiply the asset's original basis times the rate factor in the *year 2* row and the *year 3* row in the following year and so on.

Example 10-4

What if: Assume that Teton holds the tangible personal property it acquired and placed in service this year until the assets are fully depreciated. Using the IRS provided tables (see Table 1) how would Teton determine its depreciation expense for years 1 through 8?

Answer: See the following table:

Depreciation Over Asset Recovery Period

Year	7-Year Office Furniture	7-Year Machinery	5-Year Delivery Truck	Yearly Total
1	$ 1,429	$ 72,879	$ 3,000	$ 77,308
2	2,449	124,899	4,800	132,148
3	1,749	89,199	2,880	93,828
4	1,249	63,699	1,728	66,676
5	893	45,543	1,728	48,164
6	892	45,492	864	47,248
7	893	45,543	N/A	46,436
8	446	22,746	N/A	23,192
Accumulated Depreciation	$10,000	$510,000	$15,000	$535,000

Half-year convention for year of disposition. Businesses often sell or dispose of assets before they fully depreciate them. Recall that the half-year convention applies in both the year of acquisition and the year of disposition. Note, however, that the tables can't anticipate when a business may dispose of an asset. Accordingly, the tables only provide depreciation percentages for assets assuming the asset won't be disposed of before it is fully depreciated. That is, for each year in the asset's recovery period, the tables provide a percentage for an entire year's worth of depreciation. So, to calculate the depreciation for the year of disposition, the business first calculates depreciation for the *entire year* as if the property had not been disposed of. Then the business applies the half-year convention by multiplying the full year's depreciation by 50 percent (one-half of a year's depreciation). Note, however, that if a business acquires and disposes of an asset in the same tax year, it is not allowed to claim any depreciation on the asset.[16]

Example 10-5

What if: Assume that Teton sells all of its office furniture in year 2 (the year after it buys it). What is Teton's depreciation for the office furniture in the year of disposition (year 2)?

Answer: $1,225, calculated using the MACRS Half-Year Convention Table as follows:

Asset	Amount	Explanation
(1) Office furniture	$10,000	Original basis.
(2) Depreciation percentage	24.49%	Seven-year property, year 2.
(3) Full year of depreciation	$ 2,449	(1) × (2).
(4) Half-year convention percentage	50%	Depreciation limit in year of disposal.
Depreciation in year of disposal	$ 1,225	(3) × (4).

What if: Assume that Teton sold all of its office furniture in year 1 (the year it bought it and placed it in service). How much depreciation expense can Teton deduct for the office furniture in year 1?

Answer: $0. A business is not allowed to claim any depreciation expense for assets it acquires and disposes of in the same year.

Mid-quarter convention. Under the mid-quarter convention, businesses treat assets *as though* they were placed in service during the middle of the *quarter* in which the business actually placed the assets into service. For example, when the mid-quarter convention applies, if a business places an asset in service on December 1 (in the fourth quarter) it must treat the asset as though it was placed in service on November 15, which is the middle of the fourth quarter. Consequently, the business would only be able to deduct one-half of a quarter's worth of depreciation in the year the asset was placed in service (depreciation for the second half of November and the entire month of December). In addition, if the mid-quarter convention applies, businesses must use the convention for all tangible personal property placed in service during the year. The IRS depreciation tables have built in the mid-quarter convention to simplify the calculations.

Businesses must use the mid-quarter convention when *more* than 40 percent of their total *tangible personal property* that they place in service during the year is placed in service during the *fourth* quarter. Thus, the steps to determine whether the mid-quarter convention applies are the following:

Step 1: Sum the total basis of the tangible personal property that was placed in service during the year.

[16]Suppose Teton sells the 5-year delivery truck in year 6 on January 5. What depreciation percentage should Teton use for purposes of determining year 6 depreciation? Teton should take one-half year's depreciation on the truck. The percentage shown in Table 1 for year 6 already reflects the half-year convention, so Teton would take $864 of depreciation regardless of when during year 6 the truck was sold.

Step 2: Sum the total basis of the tangible personal property that was placed in service in the fourth quarter.

Step 3: Divide the outcome of Step 2 by the outcome of Step 1. If the quotient is greater than 40 percent, the business must use the mid-quarter convention to determine the depreciation for all tangible personal property the business placed in service during the year. Otherwise, the business uses the half-year convention for depreciating this property.

In accordance with Reg. §1.168(d)-1(b)(4), property expensed under §179 (discussed later in the chapter) is not included in the numerator or denominator of the mid-quarter test. The mid-quarter test is applied after the §179 expense but before bonus depreciation.

Example 10-6

The following excerpt from the base scenario in Exhibit 10-5 provides the information we need to determine if Teton must use the mid-quarter convention to compute depreciation:

Asset	Date Acquired	Quarter Acquired	Cost Basis
Office furniture	2/3/15	First	$ 10,000
Machinery	7/22/15	Third	510,000
Delivery truck	8/17/15	Third	15,000
Total personal property			**$535,000**

Is Teton required to use the mid-quarter convention to depreciate its personal property?

Answer: No. See computation below.

Description	Amount	Explanation
(1) Total basis of tangible personal property placed in service during year	$535,000	
(2) Total basis of tangible personal property placed in service in fourth quarter	0	
(3) Percentage of basis of total tangible personal property placed in service during fourth quarter	0%	(2)/(1).

Teton is not required to use the mid-quarter convention because it did not place more than 40 percent of its assets in service during the fourth quarter. (In fact, Teton did not place any assets in service in the fourth quarter.) Consequently, Teton will use the half-year convention to calculate its depreciation expense.

THE KEY FACTS

Mid-Quarter Convention

- The mid-quarter convention is required when more than 40 percent of a taxpayer's personal property placed in service during the year was placed during the fourth quarter.
- Each quarter has its own depreciation table. Once you begin using a table, you must use the table over the asset's whole life.
- If an asset is disposed of before it is fully depreciated, use the formula given to determine the allowable depreciation in the year of disposition.

Example 10-7

What if: Let's replace the facts from the base scenario presented in Exhibit 10-5 with the following alternative scenario 1 facts. In this alternative set of facts, we assume the machinery was acquired during the fourth quarter on October 25 as follows:

Asset	Date Acquired	Quarter Acquired	Cost Basis
Office furniture	2/3/15	First	$ 10,000
Delivery truck	8/17/15	Third	15,000
Machinery	10/25/15	Fourth	510,000
Total personal property			**$535,000**

(continued on page 10-12)

Under alternative scenario 1, is Teton required to use the mid-quarter convention?

Answer: Yes. Of the personal property it placed in service during the year, it placed 95.3 percent in service in the last quarter (this is greater than 40 percent). See the calculations below:

Description	Amount	Explanation
(1) Cost of all personal property placed in service during current year.	$535,000	
(2) Cost of personal property placed in service in the fourth quarter during current year.	510,000	
(3) Percentage of all personal property placed in service during current year that was placed in service in the fourth quarter.	95.3%	(2)/(1).

What if: Assume that Teton also placed in service on July 1 a building costing $1,000,000. Is Teton subject to the mid-quarter convention?

Answer: Yes. Because the building is real property (not personal property), it is not included in the mid-quarter calculation. The calculation is exactly the same as the calculation in alternative scenario 1 above.

Applying the Mid-Quarter Convention When the mid-quarter convention applies, the process for computing depreciation is the same as it is when the half-year convention applies, except that businesses use a different set of depreciation tables (a separate table for each quarter). After categorizing the assets by recovery period and grouping them into quarters, businesses consult the Mid-Quarter Convention Tables 2a–d in the appendix to this chapter to determine the depreciation rate for each asset group.

The depreciation expense for an asset is the product of the asset's original basis and the percentage from the table.

Example 10-8

What if: For this example, we assume the facts from alternative scenario 1 presented in Example 10-7 (see table below). What is Teton's year 1 depreciation expense for its personal property additions under the alternative scenario 1 presented in Example 10-7?

Answer: $22,957, computed as follows:

Asset	Purchase Date	Quarter	Original Basis	Rate	Depreciation
Office furniture (7-year)	February 3	First	$ 10,000	25.00%	$ 2,500
Delivery truck (5-year)	August 17	Third	15,000	15.00%	2,250
Machinery (7-year)	October 25	Fourth	510,000	3.57%	18,207
					$22,957

The office furniture factor of 25.00 percent is located in Table 2a. See the columns for property placed into service during the first quarter (first two columns), select the 7-year recovery period column (last column), and the year 1 row. The process for determining the rate factor for the delivery truck and machinery follows the same methodology using Tables 2c and 2d, respectively.

Teton's $77,308 depreciation expense under the half-year convention (see Example 10-3) is significantly higher than its $22,957 depreciation expense under the mid-quarter convention (see Example 10-8). Why the big disparity? Because the (high cost) machinery was placed into service during the fourth quarter and thus generated significantly less current depreciation expense (one-half of one quarter's depreciation) than it would have under the half-year convention. It is important to note, however, that when using the mid-quarter convention, assets placed in service in the first or second quarter will generate more depreciation than they would have under the half-year convention (10.5/12ths and 7.5/12ths of a full year, respectively). However, because the mid-quarter convention only applies when a large percentage of the cost of the assets was placed in service in the fourth quarter, the mid-quarter convention tends to generate less overall depreciation expense for new additions than the half-year convention.

The process for calculating depreciation for assets in years after the year of acquisition under the mid-quarter convention is nearly identical to the process we described for making this computation under the half-year convention. The only difference is that the business looks to the MACRS Mid-Quarter Convention Table (Table 2 in the chapter appendix) for the appropriate quarter rather than the MACRS Half-Year Convention Table (Table 1 in the chapter appendix).

Example 10-9

What if: Assume that Teton held and fully depreciated the tangible personal property it placed in service this year under the mid-quarter convention (alternative scenario 1). What would be Teton's depreciation expense for its personal property additions for years 1 through 8 using the mid-quarter tables provided in the appendix at the end of this chapter?

Answer: See table below*:

Year	7-Year Office Furniture 1st Quarter	5-Year Delivery Truck 3rd Quarter	7-Year Machinery 4th Quarter	Yearly Total
1	$ 2,500	$ 2,250	$ 18,207	$ 22,957
2	2,143	5,100	140,505	147,748
3	1,531	3,060	100,368	104,959
4	1,093	1,836	71,706	74,635
5	875	1,695	51,204	53,774
6	874	1,059	44,523	46,456
7	875	N/A	44,523	45,398
8	109	N/A	38,964	39,073
	$10,000	$15,000	$510,000	$535,000

*See Table 2; the depreciation is calculated by multiplying the applicable rate by the cost basis.

Mid-quarter convention for year of disposition. Calculating depreciation expense in the year of sale or disposition is a bit more involved when the mid-quarter convention applies than when it does not. When the mid-quarter convention applies, the asset is treated as though it is sold in the middle of the quarter of which it was actually sold. The process for calculating mid-quarter convention depreciation for the year of sale is exactly the same as the process for using the half-year convention, except that *instead of* multiplying the full year's depreciation by 50 percent, the business multiplies the amount of depreciation it would have been able to claim on the asset if it had not sold the asset (a full year's depreciation) by the applicable percentage in Exhibit 10-6.[17]

[17]Suppose Teton sells the 5-year delivery truck in year 6 on January 5 after using the mid-quarter convention as in example 10-9. What depreciation percentage should Teton use for purposes of determining year 6 depreciation? Teton should be allowed 1/2 of a quarter's depreciation in year 6. The calculation of this amount is complicated by the mid-quarter convention because the 3rd quarter depreciation percentage for a 5-year asset in year 6 using Table 2c shows 7.06 percent. This amount, however, is the depreciation rate for 2 1/2 quarters representing the remaining depreciation in the final year of the asset's recovery period. Teton will be allowed $212 of depreciation in the year of disposition determined as $15,000 multiplied by 1.412 percent (7.06%/2.5 quarters × .5 quarters = 1.412%).

EXHIBIT 10-6 Mid-Quarter Convention Percentage of Full Year's Depreciation in Year of Disposition

Quarter of Disposition	Percentage	Calculation*
First	12.5%	1.5/12
Second	37.5	4.5/12
Third	62.5	7.5/12
Fourth	87.5	10.5/12

*The calculation is the number of months the taxpayer held or is deemed to have held the asset in the year of disposition divided by 12 months in the year.

Example 10-10

What if: Assume that Teton depreciates its personal property under the mid-quarter convention (alternative scenario 1, see Example 10-5) and that it sells its office furniture in the third quarter of year 2. The office furniture ($10,000 original basis) was placed into service during the first quarter of year 1 and has a seven-year recovery period. What depreciation expense can Teton deduct for the office furniture in year 2, the year of sale?

Answer: $1,339. Computed as follows:

Description	Amount	Explanation
(1) Original basis	$10,000	Example 10-7.
(2) Year 2 depreciation percentage	21.43%	Table 2a, mid-quarter, first quarter table, 7-year property, year 2.
(3) Full year 2 depreciation	2,143	(1) × (2).
(4) Percentage of full year's depreciation in year of disposition if mid-quarter convention applies	62.5%	From Exhibit 10-6; asset disposed of in third quarter.
Depreciation in year of disposition	$ 1,339	(3) × (4).

What if: Assume Teton disposed of the office furniture on January 2 of year 2. How much depreciation expense would it be able to claim on the furniture in year 2?

Answer: $268 ($2,143 full year's depreciation × 12.5% from Exhibit 10-6).

THE KEY FACTS

Real Property Depreciation

- Real property is depreciated using the straight-line method.
- Real property uses the mid-month convention.
- Residential property has a recovery period of 27.5 years.
- Nonresidential property placed in service on or after May 13, 1993, has a life of 39 years.

Real Property

For depreciation purposes, real property is classified as land, *residential rental* property, or *nonresidential property*. Land is nondepreciable. Residential rental property consists of dwelling units such as houses, condominiums, and apartment complexes. Residential property has a 27.5-year recovery period. Nonresidential property consists of all other buildings (office buildings, manufacturing facilities, shopping malls, and the like). Nonresidential property placed in service on or after May 13, 1993, has a 39-year recovery period and nonresidential property placed in service after December 31, 1986, and before May 13, 1993, has a 31.5-year recovery period. Exhibit 10-7 summarizes the recovery periods for real property.

If a building is substantially improved (not a minor repair) at some point after the initial purchase, the building addition is treated as a new asset with the same recovery period of the original building. For example, if Teton expanded its warehouse 10 years after the building was placed in service, the expansion or building addition would be depreciated as a *new, separate* asset over 39 years because it is nonresidential property.

EXHIBIT 10-7 Recovery Period for Real Property

Asset Description (summary from Rev. Proc. 87-57)	Recovery Period
Residential	27.5 years
Nonresidential property placed in service on or after May 13, 1993	39 years
Nonresidential property placed in service before May 13, 1993	31.5 years

An important area of tax practice related to real property is cost segregation. This practice attempts to partition or divide the costs of a building into two or more categories. The first category is the building itself, which has a recovery period as noted in Exhibit 10-7. The second category is building components (tangible personal property associated with the building such as electrical and plumbing fixtures that have a shorter recovery period and accelerated depreciation method). Cost segregation utilizes engineers and construction experts who divide the costs between real and tangible personal property. This can generate significant tax savings due to the difference in the present value of the tax savings from the accelerated depreciation deductions associated with personal property relative to real property.

Applicable Method All depreciable real property is depreciated for tax purposes using the straight-line method. This is generally consistent with depreciation methods used for financial accounting purposes.

Applicable Convention All real property is depreciated using the mid-month convention. The **mid-month convention** allows the owner of real property to expense one-half of a month's depreciation for the month in which the property was placed in service (and in the month of the year it is sold as well). This is true regardless of whether the asset was placed in service at the beginning or at the end of the month. For example, if Teton placed its warehouse into service on May 1 (or on *any* other day in May), it would deduct *one-half* a month's depreciation for May and then full depreciation for the months June through December.

Depreciation Tables Just as it does for personal property, the IRS provides depreciation tables for real property. The depreciation tables for 27.5 years, 31.5 years, and 39 years real property are reproduced as Tables 3, 4, and 5, respectively, in this chapter's appendix. The percentage of the asset's original basis that is depreciated in a particular year is located at the intersection of the month the asset was placed in service (column) and the year of depreciation (row—first, second, etc.).

Example 10-11

As indicated in Example 10-1, Teton's basis in the warehouse it purchased on May 1 of year 1 is $275,000. What is Teton's year 1 depreciation on its warehouse?

Answer: $4,414, computed as follows:

Asset	Method	Recovery Period	Date Placed in Service	(1) Basis	(2) Rate*	(1) × (2) Depreciation
Warehouse	SL	39	May 1	$275,000	1.605%	$4,414

(continued on page 10-16)

What if: What would be Teton's year 1 depreciation expense if the building was not a warehouse but was an apartment building that it rented to Teton's employees?

Answer: $6,251, computed as follows:

Asset	Method	Recovery Period	Date Placed in Service	(1) Basis	(2) Rate†	(1) × (2) Depreciation
Apt. Bldg.	SL	27.5	May 1	$275,000	2.273%	$6,251

*The 1.605 percent tax rate factor for the year is found in the 39-year table (Table 5, in the appendix to this chapter) in the fifth column (fifth month) and first row (first year).

† The 2.273 percent tax rate factor for the year is found in the 27.5-year table (Table 4, in the appendix to this chapter) in the fifth column (fifth month) and first row (first year).

When using depreciation tables for real property it is important to stay in the month column corresponding with the month the property was originally placed in service.[18] Thus, to calculate depreciation for a piece of real property placed in service in May (the fifth month), businesses will *always* (for each year of depreciation) find the current year rate factor in the fifth column for that asset. This is true even if the asset is sold in a subsequent year in July (it's easy to make the mistake of using the seventh column to calculate the depreciation for the year of disposition in this situation).

Mid-month convention for year of disposition. Businesses deduct one-half of a month's depreciation in the month they sell or otherwise dispose of real property. For example, if Teton sold its warehouse on March 5 of year 2, it would deduct two and one-half months of depreciation in that year for the warehouse (depreciation for January, February, and one-half of March). Calculating depreciation expense in the year of sale or disposition for mid-month convention assets is similar to the calculation under the mid-quarter convention. When the mid-month convention applies, the asset is treated as though it is sold in the *middle of the month* of which it was actually sold. The simplest process for calculating mid-month convention depreciation for the year of sale consists of the following four steps:

Step 1: Determine the amount of depreciation expense for the asset as if the asset was held for the entire year.

Step 2: Subtract one-half of a month from the month in which the asset was sold (if sold in third month, subtract .5 from 3 to get 2.5). (Subtract half of a month because the business is treated as though the asset was disposed of in the middle of the third month—not the end.)

Step 3: Divide the amount determined in Step 2 by 12 months (2.5/12). This is the fraction of the full year's depreciation the business is eligible to deduct.

Step 4: Multiply the Step 3 outcome by the full depreciation determined in Step 1.

These steps are summarized in the following formula:

Mid-month depreciation for year of disposition

$$= \text{Full year's depreciation} \times \frac{(\text{Month in which asset was disposed of } -.5)}{12}$$

[18]Failure to do so will result in the wrong depreciation expense and is technically a change in accounting method (which requires filing of a Form 3115 with the IRS).

Example 10-12

What if: Assume that Teton sells its warehouse on March 5 in year 2 (the year after Teton buys it). What is Teton's depreciation for the warehouse in the year of disposition (year 2)?

Answer: $1,469, computed using the four-step procedure outlined above as follows.

Step 1: Determine full year's depreciation: $275,000 × 2.564%* = $7,051

Step 2: 3 (month sold) − .5 = 2.5

Step 3: 2.5/12

Step 4: $7,051 × 2.5/12 = $1,469 (see formula above).

*The 2.564 percent rate factor (full year percentage) in Step 1 is obtained from the MACRS Mid-Month Table for 39-year property (Table 5) placed in service during the fifth month (year 2 row).

Special Rules Relating to Cost Recovery

LO 10-3

In addition to the basic MACRS rules, several additional provisions examining the cost recovery of tangible personal property. Congress often uses these special rules for economic stimulus or to curb perceived taxpayer abuses. At the time we went to press, it was unclear whether Congress would extend the higher 2014 limits for these provisions to 2015. If the 2014 limits are not extended to 2015, the limits will decrease significantly. Throughout our main discussion, we assume that the 2014 limits are extended to 2015. However, we also provide examples illustrating how same calculations will be made if Congress does not extend the 2014 limits into 2015.

Immediate Expensing Policy makers created an important tax incentive designed to help small businesses purchasing new or used tangible personal property. This incentive is commonly referred to as the **§179 expense** or *immediate expensing* election.[19] As discussed earlier in the chapter, businesses must generally depreciate assets over the assets' recovery periods. However, under §179, businesses may elect to immediately expense up to $500,000 of tangible personal property placed in service during 2015 (assuming the 2014 limits are extended to 2015).[20,21] Businesses can also use immediate expensing (up to $250,000) for qualified real property (qualified leasehold improvements, qualified retail improvements, and qualified restaurant property). They may also elect to deduct less than the maximum. When businesses elect to deduct a certain amount of §179 expense, they immediately expense all or a portion of an asset's basis or several assets' bases. To reflect this immediate depreciation expense, they must reduce the basis of the asset or assets (to which they applied the expense) *before* they compute the MACRS depreciation expense (from the tables).

Example 10-13

What if: Assume Teton is eligible for and elects to immediately deduct $80,000 of §179 expense against the basis of the machinery. (Note that Teton could have elected to deduct up to $500,000.) What is the amount of Teton's current year depreciation expense, including regular MACRS depreciation and the §179 expense on its machinery (assuming half-year convention applies)?

(continued on page 10-18)

[19]Intangibles and tangible personal property that are used less than 50 percent for business and most real property are not eligible for immediate expensing.

[20]The maximum allowable expense under §179 is indexed for inflation and changes annually. Generally, the annual amount is released in a Revenue Procedure at the beginning of the taxable year. However, in recent years Congress has passed new legislation to enact the expense amounts under §179.

[21]These maximum amounts are per tax return. Thus, if an individual has multiple businesses with asset acquisitions, the taxpayer may only deduct up to these maximum amounts for the combined businesses.

Answer: $141,447, computed as follows:

Description	Amount	Explanation
(1) Machinery	$510,000	Example 10-1.
(2) §179 expense	$ 80,000	
(3) Remaining basis in machinery	$430,000	(1) − (2).
(4) MACRS depreciation rate for 7-year machinery	14.29%	Rate from Table 1.
(5) MACRS depreciation expense on machinery	$ 61,447	(3) × (4).
Total depreciation on machinery	$141,447	(2) + (5).

What if: Assume that Teton was eligible for and elected to claim the maximum amount of §179 expense. What would be its total current-year depreciation expense, including MACRS depreciation and §179 expense (assuming half-year convention applies)?

Answer: $501,429, computed as follows:

Description	Amount	Explanation
(1) Machinery	$510,000	Example 10-1.
(2) §179 expense	$500,000	Maximum expense in 2015.
(3) Remaining basis in machinery	$ 10,000	(1) − (2).
(4) MACRS depreciation rate for 7-year machinery	14.29%	Rate from Table 1.
(5) MACRS depreciation expense on machinery	$ 1,429	(3) × (4).
Total depreciation on machinery	$501,429	(2) + (5).

Limits on immediate expensing. The maximum amount of §179 expense a business may elect to claim for the year is subject to a phase-out limitation. Under the phase-out limitation, businesses must reduce the $500,000 maximum available expense dollar for dollar for the amount of *tangible personal property* purchased and placed in service during 2015 *over* a $2,000,000 threshold (assuming the 2014 limits are extended to 2015).[22] Thus if a business places $2,500,000 ($2,000,000 threshold plus $500,000) or more of tangible personal property into service during 2015, its maximum available §179 expense for the year is $0. The phased-out portion of the maximum expense disappears and does *not* carry over to another year.

Example 10-14

What if: Let's assume that during 2015, Teton placed into service $2,100,000 of machinery (up from the base scenario amount of $510,000), $10,000 of office furniture, and a $15,000 truck for a total of $2,125,000 tangible *personal* property placed in service for the year. What is Teton's maximum §179 expense after applying the phase-out limitation?

[22]The threshold under §179 is indexed for inflation and changes annually. Generally, the annual amount is released in a Revenue Procedure at the beginning of the taxable year.

Answer: $375,000 computed as follows:

Description	Amount	Explanation
(1) Property placed in service in 2015	$2,125,000	
(2) Threshold for §179 phase-out	2,000,000	2015 amount [§179(b)(1)].
(3) Phase-out of maximum §179 expense	$ 125,000	(1) − (2) (permanently disallowed).
(4) Maximum §179 expense before phase-out	$ 500,000	§179(b)(2).
(5) Phase-out of maximum §179 expense	125,000	From (3).
Maximum §179 expense after phase-out*	$ 375,000	(4) − (5).

*Note that this is the maximum expense after phase-out but *before* the taxable income limitation we discuss next.

What if: Assume further that Teton acquired and placed in service a warehouse costing $275,000. Taking the warehouse into account, what is Teton's maximum §179 expense after the phase-out?

Answer: $375,000. The same answer as above. The phase-out is based on the amount of tangible personal property placed in service during the year. Because the warehouse is *real property* (not qualified), its acquisition has no effect on Teton's maximum §179 expense.

Businesses may elect to claim the §179 expense for the year up to the maximum amount available (after computing the phase-out—see the previous example). When a business elects to claim a certain amount of §179 expense, it must reduce the basis of the asset(s) to which the expense is applied. It then computes regular depreciation on the remaining basis after reducing the basis of the asset(s) for the §179 expense.

The business's *deductible* §179 expense is limited to the taxpayer's business income after deducting all expenses (including regular depreciation expense) except the §179 expense. Consequently, the §179 expense cannot create or extend a business's net operating loss. Taxpayers' business income includes income from all businesses. For example, a sole-proprietor's business income for purposes of §179 would include not only the income from all Schedules C but also from regular wages. If a business claims more §179 expense than it is allowed to deduct due to the taxable income limitation, it carries the excess forward (indefinitely) and deducts it in a subsequent year, subject to the taxable income limitation (but not the phase-out limitation) in the subsequent year.[23]

Example 10-15

What if: Let's assume the facts of the previous example, where Teton's maximum §179 expense after applying the phase-out limitation is $375,000. Also assume that Teton elects to claim the entire $375,000 expense and it chooses to apply it against the machinery. Further assume that Teton reports $296,503 of taxable income before deducting any §179 expense and depreciation. What amount of total depreciation (including §179 expense) is Teton able to deduct on the machinery for the year?

(continued on page 10-20)

[23]Businesses typically elect only to expense the currently deductible amount since the taxable income limitation may also limit their §179 expense in future years just as it does for the current year.

Answer: $296,503 computed as follows:

Description	Amount	Explanation
(1) Machinery	$2,100,000	Example 10-14.
(2) Elected §179 expense	375,000	
(3) Remaining basis	1,725,000	(1) − (2).
(4) MACRS depreciation rate for 7-year machinery, year 1	14.29%	See Table 1.
(5) MACRS deprecation expense on machinery	$ 246,503	(3) × (4).
(6) Deductible §179 expense	50,000	Taxable income limitation ($296,503 − $249,503).
(7) Total depreciation expense on machinery for the year	296,503	(5) + (6).
(8) Excess §179 expense	325,000	(2) − (6).

What is the amount of Teton's excess §179 expense (elected expense in excess of the deductible amount due to the taxable income limitation), and what does it do with it for tax purposes?

Answer: $325,000. See the above table for the computation (line 8). Teton carries this $325,000 excess §179 expense forward to future years and may deduct it subject to the taxable income limitation. Note that the depreciable basis of the machinery remaining after the §179 expense is $1,725,000 because the depreciable basis is reduced by the full $375,000 of §179 expense claimed even though the deductible §179 expense was limited to $50,000 in the current year.

Effect of Congress not extending the §179 provisions. Our prior discussion assumes Congress will extend the 2014 §179 limits to 2015. However, as of press time, the limits had not been extended. If Congress does not act to extend the 2014 limits to to 2015, the maximum amount businesses would be allowed to immediately expense would drop to $25,000 subject to a property phase-out threshold beginning at $200,000. Example 10-16 illustrates the effect of the reduction of the §179 expensing provision.

Example 10-16

What if: Suppose the maximum §179 expense is $25,000 for 2015, what is Teton's maximum amount of §179 expense on the following assets (same as in Exhibit 10-5) after applying the phase-out limitation of $200,000?

Asset	Date Placed in Service	Original Basis
Office furniture	February 3	$ 10,000
Machinery	July 22	510,000
Used delivery truck	August 17	15,000
Total		$535,000

Answer: $-0-, computed as follows:

Description	Amount	Explanation
(1) Maximum §179 expense for 2015	$ 25,000	Assuming Congress does not extend provision.
(2) Property placed in service in 2015	$535,000	
(3) Threshold for §179 phase-out	200,000	
(4) Phase-out of maximum §179 expense	$ 25,000	Lesser of (1) or (2) − (3).
Maximum §179 expense after phase-out	$ -0-	(1) − (4).

What if: Suppose Teton places only $150,000 of machinery into service on May 12. What would be its total depreciation expense, including MACRS depreciation and §179 expense for the year?

Answer: $42,863, computed as follows:

Description	Amount	Explanation
(1) Machinery	$150,000	
(2) §179 expense	25,000	Not subject to phase-out since machinery placed in service is below threshold amount of $200,000.
(3) Remaining basis in machinery	125,000	(1) − (2).
(4) MACRS depreciation rate for 7-year machinery	14.29%	Rate from Table 1.
(5) MACRS depreciation expense on machinery	17,863	(3) × (4).
Total depreciation on machinery	$ 42,863	(2) + (5).

THE KEY FACTS

§179 Expenses

- $500,000 of tangible personal property can be immediately expensed in 2015 (assuming 2014 amounts are extended to 2015).
- Businesses are eligible for the full amount of this expense when tangible personal property placed in service is less than $2,000,000 (assuming 2014 amounts are extended to 2015). Beginning at $2,000,000, the §179 expense is phased out, dollar-for-dollar. When assets placed in service reach $2,500,000, no §179 expense can be taken.
- §179 expenses are also limited to a business's taxable income before the §179 expense. §179 expenses cannot create losses.

Choosing the assets to immediately expense. Businesses qualifying for immediate expensing are allowed to choose the asset or assets (from tangible personal property placed in service during the year) they immediately expense under §179. If a business's objective is to maximize its current depreciation expense and the half-year convention applies, it should immediately expense the asset with the lowest first-year cost recovery percentage including bonus depreciation (discussed in the next section). For example, looking at Tables 2a and 2c in the chapter appendix, if a business had to choose between immediately expensing seven-year property placed in service in the first quarter or five-year property placed in service in the third quarter, which asset should it elect to expense under §179 if it wanted to maximize its current year depreciation expense? The five-year asset because its first year depreciation percentage is 15 percent, while the seven-year asset's first year depreciation percentage is 25 percent. Finally, it is important to note that businesses reduce the basis of the assets for the §179 expense before computing whether the mid-quarter convention applies.[24]

Example 10-17

What if: Let's assume that Teton placed into service on June 1, five-year property costing $600,000 and seven-year property costing $600,000. Further assume that Teton is not subject to the taxable income limitation for the §179 expense. What is Teton's depreciation expense (including §179 expense) if it elects to apply the full §179 expense against the five-year property (Scenario A)? What is its depreciation expense if it applies it against its seven-year property (Scenario B)? (Assume the 2013 limits are extended to 2015.)

(continued on page 10-22)

[24]Treasury Regulation §1.168(d)-1(b)(4)(i).

Answer: $605,740 if it applies the §179 to the five-year property (Scenario A) and $634,290 if it applies it to the seven-year property (Scenario B). See the computations below:

Description	(Scenario A) §179 Expense on 5-year Property	(Scenario B) §179 Expense on 7-year Property	Explanation
(1) Original basis	$600,000	$600,000	
(2) Elected §179 expense	500,000	500,000	Maximum expense.
(3) Remaining basis	100,000	100,000	(1) − (2).
(4) MACRS depreciation rate	20%	14.29%	See Table 1.
(5) MACRS depreciation expense	$ 20,000	$ 14,290	(3) × (4).
(6) Deductible §179 expense	500,000	500,000	Example 10-14.
(7) MACRS depreciation on other property	85,740	120,000	This is the depreciation on the $600,000 seven-year property in the five-year column and on the $600,000 five-year property in the seven-year column.
Total depreciation expense	$ 605,740	$634,290	(5) + (6) + (7).

Note that Teton deducts $28,550 more in depreciation expense if it applies the §179 expense to the seven-year property.

What if: Assume the same facts, except that Teton placed the five-year property in service on December 1. Absent any §179 expense, Teton would be subject to the mid-quarter convention because 50 percent of its tangible personal property was placed in service in the fourth quarter. Assuming Teton wanted to avoid the mid-quarter convention, how should it apply its §179 expense?

Answer: It should apply the §179 expense against the five-year property. By doing so, the basis of the assets placed in service in the fourth quarter is $100,000 ($600,000 minus $500,000 §179 expense) and the basis of the assets placed in service in total is $700,000 ($600,000 7-year property + $100,000 5-year property). Thus, the percentage of tangible personal property placed in service in the fourth quarter is 14.3 percent ($100,000/$700,000) and the mid-quarter convention does not apply. If, however, it applies the §179 expense against the seven-year property, the mid-quarter convention would apply because the percentage of tangible personal property placed in service in the fourth quarter increases to 85.7 percent ($600,000/$700,000). Because this exceeds 40 percent, the mid-quarter convention applies. Teton could also expense just enough five-year property to avoid the mid-quarter convention and elect the rest of the §179 expense against the seven-year property to maximize its total depreciation.

Bonus depreciation.[25] To stimulate the economy, policy makers occasionally implement **bonus depreciation.**[26] Taxpayers can immediately expense 50 percent of qualified property. Qualified property must have a recovery period of 20 years or less (no real property) and the original use of the property must commence with the taxpayer (the property must be new rather than used), and the property must be placed in service during 2015.[27] The bonus depreciation is calculated after the §179 expense

[25]Although, as of press time, the bonus depreciation provisions from 2014 were scheduled to expire in 2015, we assume Congress will extend the bonus depreciation rules to 2015 in order to illustrate the tax consequences of bonus depreciation.

[26]§168(k)(2)(6). Bonus depreciation, if applicable, is also allowable for purposes of the AMT.

[27]§168(k)(2)(A)(iv).

but before regular MACRS depreciation.[28] Taxpayers may elect not to take bonus depreciation by attaching a statement to their tax return indicating they are electing to not claim bonus depreciation.

Example 10-18

What if: Assume that Teton elected bonus depreciation for the tangible personal property acquired in Exhibit 10-5.

Asset	Date Acquired	Quarter Acquired	Cost Basis	Recovery Period
Office furniture	2/3/15	1st	$ 10,000	7
Machinery	7/22/15	3rd	510,000	7
Delivery truck	8/17/15	3rd	15,000	5
Total			$535,000	

Assuming Teton elects no §179 expense, what is Teton's bonus depreciation?

Answer: $260,000 computed as follows:

Description	Amount	Explanation
(1) Qualified property	$520,000	
(2) Bonus depreciation rate	50%	§168(k)(1)(A).
Bonus depreciation	$260,000	(1) × (2).

Note that the delivery truck is not eligible for bonus depreciation because it is used property.

What if: Assuming Teton elects the maximum §179 expense, what is Teton's bonus depreciation?

Answer: $17,500 computed as follows:

Description	Amount	Explanation
(1) §179 qualified property	$535,000	
(2) §179 expense	500,000	Maximum expense assuming the 2014 amounts are extended to 2015.
(3) Remaining basis	35,000	(1) − (2).
(4) Remaining amount eligible for bonus depreciation	35,000	Remaining amount relates to the office furniture and machinery. Since the truck is used and not eligible for bonus depreciation, we would apply the §179 expense to the truck to maximize the current year depreciation deduction.
(5) Bonus depreciation rate	50%	§168(k)(1)(A).
(6) Bonus depreciation	$ 17,500	(4) × (5).

What if: Suppose Congress does not extend bonus depreciation to 2015 and that it does not extend the 2014 limits for the §179 provisions to 2015. What is the amount of Teton's total depreciation expense for the year?

Answer: $77,308, computed as follows:

Asset	(1) Original Basis	(2) Rate	(1) × (2) Depreciation
Office furniture	$ 10,000	14.29%	$ 1,429
Machinery	510,000	14.29	72,879
Used delivery truck	15,000	20.00	3,000
Total			$77,308

[28]Reg. §1.168(k)-1(a)(2)(iii) and Reg. §1.168(k)-1(d)(3) Example (2).

Teton is not eligible for §179 expense because it has placed $535,000 of qualified assets into service during the year. This amount exceeds the threshold amount of $200,000 by more than $25,000 so Teton's §179 is $-0-. In addition, if Congress does not extend the bonus depreciation provision, Teton's depreciation will be limited to MACRS depreciation only.

THE KEY FACTS

Listed Property

- When an asset is used for both personal and business use, calculate the business-use percentage.
- If the business-use percentage is above 50 percent, the allowable depreciation is limited to the business-use percentage.
- If a listed property's business-use percentage ever falls below 50 percent, depreciation for all previous years is retroactively restated using MACRS straight-line method.

TAXES IN THE REAL WORLD What a Difference a Day (or Few) Makes

Taxpayers may begin taking depreciation deductions on their tax returns for business assets "placed in service" during the taxable year. As one taxpayer recently found out, determining when an asset is placed in service is not as simple as purchasing and using an asset. Michael Brown, a wealthy insurance salesman, purchased a $22 million Bombardier Challenger 604 airplane for use in his business. He took possession of the plane on December 30, 2003, and flew the plane across the country on business trips before the end of the year. Accordingly, Brown claimed about $11 million of bonus depreciation on his 2003 tax return. In January 2004, the plane was grounded for a period of time while a conference table and a display screen were added at an additional cost of $500,000. These improvements were "needed" and "required" for his insurance business according to Brown.

The IRS challenged Brown's bonus depreciation deduction claiming that the plane was not "placed in service" in 2003. The issue is when the plane was regularly available for use in its specifically intended function. Per Brown's testimony, he insisted on having the conference table and display screen so he could conduct business on the plane. Because of this testimony that determined the plane's specifically intended function, the Tax Court denied the bonus depreciation deduction for 2003.

The outcome of this case illustrates the importance of determining the specific function for an asset and whether seemingly minor (2 percent) upgrades can make the asset substantially unavailable for its specifically intended function. It seems the taxpayer's own testimony of the plane's specifically intended function drove the Tax Court's decision to disallow the bonus depreciation deduction.

Source: Brown, T. C. Memo. 2013-275.

Listed Property Most business-owned assets are used for business rather than personal purposes. For example, Weyerhaeuser employees probably have little or no personal interest in using Weyerhaeuser's timber-harvesting equipment during their free time. In contrast, business owners and employees may find some business assets, such as company automobiles or laptop computers, conducive for personal use.

Business assets that tend to be used for both business and personal purposes are referred to as **listed property.** For example, automobiles, other means of transportation (planes, boats, and recreation vehicles), computer equipment, and even digital cameras are considered to be listed property. The tax law limits the allowable depreciation on listed property to the portion of the asset used for business purposes.

How do taxpayers compute depreciation for listed property? First, they must determine the percentage of business vs. personal use of the asset for the year. If the business-use percentage for the year *exceeds* 50 percent, the deductible depreciation is limited to the full annual depreciation multiplied by the *business-use* percentage for the year. Listed property used in trade or business more than 50 percent is eligible for the §179 expensing election and bonus depreciation (if bonus depreciation is applicable for year asset was placed into service).

Example 10-19

What if: Assume that, in addition to the assets Teton purchased in the base scenario presented in Exhibit 10-5, it also purchased a new computer projector for $2,000 that its employees use for business presentations on weekdays. On weekends, Steve uses the projector as an integral part of his high-definition home theater system. Since the computer projector is listed property, Teton must assess the business-use percentage to properly calculate its deductible depreciation for the projector. Assuming that Teton determines the business-use percentage to be 75 percent, what is Teton's depreciation deduction on the projector for the year (ignoring bonus depreciation and §179 expensing)?

Answer: $300, computed as follows:

Description	Amount	Explanation
(1) Original basis of projector	$2,000	
(2) MACRS depreciation rate	20%	5-year property, year 1, half-year convention.
(3) Full MACRS depreciation expense	$ 400	(1) × (2).
(4) Business-use percentage	75%	
Depreciation deduction for year	$ 300	(3) × (4).

When the business-use percentage of an asset is 50 percent or less, the business must compute depreciation for the asset using the MACRS *straight-line* method over the MACRS ADS (alternative depreciation system) recovery period.[29] For five-year assets such as automobiles and computers, the assets on which the personal use limitation is most common, the MACRS ADS recovery period is also five years. However, for seven-year assets, the ADS recovery period is generally 10 years.[30]

If a business initially uses an asset more than 50 percent of the time for business (and appropriately adopts the 200 percent declining balance method) but subsequently its business use drops to 50 percent or below, the *depreciation expense for all prior years must be recomputed* as if it had been using the straight-line depreciation over the ADS recovery period the entire time. It must then recapture any excess accelerated depreciation it deducted over the straight-line depreciation it should have deducted by adjusting the current year depreciation. In practical terms, the business can use the following five steps to determine its current depreciation expense for the asset:

Step 1: Compute depreciation for the year it drops to 50 percent or below using the straight-line method (this method also applies to all subsequent years).

Step 2: Compute the amount of depreciation the taxpayer would have deducted if the taxpayer had used the straight-line method over the ADS recovery period for all prior years (recall that depreciation is limited to the business-use percentage in those years).

Step 3: Compute the amount of depreciation the taxpayer had actually deducted on the asset for all prior years.

Step 4: Subtract the amount from Step 2 from the amount in Step 3. The difference is the prior year accelerated depreciation in excess of straight-line depreciation.

Step 5: Subtract the excess accelerated depreciation determined in Step 4 from the current year straight-line depreciation in Step 1. This is the business's allowable depreciation expense on the asset for the year. If the prior year excess depreciation from Step 4 exceeds the current year straight-line depreciation in Step 1, the business is not allowed to deduct any depreciation on the asset for the year and must actually recognize additional ordinary income for the amount of the excess.

This five-step process is designed to place the business in the same position it would have been in if it had used straight-line depreciation during all years of the asset's life.

[29]This is the alternative recovery period listed in Rev. Proc. 87-56. See §168(g)(3)(C) and Reg. §1.280F-3T(d)(1).

[30]However, there are exceptions to this general rule. For example, the ADS recovery period for certain machinery for food and beverages is 12 years and the ADS recovery period for machinery for tobacco products is 15 years. Thus, it is important to check Rev. Proc. 87-56 to verify the ADS recovery period in these situations.

Example 10-20

What if: Assume that, consistent with the previous example, in year 1 Teton used the projector 75 percent of the time for business purposes and deducted $300 depreciation expense on the projector. However, in year 2, Teton's business-use percentage falls to 40 percent. What is Teton's depreciation deduction for the projector in year 2?

Answer: $10, computed using the five-step process described above as follows:

Description	Amount	Explanation*
(1) Straight-line depreciation in current year	$160	$2,000/5 years × 40 percent business use percentage (Step 1).
(2) Prior year straight-line depreciation	150	$2,000/5 × 50 percent (half-year convention) × 75 percent business-use percentage (Step 2).
(3) Prior year accelerated depreciation	300	Example 10-19 (prior example) (Step 3).
(4) Excess accelerated depreciation	150	(3) − (2) (Step 4).
Allowable current year depreciation	**$ 10**	(1) − (4) (Step 5).

*Note that the MACRS ADS recovery period (five years) for computers and peripherals (qualified technological equipment) is the same as the standard MACRS recovery period (five years).

What if: Now assume that, in year 1 Teton used the projector 85 percent of the time for business purposes and deducted $340 depreciation expense on the projector. However, in year 2, Teton's business-use percentage falls to 40 percent. What is Teton's depreciation deduction for the projector in year 2?

Answer: $0 depreciation deduction and $10 of ordinary income because excess accelerated depreciation exceeds current year straight-line depreciation, computed as follows:

Description	Amount	Explanation
(1) Straight-line depreciation in current year	$160	$2,000/5 years × 40 percent business use.
(2) Prior year straight-line depreciation	170	$2,000/5 × 50 percent (half-year convention) × 85 percent business-use percentage.
(3) Prior year accelerated depreciation	340	Example 10-19 (prior example, if 85%).
(4) Excess accelerated depreciation	170	(3) − (2).
Allowable current year depreciation (income)	**($10)**	(1) − (4).

TAXES IN THE REAL WORLD Do Depreciation Tax Incentives Work?

U.S. companies have been hoarding cash to the tune of $1.64 trillion as of the 2013 year-end according to a Moody's Investors Services report. One way the government tries to stimulate business spending is through generous depreciation provisions such as bonus depreciation and §179 immediate expensing provisions. So do these provisions really work?

A survey conducted by Bloomberg BNA, a tax and accounting software vendor, says not really. The survey found that just 10 percent of CFOs, controllers, and tax directors of companies with average revenues of $7.5 billion per year expect their 2014 capital expenditures to change because of the expiration of the bonus depreciation and §179 incentives. A majority of respondents to the survey were even more specific by saying that even if the currently available tax incentives could reduce their total cost of capital by 10 percent, their companies would not increase their capital expenditures.

Bloomberg BNA concludes that "Bonus depreciation and Section 179 expensing, while welcomed by the business community, is not viewed by a majority of that same community as an economic stimulus that drives business decisions."

Source: Bloomberg BNA "US Corporate Capital Expenditures: Consciously Uncoupled from Federal Tax Incentives" http://forms.bnasoftware.com/MTC_Common/mtcURLSrv.aspx?ID=13723&Key=ECEDF59D-C244-4682-B6EF-8278126A6F67&URLID=30222&mtcPromotion=20490

Luxury Automobiles As we discussed in Chapter 9, §162 limits business deductions to those considered to be "ordinary, necessary, and reasonable" to prevent subsidizing (giving a tax deduction for) unwarranted business expenses. Although these terms are subject to interpretation, most taxpayers agree that for purposes of simply transporting passengers for business-related purposes, the cost of acquiring and using a Ford Focus is more likely to be ordinary, necessary, and reasonable than the cost of acquiring and using a Ferrari California—although perhaps not as exhilarating. Since either vehicle should be able to transport an employee or business owner from the office to a business meeting, the Ford Focus should be just as effective at accomplishing the business purpose as the Ferrari. If this is true, why should the government help taxpayers pay for expensive cars with tax savings from large depreciation deductions associated with automobiles? Congress decided it shouldn't. Therefore, with certain exceptions we discuss below, the tax laws generally limit the annual depreciation expense for automobiles.[31] Each year, the IRS provides a maximum depreciation schedule for automobiles placed in service during that particular year.[32] For 2010 through 2014, taxpayers are allowed to expense $8,000 of bonus depreciation above the otherwise allowable maximum depreciation (maximum depreciation of $11,160 for automobiles placed in service in 2012 through 2014); however, as of press date the bonus depreciation provisions have not been extended to 2015.[33] Exhibit 10-8 summarizes these schedules for automobiles placed in service for each year from 2015 back to 2012.

THE KEY FACTS

Luxury Vehicles

- Depreciation on automobiles weighing less than 6,000 lbs. is subject to luxury auto provisions.
- Luxury automobiles have a maximum depreciation limit for each year.
- Listed property rules are also applicable to luxury automobiles.

EXHIBIT 10-8 Automobile Depreciation Limits

Recovery Year	Year Placed in Service			
	2015	2014	2013	2012
1	3,160*	3,160*	3,160*	3,160*
2	5,100	5,100	5,100	5,100
3	3,050	3,050	3,050	3,050
4 and after	1,875	1,875	1,875	1,875

*$8,000 additional depreciation is allowed when bonus depreciation is elected. If the 2014 bonus depreciation provisions are not extended to 2015, the $8,000 additional amount would not apply for those years.

Businesses placing automobiles into service during the year determine depreciation expense for the automobiles by first computing the regular MACRS depreciation expense (using the appropriate convention). They then compare it to the maximum depreciation amount for the first year of the recovery period based on the IRS-provided tables. Businesses are allowed to deduct the lesser of the two. If the automobile depreciation limits apply in the first year, the taxpayer must use the IRS maximum automobile depreciation table to compute depreciation for the asset(s) in all

[31]The passenger automobile definition excludes vehicles that charge for transportation such as taxi cabs, limousines, and hearses. It also excludes delivery trucks and vans. The tax law also limits the deduction for leased autos, which closed the leasing loophole that circumvented the luxury auto depreciation rules.

[32]These limitations are indexed for inflation and change annually. Revenue Procedure 2015-19 includes the 2015 limitations for automobiles and also provides slightly higher limits for hybrids, trucks, and SUVs.

[33]§168(k)(2)(F)(i).

subsequent years. In 2015, if the half-year convention applies, the table limits the depreciation on automobiles placed in service during the year costing more than $15,800.[34] Automobiles to which the depreciation limits apply are commonly referred to as **luxury automobiles.**[35] For any two such luxury cars—say, a 2016 Honda Civic and a 2016 Porsche 911—the annual depreciation limit is the same, regardless of the cost of the vehicles. The only difference is the length of time it will take to fully depreciate the vehicle.

Example 10-21

What is the maximum annual depreciation expense available for 2015 (year 1) on a 2016 Honda Civic costing $15,860 and a 2016 Porsche 911 costing $97,400 (ignoring bonus depreciation)?

Answer: $3,160 for both. See the following depreciation schedules for each automobile.

Luxury Auto Depreciation

Year/Make	2016 Honda Civic	2016 Porsche 911
Model	DX 2dr Coupe	Carrera 4S
Price	$15,860	$97,400
Depreciation		
Year 1	$ 3,160	$ 3,160
Year 2	5,100	5,100
Year 3	3,050	3,050
Year 4	1,875	1,875
Year 5	1,875	1,875
Year 6	800	1,875
Years 7–48		1,875
Year 49		1,715

Given the maximum deduction limitations, the depreciation of the Honda and Porsche are identical in years 1–5. However, beginning in year 6 the Porsche is depreciated at a maximum of $1,875 per year until fully depreciated in year 49—however, it is unlikely the business will actually hold the Porsche through year 49.

The luxury automobile limitations don't apply to vehicles weighing more than 6,000 pounds. Thus, businesses owning these vehicles are allowed to claim §179, bonus, and regular MACRS depreciation expense for these vehicles.[36]

Just like businesses using other types of listed property, businesses using luxury automobiles for business and personal purposes may only deduct depreciation on the asset to the extent of business use. Business use is determined by miles driven for business purposes relative to total miles driven for the year.[37] Consequently, if a business places a luxury automobile into service in 2015 and uses the automobile 90 percent of the time for business purposes during the year (9,000 miles for business and 1,000 miles of personal use), the owner's depreciation (ignoring bonus depreciation) on the auto for the year is limited to $2,844 (year 1 full depreciation of $3,160 × 90 percent business use—see Exhibit 10-8).[38] Further, if the business use falls to

[34]In 2015, the full first-year depreciation on an automobile costing $15,800 is $3,160 ($15,800 × 20%). This is the amount of the first year limit for automobiles placed in service in 2015.

[35]Correspondingly, the depreciation limits on automobiles are commonly referred to as the *luxury auto depreciation limits.*

[36]§280F(d)(5)(A).

[37]As an alternative to deducting depreciation expense and other costs of operating an automobile, taxpayers using automobiles for both personal and business purposes may deduct a standard mileage rate for each mile of business use. In 2015 the business mileage rate is 57.5 cents per mile.

[38]Even if the business-use percentage multiplied by the MACRS depreciation is greater than the $3,160 maximum, the depreciation amount is limited to the maximum depreciation amount times the business-use percentage.

50 percent or less in any subsequent year, just as with other listed property, the taxpayer must use the straight-line method of depreciation and reduce depreciation expense by the amount of excess accelerated depreciation (see Example 10-20). However, because straight-line depreciation is also limited by the luxury auto depreciation limits, it may turn out that the business doesn't have any excess accelerated depreciation.

Are businesses allowed to deduct §179 expensing on luxury automobiles? Yes, but the maximum depreciation *including* §179 expense (but excluding the additional $8,000 bonus depreciation) is subject to the luxury auto limits ($3,160 for 2015). Thus, using the §179 expense on a luxury auto is unlikely to provide any tax benefit beyond the regular depreciation for most automobiles. However, businesses may deduct $25,000 of §179 expense for trucks and SUVs weighing over 6,000 pounds. This $25,000 is part of the overall $500,000 maximum §179 amount. Some companies use tax benefits to sell customers on purchasing these types of automobiles.

Depreciation for the Alternative Minimum Tax

Both individuals and corporations are subject to tax under the alternative minimum tax (AMT) system. In determining their alternative minimum taxable income, individuals and corporations may be required to recalculate their depreciation expense. For AMT purposes, the allowable recovery period and conventions are the same for all depreciable assets as they are for regular tax purposes.[39] However, for AMT purposes, businesses are not allowed to use the 200 percent declining balance method to depreciate tangible personal property. Rather, they must choose from the 150 percent declining balance method or the straight-line method to depreciate the property for AMT purposes. The difference between regular tax depreciation and AMT depreciation is an adjustment that is either added to or subtracted from regular taxable income in computing the alternative minimum tax base.[40] In contrast, the §179 expense is equally deductible for both regular tax and AMT purposes. Depreciation of real property is the same for both regular tax and AMT purposes.

Depreciation Summary

Teton's depreciation for the year is summarized in Exhibit 10-9, and Exhibit 10-10 presents Teton's depreciation expense as it would be reported on its tax return on Form 4562 (this assumes Teton elected out of bonus depreciation).

EXHIBIT 10-9 Tax Depreciation Expense Summary

Asset	Original Basis	§179 Expense	Remaining Basis*	Depreciation Expense	Reference
Machinery	$510,000	$80,000	$430,000	$ 61,447	Example 10-13 (What-if scenario).
Office furniture	10,000		10,000	1,429	Example 10-3.
Delivery truck	15,000	0	15,000	3,000	Example 10-3.
Warehouse	275,000	N/A	275,000	4,414	Example 10-11.
Land	75,000	N/A	75,000	0	N/A.
§179 Expense				80,000	Example 10-13.
Total Depreciation Expense				$150,290	

*Note that Teton's remaining basis is the original cost less the §179 expense.

[39]This is true for assets placed in service after 1998.

[40]If the taxpayer elected either the 150 percent declining balance or the straight-line method for regular tax depreciation of tangible personal property, then there is no AMT adjustment with respect to that property.

EXHIBIT 10-10 Teton's Form 4562 Parts I-IV for Depreciation (Assumes $100,000 of taxable income before the §179 expense)

Form **4562** | **Depreciation and Amortization** (Including Information on Listed Property) | OMB No. 1545-0172

Department of the Treasury Internal Revenue Service (99)

▶ Attach to your tax return.

▶ Information about Form 4562 and its separate instructions is at *www.irs.gov/form4562.*

2014 Attachment Sequence No. **179**

Name(s) shown on return	Business or activity to which this form relates	Identifying number

Part I **Election To Expense Certain Property Under Section 179**
Note: *If you have any listed property, complete Part V before you complete Part I.*

1	Maximum amount (see instructions)	1	500,000
2	Total cost of section 179 property placed in service (see instructions)	2	535,000
3	Threshold cost of section 179 property before reduction in limitation (see instructions)	3	2,000,000
4	Reduction in limitation. Subtract line 3 from line 2. If zero or less, enter -0-	4	0
5	Dollar limitation for tax year. Subtract line 4 from line 1. If zero or less, enter -0-. If married filing separately, see instructions	5	500,000

6 (a) Description of property	(b) Cost (business use only)	(c) Elected cost
Machinery	510,000	80,000
7 Listed property. Enter the amount from line 29	7	

8	Total elected cost of section 179 property. Add amounts in column (c), lines 6 and 7	8	80,000
9	Tentative deduction. Enter the **smaller** of line 5 or line 8	9	80,000
10	Carryover of disallowed deduction from line 13 of your 2013 Form 4562	10	
11	Business income limitation. Enter the smaller of business income (not less than zero) or line 5 (see instructions)	11	100,000
12	Section 179 expense deduction. Add lines 9 and 10, but do not enter more than line 11	12	80,000
13	Carryover of disallowed deduction to 2015. Add lines 9 and 10, less line 12 ▶ 13		

Note: *Do not use Part II or Part III below for listed property. Instead, use Part V.*

Part II **Special Depreciation Allowance and Other Depreciation (Do not** include listed property.**)** (See instructions.)

14	Special depreciation allowance for qualified property (other than listed property) placed in service during the tax year (see instructions)	14	
15	Property subject to section 168(f)(1) election	15	
16	Other depreciation (including ACRS)	16	

Part III **MACRS Depreciation (Do not** include listed property.**)** (See instructions.)

Section A

17	MACRS deductions for assets placed in service in tax years beginning before 2014	17	
18	If you are electing to group any assets placed in service during the tax year into one or more general asset accounts, check here ▶ ☐		

Section B—Assets Placed in Service During 2014 Tax Year Using the General Depreciation System

(a) Classification of property	(b) Month and year placed in service	(c) Basis for depreciation (business/investment use only—see instructions)	(d) Recovery period	(e) Convention	(f) Method	(g) Depreciation deduction
19a 3-year property						
b 5-year property		15,000	5-year	HY	DDB	3,000
c 7-year property		440,000	7-year	HY	DDB	62,876
d 10-year property						
e 15-year property						
f 20-year property						
g 25-year property			25 yrs.		S/L	
h Residential rental property			27.5 yrs.	MM	S/L	
			27.5 yrs.	MM	S/L	
i Nonresidential real property	May 2014	275,000	39 yrs.	MM	S/L	4,414
				MM	S/L	

Section C—Assets Placed in Service During 2014 Tax Year Using the Alternative Depreciation System

20a Class life					S/L	
b 12-year			12 yrs.		S/L	
c 40-year			40 yrs.	MM	S/L	

Part IV **Summary** (See instructions.)

21	Listed property. Enter amount from line 28	21	
22	**Total.** Add amounts from line 12, lines 14 through 17, lines 19 and 20 in column (g), and line 21. Enter here and on the appropriate lines of your return. Partnerships and S corporations—see instructions	22	150,290
23	For assets shown above and placed in service during the current year, enter the portion of the basis attributable to section 263A costs	23	

For Paperwork Reduction Act Notice, see separate instructions. Cat. No. 12906N Form **4562** (2014)

AMORTIZATION

LO 10-4

Businesses recover the cost of intangible assets through amortization rather than depreciation expense. Intangible assets in the form of capitalized expenditures, such as capitalized **research and experimentation (R&E) costs** or **covenants not to compete,** do not have physical characteristics. Nonetheless, they may have determinable lives. While research and experimentation costs may have an indeterminate life, a covenant not to compete, for example, would have a life equal to the stated term of the contractual agreement. When the life of intangible assets cannot be determined, taxpayers recover the cost of the assets when they dispose of them—unless they are assigned a specific tax recovery period.

For tax purposes, an intangible asset can be placed into one of the following four general categories:

1. §197 purchased intangibles.
2. Start-up expenditures and organizational costs.
3. Research and experimentation costs.
4. Patents and copyrights.

Businesses amortize all intangible assets in these categories using the straight-line method for both book and tax purposes.

Section 197 Intangibles

THE KEY FACTS

§197 Intangible Assets

- Purchased intangibles are amortized over a period of 180 months, regardless of their explicitly stated lifetimes.
- The full-month convention applies to amortizable assets.

When a business purchases the *assets* of another business for a single purchase price, the business must determine the basis of each of the assets it acquired in the transaction. To determine basis, the business must allocate a portion of the purchase price to each of the individual assets acquired in the transaction. Generally, under this approach, each asset acquired in the purchase (cash, machinery, and real property, for example) takes a basis equal to its fair market value. However, some of the assets acquired in the transaction may not appear on the seller's balance sheet. In fact, a substantial portion of a business's value may exist in the form of intangible assets such as customer lists, patents, trademarks, trade names, goodwill, going-concern value, covenants not to compete, and so forth. Nearly all of these assets are amortized according to §197 of the Internal Revenue Code—hence, they are often referred to **§197 purchased intangibles.** According to §197, these assets have a recovery period of 180 months (15 years), *regardless of their actual life*.[41] For example, when a business buys an existing business, the owner selling the business often signs a covenant not to compete for a specified period such as five years.[42] Even though a five-year covenant not to compete clearly has a fixed and determinable life, it must be amortized over 180 months (15 years). The **full-month convention** applies to the amortization of purchased intangibles. This convention allows taxpayers to deduct an entire month's worth of amortization for the month of purchase and all subsequent months in the year. The full-month convention also applies in the month of sale or disposition.[43]

[41]§197 was Congress's response to taxpayers manipulating the valuation and recovery periods assigned to these purchased intangibles.

[42]A covenant not to compete is a contract between the seller of a business and its buyer that the seller will not operate a similar business that would compete with the previous business for a specified period of time.

[43]Reg. §1.197-2(g)(1)(i) illustrates the special rules that apply when a taxpayer sells a §197 intangible or the intangible becomes worthless and the taxpayer's basis in the asset exceeds the sale proceeds (if any). A business may recognize a loss on the sale or disposition only when the business does not hold any other §197 assets that the business acquired in the *same initial transaction*. Otherwise, the taxpayer may not deduct the loss on the sale or disposition until the business sells or disposes of *all* of the other §197 intangibles that it purchased in the same initial transaction. The same loss disallowance rule applies if a §197 intangible expires before it is fully amortized.

Example 10-22

What if: Assume that at the beginning of year 1, Teton acquires a competitor's assets for $350,000.[44] Of the $350,000 purchase price, $125,000 is allocated to tangible assets and $225,000 is allocated to § 197 intangible assets (patent, goodwill, and a customer list with a three-year life).[45] For each of the first three years, Teton would deduct one-fifteenth of the basis of each asset as amortization expense. What is Teton's accumulated amortization and remaining basis in each of these § 197 intangibles after three years?

Answer: See the table below:

Description	Patent	Goodwill	Customer List
Basis	$25,000	$150,000	$50,000
Accumulated amortization (3/15ths of original basis)	(5,000)	(30,000)	(10,000)
Remaining basis	$20,000	$120,000	$40,000

When a taxpayer sells a §197 intangible for more than its basis, the taxpayer recognizes gain. We describe how to characterize this type of gain in the next chapter.

Organizational Expenditures and Start-Up Costs

Organizational expenditures include expenditures to form and organize a business in the form of a corporation or a partnership.[46] Organizational expenditures typically include costs of organizational meetings, state fees, accounting service costs incident to organization, and legal service expenditures such as document drafting, taking minutes of organizational meetings, and creating terms of the original stock certificates. These costs are generally incurred prior to the starting of business (or shortly thereafter) but relate to creating the business entity. The costs of selling or marketing stock do *not* qualify as organizational expenditures and cannot be amortized.[47]

Example 10-23

What if: Suppose Teton was organized as a corporation rather than a sole proprietorship (recall that sole proprietorships cannot expense organizational expenditures). Steve paid $35,000 of legal costs to Scott, Tang, and Malan to draft the corporate charter and articles of incorporation; $10,000 to Harvey and Stratford for accounting fees related to the organization; and $7,000 for organizational meetings, $5,000 for stock issuance costs, and $1,000 for state fees related to the incorporation. What amounts of these expenditures qualify as organizational costs?

Answer: $53,000 computed as follows (with the exception of the stock issuance costs, each of Teton's expenses qualify as amortizable organizational expenditures):

[44] If a business acquires another business's stock (rather than assets) there is no goodwill assigned for tax purposes, and the purchase price simply becomes the basis of the stock purchased.

[45] A customer base is the value assigned to current customers (i.e., the lists that will allow the new owner to capture future benefits from the current customers).

[46] §248 for corporations and §709 for partnerships. Sole proprietorships cannot deduct organizational expenditures.

[47] These syndication costs are capitalized and deducted on the final tax return a business files.

Description	Qualifying Organizational Expenditures
Legal drafting of corporate charter and articles of incorporation	$35,000
Accounting fees related to organization	10,000
Organizational meetings	7,000
Stock issuance costs	0
State incorporation fees	1,000
Totals	$53,000

THE KEY FACTS

Organizational Expenditures and Start-Up Costs

- Taxpayers may immediately expense up to $5,000 of organizational expenditures and $5,000 of start-up costs.
- The immediate expense rule has a dollar-for-dollar phase-out that begins at $50,000 for organizational expenditures and for start-up costs. Thus, when organizational expenditures or start-up costs exceed $55,000 there is no immediate expensing.

Businesses may *immediately expense* up to $5,000 of organizational expenditures.[48] However, businesses incurring more than $50,000 in organizational expenditures must phase-out (reduce) the $5,000 immediate expense amount dollar for dollar for expenditures exceeding $50,000. Thus, businesses incurring at least $55,000 of organizational expenditures are not allowed to immediately expense any of the expenditures.

Example 10-24

What if: Suppose Teton is a corporation and it wants to maximize its current year organizational expenditure deduction. As described in Example 10-23, Teton incurred $53,000 of organizational expenditures in year 1. How much of the organizational expenditures can Teton immediately expense in year 1?

Answer: $2,000, computed as follows:

Description	Amount	Explanation
(1) Maximum immediate expense	$ 5,000	§248(a)(1).
(2) Total organizational expenditures	53,000	Example 10-23.
(3) Phase-out threshold	50,000	§248(a)(1)(B).
(4) Immediate expense phase-out	3,000	(2) − (3).
(5) Allowable immediate expense	**2,000**	(1) − (4), but not below zero.
Remaining organizational expenditures	$51,000*	(2) − (5).

What if: Assuming that Teton is a corporation and that it incurred $41,000 of organizational expenditures in year 1, how much of the organizational expenditures could Teton immediately expense in year 1?

Answer: $5,000, computed as follows:

Description	Amount	Explanation
(1) Maximum immediate expense	$ 5,000	§248(a)(1).
(2) Total organizational expenditures	41,000	
(3) Phase-out threshold	50,000	§248(a)(1)(B).
(4) Immediate expense phase-out	0	(2) − (3), limit to zero.
(5) Allowable immediate expense	**5,000**	(1) − (4).
Remaining organizational expenditures	$36,000*	(2) − (5).

(*continued on page 10-34*)

[48]§248(a)(1) for corporations or §709 for partnerships.

What if: Assuming that Teton is a corporation and it incurred $60,000 of organizational expenditures in year 1, how much of the organizational expenditures could Teton immediately expense in year 1?

Answer: $0, computed as follows:

Description	Amount	Explanation
(1) Maximum immediate expense	$ 5,000	§248(a)(1).
(2) Total organizational expenditures	60,000	
(3) Phase-out threshold	50,000	§248(a)(1)(B).
(4) Immediate expense phase-out	10,000	(2) − (3).
(5) Allowable immediate expense	**0**	(1) − (4).
Remaining organizational expenditures	$60,000*	(2) − (5).

*As we discuss below, Teton amortizes the remaining organizational costs.

Businesses amortize organizational expenditures that they do not immediately expense using the straight-line method over a recovery period of 15 years (180 months).

Example 10-25

What if: Assume Teton is a corporation and it amortizes the $51,000 of organizational expenditures remaining after it immediately expenses $2,000 of the costs (see Example 10-24). If Teton began business on February 1 of year 1, how much total cost recovery expense for the organizational expenditures is Teton able to deduct in year 1?

Answer: $5,117, computed as follows:

Description	Amount	Explanation
(1) Total organizational expenditures	$53,000	Example 10-22.
(2) Amount immediately expensed	2,000	Example 10-23.
(3) Expenditures subject to straight-line amortization	$51,000	(1) − (2).
(4) Recovery period in months	180	15 years §248(a)(2).
(5) Monthly straight-line amortization	283.33	(3)/(4).
(6) Teton business months during year 1	× 11	February through December.
(7) Year 1 straight-line amortization	3,117	(5) × (6).
Total year 1 cost recovery expense for organizational expenditures.	**$ 5,117**	(2) + (7).

Start-up costs are costs businesses incur to, not surprisingly, start up a business.[49] Start-up costs apply to all types of business forms.[50] These costs include costs associated with investigating the possibilities of and actually creating or acquiring a trade or business. For example, costs Teton incurs in deciding whether to locate the business in Cody, Wyoming, or Bozeman, Montana, are start-up costs. Start-up costs also include costs that would normally be deductible as ordinary business expenses except that they don't qualify as business expenses because they are incurred before the trade or business activity actually begins. For example, costs Teton incurs to train its employees before the business begins are start-up costs. The rules for immediately expensing and amortizing start-up costs are the same as those for immediately expensing and amortizing organizational expenditures. Consequently, businesses incurring at least $55,000 of start-up costs are not allowed to immediately expense any of the costs. The limitations are computed separately for organizational expenditures and for start-up costs.

[49]§195.

[50]Recall that rules for amortizing organizational expenditures apply only to corporations and partnerships.

Consequently, a business could immediately expense $5,000 of organizational expenditures and $5,000 of start-up costs in its first year of business.

Example 10-26

What if: Assume that in January of year 1 (before it began business on February 1) Teton spent $4,500 investigating the climbing hardware market, creating company logos, and determining the locations for both the office and manufacturing facility. The $4,500 of expenditures qualifies as start-up costs. How much of the $4,500 of start-up costs is Teton allowed to immediately expense?

Answer: All $4,500. Teton is allowed to immediately expense the entire $4,500 because its total start-up costs do not exceed $50,000. Teton could have immediately expensed up to $5,000 of start-up costs as long as its total start-up costs did not exceed $50,000.

Exhibit 10-11 illustrates the timing of organizational expenditures, start-up costs, and normal trade or business expenses.

EXHIBIT 10-11 **Summary of Timing for Organizational Expenditures, Start-Up Costs, and Normal Trade or Business Expenses**

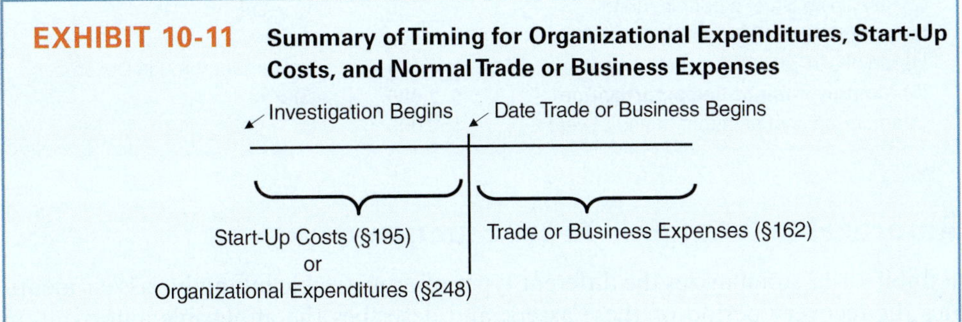

Research and Experimentation Expenditures

To stay competitive, businesses often invest in activities they believe will generate innovative products or significantly improve their current products or processes. These research and experimentation costs include expenditures for research laboratories including salaries, materials, and other related expenses. Businesses may immediately expense these costs or they may *elect* to capitalize these costs and amortize them using the straight-line method over the determinable useful life or, if there is no determinable useful life, over a period of not less than 60 months, beginning in the month benefits are first derived from the research.[51] However, if a business elects to capitalize and amortize the costs, it must stop amortizing the costs if and when the business receives a patent relating to the expenditures. When the business obtains a patent, it adds any remaining basis in the costs to the basis of the patent and it amortizes the basis of the patent over the patent's life (see discussion below).

Patents and Copyrights

The manner in which a business amortizes a patent or copyright depends on whether the business directly purchases the patent or copyright or whether it self-creates the intangibles. Businesses directly purchasing patents or copyrights (not in an asset acquisition to which §197 applies) amortize the cost over the remaining life of the patents or copyrights.[52] Businesses receiving "self-created" patents or copyrights amortize the cost or basis of the self-created intangible assets over their legal lives. The costs included in the basis

[51]See §174. High tax rate taxpayers may choose to deduct these costs while low tax rate taxpayers may prefer to capitalize and amortize them so that they will have more future deductions when they generate more income. There is also the research and experimentation credit which is available to some businesses.

[52]§167(f).

of a self-created patent or copyright include legal costs, fees, and, as we discussed above, unamortized research and experimentation expenditures associated with the creation of the patent or copyright. However, because the patent approval process is slow, the unamortized research and experimentation costs included in the patent's basis are likely to be relatively small because, with a five-year recovery period, the research and experimentation costs would likely be mostly or even fully amortized by the time the patent is approved.

Example 10-27

In September of year 1, Teton purchased a patent with a remaining life of 10 years from Chouinard Equipment for $60,000. What amount of amortization expense is Teton allowed to deduct for the patent in year 1?

Answer: $2,000, computed as follows:

Description	Amount	Explanation
(1) Cost of patent	$60,000	
(2) Remaining life of patent in months	120	10 years.
(3) Monthly amortization	$ 500	(1)/(2).
(4) Months in year 1 Teton held patent	× 4	September through December.
(5) Monthly straight-line amortization	**$ 2,000**	(3) × (4).
Unamortized cost of patent at end of year 1	$58,000	(1) − (5).

Amortizable Intangible Asset Summary

Exhibit 10-12 summarizes the different types of amortizable intangible assets, identifies the recovery period of these assets, and describes the applicable amortization method for each asset. Exhibit 10-12 also identifies the applicable convention for each type of amortizable intangible asset and identifies the financial accounting treatment for recovering the cost of the intangible assets under GAAP.

EXHIBIT 10-12 Summary of Amortizable Assets

Asset Description	Recovery Period (months)	Applicable Method	Applicable Convention	Financial Accounting Treatment
§197 purchased intangibles including goodwill, trademarks, patents, and covenants not to compete.[53]	180	Straight-line	Full-month beginning with month of purchase.	ASC 350 tests for annual impairment.
Organizational expenditures and start-up costs are required to be capitalized.	180	Straight-line	Full-month in month business begins.	AICPA SOP 98-5.
Research and experimentation costs that are capitalized.	Determinable useful life, or 60 (not less than); ceases when patent is issued.	Straight-line	Full-month in first month that benefits from research are obtained.	Expensed.
Self-created patents and copyrights.	Actual life.	Straight-line	Full-month month intangible is obtained.	Expensed.
Purchased patents and copyrights.	Remaining life.	Straight-line	Full-month in month intangible is obtained.	Expensed.

[53]A patent or copyright that is part of a basket purchase (several assets together) is treated as a §197 intangible. A patent or copyright that is purchased separately is simply amortized over its remaining life (§167(f)).

Exhibit 10-13 presents Teton's amortization expense as it would be reported on its tax return on Form 4562 (the exhibit assumes that Teton is a corporation so it can amortize organizational expenditures).

EXHIBIT 10-13 Teton Form 4562, Part VI Amortization of Organizational Expenditures and Patent

Part VI Amortization

(a) Description of costs	(b) Date amortization begins	(c) Amortizable amount	(d) Code section	(e) Amortization period or percentage	(f) Amortization for this year
42 Amortization of costs that begins during your 2014 tax year (see instructions):					
Organizational expenditures	**2/1/2015**	**53,000**	**243**	**15 years**	**5,117**
Patents	**9/1/2015**	**60,000**	**167**	**10 years**	**2,000**
43 Amortization of costs that began before your 2014 tax year				**43**	
44 Total. Add amounts in column (f). See the instructions for where to report				**44**	**7,117**

Form **4562** (2014)

continued from page 10-1 . . .

Teton was developing some additional employee parking on a lot adjacent to the warehouse when the excavation crew discovered a small gold deposit. Steve called his friend Ken, who had some experience in mining precious metals, to see what Ken thought of the find. Ken was impressed and offered Steve $150,000 for the rights to the gold. Steve accepted the offer on Teton's behalf. ■

LO 10-5

DEPLETION

Depletion is the method taxpayers use to recover their capital investment in natural resources. Depletion is a particularly significant deduction for businesses in the mining, oil and gas, and forestry industries. These businesses generally incur depletion expense as they use the natural resource. Specifically, businesses compute annual depletion expense under both the cost and percentage depletion methods and they deduct the larger of the two.[54]

Under **cost depletion,** taxpayers must estimate or determine the number of units or reserves (tons of coal, barrels of oil, board feet of timber, for example) that remain at the beginning of the year and allocate a pro rata share of that basis to each unit that is extracted during the year.[55]

Example 10-28

Ken's cost basis in the gold is the $150,000 he paid for it. Based on a mining engineer's estimate that the gold deposit probably holds 1,000 ounces of gold, Ken can determine his cost depletion. What is Ken's cost depletion for year 1 and year 2, assuming he extracts 300 and 700 ounces of gold in year 1 and year 2, respectively?

(continued on page 10-38)

[54]Depletion of timber and major integrated oil companies must be calculated using only the cost depletion method (no percentage depletion is available).

[55]§612.

THE KEY FACTS

Depletion

- Cost depletion involves estimating resource reserves and allocating a pro-rata share of basis based on the number of units extracted.
- Percentage depletion is determined by a statutory percentage of gross income that is permitted to be expensed each year. Different resources have different statutory percentages (i.e., gold, tin, coal).
- Taxpayers may expense the larger of cost or percentage depletion.

Answer: $45,000 in year 1 and $105,000 in year 2, computed as follows:

Description	Amount	Explanation
(1) Cost basis in gold	$150,000	
(2) Estimated ounces of gold	1,000	
(3) Per ounce cost depletion rate	150	(1)/(2).
(4) Year 1 ounces extracted	300	
(5) Year 1 cost depletion	**$ 45,000**	(3) × (4).
(6) Basis remaining after year 1 depletion	105,000	(1) − (5).
(7) Year 2 ounces extracted	700	
(8) Year 2 cost depletion	**$105,000**	(7) × (3).
Basis remaining after year 2 depletion	$ 0	(6) − (8).

Ken is not eligible for cost depletion after year 2 because as of the end of year 2, his cost basis has been reduced to $0.

Because the cost depletion method of depletion requires businesses to estimate the number of units of the resource they will actually extract, it is possible that their estimate will prove to be inaccurate. If they underestimate the number of units, they will fully deplete the cost basis of the resource before they have fully extracted the resource. Once they have recovered the entire cost basis of the resource, businesses are not allowed to use cost depletion to determine depletion expense. Businesses, however, may continue to use percentage depletion (see discussion below). If a business overestimates the number of units to be extracted, it will still have basis remaining after the resource has been fully extracted. In these situations, the business would deduct the unrecovered basis once it had sold all the remaining units.

The amount of **percentage depletion** for a natural resource business activity is determined by multiplying the *gross income* from the resource extraction activity by a fixed percentage based on the type of natural resource as indicated in Exhibit 10-14.[56]

EXHIBIT 10-14 Applicable Percentage Depletion Rates

Statutory Percentage	Natural Resources (Partial list)
5 percent [§613(b)(6)]	Gravel, pumice, and stone.
14 percent [§613(b)(3)]	Asphalt rock, clay, and other metals.
15 percent [§613(b)(2)]	Gold, copper, oil shale, and silver.
15 percent [§613A(c)(1)]	Domestic oil and gas
22 percent [§613(b)(1)]	Platinum, sulfur, uranium, and titanium.

In many cases, percentage depletion may generate *larger* depletion deductions than does cost depletion. Recall that taxpayers are allowed to deduct the greater of cost or percentage depletion. Businesses reduce their cost basis in the resource when they deduct percentage depletion. However, once the cost basis is exhausted, they are allowed to continue to deduct percentage (but not cost) depletion. This provides a potentially significant governmental subsidy to extraction businesses that have completely recovered their costs in a natural resource.[57]

It is important to note that businesses deduct percentage depletion when they *sell* the natural resource and they deduct cost depletion in the year they *produce* or extract the natural resource. Also, percentage depletion cannot exceed 50 percent (100 percent in the case of oil and gas properties) of the *taxable income* from the

[56]§613.

[57]Percentage depletion in excess of basis is an AMT preference item.

natural resource business activity before considering the depletion expense, while cost depletion has no such limitation.

Example 10-29

In Example 10-28, Ken determined his cost depletion expense for the gold. However, because he is allowed to deduct the greater of cost or percentage depletion each year, he set out to determine his percentage depletion for year 2. Assuming that Ken has gross (taxable) income from the gold mining activity before depletion expense of $200,000 ($50,000), $600,000 ($450,000), and $600,000 ($500,000) in year 1, year 2, and year 3, respectively, what is his percentage depletion expense for each of these three years?

Answer: $25,000, $90,000, and $90,000 for years 1, 2, and 3, respectively, computed as follows:

	Year 1	Year 2	Year 3	Explanation
(1) Taxable income from activity (before depletion expense)	$ 50,000	$450,000	$500,000	
(2) Gross income	$200,000	$600,000	$600,000	
(3) Percentage	× 15%	× 15%	× 15%	Exhibit 10-14.
(4) Percentage depletion expense before limit	$ 30,000	$ 90,000	$ 90,000	(2) × (3).
(5) 50 percent of taxable income limitation	$ 25,000	$225,000	$250,000	(1) × 50%.
Allowable percentage depletion	**$ 25,000**	**$ 90,000**	**$ 90,000**	Lesser of (4) or (5).

Finally, as we discussed above, a business's depletion expense deduction is the greater of either the annual cost or percentage depletion.

Example 10-30

Based on his computations of cost depletion and percentage depletion, Ken was able to determine his deductible depletion expense. Using the cost and percentage depletion computations from Examples 10-28 and 10-29, what is Ken's deductible depletion expense for years 1, 2, and 3?

Answer: $45,000 for year 1, $105,000 for year 2, and $90,000 for year 3, computed as follows:

Tax Depletion Expense	Year 1	Year 2	Year 3	Explanation
(1) Cost depletion	$45,000	$105,000	$ 0	Example 10-28.
(2) Percentage depletion	25,000	90,000	90,000	Example 10-29.
Allowable expense	45,000	105,000	90,000	Greater of (1) or (2).

CONCLUSION

This chapter describes and discusses how businesses recover the costs of their tangible and intangible assets. Cost recovery expenses are important because they represent a significant tax deduction for many businesses. Businesses must routinely make choices that affect the amount and timing of these deductions. Further understanding cost recovery basics helps businesses determine how to compute and characterize gain and loss they recognize when they sell or otherwise dispose of business assets. We address the interaction between cost recovery expenses and gain and loss on property dispositions in the next chapter.

Appendix MACRS Tables

TABLE 1 MACRS Half-Year Convention

	Depreciation Rate for Recovery Period					
Year	3-year	5-year	7-year	10-year	15-year	20-year
1	33.33	20.00	14.29	10.00	5.00	3.750
2	44.45	32.00	24.49	18.00	9.50	7.219
3	14.81	19.20	17.49	14.40	8.55	6.677
4	7.41	11.52	12.49	11.52	7.70	6.177
5		11.52	8.93	9.22	6.93	5.713
6		5.76	8.92	7.37	6.23	5.285
7			8.93	6.55	5.90	4.888
8			4.46	6.55	5.90	4.522
9				6.56	5.91	4.462
10				6.55	5.90	4.461
11				3.28	5.91	4.462
12					5.90	4.461
13					5.91	4.462
14					5.90	4.461
15					5.91	4.462
16					2.95	4.461
17						4.462
18						4.461
19						4.462
20						4.461
21						2.231

TABLE 2a MACRS Mid-Quarter Convention: *For property placed in service during the first quarter*

	Depreciation Rate for Recovery Period	
Year	5-year	7-year
1	35.00%	25.00%
2	26.00	21.43
3	15.60	15.31
4	11.01	10.93
5	11.01	8.75
6	1.38	8.74
7		8.75
8		1.09

TABLE 2b **MACRS Mid-Quarter Convention:** *For property placed in service during the second quarter*

Depreciation Rate for Recovery Period		
Year	**5-year**	**7-year**
1	25.00%	17.85%
2	30.00	23.47
3	18.00	16.76
4	11.37	11.97
5	11.37	8.87
6	4.26	8.87
7		8.87
8		3.34

TABLE 2c **MACRS Mid-Quarter Convention:** *For property placed in service during the third quarter*

Depreciation Rate for Recovery Period		
Year	**5-year**	**7-year**
1	15.00%	10.71%
2	34.00	25.51
3	20.40	18.22
4	12.24	13.02
5	11.30	9.30
6	7.06	8.85
7		8.86
8		5.53

TABLE 2d **MACRS-Mid Quarter Convention:** *For property placed in service during the fourth quarter*

Depreciation Rate for Recovery Period		
Year	**5-year**	**7-year**
1	5.00%	3.57%
2	38.00	27.55
3	22.80	19.68
4	13.68	14.06
5	10.94	10.04
6	9.58	8.73
7		8.73
8		7.64

TABLE 3 **Residential Rental Property Mid-Month Convention Straight Line—27.5 Years**

	Month Property Placed in Service											
Year	**1**	**2**	**3**	**4**	**5**	**6**	**7**	**8**	**9**	**10**	**11**	**12**
1	3.485%	3.182%	2.879%	2.576%	2.273%	1.970%	1.667%	1.364%	1.061%	0.758%	0.455%	0.152%
2–9	3.636	3.636	3.636	3.636	3.636	3.636	3.636	3.636	3.636	3.636	3.636	3.636
10	3.637	3.637	3.637	3.637	3.637	3.637	3.636	3.636	3.636	3.636	3.636	3.636
11	3.636	3.636	3.636	3.636	3.636	3.636	3.637	3.637	3.637	3.637	3.637	3.637
12	3.637	3.637	3.637	3.637	3.637	3.637	3.636	3.636	3.636	3.636	3.636	3.636
13	3.636	3.636	3.636	3.636	3.636	3.636	3.637	3.637	3.637	3.637	3.637	3.637
14	3.637	3.637	3.637	3.637	3.637	3.637	3.636	3.636	3.636	3.636	3.636	3.636
15	3.636	3.636	3.636	3.636	3.636	3.636	3.637	3.637	3.637	3.637	3.637	3.637
16	3.637	3.637	3.637	3.637	3.637	3.637	3.636	3.636	3.636	3.636	3.636	3.636
17	3.636	3.636	3.636	3.636	3.636	3.636	3.637	3.637	3.637	3.637	3.637	3.637
18	3.637	3.637	3.637	3.637	3.637	3.637	3.636	3.636	3.636	3.636	3.636	3.636
19	3.636	3.636	3.636	3.636	3.636	3.636	3.637	3.637	3.637	3.637	3.637	3.637
20	3.637	3.637	3.637	3.637	3.637	3.637	3.636	3.636	3.636	3.636	3.636	3.636
21	3.636	3.636	3.636	3.636	3.636	3.636	3.637	3.637	3.637	3.637	3.637	3.637
22	3.637	3.637	3.637	3.637	3.637	3.637	3.636	3.636	3.636	3.636	3.636	3.636
23	3.636	3.636	3.636	3.636	3.636	3.636	3.637	3.637	3.637	3.637	3.637	3.637
24	3.637	3.637	3.637	3.637	3.637	3.637	3.636	3.636	3.636	3.636	3.636	3.636
25	3.636	3.636	3.636	3.636	3.636	3.636	3.637	3.637	3.637	3.637	3.637	3.637
26	3.637	3.637	3.637	3.637	3.637	3.637	3.636	3.636	3.636	3.636	3.636	3.636
27	3.636	3.636	3.636	3.636	3.636	3.636	3.637	3.637	3.637	3.637	3.637	3.637
28	1.97	2.273	2.576	2.879	3.182	3.485	3.636	3.636	3.636	3.636	3.636	3.636
29							0.152	0.455	0.758	1.061	1.364	1.667

TABLE 4 **Nonresidential Real Property Mid-Month Convention Straight Line—31.5 Years (for assets placed in service before May 13, 1993)**

	Month Property Placed in Service											
Year	**1**	**2**	**3**	**4**	**5**	**6**	**7**	**8**	**9**	**10**	**11**	**12**
1	3.042%	2.778%	2.513%	2.249%	1.984%	1.720%	1.455%	1.190%	0.926%	0.661%	0.397%	0.132%
2–7	3.175	3.175	3.175	3.175	3.175	3.175	3.175	3.175	3.175	3.175	3.175	3.175
8	3.175	3.174	3.175	3.174	3.175	3.174	3.175	3.175	3.175	3.175	3.175	3.175
9	3.174	3.175	3.174	3.175	3.174	3.175	3.174	3.175	3.174	3.175	3.174	3.175
10	3.175	3.174	3.175	3.174	3.175	3.174	3.175	3.174	3.175	3.174	3.175	3.174
11	3.174	3.175	3.174	3.175	3.174	3.175	3.174	3.175	3.174	3.175	3.174	3.175
12	3.175	3.174	3.175	3.174	3.175	3.174	3.175	3.174	3.175	3.174	3.175	3.174
13	3.174	3.175	3.174	3.175	3.174	3.175	3.174	3.175	3.174	3.175	3.174	3.175
14	3.175	3.174	3.175	3.174	3.175	3.174	3.175	3.174	3.175	3.174	3.175	3.174
15	3.174	3.175	3.174	3.175	3.174	3.175	3.174	3.175	3.174	3.175	3.174	3.175
16	3.175	3.174	3.175	3.174	3.175	3.174	3.175	3.174	3.175	3.174	3.175	3.174
17	3.174	3.175	3.174	3.175	3.174	3.175	3.174	3.175	3.174	3.175	3.174	3.175
18	3.175	3.174	3.175	3.174	3.175	3.174	3.175	3.174	3.175	3.174	3.175	3.174
19	3.174	3.175	3.174	3.175	3.174	3.175	3.174	3.175	3.174	3.175	3.174	3.175
20	3.175	3.174	3.175	3.174	3.175	3.174	3.175	3.174	3.175	3.174	3.175	3.174
21	3.174	3.175	3.174	3.175	3.174	3.175	3.174	3.175	3.174	3.175	3.174	3.175
22	3.175	3.174	3.175	3.174	3.175	3.174	3.175	3.174	3.175	3.174	3.175	3.174
23	3.174	3.175	3.174	3.175	3.174	3.175	3.174	3.115	3.174	3.175	3.174	3.175
24	3.175	3.174	3.175	3.174	3.175	3.174	3.175	3.174	3.175	3.174	3.175	3.174
25	3.174	3.175	3.174	3.175	3.174	3.175	3.174	3.175	3.174	3.175	3.174	3.175
26	3.175	3.174	3.175	3.174	3.175	3.174	3.175	3.174	3.175	3.174	3.175	3.174
27	3.174	3.175	3.174	3.175	3.174	3.175	3.174	3.175	3.174	3.175	3.174	3.175
28	3.175	3.174	3.175	3.174	3.175	3.174	3.175	3.174	3.175	3.174	3.175	3.174
29	3.174	3.175	3.174	3.175	3.174	3.175	3.174	3.175	3.174	3.175	3.174	3.175
30	3.175	3.174	3.175	3.174	3.175	3.174	3.175	3.174	3.175	3.174	3.175	3.174
31	3.174	3.175	3.174	3.175	3.174	3.175	3.174	3.175	3.174	3.175	3.174	3.175
32	1.720	1.984	2.249	2.513	2.778	3.042	3.175	3.174	3.175	3.174	3.175	3.174
33							0.132	0.397	0.661	0.926	1.190	1.455

TABLE 5 **Nonresidential Real Property Mid-Month Convention Straight Line—39 Years (for assets placed in service on or after May 13, 1993)**

	Month property placed in service											
Year	**1**	**2**	**3**	**4**	**5**	**6**	**7**	**8**	**9**	**10**	**11**	**12**
1	2.461%	2.247%	2.033%	1.819%	1.605%	1.391%	1.177%	0.963%	0.749%	0.535%	0.321%	0.107%
2–39	2.564	2.564	2.564	2.564	2.564	2.564	2.564	2.564	2.564	2.564	2.564	2.564
40	0.107	0.321	0.535	0.749	0.963	1.177	1.391	1.605	1.819	2.033	2.247	2.461

Summary

LO 10-1 Explain the concept of basis and adjusted basis and describe the cost recovery methods used under the tax law to recover the cost of personal property, real property, intangible assets, and natural resources.

- Tangible personal and real property (depreciation), intangibles (amortization), and natural resources (depletion) are all subject to cost recovery.
- An asset's basis is the amount that is subject to cost recovery. Generally, an asset's initial basis is its purchase price, plus the cost of any other expenses incurred to get the asset in working condition.
- The taxpayer's basis of assets acquired in a nontaxable exchange is the same basis the taxpayer transferred to acquire the property received.
- Expenditures on an asset are either expensed currently or capitalized as a new asset. Expenditures for routine or general maintenance of the asset are expensed currently. Expenditures that extend the useful life of the asset are capitalized.
- When acquiring a business and purchasing a bundle of property, the basis of each asset is determined as the fair market value of the asset.

LO 10-2 Determine the applicable cost recovery (depreciation) life, method, and convention for tangible personal and real property and calculate the deduction allowable under basic MACRS.

- Tax depreciation is currently calculated under the Modified Accelerated Cost Recovery System (MACRS).
- MACRS for tangible personal property is based upon recovery period (Rev. Proc. 87-56), method (200 percent declining balance, 150 percent declining balance, and straight-line), and convention (half-year or mid-quarter).
- Real property is divided into two groups for tax purposes: residential rental and nonresidential. The recovery period is 27.5 years for residential property and 31.5 years or 39 years for nonresidential property, depending on when the property was placed in service. The depreciation method is straight-line and the convention is mid-month.

LO 10-3 Explain the additional special cost recovery rules (§179, bonus, listed property) and calculate the deduction allowable under these rules.

- §179 allows taxpayers to expense tangible personal property. The expense is limited by the amount of property placed in service and taxable income.
- Bonus depreciation allows taxpayers to immediately expense 50 percent of qualified property in the year of acquisition.
- Listed property includes automobiles, other means of transportation, and computer equipment. Depreciation is limited to the expense multiplied by business-use percentage. Special rules apply if business use is less than 50 percent.
- Additional limitations apply to luxury automobiles.

LO 10-4 Explain the rationale behind amortization, describe the four categories of amortizable intangible assets, and calculate amortization expense.

- Intangible assets (such as patents, goodwill, and trademarks) have their costs recovered through amortization.
- Intangible assets are amortized (straight-line method) using the full-month convention.
- Intangibles are divided into four types (§197 purchased intangibles, start-up costs and organizational expenditures, research and experimentation, and self-created intangibles).

LO 10-5 Explain cost recovery of natural resources and the allowable depletion methods.

- Depletion allows a taxpayer to recover his or her capital investment in natural resources.
- Two methods of depletion are available, and the taxpayer must calculate both and take the one that results in the larger depletion deduction each year.
- Cost depletion allows taxpayers to estimate number of units and then allocate a pro rata share of the basis to each unit extracted during the year.
- Percentage depletion allows the taxpayer to take a statutory determined percentage of gross income as an expense. Deductions are not limited to basis.

KEY TERMS

Accelerated Cost Recovery System (ACRS) (10-5)
adjusted basis (10-3)
amortization (10-2)
bonus depreciation (10-22)
cost depletion (10-37)
cost recovery (10-2)
covenant not to compete (10-31)
depletion (10-2)
depreciation (10-2)
full-month convention (10-31)
half-year convention (10-8)
intangible assets (10-2)
listed property (10-24)
luxury automobile (10-28)
mid-month convention (10-15)
mid-quarter convention (10-8)
Modified Accelerated Cost Recovery System (MACRS) (10-5)
organizational expenditures (10-32)
percentage depletion (10-38)
personal property (10-5)
real property (10-5)
recovery period (10-5)
research and experimentation (R&E) costs (10-31)
§179 expense (10-17)
§197 purchased intangibles (10-31)
start-up costs (10-34)
tax basis (10-3)

DISCUSSION QUESTIONS

1. Explain the reasoning why the tax laws require the cost of certain assets to be capitalized and recovered over time rather than immediately expensed. LO 10-1
2. Explain the differences and similarities between personal property, real property, intangible property, and natural resources. Also, provide an example of each type of asset. LO 10-1
3. Explain the similarities and dissimilarities between depreciation, amortization, and depletion. Describe the cost recovery method used for each of the four asset types (personal property, real property, intangible property, and natural resources). LO 10-1
4. Is an asset's initial or cost basis simply its purchase price? Explain. LO 10-1
5. Compare and contrast the basis of property acquired via purchase, conversion from personal use to business or rental use, a nontaxable exchange, gift, and inheritance. LO 10-1
6. Explain why the expenses incurred to get an asset in place and operable should be included in the asset's basis. LO 10-1
7. Graber Corporation runs a long-haul trucking business. Graber incurs the following expenses: replacement tires, oil changes, and a transmission overhaul. Which of these expenditures may be deducted currently and which must be capitalized? Explain. LO 10-1
8. MACRS depreciation requires the use of a recovery period, method, and convention to depreciate tangible personal property assets. Briefly explain why each is important to the calculation. LO 10-2
9. Can a taxpayer with very little current year income choose to not claim any depreciation expense for the current year and thus save depreciation deductions for the future when the taxpayer expects to be more profitable? LO 10-2
10. What depreciation methods are available for tangible personal property? Explain the characteristics of a business likely to adopt each method. LO 10-2 planning
11. If a business places several different assets in service during the year, must it use the same depreciation method for all assets? If not, what restrictions apply to the business's choices of depreciation methods? LO 10-2
12. Describe how you would determine the MACRS recovery period for an asset if you did not already know it. LO 10-2

research LO 10-2 13. Compare and contrast the recovery periods used by MACRS and those used under generally accepted accounting principles (GAAP).

LO 10-2 14. What are the two depreciation conventions that apply to tangible personal property under MACRS? Explain why Congress provides two methods.

LO 10-2 15. A business buys two identical tangible personal property assets for the same identical price. It buys one at the beginning of the year and one at the end of the year. Under what conditions would the taxpayer's depreciation on each asset be exactly the same? Under what conditions would it be different?

LO 10-2 16. AAA Inc. acquired a machine in year 1. In May of year 3, it sold the asset. Can AAA find its year 3 depreciation percentage for the machine on the MACRS table? If not, what adjustment must AAA make to its full year depreciation percentage to determine its year 3 depreciation?

LO 10-2 17. There are two recovery period classifications for real property. What reasons might Congress have to allow residential real estate a shorter recovery period than nonresidential real property?

LO 10-2 18. Discuss why Congress has instructed taxpayers that real property be depreciated using the mid-month convention as opposed to the half-year or mid-quarter conventions used for tangible personal property.

LO 10-2 research 19. If a taxpayer has owned a building for 10 years and decides that it should make significant improvements to the building, what is the recovery period for the improvements?

LO 10-2 20. Compare and contrast the differences between computing depreciation expense for tangible personal property and depreciation expense for real property under both the regular tax and alternative tax systems.

LO 10-3 21. Discuss why a small business might be able to deduct a greater percentage of the assets it places in service during the year than a larger business.

LO 10-3 22. Explain the two limitations placed on the §179 deduction. How are they similar? How are they different?

LO 10-3 23. Compare and contrast the types of businesses that would benefit from and those that would not benefit from the §179 expense.

LO 10-3 24. What strategies will help a business maximize its current depreciation deductions (including §179)? Why might a taxpayer choose not to maximize its current depreciation deductions?

LO 10-3 25. Why might a business elect only the §179 expense it can deduct in the current year rather than claiming the full amount available?

LO 10-3 26. Describe assets that are considered to be listed property. Why do you think the Internal Revenue Service requires them to be "listed"?

LO 10-3 27. Are taxpayers allowed to claim depreciation expense on assets they use for both business and personal purposes? What are the tax consequences if the business use drops from above 50 percent in one year to below 50 percent in the next?

LO 10-3 28. Discuss why Congress limits the amount of depreciation expense businesses may claim on certain automobiles.

LO 10-3 29. Compare and contrast how a Land Rover SUV and a Mercedes Benz sedan are treated under the luxury auto rules. Also include a discussion of the similarities and differences in available §179 expense.

LO 10-4 30. What is a §197 intangible? How do taxpayers recover the costs of these intangibles? How do taxpayers recover the cost of a §197 intangible that expires (such as a covenant not to compete)?

31. Compare and contrast the tax and financial accounting treatment of goodwill. Are taxpayers allowed to deduct amounts associated with self-created goodwill? LO 10-4

32. Compare and contrast the similarities and differences between organizational expenditures and start-up costs for tax purposes. LO 10-4

33. Discuss the method used to determine the amount of organizational expenditures or start-up costs that may be immediately expensed in the year a taxpayer begins business. LO 10-4

34. Explain the amortization convention applicable to intangible assets. LO 10-4

35. Compare and contrast the recovery periods of §197 intangibles, organizational expenditures, start-up costs, and research and experimentation expenses. LO 10-4

36. Compare and contrast the cost and percentage depletion methods for recovering the costs of natural resources. What are the similarities and differences between the two methods? LO 10-5

37. Explain why percentage depletion has been referred to as a government subsidy. LO 10-5

PROBLEMS

All applicable problems are available with McGraw-Hill's *Connect*® *Accounting*.

38. Jose purchased a delivery van for his business through an online auction. His winning bid for the van was $24,500. In addition, Jose incurred the following expenses before using the van: shipping costs of $650; paint to match the other fleet vehicles at a cost of $1,000; registration costs of $3,200, which included $3,000 of sales tax and a registration fee of $200; wash and detailing for $50; and an engine tune-up for $250. What is Jose's cost basis for the delivery van? LO 10-1

39. Emily purchased a building to store inventory for her business. The purchase price was $760,000. Beyond this, Emily incurred the following necessary expenses to get the building ready for use: $10,000 to repair the roof (does not extend the roof life), $5,000 to make the interior suitable for her finished goods, and $300 in legal fees. What is Emily's cost basis in the new building? LO 10-1

40. Dennis contributed business assets to a new business in exchange for stock in the company. The exchange did not qualify as a nontaxable exchange. The fair market value of these assets was $287,000 on the contribution date. Dennis's original basis in the assets he contributed was $143,000, and the accumulated depreciation on the assets was $78,000. LO 10-1
    a) What is the business's basis in the assets it received from Dennis?
    b) What would be the business's basis if the transaction qualified as a nontaxable exchange?

41. Brittany started a law practice as a sole proprietor. She owned a computer, printer, desk, and file cabinet she purchased during law school (several years ago) that she is planning to use in her business. What is the depreciable basis that Brittany should use in her business for each asset, given the following information? LO 10-1

Asset	Purchase Price	FMV at Time Converted to Business Use
Computer	$2,500	$ 800
Printer	300	150
Desk	1,200	1,000
File cabinet	200	225

LO 10-1 42. Meg O'Brien received a gift of some small-scale jewelry manufacturing equipment that her father had used for personal purposes for many years. Her father originally purchased the equipment for $1,500. Because the equipment is out of production and no longer available, the property is currently worth $4,000. Meg has decided to begin a new jewelry manufacturing trade or business. What is her depreciable basis for depreciating the equipment?

LO 10-1 43. Gary inherited a Maine summer cabin on 10 acres from his grandmother. His grandparents originally purchased the property for $500 in 1950 and built the cabin at a cost of $10,000 in 1965. His grandfather died in 1980 and when his grandmother recently passed away, the property was appraised at $500,000 for the land and $700,000 for the cabin. Since Gary doesn't currently live in New England, he decided that it would be best to put the property to use as a rental. What is Gary's basis in the land and in the cabin?

LO 10-1 44. Wanting to finalize a sale before year-end, on December 29, WR Outfitters sold to Bob a warehouse and the land for $125,000. The appraised fair market value of the warehouse was $75,000, and the appraised value of the land was $100,000.

a) What is Bob's basis in the warehouse and in the land?

b) What would be Bob's basis in the warehouse and in the land if the appraised value of the warehouse is $50,000, and the appraised value of the land is $125,000?

c) Which appraisal would Bob likely prefer?

LO 10-2 45. At the beginning of the year, Poplock began a calendar-year dog boarding business called Griff's Palace. Poplock bought and placed in service the following assets during the year:

Asset	Date Acquired	Cost Basis
Computer equipment	3/23	$ 5,000
Dog grooming furniture	5/12	7,000
Pickup truck	9/17	10,000
Commercial building	10/11	270,000
Land (one acre)	10/11	80,000

Assuming Poplock does not elect §179 expensing or bonus depreciation, answer the following questions:

a) What is Poplock's year 1 depreciation expense for each asset?

b) What is Poplock's year 2 depreciation expense for each asset?

LO 10-2 46. DLW Corporation acquired and placed in service the following assets during the year:

Asset	Date Acquired	Cost Basis
Computer equipment	2/17	$ 10,000
Furniture	5/12	17,000
Commercial building	11/1	270,000

Assuming DLW does not elect §179 expensing or bonus depreciation, answer the following questions:

a) What is DLW's year 1 cost recovery for each asset?

b) What is DLW's year 3 cost recovery for each asset if DLW sells all of these assets on 1/23 of year 3?

47. At the beginning of the year, Dee began a calendar-year business and placed in service the following assets during the year: LO 10-2

Asset	Date Acquired	Cost Basis
Computer equipment	3/23	$ 5,000
Furniture	5/12	7,000
Pickup truck	11/15	10,000
Commercial building	10/11	270,000

Assuming Dee does not elect §179 expensing or bonus depreciation, answer the following questions:

a) What is Dee's year 1 cost recovery for each asset?

b) What is Dee's year 2 cost recovery for each asset?

48. Evergreen Corporation (calendar-year-end) acquired the following assets during the current year (ignore §179 expense and bonus depreciation for this problem): 

Asset	Placed in Service Date	Original Basis
Machinery	October 25	$ 70,000
Computer equipment	February 3	10,000
Used delivery truck*	August 17	23,000
Furniture	April 22	150,000

*The delivery truck is not a luxury automobile.

a) What is the allowable MACRS depreciation on Evergreen's property in the current year?

b) What is the allowable MACRS depreciation on Evergreen's property in the current year if the machinery had a basis of $170,000 rather than $70,000?

49. Convers Corporation (June 30 year-end) acquired the following assets during the current tax year (ignore §179 expense and bonus depreciation for this problem): 

Asset	Placed in Service Date	Original Basis
Machinery	October 25	$ 70,000
Computer equipment	February 3	10,000
Used delivery truck*	March 17	23,000
Furniture	April 22	150,000
Total		$253,000

*The delivery truck is not a luxury automobile.

What is the allowable MACRS depreciation on Convers' property in the current year?

50. Harris Corp. is a technology start-up and is in its second year of operations. The company didn't purchase any assets this year but purchased the following assets in the prior year: 

Asset	Placed in Service	Basis
Office equipment	August 14	$10,000
Manufacturing equipment	April 15	68,000
Computer system	June 1	16,000
Total		$94,000

Harris did not know depreciation was tax deductible until it hired an accountant this year and didn't claim any depreciation expense in its first year of operation.

a) What is the maximum amount of depreciation expense Harris Corp. can deduct in its second year of operation (ignore bonus and §179 expense)?

b) What is the basis of the office equipment at the end of the second year?

LO 10-2 planning

51. Parley needs a new truck to help him expand Parley's Plumbing Palace. Business has been booming and Parley would like to accelerate his tax deductions as much as possible (ignore §179 expense and bonus depreciation for this problem). On April 1, Parley purchased a new delivery van for $25,000. It is now September 26 and Parley, already in need of another vehicle, has found a deal on buying a truck for $22,000 (all fees included). The dealer tells him if he doesn't buy the truck (Option 1), it will be gone tomorrow. There is an auction (Option 2) scheduled for October 5 where Parley believes he can get a similar truck for $21,500, but there is also a $500 auction fee.

a) Which option allows Parley to generate more depreciation expense deductions this year (the vehicles are not considered to be luxury autos)?

b) Assume the original facts, except that the delivery van was placed in service one day earlier on March 31 rather than April 1. Which option generates more depreciation expense?

LO 10-2

52. Way Corporation disposed of the following tangible personal property assets in the current year. Assume that the delivery truck is not a luxury auto. Calculate Way Corporation's 2015 depreciation expense (ignore §179 expense and bonus depreciation for this problem).

Asset	Date Acquired	Date Sold	Convention	Original Basis
Furniture (7-year)	5/12/11	7/15/15	HY	$ 55,000
Machinery (7-year)	3/23/12	3/15/15	MQ	72,000
Delivery truck* (5-year)	9/17/13	3/13/15	HY	20,000
Machinery (7-year)	10/11/14	8/11/15	MQ	270,000
Computer (5-year)	10/11/15	12/15/15	HY	80,000

*Used 100 percent for business.

LO 10-2

53. On November 10 of year 1 Javier purchased a building, including the land it was on, to assemble his new equipment. The total cost of the purchase was $1,200,000; $300,000 was allocated to the basis of the land and the remaining $900,000 was allocated to the basis of the building.

a) Using MACRS, what is Javier's depreciation expense on the building for years 1 through 3?

b) What would be the year 3 depreciation expense if the building was sold on August 1 of year 3?

c) Answer the question in part (a), except assume the building was purchased and placed in service on March 3 instead of November 10.

d) Answer the question in part (a), except assume that the building is residential property.

e) What would be the depreciation for 2015, 2016, and 2017 if the property were nonresidential property purchased and placed in service November 10, 1998 (assume the same original basis)?

LO 10-2

54. Carl purchased an apartment complex for $1.1 million on March 17 of year 1. $300,000 of the purchase price was attributable to the land the complex sits on. He also installed new furniture into half of the units at a cost of $60,000.

a) What is Carl's allowable depreciation expense for his real property for years 1 and 2?

b) What is Carl's allowable depreciation expense for year 3 if the real property is sold on January 2 of year 3?

55. AMP Corporation (calendar-year-end) has 2015 taxable income of $900,000 before the §179 expense. During 2015, AMP acquired the following assets: LO 10-2 LO 10-3

Asset	Placed in Service	Basis
Machinery	September 12	$1,550,000
Computer equipment	February 10	365,000
Office building	April 2	480,000
Total		$2,395,000

a) What is the maximum amount of §179 expense AMP may deduct for 2015 (assume the 2014 §179 limits are extended to 2015)?

b) What is the maximum total depreciation expense, including §179 expense, that AMP may deduct in 2015 on the assets it placed in service in 2015 assuming no bonus depreciation (assume the 2014 §179 limits are extended to 2015)?

56. Assume that TDW Corporation (calendar-year-end) has 2015 taxable income of $650,000 before the §179 expense and acquired the following assets during 2015: LO 10-2 LO 10-3

Asset	Placed in Service	Basis
Machinery	October 12	$1,270,000
Computer equipment	February 10	263,000
Furniture	April 2	880,000
Total		$2,413,000

a) What is the maximum amount of §179 expense TDW may deduct for 2015 (assume the 2014 §179 limits are extended to 2015)?

b) What is the maximum total depreciation expense, including §179 expense, that TDW may deduct in 2015 on the assets it placed in service in 2015 assuming no bonus depreciation (assume the 2014 §179 limits are extended to 2015)?

57. Assume that Timberline Corporation has 2015 taxable income of $240,000 before the §179 expense (assume the 2014 §179 limits are extended to 2015). LO 10-2 LO 10-3

Asset	Purchase Date	Basis
Furniture (7-year)	December 1	$350,000
Computer equipment (5-year)	February 28	90,000
Copier (5-year)	July 15	30,000
Machinery (7-year)	May 22	480,000
Total		$950,000

a) What is the maximum amount of §179 expense Timberline may deduct for 2015? What is Timberline's §179 carryforward to 2016, if any?

b) What would Timberline's maximum depreciation expense be for 2015 assuming no bonus depreciation?

c) What would Timberline's maximum depreciation expense be for 2015 if the furniture cost $2,000,000 instead of $350,000 and assuming no bonus depreciation?

58. Dain's Diamond Bit Drilling purchased the following assets this year. Assume its taxable income for the year was $53,000 before deducting any §179 expense LO 10-2 LO 10-3

(assume no bonus depreciation but assume that the 2014 §179 limits are extended to 2015).

Asset	Purchase Date	Original Basis
Drill bits (5-year)	January 25	$ 90,000
Drill bits (5-year)	July 25	95,000
Commercial building	April 22	220,000

a) What is the maximum amount of §179 expense Dain may deduct for the year?
b) What is Dain's maximum depreciation expense for the year (including §179 expense)?
c) If the January drill bits' original basis was $2,375,000, what is the maximum amount of §179 expense Dain may deduct for the year?
d) If the January drill bits' basis was $2,495,000, what is the maximum amount of §179 expense Dain may deduct for the year?

59. Assume that ACW Corporation has 2015 taxable income of $1,000,000 before the §179 expense and acquired the following assets during 2015 (assume no bonus depreciation but assume that the 2014 §179 limits are extended to 2015).

Asset	Placed in Service	Basis
Machinery	September 12	$ 470,000
Computer equipment	February 10	70,000
Delivery truck	August 21	93,000
Qualified leasehold improvements	April 2	380,000
Total		$1,013,000

a) What is the maximum amount of §179 expense ACW may deduct for 2015?
b) What is the maximum *total* depreciation expense that ACW may deduct in 2015 on the assets it placed in service in 2015?

60. Chaz Corporation has taxable income in 2015 of $312,000 before the §179 expense and acquired the following assets during the year:

Asset	Placed in Service	Basis
Office furniture	September 12	$1,280,000
Computer equipment	February 10	930,000
Delivery truck	August 21	68,000
Total		$2,278,000

What is the maximum *total* depreciation expense that Chaz may deduct in 2015 (assume that the 2014 §179 limits and bonus depreciation are extended to 2015)?

61. Woolard Inc. has taxable income in 2015 of $150,000 before any depreciation deductions (§179, bonus, or MACRS) and acquired the following assets during the year:

Asset	Placed in Service	Basis
Office furniture (used)	March 20	$600,000

a) If Woolard elects $50,000 of §179, what is Woolard's total depreciation deduction for the year (assume that bonus depreciation and 2014 §179 limits are extended to 2015)?
b) If Woolard elects the maximum amount of §179 for the year, what is the amount of deductible §179 expense for the year? What is the *total* depreciation expense that Woolard may deduct in 2015? What is Woolard's §179 carryforward

amount to next year, if any (assume that bonus depreciation and 2014 §179 limits are extended to 2015)?

c) Woolard is concerned about future limitations on its §179 expense. How much §179 expense should Woolard expense this year if it wants to maximize its depreciation this year and avoid any carryover to future years (assume that bonus depreciation and 2014 §179 limits are extended to 2015)?

62. Assume that Sivart Corporation has 2015 taxable income of $750,000 before the §179 expense and acquired the following assets during 2015: LO 10-2 LO 10-3 planning

Asset	Placed in Service	Basis
Machinery	October 12	$1,440,000
Computer equipment	February 10	70,000
Delivery Truck-used	August 21	93,000
Furniture	April 2	310,000
Total		$1,913,000

a) What is the maximum amount of §179 expense Sivart may deduct for 2015 (assume that bonus depreciation and 2014 §179 limits are extended to 2015)?

b) What is the maximum *total* depreciation expense (§179, bonus, MACRS) that Sivart may deduct in 2015 on the assets it placed in service in 2015 (assume that bonus depreciation and 2014 §179 limits are extended to 2015)?

63. Acorn Construction (calendar year-end C-corporation) has had rapid expansion during the last half of the current year due to the housing market's recovery. The company has record income and would like to maximize its cost recovery deduction for the current year. Acorn provided you with the following information:

Asset	Placed in Service	Basis
New equipment and tools	August 20	$ 800,000
Used light duty trucks	October 17	1,200,000
Used machinery	November 6	525,000
Total		$2,525,000

a) What is Acorn's maximum cost recovery deduction in the current year assuming that bonus depreciation and 2014 §179 limits are extended to 2015?

b) What planning strategies would you advise Acorn to consider?

64. Phil owns a ranch business and uses four-wheelers to do much of his work. Occasionally, though, he and his boys will go for a ride together as a family activity. During year 1, Phil put 765 miles on the four-wheeler that he bought on January 15 for $6,500. Of the miles driven, only 175 miles were for personal use. Assume four-wheelers qualify to be depreciated according to the five-year MACRS schedule and the four-wheeler was the only asset Phil purchased this year. LO 10-3

a) Calculate the allowable depreciation for year 1 (ignore the §179 expense and bonus depreciation).

b) Calculate the allowable depreciation for year 2 if total miles were 930 and personal use miles were 400 (ignore the §179 expense and bonus depreciation).

65. Assume that Ernesto purchased a laptop computer on July 10 of year 1 for $3,000. In year 1, 80 percent of his computer usage was for his business and 20 percent was for computer gaming with his friends. This was the only asset LO 10-3

he placed in service during year 1. Ignoring any potential §179 expense and bonus depreciation, answer the questions for each of the following alternative scenarios:

a) What is Ernesto's depreciation deduction for the computer in year 1?

b) What would be Ernesto's depreciation deduction for the computer in year 2 if his year 2 usage was 75 percent business and 25 percent for computer gaming?

c) What would be Ernesto's depreciation deduction for the computer in year 2 if his year 2 usage was 45 percent business and 55 percent for computer gaming?

d) What would be Ernesto's depreciation deduction for the computer in year 2 if his year 2 usage was 30 percent business and 70 percent for computer gaming?

LO 10-3

66. Lina purchased a new car for use in her business during 2015. The auto was the only business asset she purchased during the year and her business was extremely profitable. Calculate her maximum depreciation deductions (including §179 expense unless stated otherwise) for the automobile in 2015 and 2016 (Lina doesn't want to take bonus depreciation for 2015 or 2016) in the following alternative scenarios (assuming half-year convention for all and that the 2014 §179 amounts are extended to 2015):

a) The vehicle cost $15,000 and business use is 100 percent (ignore §179 expense).

b) The vehicle cost $40,000, and business use is 100 percent.

c) The vehicle cost $40,000, and she used it 80 percent for business.

d) The vehicle cost $40,000, and she used it 80 percent for business. She sold it on March 1 of year 2.

e) The vehicle cost $40,000, and she used it 20 percent for business.

f) The vehicle cost $40,000, and is an SUV that weighed 6,500 pounds. Business use was 100 percent.

LO 10-2 LO 10-3

67. Burbank Corporation (calendar-year end) acquired the following property this year:

Asset	Placed in Service	Basis
Used copier	February 12	$ 7,800
New computer equipment	June 6	14,000
Furniture	July 15	32,000
New delivery truck	October 28	19,000
Luxury auto	December 31	60,000
Total		$132,800

a) Assuming no bonus or §179 expense, what is Burbank's maximum cost recovery deduction for this year?

b) Assuming Burbank would like to maximize its cost recovery deductions by electing bonus and §179 expense, which assets should Burbank immediately expense? Assume the 2014 §179 expense limits and bonus depreciation are extended to this year.

c) What is Burbank's maximum cost recovery deduction this year assuming it elects §179 expense and bonus depreciation? Assume the 2014 §179 expense limits and bonus depreciation are extended to this year.

LO 10-3

68. Paul Vote purchased the following assets this year (ignore §179 expensing and bonus depreciation when answering the questions below):

Asset	Purchase Date	Basis
Machinery	May 12	$ 23,500
Computers	August 13	20,000
Warehouse	December 13	180,000

a) What is Paul's allowable MACRS depreciation expense for the property?

b) What is Paul's allowable alternative minimum tax (AMT) depreciation expense for the property? You will need to find the AMT depreciation tables to compute the depreciation.

69. After several profitable years running her business, Ingrid decided to acquire the assets of a small competing business. On May 1 of year 1, Ingrid acquired the competing business for $300,000. Ingrid allocated $50,000 of the purchase price to goodwill. Ingrid's business reports its taxable income on a calendar-year basis. LO 10-4

a) How much amortization expense on the goodwill can Ingrid deduct in year 1, year 2, and year 3?

b) In lieu of the original facts, assume that Ingrid purchased only a phone list with a useful life of 5 years for $10,000. How much amortization expense on the phone list can Ingrid deduct in year 1, year 2, and year 3?

70. Juliette formed a new business to sell sporting goods this year. The business opened its doors to customers on June 1. Determine the amount of start-up costs Juliette can immediately expense (not including the portion of the expenditures that are amortized over 180 months) this year in the following alternative scenarios: LO 10-4

a) She incurred start-up costs of $2,000.

b) She incurred start-up costs of $45,000.

c) She incurred start-up costs of $53,500.

d) She incurred start-up costs of $63,000.

e) How would you answer parts (a) through (d) if she formed a partnership or a corporation and she incurred the same amount of organizational expenditures rather than start-up costs (how much of the organizational expenditures would be immediately deductible)?

71. Nicole organized a new corporation. The corporation began business on April 1 of year 1. She made the following expenditures associated with getting the corporation started: LO 10-4

Expense	Date	Amount
Attorney fees for articles of incorporation	February 10	$32,000
March 1–March 30 wages	March 30	4,500
March 1–March 30 rent	March 30	2,000
Stock issuance costs	April 1	20,000
April 1–May 30 wages	May 30	12,000

a) What is the total amount of the start-up costs and organizational expenditures for Nicole's corporation?

b) What amount of the start-up costs and organizational expenditures may the corporation immediately expense in year 1 (excluding the portion of the expenditures that are amortized over 180 months)?

c) What amount can the corporation deduct as amortization expense for the organizational expenditures and for the start-up costs for year 1 (not including the amount determined in part b)?

d) What would be the total allowable organizational expenditures, if Nicole started a sole proprietorship instead?

72. Bethany incurred $20,000 in research and experimental costs for developing a specialized product during July of year 1. Bethany went through a lot of trouble and spent $10,000 in legal fees to receive a patent for the product in August of year 3. Bethany expects the patent to have a remaining useful life of 10 years. LO 10-4

a) What amount of research and experimental expenses for year 1, year 2, and year 3 may Bethany deduct if she elects to amortize the expenses over 60 months?

b) How much *patent* amortization expense would Bethany deduct in year 3 assuming she elected to amortize the research and experimental costs over 60 months?

c) If Bethany chose to capitalize but *not* amortize the research and experimental expenses she incurred in year 1, how much patent amortization expense would Bethany deduct in year 3?

LO 10-5

73. Last Chance Mine (LC) purchased a coal deposit for $750,000. It estimated it would extract 12,000 tons of coal from the deposit. LC mined the coal and sold it, reporting gross receipts of $1 million, $3 million, and $2 million for years 1 through 3, respectively. During years 1–3, LC reported net income (loss) from the coal deposit activity in the amount of ($20,000), $500,000, and $450,000, respectively. In years 1–3, LC actually extracted 13,000 tons of coal as follows:

(1) Tons of Coal	(2) Basis	Depletion (2)/(1) Rate	Tons Extracted per Year Year 1	Year 2	Year 3
12,000	$750,000	$62.50	2,000	7,200	3,800

a) What is Last Chance's cost depletion for years 1, 2, and 3?

b) What is Last Chance's percentage depletion for each year (the applicable percentage for coal is 10 percent)?

c) Using the cost and percentage depletion computations from the previous parts, what is Last Chance's actual depletion expense for each year?

COMPREHENSIVE PROBLEMS

All applicable problems are available with McGraw-Hill's *Connect® Accounting.*

74. Back in Boston, Steve has been busy creating and managing his new company, Teton Mountaineering (TM), which is based out of a small town in Wyoming. In the process of doing so, TM has acquired various types of assets. Below is a list of assets acquired during 2014:

Asset	Cost	Date Placed in Service
Office furniture	$ 10,000	02/03/2014
Machinery	560,000	07/22/2014
Used delivery truck*	15,000	08/17/2014

*Not considered a luxury automobile, thus not subject to the luxury automobile limitations.

During 2014, TM had huge success (and had no §179 limitations) and Steve acquired more assets the next year to increase its production capacity. These are the assets acquired during 2015:

Asset	Cost	Date Placed in Service
Computers & Info. System	$ 40,000	03/31/2015
Luxury Auto†	80,000	05/26/2015
Assembly Equipment	475,000	08/15/2015
Storage Building	400,000	11/13/2015

†Used 100% for business purposes.

TM generated a taxable income in 2015 before any §179 expense of $732,500 (assume bonus depreciation and the 2014 §179 limitations are extended to 2015).

Required

a) Compute maximum 2014 depreciation deductions including §179 expense (ignoring bonus depreciation).

b) Compute maximum 2015 depreciation deductions including §179 expense (ignoring bonus depreciation).

c) Compute maximum 2015 depreciation deductions including §179 expense, but now assume that Steve would like to take bonus depreciation.

d) Ignoring part (c), now assume that during 2015, Steve decides to buy a competitor's assets for a purchase price of $350,000. Compute maximum 2015 cost recovery including §179 expense (ignoring bonus depreciation). Steve purchased the following assets for the lump-sum purchase price.

Asset	Cost	Date Placed in Service
Inventory	$ 20,000	09/15/2015
Office furniture	30,000	09/15/2015
Machinery	50,000	09/15/2015
Patent	98,000	09/15/2015
Goodwill	2,000	09/15/2015
Building	130,000	09/15/2015
Land	20,000	09/15/2015

e) Complete Part I of Form 4562 for part (b).

75. While completing undergraduate school work in information systems, Dallin Bourne and Michael Banks decided to start a business called ISys Answers, which was a technology support company. During year 1, they bought the following assets and incurred the following fees at start-up:

Year 1 Assets	Purchase Date	Basis
Computers (5-year)	October 30, Y1	$15,000
Office equipment (7-year)	October 30, Y1	10,000
Furniture (7-year)	October 30, Y1	3,000
Start-up costs	October 30, Y1	17,000

In April of year 2, they decided to purchase a customer list from a company started by fellow information systems students preparing to graduate who provided virtually the same services. The customer list cost $10,000 and the sale was completed on April 30. During their summer break, Dallin and Michael passed on internship opportunities in an attempt to really grow their business into something they could do full-time after graduation. In the summer, they purchased a small van (for transportation, not considered a luxury auto) and a pinball machine (to help attract new employees). They bought the van on June 15, Y2, for $15,000 and spent $3,000 getting it ready to put into service. The pinball machine cost $4,000 and was placed in service on July 1, Y2.

Year 2 Assets	Purchase Date	Basis
Van	June 15, Y2	$18,000
Pinball machine (7-year)	July 1, Y2	4,000
Customer list	April 30, Y2	10,000

Assume that ISys Answers does not claim any §179 expense or bonus depreciation.

a) What are the maximum cost recovery deductions for ISys Answers for Y1 and Y2?

b) Complete ISys Answers' Form 4562.

c) What is ISys Answers' basis in each of its assets at the end of Y2?

76. Diamond Mountain was originally thought to be one of the few places in North America to contain diamonds, so Diamond Mountain Inc. (DM) purchased the land for $1,000,000. Later, DM discovered that the only diamonds on the mountain had been planted there and the land was worthless for mining. DM engineers discovered a new survey technology and discovered a silver deposit estimated at 5,000 pounds on Diamond Mountain. DM immediately bought new drilling equipment and began mining the silver.

In years 1–3 following the opening of the mine, DM had net (gross) income of $200,000 ($700,000), $400,000 ($1,100,000), and $600,000 ($1,450,000), respectively. Mining amounts for each year were as follows: 750 pounds (year 1), 1,450 pounds (year 2), and 1,800 pounds (year 3). At the end of year 2, engineers used the new technology (which had been improving over time) and estimated there was still an estimated 6,000 pounds of silver deposits.

DM also began a research and experimentation project with the hopes of gaining a patent for its new survey technology. Diamond Mountain Inc. chooses to capitalize research and experimentation expenditures and amortize the costs over 60 months or until it obtains a patent on its technology. In March of year 1, DM spent $95,000 on research and experimentation. DM spent another $75,000 in February of year 2 for research and experimentation. In September of year 2, DM paid $20,000 of legal fees and was granted the patent in October of year 2 (the entire process of obtaining a patent was unusually fast).

Answer the following questions regarding DM's activities (assume that DM tries to maximize its deductions if given a choice).

a) What is DM's depletion expense for years 1–3?

b) What is DM's research and experimentation amortization for years 1 and 2?

c) What is DM's basis in its patent and what is its amortization for the patent in year 2?

chapter

11 Property Dispositions

Learning Objectives

Upon completing this chapter, you should be able to:

LO 11-1 Calculate the amount of gain or loss recognized on the disposition of assets used in a trade or business.

LO 11-2 Describe the general character types of gain or loss recognized on property dispositions.

LO 11-3 Explain the rationale for and calculate depreciation recapture.

LO 11-4 Describe the tax treatment of unrecaptured §1250 gains and determine the character of gains on property sold to related parties.

LO 11-5 Describe the tax treatment of §1231 gains or losses, including the §1231 netting process.

LO 11-6 Explain common exceptions to the general rule that realized gains and losses are recognized currently.

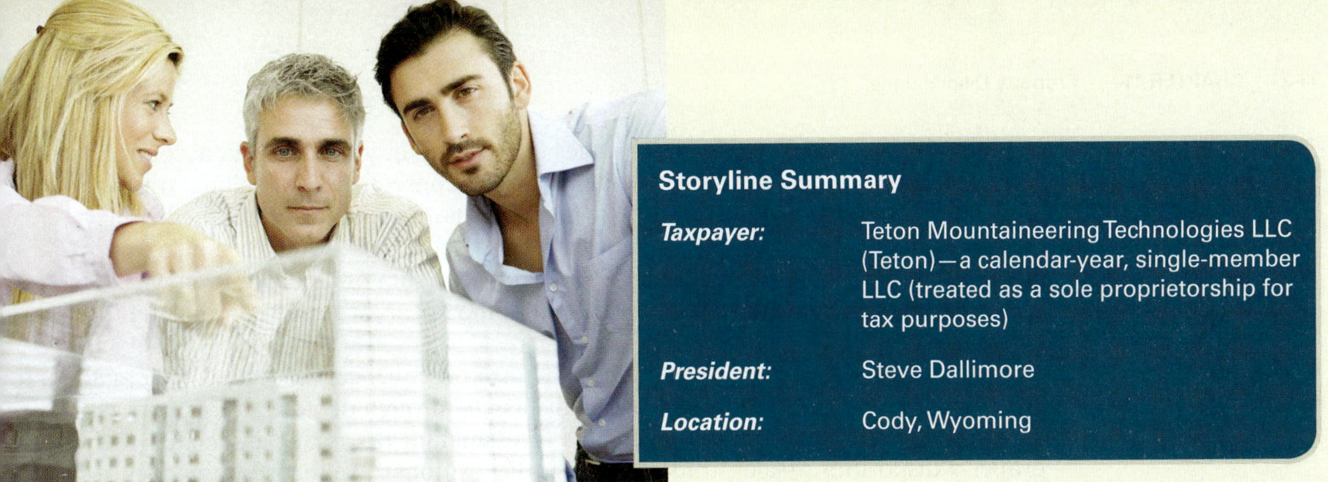

© BananaStock/Jupiterimages

Storyline Summary

Taxpayer:	Teton Mountaineering Technologies LLC (Teton)—a calendar-year, single-member LLC (treated as a sole proprietorship for tax purposes)
President:	Steve Dallimore
Location:	Cody, Wyoming

By most measures, Teton Mountaineering Technologies LLC (Teton) has become a success with sponsored climbers summiting the world's highest peaks, satisfied customers creating brand loyalty, and profitability improving steadily. However, after several years of operation, some of Teton's machinery is wearing out and must be replaced. Further, because Teton has outgrown its manufacturing capacity, Steve is considering whether to expand the company's current facility or sell it and build a new one in a different location. Steve would like to know how any asset dispositions will affect Teton's tax bill.

Steve has found a willing buyer for Teton's machinery, and he has options for trading the equipment. For tax purposes, does it matter whether he sells or trades the equipment? Steve also has questions about how to best manage Teton's acquisitions and dispositions of real property. It all seems a bit overwhelming. . . . He picks up the phone and dials his tax accountant's number. ■

You can imagine why Steve might be eager to reach his accountant. Tax accounting widely impacts business decisions: What are the tax consequences of selling, trading, or even abandoning business assets? Are the tax consequences the same whether taxpayers sell machinery, inventory, or investment assets? Does it matter for tax purposes whether Teton is structured as a sole proprietorship or a corporation when it sells its warehouse? If Steve sells his personal sailboat, car, or furniture, what are the tax consequences?

In the previous chapter we explained the tax consequences associated with purchasing assets and recovering the cost of the assets through depreciation, amortization, or depletion. This chapter explores fundamental tax issues associated with property dispositions (sales, trades, or other dispositions). We focus on the disposition of tangible assets, but the same principles apply to the sale of intangible assets and natural resources.

LO 11-1

DISPOSITIONS

Taxpayers can dispose of assets in many ways. For example, a taxpayer could sell an asset, donate it to charity, trade it for a similar asset, take it to the landfill, or have it destroyed in a natural disaster. No matter how it is accomplished, every asset disposition triggers a realization event for tax purposes. To calculate the amount of gain or loss taxpayers realize when they sell assets, they must determine the amount realized on the sale and the *adjusted basis* of each asset they are selling.

Amount Realized

Simply put, the **amount realized** by a taxpayer from the sale or other disposition of an asset is everything of *value* received from the buyer *less* any selling costs.[1] Although taxpayers typically receive cash when they sell property, they may also accept marketable securities, notes receivable, similar assets, or any combination of these items as payment. Additionally, taxpayers selling assets such as real property subject to loans or mortgages may receive some debt relief and would increase their amount realized by the amount of debt relief (the buyer's assumption of the seller's liability increases the seller's amount realized). The amount realized computation is captured in the following formula:

Amount realized = Cash received + Fair market value of other property
+ Buyer's assumption of liabilities − Seller's expenses

Example 11-1

Teton wants to upgrade its old manufacturing machinery that is wearing out. On November 1 of the current year, Teton sells the old machinery for $130,000 cash and marketable securities valued at $70,500. Teton paid a broker $500 to find a buyer. What is Teton's amount realized on the sale of the machinery?

Answer: $200,000, computed as follows:

Description	Amount	Explanation
(1) Cash received	$130,000	
(2) Marketable securities received	70,500	
(3) Broker commission paid	(500)	
Amount realized	$200,000	(1) + (2) + (3).

[1]*S.C. Chapin*, CA-8, 50-1 USTC ¶9171.

Determination of Adjusted Basis

In the previous chapter, we discussed the basis for cost recovery and focused on purchased assets in which the initial basis is the asset's cost. However, taxpayers may acquire assets without purchasing them. For example a taxpayer may acquire an asset as a gift or as an inheritance. In either case, the taxpayer does not purchase the asset, so the taxpayer's initial basis in the asset must be computed as something other than purchase price. Although there are many situations when an asset's initial basis is not the asset's cost, we focus on three cases: gifts, inherited assets, and property converted from personal use to business use.

Gifts. A gift is defined as a transfer of property proceeding from a detached and disinterested generosity, out of affection, respect, admiration, charity, or like impulses.[2] The initial basis of gift property to a recipient (donee) depends on whether the value of the asset exceeds the donor's basis on the date of the gift. If the fair market value of the asset on the date of the gift is greater than the donor's basis, then the asset's initial basis to the recipient of the gift will be the same as the donor's basis.[3] That is, the donor's basis carries over to the donee.

If the asset has declined in value since the donor acquired it (fair market value at the date of the gift is less than the donor's basis), then special dual basis rules apply. A dual basis means that the gift property has one basis to the donee for determining gains and a different basis for determining losses when the donee disposes of the property. Thus, the basis of gifted property that has declined in value depends on the sales price of the asset subsequent to the gift. The donee uses the carryover basis if the asset is sold for a gain, whereas the donee uses the fair market value at the date of the gift if the asset sells for a loss.[4] If the asset sells at a price between the donor's basis and the fair market value at the date of the gift, then the donee's basis at the time of the sale is assumed to equal the selling price so the donee does not recognize gain or loss on the sale. The dual basis rule prevents the transfer of unrealized losses from one taxpayer to another by gift.

Inherited Property. For inherited property, the general rule is that the heir's basis in property passing from a decedent to the heir is the fair market value on the date of the decedent's death.[5] The holding period of inherited property is deemed to be long-term regardless of how long the heir owns the property.[6]

Property Converted from Personal Use to Business Use. In order to prevent taxpayers from converting nondeductible personal losses to business losses, special basis rules apply when property is converted from personal use to business use. The basis for determining the gain or loss on the sale of converted property depends on whether the property appreciated or declined in value during the time the property was used personally. That is, if the fair market value at the date of the conversion is greater than the taxpayer's basis in the property, then the taxpayer will use the lower taxpayer basis to calculate gain or loss at disposition. However, if the fair market value at the date of conversion is below the taxpayer's basis, the basis for calculating loss will be the fair market value at the date of conversion. After conversion, the taxpayer adjusts the loss

[2]Comr. v. Duberstein, 363 U.S. 278 (1960), rev'g 265 F.2d 28 (6th Cir. 1959), rev'g T. C. Memo 1958–4.

[3]§1015(a). The basis to the donee may be increased if the donor is required to pay gift tax on the gift.

[4]The holding period of the asset also depends on whether the gift property subsequently sells for a gain or loss. If the donor's basis is used to determine the gain, the holding period includes that of the donor. If the fair market value at the date of the gift is used to figure the loss, the holding period starts on the date of the gift.

[5]§1014(a)(1). An alternate valuation date may be used to determine the basis to the heirs if elected by the estate.

[6]§1223(9).

basis and the gain basis for depreciation deductions from the date of conversion to the date of disposition. As discussed in Chapter 10, the taxpayer uses the basis for loss in calculating depreciation deductions. If the property later sells for an amount that falls between the basis for gain and the basis for loss, the basis for the sale is treated as the sales price so that the taxpayer does not recognize gain or loss on the sale.[7]

Example 11-2

Assume that Steve received a desk from his grandfather on January 8. On the date of the gift, the desk was worth $15,000. Steve's grandfather originally purchased the desk 10 years earlier for $10,000. What is Steve's initial basis in the desk?

Answer: Since the desk had appreciated in value while Steve's grandfather owned it, Steve's initial basis is a carryover basis of $10,000.

What if: Assume that on the date of the gift, the fair market value of the desk was $8,000. What is Steve's initial basis in the desk?

Answer: Steve's initial basis depends on the price for which he later sells the desk. If Steve subsequently sells the desk at a price greater than $10,000, his initial basis is the $10,000 carryover basis. If he sells the desk at a price less than $8,000, his basis is $8,000, the fair market value at the date of the gift. If he sells the desk for a price in between $10,000 and $8,000, his basis is the sales price.

What if: Assume that Steve inherited the desk from his grandfather on January 8. What is Steve's initial basis if the fair market value was (a) $15,000 and (b) $8,000 at the time of his grandfather's death?

Answer: Steve's initial basis is the fair market value at the date of his grandfather's death regardless of whether the value is greater or less than his grandfather's original cost. If the fair market value was $15,000, Steve's initial basis is $15,000. If the fair market value is $8,000, Steve's initial basis is $8,000.

What if: Assume Steve owns some mountaineering equipment that he uses personally and purchased two years ago for $4,000. On March 20, he converts the equipment into business use property when the fair market value of the equipment is $5,000. What is Steve's initial basis in the equipment for business purposes?

Answer: Because the equipment appreciated in value before Steve converted it to business use, his basis is his original cost of $4,000. Steve uses the $4,000 as his initial basis for calculating cost recovery and determining his adjusted basis when he sells or otherwise disposes of the equipment.

What if: Assume that the equipment that Steve converts from personal to business use has a fair market value of $3,000 at the date of conversion. What is Steve's initial basis in the equipment for business purposes?

Answer: The equipment declined in value before Steve converted it to business use. In order to prevent Steve from converting his $1,000 personal loss into a business loss, his initial basis for business purposes will depend on whether he subsequently sells the equipment at a gain or loss. His initial basis for loss (and cost recovery) is the $3,000 fair market value at the conversion date. His initial basis for gain is his $4,000 original cost.

What if: Assume that the equipment that Steve converts from personal to business use has a fair market value of $3,000 at the date of conversion. Two years later, after taking $500 of depreciation deductions, he sells the equipment for $3,300. What is Steve's adjusted basis in the equipment for purposes of determining the gain or loss on the disposition?

Answer: Steve's initial basis for loss was the $3,000 fair market value at the conversion date, and his initial basis for gain was $4,000 original cost. At the time of the sale, the adjusted basis for loss is $2,500, and the adjusted basis for gain is $3,500. Because the sales price falls between the adjusted basis for gain and the adjusted basis for loss, the adjusted basis is assumed to be equal to the sales price of $3,300.

[7]Reg. §1.165-9(b)(2) and Reg. §1.167(g)-1.

The **adjusted basis** for determining the gain or loss on the sale of an asset is the initial basis (however determined) reduced by depreciation or other types of cost recovery deductions allowed (or allowable) on the property. The adjusted basis of an asset can be determined using the following formula:

Adjusted basis = Initial basis − Cost recovery allowed (or allowable)

Example 11-3

To determine its realized gain or loss on the sale, Teton must calculate the adjusted basis of the machinery it sold in Example 11-1 for $200,000. Teton originally purchased the machinery for $510,000 three years ago. For tax purposes, Teton depreciated the machinery using MACRS (seven-year recovery period, 200 percent declining balance method, and half-year convention). The machinery's adjusted basis at the time of the sale is $191,173, computed as follows:

Description	Tax	Explanation
(1) Original basis	$510,000	Example 10-1.
(2) Year 1	(72,879)	Example 10-4.
(3) Year 2	(124,899)	Example 10-4.
(4) Year 3	(89,199)	Example 10-4.
(5) Year 4	(31,850)	$63,699 (Example 10-4) × 50% (half-year convention).
(6) Accumulated depreciation	(318,827)	(2) + (3) + (4) + (5).
Adjusted basis	$191,173	(1) + (6).

Because businesses generally use more highly accelerated depreciation methods for tax purposes than they do for book purposes, the tax-adjusted basis of a particular asset is likely to be lower than the book-adjusted basis.

Realized Gain or Loss on Disposition

The amount of gain or loss taxpayers realize on a sale or other disposition of assets is simply the amount they realize minus their adjusted basis in the disposed assets.[8] The formula for computing **realized gain or loss** is as follows:

Gain or (loss) realized = Amount realized − Adjusted basis

Example 11-4

In Example 11-1, we learned that Teton sold machinery for a total amount realized of $200,000, and in Example 11-3 we learned that its basis in the machinery was $191,173. What is Teton's realized gain or loss on the sale of the machinery?

Answer: $8,827, computed as follows:

Description	Amount	Explanation
(1) Amount realized	$200,000	Example 11-1.
(2) Adjusted basis	(191,173)	Example 11-3.
Gain realized	**$ 8,827**	(1) + (2).

Exhibit 11-1 details the important formulas necessary to determine realized tax gains and losses.

[8]§1001(a).

EXHIBIT 11-1 Summary of Formulas for Computing Gain or Loss Realized on an Asset Disposition

- Gain (loss) realized = Amount realized − Adjusted basis; where
  - Amount realized = Cash received + Fair market value of other property + Buyer's assumption of seller's liabilities − Seller's expenses
  - Adjusted basis = Initial basis − Cost recovery deductions

So far, our examples have used one of Teton's asset sales to demonstrate how to compute gain or loss realized when property is sold. However, as we describe in Exhibit 11-2, Teton disposed of several assets during the year. We refer to this exhibit throughout the chapter as a reference point for discussing the tax issues associated with property dispositions.

EXHIBIT 11-2 Teton's Asset Dispositions* Realized Gain (Loss) for Tax Purposes

Asset	(1) Amount Realized	(2) Initial Basis	(3) Accumulated Depreciation	(4) [(2) − (3)] Adjusted Basis	(5) [(1) − (4)] Gain (Loss) Realized
Machinery	$200,000	$510,000	$318,827	$191,173	$ 8,827
Office furniture	12,000	10,000	7,000	3,000	9,000
Delivery truck	2,000	15,000	10,500	4,500	(2,500)
Warehouse	350,000	275,000	15,000	260,000	90,000
Land	175,000	75,000	0	75,000	100,000
Total gain realized					$205,327

*These are the assets initially purchased by Teton in Example 10-1. Chapter 11 generally assumes that Teton has been in business for four years. For simplicity, this chapter assumes Teton did not previously elect any §179 immediate expensing or bonus depreciation.

THE KEY FACTS

- Realized gain or loss.
  - Amount realized less adjusted basis.
- Recognized gain or loss.
  - A realized gain or loss reported on the taxpayer's current year return.

Recognized Gain or Loss on Disposition

As a general rule, taxpayers realizing gains and losses during a year must recognize the gains or losses. **Recognized gains or losses** are gains (losses) that increase (decrease) taxpayers' gross income.[9] Thus, taxpayers must report recognized gains and losses on their tax returns. Although taxpayers must immediately recognize the vast majority of realized gains and losses, in certain circumstances they may be allowed to defer recognizing gains to subsequent periods, or they may be allowed to permanently exclude the gains from taxable income. However, taxpayers may also be required to defer losses to later periods and, in more extreme cases, they may have their realized losses permanently disallowed. We address certain nonrecognition provisions later in the chapter.

LO 11-2

CHARACTER OF GAIN OR LOSS

In order to determine how a recognized gain or loss affects a taxpayer's income tax liability, the taxpayer must determine the *character* or type of gain or loss recognized. Ultimately, every gain or loss is characterized as either ordinary or capital (long-term or short-term). As described below, businesses may recognize certain gains or losses (known as §1231) on property dispositions that require some intermediary steps, but even the §1231 gains or losses are eventually characterized as ordinary or capital (long-term). The character of a gain or loss is important because gains and losses of

[9]Recall under the return of capital principle we discussed in Chapter 5, when a taxpayer sells an asset, the taxpayer's adjusted basis is a return of capital and not a deductible expense.

different characters are treated differently for tax purposes. For example, ordinary income (loss) is generally taxed at ordinary rates (fully deductible against ordinary income). However, capital gains may be taxed at preferential (lower) rates while deductions for capital losses are subject to certain restrictions. The character of the gains or losses taxpayers recognize when they sell assets depends on the character of the assets they are selling. The character of an asset depends on how the taxpayer used the asset and how long the taxpayer owned the asset (the holding period) before selling it.

In general terms, property may be used in a trade or business, treated as inventory or accounts receivable of a business, held for investment, or used for personal purposes. The holding period may be short-term (one year or less) or long-term (more than a year). Exhibit 11-3 provides a matrix of the character of assets (ordinary, capital, or §1231) depending on how taxpayers used the assets and the length of time they held the property before selling it.

THE KEY FACTS

Character of Assets

- Ordinary assets
  - Assets created or used in a taxpayer's trade or business.
  - Business assets held for one year or less.
- Capital assets
  - Assets held for investment purposes.
  - Assets held for personal-use purposes.
- §1231 assets
  - Depreciable assets and land used in a trade or business held for *more* than one year.

EXHIBIT 11-3 Character of Assets Depending on Property Use and Holding Period

	Property Use		
Holding Period	**Trade or Business**	**Investment or Personal-Use Assets***	**Inventory and Accounts Receivable**
Short-term (one year or less)	Ordinary	Short-term capital	Ordinary
Long-term (more than one year)	§1231†	Long-term capital	Ordinary

*Gains on the sale of personal-use assets are taxable capital gains, but losses on the sale of personal-use assets are not deductible.

†As we describe later in the chapter, gain or loss is eventually characterized as ordinary or capital (long-term).

Ordinary Assets

Ordinary assets are generally assets created or used in a taxpayer's trade or business. For example, inventory is an **ordinary asset** because it is held for sale to customers in the ordinary course of business. Accounts receivable are ordinary assets because receivables are generated from the sale of inventory or business services. Other assets used in a trade or business such as machinery and equipment are also considered to be ordinary assets if they have been used in a business for *one year or less*. For example, if Teton purchased a forklift for the warehouse but sold it six months later, the gain or loss would be ordinary. When taxpayers sell ordinary assets at a gain, they recognize an ordinary gain that is taxed at ordinary rates. When taxpayers sell ordinary assets at a loss, they deduct the loss against other ordinary income.

Capital Assets

A **capital asset** is generally something held for investment (stocks and bonds), for the **production of income** (a for-profit activity that doesn't rise to the level of a trade or business), or for personal use (your car, house, or personal computer).[10] Whether an asset qualifies as a capital asset depends on the purpose for which the taxpayer uses the asset. Thus, the same asset may be considered a capital asset to one taxpayer and an ordinary asset to another taxpayer. For example, a piece of land held as an investment because it is expected to appreciate in value over time is a capital asset to that taxpayer. However, the same piece of land held as inventory by a real estate developer would be an ordinary asset. Finally, the same piece of land would be a §1231 asset if the taxpayer held it for more than one year and used it in a trade or business (e.g., as a parking lot).

[10]§1221 defines what is not a capital asset. Broadly speaking, a *capital asset* is any property *other than* property used in a trade or business (e.g., inventory, manufacturing equipment) or accounts (or notes) receivable acquired in a business from the sale of services or property.

Individual taxpayers generally prefer capital gains to ordinary income because certain capital gains are taxed at lower rates and capital gains may offset capital losses that cannot be deducted against ordinary income. Individuals also prefer ordinary losses to capital losses because ordinary losses are deductible without limit, while individuals may deduct only $3,000 of net capital losses against ordinary income each year. Corporate taxpayers may prefer capital gains to ordinary income because capital gains may offset capital losses that they would not be allowed to offset otherwise. Corporations are not allowed to offset any net capital losses, but they are allowed to carry capital losses back three years and forward five years. Exhibit 11-4 reviews the treatment of capital gains and losses for individuals and corporations.

EXHIBIT 11-4 Review of Capital Gains and Losses

Taxpayer Type	Preferential Rates	Loss Limitations
Individuals	• Net capital gains on assets held more than one year are taxed at 15 percent (0 percent to the extent the gain would have been taxed at a 15 percent or lower rate if it were ordinary income and 20 percent to the extent the gain would have been taxed at 39.6 percent if it were ordinary income). • Unrecaptured §1250 gains on real property held more than one year are taxed at a maximum rate of 25 percent. • Net gains on collectibles held for more than a year are taxed at a maximum rate of 28 percent. • Net capital gains on assets held one year or less are taxed at ordinary rates.	• Individuals may annually deduct up to $3,000 of net capital losses against ordinary income. • Losses carried forward indefinitely but not carried back.
Corporations	• No preferential rates, taxed at ordinary rates.	• No offset against ordinary income. • Net capital losses can generally be carried back three years and forward five years to offset net capital gains in those years.

§1231 Assets

Section 1231 assets are depreciable assets and land used in a trade or business (including rental property) held by taxpayers for *more* than one year.[11] At a general level, when a taxpayer sells a §1231 asset, the taxpayer recognizes a §1231 gain or loss. As discussed above, however, ultimately §1231 gains or losses are characterized as ordinary or capital on a taxpayer's return. When taxpayers sell multiple §1231 assets during the year, they combine or "net" their §1231 gains and §1231 losses together. If the netting results in a net §1231 gain, the net gain is treated as a long-term capital gain. If the netting results in a net §1231 loss, the net loss is treated as an ordinary loss. Because net §1231 gains are treated as capital gains and §1231 losses are treated as ordinary losses, §1231 assets are tax favored relative to other types of assets.

As we discuss below, §1231 gains on individual depreciable assets may be recharacterized as ordinary income under the depreciation recapture rules. However,

[11]As noted above, property used in a trade or business and held for *one year or less* is ordinary income property.

because land is not depreciable, when taxpayers sell or otherwise dispose of land that qualifies as §1231 property, the gain or loss from the sale is always characterized as §1231 gain or loss. Thus, we refer to land as a pure §1231 asset.

Example 11-5

In order to acquire another parcel of land to expand its manufacturing capabilities, Teton sold five acres of land that it has been using in its trade or business for $175,000. Teton purchased the land several years ago for $75,000. What is the amount and character of Teton's gain recognized on the land?

Answer: $100,000 §1231 gain, calculated as follows:

Description	Amount	Explanation
(1) Amount realized	$175,000	
(2) Original basis and current adjusted basis	75,000	
Gain (Loss) realized and recognized	**$100,000**	(1) − (2) §1231 gain.

What if: Assume that Teton sold the land for $50,000. What would be the character of the ($25,000) loss it would recognize?

Answer: §1231 loss.

What if: Assume that the land was the only asset Teton sold during the year. How would the §1231 gain or §1231 loss on the sale ultimately be characterized on its tax return?

Answer: If Teton recognized a §1231 gain on the sale, it would be characterized as a long-term capital gain on its return. If Teton recognized a §1231 loss on the sale, it would be characterized as an ordinary loss.

DEPRECIATION RECAPTURE

LO 11-3

Although Congress intended for businesses to receive favorable treatment on economic gains from the economic *appreciation* of §1231 assets, it did not intend for this favorable treatment to apply to gains that were created artificially through depreciation deductions that offset ordinary income. For example, if a taxpayer purchases an asset for $100 and sells it three years later for the same amount, we would generally agree that there is no economic gain on the disposition of the asset. However, if the taxpayer claimed depreciation deductions of $70 during the three years of ownership, the taxpayer would recognize a $70 gain on the disposition simply because the depreciation deductions reduced the asset's adjusted basis. Depreciation is an ordinary deduction that offsets income that would otherwise be taxed at ordinary rates. Absent tax rules to the contrary, the gain recognized by the taxpayer upon the sale of the asset would be treated as long-term capital gain and would be taxed at a preferential rate (for individuals). Thus, depreciation deductions save taxes at the ordinary rate but the gains created by depreciation would generate income taxed at a preferential rate. This potential asymmetrical treatment led Congress to implement the concept of **depreciation recapture.** Depreciation recapture potentially applies to gains (but not losses) on the sale of depreciable or amortizable business property. When depreciation recapture applies, it changes the character of the gain on the sale of a §1231 asset (all or a portion of the gain) from §1231 gain into ordinary income. Note, however, that depreciation recapture does not affect losses recognized on the disposition of §1231 assets.

The method for computing the amount of depreciation recapture depends on the type of §1231 asset the taxpayer is selling (personal property or real property). As presented in Exhibit 11-5, §1231 assets can be categorized as pure §1231 assets (land), §1245 assets (personal property), or §1250 assets (real property). Whether personal or real property is sold, it is important to understand that depreciation recapture changes only the *character* but not the *amount* of gain recognized.

EXHIBIT 11-5 §1231 Asset Types

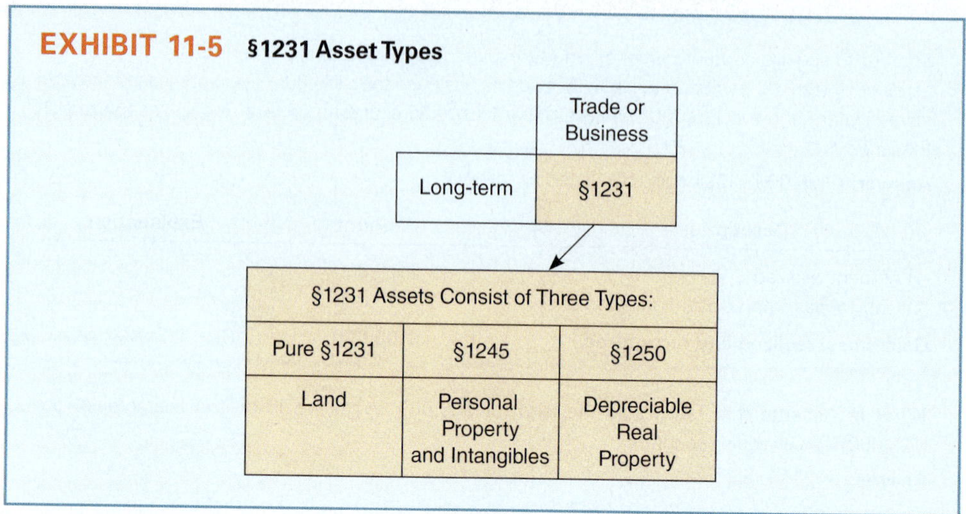

THE KEY FACTS

§1245 Assets

- Personal property and amortizable intangible assets are §1245 assets.
- The lesser of (1) gain recognized or (2) accumulated depreciation is recaptured (characterized) as ordinary income under §1245.
- Any remaining gain is §1231 gain.
- There is no depreciation recapture on assets sold at a loss.

§1245 Property

Tangible personal property (machinery, equipment, and automobiles) and amortizable intangible property (patents, copyrights, and purchased goodwill) are a subset of §1231 property known as **§1245 property.**[12] The gain from the sale of §1245 property is characterized as ordinary income to the extent the gain was created by depreciation or amortization deductions. The amount of *ordinary income* (§1245 depreciation recapture) taxpayers recognize when they sell §1245 property is the lesser of (1) recognized gain on the sale *or* (2) total accumulated depreciation (or amortization) on the asset.[13] The remainder of any recognized gain is characterized as §1231 gain.[14] The sum of the ordinary income (due to depreciation recapture) and the §1231 gain on the sale equals the *total* gain recognized because depreciation recapture changes only the character of the gain, not the amount.

When taxpayers sell or dispose of §1245 property, they encounter one of the following three scenarios involving gain or loss:

Scenario 1: They recognize a gain created solely through depreciation deductions.

Scenario 2: They recognize a gain created through both depreciation deductions and actual asset appreciation.

Scenario 3: They recognize a loss.

[12]An exception in the law is that §1245 property also includes nonresidential real property placed in service between 1981 and 1986 (ACRS) for which the taxpayer elected accelerated depreciation.

[13]§1245 recapture is commonly referred to as "full" depreciation recapture because it may cause a taxpayer to recapture the entire accumulated depreciation amount as ordinary income. §1245 recapture applies notwithstanding any other provision of the Internal Revenue Code (depreciation recapture trumps all other tax rules).

[14]As a practical matter, taxpayers are unlikely to recognize any §1231 gain on the disposition of personal property because the real economic value of most tangible personal property does not increase over time as the property is used.

The following discussion considers each of these scenarios.

Scenario 1: Gain Created Solely through Cost Recovery Deductions Most §1231 assets that experience wear and tear or obsolescence generally do not appreciate in value. Thus, when a taxpayer sells these types of assets at a gain, the gain is usually created because the taxpayer's depreciation deductions associated with the asset reduced the asset's adjusted basis faster than the real decline in the asset's economic value. In other words, the entire gain is artificially generated through depreciation the taxpayer claims before disposing of the asset. That is, absent depreciation deductions, the taxpayer would recognize a loss on the sale of the asset. Therefore, the entire gain on the disposition is recaptured (or characterized) as ordinary income under §1245 (recall that without depreciation recapture the gain would be §1231 gain, which can generate long-term capital gain and could create a double benefit for the taxpayer: ordinary depreciation deductions and capital gain upon disposition).

Example 11-6

As indicated in Exhibit 11-2, Teton sold machinery for $200,000. What is the amount and character of the gain Teton recognizes on the sale?

Answer: $8,827 of ordinary income under the §1245 depreciation recapture rules and $0 of §1231 gain, computed as follows:

Machinery Sale: Scenario 1
(Original scenario sales price = $200,000)

Description	Amount	Explanation
(1) Amount realized	$200,000	Exhibit 11-2.
(2) Original basis	510,000	Exhibit 11-2.
(3) Accumulated depreciation	318,827	Exhibit 11-2.
(4) Adjusted basis	191,173	(2) – (3).
(5) Gain (loss) recognized	8,827	(1) – (4).
(6) Ordinary income (§1245 depreciation recapture)	**$ 8,827**	Lesser of (3) or (5).
§1231 gain	**0**	(5) – (6).

Note that in this situation, because Teton's entire gain is created through depreciation deductions, the entire gain is treated as ordinary income under §1245.

What if: What would be the amount and character of Teton's gain without the depreciation recapture rules?

Answer: $8,827 of §1231 gain. Note that the recapture rules change the character of the gain but not the amount of the gain.

Scenario 2: Gain Due to Both Cost Recovery Deductions and Asset Appreciation Assets subject to cost recovery deductions may actually *appreciate* in value over time. When these assets are sold, the recognized gain must be divided into ordinary gain from depreciation recapture and §1231 gain. The portion of the gain created through cost recovery deductions is **recaptured** as ordinary income. The remaining gain (the gain due to economic appreciation) is §1231 gain.

Example 11-7

What if: Let's assume the same facts as in the previous example and in Exhibit 11-2, except that Teton sells the machinery for $520,000. What is the amount and character of the gain Teton would recognize on this sale?

Answer: $318,827 of ordinary income under the §1245 depreciation recapture rules and $10,000 of §1231 gain due to the asset's economic appreciation, computed as follows:

Machinery Sale: Scenario 2
(Assumed sales price = $520,000)

Description	Amount	Explanation
(1) Amount realized	$520,000	
(2) Original basis	510,000	Exhibit 11-2.
(3) Accumulated depreciation	$318,827	Exhibit 11-2.
(4) Adjusted basis	191,173	(2) – (3).
(5) Gain (loss) recognized	328,827	(1) – (4).
(6) Ordinary income (§1245 depreciation recapture)	**$318,827**	Lesser of (3) or (5).
§1231 gain	**$ 10,000**	(5) – (6).

Note that taxpayers can quickly determine their §1231 gain (if any) when they sell §1245 property by subtracting the asset's *original* basis from the amount realized. In Scenario 2, presented above (Example 11-7), the §1231 gain is $10,000 ($520,000 amount realized less the $510,000 original basis).

Scenario 3: Asset Sold at a Loss Many §1231 assets, such as computer equipment or automobiles, tend to decline in value faster than the corresponding depreciation deductions reduce the asset's adjusted basis. When taxpayers sell or dispose of these assets before the assets are fully depreciated, they recognize a loss on the disposition. Because the depreciation recapture rules don't apply to losses, taxpayers selling §1245 property at a loss recognize §1231 loss.

Example 11-8

What if: Let's assume the same facts as in Example 11-6 and in Exhibit 11-2, except that Teton sells the machinery for $180,000. What is the amount and character of the gain or loss Teton would recognize on this sale?

Answer: A $11,173 §1231 loss, computed as follows:

Machinery Sale: Scenario 3
(Assumed sales price = $180,000)

Description	Amount	Explanation
(1) Amount realized	$180,000	
(2) Original basis	510,000	Exhibit 11-2.
(3) Accumulated depreciation	318,827	Exhibit 11-2.
(4) Adjusted basis	191,173	(2) – (3).
(5) Gain (loss) recognized	(11,173)	(1) – (4).
(6) Ordinary income (§1245 depreciation recapture)	0	Lesser of (3) or (5) (limited to $0).
§1231 (loss)	**($11,173)**	(5) – (6).

Exhibit 11-6 graphically illustrates the §1245 depreciation recapture computations for the machinery sold in Scenarios 1, 2, and 3, presented in Examples 11-6, 11-7, and 11-8, respectively.[15]

EXHIBIT 11-6 Machinery §1245 Depreciation Recapture Scenarios 1, 2, and 3

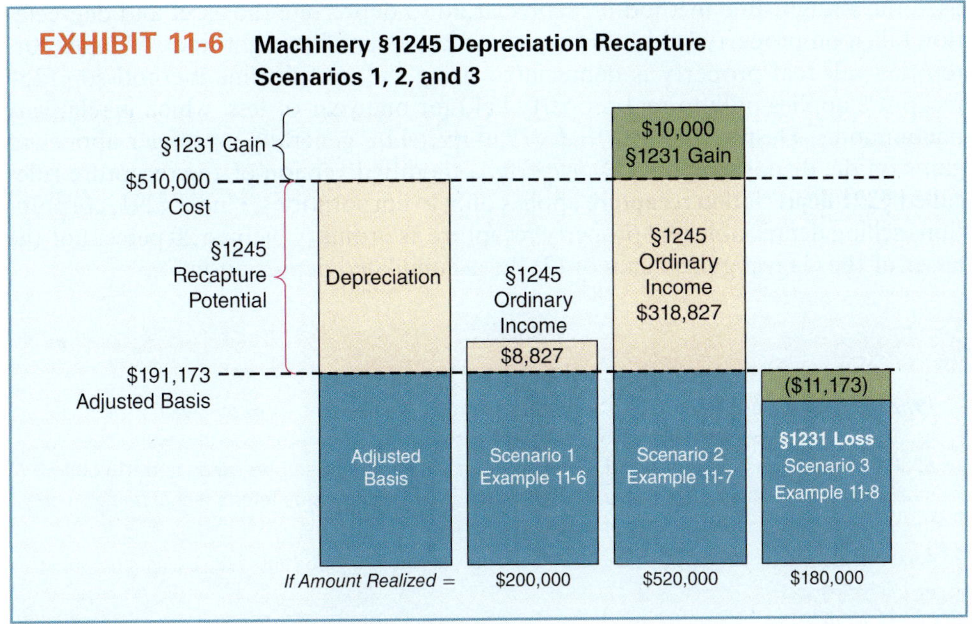

Example 11-9

In Example 11-6 (Scenario 1), we characterized the gain Teton recognized when it sold its machinery. For completeness, let's characterize the gain or loss Teton recognized on the other two §1245 assets it sold during the year (see Exhibit 11-2). Teton sold its office furniture for $12,000 and its delivery truck for $2,000. What is the amount and character of gain or loss Teton recognizes on the sales of the office furniture and delivery truck?

Answer: Office furniture: $7,000 ordinary income and $2,000 §1231 gain. Delivery truck: $2,500 §1231 loss.

The computations supporting the answers are as follows:

Description	Office Furniture	Delivery Truck	Explanation
(1) Amount realized	$12,000	$ 2,000	Exhibit 11-2.
(2) Original basis	10,000	15,000	Exhibit 11-2.
(3) Accumulated depreciation	7,000	10,500	Exhibit 11-2.
(4) Adjusted basis	3,000	4,500	(2) − (3).
(5) Gain (loss) recognized	9,000	(2,500)	(1) − (4).
(6) Ordinary income (§1245 depreciation recapture)	**7,000**	**0**	Lesser of (3) or (5), limited to $0.
§1231 gain (loss)	**2,000**	**(2,500)**	(5) − (6).

§1250 Depreciation Recapture for Real Property

Depreciable real property, such as an office building or a warehouse, sold at a gain is *not* subject to §1245 depreciation recapture. Rather, it is subject to a different type of recapture called §1250 depreciation recapture. Thus, depreciable real property is

[15]The authors thank PwC for allowing us to use these figures.

frequently referred to as **§1250 property.** Under §1250, when depreciable real property is sold at a gain, the amount of gain recaptured as ordinary income is limited to *additional* depreciation, defined as the excess of *accelerated* depreciation deductions on the property over the amount that would have been deducted if the taxpayer had used the straight-line method of depreciation to depreciate the asset and depreciation taken on property held for one year or less (even if straight-line).[16] Under current law, all real property is depreciated using the straight-line method so §1250 recapture applies only to real property held for one year or less, which is relatively uncommon.[17] Despite the fact that *§1250 recapture* generally no longer applies to gains on the disposition of real property, a modified version of the recapture rules called **§291 depreciation recapture** applies only to corporations. Under §291, corporations selling depreciable real property recapture as ordinary income 20 percent of the lesser of the (1) recognized gain or (2) the accumulated depreciation.

Example 11-10

What if: Suppose that Teton was organized as a corporation and that, as described in Exhibit 11-2, it sold its existing warehouse. Let's assume the same facts: that Teton sold the warehouse for $350,000, that it initially purchased the warehouse for $275,000, and has deducted $15,000 of straight-line depreciation deductions as of the date of the sale. What is Teton's recognized gain on the sale and what is the character of its gain on the sale?

Answer: $90,000 gain recognized; $3,000 ordinary income and $87,000 §1231 gain, computed as follows:

Description	Amount	Explanation
(1) Amount realized	$350,000	Exhibit 11-2.
(2) Original basis	275,000	Exhibit 11-2.
(3) Accumulated depreciation	15,000	Exhibit 11-2.
(4) Adjusted basis	260,000	(2) − (3).
(5) Gain (Loss) recognized	90,000	(1) − (4).
(6) Lesser of accumulated depreciation or recognized gain	15,000	Lesser of (3) or (5).
(7) §291 recapture (ordinary income)	$ 3,000	20% × (6).
§1231 gain	$ 87,000	(5) − (7).

LO 11-4

OTHER PROVISIONS AFFECTING THE RATE AT WHICH GAINS ARE TAXED

Other provisions, other than depreciation recapture, may affect the rate at which taxpayer gains are taxed. The first potentially applies when individuals sell §1250 property at a gain, and the second potentially applies when taxpayers sell property to related parties at a gain.

Unrecaptured §1250 Gain for Individuals

Except for assets held 12 months or less, neither corporations nor individuals recognize §1250 recapture on the sale of §1250 property when sold at a gain. Instead,

[16]§1250 recapture is commonly referred to as *partial depreciation recapture.*

[17]Accelerated depreciation was allowed for real property placed in service before 1987. Such property had a maximum recovery period of 19 years, which means that as of 2005 all of this property is now fully depreciated under both the accelerated and straight-line depreciation methods.

corporations recognize §291 recapture as ordinary income on the sale of these assets. Individuals, however, do not recognize ordinary income from the sale of §1250 property when held long term. Rather, individual taxpayers treat a gain resulting from the disposition of §1250 property as a §1231 gain and combine it with other §1231 gains and losses to determine whether a net §1231 gain or a net §1231 loss results for the year.

If, after the §1231 netting process (described below), the gain on the sale of the §1250 property is ultimately determined to be a long-term capital gain, the taxpayer must determine the rate at which the gain will be taxed. Tax policy makers determined that the portion of the gain caused by depreciation deductions reducing the basis (called **unrecaptured §1250 gain**) should be taxed at a maximum rate of 25 percent (taxed at the ordinary rate if the ordinary rate is lower than 25 percent) and not the 0/15/20 percent rate generally applicable to other types of long-term capital gains. Consequently, when an individual sells §1250 property at a gain, the amount of the gain taxed at a maximum rate of 25 percent is the *lesser* of the (1) recognized gain or (2) the accumulated depreciation on the asset.[18] The remainder of the gain is taxed at a maximum rate of 0/15/20 percent.[19]

Example 11-11

Teton bought its warehouse for $275,000, depreciated it $15,000, and sold it for $350,000. What is the amount and character of the gain Teton (and thus Steve) reports on the sale (recall that income of sole proprietorships is taxed directly to the owner of the business)?

Answer: $90,000 of §1231 gain, which includes $15,000 of unrecaptured §1250 gain, computed as follows:

Description	Amount	Explanation
(1) Amount realized	$350,000	
(2) Original basis	275,000	
(3) Accumulated depreciation	15,000	
(4) Adjusted basis	260,000	(2) − (3).
(5) Gain (Loss) recognized	90,000	(1) − (4).
(6) Unrecaptured §1250 gain	15,000	Lesser of (3) or (5).
(7) Remaining §1231 gain	75,000	(5) − (6).
Total §1231 gain	**$ 90,000**	(6) + (7).

What if: Suppose Steve's marginal ordinary tax rate is 35 percent. What amount of tax will he pay on the gain (assuming no other asset dispositions)?

Answer: $15,000, computed as follows:

Description	(1) Gain	(2) Rate	(1) × (2) Tax	Explanation
Long-term capital gain (unrecaptured §1250 gain portion)	$15,000	25%	$ 3,750	This is the gain due to depreciation deductions.
Long-term capital gain (15 percent portion)	75,000	15%	11,250	Taxed at 15 percent because Steve is in the 35% tax bracket.
Totals	$90,000		$15,000	

Because Steve did not sell any other §1231 assets during the year, the entire §1231 gain is treated as a long-term capital gain that is split into a portion taxed at 25 percent and a portion taxed at 15 percent.

THE KEY FACTS

Unrecaptured §1250 Gains

- Depreciable real property sold at a gain is §1250 property but is no longer subject to §1250 recapture unless it is held 12 months or less.
- The lesser of the (1) recognized gain or (2) accumulated depreciation on the assets is called *unrecaptured* §1250 gain.
- Unrecaptured §1250 gain is §1231 gain that, if ultimately characterized as a long-term capital gain, is taxed at a maximum rate of 25 percent.

[18]The amount taxed at a maximum rate of 25 percent cannot exceed the amount of the taxpayer's net §1231 gain.

[19]These rates (25 or 0/15/20 percent) apply to net §1231 gains after a netting process for capital gains, which we discussed in Chapter 7.

THE KEY FACTS

§1239 Related-Person Transactions

- All gain recognized from selling property that is a depreciable asset to a related buyer is ordinary income (regardless of the character of the asset to the seller).
- Related persons are defined in §1239 and include
  - An individual and the individual's controlled corporation or partnership.
  - A taxpayer and any trust in which the taxpayer (or spouse) is a beneficiary.

Characterizing Gains on the Sale of Depreciable Property to Related Persons

Under §1239, when a taxpayer sells property to a *related person* and the property is depreciable property to the *buyer*, the entire gain on the sale is characterized as ordinary income to the *seller*.[20] Without this provision, related taxpayers could create tax savings by currently generating capital or §1231 gains through selling appreciated assets to related persons who would receive future ordinary deductions through depreciation expense on the basis of the property (stepped up to fair market value through the sale) acquired in the transaction.

The §1239 recapture provision is different from depreciation recapture in the sense that the seller is required to recognize ordinary income *for depreciation deductions the buyer will receive in the future,* while depreciation recapture requires taxpayers to recognize ordinary income *for depreciation deductions they have received in the past.* In both cases, however, the tax laws are designed to provide symmetry between the character of deductions an asset generates and the character of income the asset generates when it is sold. When depreciation recapture and the §1239 recapture provision apply to the same gain, the depreciation recapture rule applies first.

For purposes of §1239, a related person includes an individual and his or her controlled (more than 50 percent owned) corporation or partnership or a taxpayer and any trust in which the taxpayer (or spouse) is a beneficiary.[21]

Example 11-12

What if: Suppose that Teton is organized as a corporation and Steve is the sole shareholder. Steve sells equipment that he was using for personal purposes to Teton for $90,000 (he originally purchased the equipment for $80,000). The equipment was a capital asset to Steve because he had been using it for personal purposes (he did not depreciate it). What is the amount and character of the gain Steve would recognize on the sale?

Answer: $10,000 of ordinary income (amount realized $90,000 − $80,000 adjusted basis). Even though Steve is selling what is a capital asset to him, because it is a depreciable asset to Teton and because Steve and Teton are considered to be related persons, Steve is required to characterize the entire amount of gain as ordinary under §1239. Without the §1239 provision, Steve would have recognized a capital gain.

Exhibit 11-7 provides a flowchart for determining the character of gains and losses on the taxable sale of assets used in a trade or business.

LO 11-5 CALCULATING NET §1231 GAINS OR LOSSES

Once taxpayers determine the amount and character of gain or loss they recognize on *each* §1231 asset they sell during the year, they still have work to do to determine whether the gains or losses will be treated as ordinary or capital. After recharacterizing §1231 gain as ordinary income under the §1245 and §291 (if applicable) depreciation recapture rules and the §1239 related-person rules, the remaining §1231 gains and losses are netted together.[22] If the gains exceed the losses, the net gain

[20]§1239. §707(b)(2) contains a similar provision for partnerships.

[21]Additional related persons for purposes of §1239 include two corporations that are members of the same controlled group, a corporation and a partnership if the same person owns more than 50 percent of both entities, two S corporations controlled by the same person, and an S corporation and a C corporation controlled by the same person.

[22]If any of the §1231 gains and losses result from casualty or theft, these gains and losses are netted together first. If a net loss results, the net loss from §1231 casualty and theft events are treated as ordinary loss. Net gains from casualty and theft are treated as other §1231 gains and continue through the normal §1231 netting process.

EXHIBIT 11-7

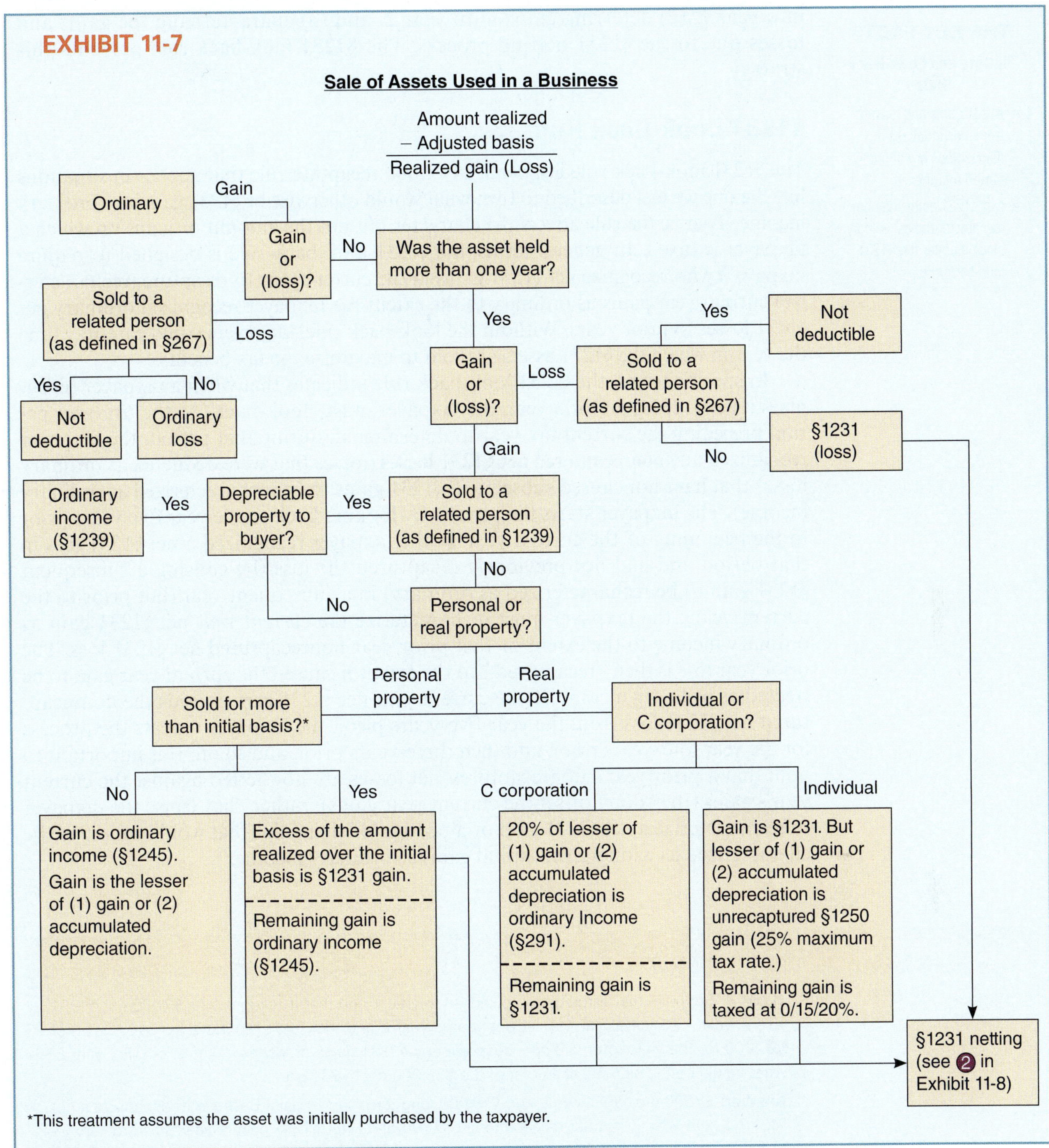

becomes a long-term capital gain (a portion of which may be taxed at the maximum rate of 25 percent). If the losses exceed the gains, the net loss is treated as an ordinary loss.

A taxpayer could gain significant tax benefits by discovering a way to have all §1231 gains treated as long-term capital gains and all §1231 losses treated as ordinary losses. The *annual* netting process makes this task impossible for a *particular* year. However, a taxpayer who owns multiple §1231 assets could sell the §1231 loss assets at the end of year 1 and the §1231 gain assets at the beginning of year 2. The taxpayer could benefit from this strategy in three ways: (1) accelerating losses

THE KEY FACTS

Netting and Look-Back Rule

- §1231 gains and losses from individual asset dispositions are annually netted together.
- Net §1231 gains may be recharacterized as ordinary income under the §1231 look-back rule.

into year 1, (2) deferring gains until year 2, and (3) characterizing the gains and losses due to the §1231 netting process. The **§1231 look-back rule** prevents this strategy.

§1231 Look-Back Rule

The §1231 look-back rule is a *nondepreciation* recapture rule that applies in situations like the one we just described to turn what would otherwise be §1231 gain into ordinary income. That is, the rule affects the character but not the amount of gains on which a taxpayer is taxed. In general terms, the §1231 look-back rule is designed to require taxpayers who recognize net §1231 gains in the current year to recapture (recharacterize) current year gains as ordinary to the extent the taxpayer recognized ordinary net §1231 losses in prior years. Without the look-back rule, taxpayers could carefully time the year in which the §1231 assets are sold to maximize the tax benefits.

In specific terms, the §1231 look-back rule indicates that when a taxpayer recognizes a net §1231 gain for a year, the taxpayer must "look-back" to the *five-year* period preceding the current tax year to determine if, during that period, the taxpayer recognized any **nonrecaptured net §1231 losses** (losses that were deducted as ordinary losses that have not caused subsequent §1231 gains to be recharacterized as ordinary income). The taxpayer starts the process by looking back to the year five years prior to the beginning of the current year. If the taxpayer recognized a net §1231 loss in that period and had not previously recaptured the loss (by causing a subsequent §1231 gain to be recharacterized as ordinary) in a subsequent year (but prior to the current year), the taxpayer must recharacterize the *current year* net §1231 gain as ordinary income to the extent of that prior year nonrecaptured net §1231 loss. The prior year loss is then "recaptured," to the extent it caused the current year gain to be treated as ordinary income. If the current year net §1231 gain exceeds the nonrecaptured net §1231 loss from the year five-years prior, the taxpayer repeats the process for the year four-years prior, and then three-years prior, and so on. It is important to note that a prior year's nonrecaptured net losses are not netted against the current year's gains (they don't offset the current year gains); rather, they cause the taxpayer to recharacterize a net §1231 gain or a portion of that gain (that would otherwise be characterized as a long-term capital gain) as ordinary income.[23]

Example 11-13

What if: Suppose that Teton began business in year 1 and that it recognized a $7,000 net §1231 loss in year 1. Assume that the current year is year 6 and that Teton reports a *net* §1231 gain of $25,000 for the year. Teton did not recognize any §1231 gains or losses in years 2–5. For year 6, what would be the ultimate character of the $25,000 net §1231 gain?

Answer: $7,000 ordinary income and $18,000 long-term capital gain. Because it recognized a net §1231 loss in year 1, it must recharacterize $7,000 of its net §1231 gain in year 6 as ordinary income. The remaining $18,000 §1231 gain is taxed as long-term capital gain.

What if: Assume the same facts as above, except that Teton also recognized a $2,000 net §1231 loss in year 5. For year 6, what would be the ultimate character of the $25,000 net §1231 gain?

Answer: $9,000 ordinary income and $16,000 long-term capital gain. Note that the overall gain is still $25,000, but to the extent of the $7,000 loss in year 1 and the $2,000 loss in year 5, the §1231 gain is recharacterized as ordinary income under the §1231 look-back rule.

[23] If the taxpayer's net §1231 gains include unrecaptured §1250 gains and other 0/15/20 percent long-term capital gains, the nonrecaptured net §1231 losses first recharacterize the unrecaptured §1250 gains as ordinary income.

ETHICS

Emma Bean operates a yoga studio and wants to sell some of her business equipment and a piece of land that is used as a parking lot. She expects to realize a $10,000 loss on the equipment and a $15,000 gain on the land. Emma has talked to her accountant and has learned about the look-back rule for §1231 property. To thwart any negative effects, she has decided to game the system and sell the land this year and then sell the equipment early next year. What do you think about her strategy to avoid the look-back rule?

As we've mentioned before, ultimately, all of a taxpayer's §1231 gains and losses must be characterized as ordinary or capital for purposes of determining a taxpayer's tax liability. Exhibit 11-8 summarizes the process of characterizing §1231 gains and losses as ordinary or capital.

EXHIBIT 11-8 §1231 Netting Process

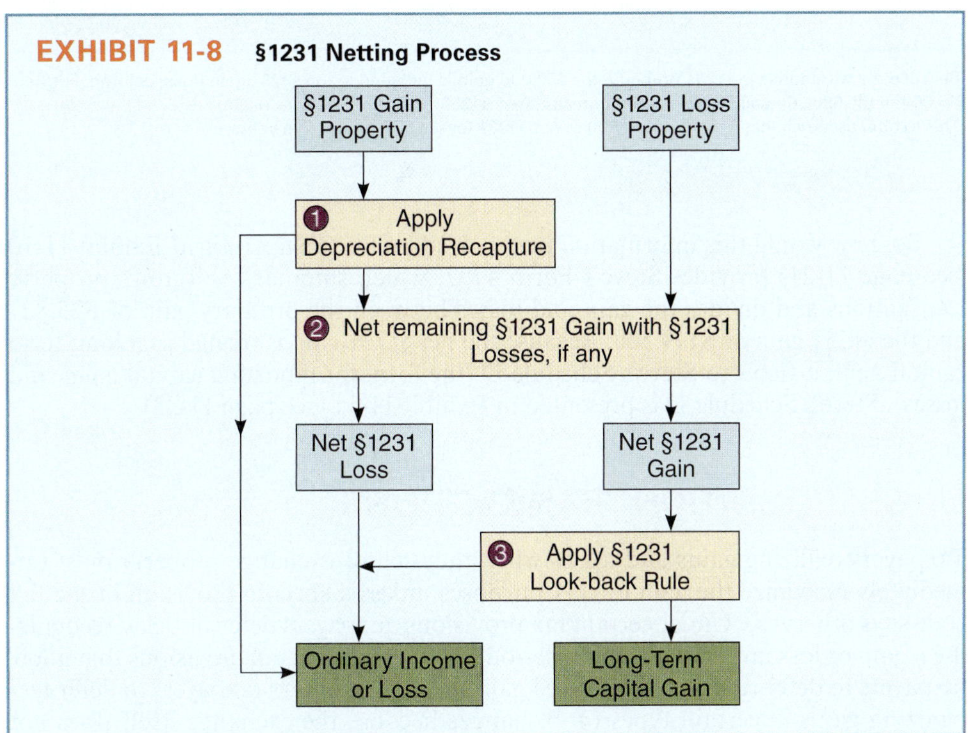

The following provides details on Steps 1–3 from Exhibit 11-8:

Step 1: Apply the *depreciation* recapture rules (and the §1239 recapture rules) to §1231 assets sold at a gain (any recaptured amounts become ordinary).

Step 2: Net the remaining §1231 gains with the §1231 losses. If the netting process yields a §1231 loss, the net §1231 loss becomes an ordinary loss.

Step 3: If the netting process produces a net §1231 gain, the taxpayer applies the §1231 look-back rule to determine if any of the remaining §1231 gain should be recharacterized as ordinary gain. Any gain remaining after applying the look-back rule is treated as long-term capital gain (including unrecaptured §1250 gain). This gain is included in the capital gains netting process, which is discussed in Chapter 7.

GAIN OR LOSS SUMMARY

As indicated in Exhibit 11-2, Teton sold several assets during the year. Exhibit 11-9 summarizes the character of the gain or loss Teton (and thus Steve) recognized on each asset sale.

EXHIBIT 11-9 Summary of Teton Gains and Losses on Property Dispositions

Asset	(1) §1245 Ordinary Gain	(2) Total Ordinary Gain	(3) §1231 Gain (Loss)	(2) + (3) Total Gain
Machinery	$ 8,827	$ 8,827	$ 0	$ 8,827
Office furniture	7,000	7,000	2,000	9,000
Delivery truck	0	0	(2,500)	(2,500)
Warehouse	0	0	90,000*	90,000
Land	0	0	100,000	100,000
§1231 look-back		10,000	(10,000)†	0
Totals	$15,827	$25,827	$179,500*	$205.327

*Because the warehouse is §1231 property, the $90,000 gain is included in the §1231 gain (loss) column. Further, $15,000 of the $90,000 gain is considered unrecaptured §1250 gain (see Example 11-11).
†This exhibit assumes that Teton had $10,000 of net §1231 losses in the prior five years.

So, how would this information be reported on Steve's tax return? Exhibit 11-10 (see page 11-21) provides Steve's Form 4797, which summarizes Teton's property transactions and divides the gain and losses between the ordinary gain of $25,827 and the §1231 gain of $179,500. Because the net §1231 gain is treated as a long-term capital gain, it flows to Steve's Schedule D (the form for reporting capital gains and losses). Steve's Schedule D is presented in Exhibit 11-11 (see page 11-23).

LO 11-6

NONRECOGNITION TRANSACTIONS

Taxpayers realizing gains and losses when they sell or exchange property must immediately recognize the gain for tax purposes unless a specific provision in the tax code says otherwise. Under certain tax provisions, taxpayers defer or delay recognizing a gain or loss until a subsequent period. We first explore tax provisions that allow taxpayers to defer recognizing realized gains. Congress allows taxpayers to defer recognizing gains in certain types of exchanges because the exchange itself does not provide the taxpayers with the wherewithal (cash) to pay taxes on the realized gain if the taxpayers were required to immediately recognize the gain. In particular, we discuss common **nonrecognition transactions** such as like-kind exchanges, involuntary conversions, installment sales, and other business-related transactions such as business formations and reorganizations.

Like-Kind Exchanges

Taxpayers involved in a business may have valid reasons to trade business assets to others for similar business assets. For example, to increase productivity a taxpayer may want to trade machinery used in the business for the latest model. As we discussed earlier in this chapter, taxpayers exchanging property *realize* gains (or losses) on exchanges just as taxpayers do by selling property for cash. However,

EXHIBIT 11-10 Teton's (On Steve's return) Form 4797

Form **4797**

Department of the Treasury
Internal Revenue Service

Sales of Business Property

(Also Involuntary Conversions and Recapture Amounts Under Sections 179 and 280F(b)(2))

▶ Attach to your tax return.

▶ Information about Form 4797 and its separate instructions is at *www.irs.gov/form4797.*

OMB No. 1545-0184

2014

Attachment Sequence No. **27**

Name(s) shown on return: Steve Dallimore (Teton Mountaineering Technologies, LLC)

Identifying number

1	Enter the gross proceeds from sales or exchanges reported to you for 2014 on Form(s) 1099-B or 1099-S (or substitute statement) that you are including on line 2, 10, or 20 (see instructions)	1	

Part I **Sales or Exchanges of Property Used in a Trade or Business and Involuntary Conversions From Other Than Casualty or Theft—Most Property Held More Than 1 Year** (see instructions)

2 (a) Description of property	(b) Date acquired (mo., day, yr.)	(c) Date sold (mo., day, yr.)	(d) Gross sales price	(e) Depreciation allowed or allowable since acquisition	(f) Cost or other basis, plus improvements and expense of sale	(g) Gain or (loss) Subtract (f) from the sum of (d) and (e)
Delivery truck	Yr 0	Yr 4	2,000	10,500	15,000	(2,500)
Land	Yr 0	Yr 4	175,000	0	75,000	100,000

3	Gain, if any, from Form 4684, line 39	3	
4	Section 1231 gain from installment sales from Form 6252, line 26 or 37	4	
5	Section 1231 gain or (loss) from like-kind exchanges from Form 8824	5	
6	Gain, if any, from line 32, from other than casualty or theft	6	92,000
7	Combine lines 2 through 6. Enter the gain or (loss) here and on the appropriate line as follows:	7	189,500
	Partnerships (except electing large partnerships) and S corporations. Report the gain or (loss) following the instructions for Form 1065, Schedule K, line 10, or Form 1120S, Schedule K, line 9. Skip lines 8, 9, 11, and 12 below.		
	Individuals, partners, S corporation shareholders, and all others. If line 7 is zero or a loss, enter the amount from line 7 on line 11 below and skip lines 8 and 9. If line 7 is a gain and you did not have any prior year section 1231 losses, or they were recaptured in an earlier year, enter the gain from line 7 as a long-term capital gain on the Schedule D filed with your return and skip lines 8, 9, 11, and 12 below.		
8	Nonrecaptured net section 1231 losses from prior years (see instructions)	8	10,000
9	Subtract line 8 from line 7. If zero or less, enter -0-. If line 9 is zero, enter the gain from line 7 on line 12 below. If line 9 is more than zero, enter the amount from line 8 on line 12 below and enter the gain from line 9 as a long-term capital gain on the Schedule D filed with your return (see instructions)	9	179,500

Part II **Ordinary Gains and Losses** (see instructions)

10 Ordinary gains and losses not included on lines 11 through 16 (include property held 1 year or less):

11	Loss, if any, from line 7	11	( )
12	Gain, if any, from line 7 or amount from line 8, if applicable	12	10,000
13	Gain, if any, from line 31	13	15,827
14	Net gain or (loss) from Form 4684, lines 31 and 38a	14	
15	Ordinary gain from installment sales from Form 6252, line 25 or 36	15	
16	Ordinary gain or (loss) from like-kind exchanges from Form 8824	16	
17	Combine lines 10 through 16	17	25,827
18	For all except individual returns, enter the amount from line 17 on the appropriate line of your return and skip lines a and b below. For individual returns, complete lines a and b below:		
a	If the loss on line 11 includes a loss from Form 4684, line 35, column (b)(ii), enter that part of the loss here. Enter the part of the loss from income-producing property on Schedule A (Form 1040), line 28, and the part of the loss from property used as an employee on Schedule A (Form 1040), line 23. Identify as from "Form 4797, line 18a." See instructions	18a	
b	Redetermine the gain or (loss) on line 17 excluding the loss, if any, on line 18a. Enter here and on Form 1040, line 14	18b	25,827

For Paperwork Reduction Act Notice, see separate instructions. Cat. No. 13086I Form **4797** (2014)

EXHIBIT 11-10 Teton's (On Steve's return) Form 4797 (*continued*)

Form 4797 (2014) Page **2**

Part III **Gain From Disposition of Property Under Sections 1245, 1250, 1252, 1254, and 1255** (see instructions)

19 (a) Description of section 1245, 1250, 1252, 1254, or 1255 property:	(b) Date acquired (mo., day, yr.)	(c) Date sold (mo., day, yr.)
A Machinery	Yr 0	Yr 4
B Office furniture	Yr 0	Yr 4
C Warehouse	Yr 0	Yr 4
D		

These columns relate to the properties on lines 19A through 19D. ▶		Property A	Property B	Property C	Property D
20 Gross sales price (**Note:** *See line 1 before completing.*)	20	200,000	12,000	350,000	
21 Cost or other basis plus expense of sale	21	510,000	10,000	275,000	
22 Depreciation (or depletion) allowed or allowable	22	318,827	7,000	15,000	
23 Adjusted basis. Subtract line 22 from line 21	23	191,173	3,000	260,000	
24 Total gain. Subtract line 23 from line 20	24	8,827	9,000	90,000	
25 **If section 1245 property:**					
a Depreciation allowed or allowable from line 22	25a	318,827	7,000		
b Enter the **smaller** of line 24 or 25a	25b	8,827	7,000		
26 **If section 1250 property:** If straight line depreciation was used, enter -0- on line 26g, except for a corporation subject to section 291.					
a Additional depreciation after 1975 (see instructions)	26a				
b Applicable percentage multiplied by the **smaller** of line 24 or line 26a (see instructions)	26b				
c Subtract line 26a from line 24. If residential rental property **or** line 24 is not more than line 26a, skip lines 26d and 26e	26c				
d Additional depreciation after 1969 and before 1976	26d				
e Enter the **smaller** of line 26c or 26d	26e				
f Section 291 amount (corporations only)	26f				
g Add lines 26b, 26e, and 26f	26g			0	
27 **If section 1252 property:** Skip this section if you did not dispose of farmland or if this form is being completed for a partnership (other than an electing large partnership).					
a Soil, water, and land clearing expenses	27a				
b Line 27a multiplied by applicable percentage (see instructions)	27b				
c Enter the **smaller** of line 24 or 27b	27c				
28 **If section 1254 property:**					
a Intangible drilling and development costs, expenditures for development of mines and other natural deposits, mining exploration costs, and depletion (see instructions)	28a				
b Enter the **smaller** of line 24 or 28a	28b				
29 **If section 1255 property:**					
a Applicable percentage of payments excluded from income under section 126 (see instructions)	29a				
b Enter the **smaller** of line 24 or 29a (see instructions)	29b				

Summary of Part III Gains. Complete property columns A through D through line 29b before going to line 30.

30 Total gains for all properties. Add property columns A through D, line 24	30	107,827
31 Add property columns A through D, lines 25b, 26g, 27c, 28b, and 29b. Enter here and on line 13	31	15,827
32 Subtract line 31 from line 30. Enter the portion from casualty or theft on Form 4684, line 33. Enter the portion from other than casualty or theft on Form 4797, line 6	32	92,000

Part IV **Recapture Amounts Under Sections 179 and 280F(b)(2) When Business Use Drops to 50% or Less** (see instructions)

		(a) Section 179	(b) Section 280F(b)(2)
33 Section 179 expense deduction or depreciation allowable in prior years	33		
34 Recomputed depreciation (see instructions)	34		
35 Recapture amount. Subtract line 34 from line 33. See the instructions for where to report	35		

Form **4797** (2014)

EXHIBIT 11-11 **Steve's Schedule D (Assumes Steve had no other capital gains and losses other than those incurred by Teton)**

SCHEDULE D (Form 1040)

Department of the Treasury Internal Revenue Service (99)

Capital Gains and Losses

▶ Attach to Form 1040 or Form 1040NR.
▶ Information about Schedule D and its separate instructions is at *www.irs.gov/scheduled*.
▶ Use Form 8949 to list your transactions for lines 1b, 2, 3, 8b, 9, and 10.

OMB No. 1545-0074

2014

Attachment Sequence No. 12

Name(s) shown on return	Your social security number
Steve Dallimore	

Part I **Short-Term Capital Gains and Losses—Assets Held One Year or Less**

See instructions for how to figure the amounts to enter on the lines below. This form may be easier to complete if you round off cents to whole dollars.	(d) Proceeds (sales price)	(e) Cost (or other basis)	(g) Adjustments to gain or loss from Form(s) 8949, Part I, line 2, column (g)	(h) Gain or (loss) Subtract column (e) from column (d) and combine the result with column (g)
1a Totals for all short-term transactions reported on Form 1099-B for which basis was reported to the IRS and for which you have no adjustments (see instructions). However, if you choose to report all these transactions on Form 8949, leave this line blank and go to line 1b .				
1b Totals for all transactions reported on Form(s) 8949 with **Box A** checked				
2 Totals for all transactions reported on Form(s) 8949 with **Box B** checked				
3 Totals for all transactions reported on Form(s) 8949 with **Box C** checked				

4 Short-term gain from Form 6252 and short-term gain or (loss) from Forms 4684, 6781, and 8824 .	4	
5 Net short-term gain or (loss) from partnerships, S corporations, estates, and trusts from Schedule(s) K-1	5	
6 Short-term capital loss carryover. Enter the amount, if any, from line 8 of your **Capital Loss Carryover Worksheet** in the instructions	6	( )
7 **Net short-term capital gain or (loss).** Combine lines 1a through 6 in column (h). If you have any long-term capital gains or losses, go to Part II below. Otherwise, go to Part III on the back	7	

Part II **Long-Term Capital Gains and Losses—Assets Held More Than One Year**

See instructions for how to figure the amounts to enter on the lines below. This form may be easier to complete if you round off cents to whole dollars.	(d) Proceeds (sales price)	(e) Cost (or other basis)	(g) Adjustments to gain or loss from Form(s) 8949, Part II, line 2, column (g)	(h) Gain or (loss) Subtract column (e) from column (d) and combine the result with column (g)
8a Totals for all long-term transactions reported on Form 1099-B for which basis was reported to the IRS and for which you have no adjustments (see instructions). However, if you choose to report all these transactions on Form 8949, leave this line blank and go to line 8b .				
8b Totals for all transactions reported on Form(s) 8949 with **Box D** checked				
9 Totals for all transactions reported on Form(s) 8949 with **Box E** checked				
10 Totals for all transactions reported on Form(s) 8949 with **Box F** checked.				

11 Gain from Form 4797, Part I; long-term gain from Forms 2439 and 6252; and long-term gain or (loss) from Forms 4684, 6781, and 8824	11	179,500
12 Net long-term gain or (loss) from partnerships, S corporations, estates, and trusts from Schedule(s) K-1	12	
13 Capital gain distributions. See the instructions	13	
14 Long-term capital loss carryover. Enter the amount, if any, from line 13 of your **Capital Loss Carryover Worksheet** in the instructions	14	( )
15 **Net long-term capital gain or (loss).** Combine lines 8a through 14 in column (h). Then go to Part III on the back	15	179,500

For Paperwork Reduction Act Notice, see your tax return instructions. Cat. No. 11338H **Schedule D (Form 1040) 2014**

taxpayers exchanging property for property are in a different situation than taxpayers selling the same property for cash. Taxpayers exchanging one piece of business property for another haven't changed their relative economic position in the sense that both before and after the exchange they hold an asset for use in their business. Further, exchanges of property do not generate the wherewithal (cash) for the taxpayers to pay taxes on the gain they realize on the exchanges. While taxpayers selling property for cash must immediately recognize gain on the sale, taxpayers exchanging property for assets other than cash must defer recognizing gain (or loss) realized on the exchange if they meet certain requirements. This type of deferred gain (or loss) transaction is commonly referred to as a **like-kind exchange** or §1031 exchange.[24]

Like-kind exchange treatment can provide taxpayers with significant tax advantages by allowing them to defer gain (and current taxes payable) that would otherwise be recognized immediately.[25] For an exchange to qualify as a like-kind exchange for tax purposes, the transaction must meet the following three criteria:

1. The property is exchanged "solely for like-kind" property.
2. Both the property given up and the property received in the exchange by the taxpayer are either "used in a trade or business" or are "held for investment," by the taxpayer.
3. The "exchange" must meet certain time restrictions.

Below, we discuss each of these requirements in detail.

THE KEY FACTS

Like-Kind Property

- Real property
  - All real property used in a trade or business or held for investment is considered "like-kind" with other real property used in a trade or business or held for investment.
- Personal property
  - Personal property is considered "like-kind" if it has the same general use and is used in a business or held for investment.
- Ineligible property
  - Inventory.
  - Most financial instruments.
  - Partnerships interests.
  - Domestic property exchanged for property used in a foreign country and all property used in a foreign country.

Definition of Like-Kind Property

The definition of like-kind property depends on whether the property exchanged is real property or tangible personal property. Generally, the definition of like-kind *real* property is much less restrictive than it is for like-kind *personal* property.

Real Property All real property is considered to be "like-kind" with any other type of real property as long as the real property is used in a trade or business or held for investment. For example, from Teton's perspective, its warehouse on 10 acres would be considered to be like-kind with a nearby condominium complex, a 20-acre parcel of raw land for sale across town, or even a Manhattan skyscraper.

Personal Property Determining what qualifies as like-kind property for tangible personal property is a little more involved. The Treasury regulations explain that tangible personal property qualifies as "like-kind" if the property transferred and the property received in the exchange is in the same general asset class in Rev. Proc. 87-56 (this is the concept we use in the previous chapter to determine the recovery period for MACRS depreciation).[26] In simpler terms, for personal property to qualify as like-kind property the property given in the exchange and the property received in the exchange must have the same general use to the taxpayer. For example, if Teton were to trade some machinery used in its manufacturing operations for some new machinery to be used in its manufacturing process, the transaction would qualify as a like-kind exchange. However, if Teton were to trade some machinery used in its manufacturing operations for a new delivery truck, the exchange would not qualify as a like-kind exchange.

[24]Like-kind exchanges are defined in §1031 of the Internal Revenue Code.

[25]In contrast, financial accounting rules require businesses to recognize (for financial accounting purposes) any gain they realize in a like-kind exchange transaction.

[26]Like-kind is defined in Reg. §1.1031(a)-2(b).

Property Ineligible for Like-Kind Treatment Certain types of property are, by definition, excluded from the definition of like-kind property and thus are not eligible for like-kind treatment.[27] This property includes inventory held for resale (including land held by a developer), most financial instruments (such as stocks, bonds, or notes), domestic property exchanged for foreign property, and partnership interests.[28]

Property Use

Even when property meets the definition of like-kind property, taxpayers can only exchange the property in a qualifying like-kind exchange if the taxpayer used the transferred property in a trade or business or for investment *and* the taxpayer will use the property received in the exchange in a trade or business or for investment. For example, Teton could exchange its warehouse on 10 acres for a 200-acre parcel of land it intends to hold as an investment in a qualifying like-kind exchange because Teton was using the warehouse in its business and it would hold the land as an investment. However, if Steve exchanged his personal-use cabin in Maine for a personal residence in Wyoming, the exchange would not qualify because Steve used the residence for personal purposes, and he would be using the Wyoming property for personal rather than business or investment purposes. In fact, even if Steve was renting his Maine cabin (it qualifies as investment property) when he exchanged it for his principal residence in Wyoming, the exchange would not qualify for like-kind exchange treatment because *both* properties (the property the taxpayer is giving up and the property the taxpayer is receiving in the exchange) must meet the use test (the personal residence does not qualify as business or investment property). Likewise, if Teton exchanged a business computer for Steve's personal use computer, Teton would qualify for like-kind exchange treatment because Teton was using its computer equipment in its business and it will use Steve's computer in its business. However, the exchange would not qualify as a like-kind exchange for Steve because Steve used the computer for personal (not business or investment) purposes. A key takeaway here is that due to the use and other requirements, one party to an exchange may qualify for like-kind treatment and the other party may not. Each party to the exchange must individually determine whether or not the exchange qualifies as a like-kind exchange to her.

Timing Requirements for a Like-Kind Exchange

Many like-kind exchanges involve a simultaneous exchange of like-kind assets. For example, Teton could take its used machinery to a dealer and pick up its new machinery at the same time. However, a simultaneous exchange may not be practical or possible. For example, taxpayers may not always be able to immediately (or even eventually) find another party who is willing to exchange properties with the taxpayer. In these situations taxpayers often use **third-party intermediaries** to facilitate like-kind exchanges. When a third party is involved, the taxpayer transfers the like-kind property to the intermediary and the intermediary sells the property and uses the proceeds to acquire the new property for the taxpayer.[29] Because the third party must sell the taxpayer's old property and locate and purchase suitable replacement property, this process is subject to delay. In these types of situations, does a delay in

THE KEY FACTS

Timing Requirements

- Like-kind property exchanges may involve intermediaries.
- Taxpayers must identify replacement like-kind property within 45 days of giving up their property.
- Like-kind property must be received within 180 days of when the taxpayer transfers property in a like-kind exchange.

[27]§1031(a)(2).

[28]Property used more than 50 percent of the time in a foreign country is not like-kind with domestic or with other foreign property.

[29]Exchanges involving third-party intermediaries are very common with real estate exchanges. For real estate, taxpayers must use a "qualified exchange intermediary," such as a title company, and cannot use a personal attorney (because attorneys are considered to be the taxpayer's agent).

the completion of the exchange disqualify an otherwise allowable like-kind exchange? Not necessarily. The tax laws do not require a simultaneous exchange of assets, but they do impose some timing requirements to ensure that a transaction is completed within a reasonable time in order to qualify as a **deferred** (not simultaneous) **like-kind exchange**—often referred to as a *Starker exchange*.[30]

The two timing rules applicable to like-kind exchanges are (1) the taxpayer must *identify* the like-kind replacement property within 45 days after transferring the property given up in the exchange, and (2) the taxpayer must receive the replacement like-kind property within 180 days (or the due date of the tax return including extensions) after the taxpayer initially transfers property in the exchange.[31] The time limits force the taxpayer to close the transaction within a specified time period, so that the taxpayers can report the tax consequences of the transaction. Exhibit 11-12 provides a diagram of a like-kind exchange involving a third-party intermediary.

EXHIBIT 11-12 Diagram of Deferred or Starker Exchange

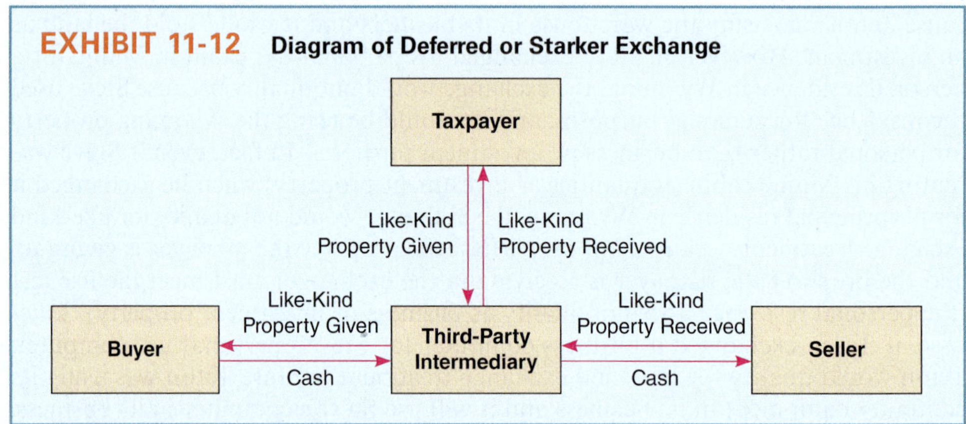

When a taxpayer fails to meet the timing requirements, the exchange fails to qualify for like-kind treatment and is thus fully taxable.

Example 11-14

What if: Suppose that on July 1 of year 1 Steve transferred a parcel of real property that he was holding as an investment to a third-party intermediary with the intention of exchanging the property for another suitable investment property. By what date does Steve need to identify the replacement property?

Answer: August 16 of year 1, which is 45 days after Steve transferred the property to the intermediary.

Assuming Steve identifies the replacement property within the 45-day time period, by what date does he need to receive the replacement property in order to qualify for like-kind exchange treatment?

Answer: December 28 of year 1, which is 180 days from July 1, the date he transferred the property to the intermediary.

[30]The term *Starker exchange* refers to a landmark court case that first allowed deferred exchanges (*T.J. Starker, Appellant v. United States of America,* 79-2 USTC ¶9541). The rules for deferred exchanges are found in §1031(a)(3). The tax laws also allow for reverse like-kind exchanges where replacement property is acquired before the taxpayer transfers the like-kind property.

[31]The taxpayer must identify at least one like-kind asset; however, since failure to obtain the asset disqualifies the transaction from having deferred like-kind exchange status, the taxpayer may identify up to three alternatives to hedge against the inability to obtain the first identified asset. Generally, a taxpayer must obtain only one to facilitate the exchange [see Reg. §1.1031(k)-1(c)(4)].

Tax Consequences When Like-Kind Property Is Exchanged Solely for Like-Kind Property

As we've discussed, when taxpayers exchanging property meet the like-kind exchange requirements, they do not recognize gain or loss on the exchange. They also establish or receive an **exchanged basis** in the like-kind property they receive. That is, they exchange the basis they had in the property given up and transfer it to the basis of the property received.[32]

Example 11-15

Teton would like to trade machinery worth $29,500 (adjusted basis of $18,742), for new machinery worth $29,500. How much gain does Teton recognize on this exchange?

Answer: $0. Teton's exchange qualifies as a like-kind exchange and the $10,758 realized gain ($29,500 amount realized minus $18,742 adjusted basis) is deferred.

What is Teton's basis in the new machinery?

Answer: $18,742, the basis it had in the old machinery it traded in.

Tax Consequences of Transfers Involving Like-Kind and Non-Like-Kind Property (Boot)

A practical problem with like-kind exchanges is that the value of the like-kind property the taxpayer transfers may differ from the value of the like-kind property the taxpayer receives in the exchange. In these situations the party transferring the lesser-valued asset must also transfer additional property to the other party to equate the values. When this additional property or **"boot"** (non-like-kind property) is transferred, the party receiving it apparently fails the first like-kind exchange requirement that like-kind property be exchanged solely for like-kind property. Nevertheless, if a taxpayer receives boot in addition to like-kind property, the transaction can still qualify for like-kind exchange treatment, but the taxpayer is required to recognize realized gain *to the extent of the boot received.*[33] As a practical matter, this means the taxpayer's recognized gain is the *lesser of* (1) gain realized or (2) boot received.

The reason a taxpayer must recognize gain is that the taxpayer is essentially selling a portion of the like-kind property for the boot in a taxable exchange. The receipt of boot triggers taxable gain (but not a taxable loss) in an otherwise qualifying like-kind exchange. If the taxpayer transfers loss property (adjusted basis is greater than fair market value) in a qualifying like-kind exchange, the taxpayer defers recognition of the loss until the taxpayer sells or disposes of the loss property in a taxable transaction—so it may be important for tax planning purposes to avoid the like-kind exchange rules if the taxpayer wishes to currently recognize the loss.[34] When a taxpayer recognizes gain in a like-kind exchange, the character of the gain depends on the character of the asset transferred by the taxpayer (the depreciation recapture rules apply when characterizing gains).

THE KEY FACTS

Like-Kind Exchanges Involving Boot

- Non-like-kind property is known as boot.
- When boot is given as part of a like-kind transaction:
  - The asset received is recorded in two parts: property received in exchange for like-kind property and property received in a sale (bought by the boot).
- When boot is received:
  - Boot received usually creates recognized gain.
  - Gain recognized is lesser of gain realized or boot received.

[32]If the asset is a depreciable asset, the taxpayer continues to depreciate the new asset as if it were the old asset.

[33]§1031(b).

[34]§1031(a) states that no gain or loss is recognized in a qualifying like-kind exchange.

Example 11-16

What if: Suppose that Teton trades its used machinery with a value of $29,500 and an adjusted basis of $18,742 ($30,615 historical cost less $11,873 of accumulated depreciation) to the dealer for new machinery valued at $27,500. To equate the value of the property exchanged, the dealer also pays Teton $2,000. What gain or loss does Teton realize on the exchange and what gain or loss does Teton recognize on the exchange?

Answer: $10,758 realized gain and $2,000 recognized gain, calculated as follows:

Description	Amount	Explanation
(1) Amount realized from machine	$27,500	
(2) Amount realized from boot (cash)	2,000	
(3) Total amount realized	29,500	(1) + (2).
(4) Adjusted basis	18,742	
(5) Gain realized	**10,758**	(3) − (4).
Gain recognized	**$ 2,000**	Lesser of (2) or (5).

What is the character of Teton's $2,000 gain?

Answer: Ordinary income. Because Teton's accumulated depreciation on the asset exceeds its $2,000 gain, Teton must treat the gain as ordinary gain under the §1245 depreciation recapture rules discussed earlier.

What if: Suppose the same facts as above, except that Teton's adjusted basis in the machinery was $29,000. What amount of gain would Teton recognize on the exchange?

Answer: $500. Teton recognizes the lesser of (1) $500 gain realized ($29,500 minus $29,000) or (2) $2,000 boot received.

When taxpayers receive like-kind property and boot in a like-kind exchange, their basis in the like-kind property is computed under §1031(d) using the following formula:

Adjusted basis of like-kind property surrendered
+ Adjusted basis of boot given
+ Gain recognized
− Fair market value of boot received
− Loss recognized
= Basis of like-kind property received

An alternative and simplified method for checking the basis calculation is to begin with the fair market value of the like-kind property received and subtract any deferred gain or add any deferred loss.

The basis of boot received in the exchange is always the boot's fair market value. This formula for computing basis ensures that the taxpayer's deferred gain or loss on the exchange (the gain or loss realized that is not recognized) is captured in the difference between the value and the basis of the new property received. Consequently, taxpayers defer realized gain or loss on qualifying like-kind exchanges; they do not exclude them. Taxpayers will ultimately recognize the gain or loss when they dispose of the new asset in a taxable transaction.[35]

[35]Additionally, the deferred gain is subject to depreciation recapture when the asset is eventually disposed of in a taxable disposition.

Example 11-17

What if: Assume the facts in the previous example where Teton traded its used machinery with a value of $29,500 and an adjusted basis of $18,742 to the dealer for new machinery valued at $27,500 and $2,000 cash. Teton recognized $2,000 on the exchange. What is Teton's basis in the new machinery it received from the dealer?

Answer: $18,742, computed as follows:

Description	Amount	Explanation
(1) Amount realized from machine	$27,500	Fair market value of new machine.
(2) Amount realized from boot (cash)	2,000	
(3) Total amount realized	29,500	(1) + (2).
(4) Adjusted basis of used machinery	18,742	
(5) Gain realized	10,758	(3) − (4).
(6) Gain recognized	$ 2,000	Lesser of (2) or (5).
(7) Deferred gain	8,758	(5) − (6).
Adjusted basis in new property	**$18,742**	(1) − (7).

THE KEY FACTS

Exchanged Basis

- The basis of like-kind property received is the fair market value of the new asset minus deferred gain or plus deferred loss on the exchange (unless boot is given).
  - When no gain is recognized on the exchange, the basis of the new property is the same as taxpayer's basis in the old like-kind property.
- The basis of boot received is the fair market value of the boot.

It is important to note that anything a taxpayer receives in an exchange other than like-kind property is considered boot. This includes cash, other property, or even the amount of a taxpayer's liability transferred to (assumed by) the other party in the exchange. For example, let's return to the previous example. If instead of paying Teton $2,000 of cash, the dealer assumed Teton's $2,000 liability secured by Teton's old machinery, the tax consequences would have been identical. The dealer relieved Teton of $2,000 of debt and the debt relief is treated the same as if the dealer had paid Teton cash and Teton had paid off its $2,000 liability. Generally, when a taxpayer both transfers and receives boot in an otherwise qualifying like-kind exchange, the taxpayer must recognize any realized gain to the extent of the boot received. That is, the taxpayer is not allowed to offset boot received with boot paid.[36] However, when the taxpayer gives and receives boot in the form of liabilities, the taxpayer is allowed to net the boot received and the boot paid.[37]

Reporting Like-Kind Exchanges

Like-kind exchange transactions are reported on Form 8824. Exhibit 11-13 presents the computations from Form 8824 reflecting the like-kind exchange of the machinery in Example 11-15.

THE KEY FACTS

Involuntary Conversions

- Gain is deferred when appreciated property is involuntarily converted in an accident or natural disaster.
- Basis of property directly converted is carried over from the old property to the new property.
- In an indirect conversion, gain recognized is the lesser of:
  - Gain realized, or
  - Amount of reimbursement the taxpayer does not reinvest in qualified property.
- Qualified replacement property must be of a similar or related use to the original property.

Involuntary Conversions

Usually, when taxpayers sell, exchange, or abandon property they intend to do so. However, sometimes taxpayers may involuntarily dispose of property due to circumstances beyond their control. Thus, the tax law refers to these types of property dispositions as **involuntary conversions.**[38] Involuntary conversions occur when property is partially or wholly destroyed by a natural disaster or accident, stolen, condemned, or seized via eminent domain by a governmental agency. Tragic examples of this include the results of the September 11, 2001, terrorist attacks and the Hurricane Katrina-related events in 2005. Even in situations when taxpayers

[36]However, Reg. §1.1031(j)-1 provides an exception where multiple like-kind exchanges are made in a single exchange.

[37]Further details of this important exception are beyond the scope of our discussion. See the examples provided in Reg. §1.1031(d)-2 for further guidance.

[38]§1033.

EXHIBIT 11-13 Form 8824, Part III (From machine exchange in Example 11-15)

Form 8824 (2014) Page 2

Name(s) shown on tax return. Do not enter name and social security number if shown on other side. | Your social security number

Steve Dallimore (Teton Mountaineering Technologies, LLC)

Part III Realized Gain or (Loss), Recognized Gain, and Basis of Like-Kind Property Received

Caution: *If you transferred **and** received **(a)** more than one group of like-kind properties or **(b)** cash or other (not like-kind) property, see **Reporting of multi-asset exchanges** in the instructions.*

Note: *Complete lines 12 through 14 **only** if you gave up property that was not like-kind. Otherwise, go to line 15.*

12	Fair market value (FMV) of other property given up	12			
13	Adjusted basis of other property given up	13			
14	Gain or (loss) recognized on other property given up. Subtract line 13 from line 12. Report the gain or (loss) in the same manner as if the exchange had been a sale			14	
	Caution: *If the property given up was used previously or partly as a home, see* **Property used as home** *in the instructions.*				
15	Cash received, FMV of other property received, plus net liabilities assumed by other party, reduced (but not below zero) by any exchange expenses you incurred (see instructions)			15	0
16	FMV of like-kind property you received			16	29,500
17	Add lines 15 and 16			17	29,500
18	Adjusted basis of like-kind property you gave up, net amounts paid to other party, plus any exchange expenses **not** used on line 15 (see instructions)			18	18,742
19	**Realized gain or (loss).** Subtract line 18 from line 17			19	10,758
20	Enter the smaller of line 15 or line 19, but not less than zero			20	
21	Ordinary income under recapture rules. Enter here and on Form 4797, line 16 (see instructions)			21	
22	Subtract line 21 from line 20. If zero or less, enter -0-. If more than zero, enter here and on Schedule D or Form 4797, unless the installment method applies (see instructions)			22	
23	**Recognized gain.** Add lines 21 and 22			23	0
24	Deferred gain or (loss). Subtract line 23 from line 19. If a related party exchange, see instructions			24	10,758
25	**Basis of like-kind property received.** Subtract line 15 from the sum of lines 18 and 23			25	18,742

experience a loss of property due to theft, disaster, or other circumstances, they might realize a gain for tax purposes if they receive replacement property or insurance proceeds in excess of their basis in the property that was stolen or destroyed.

Taxpayers may experience a tremendous financial hardship if they were required to recognize the realized gain in these circumstances. For example, let's consider a business that acquired a building for $100,000. The building appreciates in value and when the building is worth $150,000 it is destroyed by fire. The building is fully insured at its replacement cost, so the business receives a check from the insurance company for $150,000. The problem for the business is that it realizes a $50,000 gain on this involuntary conversion ($150,000 insurance proceeds minus $100,000 basis in property without considering depreciation). Assuming the business's income is taxed at a 30 percent marginal rate, it must pay $15,000 of tax on the insurance money it receives. This leaves the business with only $135,000 to replace property worth $150,000. This hardly seems equitable. Congress provides special tax laws to allow taxpayers to defer the gains on such *involuntary* conversions.

Taxpayers may defer realized gains on both direct and indirect involuntary conversions. **Direct conversions** involve taxpayers receiving a direct property replacement for the involuntarily converted property. For example, a municipality that is widening its streets may seize land from a taxpayer through its eminent domain and compensate the taxpayer with another parcel of similar value. In this case, the taxpayer would not recognize gain on the exchange of property and would take an adjusted basis in the new parcel of land equal to the taxpayer's basis in the land that was claimed by the municipality. Just as with like-kind exchanges, an exchanged basis

(basis of old property exchanged for basis of new property) ensures that the gain built into the new property (fair market value minus adjusted basis) includes the same gain that was built into the old property.

Indirect conversions involve taxpayers receiving money for the involuntarily converted property through insurance reimbursement or some other type of settlement. Taxpayers meeting the involuntary conversion requirements may *elect* to either recognize or defer realized gain on the conversions. Indirect conversions are more common than direct conversions. Taxpayers can defer realized gains on indirect conversions *if* they acquire **qualified replacement property** within a prescribed time limit, which is generally two years (three years in case of condemnation) after the close of the tax year in which they receive the proceeds.[39]

For both personal and real property, qualified replacement property for an involuntary conversion is defined more narrowly than is like-kind property in a like-kind exchange. The property must be similar *and* related in service or use to qualify.[40] For example, a bowling alley is not qualified replacement property for a pool hall, even though both are real properties used for entertainment purposes. This is stricter than the like-kind exchange rules that would allow the bowling alley to be exchanged for any other real property including a pool hall. Taxpayers recognize realized gain to the extent that they do not reinvest the reimbursement proceeds in qualified property. However, just as in like-kind exchanges, taxpayers do not recognize more gain than they realize on involuntary conversions. That is, a taxpayer's recognized gain on an involuntary conversion can be determined by the following formula: Recognized gain on involuntary conversion = the *lesser of* (1) the gain realized on the conversion or (2) the amount of reimbursement the taxpayer does *not reinvest* in qualified property.

The character of any gain recognized in an involuntary conversion depends on the nature of the asset that was converted—including depreciation recapture if applicable. The basis of the replacement property in an involuntary conversion is calculated in the same way it is for like-kind exchange property. That is, the basis of the replacement property is the fair market value of the new property minus the deferred gain on the conversion.

Example 11-18

What if: Assume that one of Teton's employees was involved in a traffic accident while driving a delivery van. The employee escaped without serious injury but the van was totally destroyed. Before the accident, Teton's delivery van had a fair market value of $15,000 and an adjusted basis of $11,000 (the cost basis was $15,000 and accumulated depreciation on the van was $4,000). Teton received $15,000 of insurance proceeds to cover the loss. Teton was considering two alternatives for replacing the van: Alternative 1 was to purchase a new delivery van for $20,000 and Alternative 2 was to purchase a used delivery van for $14,000. What gain or loss does Teton recognize under Alternative 1 and Alternative 2?

Answer: $0 gain recognized under Alternative 1 and $1,000 gain recognized under Alternative 2 (see computations below). Teton qualifies for a deferral because the new property (delivery van) has a similar and related use to the old property (delivery van). But it must recognize gain under Alternative 2 because it did not reinvest all of the insurance proceeds in a replacement van.

(continued on page 11-32)

[39]§1033(a)(2)(B). The time period varies depending on the type of property converted. Additionally, the IRS may consent to an extension of the time period for replacement.

[40]The similar and related-use test has been developed through a variety of administrative pronouncements and judicial law.

What is Teton's basis in the replacement property it acquired under Alternative 1 and Alternative 2?

Answer: $16,000 in Alternative 1 and $11,000 in Alternative 2, computed as follows:

Description	Alternative 1 Amount	Alternative 2 Amount	Explanation
(1) Amount realized	$15,000	$15,000	
(2) Adjusted basis	11,000	11,000	
(3) Gain realized	4,000	4,000	(1) − (2).
(4) Insurance proceeds	15,000	15,000	
(5) Proceeds reinvested	15,000	14,000	
(6) Amount not reinvested	0	1,000	(4) − (5).
(7) Gain recognized	**0**	**1,000**	Lesser of (3) or (6).*
(8) Deferred gain	4,000	3,000	(3) − (7).
(9) Value of replacement property	20,000	14,000	
Basis of replacement property	**16,000**	**11,000**	(9) − (8).

*The character of the $1,000 recognized gain is ordinary income under §1245 (lesser of gain recognized or accumulated depreciation).

Involuntary conversions share several similar concepts with like-kind exchanges such as the concept of qualified property, time period restrictions, the method of computing gain recognized (lesser of realized gain or cash received in addition to qualifying property), and basis calculation (gain or loss from old property remains built into new property). However, one important difference between the two is that taxpayers experiencing a loss from involuntary conversion may immediately deduct the loss as a casualty loss (either personal or business depending on the nature of the loss).

TAXES IN THE REAL WORLD Weather Break

Weather conditions across the country have caused hardship to many cattle farmers. Drought in the Southwest or floods in the Plains could cause cattle farmers to sell more of their herds than normal because they may not have enough crops to feed the livestock. To aid these farmers, the IRS offers relief in the form of an election to postpone recognizing gain from the sale of livestock sold due to weather-related conditions. What's the catch? The livestock must be replaced within a two-year period. In essence, the IRS allows cattle farmers to take advantage of the §1033 (involuntary conversion) rules.

As an alternative, if a taxpayer sells livestock because of weather conditions, he or she may be able to defer reporting the sale of the livestock for a one-year period. As a result of these two possibilities, cattle farmers may need to consider whether they will replace the livestock to take advantage of the involuntary conversion provision or whether the one-year deferral will better suit their plans.

THE KEY FACTS

Installment Sales

- Sale of property where the seller receives at least one payment in a taxable year subsequent to the year of disposition of the property.
- Must recognize a portion of gain on each installment payment received.
- Gains from installment sales are calculated as follows:

  Gross profit percentage = Gross profit/Contract price.

  Gain recognized = Gross profit percentage × Payment received in the year.
- Inventory, marketable securities, and depreciation recapture cannot be accounted for under installment sale rules.
- Does not apply to losses.

Installment Sales

In general, when taxpayers sell property for cash and collect the entire sale proceeds in one lump-sum payment, they immediately recognize gain or loss for tax purposes. However, taxpayers selling property don't always collect the sale proceeds in one lump sum from the buyer. For example, the buyer may make a down payment in the year of sale and then agree to pay the remainder of the sale proceeds over a period of time. This type of arrangement is termed an **installment sale.** Technically, an installment sale is any sale of property where the seller receives at least one payment in a taxable year subsequent to the year of disposition of the property.[41] Taxpayers selling property via an installment sale realize gains to the extent the selling price (the amount realized) exceeds their adjusted basis in the property sold. The installment

[41]§453(b)(1).

sale rules stay true to the wherewithal-to-pay concept and allow taxpayers selling property in this manner to use the installment method of recognizing *gain* on the sale over time.[42] The installment method does not apply to property sold at a loss. Under the installment method taxpayers determine the amount of realized gain on the transaction, and they recognize the gain pro rata as they receive the installment payments. So, by the time they have received all of the installment payments, they will have recognized all of the initial realized gain.[43] For financial accounting purposes, businesses selling property on an installment basis generally immediately recognize the realized gain on their financial statements.[44]

To determine the amount of gain the taxpayer (seller) must recognize on each installment payment received, the seller must compute the gross profit percentage on the transaction. The gross profit percentage is calculated as follows:

$$\text{Gross profit percentage} = \frac{\text{Gross profit}}{\text{Contract price}}$$

The gross profit percentage indicates the percentage of the contract price that will ultimately be recognized as gain. Gross profit is calculated as the sales price minus the adjusted basis of the property being sold. The contract price is the sales price less the seller's liabilities that are assumed by the buyer. To determine the portion of a particular payment that is currently recognized as gain, the seller multiplies the amount of the payments received during the year (including the year of sale) by the gross profit percentage (note that once established, the gross profit percentage does not change). Similar to fully taxable transactions, the character of gain taxpayers recognize using the installment method is determined by the character of the asset sold.

Example 11-19

What if: Suppose Teton decides to sell 5 acres of land adjacent to the warehouse for $100,000. The cost basis for the land is $37,500. Teton agrees to sell the property for four equal payments of $25,000—one now (in year 1) and the other three on January 1 of the next three years—plus interest. What amount of gain does Teton realize on the sale and what amount of gain does it recognize in year 1?

Answer: The realized gain on the transaction is $62,500 ($100,000 amount realized less $37,500 adjusted basis), and the year 1 recognized gain is $15,625, computed as follows:

Description	Amount	Explanation
(1) Sales price	$100,000	
(2) Adjusted basis	37,500	
(3) Gross profit	$ 62,500	(1) − (2).
(4) Contract price	$100,000	(1) − assumed liabilities (-0-).
(5) Gross profit percentage	62.5%	(3)/(4).
(6) Payment received in year 1	$ 25,000	
Gain recognized in year 1	**$ 15,625**	(5) × (4).

Because Teton used the land in its trade or business and it held the land for more than a year, the character of the gain is §1231 gain.

[42]Technically, a taxpayer selling property on an installment basis at a gain is required to use the installment method of reporting the recognized gain from the transaction. However, taxpayers are allowed to *elect* out of using the installment method §453(d).

[43]Because the seller in an installment sale is essentially lending money to the buyer, the buyer makes the required installment payments to the seller and the buyer pays interest to the seller for the money the buyer is borrowing. Any interest income received by the seller is immediately taxable as ordinary income. Special rules apply regarding interest for installment sales of more than $150,000 (see §453A).

[44]One exception is that the installment sale method similar to the tax installment method is used for financial accounting purposes when there is doubt that the business will collect the receivable.

The formula for determining the basis of an installment note receivable is (1 – gross profit percentage) × remaining payments on note. Because the gross profit percentage reflects the percentage of the installment payments that will be recognized as gain, (1 – gross profit percentage) is the percentage that is not recognized as gain because it reflects a return of capital (basis).

Gains Ineligible for Installment Reporting

Not all gains are eligible for installment sale reporting. Taxpayers selling marketable securities or inventory on an installment basis may not use the installment method to report gain on the sales. Similarly, any depreciation recapture (including §1245, §1250, and §291 depreciation recapture) is not eligible for installment reporting and must be recognized in the year of sale.[45] However, the §1231 gain remaining after the depreciation recapture can be recognized using the installment method. To ensure that any depreciation recapture is not taxed twice (once immediately and then a second time as payments are received), immediately taxable recapture-related gains are *added to* the adjusted basis of the property sold to determine the gross profit percentage. The increase in basis reduces the gain realized, which also reduces the gross profit percentage and the amount of future gain that will ultimately be recognized as the taxpayer receives the installment payments.

Example 11-20

What if: Assume that Teton agrees to sell some of its machinery for $90,000 for two equal payments of $45,000 plus interest. Teton's original basis was $80,000 and accumulated depreciation on the machinery was $30,000. Teton will receive one payment in year 1 (the current year) and the other payment in year 2. What is the amount and character of the gain Teton recognizes on the sale in year 1?

Answer: $30,000 ordinary income and $5,000 of §1231 gain, computed as follows:

Description	Amount	Explanation
(1) Sales price	$90,000	
(2) Original basis	80,000	
(3) Accumulated depreciation	(30,000)	
(4) Adjusted basis	50,000	(2) + (3).
(5) Realized gain (loss)	$40,000	(1) – (4).
(6) Ordinary income from depreciation recapture (not eligible for installment reporting)	**30,000**	Ordinary income. Lesser of (3) or (5).
(7) Gain eligible for installment reporting	$10,000	(5) – (6).
(8) Contract price	$90,000	(1) – assumed liabilities (-0-)
(9) Gross profit percentage	11.11%	(7)/(8)
(10) Payment received in year 1	$45,000	
Installment gain recognized in year 1	**$ 5,000**	(10) × (9) §1231 gain.

What is the amount and character of the gain Teton recognized upon receipt of the payment in year 2?

Answer: $5,000 of §1231 gain ($45,000 payment received times the gross profit percentage of 11.11 percent).

Other Nonrecognition Provisions

There are several tax law provisions that allow businesses to change the form or organization of their business while deferring the realized gains for tax purposes. For

[45]§453(i).

example, a sole proprietor can form his business as a corporation or contribute assets to an existing corporation and defer the gain realized on the exchange of assets for an ownership interest in the business entity.[46] Without the nonrecognition provision, the tax cost of forming a corporation may be large enough to deter taxpayers from doing so. Nonrecognition rules also apply to taxpayers forming partnerships or contributing assets to partnerships.[47] In still other corporate transactions, such as mergers, divisions (spin-offs or split-ups), or reorganizations, corporations can often do so in tax deferred transactions.[48] While these transactions generally result in deferred gain or loss for the involved parties, the specific details of these topics can easily fill chapters worth of material, and are not considered further in this chapter.

THE KEY FACTS

Related-Person Losses

- Related persons are defined in §267 and include certain family members, related corporations, and other entities.
- Losses on sales to related persons are not deductible by the seller.
- The related person may deduct the previously disallowed loss *to the extent of the gain* on the sale to the unrelated third person.

Related-Person Loss Disallowance Rules

Taxpayers selling business or investment property at a loss to unrelated persons are generally able to deduct the loss.[49] This makes sense in most situations because taxpayers are selling the property for less than their remaining investment (adjusted basis) in the property, and after the sale, the taxpayer's investment in the property is completely terminated. In contrast, when a taxpayer sells property at a loss to a related person, she effectively retains some element of control over the property through the related person. Consistent with this idea, §267(a) disallows recognition of losses on sales to related persons. Under §267, related persons include individuals with family relationships including siblings, spouses, ancestors, and lineal descendants. Related persons also include an individual and a corporation if the individual owns more than 50 percent of the stock of the corporation.[50]

Example 11-21

What if: Suppose Teton is formed as a corporation and Steve is its sole shareholder. Teton is looking to make some long-term investments to fund its anticipated purchase of a new manufacturing facility. Steve currently owns 1,000 shares of stock in his previous company Northeastern Corp., which he intends to sell in the near future. Steve initially paid $40 a share for the stock but the stock is currently valued at $30 a share. While Steve believes the stock has good long-term potential, he needs cash now to purchase a personal residence in Cody, Wyoming. Steve believes selling the shares to Teton makes good sense because he can deduct the loss and save taxes now and Teton can benefit from the expected long-term appreciation of the stock. If Steve sells 1,000 shares of Northeastern Corp. stock to Teton for $30 per share, what amount of loss will he realize and what amount of loss will he recognize for tax purposes?

Answer: $10,000 loss realized and $0 loss recognized, determined as follows:

Description	Amount	Explanation
(1) Amount realized on sale	$30,000	(1,000 × $30).
(2) Adjusted basis in stock	40,000	(1,000 × $40).
(3) Loss realized on sale	**($10,000)**	(1) – (2).
Loss recognized on sale	**$ 0**	Losses on sales to related persons are disallowed.

Because Steve owns more than 50 percent of Teton (he owns 100 percent), Steve and Teton are considered to be related persons. Consequently, Steve is not allowed to recognize any loss on the sale.

[46]§351.

[47]§721.

[48]§368 contains the numerous variations and requirements of these tax-deferred reorganizations.

[49]Capital losses are subject to certain limitations for individuals and corporate taxpayers (§1211).

[50]§267(a). The related-person rules include both direct ownership as well as indirect ownership (ownership attributed to the taxpayer from related persons). See §267(c) for a description of the indirect ownership rules.

Although taxpayers are not allowed to immediately deduct losses when they sell property to the related person, the related-person buyer may be able to subsequently deduct the disallowed loss by selling the property to an *unrelated* third party at a gain. The rules follow:

- If the related buyer sells the property at a gain (the related-person buyer sells it for more than she purchased it for) greater than the disallowed loss, the entire loss that was disallowed for the related-person seller is deductible by the buyer.
- If the related-person buyer subsequently sells the property and the related-person seller's disallowed loss exceeds the related person's gain on the subsequent sale, the related-person buyer may only deduct or offset the previously disallowed loss *to the extent of the gain* on the sale to the unrelated third party—the remaining disallowed loss expires unused.
- If the related-person buyer sells the property for less than her purchase price from the related seller, the disallowed loss expires unused.

Example 11-22

What if: Let's return to the previous example where Steve sold 1,000 shares of Northeastern Corp. stock to Teton (a corporation) for $30,000. As we discovered in that example, Steve realized a $10,000 loss on the sale, but he was not allowed to deduct it because Steve and Teton are related persons. Let's assume that a few years after Teton purchased the stock from Steve, Teton sells the Northeastern Corp. stock to an unrelated third party. What gain or loss does *Teton* recognize when it sells the stock in each of three scenarios, assuming it sells the stock for $37,000 in Scenario 1, $55,000 in Scenario 2, and $25,000 in Scenario 3?

Answer: $0 gain or loss in Scenario 1, $15,000 gain in Scenario 2, and $5,000 loss in Scenario 3, computed as follows:

Description	Scenario 1	Scenario 2	Scenario 3	Explanation
(1) Amount realized	$37,000	$55,000	$25,000	
(2) Adjusted basis	30,000	30,000	30,000	Example 11-21 (Teton's purchase price).
(3) Realized gain (loss)	7,000	25,000	(5,000)	(1) − (2).
(4) Benefit of Steve's ($10,000) disallowed loss	(7,000)	(10,000)	0	Loss benefit limited to realized gain.
Recognized gain (loss)	**$ 0**	**$15,000**	**($5,000)**	(3) + (4).

In Scenario 1 $3,000 of Steve's $10,000 remaining disallowed loss expires unused. In Scenario 3, Steve's entire $10,000 disallowed loss expires unused.

CONCLUSION

This chapter describes and discusses the tax consequences associated with sales and other types of property dispositions. We've learned how to determine the amount of gain or loss taxpayers recognize when they sell or otherwise dispose of property, and we've learned how to determine the character of these gains and losses. Tax accountants who understand the rules and concepts of property dispositions are able to comply with the tax law and advise clients of potential tax-planning opportunities and avoid pitfalls associated with various nonrecognition provisions.

Summary

Calculate the amount of gain or loss recognized on the disposition of assets used in a trade or business. **LO 11-1**

- Dispositions occur in the form of sales, trades, or other realization events.
- Gain realized is the amount realized less the adjusted basis of an asset.
- Amount realized is everything of value received in the transaction less any selling costs.
- Adjusted basis is the historical cost or basis of an asset less any cost recovery deductions applied against the asset.
- Gain realized on asset dispositions is not always recognized.

Describe the general character types of gain or loss recognized on property dispositions. **LO 11-2**

- Recognized gains must be characterized as ordinary, capital, or §1231. An asset's character is a function of the asset's use and holding period.
- Ordinary assets are derived from normal transactions of the business (revenues and accounts receivable), sale of short-term trade or business assets, and depreciation recapture.
- Capital assets are assets that are held either for investment or for personal use (a taxpayer's principal residence).
- §1231 assets consist of property used in a taxpayer's trade or business that has been held for more than one year.
- Net §1231 gains are treated as long-term capital gains and net §1231 losses are treated as ordinary losses.

Explain the rationale for and calculate depreciation recapture. **LO 11-3**

- §1231 assets, other than land, are subject to cost recovery deductions (depreciation), which generate ordinary deductions.
- Gains that are created through depreciation deductions are subject to depreciation recapture. Any remaining gain is §1231 gain.
- Depreciation recapture does not change the amount of the gain but simply converts or recharacterizes the gain from §1231 to ordinary.
- Different recapture rules apply to tangible personal property (§1245) and real property (§291 for corporations only and §1250).

Describe the tax treatment of unrecaptured §1250 gains and determine the character of gains on property sold to related parties. **LO 11-4**

- When individuals sell §1250 property at a gain, the portion of the gain generated by depreciation deductions is called unrecaptured §1250 gain.
- This gain is a §1231 gain that, if treated as a capital gain after the §1231 netting process, flows into the capital gain/loss process (Chapter 11) and is taxed at a maximum rate of 25 percent.
- If a taxpayer sells an asset at a gain to a related person and the asset is a depreciable asset to the related person, the seller must characterize the entire gain as ordinary income.

Describe the tax treatment of §1231 gains or losses, including the §1231 netting process. **LO 11-5**

- After applying the depreciation recapture rules, taxpayers calculate the net §1231 gain or loss.
- If a net §1231 loss results, the loss will become ordinary and offset ordinary income.
- If a net §1231 gain results, the §1231 look-back rule must be applied.
- After applying the look-back rule, any remaining net §1231 gain is a long-term capital gain.

Explain common exceptions to the general rule that realized gains and losses are recognized currently. **LO 11-6**

- Like-kind exchanges involve trading or exchanging business assets for similar business assets. The gain is deferred unless boot or non-like-kind property is received.

- Involuntary conversions are the losses on property through circumstances beyond taxpayers' control. Reasons include natural disasters, accidents, theft, or condemnation.
- Installment sales occur when any portion of the amount realized is received in a year subsequent to the disposition.
- §267 related-person losses are disallowed but the related-person buyer may be able to deduct the disallowed loss if she subsequently sells the property at a gain.

KEY TERMS

adjusted basis (11-5)
amount realized (11-2)
boot (11-27)
capital asset (11-7)
deferred like-kind exchange (11-26)
depreciation recapture (11-9)
direct conversion (11-30)
exchanged basis (11-27)
indirect conversion (11-31)
installment sale (11-32)
involuntary conversion (11-29)
like-kind exchange (11-24)
nonrecaptured net §1231 losses (11-18)
nonrecognition transaction (11-20)
ordinary asset (11-7)
production of income (11-7)
qualified replacement property (11-31)
realized gain or loss (11-5)
recapture (11-11)
recognized gain or loss (11-6)
§291 depreciation recapture (11-14)
§1231 assets (11-8)
§1231 look-back rule (11-18)
§1245 property (11-10)
§1250 property (11-14)
third-party intermediaries (11-25)
unrecaptured §1250 gain (11-15)

DISCUSSION QUESTIONS

LO 11-1 1. Compare and contrast different ways in which a taxpayer triggers a realization event by disposing of an asset.

LO 11-1 2. Potomac Corporation wants to sell a warehouse that it has used in its business for 10 years. Potomac is asking $450,000 for the property. The warehouse is subject to a mortgage of $125,000. If Potomac accepts Wyden Inc.'s offer to give Potomac $325,000 in cash and assume full responsibility for the mortgage on the property, what amount does Potomac realize on the sale?

LO 11-1 3. Montana Max sells a 2,500-acre ranch for $1,000,000 in cash, a note receivable of $1,000,000, and debt relief of $2,400,000. He also pays selling commissions of $60,000. In addition, Max agrees to build a new barn on the property (cost $250,000) and spend $100,000 upgrading the fence on the property before the sale. What is Max's amount realized on the sale?

LO 11-1 4. Hawkeye sold farming equipment for $55,000. It bought the equipment four years ago for $75,000, and it has since claimed a total of $42,000 in depreciation deductions against the asset. Explain how to calculate Hawkeye's adjusted basis in the farming equipment.

LO 11-1 5. When a taxpayer sells an asset, what is the difference between realized and recognized gain or loss on the sale?

LO 11-2 6. What does it mean to characterize a gain or loss? Why is characterizing a gain or loss important?

LO 11-2 7. Explain the difference between ordinary, capital, and §1231 assets.

LO 11-2 8. Discuss the reasons why individuals generally prefer capital gains over ordinary gains. Explain why corporate taxpayers might prefer capital gains over ordinary gains.

LO 11-2 9. Dakota Conrad owns a parcel of land he would like to sell. Describe the circumstances in which the sale of the land would generate §1231 gain or loss, ordinary gain or loss, or capital gain or loss. Also, describe the circumstances where Dakota would not be allowed to deduct a loss on the sale.

10. Lincoln has used a piece of land in her business for the past five years. The land qualifies as §1231 property. It is unclear whether Lincoln will have to recognize a gain or loss when she eventually sells the asset. She asks her accountant how the gain or loss would be characterized if she decides to sell. Her accountant said that selling §1231 assets gives sellers "the best of both worlds." Explain what her accountant means by "the best of both worlds." LO 11-2
11. Explain Congress's rationale for depreciation recapture. LO 11-3
12. Compare and contrast §1245 recapture and §1250 recapture. LO 11-3
13. Why is depreciation recapture not required when assets are sold at a loss? LO 11-3
14. What are the similarities and differences between the tax benefit rule and depreciation recapture? LO 11-3
15. Are both corporations and individuals subject to depreciation recapture when they sell depreciable real property at a gain? Explain. LO 11-3 LO 11-4
16. How is unrecaptured §1250 gain for individuals similar to depreciation recapture? How is it different? LO 11-4
17. Explain why gains from depreciable property sold to a related taxpayer are treated as ordinary income under §1239. LO 11-4
18. Bingaman Resources sold two depreciable §1231 assets during the year. One asset resulted in a large gain (the asset was sold for more than it was purchased for) and the other in a small loss. Describe the §1231 netting process for Bingaman. LO 11-5
19. Jeraldine believes that when the §1231 look-back rule applies, the taxpayer deducts a §1231 loss in a previous year against §1231 gains in the current year. Explain whether Jeraldine's description is correct. LO 11-5
20. Explain the purpose behind the §1231 look-back rule. LO 11-5
21. Does a taxpayer apply the §1231 look-back rule in a year when the taxpayer recognizes a net §1231 loss? Explain. LO 11-5
22. Describe the circumstances in which an individual taxpayer with a net §1231 gain will have different portions of the gain taxed at different rates. LO 11-4 LO 11-5
23. Rocky and Bullwinkle Partnership sold a parcel of land during the current year and realized a gain of $250,000. Rocky and Bullwinkle did not recognize gain related to the sale of the land on its tax return. Is this possible? Explain how a taxpayer could realize a gain but not recognize it. LO 11-6
24. Why does the tax code allow taxpayers to defer gains on like-kind exchanges? How do the tax laws ensure that the gains (or losses) are deferred and not permanently excluded from a taxpayer's income? LO 11-6
25. Compare and contrast the like-kind property requirements for real property and for personal property for purposes of qualifying for a like-kind exchange. Explain whether a car held by a corporation for delivering documents will qualify as like-kind property with a car held by an individual for personal use. LO 11-6
26. Salazar Inc., a Colorado company, is relocating to a nearby town. It would like to trade its real property for some real property in the new location. While Salazar has found several prospective buyers for its real property and has also located several properties that are acceptable in the new location, it cannot find anyone that is willing to trade Salazar Inc. for its property in a like-kind exchange. Explain how a third-party intermediary could facilitate Salazar's like-kind exchange. LO 11-6
27. Minuteman wants to enter into a like-kind exchange by exchanging its old New England manufacturing facility for a ranch in Wyoming. Minuteman is using a third-party intermediary to facilitate the exchange. The purchaser of the manufacturing facility wants to complete the transaction immediately but, for various reasons, the ranch transaction will not be completed for three to four months. Will this delay cause a problem for Minuteman's desire to accomplish this through a like-kind exchange? Explain. LO 11-6

LO 11-6 28. Olympia Corporation, of Kittery, Maine, wants to exchange its manufacturing machinery for Bangor Company's machinery. Both parties agree that Olympia's machinery is worth $100,000 and that Bangor's machinery is worth $95,000. Olympia would like the transaction to qualify as a like-kind exchange. What could the parties do to equalize the value exchanged but still allow the exchange to qualify as a like-kind exchange? How would the necessary change affect the tax consequences of the transaction?

LO 11-6 29. Compare and contrast the similarities and differences between like-kind exchanges and involuntary conversions for tax purposes.

LO 11-6 30. What is an installment sale? How do the tax laws ensure that taxpayers recognize all the gain they realize on an installment sale? How is depreciation recapture treated in an installment sale? Explain the gross profit ratio and how it relates to gains recognized under installment method sales.

LO 11-6 31. Mr. Kyle owns stock in a local publicly traded company. Although the stock price has declined since he purchased it two years ago, he likes the long-term prospects for the company. If Kyle sells the stock to his sister because he needs some cash for a down payment on a new home, is the loss deductible? If Kyle is right and the stock price increases in the future, how is his sister's gain computed if she sells the stock?

PROBLEMS

All applicable problems are available with McGraw-Hill's *Connect® Accounting.*

LO 11-1 32. Rafael sold an asset to Jamal. What is Rafael's amount realized on the sale in each of the following alternative scenarios?

a) Rafael received $80,000 of cash and a vehicle worth $10,000. Rafael also pays $5,000 in selling expenses.

b) Rafael received $80,000 of cash and was relieved of a $30,000 mortgage on the asset he sold to Jamal. Rafael also paid a commission of $5,000 on the transaction.

c) Rafael received $20,000 of cash, a parcel of land worth $50,000, and marketable securities of $10,000. Rafael also paid a commission of $8,000 on the transaction.

LO 11-1 33. Alan Meer inherits a hotel from his grandmother, Mary, on February 11 of the current year. Mary bought the hotel for $730,000 three years ago. Mary deducted $27,000 of cost recovery on the hotel before her death. The fair market of the hotel in February is $725,000. (Assume that the alternative valuation date is not used.)

a) What is Alan's adjusted basis in the hotel?

b) If the fair market value of the hotel at the time of Mary's death was $500,000, what is Alan's basis?

LO 11-1 34. Shasta Corporation sold a piece of land to Bill for $45,000. Shasta bought the land two years ago for $30,600. What gain or loss does Shasta realize on the transaction?

LO 11-1 35. Lassen Corporation sold a machine to a machine dealer for $25,000. Lassen bought the machine for $55,000 and has claimed $15,000 of depreciation expense on the machine. What gain or loss does Lassen realize on the transaction?

LO 11-1 LO 11-2 36. Hannah Tywin owns 100 shares of MM Inc. stock. She sells the stock on December 11 for $25 per share. She received the stock as a gift from her Aunt Pam on March 20 of this year when the fair market value of the stock was $18 per share. Aunt Pam originally purchased the stock seven years ago at a price of $12 per share. What is the amount and character of Hannah's recognized gain on the stock?

37. On September 30 of last year, Rex received some investment land from Holly as a gift. Holly's adjusted basis was $50,000 and the land was valued at $40,000 at the time of the gift. Holly acquired the land five years ago. What is the amount and character of Rex's recognized gain (loss) if he sells the land on May 12 this year at the following prices? LO 11-1 LO 11-2

a) $32,000
b) $70,000
c) $45,000

38. Franco converted a building from personal to business use in May 2013 when the fair market value was $55,000. He purchased the building in July 2010 for $80,000. On December 15 of this year, Franco sells the building for $40,000. On the date of sale, the accumulated depreciation on the building was $5,565. What is Franco's recognized gain or loss on the sale? LO 11-1 LO 11-2

39. Identify each of White Corporation's following assets as an ordinary, capital, or §1231 asset. LO 11-2

a) Two years ago, White used its excess cash to purchase a piece of land as an investment.
b) Two years ago, White purchased land and a warehouse. It uses these assets in its business.
c) Manufacturing machinery White purchased earlier this year.
d) Inventory White purchased 13 months ago but is ready to be shipped to a customer.
e) Office equipment White has used in its business for the past three years.
f) 1,000 shares of stock in Black corporation that White purchased two years ago because it was a good investment.
g) Account receivable from a customer with terms 2/10 net 30.
h) Machinery White held for three years and then sold at a loss of $10,000.

40. In year 0, Canon purchased a machine to use in its business for $56,000. In year 3, Canon sold the machine for $42,000. Between the date of the purchase and the date of the sale, Canon depreciated the machine by $32,000. LO 11-3 LO 11-4

a) What is the amount and character of the gain Canon will recognize on the sale, assuming that it is a partnership?
b) What is the amount and character of the gain Canon will recognize on the sale, assuming that it is a corporation?
c) What is the amount and character of the gain Canon will recognize on the sale, assuming that it is a corporation and the sale proceeds were increased to $60,000?
d) What is the amount and character of the gain Canon will recognize on the sale, assuming that it is a corporation and the sale proceeds were decreased to $20,000?

41. In year 0, Longworth Partnership purchased a machine for $40,000 to use in its business. In year 3, Longworth sold the machine for $35,000. Between the date of the purchase and the date of the sale, Longworth depreciated the machine by $22,000. LO 11-3 LO 11-4

a) What is the amount and character of the gain (loss) Longworth will recognize on the sale?
b) What is the amount and character of the gain (loss) Longworth will recognize on the sale if the sale proceeds were increased to $45,000?
c) What is the amount and character of the gain (loss) Longworth will recognize on the sale if the sale proceeds were decreased to $15,000?

LO 11-3 LO 11-4

42. On August 1 of year 0, Dirksen purchased a machine for $20,000 to use in its business. On December 4 of year 0, Dirksen sold the machine for $18,000.
    a) What is the amount and character of the gain or loss Dirksen will recognize on the sale?
    b) What is the amount and character of the gain or loss Dirksen will recognize on the sale if the machine was sold on January 15 of year 1 instead?

LO 11-3 LO 11-4

43. Rayburn Corporation has a building that it bought during year 0 for $850,000. It sold the building in year 5. During the time it held the building Rayburn depreciated it by $100,000. What is the amount and character of the gain or loss Rayburn will recognize on the sale in each of the following alternative situations?
    a) Rayburn receives $840,000.
    b) Rayburn receives $900,000.
    c) Rayburn receives $700,000.

LO 11-3 LO 11-4

44. Moran owns a building he bought during year 0 for $150,000. He sold the building in year 6. During the time he held the building he depreciated it by $32,000. What is the amount and character of the gain or loss Moran will recognize on the sale in each of the following alternative situations?
    a) Moran received $145,000.
    b) Moran received $170,000.
    c) Moran received $110,000.

LO 11-3 LO 11-4 LO 11-5 planning

45. Hart, an individual, bought an asset for $500,000 and has claimed $100,000 of depreciation deductions against the asset. Hart has a marginal tax rate of 30 percent. Answer the questions presented in the following alternative scenarios (assume Hart had no property transactions other than those described in the problem):
    a) What is the amount and character of Hart's recognized gain if the asset is tangible personal property sold for $450,000? What effect does the sale have on Hart's tax liability for the year?
    b) What is the amount and character of Hart's recognized gain if the asset is tangible personal property sold for $550,000? What effect does the sale have on Hart's tax liability for the year?
    c) What is the amount and character of Hart's recognized gain if the asset is tangible personal property sold for $350,000? What effect does the sale have on Hart's tax liability for the year?
    d) What is the amount and character of Hart's recognized gain if the asset is a nonresidential building sold for $450,000? What effect does the sale have on Hart's tax liability for the year?
    e) Now assume that Hart is a corporation. What is the amount and character of its recognized gain if the asset is a nonresidential building sold for $450,000? What effect does the sale have on Hart's tax liability for the year (assume the same 30 percent marginal tax rate)?
    f) Now assuming that the asset is real property, which entity type should be used to minimize the taxes paid on real estate gains?

LO 11-4

46. Luke sold a building and the land on which the building sits to his wholly owned corporation, Studemont Corp. at fair market value. The fair market value of the building was determined to be $325,000; Luke built the building several years ago at a cost of $200,000. Luke had claimed $45,000 of depreciation expense on the building. The fair market value of the land was determined to be $210,000 at the time of the sale; Luke purchased the land many years ago for $130,000.
    a) What is the amount and character of Luke's recognized gain or loss on the building?
    b) What is the amount and character of Luke's recognized gain or loss on the land?

47. Buckley, an individual, began business two years ago and has never sold a §1231 asset. Buckley owned each of the assets since he began the business. In the current year, Buckley sold the following business assets: LO 11-5

Asset	Original Cost	Accumulated Depreciation	Gain/Loss
Computers	$ 6,000	$ 2,000	($3,000)
Machinery	10,000	4,000	(2,000)
Furniture	20,000	12,000	7,000
Building	100,000	10,000	(1,000)

Assuming Buckley's marginal ordinary income tax rate is 35 percent, answer the questions for the following alternative scenarios:

a) What is the character of Buckley's gains or losses for the current year? What effect do the gains and losses have on Buckley's tax liability?

b) Assume that the amount realized increased so that the building was sold at a $6,000 gain instead. What is the character of Buckley's gains or losses for the current year? What effect do the gains and losses have on Buckley's tax liability?

c) Assume that the amount realized increased so that the building was sold at a $15,000 gain instead. What is the character of Buckley's gains or losses for the current year? What effect do the gains and losses have on Buckley's tax liability?

48. Lily Tucker (single) owns and operates a bike shop as a sole proprietorship. This year, she sells the following long-term assets used in her business: LO 11-3 LO 11-4 LO 11-5

Asset	Sales Price	Cost	Accumulated Depreciation
Building	$230,000	$200,000	$52,000
Equipment	80,000	148,000	23,000

Lily's taxable income before these transactions is $160,500. What are Lily's taxable income and tax liability for the year?

49. Shimmer Inc. is a calendar-year-end, accrual-method corporation. This year, it sells the following long-term assets: LO 11-3 LO 11-4 LO 11-5

Asset	Sales Price	Cost	Accumulated Depreciation
Building	$650,000	$642,000	$37,000
Sparkle Corporation stock	130,000	175,000	n/a

Shimmer does not sell any other assets during the year, and its taxable income before these transactions is $800,000. What are Shimmer's taxable income and tax liability for the year?

50. Aruna, a sole proprietor, wants to sell two assets that she no longer needs for her business. Both assets qualify as §1231 assets. The first is machinery and will generate a $10,000 §1231 loss on the sale. The second is land that will generate a $7,000 §1231 gain on the sale. Aruna's ordinary marginal tax rate is 30 percent. LO 11-5 planning

a) Assuming she sells both assets in December of year 1 (the current year), what effect will the sales have on Aruna's tax liability?

b) Assuming that Aruna sells the land in December of year 1 and the machinery in January of year 2, what effect will the sales have on Aruna's tax liability for each year?

c) Explain why selling the assets in separate years will result in greater tax savings for Aruna.

LO 11-5

51. Bourne Guitars, a corporation, reported a $157,000 net §1231 gain for year 6.

a) Assuming Bourne reported $50,000 of nonrecaptured net §1231 losses during years 1–5, what amount of Bourne's net §1231 gain for year 6, if any, is treated as ordinary income?

b) Assuming Bourne's nonrecaptured net §1231 losses from years 1–5 were $200,000, what amount of Bourne's net §1231 gain for year 6, if any, is treated as ordinary income?

LO 11-5
planning

52. Tonya Jefferson, a sole proprietor, runs a successful lobbying business in Washington, DC. She doesn't sell many business assets, but she is planning on retiring and selling her historic townhouse, from which she runs her business, in order to buy a place somewhere sunny and warm. Tonya's townhouse is worth $1,000,000 and the land is worth another $1,000,000. The original basis in the townhouse was $600,000, and she has claimed $250,000 of depreciation deductions against the asset over the years. The original basis in the land was $500,000. Tonya has located a buyer that would like to finalize the transaction in December of the current year. Tonya's marginal ordinary income tax rate is 35 percent.

a) What amount of gain or loss does Tonya recognize on the sale? What is the character of the gain or loss? What effect does the gain or loss have on her tax liability?

b) In addition to the original facts, assume that Tonya reports the following nonrecaptured net §1231 loss:

Year	Net §1231 Gains/(Losses)
Year 1	($200,000)
Year 2	0
Year 3	0
Year 4	0
Year 5	0
Year 6 (current year)	?

What amount of gain or loss does Tonya recognize on the sale? What is the character of the gain or loss? What effect does the gain or loss have on her year 6 (the current year) tax liability?

c) As Tonya's tax advisor, you suggest that Tonya sell the townhouse in year 7 in order to reduce her taxes. What amount of gain or loss does Tonya recognize on the sale in year 7?

LO 11-5

53. Morgan's Water World (MWW), an LLC, opened several years ago and reports the following net §1231 gains and losses since it began business.

Year	Net §1231 Gains/(Losses)
Year 1	($11,000)
Year 2	5,000
Year 3	(21,000)
Year 4	(4,000)
Year 5	17,000
Year 6	(43,000)
Year 7 (current year)	113,000

What amount, if any, of the year 7 $113,000 net §1231 gain is treated as ordinary income?

54. Hans runs a sole proprietorship. Hans reported the following net §1231 gains and losses since he began business: LO 11-5

Year	Net §1231 Gains/(Losses)
Year 1	($65,000)
Year 2	15,000
Year 3	0
Year 4	0
Year 5	10,000
Year 6	0
Year 7 (current year)	50,000

a) What amount, if any, of the year 7 (current year) $50,000 net §1231 gain is treated as ordinary income?

b) Assume that the $50,000 net §1231 gain occurs in year 6 instead of year 7. What amount of the gain would be treated as ordinary income in year 6?

55. Independence Corporation needs to replace some of the assets used in its trade or business and is contemplating the following exchanges: LO 11-6

Exchange	Asset Given Up by Independence	Asset Received by Independence
a	Band saw	Band saw
b	Machinery used in textiles	Machinery used for wood working
c	Passenger automobile used for deliveries	Heavy duty van that seats two and has a large cargo box
d	Large warehouse on two acres	Small warehouse on twenty-two acres
e	Office building in Green Bay, WI, used in the business	Apartment complex in Newport Beach, CA, that will be held as an investment

Determine whether each exchange qualifies as a like-kind exchange. Also, explain the rationale for why each qualifies or does not qualify as a like-kind exchange.

56. Kase, an individual, purchased some property in Potomac, Maryland, for $150,000 approximately 10 years ago. Kase is approached by a real estate agent representing a client who would like to exchange a parcel of land in North Carolina for Kase's Maryland property. Kase agrees to the exchange. What is Kase's realized gain or loss, recognized gain or loss, and basis in the North Carolina property in each of the following alternative scenarios? LO 11-6

a) The transaction qualifies as a like-kind exchange and the fair market value of each property is $675,000.

b) The transaction qualifies as a like-kind exchange and the fair market value of each property is $100,000.

57. Longhaul Trucking traded two small trucks (each had a 10,000-pound gross weight) for one large truck (18,000-pound gross weight). Do the trucks qualify as like-kind property? (*Hint:* Because the trucks are tangible personal property they must be the same asset class to be like-kind assets. Use Rev. Proc. 87-56 to determine the asset classes for the trucks.) LO 11-6

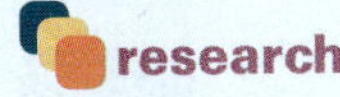

58. Twinbrook Corporation needed to upgrade to a larger manufacturing facility. Twinbrook first acquired a new manufacturing facility for $2,100,000 cash, and then transferred the facility it was using (building and land) to White Flint Corporation for $2,000,000 three months later. Does the exchange qualify for like-kind exchange treatment? (*Hint:* Examine Revenue Procedures 2000-37 and 2004-51.) If not, can you propose a change in the transaction that will allow it to qualify? LO 11-6

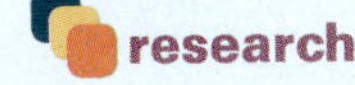

LO 11-6 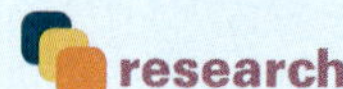

59. Woodley Park Corporation currently owns two parcels of land (parcel 1 and parcel 2). It owns a warehouse facility on parcel 1. Woodley needs to acquire a new and larger manufacturing facility. Woodley was approached by Blazing Fast Construction (who specializes in prefabricated warehouses) about acquiring Woodley's existing warehouse on parcel 1. Woodley indicated that it prefers to exchange its existing facility for a new and larger facility in a qualifying like-kind exchange. Blazing Fast indicated that it could construct a new manufacturing facility on parcel 2 to Woodley's specification within four months. Woodley and Blazing Fast agreed to the following arrangement. First, Blazing Fast would construct the new warehouse on parcel 2 and then relinquish the property to Woodley within four months. Woodley would then transfer the warehouse facility and land parcel 1 to Blazing Fast. All of the property exchanged in the deal was identified immediately and the construction was completed within 180 days. Does the exchange of the new building for the old building and parcel 1 qualify as a like-kind exchange (see *DeCleene v. Commissioner,* 115 TC 457)?

LO 11-6

60. Metro Corp. traded machine A for machine B. Metro originally purchased machine A for $50,000 and machine A's adjusted basis was $25,000 at the time of the exchange. What is Metro's realized gain or loss, recognized gain or loss, and adjusted basis in machine B in each of the following alternative scenarios?
   a) The fair market value of machine A and of machine B is $40,000 at the time of the exchange. The exchange does not qualify as a like-kind exchange.
   b) The fair market value of machine A and of machine B is $40,000. The exchange qualifies as a like-kind exchange.
   c) The fair market value of machine A is $35,000 and machine B is valued at $40,000. Metro exchanges machine A and $5,000 cash for machine B. Machine A and machine B are like-kind property.
   d) The fair market value of machine A is $45,000 and Metro trades machine A for machine B valued at $40,000 and $5,000 cash. Machine A and machine B are like-kind property.

LO 11-6

61. Prater Inc. enters into an exchange in which it gives up its warehouse on 10 acres of land and receives a tract of land. A summary of the exchange is as follows:

Transferred	FMV	Original Basis	Accumulated Depreciation
Warehouse	$300,000	$225,000	$45,000
Land	50,000	50,000	
Mortgage on warehouse	30,000		
Cash	20,000	20,000	

Assets Received	FMV
Land	$340,000

What is Prater's realized and recognized gain on the exchange and its basis in the assets it received in the exchange?

LO 11-6

62. Baker Corporation owned a building located in Kansas. Baker used the building for its business operations. Last year a tornado hit the property and completely destroyed it. This year, Baker received an insurance settlement. Baker had originally purchased the building for $350,000 and had claimed a total of $100,000 of depreciation deductions against the property. What is Baker's realized and recognized gain or (loss) on this transaction and what is its basis in the new building in the following alternative scenarios?
   a) Baker received $450,000 in insurance proceeds and spent $450,000 rebuilding the building during the current year.

b) Baker received $450,000 in insurance proceeds and spent $500,000 rebuilding the building during the current year.

c) Baker received $450,000 in insurance proceeds and spent $400,000 rebuilding the building during the current year.

d) Baker received $450,000 in insurance proceeds and spent $450,000 rebuilding the building during the next three years.

63. Russell Corporation sold a parcel of land valued at $400,000. Its basis in the land was $275,000. For the land, Russell received $50,000 in cash in year 0 and a note providing that Russell will receive $175,000 in year 1 and $175,000 in year 2 from the buyer. **LO 11-6**

a) What is Russell's realized gain on the transaction?

b) What is Russell's recognized gain in year 0, year 1, and year 2?

64. In year 0, Javens Inc. sold machinery with a fair market value of $400,000 to Chris. The machinery's original basis was $317,000 and Javens's accumulated depreciation on the machinery was $50,000, so its adjusted basis to Javens was $267,000. Chris paid Javens $40,000 immediately (in year 0) and provided a note to Javens indicating that Chris would pay Javens $60,000 a year for six years beginning in year 1. What is the amount and character of the gain that Javens will recognize in year 0? What amount and character of the gain will Javens recognize in years 1 through 6? **LO 11-6**

65. Ken sold a rental property for $500,000. He received $100,000 in the current year and $100,000 each year for the next four years. $400,000 of the sales price was allocated to the building and the remaining $100,000 was allocated to the land. Ken purchased the property several years ago for $300,000. When he initially purchased the property, he allocated $225,000 of the purchase price to the building and $75,000 to the land. Ken has claimed $25,000 of depreciation deductions over the years against the building. Ken had no other sales of §1231 or capital assets in the current year. For the year of the sale, determine Ken's recognized gain or loss, the character of Ken's gain, and calculate Ken's tax due because of the sale (assuming his marginal ordinary tax rate is 35 percent). (*Hint:* See the examples in Reg. §1.453-12.) **LO 11-6** research

66. Hillary is in the leasing business and faces a marginal tax rate of 35 percent. She has leased equipment to Whitewater Corporation for several years. Hillary bought the equipment for $50,000 and claimed $20,000 of depreciation deductions against the asset. The lease term is about to expire and Whitewater would like to acquire the equipment. Hillary has been offered two options to choose from: **LO 11-6** planning

Option	Details
Like-kind exchange	Whitewater would provide Hillary with like-kind equipment. The like-kind equipment has a fair market value of $35,000.
Installment sale	Whitewater would provide Hillary with two payments of $19,000. She would use the proceeds to purchase equipment that she could also lease.

Ignoring time value of money, which option provides the greatest after-tax value for Hillary, assuming she is indifferent between the proposals based on nontax factors?

67. Deirdre sold 100 shares of stock to her brother, James, for $2,400. Deirdre purchased the stock several years ago for $3,000. **LO 11-6**

a) What gain or loss does Deirdre recognize on the sale?

b) What amount of gain or loss does James recognize if he sells the stock for $3,200?

c) What amount of gain or loss does James recognize if he sells the stock for $2,600?

d) What amount of gain or loss does James recognize if he sells the stock for $2,000?

COMPREHENSIVE PROBLEMS

All applicable problems are available with McGraw-Hill's *Connect*® *Accounting*.

68. Two years ago, Bethesda Corporation bought a delivery truck for $30,000 (not subject to the luxury auto depreciation limits). Bethesda used MACRS 200 percent declining balance and the half-year convention to recover the cost of the truck, but it did not elect §179 expensing or any eligible bonus depreciation. Answer the questions for the following alternative scenarios.
    a) Assuming Bethesda used the truck until March of year 3, what depreciation expense can it claim on the truck for years 1 through 3?
    b) Assume that Bethesda claimed $18,500 of depreciation expense on the truck before it sold it in year 3. What is the amount and character of the gain or loss if Bethesda sold the truck in year 3 for $17,000, and incurred $2,000 of selling expenses on the sale?
    c) Assume that Bethesda claimed $18,500 of depreciation expense on the truck before it sold it in year 3. What is the amount and character of the gain or loss if Bethesda sold the truck in year 3 for $35,000, and incurred $3,000 of selling expenses on the sale?
69. Hauswirth Corporation sold (or exchanged) some manufacturing equipment in year 0. Hauswirth bought the machinery several years ago for $65,000 and it has claimed $23,000 of depreciation expense against the equipment.
    a) Assuming that Hauswirth receives $50,000 in cash for the equipment, compute the amount and character of Hauswirth's recognized gain or loss on the sale.
    b) Assuming that Hauswirth receives like-kind equipment with a fair market value of $50,000 in exchange for its equipment, compute Hauswirth's gain realized, gain recognized, deferred gain, and basis in the new equipment.
    c) Assuming that Hauswirth receives $20,000 in cash in year 0 and a $50,000 note receivable that is payable in year 1, compute the amount and character of Hauswirth's gain in year 0 and in year 1.

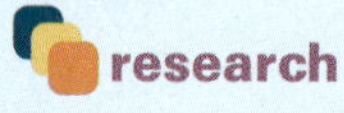

70. Fontenot Corporation sold some machinery to its majority owner Gray (an individual who owns 60 percent of Fontenot). Fontenot purchased the machinery for $100,000 and has claimed a total of $40,000 of depreciation expense deductions against the property. Gray will provide Fontenot with $10,000 of cash today and provide a $100,000 note that will pay Fontenot $50,000 one year from now and $50,000 two years from now.
    a) What gain does Fontenot realize on the sale?
    b) What is the amount and character of the gain that Fontenot must recognize in the year of sale (if any) and each of the two subsequent years? (*Hint:* Use the Internal Revenue Code and start with §453; please give appropriate citations.)

71. Moab Inc. manufactures and distributes high-tech biking gadgets. It has decided to streamline some of its operations so that it will be able to be more productive and efficient. Because of this decision it has entered into several transactions during the year.

    Part (1) Determine the gain/loss realized and recognized in the current year for each of these events. Also determine whether the gain/loss recognized will be §1231, capital, or ordinary.

    a) Moab Inc. sold a machine that it used to make computerized gadgets for $27,300 cash. It originally bought the machine for $19,200 three years ago and has taken $8,000 depreciation.
    b) Moab Inc. held stock in ABC Corp., which had a value of $12,000 at the beginning of the year. That same stock had a value of $15,230 at the end of the year.
    c) Moab Inc. sold some of its inventory for $7,000 cash. This inventory had a basis of $5,000.

d) Moab Inc. disposed of an office building with a fair market value of $75,000 for another office building with a fair market value of $55,000 and $20,000 in cash. It originally bought the office building seven years ago for $62,000 and has taken $15,000 in depreciation.

e) Moab Inc. sold some land held for investment for $28,000. It originally bought the land for $32,000 two years ago.

f) Moab Inc. sold another machine for a note payable in four annual installments of $12,000. The first payment was received in the current year. It originally bought the machine two years ago for $32,000 and has claimed $9,000 in depreciation expense against the machine.

g) Moab Inc. sold stock it held for eight years for $2,750. It originally purchased the stock for $2,100.

h) Moab Inc. sold another machine for $7,300. It originally purchased this machine six months ago for $9,000 and has claimed $830 in depreciation expense against the asset.

Part (2) From the recognized gains/losses determined in part 1, determine the net §1231 gain/loss and the net ordinary gain/loss Moab will recognize on its tax return. Moab Inc. also has $2,000 of nonrecaptured net §1231 losses from previous years.

Part (3) Complete Moab Inc.'s Form 4797 for the year.

72. Vertovec Inc., a large local consulting firm in Utah, hired several new consultants from out of state last year to help service their expanding list of clients. To aid in relocating the consultants, Vertovec Inc. purchased the consultants' homes in their prior location if the consultants were unable to sell their homes within 30 days of listing them for sale. Vertovec Inc. bought the homes from the consultants for 5 percent less than the list price and then continued to list the homes for sale. Each home Vertovec Inc. purchased was sold at a loss. By the end of last year, Vertovec had suffered a loss totaling $250,000 from the homes. How should Vertovec treat the loss for tax purposes? Write a memo to Vertovec Inc. explaining your findings and any planning suggestions that you may have if Vertovec Inc. continues to offer this type of relocation benefit to newly hired consultants.

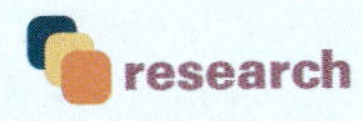

73. WAR (We Are Rich) has been in business since 1982. WAR is an accrual method sole proprietorship that deals in the manufacturing and wholesaling of various types of golf equipment. Hack & Hack CPAs have filed accurate tax returns for WAR's owner since WAR opened its doors. The managing partner of Hack & Hack (Jack) has gotten along very well with the owner of WAR – Mr. Someday Woods (single). However, in early 2015, Jack Hack and Someday Woods played a round of golf and Jack, for the first time ever, actually beat Mr. Woods. Mr. Woods was so upset that he fired Hack & Hack and has hired you to compute his 2015 taxable income. Mr. Woods was able to provide you with the following information from prior tax returns. The taxable income numbers reflect the results from all of Mr. Wood's activities *except for the items separately stated*. You will need to consider how to handle the separately stated items for tax purposes. Also, note that the 2010–2014 numbers do not reflect capital loss carryovers.

	2010	2011	2012	2013	2014
Ordinary taxable income	$4,000	$ 2,000	$94,000	$170,000	$250,000
Other items not included in ordinary taxable income					
Net gain (loss) on disposition of §1231 assets	$3,000	10,000		($6,000)	
Net long-term capital gain (loss) on disposition of capital assets	($15,000)	$ 1,000	($7,000)		($7,000)

In 2015, Mr. Woods had taxable income in the amount of $460,000 *before* considering the following events and transactions that transpired in 2015:

a) On January 1, 2015, WAR purchased a plot of land for $100,000 with the intention of creating a driving range where patrons could test their new golf equipment. WAR never got around to building the driving range; instead, WAR sold the land on October 1, 2015, for $40,000.

b) On August 17, 2015, WAR sold its golf testing machine, "Iron Byron" and replaced it with a new machine "Iron Tiger." "Iron Byron" was purchased and installed for a total cost of $22,000 on February 5, 2011. At the time of sale, "Iron Byron" had an adjusted tax basis of $4,000. WAR sold "Iron Byron" for $25,000.

c) In the months October through December 2015, WAR sold various assets to come up with the funds necessary to invest in WAR's latest and greatest invention–the three dimple golf ball. Data on these assets are provided below:

Asset	Placed in Service (or purchased)	Sold	Initial Basis	Accumulated Depreciation	Selling Price
Someday's black leather sofa (used in office)	4/4/14	10/16/15	$ 3,000	$ 540	$ 2,900
Someday's office chair	3/1/13	11/8/15	$ 8,000	$3,000	$ 4,000
Marketable securities	2/1/12	12/1/15	$12,000	$ 0	$20,000
Land held for investment	7/1/14	11/29/15	$45,000	$ 0	$48,000
Other investment property	11/30/13	10/15/15	$10,000	$ 0	$ 8,000

d) Finally, on May 7, 2015, WAR decided to sell the building where they tested their plutonium shaft, lignite head drivers. WAR purchased the building on January 5, 2003, for $190,000 ($170,000 for the building, $20,000 for the land). At the time of the sale, the accumulated depreciation on the building was $50,000. WAR sold the building (with the land) for $300,000. The fair market value of the land at the time of sale was $45,000.

Part 1: Compute Mr. Woods's taxable income *after* taking into account the transactions described above.

Part 2: Compute Mr. Woods's tax liability for the year. (Ignore any net investment income tax for the year.)

Part 3: Complete Mr. Woods's Form 8949, Schedule D, and Form 4797 (use the most current version of these schedules) to be attached to his Form 1040. Assume that asset bases are not reported to the IRS.

74. Fizbo Corporation is in the business of breeding and racing horses. Fizbo has taxable income of $5,000,000 other than from these transactions. It has nonrecaptured §1231 losses of $10,000 from 2011 and $13,000 from 2009.

Consider the following transactions that occur during 2015:

a) A building with an adjusted basis of $300,000 is totally destroyed by fire. Fizbo receives insurance proceeds of $400,000, but does not plan to replace the building. The building was built 12 years ago at a cost of $420,000 and was used to provide lodging for employees.

b) Fizbo sells four acres of undeveloped farmland (used for grazing) for $50,000. Fizbo purchased the land 15 years ago for $15,000.

c) Fizbo sells a racehorse for $250,000. The racehorse was purchased four years ago for $200,000. Total depreciation taken on the racehorse was $160,000.

d) Fizbo exchanges equipment that was purchased three years ago for $300,000 for $100,000 of IBM common stock. The adjusted basis of the equipment is

$220,000. If straight-line depreciation had been used, the adjusted basis would be $252,000.

e) On November 1, Fizbo sold XCON stock for $50,000. Fizbo had purchased the stock on December 12, 2014 for $112,000.

Part 1: After ALL netting is complete, what is Fizbo's total amount of income from these transactions to be treated as ordinary income or loss? What is its capital gain or loss?

Part 2: What is Fizbo's taxable income for the year after including the effects of these transactions?

chapter

12 Compensation

Learning Objectives

Upon completing this chapter, you should be able to:

LO 12-1 Discuss and explain the tax implications of compensation in the form of salary and wages from the employee's and employer's perspectives.

LO 12-2 Describe and distinguish the tax implications of various forms of equity-based compensation from the employer's and employee's perspectives.

LO 12-3 Compare and contrast taxable and nontaxable fringe benefits and explain the employee and employer tax consequences associated with fringe benefits.

© image 100/Jupiterimages

Storyline Summary

Taxpayers:	Julie and Ethan Clark
Location:	San Diego, California
Employment status:	Julie—mid-level executive for Premier Computer Corporation (PCC); current salary $240,000 Ethan—mechanical engineer; current salary $70,000
Filing status:	Married filing jointly
Dependents:	Two children
Marginal ordinary tax rate:	40 percent
Current situation:	Julie is considering an offer for the vice president of marketing position with Technology Products Inc (TPI).

Julie and Ethan Clark and their two children have been settled into their life in San Diego, California, for some time. Julie has decided her career is at a crossroads. On the one hand, her employment as a mid-level executive for Premier Computer Corporation (PCC) is going well, but the work is not as challenging as it used to be. She suspects that, given her skills and abilities, she could put her career on the fast track with the right opportunity, engaging in more fulfilling work and gaining a significant increase in compensation.

Julie was sitting at her desk contemplating her career when she received yet another call from a corporate headhunter. While she usually quickly dismisses such calls, this time her interest and curiosity were piqued and she gave her full attention. He asked if she had any interest in a vice president of marketing position with a publicly traded company located nearby. After the headhunter answered a few of her questions, Julie gave him the go-ahead to set up an interview.

A couple of weeks later, Julie had been through two rounds of interviews for the marketing VP position when she received a call informing her that she was the one Technology Products Inc. (TPI) wanted for the job and that an offer letter with the details was on its way. The letter indicated TPI was offering a $280,000 salary (a significant increase from her current salary). TPI was also offering her a choice of certain types of equity-based compensation and some attractive fringe benefits. While excited by the letter, Julie knew she needed to learn more about the equity-based compensation alternatives and the other forms of compensation TPI was offering before she could adequately evaluate the offer and reach her decision.

to be continued . . .

As TPI's letter to Julie illustrates, employers are able to offer many different forms of compensation to employees. They can also pay some compensation now and defer some to the future. Each type of compensation has unique tax and nontax consequences.

This chapter addresses the tax and nontax consequences of *current* compensation packages from both the employee's and the employer's perspective. The next chapter addresses *future* compensation.

LO 12-1

SALARY AND WAGES

Current compensation paid to **employees** in the form of **salary** and **wages,** usually paid in cash, has tax consequences to both employees and employers. Below, we address the tax (and nontax) considerations of salary and wages from the employee's perspective followed by the employer's perspective.

Employee Considerations for Salary and Wages

Employees receiving salary generally earn a fixed amount of compensation for the year no matter how many hours they work. In addition, salaried employees may be eligible for bonuses based on satisfying certain criteria. In contrast, employees receiving wages generally get paid by the hour. Salary, bonus, and wages are taxed to employees as ordinary income. Employees generally report income from salary and wages as they receive it.[1] As we discussed in detail in Chapter 8, employees must pay **FICA taxes** on their wages.[2] FICA tax consists of both a Social Security and a Medicare component.

At the end of each year, employees receive a **Form W-2** (see Exhibit 12-1) from their employers summarizing their salary or wage compensation and the various withholding amounts made during the year.[3] Employees simply report their wages on Page 1, line 7 of the 1040 federal tax return and report their income taxes withheld on line 62 of Page 2. Self-employed taxpayers receive a Form 1099 indicating the compensation they received, which they report on Schedule C.

THE KEY FACTS

Employment-Related Forms

- **Form W-2**
  - Summarizes an employee's taxable salary and wages.
  - Provides annual federal and state withholding information.
  - Generated by employer on an annual basis.
- **Form W-4**
  - Supplies an employee's withholding information to employer.
  - Generated by employee.
  - Numbers reported on form remain constant unless employee makes changes.
- **Form 1099**
  - Summarizes an independent contractor's or nonemployee's taxable compensation.
  - Generated by person or entity paying the compensation.

Tax Withholding

When employees begin employment with a firm, they complete a **Form W-4** to supply the information the firm needs in order to withhold the correct amount of tax from each paycheck. Specifically, employees use Form W-4 to indicate (1) whether to withhold at the single rate or at the lower married rate, (2) the number of withholding allowances the employee chooses to claim (the more withholding allowances claimed, the less the withholding amount), and (3) whether the employee wants an additional amount of tax withheld each period above the amount based on the number of allowances claimed.

In general, the withholding tables are designed so that employers will withhold taxes fairly close to the amount of the taxpayer's actual tax liability—provided the employee claims the same number of withholding allowances on her W-4 as the number of personal and dependency exemptions she claims on her tax return. However, there are special circumstances in which this general rule does not hold. Taxpayers who itemize deductions, have deductible losses, file jointly with an

[1]Reg. §1.451-1(a).

[2]FICA stands for Federal Insurance Contributions Act.

[3]Compensation received by taxpayers who are self-employed is not considered to be salary and wages.

The 2015 Form W-2 was unavailable at press time. Please visit the IRS website (www.irs.gov) for the final 2015 form.

EXHIBIT 12-1 2014 Form W-2

	a Employee's social security number	OMB No. 1545-0008	Safe, accurate, FAST! Use IRS e-file	Visit the IRS website at www.irs.gov/efile
b Employer identification number (EIN)			1 Wages, tips, other compensation	2 Federal income tax withheld
c Employer's name, address, and ZIP code			3 Social security wages	4 Social security tax withheld
			5 Medicare wages and tips	6 Medicare tax withheld
			7 Social security tips	8 Allocated tips
d Control number			9	10 Dependent care benefits
e Employee's first name and initial	Last name	Suff.	11 Nonqualified plans	12a See instructions for box 12 Code
			13 Statutory employee ☐ Retirement plan ☐ Third-party sick pay ☐	12b Code
			14 Other	12c Code
				12d Code
f Employee's address and ZIP code				

15 State	Employer's state ID number	16 State wages, tips, etc.	17 State income tax	18 Local wages, tips, etc.	19 Local income tax	20 Locality name

Form **W-2** **Wage and Tax Statement** **2015** Department of the Treasury—Internal Revenue Service

Copy B—To Be Filed With Employee's FEDERAL Tax Return.
This information is being furnished to the Internal Revenue Service.

employed spouse, or have other special tax circumstances may need to adjust the number of withholding allowances claimed to have the desired amount of taxes withheld.[4]

Employer Considerations for Salary and Wages

Storyline Summary

Taxpayer:	TPI Corporation
Location:	San Diego, California
Ownership:	Publicly traded corporation
Industry:	Manufacturer of high-technology products
CEO:	Daniel Hewitt
Marginal tax rate:	35 percent
Current Situation:	Recruiting Julie Clark for VP of marketing position

[4]See IRS publication 505 "Tax Withholding and Estimated Tax" for other circumstances.

THE KEY FACTS

Compensation Deductibility for Accrual-Basis Taxpayers

- Compensation expense accrued at end of year is deductible in year accrued if:
  - Paid to an *unrelated* party within 2½ months of year-end.
- Compensation expense accrued at end of year is not *deductible when paid* if:
  - Paid to *related* party owning > 50 percent of corporate employer.

Deductibility of Salary Payments Employers computing taxable income under the cash method of accounting generally deduct salary and wages when they pay the employee.[5] Employers computing taxable income under the accrual method generally deduct wages payable to employees as the employees earn the wages.[6] This general rule holds even in situations when the employer accrues compensation expense in one year but actually pays the employee in the subsequent year, as long as the company makes the payment within 2½ months after the employer's year-end. If the employer pays the employee more than 2½ months after the employer's year-end, the wages are considered deferred compensation and are not deductible by the employer until the employee recognizes the salary as income (receives payment).[7] Because most employers pay regular salary and wages to employees each month (or more frequently), the 2½ month rule is likely to be more of an issue for accrued compensation, such as one-time year-end bonuses, than it is for normal wages.

In situations when the employer and employee are "related" parties, special rules apply. In this context, the definition of related parties includes an employee/shareholder who owns more than 50 percent of the value of the employer corporation.[8] When the corporation and employee/shareholder are related parties, a corporation is not allowed to deduct the compensation expense until the employee/shareholder (related party) includes the payment in income.[9] Therefore, for an accrual-method company paying compensation, such as wages or a bonus, to a related employee, the 2½ month rule does not apply. Because related parties are theoretically considered to be the same taxpayer to some extent, the tax laws limit their ability to accelerate deductions and enjoy the immediate tax benefits, while at the same time deferring income and delaying the payment of taxes.

The after-tax cost of providing this salary is generally much less than the before-tax cost.[10] The formula for computing the after-tax cost of the salary (the cost after subtracting the tax savings from the deduction), or any deductible expense, for that matter, is as follows:

Deductible expenditure × (1 − Marginal tax rate)

Example 12-1

What is PCC's before-tax and after-tax costs of paying Julie a $240,000 salary? (Note that PCC's marginal tax rate is 35 percent.)

Answer: $240,000 before taxes and $156,000 after taxes, computed as follows:

Description	Amount	Explanation
Before tax cost of salary:		
(1) Compensation	$240,000	
(2) (1 − marginal tax rate)	× 65%	(1 − 35%).
After-tax cost of salary	**$156,000**	(1) × (2).

[5]Reg. §1.461-1(a)(1).

[6]Reg. §1.461-1(a)(2). See Chapter 9 for a detailed discussion of the cash and accrual accounting methods.

[7]Reg. §1.404(b)-1T(A-2). We discuss tax issues and consequences relating to deferred compensation in Chapter 13.

[8]See §267(b) for the complete definition of "related" parties.

[9]§267(a)(2).

[10]As discussed in Chapter 8, employers are required to pay FICA taxes on employees' compensation. Employers may also be required to pay other expenses based on employee wages such as workers' compensation insurance.

TAXES IN THE REAL WORLD Are CEOs Rewarded for Tax Dodging?

In August of 2011, the Institute for Policy Studies reported that 25 U.S. companies paid their CEOs more than they paid the U.S. government in taxes. The list of companies includes: International Paper, General Electric, Verizon, Boeing, and Ford Motor Company. On average, the companies reported $1.6 billion in profits and $16.7 million in executive compensation. In total, the companies also reported 556 subsidiaries located in tax havens, $12.6 million in campaign contributions, and $129 million in lobbying expenditures (campaign contributions and lobbying expenditures are nondeductible for tax). On average, these CEOs were paid $5.9 million more than average of CEOs comprising the S&P 500.

Limits on salary deductibility. Employers are generally allowed to deduct reasonable compensation paid to employees.[11] Determining whether compensation is reasonable in amount is a **facts and circumstances test** that involves considering the duties of the employee, the complexities of the business, and the amount of salary compared with the income of the business among other things. The amount of salary in excess of the amount considered reasonable is not deductible. The reasonable compensation limit typically applies to closely held businesses where the employee is also an owner of the company or the employee is a relative of the business owner. For publicly traded corporations, another limitation applies that is generally more restrictive than the reasonableness limitation.

THE KEY FACTS

Limits on Salary Deductibility of Publicly Traded Corporations

- $1,000,000 maximum annual compensation deduction per person.
  - Limit applies to CEO and three other highest compensated officers (not including the CFO).
  - Does not apply to performance-based compensation.

Responding to a growing public perception that executives of publicly traded corporations were being overpaid at the expense of shareholders and that the government was subsidizing (paying a part of) the excess by allowing corporations to deduct the high salaries, in 1993 Congress enacted §162(m) of the Internal Revenue Code.[12] This provision limits the deduction for compensation paid by publicly traded corporations to covered employees to $1 million per year. Covered employees include the principal executive officer (CEO) and the next three highest paid officers [not including the principal financial officer (CFO)].[13] However, certain exceptions allow companies to pay and deduct compensation in excess of the $1 million limit. For example, the limit does not apply to compensation based on (1) performance (this is the most significant of the exceptions in terms of dollars and frequency of application), (2) commissions, (3) contributions to qualified retirement plans, or (4) other tax-free benefits.

While most publicly traded corporations are aware of and are sensitive to the limitation, they may take different approaches in dealing with it. For example, as described in the excerpt from its proxy statement (see Exhibit 12-2), Callaway Golf attempts to maximize its compensation deduction, yet it acknowledges that there are situations when, in order to achieve its nontax goals, it may provide compensation to executives that is not deductible.

[11]As we discussed in Chapter 9, all business expenses (not just compensation) must be reasonable in amount to be fully deductible.

[12]Nelson, Daniel, "Section 162(m) Revisited," *Tax Notes Today,* January 10, 2005, pp. 8–22.

[13]Notice 2007-49. Section 162(m) defines "covered employees" as the CEO and the four most highly compensated officers (as of the end of the year). In providing this definition, Section 162(m) references and relies on executive compensation rules provided in the Securities Exchange Act of 1934. In September of 2006, the SEC modified the executive compensation disclosure rules referenced in Section 162(m). Nevertheless, Section 162(m) has not been updated to reflect this change. To resolve the inconsistency in the definition of "covered employee" between the language in Section 162(m) and the modified executive compensation rules, the IRS issued Notice 2007-49.

EXHIBIT 12-2 Excerpt from Callaway Golf's 2014 Proxy Statement

The tax deductibility of compensation should be maximized where appropriate.

To the extent consistent with the Company's compensation strategy, the Company seeks to maximize the deductibility for tax purposes of all elements of compensation. In designing and approving the Company's executive compensation plans, the Compensation Committee considers the effect of all applicable tax regulations, including Section 162(m) of the Internal Revenue Code, which generally disallows a tax deduction to public corporations for nonqualifying compensation in excess of $1.0 million paid to the chief executive officer or certain of the Company's other executive officers. Although maximizing the tax deductibility of compensation is an important consideration, the Compensation Committee may from time to time approve compensation that does not qualify for deductibility where it is appropriate to do so in light of other compelling interests or objectives. In addition, because of ambiguities and uncertainties as to the application and interpretation of Section 162(m) and related regulations, and the fact that such regulations and interpretations may change from time to time (with potentially retroactive effect), no assurance can be given that compensation intended to satisfy the requirements for deductibility under Section 162(m) will in fact do so.

In contrast, State Street Corporation takes a slightly different approach. As indicated in the following excerpt from its proxy statement (see Exhibit 12-3), State Street caps its salaries at $1 million. Apparently, the firm wants to make sure salaries paid to executives are fully deductible.

EXHIBIT 12-3 Excerpt from State Street Bank's 2014 Proxy Statement

Tax Deductibility of Executive Compensation

Section 162(m) of the U.S. Internal Revenue Code, or Section 162(m), generally limits to $1 million the U.S. federal income tax deductibility of compensation paid in one year to any one of a group of specified employees, including our NEOs (other than our chief financial officer). Performance-based compensation is not subject to the limits on deductibility of Section 162(m), provided such compensation meets specified requirements, including shareholder approval of material terms of compensation. The Compensation Committee considers tax deductibility in making compensation decisions, to the extent deductibility is reasonably practicable and consistent with our other compensation objectives.

The difference in philosophy between Callaway and State Street may be driven by nontax considerations. To be deductible, compensation to executives in excess of $1 million generally must be performance-based. This means that the executives bear the risk that they won't receive the additional compensation if certain performance benchmarks, like stock-price targets, aren't met. Some companies may decide they don't want their executives to shoulder this risk, so they pay them salaries in excess of the deductible amount to guarantee a certain level of compensation. Companies may also decide to cap executive salaries at $1 million just to avoid the public perception that they are being fiscally irresponsible by paying more than the deductibility limits.

Example 12-2

Several years ago, TPI was actively searching for a new CEO. The board of directors eventually chose Daniel Hewitt. During negotiations, Daniel indicated he wanted a $2 million salary (Option 1) in addition to the equity-based compensation the board was offering. While this level of salary could be considered reasonable, the board of directors was concerned about the $1 million limitation on deductible salary, so the board offered an alternative proposal. Under this proposal, TPI would pay Daniel a $1 million salary and offer him an additional $1.2 million bonus, contingent on achieving realistic financial performance goals for TPI (Option 2). Confident he could meet the financial goals, Daniel accepted the offer. Assuming the performance goals are met, what is TPI's after-tax cost of providing the current year compensation under Option 1 and Option 2?

Answer: $1,650,000 under Option 1 and $1,430,000 under Option 2, computed as follows:

	Option 1 ($2,000,000 salary $0 bonus)	Option 2 ($1,000,000 salary $1,200,000 bonus)	Explanation
Before-tax cost:			
(1) Total compensation	$2,000,000	$2,200,000	Salary + bonus.
(2) Deductible amount	$1,000,000	$2,200,000	Option 1: $1M salary not deductible.
(3) Marginal tax rate	× 35%	× 35%	
(4) Tax savings from compensation deduction	$ 350,000	$ 770,000	(2) × (3).
After-tax cost	$1,650,000	$1,430,000	(1) − (4).

Assuming the performance goals are met, both parties benefit from the arrangement. Daniel prefers Option 2 because it provides him with $200,000 more of before-tax compensation ($2.2M − $2M). TPI also prefers Option 2 because it costs $220,000 less after taxes than Option 1 ($1,650,000 − $1,430,000). Of course, Daniel is the one who must bear the risk of the contingent compensation in Option 2, so he must consider this risk before accepting the offer.

As this example illustrates, the $1 million deduction limitation can have a considerable impact on the after-tax cost of providing compensation to corporate executives. However, employers frequently utilize the options described above to craft offers that meet the needs of both parties.

LO 12-2

EQUITY-BASED COMPENSATION

continued from page 12-1...

As she read TPI's offer letter more carefully, Julie discovered that on the first day of January following her acceptance of the offer, she would be granted 10,000 shares of restricted stock, 50 incentive stock options (ISOs), and 200 nonqualified options (NQOs). Each of the ISOs and NQOs gives her the right to purchase 100 shares of stock at a fixed price equal to the market value of TPI stock on the date of grant. As she read on, Julie noticed that she would not be able to exercise either type of stock option (i.e., purchase TPI stock for the exercise price stated in the options) until the options vested (the options become hers when they vest), which will be two years from the grant date. Further, Julie understood that, after the restricted stock vests (one year from the grant date on January 1), she would be free to do what she wanted with it. The last detail Julie noticed when reading this part of the offer letter was that both types of options will expire 10 years from the grant date. She understood this to mean that if she did not exercise her options sometime before their expiration date, she would lose them.

Although it was obvious to Julie that the value of the options and restricted stock would increase as the share price of TPI increased from the current share price of $5 per share, she remained unsure about the terminology used in this section of the letter, and she realized she needed to know more about the economic and tax implications of stock options and restricted stock before making her decision.

to be continued...

THE KEY FACTS

Equity-Based Compensation

- Stock Options
  - Allow employees to purchase stock at a discount.
- Restricted Stock
  - Form of compensation that provides actual stock ownership to employee after restrictions lapse.

Equity-based compensation such as stock options and restricted stock provides risks and potential rewards not available with other forms of compensation. If the employer's stock price increases after it grants options and restricted stock, employees can be rewarded handsomely. On the other hand, if employer stock prices don't increase, the value of restricted stock will be limited and stock options will expire worthless.

Employers use equity-based compensation, in part, to motivate their employees to take ownership in their companies. When employees hold employer options and stock, their compensation is more directly tied to the fortunes of their employer and its shareholders—employees' compensation increases in tandem with their employer's stock price. This philosophy is reflected in an excerpt from Adobe's proxy statement presented in Exhibit 12-4.

EXHIBIT 12-4 Excerpt from Adobe's 2014 Proxy Statement

Goals of Equity Compensation

We use equity compensation to motivate and reward strong corporate performance and to retain valued NEOs. We also use equity incentive awards as a means to attract and recruit qualified executives. We believe that equity awards serve to align the interest of our NEOs with those of our stockholders by rewarding them for stock price growth and the achievement of key operational goals. By having a significant majority of our NEOs' target TDC payable in the form of equity and, thus, subject to higher risk and longer vesting than cash compensation, our NEOs are motivated to align themselves with our stockholders by taking actions that will benefit Adobe and its stockholders in the long term.

THE KEY FACTS

Stock Option Terminology

- *Incentive stock options* satisfy certain tax code requirements to provide favorable tax treatment to employees.
- *Nonqualified stock options* are any options that don't meet the requirements for being classified as incentive stock options.
- The *grant date* is the date employees are initially allocated stock options.
- The *exercise date* is the date that employees purchase stock using their options.
- The *exercise price* (or strike price) is the amount paid to acquire shares with stock options.
- The *bargain element* is the difference between the fair market value of stock and the exercise price on the exercise date.
- The *vesting date* is the time when stock options granted can be exercised.

In addition to its motivational effects, equity-based compensation has traditionally brought employers cash flow benefits as well. How? Unless employers purchase their own stock in a market transaction to satisfy option exercises and stock grants, there are no cash outflows associated with this form of compensation. In fact, employers actually *receive* cash from their employees in the amount of the exercise price on the options exercised. There are a couple of downsides to this benefit, however. First, employers experience the opportunity cost of selling shares at a discounted price to employees rather than selling the shares at fair market value on the open market. Second, because employers must issue new shares to satisfy option exercises and stock grants, the total number of shares outstanding increases, and, therefore, earnings per share are diluted, which is a detriment to existing shareholders. The only way for employers to mitigate this problem without increasing earnings is to use their cash reserves to acquire their own shares to satisfy the options exercise.[14] However, from a cash-flow perspective, this is no different than paying cash compensation.

Stock Options

As a form of equity-based compensation, stock options have two important characteristics: (1) employees must use cash to purchase the employer's stock once they are allowed to exercise the options and (2) employees often never exercise options when share prices are depressed. When stock options **vest,** employees are legally entitled to buy or exercise employer stock at a stipulated price, referred to as the **exercise price** or **strike price.** Options may be exercised anytime between the vesting date and the expiration date of the options.[15] If the share price does not go above the exercise

[14]Because earnings per share is calculated by dividing earnings by the number of shares of stock outstanding, for a given level of earnings, earnings per share could even increase when new shares are issued to satisfy option exercises if earnings increase by an amount that more than offsets the effect of issuing new shares into the market.

[15]Vesting dates are frequently specified as future calendar dates or they may be triggered when certain events occur (i.e., predefined performance objectives are met, or the company has been sold).

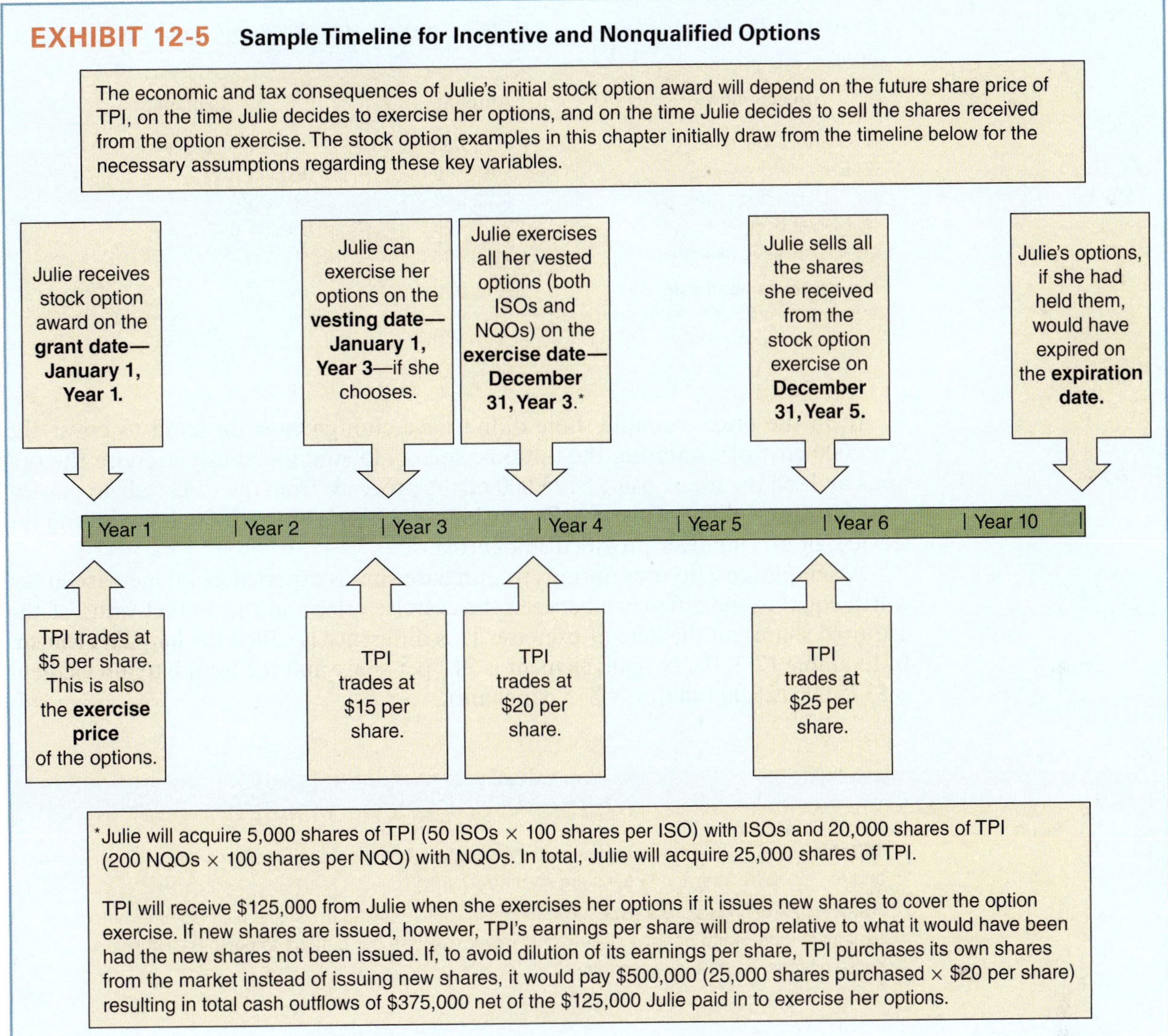

price at some point during this interval, employees will not exercise their options and the options will expire without providing them any benefit.

EXHIBIT 12-5 Sample Timeline for Incentive and Nonqualified Options
The economic and tax consequences of Julie's initial stock option award will depend on the future share price of TPI, on the time Julie decides to exercise her options, and on the time Julie decides to sell the shares received from the option exercise. The stock option examples in this chapter initially draw from the timeline below for the necessary assumptions regarding these key variables.
Julie receives stock option award on the grant date—January 1, Year 1.
Julie can exercise her options on the vesting date—January 1, Year 3—if she chooses.
Julie exercises all her vested options (both ISOs and NQOs) on the exercise date—December 31, Year 3.*
Julie sells all the shares she received from the stock option exercise on December 31, Year 5.
Julie's options, if she had held them, would have expired on the expiration date.
| Year 1 | Year 2 | Year 3 | Year 4 | Year 5 | Year 6 | Year 10
TPI trades at $5 per share. This is also the exercise price of the options.
TPI trades at $15 per share.
TPI trades at $20 per share.
TPI trades at $25 per share.
*Julie will acquire 5,000 shares of TPI (50 ISOs × 100 shares per ISO) with ISOs and 20,000 shares of TPI (200 NQOs × 100 shares per NQO) with NQOs. In total, Julie will acquire 25,000 shares of TPI.
TPI will receive $125,000 from Julie when she exercises her options if it issues new shares to cover the option exercise. If new shares are issued, however, TPI's earnings per share will drop relative to what it would have been had the new shares not been issued. If, to avoid dilution of its earnings per share, TPI purchases its own shares from the market instead of issuing new shares, it would pay $500,000 (25,000 shares purchased × $20 per share) resulting in total cash outflows of $375,000 net of the $125,000 Julie paid in to exercise her options.

As suggested in Exhibit 12-5, the future value of stock option awards will depend on the exercise price, the company's future share price, the exercise date of the options, and the timing for selling the shares received from the **option exercise.**

Example 12-3

Given the assumptions in the stock option timeline shown in Exhibit 12-5 (above), how much will it cost Julie to exercise all of her options at the end of year 3 (before taxes), and how much will she have if she were to immediately sell the acquired shares (before taxes)?[16]

(continued on page 12-10)

[16]According to the facts presented in Exhibit 12-5, Julie could have exercised her options as early as the vesting date for her options at the end of year 2. We assume she waits one year to exercise her options to better illustrate the implications of deferring the option exercise beyond the vesting date. In reality, it is quite common for employees to exercise their stock options on the vesting date.

Answer: $125,000 cost to exercise; $375,000 remaining after sale before taxes, calculated as follows:

Description	Amount	Explanation
(1) Shares acquired	25,000	(20,000 NQOs and 5,000 ISOs).
(2) Exercise price	$ 5	Exhibit 12-5.
(3) Cash needed to exercise	$125,000	(1) × (2).
(4) Market price	$ 20	Exhibit 12-5.
(5) Market value of shares	$500,000	(1) × (4).
Net proceeds upon sale	$375,000	(5) − (3).

If, in the prior example, Julie didn't have enough cash on hand to cover the $125,000 cost of exercising the options, she could simultaneously exercise the options and sell the stock, using $125,000 of the proceeds from the stock sale to pay for exercising the options. This so-called cashless exercise is typically facilitated using the services of an employer-provided stockbroker.

An employee who uses options to purchase shares experiences an increase in net worth equal to the difference between the exercise price and the market value of the acquired shares on the date of exercise. This difference is called the **bargain element.** In Example 12-3, the bargain element is $15 per share and the total bargain element is $375,000 (25,000 shares × $15 per share).

Example 12-4

What if: What is Julie's economic loss from her stock options if the TPI shares fall to $3 per share and remain there after the options are granted?

Answer: Zero. If TPI's stock price never increases above the $5 per share exercise price before the expiration date of the options, Julie would never exercise her options to purchase TPI shares, and those options would expire worthless.

Employee Considerations for Stock Options

Stock options are classified for tax purposes as either **nonqualified stock options** (NQOs) or **incentive stock options** (ISOs). They differ in terms of when and how the bargain element is taxed. To appreciate these differences, it's important to understand what happens on the **grant date,** the **vesting date,** the **exercise date,** and the date the shares are ultimately sold.

For either type of option, employees experience no tax consequences on the grant date and vesting date. However, when they exercise *nonqualified* stock options, employees report ordinary income equal to the total bargain element on the shares of stock acquired (as if they were sold)—whether they hold the shares or sell them immediately.[17] A taxpayer's basis in nonqualified stock options acquired is the fair market value on the date of exercise. Thus the basis includes the exercise price plus the ordinary income the taxpayer recognizes on the exercise (the bargain element). In contrast, when *incentive* stock options are exercised, employees don't report any income for regular tax purposes (as long as they don't immediately sell

[17]The bargain element income is reflected on employees' Form W-2 and the applicable income and payroll taxes are withheld.

their shares). Their basis in shares acquired with ISOs is the exercise price. The holding period for stock shares acquired with NQOs and ISOs begins on the exercise date.

When taxpayers exercise incentive stock options, the bargain element is added to their alternative minimum taxable income. This increases the likelihood that taxpayers exercising incentive stock options will be required to pay the alternative minimum tax—this is almost always true if the bargain element is large. We discuss the alternative minimum tax in Chapter 9.

Example 12-5

On the date Julie exercises her options (Example 12-3), she acquires 20,000 shares of TPI with NQOs (200 NQOs × 100 shares per NQO) and 5,000 shares with ISOs (50 ISOs × 100 shares per ISO). Given that the bargain element for each share she purchased is $15, how much income will Julie report on the day she exercises the options?

Answer: $300,000 ordinary income from the NQOs, calculated below, and $0 for the ISOs (she must include the bargain element of $75,000 on the 5,000 ISOs in her AMT calculation).

Description	Amount	Explanation
(1) Shares acquired with NQOs	20,000	
(2) Market price per share	$ 20	Exhibit 12-5.
(3) Exercise price	5	Exhibit 12-5.
(4) Bargain element per share	$ 15	(2) − (3).
Bargain element (ordinary income)	$300,000	(1) × (4).

What is Julie's basis in the 20,000 shares she acquired with NQOs?

Answer: $400,000. [$100,000 (20,000 shares × $5 per share exercise price) + $300,000 (bargain element taxed as ordinary income).]

What is Julie's basis in the 5,000 shares she acquired through ISOs?

Answer: $25,000. (5,000 shares acquired × $5 per share exercise price.)

Once they've exercised their stock options, employees face different choices depending on the type of option. Employees who purchase stock with NQOs and retain the stock are in the same position for tax purposes as any other investor: Their basis in the stock is the fair market value on the date they exercised the options (this is the exercise price of the stock plus the bargain element), and any *future* appreciation or depreciation of the stock will be treated for tax purposes as either short-term or long-term capital gain(s) or loss(es) depending on the holding period, which begins on the date of exercise. Moreover, employees using NQOs to purchase employer stock are also in the same economic position as any other investor in that the value of the stock is subject to investment risk (the risk that the value of the stock will go down). To avoid overweighting their investment portfolios with a single stock, employees exercising NQOs often immediately sell all or a significant portion of the shares acquired on the exercise date, a practice referred to as a **same-day sale.**[18]

[18]In addition to limiting investment risk, employees also engage in same-day sales to cover all or a portion of the exercise price associated with the options exercised, to pay the taxes triggered when nonqualified options are exercised, and to fund planned purchases.

Example 12-6

THE KEY FACTS

Nonqualified Stock Options (NQOs)

- No tax consequences on grant date.
- On exercise date, bargain element is treated as ordinary (compensation) income to employee.
  - Employee holds stock with holding period beginning on date of exercise.
- Employers deduct bargain element as compensation expense on exercise date.

What if: Suppose that five years after Julie exercised her NQOs and acquired 20,000 TPI shares with a basis of $20 per share, she sold all of the shares for $25 per share. What is the amount and character of the gain she will recognize on the sale?

Answer: $100,000 long-term capital gain, calculated as follows:

Description	Amount	Explanation
(1) Amount realized (sale proceeds)	$500,000	(20,000 × $25).
(2) Tax basis	400,000	Example 12-5.
Long-term capital gain recognized	$100,000	(1) − (2).

What if: If Julie sold the shares for $25 per share six months after she exercised them, what is the character of the $100,000 gain she recognized on the sale?

Answer: Short-term capital gain because she held the shares for one year or less before selling.

Employees who acquire shares through the exercise of ISOs also have an additional tax benefit: if they hold such shares *for at least two years after the grant date and one year after the exercise date,* they will not be taxed until they sell the stock.[19] When they sell, employees will treat the difference between the sale proceeds and the tax basis (the exercise price) as a long-term capital gain in the year of disposition. Thus, employees prefer ISOs to NQOs.

Example 12-7

What if: Suppose that five years after Julie exercised her ISOs and acquired 5,000 TPI shares with a basis of $5 per share, she sold all of the shares for $25 per share. What is the amount and character of the gain she will recognize on the sale?

Answer: Julie will recognize a $100,000 long-term capital gain, calculated as follows:

Description	Amount	Explanation
(1) Amount realized	$125,000	(5,000 × $25).
(2) Tax basis	25,000	Example 12-5.
Long-term capital gain recognized	$100,000	(1) − (2).

If the two-year and one-year requirements are not met, the premature sale of stock is classified as a **disqualifying disposition,** and the bargain element is taxed at the time of sale *as if* the option had been an NQO. Thus, when holders of ISOs execute same-day sales, they forgo the benefit of taxing the bargain element at lower capital gains rates—but they do so in order to eliminate the investment risk they would otherwise have to bear if they attempted to satisfy the two-year and one-year holding period requirements.

Example 12-8

What if: Assume that Julie exercised her ISOs and executed a same-day sale of the 5,000 shares on the vesting date (January 1, year 3) when the share price was $15, what is the amount and character of income she will recognize on these transactions?

[19]§422(a)(1).

Answer: $50,000 ordinary income. Because Julie's sale is a disqualifying disposition, the transactions are recast as though she exercised nonqualified options. See computations below.

Description	Amount	Explanation
(1) Shares acquired with ISOs that were disqualified (became NQOs)	5,000	
(2) Market price per share	$ 15	
(3) Exercise price	5	Exhibit 12-5.
(4) Bargain element per share	$ 10	(2) − (3).
Bargain element (ordinary income)	$50,000	(1) × (4).

THE KEY FACTS

Incentive Stock Options (ISOs)

- No tax consequences on grant date.
- No tax consequences on exercise date if employee holds for two years after grant date and one year after exercise date.
  - If holding requirements are not met (if there is a disqualifying disposition), option becomes an NQO.
- When employee sells stock, employee recognizes long-term capital gain on difference between selling price and exercise price.
- No deduction for employers unless employee doesn't meet holding requirements.

TAXES IN THE REAL WORLD Stock Options

Sometimes, stock option compensation is the icing on the cake. Other times, options are the entire cake. According to Oracle Corporation's 2014 proxy statement, it paid founder and CEO Larry Ellison an entire $1 in cash ($1 is not a misprint) and stock options worth more than $67 million. No need to pay taxes on the compensation now; once the shares vest, Mr. Ellison can choose when to exercise the shares and, consequently, time his tax payments as well.

Source: Oracle Corporation 2014 Proxy Statement.

Employer Considerations for Stock Options As is true for employees, an employer's tax treatment of stock options depends on whether the options are NQOs or ISOs.

Nonqualified options. With NQOs, employers deduct the bargain element that employees recognize as income when the employees exercise the NQOs. From the employer's perspective, no other date is relevant for tax purposes.

Example 12-9

What if: Suppose that in year 3, Julie exercises NQOs to acquire 20,000 shares of TPI, and she reports $300,000 of ordinary income for the bargain element of the exercise (see Example 12-5). How much compensation expense for Julie's stock option exercise can TPI deduct in year 3?

Answer: $300,000. TPI can deduct the bargain element of Julie's exercise.

Note that this tax deduction is not tied to a cash payment. Thus, unless employers purchase their own shares to satisfy their employees' stock option exercises, they'll be entitled to a tax deduction without incurring any cash outflow.

Another important tax benefit associated with NQOs derives from the fact that income from NQOs is usually viewed as performance-based compensation. As a result, employers frequently use these options to circumvent the $1,000,000 deduction limitation imposed by §162(m). In fact, the stock option income of key executives at publicly traded companies usually dwarfs their cash salaries.

Incentive stock options. Employers typically don't view incentive stock options as favorably as NQOs, because (1) ISOs don't provide them with the same tax benefits (no tax deduction) and (2) the IRS regulatory requirements for ISOs can be cumbersome. That is, as long as the employee doesn't sale the stock in a disqualifying disposition, the employer does not get a tax deduction for ISOs. For this reason, firms with high marginal tax rates may lose significant tax benefits by issuing ISOs rather than NQOs. On the other hand, start-up companies or firms with net operating losses may actually benefit by issuing ISOs instead of NQOs. Due to their low or nonexistent marginal tax rates, companies in this position may not lose tax benefits by granting ISOs; however, because of the potential tax benefits ISOs provide to their employees relative to NQOs, they may be able to persuade their employees to accept relatively fewer ISOs.

ETHICS

Many companies use stock options as a form of equity compensation—to motivate executives and key employees. Some stock option issuers have either back dated and/or repriced stock options. Backdating is an illegal practice where a company, after-the-fact, chooses a date (timed retroactively) where the stock price was at its lowest point in order to maximize executive compensation. Stock option repricing is used when stock options are underwater (the market price is below the strike price). Repricing simply resets the strike price to a price below the current market price. While backdating options is illegal and obviously unethical, what do you think about the practice of repricing stock options?

Accounting issues. Historically, a major reason that companies used stock options to compensate their employees was the favorable accounting treatment stock options were afforded. Before 2006, companies were not required to reflect stock options as an expense in their financial statements. Thus, before 2006, companies that used stock options in lieu of cash salaries typically reported higher earnings than equally situated firms that were not heavy users of stock options. To increase the comparability of financial statements as well as to ensure that the true cost of stock options would be reflected in the financial statements, the FASB mandated the expensing of stock options for financial accounting purposes for years beginning on or after January 1, 2006.[20] Under the new rules, firms must measure the economic value of options on the grant date and then amortize this cost on a straight-line basis over the vesting period of the options.[21]

Example 12-10

What if: Assume that an accounting employee benefits specialist calculated the economic value of Julie's stock option grant (NQOs and ISOs) to be $32,000. Also assume that Julie's options vest 50 percent in year 1 (the year of the grant) and 50 percent in year 2. What compensation expense for book purposes would TPI report for Julie's stock options in year 1 and year 2?

Answer: $16,000 ($32,000 × 50%) in year 1 and $16,000 in year 2.

THE KEY FACTS

Stock Option Expense: GAAP vs. Tax

- For tax purposes, employers deduct the bargain element of NQOs on exercise date but receive no tax deduction for ISOs unless they become disqualified.
- For GAAP purposes, employers expense the estimated value of the option pro rata over the vesting period.

As you probably realize by now, the tax rules governing the treatment of stock options differ markedly from generally accepted accounting principles in terms of both the amount and the timing of the stock option expense. To compare the tax and book treatment, we present TPI's book expense and tax deduction resulting from its stock option grant to Julie (given prior assumptions) in Exhibit 12-6.

The tremendous difference between the book and tax numbers presented in Exhibit 12-6 is driven by the increase in TPI's share price, from $5 on the date of

[20]Accounting Standards Codification (ASC) 718, Stock Compensation.

[21]Although the exercise price of compensatory stock options typically equals the stock price on the date of grant, compensatory options are, nevertheless, economically valuable on the grant date. They have economic value because the stock price may eventually exceed the exercise price before the options expire. To determine economic value, firms typically use either the Black-Scholes option pricing model or the binomial option pricing model.

EXHIBIT 12-6 **TPI's Tax Deductions and Book Expense from Stock Option Grant to Julie**

	Tax Deduction if Stock Price Increases	Tax Deduction if Stock Price Decreases	Book Expense
Year 1	$ 0	$0	$16,000
Year 2	0	0	16,000
Year 3	300,000	0*	0

*There would be no exercise because the exercise price exceeds the stock price.

grant to $20 on the date of exercise. The economic valuation of the stock options used to determine the book expense did not anticipate the extent of the stock appreciation before exercise.

Restricted Stock

Like stock options described above, **restricted stock** can't be sold or otherwise treated as owned by employees until they legally have the right to sell the shares on the vesting date. However, unlike the stock acquired through options exercises, employees receive restricted stock on the vesting date *without having to pay for it,* after which they can either sell it immediately or retain it.

As indicated in the timeline in Exhibit 12-7, the initial value of an employee's restricted stock award depends on the share price of the stock on the vesting date.

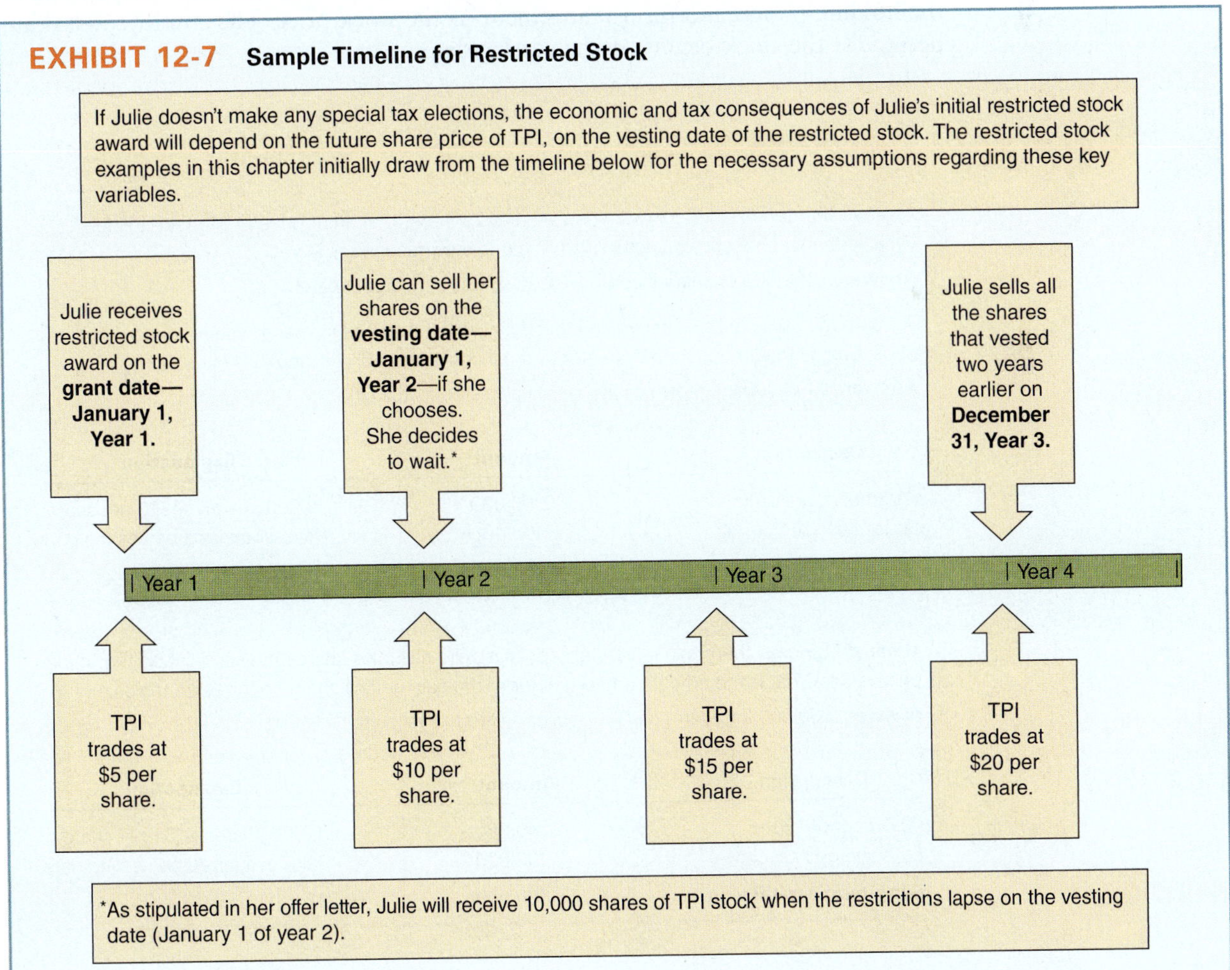

EXHIBIT 12-7 Sample Timeline for Restricted Stock
If Julie doesn't make any special tax elections, the economic and tax consequences of Julie's initial restricted stock award will depend on the future share price of TPI, on the vesting date of the restricted stock. The restricted stock examples in this chapter initially draw from the timeline below for the necessary assumptions regarding these key variables.
Julie receives restricted stock award on the grant date—January 1, Year 1.
Julie can sell her shares on the vesting date—January 1, Year 2—if she chooses. She decides to wait.*
Julie sells all the shares that vested two years earlier on December 31, Year 3.
Year 1
Year 2
Year 3
Year 4
TPI trades at $5 per share.
TPI trades at $10 per share.
TPI trades at $15 per share.
TPI trades at $20 per share.
*As stipulated in her offer letter, Julie will receive 10,000 shares of TPI stock when the restrictions lapse on the vesting date (January 1 of year 2).

Example 12-11

Given the assumptions regarding the restricted stock in Exhibit 12-7, by how much would Julie's wealth increase on the vesting date?

Answer: Julie's wealth would increase by $100,000 (10,000 shares × $10 per share).

What if: Assuming that the stock decreased to $3 per share on the vesting date, by how much would Julie's wealth increase or decrease on the vesting date?

Answer: $30,000 increase ($3 × 10,000). Until the vesting date, Julie was not entitled to any economic benefit from the restricted stock. On the vesting date, however, she is entitled to stock valued at $30,000. Thus, the vesting of Julie's restricted stock increases her wealth even if the stock price decreases between the grant date and vesting date (unlike options that would be worthless).

THE KEY FACTS

Restricted Stock *without* §83(b) Election

- No tax consequences on grant date.
- Employee recognizes ordinary income on fair market value of stock on vesting date.
- Holding period for stock begins on vesting date.
- Employer deducts fair market value of stock on vesting date.

Employee Considerations for Restricted Stock Restricted stock is taxed like NQOs with two important distinctions: while employees receiving NQOs are taxed at ordinary rates on the bargain element of the shares when they exercise their options, employees receiving restricted stock are taxed on the *full fair market value* of the shares *on the date the restricted stock vests.* They are taxed on the fair market value of the stock because they are entitled to receive the stock without any payment requirements (contrast this with the exercise price paid for stock options). Any subsequent appreciation in the value of the stock is taxed as either long-term or short-term capital gain(s) or loss(es) when the taxpayer sells the stock, depending on the holding period and future movement of the stock price. The employee's holding period for the stock begins on the vesting date.

Example 12-12

Assume that the restricted stock vests in year 2 when the market price is $10 (see Exhibit 12-7). What is the amount and character of the income Julie recognizes in year 2?

Answer: $100,000 ordinary income (10,000 shares × $10 per share).

Assume the same facts as above and that Julie sells the shares in year 4 when the market price is $20? What is the amount and character of the income she will recognize on the sale?

Answer: $100,000 long-term capital gain, calculated as follows:

Description	Amount	Explanation
(1) Amount realized	$200,000	10,000 shares × $20 per share.
(2) Tax basis	100,000	Gain recognized on vesting date.
Long-term capital gain	$100,000	(1) − (2).

What if: Assume the original facts except that Julie sells the shares in year 4 when the market price is $4. What is the amount and character of the gain or loss she recognizes on the sale?

Answer: $60,000 long-term capital loss, calculated as follows:

Description	Amount	Explanation
(1) Amount realized	$ 40,000	10,000 shares × $4 per share.
(2) Adjusted basis	100,000	Gain recognized on vesting date.
Long-term capital loss	($60,000)	(1) − (2).

§83(b) election. The tax laws allow employees who receive restricted stock to make a tax election that can significantly change the tax consequences by treating the stock nearly the same as vested stock. Up until 30 days after the grant date, employees can make what is known as an **§83(b) election;** once made, however, this election is irrevocable. If the employee makes the §83(b) election, the value of the restricted stock is taxed on the grant date rather than the date on which the stock vests. The effect of the election is to accelerate the tax on the market value of the restricted shares—which, you'll recall from Chapter 3, is usually not desirable from a tax planning perspective. However, if the employee expects the share price to increase after the grant date, making the election converts ordinary income to long-term capital gain (which, assuming the shares are held for more than one year after the grant date, results in a preferential tax rate when the taxpayer sells the shares). Without the §83(b) election, the employee reports no income when the shares are granted, but is taxed on their fair market value at ordinary rates when the stock vests. With the §83(b) election, the employee simply pays tax at ordinary rates on the market value of the shares at the grant date.

THE KEY FACTS

Restricted Stock *with* Section §83(b) Election

- On grant date, employee recognizes market value ofstock as ordinary income.
- Employee takes fair market value basis in stock.
- Holding period for stock begins on grant date.
- If employee never vests, no deduction for basis in stock.
- Employer deducts value of stock on grant date.

Example 12-13

What if: How much tax on the restricted stock would Julie pay in year 1 if she does not make an §83(b) election?

Answer: $0. The stock has not vested yet so she has no income.

What if: How much tax on the restricted stock would Julie pay in year 1 if she makes an §83(b) election?

Answer: $20,000 [$50,000 ordinary income (10,000 shares × $5 per share) × 40 percent marginal ordinary tax rate].

What if: How much tax would Julie pay in year 2 on the restricted stock (the year the restricted stock vests) if she did *not* make an §83(b) election in year 1 (the stock is trading at $10 a share on the vesting date)?

Answer: $40,000 [$100,000 ordinary income (10,000 shares × $10 per share) × 40 percent marginal ordinary tax rate].

What if: How much tax would Julie pay in year 2 on the restricted stock if she made the §83(b) election in year 1?

Answer: $0. With the §83(b) election, Julie treated the stock as though it vested in year 1, not year 2, so she does not have a taxable event in year 2 when the stock actually vests.

What if: How much tax would Julie pay in year 4 on the restricted stock when she sells the stock for $20 a share (on December 31) if she did *not* make the §83(b) election in year 1?

Answer: $20,000 [$200,000 (10,000 × $20) − $100,000 tax basis (fair market value on vesting date in year 2) − $100,000. $100,000 × 20 percent long-term capital gains rate = $20,000].

What if: How much tax would Julie pay in year 4 on the restricted stock when she sells the stock for $20 a share (on December 31) if she made the §83(b) election in year 1?

Answer: $30,000 [$200,000 (10,000 × $20) − $50,000 tax basis (fair market value in year 1 when made §83(b) election) = $150,000. $150,000 × 20 percent long-term capital gains rate = $30,000].

Given the analyses above, what amount of taxes would Julie save by making the §83(b) election (ignore time value of money)?

(continued on page 12-18)

Answer: $10,000 ($50,000 with election; $60,000 without), computed as follows:

Taxes Payable		
Description	**With Election**	**Without Election**
Year 1 taxes on ordinary income	$20,000	$ 0
Year 2 taxes on ordinary income	0	40,000
Year 4 taxes on long-term capital gains	30,000	20,000
Total taxes	$50,000	$60,000

Note that Julie reduces her taxable income because the election allowed her to convert $50,000 in income from ordinary income taxed at 40 percent into long-term capital gain taxed at 20 percent.

Also note that this computation overstates to some degree the benefits of making the §83(b) election because it ignores the time value of money. In order to have a greater portion of her gains taxed at the preferential capital gain rates, Julie gave up some tax deferral when she accelerated $50,000 of income from year 4 into year 1.

Employees making the §83(b) election essentially trade off some additional current tax now in order to convert ordinary income into a long-term capital gain later. Accordingly, the §83(b) election is advisable when the potential for growth in the stock value is high and the amount of additional current tax is manageable. If an employee makes an §83(b) election and then forfeits the stock for any reason, the employee cannot deduct the loss on the forfeiture.[22] Thus, the risk of making the election is that if the employee forfeits the stock, tax would have been paid on value never received.

Employer Considerations for Restricted Stock Like the tax treatment of NQOs, the employer's deduction for restricted stock equals the amount of ordinary income reported by its employees. The timing of the deduction is determined by the employee's decision regarding the §83(b) election. If the employee makes an §83(b) election, the employer claims the deduction in the year the restricted stock is granted. Otherwise, the employer claims a deduction when the restrictions lapse. Some employers believe that restricted stock is a superior form of compensation to stock options. See Apple Inc.'s proxy statement in Exhibit 12-8.

EXHIBIT 12-8 Excerpt from Apple Inc.'s 2014 Proxy Statement

The Role of Long-Term Equity Awards

Emphasis on RSUs. The Company has traditionally believed that long-term equity awards in the form of RSUs are the most effective way to attract and retain a talented executive team and align executives' interests with those of shareholders. Accordingly, the Company's executive compensation program in recent years has been weighted considerably toward long-term equity awards rather than cash compensation. The Company believes RSUs create incentives for performance and further align executives' interests with those of shareholders because an RSU's value increases or decreases in conjunction with the Company's stock price. As explained in more detail above, the Company is committed to including performance criteria in a portion of the equity awards it grants to executive officers in the future. At Mr. Cook's request, the Compensation Committee began this initiative in 2013 by amending his 2011 RSU award to include performance-based vesting conditions.

The accounting treatment for restricted stock is similar to the accounting treatment for stock options.[23] If restricted stock grants vest over time, the value of restricted stock on the *date of grant* is expensed pro rata over the vesting period.

[22]Reg. §1.83-2(a).
[23]ASC 718.

Example 12-14

What if: Given the assumptions in Exhibit 12-7, what amount can TPI deduct for tax purposes in year 1 and in year 2 assuming Julie does *not* make an §83(b) election?

Answer: $0 in year 1 and $100,000 in year 2 (10,000 shares of restricted stock vested × $10 per share market price at vesting date).

What if: What amount can TPI deduct in year 1 and in year 2 if Julie *does* make an §83(b) election?

Answer: $50,000 in year 1 (10,000 shares of restricted stock awarded × $5 per share market price on the grant date) and $0 in year 2.

What amount is TPI's compensation expense for financial accounting purposes for Julie's restricted stock in year 1 and in year 2?

Answer: $50,000 book expense in year 1. Because the value of Julie's restricted stock award on the date of grant is $50,000, TPI expenses the award on its books over the vesting period, which in this case is just one year (it has a one-year vesting period).

Equity-Based Compensation Summary

To summarize our discussion of the tax treatment of equity-based compensation, Exhibit 12-9 highlights the general tax treatment of NQOs, ISOs, and restricted stock on a per share basis from both employee and employer perspectives given an arbitrary time series of share prices. In addition to future share prices, the exhibit assumes options are exercisable for the share price on the grant date.

THE KEY FACTS

Restricted Stock Expense: GAAP vs. Tax

- For tax purposes, employers deduct the market value of stock when the employee recognizes income. For GAAP purposes, employers deduct the grant date value over the vesting period.

EXHIBIT 12-9 Reportable Income and Deductions from Equity-Based Compensation (for given time frame and stock prices)

	Party Affected	NQOs	ISOs	Restricted Stock
Grant date–year 1 Stock (exercise) price = $1/share	Employee	No effect	No effect	No effect
	Employer	No effect	No effect	No effect
Vesting date–year 4 Stock price = $6/share	Employee	No effect	No effect	$6/share ordinary income
	Employer	No effect	No effect	$6/share ordinary deduction
Exercise date for options–year 6 Stock price = $11/share	Employee	$10/share ordinary income	No effect*	N/A
	Employer	$10/share ordinary deduction	No effect	N/A
Sale date–year 8 Stock price = $16/share	Employee	$5/share LT capital gain	$15/share LT capital gain	$10/share Capital gain
	Employer	No effect	No effect	No effect

*$10 per share is included in alternative minimum taxable income.

LO 12-3

FRINGE BENEFITS

continued from page 12-7. . .

The final section of TPI's offer letter indicated Julie would receive fringe benefits in the form of health and dental insurance (value of $18,000), $750,000 of group-term life insurance, a biennial $30,000 automobile allowance, monthly parking, and a flexible spending account for medical expenses. ■

Employees generally receive most of their compensation in the form of cash salary or wages. However, employers often provide noncash benefits to employees in addition to their cash compensation. These **fringe benefits** range from the common (health insurance) to the exotic (use of a corporate aircraft). As a general rule, because fringe benefits are employee compensation, they are taxable to the employee on receipt. In fact, fringe benefits are specifically mentioned in the definition of gross income. As we indicated in Chapter 5, IRC §61(a) indicates that, "gross income means all income from whatever source derived, including . . . (1) Compensation for services, including fees, commissions, *fringe benefits,* and similar items (emphasis added)." This definition of income notwithstanding, the tax laws specifically *exclude* certain fringe benefits from an employee's gross income. Thus, some fringe benefits are taxable and others are not.

Taxable Fringe Benefits

THE KEY FACTS

Taxable Fringe Benefits

- Employees recognize compensation income on all benefits received unless specifically excluded by tax laws.
- Employees treat benefits received like taxable cash compensation.
- Employer deducts cost and pays employer's share of FICA taxes on benefit.

Taxable fringe benefits are fringe benefits not specifically excluded from gross income. Congress views many of the taxable fringe benefits as luxuries and chooses not to subsidize them. Taxable fringe benefits include such things as below-market interest rate loans (see discussion in Chapter 5), gym memberships, season tickets to the local NBA team, an automobile allowance for a personal automobile, or anything else not specifically excluded by the tax laws. Employers generally provide taxable fringe benefits to executives and higher-salaried employees rather than to the rank-and-file employees.

Employee Considerations for Taxable Fringe Benefits From an employee's perspective, taxable fringe benefits are treated just like cash. Employees recognize ordinary compensation income when they receive taxable benefits and, just as they do with salary, pay FICA taxes on the value of the benefit. As a result, taxable fringe benefits cost employees the amount of tax they must pay on the benefits.

Example 12-15

Julie's offer includes a biennial auto allowance of up to $30,000. That is, every other year, TPI will reimburse Julie for an automobile purchase up to $30,000. TPI provides this benefit to executives that interact with the public on a regular basis. Julie purchases a Toyota 4Runner with a retail price of $35,000. What tax is Julie required to pay if she uses the allowance to apply toward the purchase? What is Julie's after-tax cost of the automobile if her marginal tax rate is 40 percent (ignoring FICA taxes)?

Answer: $12,000 in income taxes and $17,000 after-tax cost, computed as follows:

Description	Amount	Explanation
(1) Fair market value of Toyota	$35,000	
(2) Automobile allowance	30,000	Taxable fringe benefit.
(3) Julie's additional cost	5,000	(1) − (2).
(4) Income tax on allowance	12,000	(2) × 40%.
Total after-tax cost	$17,000	(3) + (4).

From Julie's perspective, this is a pretty good deal—particularly if she was willing to pay the market price for the car.

Employees may prefer a taxable benefit to an equivalent amount of cash when they benefit from employer-provided quantity or group discounts associated with the benefit. For example, many companies provide (pay premiums for) **group-term life insurance** as a fringe benefit, in part, because they can purchase the insurance at a lower rate than employees can purchase it individually. However, employees must recognize a certain amount of gross income when employers pay life insurance premiums for the employee for policies with a death benefit in excess of $50,000.[24] Consequently, a portion of the group-term life insurance benefit is taxable and a portion is nontaxable. In these circumstances, the employer determines the employee's taxable amount using a table provided in the Treasury Regulations. An excerpt of this table is provided in Exhibit 12-10.[25] To compute the annual taxable benefit, taxpayers use the following steps:

Step 1: Subtract $50,000 from the death benefit of their employer-provided group-term life insurance policy.

Step 2: Divide the Step 1 result by $1,000.

Step 3: Multiply the result from Step 2 by the cost per $1,000 of protection for one month from the table (Exhibit 12-10) based on the taxpayer's age.

Step 4: Multiply the outcome of Step 3 by the number of months the benefit was received during the taxable year.

EXHIBIT 12-10 Uniform Premiums for $1,000 of Group-Term Life Insurance Protection

5-year Age Bracket	Cost per $1,000 of Protection for One Month
Under 25	$0.05
25 to 29	.06
30 to 34	.08
35 to 39	.09
40 to 44	.10
45 to 49	.15
50 to 54	.23
55 to 59	.43
60 to 64	.66
65 to 69	1.27
70 and above	2.06

Example 12-16

Julie's offer from TPI includes $750,000 of group-term life insurance. TPI's cost to provide Julie the insurance is $500 per year. If Julie were to purchase the insurance herself she would pay $2,000 per year. Assume that Julie is 37 years old. Based on the Treasury's table (see Exhibit 12-10), the monthly premium per $1,000 of insurance is $.09 cents. What is Julie's taxable compensation from receiving the group-term life benefit? What does this benefit cost Julie (ignoring FICA taxes)?

(continued on page 12-22)

[24]§79.

[25]Reg. §1.79-3(d)(2) provides an age-based table and instructions to calculate the employee's includable amount.

Answer: $756 of taxable compensation and $302 cost (all taxes). Julie's cost is the income and Medicare taxes she must pay on the compensation, calculated as follows:

Group-Term Life Insurance Description	Amount	Explanation
(1) Insurance coverage	$750,000	Provided by employer.
(2) Excluded coverage	(50,000)	Nontaxable portion.
(3) Taxable benefit	$700,000	(1) + (2) (Step 1).
(4) Divide by 1,000	1,000	Divide by 1,000 (Step 2).
(5) Result of Step 2	700	(3)/(4).
(6) Monthly cost per $1,000	× 0.09	Taxable portion per $1,000 from Exhibit 12-10.
(7) Monthly benefit	$ 63	(5) × (6), (Step 3).
(8) Months	× 12	Annualize monthly taxable amount.
(9) Annual taxable benefit	$ 756	(7) × (8), (Step 4).
Income taxes	$ 302	(9) × 40%.

Note that Julie's income is not based on TPI's actual cost ($500) of providing the policy.

Taxpayers receiving taxable fringe benefits may experience some financial strain because they must pay the tax on the benefits. Frequently, when corporations provide taxable fringe benefits to senior executives, they also provide the executives enough cash to cover the taxes so the benefit(s) costs the executive nothing.[26] This is commonly referred to as a *gross-up.* For example, GE's 2014 proxy statement reveals that it made payments of $4,057,598 to Daniel C. Heintzelman, its vice chairman, and indicates that the additional cash is for "Expatriate Tax Benefits."[27] Employees can choose to forgo a benefit if they prefer not to pay taxes on it.

Employer Considerations for Taxable Fringe Benefits Like employees, employers treat taxable fringe benefits just like cash compensation. That is, the employer has an outlay for the cost of the benefit and deducts its *cost* of the benefit, *not the value* of the benefit to the employee.[28] As we mention above, employers are often able to purchase fringe benefits at a lower cost than individual employees can. For example, employers may receive a group discount for purchasing life insurance, automobiles, financial or tax planning services, or accident insurance.

Example 12-17

In Example 12-16, TPI provided Julie with $750,000 of group-term life insurance. Its cost of providing the entire $750,000 of coverage is $500 per year. If Julie were to purchase the policy herself, it would cost her $2,000 per year. Assuming TPI's marginal tax rate is 35 percent, what is TPI's after-tax cost of the partially taxable group-term life insurance benefit it provided to Julie?

[26]Companies generally choose a formula to determine how much cash (gross-up) they need to pay the employee in addition to the taxable benefit to ensure the benefit costs the employee nothing.

[27]This amount represents the tax gross-up payments made on behalf of Mr. Heintzelman in connection with his non-permanent relocation, at the company's request, to Florence, Italy, consistent with the company's policy for all employees

[28]The employer also has an outlay for the cost of the employer's share of FICA taxes on the taxable portion of benefits it provides to employees and receives a deduction for the FICA taxes paid.

Answer: TPI's after-tax cost of the benefit provided is $325, calculated as follows:

Description	Amount	Explanation
(1) Cost of policy	$500	
(2) Income tax benefit	(175)	(1) × 35%.
Total after-tax cost	$325	(1) + (2).

Finally, employers may discriminate between employees when providing taxable benefits. That is, they can select which employees receive the taxable benefits and which do not. Not surprisingly, the more highly compensated employees tend to receive these benefits. For example, as described in an excerpt from Walmart's proxy statement in Exhibit 12-11, Walmart's perquisite and supplemental benefits provide certain officers with use of the company aircraft and home security systems. Walmart is unlikely to offer these same benefits to its hourly sales associates.

TAXES IN THE REAL WORLD Fringe Benefits

Google Takes Off

Google's stock price isn't the only thing that has taken off; its executive usage of aircraft paid for by the company has as well. According to two excerpts from Google's 2014 Proxy Statement this amount exceeds $1 million.

> In 2013, we paid for personal security for Eric and amounts related to the personal use of non-commercial aircraft for Eric, Patrick, Nikesh, and David. Pursuant to our Non-Commercial Aircraft Policy, executives and their guests may use company aircraft with appropriate approvals.

Corporate Use of Personal Aircraft

Eric beneficially owns 100% of one aircraft and 33% of another aircraft, both of which are used by Eric and our other executive officers from time to time for business trips. The reimbursement rate for use of these aircraft is $7,500 per hour. The board of directors approved this hourly reimbursement rate based upon a competitive analysis of comparable chartered aircraft that, as our board of directors determined, is at or below market rates for the charter of similar aircraft. In 2013, we used these aircraft for business-related travel services for certain of our executive officers, including Eric, and reimbursed Eric approximately $1,398,750. Due to the fact that the $7,500 hourly rate paid for the use of these aircraft is less than the actual operational costs incurred by Eric as owner of these aircraft, Eric does not profit from the use of these aircraft.

EXHIBIT 12-11 Excerpt from Walmart's 2014 Proxy Statement

What perquisites and other benefits do our NEOs receive?

Our NEOs receive a limited number of perquisites and supplemental benefits. We cover the cost of annual physical examinations for our NEOs and provide each NEO with personal use of our aircraft for a limited number of hours each year. Our NEOs also receive company-paid life and accidental death and dismemberment insurance. Additionally, our NEOs are entitled to benefits available to officers generally, such as participation in the Deferred Compensation Matching Plan, and benefits available to Associates generally, including a Walmart discount card, a limited 15 percent match of purchases of Shares through our Stock Purchase Plan, participation in our 401(k) Plan, medical benefits, and foreign business travel insurance. We provide these perquisites and supplemental benefits to attract talented executives to our company and to retain our current executives, and we believe their limited cost is outweighed by these benefits to our company.

Nontaxable Fringe Benefits

For policy reasons, Congress specifically excludes certain fringe benefits, such as health insurance, from employees' gross income to encourage employers to provide the benefits.[29] We refer to excluded benefits as **nontaxable fringe benefits.** Other nontaxable fringe benefits enable taxpayers to become or stay employed, including meals or lodging for the convenience of the employer, educational assistance, dependent-care benefits, moving expense benefits, and transportation-related benefits. Finally, some benefits are excluded for simplicity's sake, such as no-additional-cost services, qualified employee discounts, and *de minimis* (small) fringe benefits. Exhibit 12-12 provides a partial list of nontaxable fringe benefits. Below, we discuss these benefits in more detail.

EXHIBIT 12-12 Common Forms of Nontaxable Fringe Benefits

Benefit	Description
Group-term life insurance (§79)	Employer-paid premiums on up to $50,000 group-term life insurance policy are excluded from employees' income.
Health benefits (§§ 105-106)	Employer-paid premiums covering health, medical, and dental insurance and the benefits provided through the insurance.
Meals or lodging for the convenience of the employer (§119)*	Meals provided on employer's premises and lodging provided by the employer as a condition of employment.
Employee educational assistance (§127)	Up to $5,250 exclusion for tuition, books, and fees. See IRS Publication 970, *Tax Benefits for Education.*
Dependent care benefits (§129)	Up to $5,000 exclusion for cost of providing care for a dependent who is under 13 years old or a dependent who is disabled.
No-additional-cost services [§132(a)(1)]	Benefits that don't cost the employer a material amount.
Qualified employee discounts [§132(a)(2)]	Reduced prices on employer's product within certain limits.
Working condition fringe benefits [§132(a)(3)]*	A benefit provided by an employer that would be deductible as an ordinary and necessary business expense by the employee if the employee rather than the employer paid the expense.
De minimis fringe benefits [§132(a)(4)]*	Relatively small and infrequently provided benefits.
Qualified transportation fringe benefits [§132(a)(5)]*	Mass transit passes up to monthly limit of $130, qualified parking up to monthly limit of $250, or use of company owned car pool vehicles (vans).
Qualified moving expense reimbursement [§132(a)(6)]*	Reimbursement for allowable moving expenses such as moving household goods and travel.
Cafeteria plans (§125)	A plan where employees can choose from among various nontaxable fringe benefits or cash. Taxable to the extent employees receive cash.

*Employer may discriminate in providing this benefit.

[29]The nontaxable fringe benefits are listed with "items specifically excluded from gross income" in §§101-140 of the Internal Revenue Code. Employers are generally prohibited from discriminating among employees with respect to nontaxable fringe benefits (they cannot offer them only to executives). This chapter indicates whether or not discrimination for a particular benefit is allowed. However, the discrimination rules are complex and vary from benefit to benefit in ways too numerous to explain in detail in this text.

Group-Term Life Insurance As we mentioned in the taxable benefits section, employees may exclude from income the employer-provided benefit for the first $50,000 of group-term life insurance.[30] Any remaining group-term life insurance benefit is taxable (see Example 12-16). An employer may not discriminate between employees in providing nontaxable group-term life insurance benefits.

Health and Accident Insurance and Benefits When employers pay for **health and accident insurance** for an employee and the employee's spouse and dependents, the employee excludes the benefit from her gross income.[31] For example, if TPI pays health premiums of $18,000 for Julie and her family, Julie is not required to include this $18,000 fringe benefit in her gross income.[32] Further, when employees receive cash reimbursements for medical care, they can exclude the reimbursement from gross income.[33] For example, if TPI reimburses Julie for $450 of medical co-payments she makes during the year, Julie excludes the $450 from gross income. Generally, employers may not discriminate between employees when providing health and accident insurance benefits.[34]

TAXES IN THE REAL WORLD Free Lunch

Apple, Google, and Facebook are famous for their cafeterias, which have been chronicled in Bon Appetit and other foodie magazines. These cafeterias are light years ahead of the dorm cafeteria you ate in as a college freshman. And better yet, they are either free or almost free for employees. However, the secret is out—and now the IRS is questioning whether these benefits are taxable or nontaxable. To be considered nontaxable, the benefit has to be provided "for the convenience of the employer" rather than as a way to attract and compensate employees. These companies are arguing that without these cafeterias employees will be away from the company premises more and lose the opportunity to talk together, both of which are detrimental to the employer. The IRS has made this issue an administrative priority; that could be bad news for those companies that have relied on such perks to lure the best and brightest employees. The result may also cost the companies and employees back taxes in the future.

Meals and Lodging for the Convenience of the Employer The value of certain meals and lodging the employer provides to an employee may be excluded from an employee's gross income if the benefit meets two criteria: (1) the meals and lodging are provided on the employer's business premises to the employee (and the employee's spouse and dependents, if any) and (2) the meals and lodging are provided for the convenience of the employer.[35] For example, employers may provide meals at their place of business so employees can continue working efficiently without taking time off to go out to eat. Accounting firms frequently provide meals to tax professionals working late during tax season. Employers are allowed to deduct the full cost of meals provided to employees for the convenience of the employer. That is, the cost is not subject to the 50 percent deductibility limitation on meals we discussed in Chapter 9.[36] Employers may generally discriminate between employees **for the convenience of the employer benefits.**

[30]§79.

[31]§106.

[32]If Julie were to purchase the health insurance with after-tax dollars the equivalent would be $30,000 [$18,000 / (1 − .4 marginal tax rate)].

[33]§105(b). Although, reimbursement in excess of costs is included in income.

[34]However, employers may exclude part-time employees from participation.

[35]§119(a)(1).

[36]§274(n).

Example 12-18

What if: Assume that last year Julie purchased 25 meals, at a cost of $500, on evenings when she worked late. Julie turned in expense reports and receipts for the meals totaling $500, which PCC reimbursed. What is the amount Julie must include in income?

Answer: Julie will not include the value of any of the overtime meals into income because they were provided for PCC's convenience.

In some situations, employers may provide lodging for employees and require employees to live on the business premises as a condition of their employment. In these cases, employees may exclude the value of the lodging from gross income.[37] For example, an employer may require an apartment complex manager to live in an apartment in the complex (free of charge) so the employee can respond to tenant needs, provide security, and handle emergencies. The apartment manager can exclude the value of the lodging from gross income.

Employee Educational Assistance Employees can exclude from income up to $5,250 of employee **educational assistance benefits** covering tuition, books, and fees.[38] Amounts received in excess of this limit are taxed as compensation to the employee. (See IRS Publication 970 for details related to education benefits.) This includes amounts employers provide for employee undergraduate- or graduate-level courses or for courses that lead to a professional degree. Amounts excluded from income cannot qualify for educational deductions or credits (such as the American opportunity and lifetime learning credits).

Dependent Care Benefits Employees can exclude up to $5,000 for benefits paid or reimbursed by employers for caring for children under age 13 or dependents or spouses who are physically or mentally unable to care for themselves.[39] Excluded amounts do not qualify for the child and dependent care credit (see Chapter 8).

No-Additional-Cost Services Employees can exclude the value of **no-additional-cost services.** These are any services employers provide to employees in the ordinary course of business that generate no substantial costs to the employer (including opportunity costs).[40] For example, airline companies can provide employees with free flight benefits on a space-available basis, hoteliers can allow employees to use vacant hotel rooms, and telephone companies can provide free basic phone service to their employees—all without the employees recognizing gross income. Exhibit 12-13 describes no-cost benefits that airline companies like JetBlue provide to their employees.[41]

EXHIBIT 12-13 Flight Benefits

JetBlue, like most other airlines, offers the following flight benefits to employees:

- Free and reduced rate standby travel on JetBlue flights.
- Discounted standby travel on other airlines.

[37]§119(a)(2).

[38]§127(a)(2). The discrimination and eligibility rules are provided in §127(b)(2).

[39]§129.

[40]§132(a)(1).

[41]See http://www.jetblue.com/work-here/benefits.aspx

Example 12-19

What if: Assume that Julie's current employer, PCC, has a division that provides wireless Internet service and virus protection software. Because PCC has such a large contract with a national provider, its contract has sufficient bandwidth to allow employees to use the service without incurring additional cost. The market value of the services is $1,080 per year. What amount of this benefit must Julie include in her gross income?

Answer: $0. Julie may exclude the value of the wireless Internet from her income because it qualifies as a no-additional-cost service under §132.

Qualified Employee Discounts Employers frequently allow employees to purchase their goods and services at a discount. Employees may exclude **qualified employee discounts** from income as long as they don't acquire *goods* at a discount greater than the average gross profit percentage for the employer's goods.[42] Employees may also exclude qualified employee discounts on *services* as long as the discount is not more than 20 percent of the price of the services that are offered to customers. This can be a fairly significant nontaxable benefit to employees, particularly for higher priced products. For example, Ford Motor Company could allow employees a substantial discount on its Ford, Lincoln, and Mercury brand cars. Also, Exhibit 12-14 presents an excerpt from the IBM website describing the IBM employee product purchase plan that allows employees to acquire home appliances at a significant discount.

EXHIBIT 12-14 **Excerpt from IBM's Website**

Employee Purchase Program

Discounted pricing for IBM U.S. and employees, their family and friends.

See www-304.ibm.com/shop/americas/content/home/store_eppus/en_US/epplogin.html

From a nontax perspective, employers can use this qualified fringe benefit to entice and retain employees who would otherwise purchase the employer's brand or product.

Example 12-20

What if: Assume that Julie's current employer, PCC, allows all employees to purchase computers (both laptops and desktops) from its retail stores at a discount. Julie purchased two computers during the current year: a laptop for $1,600 (retails for $2,100, with a cost to PCC of $1,500) and a desktop for $1,300 (retails for $1,800, with a cost of $1,250). Julie saved $500 ($2,100 − $1,600) on the laptop and $500 ($1,800 − $1,300) on the desktop. What amount of the savings must Julie include in her gross income?

Answer: Julie can exclude the entire savings from her income because the savings are a qualified employee discount under §132.

What if: Suppose that the laptop Julie purchased for $1,600 has a cost of $1,700 (instead of $1,500 as stated above). What amount of the tax savings on the laptop must Julie include in her gross income?

Answer: $100. Because Julie's cost of the computer is $100 less than PCC's cost, Julie must include $100 in her gross income.

What if: Assume that Julie's current employer, PCC, allows all employees to receive one free computer each year. Julie selected the laptop (retails for $2,100, with a cost to PCC of $1,500) as her free computer. What amount must PCC include in Julie's gross income?

Answer: $1,500. Julie's cost of the computer ($0) is $1,500 less than PCC's cost. Therefore, she must include $1,500 in income. Employee discounts only qualify as a qualified employee discount under §132 to the extent they don't exceed the employer's cost.

[42]§132(a)(2).

Working Condition Fringe Benefits Employees may exclude from income any benefit or reimbursement of a benefit provided by an employer that would be deductible as an ordinary and necessary expense by the employee if the employee rather than the employer paid the expense (or the employer did not reimburse the employee). For example, if a company or firm reimburses its employees for professional licensing costs or dues (CPA or bar fees or AICPA dues), the reimbursement may be excluded from an employee's income.[43] Additionally, telephones or computers provided to employees for business use may be excluded. Employers may discriminate between employees with respect to **working condition fringe benefits.**

Example 12-21

What if: Assume that Julie's employer reimburses executives for business-related continuing education courses as well as travel costs related to such education. Julie attended a certificate (nondegree program) course at the University of Chicago this year. Her costs were as follows: $2,500 for the course, $600 for airfare, $800 for hotels, and $200 for books and course materials. PCC reimbursed Julie for the entire $4,100 ($2,500 + $600 + $800 + $200). What amount of the reimbursement must Julie include in her gross income?

Answer: $0. The reimbursement qualifies as a working condition fringe benefit under §132.

What if: Assume that Ethan's employer allows all of its engineers to take home products for consumer testing and evaluation. For example, Ethan is currently designing a new disc brake system for mountain bikes. So Ethan is allowed to check out up to three mountain bikes at a time to see how various different brake systems work. The annual rental value of products Ethan uses is $2,500. What amount of the annual rental value must Ethan include in his gross income?

Answer: $0. The value of the consumer testing products is an excludible working condition fringe benefit under §132.

***De Minimis* Fringe Benefits** Employees can also exclude from income occasional or incidental ***de minimis* fringe benefits** (very small).[44] These typically include occasional personal use of a copy machine, company-sponsored picnics, noncash traditional holiday gifts (Thanksgiving turkey or Christmas ham), and occasional tickets to sporting or theatrical events. Employers are allowed to discriminate between employees when providing *de minimis* fringe benefits. Who do you think gets to use a company's NBA tickets—the new employee or the boss?

Qualified Transportation Fringe Employees may exclude from income the value of certain transportation benefits they receive from employers, whether employers pay for these benefits directly or reimburse employees for the transportation costs.[45] These **qualified transportation fringe benefits** eligible for exclusion include the value of company-owned car pool vehicles for commuting to and from work, the cost of mass transit passes, and the cost of qualified parking near the work place. In 2015, the maximum exclusion for the car pool vehicle and mass transit pass is $130 per month and the maximum exclusion for the qualified parking benefit is $250 per month.

Qualified Moving Expense Reimbursement Employees receiving payments (or reimbursements) from employers for **qualified moving expense reimbursements** may exclude the payments from gross income to the extent that they do not deduct the moving expenses.[46] As we discussed in Chapter 6, qualified moving expenses

[43]Employees can exclude reimbursements from their income if they properly document their expenses through expense reports, mileage logs, and receipts.

[44]§132(a)(4).

[45]§132(f)(1).

[46]§132(a)(6).

include the cost of moving household items and travel, including lodging, for the employee and dependents as long as the employee's move meets certain distance and length of employment tests. Employees are, however, taxed on payments they receive from employers for house-hunting trips, temporary housing allowances, and reimbursements for expenses related to the sale of their prior residence.

Cafeteria Plans and Flexible Spending Accounts (FSAs) Employers choose the benefits they make available to employees. Some employers offer a standard package of benefits that employees can either take or leave. Standard benefits typically include health and dental insurance for the employee and family, dependent care benefits, and group-term life insurance for the employee. However, a standard benefit plan is not optimal for all employees because each employee has individual needs. So how can employers tailor their benefits to the needs of employees? The answer is cafeteria plans and flexible spending accounts.

Under a **cafeteria plan,** employers determine the total cost of benefits they are willing to provide for each employee. Each employee then either chooses (or buys) benefits up to the determined amount from a menu of nontaxable fringe benefits or may receive a cash equivalent in lieu of forgone benefits.[47] However, cash received from a cafeteria plan is taxable compensation to employees. Cafeteria plans are popular because each employee may desire different types of nontaxable fringe benefits. For example, if an employer provides $3,000 of dependent care benefits to every employee, the benefits would be worthless to employees without dependents. Through a cafeteria plan, employees can select the benefits best suited to their needs. For example, instead of selecting dependent care benefits, an employee with no dependents could choose any combination of nontaxable benefits such as dental insurance, educational benefits, or cash if none of the benefits are desirable.

Employers can also offer **flexible spending accounts (FSAs),** which allow employees to set aside a portion of their before-tax salary for payment of either health and/or dependent-care benefits. These plans allow employees to set aside either employee contributions (on a before-tax basis) or employer contributions (a leftover cafeteria plan amount) to pay for medical-related expenses (such as co-payments and prescriptions) or dependent care. The Patient Protection and Affordable Care Act reduces the limit for medical-related expenses to $2,550 in 2015. Generally, amounts placed in flexible spending accounts must be used for qualifying benefits during the FSA plan year (which is often the calendar year). However, employers may allow employees to use the remaining balance from one year within the first two and a half months of the next FSA plan year.[48] Any remaining balance is forfeited by the employee.

THE KEY FACTS

Nontaxable Fringe Benefits

- Specifically identified in the Code.
- Employee excludes benefit from taxable income.
- Employer deducts cost when benefit is paid.

Employee and Employer Considerations for Nontaxable Fringe Benefits Nontaxable fringe benefits are very attractive to employees because their after-tax cost of these benefits is zero.[49] They do not pay for the benefits and they are not taxed on the value of the benefits they receive. In contrast to taxable fringe benefits, nontaxable fringe benefits cannot, with a few exceptions noted above, be provided on a discriminatory basis (may not be provided to some employees and not others). Employers deduct the cost of providing the benefits, which (thanks to group or quantity discounts) can be considerably lower than the cost to the employee of

[47]§125.

[48]Employers can elect to allow employees to use funds set aside for one year until March 15 of the following year under Notice 2005-42. If employers don't make the election, employees must use their account balance by December 31 of the current year or they lose it after year-end.

[49]Furthermore, there are nontax reasons for employees to value nontaxable benefits, such as the fact that many employer-provided group health insurance plans allow for preexisting health conditions, whereas employees may not be able to obtain health insurance plans that cover preexisting health conditions on their own.

purchasing the benefit(s) separately. IRS publication 15-B "Employer's Tax Guide to Fringe Benefits" (available at www.IRS.gov) provides tax guidance for employers providing fringe benefits.

Tax Planning with Fringe Benefits

The fact that employees can exclude nontaxable fringe benefits from gross income, while employers can deduct the cost of providing them (just as they deduct the cost of taxable fringe benefits), gives rise to compensation-related tax-planning opportunities that may benefit both employee and employer.

Example 12-22

TPI proposed to reimburse Julie $200 a month for her parking costs. What amount of this reimbursement would be a nontaxable qualified transportation fringe to Julie?

Answer: All $2,400. Julie can exclude up to $250 per month ($3,000 per year) as a qualified transportation fringe.

What if: Assume that TPI would not reimburse Julie's parking costs unless Julie is willing to accept a reduction in salary. Assuming Julie is subject to a 40 percent marginal tax rate, how much salary should Julie be willing to forgo to receive the $2,400 of nontaxable parking benefits?

Answer: $4,000, computed as follows:

Description	Amount	Explanation
(1) Annual fringe benefit	$2,400	
(2) Marginal ordinary tax rate	40%	
Before-tax compensation required to pay for annual fringe benefit	$4,000	(1)/[1 − (2)].

Example 12-23

What if: Assume that instead of a parking benefit, TPI would pay Julie $4,000 of salary that she would use to pay for her parking. What would be TPI's after-tax cost of paying $4,000 of salary to Julie assuming its marginal tax rate is 35 percent?

Answer: $2,600, calculated as follows:

Description	Amount	Explanation
(1) Taxable salary paid	$4,000	
(2) Income tax benefit	(1,400)	(1) × 35%.
Total after-tax cost of salary	$2,600	(1) + (2).

What if: Assume that TPI were to provide Julie $2,400 of qualified transportation fringe benefits in the form of parking. What would be its after-tax cost of paying the $2,400 nontaxable fringe benefit to Julie assuming its marginal tax rate is 35 percent?

Answer: $1,560, calculated as follows:

Description	Amount	Explanation
(1) Nontaxable fringe benefit paid	$2,400	
(2) Income tax benefit	(840)	(1) × 35%
Total after-tax cost of nontaxable benefit	$1,560	(1) + (2).

Can an employer and an employee work together to implement the conversion tax planning strategy to make both the employee and employer better off by substituting desired nontaxable fringe benefits for taxable salary in the compensation package? The answer is yes!

Example 12-24

What if: As shown in Example 12-22, Julie is indifferent between receiving (1) $4,000 in salary or (2) $2,400 in nontaxable parking benefits. Consequently, if TPI paid Julie $2,400 in nontaxable benefits and any amount of additional salary, she would be better off than she would be by receiving no parking and $4,000 in salary. As shown in Example 12-23, TPI would be better off after taxes by providing Julie with (1) $2,400 in nontaxable benefits (cost of $1,560) rather than (2) salary of $4,000 (after-tax cost of $2,600). What amount of salary could TPI provide in addition to the $2,400 of nontaxable benefits to make it indifferent between providing the parking and the additional salary or providing salary of $4,000?

Answer: $1,600 additional salary for indifference, calculated as follows:

Description	Amount	Explanation
(1) After-tax cost of salary	$2,600	Example 12-23.
(2) After-tax cost of fringe benefit	1,560	Example 12-23.
(3) After-tax cost of additional salary	$1,040	(1) − (2).
(4) After-tax cost percentage	65%	(1 − .35).
Additional before-tax salary	$1,600	(3)/(4).

To summarize, if TPI pays Julie's parking costs and provides her with additional salary of any amount below $1,600, it will be better off than it would be by not providing the parking and paying her $4,000 in salary. Julie is better off if TPI pays her parking and gives her any additional salary than she is if it doesn't pay her parking but pays her $4,000 of salary.

Fringe Benefits Summary

Fringe benefits, both taxable and nontaxable, can make up a significant portion of an employee's compensation. Fringe benefits are taxable unless the tax laws specifically exclude them from gross income. Taxable fringe benefits usually represent a luxury perk, while nontaxable fringe benefits are generally excluded for public policy reasons. At this point, you should be able to distinguish between taxable and nontaxable fringe benefits. Exhibit 12-15 presents an excerpt from Disney Company's proxy statement. Read through the excerpt and see if you can determine which of the benefits Mr. Iger received are taxable and which are nontaxable.

Mr. Iger's taxable benefits include the personal air travel, security, health club membership, annual physical exam, reimbursement for financial consulting, and perhaps part of the group-term life insurance. Mr. Iger's nontaxable benefits include theme park access (a no-additional-cost service), merchandise discounts (qualified employee discount), occasional sporting events (*de minimis* fringe benefit), educational expense reimbursements, health insurance, and group-term life insurance (some of this coverage may be taxable).

Recall the fringe benefits included in Julie's offer letter: health insurance (valued at $18,000), $750,000 of group-term life insurance, and a flexible spending account (no amounts given; assume she elects $1,500). She also received an annual parking benefit of $2,400. Which benefits are taxable and which are nontaxable? Exhibit 12-16 summarizes how each of these benefits is classified for tax purposes, Julie's after-tax benefit, and TPI's after-tax cost.

EXHIBIT 12-15 Excerpt from Disney Company's 2014 Proxy Statement Dealing with Fringe Benefits

The following table identifies the incremental cost of each perquisite or personal benefit that exceeded the greater of $25,000 or 10% of the total amount of perquisites and personal benefits for a named executive officer in fiscal 2013.

Fiscal 2013 Perquisites and Personal Benefits

Executive	Year	Personal Air Travel	Security	Other	Total
Robert A. Iger	2013	$332,808	$584,075	$30,730	$947,613

The incremental cost to the Company of the items specified above was determined as follows:

- Personal air travel: the actual catering costs, landing and ramp fees, fuel costs and lodging costs incurred by flight crew plus a per hour charge based on the average hourly maintenance costs for the aircraft during the year for flights that were purely personal in nature, and a pro rata portion of catering costs where personal guests accompanied a named executive officer on flights that were business in nature. Where a personal flight coincided with the positioning of an aircraft following a business flight, only the incremental costs of the flight compared to an immediate repositioning of the aircraft are included. As noted on page 24, above, Mr. Iger is required for security reasons to use corporate aircraft for all of his personal travel.
- Security: the actual costs incurred by the Company for providing security equipment and services.

The "Other" column in the table above includes, to the extent a named executive officer elected to receive any of these benefits, the incremental cost to the Company of the vehicle benefit, personal air travel where the cost to the Company was less than $25,000, reimbursement of up to $450 for health club membership or exercise equipment and reimbursement of expenses for financial consulting.

The named executive officers also were eligible to receive the other benefits described in *the Compensation Discussion and Analysis* under the discussion of *"Benefits and Perquisites"* in the *"Compensation Program Elements"* section, which involved no incremental cost to the Company or are offered through group life, health or medical reimbursement plans that are available generally to all of the Company's salaried employees.

EXHIBIT 12-16 Summary of Julie's Nonsalary Benefits from TPI

Benefit	Nontaxable Fringe	Taxable Fringe	Employee After-Tax Benefit	Employer After-Tax Cost
Auto allowance		X	**$18,000** ($30,000 − $12,000) (Example 12-15)	**$19,500** [$30,000 × (1 − .35)]
Health and dental insurance	X		**$18,000** [$18,000 × (1 − .0)]	**$11,700** [$18,000 × (1 − .35)]
Flexible spending account	X		**$1,500** [$1,500 × (1 − .0)]	**$975** [$1,500 × (1 − .35)]
Parking reimbursement	X		**$2,400** [$2,400 × (1 − .0)] (Example 12-22)	**$1,560** [$2,400 × (1 − .35)] (Example 12-23)
Group-term life insurance	X	X	**$1,698** ($2,000 − $302)* (Examples 12-16, 17)	**$325** [$500 × (1 − .35)] (Example 12-17)
Total			**$41,598**	**$34,060**

*This is the fair market value of the benefit less the actual taxes payable by Julie.

CONCLUSION

Individuals and employers routinely make choices involving compensation issues. As they do so, they must understand how alternative forms of compensation are taxed. In this chapter, we have discussed the tax compliance and planning implications associated with common types of payment including salary and wages, equity-based compensation (such as stock options and restricted stock), and taxable and nontaxable fringe benefits from both employee and employer perspectives. Throughout, we have emphasized that both tax and nontax issues must be considered in the broader context of compensation planning. Armed with the information provided in this chapter, future employees and employers can approach the compensation decisions they will undoubtedly face with more confidence and insight.

Summary

Discuss and explain the tax implications of compensation in the form of salary and wages from the employee's and employer's perspectives. **LO 12-1**

- Employees are taxed on salary at ordinary income rates.
- Employees use Form W-4 to supply their employer with withholding information. Employees can use the W-4 to manage withholding throughout the year because withholding is treated as though it is withheld evenly throughout the year for estimated tax purposes.
- Cash-method employers deduct wages when paid. Accrual-method employers deduct wages when accrued as long as the wages are paid within 2.5 months of year-end. If paid after 2.5 months of year-end, wages are deductible when the employee recognizes the income (when paid). When an employer accrues wages to a related-party employee (more than 50 percent ownership), the wages are not deductible until the employee recognizes the income (when paid).
- Employers' after-tax cost of wages is the cost of the wages minus the tax benefit of the deduction for the wages.
- For publicly traded corporations, the tax deduction for nonperformance-based compensation paid to the CEO and for other most highly compensated officers is limited to $1,000,000 per year per individual.

Describe and distinguish the tax implications of various forms of equity-based compensation from the employee's and employer's perspectives. **LO 12-2**

- Stock options and restricted stock are common forms of equity-based compensation. Although both reward employees for increases in the stock price of their employers, there are fundamental economic differences between them.
- Stock options are treated as either nonqualified or incentive stock options for tax purposes.
- Employees recognize ordinary income equal to the bargain element on NQOs when they are exercised. Employers are able to deduct the bargain element when NQOs are exercised. Any appreciation in the value of shares subsequent to the exercise of NQOs is treated as capital gain by employees when the shares are sold.
- If certain holding period requirements are met, employees exercising ISOs don't recognize any income until the shares received from the exercised options are sold. When the shares are sold, the difference between the exercise price and the share price is long-term capital gain (assuming appreciation). Employers are not permitted a deduction for ISOs.
- Generally, employees prefer ISOs and employers prefer NQOs because of differences in the way the two types of options are taxed.
- Employers treat stock options differently for book and tax purposes.

- Employees recognize ordinary income from restricted stock equal to the fair market value of the stock on the vesting date. Employers receive a corresponding tax deduction.
- Employees may elect to recognize taxable income from restricted stock on the date it is received rather than on the vesting date if they make an §83(b) election. Although this election accelerates the recognition of income, it gives the employee the ability to convert ordinary income from further appreciation into a capital gain.

LO 12-3 Compare and contrast taxable and nontaxable fringe benefits and explain the employee and employer tax consequences associated with fringe benefits.

- Fringe benefits are taxable to the employee unless the Code specifically excludes the benefit from gross income. Taxable fringe benefits are generally luxury perks, such as corporate air travel and security.
- Nontaxable fringe benefits include up to $50,000 of group-term life insurance, health benefits, meals and lodging for the convenience of the employer, educational assistance, dependent care benefits, qualified employee discounts, and qualified transportation benefits (among others).

KEY TERMS

bargain element (12-10)
cafeteria plan (12-29)
***de minimis* fringe benefit (12-28)**
disqualifying disposition (12-12)
educational assistance benefit (12-26)
employee (12-2)
exercise date (12-10)
exercise price (12-8)
facts and circumstances test (12-5)
FICA taxes (12-2)
flexible spending account (FSA) (12-29)
for the convenience of the employer benefits (12-25)
Form W-2 (12-2)
Form W-4 (12-2)
fringe benefits (12-20)
grant date (12-10)
group-term life insurance (12-21)
health and accident insurance (12-25)
incentive stock option (12-10)
no-additional-cost services (12-26)
nonqualified stock option (12-10)
nontaxable fringe benefit (12-24)
option exercise (12-9)
qualified employee discount (12-27)
qualified moving expense reimbursement (12-28)
qualified transportation fringe benefit (12-28)
restricted stock (12-15)
salary (12-2)
same-day sale (12-11)
§83(b) election (12-17)
strike price (12-8)
taxable fringe benefit (12-20)
vest (12-8)
vesting date (12-10)
wages (12-2)
working condition fringe benefit (12-28)

DISCUSSION QUESTIONS

LO 12-1 1. Nicole and Braxton are each 50 percent shareholders of NB Corporation. Nicole is also an employee of the corporation. NB is a calendar-year taxpayer and uses the accrual method of accounting. The corporation pays its employees monthly on the first day of the month after the salary is earned by the employees. What issues must NB consider with respect to the deductibility of the wages it pays to Nicole if Nicole is Braxton's sister? What issues arise if Nicole and Braxton are unrelated?

LO 12-1 2. Holding all else equal, does an employer with a higher marginal tax rate or lower marginal tax rate have a lower after-tax cost of paying a particular employee's salary? Explain.

LO 12-1 3. What are nontax reasons for why a corporation may choose to cap its executives' salaries at $1 million?

LO 12-1 4. What are tax reasons why a corporation may choose to cap its executives' salaries at $1 million?

5. Lea is a highly paid executive with MCC Inc., a publicly traded corporation. What are the circumstances under which MCC will be able to deduct more than $1 million of compensation paid to Lea during the year? LO 12-1
6. From an *employee* perspective, how are ISOs treated differently than NQOs for tax purposes? In general, for a given number of options, which type of stock option should employees prefer? LO 12-2
7. From an *employer* perspective, how are ISOs treated differently than NQOs for tax purposes? In general, for a given number of options, which type of stock option should employers prefer? LO 12-2
8. Why do employers use stock options in addition to salary to compensate their employees? For employers, are stock options treated more favorably than salary for tax purposes? Explain. LO 12-2
9. What is a "disqualifying disposition" of ISOs, and how does it affect employees who have exercised ISOs? LO 12-2
10. Compare and contrast how employers record book and tax expense for stock options. LO 12-2
11. How is the tax treatment of restricted stock different from that of NQOs? How is it similar? LO 12-2
12. Matt just started work with Boom Zoom Inc., a manufacturer of credit-card-sized devices for storing and playing back music. Due to the popularity of its devices, analysts expect Boom Zoom's stock price to increase dramatically. In addition to his salary, Matt received Boom Zoom restricted stock. How will Matt's restricted stock be treated for tax purposes? Should Matt consider making the §83(b) election? What are the factors he should consider in making this decision? From a tax perspective, would this election help or hurt Boom Zoom? LO 12-2
13. What risks do employees making an §83(b) election on a restricted stock grant assume? LO 12-2
14. Explain the differences and similarities between fringe benefits and salary as forms of compensation. LO 12-3
15. When an employer provides group-term life insurance for an employee, what are the tax consequences to the employee? What are the tax consequences for the employer? LO 12-3
16. Compare and contrast the employer's tax consequences of providing taxable versus nontaxable fringe benefits. LO 12-3
17. Mike is working his way through college and trying to make ends meet. Tara, a friend, is graduating soon and tells Mike about a really great job opportunity. She is the onsite manager for an apartment complex catering to students. The job entails working in the office for about 10 hours a week, collecting rent each month, and answering after-hours emergency calls. The pay is $10 per hour, plus a rent-free apartment (worth about $500 per month). Tara then tells him the best part: the rent-free apartment is tax-free. Knowing that you are a tax student, Mike asks you if the rent-free apartment is really tax-free or if Tara is mistaken. Explain to Mike whether the compensation for the apartment is really a nontaxable fringe benefit. LO 12-3
18. Assume that your friend has accepted a position working as an accountant for a large automaker. As a signing bonus, the employer provides the traditional cash incentive but also provides the employee with a vehicle not to exceed a retail price of $25,000. Explain to your friend whether the value of the vehicle is included, excluded, or partially included in the employee's gross income. LO 12-3

LO 12-3 19. Explain why an employee might accept a lower salary to receive a nontaxable fringe benefit. Why might an employee not accept a lower salary to receive a nontaxable fringe benefit?

LO 12-3 20. Describe a cafeteria plan and discuss why an employer would provide a cafeteria plan for its employees.

LO 12-3 21. Explain why Congress allows employees to receive certain fringe benefits tax-free but others are taxable.

LO 12-3 22. Explain the policy reason for including the value of country club memberships provided to an executive as a taxable fringe benefit.

LO 12-3 23. Describe the circumstances in which an employee may not value a nontaxable fringe benefit.

PROBLEMS

All applicable problems are available with McGraw-Hill's *Connect*® *Accounting*.

LO 12-1 24. North Inc. is a calendar-year, accrual-basis taxpayer. At the end of year 1, North accrued and deducted the following bonuses for certain employees for financial accounting purposes.

- $7,500 for Lisa Tanaka, a 30 percent shareholder.
- $10,000 for Jared Zabaski, a 35 percent shareholder.
- $12,500 for Helen Talanian, a 20 percent shareholder.
- $5,000 for Steve Nielson, a 0 percent shareholder.

Unless stated otherwise, assume these shareholders are unrelated.

How much of the accrued bonuses can North Inc. deduct in year 1 under the following alternative scenarios?

a) North paid the bonuses to the employees on March 1 of year 2.

b) North paid the bonuses to the employees on April 1 of year 2.

c) North paid the bonuses to employees on March 1 of year 2 and Lisa and Jared are related to each other, so they are treated as owning each other's stock in North.

d) North paid the bonuses to employees on March 1 of year 2 and Lisa and Helen are related to each other, so they are treated as owning each other's stock in North.

LO 12-1 25. Jorgensen High Tech Inc. is a calendar-year, accrual-method taxpayer. At the end of year 1, Jorgensen accrued and deducted the following bonuses for certain employees for financial accounting purposes.

- $40,000 for Ken.
- $30,000 for Jayne.
- $20,000 for Jill.
- $10,000 for Justin.

How much of the accrued bonuses can Jorgensen deduct in year 1 under the following alternative scenarios?

a) Jorgensen paid the bonuses to the employees on March 1 of year 2.

b) Jorgensen paid the bonuses to the employees on April 1 of year 2.

c) Jorgensen paid the bonuses to employees on March 1 of year 2, and there is a requirement that the employee remain employed with Jorgensen on the payment date to receive the bonus.

d) Jorgensen paid the bonuses to employees on March 1 of year 2, and there is a requirement that the employee remain employed with Jorgensen on the payment date to receive the bonus; if not, the forfeited bonus is reallocated to the other employees.

26. Lynette is the CEO of publicly traded TTT Corporation and earns a salary of $200,000 in the current year. Assume TTT has a 35 percent marginal tax rate. LO 12-1

    a) What is TTT Corporation's after-tax cost of paying Lynette's salary?

27. Marcus is the CEO of publicly traded ABC Corporation and earns a salary of $1,500,000. Assume ABC has a 35 percent marginal tax rate. LO 12-1

    a) What is ABC's after-tax cost of paying Marcus's salary?

    b) Now assume that Marcus, in addition to the $1.5 million salary, earns a performance-based bonus of $500,000. What is ABC's after-tax cost of paying Marcus's salary?

28. Ramon has finally arrived. He has interviewed for the CEO position with MMM Corporation. They have presented him with two alternative compensation offers. Alternative 1 is for a straight salary of $2,500,000. Option 2 is for a salary of $1,000,000 and performance-based compensation of up to $2,000,000. Assume that Ramon has a marginal tax rate of 40 percent, MMM has a marginal tax rate of 35 percent. Answer the questions under each of the following alternative scenarios. LO 12-1 planning

    a) If Ramon is 100 percent certain he can meet the qualifications for the full performance-based compensation, which offer should he choose?

    b) If Ramon believes there is only a 20 percent chance that he can meet the performance-based requirements, which offer should he choose (assume he is risk neutral)?

    c) What is MMM's after-tax cost of providing Ramon with Option 1?

    d) What is MMM's expected after-tax cost of providing Ramon with Option 2 if it believes there is a 40 percent chance Ramon will qualify for the performance-based compensation?

29. Cammie received 100 NQOs (each option provides a right to purchase 10 shares of MNL stock for $10 per share) at the time she started working for MNL Corporation four years ago when MNL's stock price was $8 per share. Now that MNL's stock price is $40 per share, she intends to exercise all of her options. After acquiring the 1,000 MNL shares with her options, she held the shares for over one year and sold them at $60 per share. LO 12-2

    a) What are Cammie's taxes due on the grant date, exercise date, and sale date, assuming her ordinary marginal rate is 30 percent and her long-term capital gains rate is 15 percent?

    b) What are MNL Corporation's tax savings on grant date, exercise date, and date of sale assuming its marginal tax rate is 35 percent?

    c) Complete Cammie's Schedule D for the year of sale.

30. Yost received 300 NQOs (each option gives Yost the right to purchase 10 shares of Cutter Corporation stock for $15 per share) at the time he started working for Cutter Corporation three years ago. Cutter's stock price was $15 per share. Yost exercises all of his options when the share price is $26 per share. Two years after acquiring the shares, he sold them at $47 per share. LO 12-2

    a) What are Yost's taxes due on the grant date, exercise date, and sale date, assuming his ordinary marginal rate is 35 percent and his long-term capital gains rate is 15 percent?

b) What are Cutter Corporation's tax consequences (amount of deduction and tax savings from deduction) on the grant date, the exercise date, and the date Yost sells the shares assuming its marginal tax rate is 25 percent?

c) Assume that Yost is cash poor and needs to perform a same-day sale in order to buy his shares. Due to his belief that the stock price is going to increase significantly, he wants to maintain as many shares as possible. How many shares must he sell in order to cover his purchase price and taxes payable on the exercise?

d) Assume that Yost's options were exercisable at $20 and expired after five years. If the stock only reached $18 dollars during its high point during the five-year period, what are Yost's tax consequences on the grant date, the exercise date, and the date the shares are sold, assuming his ordinary marginal rate is 35 percent and his long-term capital gains rate is 15 percent?

LO 12-2

31. Haven received 200 NQOs (each option gives him the right to purchase 20 shares of Barlow Corporation stock for $7 per share) at the time he started working for Barlow Corporation three years ago when its stock price was $7 per share. Now that Barlow's share price is $50 per share, he intends to exercise all of his options. After acquiring the 4,000 Barlow shares with his options, he intends to hold the shares for more than one year and then sell the shares when the price reaches $75 per share.

a) What are Haven's taxes due on the grant date, exercise date, and sale date, assuming his ordinary marginal rate is 30 percent and his long-term capital gains rate is 15 percent?

b) What are the cash flow effects for Barlow Corporation resulting from Haven's option exercise if Barlow's marginal tax rate is 35 percent?

LO 12-2

32. Mark received 10 ISOs (each option gives him the right to purchase 10 shares of Hendricks Corporation stock for $5 per share) at the time he started working for Hendricks Corporation five years ago when Hendricks' stock price was $5 per share. Now that Hendricks' share price is $35 per share, he intends to exercise all options and hold all of his shares for more than one year. Assume that more than a year after exercise, Mark sells the stock for $35 a share.

a) What are Mark's taxes due on the grant date, the exercise date, and the date he sells the shares, assuming his ordinary marginal rate is 30 percent and his long-term capital gains rate is 15 percent?

b) What are Hendricks' tax consequences on the grant date, the exercise date, and the date Mark sells the shares assuming its marginal tax rate is 25 percent?

LO 12-2

33. Antonio received 40 ISOs (each option gives him the right to purchase 20 shares of Zorro stock for $3 per share) at the time he started working for Zorro Corporation six years ago. Zorro's stock price was $3 per share at the time. Now that Zorro's stock price is $50 per share, he intends to exercise all of his options and immediately sell all the shares he receives from the options exercise.

a) What are Antonio's taxes due on the grant date, the exercise date, and the date the shares are sold, assuming his ordinary marginal rate is 30 percent and his long-term capital gains rate is 15 percent?

b) What are Zorro's tax consequences on the grant date, the exercise date, and the date Antonio sells the shares assuming its marginal tax rate is 25 percent?

c) What are the cash flow effects of these transactions to Antonio, assuming his ordinary marginal rate is 25 percent and his long-term capital gains rate is 15 percent?

d) What are the cash flow effects to Zorro Corporation resulting from Antonio's option exercise if Zorro's marginal tax rate is 35 percent?

34. Harmer Inc. is now a successful company. In the early days (before it became profitable), it issued ISOs to its employees. Now Harmer is trying to decide whether to issue NQOs or ISOs to its employees. Initially, Harmer would like to give each employee 20 options (each option allows the employee to acquire one share of Harmer stock). For purposes of this problem, assume that the options are exercised in three years (*three years from now*) and that the underlying stock is sold in five years (*five years from now*). Assume that taxes are paid at the same time the income generating the tax is recognized. Also assume the following facts: LO 12-2 planning

- The after-tax discount rate for both Harmer Inc. and its employees is 10 percent.
- Corporate tax rate is 35 percent.
- Personal (employee) ordinary income rate is 40 percent.
- Personal (employee) long-term capital gains rate is 20 percent.
- Exercise price of the options is $7.
- Market price of Harmer at date of grant is $5.
- Market price of Harmer at date of exercise is $25.
- Market price of Harmer at date of sale is $35.

Answer the following questions:

a) Considering these facts, which type of option plan, NQO or ISO, should Harmer Inc. prefer? Explain.
b) Assuming Harmer issues NQOs, what is Harmer's tax benefit from the options for each employee in the year each employee exercises the NQOs?
c) Assuming Harmer issues ISOs, what is the tax benefit to Harmer in the year the ISOs are exercised?
d) Which type of option plan should Harmer's employees prefer?
e) What is the present value of each employee's after-tax cash flows from year 1 through year 5 if the employees receive ISOs?
f) What is the present value of each employee's after-tax cash flows from year 1 through year 5 if the employees receive NQOs?
g) How many NQOs would Harmer have to grant to keep its employees indifferent between NQOs and 20 ISOs?

35. On January 1, year 1, Dave received 1,000 shares of restricted stock from his employer, RRK Corporation. On that date, the stock price was $7 per share. Dave's restricted shares will vest at the end of year 2. He intends to hold the shares until the end of year 4 when he intends to sell them to help fund the purchase of a new home. Dave predicts the share price of RRK will be $30 per share when his shares vest and will be $40 per share when he sells them. LO 12-2

a) If Dave's stock price predictions are correct, what are the taxes due on these transactions to Dave if his ordinary marginal rate is 30 percent and his long-term capital gains rate is 15 percent?
b) If Dave's stock price predictions are correct, what are the tax consequences of these transactions to RRK if its marginal rate is 35 percent?

36. On January 1, year 1, Dave received 1,000 shares of restricted stock from his employer, RRK Corporation. On that date, the stock price was $7 per share. On receiving the restricted stock, Dave made the §83(b) election. Dave's restricted shares will vest at the end of year 2. He intends to hold the shares until the end of year 4 when he intends to sell them to help fund the purchase of a new home. Dave predicts the share price of RRK will be $30 per share when his LO 12-2

shares vest and will be $40 per share when he sells them. Assume that Dave's price predictions are correct and answer the following questions:

a) What are Dave's taxes due if his ordinary marginal rate is 30 percent and his long-term capital gains rate is 15 percent?

b) What are the tax consequences of these transactions to RRK if its marginal rate is 35 percent?

LO 12-2

37. On January 1, year 1, Jessica received 10,000 shares of restricted stock from her employer, Rocket Corporation. On that date, the stock price was $10 per share. On receiving the restricted stock, Jessica made the §83(b) election. Jessica's restricted shares will all vest at the end of year 4. After the shares vest, she intends to sell them immediately to fund an around-the-world cruise. Unfortunately, Jessica decided that she couldn't wait four years and she quit her job to start her cruise on January 1, year 3.

a) What are Jessica's taxes due in year 1 assuming her marginal tax rate is 33 percent and her long-term capital gains rate is 15 percent?

b) What are Jessica's taxes due in year 3 assuming her marginal tax rate is 33 percent and her long-term capital gains rate is 15 percent?

LO 12-2

38. On May 1, year 1, Anna received 5,000 shares of restricted stock from her employer, Jarbal Corporation. On that date, the stock price was $5 per share. On receiving the restricted stock, Anna made the §83(b) election. Anna's restricted shares will all vest on May 1, year 3. After the shares vest, she intends to sell them immediately to purchase a condo. True to her plan, Anna sold the shares immediately after they were vested.

a) What is Anna's ordinary income in year 1?

b) What is Anna's gain or loss in year 3 if the stock is valued at $1 per share on the day the shares vest?

c) What is Anna's gain or loss in year 3 if the stock is valued at $9 per share on the day the shares vest?

d) What is Anna's gain or loss in year 3 if the stock is valued at $5 per share on the day the shares vest?

LO 12-2
planning

39. On January 1, year 1, Tyra started working for Hatch Corporation. New employees must choose immediately between receiving seven NQOs (each NQO provides the right to purchase for $5 per share 10 shares of Hatch stock) or 50 restricted shares. Hatch's stock price is $5 on Tyra's start date. Either form of equity-based compensation will vest in two years. Tyra believes that the stock will be worth $15 per share in two years and $25 in four years when she will sell the stock. Tyra's marginal tax rate is 30 percent and her long-term capital gains rate is 15 percent. Assuming that Tyra's price predictions are correct, answer the following questions (ignore present value, use nominal dollars):

a) What are the cash-flow effects to Tyra in the year she receives the options, the year the options vest and she exercises the options, and in the year she sells the stock if she chooses the NQOs?

b) What are the cash-flow effects to Tyra in the year she receives the restricted stock, in the year the stock vests, and in the year she sells the stock if Tyra chooses the restricted stock?

c) What are the cash-flow effects to Tyra in the year she receives the restricted stock, the year the stock vests, and the year she sells the stock if she makes an §83(b) election?

d) What recommendation would you give Tyra? Explain.

40. Nicole's employer, Poe Corporation, provides her with an automobile allowance of $20,000 every other year. Her marginal tax rate is 30 percent. Poe Corporation has a marginal tax rate of 35 percent. Answer the following questions relating to this fringe benefit. LO 12-3

    a) What is Nicole's after-tax benefit if she receives the allowance this year?

    b) What is Poe's after-tax cost of providing the auto allowance?

41. Bills Corporation runs a defense contracting business that requires security clearance. To prevent unauthorized access to its materials, Bills requires its security personnel to be on duty except for a 15-minute break every two hours. Since the nearest restaurants are a 25-minute round trip, Bills provides free lunches to its security personnel. Bills has never included the value of these meals in its employees' compensation. Bills is currently under audit, and the IRS agent wants to deny Bills a deduction for past meals. The agent also wants Bills to begin including the value of the meals in employee compensation starting with the current year. As Bills's tax advisor, give it a recommendation on whether to appeal the agent's decision. (*Hint:* See *Boyd Gaming Corp.*, CA-9, 99-1 USTC ¶50,530 (Acq.), 177 F3d 1096.) LO 12-3

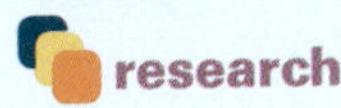

42. Lars Osberg, a single taxpayer with a 35 percent marginal tax rate, desires health insurance. The health insurance would cost Lars $8,500 to purchase if he pays for it himself (Lars's AGI is too high to receive any tax deduction for the insurance as a medical expense). Volvo, Lars's employer, has a 40 percent marginal tax rate. Answer the following questions about this benefit. LO 12-3 planning

    a) What is the maximum amount of before-tax salary Lars would give up to receive health insurance from Volvo?

    b) What would be the after-tax cost to Volvo to provide Lars with health insurance if it could purchase the insurance through its group plan for $5,000?

    c) Assume that Volvo could purchase the insurance for $5,000. Lars is interested in getting health insurance and he is willing to receive a lower salary in exchange for the health insurance. What is the least amount by which Volvo would be willing to reduce Lars's salary while agreeing to pay his health insurance?

    d) Will Volvo and Lars be able to reach an agreement by which Volvo will provide Lars with health insurance?

43. Seiko's current salary is $85,000. Her marginal tax rate is 30 percent and she fancies European sports cars. She purchases a new auto each year. Seiko is currently a manager for an office equipment company. Her friend, knowing of her interest in sports cars, tells her about a manager position at the local BMW and Porsche dealer. The new position pays only $75,000 per year, but it allows employees to purchase one new car per year at a discount of $15,000. This discount qualifies as a nontaxable fringe benefit. In an effort to keep Seiko as an employee, her current employer offers her a $10,000 raise. Answer the following questions about this analysis. LO 12-3 planning

    a) What is the annual after-tax cost to her current employer (office equipment company that has a 35 percent marginal tax rate) to provide Seiko with the $10,000 increase in salary?

    b) Financially, which offer is better for Seiko on an after-tax basis and by how much? (Assume that Seiko is going to purchase the new car whether she switches jobs or not.)

    c) What salary would Seiko need to receive from her current employer to make her financially indifferent (after taxes) between receiving additional salary from her current employer and accepting a position at the auto dealership?

LO 12-1 LO 12-3 44. JDD Corporation provides the following benefits to its employee, Ahmed (age 47):

Salary	$300,000
Health insurance	10,000
Dental insurance	2,000
Life insurance	3,000
Dependent care	5,000
Professional dues	500
Personal use of company jet	200,000

Assume the life insurance is a group-term life insurance policy that provides $200,000 of coverage for Ahmed.

a) Assuming Ahmed is subject to a marginal tax rate of 30 percent, what is his after-tax benefit of receiving each of these benefits?

LO 12-3 45. Gray's employer is now offering group-term life insurance. The company will provide each employee with $100,000 of group-term life insurance. It costs Gray's employer $300 to provide this amount of insurance to Gray each year. Assuming that Gray is 52 years old, determine the monthly premium that Gray must include in gross income as a result of receiving the group-term life benefit.

LO 12-3 46. Brady graduated from SUNY New Paltz with his bachelor's degree recently. He works for Makarov & Company CPAs. The firm pays his tuition ($10,000 per year) for him so that he can receive his Master of Science in Taxation, which will qualify him to sit for the CPA exam. How much of the $10,000 tuition benefit does Brady need to include in gross income?

LO 12-3 47. Meg works for Freedom Airlines in the accounts payable department. Meg and all other employees receive free flight benefits (for the employee, family, and 10 free buddy passes for friends per year) as part of its employee benefits package. If Meg uses 30 flights with a value of $12,350 this year, how much must she include in her compensation this year?

LO 12-3 research 48. Sharmilla works for Shasta Lumber, a local lumber supplier. The company annually provides each employee with a Shasta Lumber shirt so that employees look branded and advertise for the business while wearing the shirts. Are Shasta's employees required to include the value of the shirts in income?

LO 12-3 research 49. LaMont works for a company in downtown Chicago. The firm encourages employees to use public transportation (to save the environment) by providing them with transit passes at a cost of $255 per month.

a) If LaMont receives one pass (worth $255) each month, how much of this benefit must he include in his gross income each year?

b) If the company provides each employee with $255 per month in parking benefits, how much of the parking benefit must LaMont include in his gross income each year?

LO 12-3 50. Jasmine works in Washington, D.C. She accepts a new position with her current firm in Los Angeles. Her employer provides the following moving benefits:

- Temporary housing for one month—$3,000.
- Transportation for her household goods—$4,500.
- Flight and hotel for a house-hunting trip—$1,750.
- Flights to Los Angeles for her and her family—$2,000.

What amount of these benefits must Jasmine include in her gross income?

LO 12-3 51. Jarvie loves to bike. In fact, he has always turned down better paying jobs to work in bicycle shops where he gets an employee discount. At Jarvie's current shop, Bad Dog Cycles, each employee is allowed to purchase four bicycles a year at a discount. Bad Dog has an average gross profit percentage on bicycles of 25 percent. During the current year, Jarvie bought the following bikes:

Description	Retail Price	Cost	Employee Price
Specialized road bike	$3,200	$2,000	$2,240
Rocky Mountain mountain bike	3,800	3,200	3,040
Trek road bike	2,700	2,000	1,890
Yeti mountain bike	3,500	2,500	2,800

a) What amount is Jarvie required to include in taxable income from these purchases?
b) What amount of deductions is Bad Dog allowed to claim from these transactions?

52. Matt works for Fresh Corporation. Fresh offers a cafeteria plan that allows each employee to receive $15,000 worth of benefits each year. The menu of benefits is as follows: LO 12-1 LO 12-3

Benefit	Cost
Health insurance—single	$ 5,000
Health insurance—with spouse	$ 8,000
Health insurance—with spouse and dependents	$11,000
Dental and vision	$ 1,500
Dependent care—any specified amount up to $5,000	Variable
Adoption benefits—any specified amount up to $5,000	Variable
Educational benefits—any specified amount (no limit)	Variable
Cash—any specified amount up to $15,000 plan benefit	Variable
401(k)—any specified amount up to $10,000	Variable

For each of the following independent circumstances, determine the amount of income Matt must recognize and the amount of deduction Fresh may claim:
a) Matt selects the single health insurance and places $10,000 in his 401(k).
b) Matt selects the single health insurance, is reimbursed $5,000 for MBA tuition, and takes the remainder in cash.
c) Matt selects the single health insurance and is reimbursed for MBA tuition of $10,000.
d) Matt gets married and selects the health insurance with his spouse and takes the rest in cash to help pay for the wedding.
e) Matt elects to take all cash.

COMPREHENSIVE PROBLEMS

All applicable problems are available with McGraw-Hill's *Connect*® *Accounting*.

53. Pratt is ready to graduate and leave College Park. His future employer (Ferndale Corp.) offers the following four compensation packages from which Pratt may choose. Pratt will start working for Ferndale on January 1, year 1.

Benefit Description	Option 1	Option 2	Option 3	Option 4
Salary	$60,000	$50,000	$45,000	$45,000
Health insurance	0	5,000	5,000	5,000
Restricted stock	0	0	1,000 shares	0
NQOs	0	0	0	100 options

Assume that the restricted stock is 1,000 shares that trade at $5 per share on the grant date (January 1, year 1) and are expected to be worth $10 per share on the vesting date at the end of year 1. Assume that the NQOs (100 options that each allow the employee to purchase 10 shares at $5 strike price). The stock trades at $5 per share on the grant date (January 1, year 1) and is expected to be worth $10 per share on the vesting date at the end of year 1. Also assume that Pratt spends on average $3,000 on health-related costs that would be covered by insurance if he has coverage. Assume that Pratt's marginal tax rate is 35 percent.

a) What is the after-tax value of each compensation package for year 1?

b) If Pratt's sole consideration is maximizing after-tax value for year 1, which scheme should he select?

c) Assuming Pratt chooses Option 3 and sells the stock on the vesting date (on the last day of year 1), complete Pratt's Schedule D for the sale of the restricted stock.

54. Santini's new contract for 2015 indicates the following compensation and benefits:

Benefit Description	Amount
Salary	$130,000
Health insurance	9,000
Restricted stock grant	2,500
Bonus	5,000
Hawaii trip	4,000
Group-term life insurance	1,600
Parking ($275 per month)	3,300

Santini is 54 years old at the end of 2015. He is single and has no dependents. Assume that the employer matches $1 for $1 for the first $6,000 that the employee contributes to his 401(k) during the year. The 100 ISOs each allow the purchase of 10 shares of stock at a strike price of $5 (also the market price on the date of grant). The ISOs vest in two years when the stock price is expected to be $15 and Santini expects to sell the shares in three years when the market price is $20. The restricted stock grant is 500 shares granted when the market price was $5 per share. Assume that the stock vests on December 31, 2015, and that the market price on that date is $7.50 per share. Also assume that Santini is willing to make any elections to reduce equity-based compensation taxes. The Hawaii trip was given to him as the outstanding sales person for 2014. The group-term life policy gives him $150,000 of coverage. Assume that Santini does not itemize deductions for the year. Determine Santini's taxable income and income tax liability for 2015.

planning 55. Sylvana is given a job offer with two alternative compensation packages to choose from. The first package offers her $250,000 annual salary with no qualified fringe benefits. The second package offers $235,000 annual salary plus health and life insurance benefits. If Sylvana were required to purchase the health and life insurance benefits herself, she would need to pay $10,000 annually after taxes. Assume her marginal tax rate is 33 percent.

a) Which compensation package should she choose and by how much would she benefit in after-tax dollars by choosing this package?

b) Assume the second package offers $240,000 plus benefits instead of $235,000 plus benefits. Which compensation package should she choose and by how much would she benefit in after-tax dollars by choosing this package?

planning 56. In 2015, Jill, age 35, received a job offer with two alternative compensation packages to choose from. The first package offers her $90,000 annual salary with no qualified fringe benefits, requires her to pay $3,500 a year for parking, and will purchase life insurance at a cost of $1,000. The second package offers $80,000 annual salary, employer-provided health insurance, annual free parking (worth $300 per month), $200,000 of life insurance (purchasing on her own would have been $1,000 annually), and free flight benefits (she figures that it will save her $5,000 per year). If Jill chooses the first package, she would purchase the health and life insurance benefits herself at a cost of $5,000 annually after taxes and spend another $5,000 in flights while traveling. Assume her marginal tax rate is 28 percent.

a) Which compensation package should she choose, and by how much would she benefit in after-tax dollars by choosing this compensation package instead of the other compensation package?

b) Assume the first package offers $100,000 salary with no qualified benefits instead of $90,000 salary plus benefits. Which compensation package should she choose, and by how much would she benefit in after-tax dollars by choosing this package?

chapter

13 Retirement Savings and Deferred Compensation

Learning Objectives

Upon completing this chapter, you should be able to:

LO 13-1 Describe the tax and nontax aspects of employer-provided defined benefit plans from both the employer's and employee's perspective.

LO 13-2 Explain and determine the tax consequences associated with employer-provided defined contribution plans, including traditional 401(k) and Roth 401(k) plans.

LO 13-3 Describe the tax implications of deferred compensation from both the employer's and employee's perspective.

LO 13-4 Determine the tax consequences of traditional and Roth Individual Retirement Accounts and explain the differences between them.

LO 13-5 Describe retirement savings options available to self-employed taxpayers and compute the limitations for deductible contributions to retirement accounts for self-employed taxpayers.

LO 13-6 Compute the saver's credit.

© Paul Bradbury/age fotostock

Storyline Summary

Taxpayer:	Tina Hillman
Location:	Chicago, Illinois
Employment status:	Graduating student about to begin career in the tax department of Corporate Business Associates
Starting salary:	$60,000 per year
Filing status:	Single
Dependents:	None
Marginal tax rate:	Current year 15 percent, next year 25 percent
Taxpayer:	Lisa Whitlark
Location:	Chicago, Illinois
Employment status:	Recently promoted to chief financial officer (CFO) for Corporate Business Associates
Salary:	$400,000
Filing status:	Married, filing jointly
Marginal tax rate:	33 percent
Dependents:	Spouse and three children
Taxpayer:	Dave Allan
Location:	Chicago, Illinois
Employment status:	Recently retired as CFO for Corporate Business Associates after 20 years of employment with the company
Salary at retirement:	$450,000
Retirement benefits:	Participant in Corporate Business Associates' defined benefit plan, 401(k) plan, and nonqualified deferred compensation plan
Filing status:	Married filing jointly
Dependents:	Spouse
Marginal tax rate:	35 percent for current year
Taxpayer:	Corporate Business Associates (CBA)
Location:	Chicago, Illinois
Marginal tax rate:	35 percent
Status:	Publicly traded corporation

Tina Hillman

Tina Hillman just completed her last exam, finally fulfilling the requirements for a bachelor's degree in accounting. It was the end of June and she would finally have some time to vacation and see her family before September when she will start her professional career working in the tax department of Corporate Business Associates (CBA). While Tina was looking forward to the time off, she was also eager to start making money instead of just spending it. She had a great experience during her internship at CBA last year. She had some challenging but enjoyable work assignments and she got along very well with the staff. Overall, she was excited about the work opportunities she would get at CBA.

Tina recently received an information packet on the benefits available to her as a CBA employee. The information indicated that Tina would be eligible to participate in CBA's 401(k) retirement plan on January 1 of next year. Tina plans on contributing to the plan as soon as she is eligible because CBA matches employee contributions to the plan such that for every dollar contributed by the employee (up to 4 percent of the employee's salary) CBA contributes two dollars. In the meantime, Tina wonders if she has any retirement savings options during the current year while waiting to become eligible to participate in CBA's plan.

Lisa Whitlark

Lisa Whitlark is finally getting used to her new responsibilities. She was recently promoted to the position of chief financial officer (CFO) for CBA. Lisa threw her name into the ring a few months ago when CBA announced that Dave Allan, the former CFO, would be retiring. Lisa had been working as CBA's tax director for the last 10 years. As a top executive of the company, Lisa is now eligible to participate in CBA's nonqualified deferred compensation program. She didn't have this option as a tax director. Lisa knows she should consider both tax and nontax factors when deciding whether and to what extent she will participate in the plan.

Dave Allan

Dave Allan couldn't believe that he was actually retiring at the end of this year. Looking back, his successful career had passed so quickly. At age 72, he is now ready to move on and spend time seeing the world with his wife. Dave's retirement plans are going to be quite expensive. Fortunately, he has accumulated substantial retirement benefits during his CBA career. Dave will be receiving retirement benefits from CBA's defined benefit plan, 401(k) plan, and nonqualified deferred compensation plan. He knows he has some choices about the timing and amounts of his distributions from these plans. Dave wants to be sure to evaluate both the tax and nontax considerations before making these decisions. ■

At different stages in their careers, taxpayers are likely to face issues similar to those confronting Tina, Lisa, and Dave. Saving for retirement is not always easy to do because it requires forgoing cash now in order to receive benefits at some point in the future. However, not saving for retirement can be a costly mistake because it's not likely that government-promised Social Security benefits alone will satisfy most taxpayers' retirement needs.[1] Many employers help employees save for retirement by sponsoring retirement plans on behalf of their employees. These plans may be "qualified" retirement plans or "nonqualified" deferred compensation plans. Qualified plans are subject to certain restrictions not applicable to nonqualified plans. Both qualified and nonqualified plans are useful tools through which employers can

[1]Under current law, the projected cost of Social Security generally increases faster than projected income because of the aging of the baby-boom generation, continuing low fertility since the baby-boom period, and increasing life expectancy. Social Security's total expenditures have exceeded noninterest income of its combined trust funds since 2010. The 2014 Social Security Trustees report projects that the Social Security Trust fund reserves will be depleted in 2033. See http://www.socialsecurity.gov/oact/TRSUM/index.html

achieve various compensation-related goals. In this chapter, we discuss the tax and nontax consequences of qualified retirement plans and nonqualified plans to both employers and to employees, including issues relating to contributions to and distributions from these plans. We also discuss individually managed retirement savings plans available to certain individual taxpayers and qualified retirement plans available to self-employed taxpayers.

EMPLOYER-PROVIDED QUALIFIED PLANS

Traditional **qualified retirement plans** grew from a congressional concern that, if unregulated, employers might not adequately fund and protect employee pension benefits and that they might be tempted to provide lavish retirement plans to highly compensated employees such as executives and business owners to the detriment of rank-and-file employees. To address these concerns, Congress mandated that employer-provided plans only receive tax-favored qualified plan status if they meet certain requirements ensuring the plan does not discriminate against rank-and-file employees and if promised benefits are secure. Over the years, the rules addressing these issues have evolved, but the concept of a qualified plan eligible for favorable tax treatment remains the same.

Employer-provided qualified plans can be generally classified as **defined benefit plans** or **defined contribution plans.** As the name suggests, defined benefit plans spell out the specific benefit the employee will receive on retirement. In contrast, defined contribution plans specify the maximum annual contributions that employers and employees may contribute to the plan. While we explore both basic plan types below, we emphasize defined contribution plans because they are much more common than defined benefit plans.

DEFINED BENEFIT PLANS

LO 13-1

Defined benefit plans are traditional pension plans used by many older and more established companies and tax-exempt organizations. These plans provide standard retirement benefits to employees based on a fixed formula. The formula to determine the standard retirement benefit is usually a function of years of service and employees' compensation levels as they near retirement. For employees who retire in 2015, the maximum annual benefit an employee can receive is the *lesser* of (1) 100 percent of the average of the employee's three highest years of compensation or (2) $210,000.[2]

Example 13-1

CBA provides a defined benefit plan for its employees. The plan uses a fixed formula to determine employee benefits. The formula specifies a benefit of 2 percent for each year of service, up to a maximum of 50 percent (25 years of service), of the average of the employee's three highest years of salary. In 2015, Dave retires from CBA. On the date of retirement, Dave had been a CBA employee for 20 years plus a couple of months. The average of his three highest years of salary was $420,000. What is Dave's annual benefit from the defined benefit plan?

Answer: $168,000 a year. The benefit is calculated by multiplying 40 percent (2 percent for each of his 20 years of service) by $420,000 (the average of his highest three years of salary).

What if: Assume the same facts except that the average of Dave's three highest years of salary was $600,000. What is the annual benefit he will receive from the plan?

Answer: $210,000. The lesser of (1) $240,000 ($600,000 × 40%) or (2) $210,000.

[2]§415(b)(1). The maximum benefit is adjusted annually for inflation.

THE KEY FACTS

Defined Benefit Plans

- Employer specifies benefit employee receives on retirement based on years of service and salary.
- Maximum annual benefit for employees who retire in 2015 is the lesser of (1) 100% of the average of the employee's three highest years of compensation or (2) $210,000.
- Employee must vest to receive benefits using
  - 5-year cliff vesting schedule
  - 7-year graded vesting schedule

Vesting

We've discussed the idea that an employee's benefit is based on the number of years she works for an employer. When an employee works for an employer for only a short time before leaving, her benefit depends on her salary, the number of full years she worked for the employer, and the employer's vesting schedule. **Vesting** is the process of becoming legally entitled to a certain right or property. Thus, a taxpayer vests in retirement benefits (becomes legally entitled to retirement benefits) as she meets certain requirements set forth by the employer. The most restrictive vesting requirements an employer can impose on a qualified defined benefit plan is either a five-year "cliff" or seven-year graded vesting schedule.[3] Under the **cliff vesting** option, after a certain period of time, benefits vest all at once. With a **graded vesting** schedule, the employee's vested benefit increases each full year she works for the employer. Exhibit 13-1 features the five-year cliff and seven-year graded vesting schedules for defined benefit plans.

EXHIBIT 13-1 Defined Benefit Plans Minimum Vesting Schedules*

Full Years of Service	5-year Cliff	7-year Graded
1	0%	0%
2	0	0
3	0	20
4	0	40
5	100	60
6	N/A	80
7	N/A	100

*Percent of employee benefit no longer subject to forfeiture.

Example 13-2

What if: CBA provides a defined benefit plan to its employees. Under the plan, employees earn a benefit equal to 2 percent for every year of service of their average salary for their three highest years of compensation. CBA implements a seven-year graded vesting schedule as part of the plan. If Tina works for CBA for four years, earning annual salaries of $60,000, $65,000, $70,000, and $75,000, and then leaves to work for another employer, what benefit would she be entitled to receive (her vested benefit)?

Answer: $2,240, computed as follows:

Description	Amount	Explanation
(1) Average of three highest years of salary	$70,000	($65,000 + 70,000 + 75,000)/3.
(2) Benefit percentage	× 8%	Four years of service × 2 percent per year.
(3) Full annual benefit	$ 5,600	(1) × (2).
(4) Vesting percentage	× 40%	Four years of service on 7-year graded vesting schedule (see Exhibit 13-1).
Vested benefit	$ 2,240	(3) × (4) Amount that she is allowed to keep.

Tina would forfeit her unvested benefit of $3,360 ($5,600 − $2,240 vested benefit).

What if: Assume the same facts except that CBA uses a five-year cliff schedule. What would be Tina's vested benefit?

Answer: $0. She did not work for CBA for five years so she would not vest in her benefits in CBA's defined benefit plan.

[3]§411(a) specifies maximum vesting periods for employer contributions to qualified plans. Employers are allowed to adopt more generous vesting requirements such as immediate vesting if they choose.

Distributions

When their benefits have vested, employees are entitled to receive future distributions according to the provisions of the plan—these distributions are taxable as ordinary income in the year received.[4] Distributions from defined benefit plans (and defined contribution plans) are subject to early distribution requirements and to minimum distribution requirements. Distributions violating these requirements are penalized. However, because defined benefit plans typically don't permit payout arrangements that would trigger the early distribution or minimum distribution penalties, these penalties are of greater concern to participants in defined contribution plans. Consequently, we address these penalties in more detail when we discuss distributions from defined contribution plans.

Nontax Considerations

From a nontax perspective, a defined benefit plan imposes administrative burdens and risks on the employer sponsoring the plan. A significant amount of work is required to track employee benefits and to compute required contributions to the plan. Because defined benefit plans require employers to provide particular benefits to employees on retirement, the employer bears the investment risk associated with investments within the plan. Beyond the additional administrative costs and risk, defined benefit plans impose significant funding costs on employers relative to alternative retirement plans. Consequently, in recent years, many employers have begun replacing defined benefit plans with defined contribution plans.

THE KEY FACTS

Defined Benefit Plans

- Employer, not employee, bears investment risk of plan.
- Early and minimum distribution rules apply, but usually not restrictive.

DEFINED CONTRIBUTION PLANS

LO 13-2

Defined contribution plans provide an alternative approach for employers to help employees save for retirement. While defined contribution plans and defined benefit plans have similar overall objectives, they are different in important ways. First, employers maintain separate accounts for *each* employee participating in a defined contribution plan. Second, defined contribution plans specify the up-front contributions the employer will make to the employee's separate account rather than specifying the ultimate benefit the employee will receive from the plan. Third, employees are frequently allowed to contribute to their own defined contribution plans, and in many instances they contribute more than their employers. Finally, employees are generally free to choose how amounts in their retirement accounts are invested. If investments in the plan perform well, employees benefit; if the investments perform poorly, employees suffer the financial consequences. Thus, relative to defined benefit plans, defined contribution plans shift the funding responsibility and investment risk from the employer to the employee.

Employers may provide different types of defined contribution plans such as 401(k) (used by for-profit companies), 403(b) plans (used by nonprofit organizations, including educational institutions), and 457 plans (used by government agencies), profit sharing plans, and money purchase pension plans.[5] Employers may even offer multiple defined contribution plans. Because of their popularity, we use 401(k) plans here to represent the general category of defined contribution plans. However, no matter what defined contribution plan(s) employers provide, employers must ensure that they meet certain requirements relating to annual contribution limits and vesting requirements. Also, to a greater extent than with defined benefit plans, *participants* in defined contribution plans must be careful to avoid the penalties associated with either early distributions or insufficient **minimum distributions** from these plans.

THE KEY FACTS

Traditional Defined Contribution Plans: Overview

- Employer specifies amount it will contribute to employee's retirement account, *not* the amount the employee will receive at retirement.
  - Employers typically match employee contributions.
- Employee chooses how funds are invested and bears market risk.

[4]Distributions of both defined benefit plans and defined contribution plans are reported to taxpayers on Form 1099R.

[5]401(k), 403(b), and 457 plans reflect the Code sections describing the plans.

Employer Matching

Employers, but not employees, typically contribute to certain defined contribution plan types such as profit sharing (contributions may be made based on a fixed formula based on profits or may be at the employer's discretion) and money purchase plans (contributions are a fixed percentage of the employee's compensation). In contrast, employees contribute to 401(k) type plans. Many employers also "match" employee contributions to these plans. When deciding whether to contribute to a 401(k) plan, employees should take into account their employer's matching policy. For companies matching employee contributions, the match can range from a small percentage (25 cents on the dollar) to a multiple of the employee's contribution. A dollar-for-dollar match gives employees a 100 percent immediate return on their contributions. Therefore, whenever possible, employees should contribute enough to receive the full match from the employer because, subject to the employer's vesting requirements, the match represents an immediate, no-risk return on the amount contributed.

Example 13-3

Tina's offer from CBA includes participation in its 401(k) plan effective the beginning of next year. The plan's formula provides that CBA will match employee contributions on a two-for-one basis up to employee contributions of 4 percent of the employee's annual salary. Next year when she's eligible, Tina will contribute 4 percent of her salary to the plan. Assuming a $60,000 salary for next year, how much will Tina contribute and how much will CBA contribute to Tina's 401(k) account?

Answer: Tina will contribute $2,400 ($60,000 × 4%) to her 401(k) account and CBA will contribute $4,800 ($2,400 × 2).

THE KEY FACTS

Traditional Defined Contribution Plans: Contribution Limits

- 2015 overall contribution limits for sum of employer and employee contributions.
  - Lesser of $53,000 ($59,000 for employees 50 years old by year-end) or 100 percent of employee's annual compensation.
- 2015 employee contribution limit to 401(k) plan:
  - $18,000 or
  - $24,000 for employees 50 years old by year-end.

Contribution Limits

For 2015, the sum of employer *and* employee contributions to an employee's defined contribution account(s) is limited to the *lesser* of (1) $53,000 ($59,000 for employees who are at least 50 years of age by the end of the year) or (2) 100 percent of the employee's compensation for the year.[6] *Employee* contributions to an employee's 401(k) account are limited to $18,000 (or $24,000 for employees that reach age 50 by the end of the year).[7] While this limit applies only to employee contributions, the $53,000 (or $59,000) limit still applies to the sum of employer and employee contributions. For example, if an employee under age 50 contributes the maximum $18,000 to her employer-sponsored 401(k) plan in 2015, the employer's contribution would be limited to $35,000 ($53,000 − $18,000).[8] Because of this limit on employer contributions, highly compensated employees may not be able to receive the full employer match available to other employees.

Example 13-4

Before Dave retires at the end of 2015 he continues to contribute to his CBA-sponsored 401(k) account. CBA matches employee contributions on a two-for-one basis up to 4 percent of the employee's salary. Dave is 72 years old at the end of the year and he earned a salary of $450,000 during the year. Dave contributed $24,000 to his 401(k) account. How much would CBA contribute to Dave's 401(k) account?

Answer: $35,000 [$59,000 (Dave is 50+ years old) minus $24,000 (Dave's contribution)]. Without the limitation, CBA would have contributed $36,000 ($450,000 × 4% × 2) to Dave's account.

[6]§415(c)(1). The amount is indexed for inflation under §415(d)(1)(C).

[7]§402(g)(1). The amount is indexed for inflation under §402(g)(4).

[8]If an employee participates in more than one defined contribution plan, these limits apply to the total employee and employer contributions to all defined contribution plans. Thus, in a situation where the employee participates in more than one defined contribution plan, the contribution limits for any one defined contribution plan may be less than the overall contribution limits described here.

What if: Assume Dave contributed $23,000 to his 401(k) account. How much would CBA contribute to his account?

Answer: $36,000. Note that this is a better deal for Dave because $59,000 ends up in his account either way, but he funded $23,000 of the contribution instead of $24,000.

Vesting

When employees contribute to defined contribution plans, they are fully vested in the accrued benefit from the contributions (employee contributions plus earnings on the contributions). However, employees vest in the accrued benefit from employer contributions (employer contributions plus earnings on the contributions) based on the employer's vesting schedule. When separate employee accounts are not maintained, the accrued benefit from employee contributions is determined by multiplying the total accrued benefit in the account by the ratio of employee contributions to total contributions (employee plus employer) to the account.[9] The accrued benefit from employer contributions is the difference between the total accrued benefit and the accrued benefit from employee contributions. The minimum vesting requirements for defined contribution plans are a bit more accelerated than the five-year cliff and seven-year graded vesting schedules applicable to defined benefit plans. For defined contribution plans, employers have the option of providing three-year cliff or six-year graded vesting. These vesting schedules are presented in Exhibit 13-2.

EXHIBIT 13-2 Defined Contribution Plans Minimum Vesting Schedules*

Full Years of Service with Employer	3-year Cliff	6-year Graded
1	0%	0%
2	0	20
3	100	40
4	N/A	60
5	N/A	80
6	N/A	100

*Percent of employer contributions no longer subject to forfeiture.

Example 13-5

What if: Suppose that in three and one-half years the balance in Tina's 401(k) account is $33,000. In total, Tina had contributed $9,000 to the account and CBA had contributed $18,000. Also assume that Tina was 40 percent vested in her accrued benefit from CBA contributions. What is Tina's vested benefit?

Answer: $19,800 [$11,000 accrued benefit from her contributions + $8,800 ($22,000 × 40%), which is 40 percent of the $22,000 accrued benefit from CBA contributions]. Tina is fully vested in the $11,000 accrued benefit from her contributions ($33,000 total accrued benefit in account × $9,000 employee contributions/$27,000 total contributions to her account) and 40 percent vested in the $22,000 accrued benefit from CBA contributions ($33,000 total accrued benefit in account minus $11,000 accrued benefit from her contributions).

THE KEY FACTS

Traditional Defined Contribution Plans: Vesting and After-Tax Cost

- Employee must vest to be entitled to employer contributions (and earnings on those contributions) using:
  - 3-year cliff vesting schedule.
  - 6-year graded vesting schedule.
- Employee contributes before-tax amounts (contributions are deductible).
- After-tax cost is before-tax contribution minus tax savings from contribution.

After-Tax Cost of Contributions

Employees effectively deduct their contributions to defined contribution plans, except for Roth 401(k) plans (discussed below), because contributions are removed from their taxable salary (they are, however, still subject to FICA taxes).[10] When

[9]§411(c).

[10]Employees pay the same FICA taxes no matter how much they contribute to defined contribution plans.

employees contribute to traditional defined contribution plan accounts, they are contributing "before-tax" dollars because the contribution represents the cost of the contribution before considering the tax savings generated by the contribution. The employee's after-tax contribution (or after-tax cost of making the contribution) is the before-tax contribution minus the tax savings generated by the contribution.

Example 13-6

Tina contributed $2,400 to her CBA-sponsored traditional 401(k) account in her first full calendar year with CBA. Given Tina's marginal tax rate of 25 percent, what is the after-tax cost of her $2,400 contribution?

Answer: $1,800 computed as follows:

Description	Amount	Explanation
(1) Before-tax contribution	$2,400	Cost of contribution before tax savings.
(2) Tax savings from contribution	(600)	$2,400 deduction × 25 percent marginal tax rate.
After-tax cost of contribution	$1,800	(1) + (2).

Distributions

When employees receive distributions from defined contribution plans (other than Roth 401(k) plans), the distributions are taxed as ordinary income. However, when employees receive distributions (or take withdrawals) from defined contribution plans either too early or too late, they must pay a penalty in addition to the ordinary income taxes they owe on the distributions. Generally, employees who receive distributions before they reach

- 59½ years of age or
- 55 years of age *and* have separated from service (retired or let go)

are subject to a 10 percent nondeductible penalty on the amount of the early distributions.

Example 13-7

What if: Assume that when she reaches 60 years of age, Lisa Whitlark retires from CBA and receives a $60,000 distribution from her 401(k) account in the year she retires. Assuming her marginal ordinary tax rate is 33 percent, what amount of tax and penalty will Lisa pay on the distribution?

Answer: $19,800 taxes ($60,000 × 33%) + $0 penalty (she is over 59½ years of age on date of distribution).

What if: Assume that when Lisa is 57 years of age and still employed by CBA, she requests and receives a $60,000 distribution from her 401(k) account. What amount of tax and penalty is Lisa required to pay on the distribution?

Answer: $19,800 taxes ($60,000 × 33%) + $6,000 penalty ($60,000 × 10%).

What if: Assume that Lisa is let go from CBA when she is 57 years old. In that same year, she requests and receives a $60,000 distribution from her 401(k) account. What amount of tax and penalty is Lisa required to pay on the distribution?

Answer: $19,800 taxes ($60,000 × 33%) + $0 penalty (she is over 55 years of age and has separated from service with CBA).

Taxpayers who fail to receive a minimum distribution for (pertaining to) a particular year are also penalized. The year for which taxpayers must receive their *first* minimum distribution is the *later* of

- The year in which the employee reaches 70½ years of age.
- The year in which the employee retires.

Taxpayers must receive their first required minimum distribution no later than April 1 of the year after the year to which the distribution pertains.[11] Taxpayers generally must receive minimum distributions for subsequent years by the end of the years to which they pertain. Thus, a retired taxpayer who turns 70½ years of age in 2015 must receive a minimum distribution for 2015 by April 1, 2016. The same taxpayer must also receive a minimum distribution for 2016 by December 31, 2016.

The amount of the minimum required distribution for a particular year is the taxpayer's account balance at the end of the year *prior to* the year to which the distribution pertains multiplied by a percentage from an IRS Uniform Lifetime Table. The percentage is based on the taxpayer's age at the end of the year to which the distribution pertains. An abbreviated version of the table is presented in Exhibit 13-3.[12]

THE KEY FACTS

Traditional Defined Contribution Plans: Distributions

- Taxed at ordinary rates.
- 10 percent penalty on early distributions.
  - Before 59½ years of age if not retired or
  - Before 55 years of age if retired.
- Minimum distribution requirements:
  - Must receive by April 1 of the later of (1) the year after the year in which taxpayer reaches 70½ years of age or (2) the year after the year in which the employee retires.
  - If retired employee waits until year after 70½ to begin receiving distributions, must receive two distributions in year of first distribution.
- 50 percent penalty on excess of required minimum distribution amounts and amount actually distributed.

EXHIBIT 13-3 Abbreviated Uniform Lifetime Table

Age of Participant	Distribution Period	Applicable Percentage*
70	27.4	3.65%
71	26.5	3.77
72	25.6	3.91
73	24.7	4.05
74	23.8	4.20
75	22.9	4.37
76	22.0	4.54
77	21.2	4.72

*The applicable percentage is calculated by dividing one by the relevant distribution period.

Example 13-8

What if: Suppose that Dave retires from CBA in 2015 at age 72 (also 72 at year-end). When must he receive his minimum distribution for 2015 from his 401(k) account?

Answer: By April 1, 2016.

What if: Assuming Dave retires in 2015 and that his 401(k) account balance on December 31, 2014, was $3,500,000, what is the amount of the minimum distribution Dave must receive by April 1, 2016?

Answer: $136,850 ($3,500,000 × 3.91%). The percentage from the IRS table for determining this minimum distribution is based on Dave's age at the end of 2015, which is 72 years old.

What if: Assuming Dave's 401(k) account balance on December 31, 2015, is $3,700,000, what is the minimum distribution for 2016 Dave must receive sometime during 2016 (in addition to the $136,850 distribution by April 1)?

Answer: $149,850 ($3,700,000 × 4.05%) for 2016 to be received in 2016.

[11]The amount of the required minimum distribution *for the year* in which a retired employee turns 70½ is the same whether the employee receives the distribution in the year she turns 70½ or whether she defers receiving the distribution until the next year (no later than April 1).

[12]See Reg. §1.401(a)(9)-9 Q&A 2 to reference the full version of the table. The table provided in this exhibit applies in most circumstances.

The consequences for failing to receive timely minimum distributions from defined contribution plans are even more severe than receiving distributions too early. Taxpayers incur a 50 percent nondeductible penalty on the amount of a minimum distribution the employee should have received but did not. For this reason, it is vital that payouts from defined contribution plans be monitored to avoid not only the 10 percent premature distribution penalty, but also the 50 percent penalty for late withdrawals.

Example 13-9

What if: In the previous example, we determined that Dave must receive a minimum distribution of $136,850 from his 401(k) account by April 1, 2016. If Dave does not receive any distribution before April 1, 2016, what penalty will he be required to pay?

Answer: $68,425 ($136,850 × 50%). This nondeductible penalty is a strong incentive to take the required minimum distributions or at least to take the penalty into consideration when developing a distribution plan.

What if: Assume that Dave received his first distribution from his 401(k) account on March 1, 2016, in the amount of $100,000. But, he did not receive any other distributions before April 1, 2016. What penalty is Dave required to pay?

Answer: $18,425 [($136,850 − $100,000) × 50%]

In contrast to defined benefit plans, defined contribution plans often provide distribution options that could trigger the penalty for premature distributions for the uninformed or unwary. For example, an employee who retires (or is fired) and takes a lump-sum distribution from her defined contribution account in a year before the year in which she turns 55 will be subject to a 10 percent early distribution penalty on the entire amount of the distribution. Employees who receive such lump-sum distributions may avoid the 10 percent penalty by electing to "roll over" (deposit) the distributions into one of the individually managed retirement plans we discuss later in this chapter.

After-Tax Rates of Return

For a given before-tax rate of return, the longer the taxpayer defers distributions from a qualified retirement account, the greater the taxpayer's after-tax rate of return on the account, because deferring the distribution reduces the present value of the taxes paid on the distribution. A taxpayer's after-tax rate of return is also sensitive to the taxpayer's marginal tax rate at the time she contributes to the plan and at the time she receives distributions from the plan. All else being equal, the higher her marginal tax rate at the time she contributes to the plan, the higher the after-tax rate of return (the higher tax rate makes the deduction more valuable), and the lower her marginal tax rate at the time she receives distributions from the plan the higher the after-tax rate of return (the lower rate reduces the taxes on the income).

Of course, any employer contributions to an employee's account, such as CBA's two-for-one matching contributions to Tina's account, significantly increases the after-tax rate of return (and after-tax accumulation) because the contributions increase the employee's after-tax proceeds, but the employee's cost of these contributions is zero.

Exhibit 13-4 summarizes the tax aspects of defined benefit and defined contribution plans.

EXHIBIT 13-4 Defined Benefit Plan vs. Defined Contribution Plan Summary

	Defined Benefit Plan	Defined Contribution Plan
Benefits	• Specifies benefit employee receives on retirement. • Maximum benefit in 2015 lesser of (1) 100 percent of average of highest three years' compensation or (2) $210,000.	• Specifies the amounts employer and employee contribute to the account. • Ultimate benefit depends on earnings on contributions.
Payout type	• Life annuity. • Lump sum distribution of the present value of standard benefit.	• Life annuity. • Lump sum. • Fixed number of years.
Funding requirements	• Employers fund increase in expected future liability each year.	• No funding requirement other than to make required contributions to employee accounts.
Employer's contributions tax deductible?	• Yes.	• Yes, but limited to 25 percent of aggregate employee annual compensation.
Employee's contributions tax deductible?	• No employee contributions.	• Yes, subject to limitations on the amount that can be contributed [$18,000 ($24,000 if 50 or older) maximum contribution to 401(k) plan in 2015].
Contribution limits	• Not applicable.	• In 2015, lesser of (1) $53,000 ($59,000 for taxpayers at least 50 years of age at end of year) and (2) 100 percent of the employee's compensation for year.
Other factors	• All employees paid from same account. • Heavy administrative burden. • Employer assumes investment risk.	• Separate accounts for each employee. • Employees make investment choices. • Employees assume investment risk.
Vesting requirements	• 5-year cliff or • 7-year graded	• 3-year cliff or • 6-year graded • Employee contributions vest immediately.
Distributions	• Taxed as ordinary income. • No 10 percent penalty if 55 years of age by year-end and retired. • Minimum distributions required by April 1 of year after the later of (1) year employee reaches 70½ or (2) year employee retires.	• Taxed as ordinary income (except Roth type accounts). • No 10 percent penalty if 55 years of age by year-end and retired. • Minimum distributions requirements same as for defined benefit plan.

Roth 401(k) Plans

Employers that provide **traditional 401(k)** plans to employees may also provide **Roth 401(k)** plans. As we discuss below, employee tax consequences for Roth 401(k) plans differ from tax consequences of other traditional defined contribution plans.

When employers provide a Roth 401(k) plan, *employees* may elect to contribute to the Roth 401(k) *instead of or in addition to* contributing to a traditional 401(k) plan. However, *employer* contributions to an employee's 401(k) account must go to the employee's *traditional* 401(k) account rather than the employee's Roth 401(k) account. Consequently, the balance in an employee's Roth 401(k) account must consist

THE KEY FACTS

Roth 401(k) Defined Contribution Plans

- Employees but not employers may contribute.
  - Employers contribute to traditional 401(k).
- Contributions are not deductible.
  - Employees contribute after-tax dollars.
  - Same contribution limits as traditional 401(k) plans.

of only the employee's contributions and the earnings on those contributions. Because employers providing Roth 401(k) plans to employees are not allowed to contribute to the Roth plans, these employers are required to maintain traditional 401(k) accounts for each employee participating in the Roth 401(k) plan.

In contrast to contributions to traditional 401(k) plans, employee contributions to Roth 401(k) accounts are *not* deductible and, therefore, do not produce any immediate tax savings for employees. Consequently, employees contributing to Roth 401(k) accounts are contributing after-tax dollars. That is, employees wanting to contribute a certain amount to a Roth 401(k) plan must earn more than that specified amount in order to have the desired contribution amount remaining *after* paying taxes on the amount they earn. For example, assume an employee with a 20 percent marginal tax rate wants to contribute $2,000 to a Roth 401(k) account. To earn the funds to make this contribution, the employee must earn $2,500 before taxes. The tax on the $2,500 of income is $500 ($2,500 × 20%). This leaves the taxpayer with $2,000 after taxes ($2,500 before taxes minus $500 in taxes) to contribute to the Roth 401(k) account.

Example 13-10

THE KEY FACTS

Roth 401(k) Defined Contribution Plans

- Qualified distributions not taxable.
  - Account open for five years.
  - Employee at least 59½ at time of distribution.
- Nonqualified distributions.
  - Distributions of account earnings taxable and subject to 10 percent penalty.
  - Distributions of contributions not taxed or penalized.
  - Distribution × ratio of contributions to account balance is nontaxable.
- After-tax return equals before-tax return.

What if: Let's assume that CBA offers a Roth 401(k) plan in addition to its traditional 401(k) plan. In her first full calendar year of employment with CBA, Tina elects to contribute 4 percent of her $60,000 salary to CBA's Roth 401(k) plan instead of CBA's traditional 401(k) plan. What is Tina's after-tax cost of this $2,400 contribution (her marginal tax rate is 25 percent)?

Answer: $2,400. Her after-tax cost is her $2,400 contribution because the contribution does not generate any tax savings.

What is Tina's before-tax cost of the contribution? That is, how much did Tina need to earn before taxes to fund the $2,400 after-tax contribution?

Answer: $3,200. Because her marginal tax rate is 25 percent, she needs to earn $3,200 before taxes [$2,400/(1 − .25)] to have $2,400 to contribute to the Roth 401(k) after taxes [$3,200 × (1 − .25)] When she contributes $2,400 *after taxes* to the Roth 401(k), she is contributing $3,200 *before taxes.*

While contributions to Roth 401(k) accounts are not deductible and, as a result, do not generate any current tax savings, *qualified* distributions from a Roth 401(k) account are excluded from gross income. Note that because these distributions are excluded from income, in contrast to traditional 401(k) distributions, qualifying Roth 401(k) distributions do not increase AGI and thus do not cause AGI-based tax benefit phase-outs (e.g., certain itemized deductions and tax credits) and they do not cause an increase in the taxation of the recipient's Social Security benefits (see Chapter 5 for discussion of taxation of Social Security benefits).

Example 13-11

What if: In the previous example, Tina contributed $2,400 after taxes to her Roth 401(k) account in her first calendar year on the job with CBA. Let's assume that Tina leaves this contribution in the account until she retires in 40 years at the age of 63, that her contribution earns an annual 8 percent before-tax rate of return, and that her marginal tax rate will be 30 percent when she receives the distribution. How much will Tina have accumulated after taxes if she withdraws the initial contribution and all the earnings on the contribution when she retires?

Answer: $52,139 ($2,400 × 1.08^{40}).

Tina's after-tax rate of return on her $2,400 after-tax contribution is exactly 8 percent, the same as the before-tax rate of return. With a Roth 401(k) the after-tax rate of return should always equal the before-tax rate of return because the after-tax cost of the contribution and the after-tax accumulation on distribution are not affected by the taxpayer's marginal tax rate at the time of contribution or at the time of distribution.

Qualified distributions from Roth 401(k) accounts are those made after the employee's account has been open for five taxable years *and* the employee is at least 59½ years of age. All other distributions are nonqualified distributions. When a taxpayer receives a *non*qualified distribution from a Roth 401(k) account, the tax consequences of the distribution depends on the extent to which the distribution is from the account earnings and the extent to which it is from the employee's contributions to the account. Nonqualified distributions of the account *earnings* are fully taxable and are subject to the 10 percent early distribution penalty. Nonqualified distributions of the taxpayer's account *contributions* are not subject to tax because the taxpayer did not deduct these amounts. If less than the entire balance in the plan is distributed, the nontaxable portion of the distribution is determined by multiplying the amount of the distribution by the ratio of account contributions to the total account balance.

Example 13-12

What if: In the previous example, Tina contributed $2,400 to CBA's Roth 401(k) plan, her account generated an 8 percent before-tax return, and she withdrew the entire balance 40 years after the contribution. Let's assume that at the end of year 6, Tina needs cash, so she withdraws $1,000 from the account when the account balance is $3,808 and her marginal tax rate is 28 percent. How much tax and penalty, if any, is Tina required to pay on this nonqualified distribution?

Answer: $104 tax and $37 penalty, computed as follows:

Description	Amount	Explanation
(1) Nondeductible contribution to Roth 401(k)	$2,400	Beginning of year 1.
(2) Account balance end of year 6	3,808	$2,400 × 1.08[6].
(3) Nonqualified distribution end of year 6	1,000	
(4) Percentage of distribution that is not taxable	63.03%	(1)/(2).
(5) Nontaxable portion of distribution	630	(3) × (4).
(6) Taxable portion of distribution	370	(3) − (5).
(7) Marginal tax rate in year 6	28%	
(8) Regular income tax on distribution	**104**	**(6) × (7).**
(9) Penalty tax percentage for early distributions	10%	
(10) Penalty tax on early distribution	**37**	**(6) × (9).**
Total tax and penalty on early distribution	$ 141	(8) + (10).

Finally, it is important to note that the minimum distribution requirements applicable to traditional 401(k) accounts also apply to Roth 401(k) accounts.

Comparing Traditional Defined Contribution Plans and Roth 401(k) Plans

We've described and discussed the tax consequences associated with participating in traditional and Roth 401(k) plans. So which is better for employees? If given a choice, which type of 401(k) plan should you contribute to? As we've discussed, current and future marginal tax rates are an important factor to consider. In general terms, the traditional 401(k) plans will generate higher (lower) after-tax rates of return than Roth 401(k) plans when taxpayers' marginal tax rates *decrease* (*increase*) from the time of contribution to the time of distribution. If marginal tax rates remain the same, 401(k) plans and Roth 401(k) plans will generate the same after-tax rate of return. It is also important to consider that qualified distributions from Roth 401(k) accounts do not increase AGI so they do not cause taxpayers to lose tax benefits that are phased-out based on an AGI threshold. Exhibit 13-5 summarizes and compares traditional 401(k) plans and Roth 401(k) plans.

EXHIBIT 13-5 **Traditional 401(k) Plan vs. Roth 401(k) Plan Summary**

	Traditional 401(k) Plans	Roth 401(k) Plans
Employer contributions allowed	• Yes.	• No.
Tax consequences to employer	• Contributions deductible when paid.	• Not applicable.
Tax consequences to employee	• Contributions are deductible.	• Contributions are not deductible.
Distributions	• Taxed as ordinary income. • No 10 percent penalty if 55 years of age at year-end and retired. • If life annuity or joint and survivor annuity no penalty even if not 55 years of age. • Minimum distributions required by April 1 of the later of (1) the year after the year in which the employee reaches 70½ or (2) the year after the year in which the employee retires. • Failure to meet minimum distribution timing and amount requirements triggers 50 percent penalty. • Nonqualified distributions (early distributions) trigger ordinary tax and penalty tax on earnings.	• Qualified distributions not taxed. • Qualified distributions when account is open for at least 5 years and employee has reached the age of 59½. • No 10 percent penalty if 55 years of age at year-end and retired. • If life annuity or joint and survivor annuity, no penalty even if not 55 years of age. • Minimum distribution requirements and penalties are the same as for traditional 401(k) plans. • If nonqualified distribution, nontaxable percentage of distribution is the ratio of contributions to total account value.

LO 13-3

NONQUALIFIED DEFERRED COMPENSATION

So far, our discussion has emphasized the tax and nontax aspects of employer-provided *qualified* defined benefit and defined contribution plans. In addition to or perhaps in lieu of these types of qualified plans, employers may offer **nonqualified deferred compensation** plans to certain employees.

Nonqualified Plans vs. Qualified Defined Contribution Plans

Deferred compensation plans permit employees to defer (or contribute) current salary in exchange for a future payment from the employer. From an employee's perspective, the tax consequences of contributions to and distributions from nonqualified plans receive tax treatment similar to qualified defined contribution plans. For example, just as with defined contribution plans, employee contributions to nonqualified deferred compensation plans (NQDC) reduce an employee's taxable income in the year of contribution.[13] Also, just as with qualified plans, employees are not taxed on the balance in their accounts until they receive distributions. Finally,

[13]Technically, employees participating in NQDC plans defer the receipt of current salary and employers credit the employee's account for the amount of the deferral. This has the same effect as if the employee had actually made a deductible contribution to her account as an employee participating in a defined contribution plan would do.

like distributions from qualified plans, distributions from nonqualified deferred compensation plans are taxed as ordinary income.

Example 13-13

CBA provides a nonqualified deferred compensation plan under which executives may elect to defer up to 10 percent of their salary. Dave Allan has been participating in the plan by deferring a portion of his salary each year for the last 15 years. The balance in his deferred compensation account is currently $2,000,000. In keeping with a fixed payment schedule Dave elected under the plan, he receives a $50,000 distribution. What amount of tax must Dave pay on the distribution (recall that his marginal tax rate is 35 percent)?

Answer: $17,500 ($50,000 × .35).

For employers, NQDC plans are treated differently than qualified plans. For example, because nonqualified plans are not subject to the same restrictive requirements pertaining to qualified plans, employers may discriminate in terms of whom they allow to participate in the plan. In fact, employers generally restrict participation in nonqualified plans to more highly compensated employees. Also, employers are not required to "fund" nonqualified plans. That is, employers are not required to formally set aside and accumulate funds specifically to pay the deferred compensation obligation when it comes due. Rather, employers typically retain funds deferred by employees under the plan, use the funds for business operations, and pay the deferred compensation out of their general funds when it becomes payable. Because employers retain, control, and generate income on funds deferred by employees under nonqualified plans, employers are allowed to *deduct only actual payments* of deferred compensation to employees. That is, employers cannot deduct the amount of deferred compensation they accrue each year. Thus, for tax purposes, an employer may not deduct the deferred compensation when an employee initially earns the compensation even though the employer becomes liable for the deferred compensation payment. In contrast, for financial accounting purposes, companies generally expense deferred compensation in the year employees earn it and record a corresponding deferred compensation liability.[14]

THE KEY FACTS

Nonqualified Deferred Compensation Plans

- Employees defer current income in exchange for future payment.
  - Employee taxed when payment received.
  - Employee generally selects deemed investment choices up front to determine return on deferral.
  - Just like traditional deferred compensation plans, after-tax rate of return depends on before-tax rate of return, marginal tax rate at time of deferral, and marginal tax rate at time of distribution.
  - Payment not guaranteed. If employer doesn't pay, employee becomes unsecured creditor.

Employee Considerations

Should employees participate in nonqualified plans when given the chance? The decision obviously involves several considerations. First, employees must decide if the benefits they expect to receive from qualified retirement plans (or other sources) will be adequate to provide for their expected costs during retirement. Next, employees should consider whether they can afford to defer current salary. This may not be a significant concern for most eligible participants, however, because nonqualified plans are generally available only to highly compensated employees who likely may not have the liquidity concerns that lower-compensated employees may face. Also, employees should consider the expected after-tax rate of return on the deferred salary relative to what they could earn on the salary by receiving it currently and personally investing it.

Generally, larger employers allow employees participating in nonqualified plans to choose how their deferred compensation will be invested from among alternative investments provided under the plan (money market, various bond funds, and stock funds among others). However, because employers *do not actually invest* compensation

[14]Employers record additional expense and liability as earnings on the deferred compensation accumulate.

deferred under the plan on the employee's behalf, the employer credits the employee's account "as if" the employee's contributions had been invested in the employee's *deemed* investment choices. The description of Coca-Cola Company's nonqualified retirement plan, presented in Exhibit 13-6, illustrates this concept:

EXHIBIT 13-6 Description of Nonqualified Retirement Plan
Excerpt from Coca-Cola Company's proxy statement

Deferred Compensation Plan. The Deferred Compensation Plan is a nonqualified and unfunded deferred compensation program offered to approximately 925 U.S. based Company employees in 2013. International Service Associates do not participate in the Deferred Compensation Plan. Eligible participants may defer up to 80% of base salary and up to 95% of their annual incentive. The Company has the benefit of full unrestricted use of all amounts deferred under the Deferred Compensation Plan until such amounts are required to be distributed to the plan participants. Gains and losses are credited based on the participant's election of a variety of deemed investment choices. The Company does not match any employee deferral or guarantee a return. Participants' accounts may or may not appreciate and may depreciate depending on the performance of their deemed investment choices. None of the deemed investment choices provide returns at above-market or preferential rates. All deferrals are paid out in cash upon distribution. Participants may schedule a distribution during employment or may opt to receive their balance after separation from service.

Just as with qualified defined contribution plans, other than Roth 401(k) plans, an employee's after-tax rate of return on deferred compensation depends on the employee's investment choices *and* on the employee's marginal tax rates at the time of the contribution and at the time of the distribution.[15]

Example 13-14

As a new executive with CBA, Lisa Whitlark is eligible to participate in its nonqualified deferred compensation plan. Recall that CBA provides a nonqualified deferred compensation plan under which executives may elect to defer up to 10 percent of their salary. In her first year with CBA, Lisa elects to defer $40,000 of salary ($400,000 × 10%) under the plan. Because her current marginal income tax rate is 33 percent, she saves $13,200 in taxes by deferring the salary ($40,000 × 33%). Consequently, her after-tax cost of deferring the compensation is $26,800 ($40,000 − $13,200). She plans to receive a distribution from the nonqualified plan in 20 years when she expects her marginal tax rate to be 28 percent. Lisa selects a stock index fund as her "deemed" investment choice. She expects the fund to provide an 8 percent before-tax rate of return on her $40,000 deferral. What will Lisa receive after taxes from her $40,000 deferral?

Answer: $134,235 after-tax accumulation, computed as follows:

Description	Amount	Explanation
Before-tax contribution	$ 40,000	Deferral of 10 percent of her current salary.
Times future value factor	$\times 1.08^{20}$	8 percent annual rate of return for 20 years.
Future value of deferred compensation	186,438	Value of deferral/distribution 20 years after deferral.
Minus: taxes payable on distribution	(52,203)	$186,438 value of account × 28 percent marginal tax rate.
After-tax proceeds from distributions	**$134,235**	Value of account minus taxes payable on distribution.

[15]As discussed previously, after-tax accumulations in Roth 401(k) accounts are not dependent on current and future marginal tax rates.

Deferring salary to a future period is potentially an effective tax planning technique, particularly when the employee anticipates her marginal tax rate to be lower in the year she will receive the deferred compensation than it is in the year she defers the salary. In fact, if employees had complete flexibility as to when they could receive distributions from deferred compensation plans, they would likely accelerate distributions from deferred compensation plans into years they knew with certainty would have relatively low marginal tax rates. This strategy is limited, however, by rules requiring employees to specify the timing of the future payments at the time they decide to participate in deferred compensation plans.[16]

Employees considering participating in nonqualified deferred compensation plans should also consider potential financial risks of doing so. Recall that employers are not required to fund nonqualified plans. So, there's always the possibility that the employer will not have the funds to pay the employee on the scheduled distribution dates (the employer becomes bankrupt). If the employer is not able to make the payments, the employee becomes an unsecured creditor of the company and may never receive the full compensation owed to her. Consequently, the employee should evaluate the financial stability of the company when deciding whether to defer compensation under the employer's plan.

Employer Considerations

It's pretty clear that nonqualified plans can provide significant benefits to employees. How might employers benefit from providing nonqualified plans? First, employers may benefit if they are able to earn a better rate of return on the deferred compensation than the rate of return they are required to pay employees participating in the plan. In addition, employers can use nonqualified plans to achieve certain compensation objectives. For example, nonqualified plans could be a component of a compensation package a company may use to attract prospective executives. Also, because deferred compensation is not deductible until it is paid, deferred compensation plans provide a potentially effective way for employers to circumvent the $1 million salary deduction limitation for executives of publicly traded corporations imposed by the **§162(m) limitation** (see Chapter 12 discussion of the limitation). That is, an employer may pay an executive $1 million of current compensation and defer compensation over $1 million to a future period. By doing this, the employer is able to deduct the full $1 million of salary and the entire amount of the deferred compensation as long as the employee has retired at the time the employer pays the deferred compensation. This is because the $1 million deductibility limitation on compensation does not apply if the executive is no longer employed by the company when the company pays the deferred compensation. However, if the executive is still an employee when the deferred compensation is paid, it is subject to the $1 million deduction limit.

Likewise, deferring compensation may be an important tax planning tool for employers in situations where their current marginal tax rates are low (employers currently experiencing net operating losses) and they expect their future marginal tax rates when deferred compensation is paid to be significantly higher (employers expect to return to profitability). In effect, deferring compensation into a year with a higher marginal tax rate increases the after-tax benefit of the compensation deduction, which reduces the after-tax cost of the compensation to the employer.

THE KEY FACTS

Nonqualified Deferred Compensation Plans

- Employer promises to pay deferred compensation at some point in future.
  - Deduct when paid to employee.
  - Not required to fund obligation.
  - Use to accomplish compensation objectives like avoid $1M deductibility limit on salary and make whole employees who are over contribution limits on qualified plans.
  - Employer's marginal tax rates at time of deferral relative to those at time of payment affect after-tax cost of providing deferred compensation relative to current compensation.

[16] §409A. These rules do provide, however, that specified payments from deferred compensation plans may commence while employees are still employed.

Exhibit 13-7 summarizes and compares qualified retirement plans and nonqualified deferred compensation plans.

EXHIBIT 13-7 Qualified Plan vs. Nonqualified Plan Summary

	Qualified Plans	Nonqualified Plans
Types	• Defined benefit (Pension). • Defined contribution (401k).	• Deferred compensation.
Requirements	• May not discriminate against "rank and file" employees of the company. • Funding or contribution requirements. • Vesting requirements.	• May discriminate. • Generally provided to executives and highly compensated. • No formal funding requirements (employee essentially unsecured creditor). • No formal vesting requirements.
Tax consequences to employers	• Immediately deduct contributions to plan (amount funded).	• No deduction until paid to employee.
Tax consequences to employees	• Employee contributions deductible unless to Roth-type account. • Employer contributions not immediately taxed. • Earnings deferred until distributed to employee. • Distributions from non-Roth plans treated as ordinary income.	• Employee contributions (or deferrals) deductible. • Taxed as ordinary income when received. • Earnings deferred until distributed to employee.

INDIVIDUALLY MANAGED QUALIFIED RETIREMENT PLANS

We've covered tax and nontax issues relating to both qualified and nonqualified employer-sponsored retirement savings plans. However, not all employers provide retirement savings plans, and when they do, some employees may not be eligible to participate, while others who are eligible may elect to not participate in these plans. The tax laws provide opportunities for these taxpayers to provide for their own retirement security through individually managed retirement plans. The **Individual Retirement Account (IRA)** is the most common of the individually managed retirement plans. Other types of individually managed plans are available to self-employed taxpayers.

LO 13-4

INDIVIDUAL RETIREMENT ACCOUNTS

Taxpayers who meet certain eligibility requirements can contribute to **traditional IRAs,** to **Roth IRAs,** or to both. Just like traditional and Roth 401(k) plans, traditional IRAs and Roth IRAs have different tax characteristics. In fact, in most respects, the tax characteristics of traditional 401(k) plans mirror those of traditional IRAs and tax characteristics of Roth 401(k) plans mirror those of Roth IRA accounts. To minimize redundancy in this section, we focus on the tax characteristics that differ between employer-sponsored 401(k) plans and self-managed IRAs.

Traditional IRAs

Contributions Deductible contributions to IRAs are *for* AGI deductions. The maximum deductible contribution for a taxpayer in 2015 depends on the taxpayer's age as follows:

- $5,500 deduction limit if the taxpayer is less than 50 years of age at year-end.[17,18]
- $6,500 deduction limit if the taxpayer is at least 50 years of age at year-end.[19]
- $0 deduction if the taxpayer is at least 70½ years of age at year end.

The deductible contribution limit may be further restricted depending on the following factors:

- Whether the taxpayer is an active participant in an employer-sponsored retirement plan.
- The taxpayer's filing status.
- The amount of the taxpayer's earned income.
- The taxpayer's AGI.

Unmarried taxpayers not participating in an employer-sponsored retirement plan may deduct IRA contributions up to the *lesser* of

- $5,500 ($6,500 for taxpayers 50+ years of age).
- Earned income.

As we discuss in Chapter 5, earned income generally includes income actually earned through the taxpayer's efforts such as wages, salaries, tips, and other employee compensation plus the amount of the taxpayer's net earnings from self-employment. Alimony income is also considered as earned income for this purpose.

THE KEY FACTS

Traditional IRAs

- 2015 Contribution limit.
  - Lesser of $5,500 or earned income.
  - Taxpayers over 50, lesser of $6,500 or earned income.
- If taxpayers participate in employer provided plan:
  - For 2015, deduction limit phased out for single taxpayers with AGI between $61,000 and $71,000 and for married filing jointly taxpayers with AGI between $98,000 and $118,000.
  - Special rules if one spouse covered by plan and other is not.

Example 13-15

In the year she graduated from college, Tina earned $25,000. She earned $5,000 in salary working part-time while she was in school and she earned $20,000 in salary working for CBA from September through December. To get an early start saving for retirement, she contributed $5,000 to a *traditional* IRA. How much of this contribution may Tina deduct?

Answer: $5,000. Because Tina is not participating in an employer-sponsored retirement plan during the current year, Tina may deduct the full $5,000 contribution as a *for* AGI deduction, reducing her AGI from $25,000 to $20,000.

For *unmarried taxpayers* who actively participate in an employer-sponsored retirement plan, the deduction limits are the same as for those who do not participate except that the maximum deduction is phased out based on the taxpayer's AGI as follows:

- No phase-out if AGI is equal to or less than $61,000.
- Proportional phase-out of full limit for AGI between $61,000 and $71,000 (The phase-out percentage is computed as follows: (AGI minus $61,000) divided by ($71,000 – $61,000) for example if AGI is $63,000, taxpayer loses 20 percent of contribution limit).
- Full phase-out (no deduction) if AGI is equal to or greater than $71,000.

[17]Lump-sum distributions from qualified plans other than Roth 401(k)s received prior to retirement are frequently rolled over into traditional IRA accounts to avoid the 10 percent premature distribution penalty and current taxation. Rollover contributions are not subject to normal contribution limits for traditional IRAs.

[18]The IRA contribution limit is indexed for inflation.

[19]The $1,000 increase in the deduction limit for older taxpayers is granted to allow taxpayers nearing retirement age to "catch up" on contributions they may have not made in previous years.

Married taxpayers can make deductible contributions to separate IRAs (IRA for each spouse), subject to limitations. If the married couple files jointly, before considering any AGI-based phase-out amounts (discussed below), the maximum deduction for the spouse with the *higher* amount of earned income is the same as it is for unmarried taxpayers [$5,500 ($6,500 if at least 50 years of age at year-end) or earned income if it is less]. However, the maximum deduction for the spouse with the *lesser* amount of earned income, is limited to the lesser of

- $5,500 ($6,500 if this spouse is age 50+) or
- Total earned income of both spouses reduced by deductible and nondeductible contributions to the other spouse's traditional IRA and by contributions to the other spouse's Roth IRA.[20]

The contribution to the lesser earning spouse's IRA is called a **spousal IRA.** The money in the account belongs to the lesser earning spouse no matter where the funds for the contribution came from.

If a spouse is an active participant in an employer's retirement plan, and the couple files jointly, the maximum deduction for that spouse is phased out based on the *couple's* AGI as follows (this phase-out applies whether the other spouse is an active participant in an employer's retirement plan or not, and it applies whether the spouse is the higher or lesser earning spouse):

- No phase-out if the couple's AGI is equal to or less than $98,000.
- Proportional phase-out of full limit for AGI between $98,000 and $118,000 (for example, if AGI is $110,000, taxpayer loses 60 percent of contribution limit).
- Full phase-out (no deduction) if AGI is equal to or greater than $118,000.

If one spouse is an active participant in an employer's retirement plan and the other is not, the deduction for the spouse who is not an active participant is phased out based on the couple's AGI as follows (the phase-out applies whether the spouse is the higher or lesser earning spouse):

- No phase-out if the couple's AGI is equal to or less than $183,000.
- Proportional phase-out of full limit for AGI between $183,000 and $193,000.
- Full phase-out (no deduction) if AGI is equal to or greater than $193,000.

Married taxpayers who file separately may also make deductible contributions to an IRA. The maximum deduction is the lesser of

- $5,500 ($6,500 if taxpayer is 50+).
- Earned income.

However, if either spouse is an active participant in an employer's retirement plan, then each spouse's deductible contribution (including the nonactive participant spouse) is phased out over the couple's AGI as follows:

- No phase-out if the taxpayer's AGI is $0 (also no tax benefit of deducting).
- Proportional phase-out of full limit for AGI between $0 and $10,000.
- Full phase-out (no deduction) if AGI is equal to or greater than $10,000.

If the couple files separate tax returns and did not live with each other at any time during the year, both spouses will be treated as unmarried taxpayers for purposes of the IRA deduction limitations. Appendix A to this chapter provides a flowchart for determining traditional IRA deduction limitations.

THE KEY FACTS

Traditional IRAs

- If taxpayer does not participate in employer provided plan but spouse does
  - Deduction limit phased out for AGI between $183,000 and $193,000.
- Distribution taxed as ordinary income
  - If distribution before taxpayer is 59½, 10 percent penalty generally applies.

[20]§219(c).

Example 13-16

In her first full calendar year working for CBA, Tina earns $60,000. Because she contributes $2,400 of her salary to CBA's 401(k) plan, her AGI is $57,600 ($60,000 − $2,400). Tina would like to make the maximum deductible contribution to her IRA. Assuming the 2015 limitations apply, how much is she allowed to deduct?

Answer: $5,500. Because Tina is a participant in CBA's retirement plan, the $5,500 deduction limit is subject to phase-out. However, because Tina's AGI is less than the beginning of the phase-out threshold ($61,000), she is allowed to deduct the maximum contribution.

What if: Assume that in her first full calendar year working for CBA, Tina earns $65,000. Because she contributes $2,400 of her salary to CBA's 401(k) plan, her AGI is $62,600 ($65,000 − $2,400). Tina would like to make the maximum deductible contribution to her IRA. How much is she allowed to deduct?

Answer: $4,620. The deductible amount before considering AGI limitations is $5,500. However, because Tina is a participant in CBA's retirement plan, the $5,500 deduction limit is subject to phase-out. Because Tina's AGI is 16 percent of the way through the $61,000 − $71,000 phase-out range for a single taxpayer [($62,600 − $61,000)/($71,000 − $61,000)], the $5,500 deductible contribution limit is reduced by 16 percent to $4,620 [$5,500 × (1 − .16)]. So, $4,620 is the maximum deductible contribution she can make to her traditional IRA.

What if: Assume that Tina is married and files a joint return with her spouse Steve. Tina participates in CBA's 401(k) plan and she receives $60,000 in salary from CBA for the year. Steve is a full-time student and is unemployed. The couple's AGI before considering IRA contributions is $60,000. What is Tina's maximum deductible IRA contribution for the year? What is Steve's maximum deductible IRA contribution for the year?

Answer: Tina's maximum deductible contribution for the year is $5,500. Because Tina is married, files a joint return, and reports AGI under $98,000 with her husband, her contribution is not phased out at all even though she is an active participant in CBA's retirement plan.

Steve's maximum deductible contribution for the year is also $5,500. Because Steve reports less earned income than Tina (in fact he doesn't report any earned income for the year), his deductible IRA contribution is limited to the lesser of (1) $5,500 or (2) $54,500 ($60,000 − $5,500) which is the couple's earned income minus Tina's deductible IRA contribution.

What if: Assume the same facts as the previous what-if example, except that Tina and Steve file separately. What is each spouse's maximum deductible IRA contribution for the year?

Answer: $0 for Tina and $0 for Steve. Tina is ineligible to make a deductible IRA contribution because the couple's AGI of $60,000 exceeds the $10,000 phase-out limit and Steve may not make a deductible contribution to the IRA for two reasons: (1) his spouse participates in an employer's retirement plan and the couple's AGI exceeds the $10,000 phase-out limit and (2) he does not report any earned income.

Nondeductible Contributions For all taxpayers, to the extent the maximum deductible contribution is phased out based on AGI, taxpayers can still make *nondeductible* contributions to reach the contribution limit (taxpayers who have reached age 70½ by year-end are not allowed to contribute to an IRA). Earned income limitations (including the spousal IRA limits) that apply to deductible IRA contributions also apply to nondeductible contributions. The earnings on nondeductible contributions grow tax-free until the taxpayer receives distributions from the IRA. On distribution, the taxpayer is taxed on the earnings generated by the nondeductible contributions but not on the actual nondeductible contributions. When taxpayers take partial distributions from an IRA to which they have made deductible and nondeductible contributions, each distribution consists of a taxable and nontaxable component. The portion of the distribution that is nontaxable is the ratio of the nondeductible contributions to the total account balance at the time of the distribution.

This is exactly the same formula used in Example 13-11 to determine the nontaxable portion of nonqualified distributions from Roth 401(k) accounts. Most taxpayers exceeding the deductibility limits on traditional IRAs would likely do better by contributing to a Roth IRA, if eligible, instead of making nondeductible contributions to traditional IRAs.

Taxpayers who are eligible to contribute to an IRA may contribute to the IRA up to the unextended tax return due date (generally, April 15 of the subsequent year). That is, as long as the taxpayer makes a contribution to the IRA by April 15 of year 2, the contribution counts as though it were made during year 1 (the prior calendar year).

Distributions Just as with traditional 401(k) plans, distributions from traditional IRAs are taxed as ordinary income to the taxpayer. Also, taxpayers withdrawing funds from traditional IRAs before reaching the age of 59½ are subject to a 10 percent early distribution penalty on the amount of the withdrawal. The IRA rules exempt certain distributions from the 10 percent penalty for early withdrawal. Among others, these distributions include proceeds distributed in the form of a life annuity (fixed payment each month or year over the taxpayer's life) and proceeds used for qualifying medical expenses, health insurance premiums for the owner, qualified higher education expenses, or first-time home purchases (limited to $10,000).[21] Taxpayers must receive their first required minimum distribution by April 1 of the year following the year in which the taxpayer reaches 70½ years of age. Because the distribution rules for traditional IRAs are so similar to the rules for traditional 401(k) accounts, taxpayers with traditional IRAs face virtually the same issues as participants in traditional 401(k) plans when planning for distributions. Thus, they should be careful to avoid the 10 percent penalty while at the same time taking similar steps to maximize the tax deferral on their traditional IRA account balances.

Roth IRAs

THE KEY FACTS

Roth IRAs

- Contributions not deductible.
- Same contribution limits as traditional IRAs but
  - For 2015, contribution phases out for AGI between $116,000 and $131,000 for unmarried taxpayers and between $183,000 and $193,000 for married filing jointly taxpayers.
- Qualified distributions not taxable.
  - To qualify, account must be open for at least five years before distribution and distribution made after taxpayer reaches 59½ years of age (among others).
- Nonqualified distributions of account earnings
  - Taxed at ordinary rates and subject to 10 percent penalty.
- Distributions first from contributions and then from account earnings.

As an alternative to traditional IRAs, taxpayers meeting certain requirements can contribute to Roth IRAs. Contributions to Roth IRAs are *not* deductible and *qualifying* distributions from Roth IRAs are *not* taxable.

Contributions Roth IRAs are subject to the same annual contribution limits as traditional IRAs [the lesser of $5,500 ($6,500 if at least age 50 at year-end) or earned income]. Further, the same spousal IRA rules that apply to traditional IRAs apply to Roth IRA contributions. These limits apply to the sum of a taxpayer's contributions to deductible IRAs, nondeductible IRAs, and Roth IRAs.

Whether or not they participate in an employer-sponsored retirement plan, the Roth IRA contribution limitation phases out as follows:

Unmarried taxpayers

- No phase-out if the taxpayer's AGI is $116,000 or below.
- Proportional phase-out of full limit for AGI between $116,000 and $131,000.
- Full phase-out (no contribution) if AGI is $131,000 or higher.

Married taxpayer filing jointly

- No phase-out if the taxpayer's AGI is $183,000 or below.
- Proportional phase-out of full limit for AGI between $183,000 and $193,000.
- Full phase-out (no contribution) if AGI is $193,000 or higher.

Married taxpayers filing separately

- No phase-out if the taxpayer's AGI is $0.
- Proportional phase-out of full limit for AGI between $0 and $10,000.
- Full phase-out (no contribution) if AGI is equal to or greater than $10,000.

Appendix B to this chapter provides a flowchart for determining Roth IRA contribution limits.

[21]§72(t). A first-time homebuyer is someone who did not own a principal residence in the two years before acquiring the new home [see §72(t)(8)(D)].

Distributions *Qualifying* distributions from Roth IRAs are not taxable. A qualifying distribution is a distribution from funds or earnings from funds in a Roth IRA *if the distribution is at least five years after the taxpayer opened the Roth IRA*[22] and the distribution meets one of the following requirements:

- Distribution is made on or after the date the taxpayer reaches 59½ years of age,
- Distribution is made to a beneficiary (or to the estate of the taxpayer) on or after the death of the taxpayer,
- Distribution is attributable to the taxpayer being disabled, or
- Distribution is used to pay qualified acquisition costs for first-time homebuyers (limited to $10,000).[23]

All other distributions are considered to be *nonqualified* distributions.

Nonqualified distributions are not necessarily taxable, however. Because taxpayers contributing to a Roth IRA contribute after-tax dollars (they don't deduct the contribution), they are able to withdraw the contributions tax-free at any time. However, *nonqualified* distributions of the *earnings* of a Roth IRA are taxable as ordinary income and subject to a 10 percent penalty. Nonqualified distributions are deemed to come

- First from the taxpayer's contributions.
- Then from the earnings after the total contributions have been distributed (note that this is different than the equivalent rule for Roth 401(k)s).

Thus, taxpayers can treat the Roth IRA as an emergency savings account to the extent of their contributions without incurring any penalties.

ETHICS

Ryan had just finished a finance class and had learned about the importance of the time value of money. With this knowledge, he wanted to start saving for retirement. Last year Ryan had a job and earned $2,000. After paying his expenses, he placed the remaining $500 in a savings account in the bank. This year, however, Ryan decided to focus on his studies so he did not earn any income. He paid his living expenses through student loans. At the end of the current year, Ryan contributed $400 to a Roth IRA. On his tax return for the year, Ryan reported $400 of self-employment income (even though he didn't earn any). Why did Ryan report this "phantom" income? What do you think of his strategy?

Example 13-17

What if: Assume that when Tina started working for CBA, she made a one-time contribution of $4,000 to a Roth IRA. Years later, she retired at the age of 65 when the value of her Roth account was $60,000. If Tina receives a $10,000 distribution from her Roth IRA, what amount of taxes (and penalty, if applicable) must she pay on the distribution (assume her ordinary marginal rate is 30 percent)?

Answer: $0 taxes and $0 penalty. Qualified Roth IRA distributions are not taxable.

What if: Assume the same facts as above, except that Tina received a $10,000 distribution when she was 57 years of age. What amount of taxes (and penalty, if applicable) is she required to pay on the distribution (assume a 30 percent ordinary marginal rate)?

Answer: $2,400 in total consisting of $1,800 in taxes ($6,000 earnings distributed × 30 percent marginal tax rate) and $600 penalty ($6,000 earnings × 10 percent penalty rate). Because Tina has not reached age 59½ at the time of the distribution, this is a nonqualified distribution. Consequently, she is taxed and penalized on the $6,000 distribution of earnings ($10,000 distribution minus $4,000 contribution).

(continued on page 13-24)

[22]The five-year period starts on January 1 of the year in which the contribution was made and ends on the last day of the fifth taxable year. See Reg §1.408A-6, Q&A2 and Q&A-5(b).

[23]§408A(d)(2).

What if: Assume that when Tina was 62 years old, she opened a Roth IRA, contributing $4,000. Three years later, Tina withdrew the entire account balance of $5,000. What amount of taxes (and penalty, if applicable) must Tina pay on the distribution (assume her marginal tax rate is 30 percent)?

Answer: $400 in total consisting of $300 taxes ($1,000 earnings × 30 percent marginal tax rate) and $100 penalty ($1,000 earnings × 10 percent penalty rate). The distribution is a nonqualified distribution because Tina did not have the Roth IRA open for five years before receiving the distribution. Consequently, she must pay taxes and penalties on the $1,000 account earnings ($5,000 − $4,000).

In contrast to taxpayers with traditional IRAs, taxpayers are *not* required to take minimum distributions from Roth IRAs. Thus, taxpayers can minimize distributions from Roth IRAs to maintain a source of tax-free income during their lifetime.

Rollover from Traditional to Roth IRA

Many taxpayers made contributions to traditional IRAs before Roth IRAs were available. Some taxpayers may have contributed to traditional IRAs and then later decided they should have contributed to a Roth IRA. The tax laws accommodate these taxpayers by allowing them to transfer funds from a traditional IRA (and other qualified defined contribution plans) to a Roth IRA.[24] This transfer of funds is called a **rollover.** When taxpayers do this, however, the entire amount taken out of the traditional IRA is taxed at ordinary rates but is not subject to the 10 percent penalty tax as long as the taxpayer contributes the *full amount* to a Roth IRA within 60 days of the withdrawal from the traditional IRA.[25]

Example 13-18

What if: Let's assume that in the year she graduated from college and began working for CBA, Tina made a fully deductible $4,000 contribution to a *traditional* IRA. Three years later, when her marginal tax rate is 25 percent, she rolls over the entire $5,000 account balance into a Roth IRA. What amount of taxes is she required to pay on the rollover?

Answer: $1,250 ($5,000 × 25%). The entire $5,000 transferred from the IRA to the Roth IRA is taxed at 25 percent but is not subject to the 10 percent early withdrawal penalty. Even though Tina pays $1,250 in taxes on the transfer, she is required to contribute $5,000 to the Roth IRA within 60 days from the time she withdraws the money from the traditional IRA.

What if: What are the tax consequences if Tina pays the $1,250 tax bill and contributes only $3,750 to the Roth IRA account?

Answer: She must pay a $125 penalty. The penalty is 10 percent of the $1,250 that she withdrew from the IRA and did not contribute to the Roth IRA ($5,000 − $3,750).

THE KEY FACTS

Roth IRAs

- Rollovers from traditional IRAs to Roth IRAs.
  - Amount withdrawn from traditional IRA fully taxable but not penalized.
  - Must contribute full amount withdrawn to Roth IRA account within 60 days of withdrawal.
  - Amounts withdrawn but not contributed subject to tax and 10 percent penalty.

Why would anyone be willing to pay taxes currently in order to avoid paying taxes later? Typically, a rollover from a traditional to a Roth IRA makes sense when a taxpayer's marginal tax rate is currently low (when the tax cost of the rollover is low) and expected to be significantly higher in the future (when the expected benefit of the rollover is high). Note that high-income taxpayers may not be allowed to contribute to Roth IRAs due to the AGI restrictions on contribution limits. However, because currently there is no AGI restriction on who may rollover funds from a traditional IRA (or other qualified defined contribution plan) into a Roth IRA, high-income taxpayers who would like to fund a Roth IRA may do so through a rollover.[26]

[24]See Notice 2009-75, 2009-39 IRB.

[25]§408(d)(3). Taxpayers who roll over funds from a traditional IRA (or other traditional retirement account) to a Roth must wait at least five years from the date of the rollover to withdraw the funds from the rollover in order to avoid a 10% penalty on the distribution (§408(d)(3)(F)).

[26]§408A(c)(3).

Comparing Traditional and Roth IRAs

So, which type of IRA is better for taxpayers? The tax considerations are very similar to those we already discussed when we compared traditional and Roth 401(k) plans. In general, after-tax returns from traditional IRAs will exceed those from Roth IRAs when marginal tax rates decline. However, after-tax rates of return from Roth IRAs will exceed those from traditional IRAs when tax rates increase.

Unrelated to marginal tax rates, Roth IRAs have other advantages relative to traditional IRAs as follows:

- Taxpayers can contribute to Roth IRAs at any age. In contrast, taxpayers are not allowed to make deductible contributions to traditional IRAs once they have reached 70½ years of age.
- The minimum distribution requirements for traditional IRAs do not apply to Roth IRAs. This provision permits owners of Roth IRAs to use their accounts to generate tax-free returns long after retirement.
- Taxpayers can withdraw their Roth contributions tax free at any time without paying tax or paying a penalty. Taxpayers who withdraw their traditional IRA contributions are taxed on the distribution and potentially penalized.

Exhibit 13-8 summarizes tax-related requirements for traditional and Roth IRAs.

EXHIBIT 13-8 Traditional IRA vs. Roth IRA Summary

	Traditional IRA	Roth IRA
Contributions requirements	• Taxpayer must not be a participant in an employer-sponsored plan or, if participating in an employer-provided plan, must meet certain income thresholds. Those above the threshold will have deductible portion of contribution phased out.	• No deduction allowed for contributions. Must meet certain income requirements to be able to contribute to a Roth IRA.
Contributions	• Deductible unless participant in employer plan and high AGI. • Nondeductible contributions allowed.	• Not deductible. • May not contribute if high AGI.
Maximum contribution	• Lesser of $5,500 per taxpayer ($6,500 for taxpayers over 50 years old) or earned income.	• Same as traditional IRA.
	• The contribution limits apply to the sum of contributions to traditional deductible IRAs, nondeductible IRAs, and Roth IRAs for the year.	• Same as traditional IRA.
	• For married couples filing jointly, contributions for the lesser earning spouse may not exceed the total earned income of both spouses reduced by deductible and nondeductible contributions to the other spouse's traditional IRA and by contributions to the other spouse's Roth IRA.	• Same as traditional IRA.
Contribution dates	• Can contribute up to unextended tax return due date—generally April 15.	• Same as traditional IRA.
Distributions	• Generally taxed as ordinary income. • If made before 59½, generally subject to 10 percent penalty. • If nondeductible contribution made, allocate distribution between taxable and nontaxable amounts similar to annuity rules. • Minimum distributions required by April 1 of the year after the year in which the taxpayer reaches 70½. • Failure to meet minimum distribution timing and amount requirements triggers 50 percent penalty.	• Qualified distributions not taxed. • Generally, distributions are qualified after account open for five years and employee has reached the age of 59½. • Nonqualified distributions not taxed to extent of prior contributions. • Nonqualified distributions of earnings subject to tax at ordinary rates and 10 percent penalty. • No minimum distribution requirements.

TAXES IN THE REAL WORLD Roth or Traditional Retirement Savings Vehicle?

With increasing budgetary deficits and the government's increasing need for revenues, one can reasonably anticipate that future tax rates will exceed current tax rates. With increasing tax rates, taxpayers should favor Roth 401k and Roth IRAs over traditional retirement savings vehicles. Yet, less than 10 percent of employees who could contribute to Roth 401k plans choose to do so and more than 15 times more taxpayers use traditional IRAs than use Roth IRAs. Why are so many more taxpayers choosing traditional retirement savings options when Roth accounts may theoretically provide a greater after-tax sum at retirement? It could be that there are not a lot of taxpayers who expect their marginal tax rates to be higher at retirement than they are now, it could be that taxpayers prefer deductible retirement savings contributions for the current tax savings, or it could be that taxpayers believe that in the future Congress may change the tax laws so that distributions from Roth accounts will become taxable. A sound response to the tax law uncertainty would be to hedge your bets and include some retirement savings in traditional accounts and some in Roth accounts so that you can adapt to changing tax laws over time.

Source: "Bad Math: Taxes Rise as Savings Fall," by Carolyn T. Geer January 20, 2013 *WSJ*.

LO 13-5

SELF-EMPLOYED RETIREMENT ACCOUNTS

THE KEY FACTS

Self-Employed Retirement Accounts

- Popular plans include SEP IRAs and individual 401(k)s.
- Similar to (non-Roth) qualified defined contribution plans.
  - Contributions deductible, distributions taxable.

We've discussed retirement savings opportunities available to employees. However, many taxpayers are self-employed small business owners who do not have access to employer-sponsored plans.[27] Moreover, individually managed retirement plans such as traditional and Roth IRAs are not particularly attractive to self-employed taxpayers due to the relatively low contribution limits on these plans. What retirement savings options, then, are available to the self-employed?

Congress created a number of retirement savings plans targeted toward self-employed taxpayers. Two of the more popular plans for the self-employed are SEP IRAs and individual (or "self-employed") 401(k) plans. These are defined contribution plans that generally work the same as employer-provided plans. That is, amounts set aside in these plans are deducted from income, earnings are free from tax until distributed, and distributions from the plans are fully taxable.[28] As we discuss below, these plans differ in terms of their annual contribution limits. They also have different nontax characteristics including their suitability for businesses with employees other than the owner and their administration costs. As you might expect, these factors come into play when self-employed small business owners choose a retirement plan.[29] We describe SEP IRAs and individual 401(k) plans below.[30]

Simplified Employee Pension (SEP) IRA

A simplified employee pension (SEP) can be administered through an individual retirement account (IRA) called a **SEP IRA.**[31] The owner of a sole proprietorship can

[27]Because sole proprietorships with self-employment income are very common, we assume in our examples and explanations here that any self-employment income originates from a sole proprietorship. In some cases, however, partners and LLC members may also have self-employment income from a partnership or LLC.

[28]"Keogh" self-employed defined benefit plans are also an option. Generally, defined benefit plans are attractive to older, self-employed individuals with profitable businesses because they allow for greater deductible contributions. However, they are usually more costly to maintain than the defined contribution plans we mention here.

[29]Many investment firms provide comparisons to help taxpayers select self-employed retirement plans. One particularly good comparison is provided by Fidelity Investments at www.fidelity.com/retirement/small-business/compare-plans-chart

[30]A Savings Incentive Match Plans for Employees (SIMPLE) IRA is another popular form of retirement plan for the self-employed. For those earning lower amounts of self-employment income, the contribution limits for a SIMPLE IRA tend to be higher than contribution limits for SEP IRAs.

[31]§408(k).

make annual contributions directly to her SEP IRA. For 2015, the annual contribution is limited to the *lesser* of

- $53,000.
- 20 percent of Schedule C net income after reducing Schedule C net income by the deduction for the employer's portion of self-employment taxes paid (50 percent of the self-employment taxes paid).[32]

Contributions can be made up to the extended due date of the tax return.[33]

Example 13-19

What if: Dave (age 64) reports Schedule C net income of $40,000 during the current year. If he sets up a SEP IRA for himself, what is the maximum contribution he may make to the plan (assuming he has no other source of employee or self-employment income)?

Answer: $7,435, computed as follows:

Description	Amount	Explanation
(1) First limit on contribution	$53,000	
(2) Schedule C net income minus the self-employment tax deduction	37,174	$40,000 − ($40,000 × .9235 × 15.3% × 50%).
(3) Percentage for limitation based on (2)	20%	
(4) Second limit on contribution	7,435	(2) × (3).
Maximum contribution	**$ 7,435**	Lesser of (1) or (4).

What if: Assume Dave is 48 years old at the end of the year. What is his maximum deductible contribution?

Answer: $7,435. Dave's maximum deductible contribution for a SEP IRA does not depend on his age.

What if: Suppose Dave reports $310,000 of Schedule C net income rather than $40,000. What is his maximum deductible contribution to his SEP IRA account?

Answer: $53,000, the lesser of (1) $53,000 or (2) $59,700 [20% × ($310,000 − (((310,000 × .9235 − $118,500) × 2.9% × 50%) + ($118,500 × 15.3% × 50%)))].

THE KEY FACTS

Self-Employed Retirement Accounts

- SEP IRA 2015 contribution limit.
    - Lesser of (1) $53,000 or (2) 20 percent of Schedule C net income (after reducing Schedule C net income by the deduction for the employer's portion of self-employment taxes paid).

Nontax Considerations If a sole proprietor has hired employees, the sole proprietor *must* contribute to the employees' respective SEP IRAs based on their compensation. Because owners may view this requirement as being too favorable to employees, this plan is best suited for sole proprietors who do not have employees or for situations where owners are willing to provide generous benefits to their employees. From an administrative perspective, SEP IRAs are easy to set up and have relatively low administrative costs from year to year.

Individual 401(k)s

Individual 401(k) plans are strictly for sole proprietors (and the spouse of the sole proprietor) who do not have employees. Under this type of plan, the sole proprietor can contribute the lesser of

- $53,000.
- 20 percent of Schedule C net income after reducing Schedule C net income by the deduction for the employer's portion of self-employment taxes paid (50 percent of self-employment taxes paid) (employer's contribution) plus an additional $18,000 (employee's contribution).

[32]Chapter 8 addresses self-employment taxes in more detail. Also note that for SEP IRAs no catch-up contributions are allowed for taxpayers 50 years and older.

[33]§404(h). This is September 15 for a calendar-year taxpayer.

Further, if the sole proprietor is at least 50 years of age by the end of the tax year, she may contribute an *additional* $6,000 as a catch-up contribution. However, total contributions may not exceed the taxpayer's Schedule C net income minus the self-employment tax deduction.

Example 13-20

THE KEY FACTS

Self-Employed Retirement Accounts

- Individual 401(k) 2015 contribution limit.
  - Lesser of (1) $53,000 or (2) 20 percent of Schedule C net income (after reducing Schedule C net income by the deduction for the employer's portion of self-employment taxes paid) plus $18,000 ($24,000 for taxpayers who are at least 50 years old at the end of the year).
  - Contribution cannot exceed Schedule C net income minus self-employment tax deduction.

What if: Suppose that Dave is 64 years old at the end of the year, reports $40,000 of Schedule C net income, and has no other sources of income. What is the maximum amount he can contribute to an individual 401(k) account?

Answer: $31,435, computed as follows:

Description	Amount	Explanation
(1) First limit on contribution	$53,000	
(2) Schedule C net income minus the self-employment tax deduction	37,174	$40,000 − ($40,000 × .9235 × 15.3% × 50%).
(3) Percentage for limitation based on (2)	20%	
(4) Limit on employer's contribution	7,435	(2) × (3).
(5) Limit on employee's contribution	18,000	
(6) Second limitation	25,435	(4) + (5).
(7) Maximum contribution before catch-up contribution	25,435	Lesser of (1) or (6).
(8) Catch-up contribution	6,000	Dave is 64 years old at year-end.
Maximum contribution	**$31,435**	(7) + (8), not to exceed (2).

Example 13-21

What if: Assume Dave is 48 years old at the end of the year, reports $40,000 of Schedule C net income, and has no other sources of income. What is his maximum deductible contribution to his individual 401(k) account?

Answer: $25,435. This is the same as the amount he could contribute as a 64-year-old (see prior example), minus the $6,000 catch-up adjustment ($31,435 − $6,000).

What if: Assume the same facts as above except that Dave (age 64) earned $10,000 of Schedule C net income rather than $40,000. What is his maximum deductible contribution to his individual 401(k)?

Answer: $9,294, computed as follows (Dave's contribution is limited to his Schedule C net income minus self-employment tax deduction):

Description	Amount	Explanation
(1) First limit on contribution	$53,000	
(2) Schedule C net income minus self-employment tax deduction	9,294	$10,000 − ($10,000 × .9235 × 15.3% × 50%).
(3) Percentage for limitation based on (2)	20%	
(4) Limit on employer's contribution	1,859	(2) × (3).
(5) Limit on employee's contribution	18,000	
(6) Second limitation	19,859	(4) + (5).
(7) Maximum contribution before catch-up contribution	19,859	Lesser of (1) or (6).
(8) Catch-up contribution	6,000	Dave is 64 years old at year-end.
Maximum contribution	**$ 9,294**	(7) + (8), not to exceed (2).

Example 13-22

What if: Assume Dave (age 64) earned $400,000 of Schedule C net income. What is his maximum deductible contribution to his individual 401(k)?

Answer: $59,000, computed as follows:

Description	Amount	Explanation
(1) First limit on contribution	$ 53,000	
(2) Schedule C net income minus self-employment tax deduction	387,297	$400,000 − [((400,000 × .9235 − 118,500) × 2.9% × 50%) + (118,500 × 15.3% × 50%)].
(3) Percentage for limitation based on (2)	20%	
(4) Limit on employer's contribution	77,459	(2) × (3).
(5) Limit on employee's contribution	18,000	
(6) Second limitation	95,459	(4) + (5).
(7) Maximum contribution before catch-up contribution	53,000	Lesser of (1) or (6).
(8) Catch-up contribution	6,000	Dave is 64 years old at year-end.
Maximum contribution	**$ 59,000**	(7) + (8), not to exceed (2).

Nontax Considerations As we mentioned above, the individual 401(k) plan is not available for sole proprietors with employees, so providing benefits to employees under the plan is not a concern. However, the administrative burden of establishing, operating, and maintaining a 401(k) plan is potentially higher than it is for the other self-employed plans.

SAVER'S CREDIT

LO 13-6

To encourage middle- and low-income taxpayers to take advantage of the retirement savings opportunities discussed in this chapter, Congress provides an additional **saver's credit** for an individual's elective contribution of up to $2,000 to any of the qualified retirement plans discussed in this chapter including employer-sponsored qualified plans, traditional and Roth IRA plans, and self-employed qualified plans. The credit is provided *in addition to* any deduction the taxpayer is allowed for contributing to a retirement account. It is calculated by multiplying the taxpayer's contribution, up to a maximum of $2,000, by the applicable percentage depending on the taxpayer's filing status and AGI. The credit is nonrefundable.[34] Exhibit 13-9 provides the applicable percentages for 2015 according to a taxpayer's filing status and AGI.[35]

THE KEY FACTS

Saver's Credit

- Credit for taxpayers contributing to qualified plan.
- Credit is based on contributions up to $2,000, taxpayer's filing status, and AGI.
  - Phased out as AGI increases.
  - Maximum credit is $1,000.
  - Unavailable for married filing jointly taxpayers with AGI over $61,000, head of household taxpayers with AGI above $45,750, and all other taxpayers with AGI above $30,500.

[34]According to §25B(g), the saver's credit is applied to the taxpayer's remaining tax liability after the application of certain other tax credits including the child tax credit and the American opportunity and lifetime learning credits.

[35]For this purpose, AGI is determined without considering the foreign earned income exclusion provided for U.S. residents living abroad under §911.

In addition to restricting the credit to taxpayers with AGI below a certain amount, the credit is also restricted to individuals who are 18 years of age or older, who are not claimed as dependents by another taxpayer, and are not students. For this purpose, students are those who are full-time students at a qualified educational organization during each of five calendar months of the taxpayer's tax year.[36] Although limited in scope, the saver's credit provides some tax benefits for those taxpayers who qualify.

EXHIBIT 13-9 2015 Applicable Percentages for Saver's Credit by Filing Status and AGI

Applicable Percentage	Joint Filers AGI	Heads of Household AGI	All Other Filers AGI
50%	0 to $36,500	0 to $27,375	0 to $18,250
20%	$36,501 to $39,500	$27,376 to $29,625	$18,251 to $19,750
10%	$39,501 to $61,000	$29,626 to $45,750	$19,751 to $30,500
No credit available	Above $61,000	Above $45,750	Above $30,500

Example 13-23

What if: Tina earned $24,000 during the year she began working for CBA. She earned $4,000 in salary working part-time while she was in school and $20,000 in salary working for CBA from September through December. To get an early start saving for retirement, assume she contributed $4,000 to a traditional IRA. Because Tina did not participate in an employer-sponsored retirement plan during the current year she may deduct the full $4,000 contribution as a *for* AGI deduction, reducing her AGI from $24,000 to $20,000. What amount of saver's credit, if any, is Tina allowed to claim, assuming she was a full-time student during four months of the year (if she were a full-time student during five months of the year she would be ineligible for the saver's credit)?

Answer: $200 ($2,000 × 10 percent applicable credit).

What if: What saver's credit may Tina claim if her AGI was $15,000?

Answer: $1,000 ($2,000 × 50 percent applicable credit).

CONCLUSION

The decisions that employees like Tina, Lisa, and Dave must deal with highlight the role that tax issues play in this important area. Employers, like their employees, must also pay careful attention to tax considerations when deciding on retirement savings vehicles to offer their employees. Further, as has been a recurring theme throughout this book, nontax issues play an equal, if not more important, role in the retirement savings decisions of both employees and employers.

[36] §152(f)(2).

Appendix A (Page 1) Traditional IRA Deduction Limitations

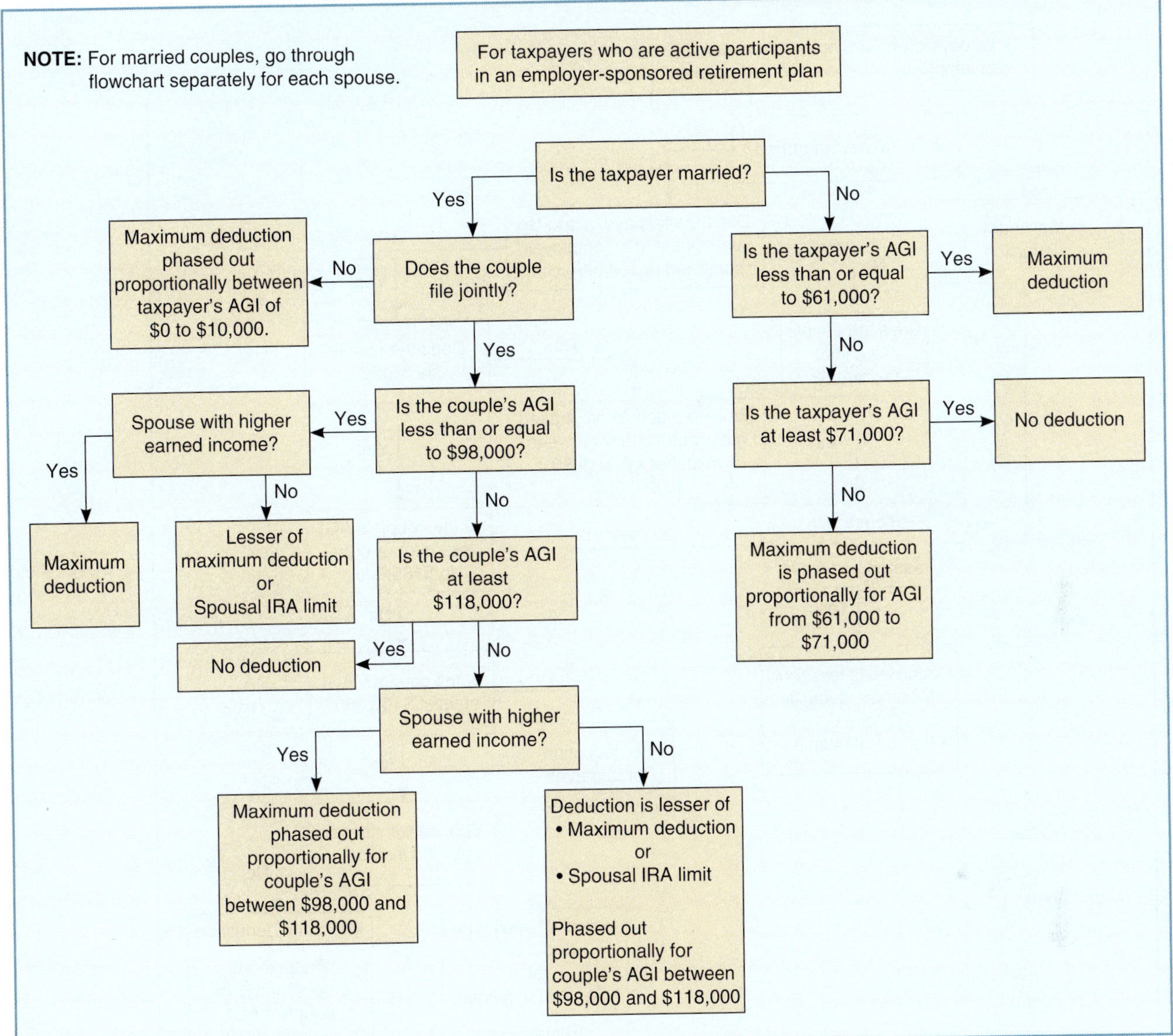
NOTE: For married couples, go through flowchart separately for each spouse.
For taxpayers who are active participants in an employer-sponsored retirement plan
Is the taxpayer married?
Yes
No
Does the couple file jointly?
No
Maximum deduction phased out proportionally between taxpayer's AGI of $0 to $10,000.
Yes
Is the couple's AGI less than or equal to $98,000?
Yes
Spouse with higher earned income?
Yes
Maximum deduction
No
Lesser of maximum deduction or Spousal IRA limit
No
Is the couple's AGI at least $118,000?
Yes
No deduction
No
Spouse with higher earned income?
Yes
Maximum deduction phased out proportionally for couple's AGI between $98,000 and $118,000
No
Deduction is lesser of
• Maximum deduction
or
• Spousal IRA limit
Phased out proportionally for couple's AGI between $98,000 and $118,000
Is the taxpayer's AGI less than or equal to $61,000?
Yes
Maximum deduction
No
Is the taxpayer's AGI at least $71,000?
Yes
No deduction
No
Maximum deduction is phased out proportionally for AGI from $61,000 to $71,000

(Page 2) Traditional IRA Deduction Limitations

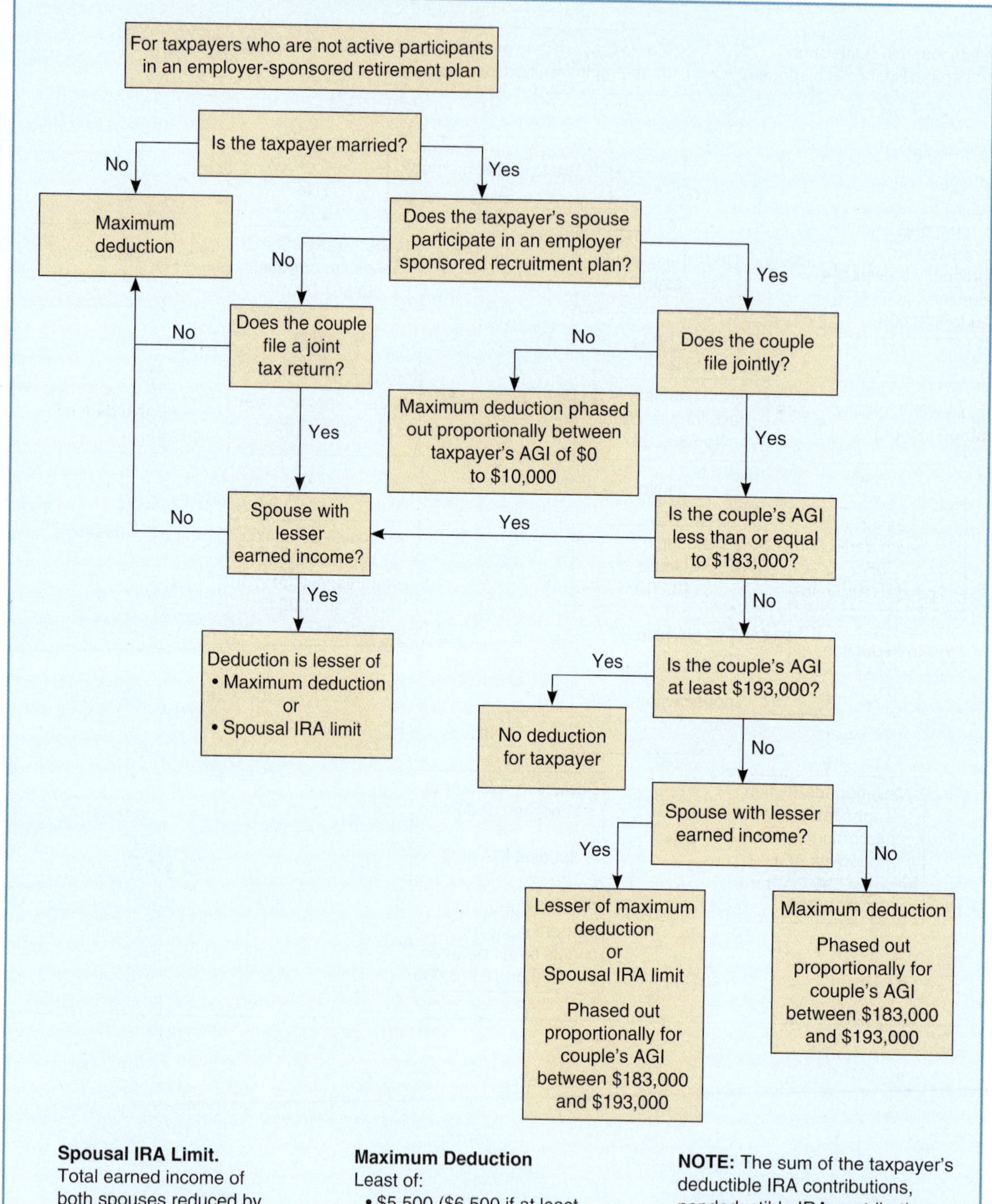

For taxpayers who are not active participants in an employer-sponsored retirement plan
Is the taxpayer married?
No
Yes
Maximum deduction
Does the taxpayer's spouse participate in an employer sponsored recruitment plan?
No
Yes
Does the couple file a joint tax return?
No
Does the couple file jointly?
No
Maximum deduction phased out proportionally between taxpayer's AGI of $0 to $10,000
Yes
Yes
No
Spouse with lesser earned income?
Yes
Is the couple's AGI less than or equal to $183,000?
Yes
No
Deduction is lesser of
• Maximum deduction
or
• Spousal IRA limit
Yes
Is the couple's AGI at least $193,000?
No deduction for taxpayer
No
Spouse with lesser earned income?
Yes
No
Lesser of maximum deduction or Spousal IRA limit
Phased out proportionally for couple's AGI between $183,000 and $193,000
Maximum deduction
Phased out proportionally for couple's AGI between $183,000 and $193,000

Spousal IRA Limit.
Total earned income of both spouses reduced by contributions to deductible IRAs, nondeductible IRA, and Roth IRA made by higher-earning spouse.

Maximum Deduction
Least of:
- $5,500 ($6,500 if at least age 50 at year-end)
- $0 if at least age 70½ at year-end
- Taxpayer's earned income for year

NOTE: The sum of the taxpayer's deductible IRA contributions, nondeductible IRA contributions, and Roth IRA contributions cannot exceed $5,500 (or $6,500 if the taxpayer is at least 50 years old at year-end).

Appendix B Roth IRA Contribution Limits

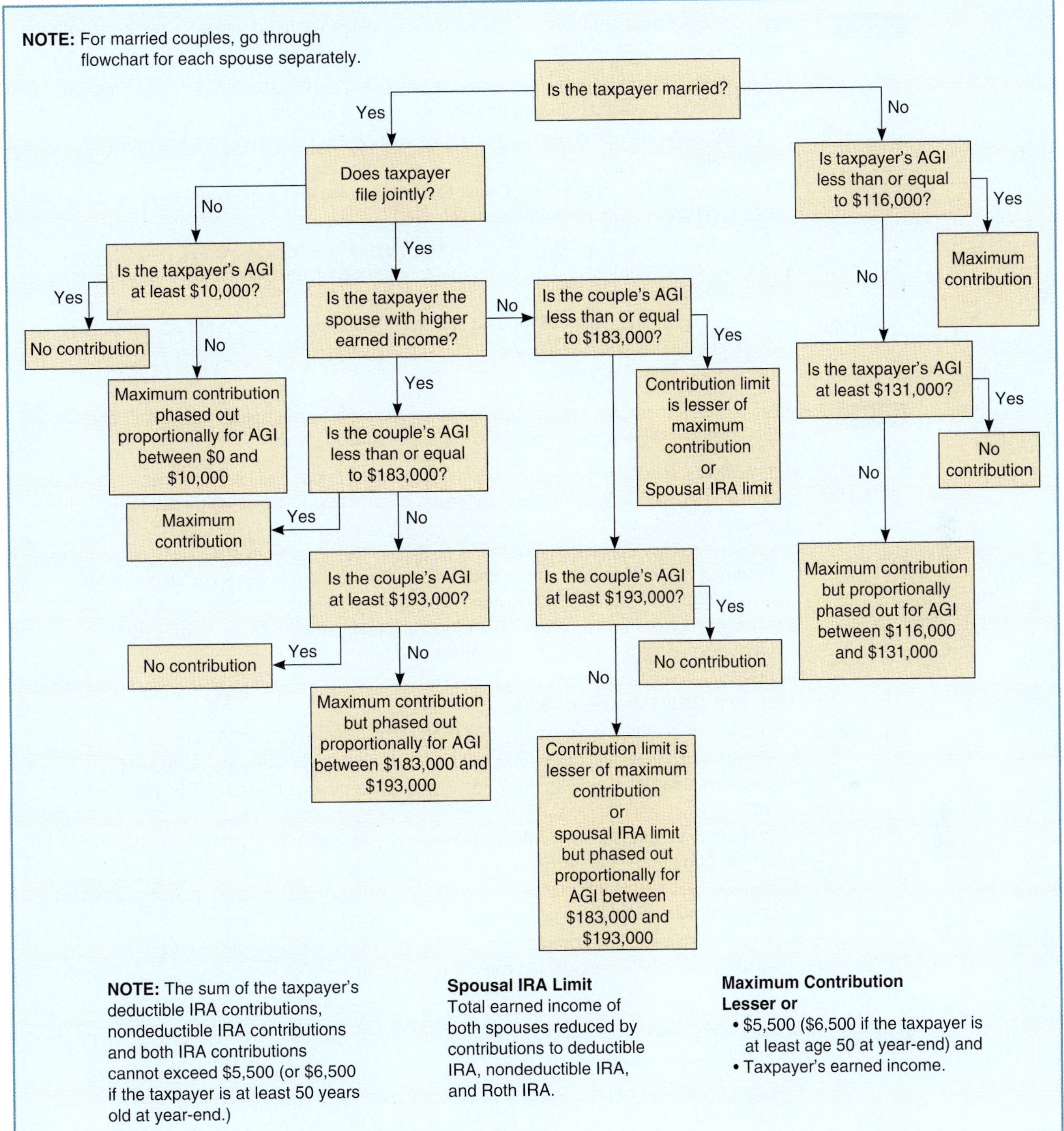

NOTE: The sum of the taxpayer's deductible IRA contributions, nondeductible IRA contributions and both IRA contributions cannot exceed $5,500 (or $6,500 if the taxpayer is at least 50 years old at year-end.)

Spousal IRA Limit
Total earned income of both spouses reduced by contributions to deductible IRA, nondeductible IRA, and Roth IRA.

Maximum Contribution Lesser or
- $5,500 ($6,500 if the taxpayer is at least age 50 at year-end) and
- Taxpayer's earned income.

Summary

LO 13-1 Describe the tax and nontax aspects of employer-provided defined benefit plans from both the employer's and employee's perspective.

- Benefits are determined based on years of service and salary. The maximum annual benefit is capped and adjusted upward annually for inflation.
- Benefits vest over time using either a five-year cliff or seven-year graded vesting schedule.
- Employers deduct cash contributions to fund the plan and employees treat cash distributions as ordinary income in the year received.
- Employers bear investment risk with defined benefit plans.
- Premature distribution and minimum distribution penalties don't typically apply to defined benefit distributions.
- Because of the high cost of funding and maintaining defined benefit plans, they are waning in popularity.

LO 13-2 Explain and determine the tax consequences associated with employer-provided defined contribution plans, including traditional 401(k) and Roth 401(k) plans.

- Employers specify the amount they will contribute to defined contribution plans instead of the annual benefit. However, employers are not permitted to contribute to Roth 401(k) plans.
- Employees may contribute to either a traditional 401(k) or Roth 401(k) account, and they determine how employer and employee contributions are invested. Employees bear investment risk with defined contribution plans.
- Annual employer and employee contributions are limited and maximum contribution amounts are adjusted annually for inflation.
- Employer contributions to traditional plans vest over time using either a three-year cliff or six-year graded vesting schedule.
- Employers deduct their contributions to traditional defined contribution plans.
- Employee contributions to traditional defined contribution plans are excluded from their taxable wages on Form W-2. Employee contributions to Roth 401(k) plans are not excluded.
- Distributions from traditional 401(k) plans are taxable at ordinary rates and qualified distributions from Roth 401(k) plans are not taxable.
- Distributions from both traditional 401(k) and Roth 401(k) plans are subject to premature and minimum distribution penalties.
- After-tax returns from Roth 401(k) plans are generally superior to those from traditional 401(k) plans when marginal tax rates are increasing.

LO 13-3 Describe the tax implications of deferred compensation from both the employer's and employee's perspective.

- Employees elect to defer current salary in exchange for promised future payments from the employer.
- Because the employer's promise of future payment is unsecured, employees recognize ordinary income when future payments are received. Employers wait to deduct payments until cash is actually paid.
- The after-tax returns and costs from deferred compensation arrangements to employees and employers depend on the current and future marginal tax rates of both the employee and employer. They also depend on the rate of return employers promise employees on deferred salary.
- Deferred compensation is often used to overcome deductibility constraints imposed on salary and qualified pension plans.

- Employees bear more risk with deferred compensation relative to other forms of retirement savings because employees are unsecured creditors of their employers.

Determine the tax consequences of traditional and Roth Individual Retirement Accounts and explain the differences between them. LO 13-4

- The same inflation-adjusted annual contribution limits apply to both traditional IRAs and Roth IRAs.
- The deduction for traditional IRA contributions is phased out for taxpayers covered by a retirement plan at work and with AGI above certain inflation-adjusted amounts. Special rules pertain for spouses not covered by an employer plan.
- The ability to contribute to a Roth IRA is phased out for individuals with AGI above certain inflation-adjusted amounts.
- Distributions from traditional IRAs are taxed at ordinary rates. A 10 percent premature distribution penalty generally applies to distributions from traditional IRAs received before age 59½.
- Distributions from Roth IRAs received after a Roth IRA account has been open for at least five years and after the recipient reaches age 59½ are not taxable. The earnings component of any distributions not meeting these requirements is generally taxable and subject to the 10 percent premature distribution penalty.
- Taxpayers generally prefer Roth IRAs to traditional IRAs when they expect their marginal tax rates to increase.

Describe retirement savings options available to self-employed taxpayers and compute the limitations for deductible contributions to retirement accounts for self-employed taxpayers. LO 13-5

- Self-employed individuals may set up their own qualified pension plans such as SEP IRAs and individual 401(k)s.
- Contribution limits generally parallel those for employer-sponsored plans, allowing self-employed individuals to have the same access to qualified plans that employees have.
- Self-employed individuals with employees may have to incur the cost of covering their employees when they establish a qualified retirement plan.

Compute the saver's credit. LO 13-6

- Individuals may receive up to a $1,000 tax credit for contributions they make to IRAs and employer-sponsored qualified plans.
- The maximum contribution eligible for the credit is $2,000, and the amount of the credit is a function of the taxpayer's filing status and AGI.

KEY TERMS

cliff vesting (13-4)
defined benefit plan (13-3)
defined contribution plan (13-3)
graded vesting (13-4)
Individual Retirement Account (IRA) (13-18)
minimum distributions (13-5)
nonqualified deferred compensation (13-14)
qualified retirement plans (13-3)
rollover (13-24)
Roth 401(k) (13-11)
Roth IRA (13-18)
saver's credit (13-29)
§162(m) limitation (13-17)
SEP IRA (13-26)
spousal IRA (13-20)
traditional 401(k) (13-11)
traditional IRA (13-18)
vesting (13-4)

DISCUSSION QUESTIONS

1. How are defined benefit plans different from defined contribution plans? How are they similar? LO 13-1 LO 13-2
2. Describe how an employee's benefit under a defined benefit plan is computed. LO 13-1
3. What does it mean to vest in a defined benefit or defined contribution plan? LO 13-1 LO 13-2

LO 13-1 LO 13-2 4. Compare and contrast the minimum vesting requirements for defined benefit plans and defined contribution plans.

LO 13-1 LO 13-2 5. What are the nontax advantages and disadvantages of defined benefit plans relative to defined contribution plans?

LO 13-1 6. Describe the maximum annual benefit that taxpayers may receive under defined benefit plans.

LO 13-1 7. Describe the distribution or payout options available to taxpayers participating in qualified defined benefit plans. How are defined benefit plan distributions to recipients taxed?

LO 13-1 LO 13-2 8. Describe the minimum distribution requirements for defined benefit plans. Are these requirements typically an item of concern for taxpayers?

LO 13-1 LO 13-2 9. Compare and contrast the employer's responsibilities for providing a defined benefit plan to employees relative to providing a defined contribution plan.

LO 13-2 10. Describe how an employee's benefit under a defined contribution plan is determined.

LO 13-2 11. Is there a limit to how much an employer and/or employee may contribute to an employee's defined contribution account(s) for the year? If so, describe the limit.

LO 13-2 12. Cami (age 52 and married) was recently let go as part of her employer's reduction in force program. Cami's annual AGI was usually around $50,000. Shortly after Cami's employment was terminated, her employer distributed the balance of her employer-sponsored 401(k) account to her. What could Cami do to avoid being assessed the 10 percent early distribution penalty?

LO 13-2 13. When may employees begin to receive defined contribution plan distributions without penalty?

LO 13-2 14. Describe the circumstances under which distributions from defined contribution plans are penalized. What are the penalties?

LO 13-2 research 15. Brady Corporation has a profit-sharing plan that allocates 10 percent of all after-tax income to employees. The profit sharing is allocated to individual employees based on relative employee compensation. The profit-sharing contributions vest to employees under a six-year graded plan. If an employee terminates his or her employment before fully vesting, the plan allocates the forfeited amounts among the remaining participants according to their account balances. Is this forfeiture allocation policy discriminatory, and will it cause the plan to lose its qualified status? Use Rev. Rul. 81-10 to help formulate your answer.

LO 13-2 16. What does it mean if an employer "matches" employee contributions to 401(k) plans?

planning LO 13-2 17. What nontax factor(s) should an employee consider when deciding whether and to what extent to participate in an employer's 401(k) plan?

LO 13-2 18. What are the differences between a traditional 401(k) and Roth 401(k) plan?

LO 13-2 19. Can employers match employee contributions to Roth 401(k) plans? Explain.

LO 13-2 20. Describe the annual limitation on employer and employee contributions to traditional 401(k) and Roth 401(k) plans.

LO 13-2 LO 13-3 21. When a company is limited by the tax laws in the amount it can contribute to an employee's 401(k) plan, what will it generally do to make the employee whole? Is this likely an issue for rank-and-file employees? Why or why not?

planning LO 13-2 22. From a tax perspective, how would taxpayers determine whether they should contribute to a traditional 401(k) or a Roth 401(k)?

LO 13-2 23. Could a taxpayer contributing to a traditional 401(k) plan earn an after-tax return *greater* than the before-tax return? Explain.

24. Explain the *tax* similarities and differences between qualified defined contribution plans and nonqualified deferred compensation plans from an *employer's* perspective. LO 13-2 LO 13-3
25. Explain the *tax* similarities and differences between qualified defined contribution plans and nonqualified deferred compensation plans from an *employee's* perspective. LO 13-2 LO 13-3
26. Explain the *nontax* similarities and differences between qualified defined contribution plans and nonqualified deferred compensation plans from an *employer's* perspective. LO 13-2 LO 13-3
27. Explain the *nontax* similarities and differences between qualified defined contribution plans and nonqualified deferred compensation plans from an *employee's* perspective. LO 13-2 LO 13-3
28. From a *tax* perspective, what issues does an employee need to consider in deciding whether to defer compensation under a nonqualified deferred compensation plan or to receive it immediately? LO 13-3 planning
29. From a *nontax* perspective, what issues does an employee need to consider in deciding whether to defer compensation under a nonqualified deferred compensation plan or to receive it immediately? LO 13-3 planning
30. What are reasons why companies provide nonqualified deferred compensation plans for certain employees? LO 13-3
31. How can companies use deferred compensation to avoid the §162(m) limitation on salary deductibility? LO 13-2 planning
32. Are companies allowed to decide who can and who cannot participate in nonqualified deferred compensation plans? Briefly explain. LO 13-3
33. How might the ultimate benefits to an employee who participates in a qualified retirement plan of a company differ from an employee who participates in a nonqualified deferred compensation plan of the company if the company experiences bankruptcy before the employee is scheduled to receive the benefits? LO 13-1 LO 13-2 LO 13-3
34. What are the primary tax differences between traditional IRAs and Roth IRAs? LO 13-4
35. Describe the circumstances in which it would be more favorable for a taxpayer to contribute to a traditional IRA rather than a Roth IRA and vice versa. LO 13-4 planning
36. What are the requirements for a taxpayer to make a deductible contribution to a traditional IRA? Why do the tax laws impose these restrictions? LO 13-4
37. What is the limitation on a deductible IRA contribution for 2015? LO 13-4
38. Compare the minimum distribution requirements for traditional IRAs to those of Roth IRAs. LO 13-4
39. How are qualified distributions from Roth IRAs taxed? How are nonqualified distributions taxed? LO 13-4
40. Explain when a taxpayer will be subject to the 10 percent penalty when receiving distributions from a Roth IRA. LO 13-4
41. Is a taxpayer who contributed to a traditional IRA able to transfer or "roll over" the money into a Roth IRA? If yes, explain the tax consequences of the transfer. LO 13-4
42. Assume a taxpayer makes a nondeductible contribution to a traditional IRA. How does the taxpayer determine the taxability of distributions from the IRA on reaching retirement? LO 13-4
43. When a taxpayer takes a nonqualified distribution from a Roth IRA, is the entire amount of the distribution treated as taxable income? LO 13-4
44. What types of retirement plans are available to self-employed taxpayers? LO 13-5
45. Compare and contrast the annual limitations on deductible contributions for self-employed taxpayers to SEP IRAs, and individual 401(k) accounts. LO 13-5

LO 13-5 46. What are the nontax considerations for self-employed taxpayers deciding whether to set up a SEP IRA or an individual 401(k)?

LO 13-6 47. What is the saver's credit and who is eligible to receive it?

LO 13-6 48. What is the maximum saver's credit available to taxpayers? What taxpayer characteristics are relevant to the determination?

LO 13-6 49. How is the saver's credit computed?

PROBLEMS

All applicable problems are available with McGraw-Hill's *Connect® Accounting*.

LO 13-1 50. Javier recently graduated and started his career with DNL Inc. DNL provides a defined benefit plan to all employees. According to the terms of the plan, for each full year of service working for the employer, employees receive a benefit of 1.5 percent of their average salary over their highest three years of compensation from the company. Employees may accrue only 30 years of benefit under the plan (45 percent). Determine Javier's annual benefit on retirement, before taxes, under each of the following scenarios:

a) Javier works for DNL for three years and three months before he leaves for another job. Javier's annual salary was $55,000, $65,000, $70,000, and $72,000 for years 1, 2, 3, and 4, respectively. DNL uses a five-year cliff vesting schedule.

b) Javier works for DNL for three years and three months before he leaves for another job. Javier's annual salary was $55,000, $65,000, $70,000, and $72,000 for years 1, 2, 3, and 4, respectively. DNL uses a seven-year graded vesting schedule.

c) Javier works for DNL for six years and three months before he leaves for another job. Javier's annual salary was $75,000, $85,000, $90,000, and $95,000 for years 4, 5, 6, and 7, respectively. DNL uses a five-year cliff vesting schedule.

d) Javier works for DNL for six years and three months before he leaves for another job. Javier's annual salary was $75,000, $85,000, $90,000, and $95,000 for years 4, 5, 6, and 7, respectively. DNL uses a seven-year graded vesting schedule.

e) Javier works for DNL for 32 years and three months before retiring. Javier's annual salary was $175,000, $185,000, and $190,000 for his final three years of employment.

LO 13-1 51. Alicia has been working for JMM Corp. for 32 years. Alicia participates in JMM's defined benefit plan. Under the plan, for every year of service for JMM she is to receive 2 percent of the average salary of her three highest years of compensation from JMM. She retired on January 1, 2015. Before retirement, her annual salary was $570,000, $600,000, and $630,000 for 2012, 2013, and 2014. What is the maximum benefit Alicia can receive in 2015?

LO 13-2
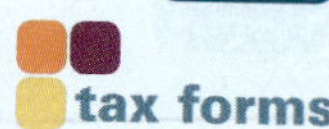
52. Kim has worked for one employer her entire career. While she was working, she participated in the employer's defined contribution plan [traditional 401(k)]. At the end of 2015, Kim retires and the balance in her defined contribution plan was $2,000,000 at the end of 2014.

a) What is Kim's minimum required distribution for 2015 in 2016 if she is 68 years old at the end of 2015?

b) What is Kim's minimum required distribution for 2015 if she turns 70½ during 2015 and she has not turned 71 years old by the end of 2015? When must she receive this distribution?

c) What is Kim's minimum required distribution for 2015 in 2016 if she is 73 years old at the end of 2015?

d) Assuming that Kim is 75 years old at the end of 2015 and that her marginal tax rate in 2015 is 33 percent, what will she have remaining after taxes if she receives only a distribution of $50,000 for 2015?

e) Complete Form 5329, page 2, to report the minimum distribution penalty in part (d). Use the most recent form available.

53. Matthew (48 at year-end) develops cutting-edge technology for SV Inc., located in Silicon Valley. In 2015, Matthew participates in SV's money purchase pension plan (a defined contribution plan) and in his company's 401(k) plan. Under the money purchase pension plan, SV contributes 15 percent of an employee's salary to a retirement account for the employee up to the amount limited by the tax code. Because it provides the money purchase pension plan, SV does not contribute to the employee's 401(k) plan. Matthew would like to maximize his contribution to his 401(k) account after SV's contribution to the money purchase plan. LO 13-2

a) Assuming Matthew's annual salary is $400,000, what amount will SV contribute to Matthew's money purchase plan? What can Matthew contribute to his 401(k) account in 2015?

b) Assuming Matthew's annual salary is $240,000, what amount will SV contribute to Matthew's money purchase plan? What can Matthew contribute to his 401(k) account in 2015?

c) Assuming Matthew's annual salary is $60,000, what amount will SV contribute to Matthew's money purchase plan? What amount can Matthew contribute to his 401(k) account in 2015?

d) Assume the same facts as part (c), except that Matthew is 54 years old at the end of 2015. What amount can Matthew contribute to his 401(k) account in 2015?

54. In 2015, Maggy (34 years old) is an employee of YBU Corp. YBU provides a 401(k) plan for all its employees. According to the terms of the plan, YBU contributes 50 cents for every dollar the employee contributes. The maximum employer contribution under the plan is 15 percent of the employee's salary (if allowed, YBU contributes until the employee has contributed 30 percent of her salary). LO 13-2 planning

a) Maggy has worked for YBU corporation for 3½ years before deciding to leave. Maggy's annual salary during this time was $45,000, $52,000, $55,000, and $60,000 (she only received half of her final year's salary). Assuming Maggy contributed 8 percent of her salary (including her 2015 salary) to her 401(k) account, what is Maggy's vested account balance when she leaves YBU (exclusive of account earnings)? Assume YBU uses three-year cliff vesting.

b) Same question as part (a), except YBU uses six-year graded vesting.

c) Maggy wants to maximize YBU's contribution to her 401(k) account in 2015. How much should Maggy contribute to her 401(k) account assuming her annual salary is $100,000 (she works for YBU for the entire year)?

d) Same question as part (c), except Maggy is 55 years old rather than 34 years old at the end of the year.

55. In 2015, Nina contributes 10 percent of her $100,000 annual salary to her 401(k) account. She expects to earn a 7 percent before-tax rate of return. Assuming she leaves this (and any employer contributions) in the account until she retires in 25 years, what is Nina's after-tax accumulation from her 2015 contributions to her 401(k) account? LO 13-2

a) Assume Nina's marginal tax rate at retirement is 30 percent.

b) Assume Nina's marginal tax at retirement is 20 percent.

c) Assume Nina's marginal tax rate at retirement is 40 percent.

LO 13-2

56. In 2015, Nitai contributes 10 percent of his $100,000 annual salary to a Roth 401(k) account sponsored by his employer, AY Inc. AY Inc. matches employee contributions dollar for dollar up to 10 percent of the employee's salary to the employee's traditional 401(k) account. Nitai expects to earn a 7 percent before-tax rate of return. Assuming he leaves his contributions in the Roth 401(k) and traditional 401(k) accounts until he retires in 25 years, what are Nitai's after-tax proceeds from the Roth 401(k) and traditional 401(k) accounts after he receives the distributions assuming his marginal tax rate at retirement is 30 percent?

LO 13-3 planning

57. Marissa participates in her employer's nonqualified deferred compensation plan. For 2015, she is deferring 10 percent of her $320,000 annual salary. Assuming this is her only source of income and her marginal income tax rate is 30 percent, how much *tax* does Marissa save in 2015 by deferring this income?

LO 13-3

58. Paris participates in her employer's nonqualified deferred compensation plan. For 2015, she is deferring 10 percent of her $320,000 annual salary. Assuming this is her only source of income and her marginal income tax rate is 30 percent, how much does deferring Paris's income save her employer (after taxes) in 2015? Paris's employer's marginal tax rate is 35 percent.

LO 13-3 planning

59. Leslie participates in IBO's nonqualified deferred compensation plan. For 2015, she is deferring 10 percent of her $300,000 annual salary. Based on her deemed investment choice, Leslie expects to earn a 7 percent before-tax rate of return on her deferred compensation, which she plans to receive in 10 years. Leslie's marginal tax rate in 2015 is 30 percent. IBO's marginal tax rate is 35 percent.
   a) Assuming Leslie's marginal tax rate in 10 years when she receives the distribution is 33 percent, what is Leslie's after-tax accumulation on the deferred compensation?
   b) Assuming Leslie's marginal tax rate in 10 years when she receives the distribution is 20 percent, what is Leslie's after-tax accumulation on the deferred compensation?
   c) Assuming IBO's cost of capital is 8 percent after taxes, how much deferred compensation should IBO be willing to pay Leslie that would make it indifferent between paying 10 percent of Leslie's current salary or deferring it for 10 years?

LO 13-3 planning

60. XYZ Corporation has a deferred compensation plan under which it allows certain employees to defer up to 40 percent of their salary for five years.
   a) Assume XYZ has a marginal tax rate of 35 percent for the foreseeable future and earns an after-tax rate of return of 8 percent on its assets. Joel Johnson, XYZ's VP of finance, is attempting to determine what amount of deferred compensation XYZ should be willing to pay in five years that would make XYZ indifferent between paying the current salary of $10,000 and paying the deferred compensation. What amount of deferred compensation would accomplish this objective?
   b) Assume Julie, an XYZ employee, has the option of participating in XYZ's deferred compensation plan. Julie's marginal tax rate is 40 percent and she expects the rate to remain constant over the next five years. Julie is trying to decide how much deferred compensation she will need to receive from XYZ in five years to make her indifferent between receiving the current salary of $10,000 and receiving the deferred compensation payment. If Julie takes the salary, she will invest it in a taxable corporate bond paying interest at 5 percent annually (after taxes). What amount of deferred compensation would accomplish this objective?

LO 13-4

61. John (age 51 and single) has earned income of $3,000. He has $30,000 of unearned (capital gain) income.
   a) If he does not participate in an employer-sponsored plan, what is the maximum deductible IRA contribution John can make in 2015?

b) If he does participate in an employer-sponsored plan, what is the maximum deductible IRA contribution John can make in 2015?

c) If he does not participate in an employer-sponsored plan, what is the maximum deductible IRA contribution John can make in 2015 if he has earned income of $10,000?

62. William is a single writer (age 35) who recently decided that he needs to save more for retirement. His 2015 AGI is $65,000 (all earned income). LO 13-4

a) If he does not participate in an employer-sponsored plan, what is the maximum deductible IRA contribution William can make in 2015?

b) If he does participate in an employer-sponsored plan, what is the maximum deductible IRA contribution William can make in 2015?

c) Assuming the same facts as in part (b), except his AGI is $75,000, what is the maximum deductible IRA contribution William can make in 2015?

63. In 2015, Susan (44 years old) is a highly successful architect and is covered by an employee-sponsored plan. Her husband, Dan (47 years old), however, is a Ph.D. student and is unemployed. Compute the maximum deductible IRA contribution for each spouse in the following alternative situations. LO 13-4

a) Susan's salary and the couple's AGI is $190,000. The couple files a joint tax return.

b) Susan's salary and the couple's AGI is $120,000. The couple files a joint tax return.

c) Susan's salary and the couple's AGI is $80,000. The couple files a joint tax return.

d) Susan's salary and her AGI is $80,000. Dan reports $5,000 of AGI (earned income). The couple files separate tax returns.

64. In 2015, Rashaun (62 years old) retired and planned on immediately receiving distributions (making withdrawals) from his traditional IRA account. The balance of his IRA account is $160,000 (before reducing it for withdrawals/distributions described below). Over the years, Rashaun has contributed $40,000 to the IRA. Of his $40,000 contributions, $30,000 was *nondeductible* and $10,000 was *deductible*. Assume Rashaun did not make any contributions to the account during 2015. LO 13-4 tax forms

a) If Rashaun currently withdraws $20,000 from the IRA, how much tax will he be required to pay on the withdrawal if his marginal tax rate is 25 percent?

b) If Rashaun currently withdraws $70,000 from the IRA, how much tax will he be required to pay on the withdrawal if his marginal tax rate is 28 percent?

c) Using the information provided in part (b), complete Form 8606, Part I, to report the taxable portion of the $70,000 distribution (withdrawal). Use 2014 forms if 2015 forms are unavailable.

65. Brooklyn has been contributing to a traditional IRA for seven years (all deductible contributions) and has a total of $30,000 in the account. In 2015, she is 39 years old and has decided that she wants to get a new car. She withdraws $20,000 from the IRA to help pay for the car. She is currently in the 25 percent marginal tax bracket. What amount of the withdrawal, after tax considerations, will Brooklyn have available to purchase the car? LO 13-4

66. Jackson and Ashley Turner (both 45 years old) are married and want to contribute to a Roth IRA for Ashley. In 2015, their AGI is $185,000. Jackson and Ashley each earned half of the income. LO 13-4

a) How much can Ashley contribute to her Roth IRA if they file a joint return?

b) How much can Ashley contribute if she files a separate return?

c) Assume that Ashley earned all of the couple's income and that she contributed the maximum amount she is allowed to contribute to a Roth IRA. What amount can be contributed to Jackson's Roth IRA?

LO 13-4

67. Harriet and Harry Combs (both 37 years old) are married and both want to contribute to a Roth IRA. In 2015, their AGI is $50,000. Harriet earned $46,000 and Harry earned $4,000.
    a) How much can Harriet contribute to her Roth IRA if they file a joint return?
    b) How much can Harriet contribute if she files a separate return?
    c) How much can Harry contribute to his Roth IRA if they file separately?

LO 13-4

68. Michael is single and 35 years old. He is a participant in his employer's sponsored retirement plan. How much can Michael contribute to a Roth IRA in each of the following alternative situations?
    a) Michael's AGI is $50,000 after he contributed $3,000 to a traditional IRA.
    b) Michael's AGI is $80,000 before any IRA contributions.
    c) Michael's AGI is $135,000 before any IRA contributions.

LO 13-4

69. George (age 42 at year-end) has been contributing to a traditional IRA for years (all deductible contributions) and his IRA is now worth $25,000. He is planning on transferring (or rolling over) the entire balance into a Roth IRA account. George's marginal tax rate is 25 percent.
    a) What are the tax consequences to George if he takes $25,000 out of the traditional IRA and puts the entire amount into a Roth IRA?
    b) What are the tax consequences to George if he takes $25,000 out of the traditional IRA, pays the taxes due from the IRA distribution, and contributes the remaining distribution to the Roth IRA?
    c) What are the tax consequences to George if he takes $25,000 out of the traditional IRA, keeps $10,000 to pay taxes and to make a down payment on a new car, and contributes the remaining distribution to the Roth IRA?

LO 13-4

70. Jimmer has contributed $15,000 to his Roth IRA and the balance in the account is $18,000. In the current year, Jimmer withdrew $17,000 from the Roth IRA to pay for a new car. If Jimmer's marginal ordinary income tax rate is 25 percent, what amount of tax and penalty, if any, is Jimmer required to pay on the withdrawal in each of the following alternative situations?
    a) Jimmer opened the Roth account 44 months before he withdrew the $17,000 and Jimmer is 62 years of age.
    b) Jimmer opened the Roth account 44 months before he withdrew the $17,000 and Jimmer is age 53.
    c) Jimmer opened the Roth account 76 months before he withdrew the $17,000 and Jimmer is age 62.
    d) Jimmer opened the Roth account 76 months before he withdrew the $17,000 and Jimmer is age 53.

LO 13-4
planning

71. John is trying to decide whether to contribute to a Roth IRA or a traditional IRA. He plans on making a $5,000 contribution to whichever plan he decides to fund. He currently pays tax at a 30 percent marginal income tax rate but he believes that his marginal tax rate in the future will be 28 percent. He intends to leave the money in the Roth IRA or traditional IRA accounts for 30 years and he expects to earn a 6 percent before-tax rate of return on the account.
    a) How much will John accumulate after taxes if he contributes to a Roth IRA (consider only the funds contributed to the Roth IRA)?
    b) How much will John accumulate after taxes if he contributes to a traditional IRA (consider only the funds contributed to the Roth IRA)?
    c) Without doing any computations, explain whether the traditional IRA or the Roth IRA will generate a greater after-tax rate of return.

72. Over the past three years, Sherry has contributed a total of $12,000 to a Roth IRA account ($4,000 a year). The current value of the Roth IRA is $16,300. In the current year, Sherry withdraws $14,000 of the account balance to purchase a car. Assuming Sherry is in a 25 percent marginal tax bracket, how much of the $14,000 withdrawal will she retain after taxes to fund her car purchase? LO 13-4

73. Seven years ago, Halle (currently age 41) contributed $4,000 to a Roth IRA account. The current value of the Roth IRA is $9,000. In the current year Halle withdraws $8,000 of the account balance to use as a down payment on her first home. Assuming Halle is in a 25 percent marginal tax bracket, how much of the $8,000 withdrawal will she retain after taxes to fund her house down payment? LO 13-4

74. Yuki (age 45 at year-end) has been contributing to a traditional IRA for years (all deductible contributions), and her IRA is now worth $50,000. She is trying to decide whether she should roll over her traditional IRA into a Roth IRA. Her current marginal tax rate is 25 percent. She plans to withdraw the entire balance of the account in 20 years and she expects to earn a before-tax rate of return of 5 percent on her retirement accounts and a 4 percent after-tax rate of return on all investments outside of her retirement accounts. For each of the following alternative scenarios, indicate how much more or less Yuki will accumulate after taxes in 20 years if she rolls over her traditional IRA into a Roth IRA. Be sure to include the opportunity cost of having to pay taxes on the rollover. LO 13-4 planning research
    a) When she withdraws the retirement funds in 20 years, she expects her marginal tax rate to be 35 percent.
    b) When she withdraws the retirement funds in 20 years, she expects her marginal tax rate to be 20 percent.
    c) Assume the same facts as in part (b), except that she earns a 3 percent after-tax rate of return on investments outside of the retirement accounts.
    d) In general terms, reconcile your answer from part (b) with your answer to part (c) (no numbers required).

75. Sarah was contemplating making a contribution to her traditional individual retirement account for 2015. She determined that she would contribute $5,500 to her IRA and she deducted $5,500 for the contribution when she completed and filed her 2015 tax return on February 15, 2016. Two months later, on April 15, Sarah realized that she had not yet actually contributed the funds to her IRA. On April 15, she went to the post office and mailed a $5,500 (for all) check to the bank holding her IRA. The bank received the payment on April 18. In which year is Sarah's $5,500 contribution deductible? LO 13-4 research

76. Elvira is a self-employed taxpayer who turns 42 years old at the end of the year (2014). In 2015, her net Schedule C income was $120,000. This was her only source of income. This year, Elvira is considering setting up a retirement plan. What is the maximum amount Elvira may contribute to the self-employed plan in each of the following situations? LO 13-5 planning
    a) She sets up a SEP IRA.
    b) She sets up an individual 401(k).

77. Hope is a self-employed taxpayer who turns 54 years old at the end of the year (2015). In 2015, her net Schedule C income was $120,000. This was her only source of income. This year, Hope is considering setting up a retirement plan. What is the maximum amount Hope may contribute to the self-employed plan in each of the following situations? LO 13-5 planning
    a) She sets up a SEP IRA.
    b) She sets up an individual 401(k).

LO 13-5

78. Rita is a self-employed taxpayer who turns 39 years old at the end of the year (2015). In 2015, her net Schedule C income was $300,000. This was her only source of income. This year, Rita is considering setting up a retirement plan. What is the maximum amount Rita may contribute to the self-employed plan in each of the following situations?
    a) She sets up a SEP IRA.
    b) She sets up an individual 401(k).

LO 13-5

79. Reggie is a self-employed taxpayer who turns 59 years old at the end of the year (2015). In 2015, his net Schedule C income was $300,000. This was his only source of income. This year, Reggie is considering setting up a retirement plan. What is the maximum amount he may contribute to the self-employed plan in each of the following situations?
    a) He sets up a SEP IRA.
    b) He sets up an individual 401(k).

LO 13-6

80. Desmond is 25 years old and he participates in his employer's 401(k) plan. During the year, he contributed $3,000 to his 401(k) account. What is Desmond's 2015 saver's credit in each of the following alternative scenarios?
    a) Desmond is not married and has no dependents. His AGI after deducting his 401(k) contribution is $34,000.
    b) Desmond is not married and has no dependents. His AGI after deducting his 401(k) contribution is $17,500.
    c) Desmond files as a head of household and has AGI of $44,000.
    d) Desmond and his wife file jointly and report an AGI of $30,000 for the year.

LO 13-6

81. Penny is 57 years old and she participates in her employer's 401(k) plan. During the year, she contributed $2,000 to her 401(k) account. Penny's AGI is $27,000 after deducting her 401(k) contribution. What is Penny's 2015 saver's credit in each of the following alternative scenarios?
    a) Penny is not married and has no dependents.
    b) Penny files as a head of household and she has three dependents.
    c) Penny files as a head of household and she has one dependent.
    d) Penny is married and files a joint return with her husband. They have three dependents.
    e) Penny files a separate tax return from her husband. She claims two dependent children on her return.

COMPREHENSIVE PROBLEMS

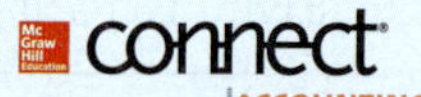

All applicable problems are available with McGraw-Hill's *Connect*® *Accounting*.

82. Jacquiline is unmarried and age 32. Even though she participates in an employer-sponsored retirement plan, Jacquiline contributed $3,000 to a traditional IRA during the year. Jacquiline files as a head of household, her AGI before the contribution is $43,000, and her marginal tax rate is 15 percent. What is the after-tax cost of her $3,000 traditional IRA contribution?

83. Ian retired in June 2014 at the age of 69 (he turned 70 in August 2014). Ian's retirement account was valued at $490,000 at the end of 2013 and $500,000 at the end of 2014. What is Ian's required minimum distribution for 2015 under each of the following alternative scenarios?
    a) Ian's retirement account is a traditional 401(k) account.
    b) Ian's retirement account is a Roth 401(k) account.

c) Ian's retirement account is a traditional IRA.

d) Ian's retirement account is a Roth IRA.

84. Alex is 31 years old and has lived in Los Alamos, New Mexico, for the last four years where he works at the Los Alamos National Laboratory (LANL). LANL provides employees with a 401(k) plan and for every $1 an employee contributes (up to 9 percent of the employee's salary) LANL contributes $3 (a 3-to-1 match). The plan provides a six-year graded vesting schedule. Alex is now in his fifth year working for LANL, and his current year salary is $150,000. Alex's marginal tax rate is 28 percent in 2015. Answer the following questions relating to Alex's retirement savings in 2015.

    a) Assume that over the past four years, Alex has contributed $45,000 to his 401(k) and his employer has contributed $115,000 to the plan. The plan has an account balance of $175,000. What is Alex's vested account balance in his 401(k)?

    b) Because Alex considers his employer's matching contributions "free money," he wants to maximize the amount of LANL's contributions. What is the least amount Alex can contribute and still maximize LANL's contribution?

    c) In need of cash to build a home theater, Alex withdrew $30,000 from his traditional 401(k) account. What amount of the withdrawal, after taxes and penalties, will Alex have available to complete his project?

    d) Assume that Alex contributes $10,000 to his traditional 401(k) account this year. Also assume that in 30 years, Alex retires (at age 61) and withdraws the $10,000 contribution made this year *and* all the earnings generated by the contribution. Also assume that his marginal tax rate at the time he retires is 25 percent. Ignore any prior or subsequent contributions to his plan. If Alex earns a 6 percent annual before-tax rate of return, what are his after-tax proceeds from the distribution?

    e) Assume that Alex is 74 years old at the end of the year, retired, and that his marginal tax rate is 25 percent. His account balance in his traditional 401(k) was $1,250,000 at the end of last year. What is the minimum distribution Alex must receive from his 401(k) account for this year? If Alex receives a $43,000 distribution from his 401(k) account (his only distribution during the year), what amount will he be able to keep after taxes and penalties (if any)?

85. Tommy (age 47) and his wife, Michelle (age 49), live in Columbus, Ohio, where Tommy works for Callahan Auto Parts (CAP) as the vice president of the brakes division. Tommy's 2015 salary is $360,000. CAP allows Tommy to participate in its nonqualified deferred compensation plan in which participants can defer 15 percent of their salary for five years. Tommy also participates in CAP's qualified 401(k) plan. Tommy's current marginal tax rate is 28 percent and CAP's current marginal tax rate is 34 percent.

    a) Assuming Tommy earns a 6 percent *after-tax* rate of return and he expects his marginal tax rate to be 30 percent in five years, what before-tax deferred compensation payment in five years would make him indifferent between receiving the deferred compensation payment or 15 percent of his salary now (ignore payroll taxes)?

    b) Assuming CAP has an 8 percent *after-tax* rate of return and expects its marginal tax rate to be 35 percent in five years, how much would it be willing to pay in five years to be indifferent between paying the deferred compensation or paying 15 percent of Tommy's salary now (ignore payroll taxes)?

c) Will Tommy and CAP be able to come to an agreement on deferring Tommy's salary?

d) Assume that Tommy and Michelle have an AGI of $99,000 before IRA deductions by either spouse. The AGI includes $10,000 that Michelle earned working part-time (but she does not participate in an employer-sponsored retirement plan). Tommy and Michelle file a joint return. What is the maximum deductible contribution Tommy and Michelle may make to a traditional IRA?

e) Tommy has a balance of $55,000 in his traditional IRA. Due to some recent tax cuts, his marginal tax rate is 20 percent, so he would like to roll his traditional IRA into a Roth IRA. What are the tax consequences to Tommy if he takes $55,000 out of the IRA, pays the taxes due from the traditional IRA distribution, and contributes the remaining distribution to the Roth IRA?

86. Gerry (age 56) and Elaine (age 54) have been married for 12 years and file a joint tax return. The couple lives in an apartment in downtown Manhattan. Gerry's father, Mortey, recently retired from Del Boca Vista Corporation (DBVC) where he worked for many years. Mortey participated in DBVC's defined benefit plan. Elaine is an editor and works for Pendent Publishing earning an annual $150,000 salary in 2015. Gerry is a self-employed standup comedian, and had net business income of $46,000 in 2015. At the advice of their neighbor, Gerry and Elaine have come to you to for help in answering several retirement savings-related questions.

a) The DBVC defined benefit plan specifies a benefit of 1.5 percent for each year of service, up to a maximum of 30 percent (20 years of service), of the average of the employee's three highest years of salary. Mortey worked for the company for 25 years and earned $75,000, $78,000, and $84,000 over his final three years of service. What is Mortey's annual benefit from DBVC's defined benefit plan?

b) Elaine has worked at Pendent Publishing since January 1, 2011. The company offers a defined contribution plan. It matches 100 percent of employee contributions to the plan up to 6 percent of her salary. Prior to 2015, Elaine had contributed $40,000 to the plan and her employer had contributed $28,000 to the plan. In 2015, Elaine contributed $17,000 to her traditional 401(k). What is the amount of her employer's matching contribution for 2015? Assuming the company uses a six-year graded vesting schedule, what is Elaine's vested balance in the plan at the end of 2015 (for simplicity, disregard the plan's earnings)?

c) Elaine tells you that her employer has offered her $30,000 in 10 years to defer 10 percent of her current salary (defer $15,000). Assuming that the couple's marginal tax rate is currently 30 percent, they earn an after-tax rate of return of 8 percent, and they expect their marginal tax rate to be 25 percent in 10 years, should Elaine accept her company's offer? What is the minimum amount she should be willing to accept (ignoring nontax factors and payroll taxes)?

d) Gerry has a SEP IRA and would like to contribute as much as possible to this account. What is the maximum contribution Gerry can make to his SEP IRA in 2015?

e) Assuming Gerry had an individual 401(k), what is the maximum amount he could contribute to the plan in 2015?

f) Gerry also has a traditional IRA with an account balance of $42,000. He would like to convert the traditional IRA to a Roth IRA. Gerry would like to pay the least amount of tax possible in rolling the account over. What is the least amount of tax Gerry will be required to pay on the rollover?

g) Assume that Gerry rolled over his traditional IRA into a Roth IRA six years ago (rather than in 2015) and that the account now has a balance of $78,000. The couple is considering buying their first home and would like to pay as much down as possible. They have heard from their friends that they can take the funds from their Roth IRA and use it to buy their first home. Are their friends correct? What would you advise them to do?

h) Assume that Gerry and Elaine made $20,000 of total contributions to their qualified retirement accounts in 2015. Also assume that their AGI is $38,000. What would be the amount of their saver's credit for 2015?

chapter

14 Tax Consequences of Home Ownership

Learning Objectives

Upon completing this chapter, you should be able to:

- **LO 14-1** Determine whether a home is considered a principal residence, a residence (not principal), or a nonresidence for tax purposes.
- **LO 14-2** Compute the taxable gain on the sale of a residence and explain the requirements for excluding gain on the sale.
- **LO 14-3** Determine the amount of allowable interest expense deductions on loans secured by a residence.
- **LO 14-4** Discuss the deductibility of real property taxes.
- **LO 14-5** Explain the tax issues and consequences associated with rental use of the home, including determining the deductibility of residential rental real estate losses.
- **LO 14-6** Describe the requirements necessary to qualify for home office deductions and compute the deduction limitations on home office deductions.

© Purestock/SuperStock

Storyline Summary

Taxpayers:	Tyler and Jasmine Jefferson
Location:	Chicago, Illinois
Employment status:	Tyler—Newly hired VP of Sales for GLO Corporation earning an annual salary of $200,000 per year. Jasmine—graphic designer, earning an annual salary of $40,000 per year.
Filing status:	Married filing jointly
Dependents:	Two children
Marginal tax rate:	28 percent

With the extra income Tyler Jefferson is earning in his new VP of Sales position for GLO Corporation, his family now has greater financial flexibility, but with the money comes new possibilities. For one, Tyler and Jasmine Jefferson would like to sell their current home and purchase a larger one closer to Tyler's work. Fortunately, the value of their home has increased considerably since they purchased it, which should allow them to make a substantial down payment on a new home. Still, they would need to acquire financing to make the purchase. Jasmine likes the idea of buying a vacation home in Scottsdale, Arizona. Besides the great weather (she and Tyler both love golf), Scottsdale has the added benefit of being near Jasmine's family. She is trying to sell the second-home idea to Tyler by suggesting that they could rent the house when they're not there to help defray the costs. Finally, Jasmine is seriously considering a transition to self-employment as a graphic designer. She believes, with her experience and contacts, she can find enough clients to keep busy most of the time—and she very much likes the idea of setting aside a room in their primary home as her workplace. ■

When making these decisions, the Jeffersons should consider the tax consequences of their actions. Will they be required to pay taxes on the gain from the sale of their current home? Will the interest expense on the new home be fully deductible? Should they pay points to obtain a lower interest rate on the home loan? What will be the after-tax cost of the loan payments? If they use a home-equity loan to cover personal expenses, is the interest expense deductible? If they borrow money to buy a vacation home, can they deduct interest on the loan? If they rent out the vacation home for part of the year, how do they account for the related income and expenses for tax purposes? If the rental of the second home generates losses, are these losses deductible? If Jasmine sets up a home office, will the Jeffersons be allowed any tax deductions for expenses relating to their home? This chapter answers these and other relevant questions for the Jeffersons and for others interested in the tax consequences of home ownership.

LO 14-1 The starting point for determining the tax consequences of home ownership is first determining whether the taxpayer owns a **dwelling unit.** A dwelling unit is property that provides a place suitable for people to occupy (live and sleep). For tax purposes, a dwelling unit includes the following:

- House
- Condominium
- Mobile home
- Boat
- Other similar property[1]

A taxpayer may acquire a dwelling unit solely for personal use, for some mixture of personal and rental use, or solely for rental use. Each year, the dwelling unit is classified as either a residence or a nonresidence (rental property) based on how the taxpayer used the unit. The dwelling unit is considered to be a residence if the taxpayer's number of personal use days of the home is more than the greater of

1. 14 days or
2. 10 percent of the number of rental days during the year.[2]

To determine whether a dwelling unit is a residence or not, the taxpayer needs to calculate the number of days the home (dwelling unit) was used for personal use during the year and the number of days the home was rented out during the year. So what counts as a day of personal use and what counts as a day of rental use? The rules for determining the days of personal use are

- The taxpayer (owner) or any other owner of the home stays in the home.
- A relative of an owner stays in the home, even if the relative pays full fair market value rent unless the home is the relative's principal residence (discussed below).
- A nonowner stays in the home under a vacation home exchange or swap arrangement.
- The taxpayer rents out the property for less than fair market value.[3]

Rental use includes the following:

- Days when the taxpayer rents out the property at fair market value.
- Days spent repairing or maintaining the home for rental use.

Days when the home is available for rent, but not actually rented out, *do not count* as either personal or rental days.

When a dwelling unit is determined to be a residence, the taxpayer must determine whether the residence is the taxpayer's **principal residence** in order to determine

[1]§280A(f)(1). A dwelling unit does not include a hotel, motel, inn, or similar establishment.

[2]§280A(d)(1).

[3]§280A(d)(2).

certain tax consequences associated with the property (for certain purposes, the taxpayer need only determine whether the property is a residence). What makes a residence a "principal" residence? When a taxpayer lives in more than one residence during the year, the determination of which residence is the principal residence depends on the facts and circumstances such as

- Amount of time the taxpayer spends at each residence during the year.
- The proximity of each residence to the taxpayer's place of employment.
- The principal place of abode (living and sleeping) of the taxpayer's immediate family.
- The taxpayer's mailing address for bills and correspondence.

Note that a taxpayer can have only one principal residence during a particular year, and the principal residence may change from year to year.

To summarize, with respect to a particular taxpayer for a particular year, a dwelling unit or home can be classified as either a

- Principal residence,
- Residence (not principal), or a
- Nonresidence (rental property).

We refer to these property classifications throughout the chapter as we describe the tax consequences of home ownership. Exhibit 14-1 lists deductions and other tax provisions available for each property type. We discuss each of these tax provisions, including limitations, throughout the chapter. Also, Appendix B at the end of this chapter provides a flowchart for determining the tax status of a dwelling unit.

EXHIBIT 14-1 Tax Provisions by Property Type

	Property Type		
Tax Provision	Principal Residence	Residence (not principal)	Nonresidence
Home mortgage interest deductions (*from* AGI)	X	X	
Home-equity interest deduction (*from* AGI)	X	X	
Real property taxes (*from* AGI deduction)	X	X	X
Deductions associated with rental use, if any (*for* AGI)	X	X	X
Exclusion of gain on sale of home	X	X*	X*
Forgiveness of debt on home foreclosure (income exclusion)†	X		

*Must have previously been a principal residence to qualify.
†This provision had not been extended to 2015 as of press time.

We begin our discussion by considering the tax consequence associated with personal use of the home. We then discuss the tax consequences of rental use of the home, and we conclude the chapter by discussing the tax consequences of business use of the home.

THE KEY FACTS

Tax and Nontax Consequences of Home Ownership

- Nontax Consequences
  - Large investment.
  - Potential for big return (or loss) on investment with use of leverage.
  - Risk of default on home loan.
  - Time and costs of maintenance.
  - Limited mobility.
- Tax Consequences
  - Interest expense deductible.
  - Gain on sale excludable.
  - Real property taxes on home deductible.
  - Rental and business-use possibilities.

PERSONAL USE OF THE HOME

To buy or to rent? This is a difficult question with no single answer. The decision to purchase a home is a significant one that involves both nontax and tax considerations. Primary nontax factors favoring home ownership include the appreciation potential for the home as an investment. As the value of the home increases so does the homeowner's net worth. A home is frequently an individual's most significant investment. Therefore, home ownership also involves significant potential risk. When real estate values decline, the owner's net worth declines as well. Homeowners borrowing funds to purchase their home can potentially achieve large returns on their investment due to the power of leverage, but a home is by no means a liquid asset. Furthermore, homeowners must assume the risk associated with the possible default on the loan. If the owner does not make the mortgage payments required by the terms of the loan, the lender may repossess the home. Homeowners also are responsible for the cost or effort required to repair, maintain, and landscape the home. Finally, because building, buying, or selling a home and moving in or out of a home are expensive and time-consuming tasks, home ownership reduces one's ability to relocate to take advantage of new opportunities.

On the tax side, the government clearly smiles on home ownership given the deductions available to homeowners that are unavailable to renters. In fact, in the government's listing of projected "tax expenditures" (tax breaks provided to taxpayers) for the years 2015–2019, the deductibility of mortgage interest on owner-occupied homes is ranked number two.[4] The projections indicate that in 2015 homeowners are expected to save nearly $75 billion in tax payments due to the mortgage interest deduction. Besides the deduction for interest payments made on home-related loans, other tax benefits of home ownership include deducting real estate taxes paid on the home, excluding gain on the sale of the home, and deducting expenses relating to business offices in the home. Homeowners also may gain tax benefits associated with owning and renting a vacation home. We address the tax consequences of home ownership throughout the remainder of the chapter.

LO 14-2 Exclusion of Gain on Sale of Personal Residence

When a taxpayer sells a personal residence, she *realizes* a gain or a loss determined by subtracting the basis of the home from the amount the taxpayer receives from the buyer (minus selling costs). The basis of the residence depends on how the taxpayer acquired the home. The general rules for determining the basis of the home are as follows:

- Purchase: the cost of the home.
- Inheritance: the fair market value of the home on the date of death.
- Gift: the donor's basis.
- Convert rental home to residence: the taxpayer's basis in the rental home at the time of the conversion.

Because a personal residence is a capital asset, the gain or loss a taxpayer realizes by selling the residence is a capital gain or loss. However, because a personal residence is a personal use asset, the loss on the sale of a personal residence is a nondeductible personal loss.[5] This is an important limitation to many taxpayers, when the housing market is depressed. When a taxpayer sells a personal residence at a gain, the tax consequences are generally more favorable. In fact, taxpayers meeting certain requirements are allowed to exclude a certain amount of realized gain on the sale. The maximum exclusion depends on filing status as follows:

- $500,000 for married filing jointly taxpayers.
- $250,000 for other taxpayers.

Gain in excess of the excludable amount generally qualifies as long-term capital gain subject to tax at preferential rates. Further, gain in excess of the exclusion amount is considered to be investment income for purposes of determining the 3.8% net investment income discussed in Chapter 8.

[4]Number one on the list is the gross income exclusion for employer-paid medical insurance premiums and medical care. See www.whitehouse.gov/sites/default/files/omb/budget/fy2015/assets/teb2015.xls (Table 14-3).

[5]§165(c).

Requirements To qualify for the exclusion, the taxpayer must meet both ownership and use tests for the residence:

> *Ownership test:* The taxpayer must have owned the property for a total of two or more years during the five-year period ending on the date of the sale. The ownership test prevents a taxpayer from purchasing a home, fixing it up, and soon thereafter selling it and excluding the gain—a real estate investment practice termed **flipping.** In these circumstances, the gain is primarily due to the taxpayer's efforts in remodeling the home, not to general appreciation in the value of the property.
>
> *Use test:* The taxpayer must have *used* the property as her principal residence (see earlier discussion) for a total of two or more years during the five-year period ending on the date of the sale. The exclusion provision was designed to provide tax benefits to homeowners rather than investors or landlords. The use test helps ensure that taxpayers using the exclusion have realized gains from selling the home they actually live in as opposed to selling an investment or rental property.

Note that the periods of ownership and use need not be continuous nor do they need to cover the same two-year period. In fact, a taxpayer could rent a home and live in it as her principal residence during 2010 and then again during 2012, purchase the home and rent it to someone else during 2013 and 2014, and then sell the home at the beginning of 2015—and *still* meet the ownership and use tests!

THE KEY FACTS

Exclusion of Gain on Sale of Personal Residence

- Must meet ownership and use tests.
  - Must own home for at least two of five years before sale.
  - Must use home as principal residence for at least two of five years before sale.
  - For married couples to qualify for maximum exclusion on a joint return, one spouse must meet ownership test and both spouses must meet use test.

Example 14-1

The Jeffersons sold their home in Denver, Colorado, before moving to Chicago. They sold the Denver home for $350,000. The Jeffersons initially purchased the home for $250,000. They owned and lived in the home (as their principal residence) for four years before selling. How much of the $100,000 gain realized on the sale ($350,000 − $250,000) are they allowed to exclude?

Answer: All $100,000. The Jeffersons qualified for the full exclusion available to married couples filing jointly because they met the ownership and use tests. Consequently, they are allowed to exclude the entire $100,000 of gain and could have excluded up to $500,000 of gain on the sale.

How do the ownership and use tests apply to married couples filing joint returns? Married couples filing joint returns are eligible for the full $500,000 exclusion if *either* spouse meets the ownership test and *both* spouses meet the principal-use test. Even if a married couple filing jointly does not qualify for the $500,000 exclusion, the couple may still claim an exclusion for up to $250,000 on their joint return if one spouse meets the ownership and use tests.

Example 14-2

What if: Suppose that when Tyler and Jasmine were married, Jasmine moved into Tyler's home located in Denver, Colorado. Tyler had purchased the home two years before the marriage. After the marriage, the couple lived in the home together as their principal residence for four years before selling the home to move to Chicago. Tyler was the sole owner of the home for the entire six years he resided in the home. Would gain on the sale of the home qualify for the $500,000 exclusion available to married couples filing jointly even though Jasmine was never an owner of the home?

Answer: Yes. Gain on the sale qualifies for the full $500,000 exclusion available to married couples filing jointly because Tyler met the ownership test, and both Tyler and Jasmine met the use test.

What if: Suppose that Tyler and Jasmine lived in the home together for only one year before selling it. Would the couple be allowed to exclude any gain on the sale?

Answer: Yes, but because only Tyler meets the ownership and use tests, they would qualify only for the $250,000 exclusion even if they file a joint return.

If a widow or widower sells a home that the surviving spouse owned and occupied with the decedent spouse (the spouse who died), the surviving spouse is entitled to the full $500,000 exclusion provided that the surviving spouse sells the home within two years after the date of death of the decedent spouse. Finally, once a taxpayer claims a home sale exclusion, she is not eligible to claim another exclusion until at least two years pass from the time of the first sale (see the hardship circumstances discussion for an exception to this general rule).

General rule exceptions for nonqualified use and for hardship circumstances. In certain circumstances, taxpayers who otherwise meet the ownership and use requirements may have their exclusion limited under a "nonqualified use" provision. In other circumstances, taxpayers who fail the ownership and/or use tests are allowed to exclude gain on the sale of their residence under a "hardship" circumstances provision. Let's first discuss the nonqualified use provision.

Under the general rules for the home sale exclusion, taxpayers could exclude gain on the sale of a vacation home or rental property (including gain accrued while it was not a principal residence) simply by moving into the property and using it as their principal residence for two years before selling it. To limit a taxpayer's ability to benefit from this strategy, the nonqualified use provision reduces the taxpayer's otherwise excludable gain on the home sale if, on or after January 1, 2009, the taxpayer used or uses the home for something other than a principal residence for a period (termed *nonqualified use*).[6] The period of nonqualified use does not include any portion of the five-year period ending on the date of the sale that is after the last date that such property is used as the principal residence of the taxpayer or the taxpayer's spouse. This exception allows the taxpayer time to sell the principal residence after moving out of it, without having to count the time the house is available for sale as nonqualified use, which would increase the amount of gain the taxpayer would be required to recognize on the sale.

If the limitation applies, the percentage of the realized gain that must be recognized is the ratio of the period of nonqualified use divided by the period of time the taxpayer owned the home (acquisition date through date of sale). Note that this provision does not reduce the maximum exclusion; it reduces the amount of realized gain eligible for exclusion.

Example 14-3

What if: Suppose the Jeffersons purchased home 1 on January 1, 2012, for $250,000. They lived in home 1 as their principal residence until January 1, 2015, when they moved into a new principal residence (home 2). They finally sold home 1 on January 1, 2017, for $350,000. What amount of the $100,000 gain on the sale of home 1 ($350,000 amount realized minus $250,000 basis) may the Jeffersons exclude from gross income?

Answer: All $100,000. The Jeffersons meet the ownership and use tests (they owned and used home 1 as their principal residence for at least two of the five years prior to January 1, 2017), so they qualify for a maximum exclusion of $500,000. Further, the gain eligible for the exclusion is *not* reduced because the Jeffersons stopped using home 1 as a principal residence after January 1, 2015, and they sold the home within five years of this date.

What if: Assume the same facts as above, except that on January 1, 2016, the Jeffersons moved back into home 1 and used it as their principal residence until they sold it for $350,000 on January 1, 2017. What amount of the $100,000 gain on the sale of home 1 may the Jeffersons exclude from income?

Answer: $80,000. The Jeffersons meet the ownership and use tests for home 1 and therefore qualify for the maximum $500,000 exclusion. However, because they stopped using the home as their principal residence for a period on or after January 1, 2009 (nonqualified use from January 1, 2015–January 1, 2016), and they used the home as their principal residence immediately before selling (January 1, 2016–January 1, 2017), the gain eligible for exclusion must be reduced. The percentage of the gain that is not eligible for exclusion is 20 percent, which is the period of nonqualified use (one year: January 1, 2016–January 1, 2017) divided by the total period of time the Jeffersons owned the home (five years: January 1, 2012–January 1, 2017). Therefore, the Jeffersons must reduce their gain eligible for exclusion by $20,000 ($100,000 gain × 20% reduction percentage), allowing them to exclude $80,000 of the $100,000 gain from gross income.

[6]§121(b) (4)[(5)].

Sometimes taxpayers are unable to meet the two-year requirements for the ownership and use tests due to unusual or hardship circumstances. For example, a taxpayer may be forced to sell his home before he meets the ownership and use requirements due to a change in employment, significant health issues, or other unforeseen financial difficulties. In such cases, the *maximum* exclusion amount ($500,000 for married filing jointly, $250,000 otherwise) is reduced based on the amount of time the taxpayer owned and used the home as a principal residence before selling. For example, if a single taxpayer owned and used a home as principal residence for six months before selling due to hardship circumstances, the maximum exclusion would be $62,500, which is one-fourth of what it would be otherwise (6 months of ownership and use divided by 24 months required under general rule multiplied by the full $250,000 exclusion for single taxpayers). The maximum exclusion available to a taxpayer selling under these circumstances is expressed in the formula presented in Exhibit 14-2.

THE KEY FACTS

Exclusion of Gain on Sale of Personal Residence

- Exclusion Amount
  - $500,000 for married couples filing joint returns.
  - $250,000 for other taxpayers.
  - Hardship provisions *maximum exclusion* = full exclusion × months of qualifying ownership and use/24 months.
  - Gain eligible for exclusion may be reduced for period of nonqualified use.

EXHIBIT 14-2 Formula for Determining Maximum Home Sale Exclusion in Hardship Circumstances

Maximum exclusion in hardship circumstances =
Full exclusion × Qualifying months/24 months, where

Full exclusion = $250,000 for single taxpayers or $500,000 for taxpayers filing a joint return.

Qualifying months = the number of months the taxpayer met the ownership and use requirements for the home before *selling* it.

24 months = the number of months taxpayer must own and use home as principal residence to qualify for the full exclusion.[7]

Finally, to qualify for the exclusion due to a change in employment, the taxpayer's new place of employment must be at least 50 miles farther from the residence that is sold than was the previous place of employment.[8] That is, the taxpayer will not qualify unless the taxpayer's commute from the old home to the new job is at least 50 miles longer than the taxpayer's commute from the old home to the old job.[9]

Example 14-4

What if: Let's assume that when the Jeffersons moved from Denver, they purchased a home in Chicago for $275,000 and moved into the home on July 1, 2014. In January of 2015, Tyler accepted a work opportunity with a different employer located in Miami, Florida. On February 1, 2015, the Jeffersons sold their home for $295,000 and permanently relocated to Miami. How much of the $20,000 realized gain ($295,000 − $275,000) on their Chicago home sale can the Jeffersons exclude from taxable income?

Answer: All $20,000. The Jeffersons lived in the home for only seven months (July 1, 2014, to February 1, 2015), so they do not meet either the ownership or the use test to qualify for the maximum exclusion. However, under the hardship provision, they are eligible for a reduced maximum exclusion computed as follows: $500,000 (maximum exclusion) × 7 (qualifying months)/24 = $145,833. Because the amount they are able to exclude ($145,833) exceeds the $20,000 gain they realized on the sale, they are able to exclude all $20,000.

(continued on page 14-8)

[7]Taxpayers may choose to use the number of days the taxpayer fully qualified for the exclusion divided by 730 days.

[8]If there is no previous place of employment, the distance between the individual's new place of employment and the residence sold must be at least 50 miles.

[9]You may recall that this is the same test required to determine if a taxpayer qualifies for moving expenses as discussed in Chapter 6.

What if: Assume the same facts, except that the Jeffersons realized a $150,000 gain on the sale of their home. How much of the realized gain would they recognize and at what rate would this gain be taxed?

Answer: $150,000 gain realized minus $145,833 exclusion = $4,167 short-term capital gain (the home is a capital asset that the Jeffersons owned for one year or less). Assuming the Jeffersons did not recognize any other capital gains during the year, the $4,167 would be taxed at the Jeffersons' 28 percent marginal tax rate.

Note, as the previous example illustrates, that under the so-called hardship provision, it is the *full exclusion* that is reduced, not necessarily the excludable gain. Consequently, if a taxpayer's gain on the sale of a residence is less than the maximum exclusion, the taxpayer may exclude the full amount of the gain.

Exclusion of Gain from Debt Forgiveness on Foreclosure of Home Mortgage Prior to 2007, if a lender foreclosed (took possession of) a taxpayer's principal residence, sold the home for less than the taxpayer's outstanding mortgage, and forgave the taxpayer of the remainder of the debt, the taxpayer was required to include the debt forgiveness in her gross income. However, through December 31, 2014 (this provision had not been extended to 2015 as of the time we went to press), taxpayers who realize income from this situation are allowed to exclude up to $2 million of debt forgiveness if the debt is secured by the taxpayer's principal residence (the principal residence is collateral for the loan) and the debt was incurred to acquire, construct, or substantially improve the home.[10] The taxpayer must apply the excluded amount of debt forgiveness income to reduce the basis of the principal residence, but not below zero.

LO 14-3

Interest Expense on Home-Related Debt

A major tax benefit of owning a home is that taxpayers are generally allowed to deduct the interest they pay on their home mortgage loans as itemized (*from* AGI) deductions. Taxpayers report these itemized deductions on Schedule A of their individual tax Form 1040. For taxpayers who itemize deductions, the mortgage interest expense can generate significant tax savings and reduce the after-tax cost of mortgage payments. Often, this deduction alone exceeds the standard deduction, thus allowing taxpayers to claim other itemized deductions.[11]

Example 14-5

During the current year, Tyler and Jasmine own a home with an average mortgage balance of $300,000. They pay interest at 6 percent annually on the loan, and they qualify to deduct the interest expense as an itemized deduction. The Jeffersons' marginal income tax rate is 28 percent, and before counting mortgage interest, their itemized deductions exceed the standard deduction. What is the before- and after-tax cost of their mortgage interest expense for the year?

Answer: $18,000 before-tax cost and $12,960 after-tax cost, computed as follows:

Description	Amount	Explanation
(1) Before-tax interest expense	$18,000	$300,000 × 6%. All deductible.
(2) Marginal tax rate	× 28%	
(3) Tax savings from interest expense	5,040	(1) × (2).
After-tax cost of interest expense	**$12,960**	(1) − (3).

Note that the $5,040 tax savings generated by the mortgage interest expense deduction reduces the after-tax cost of their monthly mortgage payment by $420 ($5,040/12).

[10]§108(a)(1)(E) and §108(h).

[11]Note that home mortgage interest deductions (including deductions for home equity interest and points) are subject to the itemized deduction phase-out for high income taxpayers. See Chapter 6 for a detailed discussion.

What if: Assume that instead of buying a home, the Jeffersons rented a home and paid $1,500 a month for rent expense. What would be the before- and after-tax cost of the $18,000 annual rental payments?

Answer: $18,000 before- and after-tax cost of rental payments. Because rental payments are not deductible, they do not generate any tax savings, so the before- and after-tax cost of the rental payments is the same.

Despite the apparent tax savings from buying versus renting a home, it is important to consider that nontax factors could favor renting over purchasing a home.

Taxpayers are allowed to deduct only "qualified" residence interest as an itemized deduction.[12] Qualified residence interest is interest paid on the principal amount of **acquisition indebtedness** and on the principal amount of **home-equity indebtedness.** Both types of indebtedness must be **secured** by a **qualified residence** to qualify. To understand what this means exactly, we need to define a few terms.

Loan secured by residence: The residence is the collateral for the loan. If the owner does not make the payments on the loan, the lender may take possession of the home to satisfy the owner's responsibility for the loan.

Qualified residence: The taxpayer's principal residence *and* one other residence (see previous discussion for definition of principal residence and of residence). For a taxpayer with *more* than two residences, which property is treated as the second qualified residence is an annual election—that is, the taxpayer can choose to deduct interest related to a particular second home one year and a different second home the next. The second residence is often a vacation home where the taxpayer resides part time.

Acquisition indebtedness: Any debt secured by a qualified residence that is incurred in acquiring, constructing, or substantially improving the residence (limited to $1,000,000, as discussed below).

Home-equity indebtedness: Any debt, except for acquisition indebtedness, secured by the taxpayer's qualified residence to *the extent it does not exceed the fair market value of the residence minus the acquisition indebtedness* (limited to $100,000, as discussed below). That is, for purposes of deducting interest, total qualifying home-related debt cannot exceed the total value of the home. The determination of the amount of home-equity debt is made at the time the loan is executed, so a subsequent decline in a home's value does not reduce the interest expense deduction.

Limitations on Home-Related Debt The tax laws *limit the amount of debt* on which taxpayers can deduct interest expense. Two separate considerations limit the amount of debt that generates qualifying residence (and thus deductible) interest: a limitation on the amount of acquisition indebtedness and a limitation on the amount of home-equity indebtedness.

Limitation on amount of acquisition indebtedness. Interest expense on up to $1,000,000 of acquisition indebtedness is deductible as qualified residence interest. Once acquisition indebtedness is established for a qualifying residence (or for the sum of two qualifying residences), only principal payments on the loan(s) can reduce it and only additional indebtedness, secured by the residence(s) *and* incurred to substantially improve the residence(s), can increase it. (Notice the requirements to use funds to *acquire or improve the residence,* a stipulation that markedly differentiates acquisition indebtedness from home-equity indebtedness.)

THE KEY FACTS

Home-Related Interest Deduction

- Deduction allowed for qualified residence interest.
  - Principal residence and one other residence.
- Acquisition Indebtedness
  - Proceeds used to acquire or substantially improve home.
  - Limited to $1,000,000.
  - Principal payments permanently reduce amount.

[12]§163(h).

When a taxpayer **refinances** a mortgage, how does the tax law treat the new loan? Assuming the taxpayer does not use the proceeds from the refinance to substantially improve her residence, the refinanced loan is treated as acquisition debt *only to the extent that the principal amount of the refinancing does not exceed the amount of the acquisition debt immediately before the refinancing*. Consequently, any amount borrowed in excess of the remaining principal on the original loan does not qualify as acquisition indebtedness. Interest on the "excess" part of this loan can only be deducted if it qualifies as home-equity indebtedness (described below).

Example 14-6

What if: Assume the Jeffersons purchased a home in Chicago costing $330,000 by making a down payment of $30,000 and taking out a $300,000 loan secured by the home. What is the Jeffersons' acquisition indebtedness?

Answer: $300,000. This is debt secured by a qualified residence that is incurred in acquiring, constructing, or substantially improving the residence.

What if: Assume that when they moved to Chicago, the Jeffersons purchased a home costing $330,000 by making a down payment of $300,000, and taking out a $30,000 loan secured by the home. During the next few years, the Jeffersons paid $10,000 of principal on the loan, thereby reducing the loan balance to $20,000. Last year, due to a decrease in interest rates and a need for cash, the Jeffersons refinanced their mortgage by taking out a loan, secured by their residence, for $150,000. With the $150,000 they paid off the $20,000 balance on the original loan and used the $130,000 of extra cash for purposes unrelated to the home. After the refinance, what is the Jeffersons' acquisition indebtedness?

Answer: $20,000, the same amount as before the refinance. The only way to increase acquisition indebtedness is to borrow money to substantially improve the home. Thus, the Jeffersons' interest deductions on the home will be limited to the interest expense on the $20,000 acquisition indebtedness plus a limited amount of home-equity indebtedness.

What if: Assume the same facts as the previous what-if example except that the Jeffersons used $40,000 of the cash from the loan to build a new garage on their property. After the refinance, what is the Jeffersons' acquisition indebtedness?

Answer: $60,000 ($20,000 original loan principal + $40,000 used to substantially improve home).

THE KEY FACTS

Home-Related Interest Deduction

- Home-Equity Indebtedness
  - Can use proceeds for any purpose.
  - Loan must be secured by equity in home (FMV > Debt).
  - $100,000 limit.

Limitation on amount of home-equity indebtedness. As noted earlier, interest on home-equity indebtedness is deductible as qualified residence interest. However, the amount of qualified home-equity indebtedness is limited to the *lesser* of (1) the fair market value of the qualified residence(s) in excess of the acquisition debt related to the residence(s) and (2) $100,000 ($50,000 for each spouse if married filing separately). Thus, a taxpayer can deduct interest on up to $100,000 of home-related debt above and beyond acquisition debt (acquisition debt is limited to $1,000,000) as long as the debt is secured by the equity in the home(s) no matter what the taxpayer does with the proceeds from the home-equity loan. However, as we note in Chapter 8, interest expense on home-equity loans not used to purchase or substantially improve the home is not deductible for AMT purposes. When deciding whether to borrow money through a home-equity loan, the taxpayer must weigh the advantage of the interest deductibility against the risk of losing her home if she does not repay the loan.

Example 14-7

What if: Assume that the Jeffersons' home is worth $400,000 and they have a balance of $290,000 on their original home loan. The Jeffersons are interested in purchasing a $50,000 Chevy Suburban. Wanting to finance the full purchase price, they ask you, their financial planner, whether they should borrow the money with a 6 percent automobile loan from their local credit union or use a home-equity loan at 8 percent to fund the purchase. Assuming their marginal tax rate is 28 percent, and that they itemize deductions, what is the after-tax interest rate for the automobile loan, and what is the after-tax interest rate for the home-equity loan?

Answer: 6 percent for the automobile loan (same as the before-tax rate because the interest is not deductible) and 5.76 percent for the home equity loan [8% × (1 − 28%)]. After taxes, the home-equity loan appears to be a much better deal than the automobile loan. Before taking out the home-equity loan, however, the Jeffersons should consider the economic consequences if they are not able to repay the loan. If they don't make the payments on the automobile loan, they may lose the automobile; if they don't make the payments on the home-equity loan, they may lose their home.

What if: If the Jeffersons wanted to tap their home-equity loan for $110,000 so that they could buy two automobiles, would they be allowed to deduct the interest on the entire loan?

Answer: No. Even though the home has $110,000 of equity ($400,000 fair market value minus $290,000 acquisition indebtedness), the cap on qualifying home-equity debt is $100,000. Consequently, the Jeffersons would be able to deduct interest on only $100,000 of the $110,000 home-equity loan.

Combined limitation on qualifying debt. What is the maximum amount of debt on which a taxpayer can deduct qualified residence interest? Because the acquisition indebtedness limit of $1,000,000 and the home-equity indebtedness limit of $100,000 are two separate limits, the maximum amount of debt on which a taxpayer may deduct qualified residence interest is $1,100,000—provided, of course, that the value of the taxpayer's qualified residence (or residences) is at least $1,100,000.

When a taxpayer's home-related debt exceeds the limitations, the amount of deductible interest can be determined in one of two ways. First, the deductible interest can be computed as the product of (1) total interest expense on debt secured by the home and (2) the ratio of **qualified debt** to total debt outstanding on the home. This average interest expense option is summarized as follows:

$$\text{Total interest expense} \times \frac{\text{Qualified debt}}{\text{Total debt}} = \text{Deductible interest}$$

The second method is based on the chronological order of when the loans were executed, rather than as a weighted average. A taxpayer can choose to deduct all interest on earlier loans up to the limit on qualifying debt. Once the limit on qualifying debt is reached, interest on debt above the limit is not deductible. Why might taxpayers opt for this ordering method? This method generates a higher deduction when the earlier loans have a higher interest rate than subsequent loans.[13]

Example 14-8

What if: Assume the Jeffersons purchased a home for $1,550,000 by paying $150,000 down and borrowing $1,400,000 with a loan secured by the home. During the year, the Jeffersons paid $84,000 in interest on the loan. What amount of interest can the Jeffersons deduct as qualified residence interest?

Answer: $66,000. The Jefferson's qualifying debt is $1,100,000. The $1,100,000 consists of $1,000,000 of acquisition indebtedness (the limit) and $100,000 of home-equity indebtedness [the Jeffersons have $150,000 of equity in their home ($1,550,000 fair market value minus $1,400,000 loan on their home). Note that the same loan can include acquisition indebtedness and home equity indebtedness. Plugging the numbers into the formula for determining deductible interest expense when total debt exceeds the qualifying debt (see above) yields the following:

$84,000 × $1,100,000/$1,400,000 = $66,000

Where the total interest expense is $84,000, the qualifying debt is $1,100,000, and total debt on the home is $1,400,000.

(continued on page 14-12)

[13]The Treasury Regulations refer to the average interest expense method as the "simplified method" and the chronological method as the "exact method." See Treas. Reg §1.163-10T(c) and (d).

What if: Assume the Jeffersons moved to Chicago several years ago and purchased a home valued at $330,000 by paying $30,000 down and funding the remaining balance with a 30-year mortgage fixed at 6 percent. By the beginning of last year the value of their home had increased to $400,000, and the principal amount of their original loan had been paid down to $290,000. In need of extra cash for anticipated expenditures unrelated to their home, the Jeffersons borrowed $70,000 at a fixed interest rate of 7 percent with a loan secured by their home. As of the beginning of this year, the value of the Jeffersons' home had increased to $420,000. With a need for still more cash, the Jeffersons decided to take out a third loan secured by their home. The Jeffersons borrowed $50,000 on the third mortgage at an annual interest rate of 9 percent. During the year, they made interest-only payments on all three loans. The interest they paid on these loans is summarized as follows:

Loan	Balance	Rate	Interest Paid
Acquisition indebtedness:			
Original home loan	$290,000	6%	$17,400
Home equity indebtedness:			
Home-equity loan 1	70,000	7	4,900
Home-equity loan 2	50,000	9	4,500
Totals	$410,000		$26,800

THE KEY FACTS

Home-Related Interest Deduction

- If combined debt exceeds limitations
  - Average method: Total interest × qualifying debt/total debt.
  - Chronological method: Deduct interest on loans based on chronological order loans were executed (FIFO).
- Acquisition debt and home-equity debt can apply to the same loan.
  - Interest-deductible loan of up to $1.1M secured by the home.

How much of the $26,800 interest expense can the Jeffersons deduct this year using the average interest expense option?

Answer: $25,493. Plugging the numbers into the formula for this option (see above) yields the following:

$$\$26,800 \times \frac{\$390,000}{\$410,000} = \$25,493$$

Where the total interest expense is $26,800, the qualifying debt is $390,000 ($290,000 acquisition indebtedness + $100,000 limit on home-equity indebtedness), and the total debt is $410,000 ($290,000 + $70,000 + $50,000).

How much of the $26,800 interest expense can the Jeffersons deduct this year using the chronological order method of determining interest expense?

Answer: $25,000. The first loan is the original home loan. Because the loan is acquisition debt and is under the $1,000,000 acquisition debt limit, the entire $17,400 interest on this loan is deductible. The second mortgage of $70,000 was executed next. Because this loan is a home-equity loan and is under the $100,000 home-equity limit, the entire $4,900 interest on this loan is deductible. Finally, the third mortgage of $50,000 was executed last. However, because only $30,000 of this debt is qualifying home-equity debt ($100,000 limit minus $70,000 second mortgage) only $2,700 of interest on this loan is deductible ($30,000 × 9%). Thus, under the chronological order option, the Jeffersons can deduct $25,000 of the interest expense ($17,400 + $4,900 + $2,700).

Note that the $25,493 interest deduction under the first option is higher than the $25,000 interest expense under the second option because the interest rate on the second home equity loan is higher than the rates on the original loan and on the first home equity loan.

Finally, even though there are separate limits on acquisition indebtedness and home-equity indebtedness, both limits can apply to the same loan.

Example 14-9

Refer back to Example 14-6 where we assumed the Jeffersons refinanced their $20,000 home loan by borrowing $150,000 against their home and paying off the original $20,000 loan. Of course, the Jeffersons can deduct interest on the $20,000 acquisition debt on the loan. How much interest on the remaining $130,000 of the loan are the Jeffersons allowed to deduct?

Answer: The Jeffersons can deduct interest on $100,000 of the remaining $130,000 loan because this is the amount that qualifies as home-equity indebtedness. Interest on the other $30,000 of loan principal is not deductible.

Assuming they paid $9,000 of interest expense on these loans during the year, the Jeffersons could deduct $7,200 of the interest, computed under the average interest rate option as follows:

$$\$9{,}000 \times \frac{\$120{,}000}{\$150{,}000} = \$7{,}200$$

Note that because in this example the Jeffersons have only one loan (part acquisition debt and part home-equity debt, and part neither), the second (chronological order) method of deducting interest expense does not apply.

Mortgage Insurance Taxpayers are allowed to deduct as qualified residence interest expense premiums paid or accrued on mortgage insurance (insurance premiums paid by the borrower to protect the lender against the borrower defaulting on the loan). To qualify, the premiums for the mortgage insurance must be paid or accrued in connection with acquisition indebtedness on a qualified residence and must be paid by December 31, 2014 (this provision had not been extended to 2015 as of press time). The deduction does not apply to mortgage insurance contracts issued before January 1, 2007. The (itemized) deduction is phased out by 10 percent for every $1,000 ($500 for married taxpayers filing separately), or fraction thereof, that the taxpayer's AGI exceeds $100,000 ($50,000 for married taxpayers filing separately).

Points A home buyer arranging financing for a home typically incurs several loan-related fees or expenses including charges for "points." A **point** is 1 percent of the principal amount of the loan. In general, borrowers pay points to lenders in exchange for reduced interest rates on loans. However, borrowers may also pay lenders for other purposes (e.g., to compensate lenders for the service of providing the loan). In order for taxpayers to deduct points, the points must be paid for a reduced interest rate (rather than for the service of providing the loans).[14] However, to minimize possible disputes regarding the deductibility of points and as a matter of administrative convenience, the IRS will treat points as deductible **qualified residence interest** if the following requirements are met:[15]

1. The **settlement statement** (see Appendix A at the end of this chapter—the settlement statement details the monies paid out and received by the buyer and seller as part of the loan transaction) must clearly designate the amounts as points payable in connection with the loan, for example as "loan origination fees," "loan discount," or "discount points." (These amounts are typically provided on lines 801 and 802 of the settlement statement.)
2. The amounts must be computed as a percentage of the stated principal amount of the loan.
3. The amounts paid must conform to an established business general practice of charging points for loans in the area in which the residence is located, and the amount of the points paid must not exceed the amount generally charged in that area.
4. The amounts must be paid in connection with the acquisition of the taxpayer's *principal residence* and the loan *must be secured by that residence* (the deduction for points is not available for points paid in connection with a loan for a second home).
5. The buyer must provide enough funds in the down payment on the home to at least equal the cost of the points (the buyer is not allowed to borrow from the lender to pay the points). However, points paid by the *seller* to the lender in connection with the taxpayer's loan are treated as paid directly by the taxpayer. Consequently, such points are generally deductible by the buyer.

[14]§461(g)(2).

[15]Rev. Proc. 94-27 1994-1 C.B. 613.

Note that points paid in *refinancing* a home loan are not immediately deductible by the homeowner. These points must be amortized and deducted on a straight-line basis over the life of the loan.[16]

Now that we understand how the tax laws treat points, let's consider the home buyer's decision of whether or not to pay points to obtain a lower interest rate on a home loan. From an economic standpoint, the buyer must choose between (1) paying extra money up front and having lower monthly mortgage payments or (2) paying less initially and having larger monthly payments.

When the taxpayer can afford to pay points, deciding whether or not to do so generally requires a "break-even" analysis. Essentially, the taxpayer determines how long it will take to recoup the after-tax cost of the point(s) through the after-tax interest savings on the loan. Generally speaking, the longer the taxpayer plans on staying in the home and maintaining the loan (not refinancing it), the more likely it is financially beneficial to pay points to obtain a lower interest rate. However, paying points can be costly if, after too short a time, the taxpayer sells the home or refinances the home loan. In these situations, the taxpayer may not reach the break-even point.

Example 14-10

Tyler and Jasmine are seeking financing for their new $800,000 home. They are paying $500,000 down and borrowing the remaining $300,000 to be paid back over 30 years. They have the choice of paying two discount points ($6,000) and getting a fixed interest rate of 5 percent or paying no discount points and getting a fixed interest rate of 6 percent. Assuming the points meet the immediate deductibility requirements, the Jeffersons' marginal tax rate is 28 percent, and they pay interest only for the first three years of the loan, what is the Jeffersons' break-even point for paying the points?

Answer: Two years, calculated as follows:

Loan summary: $300,000; 6 percent rate with no points. 5 percent rate with two points ($6,000). Assume the Jeffersons pay interest only for the first three years.

Description	Amounts	Calculation
(1) Initial cash outflow from paying points	($6,000)	$300,000 × 2%.
(2) Tax benefit from deducting points	1,680	(1) × 28%.
(3) After-tax cost of points	(4,320)	(1) + (2).
(4) Before-tax *savings per year* from 5% vs. 6% interest rate	3,000	$300,000 × (6% − 5%).
(5) *Forgone tax benefit per year* of higher interest rate	(840)	(4) × 28%.
(6) After-tax savings per year of 5% vs. 6% interest rate	$2,160	(4) + (5).
Break-even point in years	2 years	(3)/(6).

The break-even analysis in Example 14-10, while a useful exercise, oversimplifies the calculations a bit. Why? It oversimplifies because it doesn't take into account the present value of the tax savings, nor does it take into account the increasing principal that would be paid on a traditional principal-and-interest-type loan. In reality, the cost of the points is immediate while the savings comes later—so the break-even point on a present value basis is likely a little longer than two years. Also, the more principal paid on the loan, the less the amount of interest paid each month—so savings from the lower interest rate declines over time, which would also extend the break-even point.

Because points paid on a refinancing are deducted over the life of the loan, the break-even point for paying points on a refinanced mortgage is longer than the break-even point for an original mortgage of the same amount.

[16]See Chapter 2 research memo and *J.R. Huntsman v. Comm.* (8 Cir., 1990), 90-2 USTC par. 50,340, rev'g 91 TC 917 (1988) for a limited exception to this rule.

Example 14-11

What if: Assume that due to recent interest rate declines, the Jeffersons have decided to refinance the $300,000 mortgage on their home with a new 30-year loan. The Jeffersons have the option of paying two discount points ($6,000) and obtaining a 5 percent interest rate or obtaining a 6 percent interest rate with no discount points. Assuming the Jeffersons' marginal tax rate is 28 percent and they pay interest only for the first three years of the loan, what is the Jeffersons' approximate break-even point for paying the points on the refinance?

Answer: 2.71 years, calculated as follows:

Loan summary: $300,000; 6 percent rate with no points. 30 years or 5 percent rate with two points ($6,000). Assume the Jeffersons pay interest only for the first three years.

Description	Points	Notes
(1) Initial cash outflow from paying points	($6,000)	$300,000 × 2%.
(2) Tax benefit from deducting points	0	
(3) After-tax cost of points	(6,000)	(1) + (2).
(4) Before-tax savings per year from 5% vs. 6% interest rate	3,000	$300,000 × (6% − 5%).
(5) Forgone tax benefit per year of higher interest payments	(840)	(4) × 28%.
(6) After-tax savings per year of 5% vs. 6% interest rate	2,160	(4) + (5).
(7) Annual tax savings from amortizing points	56	(1)/30 years × 28%.
(8) Annual after-tax cash flow benefit of paying points	$2,216	(6) + (7).
Break-even point in years	2.71 years	(3)/(8).

The reason for the longer break-even point is that the points effectively cost more because they are not immediately deductible in a refinance.

Real Property Taxes

LO 14-4

Owners of personal residences and other types of real estate such as land, rental properties, business buildings, and other types of real property are generally required to pay **real property taxes.** These taxes are assessed by local governments and are based on the fair market value of the property.[17] Real property taxes support general public welfare by providing funding for public needs such as schools and roads.

Local governments set the tax rates applied to the value of the property annually based on financial needs for the year. The applicable rates may depend on the type of real estate. For example, the tax rate for real estate used in a business may be higher than the rates for residential real property. Real property tax payments are deductible by taxpayers conducting self-employment activities against business income as *for* AGI deductions, by landlords against rental income as *for* AGI deductions, and by individuals as itemized deductions.[18]

Taxpayers are not allowed to deduct fees paid for setting up water and sewer services, and assessments for local benefits such as streets and sidewalks.[19] Taxpayers generally add these expenditures to the basis of their property.

Frequently, homeowners pay their real estate taxes through an **escrow** (holding) **account** with their mortgage lender. Each monthly payment to the lender includes an amount that represents roughly one-twelfth of the anticipated real property taxes for the year. The actual tax payment (or payments if the taxes are due more than once a year) is made by the mortgage company with funds accumulated in the escrow account. When does the homeowner get to deduct the property taxes? The homeowner gets to deduct the property taxes when the actual taxes are paid to the taxing jurisdiction, not when the homeowner makes payments for taxes to the escrow account.

THE KEY FACTS

Real Estate Taxes

- Applies to homes, land, business buildings, and other types of real estate.
- Homeowners frequently pay real property tax bill to escrow account.
  - Deduction timing based on payment of taxes to governmental body and not escrow account.
- When homeowners sell home during year.
  - Deduction is based on proportion of year taxpayer lived in home no matter who actually pays tax.

[17]Local governments tend to understate the fair market value of property when appraising it to minimize the chances that the taxpayer will contest the appraisal.

[18]Note that real property taxes that are itemized deductions are subject to the overall itemized deduction phase-out discussed in Chapter 6.

[19]Reg. §1.164-4(a).

Because property taxes are generally payable to the government only once or twice a year, who is responsible for paying the taxes when an owner sells a personal residence or another type of real estate during the year? Is the owner at the time the taxes are due responsible for paying the full amount of the taxes? Does the person who makes the tax payment also receive the corresponding tax deduction? In most situations, the buyer and seller divide the responsibility for the tax payments based on the portion of the property tax year that each party held the property. This allocation of taxes between buyer and seller is generally spelled out on the settlement statement when the sale becomes final (see Appendix A to this chapter for a sample settlement statement for the Jeffersons). For tax purposes, it doesn't matter who actually pays the tax, although generally the current owner has the responsibility to do so. As long as the taxes are paid, the tax deduction is based on the relative amount of time each party owned the property during the year (or period over which the property taxes are payable).[20]

Example 14-12

On February 1, Tyler and Jasmine purchased a new home for $800,000. At the time of the purchase, it was estimated that the property tax bill on the home for the year would be $12,000 ($800,000 × 1.5%). Assuming the tax bill is paid and that the property tax bill is based on a calendar year, how much will the Jeffersons *deduct* in property taxes for the year?

Answer: $11,000. Because the seller lived in the home for one-twelfth of the year (January) and the Jeffersons lived in the home for eleven-twelfths of the year (February through December), the seller will deduct $1,000 of the property taxes (one-twelfth) and the Jeffersons will deduct $11,000 (eleven-twelfths) as an itemized deduction.

LO 14-5

RENTAL USE OF THE HOME

THE KEY FACTS

Rental Use of the Home

- Tax treatment depends on amount of personal and rental use. The three categories are:
  1) Residence with minimal rental use (personal residence)
  2) Residence with significant rental use (vacation home)
  3) Nonresidence (rental property)

A taxpayer with the financial wherewithal to do so may purchase a second home as a vacation home, a rental property, or a combination of the two. A taxpayer may own a second home outright or may share ownership with others through a timeshare or fractional ownership arrangement. The nontax benefits of owning a second home include a fixed vacation destination, the ability to trade the use of the home with an owner of a home in a different destination, the opportunity for generating income through rentals, and the potential appreciation of the second home as an investment. The nontax costs of owning a second home include the initial cost of the home, the extra cost of maintaining the home, the hassle of dealing with renters or property managers, and the downside risk associated with holding the second home as an investment.

The tax consequences of owning a second home depends on whether the home qualifies as a residence (see discussion at the beginning of the chapter) and on the number of days the taxpayer rents out the home. The home is categorized in one of three ways:

1. Residence with minimal rental use (rents home for 14 or fewer days).
2. Residence with significant rental use (rents home for 15 or more days).
3. Nonresidence.

THE KEY FACTS

Rental Use of the Home

- Residence with minimal rental use.
  - Taxpayer lives in the home at least 15 days and rents it 14 days or fewer.
  - Exclude all rental income.
  - Don't deduct rental expenses.

Recall that, as we discussed earlier in the chapter, a property is considered a "residence" for tax purposes if the taxpayer uses the home for personal purposes for *more than* the greater of 14 days or 10 percent of the number of rental days during the year. For example, if a taxpayer rents her home for 200 days and uses it for personal purposes for 21 days or more, the home is considered to be a residence for tax purposes. If the same taxpayer used the home for personal purposes for 20 days, the home would be considered a nonresidence for tax purposes.

[20]The seller gets a deduction for the taxes allocable for the period of time up to and including the day *before* the date of the sale. The taxes allocable to the day of the sale through the end of the property tax year are deductible by the buyer. See §164(d).

Residence with Minimal Rental Use

The law is simple for homeowners who rent a home that qualifies as a residence for a minimal amount of time during the year. That is, they live in it for at least 15 days and they rent it for 14 or fewer days. Taxpayers are not required to include the gross receipts in rental income and are not allowed to deduct any expenses related to the rental.[21] The owner is, however, allowed to deduct qualified residence interest and real property taxes on the second home as itemized deductions.

Example 14-14

The Jeffersons purchased a vacation home in a golf community in Scottsdale, Arizona, in January. They spent 10 days vacationing in the home in early March and another 15 days vacationing in the home in mid-December. In early February, they rented the home for 14 days to a group of golfers who were in town to attend a PGA Tour golf tournament and to play golf. The Jeffersons received $6,000 in rent from the group, and the Jeffersons incurred $1,000 of expenses relating to the rental home. The Jeffersons did not rent the property again for the rest of the year. How much will the $5,000 net income from the rental increase their taxable income?

Answer: Zero! Because the Jeffersons lived in the home for 14 or fewer days (25 days) and rented the home for fewer than 15 days (14 days) during the year, they do not report the rental income to the IRS, and they do not deduct expenses associated with the rental. The Jeffersons saved $1,400 in taxes by excluding the $5,000 of net rental income ($5,000 net income × 28 percent marginal tax rate). Note that the Jeffersons can also deduct the mortgage interest and real property taxes on the property for the *full year* as itemized deductions.

ETHICS

Carey and Pat were good friends and neighbors in an upscale neighborhood near several highly rated golf courses in Arizona. During the winter, both Carey and Pat decided to rent their homes (at a premium) to groups of golfers from the New York area who want to get out of the snow and enjoy sunshine and golf for a couple of weeks during the winter. While their homes were rented, Carey and Pat vacationed together in Cancun. In January 2015, Carey rented his home for 14 days and received $14,000 in rent. Pat also rented his home for the same 14 days and received $16,000 in rent. Near the end of the 14-day rental period, Pat got a call from the renters who wanted to extend their stay for one day. Pat agreed to the extension and charged the group $2,000 for the extra day. When preparing his 2015 tax return, Pat discovered that taxpayers who rent their home for more than 14 days are required to report all of their rental income on their tax returns. Pat didn't think it was fair that he had to pay taxes on the rental income while Carey did not just because Pat rented his home for one more day than Carey in 2015. Consequently, Pat decided that he rented his property for 14 days and gave the renters the last day for free. What do you think about Pat's approach to solving his tax problem?

TAXES IN THE REAL WORLD Extreme Tax Savings Strategy?

Newsweek reports that *Extreme Makeover: Home Edition* signs a contract with the contestants to rent the home from the contestant for 10 days. The "makeover" or improvements of the home take the place of rental payments. Because the rental period is less than 15 days, the value of the improvements, which would otherwise be taxable income, is not reported as taxable income by the contestant.[22]

(continued on page 14-18)

[21] §280A(g).

[22] D. McGinn, "Television: Tax Trouble for ABC's 'Extreme' Winners?" *Newsweek*, May 17, 2004, p. 12.

THE KEY FACTS

Rental Use of the Home

- Residence with significant rental use.
  - Rental use is 15 days or more and personal use exceeds the greater of (1) 14 days or (2) 10% of rental days.
  - Deduct direct rental expenses such as advertising and realtor commissions.
  - Allocate home-related expenses between rental use and personal use.
  - Interest and taxes allocated to personal use deducted as itemized deductions and all other expenses allocated to personal use not deductible.
  - IRS method allocates interest and taxes to rental use based on rental use to total use for the year while Tax Court method allocates to rental use based on rental use to total days in entire year.
  - Rental deductions other than tier-1 expenses limited to gross rental revenue. When limited, deduct tier 1 (interest and taxes) first, then tier 2 (all expenses except interest, taxes, and depreciation), and then tier 3 (depreciation).

Note that this appears to be a fairly aggressive interpretation of the tax law in this situation. In fact, the IRS has suggested in a nonbinding information letter that "to the extent that the value of the improvements constitutes a prize or an award . . . it cannot also be considered rent, and therefore could not qualify for the exclusion from gross income under §280A(g) of the Code."[23]

A taxpayer with a strategically located second (or even first) home can take advantage of this favorable tax rule by renting the property and excluding potentially large rental payments from those in town to attend high-profile events such as the Olympics, the Masters golf tournament, the Super Bowl, and Mardi Gras.

Residence with Significant Rental Use (Vacation Home)

When a home qualifies as a residence and the taxpayer rents out the home for 15 days or more the rental revenue is included in gross income, expenses to obtain tenants (advertising and realtor commissions) are fully deductible as direct rental expenses, and expenses relating to the home are allocated between personal and rental use. The expenses allocated to personal use are not deductible unless they are deductible under nonrental tax provisions as itemized deductions. (The most common of these deductions are mortgage interest and real property taxes but this also includes casualty losses on the home.)

When the gross rental revenue exceeds the sum of the direct rental expenses and the expenses allocated to the rental use of the home, the taxpayer is allowed to deduct the expenses in full. However, when these expenses exceed the rental revenue, the deductibility of the expenses is limited. In these situations, taxpayers divide the rental expenses into one of three categories or "tiers." The tier 1, 2, and 3 expenses for rental property are described in Exhibit 14-3.

The taxpayer first deducts tier 1 (expenses to obtain tenants and mortgage interest and real property taxes allocated to rental use[24]) expenses in full. This is true even

EXHIBIT 14-3 Rental Expenses by Tier and Deduction Sequence

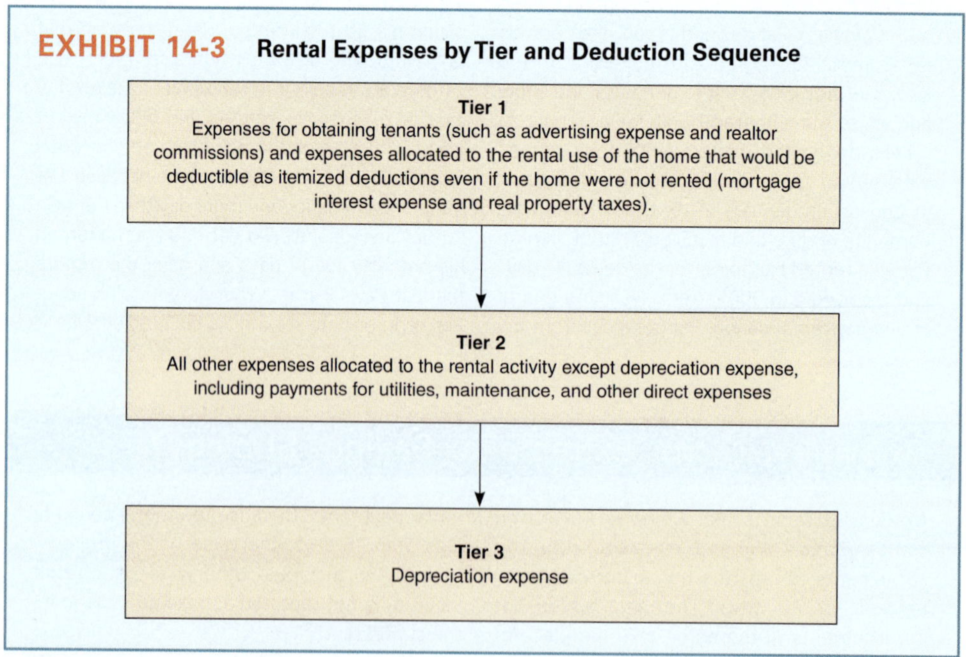

Tier 1
Expenses for obtaining tenants (such as advertising expense and realtor commissions) and expenses allocated to the rental use of the home that would be deductible as itemized deductions even if the home were not rented (mortgage interest expense and real property taxes).
Tier 2
All other expenses allocated to the rental activity except depreciation expense, including payments for utilities, maintenance, and other direct expenses
Tier 3
Depreciation expense

[23]INFO 2006-12, release date March 31, 2006.

[24]Technically, expenses to obtain tenants (advertising and realtor commissions) are a reduction in gross rental income for tax purposes. However, we classify them as tier 1 expenses to simplify the discussion.

when tier 1 expenses exceed the gross rental revenue.[25] Second, the taxpayer deducts tier 2 expenses.[26] However, the tier 2 expense deductions are limited to the gross rental revenue in excess of tier 1 expenses. Any tier 2 expenses not deducted in the current year due to the income limitation are suspended and carried forward to the next year. Finally, the taxpayer deducts tier 3 expense (depreciation calculated using the straight-line method over 27.5 years). The tier 3 expense deduction is limited to the gross rental revenue in excess of tier 1 and tier 2 expenses. Any tier 3 expenses not deductible because of the income limitation are suspended and carried forward to the subsequent year. The nondeductible tier 3 expense does not reduce the basis in the home. In general terms, this deduction sequence is unfavorable for taxpayers, because it is designed to maximize taxpayer deductions for expenses that would be deductible even without any rental use of the home (most commonly mortgage interest and real property taxes) and to minimize the allowable depreciation deductions for the home.

As we mentioned above, expenses associated with the rental use of the home must be allocated between rental use and personal use of the home. These expenses are *generally* allocated to rental use based on the ratio of the number of days of rental use to the total number of days the property was used for rental and personal purposes (see Exhibit 14-4). All expenses not allocated to rental use are allocated to personal use.

EXHIBIT 14-4 Tax Court vs. IRS Method of Allocating Expenses

Rental Allocation	IRS Method	Tax Court Method
Mortgage interest and property taxes (tier 1 expenses)	Expense × $\frac{\text{Total rental days}}{\text{Total days used}}$	Expense × $\frac{\text{Total rental days}}{\text{Days in year}}$
All other expenses	Expense × $\frac{\text{Total rental days}}{\text{Total days used}}$	Expense × $\frac{\text{Total rental days}}{\text{Total days used}}$

The only potential exception to the general allocation rule involves the allocation of mortgage interest expense and real property taxes (both tier 1 expenses). The IRS and the Tax Court disagree on how to allocate these particular expenses. The IRS allocates these expenses the same way as all other expenses. However, the Tax Court allocates *interest* and *taxes* to rental use based on the ratio of days that the property was rented over the *number of days in the year*, rather than the number of days the property was used for any purpose during the year.[27] The **IRS** and **Tax Court allocation methods** are described in Exhibit 14-4.

The Tax Court justifies its approach by pointing out that interest expense and property taxes accrue over the entire year regardless of the level of personal or rental use. The Tax Court method generally favors the taxpayer because it tends to allocate less interest expense and real property taxes to the rental use, which reduces the tier 1 expenses and allows more tier 2 and tier 3 expenses to be deducted when the gross

[25]The rental activity associated with a home falling into the residence with significant rental use category is not considered to be a passive activity, so income or loss generated from the activity is not considered to be passive income or passive loss [§469(j)]. See discussion of passive loss rules below.

[26]§280A(c)(5). Also see IRS Publication 527, "Residential Rental Property (Including Rental of Vacation Homes)."

[27]The Tax Court method of allocating these expenses is also referred to as the Bolton method after the taxpayer in the court case in which the Tax Court approved this method of allocating deductions. While the court case initially was tried in the Tax Court, the decision in favor of the taxpayer was appealed to the Ninth Circuit Court that also ruled in favor of the taxpayer and sanctioned the use of the Tax Court or Bolton method of allocating interest expense. *Bolton v. Commissioner,* 82-2 USTC §9699 (CA 9), Affirming Tax Court, 77 TC 104.

income limitation applies. That is, the sum of the taxpayer's deductible personal (*from* AGI) and rental expenses (*for* AGI) associated with the rental home under the Tax Court method generally will exceed the sum of personal (*from* AGI) and rental expenses (*for* AGI) associated with the home under the IRS method when the gross income limitation applies. This is because the taxpayer does not lose deductions for the extra interest and real property taxes allocated to personal use under the Tax Court method because these expenses are allowed as itemized deductions on Schedule A.

Example 14-15

At the beginning of the year, the Jeffersons purchased a vacation home in Scottsdale, Arizona, for $500,000 ($400,000 for the building and $100,000 for the land). They paid $200,000 down and financed the remaining $300,000 with a 6 percent mortgage secured by the home. During the year, the Jeffersons used the home for personal purposes for 30 days and rented the home for 200 days. Thus, the home falls in the residence with significant rental use category. They received $37,500 of rental revenue and incurred $500 of rental advertising expenses. How are their expenses allocated to the rental use under the IRS and Tax Court methods?

Answer: See the following summary of allocation of expenses associated with the home:

Allocation Method to Rental Use

Expense	Amount	Tier	IRS Method (200/230)	Tax Court Method (200/365 Tier 1 200/230 other)
Advertising*	$ 500	1	$ 500	$ 500
Interest	18,000	1	15,652	9,863
Real estate taxes	5,000	1	4,348	2,740
Total tier 1 expenses	**$23,500**	**1**	**$20,500**	**$13,103**
Utilities	4,500	2	3,913	3,913
Repairs	1,800	2	1,565	1,565
Insurance	3,500	2	3,043	3,043
Maintenance	3,200	2	2,783	2,783
Total tier 2 expenses	**$13,000**	**2**	**$11,304**	**$11,304**
Tier 3: Depreciation	**13,939**	**3**	**$12,121**	**$12,121**
Total expenses	$50,439			

*Advertising is a direct expense of the rental so it is fully deductible against rental revenue.

Net income from rental	IRS Method	Tax Court Method
Rental receipts	$37,500	$37,500
Less tier 1 expenses	(20,500)	(13,103)
Income after tier 1 expenses	17,000	24,397
Less tier 2 expenses	(11,304)	(11,304)
Income after tier 2 expenses	5,696	13,093
Less: tier 3 expenses	(5,696)	(12,121)
Taxable rental income	**$ 0**	**$ 972**
Deductible personal expenses (interest and property taxes)	$ 3,000	$ 10,397
Deductible rental expenses (sum of tier 1, 2, and 3 expenses)	37,500	36,528
Total personal and rental expenses	**$40,500**	**$46,925**

Note that under the Tax Court method, the Jeffersons are able to deduct $7,397 ($10,397 minus $3,000) more in itemized deductions for interest and real property taxes than they do under the IRS method, and they deduct $972 ($37,500 minus $36,528) fewer rental expenses (*for* AGI) under the Tax Court method relative to the IRS method. In total, the Jeffersons are allowed to deduct $6,425 more in total deductions under the Tax Court method than the IRS method in the current year ($46,925 minus $40,500). However, under the IRS method, the Jeffersons are allowed to carry forward to next year the $6,425 in depreciation expense that they were not allowed to deduct in the current year ($12,121 − $5,696). Under the Tax Court method, they were able to deduct all of their expenses so they do not carry forward any expenses to future years.

Taxpayers would report their rental activities on Schedule E of Form 1040. The deductible tier 1, tier 2, and tier 3 expenses are *for* AGI deductions. Exhibit 14-5 displays the completed Schedule E for the Jefferson's Scottsdale vacation home using the Tax Court method. Note that net rental income is considered to be investment income for purposes of determining the 3.8% net investment income tax discussed in Chapter 8.

THE KEY FACTS

Rental Use of the Home

- Nonresidence.
  - Rental use is at least one day and personal use is no more than the *greater* of (1) 14 days or (2) 10 percent of rental days.
  - Allocate expenses to rental and personal use.
  - Rental deductions in excess of rental income are deductible subject to passive loss limitation rules.
  - Interest expense allocated to personal use not deductible.

Nonresidence (Rental Property)

For property in this category, the taxpayer includes the rental revenue in gross income and deducts all rental expenses *allocated to the rental use* of the property as *for* AGI deductions (all on Schedule E). When the property is used for even a day for personal purposes, the expenses must be allocated between the rental usage and the personal usage.[28] In this situation, however, the law does *not allow* the taxpayer to deduct mortgage interest not allocated to rental use because the taxpayer does not meet the minimum amount of personal use required for the deduction (the home is not a qualified residence—see prior discussion). However, the taxpayer is still allowed to deduct, as an itemized deduction, real property taxes not allocated to the rental. In contrast to the residence with significant rental use category, if the rental expenses exceed the gross income from the home in this category, the deductibility of the loss is not subject to a gross income limitation but it is subject to the passive activity restrictions discussed below.[29]

Example 14-16

What if: Suppose that at the beginning of the year, the Jeffersons purchased a vacation home in Scottsdale, Arizona, for $400,000. They paid $100,000 down and financed the remaining $300,000 with a 6 percent mortgage secured by the home. During the year, the Jeffersons *did not use the home for personal purposes* and they rented the home for 200 days. They received $37,500 in gross rental revenue for the year and incurred $50,439 of expenses relating to the rental property. How much can the Jeffersons deduct in this situation?

Answer: The good news is that the deductions are not limited to gross income from the rental so they can deduct all $50,439, generating a $12,939 loss on the property ($37,500 − $50,439). The bad news is that, as we discuss below, the loss may not be immediately deductible due to the passive activity loss limitations.

[28]§280A(e).

[29]If the home rental is deemed to be a not-for-profit activity, the loss is subject to the hobby loss rules in §183.

EXHIBIT 14-5 Jeffersons' Schedule E for Vacation Home Rental

SCHEDULE E (Form 1040)
Department of the Treasury Internal Revenue Service (99)

Supplemental Income and Loss
(From rental real estate, royalties, partnerships, S corporations, estates, trusts, REMICs, etc.)
▶ Attach to Form 1040, 1040NR, or Form 1041.
▶ Information about Schedule E and its separate instructions is at *www.irs.gov/schedulee.*

OMB No. 1545-0074
2014
Attachment Sequence No. 13

Name(s) shown on return: Tyler and Jasmine Jefferson
Your social security number: 321-54-9876

Part I **Income or Loss From Rental Real Estate and Royalties** **Note.** If you are in the business of renting personal property, use **Schedule C** or **C-EZ** (see instructions). If you are an individual, report farm rental income or loss from **Form 4835** on page 2, line 40.

A Did you make any payments in 2014 that would require you to file Form(s) 1099? (see instructions) ☐ Yes ☑ No
B If "Yes," did you or will you file required Forms 1099? ☐ Yes ☐ No

1a	Physical address of each property (street, city, state, ZIP code)
A	3 Hole-in-One Blvd. Scottsdale, Arizona 85262
B	
C	

1b	Type of Property (from list below)		Fair Rental Days	Personal Use Days	QJV
A	1	A	200	30	☐
B		B			☐
C		C			☐

2 For each rental real estate property listed above, report the number of fair rental and personal use days. Check the **QJV** box only if you meet the requirements to file as a qualified joint venture. See instructions.

Type of Property:
1 Single Family Residence 2 Multi-Family Residence 3 Vacation/Short-Term Rental 4 Commercial 5 Land 6 Royalties 7 Self-Rental 8 Other (describe)

Income:	**Properties:**	A	B	C
3 Rents received	3	37,500		
4 Royalties received	4			
Expenses:				
5 Advertising	5	500		
6 Auto and travel (see instructions)	6			
7 Cleaning and maintenance	7	2,783		
8 Commissions	8			
9 Insurance	9	3,043		
10 Legal and other professional fees	10			
11 Management fees	11			
12 Mortgage interest paid to banks, etc. (see instructions)	12	9,863		
13 Other interest	13			
14 Repairs	14	1,565		
15 Supplies	15			
16 Taxes	16	2,740		
17 Utilities	17	3,913		
18 Depreciation expense or depletion	18	12,121		
19 Other (list) ▶	19			
20 Total expenses. Add lines 5 through 19	20	36,528		
21 Subtract line 20 from line 3 (rents) and/or 4 (royalties). If result is a (loss), see instructions to find out if you must file **Form 6198**	21	972		
22 Deductible rental real estate loss after limitation, if any, on **Form 8582** (see instructions)	22	( )	( )	( )

23a Total of all amounts reported on line 3 for all rental properties	23a	37,500
b Total of all amounts reported on line 4 for all royalty properties	23b	
c Total of all amounts reported on line 12 for all properties	23c	9,863
d Total of all amounts reported on line 18 for all properties	23d	12,121
e Total of all amounts reported on line 20 for all properties	23e	36,528
24 **Income.** Add positive amounts shown on line 21. **Do not** include any losses	24	972
25 **Losses.** Add royalty losses from line 21 and rental real estate losses from line 22. Enter total losses here	25	( )
26 **Total rental real estate and royalty income or (loss).** Combine lines 24 and 25. Enter the result here. If Parts II, III, IV, and line 40 on page 2 do not apply to you, also enter this amount on Form 1040, line 17, or Form 1040NR, line 18. Otherwise, include this amount in the total on line 41 on page 2	26	972

For Paperwork Reduction Act Notice, see the separate instructions. Cat. No. 11344L **Schedule E (Form 1040) 2014**

Exhibit 14-6 summarizes the tax rules relating to a home used for rental purposes depending on the extent of rental (and personal use). Appendix B to this chapter provides a flowchart summarizing the implementation of these rules.

Losses on Rental Property A rental property can be a great investment that gets the best of all worlds. It could (1) appreciate in value, (2) produce annual positive cash flow (rental receipts exceed expenses other than depreciation), and (3) generate tax losses that reduce the taxes the owner is required to pay on other sources of income. Consider the Jeffersons' second-home property, purchased for $500,000 and used primarily as a rental home (see Example 14-15), which we'll assume has appreciated to $540,000 by the end of 2015. The property has appreciated by $40,000, produced a positive cash flow of $1,000 [$37,500 rental income minus expenses other than depreciation of $36,500 ($50,439 total expenses minus depreciation expense of $13,939)], and generated a net tax loss of $12,939. This tax loss apparently saves the Jeffersons $3,623 in taxes [($12,939) × 28% marginal tax rate].

Thus, the increase in the Jeffersons' wealth from their second-home investment for the year appears to be $44,623 ($40,000 appreciation + $1,000 rental cash flow + $3,623 tax savings). But as noted elsewhere in this text, when a tax outcome seems too good to be true, it usually is. Read on.

Passive activity loss rules. In Chapter 7, we introduced the **passive activity loss** rules that indicate taxpayers may only deduct passive losses for a year to the extent of their passive income. We also learned that, by definition, a rental activity (including a second home rental that falls in the nonresidence category) is considered to be a passive activity.[30] Because they are passive losses, losses from rental property are generally not allowed to offset other ordinary or investment type income. However, as we also discussed in Chapter 7, a taxpayer who is an **active participant in a rental activity** may be allowed to deduct up to $25,000 of the rental loss against nonpassive income.[31] Consistent with a number of tax benefits, the exception amount for active owners is phased out as income increases: the $25,000 maximum exception amount is phased out by 50 cents for every dollar the taxpayer's adjusted gross income (before considering the rental loss) exceeds $100,000. Consequently, the entire $25,000 is phased out when the taxpayer's adjusted gross income reaches $150,000.

Example 14-17

Suppose the Jeffersons incurred a $12,939 passive loss from their Scottsdale rental home (described in the previous example), and they did not receive any passive income during the year. Assuming their current year AGI is $250,000 and that they are considered to be active participants in the rental activity, how much of the rental loss are the Jeffersons allowed to deduct this year under the rental real estate exception to the passive activity loss rules?

Answer: $0. Because their adjusted gross income exceeds $150,000, the $25,000 deduction exception to the passive activity loss rules is completely phased out. Consequently, the Jeffersons are not allowed to deduct any of the $12,939 rental loss for the year.

What if: How much of the $12,939 loss could the Jeffersons deduct for the year if their adjusted gross income (before considering the rental loss) was $120,000?

Answer: They could deduct the entire $12,939 loss. The $25,000 exception amount would be reduced by a $10,000 phase-out [50 cents × ($120,000 − $100,000)]. The maximum amount of the rental loss that can offset ordinary income would therefore be reduced from $25,000 to $15,000 ($25,000 − $10,000 phased out). However, because their loss is less than $15,000, they may deduct the entire $12,939 rental loss against their other sources of income for the year.

[30]Recall that second homes falling in the significant personal and rental use category are not passive activities. See §469(j).

[31]§469(i).

THE KEY FACTS

Rental Losses

- Losses on home rentals in nonresidence use category are passive losses.
- Passive loss rules generally limit deductions for losses from passive activities such as rental to passive income from other sources.
  - Passive losses in excess of passive income are suspended and deductible against passive income in the future or when the taxpayer sells the passive activity generating the loss.
- Rental real estate exception to passive loss rules
  - Applies to active participants in rental property.
  - Deduct up to $25,000 of rental real estate loss against ordinary income.
  - $25,000 maximum deduction phased out by 50 cents for every dollar of AGI over $100,000 (excluding the rental loss deduction). Fully phased out at $150,000 of AGI.

EXHIBIT 14-6 Summary of Tax Rules Relating to Home Used for Rental Purposes

	Residence with Minimal Rental Use	Residence with Significant Rental Use	Nonresidence
Classification test	Reside in home for at least 15 days and rent home for 14 or fewer days during the year.	Rent home for 15 days or more and use home for personal purposes for more than the greater of (1) 14 days or (2) 10 percent of the total rental days.	Rent home for at least one day, and personal use does not exceed the greater of (1) 14 days or (2) 10 percent of the rental days.
Rental revenue	Exclude from gross income.	Include in gross income)	Include in gross income.
Direct rental expenses unrelated to home use	Not deductible.	Fully deductible for AGI (loss not subject to passive activity loss rules).	Deductible for AGI but subject to passive activity loss rules.
Treatment of mortgage interest and real property taxes	Deductible as itemized deductions.	Allocate between personal-use days and rental days; interest and taxes allocated to rental days are deductible as rental expenses; interest and taxes allocated to personal-use days are deductible as itemized deductions.	Allocated between personal-use days and rental days; interest and taxes allocated to rental days are deductible as rental expenses; taxes allocated to personal-use days are deductible as itemized deductions; interest allocated to personal-use days is not deductible.
Treatment of all other expenses	Not deductible.	Allocate between personal-use days and rental days; expenses allocated to personal-use days are not deductible; expenses allocated to rental days are deductible as rental expenses to the extent of rental revenue minus sum of direct rental expenses and rental mortgage interest and real property taxes; when expenses allocated to rental days exceed the rental income.	Allocated between personal-use days and rental days; expenses allocated to personal-use days are not deductible; expenses allocated to rental days are deductible and can generate loss but loss is subject to passive activity loss rules.
Excess expenses	Not applicable.	Rental expenses in excess of rental income minus sum of direct rental expenses and rental mortgage interest expense and real property taxes are carried forward to the next year.	Not applicable; rental expenses are deductible, even if they create a rental loss.

Are passive losses from rental real estate activities that taxpayers are not allowed to deduct in the current year permanently disallowed? No, these losses are suspended until the taxpayer generates passive income or until the taxpayer sells the property that generated the passive loss. On the sale, in addition to reporting gain or loss from the sale of the property, the taxpayer will be allowed to deduct suspended passive losses against ordinary income.

BUSINESS USE OF THE HOME

LO 14-6

Because a personal residence is a personal use asset, utility payments and depreciation due to wear and tear are not deductible expenses. However, taxpayers who use their home—or at least part of their home—for business purposes may be able to deduct expenses associated with their home use if they meet certain stringent requirements.[32]

To qualify for **home office deductions,** a taxpayer must use her home—or part of her home—*exclusively and regularly* as either

1. The principal place of business for any of the taxpayer's trade or businesses, or
2. As a place to meet with patients, clients, or customers in the normal course of business.

Taxpayers fail the exclusive use test if they use the area of the home in question for both business and personal purposes.

Example 14-18

What if: Jasmine recently quit her job as an employee for an advertising firm because, with the move to the new home, the commute was too long. She has decided to go it alone as a self-employed graphic designer. She uses a large room in the basement of the Jeffersons' new home as her office. The room has been wired for all of her office needs. Once or twice a week, Tyler sits at the desk in the room and surfs the web to read up on his favorite sports teams. Is the office space eligible for a home office deduction?

Answer: No. The office is not used exclusively for Jasmine's business.

The exclusive use rule does not apply if the taxpayer either

- Uses part of the home for the storage of inventory or product samples.
- Uses part of the home as a day care facility.

When a taxpayer has more than one business location, including the home, which is her principal place of business? This is a facts-and-circumstances determination based upon

- The relative importance of the activities performed at each place where the taxpayer conducts business (more income from an activity generally means it's a more important activity) and
- The total time spent doing work at each location.

However, by definition, a taxpayer's principal place of business also includes the place of business used by the taxpayer for the administrative or management activities of the taxpayer's trade or business if there is no other fixed location of the trade or business where the taxpayer conducts substantial administrative or management activities of the trade or business.[33]

If a taxpayer meets with clients or patients in her home during the normal course of business, she qualifies for the home office deduction even if the home is not her

[32]§280A. If taxpayers rent the home they occupy and they meet the requirements for business use of the home, they can deduct part of the rent they pay. To determine the amount of the deduction, multiply the rental payment by the percentage of the home used for business purposes.

[33]§280A(c)(1).

principal place of business. However, the clients or patients must visit the taxpayer's home *in person*. Communication through telephone calls or other types of communication technology does not qualify.

Example 14-19

What if: Jasmine recently quit her job as an employee for an advertising firm because, with the move to the new home, the commute was too long. She has decided to go it alone as a self-employed graphic designer. She uses a large room in the basement of the Jeffersons' new home as her office. The room has been wired for all of her office needs. The Jeffersons use the room exclusively for Jasmine's graphic design business use. Does this space qualify for the home office deduction?

Answer: Yes. While Jasmine will spend a good deal of time meeting with clients on location, she has no other fixed location for her trade or business. Further, the office is used exclusively for business purposes. Consequently, the Jeffersons qualify for the home office deduction subject to certain limitations described below.

THE KEY FACTS

Home Office Deduction

- Deductibility limits on expenses allocated to office.
  - If employee, expenses deducted as unreimbursed employee business expenses.
  - If self-employed, deducted for AGI but deductions may be subject to income limitation.
  - If deduction is limited by income limitation, apply the same tiered system as used for rental property when tier 2 and tier 3 deductions are limited to gross rental income minus tier 1 expenses.
- Taxpayers can elect simplified method to report home office expenses.
  - Business use square footage (limited to 300 sq. feet) × $5 per square foot.
  - Deduction limited to gross business revenue (minus business expenses unrelated to home).
  - No carryover of excess deduction to subsequent year.
  - Deduct all property taxes and mortgage interest as itemized deductions.
  - Do not deduct depreciation expense so basis in home is unaffected by home office expense deduction (under the simplified method).

Finally, note that an *employee* (not a self-employed taxpayer) who otherwise meets these requirements qualifies for home office deductions only if

- The employee's use of the home is considered to be for the convenience of the employer and not just something that is helpful or useful for the employer, and
- The employee does not rent part of the home to the employer.

Generally, with such strict requirements, only self-employed taxpayers and employees such as outside salespersons or full-time telecommuters who have no office space anywhere except at home can qualify for the deductions.[34]

TAXES IN THE REAL WORLD If You Want the Bathroom to Qualify as a Home Office, You Better Lock It and Keep the Key

The IRS and a taxpayer with seven years of IRS work experience recently did battle over home office expenses in the Tax Court. The taxpayer operates an accounting business, and he uses a bedroom in his residence exclusively for his accounting business. The taxpayer included the bathroom adjacent to the bedroom in his home office square footage. However, because the taxpayer testified that his children and personal guests occasionally used the bathroom, the Tax Court determined that the bathroom was not used exclusively for business purposes (the children and personal guests may beg to differ), and it disallowed the expenses associated with the bathroom square footage. See *Luis Bulas*, T.C. Memo. 2011-201 (2011).

Direct vs. Indirect Expenses

When a taxpayer qualifies for home office deductions the deductions are limited to expenses that are related—either directly or indirectly—to the business. Direct expenses are expenses incurred in maintaining the room or part of the home that is set aside for business use. Direct expenses include painting or costs of other repairs to the area of the home used for business.[35] These expenses are deductible in full as home office expenses. Indirect expenses are expenses incurred in maintaining and using

[34]IRS Publication 587 Business Use of Your Home, page 4, provides a flowchart for determining whether taxpayers are allowed to deduct home office expenses.

[35]The basic local telephone service charge, including taxes, for the first telephone line into a home is a nondeductible personal expense. However, charges for business long-distance phone calls on that line, as well as the cost of a second line into the home used exclusively for business, are deductible business expenses. However, these expenses are not deducted as home office expenses. Rather, these expenses are deducted separately on the appropriate form or schedule. Taxpayers filing Schedule C (Form 1040), would deduct these expenses as utilities.

the home. Indirect expenses include insurance, utilities, interest, real property taxes, general repairs, and depreciation on the home as if it were used entirely for business purposes. Depreciation on the home is calculated using nonresidential real property depreciation tables (straight-line depreciation over 39 years). In contrast to direct expenses, only indirect expenses *allocated* to the home office space are deductible.

How do taxpayers allocate indirect expenses to the home office space? If the rooms in the home are roughly of equal size, the taxpayer may allocate the indirect expenses to the business portion of the home based on the number of rooms. In a 10-room home, a taxpayer using one room for qualifying business use is allowed to deduct 10 percent of the indirect expenses. Alternatively, the taxpayer may allocate indirect expenses based on the amount of the space or square footage of the business-use room relative to the total square footage in the home. If the home is 5,000 square feet and the home office is 250 square feet, the taxpayer may deduct 5 percent of the indirect expenses. Unrelated expenses such as painting a room not used for business purposes are not deductible.

The IRS has also sanctioned an optional simplified method for computing home office expenses.[36] Under the simplified method, taxpayers are not allowed to deduct any *actual* expenses relating to qualified business use of the home (including depreciation). Instead, taxpayers electing the simplified method deduct the allowable business use square footage of the office (not to exceed 300 square feet) multiplied by $5 per square foot. Thus, this method generates a maximum deduction of $1,500 (300 square feet × $5 per square foot). In addition, taxpayers using this method are allowed to deduct all of their home mortgage interest and real property taxes as itemized deductions on Schedule A. Taxpayers may choose from year to year whether to use the simplified method or the actual expense method.

- Depreciation expense
  - Reduces basis in home.
  - Gain on sale due to depreciation is ineligible for exclusion.
  - This gain is taxed at a maximum 25 percent rate as unrecaptured §1250 gain.

Example 14-20

The Jeffersons moved into their new $800,000, 6,000-square-foot home on February 1 (The home building was valued at $600,000, and the land was valued at $200,000.) Jasmine quit her job and set up a 420-square-foot home office in the basement on that same date. Through the end of the calendar year, the Jeffersons incurred several expenses relating to their home (see table below). Assuming they qualify for the home office deduction, they would sum the direct expenses and the indirect expenses allocated to the office. They would allocate the indirect expenses based on the square footage of the office compared to the rest of the home. Using the actual expense method, what amount of home-related expenses would qualify as home office expenses?

Answer: $4,575. See allocation below. All direct expenses and 7 percent of the indirect expenses would be allocated to the home office (420 office square footage/6,000 home square footage). The Jeffersons would allocate the expenses as follows:

Total Expense	Type	(A) Amount	(B) Office %	(A) × (B) Home Office Expense
Painting office	Direct	$ 200	100%	$ 200
Real property taxes	Indirect	11,000	7	770
Home interest expense	Indirect	27,917	7	1,954
Electricity	Indirect	2,600	7	182
Gas and other utilities	Indirect	2,500	7	175
Homeowner's insurance	Indirect	5,000	7	350
Depreciation	Indirect	13,482	7	944
Total expenses		$62,699		**$4,575**

(continued on page 14-28)

[36]Rev. Proc. 2013-13.

The expenses attributable to the home office are deductible subject to the limitations discussed below. Also, as discussed below, the Jeffersons are able to deduct the real property taxes and home interest expense not allocated to the home office as itemized deductions.

What if: Suppose Jasmine elects to use the simplified method for determining home office expenses. What would be the amount of their home office expenses?

Answer: $1,500 (300 square feet × $5 per square foot). Even though the Jeffersons' home office is 420 square feet, for purposes of the home office expense under the simplified method, the square footage is limited to 300 square feet.

What if: Suppose the Jeffersons elect to use the simplified method for home office expenses. What amount of home mortgage interest expenses and real property taxes would they be able to deduct on Schedule A as itemized deductions?

Answer: Home mortgage interest expense $27,917; Real property taxes $11,000. They are allowed to deduct all of these expenses as itemized deductions.

Limitations on Deductibility of Expenses

The process for determining the amount of deductible home office expenses, under the actual expense method, is similar to the process used to determine the deductions for vacation homes. Gross revenue from the business is included in gross income, business expenses unrelated to the home are fully deductible (on Schedule C of Form 1040), and expenses relating to the home are allocated between business (direct and indirect expenses) and nonbusiness use of the home (see above for discussion regarding allocating expenses). The expenses allocated to nonbusiness use are not deductible unless they are deductible under nonbusiness tax provisions as itemized deductions (such as mortgage interest expense and real property taxes).

When gross business revenue exceeds the sum of business expenses unrelated to the home and business expenses relating to the home, the business expenses relating to the home business are deductible in full. However, when these expenses exceed the gross business revenue, deductibility of the expenses is limited. In these situations, taxpayers divide business expenses associated with the home office into one of three categories or "tiers." Tier 1 expenses consist of mortgage interest and real property taxes allocated to the business use of the home. Tier 2 expenses consist of all other expenses allocated to the business use of the home except for depreciation. Tier 3 expense consists of depreciation.

To determine the home office deduction, the taxpayer uses a process very similar to the process to determine the deductible expenses for a vacation home described in the previous section. The taxpayer first deducts tier 1 expenses in full even when tier 1 expenses exceed gross net Schedule C income (before home office expenses).[37] Second, the taxpayer deducts tier 2 expenses. However, the amount of the deductible tier 2 expenses is limited to net Schedule C income minus tier 1 expenses. Any tier 2 expenses not deductible due to the income limitation are suspended and carried forward to the next year, subject to the same limitations. Finally, the taxpayer deducts tier 3 expense. However, the amount of the deductible tier 3 expense is limited to net Schedule C income (before home office expenses) minus tier 1 and deductible tier 2 expenses. The nondeductible portion of tier 3 expense is carried forward to the next year, subject to the same limitations.

Under the simplified method, the expense, as calculated by multiplying the square footage by the $5 application rate, is limited to gross business revenue for the year (reduced by business expenses unrelated to business use of the home). Further,

[37]§280A(c)(5).

taxpayers using the simplified method in a particular year may not deduct expenses carried over to that year under the actual expense method. However, disallowed expenses under the actual expense method can be carried over to a subsequent year in which the taxpayer uses the actual expense method for determining the home office expense deduction.

Example 14-21

For the year, Jasmine generated $4,000 of gross revenue from her graphic design business. Her home office expenses before limitation total $4,575 (see previous example). The expenses consist of painting office $200, real property taxes $770, home interest expense $1,954, electricity $182, gas and other utilities $175, homeowner's insurance $350, and depreciation $944. What is the total amount of tier 1, tier 2, and tier 3 expenses?

Answer: Tier 1 expenses $2,724 (real property taxes $770 and home interest expense of $1,954); tier 2 expenses $907 (painting office $200, electricity $182, gas and other utilities $175, and homeowner's insurance $350); tier 3 expense $944 (depreciation).

What is Jasmine's net income from the business and what expenses, if any, will she carry over to next year?

Answer: $0 net income and carry over $575 of depreciation expense, determined as follows:

	Net Income from Business
Gross business receipts	$4,000
Less: Tier 1 expenses	(2,724)
Income after tier 1 expenses	1,276
Less: Tier 2 expenses	(907)
Income after tier 2 expenses	369
Less: Tier 3 expenses	(369)
Taxable business income	$ 0

Due to the taxable income limitation, Jasmine was allowed to deduct only $369 of the $944 depreciation expense. She will carry over the remaining $575 ($944 minus $369) to next year to deduct as a home office expense subject to the same limitations.

What if: Suppose Jasmine uses the simplified method of determining home office expenses. What amount of the $1,500 expense (300 square feet × $5 application rate) would she be allowed to deduct?

Answer: All $1,500, because the home office expense is less than the $4,000 gross revenue from the business (there were no business expenses unrelated to business use of of the home).

What if: Assume the same facts as in the previous what if example except that gross revenue from the business was $2,000 and that Jasmine claimed $800 of advertising expense for her business. What amount of the $1,500 home office expense would Jasmine be allowed to deduct?

Answer: $1,200 ($2,000 minus $800). The home office expense deduction under the simplified method is limited to gross income from the business ($2,000) minus business expenses unrelated to the home ($800 advertising expense). Jasmine is not allowed to carry over the $300 nondeductible portion of the expense to a subsequent year ($1,500 total expense minus $1,200 deductible expense).

It is important to note that, when a taxpayer deducts depreciation as a home office expense using the actual expense method, the depreciation expense reduces the taxpayer's basis in the home. Consequently, when the taxpayer sells the home, the gain on the sale will be greater than it would have been had the taxpayer not deducted depreciation expense. Further, the gain on the sale of the home attributable to the depreciation deductions is *not* eligible to be excluded under the home sale exclusion provisions. Rather, this gain is treated as unrecaptured §1250 gain and is subject to a maximum 25 percent tax rate (see Chapter 11 for detailed discussion of unrecaptured §1250 gain).

Example 14-22

At the beginning of the year, the Jeffersons' basis in their home was $800,000. Jasmine's first-year home office deductions included $369 in depreciation expense. What is their adjusted basis in the home at the end of the year?

Answer: The depreciation deduction reduces the basis to $799,631 ($800,000 minus $369).

What if: Now, suppose that after the Jeffersons meet the ownership and use tests for the home sale exclusion, they sell the home for $900,000. Assume the only depreciation expense the Jeffersons have deducted is the $369 they deducted in the year they bought the home. Consequently, their adjusted basis in the home on the date of sale was $799,631 and they realize a gain of $100,369 on the sale. How much of the gain are they allowed to exclude?

Answer: They can exclude $100,000 of gain. However, they are not allowed to exclude the remaining $369 gain caused by the depreciation expense for the home office. The Jeffersons must pay $92 of tax on the gain ($369 × 25% unrecaptured §1250 gain).

Taxpayers using the simplified method are not allowed to deduct depreciation expense. Consequently, the simplified method does not affect the taxpayer's adjusted basis in the home. However, if a taxpayer switches from the simplified method in one year to the actual expense method in a subsequent year, the taxpayer is required to use modified depreciation tables to compute depreciation expense under the actual expense method.

Allowing taxpayers to deduct part of their home-related expenses as business expenses creates temptations for taxpayers to deduct home-related expenses that don't meet the requirements. Not surprisingly, the IRS is very concerned about taxpayers inappropriately deducting expenses relating to their home. Consequently, expenses for business use of the home are some of the most highly scrutinized deductions available to taxpayers. Self-employed taxpayers using the actual expense method must file a separate Form 8829 "Expenses for Business Use of Your Home" when deducting home office expenses on a tax return. Taxpayers using the simplified method file a different form that was not yet available at press time. With the high level of scrutiny applied to home office expenses, taxpayers should be sure to have documentation available to support their deductions. Exhibit 14-7 includes Form 8829 for Jasmine taken from Examples 14-20 and 14-21.

CONCLUSION

When deciding whether to invest in a home as a primary residence, a vacation home, or even a rental home, prospective owners should consider both nontax and tax factors relating to the ownership of the property. The tax code includes several provisions favorable to homeowners. This chapter is intended to provide current and prospective homeowners with enough insight on tax and nontax consequences of home ownership to allow them to make informed investment and compliance decisions when applicable.

EXHIBIT 14-7

Form **8829** — Department of the Treasury, Internal Revenue Service (99)

Expenses for Business Use of Your Home

▶ File only with Schedule C (Form 1040). Use a separate Form 8829 for each home you used for business during the year.

▶ Information about Form 8829 and its separate instructions is at *www.irs.gov/form8829.*

OMB No. 1545-0074 — **2014** — Attachment Sequence No. **176**

Name(s) of proprietor(s): Jasmine Jefferson | Your social security number: 674-65-6564

Part I — Part of Your Home Used for Business

	Line				Line	Amount
1	Area used regularly and exclusively for business, regularly for daycare, or for storage of inventory or product samples (see instructions)				1	420
2	Total area of home				2	6,000
3	Divide line 1 by line 2. Enter the result as a percentage				3	7 %
	For daycare facilities not used exclusively for business, go to line 4. All others, go to line 7.					
4	Multiply days used for daycare during year by hours used per day	4	hr.			
5	Total hours available for use during the year (365 days x 24 hours) (see instructions)	5	8,760 hr.			
6	Divide line 4 by line 5. Enter the result as a decimal amount	6	.			
7	Business percentage. For daycare facilities not used exclusively for business, multiply line 6 by line 3 (enter the result as a percentage). All others, enter the amount from line 3 ▶				7	7 %

Part II — Figure Your Allowable Deduction

			(a) Direct expenses	(b) Indirect expenses		
8	Enter the amount from Schedule C, line 29, **plus** any gain derived from the business use of your home, **minus** any loss from the trade or business not derived from the business use of your home (see instructions)				8	4,000
	See instructions for columns (a) and (b) before completing lines 9–21.					
9	Casualty losses (see instructions)	9				
10	Deductible mortgage interest (see instructions)	10		27,917		
11	Real estate taxes (see instructions)	11		11,000		
12	Add lines 9, 10, and 11	12		38,917		
13	Multiply line 12, column (b) by line 7		13	2,724		
14	Add line 12, column (a) and line 13				14	2,724
15	Subtract line 14 from line 8. If zero or less, enter -0-				15	1,276
16	Excess mortgage interest (see instructions)	16				
17	Insurance	17		5,000		
18	Rent	18				
19	Repairs and maintenance	19	200			
20	Utilities	20		5,100		
21	Other expenses (see instructions)	21				
22	Add lines 16 through 21	22	200	10,100		
23	Multiply line 22, column (b) by line 7		23	707		
24	Carryover of prior year operating expenses (see instructions)		24			
25	Add line 22, column (a), line 23, and line 24				25	907
26	Allowable operating expenses. Enter the **smaller** of line 15 or line 25				26	907
27	Limit on excess casualty losses and depreciation. Subtract line 26 from line 15				27	369
28	Excess casualty losses (see instructions)		28			
29	Depreciation of your home from line 41 below		29	944		
30	Carryover of prior year excess casualty losses and depreciation (see instructions)		30			
31	Add lines 28 through 30				31	944
32	Allowable excess casualty losses and depreciation. Enter the **smaller** of line 27 or line 31				32	369
33	Add lines 14, 26, and 32				33	4,000
34	Casualty loss portion, if any, from lines 14 and 32. Carry amount to **Form 4684** (see instructions)				34	
35	**Allowable expenses for business use of your home.** Subtract line 34 from line 33. Enter here and on Schedule C, line 30. If your home was used for more than one business, see instructions ▶				35	4,000

Part III — Depreciation of Your Home

36	Enter the **smaller** of your home's adjusted basis or its fair market value (see instructions)	36	800,000
37	Value of land included on line 36	37	200,000
38	Basis of building. Subtract line 37 from line 36	38	600,000
39	Business basis of building. Multiply line 38 by line 7	39	42,000
40	Depreciation percentage (see instructions)	40	2.247 %
41	Depreciation allowable (see instructions). Multiply line 39 by line 40. Enter here and on line 29 above	41	944

Part IV — Carryover of Unallowed Expenses to 2015

42	Operating expenses. Subtract line 26 from line 25. If less than zero, enter -0-	42	
43	Excess casualty losses and depreciation. Subtract line 32 from line 31. If less than zero, enter -0-	43	575

For Paperwork Reduction Act Notice, see your tax return instructions. Cat. No. 13232M Form **8829** (2014)

Appendix A Sample Settlement Statement for the Jeffersons (page 1)

A. **Settlement Statement** — U.S. Department of Housing and Urban Development — OMB Approval No. 2502-0265

B. Type of Loan

1. ☐ FHA 2. ☐ FmHA 3. ☑ Conv. Unins. 4. ☐ VA 5. ☐ Conv. Ins.	6. File Number: 1355	7. Loan Number: 6788	8. Mortgage Insurance Case Number:

C. Note: This form is furnished to give you a statement of actual settlement costs. Amounts paid to and by the settlement agent are shown. Items marked "(p.o.c.)" were paid outside the closing; they are shown here for informational purposes and are not included in the totals.

D. Name & Address of Borrower:	E. Name & Address of Seller:	F. Name & Address of Lender:
Tyler Jefferson Jasmine Jefferson 225 El Tejon Dr. Chicago, IL 60612	Ian Sabin 525 Roberts Ln. Glencoe, IL 60022	125 Decatur St. Chicago, IL 60612

G. Property Location:	H. Settlement Agent:	
225 El Tejon Dr. Chicago, IL 60612 Lot 1, Block 2, Dozier Estates Cook County, Illinois	Beardsley Settlement Group Place of Settlement: 425 McCray St. Chicago, IL 60612	I. Settlement Date: 1/31/2015

J. Summary of Borrower's Transaction		K. Summary of Seller's Transaction	
100. Gross Amount Due From Borrower		**400. Gross Amount Due To Seller**	
101. Contract sales price	800,000.00	401. Contract sales price	800,000.00
102. Personal property		402. Personal property	
103. Settlement charges to borrower (line 1400)	28,116.00	403.	
104.		404.	
105.		405.	
Adjustments for items paid by seller in advance		**Adjustments for items paid by seller in advance**	
106. City/town taxes to		406. City/town taxes to	
107. County taxes to		407. County taxes to	
108. Assessments to		408. Assessments to	
109.		409.	
110.		410.	
111.		411.	
112.		412.	
120. Gross Amount Due From Borrower	828,116.00	**420. Gross Amount Due To Seller**	800,000.00
200. Amounts Paid By Or In Behalf Of Borrower		**500. Reductions In Amount Due To Seller**	
201. Deposit or earnest money	20,000.00	501. Excess deposit (see instructions)	
202. Principal amount of new loan(s)	300,000.00	502. Settlement charges to seller (line 1400)	48,260.00
203. Existing loan(s) taken subject to		503. Existing loan(s) taken subject to	
204.		504. Payoff of first mortgage loan	
205.		505. Payoff of second mortgage loan	
206.		506.	
207.		507.	
208.		508.	
209.		509.	
Adjustments for items unpaid by seller		**Adjustments for items unpaid by seller**	
210. City/town taxes to		510. City/town taxes to	
211. County taxes 1/1/2015 to 1/31/2015	1,000.00	511. County taxes 1/1/2015 to 1/31/2015	1,000.00
212. Assessments to		512. Assessments to	
213.		513.	
214.		514.	
215.		515.	
216.		516.	
217.		517.	
218.		518.	
219.		519.	
220. Total Paid By/For Borrower	321,000.00	**520. Total Reduction Amount Due Seller**	49,260.00
300. Cash At Settlement From/To Borrower		**600. Cash At Settlement To/From Seller**	
301. Gross Amount due from borrower (line 120)	828,116.00	601. Gross amount due to seller (line 420)	800,000.00
302. Less amounts paid by/for borrower (line 220)	(321,000.00)	602. Less reductions in amt. due seller (line 520)	(49,260.00)
303. Cash ☑ **From** ☐ **To Borrower**	507,116.00	**603. Cash** ☑ **To** ☐ **From Seller**	750,740.00

Section 5 of the Real Estate Settlement Procedures Act (RESPA) requires the following: • HUD must develop a Special Information Booklet to help persons borrowing money to finance the purchase of residential real estate to better understand the nature and costs of real estate settlement services; • Each lender must provide the booklet to all applicants from whom it receives or for whom it prepares a written application to borrow money to finance the purchase of residential real estate; • Lenders must prepare and distribute with the Booklet a Good Faith Estimate of the settlement costs that the borrower is likely to incur in connection with the settlement. These disclosures are manadatory.

Section 4(a) of RESPA mandates that HUD develop and prescribe this standard form to be used at the time of loan settlement to provide full disclosure of all charges imposed upon the borrower and seller. These are third party disclosures that are designed to provide the borrower with pertinent information during the settlement process in order to be a better shopper.

The Public Reporting Burden for this collection of information is estimated to average one hour per response, including the time for reviewing instructions, searching existing data sources, gathering and maintaining the data needed, and completing and reviewing the collection of information.

This agency may not collect this information, and you are not required to complete this form, unless it displays a currently valid OMB control number.

The information requested does not lend itself to confidentiality.

Previous editions are obsolete — Page 1 of 2 — form **HUD-1** (3/86) ref Handbook 4305.2

(page 2)

L. Settlement Charges		Paid From Borrowers Funds at Settlement	Paid From Seller's Funds at Settlement
700. Total Sales/Broker's Commission based on price $ 800,000.00 @ 6.000 % =	48,000.00		
Division of Commission (line 700) as follows:			
701. $ 24,000.00 to Selling Agent Co.			
702. $ 24,000.00 to Listing Agent Co.			
703. Commission paid at Settlement			48,000.00
704.			
800. Items Payable In Connection With Loan			
801. Loan Origination Fee 1.000 %		3,000.00	
802. Loan Discount 2.000 %		6,000.00	
803. Appraisal Fee to Drumgoole Apraisal Co.		400.00	
804. Credit Report to O'Brien Credit Check Inc.		40.00	
805. Lender's Inspection Fee			
806. Mortgage Insurance Application Fee to			
807. Assumption Fee			
808.			
809.			
810.			
811.			
900. Items Required By Lender To Be Paid In Advance			
901. Interest from 1/31/2015 to 2/10/2015 @$ 41.10 /day		411.00	
902. Mortgage Insurance Premium for months to			
903. Hazard Insurance Premium for years to			
904. years to			
905.			
1000. Reserves Deposited With Lender			
1001. Hazard insurance 2 months@$ 100.00 per month		200.00	
1002. Mortgage insurance months@$ per month			
1003. City property taxes months@$ per month			
1004. County property taxes 11 months@$ 1,000.00 per month		11,000.00	
1005. Annual assessments months@$ per month			
1006. months@$ per month			
1007. months@$ per month			
1008. months@$ per month			
1100. Title Charges			
1101. Settlement or closing fee to Beardsley Settlement Group		300.00	
1102. Abstract or title search to			
1103. Title examination to Title Examination Inc.		250.00	
1104. Title insurance binder to			
1105. Document preparation to Buckles & Pitts, L.L.P			200.00
1106. Notary fees to			
1107. Attorney's fees to			
(includes above items numbers:)			
1108. Title insurance to Title Insurance Co.		3,250.00	
(includes above items numbers:)			
1109. Lender's coverage $			
1110. Owner's coverage $			
1111.			
1112.			
1113.			
1200. Government Recording and Transfer Charges			
1201. Recording fees: Deed $ 40.00 ; Mortgage $ 50.00 ; Releases $		90.00	
1202. City/county tax/stamps: Deed $ 450.00 ; Mortgage $ 350.00		800.00	
1203. State tax/stamps: Deed $ 1,250.00 ; Mortgage $ 1,000.00		2,250.00	
1204.			
1205.			
1300. Additional Settlement Charges			
1301. Survey to Beardsley Settlement Group		125.00	
1302. Pest inspection to Clark's Pest Control			60.00
1303.			
1304.			
1305.			
1400. Total Settlement Charges (enter on lines 103, Section J and 502, Section K)		28,116.00	48,260.00

Previous editions are obsolete

Page 2 of 2

form **HUD-1** (3/86)
ref Handbook 4305.2

Appendix B Flowchart of Tax Rules Relating to Home Used for Rental Purposes (page 1)

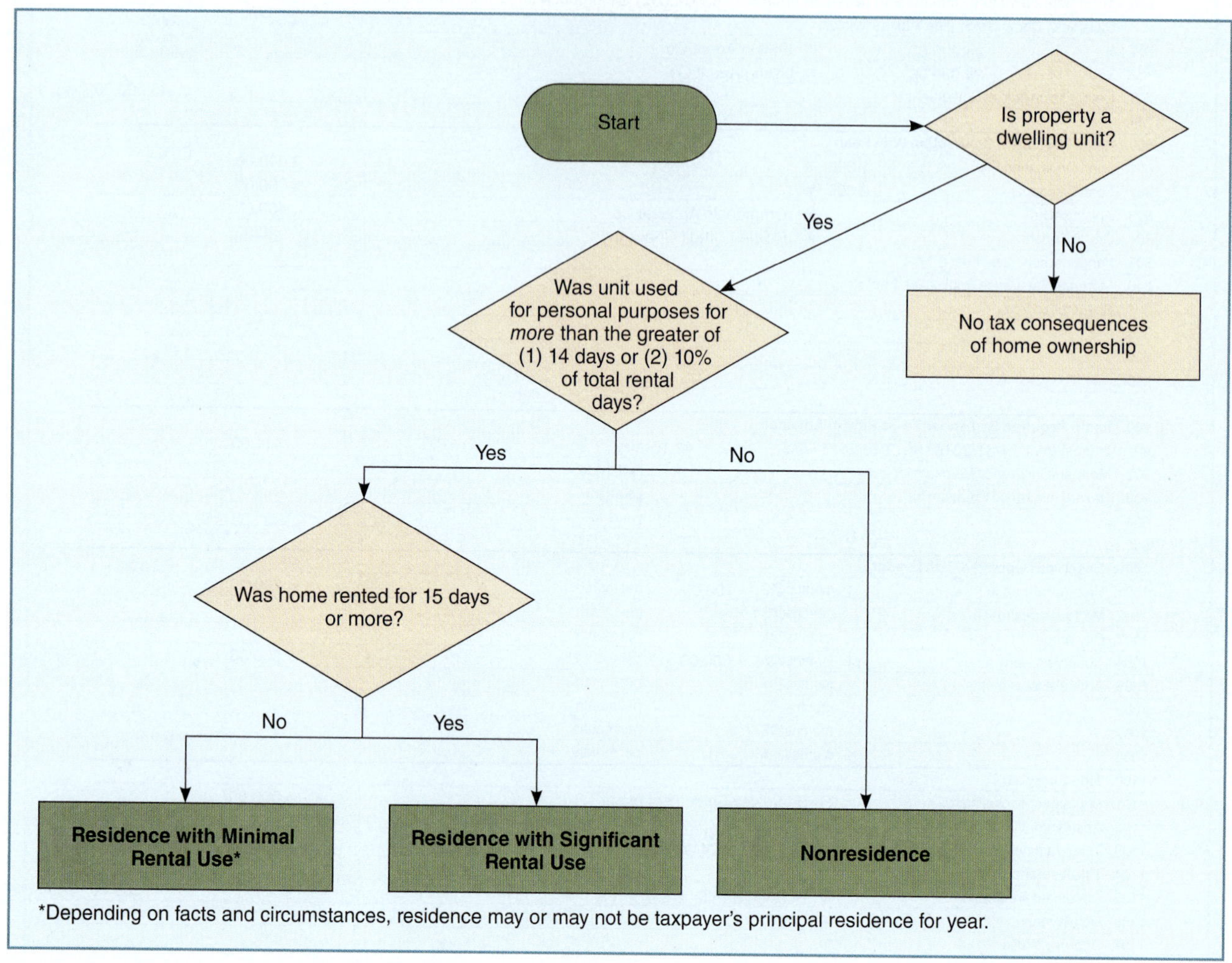

*Depending on facts and circumstances, residence may or may not be taxpayer's principal residence for year.

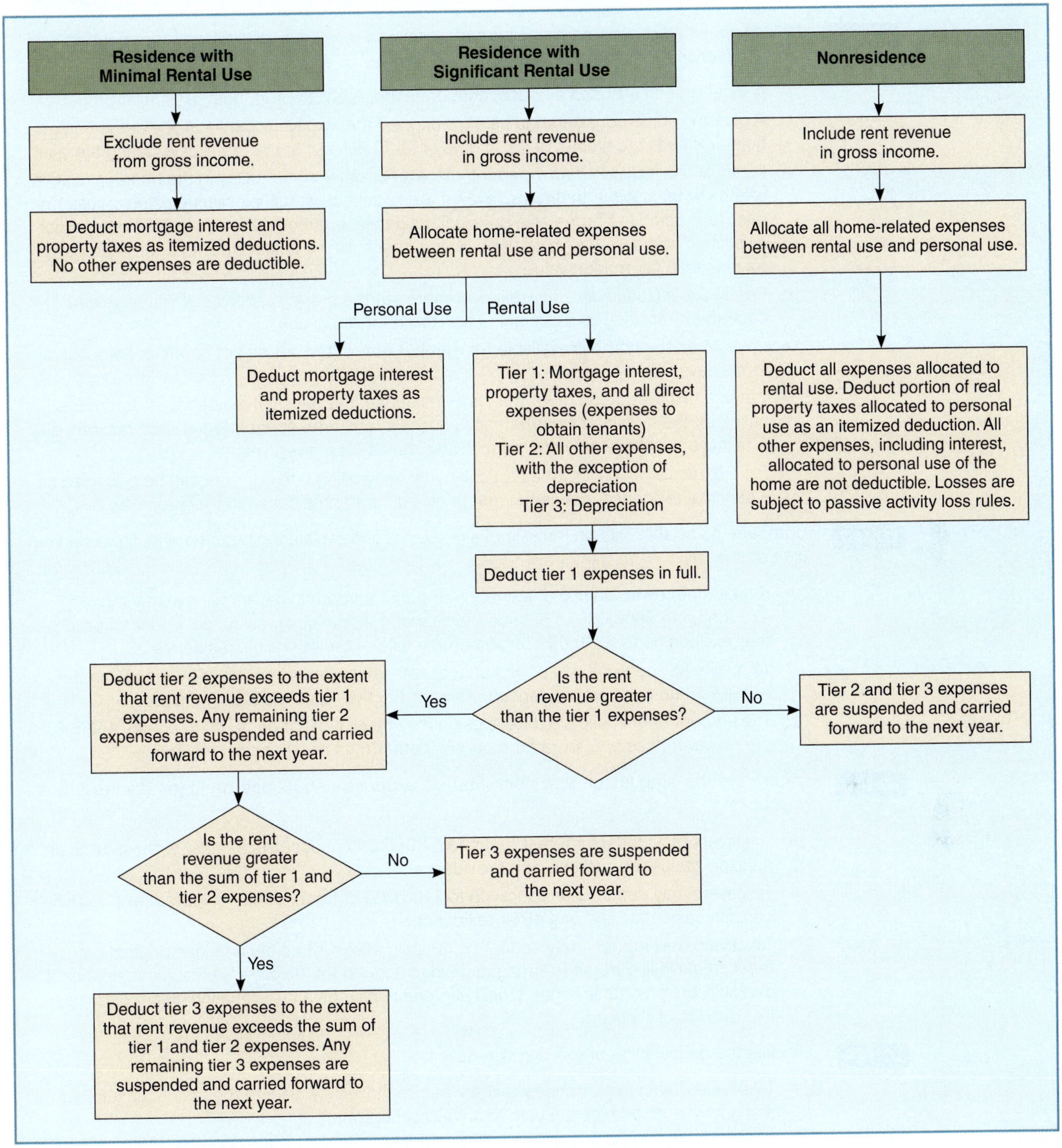

Residence with Minimal Rental Use

Exclude rent revenue from gross income.

Deduct mortgage interest and property taxes as itemized deductions. No other expenses are deductible.

Residence with Significant Rental Use

Include rent revenue in gross income.

Allocate home-related expenses between rental use and personal use.

Personal Use

Deduct mortgage interest and property taxes as itemized deductions.

Rental Use

Tier 1: Mortgage interest, property taxes, and all direct expenses (expenses to obtain tenants)
Tier 2: All other expenses, with the exception of depreciation
Tier 3: Depreciation

Deduct tier 1 expenses in full.

Is the rent revenue greater than the tier 1 expenses?

No: Tier 2 and tier 3 expenses are suspended and carried forward to the next year.

Yes: Deduct tier 2 expenses to the extent that rent revenue exceeds tier 1 expenses. Any remaining tier 2 expenses are suspended and carried forward to the next year.

Is the rent revenue greater than the sum of tier 1 and tier 2 expenses?

No: Tier 3 expenses are suspended and carried forward to the next year.

Yes: Deduct tier 3 expenses to the extent that rent revenue exceeds the sum of tier 1 and tier 2 expenses. Any remaining tier 3 expenses are suspended and carried forward to the next year.

Nonresidence

Include rent revenue in gross income.

Allocate all home-related expenses between rental use and personal use.

Deduct all expenses allocated to rental use. Deduct portion of real property taxes allocated to personal use as an itemized deduction. All other expenses, including interest, allocated to personal use of the home are not deductible. Losses are subject to passive activity loss rules.

Summary

LO 14-1 Determine whether a home is considered a principal residence, a residence (not principal), or a nonresidence for tax purposes.

- A dwelling unit includes a house, condominium, mobile home, boat, or similar property.
- A dwelling unit is considered to be a residence if the taxpayer's personal use of the unit or home exceeds the greater of (1) 14 days or (2) 10 percent of the rental days during the year.
- Personal use includes days when the taxpayer or other owners stay in the home, a relative of the owner stays in the home, even if the relative pays full fair market value unless the relative is using the home as a principal residence, a nonowner stays in the home under a vacation home exchange or swap arrangement, or the taxpayer rents out the property for less than fair market value.
- Rental use includes days the taxpayer rents out the property at fair market value and days spent repairing or maintaining the home for rental use.
- Days when the home is available for rent but not rented out do not count as personal or rental days.
- When a taxpayer owns more than one residence, the principal residence is determined based on the facts and circumstances such as total time spent living in each residence. A taxpayer can have only one principal residence for a given year.
- For a particular taxpayer for a particular year, a dwelling unit or home can be classified as a principal residence, residence (not principal), or nonresidence (rental property).

LO 14-2 Compute the taxable gain on the sale of a residence and explain the requirements for excluding gain on the sale.

- If they meet ownership and use requirements, married taxpayers filing jointly may exclude up to $500,000 of gain on the sale of their principal residence. Other taxpayers may exclude up to $250,000 of gain on the sale of their principal residence.
- To qualify for the exclusion on the sale of real estate, taxpayers must own and use the home as their principal residence for two of the five years preceding the sale.
- The amount of gain eligible for exclusion may be reduced if on or after January 1, 2009, the taxpayer uses the home for a purpose other than as a principal residence.

LO 14-3 Determine the amount of allowable interest expense deductions on loans secured by a residence.

- Taxpayers may deduct interest on up to $1,000,000 of acquisition indebtedness of their principal residence and one other residence.
- Taxpayers may deduct interest on up to $100,000 of home-equity indebtedness on their principal residence and one other residence.
- Taxpayers may immediately deduct points paid (discount points and loan origination fees) on qualifying home mortgages used to acquire the taxpayer's principal residence if certain requirements are met. Qualifying points paid on a loan refinancing are deductible over the life of the loan.

LO 14-4 Discuss the deductibility of real property taxes.

- Taxpayers deduct real property taxes when the taxes are paid to the taxing jurisdiction and not when the taxes are paid to an escrow account.
- When a piece of real property is sold during the year, the property tax deduction for the property is allocated to the buyer and seller based on the portion of the year that each held the property no matter who pays the taxes.

LO 14-5 Explain the tax issues and consequences associated with rental use of the home, including determining the deductibility of residential rental real estate losses.

- Taxpayers who live in a home for 15 days or more and rent the home out for 14 days or less (a residence with minimal rental use) do not include gross rental receipts in taxable income and do not deduct rental expenses.
- Taxpayers who both reside in and rent out a home for a significant portion of the year (a residence with significant rental use) include rental revenue in gross income,

deduct direct rental expenses not relating to the home (expenses to obtain tenants), and allocate home-related expenses between personal use and rental use of the home. They deduct mortgage interest expense and real property taxes allocated to the rental use of the home as *for* AGI deductions and the mortgage interest expense and real property taxes allocated to the personal use of the home as itemized deductions. The remaining deductions allocated to the rental use of the home are deductible in a particular sequence and the amount of these deductions cannot exceed rental revenue in excess of direct rental expenses and rental mortgage interest and real property taxes.

- Net rental income reported on Schedule E is subject to the 3.8% net investment income tax discussed in Chapter 8. This tax applies to net investment income for high income taxpayers.
- Taxpayers who rent a home with minimal or no personal use (nonresidence) include rental receipts in income and deduct all rental expenses. In this situation expenses exceeding income are subject to the passive activity loss rules.
- Taxpayers may be able to deduct up to $25,000 of passive loss on their rental home if they are active participants with respect to the property. This deduction is phased out for taxpayers with adjusted gross income between $100,000 and $150,000.

Describe the requirements necessary to qualify for home office deductions and compute the deduction limitations on home office deductions. LO 14-6

- To deduct expenses relating to a home office, the taxpayer must use the home exclusively and regularly for business purposes.
- Home-related expenses are allocated between business expenses and personal expenses based on the size of the office relative to the size of the home.
- Mortgage interest and real property taxes allocated to business use of the home are deductible in full without regard to the income of the business.
- Other expenses allocated to the business use of the home are deducted in a particular sequence. The deduction for these expenses cannot exceed the taxpayer's net Schedule C income (before home office expenses) minus the mortgage interest and real property taxes allocated to business use of the home.
- Taxpayers electing the simplified method for claiming home office expenses may deduct $5 per square foot up to 300 square feet.

KEY TERMS

acquisition indebtedness (14-9)
active participant in a rental activity (14-23)
dwelling unit (14-2)
escrow account (14-15)
flipping (14-5)
home-equity indebtedness (14-9)
home office deductions (14-25)
IRS allocation method (14-19)
passive activity income or loss (14-23)
point (14-13)
principal residence (14-2)
qualified debt (14-11)
qualified residence (14-9)
qualified residence interest (14-13)
real property taxes (14-15)
refinance (14-10)
secured loan (14-9)
settlement statement (14-13)
Tax Court allocation method (14-19)

DISCUSSION QUESTIONS

1. How does a taxpayer determine whether a dwelling unit is treated as a residence or nonresidence for tax purposes? LO 14-1
2. Does a residence for tax purposes need to be situated at a fixed location? Explain. LO 14-1
3. When determining whether a dwelling unit is treated as a residence or a non-residence for tax purposes, what constitutes a day of personal use and what constitutes a day of rental use? LO 14-1
4. A taxpayer owns a home in Salt Lake City, Utah, and a second home in St. George, Utah. How does the taxpayer determine which home is her principal residence for tax purposes? LO 14-1

LO 14-2 5. What are the ownership and use requirements a taxpayer must meet to qualify for the exclusion of gain on the sale of a residence?

LO 14-2 6. Under what circumstances, if any, can a taxpayer fail to meet the ownership and use requirements but still be able to exclude all of the gain on the sale of a principal residence?

LO 14-2 7. Under what circumstances can a taxpayer meet the ownership and use requirements for a residence but still not be allowed to exclude all realized gain on the sale of the residence?

LO 14-2 8. A taxpayer purchases and lives in a home for a year. The home appreciates in value by $50,000. The taxpayer sells the home after her employer transfers her to an office in a nearby city. The taxpayer buys a new home. What information do you need to obtain to determine whether the taxpayer is allowed to exclude the gain on the sale of the first home?

LO 14-3 9. Juanita owns a principal residence in New Jersey, a cabin in Montana, and a houseboat in Hawaii. All of these properties have mortgages on which Juanita pays interest. What limits, if any, apply to Juanita's mortgage interest deductions? Explain whether deductible interest is deductible *for* AGI or *from* AGI.

LO 14-3 10. Barbi really wants to acquire an expensive automobile (perhaps more expensive than she can really afford). She has two options. Option 1: finance the purchase with an automobile loan from her local bank at a 7 percent interest rate, or Option 2: finance the purchase with a home-equity loan at a rate of 7 percent. Compare and contrast the tax and nontax factors Barbi should consider before deciding which loan to use to pay for the automobile. Barbi typically has more itemized deductions than the standard deduction amount.

LO 14-3 11. Lars and Leigha saved up for years before they purchased their dream home. They were considering (1) using all of their savings to make a large down payment on the home (90 percent of the value of the home) and barely scraping by without the backup savings, or (2) making a more modest down payment (50 percent of the value of the loan) and holding some of the savings in reserve as needed if funds get tight. They decided to go with the large down payment because they figured they could always refinance the home to pull some equity out of the home if things got tight. What advice would you give them about the tax consequences of their decision?

LO 14-3 12. How are acquisition indebtedness and home-equity indebtedness similar? How are they dissimilar?

LO 14-3 13. Why might it be good advice from a tax perspective to think hard before deciding to quickly pay down mortgage debt?

LO 14-3 14. Can portions of one loan secured by a residence consist of both acquisition indebtedness and home-equity indebtedness? Explain.

LO 14-3 15. When a taxpayer has multiple loans secured by her residence that in total exceed the limits for deductibility, how does the taxpayer determine the amount of the deductible interest expense?

LO 14-3 16. Compare and contrast the characteristics of a deductible point from a nondeductible point on a first home mortgage.

LO 14-3 17. Is the break-even period generally longer for points paid to reduce the interest rate on initial home loans or points paid for the same purpose on a refinance? Explain.

planning LO 14-3 18. Under what circumstances is it likely economically beneficial to pay points to reduce the interest rate on a home loan?

LO 14-3 19. Harry decides to finance his new home with a 30-year fixed mortgage. Because he figures he will be in this home for a long time he decides to pay a fully deductible discount point on his mortgage to reduce the interest rate. Assuming Harry itemizes deductions and has a constant marginal tax rate over time, will the time required to recover the cost of the discount point be shorter or longer if Harry makes extra principal payments starting in the first year than it would be if he does not make any extra principal payments? Explain.

20. Consider the settlement statement in Appendix A to this chapter. What amounts on the statement are the Jeffersons allowed to deduct on their 2015 tax return? Indicate the settlement statement line number for each deductible amount (discuss any issues that must be addressed to determine deductibility) and label each deduction as a *for* AGI deduction or as a *from* AGI deduction. LO 14-3 LO 14-4

21. A taxpayer sold a piece of real property in year 1. The amount of year 1 real property taxes was estimated at the closing of the sale and the amounts were allocated between the buyer and the taxpayer. At the end of year 1, the buyer receives a property tax bill that turns out to be higher than the estimate. After paying the tax bill, the buyer contacts the taxpayer at the beginning of year 2 and asks the taxpayer to pay the taxpayer's share of the shortfall. The taxpayer sends a check to the buyer. Should the taxpayer be concerned that she won't get to deduct the extra tax payment because it was paid to the buyer and not to the taxing jurisdiction? Explain. LO 14-4

22. Is a homeowner allowed a property tax deduction for amounts included in the monthly mortgage payment that are earmarked for property taxes? Explain. LO 14-4

23. Is it possible for a taxpayer to receive rental income that is not subject to taxation? Explain. LO 14-5 planning

24. Halle just acquired a vacation home. She plans on spending several months each year vacationing in the home and on renting the property for the rest of the year. She is projecting tax losses on the rental portion of the property for the year. She is not too concerned about the losses because she is confident she will be able to use the losses to offset her income from other sources. Is her confidence misplaced? Explain. LO 14-5

25. A taxpayer stays in a second home for the entire month of September. He would like the home to fall into the residence with significant rental use category for tax purposes. What is the maximum number of days he can rent out the home and have it qualify? LO 14-5 planning

26. Compare and contrast the IRS method and the Tax Court method for allocating expenses between personal use and rental use for vacation homes. Include the Tax Court's justification for departing from the IRS method in your answer. LO 14-5

27. In what circumstances is the IRS method for allocating expenses between personal use and rental use for second homes more beneficial to a taxpayer than the Tax Court method? LO 14-5

28. Under what circumstances would a taxpayer who generates a loss from renting a home that is not a residence be able to fully deduct the loss? What potential limitations apply? LO 14-5

29. Describe the circumstances in which a taxpayer acquires a home and rents it out and is not allowed to deduct a portion of the interest expense on the loan the taxpayer used to acquire the home. LO 14-5

30. Is it possible for a rental property to generate a positive annual cash flow and at the same time produce a loss for tax purposes? Explain. LO 14-5

31. How are the tax issues associated with home offices and vacation homes used as rentals similar? How are the tax issues or requirements dissimilar? LO 14-5 LO 14-6

32. Are employees or self-employed taxpayers more likely to qualify for the home office deduction? Explain. LO 14-6

33. Compare and contrast the manner in which employees and employers report home office deductions on their tax returns. LO 14-6

LO 14-6 34. For taxpayers qualifying for home office deductions, what are considered to be indirect expenses of maintaining the home? How are these expenses allocated to personal and home office use? Can taxpayers choose to calculate home office expenses without regard to actual expenses allocated to the home office? Explain.

LO 14-6 35. What limitations exist for self-employed taxpayers in deducting home office expenses, and how does the taxpayer determine which expenses are deductible and which are not in situations when the overall amount of the home office deduction is limited?

LO 14-2 LO 14-6 36. A self-employed taxpayer deducts home office expenses including depreciation expense. The taxpayer then sells the home at a $100,000 gain. Assuming the taxpayer meets the ownership and use tests, does the full gain qualify for exclusion? Explain.

PROBLEMS

All applicable problems are available with McGraw-Hill's *Connect® Accounting*.

LO 14-1 37. Several years ago, Junior acquired a home that he vacationed in part of the time and rented out part of the time. During the current year Junior:

- Personally stayed in the home for 22 days.
- Rented it to his favorite brother at a discount for 10 days.
- Rented it to his least favorite brother for 8 days at the full market rate.
- Rented it to his friend at a discounted rate for 4 days.
- Rented the home to third parties for 58 days at the market rate.
- Did repair and maintenance work on the home for 2 days.
- Marketed the property and made it available for rent for 150 days during the year (in addition to the days mentioned above).

How many days of personal use and how many days of rental use did Junior experience on the property during the year?

LO 14-1 38. Lauren owns a condominium. In each of the following alternative situations, determine whether the condominium should be treated as a residence or nonresidence for tax purposes.

a) Lauren lives in the condo for 19 days and rents it out for 22 days.
b) Lauren lives in the condo for 8 days and rents it out for 9 days.
c) Lauren lives in the condo for 80 days and rents it out for 120 days.
d) Lauren lives in the condo for 30 days and rents it out for 320 days.

LO 14-2 39. Steve and Stephanie Pratt purchased a home in Spokane, Washington, for $400,000. They moved into the home on February 1 of year 1. They lived in the home as their primary residence until June 30 of year 5, when they sold the home for $700,000.

a) What amount of gain on the sale of the home are the Pratts required to include in taxable income?
b) Assume the original facts, except that Steve and Stephanie lived in the home until January 1 of year 3 when they purchased a new home and rented out the original home. They finally sell the original home on June 30 of year 5 for $700,000. Ignoring any issues relating to depreciation taken on the home while it was being rented, what amount of realized gain on the sale of the home are the Pratts required to include in taxable income?
c) Assume the same facts as in part (b), except that the Pratts lived in the home until January of year 4 when they purchased a new home and rented out the first home. What amount of realized gain on the sale of the home will the Pratts include in taxable income if they sell the first home on June 30 of year 5 for $700,000?

d) Assume the original facts, except that Stephanie moved in with Steve on March 1 of year 3 and the couple was married on March 1 of year 4. Under state law, the couple jointly owned Steve's home beginning on the date they were married. On December 1 of year 3, Stephanie sold her home that she lived in before she moved in with Steve. She excluded the entire $50,000 gain on the sale on her individual year 3 tax return. What amount of gain must the couple recognize on the sale in June of year 5?

40. Steve and Stephanie Pratt purchased a home in Spokane, Washington, for $400,000. They moved into the home on February 1 of year 1. They lived in the home as their primary residence until November 1 of year 1, when they sold the home for $500,000. The Pratts' marginal ordinary tax rate is 35 percent. LO 14-2

a) Assume that the Pratts sold their home and moved because they don't like their neighbors. How much gain will the Pratts recognize on their home sale? At what rate, if any, will the gain be taxed?

b) Assume the Pratts sell the home because Stephanie's employer transfers her to an office in Utah. How much gain will the Pratts recognize on their home sale?

c) Assume the same facts as in part (b), except that the Pratts sell their home for $700,000. How much gain will the Pratts recognize on the home sale?

d) Assume the same facts as part (b), except that on December 1 of year 0 the Pratts sold their home in Seattle and excluded the $300,000 gain from income on their year 0 tax return. How much gain will the Pratts recognize on the sale of their Spokane home?

41. Steve Pratt, who is single, purchased a home in Spokane, Washington, for $400,000. He moved into the home on February 1 of year 1. He lived in the home as his primary residence until June 30 of year 5, when he sold the home for $700,000. LO 14-2

a) What amount of gain will Steve be required to recognize on the sale of the home?

b) Assume the original facts, except that the home is Steve's vacation home and he vacations there four months each year. Steve does not ever rent the home to others. What gain must Steve recognize on the home sale?

c) Assume the original facts, except that Steve married Stephanie on February 1 of year 3 and the couple lived in the home until they sold it in June of year 5. Under state law, Steve owned the home by himself. How much gain must Steve and Stephanie recognize on the sale (assume they file a joint return in year 5).

42. Celia has been married to Daryl for 52 years. The couple has lived in their current home for the last 20 years. In October of year 0, Daryl passed away. Celia sold their home and moved into a condominium. What is the maximum exclusion Celia is entitled to if she sells the home on December 15 of year 1? LO 14-2

43. Sarah single purchased a home on January 1, 2008, for $600,000. She eventually sold the home for $800,000. What amount of the $200,000 gain on the sale does Sarah recognize in each of the following alternative situations? LO 14-2

a) Sarah used the home as her principal residence through December 31, 2013. She used the home as a vacation home from January 1, 2014, until she sold it on January 1, 2016.

b) Sarah used the property as a vacation home through December 31, 2013. She then used the home as her principal residence from January 1, 2014, until she sold it on January 1, 2016.

c) Sarah used the home as a vacation home from January 1, 2008, until January 1, 2015. She used the home as her principal residence from January 1, 2015, until she sold it on January 1, 2016.

d) Sarah used the home as a vacation home from January 1, 2008, through December 31, 2009. She used the home as her principal residence from January 1, 2009, until she sold it on January 1, 2015.

LO 14-2 44. Troy (single) purchased a home in Hopkinton, MA, on January 1, 2007, for $300,000. He sold the home on January 1, 2015, for $320,000. How much gain must Troy recognize on his home sale in each of the following alternative situations?

a) Troy rented the home out from January 1, 2007, through November 30, 2008. He lived in the home as his principal residence from December 1, 2008, through the date of sale. Assume accumulated depreciation on the home at the time of sale was $7,000.

b) Troy lived in the home as his principal residence from January 1, 2007, through December 31, 2010. He rented the home from January 1, 2011, through the date of the sale. Assume accumulated depreciation on the home at the time of sale was $2,000.

c) Troy lived in the home as his principal residence from January 1, 2007, through December 31, 2012. He rented out the home from January 1, 2013, through the date of the sale. Assume accumulated depreciation on the home at the time of sale was $0.

d) Troy rented the home from January 1, 2007, through December 31, 2010. He lived in the home as his principal residence from January 1, 2011, through December 31, 2011. He rented out the home from January 1, 2012, through December 31, 2012, and lived in the home as his principal residence from January 1, 2013, through the date of the sale. Assume accumulated depreciation on the home at the time of sale was $0.

LO 14-3 45. Javier and Anita Sanchez purchased a home on January 1, 2015, for $500,000 by paying $200,000 down and borrowing the remaining $300,000 with a 7 percent loan secured by the home. The loan requires interest-only payments for the first five years. The Sanchezes would itemize deductions even if they did not have any deductible interest. The Sanchezes' marginal tax rate is 30 percent.

a) What is the after-tax cost of the interest expense to the Sanchezes in 2015?

b) Assume the original facts, except that the Sanchezes rent a home and pay $21,000 in rent during the year. What is the after-tax cost of their rental payments in 2015?

c) Assuming the interest expense is their only itemized deduction for the year and that Javier and Anita file a joint return, have great eyesight, and are under 60 years of age, what is the after-tax cost of their 2015 interest expense?

LO 14-3 46. Javier and Anita Sanchez purchased a home on January 1 of year 1 for $500,000 by paying $50,000 down and borrowing the remaining $450,000 with a 7 percent loan secured by the home. The loan requires interest-only payments for the first five years. The Sanchezes would itemize deductions even if they did not have any deductible interest.

a) Assume the Sanchezes also took out a second loan (on the same day as the first loan) secured by the home for $80,000 to fund expenses unrelated to the home. The interest rate on the second loan is 8 percent. The Sanchezes make interest-only payments on the loan in year 1. What is the maximum amount of their deductible interest expense (on both loans combined) in year 1?

b) Assume the original facts and that the Sanchezes take out a second loan (on the same day as the first loan) secured by the home in the amount of $50,000 to fund expenses unrelated to the home. The interest rate on the second loan is 8 percent. The Sanchezes make interest-only payments during the year. What is the maximum amount of their deductible interest expense in year 1 on both loans combined?

LO 14-3 47. Javier and Anita Sanchez purchased a home on January 1 of year 1 for $500,000 by paying $200,000 down and borrowing the remaining $300,000 with a 7 percent loan secured by the home. The loan requires interest-only payments for the first five years. The Sanchezes would itemize deductions even if they did not have any deductible interest. On January 1, the Sanchezes also borrowed money on a second loan secured by the home for $75,000. The interest rate on the loan is 8 percent and the Sanchezes make interest-only payments in year 1 on the second loan.

a) Assuming the Sanchezes use the second loan to landscape the yard to their home, what is the maximum amount of interest expense (on both loans combined) they are allowed to deduct in year 1?
b) Assume the original facts and that the Sanchezes use the $75,000 loan proceeds for an extended family vacation. What is the maximum amount of interest expense (on both loans combined) they are allowed to deduct in year 1?
c) Assume the original facts, except that the Sanchezes borrow $120,000 on the second loan and they use the proceeds for an extended family vacation and other personal expenses. What is the maximum amount of interest expense (on both loans combined) they are allowed to deduct in year 1?

48. Lewis and Laurie are married and jointly own a home valued at $240,000. They recently paid off the mortgage on their home. In need of cash for personal purposes unrelated to the home, the couple borrowed money from the local credit union. How much interest may the couple deduct in each of the following alternative situations? (Assume they itemize deductions no matter the amount of interest.) LO 14-3
   a) The couple borrows $40,000, and the loan is secured by their home. The couple pays $1,600 interest on the loan during the year, and the couple files a joint return.
   b) The couple borrows $10,000 unsecured from the credit union. The couple pays $900 interest on the loan during the year, and the couple files a joint return.
   c) The couple borrows $110,000, and the loan is secured by their home. The couple pays $5,200 interest on the loan during the year, and the couple files a joint return.
   d) The couple borrows $110,000, and the loan is secured by their home. The couple pays $5,200 interest on the loan during the year, and the couple files separate tax returns.

49. On January 1 of year 1, Arthur and Aretha Franklin purchased a home for $1.5 million by paying $200,000 down and borrowing the remaining $1.3 million with a 7 percent loan secured by the home. LO 14-3
   a) What is the amount of the interest expense the Franklins may deduct in year 1?
   b) Assume that in year 2, the Franklins pay off the entire loan but at the beginning of year 3, they borrow $300,000 secured by the home at a 7 percent rate. They make interest-only payments on the loan during the year. What amount of interest expense may the Franklins deduct in year 3 on this loan (the Franklins do not use the loan proceeds to improve the home)?
   c) Assume the same facts as in (b), except that the Franklins borrow $80,000 secured by their home. What amount of interest expense may the Franklins deduct in year 3 on this loan (the Franklins do not use the loan proceeds to improve the home)?

50. In year 0, Eva took out a $50,000 home-equity loan from her local credit union. At the time she took out the loan, her home was valued at $350,000. At the time of the loan, Eva's original mortgage on the home was $265,000. At the end of year 1, her original mortgage is $260,000. Unfortunately for Eva, during year 1, the value of her home dropped to $280,000. Consequently, as of the end of year 1, Eva's home secured $310,000 of home-related debt but her home is only valued at $280,000. Assuming Eva paid $15,000 of interest on the original mortgage and $3,500 of interest on the home-equity loan during the year, how much qualified residence interest can Eva deduct in year 1? LO 14-3

LO 14-3

51. On January 1 of year 1, Jason and Jill Marsh acquired a home for $500,000 by paying $400,000 down and borrowing $100,000 with a 7 percent loan secured by the home. On January 1 of year 2, the Marshes needed cash so they refinanced the original loan by taking out a new $250,000 7 percent loan. With the $250,000 proceeds from the new loan, the Marshes paid off the original $100,000 loan and used the remaining $150,000 to fund their son's college education.
   a) What amount of interest expense on the refinanced loan may the Marshes deduct in year 2?
   b) Assume the original facts, except that the Marshes use the $150,000 cash from the refinancing to add two rooms and a garage to their home. What amount of interest expense on the refinanced loan may the Marshes deduct in year 2?

LO 14-3
planning

52. On January 1 of year 1 Brandon and Alisa Roy purchased a home for $1.5 million by paying $500,000 down and borrowing the remaining $1 million with a 7 percent loan secured by the home. Later the same day, the Roys took out a second loan, secured by the home, in the amount of $300,000.
   a) Assuming the interest rate on the second loan is 8 percent, what is the maximum amount of interest expense the Roys may deduct on these two loans (combined) in year 1?
   b) Assuming the interest rate on the second loan is 6 percent, what is the maximum amount of interest expense the Roys may deduct on these two loans (combined) in year 1?

LO 14-3
research

53. Jennifer has been living in her current principal residence for three years. Six months ago Jennifer decided that she would like to purchase a second home near a beach so she can vacation there for part of the year. Despite her best efforts, Jennifer has been unable to find what she is looking for. Consequently, Jennifer recently decided to change plans. She purchased a parcel of land for $200,000 with the intention of building her second home on the property. To acquire the land, she borrowed $200,000 secured by the land. Jennifer would like to know whether the interest she pays on the loan before construction on the house is completed is deductible as mortgage interest.
   a) How should Jennifer treat the interest if she has begun construction on the home and plans to live in the home in 12 months from the time construction began?
   b) How should Jennifer treat the interest if she hasn't begun construction on the home but plans to live in the home in 15 months?
   c) How should Jennifer treat the interest if she has begun construction on the home but doesn't plan to live in the home for 37 months from the time construction began?

LO 14-3
planning

54. Rajiv and Laurie Amin are recent college graduates looking to purchase a new home. They are purchasing a $200,000 home by paying $20,000 down and borrowing the other $180,000 with a 30-year loan secured by the home. The Amins have the option of (1) paying no discount points on the loan and paying interest at 8 percent or (2) paying one discount point on the loan and paying interest of 7.5 percent. Both loans require the Amins to make interest-only payments for the first five years. Unless otherwise stated, the Amins itemize deductions irrespective of the amount of interest expense. The Amins are in the 25 percent marginal ordinary income tax bracket.
   a) Assuming the Amins *do not itemize deductions,* what is the break-even point for paying the point to get a lower interest rate?
   b) Assuming the Amins do itemize deductions, what is the break-even point for paying the point to get a lower interest rate?

c) Assume the original facts, except that the amount of the loan is $300,000. What is the break-even point for the Amins for paying the point to get a lower interest rate?

d) Assume the original facts, except that the $180,000 loan is a refinance instead of an original loan. What is the break-even point for paying the point to get a lower interest rate?

e) Assume the original facts, except that the amount of the loan is $300,000 and the loan is a refinance and not an original loan. What is the break-even point for paying the point to get a lower interest rate?

55. In year 1, Peter and Shaline Johnsen moved into a home in a new subdivision. Theirs was one of the first homes in the subdivision. In year 1, they paid $1,500 in real property taxes to the state government, $500 to the developer of the subdivision for an assessment to pay for the sidewalks, and $900 for real property taxes on land they hold as an investment. What amount of property taxes are the Johnsens allowed to deduct assuming their itemized deductions exceed the standard deduction amount before considering any property tax deductions? LO 14-4

56. Jesse Brimhall is single. In 2015, his itemized deductions were $4,000 before considering any real property taxes he paid during the year. Jesse's adjusted gross income was $70,000 (also before considering any property tax deductions). In 2015, he paid real property taxes of $3,000 on property 1 and $1,200 of real property taxes on property 2. LO 14-4

a) If property 1 is Jesse's primary residence and property 2 is his vacation home (he does not rent it out at all), what is his taxable income after taking property taxes into account?

b) If property 1 is Jesse's business building (he owns the property) and property 2 is his primary residence, what is his taxable income after taking property taxes into account?

c) If property 1 is Jesse's primary residence and property 2 is a parcel of land he holds for investment, what is his taxable income after taking property taxes into account?

57. Craig and Karen Conder purchased a new home on May 1 of year 1 for $200,000. At the time of the purchase, it was estimated that the real property tax rate for the year would be 1 percent of the property's value. How much in property taxes on the new home are the Conders allowed to deduct under each of the following circumstances (the Conders' itemized deductions exceed the standard deduction before considering property taxes)? LO 14-4

a) The property tax estimate proves to be accurate. The seller and the Conders paid their share of the tax. The full property tax bill is paid to the taxing jurisdiction by the end of the year.

b) The actual property tax bill turns out to be 1.05 percent of the property's value. The Conders' paid their share of the estimated tax bill and the entire difference between the 1 percent estimate and the 1.05 percent actual tax bill and the seller paid the rest. The full property tax bill is paid to the taxing jurisdiction by the end of the year.

c) The actual property tax bill turns out to be .95 percent of the property's value. The seller paid their share of taxes based on the 1 percent estimate and the Conders paid the difference between what the seller paid and the amount of the final tax bill. The full property tax bill is paid to the taxing jurisdiction by the end of the year.

58. Kirk and Lorna Newbold purchased a new home on August 1 of year 1 for $300,000. At the time of the purchase, it was estimated that the real property tax rate for the year would be .5 percent of the property's value. Because the LO 14-4

taxing jurisdiction collects taxes on a July 1 year-end, it was estimated that the Newbolds would be required to pay $1,375 in property taxes for the property tax year relating to August through June of year 2 ($300,000 × .005 × 11/12). The seller would be required to pay the $125 for July of year 1. Along with their monthly payment of principal and interest, the Newbolds paid $125 to the mortgage company to cover the property taxes. The mortgage company placed the money in escrow and used the funds in the escrow account to pay the property tax bill in July of year 2. The Newbold's itemized deductions exceed the standard deduction before considering real property taxes.

a) How much in real property taxes can the Newbolds deduct for year 1?
b) How much in real property taxes can the Newbolds deduct for year 2?
c) Assume the original facts, except that the Newbolds were not able to collect $125 from the seller for the property taxes for July of year 1. How much in real property taxes can the Newbolds deduct for year 1 and year 2?
d) Assume the original facts, except that the tax bill for July 1 of year 1 through June 30 of year 2 turned out to be $1,200 instead of $1,500. How much in real property taxes can the Newbolds deduct in year 1 and year 2?

59. Jenae and Terry Hutchings own a parcel of land as tenants by entirety. That is, they both own the property but when one of them dies the other becomes the sole owner of the property. For nontax reasons, Jenae and Terry decide to file separate tax returns for the current year. Jenae paid the entire $3,000 property tax bill for the land. How much of the $3,000 property tax payment is each spouse entitled to deduct in the current year?

research

60. Dillon rented his personal residence at Lake Tahoe for 14 days while he was vacationing in Ireland. He resided in the home for the remainder of the year. Rental income from the property was $6,500. Expenses associated with use of the home for the entire year were as follows:

Real property taxes	$ 3,100
Mortgage interest	12,000
Repairs	1,500
Insurance	1,500
Utilities	3,900
Depreciation	13,000

a) What effect does the rental have on Dillon's AGI?
b) What effect does the rental have on Dillon's itemized deductions?

Use the following facts to answer problems 61 and 62.

Natalie owns a condominium near Cocoa Beach in Florida. This year, she incurs the following expenses in connection with her condo:

Insurance	$1,000
Advertising expense	500
Mortgage interest	3,500
Property taxes	900
Repairs & maintenance	650
Utilities	950
Depreciation	8,500

During the year, Natalie rented out the condo for 75 days, receiving $10,000 of gross income. She personally used the condo for 35 days during her vacation.

LO 14-5

61. Assume Natalie uses the IRS method of allocating expenses to rental use of the property.

a) What is the total amount of *for* AGI (rental) deductions Natalie may deduct in the current year related to the condo?

b) What is the total amount of itemized deductions Natalie may deduct in the current year related to the condo?

c) If Natalie's basis in the condo at the beginning of the year was $150,000, what is her basis in the condo at the end of the year?

d) Assume that gross rental revenue was $2,000 (rather than $10,000). What amount of *for* AGI deductions may Natalie deduct in the current year related to the condo?

e) Using the original facts, complete Natalie's Form 1040, Schedule E, for this property. Also, partially complete Natalie's 1040, Schedule A, to include her *from* AGI deductions related to the condo.

62. Assume Natalie uses the *Tax Court* method of allocating expenses to rental use of the property. LO 14-5

a) What is the total amount of *for* AGI (rental) deductions Natalie may deduct in the current year related to the condo?

b) What is the total amount of itemized deductions Natalie may deduct in the current year related to the condo?

c) If Natalie's basis in the condo at the beginning of the year was $150,000, what is her basis in the condo at the end of the year?

d) Assume that gross rental revenue was $2,000 (rather than $10,000). What amount of *for* AGI deductions may Natalie deduct in the current year related to the condo?

Use the following facts to answer problems 63, 64, and 65.

Alexa owns a condominium near Cocoa Beach in Florida. This year, she incurs the following expenses in connection with her condo:

Insurance	$2,000
Mortgage interest	6,500
Property taxes	2,000
Repairs & maintenance	1,400
Utilities	2,500
Depreciation	14,500

During the year, Alexa rented out the condo for 100 days. She did not use the condo at all for personal purposes during the year. Alexa's AGI from all sources other than the rental property is $200,000. Unless otherwise specified, Alexa has no sources of passive income.

63. Assume Alexa receives $30,000 in gross rental receipts. LO 14-5

a) What effect do the expenses associated with the property have on her AGI?

b) What effect do the expenses associated with the property have on her itemized deductions?

64. Assuming Alexa receives $20,000 in gross rental receipts, answer the following questions: LO 14-5

a) What effect does the rental activity have on her AGI for the year?

b) Assuming that Alexa's AGI from other sources is $90,000, what effect does the rental activity have on Alexa's AGI? Alexa makes all decisions with respect to the property.

c) Assuming that Alexa's AGI from other sources is $120,000, what effect does the rental activity have on Alexa's AGI? Alexa makes all decisions with respect to the property.

d) Assume that Alexa's AGI from other sources is $200,000. This consists of $150,000 salary, $10,000 of dividends, and $25,000 of long-term capital gain, and net rental income from another rental property in the amount of $15,000. What effect does the Cocoa Beach Condo rental activity have on Alexa's AGI?

65. Assume that in addition to renting the condo for 100 days, Alexa uses the condo for eight days of personal use. Also assume that Alexa receives $30,000 of gross rental receipts. Answer the following questions:
   a) What is the total amount of *for* AGI deductions relating to the condo that Alexa may deduct in the current year? Assume she uses the IRS method of allocating expenses between rental and personal days.
   b) What is the total amount of *from* AGI deductions relating to the condo that Alexa may deduct in the current year? Assume she uses the IRS method of allocating expenses between rental and personal days.
   c) Would Alexa be better or worse off after taxes in the current year if she uses the Tax Court method of allocating expenses?

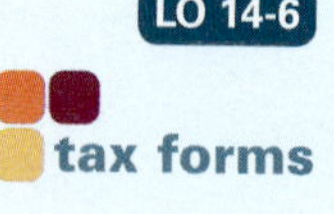

66. Brooke owns a sole proprietorship in which she works as a management consultant. She maintains an office in her home where she meets with clients, prepares bills, and performs other work-related tasks. The home office is 300 square feet and the entire house is 4,500 square feet. Brooke incurred the following home-related expenses during the year. Unless indicated otherwise, assume Brooke uses the actual expense method to compute home office expenses.

Real property taxes	$ 3,600
Interest on home mortgage	14,000
Operating expenses of home	5,000
Depreciation	12,000
Repairs to home theater room	1,000

   a) What amount of each of these expenses is allocated to the home office?
   b) What are the total amounts of tier 1, tier 2, and tier 3 expenses, respectively, allocated to the home office?
   c) If Brooke reported $2,000 of Schedule C net income before the home office expense deduction, what is the amount of her home office expense deduction and what home office expenses, if any, would she carry over to next year?
   d) Assuming Brooke reported $2,000 of Schedule C income before the home office expense deduction, complete Form 8829 for Brooke's home office expense deduction. Also assume the value of the home is $500,000 and the adjusted basis of the home (exclusive of land) is $468,019.
   e) Assume that Brooke uses the simplified method for computing home office expenses. If Brooke reported $2,000 of Schedule C net income before the home office expense deduction, what is the amount of her home office expense deduction and what home office expenses, if any, would she carry over to next year?

Use the following facts to answer problems 67 and 68.

Rita owns a sole proprietorship in which she works as a management consultant. She maintains an office in her home (500 square feet) where she meets with clients, prepares bills, and performs other work-related tasks. Her business expenses, other than home office expenses, total $5,600. The following home-related expenses have been allocated to her home office under the actual expense method for calculating home office expenses.

Real property taxes	$1,600
Interest on home mortgage	5,100
Operating expenses of home	800
Depreciation	1,600

Also, assume that not counting the sole proprietorship, Rita's AGI is $60,000.

67. Assume Rita's consulting business generated $15,000 in gross income. LO 14-6 planning
   a) What is Rita's home office deduction for the current year?
   b) What would Rita's home office deduction be if her business generated $10,000 of gross income instead of $15,000? (Answer for both the actual expense method and the simplified method.)
   c) Given the original facts, what is Rita's AGI for the year?
   d) Given the original facts, what types and amounts of expenses will she carry over to next year?

68. Assume Rita's consulting business generated $13,000 in gross income for the current year. Further, assume Rita uses the actual expense method for computing her home office expense deduction. LO 14-6
   a) What is Rita's home office deduction for the current year?
   b) What is Rita's AGI for the year?
   c) Assume the original facts, except that Rita is an employee and not self-employed. (She uses the home office for the convenience of her employer.) Consequently, she does not receive any gross income from the (sole proprietorship) business and she does not incur any business expenses unrelated to the home office. Finally, her AGI is $60,000 consisting of salary from her work as an employee. What effect do her home office expenses have on her itemized deductions?
   d) Assuming the original facts, what types and amounts of expenses will she carry over to next year?

69. Alisha, who is single, owns a sole proprietorship in which she works as a management consultant. She maintains an office in her home where she meets with clients, prepares bills, and performs other work-related tasks. She purchased the home at the beginning of year 1 for $400,000. Since she purchased the home and moved into it she has been able to deduct $10,000 of depreciation expenses to offset her consulting income. At the end of year 3, Alisha sold the home for $500,000. What is the amount of taxes Alisha will be required to pay on the gain from the sale of the home? Alisha's ordinary marginal tax rate is 30 percent. LO 14-2 LO 14-6

COMPREHENSIVE PROBLEMS

All applicable problems are available with McGraw-Hill's *Connect® Accounting*.

70. Derek and Meagan Jacoby recently graduated from State University and Derek accepted a job in business consulting while Meagan accepted a job in computer programming. Meagan inherited $75,000 from her grandfather who recently passed away. The couple is debating whether they should buy or rent a home. They located a rental home that meets their needs. The monthly rent is $2,250. They also found a three-bedroom home that would cost $475,000 to purchase. The Jacobys could use Meagan's inheritance for a down payment on the home. Thus, they would need to borrow $400,000 to acquire the home. They have the option of paying two discount points to receive a fixed interest rate of 4.5 percent on the loan or paying no points and receiving a fixed interest rate of 5.75 percent for a 30-year fixed loan. planning

    Though anything could happen, the couple expects to live in the home for no more than five years before relocating to a different region of the country. Derek and Meagan don't have any school-related debt, so they will save the $75,000 if they don't purchase a home. Also, consider the following information:

- The couple's marginal tax rate is 25 percent.
- Regardless of whether they buy or rent, the couple will itemize their deductions.

- If they buy, the Jacobys would purchase and move into the home on January 1, 2015.
- If they buy the home, the property taxes for the year are $3,600.
- Disregard loan-related fees not mentioned above.
- If the couple does not buy a home, they will put their money into their savings account where they earn 5 percent annual interest.
- Assume that all unstated costs are equal between the buy and rent option.

Required:

Help the Jacobys with their decisions by answering the following questions:

a) If the Jacobys decide to rent the home, what is their after-tax cost of the rental for the first year (include income from the savings account in your analysis)?

b) What is the approximate break-even point in years (or months) for paying the points to receive a reduced interest rate (to simplify this computation, assume the Jacobys will make interest-only payments, and ignore the time value of money)?

c) What is the after-tax cost (in interest and property taxes) of living in the home for 2015? Assume that the Jacobys' interest rate is 5.75 percent, they do not pay discount points, they make interest-only payments for the first year, and the value of the home does not change during the year.

d) Assume that on March 1, 2015, the Jacobys sold their home for $525,000, so that Derek and Meagan could accept job opportunities in a different state. The Jacobys used the sale proceeds to (1) pay off the $400,000 principal of the mortgage, (2) pay a $10,000 commission to their real estate broker, and (3) make a down payment on a new home in the different state. However, the new home cost only $300,000. What gain or loss do the Jacobys realize and recognize on the sale of their home and what amount of taxes must they pay on the gain, if any (assume they make interest only payments on the loan)?

e) Assume the same facts as in part (d), except that the Jacobys sell their home for $450,000 and they pay a $7,500 commission. What effect does the sale have on their 2015 income tax liability? Recall that the Jacobys are subject to an ordinary marginal tax rate of 25 percent and assume that they do not have any other transactions involving capital assets in 2015.

71. James and Kate Sawyer were married on New Year's Eve of 2014. Before their marriage, Kate lived in New York and worked as a hair stylist for one of the city's top salons. James lives in Atlanta where he works for a public accounting firm earning an annual salary of $100,000. After their marriage, Kate left her job in New York and moved into the couple's newly purchased 3,200-square-foot home in Atlanta. Kate incurred $2,200 of qualified moving expenses. The couple purchased the home on January 3, 2015, by paying $100,000 down and obtaining a $240,000 mortgage for the remainder. The interest rate on this loan was 7 percent and the Sawyers made interest-only payments on the loan through June 30, 2015 (assume they paid exactly one-half of a year's worth of interest on this loan by June 30). On July 1, 2015, because the value of their home had increased to $400,000, the Sawyers were in need of cash, and interest rates had dropped, the Sawyers refinanced their home loan. On the refinancing, they borrowed $370,000 at 6 percent interest. They made interest-only payments on the home loan through the end of the year and they spent $20,000 of the loan proceeds improving their home (assume they paid exactly one-half of a year's worth of interest on this loan by year end).

Kate wanted to try her hand at making it on her own in business, and with James's help, she started Kate's Beauty Cuts LLC. She set up shop in a 384-square-foot corner room of the couple's home and began to get it ready for business. The room conveniently had a door to the outside providing customers direct access to the shop. Kate paid $2,100 to have the carpet replaced with a tile floor. She also paid $1,200 to have the room painted with vibrant colors, and $650 to have the room rewired for appropriate lighting. Kate ran an ad in the local newspaper and officially opened her shop on January 24, 2015. By the end of the year, Kate's Beauty Cuts LLC generated $40,000 of *net* income before considering the home office deduction. The Sawyers incurred the following home-related expenditures during 2015:

- $4,200 of real property taxes.
- $2,000 for homeowner's insurance.
- $2,400 for electricity.
- $1,500 for gas and other utilities.

They determined depreciation expense for their entire house was $8,364.

Also, on March 2, Kate was able to finally sell her one-bedroom Manhattan condominium for $478,000. She purchased the condo, which she had lived in for six years prior to her marriage, for $205,000.

Kate owns a vacation home in Myrtle Beach, South Carolina. She purchased the home several years ago, largely as an investment opportunity. To help cover the expenses of maintaining the home, James and Kate decided to rent the home out. They rented the home for a total of 106 days at fair market value (this included eight days that they rented the home to James's brother Jack). In addition to the 106 days, Kate allowed a good friend and customer, Clair, to stay in the home for half-price for two days. James and Kate stayed in the home for six days for a romantic getaway and another three days in order to do some repair and maintenance work on the home. The rental revenues from the home in 2015 were $18,400. The Sawyers incurred the following expenses associated with the home.

- $9,100 of interest expense.
- $3,400 of real property taxes.
- $1,900 for homeowner's insurance.
- $1,200 for electricity.
- $1,600 for gas, other utilities, and landscaping.
- $5,200 for depreciation.

Required:

Determine the Sawyer's taxable income for 2015. Disregard self-employment taxes for Kate. Assume the couple paid $4,400 in state income taxes and files a joint return. The Sawyers would like to use the method for determining deductible home office expenses and the method for allocating expenses to the rental that minimize their overall taxable income for the year.

Appendix A

Tax Forms

All tax forms can be obtained from the IRS website: www.irs.gov.

Form **1040** Department of the Treasury—Internal Revenue Service (99)
U.S. Individual Income Tax Return **2014** OMB No. 1545-0074 IRS Use Only—Do not write or staple in this space.

For the year Jan. 1–Dec. 31, 2014, or other tax year beginning , 2014, ending , 20 See separate instructions.

Your first name and initial	Last name		Your social security number
If a joint return, spouse's first name and initial	Last name		Spouse's social security number
Home address (number and street). If you have a P.O. box, see instructions.		Apt. no.	▲ Make sure the SSN(s) above and on line 6c are correct.
City, town or post office, state, and ZIP code. If you have a foreign address, also complete spaces below (see instructions).			**Presidential Election Campaign** Check here if you, or your spouse if filing jointly, want $3 to go to this fund. Checking a box below will not change your tax or refund. ☐ You ☐ Spouse
Foreign country name	Foreign province/state/county	Foreign postal code	

Filing Status

Check only one box.

1 ☐ Single
2 ☐ Married filing jointly (even if only one had income)
3 ☐ Married filing separately. Enter spouse's SSN above and full name here. ▶
4 ☐ Head of household (with qualifying person). (See instructions.) If the qualifying person is a child but not your dependent, enter this child's name here. ▶
5 ☐ Qualifying widow(er) with dependent child

Exemptions

6a ☐ **Yourself.** If someone can claim you as a dependent, **do not** check box 6a . . . . .
b ☐ **Spouse** . . . .

Boxes checked on 6a and 6b

c **Dependents:** (1) First name Last name	(2) Dependent's social security number	(3) Dependent's relationship to you	(4) ✓ if child under age 17 qualifying for child tax credit (see instructions)
			☐
			☐
			☐
			☐

If more than four dependents, see instructions and check here ▶ ☐

No. of children on 6c who:
• lived with you
• did not live with you due to divorce or separation (see instructions)

Dependents on 6c not entered above

d Total number of exemptions claimed . . . . Add numbers on lines above ▶

Income

Attach Form(s) W-2 here. Also attach Forms W-2G and 1099-R if tax was withheld.

If you did not get a W-2, see instructions.

7	Wages, salaries, tips, etc. Attach Form(s) W-2		7
8a	**Taxable** interest. Attach Schedule B if required		8a
b	**Tax-exempt** interest. **Do not** include on line 8a	8b	
9a	Ordinary dividends. Attach Schedule B if required		9a
b	Qualified dividends	9b	
10	Taxable refunds, credits, or offsets of state and local income taxes		10
11	Alimony received		11
12	Business income or (loss). Attach Schedule C or C-EZ		12
13	Capital gain or (loss). Attach Schedule D if required. If not required, check here ▶ ☐		13
14	Other gains or (losses). Attach Form 4797		14
15a	IRA distributions 15a	b Taxable amount	15b
16a	Pensions and annuities 16a	b Taxable amount	16b
17	Rental real estate, royalties, partnerships, S corporations, trusts, etc. Attach Schedule E		17
18	Farm income or (loss). Attach Schedule F		18
19	Unemployment compensation		19
20a	Social security benefits 20a	b Taxable amount	20b
21	Other income. List type and amount		21
22	Combine the amounts in the far right column for lines 7 through 21. This is your **total income** ▶		22

Adjusted Gross Income

23	Educator expenses	23	
24	Certain business expenses of reservists, performing artists, and fee-basis government officials. Attach Form 2106 or 2106-EZ	24	
25	Health savings account deduction. Attach Form 8889	25	
26	Moving expenses. Attach Form 3903	26	
27	Deductible part of self-employment tax. Attach Schedule SE	27	
28	Self-employed SEP, SIMPLE, and qualified plans	28	
29	Self-employed health insurance deduction	29	
30	Penalty on early withdrawal of savings	30	
31a	Alimony paid **b** Recipient's SSN ▶	31a	
32	IRA deduction	32	
33	Student loan interest deduction	33	
34	Tuition and fees. Attach Form 8917	34	
35	Domestic production activities deduction. Attach Form 8903	35	
36	Add lines 23 through 35		36
37	Subtract line 36 from line 22. This is your **adjusted gross income** ▶		37

For Disclosure, Privacy Act, and Paperwork Reduction Act Notice, see separate instructions. Cat. No. 11320B Form **1040** (2014)

Form 1040 (2014) Page 2

Tax and Credits	38	Amount from line 37 (adjusted gross income)			38
	39a	Check if: ☐ **You** were born before January 2, 1950, ☐ Blind. ☐ **Spouse** was born before January 2, 1950, ☐ Blind. } **Total boxes checked ▶ 39a** ☐			
	b	If your spouse itemizes on a separate return or you were a dual-status alien, check here▶ 39b☐			
Standard Deduction for— • People who check any box on line 39a or 39b **or** who can be claimed as a dependent, see instructions. • All others: Single or Married filing separately, $6,200 Married filing jointly or Qualifying widow(er), $12,400 Head of household, $9,100	40	**Itemized deductions** (from Schedule A) **or** your **standard deduction** (see left margin)			40
	41	Subtract line 40 from line 38			41
	42	**Exemptions.** If line 38 is $152,525 or less, multiply $3,950 by the number on line 6d. Otherwise, see instructions			42
	43	**Taxable income.** Subtract line 42 from line 41. If line 42 is more than line 41, enter -0-			43
	44	**Tax** (see instructions). Check if any from: **a** ☐ Form(s) 8814 **b** ☐ Form 4972 **c** ☐			44
	45	**Alternative minimum tax** (see instructions). Attach Form 6251			45
	46	Excess advance premium tax credit repayment. Attach Form 8962			46
	47	Add lines 44, 45, and 46 ▶			47
	48	Foreign tax credit. Attach Form 1116 if required	48		
	49	Credit for child and dependent care expenses. Attach Form 2441	49		
	50	Education credits from Form 8863, line 19	50		
	51	Retirement savings contributions credit. Attach Form 8880	51		
	52	Child tax credit. Attach Schedule 8812, if required	52		
	53	Residential energy credits. Attach Form 5695	53		
	54	Other credits from Form: **a** ☐ 3800 **b** ☐ 8801 **c** ☐	54		
	55	Add lines 48 through 54. These are your **total credits**			55
	56	Subtract line 55 from line 47. If line 55 is more than line 47, enter -0- ▶			56
Other Taxes	57	Self-employment tax. Attach Schedule SE			57
	58	Unreported social security and Medicare tax from Form: **a** ☐ 4137 **b** ☐ 8919			58
	59	Additional tax on IRAs, other qualified retirement plans, etc. Attach Form 5329 if required			59
	60a	Household employment taxes from Schedule H			60a
	b	First-time homebuyer credit repayment. Attach Form 5405 if required			60b
	61	Health care: individual responsibility (see instructions) Full-year coverage ☐			61
	62	Taxes from: **a** ☐ Form 8959 **b** ☐ Form 8960 **c** ☐ Instructions; enter code(s)			62
	63	Add lines 56 through 62. This is your **total tax** ▶			63
Payments	64	Federal income tax withheld from Forms W-2 and 1099	64		
If you have a qualifying child, attach Schedule EIC.	65	2014 estimated tax payments and amount applied from 2013 return	65		
	66a	**Earned income credit (EIC)**	66a		
	b	Nontaxable combat pay election 66b			
	67	Additional child tax credit. Attach Schedule 8812	67		
	68	American opportunity credit from Form 8863, line 8	68		
	69	Net premium tax credit. Attach Form 8962	69		
	70	Amount paid with request for extension to file	70		
	71	Excess social security and tier 1 RRTA tax withheld	71		
	72	Credit for federal tax on fuels. Attach Form 4136	72		
	73	Credits from Form: **a** ☐ 2439 **b** ☐ Reserved **c** ☐ Reserved **d** ☐	73		
	74	Add lines 64, 65, 66a, and 67 through 73. These are your **total payments** ▶			74
Refund	75	If line 74 is more than line 63, subtract line 63 from line 74. This is the amount you **overpaid**			75
	76a	Amount of line 75 you want **refunded to you.** If Form 8888 is attached, check here ▶☐			76a
Direct deposit? See instructions.	▶ b	Routing number ▶ c Type: ☐ Checking ☐ Savings			
	▶ d	Account number			
	77	Amount of line 75 you want **applied to your 2015 estimated tax** ▶	77		
Amount You Owe	78	**Amount you owe.** Subtract line 74 from line 63. For details on how to pay, see instructions ▶			78
	79	Estimated tax penalty (see instructions)	79		

Third Party Designee

Do you want to allow another person to discuss this return with the IRS (see instructions)? ☐ **Yes.** Complete below. ☐ **No**

Designee's name ▶ Phone no. ▶ Personal identification number (PIN) ▶

Sign Here

Joint return? See instructions. Keep a copy for your records.

Under penalties of perjury, I declare that I have examined this return and accompanying schedules and statements, and to the best of my knowledge and belief, they are true, correct, and complete. Declaration of preparer (other than taxpayer) is based on all information of which preparer has any knowledge.

Your signature	Date	Your occupation	Daytime phone number
Spouse's signature. If a joint return, **both** must sign.	Date	Spouse's occupation	If the IRS sent you an Identity Protection PIN, enter it here (see inst.)

Paid Preparer Use Only

Print/Type preparer's name	Preparer's signature	Date	Check ☐ if self-employed	PTIN
Firm's name ▶			Firm's EIN ▶	
Firm's address ▶			Phone no.	

SCHEDULE A (Form 1040)

Department of the Treasury Internal Revenue Service (99)

Itemized Deductions

▶ Information about Schedule A and its separate instructions is at *www.irs.gov/schedulea*.

▶ Attach to Form 1040.

OMB No. 1545-0074

2014

Attachment Sequence No. **07**

Name(s) shown on Form 1040 | **Your social security number**

Medical and Dental Expenses

Caution. Do not include expenses reimbursed or paid by others.

1 Medical and dental expenses (see instructions) . . . . . . | 1

2 Enter amount from Form 1040, line 38 | 2

3 Multiply line 2 by 10% (.10). But if either you or your spouse was born before January 2, 1950, multiply line 2 by 7.5% (.075) instead | 3

4 Subtract line 3 from line 1. If line 3 is more than line 1, enter -0- . . . . | 4

Taxes You Paid

5 State and local **(check only one box):**
- a ☐ Income taxes, **or**
- b ☐ General sales taxes } . . . . | 5

6 Real estate taxes (see instructions) . . . . | 6

7 Personal property taxes . . . . | 7

8 Other taxes. List type and amount ▶ ________ | 8

9 Add lines 5 through 8 . . . . | 9

Interest You Paid

Note. Your mortgage interest deduction may be limited (see instructions).

10 Home mortgage interest and points reported to you on Form 1098 | 10

11 Home mortgage interest not reported to you on Form 1098. If paid to the person from whom you bought the home, see instructions and show that person's name, identifying no., and address ▶ ________ | 11

12 Points not reported to you on Form 1098. See instructions for special rules . . . . | 12

13 Mortgage insurance premiums (see instructions) . . . . . . | 13

14 Investment interest. Attach Form 4952 if required. (See instructions.) | 14

15 Add lines 10 through 14 . . . . | 15

Gifts to Charity

If you made a gift and got a benefit for it, see instructions.

16 Gifts by cash or check. If you made any gift of $250 or more, see instructions . . . . | 16

17 Other than by cash or check. If any gift of $250 or more, see instructions. You **must** attach Form 8283 if over $500 . . . | 17

18 Carryover from prior year . . . . | 18

19 Add lines 16 through 18 . . . . | 19

Casualty and Theft Losses

20 Casualty or theft loss(es). Attach Form 4684. (See instructions.) . . . . | 20

Job Expenses and Certain Miscellaneous Deductions

21 Unreimbursed employee expenses—job travel, union dues, job education, etc. Attach Form 2106 or 2106-EZ if required. (See instructions.) ▶ ________ | 21

22 Tax preparation fees . . . . | 22

23 Other expenses—investment, safe deposit box, etc. List type and amount ▶ ________ | 23

24 Add lines 21 through 23 . . . . | 24

25 Enter amount from Form 1040, line 38 | 25

26 Multiply line 25 by 2% (.02) . . . . | 26

27 Subtract line 26 from line 24. If line 26 is more than line 24, enter -0- . . . . | 27

Other Miscellaneous Deductions

28 Other—from list in instructions. List type and amount ▶ ________ | 28

Total Itemized Deductions

29 Is Form 1040, line 38, over $152,525?
- ☐ **No.** Your deduction is not limited. Add the amounts in the far right column for lines 4 through 28. Also, enter this amount on Form 1040, line 40.
- ☐ **Yes.** Your deduction may be limited. See the Itemized Deductions Worksheet in the instructions to figure the amount to enter. } . . | 29

30 If you elect to itemize deductions even though they are less than your standard deduction, check here . . . . ▶ ☐

For Paperwork Reduction Act Notice, see Form 1040 instructions. Cat. No. 17145C **Schedule A (Form 1040) 2014**

SCHEDULE B
(Form 1040A or 1040)

Department of the Treasury
Internal Revenue Service (99)

Interest and Ordinary Dividends

▶ Attach to Form 1040A or 1040.
▶ Information about Schedule B and its instructions is at *www.irs.gov/scheduleb*.

OMB No. 1545-0074
2014
Attachment Sequence No. 08

Name(s) shown on return | Your social security number

Part I Interest

(See instructions on back and the instructions for Form 1040A, or Form 1040, line 8a.)

Note. If you received a Form 1099-INT, Form 1099-OID, or substitute statement from a brokerage firm, list the firm's name as the payer and enter the total interest shown on that form.

			Amount
1	List name of payer. If any interest is from a seller-financed mortgage and the buyer used the property as a personal residence, see instructions on back and list this interest first. Also, show that buyer's social security number and address ▶	1	
2	Add the amounts on line 1	2	
3	Excludable interest on series EE and I U.S. savings bonds issued after 1989. Attach Form 8815	3	
4	Subtract line 3 from line 2. Enter the result here and on Form 1040A, or Form 1040, line 8a ▶	4	

Note. If line 4 is over $1,500, you must complete Part III.

Part II Ordinary Dividends

(See instructions on back and the instructions for Form 1040A, or Form 1040, line 9a.)

Note. If you received a Form 1099-DIV or substitute statement from a brokerage firm, list the firm's name as the payer and enter the ordinary dividends shown on that form.

			Amount
5	List name of payer ▶	5	
6	Add the amounts on line 5. Enter the total here and on Form 1040A, or Form 1040, line 9a ▶	6	

Note. If line 6 is over $1,500, you must complete Part III.

Part III Foreign Accounts and Trusts

(See instructions on back.)

You must complete this part if you **(a)** had over $1,500 of taxable interest or ordinary dividends; **(b)** had a foreign account; or **(c)** received a distribution from, or were a grantor of, or a transferor to, a foreign trust.

		Yes	No
7a	At any time during 2014, did you have a financial interest in or signature authority over a financial account (such as a bank account, securities account, or brokerage account) located in a foreign country? See instructions		
	If "Yes," are you required to file FinCEN Form 114, Report of Foreign Bank and Financial Accounts (FBAR), to report that financial interest or signature authority? See FinCEN Form 114 and its instructions for filing requirements and exceptions to those requirements		
b	If you are required to file FinCEN Form 114, enter the name of the foreign country where the financial account is located ▶		
8	During 2014, did you receive a distribution from, or were you the grantor of, or transferor to, a foreign trust? If "Yes," you may have to file Form 3520. See instructions on back		

For Paperwork Reduction Act Notice, see your tax return instructions. Cat. No. 17146N **Schedule B (Form 1040A or 1040) 2014**

SCHEDULE C (Form 1040)

Department of the Treasury Internal Revenue Service (99)

Profit or Loss From Business

(Sole Proprietorship)

▶ Information about Schedule C and its separate instructions is at *www.irs.gov/schedulec*.

▶ Attach to Form 1040, 1040NR, or 1041; partnerships generally must file Form 1065.

OMB No. 1545-0074

2014

Attachment Sequence No. **09**

Name of proprietor | **Social security number (SSN)**

A Principal business or profession, including product or service (see instructions) | **B Enter code from instructions** ▶

C Business name. If no separate business name, leave blank. | **D Employer ID number (EIN),** (see instr.)

E Business address (including suite or room no.) ▶

City, town or post office, state, and ZIP code

F Accounting method: **(1)** ☐ Cash **(2)** ☐ Accrual **(3)** ☐ Other (specify) ▶

G Did you "materially participate" in the operation of this business during 2014? If "No," see instructions for limit on losses . ☐ Yes ☐ No

H If you started or acquired this business during 2014, check here . . . ▶ ☐

I Did you make any payments in 2014 that would require you to file Form(s) 1099? (see instructions) . . . ☐ Yes ☐ No

J If "Yes," did you or will you file required Forms 1099? . . . ☐ Yes ☐ No

Part I Income

1	Gross receipts or sales. See instructions for line 1 and check the box if this income was reported to you on Form W-2 and the "Statutory employee" box on that form was checked . . . ▶ ☐	1	
2	Returns and allowances . . .	2	
3	Subtract line 2 from line 1 . . .	3	
4	Cost of goods sold (from line 42) . . .	4	
5	**Gross profit.** Subtract line 4 from line 3 . . .	5	
6	Other income, including federal and state gasoline or fuel tax credit or refund (see instructions) . . .	6	
7	**Gross income.** Add lines 5 and 6 . . . ▶	7	

Part II Expenses. Enter expenses for business use of your home **only** on line 30.

8	Advertising . . .	8		18	Office expense (see instructions)	18	
9	Car and truck expenses (see instructions). . .	9		19	Pension and profit-sharing plans .	19	
10	Commissions and fees .	10		20	Rent or lease (see instructions):		
11	Contract labor (see instructions)	11		a	Vehicles, machinery, and equipment	20a	
12	Depletion . . .	12		b	Other business property . . .	20b	
13	Depreciation and section 179 expense deduction (not included in Part III) (see instructions) . . .	13		21	Repairs and maintenance . . .	21	
				22	Supplies (not included in Part III) .	22	
				23	Taxes and licenses . . .	23	
14	Employee benefit programs (other than on line 19) . .	14		24	Travel, meals, and entertainment:		
				a	Travel . . .	24a	
15	Insurance (other than health)	15		b	Deductible meals and entertainment (see instructions) .	24b	
16	Interest:			25	Utilities . . .	25	
a	Mortgage (paid to banks, etc.)	16a		26	Wages (less employment credits) .	26	
b	Other . . .	16b		27a	Other expenses (from line 48) . .	27a	
17	Legal and professional services	17		b	**Reserved for future use** . . .	27b	

28	**Total expenses** before expenses for business use of home. Add lines 8 through 27a . . . ▶	28	
29	Tentative profit or (loss). Subtract line 28 from line 7 . . .	29	
30	Expenses for business use of your home. Do not report these expenses elsewhere. Attach Form 8829 unless using the simplified method (see instructions). **Simplified method filers only:** enter the total square footage of: (a) your home: ______ and (b) the part of your home used for business: ______ . Use the Simplified Method Worksheet in the instructions to figure the amount to enter on line 30 . . .	30	
31	**Net profit or (loss).** Subtract line 30 from line 29. • If a profit, enter on both **Form 1040, line 12** (or **Form 1040NR, line 13**) and on **Schedule SE, line 2.** (If you checked the box on line 1, see instructions). Estates and trusts, enter on **Form 1041, line 3.** • If a loss, you **must** go to line 32.	31	

32 If you have a loss, check the box that describes your investment in this activity (see instructions).

- If you checked 32a, enter the loss on both **Form 1040, line 12,** (or **Form 1040NR, line 13**) and on **Schedule SE, line 2.** (If you checked the box on line 1, see the line 31 instructions). Estates and trusts, enter on **Form 1041, line 3.**
- If you checked 32b, you **must** attach **Form 6198.** Your loss may be limited.

32a ☐ All investment is at risk.
32b ☐ Some investment is not at risk.

For Paperwork Reduction Act Notice, see the separate instructions. Cat. No. 11334P **Schedule C (Form 1040) 2014**

Schedule C (Form 1040) 2014 Page **2**

Part III Cost of Goods Sold (see instructions)

33 Method(s) used to value closing inventory: **a** ☐ Cost **b** ☐ Lower of cost or market **c** ☐ Other (attach explanation)

34 Was there any change in determining quantities, costs, or valuations between opening and closing inventory? If "Yes," attach explanation . . . ☐ **Yes** ☐ **No**

35	Inventory at beginning of year. If different from last year's closing inventory, attach explanation . . .	35	
36	Purchases less cost of items withdrawn for personal use . . .	36	
37	Cost of labor. Do not include any amounts paid to yourself . . .	37	
38	Materials and supplies . . .	38	
39	Other costs . . .	39	
40	Add lines 35 through 39 . . .	40	
41	Inventory at end of year . . .	41	
42	**Cost of goods sold.** Subtract line 41 from line 40. Enter the result here and on line 4 . . .	42	

Part IV Information on Your Vehicle. Complete this part **only** if you are claiming car or truck expenses on line 9 and are not required to file Form 4562 for this business. See the instructions for line 13 to find out if you must file Form 4562.

43 When did you place your vehicle in service for business purposes? (month, day, year) ▶ ____ / ____ / ____

44 Of the total number of miles you drove your vehicle during 2014, enter the number of miles you used your vehicle for:

a Business ____________ **b** Commuting (see instructions) ____________ **c** Other ____________

45 Was your vehicle available for personal use during off-duty hours? . . . ☐ **Yes** ☐ **No**

46 Do you (or your spouse) have another vehicle available for personal use?. . . ☐ **Yes** ☐ **No**

47a Do you have evidence to support your deduction? . . . ☐ **Yes** ☐ **No**

b If "Yes," is the evidence written? . . . ☐ **Yes** ☐ **No**

Part V Other Expenses. List below business expenses not included on lines 8–26 or line 30.

48 **Total other expenses.** Enter here and on line 27a . . . 48	

SCHEDULE D
(Form 1040)

Department of the Treasury
Internal Revenue Service (99)

Capital Gains and Losses

▶ Attach to Form 1040 or Form 1040NR.
▶ Information about Schedule D and its separate instructions is at *www.irs.gov/scheduled*.
▶ Use Form 8949 to list your transactions for lines 1b, 2, 3, 8b, 9, and 10.

OMB No. 1545-0074

2014

Attachment Sequence No. **12**

Name(s) shown on return

Your social security number

Part I Short-Term Capital Gains and Losses—Assets Held One Year or Less

See instructions for how to figure the amounts to enter on the lines below. This form may be easier to complete if you round off cents to whole dollars.	(d) Proceeds (sales price)	(e) Cost (or other basis)	(g) Adjustments to gain or loss from Form(s) 8949, Part I, line 2, column (g)	(h) Gain or (loss) Subtract column (e) from column (d) and combine the result with column (g)
1a Totals for all short-term transactions reported on Form 1099-B for which basis was reported to the IRS and for which you have no adjustments (see instructions). However, if you choose to report all these transactions on Form 8949, leave this line blank and go to line 1b .				
1b Totals for all transactions reported on Form(s) 8949 with **Box A** checked				
2 Totals for all transactions reported on Form(s) 8949 with **Box B** checked				
3 Totals for all transactions reported on Form(s) 8949 with **Box C** checked				

4 Short-term gain from Form 6252 and short-term gain or (loss) from Forms 4684, 6781, and 8824 .	4	
5 Net short-term gain or (loss) from partnerships, S corporations, estates, and trusts from Schedule(s) K-1	5	
6 Short-term capital loss carryover. Enter the amount, if any, from line 8 of your **Capital Loss Carryover Worksheet** in the instructions	6	( )
7 **Net short-term capital gain or (loss).** Combine lines 1a through 6 in column (h). If you have any long-term capital gains or losses, go to Part II below. Otherwise, go to Part III on the back	7	

Part II Long-Term Capital Gains and Losses—Assets Held More Than One Year

See instructions for how to figure the amounts to enter on the lines below. This form may be easier to complete if you round off cents to whole dollars.	(d) Proceeds (sales price)	(e) Cost (or other basis)	(g) Adjustments to gain or loss from Form(s) 8949, Part II, line 2, column (g)	(h) Gain or (loss) Subtract column (e) from column (d) and combine the result with column (g)
8a Totals for all long-term transactions reported on Form 1099-B for which basis was reported to the IRS and for which you have no adjustments (see instructions). However, if you choose to report all these transactions on Form 8949, leave this line blank and go to line 8b .				
8b Totals for all transactions reported on Form(s) 8949 with **Box D** checked				
9 Totals for all transactions reported on Form(s) 8949 with **Box E** checked				
10 Totals for all transactions reported on Form(s) 8949 with **Box F** checked.				

11 Gain from Form 4797, Part I; long-term gain from Forms 2439 and 6252; and long-term gain or (loss) from Forms 4684, 6781, and 8824	11	
12 Net long-term gain or (loss) from partnerships, S corporations, estates, and trusts from Schedule(s) K-1	12	
13 Capital gain distributions. See the instructions	13	
14 Long-term capital loss carryover. Enter the amount, if any, from line 13 of your **Capital Loss Carryover Worksheet** in the instructions	14	( )
15 **Net long-term capital gain or (loss).** Combine lines 8a through 14 in column (h). Then go to Part III on the back	15	

Part III **Summary**

16	Combine lines 7 and 15 and enter the result	**16**	
	• If line 16 is a **gain,** enter the amount from line 16 on Form 1040, line 13, or Form 1040NR, line 14. Then go to line 17 below. • If line 16 is a **loss,** skip lines 17 through 20 below. Then go to line 21. Also be sure to complete line 22. • If line 16 is **zero,** skip lines 17 through 21 below and enter -0- on Form 1040, line 13, or Form 1040NR, line 14. Then go to line 22.		
17	Are lines 15 and 16 **both** gains? ☐ **Yes.** Go to line 18. ☐ **No.** Skip lines 18 through 21, and go to line 22.		
18	Enter the amount, if any, from line 7 of the **28% Rate Gain Worksheet** in the instructions . . ▶	**18**	
19	Enter the amount, if any, from line 18 of the **Unrecaptured Section 1250 Gain Worksheet** in the instructions . . . . ▶	**19**	
20	Are lines 18 and 19 **both** zero or blank? ☐ **Yes.** Complete the **Qualified Dividends and Capital Gain Tax Worksheet** in the instructions for Form 1040, line 44 (or in the instructions for Form 1040NR, line 42). **Do not** complete lines 21 and 22 below. ☐ **No.** Complete the **Schedule D Tax Worksheet** in the instructions. **Do not** complete lines 21 and 22 below.		
21	If line 16 is a loss, enter here and on Form 1040, line 13, or Form 1040NR, line 14, the **smaller** of: • The loss on line 16 or • ($3,000), or if married filing separately, ($1,500) }	**21**	( )
	Note. When figuring which amount is smaller, treat both amounts as positive numbers.		
22	Do you have qualified dividends on Form 1040, line 9b, or Form 1040NR, line 10b? ☐ **Yes.** Complete the **Qualified Dividends and Capital Gain Tax Worksheet** in the instructions for Form 1040, line 44 (or in the instructions for Form 1040NR, line 42). ☐ **No.** Complete the rest of Form 1040 or Form 1040NR.		

Form **8949**

Department of the Treasury
Internal Revenue Service

Sales and Other Dispositions of Capital Assets

▶ Information about Form 8949 and its separate instructions is at *www.irs.gov/form8949*.
▶ File with your Schedule D to list your transactions for lines 1b, 2, 3, 8b, 9, and 10 of Schedule D.

OMB No. 1545-0074
2014
Attachment Sequence No. **12A**

Name(s) shown on return | **Social security number or taxpayer identification number**

Before you check Box A, B, or C below, see whether you received any Form(s) 1099-B or substitute statement(s) from your broker. A substitute statement will have the same information as Form 1099-B. Either may show your basis (usually your cost) even if your broker did not report it to the IRS. Brokers must report basis to the IRS for most stock you bought in 2011 or later (and for certain debt instruments you bought in 2014 or later).

Part I **Short-Term.** Transactions involving capital assets you held 1 year or less are short term. For long-term transactions, see page 2.

Note. You may aggregate all short-term transactions reported on Form(s) 1099-B showing basis was reported to the IRS and for which no adjustments or codes are required. Enter the total directly on Schedule D, line 1a; you are not required to report these transactions on Form 8949 (see instructions).

You *must* check Box A, B, *or* C below. Check only one box. If more than one box applies for your short-term transactions, complete a separate Form 8949, page 1, for each applicable box. If you have more short-term transactions than will fit on this page for one or more of the boxes, complete as many forms with the same box checked as you need.

☐ **(A)** Short-term transactions reported on Form(s) 1099-B showing basis was reported to the IRS (see **Note** above)
☐ **(B)** Short-term transactions reported on Form(s) 1099-B showing basis was **not** reported to the IRS
☐ **(C)** Short-term transactions not reported to you on Form 1099-B

1 (a) Description of property (Example: 100 sh. XYZ Co.)	(b) Date acquired (Mo., day, yr.)	(c) Date sold or disposed (Mo., day, yr.)	(d) Proceeds (sales price) (see instructions)	(e) Cost or other basis. See the **Note** below and see *Column (e)* in the separate instructions	**Adjustment, if any, to gain or loss.** If you enter an amount in column (g), enter a code in column (f). **See the separate instructions.** (f) Code(s) from instructions	(g) Amount of adjustment	(h) **Gain or (loss).** Subtract column (e) from column (d) and combine the result with column (g)
2 Totals. Add the amounts in columns (d), (e), (g), and (h) (subtract negative amounts). Enter each total here and include on your Schedule D, **line 1b** (if **Box A** above is checked), **line 2** (if **Box B** above is checked), or **line 3** (if **Box C** above is checked) ▶							

Note. If you checked Box A above but the basis reported to the IRS was incorrect, enter in column (e) the basis as reported to the IRS, and enter an adjustment in column (g) to correct the basis. See *Column (g)* in the separate instructions for how to figure the amount of the adjustment.

For Paperwork Reduction Act Notice, see your tax return instructions. Cat. No. 37768Z Form **8949** (2014)

Form 8949 (2014) Attachment Sequence No. **12A** Page **2**

Name(s) shown on return. Name and SSN or taxpayer identification no. not required if shown on other side	**Social security number or taxpayer identification number**

Before you check Box D, E, or F below, see whether you received any Form(s) 1099-B or substitute statement(s) from your broker. A substitute statement will have the same information as Form 1099-B. Either may show your basis (usually your cost) even if your broker did not report it to the IRS. Brokers must report basis to the IRS for most stock you bought in 2011 or later (and for certain debt instruments you bought in 2014 or later).

Part II **Long-Term.** Transactions involving capital assets you held more than 1 year are long term. For short-term transactions, see page 1.

Note. You may aggregate all long-term transactions reported on Form(s) 1099-B showing basis was reported to the IRS and for which no adjustments or codes are required. Enter the total directly on Schedule D, line 8a; you are not required to report these transactions on Form 8949 (see instructions).

You *must* check Box D, E, *or* F below. Check only one box. If more than one box applies for your long-term transactions, complete a separate Form 8949, page 2, for each applicable box. If you have more long-term transactions than will fit on this page for one or more of the boxes, complete as many forms with the same box checked as you need.

☐ **(D)** Long-term transactions reported on Form(s) 1099-B showing basis was reported to the IRS (see **Note** above)
☐ **(E)** Long-term transactions reported on Form(s) 1099-B showing basis was **not** reported to the IRS
☐ **(F)** Long-term transactions not reported to you on Form 1099-B

1 (a) Description of property (Example: 100 sh. XYZ Co.)	(b) Date acquired (Mo., day, yr.)	(c) Date sold or disposed (Mo., day, yr.)	(d) Proceeds (sales price) (see instructions)	(e) Cost or other basis. See the **Note** below and see *Column (e)* in the separate instructions	**Adjustment, if any, to gain or loss.** If you enter an amount in column (g), enter a code in column (f). **See the separate instructions.** (f) Code(s) from instructions	(g) Amount of adjustment	(h) **Gain or (loss).** Subtract column (e) from column (d) and combine the result with column (g)
2 Totals. Add the amounts in columns (d), (e), (g), and (h) (subtract negative amounts). Enter each total here and include on your Schedule D, **line 8b** (if **Box D** above is checked), **line 9** (if **Box E** above is checked), or **line 10** (if **Box F** above is checked) ▶							

Note. If you checked Box D above but the basis reported to the IRS was incorrect, enter in column (e) the basis as reported to the IRS, and enter an adjustment in column (g) to correct the basis. See *Column (g)* in the separate instructions for how to figure the amount of the adjustment.

SCHEDULE E (Form 1040)

Department of the Treasury
Internal Revenue Service (99)

Supplemental Income and Loss

(From rental real estate, royalties, partnerships, S corporations, estates, trusts, REMICs, etc.)

▶ Attach to Form 1040, 1040NR, or Form 1041.

▶ Information about Schedule E and its separate instructions is at *www.irs.gov/schedulee.*

OMB No. 1545-0074

2014

Attachment Sequence No. 13

Name(s) shown on return | Your social security number

Part I **Income or Loss From Rental Real Estate and Royalties** **Note.** If you are in the business of renting personal property, use **Schedule C** or **C-EZ** (see instructions). If you are an individual, report farm rental income or loss from **Form 4835** on page 2, line 40.

A Did you make any payments in 2014 that would require you to file Form(s) 1099? (see instructions) ☐ Yes ☐ No

B If "Yes," did you or will you file required Forms 1099? ☐ Yes ☐ No

1a	Physical address of each property (street, city, state, ZIP code)
A	
B	
C	

1b	Type of Property (from list below)	2 For each rental real estate property listed above, report the number of fair rental and personal use days. Check the **QJV** box only if you meet the requirements to file as a qualified joint venture. See instructions.		Fair Rental Days	Personal Use Days	QJV
A			A			☐
B			B			☐
C			C			☐

Type of Property:

1 Single Family Residence
2 Multi-Family Residence
3 Vacation/Short-Term Rental
4 Commercial
5 Land
6 Royalties
7 Self-Rental
8 Other (describe)

Income:	**Properties:**		A	B	C
3	Rents received	3			
4	Royalties received	4			
Expenses:					
5	Advertising	5			
6	Auto and travel (see instructions)	6			
7	Cleaning and maintenance	7			
8	Commissions.	8			
9	Insurance	9			
10	Legal and other professional fees	10			
11	Management fees	11			
12	Mortgage interest paid to banks, etc. (see instructions)	12			
13	Other interest.	13			
14	Repairs.	14			
15	Supplies	15			
16	Taxes	16			
17	Utilities.	17			
18	Depreciation expense or depletion	18			
19	Other (list) ▶	19			
20	Total expenses. Add lines 5 through 19	20			
21	Subtract line 20 from line 3 (rents) and/or 4 (royalties). If result is a (loss), see instructions to find out if you must file **Form 6198**	21			
22	Deductible rental real estate loss after limitation, if any, on **Form 8582** (see instructions)	22	( )	( )	( )

23a	Total of all amounts reported on line 3 for all rental properties	23a	
b	Total of all amounts reported on line 4 for all royalty properties	23b	
c	Total of all amounts reported on line 12 for all properties	23c	
d	Total of all amounts reported on line 18 for all properties	23d	
e	Total of all amounts reported on line 20 for all properties	23e	
24	**Income.** Add positive amounts shown on line 21. **Do not** include any losses	24	
25	**Losses.** Add royalty losses from line 21 and rental real estate losses from line 22. Enter total losses here	25	( )
26	**Total rental real estate and royalty income or (loss).** Combine lines 24 and 25. Enter the result here. If Parts II, III, IV, and line 40 on page 2 do not apply to you, also enter this amount on Form 1040, line 17, or Form 1040NR, line 18. Otherwise, include this amount in the total on line 41 on page 2	26	

For Paperwork Reduction Act Notice, see the separate instructions. Cat. No. 11344L **Schedule E (Form 1040) 2014**

Schedule E (Form 1040) 2014 Attachment Sequence No. 13 Page 2

Name(s) shown on return. Do not enter name and social security number if shown on other side. | Your social security number

Caution. The IRS compares amounts reported on your tax return with amounts shown on Schedule(s) K-1.

Part II Income or Loss From Partnerships and S Corporations

Note. If you report a loss from an at-risk activity for which **any** amount is **not** at risk, you **must** check the box in column **(e)** on line 28 and attach **Form 6198.** See instructions.

27 Are you reporting any loss not allowed in a prior year due to the at-risk, excess farm loss, or basis limitations, a prior year unallowed loss from a passive activity (if that loss was not reported on Form 8582), or unreimbursed partnership expenses? If you answered "Yes," see instructions before completing this section. ☐ **Yes** ☐ **No**

28	(a) Name	(b) Enter **P** for partnership; **S** for S corporation	(c) Check if foreign partnership	(d) Employer identification number	(e) Check if any amount is not at risk
A			☐		☐
B			☐		☐
C			☐		☐
D			☐		☐

	Passive Income and Loss		Nonpassive Income and Loss		
	(f) Passive loss allowed (attach **Form 8582** if required)	(g) Passive income from **Schedule K-1**	(h) Nonpassive loss from **Schedule K-1**	(i) Section 179 expense deduction from **Form 4562**	(j) Nonpassive income from **Schedule K-1**
A					
B					
C					
D					
29a Totals					
b Totals					

30 Add columns (g) and (j) of line 29a	30	
31 Add columns (f), (h), and (i) of line 29b	31	( )
32 **Total partnership and S corporation income or (loss).** Combine lines 30 and 31. Enter the result here and include in the total on line 41 below	32	

Part III Income or Loss From Estates and Trusts

33	(a) Name	(b) Employer identification number
A		
B		

	Passive Income and Loss		Nonpassive Income and Loss	
	(c) Passive deduction or loss allowed (attach **Form 8582** if required)	(d) Passive income from **Schedule K-1**	(e) Deduction or loss from **Schedule K-1**	(f) Other income from **Schedule K-1**
A				
B				
34a Totals				
b Totals				

35 Add columns (d) and (f) of line 34a	35	
36 Add columns (c) and (e) of line 34b	36	( )
37 **Total estate and trust income or (loss).** Combine lines 35 and 36. Enter the result here and include in the total on line 41 below	37	

Part IV Income or Loss From Real Estate Mortgage Investment Conduits (REMICs)—Residual Holder

38 (a) Name	(b) Employer identification number	(c) Excess inclusion from **Schedules Q,** line 2c (see instructions)	(d) Taxable income (net loss) from **Schedules Q,** line 1b	(e) Income from **Schedules Q,** line 3b

39 Combine columns (d) and (e) only. Enter the result here and include in the total on line 41 below	39	

Part V Summary

40 Net farm rental income or (loss) from **Form 4835**. Also, complete line 42 below	40	
41 **Total income or (loss).** Combine lines 26, 32, 37, 39, and 40. Enter the result here and on Form 1040, line 17, or Form 1040NR, line 18 ▶	41	

42 **Reconciliation of farming and fishing income.** Enter your **gross** farming and fishing income reported on Form 4835, line 7; Schedule K-1 (Form 1065), box 14, code B; Schedule K-1 (Form 1120S), box 17, code V; and Schedule K-1 (Form 1041), box 14, code F (see instructions)	42	
43 **Reconciliation for real estate professionals.** If you were a real estate professional (see instructions), enter the net income or (loss) you reported anywhere on Form 1040 or Form 1040NR from all rental real estate activities in which you materially participated under the passive activity loss rules	43	

Schedule E (Form 1040) 2014

SCHEDULE SE (Form 1040)

Department of the Treasury
Internal Revenue Service (99)

Self-Employment Tax

▶ **Information about Schedule SE and its separate instructions is at** ***www.irs.gov/schedulese.***

▶ **Attach to Form 1040 or Form 1040NR.**

OMB No. 1545-0074

2014

Attachment Sequence No. **17**

Name of person with **self-employment** income (as shown on Form 1040 or Form 1040NR) | Social security number of person with **self-employment** income ▶

Before you begin: To determine if you must file Schedule SE, see the instructions.

May I Use Short Schedule SE or Must I Use Long Schedule SE?

Note. Use this flowchart **only if** you must file Schedule SE. If unsure, see *Who Must File Schedule SE* in the instructions.

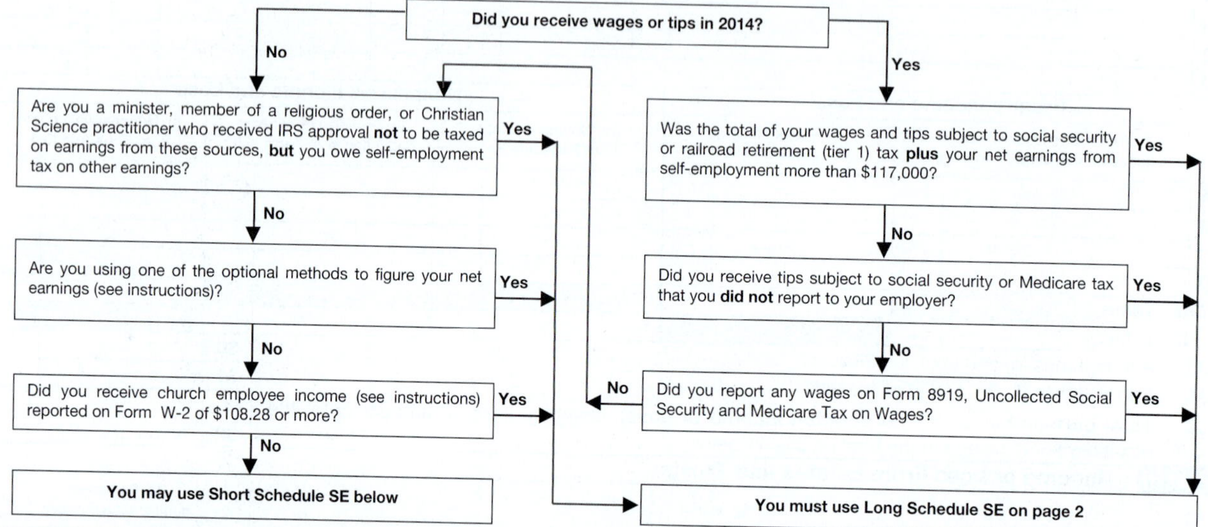

Did you receive wages or tips in 2014?
No
Yes
Are you a minister, member of a religious order, or Christian Science practitioner who received IRS approval not to be taxed on earnings from these sources, but you owe self-employment tax on other earnings?
Yes
No
Are you using one of the optional methods to figure your net earnings (see instructions)?
Yes
No
Did you receive church employee income (see instructions) reported on Form W-2 of $108.28 or more?
Yes
No
You may use Short Schedule SE below
Was the total of your wages and tips subject to social security or railroad retirement (tier 1) tax plus your net earnings from self-employment more than $117,000?
Yes
No
Did you receive tips subject to social security or Medicare tax that you did not report to your employer?
Yes
No
Did you report any wages on Form 8919, Uncollected Social Security and Medicare Tax on Wages?
No
Yes
You must use Long Schedule SE on page 2

Section A—Short Schedule SE. Caution. Read above to see if you can use Short Schedule SE.

Line	Description	Box	Amount
1a	Net farm profit or (loss) from Schedule F, line 34, and farm partnerships, Schedule K-1 (Form 1065), box 14, code A	1a	
b	If you received social security retirement or disability benefits, enter the amount of Conservation Reserve Program payments included on Schedule F, line 4b, or listed on Schedule K-1 (Form 1065), box 20, code Z	1b	( )
2	Net profit or (loss) from Schedule C, line 31; Schedule C-EZ, line 3; Schedule K-1 (Form 1065), box 14, code A (other than farming); and Schedule K-1 (Form 1065-B), box 9, code J1. Ministers and members of religious orders, see instructions for types of income to report on this line. See instructions for other income to report	2	
3	Combine lines 1a, 1b, and 2	3	
4	Multiply line 3 by 92.35% (.9235). If less than $400, you do not owe self-employment tax; **do not** file this schedule unless you have an amount on line 1b . . . . . ▶ **Note.** If line 4 is less than $400 due to Conservation Reserve Program payments on line 1b, see instructions.	4	
5	**Self-employment tax.** If the amount on line 4 is: • $117,000 or less, multiply line 4 by 15.3% (.153). Enter the result here and on **Form 1040, line 57,** or **Form 1040NR, line 55** • More than $117,000, multiply line 4 by 2.9% (.029). Then, add $14,508 to the result. Enter the total here and on **Form 1040, line 57,** or **Form 1040NR, line 55**	5	
6	**Deduction for one-half of self-employment tax.** Multiply line 5 by 50% (.50). Enter the result here and on **Form 1040, line 27,** or **Form 1040NR, line 27** 6		

For Paperwork Reduction Act Notice, see your tax return instructions. Cat. No. 11358Z **Schedule SE (Form 1040) 2014**

Schedule SE (Form 1040) 2014 | Attachment Sequence No. **17** | Page **2**

Name of person with **self-employment** income (as shown on Form 1040 or Form 1040NR)	Social security number of person with **self-employment** income ▶	

Section B—Long Schedule SE

Part I Self-Employment Tax

Note. If your only income subject to self-employment tax is **church employee income,** see instructions. Also see instructions for the definition of church employee income.

A	If you are a minister, member of a religious order, or Christian Science practitioner **and** you filed Form 4361, but you had $400 or more of **other** net earnings from self-employment, check here and continue with Part I . . . . ▶ ☐			
1a	Net farm profit or (loss) from Schedule F, line 34, and farm partnerships, Schedule K-1 (Form 1065), box 14, code A. **Note.** Skip lines 1a and 1b if you use the farm optional method (see instructions)	1a		
b	If you received social security retirement or disability benefits, enter the amount of Conservation Reserve Program payments included on Schedule F, line 4b, or listed on Schedule K-1 (Form 1065), box 20, code Z	1b	(	)
2	Net profit or (loss) from Schedule C, line 31; Schedule C-EZ, line 3; Schedule K-1 (Form 1065), box 14, code A (other than farming); and Schedule K-1 (Form 1065-B), box 9, code J1. Ministers and members of religious orders, see instructions for types of income to report on this line. See instructions for other income to report. **Note.** Skip this line if you use the nonfarm optional method (see instructions)	2		
3	Combine lines 1a, 1b, and 2	3		
4a	If line 3 is more than zero, multiply line 3 by 92.35% (.9235). Otherwise, enter amount from line 3 **Note.** If line 4a is less than $400 due to Conservation Reserve Program payments on line 1b, see instructions.	4a		
b	If you elect one or both of the optional methods, enter the total of lines 15 and 17 here . .	4b		
c	Combine lines 4a and 4b. If less than $400, **stop**; you do not owe self-employment tax. **Exception.** If less than $400 and you had **church employee income,** enter -0- and continue ▶	4c		
5a	Enter your **church employee income** from Form W-2. See instructions for definition of church employee income . . . **5a**			
b	Multiply line 5a by 92.35% (.9235). If less than $100, enter -0-	5b		
6	Add lines 4c and 5b	6		
7	Maximum amount of combined wages and self-employment earnings subject to social security tax or the 6.2% portion of the 7.65% railroad retirement (tier 1) tax for 2014	7	117,000	00
8a	Total social security wages and tips (total of boxes 3 and 7 on Form(s) W-2) and railroad retirement (tier 1) compensation. If $117,000 or more, skip lines 8b through 10, and go to line 11 **8a**			
b	Unreported tips subject to social security tax (from Form 4137, line 10) **8b**			
c	Wages subject to social security tax (from Form 8919, line 10) **8c**			
d	Add lines 8a, 8b, and 8c	8d		
9	Subtract line 8d from line 7. If zero or less, enter -0- here and on line 10 and go to line 11 . ▶	9		
10	Multiply the **smaller** of line 6 or line 9 by 12.4% (.124)	10		
11	Multiply line 6 by 2.9% (.029)	11		
12	**Self-employment tax.** Add lines 10 and 11. Enter here and on **Form 1040, line 57,** or **Form 1040NR, line 55**	12		
13	**Deduction for one-half of self-employment tax.** Multiply line 12 by 50% (.50). Enter the result here and on **Form 1040, line 27,** or **Form 1040NR, line 27** **13**			

Part II Optional Methods To Figure Net Earnings (see instructions)

	Farm Optional Method. You may use this method **only** if **(a)** your gross farm income[1] was not more than $7,200, **or (b)** your net farm profits[2] were less than $5,198.			
14	Maximum income for optional methods	14	4,800	00
15	Enter the **smaller** of: two-thirds (2/3) of gross farm income[1] (not less than zero) **or** $4,800. Also include this amount on line 4b above	15		
	Nonfarm Optional Method. You may use this method **only** if **(a)** your net nonfarm profits[3] were less than $5,198 and also less than 72.189% of your gross nonfarm income,[4] **and (b)** you had net earnings from self-employment of at least $400 in 2 of the prior 3 years. **Caution.** You may use this method no more than five times.			
16	Subtract line 15 from line 14	16		
17	Enter the **smaller** of: two-thirds (2/3) of gross nonfarm income[4] (not less than zero) **or** the amount on line 16. Also include this amount on line 4b above	17		

[1] From Sch. F, line 9, and Sch. K-1 (Form 1065), box 14, code B.

[2] From Sch. F, line 34, and Sch. K-1 (Form 1065), box 14, code A—minus the amount you would have entered on line 1b had you not used the optional method.

[3] From Sch. C, line 31; Sch. C-EZ, line 3; Sch. K-1 (Form 1065), box 14, code A; and Sch. K-1 (Form 1065-B), box 9, code J1.

[4] From Sch. C, line 7; Sch. C-EZ, line 1; Sch. K-1 (Form 1065), box 14, code C; and Sch. K-1 (Form 1065-B), box 9, code J2.

Schedule SE (Form 1040) 2014

Appendix B

Tax Terms Glossary

§83(b) election a special tax election that employees who receive restricted stock or other property with ownership restrictions can make to accelerate income recognition from the normal date when restrictions lapse to the date when the restricted stock or other property is granted. The election also accelerates the employer's compensation deduction related to the restricted stock or other property.

§1231 assets depreciable or real property used in a taxpayer's trade or business owned for more than one year.

§1231 look-back rule a tax rule requiring taxpayers to treat current year net §1231 gains as ordinary income when the taxpayer has deducted a §1231 loss as an ordinary loss in the five years preceding the current tax year.

§1245 property tangible personal property and intangible property subject to cost recovery deductions.

§1250 property real property subject to cost recovery deductions.

§162(m) limitation the $1 million deduction limit on nonperformance based salary paid to certain key executives.

§179 election an incentive for small businesses that allows them to immediately expense a certain amount of tangible personal property placed in service during the year.

§197 purchased intangibles intangible assets that are purchased that must be amortized over 180 months regardless of their actual useful lives.

§291 depreciation recapture the portion of a corporate taxpayer's gain on real property that is converted from §1231 gain to ordinary income.

§338 election an election by a corporate buyer of 80-percent-or-more of a corporation's stock to treat the acquisition as an asset acquisition and not a stock acquisition.

§338(h)(10) election a joint election by the corporate buyer and corporate seller of the stock of a subsidiary of the seller to treat the acquisition as a sale of the subsidiary's assets by the seller to the buyer.

§481 adjustment a change to taxable income associated with a change in accounting methods.

12-month rule regulation that allows prepaid business expenses to be currently deducted when the contract does not extend beyond 12 months and the contract period does not extend beyond the end of the tax year following the year of the payment.

30-day letter the IRS letter received after an audit that instructs the taxpayer that he or she has 30 days to either (1) request a conference with an appeals officer or (2) agree to the proposed adjustment.

90-day letter the IRS letter received after an audit and receipt of the 30-day letter that explains that the taxpayer has 90 days to either (1) pay the proposed deficiency or (2) file a petition in the U.S. Tax Court to hear the case. The 90-day letter is also known as the *statutory notice of deficiency*.

A

Abandoned spouse a married taxpayer who lives apart from his or her spouse for the last six months of the year (excluding temporary absences), who files a tax return separate from his or her spouse, and who maintains a household for a qualifying child.

Accelerated Cost Recovery System (ACRS) the depreciation system enacted by Congress in 1981 that is based on the concept of set recovery periods and accelerated depreciation methods.

Accountable plan an employer's reimbursement plan under which employees must submit documentation supporting expenses to receive reimbursement and reimbursements are limited to legitimate business expenses.

Accounting method the procedure for determining the taxable year in which a business recognizes a particular item of income or deduction thereby dictating the timing of when a taxpayer reports income and deductions.

Accounting period a fixed period in which a business reports income and deductions, generally referred to as a tax year.

Accrual method a method of accounting that generally recognizes income in the period earned and recognizes deductions in the period that liabilities are incurred.

Accrued market discount a ratable amount of the market discount at the time of purchase (based on the number of days the bond is held over the number of days until maturity when the bond is purchased) that is treated as interest income when a bond with market discount is sold before it matures.

Acquiescence issued after the IRS loses a trial-level or circuit court case when the IRS has decided to follow the court's adverse ruling in the future. It does not mean that the IRS agrees with the court's ruling. Instead, it simply means that the IRS will no longer litigate this issue.

Acquisition indebtedness debt secured by a qualified residence that is incurred in acquiring, constructing, or substantially improving the residence.

Action on decision an IRS pronouncement that explains the background reasoning behind an IRS acquiescence or nonacquiescence.

Active participant in a rental activity an individual who owns at least 10% of a rental property and participates in the process of making management decisions, such as approving new tenants, deciding on rental terms, and approving repairs and capital expenditures.

Ad valorem tax a tax based on the value of property.

Adjusted basis see adjusted tax basis.

Adjusted gross income (AGI) gross income less deductions for AGI. AGI is an important reference point that is often used in other calculations.

Adjusted tax basis the taxpayer's acquisition basis (for example, cost) plus capital improvements less depreciation or amortization.

After-tax rate of return a taxpayer's before-tax rate of return on an investment minus the taxes paid on the income from the investment. The formula for an after-tax rate of return that is taxed annually is the before-tax rate of return × (1 − marginal tax rate) [i.e., $r = R \times (1 - t)$]. A taxpayer's after-tax rate of return on an investment held for more than one tax period is $r = (FV/I)^{1/n} - 1$, where r is the after-tax rate of return, FV is the after-tax future value of the investment, I is the original investment amount, and n is the number of periods the investment is held.

Alimony a support payment of cash made to a former spouse. The payment must be made under a written separation agreement or divorce decree that does not designate the payment as something other than alimony, the payment must be made when the spouses do not live together, and the payments must cease no later than when the recipient dies.

All-events test requires that income or expenses are recognized when (1) all events have occurred that determine or fix the right to receive the income or liability to make the payments and (2) the amount of the income or expense can be determined with reasonable accuracy.

All-inclusive income concept a definition of income that says that gross income means all income from whatever source derived.

Allowance method bad debt expense is based on an estimate of the amount of the bad debts in accounts receivable at year-end.

Alternative minimum tax a tax on a broader tax base than the base for the "regular" tax; the additional tax paid when the tentative minimum tax (based on the alternative minimum tax base) exceeds the regular tax (based on the regular tax base). The alternative minimum tax is designed to require taxpayers to pay some minimum level of tax even when they have low or no regular taxable income as a result of certain tax breaks in the tax code.

Alternative minimum tax adjustments adjustments (positive or negative) to regular taxable income to arrive at the alternative minimum tax base.

Alternative minimum tax base (AMT base) alternative minimum taxable income minus the alternative minimum tax exemption.

Alternative minimum tax exemption a deduction to determine the alternative minimum tax base that is phased out based on alternative minimum taxable income.

Alternative minimum tax system a secondary or parallel tax system calculated on an *alternative* tax base that more closely reflects economic income than the regular income tax base. The system was designed to ensure that taxpayers generating economic income pay some *minimum* amount of income tax each year.

Amortization the method of recovering the cost of intangible assets over a specific time period.

Amount realized the value of everything received by the seller in a transaction (cash, FMV of other property, and relief of liabilities) less selling costs.

Annotated tax service a tax service arranged by code section. For each code section, an annotated service includes the code section; a listing of the code section history; copies of congressional committee reports that explain changes to the code section; a copy of all the regulations issued for the specific code section; the service's unofficial explanation of the code section; and brief summaries (called annotations) of relevant court cases, revenue rulings, revenue procedures, and letter rulings that address issues specific to the code section.

Annuity a stream of equal payments over time.

Arm's length amount price in transactions among unrelated taxpayers, where each transacting party negotiates for his or her own benefit.

Arm's-length transaction transactions among unrelated taxpayers, where each transacting party negotiates for his or her own benefit.

Assignment of income doctrine the judicial doctrine holding that earned income is taxed to the taxpayer providing the service, and that income from property is taxed to the individual who owns the property when the income accrues.

At-risk amount an investor's risk of loss in a worst-case scenario. In a partnership, an amount generally equal to a partner's tax basis exclusive of the partner's share of nonrecourse debt.

Average tax rate a taxpayer's average level of taxation on each dollar of taxable income. Specifically,

$$\text{Average tax rate} = \frac{\textit{Total tax}}{\textit{Taxable income}}$$

B

Bargain element (of stock options) the difference between the fair market value of the employer's stock and the amount employees pay to acquire the employer's stock.

Barter clubs organizations that facilitate the exchange of rights to goods and services between members.

Basis a taxpayer's unrecovered investment in an asset that provides a reference point for measuring gain or loss when an asset is sold.

Before-tax rate of return a taxpayer's rate of return on an investment before paying taxes on the income from the investment.

Bond a debt instrument issued for a period of more than one year with the purpose of raising capital by borrowing.

Bond discount the result of issuing bonds for less than their maturity value.

Bond premium the result of issuing bonds for more than their maturity value.

Bonus depreciation additional depreciation allowed in the acquisition year for new tangible personal property with a recovery period of 20 years or less.

Boot property given or received in an otherwise nontaxable transaction such as a like-kind exchange that may trigger gain to a party to the transaction.

Bracket a subset (or portion) of the tax base subject to a specific tax rate. Brackets are common to graduated taxes.

Bunching itemized deductions a common planning strategy in which a taxpayer pays two year's worth of itemized expenses in one year to exceed the standard deduction in that year.

Business activity a profit-motivated activity that requires a relatively high level of involvement or effort from the taxpayer to generate income.

Business income income derived from business activities.

Business purpose doctrine the judicial doctrine that allows the IRS to challenge and disallow business expenses for transactions with no underlying business motivation.

Business tax credits nonrefundable credits designed to provide incentives for taxpayers to hire certain types of individuals or to participate in certain business activities.

C

Cafeteria plan an employer plan that allows employees to choose benefits from a menu of nontaxable fringe benefits or receive cash compensation in lieu of the benefits.

Capital asset in general, an asset other than an asset used in a trade or business or an asset such as an account or note receivable acquired in a business from the sale of services or property.

Capital gain property any asset that would have generated a long-term capital gain if the taxpayer had sold the property for its fair market value.

Capitalization recording an expenditure as an asset on the balance sheet rather than expensing it immediately.

Cash method the method of accounting that recognizes income in the period in which cash, property, or services are received and recognizes deductions in the period paid.

Cash surrender value the amount, if any, the owner of a life insurance policy receives when the policy is cashed in before the death of the insured individual.

Casualty an unexpected, unforeseen event driven by forces outside the control of the taxpayer (such as "fire, storm, or shipwreck" or other event or theft) that damages or destroys a taxpayer's property.

Casualty loss a loss arising from a *sudden, unexpected,* or *unusual* event such as a "fire, storm, or shipwreck" or loss from theft.

Ceiling limitations that are maximum amounts for adjustments to taxable income (or credits). The amounts in excess of the ceiling are either lost or carried to another tax year.

Certainty one of the criteria used to evaluate tax systems. Certainty means taxpayers should be able to determine when, where, and how much tax to pay.

Certificate of deposit an interest-bearing debt instrument offered by banks and savings and loans. Money removed from the CD before maturity is subject to a penalty.

Character of income determines the rate at which income will be taxed. Common income characters (or types of income) include tax-exempt, ordinary, and capital.

Circular 230 regulations issued by the IRS that govern tax practice and apply to all persons practicing before the IRS. There are three parts of Circular 230: Subpart A describes who may practice before the IRS (e.g., CPAs, attorneys, enrolled agents) and what practicing before the IRS means (tax return preparation, representing clients before the IRS, etc.). Subpart B describes the duties and restrictions that apply to individuals governed by Circular 230. Subpart C explains disciplinary proceedings for practitioners violating the Circular 230 provisions.

Citator a research tool that allows one to check the status of several types of tax authorities. A citator can be used to review the history of the case to find out, for example, whether it was subsequently appealed and overturned, and to identify subsequent cases that cite the case. Citators can also be used to check the status of revenue rulings, revenue procedures, and other IRS pronouncements.

Civil penalties monetary penalties imposed when tax practitioners or taxpayers violate tax statutes without reasonable cause—for example, as the result of negligence, intentional disregard of pertinent rules, willful disobedience, or outright fraud.

Claim of right doctrine judicial doctrine that states that income has been realized if a taxpayer receives income and there are no restrictions on the taxpayer's use of the income (for example, the taxpayer does not have an obligation to repay the amount).

Cliff vesting a qualified plan provision allowing for benefits to vest all at once after a period of time has passed.

Collectibles a work of art, a rug or antique, a metal or gem, a stamp or coin, an alcoholic beverage, or other similar items held for investment for more than one year.

Community-property states nine states (Arizona, California, Idaho, Louisiana, Nevada, New Mexico, Texas, Washington, and Wisconsin) that automatically equally divide the ownership of property acquired by either spouse during a marriage.

Community property systems systems in which state laws dictate how the income and property is legally shared between a husband and a wife.

Commuting traveling from a personal residence to the place of business.

Constructive receipt doctrine the judicial doctrine that provides that a taxpayer must recognize income when it is actually or constructively received. Constructive receipt is deemed to have occurred if the income has been credited to the taxpayer's account or if the income is unconditionally available to the taxpayer, the taxpayer is aware of the income's availability, and there are no restrictions on the taxpayer's control over the income.

Convenience one of the criteria used to evaluate tax systems. Convenience means a tax system should be designed to facilitate the collection of tax revenues without undue hardship on the taxpayer or the government.

Correspondence examination an IRS audit conducted by mail and generally limited to one or two items on the taxpayer's return. Among the three types of audits, correspondence audits are generally the most common, the most narrow in scope, and least complex. The IRS typically requests supporting documentation for one or more items on the taxpayer's return (e.g., documentation of charitable contributions deducted).

Cost depletion the method of recovering the cost of a natural resource that allows a taxpayer to estimate or determine the number of units that remain in the resource at the beginning of the year and allocate a pro rata share of the remaining basis to each unit of the resource that is extracted or sold during the year.

Cost recovery the method by which a company expenses the cost of acquiring capital assets. Cost recovery can take the form of depreciation, amortization, or depletion.

Coupon rate the interest rate expressed as a percentage of the face value of the bond.

Covenant not to compete a contractual promise to refrain from conducting business or professional activities similar to those of another party.

Criminal penalties penalties commonly charged in tax evasion cases (i.e., willful intent to defraud the government). They are imposed only after normal due process, including a trial. Compared to civil cases, the standard of conviction is higher in a criminal trial (beyond a reasonable doubt). However, the penalties are also much higher, such as fines up to $100,000 for individuals plus a prison sentence.

Current income tax expense or benefit the amount of taxes paid or payable (refundable) in the current year.

Current tax liability or asset the amount of taxes payable or refundable in the current year.

***De minimis* fringe benefit** a nontaxable fringe benefit that allows employees to receive occasional or incidental benefits tax free.

Deceased spousal unused exclusion amount of unused unified credit from predeceased spouse.

Deductions amounts that are subtracted from reduced gross income in calculating taxable income.

Deductions above the line *for* AGI deductions or deductions subtracted from gross income to determine AGI.

Deductions below the line *from* AGI deductions or deductions subtracted from AGI to calculate taxable income.

Deductions *for* AGI deductions that are subtracted from gross income to determine AGI.

Deductions *from* AGI deductions subtracted from AGI to calculate taxable income.

Deferral items, deferred income, or deferrals realized income that will be taxed as income in a subsequent year.

Deferral method recognizes income from advance payments for goods by the earlier of (1) when the business would recognize the income for tax purposes if it had not received the *advance* payment or (2) when it recognizes the income for financial reporting purposes.

Deferred like-kind exchange a like-kind exchange where the taxpayer transfers like-kind property before receiving the like-kind property in exchange. The property to be received must be identified within 45 days and received within 180 days of the transfer of the property given up.

Deferred tax asset the expected future tax benefit attributable to deductible temporary differences and carryforwards.

Deferred tax liability the expected future tax cost attributable to taxable temporary differences.

Defined benefit plan employer-provided qualified plans that spell out the specific benefit employees will receive on retirement.

Defined contribution plan employer-provided qualified plans that specify the maximum annual contributions employers and/or employees may contribute to the plan.

Dependency exemption a fixed deduction allowed for each individual who qualifies as a "dependent" of the taxpayer.

Dependent a person for whom a taxpayer may claim a dependency exemption. To qualify as a dependent a person must be a qualifying child or qualifying relative of the taxpayer.

Dependent care benefit a nontaxable fringe benefit that allows employees to receive up to $5,000 of care for children under age 13 or for a spouse or other dependent with physical needs.

Depletion the cost recovery method to allocate the cost of natural resources as they are removed.

Depreciation the cost recovery method to allocate the cost of tangible personal and real property over a specific time period.

Depreciation recapture the conversion of §1231 gain into ordinary income on a sale (or exchange) based on the amount of accumulated depreciation on the property at the time of sale or exchange.

Determination letters rulings requested by the taxpayer, issued by local IRS directors, and generally not controversial. An example of a determination letter is the request by an employer for the IRS to rule that the taxpayer's retirement plan is a "qualified plan."

DIF (Discriminant Function) system the DIF system assigns a score to each tax return that represents the probability that the tax liability on the return has been underreported (a higher score = a higher likelihood of underreporting). The IRS derives the weights assigned to specific tax return attributes from historical IRS audit adjustment data from the National Research Program. The DIF system then uses these (undisclosed) weights to score each tax return based on the tax return's characteristics. Returns with higher DIF scores are then reviewed to determine if an audit is the best course of action.

Direct conversion when a taxpayer receives noncash property as a replacement for property damaged or destroyed in an involuntary conversion rather than a cash payment.

Direct write-off method required method for deducting bad debts for tax purposes. Under this method, businesses deduct bad debt only when the debt becomes wholly or partially worthless.

Disability insurance sometimes called sick pay or wage replacement insurance. It pays the insured for wages lost due to injury or disability.

Discharge of indebtedness debt forgiveness.

Discount factor the factor based on the taxpayer's rate of return that is used to determine the present value of future cash inflows (e.g., tax savings) and outflows (taxes paid).

Disqualifying disposition the sale of stock acquired using incentive stock options prior to satisfying certain holding period requirements. Failing to satisfy the holding period requirements converts the options into nonqualified stock options.

Dividend a distribution to shareholders of money or property from the corporation's earnings and profits.

Document perfection program a program under which all tax returns are checked for mathematical and tax calculation errors.

Domestic production activities deduction (DPAD) a deduction for businesses that manufacture goods in the United States.

Donee person receiving a gift.

Donor person making a gift.

Dwelling unit property that provides a place suitable for people to occupy (live and sleep).

Dynamic forecasting the process of forecasting tax revenues that incorporates into the forecast how taxpayers may alter their activities in response to a tax law change.

E

Earmarked tax a tax assessed for a specific purpose (e.g., for education).

Earned income compensation and other forms of income received for providing goods or services in the ordinary course of business.

Earned income credit a refundable credit designed to help offset the effect of employment taxes on compensation paid to low-income taxpayers and to encourage lower income taxpayers to seek employment.

Economic performance test the third requirement that must be met for an accrual method taxpayer to deduct an expense currently. The specific event that satisfies the economic performance test varies based on the type of expense.

Economy one of the criteria used to evaluate tax systems. Economy means a tax system should minimize its compliance and administration costs.

Educational assistance benefit a nontaxable fringe benefit that allows an employer to provide a certain amount of education benefits on an annual basis.

Effective tax rate the taxpayer's average rate of taxation on each dollar of total income (taxable and nontaxable income). Specifically,

$$\text{Effective tax rate} = \frac{\textit{Total tax}}{\textit{Total income}}$$

Employee a person who is hired to provide services to a company on a regular basis in exchange for compensation and who does not provide these services as part of an independent business.

Employment taxes taxes consisting of the Old Age, Survivors, and Disability Insurance (OASDI) tax, commonly called the Social Security tax, and the Medical Health Insurance (MHI) tax known as the Medicare tax.

Equity one of the criteria used to evaluate a tax system. A tax system is considered fair or equitable if the tax is based on the taxpayer's ability to pay; taxpayers with a greater ability to pay tax, pay more tax.

Escrow account (mortgage-related) a holding account with a taxpayer's mortgage lender. The taxpayer makes mortgage payments to the lender that include payment for the interest and principal and payments for property taxes. The lender maintains the payments for property taxes in the escrow account and uses the funds in the account to pay the property taxes when the taxes are due.

Estate fiduciary legal entity that comes into existence upon a person's death and is empowered by the probate court to gather and transfer the decedent's real and personal property.

Estimated tax payments quarterly tax payments that a taxpayer makes to the government if the tax withholding is insufficient to meet the taxpayer's tax liability.

Exchanged basis the basis of an asset received in a nontaxable exchange. An exchanged basis is generally the basis of the asset given up in a nontaxable exchange. Exchanged basis may also be referred to as a *substituted basis.*

Excise taxes taxes levied on the retail sale of particular products. They differ from other taxes in that the tax base for an excise tax typically depends on the *quantity* purchased, rather than a monetary amount.

Excluded income or exclusions realized income that is exempted from income taxation.

Ex-dividend date the relevant date for determining who receives a dividend from a stock. Anyone purchasing stock before this date will receive current dividends. Otherwise, the purchaser must wait until subsequent dividends are declared before receiving them.

Executor the person who takes responsibility for collecting the assets of the decedent, paying the decedent's debts, and distributing the remaining assets to the rightful heirs.

Exemption a fixed income tax deduction a taxpayer may claim for each person who qualifies as a dependent of the taxpayer. This includes the taxpayer (and spouse on a joint return) who does not qualify as a dependent of another.

Exercise date the date employees use their stock options to acquire employer stock at a discounted price.

Exercise price the price at which holders of stock options may purchase stock in the corporation issuing the option.

Explicit tax a tax directly imposed by a government.

F

Face value a specified final amount paid to the owner of a coupon bond on the date of maturity. The face value is also known as the maturity value.

Facts and circumstances test a test used to make subjective determination such as whether the amount of salary paid to an employee is reasonable. The test requires the taxpayer and the IRS to consider all the relevant facts and circumstances surrounding the situation in order to make a decision. The relevant facts and circumstance are situation specific.

Federal short-term interest rate the quarterly interest rate used to determine the interest charged for tax underpayments (federal short-term rate plus 3 percent).

FICA taxes FICA (Federal Insurance Contribution Act) taxes are a term used to denote both the Social Security and Medicare taxes upon earned income. For self-employed taxpayers, the terms "FICA tax" and "self-employment tax" are synonymous.

Field examination the least common audit. The IRS conducts these audits at the taxpayer's place of business or the location where the taxpayer's books, records, and source documents are maintained. Field examinations are generally the broadest in scope and most complex of the three audit types. They can last many months to multiple years and generally are limited to business returns and the most complex individual returns.

FIFO first-in, first-out method; an accounting method that values the cost of assets sold under the assumption that the assets are sold in the order purchased (i.e., first purchased, first sold).

Filing status filing status places taxpayers into one of five categories (married filing jointly, married filing separately, qualifying widow or widower, head of household, and single) by marital status and family situation as of the end of the year. Filing status determines whether a taxpayer must file a tax return, appropriate tax rate schedules, standard deduction amounts, and several deduction and credit limitation thresholds.

Final regulations regulations that have been issued in final form, and thus, until revoked, they represent the Treasury's interpretation of the Code.

First-in, first-out (FIFO) method an accounting method that values the cost of assets sold under the assumption that the assets are sold in the order purchased (i.e., first purchased, first sold).

Fiscal year a year that ends the last day of a month other than December.

Fixed and determinable, annual or periodic income U.S. source passive income earned by a nonresident.

Flat tax a tax in which a single tax rate is applied throughout the tax base.

Flexible spending account a plan that allows employees to contribute before-tax dollars that may be used for unreimbursed medical expenses or dependent care.

Flipping a term used to describe the real estate investment practice of acquiring a home, repairing or remodeling the home, and then immediately, or soon thereafter, selling it (presumably at a profit).

Floor limitation a minimum amount that an expenditure (or credit or other adjustment to taxable income) must meet before any amount is allowed.

Flow-through entities legal entities like partnerships, limited liability companies, and S corporations that do not pay income tax. Income and losses from flow-through entities are allocated to their owners.

For the convenience of the employer benefits nontaxable benefits employers provide to employees and employee spouses or dependents in the form of meals or lodging if provided on the employer's premises and are provided for a purpose that is helpful or convenient for the employer.

Form W-2 used to report wages paid to employees and the taxes withheld from them. The form is also used to report FICA taxes to the Social Security Administration.

Form W-4 a form used by a taxpayer to supply her employer with the information necessary to determine the amount of tax to withhold from each paycheck.

Fringe benefits noncash benefit provided to an employee as a form of compensation. As a general rule, fringe benefits are taxable. However, certain fringe benefits are excluded from gross income.

Full-inclusion method the method for accounting for advance payments for goods that requires that businesses immediately recognize advance payments as taxable income.

Full-month convention a convention that allows owners of intangibles to deduct an entire month's amortization in the month of purchase and month of disposition.

G

Gift a transfer of property where no, or inadequate, consideration is paid for the property.

Golsen rule the rule that states that the U.S. Tax Court will abide by the circuit court's rulings that has appellate jurisdiction for a case.

Graded vesting a qualified plan rule that requires an increasing percentage of plan benefits to vest with each additional year of employment.

Graduated taxes taxes in which the tax base is divided into a series of monetary amounts, or brackets, where each successive bracket is taxed at a different (gradually higher or gradually lower) percentage rate.

Grant date (stock options) the date on which employees receive stock options to acquire employer stock at a specified price.

Gross income realized income reduced for any excluded or deferred income.

Group-term life insurance term life insurance provided by an employer to a group of employees.

H

Half-year convention a depreciation convention that allows owners of tangible personal property to take one-half of a year's worth of depreciation in the year of purchase and in the year of disposition regardless of when the asset was actually placed in service or sold.

Head of household one of five primary filing statuses. A taxpayer may file as head of household if s/he is unmarried as of the end of the year *and* pays more than half of the cost to maintain a household for a qualifying person who lives with the taxpayer for more than half of the year; or, s/he pays more than half the costs to maintain a household for a parent who qualifies as the taxpayer's dependent.

Hobby a revenue-generating activity that is motivated by personal motives rather than profit objectives.

Home-equity indebtedness debt (except for acquisition indebtedness) secured by the taxpayer's qualified residence to the extent it does not exceed the fair market value of the residence over the acquisition indebtedness. Interest paid on up to $100,000 of home-equity indebtedness is allowed as an itemized deduction.

Home office deduction deductions relating to the use of an office in the home. A taxpayer must meet strict requirements to qualify for the deduction.

Horizontal equity one of the dimensions of equity. Horizontal equity is achieved if taxpayers in similar situations pay the same tax.

I

Impermissible accounting method an accounting method prohibited by tax laws.

Implicit tax indirect taxes that result from a tax advantage the government grants to certain transactions to satisfy social, economic, or other objectives. They are defined as the reduced before-tax return that a tax-favored asset produces because of its tax-advantaged status.

Imputed income income from an economic benefit the taxpayer receives indirectly rather than directly. The amount of the income is based on comparable alternatives.

Incentive stock option a type of stock option that allows employees to defer the bargain element for regular tax purposes until the stock acquired from option exercises is sold. The bargain element is taxed at capital gains rates provided the stock is retained long enough to satisfy certain holding period requirements. Employers cannot deduct the bargain element as compensation expense.

Income effect one of the two basic responses that a taxpayer may have when taxes increase. The income effect predicts that when taxpayers are taxed more (e.g., tax rate increases from 25 to 28 percent), they will work harder to generate the same after-tax dollars.

Income tax a tax in which the tax base is income. Income taxes are imposed by the federal government and by most states.

Independent contractor a person who provides services to another entity, usually under terms specified in a contract. The independent contractor has more control over how and when to do the work than does an employee.

Indirect conversion the receipt of money or other property as a replacement for property that was destroyed or damaged in an involuntary conversion.

Individual retirement account (IRA) a tax-advantaged account in which individuals who have earned income can save for retirement.

Information matching program a program that compares the taxpayer's tax return to information submitted to the IRS from other taxpayers (e.g., banks, employers, mutual funds, brokerage companies, mortgage companies). Information matched includes items such as wages (e.g., Form W-2 submitted by employers), interest income (e.g., Form 1099-INT submitted by banks), dividend income (e.g., Form 1099-DIV submitted by brokerage companies), and so forth.

Inheritance a transfer of property when the owner is deceased (the transfer is made by the decedent's estate).

Inside tax basis the tax basis of an entity's assets and liabilities.

Installment sale a sale for which the taxpayer receives payment in more than one period.

Intangible assets assets that do not have physical characteristics. Examples include goodwill, covenants not to compete, organizational expenditures, and research and experimentation expenses.

Internal Revenue Code of 1986 the codified tax laws of the United States. Although the Code is frequently revised, there have only been three different codes since the Code was created in 1939 (i.e., the IRC of 1939, IRC of 1954, and IRC of 1986).

Interpretative regulations the most common regulation; they represent the Treasury's interpretation of the Code and are issued under the Treasury's general authority to interpret the Code.

Investment activities a profit-seeking activity that is intermittent or occasional in frequency including the production or collection of income or the management, conservation, or maintenance of property held for the production of income.

Investment expenses expenses such as safe deposit rental fees, attorney fees, and accounting fees that are necessary to produce portfolio income. Investment expenses are allowed for individuals as miscellaneous itemized deductions subject to the 2 percent of AGI floor limitation.

Investment income income received from portfolio type investments. Portfolio income includes capital gains and losses, interest, dividend, annuity, and royalty income not derived in the ordinary course of a trade or business. When computing the deductibility of investment interest expense, however, capital gains and dividends subject to the preferential tax rate are not treated as investment income unless the taxpayer elects to have this income taxed at ordinary tax rates.

Investment interest expense interest paid on borrowings or loans that are used to fund portfolio investments. Individuals are allowed an itemized deduction for qualified investment interest paid during the year.

Involuntary conversion a direct or indirect conversion of property through natural disaster, government condemnation, or accident that allows a taxpayer to defer realized gain if certain requirements are met.

IRS allocation method allocates expenses associated with rental use of the home between rental use and personal use. The percentage of total expenses allocated to rental use is the ratio of the number of rental use days for the property to the total days the property was used during the year.

Itemized deductions certain types of expenditures that Congress allows taxpayers to deduct as from AGI deductions.

J

Joint tenancy with the right of survivorship title to property that provides the co-owners with equal rights to it and that automatically transfers to the survivor at the death of a co-owner.

K

Kiddie tax a tax imposed at the parent's marginal rate on a child's unearned income.

L

Late filing penalty a penalty assessed if a taxpayer does not file a tax return by the required date (the original due date plus extension).

Legislative grace the concept that taxpayers receive certain tax benefits only because Congress writes laws that allow taxpayers to receive the tax benefits.

Legislative regulations the rarest type of regulation, issued when Congress specifically directs the Treasury Department to create regulations to address an issue in an area of law. In these instances, the Treasury is actually writing the law instead of interpreting the Code. Because legislative regulations actually represent tax law instead of an interpretation of tax law, legislative regulations have more authoritative weight than interpretative and procedural regulations.

LIFO last-in, first-out method; an accounting method that values the cost of assets sold under the assumption that assets are sold in the reverse order in which they are purchased (i.e., last purchased, first sold).

Like-kind exchange a nontaxable (or partially taxable) trade or exchange of assets that are similar or related in use.

Listed property business assets that are often used for personal purposes. Depreciation on listed property is limited to the business use portion of the asset.

Local tax taxes imposed by local governments (cities, counties, school districts, etc.).

Long-term capital gain property property that would generate long-term capital gain if it were sold. This includes capital assets held for more than a year.

Long-term capital gains or losses gains or losses from the sale of capital assets held for more than 12 months.

Luxury automobile an automobile on which the amount of annual depreciation expense is limited because the cost of the automobile exceeds a certain threshold. The definition excludes vehicles with gross vehicle weight exceeding 6,000 pounds.

M

Marginal tax rate the tax rate that applies to the *next additional increment* of a taxpayer's taxable income (or to deductions). Specifically,

$$\text{Marginal tax rate} = \frac{\Delta\,Tax}{\Delta\,Taxable\ income}$$

$$= \frac{(New\ total\ tax - Old\ total\ tax)}{(New\ taxable\ income - Old\ taxable\ income)}$$

where "old" refers to the current tax and "new" refers to the revised tax after incorporating the additional income (or deductions) in question.

Marital deduction the deduction for transfers of qualified property to a spouse.

Market discount the difference between the amount paid for a bond in a market purchase rather than at original issuance when the amount paid is less than the maturity value of the bond.

Market premium the difference between the amount paid for a bond in a market purchase rather than at original issuance when the amount paid is greater than the maturity value of the bond.

Marriage benefit the tax savings married couples receive by filing a joint return relative to the tax they would have paid had they each filed as single taxpayers. This typically occurs when one spouse is either not working or earns significantly less than the other spouse.

Marriage penalty the extra tax cost a married couple pays by filing a joint return relative to what they would have paid had they each filed as single taxpayers. This typically occurs when both spouses earn approximately the same amount of income.

Married filing jointly one of five primary filing statuses. A taxpayer may file jointly if s/he is legally married as of the end of the year (or one spouse died during the year and the surviving spouse did not remarry) and both spouses agree to jointly file. Married couples filing joint returns combine their income and deductions and share joint and several liability for the resulting tax.

Married filing separately one of five primary filing statuses. When married couples file separately, each spouse reports the income he or she received during the year and the deductions he or she paid on a tax return separate from the other spouse.

Maturity the amount of time to the expiration date, or maturity date, of a debt instrument. The maturity of a debt instrument is generally the life of the instrument at which a payment of the face value is due or the instrument terminates.

Maturity value the amount paid to a bondholder when the bond matures and the bondholder redeems the bond for cash.

Medicare tax the Medical Health Insurance (MHI) tax. This tax helps pay medical costs for qualifying individuals. The Medicare tax rate for employees is 1.45% on salary or wages up to $200,000 ($125,000 for married filing separate; $250,000 of combined salary or wages for married filing joint) and is 2.35% on salary or wages in excess of $200,000 ($125,000 for married filing separate; $250,000 of combined salary or wages for married filing joint). For employers, the Medicare tax rate is 1.45% of employee salary or wages, regardless of the amount of salary or wages. Self-employed taxpayers pay both the employee and employer Medicare tax.

Mid-month convention a convention that allows owners of real property to take one-half of a month's depreciation during the month when the property was placed in service and in the month it was disposed of.

Mid-quarter convention a depreciation convention for tangible personal property that allows for one-half of a quarter's worth of depreciation in the quarter of purchase and in the quarter of disposition. This convention must be used when more than 40% of tangible personal property is placed into service in the fourth quarter of the tax year.

Minimum tax credit credit available in certain situations for the alternative minimum tax paid. The credit can be used only when the regular tax exceeds the tentative minimum tax.

Miscellaneous itemized deductions deductions representing the sum of certain itemized deductions, such as unreimbursed employee business expenses, investment expenses, and tax preparation fees, that are subject to a special floor limitation.

Mixed-motive expenditures activities that involve a mixture of business and personal objectives.

Modified Accelerated Cost Recovery System (MACRS) the current tax depreciation system for tangible personal and real property. Depreciation under MACRS is calculated by finding the depreciation method, the recovery period, and the applicable convention.

Municipal bond the common name for state and local government debt.

Mutual fund a diversified portfolio of securities owned and managed by a regulated investment company.

N

Net capital gain the net gain resulting when taxpayers combine net long-term capital gains with net short-term capital losses.

Net earnings from self-employment the amount of earnings subject to self-employment income taxes. The amount is 92.35% of the net income from a taxpayer's Schedule C (for self-employed taxpayers).

Net investment income (for determining deductibility of investment interest expense) gross investment income reduced by deductible investment expenses.

Net investment income tax a 3.8% tax on the lesser of (a) net investment income or (b) the excess of modified adjusted gross income over $250,000 for married-joint filers and surviving spouses, $125,000 for married-separate filers, and $200,000 for other taxpayers.

Net long-term capital gain the net gain resulting when taxpayers combine long-term capital gains and losses for the year.

Net long-term capital loss the net loss resulting when taxpayers combine long-term capital gains and losses for the year.

Net passive investment income passive investment income less any expenses connected with producing it.

Net short-term capital gain the net gain resulting when taxpayers combine short-term capital gains and losses for the year.

Net short-term capital loss the net loss resulting when taxpayers combine short-term capital gains and losses for the year.

Net unearned income unearned income in excess of a specified threshold amount of a child under the age of 19 or under the age of 24 if a full-time student.

No-additional-cost services a nontaxable fringe benefit that provides employer services to employees with little cost to the employer (e.g., airline tickets or phone service).

Nonacquiescence issued after the IRS loses a trial-level or circuit court case when the IRS has decided to continue to litigate this issue.

Nonperformance based compensation compensation paid to an employee that does not depend on the employee's performance or the corporation's performance or success. It usually is straight salary.

Nonqualified deferred compensation compensation provided for under a nonqualified plan allowing employees to defer compensation to a future period.

Nonqualified stock option a type of stock option requiring employees to treat the bargain element from options exercised as ordinary income in the tax year options are exercised. Correspondingly, employers may deduct the bargain element as compensation expense in the tax year options are exercised.

Nonrecaptured net §1231 losses a net §1231 loss that is deducted as an ordinary loss in one year and has not caused subsequent §1231 gain to be taxed as ordinary income.

Nonrecognition provisions tax laws that allow taxpayers to permanently exclude income from taxation or to defer recognizing realized income until a subsequent period.

Nonrecognition transaction a transaction where at least a portion of the realized gain or loss is not currently recognized.

Nonrefundable credits tax credits that reduce a taxpayer's gross tax liability but are limited to the amount of gross tax liability. Any credit not used in the current year is lost.

Nonservice partner a partner who receives a partnership interest in exchange for property rather than services.

Nontaxable fringe benefit an employer provided benefit that may be excluded from an employee's income.

O

Office examination the second most common audit. As the name suggests, the IRS conducts these audits at the local IRS office. These audits are typically broader in scope and more complex than correspondence examinations. Small businesses, taxpayers operating sole proprietorships, and middle- to high-income individual taxpayers are more likely, if audited, to have office examinations.

Operating income the annual income from a trade or business or rental activity.

Operating loss the annual loss from a trade or business or rental activity.

Option exercise the use of a stock option to acquire employer stock at a specified price.

Ordinary asset an asset created or used in a taxpayer's trade or business (e.g., accounts receivable or inventory) that generates ordinary income (or loss) on disposition.

Ordinary income property property that if sold would generate income taxed at ordinary rates.

Ordinary and necessary expense interpreted as an expense that is normal or appropriate and that is helpful or conducive to the business activity.

Original issue discount a type of bond issued for less than the maturity or face value of the bond.

P

PAL an acronym for "passive activity loss." Losses allocated to partners who are not material participants in the partnership are passive activity losses.

Passive activity an activity in which the taxpayer does not materially participate.

Passive activity income or loss income or loss from an activity in which the taxpayer does not materially participate.

Passive activity loss rules tax rules designed to limit taxpayers' ability to deduct losses from activities in which they don't materially participate against income from other sources.

Passive category income foreign source personal holding company income such as interest, dividends, rents, royalties, annuities, and gains from sale of certain assets that is combined in computing the FTC limitation.

Passive investments direct or indirect investments (other than through a C corporation) in a trade or business or rental activity in which the taxpayer does not materially participate.

Payment liability liabilities of accrual method businesses for which economic performance occurs when the business actually *pays* the liability for, among others: worker's compensation; tort; breach of contract or violation of law; rebates and refunds; awards, prizes, and jackpots; insurance, warranties, and service contracts provided *to* the business; and taxes.

Percentage depletion a method of recovering the cost of a natural resource that allows a taxpayer to recover or expense an amount based on a statutorily determined percentage.

Permissible accounting method accounting method allowed under the tax law. Permissible accounting methods are adopted the first time a taxpayer uses the method on a tax return.

Person an individual, trust, estate, partnership, association, company, or corporation.

Personal exemption a fixed deduction allowed for an individual taxpayer, and spouse if filing a joint tax return.

Personal expenses expenses incurred for personal motives. Personal expenses are not deductible for tax purposes.

Personal property all tangible property other than real property.

Personal property tax a tax on the fair market value of all types of tangible and intangible property, except real property.

Phase-outs limitations that gradually eliminate deductions, credits, or other adjustments to taxable income typically done ratably over a phase-out range (based on AGI or related income measure).

Point one percent of the principal amount of a loan. A home buyer might pay points to compensate the lender for services or for a lower interest rate.

Portfolio investments investments producing dividends, interest, royalties, annuities, or capital gains.

Positive basis adjustment (for special basis adjustment purposes) the sum of the gain recognized by the owners receiving distributed property and the amount of any required basis reduction.

Preferential tax rate tax rates lower than the tax rate applied to ordinary income.

Preferentially taxed income income taxed at a preferential rate such as long-term capital gains and qualified dividends.

Present interest right to presently enjoy property or receive income from the property.

Present value the concept that $1 today is worth more than $1 in the future. For example, assuming an investor can earn a 5% after-tax return, $1 invested today should be worth $1.05 in one year. Hence, $1 today is equivalent to $1.05 in one year.

Primary authority official sources of the tax law generated by the legislative branch (i.e., statutory authority issued by Congress), judicial branch (i.e., rulings by the U.S. District Court, U.S. Tax Court, U.S. Court of Federal Claims, U.S. Circuit Court of Appeals, or U.S. Supreme Court), or executive/administrative branch (i.e., Treasury or IRS pronouncements).

Principal residence the main place of residence for a taxpayer during the taxable year.

Private letter rulings IRS pronouncements issued in response to a taxpayer request for a ruling on specific issues for the taxpayer. They are common for proposed transactions with potentially large tax implications. For the requesting taxpayer, a private letter ruling has very high authority. For all other taxpayers, private letter rulings have little authoritative weight.

Private nonoperating foundations privately sponsored foundations that disburse funds to other charities.

Private operating foundations privately sponsored foundations that actually fund and conduct charitable activities.

Procedural regulations regulations that explain Treasury Department procedures as they relate to administering the Code.

Progressive tax rate structure a tax rate structure that imposes an increasing marginal tax rate as the tax base increases. As the tax base increases, both the marginal tax rate and the taxes paid increase.

Proportional tax rate structure also known as a flat tax, this tax rate structure imposes a constant tax rate throughout the tax base. As the tax base increases, the taxes paid increase proportionally.

Proposed regulations regulations issued in proposed form; they do not carry the same authoritative weight as temporary or final regulations. All regulations are issued in proposed form first to allow public comment on them.

Q

Qualified debt (for mortgage interest expense deduction purposes) the amount of debt on which qualified residence interest is paid. This includes debt up to $1,000,000 of acquisition indebtedness and up to $100,000 of home-equity indebtedness.

Qualified dividends paid by domestic or certain qualified foreign corporations that are eligible for lower capital gains rates.

Qualified educational expenses consist of tuition and related costs for enrolling the taxpayer, spouse, or a dependent at a post-secondary institution of higher education.

Qualified educational loans loans whose proceeds are used to pay qualified education expenses.

Qualified employee discount a nontaxable fringe benefit that provides employer goods at a discount (but not below the employer's cost) and services to employees at up to a 20% discount.

Qualified moving expense reimbursement a nontaxable fringe benefit that allows employers to pay moving-related expenses on behalf of employees.

Qualified nonrecourse financing nonrecourse debt secured by real property from a commercial lender unrelated to the borrower.

Qualified production activities income (QPAI) the *net* income from selling or leasing property that was manufactured in the United States.

Qualified replacement property property acquired to replace property damaged or destroyed in an involuntary conversion. It must be of a similar or related use to the original property even if the replacement property is real property (rental real estate for rental real estate).

Qualified residence the taxpayer's principal residence and one other residence.

Qualified residence interest interest paid on acquisition indebtedness and on home-equity indebtedness that is secured by a qualified residence.

Qualified retirement accounts plans meeting certain requirements that allow compensation placed in the account to be tax deferred until the taxpayer withdraws money from the account.

Qualified retirement plans employer-sponsored retirement plans that meet government-imposed funding and antidiscrimination requirements.

Qualified small business stock stock received at original issue from a corporation with a gross tax basis in its assets both before and after the issuance of no more than $50,000,000 and with 80% of the value of its assets used in the active conduct of certain qualified trades or businesses.

Qualified transportation fringe benefit a nontaxable fringe benefit provided by employers in the form of mass transit passes, parking, or vanpool benefits.

Qualified tuition program (529 plans) a state-sponsored program designed to help parents finance education expenses by generating tax-free income. 529 plans are administered by certain investment companies and are subject to contribution requirements and investment guidelines.

Qualifying child an individual who qualifies as a dependent of a taxpayer by meeting a relationship, age, residence, and support test with respect to the taxpayer.

Qualifying relative an individual who is not a qualifying child of another taxpayer and who meets a relationship, support, and gross income test may qualify to be a dependent of another taxpayer.

Qualifying widow or widower one of five primary filing statuses. Applies for up to two years after the year in which the taxpayer's spouse dies (the taxpayer files married filing jointly in the year of the spouse's death) as long as the taxpayer remains unmarried and maintains a household for a dependent child.

Question of fact a research question that hinges upon the facts and circumstances of the taxpayer's transaction.

Question of law a research question that hinges upon the interpretation of the law, such as interpreting a particular phrase in a code section.

R

Real property land and structures permanently attached to land.

Real property tax a tax on the fair market value of land and structures permanently attached to land.

Realization gain or loss that results from an exchange of property rights in a transaction.

Realization principle the proposition that income only exists when there is a transaction with another party resulting in a measurable change in property rights.

Realized gain or loss the difference between the amount realized and the adjusted basis of an asset sold or otherwise disposed of.

Realized income income generated in a transaction with a second party in which there is a measurable change in property rights between parties.

Reasonable in amount an expenditure is reasonable when the amount paid is not extravagant nor exorbitant.

Recapture the recharacterization of income from capital gain to ordinary income.

Recognition gain or loss included in the computation of taxable income.

Recognized gain or loss the gain or loss included in gross income on a taxpayer's tax return. This is usually the realized gain or loss unless a nonrecognition provision applies.

Recovery period a length of time prescribed by statute in which business property is depreciated or amortized.

Recurring item an election under economic performance to currently deduct an accrued liability if the liability is expected to persist in the future and is either not material or a current deduction better matches revenue.

Refinance when a taxpayer pays off a current loan with the proceeds of a second loan.

Refundable credits credits that are not limited to the amount of the gross tax liability. If the credit exceeds the gross tax liability, the taxpayer receives a refund for the excess credit.

Regressive tax rate structure a tax rate structure that imposes a decreasing marginal tax rate as the tax base increases. As the tax base increases, the taxes paid increase, but the marginal tax rate decreases.

Regulations the Treasury Department's official interpretation of the Internal Revenue Code. Regulations are the highest authority issued by the IRS.

Related-party transaction financial activities among family members, among owners and their businesses, or among businesses owned by the same owners.

Research and experimentation costs expenses for research including costs of research laboratories (salaries, materials, and other related expenses). Taxpayers can elect to amortize research and development costs over not less than 60 months from the time benefits are first derived from the research.

Restricted stock stock employees receive as compensation that may only be sold after the passage of time or after certain performance targets are achieved. Because employees are not entitled to immediately sell the restricted stock they receive, the value of the stock is generally not taxable to employees or deductible by employers until the selling restrictions lapse.

Return of capital the portion of proceeds from a sale (or distribution) representing a return of the original cost of the underlying property.

Revenue procedures second in administrative authoritative weight after regulations. Revenue procedures are much more detailed than regulations and explain in greater detail IRS practice and procedures in administering the tax law. Revenue procedures have the same authoritative weight as revenue rulings.

Revenue rulings second in administrative authoritative weight after regulations. Revenue rulings address the specific application of the Code and regulations to a specific factual situation. Revenue rulings have the same authoritative weight as revenue procedures.

Rollover a transfer of funds from a qualified retirement plan to another qualified retirement plan, from a qualified retirement plan to a Roth or traditional IRA, or from a traditional IRA to a Roth IRA.

Roth 401(k) a type of defined contribution plan that allows employees to contribute on an after-tax basis and receive distributions tax free.

Roth IRA an individually managed retirement plan permitting individuals to contribute on an after-tax basis and receive distributions tax free.

Roth qualified retirement plans retirement plans meeting the requirements for qualified plans but not allowing employees a current deduction for contributions. Distributions from Roth qualified retirement plans are tax free.

Royalties payments taxpayers receive for allowing others to use their tangible or intangible property.

Safe-harbor provision provision of the tax law that reduces or eliminates a taxpayer's liability under the law if the taxpayer meets certain requirements.

Salary a fixed regular payment by an employer to an employee in exchange for the employee's services which is usually paid on a monthly basis, but typically expressed as an annual amount.

Sales tax a tax imposed on the retail sales of goods (plus certain services). Retailers are responsible for collecting and remitting the tax; typically sales tax is collected at the point of sale.

Same-day sale a phrase used to describe a situation where a taxpayer exercises stock options and then immediately sells the stock received through the option exercise.

Schedule C a schedule on which a taxpayer reports the income and deductions for a sole-proprietorship.

Secondary authority unofficial tax authorities that interpret and explain the primary authorities, such as tax research services, tax articles, newsletters, and textbooks. Secondary authorities may be very helpful in understanding a tax issue, but they hold little weight in a tax dispute (hence, the term *unofficial* tax authorities).

Secured loan a loan for which property is used as collateral for the loan. If the loan goes into default, the lender is only allowed to take possession of the property securing the loan.

Security a financial instrument including an equity interest in business organizations and creditor interests such as savings accounts, notes, and bonds.

Self-employment taxes Social Security and Medicare taxes paid by the self-employed on a taxpayer's net earnings from self-employment. For self-employed taxpayers, the terms "self-employment tax" and "FICA tax" are synonymous.

SEP IRA a simplified employee pension that can be administered through an individual retirement account.

Settlement statement a statement that details the monies paid out and received by the buyer and seller in a real estate transaction.

Short-term capital gains or losses gains or losses from the sale of capital assets held for one year or less.

Sin taxes taxes imposed on the purchase of goods (e.g., alcohol, tobacco products, etc.) that are considered socially less desirable.

Single one of five primary statuses available. A taxpayer files as single if s/he is unmarried as of the end of the year and does not qualify for any of the other filing statuses. A taxpayer is considered single if s/he is unmarried or legally separated from his or her spouse under a divorce or separate maintenance decree.

Social Security Tax the Old Age, Survivors, and Disability Insurance (OASDI) tax. The tax is intended to provide basic pension coverage for the retired and disabled. Employees pay Social Security tax at a rate of 6.2% (4.2% in 2011 and 2012) on the wage base (employers also pay 6.2%). Self-employed taxpayers are subject to a Social Security tax at a rate of 12.4% (10.4% in 2011 and 2012) on their net earnings from self-employment. The base on which Social Security taxes are paid is limited to an annually determined amount of wages and/or net earnings from self-employment.

Specific identification method an elective method for determining the cost of an asset sold. Under this method, the taxpayer specifically chooses the assets that are to be sold.

Spot rate the foreign currency exchange rate on a specific day.

Spousal IRA an IRA account for the spouse with the lesser amount of earned income. Contributions in this account belong to this spouse no matter where the funds for the contribution came from.

Standard deduction a fixed deduction offered in lieu of itemized deductions. The amount of the standard deduction depends on the taxpayer's filing status.

Stare decisis a doctrine meaning that a court will rule consistently with (a) its previous rulings (i.e., unless, due to evolving interpretations of the tax law over time, it decides to overturn an earlier decision) and (b) the rulings of higher courts with appellate jurisdiction (i.e., the courts its cases are appealed to).

Start-up costs expenses that would be classified as business expenses except that the expenses are incurred before the business begins.

These costs are generally capitalized and amortized over 180 months, but limited immediate expensing may be available.

State tax a tax imposed by one of the 50 U.S. states.

Statements on Standards for Tax Services (SSTS) standards of practice for tax professionals issued by the AICPA. Currently, there are seven SSTS that describe the tax professional standards when recommending a tax return position, answering questions on a tax return, preparing a tax return using data supplied by a client, using estimates on a tax return, taking a tax return position inconsistent with a previous year's tax return, discovering a tax return error, and giving tax advice to taxpayers.

Static forecasting the process of forecasting tax revenues based on the existing state of transactions while ignoring how taxpayers may alter their activities in response to a tax law change.

Statute of limitations defines the period in which the taxpayer can file an amended tax return or the IRS can assess a tax deficiency for a specific tax year. For both amended tax returns filed by a taxpayer and proposed tax assessments by the IRS, the statute of limitations generally ends three years from the *later* of (1) the date the tax return was actually filed or (2) the tax return's original due date.

Step-transaction doctrine judicial doctrine that allows the IRS to collapse a series of related transactions into one transaction to determine the tax consequences of the transaction.

Stock dividend a dividend made by a corporation of its own stock.

Student loans loans where the proceeds are used for qualified educational expenses, but do not include home-equity loans.

Substance-over-form doctrine judicial doctrine that allows the IRS to consider the transaction's substance regardless of its form and, where appropriate, reclassify the transaction according to its substance.

Substantial authority the standard used to determine whether a tax practitioner may recommend and a taxpayer may take a tax return position without being subject to IRS penalty under IRC §6694 and IRC §6662, respectively. A good CPA evaluates whether supporting authority is substantial or not based upon the supporting and opposing authorities' weight and relevance. Substantial authority suggests that the probability that the taxpayer's position is sustained upon audit or litigation is in the 35 to 40 percent range or above.

Substitution effect one of the two basic responses that a taxpayer may have when taxes increase. The substitution effect predicts that, when taxpayers are taxed more, rather than work more, they will substitute nontaxable activities (e.g., leisure pursuits) for taxable ones because the marginal value of taxable activities has decreased.

Sufficiency a standard for evaluating a good tax system. Sufficiency is defined as assessing the aggregate size of the tax revenues that must be generated and ensuring that the tax system provides these revenues.

T

Tax a payment required by a government that is unrelated to any specific benefit or service received from the government.

Tax avoidance the legal act of arranging one's transactions or affairs to reduce taxes paid.

Tax base the item that is being taxed (e.g., purchase price of a good, taxable income, etc.).

Tax basis the amount of a taxpayer's unrecovered cost of or investment in an asset. *See also* adjusted tax basis.

Tax benefit rule holds that a refund of an amount deducted in a previous period is only included in income to the extent that the deduction reduced taxable income.

Tax bracket a range of taxable income taxed at a specified rate.

Tax Court allocation method allocates expenses associated with rental use of the home between to rental use and personal use. Property taxes and mortgage interest are allocated to rental use of the home based on the ratio of the number of rental use days to the total days in the year. All other expenses are allocated to rental use based on the ratio of the number of rental use days to total days the property was used during the year.

Tax credits items that directly reduce a taxpayer's tax liability.

Tax evasion the willful attempt to defraud the government (i.e., by not paying taxes legally owed). Tax evasion falls outside the confines of legal tax avoidance.

Tax haven generally, a country offering very favorable tax laws for foreign businesses and individuals.

Tax rate the level of taxes imposed on the tax base, usually expressed as a percentage.

Tax rate schedule a schedule of progressive tax rates and the income ranges to which the rates apply that a taxpayer may use to compute her gross tax liability.

Tax shelter an investment or other arrangement designed to produce tax benefits without any expectation of economic profits.

Tax tables IRS-provided tables that specify the federal income tax liability for individuals with taxable income within a specific range. The tables differ by filing status and reflect tax rates that increase with taxable income.

Tax treaties agreements negotiated between countries that describe the tax treatment of entities subject to tax in both countries (e.g., U.S. citizens earning investment income in Spain). The U.S. president has the authority to enter into a tax treaty with another country after receiving the Senate's advice.

Tax year a fixed period in which a business reports income and deductions generally referred to as an accounting period.

Taxable fringe benefit a noncash fringe benefit provided by employers to an employee that is included in taxable income (e.g., auto allowance or group-term life over $50,000).

Taxable gifts the amount left after adjusting current gifts for gift splitting, annual exclusions, the marital deduction, and the charitable deduction.

Taxable income the tax base for the individual income tax.

Technical advice memorandum ruling issued by the IRS national office, requested by an IRS agent, and generally for a completed transaction.

Temporary regulations regulations issued with a limited life (three years for regulations issued after November 20, 1988). During their life, temporary regulations carry the same authoritative weight as final regulations.

Tenancy by the entirety ownership by husband and wife similar to joint tenancy with right of survivorship.

Tenancy in common ownership in which owners hold divided rights to property and have the ability to transfer these rights during their life or upon their death.

Tentative minimum tax the tax on the AMT tax base under the alternative minimum tax system.

Term insurance a form of life insurance without an investment or savings feature.

Third-party intermediaries people or organizations that facilitate the transfer of property between taxpayers in a like-kind exchange. Typically, the intermediary receives the cash from selling the property received from the taxpayer and uses it to acquire like-kind property identified by the taxpayer.

Topical tax service a tax service arranged by subject (i.e., topic). For each topic, topical services identify tax issues that relate to each topic, and then explain and cite authorities relevant to the issue (code sections, regulations, court cases, revenue rulings, etc.).

Trade or business a profit-motivated activity characterized by a sustained, continuous, high level of individual involvement or effort.

Traditional 401(k) a popular type of defined contribution plan with before-tax employee and employer contributions and taxable distributions.

Traditional IRA an individually managed retirement account with deductible contributions and taxable distributions.

Transfer taxes taxes on the transfer of wealth from one taxpayer to another. The estate and gift taxes are two examples of transfer taxes.

Travel expenses expenditures incurred while "away from home overnight," including the cost of transportation, meals, lodging, and incidental expenses.

Treasury bond a debt instrument issued by the U.S. Treasury at face value, at a discount, or at a premium, with a set interest rate and maturity date that pays interest semiannually. Treasury bonds have terms of 30 years.

Treasury note a debt instrument issued by the U.S. Treasury at face value, at a discount, or at a premium, with a set interest rate and maturity date that pays interest semiannually. Treasury notes have terms of 2, 5, or 10 years.

U

Uncertain tax positions a tax return position for which a corporation does not have a high degree of certainty as to its tax consequences.

Underpayment penalty the penalty that applies when taxpayers fail to adequately prepay their tax liability. The underpayment penalty is determined by multiplying the federal short-term interest rate plus three percentage points by the amount of tax underpayment per quarter.

Unearned income income from property that accrues as time passes without effort on the part of the owner of the property.

Unemployment tax the tax that pays for temporary unemployment benefits for individuals terminated from their jobs without cause.

Uniform cost capitalization rules (UNICAP rules) specify that inventories must be accounted for using full absorption rules to allocate the indirect costs of productive activities to inventory.

Unrealized receivables any rights to receive payment for (1) goods delivered, or to be delivered, or (2) services rendered, or to be rendered. Unrealized receivables also include other assets to the extent that they would produce ordinary income if sold for their fair market value.

Unrecaptured §1250 gain a gain from the sale of real estate held by a noncorporate taxpayer for more than one year in a trade or business or as rental property attributable to tax depreciation deducted at ordinary tax rates. This gain is taxable at a maximum 25% capital gains rate.

U.S. Circuit Courts of Appeal the first level of appeals courts after the trial-level courts. There are 13 U.S. Circuit Courts of Appeal; one for the Federal Circuit and 12 assigned to hear cases that originated from a specific circuit (e.g., the 11th Circuit Court of Appeals only hears cases originating within the 11th Circuit).

U.S. Constitution the founding law of the United States, ratified in 1789.

U.S. Court of Federal Claims one of the three trial-level courts. It is a national court that only hears monetary claims against the federal government.

U.S. District Court one of three trial-level courts. It is the only court that allows a jury trial. There is at least one district court in each state.

U.S. savings bonds debt instruments issued by the U.S. Treasury at face value or at a discount, with a set maturity date. Interest earned from U.S. bonds is paid either at maturity or when the bonds are converted to cash before maturity.

U.S. Supreme Court the highest court in the United States. The Supreme Court hears only a few tax cases a year with great significance to a broad cross-section of taxpayers or cases litigating issues in which there has been disagreement among the circuit courts. For most tax cases, the Supreme Court refuses to hear the case (i.e., the *writ of certiorari* is denied) and, thus, litigation ends with the circuit court decision.

U.S. Tax Court a national court that only hears tax cases and where the judges are tax experts. The U.S. Tax Court is the only court that allows tax cases to be heard *before* the taxpayer pays the disputed liability and the only court with a small claims division (hearing claims involving disputed liabilities of $50,000 or less).

Use tax a tax imposed on the retail price of goods owned, possessed, or consumed within a state that were *not* purchased within the state.

V

Valuation allowance the portion of a deferred tax asset for which management determines it is more likely than not that a tax benefit will not be realized on a future tax return.

Value-added tax a tax imposed on the producer of goods (and services) on the value of goods (services) added at each stage of production. Value-added taxes are common in Europe.

Vertical equity one of the dimensions of equity. Vertical equity is achieved when taxpayers with greater ability to pay tax, pay more tax relative to taxpayers with a lesser ability to pay tax.

Vest to become legally entitled to receive a particular benefit without risk of forfeiture; to gain ownership.

Vesting date the date on which the taxpayer becomes legally entitled to receive a particular benefit without risk of forfeiture.

Vesting period period of employment over which employees earn the right to own and exercise stock options.

W

Wages a payment by an employer to an employee in exchange for the employee's services which is typically expressed in hourly, daily, or piecework rate.

Wash sale the sale of an investment if that same investment (or substantially identical investment) is purchased within 30 days before or after the sale date. Losses on wash sales are deferred.

Wherewithal to pay the ability or resources to pay taxes due from a particular transaction.

Whole life insurance a form of life insurance with an investment or savings component.

Willing-buyer, willing-seller rule the guideline for determining fair market value as "the price at which such property would change hands between a willing buyer and a willing seller, neither being under any compulsion to buy or to sell, and both have reasonable knowledge of the relevant facts."

Withholdings taxes collected and remitted to the government by an employer from an employee's wages.

Working condition fringe benefit a nontaxable fringe benefit provided by employers that would be deductible as an ordinary and necessary business expense if paid by an employee (e.g., reimbursement for professional dues).

Writ of certiorari a document filed to request the U.S. Supreme Court to hear a case.

Z

Zero coupon bond a type of bond issued at a discount that pays interest only at maturity.

Appendix C

Ten additional Comprehensive Tax Return problems—covering individual, corporation, partnership and S corporation tax returns, can be found in the *Connect Library*.

Comprehensive Tax Return Problems

INDIVIDUAL TAX RETURN PROBLEM 1

Required:

- Use the following information to complete Keith and Jennifer Hamilton's 2014 federal income tax return. If information is missing, use reasonable assumptions to fill in the gaps.
- Form 1040, supporting schedules, and instructions to the forms and schedules can be found at the IRS website (www.irs.gov).

Facts:

1. Keith Hamilton is employed as an airline pilot for Flyby Airlines in Las Vegas, NV. Jennifer is employed as a teacher's assistant at Small World Elementary School, in Henderson, NV. Keith and Jennifer live in a home they purchased this year. Keith and Jennifer have three children who lived with them all year, Joshua (17), Danielle (14), and Sara (10). Keith and Jennifer provided the following personal information:
   - Keith and Jennifer do not want to contribute to the presidential election campaign.
   - Keith and Jennifer do not claim itemized deductions.
   - Keith and Jennifer live at 3678 Blue Sky Drive, Henderson, NV 89052.
   - Keith's birthday is 10/12/1969 and his Social Security number is 535-22-4466.
   - Jennifer's birthday is 7/16/1972 and her Social Security number is 535-44-2255.
   - Joshua's birthday is 6/30/1997 and his Social Security number is 454-54-5454.
   - Danielle's birthday is 8/12/2000 and her Social Security number is 343-43-4343.
   - Sara's birthday is 5/13/2004 and her Social Security number is 232-32-3232.

2. Keith received the following Form W-2 for 2014 from Flyby Airlines.

22222 Void ☐	a Employee's social security number 535-22-4466	For Official Use Only ► OMB No. 1545-0008	
b Employer identification number (EIN) 91-0001002		1 Wages, tips, other compensation 163,645.00	2 Federal income tax withheld 31,000.00
c Employer's name, address, and ZIP code Flyby Airlines 375 West Flight Blvd. Las Vegas, NV 89119		3 Social security wages 117,000.00	4 Social security tax withheld 7,254.00
		5 Medicare wages and tips 178,645.00	6 Medicare tax withheld 2,590.35
		7 Social security tips	8 Allocated tips
d Control number		9	10 Dependent care benefits
e Employee's first name and initial	Last name Suff.	11 Nonqualified plans	12a See instructions for box 12 D 15,000
Keith Hamilton 3678 Blue Sky Drive Henderson, NV 89052		13 Statutory employee ☐ Retirement plan ☒ Third-party sick pay ☐	12b
		14 Other	12c
f Employee's address and ZIP code			12d

15 State	Employer's state ID number	16 State wages, tips, etc.	17 State income tax	18 Local wages, tips, etc.	19 Local income tax	20 Locality name
NV	987654321	163,645.00	0.00			

Form **W-2** Wage and Tax Statement **2014**

Department of the Treasury—Internal Revenue Service

For Privacy Act and Paperwork Reduction Act Notice, see the separate instructions.

Cat. No. 10134D

Copy A For Social Security Administration — Send this entire page with Form W-3 to the Social Security Administration; photocopies are **not** acceptable.

Do Not Cut, Fold, or Staple Forms on This Page

3. Jennifer received the following Form W-2 for 2014 from Small World Elementary School.

22222 Void ☐	a Employee's social security number 535-44-2255	For Official Use Only ► OMB No. 1545-0008	
b Employer identification number (EIN) 91-0001003		1 Wages, tips, other compensation 36,825.00	2 Federal income tax withheld 5,524.00
c Employer's name, address, and ZIP code Small World Elementary School 333 Tiny Tot Lane Henderson, NV 89053		3 Social security wages 39,825.00	4 Social security tax withheld 2,469.15
		5 Medicare wages and tips 39,825.00	6 Medicare tax withheld 577.46
		7 Social security tips	8 Allocated tips
d Control number		9	10 Dependent care benefits
e Employee's first name and initial	Last name Suff.	11 Nonqualified plans	12a See instructions for box 12 D 3,000
Jennifer Hamilton 3678 Blue Sky Drive Henderson, NV 89052		13 Statutory employee ☐ Retirement plan ☒ Third-party sick pay ☐	12b
		14 Other	12c
f Employee's address and ZIP code			12d

15 State	Employer's state ID number	16 State wages, tips, etc.	17 State income tax	18 Local wages, tips, etc.	19 Local income tax	20 Locality name
NV	123456789	36,825.00	0.00			

Form **W-2** Wage and Tax Statement **2014**

Department of the Treasury—Internal Revenue Service

For Privacy Act and Paperwork Reduction Act Notice, see the separate instructions.

Cat. No. 10134D

Copy A For Social Security Administration — Send this entire page with Form W-3 to the Social Security Administration; photocopies are **not** acceptable.

Do Not Cut, Fold, or Staple Forms on This Page

4. During 2014, Keith and Jennifer received $550 in interest from Las Vegas municipal bonds, $1,070 interest from U.S. Treasury bonds, and $65 from their savings account at SCD Credit Union. Keith and Jennifer are joint owners of the Las Vegas city bonds and the U.S. Treasury bonds. They have a joint savings account at SCD Credit Union.

5. On January 21, 2014, Jennifer was involved in a car accident. Because the other driver was at fault, the other driver's insurance company paid Jennifer $1,350 for medical expenses relating to her injuries from the accident and $300 for emotional distress from the accident. She received payment on March 15, 2014.
6. Keith's father died on November 15, 2013. Keith received a $100,000 death benefit from his father's life insurance policy on February 8, 2014.
7. On February 15, 2014, Keith hurt his arm on a family skiing trip in Utah and was unable to fly for two weeks. He received $4,000 for disability pay from his disability insurance policy. He received the check on March 2, 2014. Flyby Airlines paid $600 in premiums on this policy during 2014. The disability insurance policy premiums are paid for by Flyby Airlines as a fully taxable fringe benefit to Keith (the premiums paid on his behalf are included in Keith's compensation amount on his W-2).
8. Jennifer's grandmother died on March 10, 2014, leaving Jennifer with an inheritance of $30,000. (She received the inheritance on May 12, 2014.) Flyby Airlines had space available on its Long Island, NY, flight and provided Keith, Jennifer, and their three children with free flights so they could attend the funeral. The value of the ticket for each passenger was $600.
9. On April 1, 2014, Jennifer slipped in the Small World Elementary lunchroom, and injured her back. Jennifer received $1,200 in worker's compensation benefits because her work-related injury caused her to miss two weeks of work. She also received a $2,645 reimbursement for medical expenses from the health insurance company. Small World Elementary pays the premiums for Jennifer's health insurance policy as a nontaxable fringe benefit.
10. On May 17, 2014, Keith and Jennifer received a federal income tax refund of $975 from their 2013 federal income tax return.
11. On June 5, 2014, Keith and Jennifer sold their home in Henderson, NV, for $510,000 (net of commissions). Keith and Jennifer purchased the home eleven years ago for $470,000. On July 12, 2014, they bought a new home for $675,000.
12. On July 25, 2014, Keith's aunt Beatrice gave Keith $18,000 because she wanted to let everyone know that Keith is her favorite nephew.
13. On September 29, 2014, Jennifer won an iPad valued at $500 in a raffle at the annual fair held at Joshua's high school.
14. Keith and Jennifer have qualifying insurance for purposes of the the Affordable Care Act (ACA).

INDIVIDUAL TAX RETURN PROBLEM 2

Required:

- Use the following information to complete Karl and Ellie Frederickson's 2014 federal income tax return. If information is missing, use reasonable assumptions to fill in the gaps.
- You may need the following forms to complete the project: Form 1040 and Schedule A. The forms, schedules, and instructions can be found at the IRS website (www.irs.gov). The instructions can be helpful in completing the forms.

Facts:

1. Karl Frederickson is employed as a human resources manager for Toys Unlimited, Inc., and Ellie is a financial planner for her mother's company, Frederickson Investments, Inc., a full-service wealth-planning firm. They provide the following information:
   - They both want to contribute to the presidential election campaign.
   - They live at 9876 Fighting Irish Lane, South Bend, IN.

- Karl's birthday is 7/17/1965 and his Social Security number is 555-12-6789.
- Ellie's birthday is 9/11/1967 and her Social Security number is 987-65-4321.
- Karl or Ellie do not have any foreign bank accounts or trusts.

2. Karl received a Form W-2 from Toys Unlimited, Inc. that contained the following information:

• Line 1 Wages, tips, other compensation:	$45,000
• Line 2 Federal income tax withheld:	7,500
• Line 3 Social Security wages:	45,000
• Line 4 Social Security tax withheld:	2,790
• Line 5 Medicare wages and tips:	45,000
• Line 6 Medicare tax withheld:	653
• Line 17 State income tax:	2,200

3. Ellie received a Form W-2 from Frederickson Investments, Inc. that contained the following information:

• Line 1 Wages, tips, other compensation:	$85,000
• Line 2 Federal income tax withheld:	12,500
• Line 3 Social Security wages:	85,000
• Line 4 Social Security tax withheld:	5,270
• Line 5 Medicare wages and tips:	85,000
• Line 6 Medicare tax withheld:	1,233
• Line 17 State income tax:	4,200

4. Karl and Ellie incurred the following medical expenses for the year:

• Transportation to Chicago for Karl's cancer treatment:	2,000 miles
• Unreimbursed hospital charges for Karl:	$6,500
• Unreimbursed prescription drug charges for Karl and Ellie:	1,750
• Unreimbursed physician charges for Karl and Ellie:	2,200
• Unreimbursed prescription glasses for Ellie:	150
• Laser hair treatment for Ellie (so that she will no longer need to shave her legs)	2,000

5. Karl and Ellie paid $12,000 of interest payments on their primary residence (acquisition debt of $225,000). They also paid $1,750 of interest expense on Ellie's car loan and $500 of interest on their Visa card.
6. Karl and Ellie paid $4,000 of real estate taxes on their home and $1,000 of real estate tax on a vacant lot they purchased with the hope of building their dream home in the future. They also paid $3,000 in sales tax on Ellie's car and other purchases and $1,000 of ad valoreum tax on their cars.
7. Karl and Ellie made the following contributions this year:

• American Red Cross	$ 200
• United Way	150
• St. Joseph's Catholic Church	8,000
• Food for the family of Hannah Barbara (a neighbor who suffered a tragic car accident this past year)	225
• Stock transfer to the University of Notre Dame (originally purchased for $1,000 in 2005)	750

8. Karl incurred $4,000 of unreimbursed meals and entertainment related to his job. Ellie incurred $1,200 of expenses for investment publications, and last year they paid their CPA $500 to prepare their tax return.

9. The roof on Karl and Ellie's house was severely damaged in a hail storm. They had to replace the roof ($7,500), which unfortunately was not covered by insurance because of their high deductible ($10,000).
10. Karl won $5,000 in the state lottery. He has been playing the lottery for years ($10 in lottery tickets every week ($520 in total) that he saves to keep track of the numbers he plays).
11. Karl and Ellie have qualifying insurance for purposes of the Affordable Care Act (ACA).

INDIVIDUAL TAX RETURN PROBLEM 3

Required:

- Use the following information to complete Rhonda Hill's 2014 federal income tax return. If information is missing, use reasonable assumptions to fill in the gaps.
- The forms, schedules, and instructions can be found at the IRS website (www.irs.gov). The instructions can be helpful in completing the forms.

Facts:

1. Rhonda Hill (unmarried) is employed as an office manager at the main office of Carter and Associates CPA firm. Rhonda lives in a home she purchased 20 years ago. Rhonda's older cousin Mabel Wright lives with Rhonda in the home. Mabel is retired and receives $2,400 of Social Security payments each year. Mabel is able to save this money because Rhonda provides all of Mabel's support. Rhonda also provided the following information:
   - Rhonda does not want to contribute to the presidential election campaign.
   - Rhonda lives at 1234 Blue Ridge Way, Tulsa, OK 74101.
   - Rhonda's birthday is 12/18/1949 and her Social Security number is 335-67-8910.
   - Mabel's birthday is 11/2/1941 and her Social Security number is 566-77-8899.
   - Rhonda does not have any foreign bank accounts or trusts.
   - Rhonda has qualifying insurance for purposes of the Affordable Care Act (ACA).
2. Rhonda received a Form W-2 from Carter and Associates (her employer) that contained the following information:

• Line 1 Wages, tips, other compensation:	$72,000
• Line 2 Federal income tax withheld:	9,300
• Line 3 Social Security wages:	72,000
• Line 4 Social Security tax withheld:	4,464
• Line 5 Medicare wages and tips:	72,000
• Line 6 Medicare tax withheld:	1,044
• Line 16 State wages, tips, etc.:	72,000
• Line 17 State income tax:	2,700

   - Carter and Associates address is 1234 CPA Way Tulsa, OK 74101; its FEIN is 91:0001002; and its State ID number is 123456678
3. Rhonda received $250 in interest from Tulsa City bonds, $120 interest from IBM bonds, and $15 from her savings account at UCU Credit Union. She also received a $460 dividend from Huggies Company and $500 from Bicker Corporation. Both dividends are qualified dividends.

4. Rhonda sold 200 shares of DM stock for $18 a share on June 15, 2014. She purchased the stock on December 12, 2009, for $10 a share. She also sold 50 shares of RSA stock for $15 a share on October 2, 2014. She purchased the stock for $65 a share on February 2, 2014. Stock basis amounts have been reported to the IRS.
5. The following is a record of the medical expense that Rhonda paid for herself during the year. The amounts reported are amounts she paid in excess of insurance reimbursements. Rhonda drove 210 miles for medical purposes in 2014.

Insurance premiums	$3,700
Prescription medications	100
Over-the-counter medications	250
Doctor and dentist visits	1,450
Eyeglasses	300
Physical therapy	200

6. Rhonda paid $2,800 in mortgage interest during the year to UCU credit union (reported to her on Form 1098). She also paid $1,200 in real property taxes during the year.
7. Rhonda contributed $2,350 to Heavenly Church during the year. Heavenly Church's address is 1342 Religion Way, Tulsa, OK 74101.

INDIVIDUAL TAX RETURN PROBLEM 4

Required:

- Use the following information to complete Phillip and Claire Dunphy's 2014 federal income tax return. If information is missing, use reasonable assumptions to fill in the gaps. Ignore the alternative minimum tax for this problem.
- Any required forms, schedules, and instructions can be found at the IRS website (www.irs.gov). The instructions can be helpful in completing the forms.

Facts:

1. Phillip and Claire are married and file a joint return. Phillip is self-employed as a real estate agent, and Claire is a flight attendant. Phillip and Claire have three dependent children. All three children live at home with Phillip and Claire for the entire year.

   The Dunphys provide you with the following additional information:

   - The Dunphys do not want to contribute to the presidential election campaign.
   - The Dunphys live at 3701 Brighton Avenue, Los Angeles, CA 90018.
   - Phillip's birthday is 11/5/1968 and his Social Security number is 321-44-5766.
   - Claire's birthday is 5/12/1971 and her Social Security number is 567-77-1258.
   - Haley's birthday is 11/6/2002 and her Social Security number is 621-18-7592.
   - Alex's birthday is 2/1/2004 and her Social Security number is 621-92-8751.
   - Luke's birthday is 12/12/2008 and his Social Security number is 621-99-9926.
   - The Dunphys do not have any foreign bank accounts or trusts.
2. Claire is a flight attendant for Western American Airlines (WAA), where she earned $57,000 in salary. WAA withheld federal income tax of $6,375, state income tax of $1,800, Los Angeles city income tax of $675, Social Security tax of $3,600, and Medicare tax of $825.
3. Phillip and Claire received $300 of interest from State Savings Bank on a joint account. They also received a qualified dividend of $395 on jointly owned stock in Xila Corporation.

4. Phillip's full-time real estate business is named "Phillip Dunphy Realty." His business is located at 645 Grove Street, Los Angeles, CA 90018, and his employer identification number is 93-3488888. Phillip's gross receipts during the year were $730,000. Phillip uses the cash method of accounting for his business. Phillip's business expenses are as follows:

Advertising	$ 5,000
Professional dues	800
Professional journals	200
Employee wages	48,000
Insurance on office contents	1,120
Accounting services	2,100
Miscellaneous office expense	500
Utilities and telephone	3,360
Payroll taxes	3,600
Depreciation	To be calculated

On March 20, Phillip moved his business out of the old offices at 1103 Allium Lane into a newly constructed and equipped office on Grove Street. Phillip sold the old office building and all its furnishings. Phillip's expenditures for the new office building are as follows:

Date Acquired	Asset	Cost
3/20	Land	$ 300,000
3/20	Office building	2,500,000
3/20	Furniture	200,000
4/1	Computer system	350,000
6/1	Artwork	150,000

Phillip computes his cost recovery allowance using MACRS. He would like to use the §179 immediate expensing, but he has elected to not claim any bonus depreciation. Phillip has never claimed §179 or bonus depreciation before. The assets Phillip sold on March 20 are as follows:

Date Acquired	Asset	Sales Price	Original Cost	Accumulated Depreciation as of Beginning of the Year
5/1/08	Office building	$940,000	$900,000	$129,825
5/1/08	Land	200,000	100,000	0
7/1/08	Furniture	50,000	239,000	206,998
8/13/10	Furniture	10,000	324,000	222,782
4/12/11	Office equipment	100,000	120,000	67,524
5/13/13	Computers	30,000	50,000	10,000

Phillip has never sold any assets relating to his business before this transaction.

5. The Dunphys sold 60 shares of Fizbo Corporation common stock on September 3, for $65 a share (minus a $50 total commission). The Dunphys purchased the stock on November 8, 2013, for $90 a share. They also sold a painting for $13,000 on March 1. Claire purchased the painting for $20,050 on September 1, 2007, as an investment.
6. The Dunphys filed their 2013 federal, state, and local returns on April 13, 2014. They paid the following additional 2013 taxes with their returns: federal income taxes of $630, state income taxes of $250, and city income taxes of $75.
7. The Dunphys made timely estimated federal income tax payments of $20,000 each quarter during 2014. They also made estimated state income tax payments of $1,000 each quarter and estimated city income tax payments of $300 each

quarter. The Dunphys made all fourth-quarter payments on December 31, 2014. They would like to receive a refund for any overpayments.

8. Phillip and Clair have qualifying insurance for purposes of the Affordable Care Act (ACA).

INDIVIDUAL TAX RETURN PROBLEM 5

Required:

- Use the following information to complete Paul and Judy Vance's 2014 federal income tax return. If information is missing, use reasonable assumptions to fill in the gaps.
- You may need the following forms and schedules to complete the project: Form 1040, Schedule A, Schedule B, Schedule C, Schedule D, Schedule E, Schedule SE, Form 2106-EZ, Form 4562 (for the dental practice), Form 4562 (for the rental property), Form 4797, Form 8863, and Form 8949. The forms, schedules, and instructions can be found at the IRS website (www.irs.gov). The instructions can be helpful in completing the forms.

Facts:

1. Paul J. and Judy L. Vance are married and file a joint return. Paul is self-employed as a dentist, and Judy is a college professor. Paul and Judy have three children. The oldest is Vince who lives at home. Vince is a law student at the University of Cincinnati and worked part-time during the year, earning $1,500, which he spent for his own support. Paul and Judy provided $6,000 toward Vince's support (including $4,000 for Vince's fall tuition). They also provided over half the support of their daughter, Joan, who is a full-time student at Edgecliff College in Cincinnati. Joan worked part-time as an independent contractor during the year, earning $3,200. Joan lived at home until she was married in December 2014. She filed a joint return with her husband, Patrick, who earned $20,000 during the year. Jennifer is the youngest and lived in the Vances' home for the entire year. The Vances provide you with the following additional information:
   - Paul and Judy would like to take advantage on their return of any educational expenses paid for their children.
   - The Vances do not want to contribute to the presidential election campaign.
   - The Vances live at 621 Franklin Avenue, Cincinnati, OH 45211.
   - Paul's birthday is 3/5/1957 and his Social Security number is 333-45-6666.
   - Judy's birthday is 4/24/1960 and her Social Security number is 566-77-8888.
   - Vince's birthday is 11/6/1991 and his Social Security number is 576-18-7928.
   - Joan's birthday is 2/1/1995 and her Social Security number is 575-92-4321.
   - Jennifer's birthday is 12/12/2002 and her Social Security number is 613-97-8465.
   - The Vances do not have any foreign bank accounts or trusts.
2. Judy is a lecturer at Xavier University in Cincinnati, where she earned $30,000. The university withheld federal income tax of $3,375, state income tax of $900, Cincinnati city income tax of $375, $1,860 of Social Security tax and $435 of Medicare tax. She also worked part of the year for Delta Airlines. Delta paid her $10,000 in salary, and withheld federal income tax of $1,125, state income tax of $300, Cincinnati city income tax of $125, Social Security tax of $620, and Medicare tax of $145.
3. The Vances received $800 of interest from State Savings Bank on a joint account. They received interest of $1,000 on City of Cincinnati bonds they bought in January with the proceeds of a loan from Third National Bank of Cincinnati.

They paid interest of $1,100 on the loan. Paul received a dividend of $540 on General Bicycle Corporation stock he owns. Judy received a dividend of $390 on Acme Clothing Corporation stock she owns. Paul and Judy received a dividend of $865 on jointly owned stock in Maple Company. All of the dividends received in 2014 are qualified dividends.

4. Paul practices under the name "Paul J. Vance, DDS." His business is located at 645 West Avenue, Cincinnati, OH 45211, and his employer identification number is 01-2222222. Paul's gross receipts during the year were $111,000. Paul uses the cash method of accounting for his business. Paul's business expenses are as follows:

Advertising	$ 1,200
Professional dues	490
Professional journals	360
Contributions to employee benefit plans	2,000
Malpractice insurance	3,200
Fine for overbilling State of Ohio for work performed on welfare patient	5,000
Insurance on office contents	720
Interest on money borrowed to refurbish office	600
Accounting services	2,100
Miscellaneous office expense	388
Office rent	12,000
Dental supplies	7,672
Utilities and telephone	3,360
Wages	30,000
Payroll taxes	2,400

In June, Paul decided to refurbish his office. This project was completed and the assets placed in service on July 1. Paul's expenditures included $8,000 for new office furniture, $6,000 for new dental equipment (seven-year recovery period), and $2,000 for a new computer. Paul elected to compute his cost recovery allowance using MACRS. He did not elect to use §179 immediate expensing, and he chose to not claim any bonus depreciation.

5. Judy's mother, Sarah, died on July 2, 2009, leaving Judy her entire estate. Included in the estate was Sarah's residence (325 Oak Street, Cincinnati, OH 45211). Sarah's basis in the residence was $30,000. The fair market value of the residence on July 2, 2009, was $155,000. The property was distributed to Judy on January 1, 2010. The Vances have held the property as rental property and have managed it themselves. From 2010 until June 30, 2014, they rented the house to the same tenant. The tenant was transferred to a branch office in California and moved out at the end of June. Since they did not want to bother finding a new tenant, Paul and Judy sold the house on June 30, 2014. They received $140,000 for the house and land ($15,000 for the land and $125,000 for the house), less a 6 percent commission charged by the broker. They had depreciated the house using the MACRS rules and conventions applicable to residential real estate. To compute depreciation on the house, the Vances had allocated $15,000 of the property's basis to the land on which the house is located. The Vances collected rent of $1,000 a month during the six months the house was occupied during the year. They incurred the following related expenses during this period:

Property insurance	$500
Property taxes	800
Maintenance	465
Depreciation (to be computed)	?

6. The Vances sold 200 shares of Capp Corporation stock on September 3, 2014, for $42 a share (minus a $50 commission). The Vances received the stock from

Paul's father on June 25, 1980, as a wedding present. Paul's father originally purchased the stock for $10 per share in 1967. The stock was valued at $14.50 per share on the date of the gift. No gift tax was paid on the gift.

7. Judy is required by Xavier University to visit several high schools in the Cincinnati area to evaluate Xavier University students who are doing their practice teaching. However, she is not reimbursed for the expenses she incurs in doing this. During the spring semester (January through April 2014), she drove her personal automobile 6,800 miles in fulfilling this obligation. Judy drove an additional 6,700 personal miles during 2014. She has been using the car since June 30, 2013. Judy uses the standard mileage method to calculate her car expenses.
8. Paul and Judy have given you a file containing the following receipts for expenditures during the year:

Prescription medicine and drugs (net of insurance reimbursement)	$ 376
Doctor and hospital bills (net of insurance reimbursement)	2,468
Penalty for underpayment of last year's state income tax	15
Real estate taxes on personal residence	4,762
Interest on home mortgage (paid to Home State Savings & Loan)	8,250
Interest on credit cards (consumer purchases)	595
Cash contribution to St. Matthew's church	3,080
Payroll deductions for Judy's contributions to the United Way	150
Professional dues (Judy)	325
Professional subscriptions (Judy)	245
Fee for preparation of 2013 tax return paid April 12, 2014	500

9. The Vances filed their 2013 federal, state, and local returns on April 12, 2014. They paid the following additional 2013 taxes with their returns: federal income taxes of $630, state income taxes of $250, and city income taxes of $75.
10. The Vances made timely estimated federal income tax payments of $1,500 each quarter during 2014. They also made estimated state income tax payments of $300 each quarter and estimated city income tax payments of $160 each quarter. The Vances made all fourth-quarter payments on December 31, 2014. They would like to receive a refund for any overpayments.
11. Paul and Judy have qualifying insurance for purposes of the Affordable Care Act (ACA).

INDIVIDUAL TAX RETURN PROBLEM 6

Required:

- Use the following information to complete Paige Turner's 2014 federal income tax return. If information is missing, use reasonable assumptions to fill in the gaps.
- Any required forms, schedules, and instructions can be found at the IRS website (www.irs.gov). The instructions can be helpful in completing the forms.

Facts:

1. Paige Turner is single and has two children from her previous marriage. Ali lives with Paige, and Paige provides more than half of her support. Leif lives with his father, Will (Lief lived with Will for all of 2014). Will provides more than half of Leif's support. Paige pays "alimony" of $400 per month to Will. The payments are to continue until Leif reaches age 18, when they will be reduced to $150. Paige provides you with the following additional information:
   - She uses the cash method of accounting and a calendar year for reporting.
   - She wishes to contribute to the presidential election campaign.
   - Paige lives at 523 Essex Street, Bangor, ME 04401.

- Paige's birthday is May 31, 1976.
- Ali's birthday is October 5, 2005.
- Leif's birthday is December 1, 2003.
- Paige's Social Security number is 007-16-4727.
- Ali's Social Security number is 005-61-7232.
- Leif's Social Security number is 004-23-3419.
- Will's Social Security number is 006-45-6333.
- She does not have any foreign bank accounts or trusts.

2. Paige is employed as a nuclear engineer with Atom Systems Consultants, Inc. (ASCI). ASCI's federal employer identification number is 79-1234466. Paige's pay stubs indicate that she had $7,230 withheld in federal taxes, $4,987 in state taxes, $4,495 in Social Security taxes, and $1,051 in Medicare taxes. ASCI has an extensive fringe benefits program for its employees.
3. Paige earned salary of $70,000 (before subtracting her 401(k) and flexible spending plan contributions). She contributed $7,000 to her 401(k) account, and she contributed $2,500 to her flexible spending account.
4. ASCI paid $397 of whole life insurance premiums to cover Paige's personal whole life insurance policy. ASCI also paid health club dues of $900 to a nearby health club on Paige's behalf.
5. Taking advantage of ASCI's educational assistance program, during the fall Paige enrolled in two graduate engineering classes at a local college. ASCI paid her tuition, fees, and other course-related costs of $2,300.
6. Paige received free parking in the company's security garage that would normally cost $200 per month.
7. Paige manages the safety program for ASCI. In recognition of her superior handling of three potential crises during the year, Paige was awarded the Employee Safety Award on December 15. The cash award was $500.
8. On January 15, 2014, Paige's father died. From her father's estate, she received stock valued at $30,000 (his basis was $12,000) and her father's house valued at $90,000 (his basis in the house was $55,000).
9. Paige owns several other investments and in February 2015 received a statement from her brokerage firm reporting the interest and dividends earned on the investments for 2014. (See Exhibit A.)
10. In addition to the investments discussed above, Paige owns 1,000 shares of Grubstake Mining & Development common stock. Grubstake is organized as an S corporation and has 100,000 shares outstanding (S corp. ID number 45-4567890). Grubstake reported taxable income of $200,000 and paid a distribution of $1.00 per share during the current year. Paige tells you that Grubstake typically does not send out its K-1 reports until late April. However, its preliminary report has been consistent with the K-1 for many years. (See Exhibit A.) Paige does not materially participate in Grubstake's activities.
11. Paige slipped on a wet spot in front of a computer store last July. She broke her ankle and was unable to work for two weeks. She incurred $1,300 in medical costs, all of which were paid by the owner of the store. The store also gave her $1,000 for pain and suffering resulting from the injury. ASCI continued to pay her salary during the two weeks she missed because of the accident. ASCI's plan also paid her $1,200 in disability pay for the time she was unable to work. Under this plan ASCI pays the premiums for the disability insurance as a taxable fringe benefit.

EXHIBIT A **Forms 1099 and 1098**

This is important tax information and is being furnished to the Internal Revenue Service.

1099-Div Dividends & Distributions

Entity	Description	Amount
General Dynamics	Gross qualified dividends	$300

1099-Int Interest

Entity	Description	Amount
New Jersey Economic Development bonds	Gross interest	$300
IBM bonds	Gross interest	700
State of Nebraska bonds	Gross interest	200

1098-Mortgage Interest Statement

Entity	Description	Amount
Sunbelt Credit Union	Mortgage interest	$7,100
Northeast Bank	Home-equity loan interest	435

Grubstake Mining & Development: preliminary report (preliminary K-1) to Paige for the 2014 tax year

Distribution to shareholder	$1,000
Ordinary income (1% of $200,000)	$2,000

12. Paige received a Form 1099-B from her broker for the sale of the following securities during 2014. The adjusted basis amounts were reported to the IRS.

Security	Sale Date	Purchase Date	Sales Price	Commission Paid on Sale	Her Basis
Nebraska state bonds	03/14/14	10/22/08	$2,300	$160	$1,890
Cassill Corp (500 shares)	10/20/14	02/19/13	$8,500	$425	$9,760

13. In addition to the taxes withheld from her salary, she also made timely estimated federal tax payments of $175 per quarter and timely estimated state income tax payments of $150 for the first three quarters. The $150 fourth-quarter state payment was made on December 28, 2014. Paige would like to receive a refund for any overpayment.

14. Because of her busy work schedule, Paige was unable to provide her accountant with the tax documents necessary for filing her 2013 state and federal income tax returns by the due date (April 15, 2013). In filing her extension on April 15, 2014, she made a federal tax payment of $750. Her return was eventually filed on June 25, 2014. In August 2014, she received a federal refund of $180 and a state tax refund of $60. Her itemized deductions for 2013 were $12,430.

15. Paige found a renter for her father's house on August 1. The monthly rent is $400, and the lease agreement is for one year. The lease requires the tenant to pay the first and last months' rent and a $400 security deposit. The security deposit is to be returned at the end of the lease if the property is in good condition. On August 1, Paige received $1,200 from the tenant per the terms of the lease agreement. In November, the plumbing froze and several pipes burst. The tenant had the repairs made and paid the $300 bill. In December, he reduced his rental payment to $100 to compensate for the plumbing

repairs. Paige provides you with the following additional information for the rental in 2014.

Property taxes	$770
Other maintenance expenses	285
Insurance expense	495
Management fee	350
Depreciation (to be computed)	?

The rental property is located at 35 Harvest Street, Orono, ME 04473. Local practice is to allocate 12 percent of the fair market value of the property to the land. (See #8.) Paige makes all decisions with respect to the property.

16. Paige paid $2,050 in real estate taxes on her principal residence. The real estate tax is used to pay for town schools and other municipal services.
17. Paige drives a 2013 Acura TL. Her car registration fee (based on the car year) is $50 and covers the period 1/1/14 through 12/31/14. In addition, she paid $280 in property tax to the state based on the book value of the car.
18. In addition to the medical costs presented in #11, Paige incurred the following unreimbursed medical costs:

Dentist	$ 310
Doctor	390
Prescription drugs	215
Over-the-counter drugs	140
Optometrist	125
Emergency room charges	440
LASIK eye surgery	2,000
Chiropractor	265

19. On March 1, Paige took advantage of low interest rates and refinanced her $75,000 home mortgage with her original lender. The new home loan is for 15 years. She paid $215 in closing costs and $1,500 in discount points (prepaid interest) to obtain the loan. The house is worth $155,000, and Paige's basis in the house is $90,000. As part of the refinancing arrangement, she also obtained a $10,000 home-equity loan. She used the proceeds from the home-equity loan to reduce the balance due on her credit cards. Paige received several Form 1098 statements from her bank for interest paid by her in 2014. Details appear below. (See also Exhibit A on page C-11.)

Primary home mortgage	$7,100
Home-equity loan	435
Credit cards	498
Car loan	390

20. On May 14, 2014, Paige contributed clothing to the Salvation Army. The original cost of the clothing was $740. She has substantiation valuing the donation at $360. The Salvation Army is located at 350 Stone Ridge Road, Bangor, ME 04401. In addition, she made the following cash contributions and received a statement from each of the following organizations acknowledging her contribution:

Larkin College	$850
United Way	125
First Methodist Church	790
Amos House (homeless shelter)	200
Local Chamber of Commerce	100

21. On April 1, 2014, Paige's house was robbed. She apparently interrupted the burglar because all that's missing is an antique brooch she inherited from her grandmother (June 12, 2006) and $300 in cash. Unfortunately, she didn't have a separate rider on her insurance policy covering the jewelry. Therefore, the insurance company reimbursed her only $500 for the brooch. Her basis in the brooch was $6,000, and its fair market value was $7,500. Her insurance policy also limits to $100 the amount of cash that can be claimed in a theft.

22. Paige sells real estate in the evening and on weekends (considered an active trade or business). She runs her business from a rental office she shares with several other realtors (692 River Road Bangor, ME 04401). The name of her business is Turner Real Estate and the federal identification number is 05-8799561. Her business code is 531210. Paige has been operating in a business-like way since 2004 and has always shown a profit. She had the following income and expenses from her business:

Commissions earned	$21,250
Expenses:	
Advertising	2,200
Telephone	95
Real estate license	130
Rent	6,000
Utilities	600

She has used her Acura TL in her business since July 1, 2014. During 2014, she properly documented 6,000 business miles (1,000 miles each month). The total mileage on her car (i.e., business- and personal-use miles) during the year was 15,000 miles (including 200 miles commuting to and from the real estate office). In 2014, Paige elects to use the standard mileage method to calculate her car expenses. She spent $45 on tolls and $135 on parking related to the real estate business.

23. Paige's company has an accountable expense reimbursement plan for employees from which Paige receives $12,000 for the following expenses:

Airfare	$4,700
Hotel	3,400
Meals	2,000
Car rentals	600
Entertainment	900
Incidentals	400

24. During 2014, Paige also paid $295 for business publications other than those paid for by her employer and $325 for a local CPA to prepare her 2013 tax return.

25. Paige has qualifying insurance for purposes of the Affordable Care Act (ACA).

Appendix D

Code Index

Page numbers followed by n refer to footnotes.

Subject Index

Page numbers followed by n refer to footnotes.

A

B

C

D

E

F

J

K

L

S

T

U

V

W

Z

2015 Federal Tax Rate Schedule

Schedule X- Single

If taxable income is over:	But not over:	The tax is:
$ 0	$ 9,225	10% of taxable income
$ 9,225	$ 37,450	$922.50 plus 15% of the excess over $9,225
$ 37,450	$ 90,750	$5,156.25 plus 25% of the excess over $37,450
$ 90,750	$189,300	$18,481.25 plus 28% of the excess over $90,750
$189,300	$411,500	$46,075.25 plus 33% of the excess over $189,300
$411,500	$413,200	$119,401.25 plus 35% of the excess over $411,500
$413,200	—	$119,996.25 plus 39.6% of the excess over $413,200

Schedule Z-Head of Household

If taxable income is over:	But not over:	The tax is:
$ 0	$ 13,150	10% of taxable income
$ 13,150	$ 50,200	$1,315.00 plus 15% of the excess over $13,150
$ 50,200	$129,600	$6,872.50 plus 25% of the excess over $50,20
$129,600	$209,850	$26,722.50 plus 28% of the excess over $129,
$209,850	$411,500	$49,192.50 plus 33% of the excess over $209,
$411,500	$439,000	$115,737.00 plus 35% of the excess over $411,
$439,000	—	$125,362.00 plus 39.6% of the excess over $4

Schedule Y-1-Married Filing Jointly of Qualifying Widow(er)

If taxable income is over:	But not over:	The tax is:
$ 0	$ 18,450	10% of taxable income
$ 18,450	$ 74,900	$1,845.00 plus 15% of the excess over $18,450
$ 74,900	$151,200	$10,312.50 plus 25% of the excess over $74,900
$151,200	$230,450	$29,387.50 plus 28% of the excess over $151,200
$230,450	$411,500	$51,577.50 plus 33% of the excess over $230,450
$411,500	$464,850	$111,324.00 plus 35% of the excess over $411,500
$464,850	—	$129,996.50 plus 39.6% of the excess over $464,850

Schedule Y-2- Married Filing Separately

If taxable income is over:	But not over:	The tax is:
$ 0	$ 9,225	10% of taxable income
$ 9,225	$ 37,450	$922.50 plus 15% of the excess over $9,225
$ 37,450	$ 75,600	$5,156.25 plus 25% of the excess over $37,450
$ 75,600	$115,225	$14,693.75 plus 28% of the excess over $75,60
$115,225	$205,750	$25,788.75 plus 33% of the excess over $115,2
$205,750	$232,425	$55,662.00 plus 35% of the excess over $205,
$232,425	—	$64,998.25 plus 39.6% of the excess over $23

2014 Federal Tax Rate Schedule

Schedule X—Single

If taxable income is over:	But not over:	The tax is:
$ 0	$ 9,075	10% of taxable income
$ 9,075	$ 36,900	$907.50 plus 15% of the excess over $9,075
$ 36,900	$ 89,350	$5,081.25 plus 25% of the excess over $36,900
$ 89,350	$186,350	$18,193.75 plus 28% of the excess over $89,350
$186,350	$405,100	$45,353.75 plus 33% of the excess over $186,350
$405,100	$406,750	$117,541.25 plus 35% of the excess over $405,100
$406,750	—	$118,118.75 plus 39.6% of the excess over $406,750

Schedule Z—Head of Household

If taxable income is over:	But not over:	The tax is:
$ 0	$ 12,950	10% of taxable income
$ 12,950	$ 49,400	$1,295.00 plus 15% of the excess over $12,950
$ 49,400	$127,550	$6,762.50 plus 25% of the excess over $49,400
$127,550	$206,600	$26,300.00 plus 28% of the excess over $127,
$206,600	$405,100	$48,434.00 plus 33% of the excess over $206,
$405,100	$432,200	$113,939.00 plus 35% of the excess over $405,
$432,200	—	$123,424.00 plus 39.6% of the excess over $432

Schedule Y-1—Married Filing Jointly or Qualifying Widow(er)

If taxable income is over:	But not over:	The tax is:
$ 0	$ 18,150	10% of taxable income
$ 18,150	$ 73,800	$1,815.00 plus 15% of the excess over $18,150
$ 73,800	$148,850	$10,162.50 plus 25% of the excess over $73,800
$148,850	$226,850	$28,925.00 plus 28% of the excess over $148,850
$226,850	$405,100	$50,765.00 plus 33% of the excess over $226,850
$405,100	$457,600	$109,587.50 plus 35% of the excess over $405,100
$457,600	—	$127,962.50 plus 39.6% of the excess over $457,600

Schedule Y-2—Married Filing Separately

If taxable income is over:	But not over:	The tax is:
$ 0	$ 9,075	10% of taxable income
$ 9,075	$ 36,900	$907.50 plus 15% of the excess over $9,075
$ 36,900	$ 74,425	$5,081.25 plus 25% of the excess over $36,900
$ 74,425	$113,425	$14,462.50 plus 28% of the excess over $74,42
$113,425	$202,550	$25,382.50 plus 33% of the excess over $113,4
$202,550	$228,800	$54,793.75 plus 35% of the excess over $202,5
$228,800	—	$63,981.25 plus 39.6% of the excess over $228